Morality in Practice

Third Edition

Morality in Practice

Third Edition

Edited by
James P. Sterba
University of Notre Dame

Wadsworth Publishing Company
Belmont, California
A division of Wadsworth, Inc.

Philosophy Editor: Kenneth King
Editorial Assistant: Cynthia Campbell
Production Editor: Richard Lynch, Bookman Productions
Print Buyer: Randy Hurst
Designer: Vargas/Williams/Design
Copy Editor: Phil Alkana
Compositor: Kachina Typesetting
Cover: Lois Stanfield

Printed in the United States of America
1 2 3 4 5 6 7 8 9 10—95 94 93 92 91

ISBN 0-534-14592-2

Library of Congress Cataloging-in-Publication Data

Morality in practice. / edited by James P. Sterba. —3rd ed.
    p.   cm.
  Includes bibliographical references.
  ISBN 0-534-14592-2
  1. Social ethics.   I. Sterba, James P.
HM216.M667   1990
170—dc20

90-36530
CIP

To Sonya, now age 10, whose growing independence helped to make this Third Edition possible

Contents

VIII. Gay and Lesbian Rights

Introduction   388

IX.   Animal Liberation and Environmental Concern

Introduction   418

Preface

Moral problems courses tend to teach themselves. It takes a really bad teacher to mess them up. Teachers can mess up a moral problems course in at least three ways:

1. By presenting just one set of views on various topics. Students appreciate the need for fair play here.
2. By encouraging students to hold a crude relativism. Students know that all moral stances are not equally good.
3. By not being relevant to student concerns. Students can reasonably expect that at least an ethics course will be relevant to their lives.

This text enables teachers to avoid (1) by presenting radically opposed selections on all topics. It enables teachers to avoid (2) by suggesting, through the introductions and through the ordering and selection of topics, how some views turn out to be more defensible than others. It enables teachers to avoid (3) by being the first moral problems text to provide readings on a broad range of standard and new topics. In fact, no other moral problems text combines such breadth and depth. In addition, it has to recommend it, the following:

New Features

1. The only moral problems text to contain a section on privacy, drug testing, and AIDS, and another on comparable worth.
2. New sections on pornography, environmental concern, and gay and lesbian rights.
3. Eleven new articles incorporated into the other sections of the anthology.

Retained Features

1. A general introduction that provides a background discussion of ethical theory as well as a justification of morality.
2. Section introductions that help to set out the framework for the discussion and criticism of the articles in each section.
3. Brief summaries at the beginning of each article that enable students to test and improve their comprehension.
4. Each section of the anthology concludes with one or more articles discussing specific practical applications.
5. Suggestions for further reading are found at the end of each section.

In putting together this third edition, I have again benefited enormously from the advice and help of many different people. Special thanks go to my colleague John Robinson, who offered many suggestions that have been incorporated into this edition. Thanks also goes to Ken King of Wadsworth Publishing Company, Richard Lynch of Bookman Productions, my wife and fellow philosopher Janet Kourany, and my colleague Michael De Paul. I would also like to thank the following reviewers: Peter de Marneffe, Arizona State University; Samuel Freeman, University of Pennsylvania; C. Lynn Fulmer, St. Mary's University; Thomas Seung, University of Texas, Austin; and Dr. Carol Skrenes, California State University, Long Beach. Work on this anthology was made possible by financial assistance from the University of Notre Dame and the MacArthur Foundation.

Morality
in
Practice

Third Edition

General Introduction

Most of us like to think of ourselves as just and moral people. To be truly such, however, we need to know something about the demands of justice and how they apply in our own particular circumstances. We should be able to assess, for example, whether our society's economic and legal systems are just—that is, whether the ways income and wealth are distributed in society as well as the methods of enforcing that distribution give people what they deserve. We should also consider whether other societal institutions, such as the military defense system, the educational system, and the foreign aid program, are truly just. Without investigating these systems and coming to an informed opinion, we cannot say with any certainty that we are just and moral persons rather than perpetrators or beneficiaries of injustice.

This anthology has been created to help you acquire some of the knowledge you will need to justify your belief that you are a just and moral person. For this purpose, the anthology contains a wide spectrum of readings on eleven important contemporary practical problems:

1. The problem of the distribution of income and wealth. (Who should control what resources within a society?)

2. The problem of distant peoples and future generations. (What obligations do we have to distant peoples and future generations?)

3. The problem of abortion and euthanasia. (Do fetuses have a right to life, and what should we do for the dying and those requiring life-sustaining medical treatment?)

4. The problem of sex equality. (Should the sexes be treated equally, and what constitutes equal treatment?)

5. The problem of affirmative action and comparable worth. (What specific policies are required to remedy discrimination and prejudice?)

6. The problem of pornography. (Should pornography be prohibited because it promotes violence against women?)

7. The problem of privacy, drug testing, and AIDS. (Do programs for drug testing and testing for AIDS violate a person's right to privacy?)

8. The problem of gay and lesbian rights. (What rights should gays and lesbians have?)

9. The problem of animal liberation and environmental concern. (What should our policies be for the treatment of animals and the environment?)

10. The problem of punishment and responsibility. (Who should be punished,
and in what should their punishment consist?)
11. The problem of national defense and
military strategy. (What are the moral
limits to national defense?)

Before you get into these problems, however,
you should know what it means to take a moral
approach to these issues and how such an
approach is justified.

The Essential Features
of a Moral Approach to
Practical Problems

To begin with, a moral approach to practical
problems must be distinguished from various
nonmoral approaches. Nonmoral approaches
to practical problems include the *legal approach*
(what the law requires with respect to this
practical problem), the *group- or self-interest
approach* (what the group- or self-interest is of
the parties affected by this problem), and the
scientific approach (how this practical problem
can best be accounted for or understood). To
call these approaches nonmoral, of course,
does not imply that they are immoral. All that
is implied is that the requirements of these
approaches may or may not accord with the
requirements of morality.

What, then, essentially characterizes a moral approach to practical problems? I suggest
that there are two essential features to such an
approach:

1. The approach is prescriptive, that is, it
issues in prescriptions, such as "do this"
and "don't do that."
2. The approach's prescriptions are acceptable to everyone affected by them.

The first feature distinguishes a moral
approach from a scientific approach because a
scientific approach is not prescriptive. The
second feature distinguishes a moral approach
from both a legal approach and a group-
or self-interest approach because the pre-

scriptions that accord best with the law or
serve the interest of particular groups or individuals may not be acceptable to everyone
affected by them.

Here the notion of "acceptable" means
"ought to be accepted" or "is reasonable to
accept" and not simply "is capable of being
accepted." Understood in this way, certain
prescriptions may be acceptable even though
they are not actually accepted by everyone
affected by them. For example, a particular
welfare program may be acceptable even
though many people oppose it because it involves an increased tax burden. Likewise, certain prescriptions may be unacceptable even
though they have been accepted by everyone
affected by them. For example, it may be that
most women have been socialized to accept
prescriptions requiring them to fill certain social roles even though these prescriptions are
unacceptable because they impose second-
class status on them.

Alternative Moral Approaches
to Practical Problems

Using the two essential features of a moral
approach to practical problems, let us consider
three principal alternative moral approaches
to practical problems: the *Utilitarian Approach,*
the *Human Nature Approach,* and the *Social Contract Approach.*[1] The basic principle of the Utilitarian Approach is:

Do those actions that maximize the net utility or satisfaction of everyone affected by
them.

The Utilitarian Approach qualifies as a moral
approach because it is prescriptive and because it can be argued that its prescriptions are
acceptable to everyone affected by them since
they take the utility or satisfaction of all those
individuals equally into account.

To illustrate, let's consider how this approach applies to the question of whether nation A should adopt a particular defense policy with respect to nation B when nation A's
choice would have the following consequences:

Nation A's Choice

	Adopt the policy	Don't adopt the policy
Net utility to A	8½ trillion units	4 trillion units
Net utility to B	−2 trillion units	2 trillion units
Total utility	6½ trillion units	6 trillion units

Given that these are all the consequences that are relevant to nation A's choice, the Utilitarian Approach favors adopting the particular defense policy. Note that in this case, the choice favoring the Utilitarian Approach does not conflict with the group-interest of nation A, although it does conflict with the group-interest of nation B.

But are such calculations of utility possible? Admittedly, they are difficult to make. At the same time, such calculations seem to serve as a basis for public discussion. President Reagan, addressing a group of black business leaders, asked whether blacks were better off because of the Great Society programs, and although many disagreed with the answer he gave, no one found his question unanswerable.[2] Thus, faced with the exigencies of measuring utility, the Utilitarian Approach simply counsels that we do our best to determine what maximizes net utility and act on the result.

The second approach to be considered is the Human Nature Approach. Its basic principle is:

Do those actions that would further one's proper development as a human being.

This approach also qualifies as a moral approach because it is prescriptive and because it can be argued that its prescriptions are acceptable to everyone affected by them.

There are, however, different versions of this approach. According to some versions, each person can determine through the use of reason his or her proper development as a human being. Other versions disagree. For example, from a Marxist perspective, many people in capitalist societies are deluded by false consciousness and will be unable to appreciate what fosters their proper development as human beings until their society is transformed economically. Similarly, many religious traditions rely on revelation to guide people in their proper development as human beings. However, although the Human Nature Approach can take these various forms, I want to focus on what is probably its philosophically most interesting form. That form specifies proper development in terms of virtuous activity and understands virtuous activity to preclude intentionally doing evil that good may come of it. In this form, the Human Nature Approach conflicts most radically with the Utilitarian Approach, which requires intentionally doing evil whenever a *greater* good would come of it.

The third approach to be considered is the Social Contract Approach. This approach has its origins in seventeenth- and eighteenth-century social contract theories, which tended to rely on actual contracts to specify moral requirements. However, actual contracts may or may not have been made, and, even if they were made, they may or may not have been moral or fair. This has led some philosophers to resort to hypothetical contracts to ground moral requirements. A difficulty with this approach is in determining under what conditions a hypothetical contract is fair and moral. Currently, the most favored Social Contract Approach is specified by the following basic principle:

Do those actions that persons behind an imaginary veil of ignorance would unanimously agree should be done.[3]

This imaginary veil extends to most particular facts about oneself—anything that would bias one's choice or stand in the way of a unanimous agreement. Accordingly, the imaginary veil of ignorance would mask one's knowledge of one's social position, talents, sex, race, and religion, but not one's knowledge of such general information as would be contained in political, social, economic, and psychological theories. The Social Contract Approach qualifies as a moral approach because it is prescriptive and because it can be argued that its prescriptions would be acceptable to everyone affected by them since they would be agreed to by everyone affected behind an imaginary veil of ignorance.

To illustrate the approach, let's return to the example of nation A and nation B used earlier. The choice facing nation A was the following:

Nation A's Choice

	Adopt the policy	*Don't adopt the policy*
Net utility to A	8½ trillion units	4 trillion units
Net utility to B	−2 trillion units	2 trillion units
Total utility	6½ trillion units	6 trillion units

Given that these are all the consequences relevant to nation A's choice, the Social Contract Approach favors rejecting the particular defense policy because persons behind the imaginary veil of ignorance would have to consider that they might turn out to be in nation B, and in that case, they would not want to be so disadvantaged for the greater benefit of those in nation A. This resolution conflicts with the resolution favored by the Utilitarian Approach and the group-interest of nation A, but not with the group-interest of nation B.

Assessing Alternative Moral Approaches

Needless to say, each of these moral approaches has its strengths and weaknesses. The main strength of the Utilitarian Approach is that once the relevant utilities are determined, there is an effective decision-making procedure that can be used to resolve all practical problems. After determining the relevant utilities, all that remains is to total the net utilities and choose the alternative with the highest net utility. The basic weakness of this approach, however, is that it does not give sufficient weight to the distribution of utility among the relevant parties. For example, consider a society equally divided between the

Privileged Rich and the Alienated Poor who face the following alternatives:

Nation A's Choice

	Alternative A	*Alternative B*
Net utility to Privileged Rich	5½ trillion units	4 trillion units
Net utility to Alienated Poor	1 trillion units	2 trillion units
Total utility	6½ trillion units	6 trillion units

Given that these are all the relevant utilities, the Utilitarian Approach favors Alternative A even though Alternative B provides a higher minimum payoff. And if the utility values for two alternatives were:

Nation A's Choice

	Alternative A	*Alternative B*
Net utility to Privileged Rich	4 trillion units	5 trillion units
Net utility to Alienated Poor	2 trillion units	1 trillion units
Total utility	6 trillion units	6 trillion units

the Utilitarian Approach would be indifferent between the alternatives, despite the fact that Alternative A again provides a higher minimum payoff. In this way, the Utilitarian Approach fails to take into account the distribution of utility among the relevant parties. All that matters for this approach is maximizing total utility, and the distribution of utility among the affected parties is taken into account only insofar as it contributes toward the attainment of that goal.

By contrast, the main strength of the Human Nature Approach in the form we are considering is that it limits the means that can be chosen in pursuit of good consequences. In particular, it absolutely prohibits intentionally doing evil that good may come of it. However, although some limit on the means available for the pursuit of good consequences seems desirable, the main weakness of this version of the Human Nature Approach is that the limit it imposes is too strong. Indeed, exceptions to this limit would seem to be justified whenever the evil to be done is:

1. Trivial (e.g., stepping on someone's foot to get out of a crowded subway).
2. Easily reparable (e.g., lying to a temporarily depressed friend to keep her from committing suicide).
3. Sufficiently outweighed by the consequences of the action (e.g., shooting one of 200 civilian hostages to prevent in the only way possible the execution of all 200).

Still another weakness of this approach is that it lacks an effective decision-making procedure for resolving practical problems. Beyond imposing limits on the means that can be employed in the pursuit of good consequences, the advocates of this approach have not agreed on criteria for selecting among the available alternatives.

The main strength of the Social Contract Approach is that like the Human Nature Approach, it seeks to limit the means available for the pursuit of good consequences. However, unlike the version of the Human Nature Approach we considered, the Social Contract Approach does not impose an absolute limit on intentionally doing evil that good may come of it. Behind the veil of ignorance, persons would surely agree that if the evil were trivial, easily reparable, or sufficiently outweighed by the consequences, there would be an adequate justification for permitting it. On the other hand, the main weakness of the Social Contract Approach is that although it provides an effective decision-making procedure for resolving some practical problems, such as the problem of how to distribute income and wealth and the problem of distant peoples and future generations, the Social Contract Approach cannot be applied to all problems. For example, it will not work for the problems of animal rights and abortion unless we assume that animals and fetuses should be behind the veil of ignorance.

So far, we have seen that prescriptivity and acceptability of prescriptions by everyone affected by them are the two essential features of a moral approach to practical problems,

and we have considered three principal alternative approaches that qualify as moral approaches to these problems. Let's now examine what reasons there are for giving a moral approach to practical problems precedence over any nonmoral approach with which it conflicts.

The Justification for Following a Moral Approach to Practical Problems

---

To begin with, the ethical egoist, by denying the priority of morality over self-interest, presents the most serious challenge to a moral approach to practical problems. Basically, that challenge takes two forms: Individual Ethical Egoism and Universal Ethical Egoism. The basic principle of Individual Ethical Egoism is:

> Everyone ought to do what is in the overall self-interest of just one particular individual.

The basic principle of Universal Ethical Egoism is:

> Everyone ought to do what is in his or her overall self-interest.

Obviously, the prescriptions deriving from these two forms of egoism would conflict significantly with prescriptions following from a moral approach to practical problems. How then can we show that a moral approach is preferable to an egoist's approach?

Individual Ethical Egoism

In Individual Ethical Egoism, all prescriptions are based on the overall interests of just one particular individual. Let's call that individual Gladys. Because in Individual Ethical Egoism Gladys's interests constitute the sole basis for determining prescriptions, there should be no problem of inconsistent prescriptions, assuming, of course, that Gladys's own particular interests are in harmony. The crucial problem for Individual Ethical Egoism, however, is justifying that only Gladys's interests count in determining prescriptions. Individual Ethical Egoism must provide at least some reason for accepting that view. Otherwise, it would be irrational to accept the theory. But what reason or reasons could serve this function? Clearly, it will not do to cite as a reason some characteristic Gladys shares with other persons because whatever justification such a characteristic would provide for favoring Gladys's interests, it would also provide for favoring the interests of those other persons. Nor will it do to cite as a reason some unique characteristic of Gladys, such as knowing all of Shakespeare's writings by heart, because such a characteristic involves a comparative element, and consequently others with similar characteristics, like knowing some or most of Shakespeare's corpus by heart, would still have some justification, although a proportionally lesser justification, for having their interests favored. But again the proposed characteristic would not justify favoring only Gladys's interests.

A similar objection could be raised if a unique relational characteristic were proposed as a reason for Gladys's special status—such as that Gladys is Seymour's wife. Because other persons would have similar but not identical relational characteristics, similar but not identical reasons would hold for them. Nor will it do to argue that the reason for Gladys's special status is not the particular unique traits that she possesses, but rather the mere fact that she has unique traits. The same would hold true of everyone else. Every individual has unique traits. If recourse to unique traits is dropped and Gladys claims that she is special simply because she is herself and wants to further her own interests, every other person could claim the same.[4]

For the Individual Ethical Egoist to argue that the same or similar reasons do *not* hold for other peoples with the same or similar characteristics to those of Gladys, she must explain *why* they do not hold. It must always be possible to understand how a characteristic serves as a reason in one case but not in another. If no explanation can be provided, and in the case of Individual Ethical Egoism none has been forthcoming, the proposed characteristic either serves as a reason in both cases or does not serve as a reason at all.

Universal Ethical Egoism

Unfortunately, these objections to Individual Ethical Egoism do not work against Universal Ethical Egoism because Universal Ethical Egoism does provide a reason why the egoist should be concerned simply about maximizing his or her own interests, which is simply that the egoist is herself and wants to further her own interests. The Individual Ethical Egoist could not recognize such a reason without giving up her view, but the Universal Ethical Egoist is willing and able to universalize her claim and recognize that everyone has a similar justification for adopting Universal Ethical Egoism.

Accordingly, the objections that typically have been raised against Universal Ethical Egoism are designed to show that the view is fundamentally inconsistent. For the purpose of evaluating these objections, let's consider the case of Gary Gyges, an otherwise normal human being who, for reasons of personal gain, has embezzled $300,000 while working at People's National Bank and is in the process of escaping to a South Sea island where he will have the good fortune to live a pleasant life protected by the local authorities and untroubled by any qualms of conscience. Suppose that Hedda Hawkeye, a fellow employee, knows that Gyges has been embezzling money from the bank and is about to escape. Suppose, further, that it is in Hawkeye's overall self-interest to prevent Gyges from escaping with the embezzled money because she will be generously rewarded for doing so by being appointed vice president of the bank. Given that it is in Gyges's overall self-interest to escape with the embezzled money, it now appears that we can derive a contradiction from the following:

1. Gyges ought to escape with the embezzled money.
2. Hawkeye ought to prevent Gyges from escaping with the embezzled money.
3. By preventing Gyges from escaping with the embezzled money, Hawkeye is preventing Gyges from doing what he ought to do.
4. One ought never to prevent someone from doing what he ought to do.

5. Therefore, Hawkeye ought not to prevent Gyges from escaping with the embezzled money.

Because premises 2 and 5 are contradictory, Universal Ethical Egoism appears to be inconsistent.

The soundness of this argument depends, however, on premise 4, and defenders of Universal Ethical Egoism believe there are grounds for rejecting this premise. For if "preventing an action" means "rendering the action impossible," it would appear that there *are* cases in which a person is justified in preventing someone else from doing what he or she ought to do. Consider, for example, the following case. Suppose Irma and Igor are both actively competing for the same position at a prestigious law firm. If Irma accepts the position, she obviously renders it impossible for Igor to obtain the position. But surely this is *not* what we normally think of as an unacceptable form of prevention. Nor would Hawkeye's prevention of Gyges's escape appear to be unacceptable. Thus, to sustain the argument against Universal Ethical Egoism, one must distinguish between acceptable and unacceptable forms of prevention and then show that the argument succeeds even for forms of prevention that a Universal Ethical Egoist would regard as unacceptable. This requires elucidating the force of "ought" in Universal Ethical Egoism.

To illustrate the sense in which a Universal Ethical Egoist claims that other persons ought to do what is in their overall self-interest, defenders often appeal to an analogy of competitive games. For example, in football a defensive player might think that the opposing team's quarterback ought to pass on third down with five yards to go, while not wanting the quarterback to do so and planning to prevent any such attempt. Or to use Jesse Kalin's example:

I may see how my chess opponent can put my king in check. This is how he ought to move. But believing that he ought to move his bishop and check my king does not commit me to wanting him to do that, nor to persuading him to do

so. What I ought to do is sit there quietly, hoping he does not move as he ought.[5]

The point of these examples is to suggest that a Universal Ethical Egoist may, like a player in a game, judge that others ought to do what is in their overall self-interest while simultaneously attempting to prevent such actions or at least refraining from encouraging them.

The analogy of competitive games also illustrates the sense in which a Universal Ethical Egoist claims that she herself ought to do what is in her overall self-interest. For just as a player's judgment that she ought to make a particular move is followed, other things being equal, by an attempt to perform the appropriate action, so likewise when a Universal Ethical Egoist judges that she ought to do some particular action, other things being equal, an attempt to perform the appropriate action follows. In general, defenders of Universal Ethical Egoism stress that because we have little difficulty understanding the implications of the use of "ought" in competitive games, we should also have little difficulty understanding the analogous use of "ought" by the Universal Ethical Egoist.

To claim, however, that the "oughts" in competitive games are analogous to the "oughts" of Universal Ethical Egoism does not mean there are no differences between them. Most importantly, competitive games are governed by moral constraints such that when everyone plays the game properly, there are acceptable moral limits as to what one can do. For example, in football one cannot poison the opposing quarterback in order to win the game. By contrast, when everyone holds self-interested reasons to be supreme, the only limit to what one can do is the point beyond which one ceases to benefit. But this important difference between "oughts" of Universal Ethical Egoism and the "oughts" found in publicly recognized activities like competitive games does not defeat the appropriateness of the analogy. That the "oughts" found in publicly recognized activities are always limited by various moral constraints (What else would get publicly recognized?) does not preclude their being a suggestive model for the unlimited action-guiding character of the "oughts" of Universal Ethical Egoism.[6]

A Standard for Reasonable Conduct

Although the most promising attempts to show that Universal Ethical Egoism is inconsistent have failed, the challenge the view presents to a moral approach to practical problems can still be turned aside. It can be shown that, although consistent, the egoist acts contrary to reason in rejecting a moral approach to practical problems. To show this, I will draw on and generalize insights we have about holding people morally responsible to arrive at what purports to be a standard for reasonable conduct that succeeds in showing that the egoist acts contrary to reason.

Now it is generally recognized that the reasons people could have acquired can be relevant when assessing their conduct from a moral perspective. In such assessments, people are said to be morally responsible even when they presently lack any moral reasons to act otherwise, provided they are morally responsible for the lack. For example, if political leaders had the capabilities and opportunities to become aware of their society's racist and sexist practices, but, in fact, failed to do so, with the consequence that they presently lack any moral reasons to oppose such practices, we would still hold them morally responsible because their lack of moral reasons is something for which they are morally responsible. Similarly, if people allow themselves to become so engrossed in advancing their own personal and family projects that they ignore the most basic needs of others and as a result come to lack any moral reasons for helping people who are truly in need, we could still hold them morally responsible in this regard.

As these examples indicate, having moral reasons to act otherwise is not necessary for imputing responsibility. Rather, what is necessary for such moral assessments is that people are or were able to acquire the relevant moral reasons. What is not so generally recognized, however, is that the reasons a person could have acquired can also be relevant when judg-

ing a person's conduct from a self-interested perspective.

Consider the following example. On the last day a house was being offered for sale, a friend of mine bought what turned out to be a termite-infested dwelling requiring several thousands of dollars in repairs. Apparently, the previous owners did not know about the termites, and my friend, having inspected the house on her own, did not think she needed to have the house inspected professionally. She now admits that she acted unreasonably in purchasing the house, but I think it is plausible to say that her action wasn't unreasonable in terms of any reasons she had when she bought the house because at that time she didn't know or have reason to believe the house had termites. Rather, her action is best seen as unreasonable in terms of the reasons she could have had at the time of purchase—reasons she would have had if only she had arranged to have the house inspected professionally.[7]

What these examples taken together appear to support is the following general standard:

A Standard for Reasonable Conduct

Reasonable conduct accords with a rational weighing of all the relevant reasons that people are or were able to acquire.

Obviously, not all the reasons people are or were able to acquire are *relevant* to an assessment of the reasonableness of their conduct. Some reasons are not important enough to be relevant to such an assessment. Relevant reasons are those that lead one to avoid significant harm to oneself (or others) or secure significant benefit to oneself (or others) at an acceptable cost to oneself (or others). Thus, the Standard for Reasonable Conduct is not concerned with the possibility of maximizing benefit or minimizing harm overall, but only with the possibility of avoiding a significant harm or securing a significant benefit at an acceptable cost.[8]

Needless to say, people do not always consider all of the reasons that are relevant for deciding what to do. In fact, they could do so only if they had already acquired all the relevant reasons. Nevertheless, reasonable conduct is ultimately determined by a rational weighing of all the relevant reasons. To fail to accord with a rational weighing of all such reasons is to act contrary to reason.[9]

Although defenders of ethical egoism certainly would not want to deny the relevance of the self-interested reasons people are or were able to acquire to the rational assessment of conduct, they might want to deny that the moral reasons people are or were able to acquire are similarly relevant. But what would be the basis for that denial? It could not be that ethical egoists fail to act on moral reasons. That would no more show the irrelevance of moral reasons to the rational assessment of conduct than the fact that pure altruists fail to act on self-interested reasons would show the irrelevance of self-interested reasons to such an assessment. To argue on such grounds simply begs the question against the opposing view. And most defenders of ethical egoism have at least tried to support the view in a non-question-begging way.

In fact, most defenders of ethical egoism have argued for egoism in its universal form, defending the principle that everyone ought to do what is in his or her overall self-interest. However, defenders of ethical egoism cannot support this principle simply by denying the relevance of moral reasons to a rational assessment of conduct any more than defenders of pure altruism can support their opposing principle that everyone ought to do what is in the overall interests of others by denying the relevance of self-interested reasons to a rational assessment of conduct. Consequently, defenders of ethical egoism have no other alternative but to grant that moral reasons are relevant to the rational assessment of conduct and then try to show that such an assessment would never rationally require us to act on moral reasons.

Unfortunately for the defenders of ethical egoism, a rational assessment of the relevant reasons does not lead to this result. On the contrary, such an assessment shows that we are rationally required to act on moral reasons. To see why this is so, two kinds of cases must be considered: cases where the relevant moral reasons and self-interested reasons conflict and cases where no such conflict exists.

It seems obvious that where there is no conflict and both reasons are conclusive, they should both be acted on. In such contexts, we should do what is favored by both morality and self-interest.

Consider the following example. Suppose that you accept a job marketing a baby formula in underdeveloped countries, where the formula is improperly used, leading to increased infant mortality.[10] Imagine that you could just as well have accepted an equally attractive and rewarding job marketing a similar formula in developed countries where the product was not misused, so that a rational weighing of the relevant self-interested reasons alone would not have favored your accepting one of these jobs over the other.[11] At the same time, there were obvious moral reasons why you should not take the first job—reasons that you presumably are or were able to acquire. Moreover, by assumption in this case, the moral reasons do not clash with the relevant self-interested reasons; they simply make a recommendation where the relevant self-interested reasons are silent. Consequently, a rational weighing of all the relevant reasons in this case could not but favor acting in accord with the relevant moral reasons.[12]

Needless to say, defenders of ethical egoism have to be disconcerted with this result because it shows that actions that accord with ethical egoism are contrary to reason at least when there are two equally good ways of pursuing one's self-interest, only one of which does not conflict with the basic requirements of morality. Note also that in cases where there are two equally good ways of fulfilling the basic requirements of morality, only one of which does not conflict with a person's overall self-interest, it is not at all disconcerting for defenders of morality to admit that we are rationally required to choose the way that does not conflict with our overall self-interest. Nevertheless, exposing this defect in ethical egoism for cases where moral reasons and self-interested reasons do not conflict would be a small victory for defenders of morality if it were not also possible to show that in cases where such reasons do conflict, moral reasons would have priority over self-interested reasons.

When rationally assessing the relevant reasons in cases of such conflict, it is best to view the conflict not as a conflict between self-interested reasons and moral reasons but rather as a conflict between self-interested reasons and altruistic reasons. Viewed in this way, three solutions are possible. First, one could say that self-interested reasons always have priority over conflicting altruistic reasons. Second, one could say just the opposite—that altruistic reasons always have priority over conflicting self-interested reasons. Third, one could say that some kind of a compromise is rationally required. In this compromise, self-interested reasons would sometimes have priority over altruistic reasons, and altruistic reasons would sometimes have priority over self-interested reasons.

Once the conflict is described in this manner, the third solution is clearly the one that is rationally required because the first and second solutions give exclusive priority to one class of relevant reasons over the other without justifying such an exclusive priority from the standpoint of the Standard for Reasonable Conduct. Only the third solution, which sometimes gives priority to self-interested reasons and sometimes gives priority to altruistic reasons, provides a non–question begging resolution from the standpoint of the Standard for Reasonable Conduct.

Consider the following example. Suppose you are in the waste disposal business and you decide to dispose of toxic wastes in a way that is cost efficient for you, but is predicted to significantly harm future generations. Imagine that there are alternative methods available for disposing of the waste that are only slightly less cost efficient and that will not cause any significant harm to future generations.[13] In this case, the Standard for Reasonable Conduct requires that you weigh your self-interested reasons, which favor the most cost-efficient method of disposing of the toxic wastes, against the relevant altruistic reasons, which favor avoiding significant harm to future generations. If we suppose that the projected loss of benefit to yourself is very slight and the projected harm to future generations very great, any acceptable general compromise between the relevant self-interested and altruistic reasons would have to favor the altruistic reasons. Hence, as judged by the Standard for Reasonable Conduct, your

method of waste disposal is contrary to the relevant reasons.

It is important to see how morality can be viewed as just such a compromise between self-interested and altruistic reasons. First, a certain amount of self-regard is morally required or at least morally acceptable. Where this is the case, the relevant self-interested reasons have priority over the relevant altruistic reasons. Second, morality obviously places limits on the extent to which people should pursue their own self-interest. Where this is the case, the relevant altruistic reasons have priority over the relevant self-interested reasons. In this way, morality can be seen as a compromise between self-interested and altruistic reasons, and the "moral reasons" that constitute that compromise can be seen as having an absolute priority over the self-interested or altruistic reasons with which they conflict.

Of course, exactly how this compromise is to be worked out is a matter of considerable debate. The Utilitarian Approach favors one sort of resolution, the Human Nature Approach another, and the Social Contract Approach yet another. However, irrespective of how this debate is best resolved, it is clear that some sort of a compromise view or moral solution is rationally preferable to either ethical egoism or pure altruism from the standpoint of the Standard for Reasonable Conduct.[14]

The Interconnectedness of Moral Solutions to Practical Problems

Given this justification for following a moral approach to practical problems, we are in a good position to begin examining the eleven practical problems covered in this anthology. Each section contains readings defending radically opposing solutions to the problem at hand, as well as one or more readings discussing specific practical applications. Working through these readings should give you a more informed view about the demands morality places on us with respect to each of these practical problems.

Even if you do not cover all of these practical problems, you should still come to appreciate why a solution to any one of them requires solutions to the others as well. That is to say, the readings on the distribution of income and wealth (in Section I) may help you to characterize a morally defensible system for distributing income and wealth within a society, but you would still not know fully how to apply such a system in a particular society without also inquiring how just that society is with respect to the other problem areas covered by this anthology.

Or suppose justice requires us to provide for the basic nutritional needs of distant peoples and future generations as well as for people within our own society. (See the readings in Section II.) Such a requirement would at least restrict the use of nonrenewable resources to satisfy the nonbasic or luxury needs of persons within our society—a use that might otherwise be permitted by a morally defensible system for distributing income and wealth within our society.

Further moral restrictions on the satisfaction of nonbasic or luxury needs could arise from a correct determination of who has a right to life. For example, if fetuses have a right to life, many of us may be morally required to sacrifice the satisfaction of certain nonbasic or luxury needs to bring fetuses to term. If, by contrast, euthanasia can be morally justified, scarce resources that are now used to sustain human life could be freed for other purposes. (See the readings in Section III.)

Justice also may demand that we sacrifice some nonbasic or luxury needs to satisfy the requirements of sex equality and remedy past discrimination and prejudice. For example, at the cost of considerable redistribution, we may be required to provide women with the same opportunities for self-development that are now open to men. (See the readings in Section IV.) We may also be required to turn away qualified candidates for medical schools and law schools so that other candidates who have suffered past injustices may be compensated by admission to these schools. (See the readings in Section V.) Obviously, a radical solu-

tion to the problem of pornography prohibiting its distribution would affect those who derive their income from that eight-billion-dollar-a-year industry. (See the readings in Section VI.) Likewise, a radical solution to the problem of privacy, drug-testing, and AIDS favoring a strong right to privacy would have a significant impact on the cost of insurance premiums as well as the incomes of those employed in drug testing. (See the readings in Section VII.) Recognition of a strong right to privacy would also result in considerable redistribution that would benefit homosexuals, by providing them with the same opportunities for self-development as heterosexuals. (See the readings in Section VIII.)

Moral restrictions on the satisfaction of nonbasic needs and even on the way basic needs are satisfied could arise from a determination of what obligations, if any, we have to animals and the environment. For example, if vegetarianism were morally required and recognized as such, the impact on our lives would be far-reaching. (See the readings in Section IX.)

Similarly, the legitimate costs of legal enforcement must ultimately enter into any calculation of who gets to keep what in society. This will require a solution to the problem of punishment and responsibility. (See the readings in Section X.)

A solution to the problem of punishment and responsibility, in turn, presupposes solutions to the other practical problems discussed in the anthology. Suppose that in a society with a just distribution of income and wealth persons who put forth their best efforts receive a yearly income of at least $15,000. (If you think a just distribution of income would provide some other amount, plug that amount in and make the corresponding adjustments in subsequent figures.) Further suppose that the society in which you and I live has an unjust distribution of income and wealth because, although there are enough resources for a just distribution, many persons who put forth their best efforts receive no more than $8,000 per year whereas others receive as much as $500,000. Let's say that your income is $500,000 and mine is only $8,000, even though I have tried every legal way to increase my income. Assume also that any resort to civil disobedience or armed revolution would be ineffectual and too costly for me personally. If I then rob you of $7,000, thus bringing my yearly income up to the just allotment of $15,000, what would a morally defensible system of punishment and responsibility do to me if I were caught? To require a punishment equal in severity to the $7,000 I took simply reinforces an unjust distribution of income and wealth. So it seems that only a fairly light punishment or no punishment at all should be required.[15] This example shows that the application of a morally defensible solution to the problem of punishment and responsibility depends on a solution to the problem of the distribution of income and wealth in a society. To know, therefore, how to apply a morally defensible system of punishment and responsibility in a particular society, you must know to what degree that society incorporates a morally defensible distribution of income and wealth.

Finally, as we in the United States are painfully aware at the present time, proposed allocations for distributing income and wealth through social welfare programs can come into conflict with proposed allocations for military defense. Many have argued that when this happens we must sacrifice social welfare programs to meet the requirements of military defense, but many other people have disagreed. Obviously, then, to know exactly how your solutions to the other problem areas treated in this anthology should be applied in a particular society, you also need to know what a morally defensible system of military defense requires for that society. (See the readings in Section XI.)

Put briefly, what is required (or permitted) by a morally defensible solution to the problem of the distribution of income and wealth within a society will depend on what is required (or permitted) by morally defensible solutions to the problems of distant peoples and future generations; abortion and euthanasia; sex equality; affirmative action and comparable worth; pornography, privacy, drug-testing, and AIDS; gay and lesbian rights; animal liberation and environmental concerns; punishment and responsibility; and national defense and military strategy.

Moreover, as we have seen in the cases of the problem of punishment, the dependency can run both ways. This means that any solution you might devise to one of these problems is only provisional until you can determine solutions to the others as well. And even if you are unable at the moment to devise solutions to all of these practical problems (because, for example, the course you are now taking is only considering some of them), you must still acknowledge that in the final analysis your solutions to these practical problems will have to be interconnected.

Note too that acknowledging the interconnectedness of the solutions to these practical problems does not presuppose a commitment to any particular political or moral ideal. For example, whether you tend to be a libertarian, a liberal, a socialist, a communitarian, or anything else, the interconnectedness of the solutions to the practical problems we are discussing still holds true. Individuals who endorse different political and moral ideals will presumably devise different solutions to these practical problems, but the solutions will still be interconnected.

Working through the readings in this anthology will not always be an easy task. Some articles will be clear on the first reading, whereas others will require closer scrutiny. You should also make sure you give each selection a fair hearing, because although some will accord with your current views, others will not. It is important that you evaluate these latter with an open mind, allowing for the possibility that after sufficient reflection you may come to view them as the most morally defensible. Indeed, to approach the selections of this anthology in any other way would surely undermine the grounds you have for thinking you are a just and moral person.

Notes

1. Obviously, other moral approaches to practical problems could be distinguished, but I think the three I will be considering reflect the range of possible approaches that are relevant to the resolution of these problems.

2. In fact, the debate as to whether blacks are better off now because of the programs of the Great Society has taken a more scholarly turn. See Charles Murray, *Losing Ground* (New York: Basic Books, 1984), and Christopher Jencks, "How Poor Are the Poor?" *New York Review of Books,* May 9, 1985.

3. See Section II of this text and my book, *The Demands of Justice* (Notre Dame: University of Notre Dame Press, 1980), especially Chapter 2.

4. For further argument on this point, see Marcus Singer, *Generalization in Ethics* (New York: Alfred A. Knopf, Inc., 1961), Chapter 2, and Alan Gewirth, "The Non-Trivializability of Universalizability," *Australasian Journal of Philosophy* (1969), pp. 123–131.

5. Jesse Kalin, "In Defense of Egoism," in *Morality and Rational Self-interest,* ed. David Gauthier (Englewood Cliffs: Prentice-Hall, Inc., 1970), pp. 73–74.

6. For additional reasons why ethical egoism is a consistent view, see my article, "Ethical Egoism and Beyond," *Canadian Journal of Philosophy* (1979), pp. 91–108.

7. Note that on the last day the house was being offered for sale, it would have been unreasonable for my acquaintance to decide to have the house inspected professionally because the inspection and the sale presumably could not have been completed in the same day.

8. Even utilitarians would find this interpretation of the Standard for Reasonable Conduct acceptable because they would not regard all failures to maximize benefits overall as unreasonable.

9. Of course, for individuals who neither possess nor have possessed the capabilities and opportunities to acquire such reasons for acting, the question of the reasonableness of their conduct simply doesn't arise. The same is true for those who have lost the capabilities and opportunities to acquire such reasons for acting through no fault of their own.

10. For a discussion of the causal links involved here, see *Marketing and Promotion of Infant Formula in Developing Countries.* Hearing before the Subcommittee on International Economic Policy and Trade of the Committee on Foreign Affairs, U.S. House of Representatives, 1980. See also Fred D. Miller, *Out of the Mouths of Babes* (Bowling Green: Bowling Green State University Press, 1983).

11. Assume that both jobs have the same beneficial effects on the interests of others.

12. I am assuming that acting contrary to reason is an important failing with respect to the requirements of reason and that there are many ways of not acting in (perfect) accord with reason that do not constitute acting contrary to reason.

13. Assume that all of these methods of waste disposal have roughly the same amount of beneficial effects on the interests of others.

14. For further argument, see my article, "Justifying Morality: The Right and the Wrong Ways," (Kurt Baier Festschift) *Syntheses* (1987).

15. For further argument, see my article, "Is There a Rationale for Punishment?" *The American Journal of Jurisprudence* (1984), pp. 29–43.

The Distribution of Income and Wealth

Basic Concepts

The problem of the distribution of income and wealth within a society has traditionally been referred to as the problem of distributive justice. Less frequently, this problem has been taken to include the distribution of other social goods (for example, political freedoms such as freedom of speech and freedom of the press), and at times it has been expanded to embrace distribution on a worldwide scale. Most philosophers, however, tend to agree that the distribution of income and wealth within a specific society is at the heart of the problem of distributive justice.

Just as traditionally, a variety of solutions have been proposed to the problem of distributive justice. Before examining some of these solutions, let's observe what they all have in common.

First, even though the solutions may differ as to exactly how much income and wealth people deserve or should rightfully possess, they all purport to tell us what people deserve or what they have a right to possess. For example, some solutions propose that people deserve to have their needs fulfilled, whereas others state that what people deserve or should rightfully possess is what they can produce by their labor.

Second, all solutions to the problem of distributive justice distinguish between justice and charity. *Justice* is what we should do as a matter of obligation or duty, whereas *charity* is what we should do if we want to choose the morally best possible action available to us. Accordingly, the demands of charity go beyond duty. In addition, failure to fulfill the demands of justice is blameworthy, violates someone's rights, and can legitimately be punished. By contrast, failure to fulfill the demands of charity, although not ideal, is not blameworthy, does not violate anyone's rights, and cannot legitimately be punished. Some solutions to the problem of distributive justice give more scope to justice and less to charity, whereas others do just the opposite.

Turning from common ground to disputed territory, solutions offered to the problem of distributive justice have appealed to a number of political ideals. In our times, libertarians have appealed to an ideal of liberty, socialists to an ideal of equality, welfare liberals to an ideal of contractual fairness, and communitarians to an ideal of the common good.

Libertarianism

Libertarians, such as John Hospers (see Selection 1), take liberty as the ultimate political ideal and typically define liberty as "the state of being unconstrained by other persons from doing what one wants." This definition limits the scope of liberty in two ways. First, not all constraints, whatever the source, count as a restriction of liberty; the constraints must come from other persons. For example, people who are constrained by natural forces from getting to the top of Mount Everest do not lack liberty in this regard. Second, the constraints must run counter to people's wants. Thus, people who do not want to hear Beethoven's Fifth Symphony do not feel their liberty is restricted when other people forbid its performance, even though the proscription does in fact constrain what they are able to do.

Of course, libertarians may argue that these constraints do restrict a person's liberty because people normally want to be unconstrained by others. But other philosophers have claimed that such constraints point to a serious defect in the libertarian's definition of liberty, which can only be remedied by defining liberty more broadly as "the state of being unconstrained by other persons from doing what one is able to do." If we apply this revised definition to the previous example, we find that people's liberty to hear Beethoven's Fifth Symphony would be restricted even if they did not want to hear it (and even if, perchance, they did not want to be unconstrained by others) because other people would still be constraining them from doing what they are able to do.

Confident that problems of defining liberty can be overcome in some satisfactory manner, libertarians go on to characterize their political ideal as requiring that each person should have the greatest amount of liberty commensurate with the same liberty for all. From this ideal, libertarians claim that a number of more specific requirements, in particular a right to life, a right to freedom of speech, press, and assembly, and a right to property can be derived.

It is important to note that the libertarian's right to life is not a right to receive from others the goods and resources necessary for preserving one's life; it is simply a right not to be killed. So understood, the right to life is not a right to welfare. In fact, there are no welfare rights in the libertarian view. Accordingly, the libertarian's understanding of the right to property is not a right to receive from others the goods and resources necessary for one's welfare, but rather a right to acquire goods and resources either by initial acquisition or by voluntary agreement.

Obviously, by defending rights such as these, libertarians can only support a limited role for government. That role is simply to prevent and punish initial acts of coercion— the only wrongful actions for libertarians.

Libertarians do not deny that it is a good thing for people to have sufficient goods and resources to meet at least their basic nutritional needs, but libertarians do deny that government has a duty to provide for such needs. Some good things, such as the provision of welfare to the needy, are requirements of charity rather than justice, libertarians claim. Accordingly, failure to make such provisions is neither blameworthy nor punishable.

A basic difficulty with the libertarian's solution to the problem of distributive justice as defended by Hospers is the claim that rights to life and property (as the libertarian understands these rights) derive from an ideal of liberty. Why should we think that an ideal of liberty requires a right to life and a right to property that excludes a right to welfare? Surely it would seem that a right to property (as the libertarian understands it) might well justify a rich person's depriving a poor person of the liberty to acquire the goods and resources necessary for meeting his or her basic nutritional needs. How then could we appeal to an ideal of liberty to justify such a deprivation? Surely we couldn't claim that such a deprivation is justified for the sake of preserving

a rich person's freedom to use the goods and resources he or she possesses to meet luxury needs. Or could we?

To deal with this difficulty, some libertarians have resorted to defining liberty in terms of rights, so that a restriction of liberty is a violation of someone's rights, usually a violation of a right to life or a right to property. But this approach gives rise to a difficulty akin to the one it seeks to resolve. How can the libertarian interpret a right to life and a right to property so as to favor a rich person's nonbasic or luxury needs rather than a poor person's basic nutritional needs? Thus, whether rights are defined in terms of liberty or liberty is defined in terms of rights, we can still question how libertarians justify their interpretation of a right to life and a right to property.

Socialist Justice

In contrast with libertarians, socialists take equality to be the ultimate political ideal and contend that the fundamental rights and duties in a society are determined by the ideal of equality. More specifically, socialists defend an ideal that calls for equality of need fulfillment. As Kai Nielsen contends (Selection 2), radical egalitarianism is justified because it produces the conditions for the most extensive satisfaction of the needs of everyone.

At first hearing, this ideal might sound simply crazy to someone brought up in a capitalist society. The obvious problem is how to get persons to put forth their best effort if income will be distributed on the basis of individual need rather than individual contribution.

The socialist answer is to make the work that must be done enjoyable in itself, as much as is possible. As a result, people will want to do the work they are capable of doing because they find it intrinsically rewarding. For a start, socialists might try to convince workers to accept lower salaries for presently existing jobs that are intrinsically rewarding. For example, they might ask top executives to work for $300,000 a year rather than $600,000. Yet socialists ultimately hope to make all jobs intrinsically as rewarding as possible so that, after people are no longer working primarily for external rewards when making their best contributions to society, distribution can proceed on the basis of need.

Socialists propose to implement their ideal of equality by giving workers democratic control over the workplace. They believe that if workers have more to say about how they do their work, they will find their work intrinsically more rewarding. As a consequence, they will be more motivated to work, because their work itself will be meeting their needs. Socialists believe that extending democracy to the workplace will necessarily lead to socialization of the means of production and the end of private property.

However, even with democratic control of the workplace, some jobs, such as collecting garbage or changing bedpans, probably can't be made intrinsically rewarding. Now what socialists propose to do with respect to such jobs is to divide them up in some equitable manner. Some people might, for example, collect garbage one day a week and then work at intrinsically rewarding jobs for the rest of the week. Others would change bedpans or do some other slop job one day a week and then work at an intrinsically rewarding job the other days of the week. By making jobs intrinsically as rewarding as possible, in part through democratic control of the workplace and an equitable assignment of unrewarding tasks, socialists believe people will contribute according to their ability even when distribution proceeds according to need.

Finally, it is important to note that the socialist ideal of equality does not accord with what exists in such countries as China or Albania. Judging the acceptability of the socialist ideal of equality by what takes place in those countries would be as unfair as judging the acceptability of the libertarian ideal of liberty by what takes place in countries like South Africa or South Korea, where citizens are arrested and imprisoned without cause. By analogy, it would be like judging the merits of college football by the way Vanderbilt's or Northwestern's teams play rather than by the way Miami's or Notre Dame's teams play. Actually, a fairer comparison would be to judge the socialist ideal of equality by what

takes place in countries like Sweden or Yugoslavia and to judge the libertarian ideal of liberty by what takes place in the United States. Even these comparisons, however, are not wholly appropriate because none of these countries fully conforms to those ideals.

To justify the ideal of equality, Kai Nielson argues that it is required by liberty or at least by a fair distribution of liberty. By "liberty" Nielson means both "positive liberty to receive certain goods" and "negative liberty not to be interfered with," so his argument from liberty will not have much weight with libertarians, who only value negative liberty. Rather, his argument is directed primarily at welfare liberals, who value both positive and negative liberty as well as a fair distribution of liberty.

Another basic difficulty with Nielson's socialist solution to the problem of distributive justice concerns the proclaimed necessity of abolishing private property and socializing the means of production. It seems perfectly possible to give workers more control over their workplace while at the same time allowing the means of production to remain privately owned. Of course, private ownership would have a somewhat different character in a society with democratic control of the workplace, but it need not cease to be private ownership. After all, private ownership would also have a somewhat different character in a society where private holdings, and hence bargaining power, were distributed more equally than is found in most capitalist societies, yet it would not cease to be private ownership. Accordingly, we could imagine a society where the means of production are privately owned but where —because ownership is so widely dispersed throughout the society (e.g., nearly everyone owns 10 shares of major industrial stock and no one more than 20 shares) and because of the degree of democratic control of the workplace—many of the valid criticisms socialists make of existing capitalist societies would no longer apply.

Welfare Liberalism

In contrast with libertarians and socialists, welfare liberals, such as John Rawls (Selection

3), take contractual fairness to be the ultimate political ideal and contend that the fundamental rights and duties in a society are those that people would agree to under fair conditions.

Note that welfare liberals do not say that the fundamental rights and duties in a society are those to which people actually do agree, because these might not be fair at all. For example, people might agree to a certain system of fundamental rights and duties only because they have been forced to do so or because their only alternative is starving to death. Thus, actual agreement is not sufficient, nor is it even necessary, for determining an adequate conception of justice. According to welfare liberals, what is necessary and sufficient is that people would agree to such rights and duties under fair conditions.

But what are fair conditions? According to John Rawls, fair conditions can be expressed by an "original position" in which people are concerned to advance their own interests behind a "veil of ignorance." The effect of the veil of ignorance is to deprive people in the original position of the knowledge they would need to advance their own interests in ways that are morally arbitrary.

Rawls presents the principles of justice he believes would be derived in the original position in two successive formulations. The first formulation is as follows:

I. Special conception of justice
   1. Each person is to have an equal right to the most extensive basic liberty compatible with a similar liberty for others.
   2. Social and economic inequalities are to be arranged so that they are (a) reasonably expected to be to everyone's advantage and (b) attached to positions and offices open to all.
II. General conception of justice
   All social values—liberty and opportunity, income and wealth, and the bases of self-respect—are to be distributed equally unless an unequal distribution of any or all of these values is to everyone's advantage.

Later these principles are more accurately formulated as:

I. Special conception of justice
   1. Each person is to have an equal right to the most extensive total system of equal basic liberties compatible with a similar system of liberty for all.
   2. Social and economic inequalities are to be arranged so that they are (a) to the greatest benefit of the least advantaged, consistent with the just savings principle, and (b) attached to offices and positions open to all under conditions of fair equality of opportunity.
II. General conception of justice
   All social goods—liberty and opportunity, income and wealth, and the bases of self-respect—are to be distributed equally unless an unequal distribution of any or all of these goods is to the advantage of the least favored.

Under both formulations, the general conception of justice differs from the special conception of justice by allowing trade-offs between liberty and other social goods. According to Rawls, persons in the original position would want the special conception of justice to be applied in place of the general conception of justice whenever social conditions allowed all representative persons to exercise their basic liberties.

Rawls holds that these principles of justice would be chosen in the original position because persons so situated would find it reasonable to follow the conservative dictates of a "maximin strategy" and thereby secure for themselves the highest minimum payoff.

Rawls's defense of a welfare liberal conception of justice has been challenged in a variety of ways. Some critics have endorsed Rawls's contractual approach while disagreeing with Rawls over what principles of justice would be derived thereby. These critics usually attempt to undermine the use of a maximin strategy in the original position.[1] Other critics, however, have found fault with the contractual approach itself. Libertarians, for example, have challenged the moral adequacy of the very ideal of contractual fairness.

This second challenge to the ideal of contractual fairness is potentially the more damaging because, if valid, it would force supporters to embrace some other political ideal. This challenge, however, fails if it can be shown that the libertarian's own ideal of liberty, when correctly interpreted, leads to much the same practical requirements as are usually associated with the welfare liberal's ideal of contractual fairness.[2]

Communitarian Justice

As one might expect, many contemporary defenders of communitarian justice regard their conception of justice as rooted in Aristotelian moral theory. Like Aristotle, communitarians endorse a fundamental contrast between human beings as they are and human beings as they could be if they realized their essential nature. Ethics is then viewed as a science that enables human beings to understand how they can make the transition from the former state to the latter. This view of ethics requires some account of potency to act and some account of the essence of human beings and the end or *telos* they seek. Moreover, for human beings to make this transition from potency to action, a particular set of virtues is needed and people who fail to acquire these virtues cannot realize their true nature and reach their true end.

Given that the communitarian conception of justice is not a widely endorsed ideal today, communitarians have frequently chosen to defend their conception by attacking other conceptions of justice, and, by and large, they have focused their attacks on the welfare liberal conception of justice.

One of the best-known attacks of this sort has been put forth by Michael J. Sandel (Selection 4). Sandel claims that a welfare liberal conception of justice is founded on an inadequate conception of the nature of persons, according to which none of the particular wants, interests, or ends that we happen to have at any given time constitute what we are essentially. According to this conception, we are independent of and prior to all such wants, interests, or ends.

Sandel claims that this conception of the nature of persons is inadequate because:

. . . we cannot regard ourselves as independent in this way without great cost to those loyalties and convictions whose moral force consists partly in the fact that living by them is inseparable from understanding ourselves as the particular persons we are—as members of this family or community or nation or people, as bearers of this history, as sons and daughters of that revolution, as citizens of this republic. Allegiances such as these are more than values I happen to have or aims I "espouse at any given time." They go beyond the obligations I voluntarily incur and the "natural duties" I owe to human beings as such. They allow that to some I owe more than justice requires or even permits, not by reason of agreements I have made but instead in virtue of those more or less enduring attachments and commitments which taken together partly define the person I am.[3]

Thus, according to Sandel, the conception of the nature of persons required by a welfare liberal conception of justice is inadequate because it fails to take into account the fact that some of our wants, interests, and ends are at least in part constitutive of what we are essentially. Without these desires, interests, and ends, we would not be the same persons we presently happen to be.

Sandel contends that welfare liberals are led to rely on this inadequate conception of persons for reasons that are fundamental to the conception of justice they want to defend. Specifically, welfare liberals want to maintain the priority of justice and more generally the priority of the right over the good. For example, according to Rawls:

The principles of right and so of justice put limits on which satisfactions have value; they impose restrictions on what are reasonable conceptions of one's good. We can express this by saying that in justice as fairness the concept of right is prior to that of the good.[4]

To support these priorities, Sandel argues that welfare liberals endorse this inadequate conception of the nature of persons. For example, Rawls argues:

> It is not our aims that primarily reveal our nature but rather the principles that we would acknowledge to govern the background conditions under which these aims are to be found and the manner in which they are to be pursued. *For the self is prior to the ends which are affirmed by it;* even a dominant end must be chosen from among numerous possibilities. . . . We should therefore reverse the relation between the right and the good proposed by teleological doctrines and view the right as prior.[5]

What this passage shows, according to Sandel, is that welfare liberals like Rawls believe that the priority of justice and the priority of the right are grounded in the priority of the self to its ends.

At first glance, Sandel's case against welfare liberalism looks particularly strong. After all, Rawls actually does say that "the self is prior to the ends which are affirmed by it" and this claim seems to express just the inadequate conception of the nature of persons that Sandel contends underlies a Welfare Liberal Conception of Justice. Nor is Rawls's claim made specifically about persons in the original position. So Sandel cannot be dismissed for failing to distinguish between the characterization of persons in the original position and the characterization of persons in ordinary life. Nevertheless, Sandel's case against welfare liberalism presupposes that there is no other plausible interpretation that can be given to Rawls's claim than the metaphysical one that Sandel favors. And unfortunately for Sandel's argument, a more plausible interpretation of Rawls's claim does appear to be available. According to this interpretation, to say that persons are prior to their ends means simply that they are morally responsible for their ends, either because they can or could have changed those ends. Of course, the degree to which people can or could have changed their ends is a matter of considerable debate, but what is clear is that it is the degree to which people can or could have changed their ends that determines the degree to which they are morally responsible for those ends.

Nor does this interpretation deny that certain ends may in fact be constitutive of the persons we are, so that if those ends were to change we would become different persons. We can see, therefore, that nothing in this interpretation of Rawls's claim presupposes a self that is metaphysically prior to its ends. Rather, the picture we are given is of a self that is responsible for its ends insofar as its ends can or could have been revised. Such a self may well be constituted by at least some of its ends, but it is only responsible for those ends to the degree to which they can or could have been revised. So the sense in which a self is prior to its ends is simply moral; insofar as its ends can or could have been revised, a self may be called upon to change them or compensate others for their effects when they turn out to be morally objectionable. Clearly, this interpretation of Rawls's claim avoids any commitment to the inadequate conception of the nature of persons that Sandel contends underlies a welfare liberal conception of justice. Of course, this does not show that a communitarian conception of justice might not in the end be the most morally defensible. It only shows that this particular communitarian attack on a welfare liberal conception of justice is not successful.

Practical Applications

The application of the ideals of libertarianism, socialism, welfare liberalism, or communitarianism to a particular society obviously has basic and far-reaching effects. These ideals have implications for constitutional structure, the control of industry, taxing policy, social welfare programs, property law, and much more. The next two readings in this section are from important United States Supreme Court decisions to which our four political ideals can be usefully related.

The U.S. Supreme Court, of course, does not view itself as directly applying one or the other of these political ideals to the laws of the land. Rather the Court views itself as deciding whether particular laws accord with the provisions of the United States Constitution.

However, most people, including Supreme Court justices, do not clearly separate their views about what are the practical applications of the political ideal they take to be the most morally defensible from their views about what sort of laws accord with the U.S. Constitution. Hence, it is frequently possible to see how commitment to a political ideal is decisive in judicial decision making.

Beyond coming to appreciate how political ideals and their presumed applications function in judicial decision making, it is important that you examine U.S. Supreme Court decisions to determine to what degree the laws of your society accord with the political ideal you take to be the most morally defensible. For you to have good reasons to believe that you are a just and moral person, you need to assess to what degree the laws and institutions of your society are just—in this case, to what degree they accord with the requirements of distributive justice. Examining the two U.S. Supreme Court decisions included in this anthology should serve this purpose well.

In the first decision (*Wyman* v. *James*), the majority of the Court decided that the rights of welfare recipients are limited in various ways and in particular that recipients are not protected against mandatory visits by caseworkers. Such a decision would surely seem justified if one believed, as libertarians do, that the provision of welfare is, at best, only a requirement of charity. Welfare liberals, socialists, and communitarians, however, would have difficulty accepting this decision, as did the dissenting justices of the Court.

In the second decision (*Plyler* v. *Doe*), the majority of the Court determined that although public education is not a right, it still cannot be denied to the children of illegal aliens because of the pivotal role of education in sustaining our political and cultural heritage. This decision has some affinity with the way welfare liberals, socialists, and communitarians would understand the practical requirements of their ideals; libertarians would probably find themselves persuaded by the arguments of the dissenting justices.

It is important to notice that you can also work backward from your considered judgments about these Supreme Court cases to the political ideal you should favor. Frequently, only by considering the practical applications of alternative political ideals can we clarify our views about which ideal is the most morally defensible.

In the final reading in this section, Peter Marin (Selection 7) paints a vivid picture of the homeless in the United States and asks the relevant question, "What does a society owe its members in trouble, and how is that debt to be paid?" Surely, at least one of our four political ideals must have an adequate answer.

Notice, too, that any fully adequate solution to the problem of distributive justice within a society presupposes a solution to the other moral problems presented in this anthology. In particular, the problem of distant peoples and future generations, which is discussed in the following section, seems to be clearly connected with the problem of distributive justice. We cannot know for sure what resources particular persons within a society should receive unless we also know what obligations persons within that society have to distant peoples and future generations.

Notes

1. See, for example, my article, "Distributive Justice," *American Journal of Jurisprudence* (1977), pp. 55–79, and John C. Harsanyi, *Essays on Ethics, Social Behavior, and Scientific Explanation* (Boston: D. Reidel Publishing Co., 1976), pp. 37–85.

2. For an argument of this sort, see my article, "A Libertarian Justification for a Welfare State," *Social Theory and Practice* (1985), pp. 285–306.

3. Michael J. Sandel, *Liberalism and the Limits of Justice* (Cambridge: Cambridge University Press, 1982), p. 179.

4. John Rawls, *A Theory of Justice* (Cambridge: Harvard University Press, 1971), p. 31.

5. Ibid, p. 560.

1. The Libertarian Manifesto

John Hospers

John Hospers explores various ways of understanding the basic libertarian thesis that every person is the owner of his or her own life. According to Hospers, such ownership entails rights to life, liberty, and property. Since these rights are violated by an initial use of force, the proper role of government is said to be limited to the retaliatory use of force against those who have initiated its use. All other possible roles for government, such as protecting individuals against themselves or requiring people to help one another, are regarded as illegitimate by the libertarian.

The political philosophy that is called libertarianism (from the Latin *libertas,* liberty) is the doctrine that every person is the owner of his own life, and that no one is the owner of anyone else's life: and that consequently every human being has the right to act in accordance with his own choices, unless those actions infringe on the equal liberty of other human beings to act in accordance with their choices.

There are several other ways of stating the same libertarian thesis:

1. *No one is anyone else's master, and no one is anyone else's slave.* Since I am the one to decide how my life is to be conducted just as you decide about yours, I have no right (even if I had the power) to make you my slave and be your master, nor have you the right to become the master by enslaving me. Slavery is *forced* servitude, and since no one owns the life of anyone else, no one has the right to enslave another. Political theories past and present have traditionally been concerned with who should be the master (usually the king, the dictator, or government bureaucracy) and who should be the slaves, and what the extent of the slavery should be. Libertarianism holds that no one has the right to use force to enslave the life of another, or any portion or aspect of that life.

From "What Libertarianism Is," in *The Libertarian Alternative* edited by Tibor Machan (1974). Reprinted by permission of the author, the editor, and Nelson-Hall Inc.

2. *Other men's lives are not yours to dispose of.* I enjoy seeing operas; but operas are expensive to produce. Opera-lovers often say, "The state (or the city, etc.) should subsidize opera, so that we can all see it. Also it would be for people's betterment, cultural benefit, etc." But what they are advocating is nothing more or less than legalized plunder. They can't pay for the productions themselves, and yet they want to see opera, which involves a large number of people and their labor; so what they are saying in effect is, "Get the money through legalized force. Take a little bit more out of every worker's paycheck every week to pay for the operas we want to see." But I have no right to take by force from the workers' pockets to pay for what I want.

Perhaps it would be better if he *did* go to see opera—then I should try to convince him to go voluntarily. But to take the money from him forcibly, because in my opinion it would be good for *him,* is still seizure of his earnings, which is plunder.

Besides, if I have the right to force him to help pay for my pet projects, hasn't he equally the right to force me to help pay for his? Perhaps he in turn wants the government to subsidize rock-and-roll, or his new car, or a house in the country? If I have the right to milk him, why hasn't he the right to milk me? If I can be a moral cannibal, why can't he too?

We should beware of the inventors of utopias. They would remake the world according to their vision—with the lives and fruits of the labor of *other* human beings. Is it someone's utopian vision that others should build pyramids to beautify the landscape? Very well, then other men should provide the labor; and if he is in a position of political power, and he can't get men to do it voluntarily, then he must *compel* them to "cooperate"—i.e. he must enslave them.

A hundred men might gain great pleasure from beating up or killing just one insignificant human being; but other men's lives are not theirs to dispose of. "In order to achieve the worthy goals of the next five-year-plan, we must forcibly collectivize the peasants . . ."; but other men's lives are not theirs to dispose of. Do you want to occupy, rent-free, the mansion that another man has worked for twenty years to buy? But other men's lives are not yours to dispose of. Do you want operas so badly that everyone is forced to work harder to pay for their subsidization through taxes? But other men's lives are not yours to dispose of. Do you want to have free medical care at the expense of other people, whether they wish to provide it or not? But this would require them to work longer for you whether they want to or not, and other men's lives are not yours to dispose of. . . .

3. *No human being should be a nonvoluntary mortgage on the life of another.* I cannot claim your life, your work, or the products of your effort as mine. The fruit of one man's labor should not be fair game for every freeloader who comes along and demands it as his own. The orchard that has been carefully grown, nurtured, and harvested by its owner should not be ripe for the plucking for any bypasser who has a yen for the ripe fruit. The wealth that some men have produced should not be fair game for looting by government, to be used for whatever purposes its representatives determine, no matter what their motives in so doing may be. The theft of your money by a robber is not justified by the fact that he used it to help his injured mother.

It will already be evident that libertarian doctrine is embedded in a view of the rights of man. Each human being has the right to live his life as he chooses, compatibly with the equal right of all other human beings to live their lives as they choose.

All man's rights are implicit in the above statement. Each man has the right to life: any attempt by others to take it away from him, or even to injure him, violates this right, through the use of coercion against him. Each man has the right to liberty: to conduct his life in accordance with the alternatives open to him without coercive action by others. And every man has the right to property: to work to sustain his life (and the lives of whichever others he chooses to sustain, such as his family) and to retain the fruits of his labor.

People often defend the rights of life and liberty but denigrate property rights, and yet the right to property is as basic as the other two: indeed, without property rights no other rights are possible. Depriving you of property is depriving you of the means by which you live. . . .

I have no right to decide how *you* should spend your time or your money. I can make that decision for myself, but not for you, my neighbor. I may deplore your choice of lifestyle, and I may talk with you about it provided you are willing to listen to me. But I have no right to use force to change it. Nor have I the right to decide how you should spend the money you have earned. I may appeal to you to give it to the Red Cross, and you may prefer to go to prize-fights. But that is your decision, and however much I may chafe about it I do not have the right to interfere forcibly with it, for example by robbing you in order to use the money in accordance with *my* choices. (If I have the right to rob you, have you also the right to rob me?)

When I claim a right, I carve out a niche, as it were, in my life, saying in effect, "This activity I must be able to perform without interference from others. For you and everyone else, this is off limits." And so I put up a "no trespassing" sign, which marks off the area of my right. Each individual's right is his "no trespassing" sign in relation to me and others. I may not encroach upon his domain any more than he upon mine, without my consent. Every right entails a duty, true—but the duty is only that of *forbearance*—that is, of *refraining* from violating the other person's right. If you have a right to life, I have no right to take your life; if you have a right to the products of your labor (property), I have no right to take it from you without your consent. The nonviolation of these rights will not guarantee you protection against natural catastrophes such as floods and earthquakes, but it will protect you against the aggressive activities *of other men.* And rights, after all, have to do with one's relations to other human beings, not with one's relations to physical nature.

Nor were these rights created by government; governments—some governments, obviously not all—*recognize* and *protect* the rights that individuals already have. Governments regularly forbid homicide and theft; and, at a more advanced stage, protect individuals against such things as libel and breach of contract. . . .

The *right to property* is the most misunderstood and unappreciated of human rights, and it is one most constantly violated by governments. "Property" of course does not mean only real estate; it includes anything you can call your own—your clothing, your car, your jewelry, your books and papers.

The right of property is not the right to just *take* it from others, for this would interfere with *their* property rights. It is rather the right to work for it, to obtain non-coercively, the money or services which you can present in voluntary exchange.

The right to property is consistently underplayed by intellectuals today, sometimes even frowned upon, as if we should feel guilty for upholding such a right in view of all the poverty in the world. But the right to property is absolutely basic. It is your hedge against the future. It is your assurance that what you have worked to earn will still be there and be yours, when you wish or need to use it, especially when you are too old to work any longer.

Government has always been the chief enemy of the right to property. The officials of government, wishing to increase their power, and finding an increase of wealth an effective way to bring this about seize some or all of what a person has earned—and since government has a monopoly of physical force within the geographical area of the nation, it has the power (but not the right) to do this. When this

happens, of course, every citizen of that country is insecure: he knows that no matter how hard he works the government can swoop down on him at any time and confiscate his earnings and possessions. A person sees his life savings wiped out in a moment when the tax-collectors descend to deprive him of the fruits of his work; or, an industry which has been fifty years in the making and cost millions of dollars and millions of hours of time and planning, is nationalized overnight. Or the government, via inflation, cheapens the currency, so that hard-won dollars aren't worth anything any more. The effect of such actions, of course, is that people lose hope and incentive: if no matter how hard they work the government agents can take it all away, why bother to work at all, for more than today's needs? Depriving people of property is *depriving them of the means by which they live*—the freedom of the individual citizen to do what he wishes with his own life and to plan for the future. Indeed only if property rights are respected is there any point to planning for the future and working to achieve one's goals. *Property rights are what makes long-range planning possible*—the kind of planning which is a distinctively human endeavor, as opposed to the day-by-day activity of the lion who hunts, who depends on the supply of game tomorrow but has no real insurance against starvation in a day or a week. Without the right to property, the right to life itself amounts to little: how can you sustain your life if you cannot plan ahead? and how can you plan ahead if the fruits of your labor can at any moment be confiscated by government? . . .

Indeed, the right to property may well be considered second only to the right to life. Even the freedom of speech is limited by considerations of property. If a person visiting in your home behaves in a way undesired by you, you have every right to evict him; he can scream or agitate elsewhere if he wishes, but not in your home without your consent. Does a person have a right to shout obscenities in a cathedral? No, for the owners of the cathedral (presumably the Church) have not allowed others on their property for that purpose; one may go there to worship or to visit, but not just for any purpose one wishes. Their property right is prior to your or my wish to scream or expectorate or write graffiti on their building. Or, to take the stock example, does a person have a right to shout "Fire!" falsely in a crowded theater? No, for the theater owner has permitted others to enter and use his property only for a specific purpose, that of seeing a film or watching a stage show. If a person heckles or otherwise disturbs other members of the audience, he can be thrown out. (In fact, he can be removed for any reason the owner chooses, provided his admission money is returned.) And if he shouts "Fire!" when there is no fire, he may be endangering other lives by causing a panic or a stampede. The right to free speech doesn't give one the right to say anything anywhere; it is circumscribed by property rights.

Again, some people seem to assume that the right to free speech (including written speech) means that they can go to a newspaper publisher and demand that he print in his newspaper some propaganda or policy statement for their political party (or other group). But of course they have no right to the use of his newspaper. Ownership of the newspaper is the product of his labor, and he has a right to put into his newspaper whatever he wants, for whatever reason. If he excludes material which many readers would like to have in, perhaps they can find it in another newspaper or persuade him to print it himself (if there are enough of them, they will usually do just that). Perhaps they can even cause his newspaper to fail. But as long as he owns it, he has the right to put in it what he wishes; what would a property right be if he could not do this? They have no right to place their material in his newspaper without his consent—not for free, nor even for a fee. Perhaps other newspapers will include it, or perhaps they can start their own newspaper (in which case they have a right to put in it what they like). If not, an option open to them would be to mimeograph and distribute some handbills.

In exactly the same way, no one has a right to "free television time" unless the owner of the television station consents to give it; it is his station, he has the property rights over it, and it is for him to decide how to dispose of his time. He may not decide wisely, but it is his right to decide as he wishes. If he makes enough unwise decisions, and courts enough

unpopularity with the viewing public or the sponsors, he may have to go out of business; but as he is free to make his own decisions, so is he free to face their consequences. (If the government owns the television station, then government officials will make the decisions, and there is no guarantee of *their* superior wisdom. The difference is that when "the government" owns the station, you are forced to help pay for its upkeep through your taxes, whether the bureaucrat in charge decides to give you television time or not.)

"But why have *individual* property rights? Why not have lands and houses owned by everybody together?" Yes, this involves no violation of individual rights, as long as everybody consents to this arrangement and no one is forced to join it. The parties to it may enjoy the communal living enough (at least for a time) to overcome certain inevitable problems: that some will work and some not, that some will achieve more in an hour than others can do in a day, and still they will all get the same income. The few who do the most will in the end consider themselves "workhorses" who do the work of two or three or twelve, while the others will be "freeloaders" on the efforts of these few. But as long as they can get out of the arrangement if they no longer like it, no violation of rights is involved. They got in voluntarily, and they can get out voluntarily; no one has used force.

"But why not say that everybody owns everything? That we *all* own everything there is?"

To some this may have a pleasant ring—but let us try to analyze what it means. If everybody owns everything, then everyone has an equal right to go everywhere, do what he pleases, take what he likes, destroy if he wishes, grow crops or burn them, trample them under, and so on. Consider what it would be like in practice. Suppose you have saved money to buy a house for yourself and your family. Now suppose that the principle, "everybody owns everything," becomes adopted. Well then, why shouldn't every itinerant hippie just come in and take over, sleeping in your beds and eating in your kitchen and not bothering to replace the food supply or clean up the mess? After all, it belongs to all of us, doesn't it? So we have just as much right to it as you, the buyer, have. What happens if we *all* want to sleep in the bedroom and there's not room for all of us? Is it the strongest who wins?

What would be the result? Since no one would be responsible for anything, the property would soon be destroyed, the food used up, the facilities nonfunctional. Beginning as a house that *one* family could use, it would end up as a house that *no one* could use. And if the principle continued to be adopted, no one would build houses any more—or anything else. What for? They would only be occupied and used by others, without remuneration.

Suppose two men are cast ashore on an island, and they agree that each will cultivate half of it. The first man is industrious and grows crops and builds a shelter, making the most of the situation with which he is confronted. The second man, perhaps thinking that the warm days will last forever, lies in the sun, picks coconuts while they last, and does a minimum of work to sustain himself. At the time of harvest, the second man has nothing to harvest, nor does he assist the first man in his labors. But later when there is a dearth of food on the island, the second man comes to the first man and demands half of the harvest as his right. But of course he has no right to the product of the first man's labors. The first man may freely choose to give part of his harvest to the second out of charity rather than see him starve; but that is just what it is—charity, not the second man's right.

How can any of man's rights be violated? Ultimately, only by the use of force. I can make suggestions to you, I can reason with you, entreat you (if you are willing to listen), but I cannot *force* you without violating your rights; only by forcing you do I cut the cord between your free decisions and your actions. Voluntary relations between individuals involve no deprivation of rights, but murder, assault, and rape do, because in doing these things I make you the unwilling victim of my actions. A man's beating his wife involves no violation of rights if she *wanted* to be beaten. *Force is behavior that requires the unwilling involvement of other persons.*

Thus the use of force need not involve the use of physical violence. If I trespass on your property or dump garbage on it, I am violating your property rights, as indeed I am when I steal your watch; although this is not force in the sense of violence, it *is* a case of your being an unwilling victim of my action. Similarly, if you shout at me so that I cannot be heard when I try to speak, or blow a siren in my ear, or start a factory next door which pollutes my land, you are again violating my rights (to free speech, to property); I am, again, an unwilling victim of your actions. Similarly, if you steal a manuscript of mine and publish it as your own, you are confiscating a piece of my property and thus violating my right to keep what is the product of my labor. Of course, if I give you the manuscript with permission to sign your name to it and keep the proceeds, no violation of rights is involved—any more than if I give you permission to dump garbage on my yard.

According to libertarianism, the role of government should be limited to the retaliatory use of force against those who have initiated its use. It should not enter into any other areas, such as religion, social organization, and economics.

Government

Government is the most dangerous institution known to man. Throughout history it has violated the rights of men more than any individual or group of individuals could do: it has killed people, enslaved them, sent them to forced labor and concentration camps, and regularly robbed and pillaged them of the fruits of their expended labor. Unlike individual criminals, government has the power to arrest and try; unlike individual criminals, it can surround and encompass a person totally, dominating every aspect of one's life, so that one has no recourse from it but to leave the country (and in totalitarian nations even that is prohibited). Government throughout history has a much sorrier record than any individual, even that of a ruthless mass murderer. The signs we see on bumper stickers are chillingly accurate: "Beware: the Government Is Armed and Dangerous."

The only proper role of government, according to libertarians, is that of the protector of the citizen against aggression by other individuals. The government, of course, should never initiate aggression; its proper role is as the embodiment of the *retaliatory* use of force against anyone who initiates its use.

If each individual had constantly to defend himself against possible aggressors, he would have to spend a considerable portion of his life in target practice, karate exercises, and other means of self-defenses, and even so he would probably be helpless against groups of individuals who might try to kill, maim, or rob him. He would have little time for cultivating those qualities which are essential to civilized life, nor would improvements in science, medicine, and the arts be likely to occur. The function of government is to take this responsibility off his shoulders: the government undertakes to defend him against aggressors and to punish them if they attack him. When the government is effective in doing this, it enables the citizen to go about his business unmolested and without constant fear for his life. To do this, of course, government must have physical power—the police, to protect the citizen from aggression within its borders, and the armed forces, to protect him from aggressors outside. Beyond that, the government should not intrude upon his life, either to run his business, or adjust his daily activities, or prescribe his personal moral code.

Government, then, undertakes to be the individual's protector; but historically governments have gone far beyond this function. Since they already have the physical power, they have not hesitated to use it for purposes far beyond that which was entrusted to them in the first place. Undertaking initially to protect its citizens against aggression, it has often itself become an aggressor—a far greater aggressor, indeed, than the criminals against whom it was supposed to protect its citizens. Governments have done what no private citizen can do: arrest and imprison individuals without a trial and send them to slave labor camps. Government must have power in order to be effective—and yet the very means by which alone it can be effective make it vulnerable to the abuse of power, leading to managing the lives of individuals and even inflicting terror upon them.

What then should be the function of government? In a word, the *protection of human rights.*

1. *The right to life:* libertarians support all such legislation as will protect human beings against the use of force by others, for example, laws against killing, attempting killing, maiming, beating, and all kinds of physical violence.
2. *The right to liberty:* there should be no laws compromising in any way freedom of speech, of the press, and peaceable assembly. There should be no censorship of ideas, books, films, or of anything else by government.
3. *The right to property:* libertarians support legislation that protects the property rights of individuals against confiscation, nationalization, eminent domain, robbery, trespass, fraud and misrepresentation, patent and copyright, libel and slander.

Someone has violently assaulted you. Should he be legally liable? Of course. He has violated one of your rights. He has knowingly injured you and since he has initiated aggression against you he should be made to expiate.

Someone has negligently left his bicycle on the sidewalk where you trip over it in the dark and injure yourself. He didn't do it intentionally; he didn't mean you any harm. Should he be legally liable? Of course; he has, however unwittingly, injured you, and since the injury is caused by him and you are the victim, he should pay.

Someone across the street is unemployed. Should you be taxed extra to pay for his expenses? Not at all. You have not injured him, you are not responsible for the fact that he is unemployed (unless you are a senator or bureaucrat who agitated for further curtailing of business, which legislation passed, with the result that your neighbor was laid off by the curtailed business). You may voluntarily wish to help him out, or better still, try to get him a job to put him on his feet again; but since you have initiated no aggressive act against him, and neither purposely nor accidentally injured him in any way, you should not be legally penalized for the fact of his unemployment.

(Actually, it is just such penalties that increase unemployment.)

One man, A, works hard for years and finally earns a high salary as a professional man. A second man, B, prefers not to work at all, and to spend wastefully what money he has (through inheritance), so that after a year or two he has nothing left. At the end of this time he has a long siege of illness and lots of medical bills to pay. He demands that the bills be paid by the government—that is, by the taxpayers of the land, including Mr. A.

But of course B has no such right. He chose to lead his life in a certain way—that was his voluntary decision. One consequence of that choice is that he must depend on charity in case of later need. Mr. A chose not to live that way. (And if everyone lived like Mr. B, on whom would he depend in case of later need?) Each has a right to live in the way he pleases, but each must live with the consequences of his own decision (which, as always, fall primarily on himself). He cannot, in time of need, claim A's beneficence as his right.

If a house-guest of yours starts to carve his initials in your walls and break up your furniture, you have a right to evict him, and call the police if he makes trouble. If someone starts to destroy the machinery in a factory, the factory-owner is also entitled to evict him and call the police. In both cases, persons other than the owner are permitted on the property only under certain conditions, at the pleasure of the owner. If those conditions are violated, the owner is entitled to use force to set things straight. The case is exactly the same on a college or university campus: if a campus demonstrator starts breaking windows, occupying the president's office, and setting fire to a dean, the college authorities are certainly within their rights to evict him forcibly; one is permitted on the college grounds only under specific conditions, set by the administration: study, peaceful student activity, even political activity if those in charge choose to permit it. If they do not choose to permit peaceful political activity on campus, they may be unwise, since a campus is after all a place where all sides of every issue should get discussed, and the college that doesn't permit this may soon lose its reputation and its students. All the same, the college official who does not permit it is quite within his rights; the students do not own the campus, nor do the hired troublemakers imported from elsewhere. In the case of a privately owned college, the owners, or whoever they have delegated to administer it, have the right to make the decisions as to who shall be permitted on the campus and under what conditions. In the case of a state university or college, the ownership problem is more complex: one could say that the "government" owns the campus or that "the people" do since they are the taxpayers who support it; but in either case, the university administration has the delegated task of keeping order, and until they are removed by the state administration or the taxpayers, it is theirs to decide who shall be permitted on campus, and what non-academic activities will be permitted to their students on the premises.

Property rights can be violated by physical trespass, of course, or by anyone entering on your property for any reason without your consent. (If you *do* consent to having your neighbor dump garbage on your yard, there is no violation of your rights.) But the physical trespass of a person is only a special case of violation of property rights. Property rights can be violated by sound-waves, in the form of a loud noise, or the sounds of your neighbor's hi-fi set while you are trying to sleep. Such violations of property rights are of course the subject of action in the courts.

But there is another violation of property rights that has not thus far been honored by the courts; this has to do with the effects of *pollution* of the atmosphere.

From the beginnings of modern air pollution, the courts made a conscious decision not to protect, for example, the orchards of farmers from the smoke of nearby factories or locomotives. They said, in effect, to the farmers: yes, your private property is being invaded by this smoke, but we hold that "public policy" is more important than private property, and public policy holds factories and locomotives to be good things. These goods were allowed to override the defense of property rights—with our consequent headlong rush into pollution disaster. The remedy is both "radical" and crystal clear, and it has nothing to do with multibillion dollar palliative programs at the expense of the taxpayers which do not even meet the real issue. The remedy is simply to enjoin anyone from injecting pollutants into the air, and thereby invading the rights of persons and property. Period. The argument that such an injunction prohibition would add to the costs of industrial production is as reprehensible as the pre-Civil War argument that the abolition of slavery would add to the costs of growing cotton, and therefore should not take place. For this means that the polluters are able to impose the high costs of pollution upon those whose property rights they are allowed to invade with impunity.[1]

What about automobiles, the chief polluters of the air? One can hardly sue every automobile owner. But one can sue the manufacturers of automobiles who do not install anti-smog devices on the cars which they distribute—and later (though this is more difficult), owners of individual automobiles if they discard the equipment or do not keep it functional.

The violation of rights does not apply only to air-pollution. If someone with a factory upstream on a river pollutes the river, anyone living downstream from him, finding his water polluted, should be able to sue the owner of the factory. In this way the price of adding the anti-pollutant devices will be the owner's responsibility, and will probably be added to the cost of the products which the factory produces and thus spread around among all consumers, rather than the entire cost being borne by the users of the river in the form of polluted water, with the consequent impossibility of fishing, swimming, and so on. In each case, pollution would be stopped at the source rather than having its ill effects spread around to numerous members of the population.

What about property which you do not work to earn, but which you *inherit* from someone else? Do you have a right to that? You have no right to it until someone decides to give it to you. Consider the man who willed it to you; it was his, he had the right to use and

dispose of it as *he* saw fit; and if he decided to give it to you, this is a windfall for you, but it was only the exercise of *his* right. Had the property been seized by the government at the man's death, or distributed among numerous other people designated by the government, it *would* have been a violation of his rights: for he, who worked to earn and sustain it, would not have been able to dispose of it according to his own judgment. If he doesn't have the right to determine who shall have it, who does?

What about the property status of your intellectual activity, such as inventions you may devise and books you write? These, of course, are your property also; they are the products of your mind; you worked at them, you created them. Prior to that, they did not exist. If you worked five years to write a book, and someone stole it and published it as his own, receiving royalties from its sales, he would have stolen your property just as surely as if he had robbed your home. The same is true if someone used and sold without your permission an invention which was the product of your labor and ingenuity.

The role of government with respect to this issue, at least most governments of the Western world, is a proper one: government protects the products of your labor from the moment they materialize. Copyright law protects your writings from piracy. In the United States, one's writings are protected for a period of twenty-seven years, and another twenty-seven if one applies for renewal of the copyright. In most other countries, they are protected for a period of fifty years after the author's death, permitting both himself and his surviving heirs to reap the fruits of his labor. After that they enter the "public domain"— that is, anyone may reprint them without your or your heirs' permission. Patent law protects your inventions for a limited period, which varies according to the type of invention. In no case are you forced to avail yourself of this protection; you need not apply for patent or copyright coverage if you do not wish to do so. But the protection of your intellectual property is there, in case you wish to use it.

What about the property status of the airwaves? Here the government's position is far more questionable. The government now claims ownership of the airwaves, leasing them to individuals and corporations. The government renews leases or refuses them depending on whether the programs satisfy authorities in the Federal Communications Commission. The official position is that "we all own the airwaves": but since only one party can broadcast on a certain frequency at a certain time without causing chaos, it is simply a fact of reality that "everyone" cannot use it. In fact the government decides who shall use the airwaves and one courts its displeasure only at the price of a revoked license. One can write without government approval, but one cannot use the airwaves without the approval of government.

What policy should have been observed with regard to the airwaves? Much the same as the policy that was followed in the case of the Homestead Act, when the lands of the American West were opening up for settlement. There was a policy of "first come, first served," with the government parcelling out a certain acreage for each individual who wanted to claim the land as his own. There was no charge for the land, but if a man had not used it and built a dwelling during the first two-year period, it was assumed that he was not homesteading and the land was given to the next man in line. The airwaves too could have been given out on a "first come, first served" basis. The first man who used a given frequency would be its owner, and the government would protect him in the use of it against trespassers. If others wanted to use the same frequency, they would have to buy it from the first man, if he was willing to sell, or try to buy another, just as one now does with the land.

Laws may be classified into three types: (1) laws protecting individuals against themselves, such as laws against fornication and other sexual behavior, alcohol, and drugs; (2) laws protecting individuals against aggressions by other individuals, such as laws against murder, robbery, and fraud; (3) laws requiring people to help one another; for example, all laws which rob Peter to pay Paul, such as welfare.

Libertarians reject the first class of laws totally. Behavior which harms no one else is strictly the individual's own affair. Thus, there should be no laws against becoming intoxicated, since whether or not to become intoxicated is the individual's own decision: but there should be laws against driving while intoxicated, since the drunken driver is a threat to every other motorist on the highway (drunken driving falls into type 2). Similarly, there should be no laws against drugs (except the prohibition of sale of drugs to minors) as long as the taking of these drugs poses no threat to anyone else. Drug addiction is a psychological problem to which no present solution exists. Most of the social harm caused by addicts, other than to themselves, is the result of thefts which they perform in order to continue their habit—and then the *legal* crime is the theft, not the addiction. The actual cost of heroin is about ten cents a shot; if it were legalized, the enormous traffic in illegal sale and purchase of it would stop, as well as the accompanying proselytization to get new addicts (to make more money for the pusher) and the thefts performed by addicts who often require eighty dollars a day just to keep up the habit. Addiction would not stop, but the crimes would: it is estimated that 75 percent of the burglaries in New York City today are performed by addicts, and all these crimes could be wiped out at one stroke through the legalization of drugs. (Only when the taking of drugs could be shown to constitute a threat to *others*, should it be prohibited by law. It is only laws protecting people against *themselves* that libertarians oppose.)

Laws should be limited to the second class only: aggression by individuals against other individuals. These are laws whose function is to protect human beings against encroachment by others; and this, as we have seen, is (according to libertarianism) the sole function of government.

Libertarians also reject the third class of laws totally: no one should be forced by law to help others, not even to tell them the time of day if requested, and certainly not to give them a portion of one's weekly paycheck. Governments, in the guise of humanitarianism, have given to some by taking from others (charging a "handling fee" in the process, which, because of the government's waste and inefficiency, sometimes is several hundred percent). And in so doing they have decreased incentive, violated the rights of individuals, and lowered the standard of living of almost everyone.

All such laws constitute what libertarians call *moral cannibalism*. A cannibal in the physical sense is a person who lives off the flesh of other human beings. A *moral* cannibal is one who believes he has a right to live off the "spirit" of other human beings—who believes that he has a moral claim on the productive capacity, time, and effort expended by others.

It has become fashionable to claim virtually everything that one needs or desires as one's *right*. Thus, many people claim that they have a right to a job, the right to free medical care, to free food and clothing, to a decent home, and so on. Now if one asks, apart from any specific context, whether it would be desirable if everyone had these things, one might well say yes. But there is a gimmick attached to each of them: *At whose expense?* Jobs, medical care, education, and so on, don't grow on trees. These are goods and services *produced only by men*. Who then is to provide them, and under what conditions?

If you have a right to a job, who is to supply it? Must an employer supply it even if he doesn't want to hire you? What if you are unemployable, or incurably lazy? (If you say "the government must supply it," does that mean that a job must be created for you which no employer needs done, and that you must be kept in it regardless of how much or little you work?) If the employer is forced to supply it at his expense even if he doesn't need you, then isn't *he* being enslaved to that extent? What ever happened to *his* right to conduct his life and his affairs in accordance with his choices?

If you have a right to free medical care, then, since medical care doesn't exist in nature as wild apples do, some people will have to supply it to you for free: that is, they will have to spend their time and money and energy taking care of you whether they want to or not. What ever happened to *their* right to conduct their lives as they see fit? Or do you have a right to violate theirs? Can there be a right to violate rights?

All those who demand this or that as a "free service" are consciously or unconsciously evading the fact that there is in reality no such thing as free services. All man-made goods and services are the result of human expenditure of time and effort. There is no such thing as "something for nothing" in this world.

If you demand something free, you are demanding that other men give their time and effort to you without compensation. If they voluntarily choose to do this, there is no problem; but if you demand that they be *forced* to do it, you are interfering with their right not to do it if they so choose. "Swimming in this pool ought to be free!" says the indignant passerby. What he means is that others should build a pool, others should provide the material, and still others should run it and keep it in functioning order, so that *he* can use it without fee. But what right has he to the expenditure of *their* time and effort? To expect something "for free" is to expect it *to be paid for by others* whether they choose to or not.

Many questions, particularly about economic matters, will be generated by the libertarian account of human rights and the role of government. Should government have a role in assisting the needy, in providing social security, in legislating minimum wages, in fixing prices and putting a ceiling on rents, in curbing monopolies, in erecting tariffs, in guaranteeing jobs, in managing the money supply? To these and all similar questions the libertarian answers with an unequivocal no.

"But then you'd let people go hungry!" comes the rejoinder. This, the libertarian insists, is precisely what would not happen; with the restrictions removed, the economy would flourish as never before. With the controls taken off business, existing enterprises would expand and new ones would spring into existence satisfying more and more consumer needs; millions more people would be gainfully employed instead of subsisting on welfare, and all kinds of research and production, released from the stranglehold of government, would proliferate, fulfilling man's needs and desires as never before. It has always been so whenever government has permitted men to be free traders on a free market. But *why* this is so, and how the free market is the best solution to all problems relating to the material aspect of man's life, is another and far longer story.

Note

1. Murray Rothbard, "The Great Ecology Issue," *The Individualist*, 2, no. 2 (Feb. 1970), p. 5.

2. Radical Egalitarianism

Kai Nielson

The fundamental requirement of radical egalitarianism is equality of basic condition for everyone. Kai Nielson justifies this requirement on the grounds that it produces the conditions for the most extensive satisfaction of everyone's needs. He also contends that radical egalitarianism is required by the moral point of view and would lead to two specific principles of justice. Finally, Nielson defends radical egalitarianism on the grounds that it is required by liberty or at least a fair distribution of liberty.

I

I have talked of equality as a right and of equality as a goal. And I have taken, as the principal thing, to be able to state what goal we are seeking when we say equality is a goal. When we are in a position actually to achieve that goal, then that same equality becomes a right. The goal we are seeking is an equality of basic condition for everyone. Let me say a bit what this is: everyone, as far as possible, should have equal life prospects, short of genetic engineering and the like and the rooting out any form of the family and the undermining of our basic freedoms. There should, where this is possible, be an equality of access to equal resources over each person's life as a whole, though this should be qualified by people's varying needs. Where psychiatrists are in short supply only people who are in need of psychiatric help should have equal access to such help. This equal access to resources should be such that it stands as a barrier to their being the sort of differences between people that allow some to be in a position to control and to exploit others; such equal access to resources should also stand as a barrier to one adult person having power over other adult persons that does not rest on the revokable consent on the part of the persons over whom he comes to have power. Where, be-

cause of some remaining scarcity in a society of considerable productive abundance, we cannot reasonably distribute resources equally, we should first, where considerations of desert are not at issue, distribute according to stringency of need, second according to the strength of unmanipulated preferences and third, and finally, by lottery. We should, in trying to attain equality of condition, aim at a condition of autonomy (the fuller and the more rational the better) for everyone and at a condition where everyone alike, to the fullest extent possible, has his or her needs and wants satisfied. The limitations on the satisfaction of people's wants should be only where that satisfaction is incompatible with everyone getting the same treatment. Where we have conflicting wants, such as where two persons want to marry the same person, the fair thing to do will vary with the circumstances. In the marriage case, freedom of choice is obviously the fair thing. But generally, what should be aimed at is having everyone have their wants satisfied as far as possible. To achieve equality of condition would be, as well, to achieve a condition where the necessary burdens of the society are equally shared, where to do so is reasonable, and where each person has an equal voice in deciding what these burdens shall be. Moreover, everyone, as much as possible, should be in a position—and should be equally in that position—to control his own life. The goals of egalitarianism are to achieve such equalities.

Minimally, classlessness is something we should all aim at if we are egalitarians. It is necessary for the stable achievement of

Abridged from *Equality and Liberty* (1985), pp. 283–292, 302–306, 309. Reprinted by permission of Rowman & Allanheld, Publishers. Notes renumbered.

equalities of the type discussed in the previous paragraph. Beyond that, we should also aim at a statusless society, though not at an undifferentiated society or a society which does not recognize merit. . . . It is only in such a classless, statusless society that the ideals of equality (the conception of equality as a very general goal to be achieved) can be realized. In aiming for a statusless society, we are aiming for a society which, while remaining a society of material abundance, is a society in which there are to be no extensive differences in life prospects between people because some have far greater income, power, authority or prestige than others. This is the *via negativia* of the egalitarian way. The *via postiva* is to produce social conditions, where there is generally material abundance, where well-being and satisfaction are not only maximized (the utilitarian thing) but, as well, a society where this condition, as far as it is achievable, is sought equally for all (the egalitarian thing). This is the underlying conception of the egalitarian commitment to equality of condition.

II

Robert Nozick asks "How do we decide how much equality is enough?"[1] In the preceding section we gestured in the direction of an answer. I should now like to be somewhat more explicit. Too much equality, as we have been at pains to point out, would be to treat everyone identically, completely ignoring their differing needs. Various forms of "barracks equality" approximating that would also be too much. Too little equality would be to limit equality of condition, as did the old egalitarianism, to achieving equal legal and political rights, equal civil liberties, to equality of opportunity and to a redistribution of gross disparities in wealth sufficient to keep social peace, the rationale for the latter being that such gross inequalities if allowed to stand would threaten social stability. This Hobbesist stance indicates that the old egalitarianism proceeds in a very pragmatic manner. Against the old egalitarianism I would argue that we must at least aim at an equality of whole life prospects, where that is

not read simply as the right to compete for scarce positions of advantage, but where there is to be brought into being the kind of equality of condition that would provide everyone equally, as far as possible, with the resources and the social conditions to satisfy their needs as fully as possible compatible with everyone else doing likewise. (Note that between people these needs will be partly the same but will still often be importantly different as well.) Ideally, as a kind of ideal limit for a society of wondrous abundance, a radical egalitarianism would go beyond that to a similar thing for wants. We should, that is, provide all people equally, as far as possible, with the resources and social conditions to satisfy their wants, as fully as possible compatible with everyone else doing likewise. (I recognize that there is a slide between wants and needs. As the wealth of a society increases and its structure changes, things that started out as wants tend to become needs, e.g., someone in the Falkland Islands might merely reasonably want an auto while someone in Los Angeles might not only want it but need it as well. But this does not collapse the distinction between wants and needs. There are things in any society people need, if they are to survive at all in anything like a commodious condition, whether they want them or not, e.g., they need food, shelter, security, companionship and the like. An egalitarian starts with basic needs, or at least with what are taken in the cultural environment in which a given person lives to be basic needs, and moves out to other needs and finally to wants as the productive power of the society increases.)

I qualified my above formulations with "as far as possible" and with "as fully as possible compatible with everyone else doing likewise." These are essential qualifications. Where, as in societies that we know, there are scarcities, even rather minimal scarcities, not everyone can have the resources or at least all the resources necessary to have their needs satisfied. Here we must first ensure that, again as far as possible, their basic needs are all satisfied and then we move on to other needs and finally to wants. But sometimes, to understate it, even in very affluent societies, everyone's needs cannot be met, or at least they cannot be equally met. In such circumstances we have to make some hard choices. I am thinking of a situation where there are not enough dialysis machines to go around so that everyone who needs one can have one. What then should we do? The thing to aim at, to try as far as possible to approximate, if only as a heuristic ideal, is the full and equal meeting of needs and wants of everyone. It is when we have that much equality that we have enough equality. But, of course, "ought implies can," and where we can't achieve it we can't achieve it. But where we reasonably can, we ought to do it. It is something that fairness requires.

The "reasonably can" is also an essential modification: we need situations of sufficient abundance so that we do not, in going for such an equality of condition, simply spread the misery around or spread very Spartan conditions around. Before we can rightly aim for the equality of condition I mentioned, we must first have the productive capacity and resource conditions to support the institutional means that would make possible the equal satisfaction of basic needs and the equal satisfaction of other needs and wants as well.

Such achievements will often not be possible; perhaps they will never be fully possible, for, no doubt, the physically handicapped will always be with us. Consider, for example, situations where our scarcities are such that we cannot, without causing considerable misery, create the institutions and mechanisms that would work to satisfy all needs, even all basic needs. Suppose we have the technology in place to develop all sorts of complicated life-sustaining machines all of which would predictably provide people with a quality of life that they, viewing the matter clearly, would rationally choose if they were simply choosing for themselves. But suppose, if we put such technologies in place, we will then not have the wherewithal to provide basic health care in outlying regions in the country or adequate educational services in such places. We should not, under those circumstances, put those technologies in place. But we should also recognize that where it becomes possible to put these technologies in place without sacrificing other more pressing needs, we should do so. The underlying egalitarian rationale is evident enough: produce the conditions for the most extensive satisfaction of needs for everyone.

Where A's need and B's need are equally important (equally stringent) but cannot both be satisfied, satisfy A's need rather than B's if the satisfaction of A's need would be more fecund for the satisfaction of the needs of others than B's, or less undermining of the satisfaction of the needs of others than B's. (I do not mean to say that that is our only criterion of choice but it is the criterion most relevant for us here.) We should seek the satisfaction of the greatest compossible set of needs where the conditions for compossibility are (a) that everyone's needs be considered, (b) that everyone's needs be *equally* considered and where two sets of needs cannot both be satisfied, the more stringent set of needs shall first be satisfied. (Do not say we have no working criteria for what they are. If you need food to keep you from starvation or debilitating malnutrition and I need a vacation to relax after a spate of hard work, your need is plainly more stringent than mine. There would, of course, be all sorts of disputable cases, but there are also a host of perfectly determinate cases indicating that we have working criteria.) The underlying rationale is to seek compossible sets of needs so that we approach as far as possible as great a satisfaction of needs as possible for everyone.

This might, it could be said, produce a situation in which very few people got those things that they needed the most, or at least wanted the most. Remember Nozick with his need for the resources of Widner Library in an annex to his house. People, some might argue, with expensive tastes and extravagant needs, say a need for really good wine, would never, with a stress on such compossibilia, get things they are really keen about.[2] Is that the kind of world we would reflectively want? Well, *if* their not getting them is the price we have to pay for everyone having their basic needs met, then it is a price we ought to pay. I am very fond of very good wines as well as fresh ripe mangos, but if the price of my having them is that people starve or suffer malnutrition in the Sahel, or indeed anywhere else, then plainly fairness, if not just plain human decency, requires that I forego them.

In talking about how much equality is enough, I have so far talked of the benefits that equality is meant to provide. But egalitarians also speak of an equal sharing of the necessary burdens of the society as well. Fairness requires a sharing of the burdens, and for a radical egalitarian this comes to an equal sharing of the burdens where people are equally capable of sharing them. Translated into the concrete this does *not* mean that a child or an old man or a pregnant woman are to be required to work in the mines or that they be required to collect garbage, but it would involve something like requiring every able bodied person, say from nineteen to twenty, to take his or her turn at a fair portion of the necessary unpleasant jobs in the world. In that way we all, where we are able to do it, would share equally in these burdens—in doing the things that none of us want to do but that we, if we are at all reasonable, recognize the necessity of having done. (There are all kinds of variations and complications concerning this— what do we do with the youthful wonder at the violin? But, that notwithstanding, the general idea is clear enough.) And, where we think this is reasonably feasible, it squares with our considered judgments about fairness.

I have given you, in effect appealing to my considered judgments but considered judgments I do not think are at all eccentric, a picture of what I would take to be enough equality, too little equality and not enough equality. But how can we know that my proportions are right? I do not think we can avoid or should indeed try to avoid an appeal to considered judgments here. But working with them there are some arguments we can appeal to to get them in wide reflective equilibrium. Suppose we go back to the formal principle of justice, namely that we must treat like cases alike. Because it does not tell us *what* are like cases, we cannot derive substantive criteria from it. But it may, indirectly, be of some help here. We all, if we are not utterly zany, want a life in which our needs are satisfied and in which we can live as we wish and do what we want to do. Though we differ in many ways, in our abilities, capacities for pleasure, determination to keep on with a job, we do not differ about wanting our needs satisfied or being able to live as we wish. Thus, *ceterus paribus*, where questions of desert, entitlement and the like do not enter, it is only fair that all of us should have our needs equally considered and that we should, again *ceterus paribus*, all be able

to do as we wish in a way that is compatible with others doing likewise. From the formal principle of justice and a few key facts about us, we can get to the claim that *ceterus paribus* we should go for this much equality. But this is the core content of a radical egalitarianism.

However, how do we know that *ceterus* is *paribus* here? What about our entitlements and deserts? Suppose I have built my house with my own hands, from materials I have purchased and on land that I have purchased and that I have lived in it for years and have carefully cared for it. The house is mine and I am entitled to keep it even if by dividing the house into two apartments greater and more equal satisfaction of need would obtain for everyone. Justice requires that such an entitlement be respected here. (Again, there is an implicit *ceterus paribus* clause. In extreme situations, say after a war with housing in extremely short supply, that entitlement could be rightly overridden.)

There is a response on the egalitarian's part similar to a response utilitarianism made to criticisms of a similar logical type made of utilitarians by pluralistic deontologists. One of the things that people in fact need, or at least reflectively firmly want, is to have such entitlements respected. Where they are routinely overridden to satisfy other needs or wants, we would *not* in fact have a society in which the needs of everyone are being maximally met. To the reply, but what if more needs for everyone were met by ignoring or overriding such entitlements, the radical egalitarian should respond that that is, given the way we are, a thoroughly hypothetical situation and that theories of morality cannot be expected to give guidance for all logically possible worlds but only for worlds which are reasonably like what our actual world is or plausibly could come to be. Setting this argument aside for the moment, even if it did turn out that the need satisfaction linked with having other things— things that involved the overriding of those entitlements—was sufficient to make it the case that more need satisfaction all around for *everyone* would be achieved by overriding those entitlements, then, for reasonable people who clearly saw that, these entitlements would not have the weight presently given to them. They either would not have the importance presently attached to them or the need for the additional living space would be so great that their being overridden would seem, everything considered, the lesser of two evils (as in the example of the postwar housing situation).

There are without doubt genuine entitlements and a theory of justice must take them seriously, but they are not absolute. If the need is great enough we can see the merit in overriding them, just as in law as well as morality the right of eminent domain is recognized. Finally, while I have talked of entitlements here, parallel arguments will go through for desert.

III

I want now to relate this articulation of what equality comes to to my radically egalitarian principles of justice. My articulation of justice is a certain spelling out of the slogan proclaimed by Marx "From each according to his ability, to each according to his needs." The egalitarian conception of society argues for the desirability of bringing into existence a world, once the springs of social wealth flow freely, in which everyone's needs are as fully satisfied as possible and in which everyone gives according to his ability. Which means, among other things, that everyone, according to his ability, shares the burdens of society. There is an equal giving and equal responsibility here according to ability. It is here, with respect to giving according to ability and with respect to receiving according to need, that a complex equality of result, i.e., equality of condition, is being advocated by the radical egalitarian. What it comes to is this: each of us, where each is to count for one and none to count for more than one, is to give according to ability and receive according to need.

My radical egalitarian principles of justice read as follows:

(1) Each person is to have an equal right to the most extensive total system of equal basic liberties and opportunities (including equal opportunities for meaningful work, for self-determination and political and

economic participation) compatible with a similar treatment of all. (This principle gives expression to a commitment to attain and/or sustain equal moral autonomy and equal self-respect.)

(2) After provisions are made for common social (community) values, for capital overhead to preserve the society's productive capacity, allowances made for differing unmanipulated needs and preferences, and due weight is given to the just entitlements of individuals, the income and wealth (the common stock of means) is to be so divided that each person will have a right to an equal share. The necessary burdens requisite to enhance human well-being are also to be equally shared, subject, of course, to limitations by differing abilities and differing situations. (Here I refer to different natural environments and the like and not to class position and the like.)

Here we are talking about equality as a right rather than about equality as a goal as has previously been the subject matter of equality in this chapter. These principles of egalitarianism spell out rights people have and duties they have under *conditions of very considerable productive abundance*. We have a right to certain basic liberties and opportunities and we have, subject to certain limitations spelled out in the second principle, a right to an equal share of the income and wealth in the world. We also have a duty, again subject to the qualifications mentioned in the principle, to do our equal share in shouldering the burdens necessary to protect us from ills and to enhance our well-being.

What is the relation between these rights and the ideal of equality of condition discussed earlier? That is a goal for which we can struggle now to bring about conditions which will some day make its achievement possible, while these rights only become rights when the goal is actually achievable. We have no such rights in slave, feudal or capitalist societies or such duties in those societies. In that important way they are not natural rights for they depend on certain social conditions and certain social structures (socialist ones) to be realizable. What we can say is that it is always desirable

that socio-economic conditions come into being which would make it possible to achieve
the goal of equality of condition so that these
rights and duties I speak of could obtain. But
that is a far cry from saying we have such
rights and duties now.

It is a corollary of this, if these radical egalitarian principles of justice are correct, that
capitalist societies (even capitalist welfare state
societies such as Sweden) and statist societies
such as the Soviet Union or the People's
Republic of China cannot be just societies or at
least they must be societies, structured as they
are, which are defective in justice. (This is not
to say that some of these societies are not juster
than others. Sweden is juster than South Africa, Canada than the United States and Cuba
and Nicaragua than Honduras and Guatema-
la.) But none of these statist or capitalist societies can satisfy these radical egalitarian
principles of justice, for equal liberty, equal
opportunity, equal wealth or equal sharing of
burdens are not at all possible in societies having their social structure. So we do not have
such rights now but we can take it as a goal that
we bring such a society into being with a commitment to an equality of condition in which
we would have these rights and duties. Here
we require first the massive development of
productive power.

The connection between equality as a goal
and equality as a right spelled out in these
principles of justice is this. The equality of
condition appealed to in equality as a goal
would, if it were actually to obtain, have to
contain the rights and duties enunciated in
those principles. There could be no equal life
prospects between all people or anything approximating an equal satisfaction of needs if
there were not in place something like the
system of equal basic liberties referred to in
the first principle. Furthermore, without the
rough equality of wealth referred to in the
second principle, there would be disparities in
power and self-direction in society which
would render impossible an equality of life
prospects or the social conditions required for
an equal satisfaction of needs. And plainly,
without a roughly equal sharing of burdens,
there cannot be a situation where everyone has
equal life prospects or has the chance equally
to satisfy his needs. The principles of radical

egalitarian justice are implicated in its conception of an ideally adequate equality of condition.

IV

The principles of radical egalitarian justice I
have articulated are meant to apply globally
and not just to particular societies. But it is
certainly fair to say that not a few would worry
that such principles of radical egalitarian justice, if applied globally, would force the people
in wealthier sections of the world to a kind of
financial hari-kari. There are millions of desperately impoverished people. Indeed millions are starving or malnourished and things
are not getting any better. People in the
affluent societies cannot but worry about
whether they face a bottomless pit. Many believe that meeting, even in the most minimal
way, the needs of the impoverished is going to
put an incredible burden on people—people
of all classes—in the affluent societies. Indeed
it will, if acted on non-evasively, bring about
their impoverishment, and this is just too
much to ask. Radical egalitarianism is forgetting Rawls' admonitions about "the strains of
commitment"—the recognition that in any rational account of what is required of us, we
must at least give a minimal healthy self-
interest its due. We must construct our moral
philosophy for human beings and not for
saints. Human nature is less fixed than conservatives are wont to assume, but it is not so
elastic that we can reasonably expect people to
impoverish themselves to make the massive
transfers between North and South—the industrialized world and the Third World—
required to begin to approach a situation
where even Rawls' principles would be in place
on a global level, to say nothing of my radical
egalitarian principles of justice.[3]

The first thing to say in response to this is
that my radical egalitarian principles are
meant actually to guide practice, to directly
determine what we are to do, only in a world
of extensive abundance where, as Marx put it,
the springs of social wealth flow freely. If such
a world cannot be attained with the undermin-

ing of capitalism and the full putting into place, stabilizing, and developing of socialist relations of production, then such radical egalitarian principles can only remain as heuristic ideals against which to measure the distance of our travel in the direction of what would be a perfectly just society.

Aside from a small capitalist class, along with those elites most directly and profitably beholden to it (together a group constituting not more than 5 percent of the world's population), there would, in taking my radical egalitarian principles as heuristic guides, be no impoverishment of people in the affluent societies, if we moved in a radically more egalitarian way to start to achieve a global fairness. There would be massive transfers of wealth between North and South, but this could be done in stages so that, for the people in the affluent societies (capitalist elites apart), there need be no undermining of the quality of their lives. Even what were once capitalist elites would not be impoverished or reduced to some kind of bleak life though they would, the incidental Spartan types aside, find their life styles altered. But their health and general well-being, including their opportunities to do significant and innovative work, would, if anything, be enhanced. And while some of the sources of their enjoyment would be a thing of the past, there would still be a considerable range of enjoyments available to them sufficient to afford anyone a rich life that could be lived with verve and zest.

A fraction of what the United States spends on defense spending would take care of immediate problems of starvation and malnutrition for most of the world. For longer range problems such as bringing conditions of life in the Third World more in line with conditions of life in Sweden and Switzerland, what is necessary is the dismantling of the capitalist system and the creation of a socio-economic system with an underlying rationale directing it toward producing for needs—everyone's needs. With this altered productive mode, the irrationalities and waste of capitalist production would be cut. There would be no more built-in obsolescence, no more merely cosmetic changes in consumer durables, no more fashion roulette, no more useless products and the like. Moreover, the enormous expenditures that go into the war industry would be a thing of the past. There would be great transfers from North to South, but it would be from the North's capitalist fat and not from things people in the North really need. (There would, in other words, be no self-pauperization of people in the capitalist world.) . . .

V

It has been repeatedly argued that equality undermines liberty. Some would say that a society in which principles like my radical egalitarian principles were adopted, or even the liberal egalitarian principles of Rawls or Dworkin were adopted, would not be a free society. My arguments have been just the reverse. I have argued that it is only in an egalitarian society that full and extensive liberty is possible.

Perhaps the egalitarian and the anti-egalitarian are arguing at cross purposes? What we need to recognize, it has been argued, is that we have two kinds of rights both of which are important to freedom but to rather different freedoms and which are freedoms which not infrequently conflict.[4] We have rights to *fair terms of cooperation* but we also have rights to *non-interference*. If a right of either kind is overridden our freedom is diminished. The reason why it might be thought that the egalitarian and the anti-egalitarian may be arguing at cross purposes is that the egalitarian is pointing to the fact that rights to fair terms of cooperation and their associated liberties require equality while the anti-egalitarian is pointing to the fact that rights to non-interference and their associated liberties conflict with equality. They focus on different liberties.

What I have said above may not be crystal clear, so let me explain. People have a right to fair terms of cooperation. In political terms this comes to the equal right of all to effective participation in government and, in more broadly social terms, and for a society of economic wealth, it means people having a right to a roughly equal distribution of the benefits and burdens of the basic social arrangements that affect their lives and for them to stand in such relations to each other such that no one has the power to dominate the life of another. By contrast, rights to non-interference come to the equal right of all to be left alone by the government and more broadly to live in a society in which people have a right peacefully to pursue their interests without interference.

The conflict between equality and liberty comes down to, very essentially, the conflicts we get in modern societies between rights to fair terms of cooperation and rights to non-interference. As Joseph Schumpeter saw and J. S. Mill before him, one could have a thoroughly democratic society (at least in conventional terms) in which rights to non-interference might still be extensively violated. A central anti-egalitarian claim is that we cannot have an egalitarian society in which the very precious liberties that go with the rights to non-interference would not be violated.

Socialism and egalitarianism plainly protect rights to fair terms of cooperation. Without the social (collective) ownership and control of the means of production, involving with this, in the initial stages of socialism at least, a workers' state, economic power will be concentrated in the hands of a few who will in turn, as a result, dominate effective participation in government. Some right-wing libertarians blind themselves to that reality, but it is about as evident as can be. Only an utter turning away from the facts of social life could lead to any doubts about this at all. But then this means that in a workers' state, if some people have capitalistic impulses, that they would have their rights peacefully to pursue their own interests interfered with. They might wish to invest, retain and bequeath in economic domains. In a workers' state these capitalist acts in many circumstances would have to be forbidden, but that would be a violation of an individual's right to non-interference and the fact, if it was a fact, that we by democratic vote, even with vast majorities, had made such capitalist acts illegal would still not make any difference because individuals' rights to non-interference would still be violated.

We are indeed driven, by egalitarian impulses, of a perfectly understandable sort, to accept interference with laissez-faire capital-

ism to protect non-subordination and non-domination of people by protecting the egalitarian right to fair terms of cooperation and the enhanced liberty that that brings. Still, as things stand, this leads inevitably to violations of the right to non-interference and this brings with it a diminution of liberty. There will be people with capitalist impulses and they will be interfered with. It is no good denying, it will be said, that egalitarianism and particularly socialism will not lead to interference with very precious individual liberties, namely with our right peacefully to pursue our interests without interference.[5]

The proper response to this, as should be apparent from what I have argued throughout, is that to live in any society at all, capitalist, socialist or whatever, is to live in a world in which there will be some restriction or other on our rights peacefully to pursue our interests without interference. I can't lecture in Albanian or even in French in a standard philosophy class at the University of Calgary, I can't jog naked on most beaches, borrow a book from your library without your permission, fish in your trout pond without your permission, take your dog for a walk without your say so and the like. At least some of these things have been thought to be things which I might peacefully pursue in my own interests. Stopping me from doing them is plainly interfering with my peaceful pursuit of my own interests. And indeed it is an infringement on liberty, an interference with my doing what I may want to do.

However, for at least many of these activities, and particularly the ones having to do with property, even right-wing libertarians think that such interference is perfectly justified. But, justified or not, they still plainly constitute a restriction on our individual freedom. However, what we must also recognize is that there will always be some such restrictions on freedom in any society whatsoever, just in virtue of the fact that a normless society, without the restrictions that having norms imply, is a contradiction in terms.[6] Many restrictions are hardly felt as restrictions, as in the attitudes of many people toward seat-belt legislation, but they are, all the same, plainly restrictions on our liberty. It is just that they are thought to be unproblematically justified.

To the question would a socialism with a radical egalitarianism restrict some liberties, including some liberties rooted in rights to noninterference, the answer is that it indeed would; but so would laissez-faire capitalism, aristocratic conceptions of justice, liberal conceptions or any social formations at all, with their associated conceptions of justice. The relevant question is which of these restrictions are justified.

The restrictions on liberty proferred by radical egalitarianism and socialism, I have argued, are justified for they, of the various alternatives, give us both the most extensive and the most abundant system of liberty possible in modern conditions with their thorough protection of the right to fair terms of cooperation. Radical egalitarianism will also, and this is central for us, protect our civil liberties and these liberties are, of course, our most basic liberties. These are the liberties which are the most vital for us to protect. What it will not do is to protect our unrestricted liberties to invest, retain and bequeath in the economic realm and it will not protect our unrestricted freedom to buy and sell. There is, however, no good reason to think that these restrictions are restrictions of anything like a basic liberty. Moreover, we are justified in restricting our freedom to buy and sell if such restrictions strengthen, rather than weaken, our total system of liberty. This is in this way justified, for only by such market restrictions can the rights of the vast majority of people to effective participation in government and an equal role in the control of their social lives be protected. I say this because if we let the market run free in this way, power will pass into the hands of a few who will control the lives of the many and determine the fundamental design of the society. The actual liberties that are curtailed in a radically egalitarian social order are inessential liberties whose restriction in contemporary circumstances enhances human well-being and indeed makes for a firmer entrenchment of basic liberties and for their greater extension globally. That is to say, we here restrict some liberty in order to attain more liberty and a more equally distributed pattern of liberty. More people will be able to do what they want and have a greater control over their own lives than in a capitalist world

order with its at least implicit inegalitarian commitments.

However, some might say I still have not faced the most central objection to radical egalitarianism, namely its statism. (I would prefer to say its putative statism.) The picture is this. The egalitarian state must be in the redistribution business. It has to make, or make sure there is made, an equal relative contribution to the welfare of every citizen. But this in effect means that the socialist state or, for that matter, the welfare state, will be deeply interventionist in our personal lives. It will be in the business, as one right-winger emotively put it, of cutting one person down to size in order to bring about that person's equality with another person who was in a previously disadvantageous position.[7] That is said to be morally objectionable and it would indeed be deeply morally objectionable in many circumstances. But it isn't in the circumstances in which the radical egalitarian presses for redistribution. (I am not speaking of what might be mere equalizing upwards.) The circumstances are these: Capitalist A gets his productive property confiscated so that he could no longer dominate and control the lives of proletarians B, C, D, E, F, and G. But what is wrong with it where this "cutting down to size"—in reality the confiscation of productive property or the taxation of the capitalist— involves no violation of A's civil liberties or the harming of his actual well-being (health, ability to work, to cultivate the arts, to have fruitful personal relations, to live in comfort and the like) and where B, C, D, E, F, and G will have their freedom and their well-being thoroughly enhanced if such confiscation or taxation occurs? Far from being morally objectionable, it is precisely the sort of state of affairs that people ought to favor. It certainly protects more liberties and more significant liberties than it undermines.

There is another familiar anti-egalitarian argument designed to establish the liberty-undermining qualities of egalitarianism. It is an argument we have touched upon in discussing meritocracy. It turns on the fact that in any society there will be both talents and handicaps. Where they exist, what do we want to do about maintaining equal distribution? Egalitarians, radical or otherwise, certainly do not want to penalize people for talent. That being so, then surely people should be allowed to retain the benefits of superior talent. But this in some circumstances will lead to significant inequalities in resources and in the meeting of needs. To sustain equality there will have to be an ongoing redistribution in the direction of the less talented and less fortunate. But this redistribution from the more to the less talented does plainly penalize the talented for their talent. That, it will be said, is something which is both unfair and an undermining of liberty.

The following, it has been argued, makes the above evident enough.[8] If people have talents they will tend to want to use them. And if they use them they are very likely to come out ahead. Must not egalitarians say they ought not to be able to come out ahead no matter how well they use their talents and no matter how considerable these talents are? But that is intolerably restrictive and unfair.

The answer to the above anti-egalitarian argument is implicit in a number of things I have already said. But here let me confront this familiar argument directly. Part of the answer comes out in probing some of the ambiguities of "coming out ahead." Note, incidentally, that (1) not all reflective, morally sensitive people will be so concerned with that, and (2) that being very concerned with that is a mentality that capitalism inculcates. Be that as it may, to turn to the ambiguities, note that some take "coming out ahead" principally to mean "being paid well for the use of those talents" where "being paid well" is being paid sufficiently well so that it creates inequalities sufficient to disturb the preferred egalitarian patterns. (Without that, being paid well would give one no relative advantage.) But, as we have seen, "coming out ahead" need not take that form at all. Talents can be recognized and acknowledged in many ways. First, in just the respect and admiration of a fine employment of talents that would naturally come from people seeing them so displayed where these people were not twisted by envy; second, by having, because of these talents, interesting and secure work that their talents fit them for and they merit in virtue of those talents. Moreover, having more money is not going to matter much—for familiar marginal utility reasons—

where what in capitalist societies would be called the welfare floors are already very high, this being made feasible by the great productive wealth of the society. Recall that in such a society of abundance everyone will be well off and secure. In such a society people are not going to be very concerned about being a little better off than someone else. The talented are in no way, in such a situation, robbed to help the untalented and handicapped or penalized for their talents. They are only prevented from amassing wealth (most particularly productive wealth), which would enable them to dominate the untalented and the handicapped and to control the social life of the world of which they are both a part. . . .

I think that the moral authority for abstract egalitarianism, for the belief that the interests of everyone matters and matters equally, comes from its being the case that it is *required by the moral point of view*.[9] What I am predicting is that a person who has a good understanding of what morality is, has a good knowledge of the facts, is not ideologically mystified, takes an impartial point of view, and has an attitude of impartial caring, would, if not conceptually confused, come to accept the abstract egalitarian thesis. I see no way of arguing someone into such an egalitarianism who does not in this general way have a love of humankind.[10] A hard-hearted Hobbesist is not reachable here. But given that a person has that love of humankind—that impartial and impersonal caring—together with the other qualities mentioned above, then, I predict, that that person would be an egalitarian at least to the extent of accepting the abstract egalitarian thesis. What I am claiming is that if these conditions were to obtain (if they ceased to be just counterfactuals), then there would be a consensus among moral agents about accepting the abstract egalitarian thesis. . . .

Notes

1. See the debate between Robert Nozick, Daniel Bell and James Tobin, "If Inequality Is Inevitable What Can Be Done About It?" *The New York Times*, January 3, 1982, p. E5. The exchange between Bell and Nozick reveals the differences

between the old egalitarianism and right-wing libertarianism. It is not only that the right and left clash but sometimes right clashes with right.

2. Amartya Sen, "Equality of What?" *The Tanner Lectures on Human Values,* vol. 1 (1980), ed. Sterling M. McMurrin (Cambridge, England: Cambridge University Press, 1980), pp. 198–220.

3. Henry Shue, "The Burdens of Justice," *The Journal of Philosophy* 80, no. 10 (October 1983): 600–601; 606–608.

4. Richard W. Miller, "Marx and Morality," in *Marxism,* eds. J. R. Pennock and J. W. Chapman, Nomos 26 (New York: New York University Press, 1983), pp. 9–11.

5. Ibid., p. 10.

6. This has been argued from both the liberal center and the left. Ralf Dahrendorf, *Essays in the Theory of Society* (Stanford, Cal.: Stanford University Press, 1968), pp. 151–178; and G. A. Cohen, "Capitalism, Freedom and the Proletariat" in *The Idea of Freedom: Essays in Honour of Isaiah Berlin,*

ed. Alan Ryan (Oxford: Oxford University Press, 1979).

7. The graphic language should be duly noted. Jan Narveson, "On Dworkinian Equality," *Social Philosophy and Policy* 1, no. 1 (autumn 1983): 4.

8. Ibid., p. 1–24.

9. Some will argue that there is no such thing as a moral point of view. My differences with him about the question of whether the amoralist can be argued into morality not withstanding, I think Kurt Baier, in a series of articles written subsequent to his *The Moral Point of View,* has clearly shown that there is something reasonably determinate that can, without ethnocentrism, be called "the moral point of view."

10. Richard Norman has impressively argued that this is an essential background assumption of the moral point of view. Richard Norman, "Critical Notice of Rodger Beehler's *Moral Life,*" *Canadian Journal of Philosophy* 11, no. 1 (March 1981): 157–183.

3. A Social Contract Perspective

John Rawls

John Rawls believes that principles of justice are those on which free and rational persons would agree if they were in an original position of equality. This original position is characterized as a hypothetical position in which persons are behind an imaginary veil of ignorance with respect to most particular facts about themselves. Rawls claims that persons in his original position would choose principles requiring equal political liberty and opportunity and the highest possible economic minimum because they would be committed to the maximin rule, which requires maximizing the minimum payoff.

My aim is to present a conception of justice which generalizes and carries to a higher level of abstraction the familiar theory of the social contract as found, say, in Locke, Rousseau,

Abridged from *A Theory of Justice* (1971), pp. 11–22, 60–65, 150–156, 302–303. Excerpted by permission of the publishers from *A Theory of Justice* by John Rawls. Cambridge, Mass.: Harvard University Press. Copyright © 1971 by the President and Fellows of Harvard College.

and Kant.[1] In order to do this we are not to think of the original contract as one to enter a particular society or to set up a particular form of government. Rather, the guiding idea is that the principles of justice for the basic structure of society are the object of the original agreement. They are the principles that free and rational persons concerned to further their own interests would accept in an initial position of equality as defining the fundamental terms of their association. These principles are to regulate all further agreements; they specify the kinds of social cooperation that can be entered into and the forms of government that can be established. This way of regarding the principles of justice I shall call justice as fairness.

Thus we are to imagine that those who engage in social cooperation choose together, in one joint act, the principles which are to assign basic rights and duties and to determine the division of social benefits. Men are to decide in advance how they are to regulate their claims against one another and what is to be the foundation charter of their society. Just as each person must decide by rational reflection what constitutes his good—that is, the system of ends which it is rational for him to pursue—so a group of persons must decide once and for all what is to count among them as just and unjust. The choice which rational men would make in this hypothetical situation of equal liberty, assuming for the present that this choice problem has a solution, determines the principles of justice.

In justice as fairness the original position of equality corresponds to the state of nature in the traditional theory of the social contract. This original position is not, of course, thought of as an actual historical state of affairs, much less as a primitive condition of culture. It is understood as a purely hypothetical situation characterized so as to lead to a certain conception of justice.[2] Among the essential features of this situation is that no one knows his place in society, his class position or social status, nor does any one know his fortune in the distribution of natural assets and abilities, his intelligence, strength, and the like. I shall even assume that the parties do not know their conceptions of the good or their special psychological propensities. The principles of justice are chosen behind a veil of ignorance. This ensures that no one is advantaged or disadvantaged in the choice of principles by the outcome of natural chance or the contingency of social circumstances. Since all are similarly situated and no one is able to design principles to favor his particular condition, the principles of justice are the result of a fair agreement or bargain. For given the circumstances of the original position, the symmetry of everyone's relations to each other, this initial situation is fair between individuals as moral persons; that is, as rational beings with their own ends and capable, I shall assume, of a sense of justice. The original position is, one might say, the appropriate initial status quo, and thus the fundamental agreements reached in it are fair. This explains the propriety of the name "justice as fairness"; it conveys the idea that the principles of justice are agreed to in an initial situation that is fair. The name does not mean that the concepts of justice and fairness are the same, any more than the phrase "poetry as metaphor" means that the concepts of poetry and metaphor are the same.

Justice as fairness begins, as I have said, with one of the most general of all choices which persons might make together, namely, with the choice of the first principles of a conception of justice which is to regulate all subsequent criticism and reform of institutions. Then, having chosen a conception of justice, we can suppose that they are to choose a constitution and a legislature to enact laws, and so on, all in accordance with the principles of justice initially agreed upon. Our social situation is just if it is such that by this sequence of hypothetical agreements we would have contracted into the general system of rules which defines it. Moreover, assuming that the original position does determine a set of principles (that is, that a particular conception of justice would be chosen), it will then be true that whenever social institutions satisfy these principles those engaged in them can say to one another that they are cooperating on terms to which they would agree if they were free and equal persons whose relations with respect to one another were fair. They could all view their arrangements as meeting the stipulations which they would acknowledge in an initial situation that embodies widely accepted and reasonable constraints on the choice of principles. The general recognition of this fact would provide the basis for a public acceptance of the corresponding principles of justice. No society can, of course, be a scheme of cooperation which men enter voluntarily in a literal sense; each person finds himself placed at birth in some particular position in some particular society, and the nature of this position materially affects his life prospects. Yet a society satisfying the principles of justice as fairness comes as close as a society can to being a voluntary scheme, for it meets the principles which free and equal persons would assent to under circumstances that are fair. In this sense its members are autonomous and the obligations they recognize self-imposed.

One feature of justice as fairness is to think of the parties in the initial situation as rational and mutually disinterested. This does not mean that the parties are egoists; that is, individuals with only certain kinds of interests, say in wealth, prestige, and domination. But they are conceived as not taking an interest in one another's interests. They are to presume that even their spiritual aims may be opposed, in the way that the aims of those of different religions may be opposed. Moreover, the concept of rationality must be interpreted as far as possible in the narrow sense, standard in economic theory, of taking the most effective means to given ends. I shall modify this concept to some extent . . . , but one must try to avoid introducing into it any controversial ethical elements. The initial situation must be characterized by stipulations that are widely accepted.

In working out the conception of justice as fairness one main task clearly is to determine which principles of justice would be chosen in the original position. To do this we must describe this situation in some detail and formulate with care the problem of choice which it presents. It may be observed, however, that once the principles of justice are thought of as arising from an original agreement in a situation of equality, it is an open question whether the principle of utility would be acknowledged. Offhand it hardly seems likely that persons who view themselves as equals, entitled to press their claims upon one another, would agree to a principle which may require lesser life prospects for some simply for the sake of a greater sum of advantages enjoyed by others. Since each desires to protect his interests, his capacity to advance his conception of the good, no one has a reason to acquiesce in an enduring loss for himself in order to bring about a greater net balance of satisfaction. In the absence of strong and lasting benevolent impulses, a rational man would not accept a basic structure merely because it maximized the algebraic sum of advantages irrespective of its permanent effects on his own basic rights and interests. Thus it seems that the principle of utility is incompatible with the conception of social cooperation among equals for mutual advantage. It appears to be inconsistent with the idea of reciprocity implicit in the notion of a well-ordered society. Or, at any rate, so I shall argue.

I shall maintain instead that the persons in the initial situation would choose two rather different principles: the first requires equality in the assignment of basic rights and duties, while the second holds that social and economic inequalities, for example, inequalities of wealth and authority, are just only if they result in compensating benefits for everyone, and in particular for the least advantaged members of society. These principles rule out justifying institutions on the grounds that the hardships of some are offset by a greater good in the aggregate. It may be expedient but it is not just that some should have less in order that others may prosper. But there is no injustice in the greater benefits earned by a few provided that the situation of persons not so fortunate is thereby improved. The intuitive idea is that since everyone's well-being depends upon a scheme of cooperation without which no one could have a satisfactory life, the division of advantages should be such as to draw forth the willing cooperation of everyone taking part in it, including those less well situated. Yet this can be expected only if reasonable terms are proposed. The two principles mentioned seem to be a fair agreement on the basis of which those better endowed, or more fortunate in their social position, neither of which we can be said to deserve, could expect the willing cooperation of others when some workable scheme is a necessary condition of the welfare of all.[3] Once we decide to look for a conception of justice that nullifies the accidents of natural endowment and the contingencies of social circumstance as counters in quest for political and economic advantage, we are led to these principles. They express the result of leaving aside those aspects of the social world that seem arbitrary from a moral point of view.

The problem of the choice of principles,

however, is extremely difficult. I do not expect the answer I shall suggest to be convincing to everyone. It is, therefore, worth noting from the outset that justice as fairness, like other contract views, consists of two parts: (1) an interpretation of the initial situation and of the problem of choice posed there, and (2) a set of principles which, it is argued, would be agreed to. One may accept the first part of the theory (or some variant thereof), but not the other, and conversely. The concept of the initial contractual situation may seem reasonable although the particular principles proposed are rejected. To be sure, I want to maintain that the most appropriate conception of this situation does lead to principles of justice contrary to utilitarianism and perfectionism, and therefore that the contract doctrine provides an alternative to these views. Still, one may dispute this contention even though one grants that the contractarian method is a useful way of studying ethical theories and of setting forth their underlying assumptions.

Justice as fairness is an example of what I have called a contract theory. Now there may be an objection to the term "contract" and related expressions, but I think it will serve reasonably well. Many words have misleading connotations which at first are likely to confuse. The terms "utility" and "utilitarianism" are surely no exception. They too have unfortunate suggestions which hostile critics have been willing to exploit; yet they are clear enough for those prepared to study utilitarian doctrine. The same should be true of the term "contract" applied to moral theories. As I have mentioned, to understand it one has to keep in mind that it implies a certain level of abstraction. In particular, the content of the relevant agreement is not to enter a given society or to adopt a given form of government, but to accept certain moral principles. Moreover, the undertakings referred to are purely hypothetical: a contract view holds that certain principles would be accepted in a well-defined initial situation.

The merit of the contract terminology is that it conveys the idea that principles of justice may be conceived as principles that would be chosen by rational persons, and that in this way conceptions of justice may be explained and justified. The theory of justice is a part, perhaps the most significant part, of the theory of rational choice. Furthermore, principles of justice deal with conflicting claims upon the advantages won by social cooperation; they apply to the relations among several persons or groups. The word "contract" suggests this plurality as well as the condition that the appropriate division of advantages must be in accordance with principles acceptable to all parties. The condition of publicity for principles of justice is also connoted by the contract phraseology. Thus, if these principles are the outcome of an agreement, citizens have a knowledge of the principles that others follow. It is characteristic of contract theories to stress the public nature of political principles. Finally there is the long tradition of the contract doctrine. Expressing the tie with this line of thought helps to define ideas and accords with natural piety. There are then several advantages in the use of the term "contract." With due precautions taken, it should not be misleading.

A final remark. Justice as fairness is not a complete contract theory. For it is clear that the contractarian idea can be extended to the choice of more or less an entire ethical system; that is, to a system including principles for all the virtues and not only for justice. Now for the most part I shall consider only principles of justice and others closely related to them; I make no attempt to discuss the virtues in a systematic way. Obviously if justice as fairness succeeds reasonably well, a next step would be to study the more general view suggested by the name "rightness as fairness." But even this wider theory fails to embrace all moral relationships, since it would seem to include only our relations with other persons and to leave out of account how we are to conduct ourselves toward animals and the rest of nature. I do not contend that the contract notion offers a way to approach these questions, which are certainly of the first importance; and I shall have to put them aside. We must recognize the limited scope of justice as fairness and of the general type of view that it exemplifies. How far its conclusions must be revised once these other matters are understood cannot be decided in advance.

The Original Position and Justification

I have said that the original position is the appropriate initial status quo which insures that the fundamental agreements reached in it are fair. This fact yields the name "justice as fairness." It is clear, then, that I want to say that one conception of justice is more reasonable than another, or justifiable with respect to it, if rational persons in the initial situation would choose its principles over those of the other for the role of justice. Conceptions of justice are to be ranked by their acceptability to persons so circumstanced. Understood in this way the question of justification is settled by working out a problem of deliberation: we have to ascertain which principles it would be rational to adopt given the contractual situation. This connects the theory of justice with the theory of rational choice.

If this view of the problem of justification is to succeed, we must, of course, describe in some detail the nature of this choice problem. A problem of rational decision has a definite answer only if we know the beliefs and interests of the parties, their relations with respect to one another, the alternatives between which they are to choose, the procedure whereby they make up their minds, and so on. As the circumstances are presented in different ways, correspondingly different principles are accepted. The concept of the original position, as I shall refer to it, is that of the most philosophically favored interpretation of this initial choice situation for the purposes of a theory of justice.

But how are we to decide what is the most favored interpretation? I assume, for one thing, that there is a broad measure of agreement that principles of justice should be chosen under certain conditions. To justify a particular description of the initial situation one shows that it incorporates these commonly shared presumptions. One argues from widely accepted but weak premises to more specific conclusions. Each of the presumptions should by itself be natural and plausible; some of

them may seem innocuous or even trivial. The aim of the contract approach is to establish that taken together they impose significant bounds on acceptable principles of justice. The ideal outcome would be that these conditions determine a unique set of principles; but I shall be satisfied if they suffice to rank the main traditional conceptions of social justice.

One should not be misled, then, by the somewhat unusual conditions which characterize the original position. The idea here is simply to make vivid to ourselves the restrictions that it seems reasonable to impose on arguments for principles of justice, and therefore on these principles themselves. Thus it seems reasonable and generally acceptable that no one should be advantaged or disadvantaged by natural fortune or social circumstances in the choice of principles. It also seems widely agreed that it should be impossible to tailor principles to the circumstances of one's own case. We should ensure further that particular inclinations and aspirations, and persons' conceptions of their good, do not affect the principles adopted. The aim is to rule out those principles that it would be rational to propose for acceptance, however little the chance of success, only if one knew certain things that are irrelevant from the standpoint of justice. For example, if a man knew that he was wealthy, he might find it rational to advance the principle that various taxes for welfare measures be counted unjust; if he knew that he was poor, he would most likely propose the contrary principle. To represent the desired restrictions one imagines a situation in which everyone is deprived of this sort of information. One excludes the knowledge of those contingencies which sets men at odds and allows them to be guided by their prejudices. In this manner the veil of ignorance is arrived at in a natural way. This concept should cause no difficulty if we keep in mind the constraints on arguments that it is meant to express. At any time we can enter the original position, so to speak, simply by following a certain procedure; namely, by arguing for principles of justice in accordance with these restrictions.

It seems reasonable to suppose that the

parties in the original position are equal. That is, all have the same rights in the procedure for choosing principles; each can make proposals, submit reasons for their acceptance, and so on. Obviously the purpose of these conditions is to represent equality between human beings as moral persons, as creatures having a conception of their good and capable of a sense of justice. The basis of equality is taken to be similarity in these two respects. Systems of ends are not ranked in value; and each man is presumed to have the requisite ability to understand and to act upon whatever principles are adopted. Together with the veil of ignorance, these conditions define the principles of justice as those which rational persons concerned to advance their interests would consent to as equals when none are known to be advantaged or disadvantaged by social and natural contingencies.

There is, however, another side to justifying a particular description of the original position. This is to see if the principles which would be chosen match our considered convictions of justice or extend them in an acceptable way. We can note whether applying these principles would lead us to make the same judgments about the basic structure of society which we now make intuitively and in which we have the greatest confidence; or whether, in cases where our present judgments are in doubt and given with hesitation, these principles offer a resolution which we can affirm on reflection. There are questions which we feel sure must be answered in a certain way. For example, we are confident that religious intolerance and racial discrimination are unjust. We think that we have examined these things with care and have reached what we believe is an impartial judgment not likely to be distorted by an excessive attention to our own interests. These convictions are provisional fixed points which we presume any conception of justice must fit. But we have much less assurance as to what is the correct distribution of wealth and authority. Here we may be looking for a way to remove our doubts. We can check an interpretation of the initial situation, then, by the capacity of its principles to accommodate our firmest convictions and to provide guidance where guidance is needed.

In searching for the most favored description of this situation we work from both ends. We begin by describing it so that it represents generally shared and preferably weak conditions. We then see if these conditions are strong enough to yield a significant set of principles. If not, we look for further premises equally reasonable. But if so, and these principles match our considered convictions of justice, then so far well and good. But presumably there will be discrepancies. In this case we have a choice. We can either modify the account of the initial situation or we can revise our existing judgments, for even the judgments we take provisionally as fixed points are liable to revision. By going back and forth, sometimes altering the conditions of the contractual circumstances, at others withdrawing our judgments and conforming them to principle, I assume that eventually we shall find a description of the initial situation that both expresses reasonable conditions and yields principles which match our considered judgments duly pruned and adjusted. This state of affairs I refer to as reflective equilibrium.[4] It is an equilibrium because at last our principles and judgments coincide; and it is reflective since we know to what principles our judgments conform and the premises of their derivation. At the moment everything is in order. But this equilibrium is not necessarily stable. It is liable to be upset by further examination of the conditions which should be imposed on the contractual situation and by particular cases which may lead us to revise our judgments. Yet for the time being we have done what we can to render coherent and to justify our convictions of social justice. We have reached a conception of the original position.

I shall not, of course, actually work through this process. Still, we may think of the interpretation of the original position that I shall present as the result of such a hypothetical course of reflection. It represents the attempt to accommodate within one scheme both reasonable philosophical conditions on principles as well as our considered judgments of justice. In arriving at the favored interpretation of the initial situation there is no point at which an appeal is made to self-evidence in the traditional sense either of general conceptions or particular convictions. I do not claim for the principles of justice proposed that they are necessary truths or derivable from such truths. A conception of justice cannot be deduced from self-evident premises or conditions on principles; instead, its justification is a matter of the mutual support of many considerations, of everything fitting together into one coherent view.

A final comment. We shall want to say that certain principles of justice are justified because they would be agreed to in an initial situation of equality. I have emphasized that this original position is purely hypothetical. It is natural to ask why, if this agreement is never actually entered into, we should take any interest in these principles, moral or otherwise. The answer is that the conditions embodied in the description of the original position are ones that we do in fact accept. Or if we do not, then perhaps we can be persuaded to do so by philosophical reflection. Each aspect of the contractual situation can be given supporting grounds. Thus what we shall do is to collect together into one conception a number of conditions on principles that we are ready upon due consideration to recognize as reasonable. These constraints express what we are prepared to regard as limits on fair terms of social cooperation. One way to look at the idea of the original position, therefore, is to see it as an expository device which sums up the meaning of these conditions and helps us to extract their consequences. On the other hand, this conception is also an intuitive notion that suggests its own elaboration, so that led on by it we are drawn to define more clearly the standpoint from which we can best interpret moral relationships. We need a conception that enables us to envision our objective from afar: the intuitive notion of the original position is to do this for us. . . .

Two Principles of Justice

I shall now state in a provisional form the two principles of justice that I believe would be chosen in the original position. In this section I wish to make only the most general comments, and therefore the first formulation of these

principles is tentative. As we go on I shall run through several formulations and approximate step by step the final statement to be given much later. I believe that doing this allows the exposition to proceed in a natural way.

The first statement of the two principles reads as follows:

First: each person is to have an equal right to the most extensive basic liberty compatible with a similar liberty for others.

Second: social and economic inequalities are to be arranged so that they are both (a) reasonably expected to be to everyone's advantage, and (b) attached to positions and offices open to all.

There are two ambiguous phrases in the second principle, namely "everyone's advantage" and "open to all." Determining their sense more exactly will lead to a second formulation of the principle. . . .

By way of general comment, these principles primarily apply, as I have said, to the basic structure of society. They are to govern the assignment of rights and duties and to regulate the distribution of social and economic advantages. As their formulation suggests, these principles presuppose that the social structure can be divided into two more or less distinct parts, the first principle applying to the one, the second to the other. They distinguish between those aspects of the social system that define and secure the equal liberties of citizenship and those that specify and establish social and economic inequalities. The basic liberties of citizens are, roughly speaking, political liberty (the right to vote and to be eligible for public office) together with freedom of speech and assembly; liberty of conscience and freedom of thought; freedom of the person along with the right to hold personal property; and freedom from arbitrary arrest and seizure as defined by the concept of the rule of law. These liberties are all required to be equal by the first principle, since citizens of a just society are to have the same basic rights.

The second principle applies, in the first

approximation, to the distribution of income and wealth and to the design of organizations that make use of differences in authority and responsibility, or chains of command. While the distribution of wealth and income need not be equal, it must be to everyone's advantage, and at the same time, positions of authority and offices of command must be accessible to all. One applies the second principle by holding positions open, and then, subject to this constraint, arranges social and economic inequalities so that everyone benefits.

These principles are to be arranged in a serial order with the first principle prior to the second. This ordering means that a departure from the institutions of equal liberty required by the first principle cannot be justified by, or compensated for, by greater social and economic advantages. The distribution of wealth and income, and the hierarchies of authority, must be consistent with both the liberties of equal citizenship and equality of opportunity.

It is clear that these principles are rather specific in their content, and their acceptance rests on certain assumptions that I must eventually try to explain and justify. A theory of justice depends upon a theory of society in ways that will become evident as we proceed. For the present, it should be observed that the two principles (and this holds for all formulations) are a special case of a more general conception of justice that can be expressed as follows:

> All social values—liberty and opportunity, income and wealth, and the bases of self-respect—are to be distributed equally unless an unequal distribution of any, or all, of these values is to everyone's advantage.

Injustice, then, is simply inequalities that are not to the benefit of all. Of course, this conception is extremely vague and requires interpretation.

As a first step, suppose that the basic structure of society distributes certain primary goods, that is, things that every rational man is presumed to want. These goods normally have a use whatever a person's rational plan of life. For simplicity, assume that the chief primary goods at the disposition of society are rights and liberties, powers and opportunities, income and wealth. (Later on . . . the primary good of self-respect has a central place.) These are the social primary goods. Other primary goods such as health and vigor, intelligence and imagination, are natural goods; although their possession is influenced by the basic structure, they are not so directly under its control. Imagine, then, a hypothetical initial arrangement in which all the social primary goods are equally distributed: everyone has similar rights and duties, and income and wealth are evenly shared. This state of affairs provides a benchmark for judging improvements. If certain inequalities of wealth and organizational powers would make everyone better off than in this hypothetical starting situation, then they accord with the general conception.

Now it is possible, at least theoretically, that by giving up some of their fundamental liberties men are sufficiently compensated by the resulting social and economic gains. The general conception of justice imposes no restrictions on what sort of inequalities are permissible; it only requires that everyone's position be improved. We need not suppose anything so drastic as consenting to a condition of slavery. Imagine instead that men forgo certain political rights when the economic returns are significant and their capacity to influence the course of policy by the exercise of these rights would be marginal in any case. It is this kind of exchange which the two principles as stated rule out; being arranged in serial order they do not permit exchanges between basic liberties and economic and social gains. The serial ordering of principles expresses an underlying preference among primary social goods. When this preference is rational so likewise is the choice of these principles in this order.

In developing justice as fairness I shall, for the most part, leave aside the general conception of justice and examine instead the special case of the two principles in serial order. The advantage of this procedure is that from the first the matter of priorities is recognized and an effort made to find principles to deal with it. One is led to attend throughout to the conditions under which the acknowledgment of the absolute weight of liberty with respect to social and economic advantages, as defined by the lexical order of the two principles, would be reasonable. Offhand, this ranking appears extreme and too special a case to be of much interest; but there is more justification for it than would appear at first sight. Or at any rate, so I shall maintain. . . . Furthermore, the distinction between fundamental rights and liberties and economic and social benefits marks a difference among primary social goods that one should try to exploit. It suggests an important division in the social system. Of course, the distinctions drawn and the ordering proposed are bound to be at best only approximations. There are surely circumstances in which they fail. But it is essential to depict clearly the main lines of a reasonable conception of justice; and under many conditions, anyway, the two principles in serial order may serve well enough. When necessary we can fall back on the more general conception.

The fact that the two principles apply to institutions has certain consequences. Several points illustrate this. First of all, the rights and liberties referred to by these principles are those that are defined by the public rules of the basic structure. Whether men are free is determined by the rights and duties established by the major institutions of society. Liberty is a certain pattern of social forms. The first principle simply requires that certain sorts of rules, those defining basic liberties, apply to everyone equally and that they allow the most extensive liberty compatible with a like liberty for all. The only reason for circumscribing the rights defining liberty and making men's freedom less extensive than it might otherwise be is that these equal rights as institutionally defined would interfere with one another.

Another thing to bear in mind is that when principles mention persons, or require that everyone gain from an inequality, the reference is to representative persons holding the various social positions, or offices, or whatever, established by the basic structure. Thus in applying the second principle I assume that it is possible to assign an expectation of well-being to representative individuals holding these positions. This expectation indicates their life prospects as viewed from their social station. In general, the expectations of representative persons depend upon the distribution of rights and duties throughout the basic structure. When this changes, expectations change. I assume, then, that expectations are connected: by raising the prospects of the representative man in one position we presumably increase or decrease the prospects of representative men in other positions. Since it applies to institutional forms, the second principle (or rather the first part of it) refers to the expectations of representative individuals. As I shall discuss below, neither principle applies to distributions of particular goods to particular individuals who may be identified by their proper names. The situation where someone is considering how to allocate certain commodities to needy persons who are known to him is not within the scope of the principles. They are meant to regulate basic institutional arrangements. We must not assume that there is much similarity from the standpoint of justice between an administrative allotment of goods to specific persons and the appropriate design of society. Our common sense intuitions for the former may be a poor guide to the latter.

Now the second principle insists that each person benefit from permissible inequalities in the basic structure. This means that it must be reasonable for each relevant representative man defined by this structure, when he views it as a going concern, to prefer his prospects with the inequality, to his prospects without it. One is not allowed to justify differences in income or organizational powers on the ground that the disadvantages of those in one position are outweighed by the greater advantages of those in another. Much less can infringements of liberty be counterbalanced in this way. Applied to the basic structure, the principle of utility would have us maximize the sum of expectations of representative men (weighted by the number of persons they represent, on the classical view); and this would permit us to compensate for the losses of some by the gains of others. Instead, the two principles require that everyone benefit from economic and social inequalities.

The Reasoning Leading to the Two Principles of Justice

It will be recalled that the general conception of justice as fairness requires that all primary social goods be distributed equally unless an unequal distribution would be to everyone's advantage. No restrictions are placed on exchanges of these goods and therefore a lesser liberty can be compensated for by greater social and economic benefits. Now looking at the situation from the standpoint of one person selected arbitrarily, there is no way for him to win special advantages for himself. Nor, on the other hand, are there grounds for his acquiescing in special disadvantages. Since it is not reasonable for him to expect more than an equal share in the division of social goods, and since it is not rational for him to agree to less, the sensible thing for him to do is to acknowledge as the first principle of justice one requiring an equal distribution. Indeed, this principle is so obvious that we would expect it to occur to anyone immediately.

Thus, the parties start with a principle establishing equal liberty for all, including equality of opportunity, as well as an equal distribution of income and wealth. But there is no reason why this acknowledgment should be final. If there are inequalities in the basic structure that work to make everyone better off in comparison with the benchmark of initial equality, why not permit them? The immediate gain which a greater equality might allow can be regarded as intelligently invested in view of its future return. If, for example, these inequalities set up various incentives which succeed in eliciting more productive efforts, a person in the original position may look upon them as necessary to cover the costs of training and to encourage effective performance. One might think that ideally individuals should want to serve one another. But since the parties are assumed not to take an interest in one another's interests, their acceptance of these inequalities is only the acceptance of the relations in which men stand in the circumstances of justice. They have no grounds for complaining of one another's mo-

tives. A person in the original position would, therefore, concede the justice of these inequalities. Indeed, it would be shortsighted of him not to do so. He would hesitate to agree to these regularities only if he would be dejected by the bare knowledge or perception that others were better situated; and I have assumed that the parties decide as if they are not moved by envy. In order to make the principle regulating inequalities determinate, one looks at the system from the standpoint of the least advantaged representative man. Inequalities are permissible when they maximize, or at least all contribute to, the long-term expectations of the least fortunate group in society.

Now this general conception imposes no constraints on what sorts of inequalities are allowed, whereas the special conception, by putting the two principles in serial order (with the necessary adjustments in meaning), forbids exchanges between basic liberties and economic and social benefits. I shall not try to justify this ordering here. . . . But roughly, the idea underlying this ordering is that if the parties assume that their basic liberties can be effectively exercised, they will not exchange a lesser liberty for an improvement in economic well-being. It is only when social conditions do not allow the effective establishment of these rights that one can concede their limitation; and these restrictions can be granted only to the extent that they are necessary to prepare the way for a free society. The denial of equal liberty can be defended only if it is necessary to raise the level of civilization so that in due course these freedoms can be enjoyed. Thus in adopting a serial order we are in effect making a special assumption in the original position, namely, that the parties know that the conditions of their society, whatever they are, admit the effective realization of the equal liberties. The serial ordering of the two principles of justice eventually comes to be reasonable if the general conception is consistently followed. This lexical ranking is the long-run tendency of the general view. For the most part I shall assume that the requisite circumstances for the serial order obtain.

It seems clear from these remarks that the two principles are at least a plausible conception of justice. The question, though, is how one is to argue for them more systematically. Now there are several things to do. One can work out their consequences for institutions and note their implications for fundamental social policy. In this way they are tested by a comparison with our considered judgments of justice. . . . But one can also try to find arguments in their favor that are decisive from the standpoint of the original position. In order to see how this might be done, it is useful as a heuristic device to think of the two principles as the maximin solution to the problem of social justice. There is an analogy between the two principles and the maximin rule for choice under uncertainty.[5] This is evident from the fact that the two principles are those a person would choose for the design of a society in which his enemy is to assign him his place. The maximin rule tells us to rank alternatives by their worst possible outcomes: we are to adopt the alternative the worst outcome of which is superior to the worst outcomes of the others. The persons in the original position do not, of course, assume that their initial place in society is decided by a malevolent opponent. As I note below, they should not reason from false premises. The veil of ignorance does not violate this idea, since an absence of information is not misinformation. But that the two principles of justice would be chosen if the parties were forced to protect themselves against such a contingency explains the sense in which this conception is the maximin solution. And this analogy suggests that if the original position has been described so that it is rational for the parties to adopt the conservative attitude expressed by this rule, a conclusive argument can indeed be constructed for these principles. Clearly the maximin rule is not, in general, a suitable guide for choices under uncertainty. But it is attractive in situations marked by certain special features. My aim, then, is to show that a good case can be made for the two principles based on the fact that the original position manifests these features to the fullest possible degree, carrying them to the limit, so to speak.

Consider the gain-and-loss table below. It represents the gains and losses for a situation which is not a game of strategy. There is no one playing against the person making the decision; instead he is faced with several possible circumstances which may or may not obtain. Which circumstances happen to exist does not depend upon what the person choosing decides or whether he announces his moves in advance. The numbers in the table are monetary values (in hundreds of dollars) in comparison with some initial situation. The gain (g) depends upon the individual's decision (d) and the circumstances (c). Thus g = f(d,c). Assuming that there are three possible decisions and three possible circumstances, we might have this gain-and-loss table.

| Decisions | Circumstances | | |
	c_1	c_2	c_3
d_1	−7	8	12
d_2	−8	7	14
d_3	5	6	8

The maximin rule requires that we make the third decision. For in this case the worst that can happen is that one gains five hundred dollars, which is better than the worst for the other actions. If we adopt one of these we may lose either eight or seven hundred dollars. Thus, the choice of d_3 maximizes f(d,c) for that value of c which for a given d, minimizes f. The term "maximin" means the *maximum minimorum;* and the rule directs our attention to the worst that can happen under any proposed course of action, and to decide in the light of that.

Now there appear to be three chief features of situations that give plausibility to this unusual rule.[6] First, since the rule takes no account of the likelihoods of the possible circumstances, there must be some reason for sharply discounting estimates of these probabilities. Offhand, the most natural rule of choice would seem to be to compute the expectation of monetary gain for each decision and then to adopt the course of action with the highest prospect. (This expectation is defined as follows: let us suppose that g_{ij} represent the numbers in the gain-and-loss table, where i is the row index and j is the column index; and let p_i, j = 1, 2, 3, be the likelihoods of the circumstances, with $\Sigma p_j = 1$. Then the expectation for the ith decision is equal to

$\Sigma p_i g_{ij}$.) Thus it must be, for example, that the situation is one in which a knowledge of likelihoods is impossible, or at best extremely insecure. In this case it is unreasonable not to be skeptical of probabilistic calculations unless there is no other way out, particularly if the decision is a fundamental one that needs to be justified to others.

The second feature that suggests the maximin rule is the following: the person choosing has a conception of the good such that he cares very little, if anything, for what he might gain above the minimum stipend that he can, in fact, be sure of by following the maximin rule. It is not worthwhile for him to take a chance for the sake of a further advantage, especially when it may turn out that he loses much that is important to him. This last provision brings in the third feature; namely, that the rejected alternatives have outcomes that one can hardly accept. The situation involves grave risks. Of course these features work most effectively in combination. The paradigm situation for following the maximin rule is when all three features are realized to the highest degree. This rule does not, then, generally apply, nor of course is it self-evident. Rather, it is a maxim, a rule of thumb, that comes into its own in special circumstances. Its application depends upon the qualitative structure of the possible gains and losses in relation to one's conception of the good, all this against a background in which it is reasonable to discount conjectural estimates of likelihoods.

It should be noted, as the comments on the gain-and-loss table say, that the entries in the table represent monetary values and not utilities. This difference is significant since for one thing computing expectations on the basis of such objective values is not the same thing as computing expected utility and may lead to different results. The essential point, though, is that in justice as fairness the parties do not know their conception of the good and cannot estimate their utility in the ordinary sense. In any case, we want to go behind de facto preferences generated by given conditions. Therefore expectations are based upon an index of primary goods and the parties make their choice accordingly. The entries in the example are in terms of money and not utility to indicate this aspect of the contract doctrine.

Now, as I have suggested, the original position has been defined so that it is a situation in which the maximin rule applies. In order to see this, let us review briefly the nature of this situation with these three special features in mind. To begin with, the veil of ignorance excludes all but the vaguest knowledge of likelihoods. The parties have no basis for determining the probable nature of their society, or their place in it. Thus they have strong reasons for being wary of probability calculations if any other course is open to them. They must also take into account the fact that their choice of principles should seem reasonable to others, in particular their descendants, whose rights will be deeply affected by it. There are further grounds for discounting that I shall mention as we go along. For the present it suffices to note that these considerations are strengthened by the fact that the parties know very little about the gain-and-loss table. Not only are they unable to conjecture the likelihoods of the various possible circumstances, they cannot say much about what the possible circumstances are, much less enumerate them and foresee the outcome of each alternative available. Those deciding are much more in the dark than the illustration by a numerical table suggests. It is for this reason that I have spoken of an analogy with the maximin rule.

Several kinds of arguments for the two principles of justice illustrate the second feature. Thus, if we can maintain that these principles provide a workable theory of social justice, and that they are compatible with reasonable demands of efficiency, then this conception guarantees a satisfactory minimum. There may be, on reflection, little reason for trying to do better. Thus much of the argument . . . is to show, by their application to the main questions of social justice, that the two principles are a satisfactory conception. These details have a philosophical purpose. Moreover, this line of thought is practically decisive if we can establish the priority of liberty, the lexical ordering of the two principles. For this priority implies that the persons in the original position have no desire to try for greater gains at the expense of the equal liberties. The minimum assured by the two principles in lexical order is not one that the parties wish to jeopardize for the sake of greater economic and social advantages. . . .

Finally, the third feature holds if we can assume that other conceptions of justice may lead to institutions that the parties would find intolerable. For example, it has sometimes been held that under some conditions the utility principle (in either form) justifies, if not slavery or serfdom, at any rate serious infractions of liberty for the sake of greater social benefits. We need not consider here the truth of this claim, or the likelihood that the requisite conditions obtain. For the moment, this contention is only to illustrate the way in which conceptions of justice may allow for outcomes which the parties may not be able to accept. And having the ready alternative of the two principles of justice which secure a satisfactory minimum, it seems unwise, if not irrational, for them to take a chance that these outcomes are not realized.

So much, then, for a brief sketch of the features of situations in which the maximin rule comes into its own and of the way in which the arguments for the two principles of justice can be subsumed under them. . . .

The Final Formulation of the Principles of Justice

. . . I now wish to give the final statement of the two principles of justice for institutions. For the sake of completeness, I shall give a full statement including earlier formulations.

First Principle
Each person is to have an equal right to the most extensive total system of equal basic liberties compatible with a similar system of liberty for all.

Second Principle
Social and economic inequalities are to be arranged so that they are both:
(a) to the greatest benefit of the least advantaged, consistent with the just savings principle, and
(b) attached to offices and positions open to all under conditions of fair equality of opportunity.

First Priority Rule (The Priority of Liberty)
The principles of justice are to be ranked in lexical order and therefore liberty can be restricted only for the sake of liberty. There are two cases:
(a) a less extensive liberty must strengthen the total system of liberty shared by all;
(b) a less than equal liberty must be acceptable to those with the lesser liberty.

Second Priority Rule (The Priority of Justice over Efficiency and Welfare)
The second principle of justice is lexically prior to the principle of efficiency and to that of maximizing the sum of advantages; and fair opportunity is prior to the difference principle. There are two cases:
(a) an inequality of opportunity must enhance the opportunities of those with the lesser opportunity;
(b) an excessive rate of saving must on balance mitigate the burden of those bearing this hardship.

General Conception
All social primary goods—liberty and opportunity, income and wealth, and the bases of self-respect—are to be distributed equally unless an unequal distribution of any or all of these goods is to the advantage of the least favored.

By way of comment, these principles and priority rules are no doubt incomplete. Other modifications will surely have to be made, but I shall not further complicate the statement of the principles. It suffices to observe that when we come to nonideal theory, we do not fall back straightway upon the general conception of justice. The lexical ordering of the two principles, and the valuations that this ordering implies, suggest priority rules which seem to be reasonable enough in many cases. By various examples I have tried to illustrate how these rules can be used and to indicate their plausibility. Thus the ranking of the principles of justice in ideal theory reflects back and guides the application of these principles to nonideal situations. It identifies which limitations need to be dealt with first. The drawback of the general conception of justice is that it lacks the definite structure of the two principles in serial order. In more extreme and tangled instances of nonideal theory there may be no alternative to it. At some point the priority of rules for nonideal cases will fail; and indeed, we may be able to find no satisfactory answer at all. But we must try to postpone the day of reckoning as long as possible, and try to arrange society so that it never comes. . . .

Notes

1. As the text suggests, I shall regard Locke's *Second Treatise of Government*, Rousseau's *The Social Contract*, and Kant's ethical works beginning with *The Foundations of the Metaphysics of Morals* as definitive of the contract tradition. For all of its greatness, Hobbes's *Leviathan* raises special problems. A general historical survey is provided by J. W. Gough, *The Social Contract*, 2nd ed. (Oxford, The Clarendon Press, 1957), and Otto Gierke, *Natural Law and the Theory of Society*, trans. with an introduction by Ernest Barker (Cambridge, The University Press, 1934). A presentation of the contract view as primarily an ethical theory is to be found in G. R. Grice, *The Grounds of Moral Judgment* (Cambridge, The University Press, 1967).

2. Kant is clear that the original agreement is hypothetical. See *The Metaphysics of Morals*, pt. I *(Rechtslehre)*, especially §§ 47, 52; and pt. II of the essay "Concerning the Common Saying: This May Be True in Theory but It Does Not Apply in Practice," in *Kant's Political Writings*, ed. Hans Reiss and trans. by H. B. Nisbet (Cambridge, The University Press, 1970), pp. 73–87. See Georges Vlachos, *La pensée politique de Kant* (Paris, Presses Universitaires de France, 1962), pp. 326–335; and J. G. Murphy, *Kant: The Philosophy of Right* (London, Macmillan, 1970), pp. 109–112, 133–136, for a further discussion.

3. For the formulation of this intuitive idea I am indebted to Allan Gibbard.

4. The process of mutual adjustment of principles and considered judgments is not peculiar to moral philosophy. See Nelson Goodman, *Fact, Fiction, and Forecast* (Cambridge, Mass., Harvard University Press, 1955), pp. 65–68, for parallel remarks concerning the justification of the principles of deductive and inductive inference.

5. An accessible discussion of this and other rules of choice under uncertainty can be found in W. J. Baumol, *Economic Theory and Operations Analysis*, 2nd ed. (Englewood Cliffs, N.J., Prentice-Hall, 1965), ch. 24. Baumol gives a geometric interpretation of these rules, including the diagram used . . . to illustrate the difference principle. See pp. 558–562. See also R. D. Luce and Howard Raiffa, *Games and Decisions* (New York, John Wiley and Sons, Inc., 1957), ch. XIII, for a fuller account.

6. Here I borrow from William Fellner, *Probability and Profit* (Homewood, Ill., Richard D. Irwin, 1965), pp. 140–142, where these features are noted.

4. Morality and the Liberal Ideal

Michael J. Sandel

Michael J. Sandel believes that recent political philosophy has offered both a utilitarian and a rights-based defense of liberalism. The utilitarian defense, which sees liberalism as maximizing the sum of utility, has even been criticized by other liberals for failing to take seriously the distinction between persons. The rights-based defense, which sees liberalism as guaranteeing each person certain rights, has been criticized for giving the self priority over its ends. According to communitarians, we cannot even conceive of ourselves as distinct from our ends.

Liberals often take pride in defending what they oppose—pornography, for example, or unpopular views. They say the state should not impose on its citizens a preferred way of life, but should leave them as free as possible to choose their own values and ends, consistent with a similar liberty for others. This commitment to freedom of choice requires liberals constantly to distinguish between permission and praise, between allowing a practice and endorsing it. It is one thing to allow pornography, they argue, something else to affirm it.

Conservatives sometimes exploit this distinction by ignoring it. They charge that those who would allow abortions favor abortion, that opponents of school prayer, oppose prayer, that those who defend the rights of Communists sympathize with their cause. And in a pattern of argument familiar in our politics, liberals reply by invoking higher principles; it is not that they dislike pornography less, but rather that they value toleration, or freedom of choice, or fair procedures more.

But in contemporary debate, the liberal rejoinder seems increasingly fragile, its moral basis increasingly unclear. Why should toleration and freedom of choice prevail when other important values are also at stake? Too often the answer implies some version of moral relativism, the idea that it is wrong to "legislate morality" because all morality is merely subjective. "Who is to say what is literature and what is filth? That is a value judgment, and whose values should decide?"

From "Morality and the Liberal Ideal," *New Republic* (May 7, 1984), pp. 15–17. Reprinted by permission of *New Republic*.

Relativism usually appears less as a claim than as a question. "Who is to judge?" But it is a question that can also be asked of the values that liberals defend. Toleration and freedom and fairness are values too, and they can hardly be defended by the claim that no values can be defended. So it is a mistake to affirm liberal values by arguing that all values are merely subjective. The relativist defense of liberalism is no defense at all.

What, then, can be the moral basis of the higher principles the liberal invokes? Recent political philosophy has offered two main alternatives—one utilitarian, the other Kantian. The utilitarian view, following John Stuart Mill, defends liberal principles in the name of maximizing the general welfare. The state should not impose on its citizens a preferred way of life, even for their own good, because doing so will reduce the sum of human happiness, at least in the long run; better that people choose for themselves, even if, on occasion, they get it wrong. "The only freedom which deserves the name," writes Mill in *On Liberty*, "is that of pursuing our own good in our own way so long as we do not attempt to deprive others of theirs, or impede their efforts to obtain it." He adds that his argument does not depend on any notion of abstract right, only on the principle of the greatest good for the greatest number. "I regard utility as the ultimate appeal on all ethical questions; but it must be utility in the largest sense, grounded on the permanent interests of man as a progressive being."

Many objections have been raised against utilitarianism as a general doctrine of moral philosophy. Some have questioned the concept of utility, and the assumption that all human goods are in principle commensurable. Others have objected that by reducing all values to preferences and desires, utilitarians are unable to admit qualitative distinctions of worth, unable to distinguish noble desires from base ones. But most recent debate has focused on whether utilitarianism offers a convincing basis for liberal principles, including respect for individual rights.

In one respect, utilitarianism would seem well suited to liberal purposes. Seeking to maximize overall happiness does not require judging people's values, only aggregating them. And the willingness to aggregate preferences without judging them suggests a tolerant spirit, even a democratic one. When people go to the polls we count their votes, whatever they are.

But the utilitarian calculus is not always as liberal as it first appears. If enough cheering Romans pack the Coliseum to watch the lion devour the Christian, the collective pleasure of the Romans will surely outweigh the pain of the Christian, intense though it be. Or if a big majority abhors a small religion and wants it banned, the balance of preferences will favor suppression, not toleration. Utilitarians sometimes defend individual rights on the grounds that respecting them now will serve utility in the long run. But this calculation is precarious and contingent. It hardly secures the liberal promise not to impose on some the values of others. As the majority will is an inadequate instrument of liberal politics—by itself it fails to secure individual rights—so the utilitarian philosophy is an inadequate foundation for liberal principles.

The case against utilitarianism was made most powerfully by Immanuel Kant. He argued that empirical principles, such as utility, were unfit to serve as basis for the moral law. A wholly instrumental defense of freedom and rights not only leaves rights vulnerable, but fails to respect the inherent dignity of persons. The utilitarian calculus treats people as means to the happiness of others, not as ends in themselves, worthy of respect.

Contemporary liberals extend Kant's argument with the claim that utilitarianism fails to take seriously the distinction between persons.

In seeking above all to maximize the general welfare, the utilitarian treats society as a whole as if it were a single person, it conflates our many, diverse desires into a single system of desires. It is indifferent to the distribution of satisfactions among persons, except insofar as this may affect the overall sum. But this fails to respect our plurality and distinctness. It uses some as means to the happiness of all, and so fails to respect each as an end in himself.

In the view of modern day Kantians, certain rights are so fundamental that even the general welfare cannot override them. As John Rawls writes in his important work, *A Theory of Justice*, "Each person possesses an inviolability founded on justice that even the welfare of society as a whole cannot override. . . . The rights secured by justice are not subject to political bargaining or to the calculus of social interests."

So Kantian liberals need an account of rights that does not depend on utilitarian considerations. More than this, they need an account that does not depend on any particular conception of the good, that does not presuppose the superiority of one way of life over others. Only a justification neutral about ends could preserve the liberal resolve not to favor any particular ends, or to impose on its citizens a preferred way of life. But what sort of justification could this be? How is it possible to affirm certain liberties and rights as fundamental without embracing some vision of the good life, without endorsing some ends over others? It would seem we are back to the relativist predicament—to affirm liberal principles without embracing any particular ends.

The solution proposed by Kantian liberals is to draw a distinction between the "right" and the "good"—between a framework of basic rights and liberties, and the conceptions of the good that people may choose to pursue within the framework. It is one thing for the state to support a fair framework, they argue, something else to affirm some particular ends. For example, it is one thing to defend the right to free speech so that people may be free to form their own opinions and choose their own ends, but something else to support it on the grounds that a life of political discussion is inherently worthier than a life unconcerned with public affairs, or on the grounds that free speech will increase the general welfare. Only the first defense is available in the Kantian view, resting as it does on the ideal of a neutral framework.

Now, the commitment to a framework neutral with respect to ends can be seen as a kind of value—in this sense the Kantian liberal is no relativist—but its value consists precisely in its refusal to affirm a preferred way of life or conception of the good. For Kantian liberals, then, the right is prior to the good, and in two senses. First, individual rights cannot be sacrificed for the sake of the general good; and second, the principles of justice that specify these rights cannot be premised on any particular vision of the good life. What justifies the rights is not that they maximize the general welfare or otherwise promote the good, but rather that they comprise a fair framework within which individuals and groups can choose their own values and ends, consistent with a similar liberty for others.

Of course, proponents of the rights-based ethic notoriously disagree about what rights are fundamental, and about what political arrangements the ideal of the neutral framework requires. Egalitarian liberals support the welfare state, and favor a scheme of civil liberties together with certain social and economic rights—rights to welfare, education, health care, and so on. Libertarian liberals defend the market economy, and claim that redistributive policies violate peoples' rights; they favor a scheme of civil liberties combined with a strict regime of private property rights. But whether egalitarian or libertarian, rights-based liberalism begins with the claim that we are separate, individual persons, each with our own aims, interests, and conceptions of the good; it seeks a framework of rights that will enable us to realize our capacity as free moral agents, consistent with a similar liberty for others.

Within academic philosophy, the last decade or so has seen the ascendance of the rights-based ethic over the utilitarian one, due in large part to the influence of Rawls's *A Theory of Justice*. The legal philosopher H. I. A. Hart recently described the shift from "the old faith that some form of utilitarianism must capture the essence of political morality" to the new faith that "the truth must lie with a doctrine of basic human rights, protecting specific basic liberties and interests of individuals. ... . Whereas not so long ago great energy and much ingenuity of many philosophers were devoted to making some form of utilitarianism work, latterly such energies and ingenuity have been devoted to the articulation of theories of basic rights."

But in philosophy as in life, the new faith becomes the old orthodoxy before long. Even as it has come to prevail over it: utilitarian rival, the rights-based ethic has recently faced a growing challenge from a different direction, from a view that gives fuller expression to the claims of citizenship and community than the liberal vision allows. The communitarian critics, unlike modern liberals, make the case for a politics of the common good. Recalling the arguments of Hegel against Kant, they question the liberal claim for the priority of the right over the good, and the picture of the freely choosing individual it embodies. Following Aristotle, they argue that we cannot justify political arrangements without reference to common purposes and ends, and that we cannot conceive of ourselves without reference to our role as citizens, as participants in a common life.

This debate reflects two contrasting pictures of the self. The rights-based ethic, and the conception of the person it embodies, were shaped in large part in the encounter with utilitarianism. Where utilitarians conflate our many desires into a single system of desire, Kantians insist on the separateness of persons. Where the utilitarian self is simply defined as the sum of its desires, the Kantian-self is a choosing self, independent of the desires and ends it may have at any moment. As Rawls writes, "The self is prior to the ends which are affirmed by it, even a dominant end must be chosen from among numerous possibilities."

The priority of the self over its ends means I am never defined by my aims and attachments, but always capable of standing back to survey and assess and possibly to revise them. This is what it means to be a free and independent self, capable of choice. And this is the vision of the self that finds expression in the ideal of the state as a neutral framework. On the rights-based ethic, it is precisely because we are essentially separate, independent selves that we need a neutral framework, a framework of rights that refuses to choose among competing purposes and ends. If the self is prior to its ends, then the right must be prior to the good.

Communitarian critics of rights-based liberalism say we cannot conceive ourselves as independent in this way, as bearers of selves wholly detached from our aims and attachments. They say that certain of our roles are partly constitutive of the persons we are—as citizens of a country, or members of a movement, or partisans of a cause. But if we are partly defined by the communities we inhabit, then we must also be implicated in the purposes and ends characteristic of those communities. As Alasdair MacIntyre writes in his book, *After Virtue*, "What is good for me has to be the good for one who inhabits these roles." Open-ended though it be, the story of my life is always embedded in the story of those communities from which I derive my identity—whether family or city, tribe or nation, party or cause. In the communitarian view, these stories make a moral difference, not only a psychological one. They situate us in the world and give our lives their moral particularity.

What is at stake for politics in the debate between unencumbered selves and situated ones? What are the practical differences between a politics of rights and a politics of the common good? On some issues, the two theories may produce different arguments for similar policies. For example, the civil rights movement of the 1960s might be justified by liberals in the name of human dignity and respect for persons, and by communitarians in the name of recognizing the full membership of fellow citizens wrongly excluded from the common life of the nation. And where liberals might support public education in hopes of equipping students to become autonomous individuals, capable of choosing their own ends and pursuing them effectively, communitarians might support public education in hopes of equipping students to become good citizens, capable of contributing meaningfully to public deliberations and pursuits.

On other issues, the two ethics might lead to different policies. Communitarians would be more likely than liberals to allow a town to ban pornographic book stores, on the grounds that pornography offends its way of life and the values that sustain it. But a politics of civic virtue does not always part company with liberalism in favor of conservative policies. For example, communitarians would be more willing than some rights-oriented liberals to see states enact laws regulating plant closings, to protect their communities from the disruptive effects of capital mobility and sudden industrial change. More generally, where the liberal regards the expansion of individual rights and entitlements as unqualified moral and political progress, the communitarian is troubled by the tendency of liberal programs to displace politics from smaller forms of association to more comprehensive ones. Where libertarian liberals defend the private economy and egalitarian liberals defend the welfare state, communitarians worry about the concentration of power in both the corporate economy and the bureaucratic state, and the erosion of those intermediate forms of community that have at times sustained a more vital public life.

Liberals often argue that a politics of the common good, drawing as it must on particular loyalties, obligations, and traditions, opens the way to prejudice and intolerance. The modern nation-state is not the Athenian polis, they point out; the scale and diversity of modern life have rendered the Aristotelian political ethic nostalgic at best and dangerous at worst. Any attempt to govern by a vision of the good is likely to lead to a slippery slope of totalitarian temptations.

Communitarians reply, rightly in my view, that intolerance flourishes most where forms of life are dislocated, roots unsettled, traditions undone. In our day, the totalitarian impulse has sprung less from the convictions of confidently situated selves than from the confusions of atomized, dislocated, frustrated selves, at sea in a world where common meanings have lost their force. As Hannah Arendt has written, "What makes mass society so difficult to bear is not the number of people involved, or at least not primarily, but the fact that the world between them has lost its power to gather them together, to relate and to separate them." Insofar as our public life has withered, our sense of common involvement diminished, we lie vulnerable to the mass politics of totalitarian solutions. So responds the party of the common good to the party of rights. If the party of the common good is right, our most pressing moral and political project is to revitalize those civic republican possibilities implicit in our tradition but fading in our time.

---

5. *Wyman, Commissioner of New York Department of Social Services v. James*

Supreme Court of the United States

The issue before the Supreme Court of the United States was whether the Fourth Amendment prohibition of unreasonable searches applies to visits by welfare caseworkers to recipients of Aid to Families with Dependent Children. The majority of the Court held that the Fourth Amendment does not apply in this case because the visitation is not forced or compelled, and even if it were, the visitation serves the state's overriding interest in the welfare of dependent children. Dissenting Justices Douglas and Marshall argued that the Fourth Amendment prohibition does apply because the visitation is forced and compelled (although not normally by a threat of a criminal penalty) and because there are other ways of protecting the state's interest in this case. Justices Douglas and Marshall also argued that the decision of the majority is inconsistent with the Supreme Court's rulings with respect to the allocation of benefits in other cases.

Mr. Justice Blackmun delivered the opinion of the Court.

This appeal presents the issue whether a beneficiary of the program for Aid to Families with Dependent Children (AFDC) may refuse a home visit by the caseworker without risking the termination of benefits.

The New York State and City social services commissioners appeal from a judgment and decree of a divided three-judge District Court. . . .

The District Court majority held that a mother receiving AFDC relief may refuse, without forfeiting her right to that relief, the periodic home visit which the cited New York statutes and regulations prescribe as a condition for the continuance of assistance under the program. The beneficiary's thesis, and that of the District Court majority, is that home visitation is a search and, when not consented to or when not supported by a warrant based on probable cause, violates the beneficiary's Fourth and Fourteenth Amendment rights.
. . .

Plaintiff Barbara James is the mother of a son, Maurice, who was born in May 1967. They reside in New York City. Mrs. James first applied for AFDC assistance shortly before Maurice's birth. A caseworker made a visit to her apartment at that time without objection. The assistance was authorized.

Two years later, on May 8, 1969, a caseworker wrote Mrs. James that she would visit her home on May 14. Upon receipt of this advice, Mrs. James telephoned the worker that, although she was willing to supply information "reasonable and relevant" to her need for public assistance, any discussion was not to take place at her home. The worker told Mrs. James that she was required by law to visit in her home and that refusal to permit the visit would result in the termination of assistance. Permission was still denied. . . .

A notice of termination issued on June 2.

Thereupon, without seeking a hearing at the state level, Mrs. James, individually and on behalf of Maurice, and purporting to act on behalf of all other persons similarly situated, instituted the present civil rights suit. . . .

When a case involves a home and some type of official intrusion into that home, as this case appears to do, an immediate and natural reaction is one of concern about Fourth Amendment rights and the protection which that Amendment is intended to afford. Its emphasis indeed is upon one of the most precious aspects of personal security in the home: "The right of the people to be secure in their persons, houses, papers, and effects. . . ." This Court has characterized that right as "basic to a free society. . . ." And over the years the Court consistently has been most protective of the privacy of the dwelling. . . .

This natural and quite proper protective attitude, however, is not a factor in this case, for the seemingly obvious and simple reason that we are not concerned here with any search by the New York social service agency in the Fourth Amendment meaning of that term. It is true that the governing statute and regulations appear to make mandatory the initial home visit and the subsequent periodic "contacts" (which may include home visits) for the inception and continuance of aid. It is also true that the caseworker's posture in the home visit is perhaps, in a sense, both rehabilitative and investigative. But this latter aspect, we think, is given too broad a character and far more emphasis than it deserves if it is equated with a search in the traditional criminal law context. We note, too, that the visitation in itself is not forced or compelled, and that the beneficiary's denial of permission is not a criminal act. If consent to the visitation is withheld, no visitation takes place. The aid then never begins or merely ceases, as the case may be. There is no entry of the home and there is no search.

If however, we were to assume that a caseworker's home visit, before or subsequent to the beneficiary's initial qualification for benefits, somehow (perhaps because the average beneficiary might feel she is in no position to refuse consent to the visit), and despite its interview nature, does possess some of the characteristics of a search in the traditional sense,

we nevertheless conclude that does not fall within the Fourth Amendment's proscription. This is because it does not descend to the level of unreasonableness. It is unreasonableness which is the Fourth Amendment's standard.

There are a number of factors that compel us to conclude that the home visit proposed for Mrs. James is not unreasonable.

The public's interest in this particular segment of the area of assistance to the unfortunate is protection and aid for the dependent child whose family requires such aid for that child. . . . The dependent child's needs are paramount, and only with hesitancy would we relegate those needs, in the scale of comparative values, to a position secondary to what the mother claims as her rights.

The agency, with tax funds provided from federal as well as from state sources, is fulfilling a public trust. The State, working through its qualified welfare agency, has appropriate and paramount interest and concern in seeing and assuring that the intended and proper objects of that tax-produced assistance are the ones who benefit from the aid it dispenses. . . .

One who dispenses purely private charity naturally has an interest in and expects to know how his charitable funds are utilized and put to work. The public, when it is the provider, rightly expects the same. . . .

We therefore conclude that the home visitation as structured by the New York statutes and regulations is a reasonable administrative tool; that it serves a valid and proper administrative purpose for the dispensation of the AFDC program; that it is not an unwarranted invasion of personal privacy; and that it violates no right guaranteed by the Fourth Amendment.

Reversed and remanded with directions to enter a judgment of dismissal.

It is so ordered. . . .

Mr. Justice Douglas, dissenting. . . .

In 1969 roughly 127 billion dollars were spent by the federal, state, and local governments on "social welfare." To farmers alone almost four billion dollars were paid, in part for not growing certain crops. . . .

Yet almost every beneficiary whether rich or poor, rural or urban, has a "house"—one of the places protected by the Fourth Amendment against "unreasonable searches and seizures." The question in this case is whether receipt of largesse from the government makes the *home* of the beneficiary subject to access by an inspector of the agency of oversight, even though the beneficiary objects to the intrusion and even though the Fourth Amendment's procedure for access to one's *house* or *home* is not followed. The penalty here is not, of course, invasion of the privacy of Barbara James, only her loss of federal or state largesse. That, however, is merely rephrasing the problem. Whatever the semantics, the central question is whether the government by force of its largesse has the power to "buy up" rights guaranteed by the Constitution. But for the assertion of her constitutional right, Barbara James in this case would have received the welfare benefit. . . .

The applicable principle, as stated in *Camara* as "justified by history and by current experience" is that "except in certain carefully defined classes of cases, a search of private property without proper consent is 'unreasonable' unless it has been authorized by a valid search warrant."

In *See* we [decided] that the "businessman, like the occupant of a residence, has a constitutional right to go about his business free from unreasonable official entries upon his private commercial property." There is not the slightest hint in *See* that the Government could condition a business license on the "consent" of the licensee to the administrative searches we held violated the Fourth Amendment. It is a strange jurisprudence indeed which safeguards the businessman at his place of work from warrantless searches but will not do the same for a mother in her *home.*

Is a search of her home without a warrant made "reasonable" merely because she is dependent on government largesse?

Judge Skelly Wright has stated the problem succinctly:

Welfare has long been considered the equivalent of charity and its recipients have been subjected to all kinds of dehumanizing experiences in the government's effort to police its welfare payments. In fact, over half a billion dollars are expended annually for administration and policing in connection with the Aid to Families with Dependent Children program. Why such large sums are necessary for administration and policing has never been adequately explained. No such sums are spent policing the government subsidies granted to farmers, airlines, steamship companies, and junk mail dealers, to name but a few. The truth is that in this subsidy area society has simply adopted a double standard, one for aid to business and the farmer and a different one for welfare. (Poverty, Minorities, and Respect for Law, 1970 Duke L. J. 425, 437–438.)

If the welfare recipient was not Barbara James but a prominent, affluent cotton or wheat farmer receiving benefit payments for not growing crops, would not the approach be different? Welfare in aid of dependent children, like social security and unemployment benefits, has an aura of suspicion. There doubtless are frauds in every sector of public welfare whether the recipient be a Barbara James or someone who is prominent or influential. But constitutional rights—here the privacy of the *home*—are obviously not dependent on the poverty or on the affluence of the beneficiary. It is the precincts of the *home* that the Fourth Amendment protects; and their privacy is as important to the lowly as to the mighty.

I would sustain the judgment of the three-judge court in the present case.

Mr. Justice Marshall, whom Mr. Justice Brennan joins, dissenting.

. . . The record plainly shows . . . that Mrs. James offered to furnish any information that the appellants desired and to be interviewed at any place other than her home. Appellants rejected her offers and terminated her benefits solely on the ground that she refused to permit a home visit. In addition, appellants make no contention that any sort of probable cause exists to suspect appellee of welfare fraud or child abuse.

Simply stated, the issue in this case is whether a state welfare agency can require all recipients of AFDC benefits to submit to warrantless "visitations" of their homes. In answering that question, the majority dodges between constitutional issues to reach a result clearly inconsistent with the decisions of this

Court. We are told that there is no such search involved in this case; that even if there were a search, it would not be unreasonable; and that even if this were an unreasonable search, a welfare recipient waives her right to object by accepting benefits. I emphatically disagree with all three conclusions. . . .

. . . In an era of rapidly burgeoning governmental activities and their concomitant inspectors, caseworkers, and researchers, a restriction of the Fourth Amendment to "the traditional criminal law context" tramples the ancient concept that a man's home is his castle. Only last Term, we reaffirmed that this concept has lost none of its vitality. . . .

. . . [I]t is argued that the home visit is justified to protect dependent children from "abuse" and "exploitation." These are heinous crimes, but they are not confined to indigent households. Would the majority sanction, in the absence of probable cause, compulsory visits to all American homes for the purpose of discovering child abuse? Or is this Court prepared to hold as a matter of constitutional law that a mother, merely because she is poor, is substantially more likely to injure or exploit her children? Such a categorical approach to an entire class of citizens would be dangerously at odds with the tenets of our democracy. . . .

Although the Court does not agree with my conclusion that the home visit is an unreasonable search, its opinion suggests that even if the visit were unreasonable, appellee has somehow waived her right to object. Surely the majority cannot believe that valid Fourth Amendment consent can be given under the threat of the loss of one's sole means of support. . . .

In deciding that the homes of AFDC recipients are not entitled to protection from warrantless searches by welfare caseworkers, the Court declines to follow prior case law and employs a rationale that, if applied to the claims of all citizens, would threaten the validity of the Fourth Amendment. . . . Perhaps the majority has explained why a commercial warehouse deserves more protection than does this poor woman's home. I am not convinced; and, therefore, I must respectfully dissent.

6. *Plyler v. Doe*

Supreme Court of the United States

The issue before the Supreme Court was whether a Texas statute that withholds from local school districts any state funds for the education of children who were not "legally admitted" into the United States and that authorizes local school districts to deny enrollment to such children violates the Equal Protection Clause of the Fourteenth Amendment. Justice Brennan, delivering the opinion of the Court, argued that the Texas statute did violate the Equal Protection Clause. He contended that although public education is not a right granted to individuals by the Constitution (Marshall dissenting), given the "pivotal role of education in sustaining our political and cultural heritage" and the economic benefits that accrue to Texas from the presence of illegal aliens, petitioners had failed to establish a legitimate state interest in denying an education to illegal aliens. In dissent, Chief Justice Burger with whom Justices White, Rehnquist, and O'Connor joined, argued that although the Texas statute is unwise and unsound, it is not unconstitutional. Burger contended that although illegal aliens are included within the category of persons protected by the Equal Protection Clause, the Texas statute does bear "a relation to a legitimate state purpose," especially in view of the fact that the federal government sees fit to exclude illegal aliens from numerous social welfare programs.

. . . In May 1975, the Texas Legislature revised its education laws to withhold from local school districts any state funds for the education of children who were not "legally admitted" into the United States. The 1975 revision also authorized local school districts to deny enrollment in their public schools to children not "legally admitted" to the country. . . . These cases involve constitutional challenges to those provisions.

[*Plyler* v. *Doe*] is a class action, filed in the United States District Court for the Eastern District of Texas in September 1977, on behalf of certain school-age children of Mexican origin residing in Smith County, Tex., who could not establish that they had been legally admitted into the United States. The action complained of the exclusion of plaintiff children from the public schools of the Tyler Independent School District. The Superintendent and members of the Board of Trustees of the School District were named as defendants; the State of Texas intervened as a party-defendant. After certifying a class consisting of all undocumented school-age children of Mexican origin residing within the School District, the District Court preliminarily enjoined defendants from denying a free education to members of the plaintiff class. In December 1977, the court conducted an extensive hearing on plaintiffs' motion for permanent injunctive relief. . . .

The District Court held that illegal aliens were entitled to the protection of the Equal Protection Clause of the Fourteenth Amendment, and that [this section] violated that Clause . . .

The Court of Appeals for the Fifth Circuit upheld the District Court's injunction. . . .

The Fourteenth Amendment provides that "[n]o State shall . . . deprive any person of life, liberty, or property, without due process of law; nor deny to *any person within its jurisdiction* the equal protection of the laws." . . . (Emphasis added.) Appellants argue at the outset that undocumented aliens, because of their immigration status, are not "persons within the jurisdiction" of the State of Texas, and that they therefore have no right to the equal protection of Texas law. We reject this argument.
. . .

. . . The Equal Protection Clause was intended to work nothing less than the abolition of all caste-based and invidious class-based legislation. That objective is fundamentally at odds with the power the State asserts here to classify persons subject to its laws as nonetheless excepted from its protection.

Although the congressional debate concerning . . . the Fourteenth Amendment was limited, that debate clearly confirms the understanding that the phrase "within its jurisdiction" was intended in a broad sense to offer the guarantee of equal protection to all within a State's boundaries, and to all upon whom the State would impose the obligations of its laws. Indeed, it appears from those debates that Congress, by using the phrase "person within its jurisdiction," sought expressly to ensure that the equal protection of the laws was provided to the alien population. Representative Bingham reported to the House the draft resolution of the Joint Committee of Fifteen on Reconstruction (H.R. 63) that was to become the Fourteenth Amendment. . . . Two days later, Bingham posed the following question in support of the resolution:

> Is it not essential to the unity of the people that the citizens of each State shall be entitled to all the privileges and immunities of citizens in the several States? Is it not essential to the unity of the Government and the unity of the people that all persons, *whether citizens or strangers, within this land,* shall have equal protection in every State in this Union in the rights of life and liberty and property?"

. . . Our conclusion that the illegal aliens who are plaintiffs in these cases may claim the benefit of the Fourteenth Amendment's guarantee of equal protection only begins the inquiry. The more difficult question is whether the Equal Protection Clause has been violated by the refusal of the State of Texas to reimburse local school boards for the education of children who cannot demonstrate that their presence within the United States is lawful, or by the imposition by those school boards of the burden of tuition on those children. It is to this question that we now turn. . . .

. . . In applying the Equal Protection Clause

to most forms of state action, we thus seek only the assurance that the classification at issue bears some fair relationship to a legitimate public purpose.

Of course, undocumented status is not irrelevant to any proper legislative goal. Nor is undocumented status an absolutely immutable characteristic since it is the product of conscious, indeed unlawful, action. But [this statute] is directed against children, and imposes its discriminatory burden on the basis of a legal characteristic over which children can have little control. It is thus difficult to conceive of a rational justification for penalizing these children for their presence within the United States. Yet that appears to be precisely the effect of [this statute].

Public education is not a "right" granted to individuals by the Constitution. *San Antonio Independent School Dist. v. Rodriguez* . . . (1973). But neither is it merely some governmental "benefit" indistinguishable from other forms of social welfare legislation. Both the importance of education is maintaining our basic institutions, and the lasting impact of its deprivation on the life of the child, mark the distinction. The "American people have always regarded education and [the] acquisition of knowledge as matters of supreme importance." *Meyer v. Nebraska* . . . (1923). We have recognized "the public schools as a most vital civic institution for the preservation of a democratic system of government," *Abington School District v. Schempp* . . . (1963) . . . and as the primary vehicle for transmitting "the values on which our society rests." *Ambach v. Norwick* . . . (1979). "[A]s . . . pointed out early in our history, . . . some degree of education is necessary to prepare citizens to participate effectively and intelligently in our open political system if we are to preserve freedom and independence." *Wisconsin v. Yoder* . . . (1972). And these historic "perceptions of the public schools as inculcating fundamental values necessary to the maintenance of a democratic political system have been confirmed by the observations of social scientists." *Ambach v. Norwick.* . . . In addition, education provides the basic tools by which individuals might lead economically productive lives to the benefit of us all. In sum, education has a fundamental role in maintaining the fabric of our society. We cannot ignore the significant social costs borne by our Nation when select groups are denied the means to absorb the values and skills upon which our social order rests.

In addition to the pivotal role of education is sustaining our political and cultural heritage, denial of education to some isolated group of children poses an affront to one of the goals of the Equal Protection Clause: the abolition of governmental barriers presenting unreasonable obstacles to advancement on the basis of individual merit. Paradoxically, by depriving the children of any disfavored group of an education, we foreclose the means by which that group might raise the level of esteem in which it is held by the majority. But more directly, "education prepares individuals to be self-reliant and self-sufficient participants in society." *Wisconsin v. Yoder.* . . . Illiteracy is an enduring disability. The inability to read and write will handicap the individual deprived of a basic education each and every day of his life. The inestimable toll of that deprivation on the social economic, intellectual, and psychological well-being of the individual, and the obstacle it poses to individual achievement, make it most difficult to reconcile the cost or the principle of a status-based denial of basic education with the framework of equality embodied in the Equal Protection Clause. What we said 28 years ago in *Brown v. Board of Education,* . . . (1954), still holds true:

Today, education is perhaps the most important function of state and local governments. Compulsory school attendance laws and the great expenditures for education both demonstrate our recognition of the importance of education to our democratic society. It is required in the performance of our most basic public responsibilities, even service in the armed forces. It is the very foundation of good citizenship. Today it is a principal instrument in awakening the child to cultural values, in preparing him for later professional training, and in helping him to adjust normally to his environment. In these days, it is doubtful that any child may reasonably be expected to succeed in life if he is denied the opportunity of an education. Such an opportunity, where the state has undertaken to provide it, is a right which must be made available to all on equal terms." . . .

... [A]ppellants appear to suggest that the State may seek to protect itself from an influx of illegal immigrants. While a State might have an interest in mitigating the potentially harsh economic effects of sudden shifts in population, [this statute] hardly offers an effective method of dealing with an urgent demographic or economic problem. There is no evidence in the record suggesting that illegal entrants impose any significant burden on the State's economy. To the contrary, the available evidence suggests that illegal aliens underutilize public services, while contributing their labor to the local economy and tax money to the state fisc. ... The dominant incentive for illegal entry into the State of Texas is the availability of employment; few if any illegal immigrants come to this country, or presumably to the State of Texas, in order to avail themselves of a free education. Thus, even making the doubtful assumption that the net impact of illegal aliens on the economy of the State is negative, we think it clear that "[c]harging tuition to undocumented children constitutes a ludicrously ineffectual attempt to stem the tide of illegal immigration," at least when compared with the alternative of prohibiting the employment of illegal aliens. ...

Accordingly, the judgment of the Court of Appeals in each of these cases is

Affirmed.

Justice *Marshall,* concurring.

While I join the Court's opinion, I do so without in any way retreating from my opinion in *San Antonio Independent School District v. Rodriguez.* ... I continue to believe that an individual's interest in education is fundamental, and that this view is amply supported "by the unique status accorded public education by our society, and by the close relationship between education and some of our most basic constitutional values." ... Furthermore, I believe that the facts of these cases demonstrate the wisdom of rejecting a rigidified approach to equal protection analysis, and of employing an approach that allows for varying levels of scrutiny depending upon "the constitutional and societal importance of the interest adversely affected and the recognized invidiousness of the basis upon which the particular classification is drawn." ... It continues

to be my view that a class-based denial of public education is utterly incompatible with the Equal Protection Clause of the Fourteenth Amendment.

Justice *Blackmun,* concurring.

I join the opinion and judgment of the Court.

Like Justice Powell, I believe that the children involved in this litigation "should not be left on the streets uneducated." ... I write separately, however, because in my view the nature of the interest at stake is crucial to the proper resolution of these cases.

The "fundamental rights" aspect of the Court's equal protection analysis—the now-familiar concept that governmental classifications bearing on certain interests must be closely scrutinized—has been the subject of some controversy. ...

[This controversy], combined with doubts about the judiciary's ability to make fine distinctions in assessing the effects of complex social policies, led the Court in *Rodriguez* to articulate a firm rule: fundamental rights are those that "explicitly or implicitly [are] guaranteed by the Constitution." ... It therefore squarely rejected the notion that "an ad hoc determination as to the social or economic importance" of a given interest is relevant to the level of scrutiny accorded classifications involving that interest, ... and made clear that "[i]t is not the province of this Court to create substantive constitutional rights in the name of guaranteeing equal protection of the laws." ...

I joined Justice Powell's opinion for the Court in *Rodriguez,* and I continue to believe that it provides the appropriate model for resolving most equal protection disputes. Classifications infringing substantive constitutional rights necessarily will be invalid, if not by force of the Equal Protection Clause, then through operation of other provisions of the Constitution. Conversely, classifications bearing on non-constitutional interests—even those involving "the most basic economic needs of impoverished human beings." ... — generally are not subject to special treatment under the Equal Protection Clause, because they are not distinguishable in any relevant way from other regulations in "the area of economics and social welfare."

With all this said, however, I believe the

Court's experience has demonstrated that the *Rodriguez* formulation does not settle every issue of "fundamental rights" arising under the Equal Protection Clause. Only a pedant would insist that there are *no* meaningful distinctions among the multitude of social and political interests regulated by the States, and *Rodriguez* does not stand for quite so absolute a proposition. To the contrary, *Rodriguez* implicitly acknowledged that certain interests, though not constitutionally guaranteed, must be accorded a special place in equal protection analysis. Thus, the Court's decisions long have accorded strict scrutiny to classifications bearing on the right to vote in state elections, and *Rodriguez* confirmed the "constitutional underpinnings of the right to equal treatment in the voting process." . . . Yet "the right to vote, *per se,* is not a constitutionally protected right." . . . Instead, regulation of the electoral process receives unusual scrutiny because "the right to exercise the franchise in a free and unimpaired manner is preservative of other basic civil and political rights." . . . In other words, the right to vote is accorded extraordinary treatment because it is, in equal protection terms, an extraordinary right: a citizen cannot hope to achieve any meaningful degree of individual political equality if granted an inferior right of participation in the political process. Those denied the vote are relegated, by state fiat, in a most basic way to second-class status. . . .

In my view, when the State provides an education to some and denies it to others, it immediately and inevitably creates class distinctions of a type fundamentally inconsistent with those purposes, mentioned above, of the Equal Protection Clause. Children denied an education are placed at a permanent and insurmountable competitive disadvantage, for an uneducated child is denied even the opportunity to achieve. And when those children are members of an identifiable group, that group—through the State's action—will have been converted into a discrete underclass. Other benefits provided by the State, such as housing and public assistance, are of course important; to an individual in immediate need, they may be more desirable than the right to be educated. But classifications involving the complete denial of education are in a

sense unique, for they strike at the heart of equal protection values by involving the State in the creation of permanent class distinctions. . . . In a sense, then, denial of an education is the analogue of denial of the right to vote: the former relegates the individual to second-class social status; the latter places him at a permanent political disadvantage.

This conclusion is fully consistent with *Rodriguez.* The Court there reserved judgment on the constitutionality of a state system that "occasioned an absolute denial of educational opportunities to any of its children," noting that "no charge fairly could be made that the system . . . fails to provide each child with an opportunity to acquire . . . basic minimal skills." . . . And it cautioned that in a case "involv[ing] the most persistent and difficult questions of educational policy, . . . [the] Court's lack of specialized knowledge and experience counsels against premature interference with the informed judgments made at the state and local levels." . . . Thus *Rodriguez* held, and the Court now reaffirms, that "a State need not justify by compelling necessity every variation in the manner in which education is provided to its population." . . . Similarly, it is undeniable that education is not a "fundamental right" in the sense that it is constitutionally guaranteed. Here, however, the State has undertaken to provide an education to most of the children residing within its borders. And, in contrast to the situation in *Rodriguez,* it does not take an advanced degree to predict the effects of a complete denial of education upon those children targeted by the State's classification. In such circumstances, the voting decisions suggest that the State must offer something more than a rational basis for its classification. . . .

Chief Justice *Burger,* with whom Justice *White,* Justice *Rehnquist,* and Justice *O'Connor* join, dissenting.

Were it our business to set the Nation's social policy, I would agree without hesitation that it is senseless for an enlightened society to deprive any children—including illegal aliens —of an elementary education. I fully agree that it would be folly—and wrong—to tolerate creation of a segment of society made up of illiterate persons, many having a limited or no command of our language. However, the Constitution does not constitute us as "Platonic Guardians" nor does it vest in this Court the authority to strike down laws because they do not meet our standards of desirable social policy, "wisdom," or "common sense." . . . We trespass on the assigned function of the political branches under our structure of limited and separated powers when we assume a policymaking role as the Court does today.

The Court makes no attempt to disguise that it is acting to make up for Congress' lack of "effective leadership" in dealing with the serious national problems caused by the influx of uncountable millions of illegal aliens across our borders. . . . The failure of enforcement of the immigration laws over more than a decade and the inherent difficulty and expense of sealing our vast borders have combined to create a grave socioeconomic dilemma. It is a dilemma that has not yet even been fully assessed, let alone addressed. However, it is not the function of the Judiciary to provide "effective leadership" simply because the political branches of government fail to do so.

The Court's holding today manifests the justly criticized judicial tendency to attempt speedy and wholesale formulation of "remedies" for the failures—or simply the laggard pace—of the political processes of our system of government. The Court employs, and in my view abuses, the Fourteenth Amendment in an effort to become an omnipotent and omniscient problem solver. That the motives for doing so are noble and compassionate does not alter the fact that the Court distorts our constitutional function to make amends for the defaults of others. . . .

The Court acknowledges that, except in those cases when state classifications disadvantage a "suspect class" or impinge upon a "fundamental right," the Equal Protection Clause permits a state "substantial latitude" in distinguishing between different groups of persons. . . . Moreover, the Court expressly—and correctly—rejects any suggestion that illegal aliens are a suspect class, . . . or that education is a fundamental right. . . . Yet by patching together bits and pieces of what might be termed quasi-suspect-class and quasi-fundamental-rights analysis, the Court spins

out a theory custom-tailored to the facts of these cases.

In the end, we are told little more than that the level of scrutiny employed to strike down the Texas law applies only when illegal alien children are deprived of a public education. . . . If ever a court was guilty of an unabashedly result-oriented approach, this case is a prime example. . . .

Once it is conceded—as the Court does—that illegal aliens are not a suspect class, and that education is not a fundamental right, our inquiry should focus on and be limited to whether the legislative classification at issue bears a rational relationship to a legitimate state purpose. . . .

It is significant that the Federal Government has seen fit to exclude illegal aliens from numerous social welfare programs, such as the food stamp program, . . . the old-age assistance, aid to families with dependent children, aid to the blind, aid to the permanently and totally disabled, and supplemental security income programs, . . . the Medicare hospital insurance benefits program, . . . and the Medicaid hospital insurance benefits for the aged and disabled program. . . . Although these exclusions do not conclusively demonstrate the constitutionality of the State's use of the same classification for comparable purposes, at the very least they tend to support the rationality of excluding illegal alien residents of a state from such programs so as to preserve the state's finite revenues for the benefit of lawful residents. . . .

Denying a free education to illegal alien children is not a choice I would make were I a legislator. Apart from compassionate considerations, the long-range costs of excluding any children from the public schools may well outweigh the costs of educating them. But that is not the issue; the fact that there are sound *policy* arguments against the Texas Legislature's choice does not render that choice an unconstitutional one. . . .

The Constitution does not provide a cure for every social ill, nor does it vest judges with a mandate to try to remedy every social problem. . . . Moreover, when this Court rushes in to remedy what it perceives to be the failings of the political processes, it deprives those processes of an opportunity to function. When the political institutions are not forced to exercise constitutionally allocated powers and responsibilities, those powers, like muscles not used, tend to atrophy. Today's cases, I regret to say, present yet another example of unwarranted judicial action which in the long run tends to contribute to the weakening of our political processes.

Congress, "vested by the Constitution with the responsibility of protecting our borders and legislating with respect to aliens," . . . bears primary responsibility for addressing the problems occasioned by the millions of illegal aliens flooding across our southern border. Similarly, it is for Congress, and not this Court, to assess the "social costs borne by our Nation when select groups are denied the means to absorb the values and skills upon

which our social order rests." . . . While the "specter of a permanent caste" of illegal Mexican residents of the United States is indeed a disturbing one, . . . it is but one segment of a larger problem, which is for the political branches to solve. I find it difficult to believe that Congress would long tolerate such a self-destructive result—that it would fail to deport these illegal alien families or to provide for the education of their children. Yet instead of allowing the political processes to run their course—albeit with some delay—the Court seeks to do Congress' job for it, compensating for congressional inaction. It is not unreasonable to think that this encourages the political branches to pass their problems to the Judiciary.

The solution to this seemingly intractable problem is to defer to the political processes, unpalatable as that may be to some.

7. Homelessness

Peter Marin

Homelessness, in itself, is nothing more than a condition visited upon men and women (and, increasingly, children) as the final stage of a variety of problems about which the word *homelessness* tells us almost nothing. Or, to put it another way, it is a catch basin into which pour all of the people disenfranchised or marginalized or scared off by processes beyond their control, those that lie close to the heart of American life. Here are the groups packed into the single category of "the homeless":

- Veterans, mainly from the war in Vietnam. In many American cities, vets make up close to 50 percent of all homeless males.
- The mentally ill. In some parts of the country, roughly a quarter of the homeless would, a couple of decades ago, have been institutionalized.

- The physically disabled or chronically ill, who do not receive any benefits or whose benefits do not enable them to afford permanent shelter.
- The elderly on fixed incomes whose funds are no longer sufficient for their needs.
- Men, women, and whole families pauperized by the loss of a job. Some 28 percent of the homeless population is composed of families with children, and 15 percent are single women.
- Single parents, usually women, without the resources or skills to establish new lives.
- Runaway children, many of whom have been abused.
- Alcoholics and those in trouble with drugs (whose troubles often begin with one of the other conditions listed here).
- Traditional tramps, hobos and transients, who have taken to the road or the streets for a variety of reasons and who prefer to be there.

You can quickly learn two things about the homeless from this list. First, you can learn that many of the homeless, before they were homeless, were people more or less like ourselves: members of the working or middle class. And you can learn that the world of the homeless has its roots in various policies, events and ways of life for which some of us are responsible and from which some of us actually prosper.

We decide, as a people, to go to war, we ask our children to kill and to die, and the result, years later, is grown men homeless on the street.

We change, with the best intentions, the laws pertaining to the mentally ill and then, without intention, neglect to provide them with services; and the result, in our streets, drives some of us crazy with rage.

We cut taxes and prune budgets, we modernize industry and shift the balance of trade, and the result of all these actions and errors can be read, sleeping form by sleeping form, on our city streets.

The liberals cannot blame the conservatives. The conservatives cannot blame the liberals. Homelessness is the sum total of our dreams, policies, intentions, errors, omissions, cruelties, kindnesses, all of it recorded, in flesh, in the life of the streets.

The homeless can be roughly divided into two groups: those who have had homelessness forced upon them and want nothing more than to escape it; and those who have at least in part chosen it for themselves, and now accept it, or in some cases embrace it.

I understand how dangerous it is to introduce the idea of choice into a discussion of homelessness. It can all too easily be used to justify indifference or brutality toward the homeless, or to argue that they are only getting what they "deserve." And yet it seems to me that it is only by taking choice into account, in all of the intricacies of its various forms and expressions, that one can really understand certain kinds of homelessness.

The fact is, many of the homeless are not only hapless victims but voluntary exiles, "domestic refugees," people who have turned not against life itself but against us, our life, American life. Look for a moment at the vets. The price of returning to America was to forget what they had seen or learned in Vietnam, to "put it behind them." But some could not do that, and the stress of trying showed up as alcoholism, broken marriages, drug addiction, crime. And it showed up too as life on the street, which was for some vets a desperate choice made in the name of life—the best they could manage.

We must learn to accept that there may indeed be people, and not only vets, who have seen so much of our world, or seen it so clearly, that to live in it becomes impossible. Here, for example, is the story of Alice, a homeless middle-aged woman in Los Angeles, where there are perhaps 50,000 homeless people, a 50 percent increase over the previous year. It was set down last year by one of my students at the University of California at Santa Barbara, where I taught for a semester. I had encouraged them to go find the homeless and listen to their stories. And so, one day, when this student saw Alice foraging in a dumpster outside a McDonald's, he stopped and talked to her:

"She told me she had led a pretty normal life as she grew up and eventually went to college. From there she went on to Chicago to teach school. She was single and lived in a small apartment.

"One night, after she got off the train after school, a man began to follow her to her apartment building. When she got to her door she saw a knife and the man hovering behind her. She had no choice but to let him in. The man raped her.

"After that, things got steadily worse. She had a nervous breakdown. She went to a mental institution for three months, and when she went back to her apartment she found her belongings gone. The landlord had sold them to cover the rent.

"She had no place to go and no job because the school had terminated her employment. She slipped into depression. She lived with friends until she could muster enough money for a ticket to Los Angeles. She said she no longer wanted to burden her friends, and that if she had to live outside, at least Los Angeles was warmer than Chicago.

"It is as if she began back then to take on the mentality of a street person. She resolved herself to homelessness. She's been out West since

1980, without a home or job. She seems happy, with her best friend being her cat. But the scars of memories still haunt her, and she is running from them, or should I say, him."

This is, in essence, the same story one hears over and over again on the street. You begin with an ordinary life; then an event occurs—traumatic, catastrophic; smaller events follow, each one deepening the original wound; finally, homelessness becomes inevitable, or begins to seem inevitable to the person involved—the only way out of an intolerable situation.

Every government program, almost every private project, is geared as much to the needs of those giving help as it is to the needs of the homeless.

Santa Barbara is as good an example as any. There are three main shelters in the city—all of them private. Between them they provide fewer than 100 beds a night for the homeless. Two of three shelters are religious in nature: the Rescue Mission and the Salvation Army. In the mission, as in most places in the country, there are elaborate and stringent rules. Beds go first to those who have not been there for two months, and you can stay for only two nights in any two-month period. No shelter is given to those who are not sober.

Even if you go to the mission only for a meal, you are required to listen to sermons and participate in prayer, and you are regularly proselytized. There are obligatory, regimented showers. You go to bed precisely at 10: lights out, no reading, no talking. After the lights go out you will find 15 men in a room with double-decker bunks. As the night progresses the room grows stuffier and hotter. Men toss, turn, cough and moan. In the morning you are awakened precisely at 5:45. Then

breakfast. At 7:30 you are back on the street.

The town's newest shelter was opened almost a year ago by a consortium of local churches. Families and those who are employed have first call on the beds—a policy that excludes the congenitally homeless. Alcohol is not simply forbidden in the shelter; those with a history of alcoholism must sign a "contract" pledging to remain sober and chemical-free. Finally, in a paroxysm of therapeutic bullying, the shelter has added a new wrinkle: If you stay more than two days you are required to fill out and then discuss with a social worker a complex form listing what you perceive as your personal failings, goals and strategies—all of this for men and women who simply want a place to lie down out of the rain.

We are moved either to "redeem" the homeless or to punish them. Perhaps there is nothing consciously hostile about it. Perhaps it is simply that as the machinery of bureaucracy cranks itself up to deal with these problems, attitudes assert themselves automatically. But whatever the case, the fact remains that almost every one of our strategies for helping the homeless is simply an attempt to rearrange the world cosmetically, in terms of how it looks and smells to us. Compassion is little more than the passion for control.

The central question emerging from all this is, What does a society owe to its members in trouble, and how is that debt to be paid? It is a question that must be answered in two parts: first, in relation to the men and women who have been marginalized against their will, and then, in a slightly different way, in relation to those who have chosen (or accept or even prize) their marginality.

Suggestions for Further Reading

Anthologies

Arthur, John, and Shaw, William. *Justice and Economic Distribution.* Englewood Cliffs: Prentice-Hall, 1978.

Garner, Richard T., and Oldenquist, Andrew.

Society and the Individual: Readings in Political and Social Philosophy. Belmont: Wadsworth Publishing Co., 1990.

Sterba, James P. *Justice: Alternative Political Perspectives.* Belmont: Wadsworth Publishing Co., 1980.

Basic Concepts

Plato. *The Republic.* Translated by Francis Cornford. New York: Oxford University Press, 1945.

Aristotle. *Nicomachean Ethics.* Translated by Martin Ostwald. Indianapolis: Bobbs-Merrill, 1962.

Pieper, Joseph. *Justice.* London: Faber and Faber, 1957.

Libertarianism

Hospers, John. *Libertarianism.* Los Angeles: Nash Publishing, 1971.

Nozick, Robert. *Anarchy, State and Utopia.* New York: Basic Books, 1974.

Machan, Tibor. *Individuals and Their Rights.* LaSalle: Open Court, 1989.

Welfare Liberalism

Mill, John Stuart. *On Liberty.* Indianapolis: Bobbs-Merrill Co., 1956.

Ackerman, Bruce A. *Social Justice in the Liberal State.* New Haven: Yale University Press, 1980.

Rawls, John. *A Theory of Justice.* Cambridge: Harvard University Press, 1971.

Singer, Peter. *Practical Ethics.* Cambridge: Cambridge University Press, 1979.

Sterba, James P. *How to Make People Just.* Totowa: Rowman and Littlefield, 1988.

Socialism

Marx, Karl. *Critique of the Gotha Program.* Edited by C. P. Dutt. New York: International Publishers, 1966.

Fisk, Milton. *Ethics and Society: A Marxist Interpretation of Value.* New York: New York University Press, 1980.

Harrington, Michael. *Socialism Past and Future.* New York: Arcade Publishing, 1989.

Heilbroner, Robert L. *Marxism For and Against.* New York: W. W. Norton & Co., 1980.

Communitarianism

Finnis, John. *Natural Law and Natural Rights.* Oxford: Clarendon Press, 1980.

MacIntyre, Alasdair. *After Virtue.* Notre Dame: University of Notre Dame Press, 1981.

Oldenquist, Andrew. *The Nonsuicidal Society.* Bloomington: University of Indiana Press, 1986.

Walzer, Michael. *The Spheres of Justice.* New York: Basic Books, 1983.

Practical Applications

Friedman, David. *The Machinery of Freedom.* 2nd edition. LaSalle: Open Court, 1989.

Gorbachev, Mikhail. *Perestroika.* New York: Harper & Row, 1987.

Timmons, William. *Public Ethics and Issues.* Belmont: Wadsworth Publishing Co., 1990.

Distant Peoples and Future Generations

Basic Concepts

The moral problem of distant peoples and future generations has only recently begun to be discussed by professional philosophers. There are many reasons for this neglect, not all of them complimentary to the philosophical profession. Suffice it to say that once it became widely recognized that modern technology could significantly benefit or harm distant peoples and future generations, philosophers could no longer ignore the importance of this moral problem.

Nevertheless, because the problem has only recently been addressed by philosophers, a generally acceptable way of even setting out the problem has yet to be developed. Unlike the problem of the distribution of income and wealth (see Section I), there is almost no common conceptual framework shared by all solutions to the problem of distant peoples and future generations. Some philosophers have even attempted to "solve" the problem, or at least part of it, by arguing that talk about "the rights of future generations" is conceptually incoherent and thus analogous to talk about "square circles." Accordingly, the key question that must be answered first is: Can we meaningfully speak of distant peoples and future generations as having rights against us or of our having obligations to them?

This question is much easier to answer with respect to distant peoples than to future generations. Few philosophers have thought that the mere fact that people are at a distance from us precludes our having any obligations to them or their having any rights against us. Some philosophers, however, have argued that our ignorance of the specific membership of the class of distant peoples does rule out these moral relationships. Yet this cannot be right, given that in other contexts we recognize obligations to indeterminate classes of people, such as a police officer's obligation to help people in distress or the obligation of food processors not to harm those who consume their products.

What does, however, seem to be a necessary requirement before distant peoples can be said to have rights against us is that we are capable of acting across the distance that separates us. (This is simply a version of the widely accepted philosophical principle that "ought implies can.") As long as this condition is met—as it typically is for people living in most technologically advanced societies—there seems to be no conceptual obstacle to claiming that distant peoples have rights against us or that we have obligations to them. Of course, showing that it is conceptually possible does not yet prove that these rights and obligations actually exist. Such proof requires a substantial moral argument.

By contrast, answering the above question with respect to future generations is much more difficult and has been the subject of considerable debate among contemporary philosophers.

One issue concerns the question whether it is logically coherent to speak of future generations as having rights now. Of course, no one who finds talk about rights to be generally meaningful should question whether we can coherently claim that future generations *will* have rights at some point in the future (specifically, when they come into existence and are no longer *future* generations). But what is questioned, since it is of considerable practical significance, is whether we can coherently claim that future generations have rights *now* when they don't yet exist.

Some philosophers, such as Richard T. De George, have argued that such claims are logically incoherent (Selection 10). According to De George, rights logically require the existence of rights holders, and obligations logically require the existence of obligation-recipients. The basic difficulty with this view is that it is in conflict with our understanding of the rights of dead people. This is because we grant that dead people can have rights even though they no longer exist. Now we could claim that the rights that we are respecting when we recognize, for example, inheritance rights are the rights of living recipients and not the rights of dead people at all. But it would be difficult to explain, using this view, how living recipients have any inheritance rights if these rights are not derived from the rights of dead people. Furthermore, when people die with the legally executed wish that their resources be used for the benefit of animals or the preservation of nonliving things, it would be quite strange to claim that the rights we are respecting when we give effect to such wishes are the rights of animals and nonliving things. It is far better to hold that dead people can have rights, even though they no longer exist, and that it is these rights that we are primarily respecting in recognizing inheritance rights. But then by parity of reasoning we should be committed to the view that future people can also have rights, even though they do not yet exist. If present existence is not required for past people to have rights, then present existence should not be required for future people to have rights.

Still another issue relevant to whether we can meaningfully speak of future generations as having rights against us or our having obligations to them concerns the referent of the term *future generations*. Most philosophers seem to agree that the class of future generations is not "the class of all persons who simply could come into existence." But there is some disagreement concerning whether we should refer to the class of future generations as "the class of persons who will definitely come into existence, assuming that there are such" or as "the class of persons we can reasonably expect to come into existence." The first approach is more "metaphysical," specifying the class of future generations in terms of what will exist; the second approach is more "epistemological," specifying the class of future generations in terms of our knowledge. Fortunately, there does not appear to be any practical moral significance to the choice of either approach.

A final issue that is relevant to whether we can meaningfully speak of future generations as having rights against us and our having obligations to them concerns whether in a given case the actions of the existing generations that affect future generations can actually benefit or harm those generations. Some philosophers would surely hold that only in cases where future generations can benefit from or be harmed by our actions can there be a question of future generations having rights against us or our having obligations to them.

Of course, no one doubts that some of our actions that affect future generations actually do benefit or harm them. For example, consider an artist who creates a great work of art that will survive for the enjoyment of future generations. Surely such a person will benefit future generations. Just as surely, future generations will be harmed by the careless manner in which many governments and private corporations today dispose of nuclear wastes and other toxic substances.

But suppose some of our actions affect future generations by affecting the membership of the class of future generations. That is, suppose our actions cause different people to be born than otherwise would have been born had we acted differently. For example, imagine that a woman is deciding whether or not to get pregnant. Because of the medication she is taking, she will give birth to a defective child if she gets pregnant now. However, if she stops taking her medication and waits three months before getting pregnant, she will almost certainly have a normal child. If the woman decides not to wait and gives birth to a defective child, has she harmed that child? If the mother had waited three months, the child she would then have given birth to would certainly have been a different child. So it does not seem that she has harmed the child to which she did give birth, provided the child's life is worth living. Some people, however, would surely think the mother was wrong not to wait and give birth to a normal child. But how can such a judgment be supported?

At the level of social choice we can also imagine a similar situation arising. Consider a developing country choosing between a laissez-faire population policy and one that restricts population growth. If the restrictive policy is followed, capital accumulation will produce general prosperity within one or two generations. If the laissez-faire policy is followed, low wages and high unemployment will continue indefinitely. Since the choice of either of these will, over time, produce different populations, those born subsequently under the laissez-faire policy could hardly claim they were harmed by the choice of that policy because they wouldn't have been born if the restricted policies had been adopted. Still, some people would surely want to claim that it was wrong for the country to pursue a laissez-faire policy. But how could such a claim be supported if no one in subsequent generations is harmed by the choice of that policy?

Contemporary philosophers have sought to deal with the question of whether we can wrong future generations without harming them in three ways. The first is simply to recommend that we "bite the bullet" and claim that "if no one is harmed, no wrong is done." This approach is not very satisfactory, however, because it flies in the face of our strong intuitions about the examples cited previously. The second approach is to claim that regardless of whether one is harmed, we still have an obligation to produce as much happiness or utility as we possibly can. Applied to our examples, this utilitarian approach would probably require the delayed pregnancy. However, it would not call for the restricted population policy because one of the generally recognized problems with this second approach is that it is said to require massive population increases that maximize happiness or utility overall, with little regard for the quality of life. The third approach adopted by contemporary philosophers is to claim that even though we don't have an obligation to produce as much happiness or utility as we possibly can, we do have an obligation to ensure that persons are only brought into existence if they are likely to have lives that are well worth living. Applied to our examples, this obligation would require both the delayed pregnancy and the restricted population policy. Some proponents of this approach, like Sterba (Selection 11), claim that we also have an obligation to bring into existence persons whose lives are well worth living; this, however, is not the general view.

Of these three approaches, the last seems to be the most promising. But exactly how to work out the details of this approach (e.g., what constitutes a life well worth living?) is still the subject of considerable debate among contemporary philosophers.

Alternative Views

Fortunately, all of these issues do not have to be resolved fully before we can profitably examine some of the practical solutions that have been proposed to the problem of distant peoples and future generations. In fact, some of the issues we've discussed lead us directly to particular solutions for this moral problem.

Not surprisingly, most of the solutions that have been proposed are analogous to the solutions we discussed with regard to the problem of the distribution of income and wealth within a society (see Section I).

As before, there is a libertarian solution. According to this view, distant peoples and future generations have no right to receive aid from persons living in today's affluent societies, but only a right not to be harmed by them. As before, these requirements are said to be derived from a political ideal of liberty. And, as before, we can question whether such an ideal actually supports these requirements.

Both Garrett Hardin and De George endorse a "no aid" view in their selections. However, neither Hardin nor De George supports his view on libertarian grounds. Without denying that there is a general obligation to help those in need, Hardin argues that helping those who live in absolute poverty in today's world would not do any good, and for *that reason* is not required. Hardin justifies this view on empirical grounds, claiming that the giving of aid would be ineffective and even counterproductive for controlling population growth. By contrast, De George supports a "no aid" view for future generations (but not for distant peoples, who he thinks do have a right to receive aid) on purely conceptual grounds, claiming that future generations cannot logically have rights against us nor we obligations to them.

We have already noted some of the difficulties with the view De George defends. Peter Singer and Sterba both challenge the empirical grounds on which Hardin's view rests. Singer claims that Hardin's view accepts the certain evil of unrelieved poverty in today's Third World countries, like Bangladesh and Somalia, to avoid the future possibility of still greater poverty in Third World countries together with deteriorating conditions in First and Second World countries. Singer argues, however, that with a serious commitment to aid from First World countries, there is a "fair chance" that Third World countries will bring their population growth under control, thus avoiding the greater evil Hardin fears. Given the likelihood of this result, Singer argues that we have no moral justification for embracing, as Hardin does, the certain evil of unrelieved poverty in today's Third World countries by denying them aid. Sterba too objects to Hardin's willingness to sacrifice existing generations for the sake of a "better future" for subsequent generations. He argues that even if Hardin were right that providing aid would reduce the "maximal sustainable yield" of the planet's resources, we still ought to provide that aid. He claims this is so even if the population level of future generations, once a rational population policy is in effect, would have to be smaller than would otherwise have been possible.

The positive solution to the problem of distant peoples and future generations defended by both Singer and Sterba can be characterized as a welfare liberal or a communitarian solution. Singer at some point would want to defend his "pro aid" view on utilitarian grounds, but in his selection (Selection 9), he tries to base his view on premises of a more general appeal. The fundamental premise he relies on is this: If we can prevent something bad without sacrificing anything of comparable significance, we ought to do it. Singer notes that libertarians, like Robert Nozick, would at least initially have difficulty accepting this premise. Nozick would surely claim that the requirement this premise imposes is at best only one of charity rather than justice, so that failing to abide by it is neither blameworthy nor punishable. Sterba, too, although he is primarily concerned with defending a "pro aid" view on the basis of a right to life and a right to fair treatment interpreted as positive rights, is sensitive to the possibility that libertarians might be able to escape from the conclusion of his argument. Consequently, he tries to show that the same conclusion follows when a right to life is interpreted as a negative right, as libertarians tend to do. But although Sterba may have secured his view against objections by libertarians, socialists would certainly not be satisfied with his defense.

A socialist solution to the problem of distant peoples and future generations would place considerable stress on the responsibility of First World countries for the situation in Third World countries. Socialists claim that much of the poverty and unemployment found in Third World countries is the result of the disruptive and exploitative influence of First World countries. For example, it is claimed that arms supplied by First World countries enable repressive regimes in Third World countries to remain in power when they would otherwise be overthrown. Under these repressive regimes, small groups of landowners and capitalists are allowed to exploit the resources in Third World countries for export markets in First World countries. As a result, most people in Third World countries are forced off the land that their forebears have farmed for generations and are required to compete for the few, frequently low-paying jobs that have been created to serve the export markets.

Nevertheless, even if socialists are right about the responsibility of First World countries for Third World poverty, it is still a further question whether the socialization of the means of production and the abolition of private property are the only viable moral responses to this situation. It certainly seems possible that some form of restricted private property system that provides for the meeting of everyone's basic needs, justified either on welfare liberal grounds or on libertarian grounds, would serve as well.

By contrast, for communitarians the key question with respect to the problem of distant peoples and future generations is whether the requirements of community are compatible with meeting the basic needs of distant peoples and future generations. Thus, communitarians need to be convinced that when the bounds of community are drawn correctly, distant peoples and future generations would in fact be included.

Practical Applications

There does not seem to be as much of a gap between the "alternative views" and the "practical applications" with respect to the problem of distant peoples and future generations as there is in the problem of the distribution of wealth and income. This is because most of the discussions of the alternative views have already taken up the question of practical application (e.g., Singer suggests as a practical application a 10 percent tithe on income in First World countries). The merit of Gus Speth's article, however, is that it focuses squarely on the question of practical application (Selection 12). After reviewing the world situation, Speth sketches a practical program involving conservation, sustainable growth, and equity. Because his program obviously involves substantial aid to Third World countries, you should not endorse such a program unless you believe that arguments such as those presented by Singer and Sterba effec-

tively counter arguments such as those presented by Hardin and De George.

Nevertheless, whatever solution to the problem of distant peoples and future generations you favor, you will still not know how goods and resources should ultimately be distributed in society unless you have a solution to the problem of abortion and euthanasia. If abortion is morally justified, perhaps we should be funding abortions so that every woman, rich or poor, can have an abortion if she wants one. And if euthanasia is morally justified, perhaps we should be reallocating resources that are now being used for the purpose of sustaining life. Appropriately, the next section of this book takes up the problem of abortion and euthanasia.

8. Lifeboat Ethics: The Case Against Helping the Poor

Garrett Hardin

Garrett Hardin argues that our first obligation is to ourselves and our posterity. For that reason, he contends, it would be foolish for rich nations to share their surplus with poor nations, whether through a World Food Bank, the exporting of technology, or unrestricted immigration. In view of the growing populations and improvident behavior of poor nations, such sharing would do no good—it would only overload the environment and lead to demands for still greater assistance in the future.

Environmentalists use the metaphor of the earth as a "spaceship" in trying to persuade countries, industries and people to stop wasting and polluting our natural resources. Since we all share life on this planet, they argue, no single person or institution has the right to destroy, waste, or use more than a fair share of its resources.

But does everyone on earth have an equal right to an equal share of its resources? The spaceship metaphor can be dangerous when

From "The Case Against Helping the Poor," *Psychology Today* (1974), pp. 38–43, 123–126. Reprinted with permission from *Psychology Today* magazine. Copyright © 1974 American Psychological Association. Addendum 1989. Reprinted by permission of the author.

used by misguided idealists to justify suicidal policies for sharing our resources through uncontrolled immigration and foreign aid. In their enthusiastic but unrealistic generosity, they confuse the ethics of a spaceship with those of a lifeboat.

A true spaceship would have to be under the control of a captain, since no ship could possibly survive if its course were determined by committee. Spaceship Earth certainly has no captain; the United Nations is merely a toothless tiger, with little power to enforce any policy upon its bickering members.

If we divide the world crudely into rich nations and poor nations, two thirds of them are desperately poor, and only one third comparatively rich, with the United States the wealthiest of all. Metaphorically each rich nation can be seen as a lifeboat full of comparatively rich people. In the ocean outside each lifeboat swim the poor of the world, who would like to get in, or at least to share some of the wealth. What should the lifeboat passengers do?

First, we must recognize the limited capacity of any lifeboat. For example, a nation's land has a limited capacity to support a population and as the current energy crisis has shown us, in some ways we have already exceeded the carrying capacity of our land.

Adrift in a Moral Sea

So here we sit, say fifty people in our lifeboat. To be generous, let us assume it has room for ten more, making a total capacity of sixty. Suppose the fifty of us in the lifeboat see 100 others swimming in the water outside, begging for admission to our boat or for handouts. We have several options: we may be tempted to try to live by the Christian ideal of being "our brother's keeper," or by the Marxist ideal of "to each according to his needs." Since the needs of all in the water are the same, and since they can all be seen as "our brothers," we could take them all into our boat, making a total of 150 in a boat designed for sixty. The boat swamps, everyone drowns. Complete justice, complete catastrophe.

Since the boat has an unused excess capacity of ten more passengers, we could admit just ten more to it. But which ten do we let in? How do we choose? Do we pick the best ten, the neediest ten, "first come, first served"? And what do we say to the ninety we exclude? If we do let an extra ten into our lifeboat, we will have lost our "safety factor," an engineering principle of critical importance. For example, if we don't leave room for excess capacity as a safety factor in our country's agriculture, a new plant disease or a bad change in the weather could have disastrous consequences.

Suppose we decide to preserve our small safety factor and admit no more to the lifeboat. Our survival is then possible, although we shall have to be constantly on guard against boarding parties.

While this last solution clearly offers the only means of our survival, it is morally abhorrent to many people. Some say they feel guilty about their good luck. My reply is simple: "Get out and yield your place to others." This may solve the problem of the guilt-ridden person's conscience, but it does not change the ethics of the lifeboat. The needy person to whom the guilt-ridden person yields his place will not himself feel guilty about his good luck. If he did, he would not climb aboard. The net result of conscience-stricken people giving up their unjustly held seats is the elimination of that sort of conscience from the lifeboat.

This is the basic metaphor within which we must work out our solutions. Let us now enrich the image, step by step, with substantive additions from the real world, a world that must solve real and pressing problems of overpopulation and hunger.

The harsh ethics of the lifeboat become even harsher when we consider the reproductive differences between the rich nations and the poor nations. The people inside the lifeboats are doubling in numbers every eighty-seven years; those swimming around outside are doubling, on the average, every thirty-five years, more than twice as fast as the rich. And since the world's resources are dwindling, the difference in prosperity between the rich and the poor can only increase.

As of 1973, the U.S. had a population of 210 million people, who were increasing by 0.8 percent per year. Outside our lifeboat, let us imagine another 210 million people, (say the combined populations of Colombia, Ecuador, Venezuela, Morocco, Pakistan, Thailand, and the Philippines) who are increasing at a rate of 3.3 percent per year. Put differently, the doubling time for this aggregate population is twenty-one years, compared to eighty-seven years for the U.S.

Multiplying the Rich and the Poor

Now suppose the U.S. agreed to pool its resources with those seven countries, with everyone receiving an equal share. Initially the ratio of Americans to non-Americans in this model would be one-to-one. But consider what the ratio would be after eighty-seven years, by which time the Americans would have doubled to a population of 420 million. By then, doubling every twenty-one years, the other group would have swollen to 354 billion. Each American would have to share the available resources with more than eight people.

But, one could argue, this discussion assumes that current population trends will continue, and they may not. Quite so. Most likely the rate of population increase will decline much faster in the U.S. than it will in the other countries, and there does not seem to be much we can do about it. In sharing with "each according to his needs," we must recognize that needs are determined by population size, which is determined by the rate of reproduction, which at present is regarded as a sovereign right of every nation, poor or not. This being so, the philanthropic load created by the sharing ethic of the spaceship can only increase.

The Tragedy of the Commons

The fundamental error of spaceship ethics, and the sharing it requires, is that it leads to what I call "the tragedy of the commons." Under a system of private property, the men who own property recognize their responsibility to care for it, for if they don't they will eventually suffer. A farmer, for instance, will allow no more cattle in a pasture than its carrying capacity justifies. If he overloads it, erosion sets in, weeds take over, and he loses the use of the pasture.

If a pasture becomes a commons open to all, the right of each to use it may not be matched by a corresponding responsibility to protect it. Asking everyone to use it with discretion will hardly do, for the considerate herdsman who refrains from overloading the commons suffers more than a selfish one who says his needs are greater. If everyone would restrain himself, all would be well; but it takes

only one less than everyone to ruin a system of voluntary restraint. In a crowded world of less than perfect human beings, mutual ruin is inevitable if there are no controls. This is the tragedy of the commons.

One of the major tasks of education today should be the creation of such an acute awareness of the dangers of the commons that people will recognize its many varieties. For example, the air and water have become polluted because they are treated as commons. Further growth in the population or per-capita conversion of natural resources into pollutants will only make the problem worse. The same holds true for the fish of the oceans. Fishing fleets have nearly disappeared in many parts of the world, technological improvements in the art of fishing are hastening the day of complete ruin. Only the replacement of the system of the commons with a responsible system of control will save the land, air, water and oceanic fisheries.

The World Food Bank

In recent years there has been a push to create a new commons called a World Food Bank, an international depository of food reserves to which nations would contribute according to their abilities and from which they would draw according to their needs. This humanitarian proposal has received support from many liberal international groups, and from such prominent citizens as Margaret Mead, U.N. Secretary General Kurt Waldheim, and Senators Edward Kennedy and George McGovern.

A world food bank appeals powerfully to our humanitarian impulses. But before we rush ahead with such a plan, let us recognize where the greatest political push comes from, lest we be disillusioned later. Our experience with the "Food for Peace program," or Public Law 480, gives us the answer. This program moved billions of dollars worth of U.S. surplus grain to food-short, population-long countries during the past two decades. But when P.L. 480 first became law, a headline in the business magazine *Forbes* revealed the real power behind it: "Feeding the World's Hungry Millions: How It Will Mean Billions for U.S. Business."

And indeed it did. In the years 1960 to 1970, U.S. taxpayers spent a total of $7.9 billion on the Food for Peace program. Between 1948 and 1970, they also paid an additional $50 billion for other economic-aid programs, some of which went for food and food-producing machinery and technology. Though all U.S. taxpayers were forced to contribute to the cost of P.L. 480, certain special interest groups gained handsomely under the program. Farmers did not have to contribute the grain; the Government, or rather the taxpayers, bought it from them at full market prices. The increased demand raised prices of farm products generally. The manufacturers of farm machinery, fertilizers and pesticides benefited by the farmers' extra efforts to grow more food. Grain elevators profited from storing the surplus until it could be shipped. Railroads made money hauling it to ports, and shipping lines profited from carrying it overseas. The implementation of P.L. 480 required the creation of a vast Government bureaucracy, which then acquired its own vested interest in continuing the program regardless of its merits.

Extracting Dollars

Those who proposed and defended the Food for Peace program in public rarely mentioned its importance to any of these special interests. The public emphasis was always on its humanitarian effects. The combination of silent selfish interests and highly vocal humanitarian apologists made a powerful and successful lobby for extracting money from taxpayers. We can expect the same lobby to push now for the creation of a World Food Bank.

However great the potential benefit to selfish interests, it should not be a decisive argument against a truly humanitarian program. We must ask if such a program would actually do more good than harm, not only momentarily but also in the long run. Those who propose the food bank usually refer to a cur-

rent "emergency" or "crisis" in terms of world food supply. But what is an emergency? Although they may be infrequent and sudden, everyone knows that emergencies will occur from time to time. A well-run family, company, organization or country prepares for the likelihood of accidents and emergencies. It expects them, it budgets for them, it saves for them.

Learning the Hard Way

What happens if some organizations or countries budget for accidents and others do not? If each country is solely responsible for its own well-being, poorly managed ones will suffer. But they can learn from experience. They may mend their ways, and learn to budget for infrequent but certain emergencies. For example, the weather varies from year to year, and periodic crop failures are certain. A wise and competent government saves out of the production of the good years in anticipation of bad years to come. Joseph taught this policy to Pharaoh in Egypt more than 2,000 years ago. Yet the great majority of the governments in the world today do not follow such a policy. They lack either the wisdom or the competence, or both. Should those nations that do manage to put something aside be forced to come to the rescue each time an emergency occurs among the poor nations?

"But it isn't their fault!" some kindhearted liberals argue. "How can we blame the poor people who are caught in an emergency? Why must they suffer for the sins of their governments?" The concept of blame is simply not relevant here. The real question is, what are the operational consequences of establishing a world food bank? If it is open to every country every time a need develops, slovenly rulers will not be motivated to take Joseph's advice. Someone will always come to their aid. Some countries will deposit food in the world food bank, and others will withdraw it. There will be almost no overlap. As a result of such solutions to food shortage emergencies, the poor countries will not learn to mend their ways, and will suffer progressively greater emergencies as their populations grow.

Population Control the Crude Way

On the average, poor countries undergo a 2.5 percent increase in population each year; rich countries, about 0.8 percent. Only rich countries have anything in the way of food reserves set aside, and even they do not have as much as they should. Poor countries have none. If poor countries received no food from the outside, the rate of their population growth would be periodically checked by crop failures and famines. But if they can always draw on a world food bank in time of need, their population can continue to grow unchecked, and so will their "need" for aid. In the short run, a world food bank may diminish that need, but in the long run it actually increases the need without limit.

Without some system of worldwide food sharing, the proportion of people in the rich and poor nations might eventually stabilize. The overpopulated poor countries would decrease in numbers, while the rich countries that had room for more people would increase. But with a well-meaning system of sharing, such as a world food bank, the growth differential between the rich and the poor countries will not only persist, it will increase. Because of the higher rate of population growth in the poor countries of the world, 88 percent of today's children are born poor, and only 12 percent rich. Year by year the ratio becomes worse, as the fast-reproducing poor outnumber the slow-reproducing rich.

A world food bank is thus a commons in disguise. People will have more motivation to draw from it than to add to any common store. The less provident and less able will multiply at the expense of the abler and more provident, bringing eventual ruin upon all who share in the commons. Besides, any system of "sharing" that amounts to foreign aid from the rich nations to the poor nations will carry the taint of charity, which will contribute little to the world peace so devoutly desired by those who support the idea of a world food bank.

As past U.S. foreign-aid programs have amply and depressingly demonstrated, international charity frequently inspires mistrust and antagonism rather than gratitude on the part of the recipient nation.

Chinese Fish and Miracle Rice

The modern approach to foreign aid stresses the export of technology and advice, rather than money and food. As an ancient Chinese proverb goes: "Give a man a fish and he will eat for a day; teach him how to fish and he will eat for the rest of his days." Acting on this advice, the Rockefeller and Ford Foundations have financed a number of programs for improving agriculture in the hungry nations. Known as the "Green Revolution," these programs have led to the development of "miracle rice" and "miracle wheat," new strains that offer bigger harvests and greater resistance to crop damage. Norman Borlaug, the Nobel Prize winning agronomist who, supported by the Rockefeller Foundation, developed "miracle wheat," is one of the most prominent advocates of a world food bank.

Whether or not the Green Revolution can increase food production as much as its champions claim is a debatable but possibly irrelevant point. Those who support this well-intended humanitarian effort should first consider some of the fundamentals of human ecology. Ironically, one man who did was the late Alan Gregg, a vice president of the Rockefeller Foundation. Two decades ago he expressed strong doubts about the wisdom of such attempts to increase food production. He likened the growth and spread of humanity over the surface of the earth to the spread of cancer in the human body, remarking that "cancerous growths demand food; but, as far as I know, they have never been cured by getting it."

Overloading the Environment

Every human born constitutes a draft on all aspects of the environment: food, air, water, forests, beaches, wildlife, scenery and solitude. Food can, perhaps, be significantly increased to meet a growing demand. But what about clean beaches, unspoiled forests, and solitude? If we satisfy a growing population's need for food, we necessarily decrease its per capita supply of the other resources needed by men.

India, for example, now has a population of 600 million, which increases by 15 million each year. This population already puts a huge load on a relatively impoverished environment. The country's forests are now only a small fraction of what they were three centuries ago, and floods and erosion continually destroy the insufficient farmland that remains. Every one of the 15 million new lives added to India's population puts an additional burden on the environment, and increases the economic and social costs of crowding. However humanitarian our intent, every Indian life saved through medical or nutritional assistance from abroad diminishes the quality of life for those who remain, and for subsequent generations. If rich countries make it possible, through foreign aid, for 600 million Indians to swell to 1.2 billion in a mere twenty-eight years, as their current growth rate threatens, will future generations of Indians thank us for hastening the destruction of their environment? Will our good intentions be sufficient excuse for the consequences of our actions?

My final example of a commons in action is one for which the public has the least desire for rational discussion—immigration. Anyone who publicly questions the wisdom of current U.S. immigration policy is promptly charged with bigotry, prejudice, ethnocentrism, chauvinism, isolationism or selfishness. Rather than encounter such accusations, one would rather talk about other matters, leaving immigration policy to wallow in the crosscurrents of special interests that take no account of the good of the whole, or the interests of posterity.

Perhaps we still feel guilty about things we said in the past. Two generations ago the popular press frequently referred to Dagos, Wops, Polacks, Chinks and Krauts, in articles about how America was being "overrun" by foreigners of supposedly inferior genetic stock. But because the implied inferiority of foreigners was used then as justification for keeping them out, people now assume that restrictive policies could only be based on such misguided notions. There are other grounds.

A Nation of Immigrants

Just consider the numbers involved. Our Government acknowledges a net inflow of 400,000 immigrants a year. While we have no hard data on the extent of illegal entries, educated guesses put the figure at about 600,000 a year. Since the natural increase (excess of births over deaths) of the resident population now runs about 1.7 million per year, the yearly gain from immigration amounts to at least 19 percent of the total annual increase, and may be as much as 37 percent if we include the estimate for illegal immigrants. Considering the growing use of birth-control devices, the potential effect of educational campaigns by such organizations as Planned Parenthood Federation of America and Zero Population Growth, and the influence of inflation and the housing shortage, the fertility rate of American women may decline so much that immigration could account for all the yearly increase in population. Should we not at least ask if that is what we want?

For the sake of those who worry about whether the "quality" of the average immigrant compares favorably with the quality of the average resident, let us assume that immigrants and nativeborn citizens are of exactly equal quality, however one defines that term. We will focus here only on quantity; and since our conclusions will depend on nothing else, all charges of bigotry and chauvinism become irrelevant.

Immigration vs. Food Supply

World food banks *move food to the people*, hastening the exhaustion of the environment of the poor countries. Unrestricted immigration, on the other hand, *moves people to the food*, thus speeding up the destruction of the environment of the rich countries. We can easily understand why poor people should want to make this latter transfer, but why should rich hosts encourage it?

As in the case of foreign-aid programs, immigration receives support from selfish interests and humanitarian impulses. The primary selfish interest in unimpeded immigration is the desire of employers for cheap labor, particularly in industries and trades that offer degrading work. In the past, one wave of foreigners after another was brought into the U.S. to work at wretched jobs for wretched wages. In recent years the Cubans, Puerto Ricans and Mexicans have had this dubious honor. The interests of the employers of cheap labor mesh well with the guilty silence of the country's liberal intelligentsia. White Anglo-Saxon Protestants are particularly reluctant to call for a closing of the doors to immigration for fear of being called bigots.

But not all countries have such reluctant leadership. Most educated Hawaiians, for example, are keenly aware of the limits of their environment, particularly in terms of population growth. There is only so much room on the islands, and the islanders know it. To Hawaiians, immigrants from the other forty-nine states present as great a threat as those from other nations. At a recent meeting of Hawaiian government officials in Honolulu, I had the ironic delight of hearing a speaker, who like most of his audience was of Japanese ancestry, ask how the country might practically and constitutionally close its doors to further immigration. One member of the audience countered: "How can we shut the doors now? We have many friends and relatives in Japan that we'd like to bring here some day so that they can enjoy Hawaii too." The Japanese-American speaker smiled sympathetically and answered: "Yes, but we have children now, and someday we'll have grandchildren too. We can bring more people here from Japan only by giving away some of the land that we hope to pass on to our grandchildren some day. What right do we have to do that?"

At this point, I can hear U.S. liberals asking: "How can you justify slamming the door once you're inside? You say that immigrants should be kept out. But aren't we all immigrants, or the descendants of immigrants? If we insist on staying, must we not admit all others?" Our craving for intellectual order leads us to seek and prefer symmetrical rules and morals: a single rule for me and everybody else; the same rule yesterday, today, and tomorrow. Justice, we feel, should not change with time and place.

We Americans of non-Indian ancestry can look upon ourselves as the descendants of thieves who are guilty morally, if not legally, of stealing this land from its Indian owners. Should we then give back the land to the now living American descendants of those Indians? However morally or logically sound this proposal may be, I, for one, am unwilling to live by it and I know no one else who is. Besides, the logical consequence would be absurd. Suppose that, intoxicated with a sense of pure justice, we should decide to turn our land over to the Indians. Since all our wealth has also been derived from the land, wouldn't we be morally obliged to give that back to the Indians too?

Pure Justice vs. Reality

Clearly, the concept of pure justice produces an infinite regression to absurdity. Centuries ago, wise men invented statutes of limitations to justify the rejection of such pure justice, in the interest of preventing continual disorder. The law zealously defends property rights, but only relatively recent property rights. Drawing a line after an arbitrary time has elapsed may be unjust, but the alternatives are worse.

We are all the descendants of thieves, and the world's resources are inequitably distributed. But we must begin the journey to tomorrow from the point where we are today. We cannot remake the past. We cannot safely divide the wealth equitably among all peoples so long as people reproduce at different rates. To do so would guarantee that our grandchildren, and everyone else's grandchildren, would have only a ruined world to inhabit.

To be generous with one's own possessions is quite different from being generous with those of posterity. We should call this point to the attention of those who, from a commendable love of justice and equality, would institute a system of the commons, either in the form of a world food bank, or of unrestricted immigration. We must convince them if we wish to save at least some parts of the world from environmental ruin.

Without a true world government to control reproduction and the use of available resources, the sharing ethic of the spaceship is impossible. For the foreseeable future, our survival demands that we govern our actions by the ethics of a lifeboat, harsh though they may be. Posterity will be satisfied with nothing less.

Addendum 1989

Can anyone watch children starve on television without wanting to help? Naturally sympathetic, a normal human being thinks that he can imagine what it is like to be starving. We all want to do unto others as we would have them do unto us.

But wanting is not doing. Forty years of activity by the U.S. Agency for International Development, as well as episodic nongovernmental attempts to feed the world's starving, have produced mixed results. Before we respond to the next appeal we should ask, "Does what we call 'aid' really help?"

Some of the shortcomings of food aid can be dealt with briefly. Waste is unavoidable: Because most poor countries have wretched transportation systems, food may sit on a dock until it rots. Then there are the corrupt politicians who take donated food away from the poor and give it to their political supporters. In Somalia in the 1980s, fully 70 percent of the donated food went to the army.

We can school ourselves to accept such losses. Panicky projects are always inefficient: Waste and corruption are par for the course. But there is another kind of loss that we cannot—in fact, we should not—accept, and that is the loss caused by the boomerang effects of philanthropy. Before we jump onto the next "feed-the-starving" bandwagon we need to understand how well-intentioned efforts can be counterproductive.

Briefly put, it is a mistake to focus only on starving people while ignoring their surroundings. Where there is great starvation there is usually an impoverished environment: poor soil, scarce water and wildly fluctuating weather. As a result, the "carrying capacity" of the environment is low. The territory simply cannot support the population that is trying to live on it. Yet if the population were much smaller, and if it would stay smaller, the people would not need to starve.

Let us look at a particular example. Nigeria, like all the central African countries, has increased greatly in population in the last quarter-century. Over many generations, Nigerians learned that their farmlands would be most productive if crop-growing alternated with "fallow years"—years in which the land was left untilled to recover its fertility.

When modern medicine reduced the death rate, the population began to grow. More food was demanded from the same land. Responding to that need, Nigerians shortened the fallow periods. The result was counterproductive. In one carefully studied village, the average fallow period was shortened from 5.3 to 1.4 years. As a result, the yearly production (averaged over both fallow and crop years) fell by 30 percent.

Are Nigerian farmers stupid? Not at all! They know perfectly well what they are doing. But a farmer whose family has grown too large for his farm has to take care of next year's need before he can provide for the future. To fallow or not to fallow translates into this choice: zero production in a fallow year or a 30 percent shortfall over the long run. Starvation cannot wait. Long-term policies have to give way to short-term ones. So the farmer plows up his overstressed fields, thus diminishing long-term productivity.

Once the carrying capacity of a territory has been transgressed, its capacity goes down, year after year. Transgression is a one-way road to ruin. Ecologists memorialize this reality with an 11th Commandment: "Thou shalt not transgress the carrying capacity."

Transgression takes many forms. Poor people are poor in energy resources. They need energy to cook their food. Where do they get it? Typically, from animal dung or trees and bushes. Burning dung deprives the soil of nitrogen. Cutting down trees and bushes deprives the land of protection against eroding rain. Soil-poor slopes cannot support a crop of fuel-plants. Once the soil is gone, water runs off the slopes faster and floods the valleys below. First poor people deforest their land, and then deforestation makes them poorer.

When Americans send food to a starving population that has already grown beyond the environment's carrying capacity we become a partner in the devastation of their land. Food from the outside keeps more natives alive; these demand more food and fuel; greater demand causes the community to transgress the carrying capacity more, and transgression results in lowering the carrying capacity. The deficit grows exponentially. Gifts of food to an overpopulated country boomerang, increasing starvation over the long run. Our choice is really between letting some die this year and letting more die in the following years.

You may protest, "That's easy enough for a well-fed American to say, but do citizens of poor countries agree?" Well, wisdom is not restricted to the wealthy. The Somali novelist Nuruddin Farrah has courageously condemned foreign gifts as being not truly aid, but a poison, because (if continued) such gifts will make Africans permanently dependent on outside aid.

The ethicist Joseph Fletcher has given a simple directive to would-be philanthropists: "Give if it helps, but not if it hurts." We can grant that giving makes the donor feel good at first—but how will he feel later when he realizes that he has harmed the receiver?

Only one thing can really help a poor country: population control. Having accepted disease control the people must now accept population control.

What the philosopher-economist Kenneth Boulding has called "lovey-dovey charity" is not enough. "It is well to remember," he said, "that the symbol of Christian love is a cross and not a Teddy bear." A good Christian should obey the 11th Commandment, refusing to send gifts that help poor people destroy the environment that must support the next generation.

---

9. The Famine Relief Argument

Peter Singer

Peter Singer argues that people in rich countries, by allowing those in poor countries to suffer and die, are actually engaged in reckless homicide. This is because people in rich countries could prevent the deaths of the poor without sacrificing anything of comparable significance. Singer considers a number of objections to his argument and finds them all wanting. Against Hardin's objection that aiding the poor now will lead to disaster in the future, Singer argues that if the right sort of aid is given conditionally, a future disaster of the sort Hardin envisions can be avoided.

From *Practical Ethics* (1979), pp. 158–181. Reprinted by permission of Cambridge University Press.

Some Facts

Consider these facts: by the most cautious estimates, 400 million people lack the calories, protein, vitamins and minerals needed for a normally healthy life. Millions are constantly hungry; others suffer from deficiency diseases and from infections they would be able to resist on a better diet. Children are worst affected. According to one estimate, 15 million children under five die every year from the combined effects of malnutrition and infection. In some areas, half the children born can be expected to die before their fifth birthday.

Nor is lack of food the only hardship of the poor. To give a broader picture, Robert McNamara, President of the World Bank, has suggested the term 'absolute poverty'. The poverty we are familiar with in industrialized nations is relative poverty—meaning that some citizens are poor, relative to the wealth enjoyed by their neighbours. People living in relative poverty in Australia might be quite comfortably off by comparison with old-age pensioners in Britain, and British old-age pensioners are not poor in comparison with the poverty that exists in Mali or Ethiopia. Absolute poverty, on the other hand, is poverty by any standard. In McNamara's words:

> Poverty at the absolute level . . . is life at the very margin of existence.
>
> The absolute poor are severely deprived human beings struggling to survive in a set of squalid and degraded circumstances almost beyond the power of our sophisticated imaginations and privileged circumstances to conceive.
>
> Compared to those fortunate enough to live in developed countries individuals in the poorest nations have
> An infant mortality rate eight times higher
> A life expectancy one-third lower
> An adult literacy rate 60% less
> A nutritional level, for one out of every two in the population, below acceptable standards; and for millions of

infants, less protein than is sufficient to permit optimum development of the brain.

And McNamara has summed up absolute poverty as:

> a condition of life so characterized by malnutrition, illiteracy, disease, squalid surroundings, high infant mortality and low life expectancy as to be beneath any reasonable definition of human decency.

Absolute poverty is, as McNamara has said, responsible for the loss of countless lives, especially among infants and young children. When absolute poverty does not cause death it still causes misery of a kind not often seen in the affluent nations. Malnutrition in young children stunts both physical and mental development. It has been estimated that the health, growth and learning capacity of nearly half the young children in developing countries are affected by malnutrition. Millions of people on poor diets suffer from deficiency diseases, like goitre, or blindness caused by a lack of vitamin A. The food value of what the poor eat is further reduced by parasites such as hookworm and ringworm, which are endemic in conditions of poor sanitation and health education.

Death and disease apart, absolute poverty remains a miserable condition of life, with inadequate food, shelter, clothing, sanitation, health services and education. According to World Bank estimates which define absolute poverty in terms of income levels insufficient to provide adequate nutrition, something like 800 million people—almost 40% of the people of developing countries—live in absolute poverty. Absolute poverty is probably the principal cause of human misery today.

This is the background situation, the situation that prevails on our planet all the time. It does not make headlines. People died from malnutrition and related diseases yesterday, and more will die tomorrow. The occasional droughts, cyclones, earthquakes and floods that take the lives of tens of thousands in one place and at one time are more newsworthy.

They add greatly to the total amount of human suffering; but it is wrong to assume that when there are no major calamities reported, all is well.

The problem is not that the world cannot produce enough to feed and shelter its people. People in the poor countries consume, on average, 400 lbs of grain a year, while North Americans average more than 2000 lbs. The difference is caused by the fact that in the rich countries we feed most of our grain to animals, converting it into meat, milk and eggs. Because this is an inefficient process, wasting up to 95% of the food value of the animal feed, people in rich countries are responsible for the consumption of far more food than those in poor countries who eat few animal products. If we stopped feeding animals on grains, soybeans and fishmeal the amount of food saved would—if distributed to those who need it—be more than enough to end hunger throughout the world.

These facts about animal food do not mean that we can easily solve the world food problem by cutting down on animal products, but they show that the problem is essentially one of distribution rather than production. The world does produce enough food. Moreover the poorer nations themselves could produce far more if they made more use of improved agricultural techniques.

So why are people hungry? Poor people cannot afford to buy grain grown by American farmers. Poor farmers cannot afford to buy improved seeds, or fertilizers, or the machinery needed for drilling wells and pumping water. Only by transferring some of the wealth of the developed nations to the poor of the underdeveloped nations can the situation be changed.

That this wealth exists is clear. Against the picture of absolute poverty that McNamara has painted, one might pose a picture of 'absolute affluence'. Those who are absolutely affluent are not necessarily affluent by comparison with their neighbours, but they are affluent by any reasonable definition of human needs. This means that they have more income than they need to provide themselves adequately with all the basic necessities of life. After buying food, shelter, clothing, necessary health services and education, the absolutely affluent are still able to spend money on luxuries. The absolutely affluent choose their food for the pleasures of the palate, not to stop hunger; they buy new clothes to look fashionable, not to keep warm; they move house to be in a better neighbourhood or have a play room for the children, not to keep out the rain; and after all this there is still money to spend on books and records, colour television, and overseas holidays.

At this stage I am making no ethical judgments about absolute affluence, merely pointing out that it exists. Its defining characteristic is a significant amount of income above the level necessary to provide for the basic human needs of oneself and one's dependents. By this standard Western Europe, North America, Japan, Australia, New Zealand and the oil-rich Middle Eastern states are all absolutely affluent, and so are many, if not all, of their citizens. The USSR and Eastern Europe might also be included on this list. To quote McNamara once more:

> The average citizen of a developed country enjoys wealth beyond the wildest dreams of the one billion people in countries with per capita incomes under $200. . . .

These, therefore, are the countries—and individuals—who have wealth which they could, without threatening their own basic welfare, transfer to the absolutely poor.

At present, very little is being transferred. Members of the Organization of Petroleum Exporting Countries lead the way, giving an average of 2.1% of their Gross National Product. Apart from them, only Sweden, The Netherlands and Norway have reached the modest UN target of 0.7% of GNP. Britain gives 0.38% of its GNP in official development assistance and a small additional amount in unofficial aid from voluntary organizations. The total comes to less than £1 per month per person, and compares with 5.5% of GNP spent on alcohol, and 3% on tobacco. Other, even wealthier nations, give still less: Germany gives 0.27%, the United States 0.22% and Japan 0.21%.

The Moral Equivalent of Murder?

If these are the facts, we cannot avoid concluding that by not giving more than we do, people in rich countries are allowing those in poor countries to suffer from absolute poverty, with consequent malnutrition, ill health and death. This is not a conclusion which applies only to governments. It applies to each absolutely affluent individual, for each of us has the opportunity to do something about the situation; for instance, to give our time or money to voluntary organizations like Oxfam, War on Want, Freedom From Hunger, and so on. If, then, allowing someone to die is not intrinsically different from killing someone, it would seem that we are all murderers.

Is this verdict too harsh? Many will reject it as self-evidently absurd. They would sooner take it as showing that allowing to die cannot be equivalent to killing than as showing that living in an affluent style without contributing to Oxfam is ethically equivalent to going over to India and shooting a few peasants. And no doubt, put as bluntly as that, the verdict *is* too harsh.

There are several significant differences between spending money on luxuries instead of using it to save lives, and deliberately shooting people.

First, the motivation will normally be different. Those who deliberately shoot others go out of their way to kill; they presumably want their victims dead, from malice, sadism, or some equally unpleasant motive. A person who buys a colour television set presumably wants to watch television in colour—not in itself a terrible thing. At worst, spending money on luxuries instead of giving it away indicates selfishness and indifference to the sufferings of others, characteristics which may be understandable but are not comparable with actual malice or similar motives.

Second, it is not difficult for most of us to act in accordance with a rule against killing people: it is, on the other hand, very difficult to obey a rule which commands us to save all the lives we can. To live a comfortable, or even luxurious life it is not necessary to kill anyone; but it is necessary to allow some to die whom we might have saved, for the money that we need to live comfortably could have been given away. Thus the duty to avoid killing is much easier to discharge completely than the duty to save. Saving every life we could would mean cutting our standard of living down to the bare essentials needed to keep us alive.* To discharge this duty completely would require a degree of moral heroism utterly different from what is required by mere avoidance of killing.

A third difference is the greater certainty of the outcome of shooting when compared with not giving aid. If I point a loaded gun at someone and pull the trigger, it is virtually certain that the person will be injured, if not killed; whereas the money that I could give might be spent on a project than turns out to be unsuccessful and helps no one.

Fourth, when people are shot there are identifiable individuals who have been harmed. We can point to them and to their grieving families. When I buy my colour television, I cannot know who my money would have saved if I had given it away. In a time of famine I may see dead bodies and grieving families on my new television, and I might not doubt that my money would have saved some of them; even then it is impossible to point to a body and say that had I not bought the set, that person would have survived.

Fifth, it might be said that the plight of the hungry is not my doing, and so I cannot be held responsible for it. The starving would have been starving if I had never existed. If I kill, however, I am responsible for my victims' deaths, for those people would not have died if I had not killed them. . . .

---

*Strictly, we would need to cut down to the minimum level compatible with earning the income which, after providing for our needs, left us most to give away. Thus if my present position earns me, say, £10,000 a year, but requires me to spend £1,000 a year on dressing respectably and maintaining a car, I cannot save more people by giving away the car and clothes if that will mean taking a job which, although it does not involve me in these expenses, earns me only £5,000.

Do the five differences not only explain, but also justify, our attitudes? Let us consider them one by one:

1. Take the lack of an identifiable victim first. Suppose that I am a travelling salesman, selling tinned food, and I learn that a batch of tins contains a contaminant, the known effect of which when consumed is to double the risk that the consumer will died from stomach cancer. Suppose I continue to sell the tins. My decision may have no identifiable victims. Some of those who eat the food will die from cancer. The proportion of consumers dying in this way will be twice that of the community at large, but which among the consumers died because they ate what I sold, and which would have contracted the disease anyway? It is impossible to tell; but surely this impossibility makes my decision no less reprehensible than it would have been had the contaminant had more readily detectable, though equally fatal, effects.

2. The lack of certainty that by giving money I could save a life does reduce the wrongness of not giving, by comparison with deliberate killing; but it is insufficient to show that not giving is acceptable conduct. The motorist who speeds through pedestrian crossings, heedless of anyone who might be on them, is not a murderer. She may never actually hit a pedestrian; yet what she does is very wrong indeed.

3. The notion of responsibility for acts rather than omissions is more puzzling. On the one hand we feel ourselves to be under a greater obligation to help those whose misfortunes we have caused. (It is for this reason that advocates of overseas aid often argue that Western nations have created the poverty of Third World nations, through forms of economic exploitation which go back to the colonial system.) On the other hand any consequentialist would insist that we are responsible for all the consequences of our actions, and if a consequence of my spending money on a luxury item is that someone dies, I am responsible for that death. It is true that the person would have died even if I had never existed, but what is the relevance of that? The fact is that I do exist, and the consequentialist will say that our responsibilities derive from the world as it is, not as it might have been.

One way of making sense of the nonconsequentialist view of responsibility is by basing it on a theory of rights of the kind proposed by John Locke or, more recently, Robert Nozick. If everyone has a right to life, and this right is a right *against* others who might threaten my life, but not a right *to* assistance from others when my life is in danger, then we can understand the feeling that we are responsible for acting to kill but not for omitting to save. The former violates the rights of others, the latter does not.

Should we accept such a theory of rights? If we build up our theory of rights by imagining, as Locke and Nozick do, individuals living independently from each other in a 'state of nature', it may seem natural to adopt a conception of rights in which as long as each leaves the other alone, no rights are violated. I might, on this view, quite properly have maintained my independent existence if I had wished to do so. So if I do not make you any worse off than you would have been if I had had nothing at all to do with you, how can I have violated your rights? But why start from such an unhistorical, abstract and ultimately inexplicable idea as an independent individual? We now know that our ancestors were social beings long before they were human beings, and could not have developed the abilities and capacities of human beings if they had not been social beings first. In any case we are not, now, isolated individuals. If we consider people living together in a community, it is less easy to assume that rights must be restricted to rights against interference. We might, instead, adopt the view that taking rights to life seriously is incompatible with standing by and watching people die when one could easily save them.

4. What of the difference in motivation? That a person does not positively wish for the death of another lessens the severity of the blame she deserves; but not by as much as our present attitudes to giving aid suggest. The behaviour of the speeding motorist is

again comparable, for such motorists usually have no desire at all to kill anyone. They merely enjoy speeding and are indifferent to the consequences. Despite their lack of malice, those who kill with cars deserve not only blame but also severe punishment.

5. Finally, the fact that to avoid killing people is normally not difficult, whereas to save all one possibly could save is heroic, must make an important difference to our attitude to failure to do what the respective principles demand. Not to kill is a minimum standard of acceptable conduct we can require of everyone; to save all one possibly could is not something that can realistically be required, especially not in societies accustomed to giving as little as ours do. Given the generally accepted standards, people who give, say, £100 a year to Oxfam are more aptly praised for above average generosity than blamed for giving less than they might. The appropriateness of praise and blame is, however, a separate issue from the rightness or wrongness of actions. The former evaluates the agent: the latter evaluates the action. Perhaps people who give £100 really ought to give at least £1,000, but to blame them for not giving more could be counterproductive. It might make them feel that what is required is too demanding, and if one is going to be blamed anyway, one might as well not give anything at all.

(That an ethic which put saving all one possibly can on the same footing as not killing would be an ethic for saints or heroes should not lead us to assume that the alternative must be an ethic which makes it obligatory not to kill, but puts us under no obligation to save anyone. There are positions in between these extremes, as we shall soon see.)

To summarize our discussion of the five differences which normally exist between killing and allowing to die, in the context of absolute poverty and overseas aid. The lack of an identifiable victim is of no moral significance, though it may play an important role in explaining our attitudes. The idea that we are directly responsible for those we kill, but not for those we do not help, depends on a questionable notion of responsibility, and may need to be based on a controversial theory of rights. Differences in certainty and motivation are ethically significant, and show that not aiding the poor is not to be condemned as murdering them; it could, however, be on a par with killing someone as a result of reckless driving, which is serious enough. Finally the difficulty of completely discharging the duty of saving all one possibly can makes it inappropriate to blame those who fall short of this target as we blame those who kill; but this does not show that the act itself is less serious. Nor does it indicate anything about those who, far from saving all they possibly can, make no effort to save anyone.

These conclusions suggest a new approach. Instead of attempting to deal with the contrast between affluence and poverty by comparing not saving with deliberate killing, let us consider afresh whether we have an obligation to assist those whose lives are in danger, and if so, how this obligation applies to the present world situation.

The Obligation to Assist

The Argument for an Obligation to Assist

The path from the library at my university to the Humanities lecture theatre passes a shallow ornamental pond. Suppose that on my way to give a lecture I notice that a small child has fallen in and is in danger of drowning. Would anyone deny that I ought to wade in and pull the child out? This will mean getting my clothes muddy, and either cancelling my lecture or delaying it until I can find something dry to change into; but compared with the avoidable death of a child this is insignificant.

A plausible principle that would support the judgment that I ought to pull the child out is this: if it is in our power to prevent something very bad happening, without thereby sacrificing anything of comparable moral significance, we ought to do it. This principle seems uncontroversial. It will obviously win the assent of consequentialists; but non-consequentialists should accept it too, because the injunction to prevent what is bad applies only when nothing comparably significant is at stake. Thus the principle cannot lead to the kinds of actions of which non-consequentialists strongly disapprove—serious violations of individual rights, injustice, broken promises, and so on. If a non-consequentialist regards any of these as comparable in moral significance to the bad thing that is to be prevented, he will automatically regard the principle as not applying in those cases in which the bad thing can only be prevented by violating rights, doing injustice, breaking promises, or whatever else is at stake. Most non-consequentialists hold that we ought to prevent what is bad and promote what is good. Their dispute with consequentialists lies in their insistence that this is not the sole ultimate ethical principle: that it is *an* ethical principle is not denied by any plausible ethical theory.

Nevertheless the uncontroversial appearance of the principle that we ought to prevent what is bad when we can do so without sacrificing anything of comparable moral significance is deceptive. If it were taken seriously and acted upon, our lives and our world would be fundamentally changed. For the principle applies, not just to rare situations in which one can save a child from a pond, but to the everyday situation in which we can assist those living in absolute poverty. In saying this I assume that absolute poverty, with its hunger and malnutrition, lack of shelter, illiteracy, disease, high infant mortality and low life expectancy, is a bad thing. And I assume that it is within the power of the affluent to reduce absolute poverty, without sacrificing anything of comparable moral significance. If these two assumptions and the principle we have been discussing are correct, we have an obligation to help those in absolute poverty which is no less strong than our obligation to rescue a drowning child from a pond. Not to help would be wrong, whether or not it is intrinsically equivalent to killing. Helping is not, as conventionally thought, a charitable act which it is praiseworthy to do, but not wrong to omit; it is something that everyone ought to do.

This is the argument for an obligation to assist. Set out more formally, it would look like this.

First premise:	If we can prevent something bad without sacrificing anything of comparable significance, we ought to do it.
Second premise:	Absolute poverty is bad.
Third premise:	There is some absolute poverty we can prevent without sacrificing anything of comparable moral significance.
Conclusion:	We ought to prevent some absolute poverty.

The first premise is the substantive moral premise on which the argument rests, and I have tried to show that it can be accepted by people who hold a variety of ethical positions.

The second premise is unlikely to be challenged. Absolute poverty is, as McNamara put it, 'beneath any reasonable definition of human decency' and it would be hard to find a plausible ethical view which did not regard it as a bad thing.

The third premise is more controversial, even though it is cautiously framed. It claims only that some absolute poverty can be prevented without the sacrifice of anything of comparable moral significance. It thus avoids the objection that any aid I can give is just 'drops in the ocean' for the point is not whether my personal contribution will make any noticeable impression on world poverty as a whole (of course it won't) but whether it will prevent some poverty. This is all the argument needs to sustain its conclusion, since the second premise says that any absolute poverty is bad, and not merely the total amount of absolute poverty. If without sacrificing anything of comparable moral significance we can provide just one family with the means to raise itself out of absolute poverty, the third premise is vindicated.

I have left the notion of moral significance unexamined in order to show that the argument does not depend on any specific values or ethical principles. I think the third premise is true for most people living in industrialized nations, on any defensible view of what is morally significant. Our affluence means that we have income we can dispose of without giving up the basic necessities of life, and we can use this income to reduce absolute poverty. Just how much we will think ourselves obliged to give up will depend on what we consider to be of comparable moral significance to the poverty we could prevent: colour television, stylish clothes, expensive dinners, a sophisticated stereo system, overseas holidays, a (second?) car, a larger house, private schools for our children. . . . For a utilitarian, none of these is likely to be of comparable significance to the reduction of absolute poverty; and those who are not utilitarians surely must, if they subscribe to the principle of universalizability, accept that at least *some* of these things are of far less moral significance than the absolute poverty that could be prevented by the money they cost. So the third premise seems to be true on any plausible ethical view—although the precise amount of absolute poverty that can be prevented before anything of moral significance is sacrificed will vary according to the ethical view one accepts. . . .

Objections to the Argument

Property Rights

Do people have a right to private property, a right which contradicts the view that they are under an obligation to give some of their wealth away to those in absolute poverty? According to some theories of rights (for instance, Robert Nozick's) provided one has acquired one's property without the use of unjust means like force and fraud, one may be entitled to enormous wealth while others starve. This individualistic conception of rights is in contrast to other views, like the early Christian doctrine to be found in the works of Thomas Aquinas, which holds that since property exists for the satisfaction of human needs, 'whatever a man has in superabundance is owed, of natural right, to the poor for their sustenance'. A socialist would also, of course, see wealth as belonging to the community rather than the individual, while utilitarians, whether socialist or not, would be prepared to override property rights to prevent great evils.

Does the argument for an obligation to assist others therefore presuppose one of these other theories of property rights, and not an individualistic theory like Nozick's? Not necessarily. A theory of property rights can insist on our *right* to retain wealth without pronouncing on whether the rich *ought* to give to the poor. Nozick, for example, rejects the use of compulsory means like taxation to redistribute income, but suggests that we can achieve the ends we deem morally desirable by voluntary means. So Nozick would reject the claim that rich people have an 'obligation' to give to the poor, in so far as this implies that the poor have a right to our aid, but might accept that giving is something we ought to do and failing to give, though within one's rights, is wrong—for rights is not all there is to ethics.

The argument for an obligation to assist can survive, with only minor modifications, even if we accept an individualistic theory of property rights. In any case, however, I do not think we should accept such a theory. It leaves too much to chance to be an acceptable ethical view. For instance, those whose forefathers happened to inhabit some sandy wastes around the Persian Gulf are now fabulously wealthy, because oil lay under those sands; while those whose forefathers settled on better land south of the Sahara live in absolute poverty, because of drought and bad harvests. Can this distribution be acceptable from an impartial point of view? If we imagine ourselves about to begin life as a citizen of either Kuwait or Chad—but we do not know which—would we accept the principle that citizens of Kuwait are under no obligation to assist people living in Chad?

Population and the Ethics of Triage

Perhaps the most serious objection to the argument that we have an obligation to assist is that since the major cause of absolute poverty is overpopulation, helping those now in poverty will only ensure that yet more people are born to live in poverty in the future.

In its most extreme form, this objection is taken to show that we should adopt a policy of 'triage'. The term comes from medical policies adopted in wartime. With too few doctors to cope with all the casualties, the wounded were divided into three categories: those who would probably survive without medical assistance, those who might survive if they received assistance, but otherwise probably would not, and those who even with medical assistance probably would not survive. Only those in the middle category were given medical assistance. The idea, of course, was to use limited medical resources as effectively as possible. For those in the first category, medical treatment was not strictly necessary; for those in the third category, it was likely to be useless. It has been suggested that we should apply the same policies to countries, according to their prospects of becoming self-sustaining. We would not aid countries which even without our help will soon be able to feed their populations. We would not aid countries which, even with our help, will not be able to limit their population to a level they can feed. We would aid those countries where our help might make the difference between success and failure in bringing food and population into balance.

Advocates of this theory are understandably reluctant to give a complete list of the countries they would place into the 'hopeless' category; but Bangladesh is often cited as an example. Adopting the policy of triage would, then, mean cutting off assistance to Bangladesh and allowing famine, disease and natural disasters to reduce the population of that country (now around 80 million) to the level at which it can provide adequately for all.

In support of this view Garrett Hardin has offered a metaphor: we in the rich nations are like the occupants of a crowded lifeboat adrift in a sea full of drowning people. If we try to save the drowning by bringing them aboard our boat will be overloaded and we shall all drown. Since it is better that some survive than none, we should leave the others to drown. In the world today, according to Hardin, 'lifeboat ethics' apply. The rich should leave the poor to starve, for otherwise the poor will drag the rich down with them.

Against this view, some writers have argued that over-population is a myth. The world produces ample food to feed its population, and could, according to some estimates, feed ten times as many. People are hungry not because there are too many but because of inequitable land distribution, the manipulation of Third World economies by the developed nations, wastage of food in the West, and so on.

Putting aside the controversial issue of the extent to which food production might one day be increased, it is true, as we have already seen, that the world now produces enough to feed its inhabitants—the amount lost by being fed to animals itself being enough to meet existing grain shortages. Nevertheless population growth cannot be ignored. Bangladesh could, with land reform and using better techniques, feed its present population of 80 million; but by the year 2000, according to World Bank estimates, its population will be 146 million. The enormous effort that will have to go into feeding an extra 66 million people, all added to the population within a quarter of a century, means that Bangladesh must develop at full speed to stay where she is. Other low income countries are in similar situations. By the end of the century, Ethiopia's population is expected to rise from 29 to 54 million; Somalia's from 3 to 7 million, India's from 620 to 958 million, Zaire's from 25 to 47 million. What will happen then? Population cannot grow indefinitely. It will be checked by a decline in birth rates or a rise in death rates. Those who advocate triage are proposing that we allow the population growth of some countries to be checked by a rise in death rates—that is, by increased malnutrition, and related diseases; by widespread famines; by increased infant mortality; and by epidemics of infectious diseases.

The consequences of triage on this scale are so horrible that we are inclined to reject it without further argument. How could we sit by our television sets, watching millions starve while we do nothing? Would not that be the end of all notions of human equality and respect for human life? Don't people have a right to our assistance, irrespective of the consequences?

Anyone whose initial reaction to triage was not one of repugnance would be an unpleasant sort of person. Yet initial reactions based on strong feelings are not always reliable guides. Advocates of triage are rightly concerned with the long-term consequences of our actions. They say that helping the poor and starving now merely ensures more poor and starving in the future. When our capacity to help is finally unable to cope—as one day it must be—the suffering will be greater than it would be if we stopped helping now. If this is correct, there is nothing we can do to prevent absolute starvation and poverty, in the long run, and so we have no obligation to assist. Nor does it seem reasonable to hold that under these circumstances people have a right to our assistance. If we do accept such a right, irrespective of the consequences, we are saying that, in Hardin's metaphor, we would continue to haul the drowning into our lifeboat until the boat sank and we all drowned.

If triage is to be rejected it must be tackled on its own ground, within the framework of consequentialist ethics. Here it is vulnerable. Any consequentialist ethics must take probability of outcome into account. A course of action that will certainly produce some benefit is to be preferred to an alternative course that may lead to a slightly larger benefit, but is equally likely to result in no benefit at all. Only if the greater magnitude of the uncertain benefit outweighs its uncertainty should we choose it. Better one certain unit of benefit than a 10% chance of 5 units; but better a 50% chance of 3 units than a single certain unit. The same principle applies when we are trying to avoid evils.

The policy of triage involves a certain, very great evil: population control by famine and disease. Tens of millions would die slowly. Hundreds of millions would continue to live in absolute poverty, at the very margin of existence. Against this prospect, advocates of the policy place a possible evil which is greater still: the same process of famine and disease, taking place in, say, fifty years time, when the world's population may be three times its present level, and the number who will die from famine, or struggle on in absolute poverty, will be that much greater. The question is: how probable is this forecast that continued assistance now will lead to greater disasters in the future?

Forecasts of population growth are notoriously fallible, and theories about the factors which affect it remain speculative. One theory, at least as plausible as any other, is that countries pass through a 'demographic transition' as their standard of living rises. When people are very poor and have no access to

modern medicine their fertility is high, but population is kept in check by high death rates. The introduction of sanitation, modern medical techniques and other improvements reduces the death rate, but initially has little effect on the birth rate. Then population grows rapidly. Most poor countries are now in this phase. If standards of living continue to rise, however, couples begin to realize that to have the same number of children surviving to maturity as in the past, they do not need to give birth to as many children as their parents did. The need for children to provide economic support in old age diminishes. Improved education and the emancipation and employment of women also reduce the birthrate, and so population growth begins to level off. Most rich nations have reached this stage, and their populations are growing only very slowly.

If this theory is right, there is an alternative to the disasters accepted as inevitable by supporters of triage. We can assist poor countries to raise the living standards of the poorest members of their population. We can encourage the governments of these countries to enact land reform measures, improve education, and liberate women from a purely childbearing role. We can also help other countries to make contraception and sterilization widely available. There is a fair chance that these measures will hasten the onset of the demographic transition and bring population growth down to a manageable level. Success cannot be guaranteed; but the evidence that improved economic security and education reduce population growth is strong enough to make triage ethically unacceptable. We cannot allow millions to die from starvation and disease when there is a reasonable probability that population can be brought under control without such horrors.

Population growth is therefore not a reason against giving overseas aid, although it should make us think about the kind of aid to give. Instead of food handouts, it may be better to give aid that hastens the demographic transition. This may mean agricultural assistance for the rural poor, or assistance with education, or the provision of contraceptive services. Whatever kind of aid proves most effective in specific circumstances, the obligation to assist is not reduced.

One awkward question remains. What should we do about a poor and already over-populated country which, for religious or nationalistic reasons, restricts the use of contraceptives and refuses to slow its population growth? Should we nevertheless offer development assistance? Or should we make our offer conditional on effective steps being taken to reduce the birthrate? To the latter course, some would object that putting conditions on aid is an attempt to impose our own ideas on independent sovereign nations. So it is—but is this imposition unjustifiable? If the argument for an obligation to assist is sound, we have an obligation to reduce absolute poverty: but we have no obligation to make sacrifices that, to the best of our knowledge, have no prospect of reducing poverty in the long run. Hence we have no obligation to assist countries whose governments have policies which will make our aid ineffective. This could be very harsh on poor citizens of these countries—for they may have no say in the government's policies—but we will help more people in the long run by using our resources where they are most effective. (The same principles may apply, incidentally, to countries that refuse to take other steps that could make assistance effective—like refusing to reform systems of land holding that impose intolerable burdens on poor tenant farmers.) . . .

Too High a Standard?

The final objection to the argument for an obligation to assist is that it sets a standard so high that none but a saint could attain it. How many people can we really expect to give away everything not comparable in moral significance to the poverty their donation could relieve? For most of us, with commonsense views about what is of moral significance, this would mean a life of real austerity. Might it not be counter-productive to demand so much? Might not people say: 'As I can't do what is morally required anyway, I won't bother to give at all.' If, however, we were to set a more realistic standard, people might make a genuine effort to reach it. Thus setting a lower standard might actually result in more aid being given.

It is important to get the status of this objection clear. Its accuracy as a prediction of human behaviour is quite compatible with the argument that we are obliged to give to the point at which by giving more we sacrifice something of comparable moral significance. What would follow from the objection is that public advocacy of this standard of giving is undesirable. It would mean that in order to do the maximum to reduce absolute poverty, we should advocate a standard lower than the amount we think people really ought to give. Of course we ourselves—those of us who accept the original argument, with its higher standard—would know that we ought to do more than we publicly propose people ought to do, and we might actually give more than we urge others to give. There is no inconsistency here, since in both our private and our public behaviour we are trying to do what will most reduce absolute poverty.

For a consequentialist, this apparent conflict between public and private morality is always a possibility, and not in itself an indication that the underlying principle is wrong. The consequences of a principle are one thing, the consequences of publicly advocating it another.

Is it true that the standard set by our argument is so high as to be counterproductive? There is not much evidence to go by, but discussions of the argument, with students and others have led me to think it might be. On the other hand the conventionally accepted standard—a few coins in a collection tin when one is waved under your nose—is obviously far too low. What level should we advocate? Any figure will be arbitrary, but there may be something to be said for a round percentage of one's income like, say, 10%—more than a token donation, yet not so high as to be beyond all but saints. (This figure has the additional advantage of being reminiscent of the ancient tithe, or tenth, which was traditionally given to the church, whose responsibilities included care of the poor in one's local community. Perhaps the idea can be revived and applied to the global community.) Some families, of course, will find 10% a considerable strain on their finances. Others may be able to give more without difficulty. No figure should be advocated as a rigid minimum or maximum; but it seems safe to advocate that those earning average or above average incomes in affluent societies, unless they have an unusually large number of dependents or other special needs, ought to give a tenth of their income to reducing absolute poverty. By any reasonable ethical standards this is the minimum we ought to do, and we do wrong if we do less.

---

10. Do We Owe the Future Anything?

Richard T. De George

Richard T. De George argues that because future generations do not exist, they do not have any rights nor do we have any correlative obligations to them. Still, De George thinks we do have an obligation to promote the continuance of the human race—but an obligation based on considerations of value rather than of rights. At the same time, he denies that we have any obligation to produce a continuously increasing standard of living.

The desire to avoid pollution—however defined—involves concern for the duration and quality of human life. Problems dealing with the quality of human life inevitably involve value judgments. And value judgments are notorious candidates for debate and disagreement. Yet in discussions on pollution the desirability of the continuance of the human race is generally taken for granted; most people feel that a continuous rise in the standard of living would be a good thing; and many express a feeling of obligation towards future generations. How well founded are these judgments? The purpose of this paper is to examine the validity and some of the implications of three statements of principles which have a direct bearing on this question and so on the debate concerning pollution and its control. The three principles are the following:

1. Only existing entities have rights.
2. Continuance of the human race is good.
3. Continuous increase in man's standard of living is good.

From "Do We Owe the Future Anything?" in Law and the Ecological Challenge (1978), pp. 180–190. Reprinted by permission of William S. Hein & Co., Inc.

I

The argument in favor of the principle that only existing entities have rights is straightforward and simple: Non-existent entities by definition do not exist. What does not exist cannot be the subject or bearer of anything. Hence it cannot be the subject or bearer of rights.

Just as non-existent entities have no rights, so it makes no sense to speak about anyone's correlative duty towards non-existent entities. Towards that which does not exist we can have no legal or moral obligation, since there is no subject or term which can be the object of that obligation. Now it is clear that unconceived possible future human beings do not exist, though we can think, e.g., of the class of human beings which will exist two hundred years from now. It follows that since this class does not (yet) exist, we cannot have any obligations to it, nor to any of its possible members. It is a presently empty class.

More generally, then, presently existing human beings have no obligation to any future-and-not-yet existing set or class of human beings. We owe them nothing and they have no legitimate claim on us for the simple reason that they do not exist. No one can legitimately defend their interests or represent their case in court or law or government, because they are not, and so have no interests or rights.

It follows from this that a great deal of contemporary talk about obligations to the future, where this means to some distant future portion of mankind, is simply confused. In dealing with questions of pollution and clean air—as well as with similar issues such as the use of irreplaceable resources—there can be no legitimate question of the **rights** of unconceived future human beings or of any supposedly correlative **obligation** of present-day human beings to them.

Some people may find this to be counterintuitive. That it is not so may perhaps become clearer if we consider what I take to be the feelings of many—if not most people with respect to the past.

Consider the general attitude towards the ancient Greeks and Romans. Did they owe us anything? Did they have any duties or obligations to us? It is clear there are no sanctions we can impose on them and no way we can enforce any obligations we may claim they had towards us. But surely even to raise the question of their obligation to us is odd. We may rejoice in what has been saved of the past and handed down to us, and we may regret that some of Plato's dialogues have been lost or that the Library at Alexandria was burned, or that Rome was sacked. But though we may regret such events and though we may judge that they were in some sense ills for mankind or the result of immoral actions, they were not immoral because of any obligation past generations had to us.

The situation is little changed if we come up to more recent—though not too recent—times. The American Founding Fathers had no obligation to us. They could scarcely have envisaged our times or have been expected to calculate the effects of their actions on us. Or consider the unrestrained slaughter of American buffalo for sport. Such action may have been immoral and a waste of a natural resource; but if it was immoral it was not because present-day Americans have any right to have inherited more buffalo than we did.

Since it is not possible to impose sanctions on past generations it makes no sense to speak of legal obligations or even of moral obligations of those generations to us. At best, as some minority groups have been arguing, we might claim that present-day beneficiaries of past injustices are obliged to make restitution to the present descendents of those who in the past suffered injustice. This is a plausible claim, and might serve as a model in the future for some portion of mankind claiming that it has a legal or moral claim against another portion for exploitation or oppression by their forefathers. Whatever the obligation to make restoration for past injustices, however, the injustice was an injustice not primarily against present generations but against those past generations whose rights were violated or whose property or lives were unjustly taken, or who were otherwise oppressed or exploited.

The situation is basically similar today vis-a-vis future generations. Our primary obligation with respect to the control of pollution or to the use of resources is to presently existing human beings rather than to possible future human beings. The best way to protect the interests of future generations—if we choose to use this language—may be to conserve the environment for ourselves. But my present point is that in dealing with questions of public policy or legislation, the primary values to be considered are those of presently existing people, and not the projected or supposed values of future generations. To argue or act as if we could know the wants or needs of generations hundreds or more years hence is to deceive ourselves, perhaps so as to have an excuse to ignore present-day wants and needs. Hence questions about the amount and kind of pollution to be tolerated, the resources to be rationed or preserved, should not be decided in terms of far distant future needs or requirements but in terms of present and near-future needs and requirements.

It is correct that for the first time in the history of mankind presently living human beings have it within their power to annihilate mankind or to use up irreplaceable resources. But these new capacities do not change the status of our responsibilities or obligations, despite the fact that they are increased. If we do annihilate mankind, it will be no injustice to those who never were and never will be. If we were foolishly to use up vital, irreplaceable resources or disrupt the ecosystem, the reason it would be wrong or bad, unjust or immoral—and so the reason why it might now be something requiring legislation to prevent—is not its effects on those who do not yet exist, but its effects on those who do.

The thrust of the principle we are considering is that present generations or individuals must be considered primary in any calculation of value with respect to either pollution control or the distribution and use of the limited resources of the earth. The rights of presently existing people carry with them the obligation to respect their rights, e.g., to enjoy at least minimal levels of food, shelter, and the like. No one and no generation is required to sacrifice itself for imaginary, non-existent generations of the future. What does have to be considered is the future of presently existing persons—infants as well as adults.

We undoubtedly feel closer to our as yet unconceived descendents—those one remove from the present generation of children—than we do to many people living in places far distant from us, with different customs and values; and if we were to choose between raising the standard of living of these to us foreign people and preserving our wealth to be shared by our descendents, we might well opt for the latter. To do so is to aggregate to ourselves the right to conserve present resources for those to whom we choose to pass them on at the expense of those presently existing who do not share them. Since, however, presently existing people have rights to the goods of the earth, there seems to be a **prima facie** obligation to attempt to raise the level of living and comfort of presently existing people, wherever they may be, rather than ignoring them and worrying only about our own future heirs. Underfed and impoverished areas of the world may require greater attention and impose greater obligations than non-existent future generations.

Insofar as modern technology is world-significant, so too are some aspects of pollution. Mercury poured into streams finds its way into the ocean and into fish caught in international waters and shipped around the world; fall-out from nuclear blasts circles the globe. If present-day legislative principles in the United States are sufficient to handle the problems posed by pollution in our own country, it is certainly not the case that there are effective means of controlling the problem internationally. The cost of pollution control prevents poorer countries from simultaneously developing their technology in order to raise their living standards and spend the money and resources necessary to curb pollution. It is in cases such as these that it becomes especially important to be conscious of the principle discussed here which emphasizes the overbearing rights of existing persons as opposed to the putative rights of nonexistent persons. . . .

Although there is no full fledged obligation to provide, e.g., clean air, for countless future generations, we will have an obligation to provide something for at least those future persons or generations for whom or for which we are rather closely responsible. Generations overlap considerably; but any group in the position to influence and change things, though it cannot be expected to be responsible for generations hundreds, much less thousands of years hence, can be expected to take into account those persons who will be alive within the next fifty or a hundred years. A large number of these people already exist; and if future generations are produced—as barring some global catastrophe they will be—they **will** have rights and these rights must be considered at least as potential rights. The amount of consideration should be proportional to the probability that they will exist, and should be considered especially by those responsible for bringing them into the world.

Furthermore, if starting from the premise that non-existent entities can have no rights it follows that presently existing persons have no correlative obligations towards them, and so no such obligations to unborn generations, this does not mean that people may not want to consider future possible generations from some point of view other than one of such obligation and take them into account in other ways and for other reasons.

Obviously men are concerned about their own futures and those of their presently existing children and of the presently acknowledged right of their children to have children; it is a claim which must be weighed. Though we cannot assume that the children of present-day children will have exactly the same desires and values as we, there is good reason to believe they will be sufficiently similar to us so that they will need fresh air, that they will not be able to tolerate excessive amounts of mercury or DDT in their food, and that they will probably share a good many of our desires. To speak of the **right** of non-existing future persons to have children in their turn is to treat them as actual. It amounts to saying that if conditions remain more or less the same and if the presently possible entities become actual, then, when they do, they will have the rights we presently attribute to actually existing persons. Our present interest in their happiness, however, is already an actual interest which must be considered and it might impel—though not strictly require—us to leave as many options open to those who will come after us as possible, consistent with taking care of our own needs and wants.

Since most people living now would consider it possible to be living twenty years hence, the conditions of life which the next as yet unborn generation will face is a condition of life which we who presently exist will also face. So with respect to at least one, two, three or perhaps four generations hence, or for roughly fifty to a hundred years hence, it can plausibly be argued that we plan not only for unborn generations but also for ourselves. Our concern for them is equally concern for ourselves. And we do have rights. If this is the case, we can legitimately think and plan and act for the future on the basis of our own concerns, which include **our** hopes and desires for our real or anticipated offspring. But we should be clear about what we are arguing, and not confuse our rights and desires with the supposed rights of non-existent entities.

II

The second principle was: Continuance of the human race is good.

What does this mean and what does it imply?

Can we give any sense to the question: how long should the human race survive? We know that some species have had their span of years on earth and have given way to other species. To ask how long the dinosaur should have survived would be an odd question; for to say that it should have survived for a shorter or longer time than it did would be to speak as if the laws of nature should have been different, or as if the dinosaur's continued existence was a good which it could have done something to prolong beyond the time that it did. It is precisely in this sense—that the survival of the human species is a good in itself and that we should do what we can to keep it going—that we say that the human race should continue to survive. To utter this is to make a value judgment and to express our feelings about the race, despite the fact that we as individuals will die. Some people speak blithely about its being better for the human species to continue for another thousand years than for another five hundred; or for 500,000 rather than 100,000, and so on. But the content which we can give to such statements—other than expressing the judgment that human life is a good in itself, at least under certain circumstances—seems minimal. For we cannot imagine what human life would be like in the far distant future, nor what we can or should do to help make it the case that one of those figures rather than the other is the one that actually becomes the case.

If tomorrow some sort of radiation from the sun were to render all human beings sterile, we could anticipate the demise of the human race as more and more of the present population died off. We could anticipate the difficulties of those who were the relatively last to die. And we could take some solace in the fact that the radiation would have been an act of God and not the result of the acts of men. The demise of the human race would in this case be similar to the extinction of the dinosaur. If a similar occurrence was the result of the acts of men, though the result would be the same, it would make more sense in the latter case than in the former to say that man should have continued longer as a species. Just as we consider murder and suicide wrong, so we consider wrong the fouling of the air or water to such an extent that it kills others or ourselves or the whole human race.

Thus, though no injustice is done to those who will never exist because of our actions, and though we do not violate any of their rights—since they have none—we can in some sense say that with the extinction of the human race there would be less value in the world than if it had continued to exist. If we have an obligation to attempt to create and preserve as much value in the world as possible, then we have an obligation to continue the human race, where this does not necessarily mean an obligation to procreate as many people as possible but to achieve as much value as possible, taking into consideration the quality of life of those who will be alive. The basis for the obligation comes not from a consideration of rights, but from a consideration of value.

Such a calculation, obviously, is something which each generation can perform only with respect to the time it is alive and able to act. It can help assure that when it dies those who are still living are in such a condition as to preserve human life and to pass it on at as high a qualitative level as possible. And if that happened consistently each year, each decade, each century, then until there was some act of God presumably man would continue indefinitely—which is a thought we may take some pleasure in contemplating, despite the fact that beyond a rather small number of years we will not be affected by whether the race continues or not.

Thus far, then, though we do not have any obligation **to** non-existent entities, we can legitimately anticipate the future needs and requirements of ourselves and of those who will probably come soon after us; furthermore, since we can make out the case that it would be good for the human race to continue, we have the obligation to do what we can to forestall its demise. This leads us to the third principle.

III

The last of the three principles I proposed at the start of this paper was: Continuous increase in man's standard of living is good. It is a principle which a large number of people seem to subscribe to, one underlying much of our industrial and technological growth and a good deal of the concern for a constantly expanding GNP. As a principle, however, it is both ambiguous and dubious.

There are at least four basic interpretations which can be given to the principle: 1) it can be taken to refer to advancement up the economic ladder by people on an individual basis; 2) it might be understood as a statement about the hopes and aims of each generation for the succeeding generation; 3) it might mean that the standard of living of at least some men should continue to rise, pushing forward the heights to which men can rise; and 4) it can be interpreted to mean that all men in a given society, or throughout the world, should be brought up to a certain constantly rising level of life.

The differences in interpretation are extremely important and both stem from and give rise to different sets of value judgments concerning production, distribution, development of resources, and expenditure of resources on pollution control.

1) The individualistic interpretation puts its emphasis on an individual's ability through work, savings, ingenuity, or other means to advance himself economically. The Horatio Alger ideal, the rise from poverty to wealth, is the model. Increasing one's standard of living became the goal of workers as expressed in the labor union movements, and its results are clearly visible in the high standard of living enjoyed by many large segments of the population in the United States and other industrialized countries. Together with this rise has come the pollution from automobiles and factories and the birth of a small counterculture which has called into question the necessity, the wisdom, and the value of a constantly rising standard of living.

The hope of a better life expresses an undeniable value when one's life is barely tolerable. It makes less sense as one's needs are more and more taken care of and the principle becomes dubious once one has achieved a certain standard of living somewhere considerably well above the minimal necessary for survival. There is a point of diminishing returns beyond which the price one has to pay in terms of energy, time, money, and resources expended does not produce correspondingly significant benefits. And if enough people reach that state, then the society's energy and efforts become counter-productive. The result we are seeing is that the attempt to achieve a constantly higher standard of living has resulted in a lower quality of life for all, partially through pollution. This fact, admittedly, is little comfort to those who have not yet arrived at a tolerable level of life and for whom the aspiration to raise their standard of living is a real good; the present point, however, is that at least beyond a certain level the principle cannot be achieved and if acted on may serve to produce more harm than good. (The related problem of inequity in a society will be considered further under the fourth interpretation.)

2) The interpretation of the principle which expresses the hope of parents that their children will have a better life than they suffers the same fate as the preceding interpretation. Where the level of life is already good, the desire that their children's be even better may well be questionable for the reasons we have already seen. Children, of course, have no right to be better off than their parents, although those who are badly off might well wish those they love to enjoy more of the goods of life than they themselves have.

If some generation is to enjoy a higher standard of living than others, however, it is not necessary that it always be some future generation. The desire that some future generation of human beings should be better off than present generations may be the desire of some members of present generations. But it is nothing owed to future generations. Some parents sacrifice themselves and deny themselves for the benefit of their children; some carefully save their wealth only to have their children squander it. In some cases such self-sacrifice is noble and evokes our praise; in others, it is foolish. But any such case of self-sacrifice is above the demands of duty, as is obvious when we see children attempting to demand such sacrifice from their parents as if it were their right. Nor does any parent or group have the right through legislation to demand such sacrifice from others for his own or for other people's children.

3) The view that at least some men should live at constantly higher levels so as to push mankind constantly forward seems hardly defensible for a number of reasons. The first is that it is difficult to describe what a constantly higher standard of living could mean for only a few since their lives are so closely connected to other men and to the energy, pollution, and population problems they all face. Secondly, standard of living is not the same as quality of life. Simple increase in the standard of living, if measured by the goods one has, simply does not make much sense beyond a certain point. For one's needs beyond that point are artificial, and it is not at all clear that satisfying them makes one happier or more comfortable or any of the other things that an increase in the standard of living is supposed to do, and for which reasons it is desired as a good. Thirdly, it can well be argued that it is unlikely that the constantly higher standard advocated for the few—if sense can be made of it—will help do anything but increase the difference between the level of life of the haves and the have-nots. If taken to mean not that a few men in an advanced industrial society should push mankind forward but that the advanced industrial societies should continue to advance at the expense of the non-industrial societies, then this seems to go clearly against the rights of the latter, and so not be a worthy end at all.

4) The fourth interpretation is the most plausible and has the most vocal defenders today. It maintains that all men in a given society (and ideally throughout the world) should be brought up to a certain constantly rising minimal level of life—at least constantly rising for the foreseeable future, given the wide distance between the level of life of the haves and the have-nots. This is the impetus behind minimum income legislation on the American domestic scene. Globally, it affects the relations between have and have-not countries, between the industrially developed and the underdeveloped countries, and is one of the bases for advocating foreign aid programs of various sorts.

The right of all men to a minimal standard of living is one that I would argue in favor of. But my present concern is to note that the right to a constantly rising minimum is contingent upon the ability of the earth and of society to provide it. If world resources are able to adequately sustain only a limited number of people, and if more than that number are born, the distribution of goods cannot extend sufficiently far; and those societies which contributed most to the overpopulation of their land and of the earth in general may well have to bear the brunt of the evil consequences.

A continuously rising standard of living therefore is never a right, not always a good, and most often simply one good to be measured against other goods and available resources.

IV

What then, if anything, do we owe future generations? We do not owe them a better life than we enjoy, nor do we owe them resources which we need for ourselves.

When dealing with renewable resources a sound principle might be that, other things being equal, they should not be used up at a faster rate than that at which they can be replaced. But when they are needed at a greater rate than that at which they can be replaced, rationing is insufficient and they raise a problem similar to that raised by non-renewable resources. One can argue that the latter should be used up sufficiently slowly so that there are always reserves; but this may mean using less and less each year or decade, despite increasing demand. An alternative is simply to use what we need, attempting to keep our needs rational, and to face crucially diminished supplies when we are forced to face them, hoping in the meantime that some substitutes will be discovered or developed.

Frequently problems of this type have been approached from a utilitarian point of view, and such an approach is instructive. Let each man count for one, the argument goes, whether he be a present man or a future man. The happiness of each is on a par as far as importance and intrinsic goodness are concerned. But increasing the sum of total happiness is better than its opposite. If by increased growth or unlimited use now of limited resources we increase our happiness by a small amount, but doom those who come after us to struggling along without some important natural resources; and if by conserving our natural resources now our happiness or at least that part which is made up of comfort is somewhat less than it could be, but the happiness of many millions or billions who come after us is greater than it would otherwise be, then the moral thing to do is to conserve our resources now and share them with future generations.

This argument presupposes first that there will be the future generations it hypothesizes, that these future generations will want pretty much the same things that we do in order to be happy, that they will not overuse the goods of the earth, and that they will not be able to find any suitable substitutes. If we saved only to have them squander, then no more good might be achieved than if we had spent liberally and they had proportionally less; or if they find, e.g., alternate energy sources, then our penury resulted in less good than there might have been.

In earlier times the ploy of this kind of argument was to trade on the happiness of countless generations in the future as a result of some sacrifice of our happiness now. But there are now a sufficient number of doubts about there being future generations, about their not finding alternative resources, and about our present sacrifices leading to their happiness (since there might be so many of them anyway) as to render the argument less convincing than it might formerly have been.

In any calculus of pleasure or good there is no necessity for future generations to enjoy a higher standard of living at the expense of present generations. If there will be a peak in the standard somewhere along the line, followed by a decline, it might just as well be the present generation which enjoys the peak through the utilization of resources, which, since limited, will be used up sooner or later. There is no greater good served by future generations being the peak since obviously when it comes to their turn, if it is improper for us to enjoy more than our successors, and if this is the proper way to feel, they should feel so also.

Both because of these considerations and because of the large number of unknowables concerning the future, short range considerations are surer and more pertinent than long range considerations. The threshold of pollution has been recently crossed so that it is now obvious that something must be done; legislation consequently is being passed. The amount and kind of pollution to be tolerated, the resources to be rationed or preserved should not be decided in terms of far distant needs or requirements but in terms of present and near-future needs and requirement.

Production involves wastes which have now reached the pollution stage. Its control is costly. The cost must be borne either by the producer (who will pass it on to the consumer) or by society at large through the taxes required, e.g., to purify water. The principle that whoever causes the pollution must pay for cleaning it up, or that no production should be allowed without the mechanism provided to prevent pollution, will make some kinds of production unprofitable. In this case, if such production is considered necessary or desirable, it will have to be subsidized. If society cannot pay for total cleanup it might have to settle for less than it would like; or it might have to give up some of its production or some of the goods to which it had become accustomed; or it might have to forego some of the products it might otherwise produce. Such choices should not be made a priori or by the fiat of government, but by the members of society at large or by as many of them interested and aware and informed enough to help in the decision making process.

There are presently available the means nationally for allocating resources and for controlling use and production through automatic market and natural mechanisms as well as through legislation. Where legislation poses the greatest difficulty is not on the national level but on the international level. For technology has brought us into one closely interdependent world faster than the social and legal mechanisms for solving the world-wide problems of resources, population, and pollution have been able to develop.

The problems posed by the ecological challenge are many and complex. But in dealing with them it should be clear that we owe nothing **to** those who do not yet and may never exist; that nonetheless we do have an obligation to promote the continuance of the human race, and so have an obligation **for** those whom we produce; that though at least minimum standards of living for all are desirable, if some generation is to enjoy the peak it need not be other generations; and that the choice of how to use our resources and continue or control our pollution depends on the price all those concerned wish to pay and the values we wish to espouse and promote.

11. The Welfare Rights of Distant Peoples and Future Generations

James P. Sterba

This article argues that welfare rights of distant peoples and future generations are justified on the basis of a right to life and a right to fair treatment. It contends that whether a right to life is interpreted as a negative right (as libertarians tend to do) or as a positive right (as welfare liberals tend to do), it is possible to show that this right justifies welfare rights, amply providing for the basic needs of distant peoples and future generations. This article discusses what is required for meeting a person's basic needs and explains how these requirements can vary from society to society and from time to time.

From "The Welfare Rights of Distant Peoples and Future Generations: Moral Side-Constraints on Social Policy," *Social Theory and Practice* (1981), pp. 99–119. Reprinted by permission of *Social Theory and Practice*.

In order to formulate social policies to deal with issues like population control, world hunger and energy consumption, we clearly need solutions to many difficult and perplexing problems. Not the least of these problems is the determination of the moral side-constraints we should observe by virtue of our relationship to persons who are separated from us in space (distant peoples) and time (future generations). In this paper I wish, firstly, to show how these side-constraints, which I shall call "the welfare rights of distant peoples and future generations," can be grounded on fundamental moral requirements to which many of us are already committed and, secondly, to determine some of the practical requirements of these side-constraints for the issues of population control and world hunger.

The Welfare Rights of Distant Peoples

It used to be argued that the welfare rights of distant peoples would eventually be met as a byproduct of the continued economic growth of the technologically developed societies of the world. It was believed that the transfer of investment and technology to the less developed societies of the world would eventually, if not make everyone well off, at least satisfy everyone's basic needs. Now we are not so sure. Presently more and more evidence points to the conclusion that without some substantial sacrifice on the part of the technologically developed societies of the world, many of the less developed societies will never be able to provide their members with even the basic necessities for survival. For example, according to a study prepared by the World Bank in 1979, depending on the growth of world trade, between 470 and 710 million people will be living in conditions of absolute poverty as the 21st century dawns, unless, that is, the technologically developed societies of the world adopt some plausible policy of redistribution.[1] Even those, like Herman Kahn, who argue that an almost utopian world situation will obtain in the distant future, still would have to admit that unless some plausible policy of redistribution is adopted, malnutrition and starvation will continue in the less developed societies for many years to come.[2] Thus, a recognition of the welfare rights of distant peoples would appear to have significant consequences for developed and underdeveloped societies alike.

Of course, there are various senses in which distant peoples can be said to have welfare rights and various moral grounds on which those rights can be justified. First of all, the welfare rights of distant peoples can be understood to be either negative rights or positive rights.[3] A negative right is a right not to be interfered with in some specific manner. For example, a right to liberty is usually understood to be a negative right; it guarantees each person the right not to have her liberty interfered with provided that she does not unjustifiably interfere with the liberty of any other person. On the other hand, a positive right is a right to receive some specific goods or services. Typical positive rights are the right to have a loan repaid and the right to receive one's just earnings. Secondly, the welfare rights of distant peoples can be understood to be either *in personam* rights or *in rem* rights. *In personam* rights are rights that hold against some specific namable person or persons while *in rem* rights hold against everyone who is in a position to abide by the rights in question. A right to liberty is usually understood to be an *in rem* right while the right to have a loan repaid or the right to receive one's just earnings are typical *in personam* rights. Finally, the rights of distant peoples can be understood to be either legal rights, that is, rights that *are enforced* by coercive sanctions, or moral rights, that is, rights that *ought to be enforced* either simply by noncoercive sanctions (for example, verbal condemnations) or by both coercive and noncoercive sanctions. Accordingly, what distinguishes the moral rights of distant peoples from the requirements of supererogation (the nonfulfillment of which is never blameworthy) is that the former but not the latter can be justifiably enforced either by noncoercive or by coercive and noncoercive sanctions. Since we will be primarily concerned with the moral rights of distant peoples to a certain minimum of welfare, hereafter "right(s)" should be understood as short for "moral right(s)."

Of the various moral grounds for justifying the welfare rights of distant peoples, quite possibly the most evident are those which appeal either to a right to life or a right to fair treatment.[4] Indeed, whether a person's right to life is interpreted as a negative right (as libertarians tend to do)[5] or as a positive right (as welfare liberals tend to do)[6], it is possible to show that the right justifies welfare rights that would amply provide for a person's basic needs. Alternatively, it is possible to justify those same welfare rights on the basis of a person's positive right to fair treatment.

Thus suppose that a person's right to life is a positive right. So understood the person's right to life would most plausibly be interpreted as a right to receive those goods and resources that are necessary for satisfying her basic needs. For a person's basic needs are those which must be satisfied in order not to seriously endanger her health or sanity. Thus receiving the goods and resources that are necessary for satisfying her basic needs would preserve a person's life in the fullest sense. And if a person's positive right to life is to be universal in the sense that it is possessed by every person (as the right to life is generally understood to be) then it must be an *in rem* right. This is because an *in rem* right, unlike an *in personam* right, does not require for its possession the assumption by other persons of any special roles or contractual obligations. Interpreted as a positive *in rem* right, therefore, a person's right to life would clearly justify the welfare rights of distant peoples to have their basic needs satisfied.

Suppose, on the other hand, that a person's right to life is a negative right. Here again, if the right is to be universal in the sense that it is possessed by all persons then it must also be an *in rem* right. So understood the right would require that everyone who is in a position to do so not interfere in certain ways with a person's attempts to meet her basic needs.

But what sort of noninterference would this right to life justify? If one's basic needs have not been met, would a person's right to life require that others not interfere with her taking the goods she needs from the surplus possessions of those who already have satisfied their own basic needs? As it is standardly interpreted, a person's negative right to life would not require such noninterference. Instead, a person's negative right to life is usually understood to be limited in such circumstances by the property rights of those who have more than enough to satisfy their own basic needs.[7] Moreover, those who claim property rights to such surplus goods and resources are usually in a position to effectively prohibit those in need from taking what they require. For surely most underdeveloped nations of the world would be able to sponsor expeditions to the American Midwest or the Australian Plains for the purpose of collecting the grain necessary to satisfy the basic needs of their citizens if they were not effectively prohibited from doing so at almost every stage of the enterprise.

But are persons with such surplus goods and resources normally justified in so prohibiting others from satisfying their basic needs? Admittedly, such persons may have contributed greatly to the value of the surplus goods and resources they possess, but why should that give them power over the life and death of those less fortunate? While their contribution may well justify favoring their nonbasic needs over the nonbasic needs of others, how could it justify favoring their nonbasic needs over the basic needs of others? After all, a person's negative right to life, being an *in rem* right, does not depend on the assumption by other persons of any special roles or contractual obligations. By contrast, property rights that are *in personam* rights require the assumption by other persons of the relevant roles and contractual obligations which constitute a particular system of acquisition and exchange, such as the role of a neighbor and the obligations of a merchant. Consequently, with respect to such property rights, it would seem that a person could not justifiably be kept from acquiring the goods and resources necessary to satisfy her basic needs by the property rights of others to surplus possessions, unless the person herself had voluntarily agreed to be so constrained by those property rights. But obviously few people would voluntarily agree to have such constraints placed upon their ability to acquire the goods and resources necessary to satisfy their basic needs. For most people their right to acquire the goods and resources necessary to satisfy their basic needs would have priority over any other person's property rights to surplus possessions, or alternatively, they would conceive of property rights such that no one could have property rights to any surplus possessions which were required to satisfy their own basic needs.

Even if some property rights could arise, as *in rem* rights by a Lockean process of mixing one's labor with previously unowned goods and resources, there would still be a need for some sort of a restriction on such appropriations. For if these *in rem* property rights are to be *moral rights* then it must be reasonable for every affected party to accept such rights, since the requirements of morality cannot be contrary to reason. Accordingly, in order to give rise to *in rem* property rights, the appropriation of previously unowned goods and resources cannot justifiably limit anyone's ability to acquire the goods and resources necessary to satisfy her basic needs, unless it would be reasonable for the person to voluntarily agree to be so constrained. But obviously it would not be reasonable for many people, particularly those whose basic needs are not being met, to voluntarily agree to be so constrained by property rights. This means that whether property rights are *in personam* rights and arise by the assumption of the relevant roles and contractual obligations or are *in rem* rights and arise by a Lockean process of mixing one's labor with previously unowned goods and resources, such rights would rarely limit a negative right to life, interpreted as an *in rem* right to noninterference with one's attempts to acquire the goods and resources necessary to satisfy one's basic needs. So interpreted, a negative right to life would clearly justify the welfare rights of distant peoples.

If we turn to a consideration of a person's right to fair treatment, a similar justification of the welfare rights of distant peoples emerges. To determine the requirements of fair treatment, suppose we employ a decision procedure analogous to the one John Rawls developed in *A Theory of Justice*.[8] Suppose, that is to say, that in deciding upon the requirements of fair treatment, we were to discount the knowledge of which particular interests happen to be our own. Since we obviously know what our particular interests are, we would

just not be taking that knowledge into account when selecting the requirements for fair treatment. Rather, in selecting these requirements, we would be reasoning from our knowledge of all the particular interests of everyone who would be affected by our decision but not from our knowledge of which particular interests happen to be our own. In employing this decision procedure, therefore, we (like judges who discount prejudicial information in order to reach fair decisions) would be able to give a fair hearing to everyone's particular interests. Assuming further that we are well-informed of the particular interests that would be affected by our decision and are fully capable of rationally deliberating with respect to that information, then our deliberations would culminate in a unanimous decision. This is because each of us would be deliberating in a rationally correct manner with respect to the same information and would be using a decision procedure leading to a uniform evaluation of the alternatives. Consequently, each of us would favor the same requirements for fair treatment.

But what requirements would we select by using this decision procedure? Since by employing this decision procedure we would not be using our knowledge of which particular interests happen to be our own, we would be quite concerned about the pattern according to which goods and resources would be distributed throughout the world. By using this decision procedure, we would reason as though our particular interests might be those of persons with the largest share of goods and resources as well as those of persons with the smallest share of goods and resources. Consequently, we would neither exclusively favor the interests of persons with the largest share of goods by endorsing an unlimited right to accumulate goods and resources nor exclusively favor the interests of persons with the smallest share of goods and resources by endorsing the highest possible minimum for those who are least advantaged. Rather we would compromise by endorsing a right to accumulate goods and resources that was limited by the guarantee of a minimum sufficient to provide each person with the goods and resources necessary to satisfy his or her basic needs.[9] It seems clear, therefore, that a right to fair treatment as captured by this Rawlsian decision procedure would also justify the welfare rights of distant peoples.

What the preceding arguments have shown is that the welfare rights of distant peoples can be firmly grounded either in each person's right to life or each person's right to fair treatment. As a result, it would be impossible for one to deny that distant peoples have welfare rights without also denying that each person has a right to life and a right to fair treatment, unless, that is, one drastically reinterprets the significance of a right to life and a right to fair treatment.[10]

The Welfare Rights of Future Generations

At first glance, the welfare rights of future generations appear to be just as firmly grounded as the welfare rights of distant peoples. For assuming that there will be future generations, then, they, like generations presently existing, will have their basic needs that must be satisfied. And just as we are now able to make provision for the basic needs of distant peoples, so likewise we are now able to make provision for the basic needs of future generations (for example, through capital investment and the conservation of resources). Consequently, it would seem that there are equally good grounds for taking into account the basic needs of future generations as there are for taking into account the basic needs of distant peoples.

But there is a problem. How can we claim that future generations *now* have rights that we make provision for their basic needs when they don't presently exist? How is it possible for persons who don't yet exist to have rights against those who do? For example, suppose we continue to use up the earth's resources at present or even greater rates, and, as a result, it turns out that the most pessimistic forecasts for the 22nd century are realized.[11] This means that future generations will face widespread famine, depleted resources, insufficient new technology to handle the crisis, and a drastic decline in the quality of life for nearly everyone. If this were to happen, could persons living in the 22nd century legitimately claim that we in the 20th century violated their rights by not restraining our consumption of the world's resources? Surely it would be odd to say that we violated their rights over one hundred years before they existed. But what exactly is the oddness?

Is it that future generations generally have no way of claiming their rights against existing generations? While this does make the recognition and enforcement of rights much more difficult (future generations would need strong advocates in the existing generations), it does not make it impossible for there to be such rights. After all, it is quite obvious that the recognition and enforcement of the rights of distant peoples is a difficult task as well.

Or is it that we don't believe that rights can legitimately exercise their influence over long durations of time? But if we can foresee and control at least some of the effects our actions will have on the ability of future generations to satisfy their basic needs then why should we not be responsible for those same effects? And if we are responsible for them then why should not future generations have a right that we take them into account?

Perhaps what troubles us is that future generations don't exist when their rights are said to demand action. But how else could persons have a right to benefit from the effects our actions will have in the distant future if they did not exist just when those effects would be felt? Those who exist contemporaneously with us could not legitimately make the same demand upon us, for they will not be around to experience those effects. Only future generations could have a right that the effects our actions will have in the distant future contribute to satisfying their basic needs. Nor need we assume that in order for persons to have rights, they must exist when their rights demand action. Thus, to say that future generations have rights against existing generations we can simply mean that there are enforceable requirements upon existing generations that would benefit or prevent harm to future generations.[12]

Yet most likely what really bothers us is that we cannot know for sure what effects our actions will have on future generations. For example, we may at some cost to ourselves conserve resources that will be of little value to future generations who have developed different technologies. Or, because we regard them as useless, we may destroy or deplete resources that future generations will find to be essential to their well-being. However, we should not allow such possibilities to blind us to the necessity for a social policy in this regard. After all, whatever we do will have its effect on future generations. The best approach, therefore, is to use the knowledge that we presently have and assume that future generations will also require those basic resources we now find to be valuable. If it turns out that future generations will require different resources to meet their basic needs from those we were led to expect, then at least we will not be blamable for acting on the basis of the knowledge we had.[13]

As in the case of the welfare rights of distant peoples, we can justify the welfare rights of future generations by appealing either to a right to life or to a right to fair treatment.

Justifying the welfare rights of future generations on the basis of a right to life presents no new problems. As we have seen, a right to life applied to distant peoples is a positive *in rem* right of existing persons to receive the goods and resources necessary to satisfy their basic needs or a negative *in rem* right of existing persons to noninterference with their attempts to acquire the goods and resources necessary to satisfy their basic needs. Accordingly, assuming that by "future generations" we mean "those whom we can reasonably expect to come into existence," then a right to life applied to future generations would be a right of persons whom we can definitely expect to exist to receive the goods and resources necessary to satisfy their basic needs or to noninterference with their attempts to acquire the goods and resources necessary to satisfy their basic needs. Understood in this way, a right to life of future generations would justify the welfare rights of future generations for much the same reasons that a right to life of distant peoples justifies the welfare rights of distant peoples. For future generations clearly have not voluntarily agreed nor would it be reasonable for them to voluntarily agree to have their ability to receive or acquire the

goods and resources necessary to satisfy their basic needs limited by the property rights of existing generations to surplus possessions. Thus a right to life of future generations, interpreted either as a positive *in rem* right or a negative *in rem* right, would clearly justify the welfare rights of future generations to have their basic needs satisfied.

To determine the requirements of fair treatment for future generations, suppose we adapt the decision procedure used before to determine the requirements of fair treatment for distant peoples. That procedure required that in reaching decisions we discount our knowledge of which particular interests happen to be our own. Yet discounting such knowledge would not be sufficient to guarantee a fair result for future generations unless we also discounted the knowledge that we are contemporaries. For otherwise, even without using our knowledge of which particular interests happen to be our own, we could unfairly favor existing generations over future generations. Employing this now modified decision procedure, we would find it rational to endorse a right to accumulate goods and resources that was limited so as to provide each generation with a minimum of goods and resources necessary to satisfy the basic needs of the persons belonging to that generation. In this way, a right to fair treatment, as captured by this decision procedure, would justify the welfare rights of future generations.

Future Generations and Population Control

The welfare rights of future generations are also closely connected with the population policy of existing generations. For example, under a population policy that places restrictions on the size of families and requires genetic screening, some persons will not be brought into existence who otherwise would have come into existence. Thus, the membership of future generations will surely be affected by whatever population policy existing generations adopt. Given that the size and genetic health of future generations will obviously affect their ability to provide for their basic needs, the welfare rights of future generations would require existing generations to adopt a population policy that takes these factors into account.

But what population policy should existing generations adopt? There are two policies that many philosophers have found attractive.[14] Each policy represents a version of utilitarianism and each has its own difficulties. One policy requires population to increase or decrease so as to produce the largest total net utility possible. The other policy requires population to increase or decrease so as to produce the highest average net utility possible. The main difficulty with the policy of total utility is that it would justify any increase in population— even if, as a result, the lives of most people were not very happy—so long as some increase in total utility were produced. On the other hand, the main difficulty with the policy of average utility is that it would not allow persons to be brought into existence—even if they would be quite happy—unless the utility of their lives were equal or greater than the average. Clearly what is needed is a policy that avoids both of these difficulties.

Peter Singer has recently proposed a population policy designed to do just that—a policy designed to restrict the increase of population more than the policy of total utility but less than the policy of average utility.[15] Singer's policy justifies increasing a population of M members to a population of $M + N$ members only if M of the $M + N$ members would have at least as much utility as the population of M members had initially.

At first it might seem that Singer's population policy provides the desired compromise. For his policy does not require increases in population to meet or surpass the average utility of the original population. Nor does his policy seem to justify every increase in population that increases total utility but only those increases that do not provide less utility to members equal in number to the original population. But the success of Singer's compromise is only apparent. As Derek Parfit has shown, Singer's policy shares with the policy of total utility the same tendency to increase population in the face of continually declining average utility.[16]

For consider a population with just two members: Abe and Edna. Imagine that Abe and Edna were deliberating whether to have a child and they calculated that if they had a child

1. the utility of the child's life would be somewhat lower than the average utility of their own lives.
2. the child would have no net effect on the total utility of their own lives taken together.

Applied to these circumstances, Singer's population policy would clearly justify bringing the child into existence. But suppose, further, that after the birth of Clyde, their first child, Abe and Edna were deliberating whether to have a second child and they calculated that if they had a second child

1. the utility of the child's life would be somewhat lower than the utility of Clyde's life.
2. the child would have no net effect on the total utility of their own lives and Clyde's taken together.

Given these circumstances, Singer's policy would again justify bringing this second child into existence. And if analogous circumstances obtained on each of the next ten occasions that Abe and Edna consider the question of whether to bring additional children into existence, Singer's population policy would continue to justify adding new children irrespective of the general decline in average utility resulting from each new addition to Abe and Edna's family. Thus Singer's policy has the same undesirable result as the policy of total utility. It avoids the severe restriction on population increase of the policy of average utility but fails to restrict existing generations from bringing into existence persons who would not be able to enjoy even a certain minimum of well-being.

Fortunately a policy with the desired restrictions can be grounded on the welfare rights of future generations. As we have seen, the welfare rights of future generations require existing generations to make provision for the basic needs of future generations. As a result, existing generations would have to evaluate their ability to provide both for their own basic needs and for the basic needs of future generations. Since existing generations by bringing persons into existence would be determining the membership of future generations, they would have to evaluate whether they are able to provide for that membership. Existing generations should not have to sacrifice the satisfaction of their basic needs for the sake of future generations, although they would be required to sacrifice some of their nonbasic needs on this account. Thus, if existing generations believe that were population to increase beyond a certain point, they would lack sufficient resources to make the necessary provision for each person's basic needs, then it would be incumbent upon them to restrict the membership of future generations so as not to exceed their ability to provide for each person's basic needs. For if the rights of future generations were respected, the membership of future generations would never increase beyond the ability of existing generations to make the necessary provision for the basic needs of future generations.

But this is to indicate only the "negative half" of the population policy that is grounded on the welfare rights of future generations, that is, the obligation to limit the size of future generations so as not to exceed the ability of existing generations to provide for the basic needs of future generations. The "positive half" of that population policy, which I have defended elsewhere,[17] is the obligation of existing generations, once their basic needs have been met, to bring into existence additional persons whose basic needs could also be met.

Thus, not only are the welfare rights of future generations clearly justified on the basis of each person's right to life and each person's right to fair treatment, but also these welfare rights in turn justify a population policy that provides an alternative to the policies of average and total utility.

Welfare Rights and Basic Needs

It has been argued that the welfare rights of distant peoples and future generations can be justified on the basis of a right to life and a right to fair treatment. Since these welfare rights are understood to be rights to receive or to acquire those goods and resources necessary for satisfying the basic needs of distant peoples and future generations, it is important to get a better understanding of what is necessary for the satisfaction of a person's basic needs in order to more fully appreciate the implications of these welfare rights.

Now a person's basic needs are those which must be satisfied in order not to seriously endanger the person's health and sanity. Thus, the needs a person has for food, shelter, medical care, protection, companionship and self-development are at least in part needs of this sort. Naturally, societies vary in their ability to satisfy a person's basic needs, but the needs themselves would not seem to be similarly subject to variation unless there were a corresponding variation in what constitutes health and sanity in different societies. Consequently, even though the criterion of need would not be an acceptable standard for distributing all social goods because, among other things, of the difficulty of determining both what a person's nonbasic needs are and how they should be arranged according to priority, the criterion does appear to be an acceptable standard for determining the minimum of goods and resources each person has a right to receive or acquire.

Actually, specifying a minimum of this sort seems to be the goal of the poverty index used in the United States since 1964.[18] This poverty index is based on the U.S. Department of Agriculture's Economy Food Plan (for an adequate diet) and on evidence showing that low income families spend about one-third of their income on food. The index is then adjusted from time to time to take into account changing prices. However, in order to accord with the goal of satisfying basic needs, the poverty index would have to be further adjusted to take into account 1) that the Economy Food Plan was developed for "temporary or emergency use" and is inadequate for a permanent diet and 2) that, according to recent evidence, low income families spend one-fourth rather than one-third of their income on food.[19]

Of course, one might think that a minimum should be specified in terms of a standard of living that is purely conventional and varies over time and between societies. Benn and Peters, following this approach, have suggested specifying a minimum in terms of the income received by the most numerous group in a society.[20] For example, in the United States today the greatest number of household units falls within the $15,000 to $24,999 bracket (in 1979 dollars).[21] Specifying a minimum in this way, however, leads to certain difficulties. Thus, suppose that the most numerous group of household units in society with the wealth of the United States fell within a $500–$999 income bracket (in 1979 dollars). Certainly, it would not thereby follow that a guarantee of $1,000 per household unit would constitute an acceptable minimum for such a society. Or suppose that the income of the most numerous group of household units in such a society fell within the $95,000–$100,000 income bracket (in 1979 dollars). Certainly, a minimum of $100,000 per household unit would not thereby be required. Moreover, there seem to be similar difficulties with any attempt to specify an acceptable minimum in a purely conventional manner.

Nevertheless, it still seems that an acceptable minimum should vary over time and between societies at least to some degree. For example, it could be argued that today a car is almost a necessity in the typical North American household, which was not true fifty years ago nor is it true today in most other areas of the world. Happily, a basic needs approach to specifying an acceptable minimum can account for such variation without introducing any variation into the definition of the basic needs themselves. Instead, variation enters into the cost of satisfying these needs at different times and in different societies.[22] For in the same society at different times and in different societies at the same time, the normal costs of satisfying a person's basic needs can and do vary considerably. These variations are due in large part to the different ways in which the most readily available means for satisfying people's basic needs are produced. For example, in more affluent societies, the most readily available means for satisfying a person's basic needs are usually processed so as to satisfy nonbasic needs at the same time that they satisfy basic needs. This processing is carried out to make the means more attractive to persons in higher income brackets who can easily afford the extra cost. As a result, the most readily available means for satisfying people's basic needs are much more costly in more affluent societies than they are in less affluent societies. This occurs most obviously with respect to the most readily available means for satisfying people's basic needs for food, shelter and transportation, but it also occurs with respect to the most readily available means for satisfying people's basic needs for companionship, self-esteem and self-development. For a person cannot normally satisfy even these latter needs in more affluent societies without participating in at least some relatively costly educational and social development practices. Accordingly, there will be considerable variation in the normal costs of satisfying a person's basic needs as a society becomes more affluent over time, and considerable variation at the same time in societies at different levels of affluence. Consequently, a basic needs approach to specifying an acceptable minimum would guarantee each person the goods and resources necessary to meet the normal costs of satisfying his basic needs in the society in which he lives.

Welfare Rights and World Hunger

We have seen that the welfare rights of distant peoples and future generations guarantee each person a minimum of goods and resources necessary to meet the normal costs of satisfying her basic needs in the society in which she lives. Let us now determine some of the practical implications of these welfare rights for the issue of world hunger.

At present there is probably a sufficient worldwide supply of goods and resources to meet the normal costs of satisfying the basic nutritional needs of all existing persons in the societies in which they live. According to the former U.S. Secretary of Agriculture, Bob Bergland,

For the past 20 years, if the available world food supply had been evenly divided and distributed, each person would have received more than the minimum number of calories.

In fact, the 4 billion people who inhabited the world in 1978 had available about one-fifth more food per person to eat than the world's 2.7 billion had 25 years ago.[23]

Other authorities have made similar assessments of the available world food supply.[24] In fact, it has been projected that if all arable land were optimally utilized a population of between 38 and 48 billion people could be supported.[25]

Needless to say, the adoption of a policy of meeting the basic nutritional needs of all existing persons would necessitate significant changes, especially in developed societies. For example, the large percentage of the U.S. population whose food consumption clearly exceeds even an adequately adjusted poverty index would have to substantially alter their eating habits. In particular, they would have to reduce their consumption of beef and pork so as to make more grain available for direct human consumption. (Presently the amount of grain fed American livestock is as much as all the people of China and India eat in a year.) Thus, at least the satisfaction of some of the nonbasic needs of the more advantaged in developed societies would have to be foregone so that the basic nutritional needs of all existing persons in developing and underdeveloped societies could be met.

Such changes, however, may still have little effect on the relative costs of satisfying people's basic needs in different societies. For even after the basic nutritional needs of all existing persons have been met, the normal costs of satisfying basic needs would still tend to be greater in developed societies than in developing and underdeveloped societies. This is because the most readily available means for satisfying basic needs in developed societies would still tend to be more processed to satisfy nonbasic needs along with basic needs. Nevertheless, once the basic nutritional needs of future generations are also taken into account, then the satisfaction of the nonbasic needs of the more advantaged in developed societies would have to be further restricted in order to preserve the fertility of cropland and other food-related natural resources for the use of future generations.[26] And once basic needs other than nutritional needs are taken into account as well, still further restrictions would be required. For example, it has been estimated that presently a North American uses fifty times more resources than an Indian. This means that in terms of resource consumption the North American continent's population is the equivalent of 12.5 billion Indians.[27] Obviously, this would have to be radically altered if the basic needs of distant peoples and future generations are to be met. Thus, eventually the practice of utilizing more and more efficient means of satisfying people's basic needs in developed societies would appear to have the effect of equalizing the normal costs of meeting people's basic needs across societies.[28]

Although the general character of the changes required to meet the basic nutritional needs of distant peoples and future generations seems clear enough, there is still the problem of deciding between alternative strategies for carrying out these changes. Since each of these strategies would impose somewhat different burdens on developed societies and different burdens on different groups within those societies, the fundamental problem is to decide exactly whose nonbasic needs should be sacrificed in order to meet the basic needs of distant peoples and future generations. While there is no easy solution to this problem, alternative strategies for meeting the basic needs of distant peoples and future generations could be fairly evaluated by means of the Rawlsian decision procedure that was used before to justify the welfare rights of distant peoples and future generations. In using this procedure, we would be deciding which particular strategy for meeting the basic needs of distant peoples and future generations would be preferred by persons who discounted the knowledge of the society to which they belonged. Thus, the particular strategies that would be selected by this decision procedure should adequately take into account the competing interests within and between existing generations and future generations.

While the requirements, with respect to world hunger, that the welfare rights of distant peoples and future generations place upon those in developed affluent societies are obviously quite severe, they are not unconditional. For those in developing and underdeveloped societies are under a corresponding obligation to do what they can to meet their own basic nutritional needs, for example, by bringing all arable land under optimal cultivation and by controlling population growth. However, we should not be unreasonable in judging what particular developing and underdeveloped societies have managed to accomplish in this regard. For in the final analysis, such societies should be judged on the basis of what they have managed to accomplish, *given the options available to them.* For example, developing and underdeveloped societies today do not have the option, which Western European societies had during most of the last two centuries, of exporting their excess population to sparsely populated and resource rich continents. In this and other respects, developing and underdeveloped societies today lack many of the options Western European societies were able to utilize in the course of their economic and social development. Consequently, in judging what developing and underdeveloped societies have managed to accomplish we must take into account the options that they actually have available to them in their particular circumstances. In practice, this will mean, for example, that it is not reasonable to expect such societies to reduce their population growth as fast as would ideally be desirable. Nevertheless, at some point, it should be reasonable to expect that all existing persons accept the population policy proposed earlier, according to which the membership of future generations would never be allowed to increase beyond the ability of existing generations to make the necessary provision for the basic needs of future generations. In the meantime, it may be necessary in order to meet the basic needs of at least a temporarily growing world population to utilize renewable resources beyond what would secure their maximal sustainable yield. (Presently, certain renewable resources, such as fishing resources, are being so utilized for far less justifiable ends.) This, of course, would have the effect of reducing the size of succeeding generations that, according to the proposed population policy, could justifiably be brought into existence. But while such an effect obviously is not ideally desirable, it surely seems morally preferable to allowing existing persons to starve to death in order to increase the size of succeeding generations that could justifiably be brought into existence.[29]

In conclusion, what has been shown is 1) that the welfare rights of distant peoples and future generations, understood as the right of distant peoples and future generations to receive or acquire the goods and resources that are necessary to meet the normal costs of satisfying their basic needs in the society in which they live, can be justified on the basis of a right to life and a right to fair treatment, and 2) that these welfare rights can be used to justify certain requirements for the issues of population control and world hunger. Thus, given the fundamental nature of the moral foundation for these welfare rights, it would be virtually impossible for many of us to consistently reject these welfare rights with their practical requirements for social policies unless we were to reject in its entirety the moral point of view.[30]

Notes

1. *The Preliminary Report of the Presidential Commission on World Hunger,* December 1979. Section II, Chapter 3.

2. Herman Kahn, William Brown and Leon Martel, *The Next 200 Years* (New York: William Morrow, 1976), Chapter 2.

3. A distinction that is similar to the distinction between positive and negative rights is the distinction between recipient and action rights. Recipient rights, like positive rights, are rights to receive some specific goods or services. However, action rights are a bit more circumscribed than negative rights. Action rights are rights to act in some specific manner, whereas negative rights include both rights of noninterference with actions (and, hence, imply action rights) and rights of noninterference with things or states of affairs (such as a right to one's good name).

Having previously used the distinction between recipient and action rights (*The Demands of*

Justice [Notre Dame: University of Notre Dame Press, 1980, Chapter 6]), in a defense of welfare rights, I now hope to show, in response to critics, particularly Jan Narveson, that the distinction between positive and negative rights can serve as well in the fuller defense of welfare rights which I am presenting in this paper.

4. For other possibilities, see Onora Nell, "Lifeboat Earth," *Philosophy and Public Affairs,* 4 (Spring 1975): 273–92; Peter Singer, "Famine, Affluence and Morality," *Philosophy and Public Affairs,* 1 (1972): 229–43.

5. See, for example, Robert Nozick, *State Anarchy and Utopia* (New York: Basic Books, 1974), p. 179n.

6. See, for example, Ronald Dworkin, "Liberalism," in *Public and Private Morality,* edited by Stuart Hampshire (Cambridge: Cambridge University Press, 1978), pp. 112–43.

7. This is why a negative right to life is usually understood to impose lesser moral requirements than a positive right to life.

8. John Rawls, *A Theory of Justice* (Cambridge: Harvard University Press, 1971). This Rawlsian decision procedure is only designed to secure a fair consideration of everyone's interests. It does not guarantee that *all* will be better off from following the moral requirements that emerge from using the procedure. Thus, some individuals may be required to make significant sacrifices, particularly during the transition to a more favored distribution of goods and resources. On this point, see *The Demands of Justice,* Chapter 4.

9. For further argument, see "Distributive Justice," *American Journal of Jurisprudence,* 55 (1977): 55–79 and *The Demands of Justice,* Chapter 2.

10. Notice that even if one interprets a right to life as simply a right not to be killed unjustly, it could still be plausibly argued that a person's right to life would normally be violated when all other legitimate opportunities for preserving his life have been exhausted if he were then *prevented* by others from taking from their surplus goods and resources what he needs to preserve his life.

11. Donella H. Meadows, Dennis L. Meadows, Jorgen Randers and William W. Behrens III, *The Limits to Growth,* second edition (New York: New American Library, 1974), Chapters 3 and 4.

12. Indeed, right claims need not presuppose that there are any rightholders either in the present or in the future, as in the case of a right not to be born and a right to be born. On this point, see my paper "Abortion, Distant Peoples and Future Generations," *The Journal of Philosophy,* 77 (1980): 424–40 and *The Demands of Justice,* Chapter 6.

13. For a somewhat opposing view, see M. P. Golding, "Obligations to Future Generations," *The Monist,* 56 (1972): 85–99.

14. See Henry Sidgwick, *The Methods of Ethics,* 7th edition, (London: Macmillan, 1907), pp. 414–16; Jan Narveson, "Moral Problems of Population," *The Monist,* 57 (1973): 62–86.

15. Peter Singer, "A Utilitarian Population Principle," in *Ethics and Population,* edited by Michael Bayles (Cambridge: Schenkman, 1976), pp. 81–99.

16. Derek Parfit, "On Doing the Best for Our Children," in *Ethics and Population,* edited by Michael Bayles, pp. 100–15.

17. See "Abortion, Distant Peoples and Future Generations," and *The Demands of Justice,* Chapter 6.

18. See *Old Age Insurance* submitted to the Joint Economic Committee of the Congress of the United States in December, 1967, p. 186, and *Statistical Abstracts of the United States for 1979,* p. 434.

19. See Sar Levitan, *Programs in Aid of the Poor* (Baltimore: Johns Hopkins University Press, 1976), pp. 2–4; David Gordon, "Trends in Poverty" in *Problems in Political Economy: An Urban Perspective,* edited by David Gordon (Lexington, Mass.: C. Heath, 1971), pp. 297–8; Arthur Simon, *Bread for the World* (New York: Paulist Press, 1975), Chapter 8.

20. S. Benn and R. S. Peters, *The Principles of Political Thought* (New York: The Free Press, 1959), p. 167.

21. *Statistical Abstracts,* p. 434.

22. See Bernard Gendron, *Technology and the Human Condition* (New York: St. Martin's Press, 1977), pp. 222–7.

23. Bob Bergland, "Attacking the Problem of World Hunger," *The National Forum* (1979), vol. 69, No. 2, p. 4.

24. Diana Manning, *Society and Food* (Sevenoaks,

Ky.: Butterworths, 1977), p. 12; Arthur Simon, *Bread for the World*, p. 14.

25. Roger Revelle, "Food and Population," *Scientific American*, 231 (September, 1974), p. 168.

26. Lester Brown, "Population, Cropland and Food Prices," *The National Forum* (1979), Vol. 69, No. 2, pp. 11–16.

27. Janet Besecker and Phil Elder, "Lifeboat Ethics: A Reply to Hardin," in *Readings in Ecology, Energy and Human Society: Contemporary Perspectives*, edited by William R. Burch, Jr. (New York: Harper and Row, 1977), p. 229.

28. There definitely are numerous possibilities for utilizing more and more efficient means of satisfying people's basic needs in developed societies. For example, the American food industry manufactured for the U.S. Agriculture Department CSM, a product made of corn, soy and dried milk, which supplied all the necessary nutrients and 70 percent of minimum calorie intake for children. Poverty children throughout the world, but not in the United States, received half a million pounds of this product from us in 1967—at a cost of two cents per day per child. See Nick Kotz, *Let Them Eat Promises* (Englewood Cliffs, N.J.: Prentice-Hall, Inc., 1969), p. 125.

29. The rejected option seems to be the one preferred by Garrett Hardin. [See his "Lifeboat Ethics: The Case Against Helping the Poor," in this anthology.]

30. Earlier versions of this paper were presented to a Conference on World Hunger held in Denver, Colorado, to the Economics Department of the University of Nebraska and to the University Seminar on Human Rights, Columbia University. I wish to thank all of those who commented on various versions of the paper, in particular, Robert Audi, Dolores Martin, Arthur Danto, Brian Barry, Jan Narveson, Paul Martin, Mark Rollins, D. Greenberg and the referees for this journal. I also want to thank the University of Notre Dame for a summer grant which enabled me to complete the penultimate draft of this paper.

---

12. Perspectives from the *Global 2000 Report*

Gus Speth

According to Gus Speth, the *Global 2000 Report* echoes a persistent warning sounded by many others in recent years: "Our international efforts to stem the spread of human poverty, hunger, and misery are not achieving their goals; the staggering growth of human population, coupled with ever-increasing human demands, are beginning to cause permanent damage to the planet's resource base." Speth argues that we must respond to this warning by getting serious about the conservation of resources and by pursuing a policy of sustainable economic development that is fair to the interests of the poor.

Throughout the past decade, a wide variety of disturbing studies and reports have been issued by the United Nations, the Worldwatch Institute, the World Bank, the International Union for the Conservation of Nature and Natural Resources, and other organizations.

From "Resources and Security: Perspectives from the *Global 2000 Report*," *World Future Society Bulletin* (1981), pp. 1–4. Reprinted by permission of *World Future Society Bulletin*.

These reports have sounded a persistent warning: our international efforts to stem the spread of human poverty, hunger and misery are not achieving their goals; the staggering growth of human population, coupled with ever-increasing human demands, are beginning to cause permanent damage to the planet's resource base.

The most recent such warning—and the one with which I am most familiar—was issued in July of 1980 by the Council of Environmental Quality and the U.S. State Department. Called *Global 2000 Report to the President*, it is the result of a three-year effort by more than a dozen agencies of the U.S. Government to make long-term projections across the range of population, resource, and environmental concerns. Given the obvious limitations of such projections, the *Global 2000 Report* can best be seen as a reconnaissance of the future. And the results of that reconnaissance are disturbing.

I feel very strongly that the *Global 2000 Report's* findings confront the United States and other nations with one of the most difficult challenges facing our planet during the next two decades—rivaling the global arms race in importance.

The Report's projections point to continued rapid population growth, with world population increasing from 4.5 billion today to more than 6 billion by 2000. More people will be added to the world's population each day in the year 2000 than were born today—about 100 million a year as compared with 75 million in 1980. Most of these additional people will live in the poorest countries, which will contain about four-fifths of the human race by the end of the century.

Unless other factors intervene, this planetary majority will see themselves growing worse off compared with those living in affluent nations. The income gap between rich and poor nations will widen, and the per capita gross national product of the less-developed countries will remain at generally low levels. In some areas—especially in parts of Latin America and East Asia—income per capita is expected to rise substantially. But gross national product in the great populous nations of South Asia—India, Bangladesh, and Pakistan—will be less than $200 per capita (in 1975 dollars) by 2000. Today, some 800 million people live in conditions of absolute poverty, their lives dominated by hunger, ill health, and the absence of hope. By 2000, if current policies remain unchanged, their number could grow by 50 percent.

While the Report projects a 90 percent increase in overall world food production in the 30 years from 1970 to 2000, a global per capita increase of less than 15 percent is projected even for the countries that are already comparatively well-fed. In South Asia, the Middle East, and the poorer countries of Africa, per capita food consumption will increase marginally at best, and in some areas may actually decline below present inadequate levels. Real prices of food are expected to double during the same 30-year period.

The pressures of population and growing human needs and expectations will place increasing strains on the Earth's natural systems and resources. The spread of desert-like conditions due to human activities now claims an area about the size of Maine each year. Croplands are lost to production as soils deteriorate because of erosion, compaction, and waterlogging and salinization, and as rural land is converted to other uses.

The increases in world food production projected by the Report are based on improvements in crop yields per acre continuing at the same rate as the record-breaking increases of the post-World War II period. These improvements depended heavily on energy-intensive technologies like fertilizer, pesticides, fuel for tractors, and power for irrigation. But the Report's projections show no relief from the world's tight energy situation. World oil production is expected to level off by the 1990s. And for the one-quarter of humanity who depend on wood for fuel, the outlook is bleak. Projected needs for wood will exceed available supplies by about 25 percent before the turn of the century.

The conversion of forested land to agricultural use and the demand for fuelwood and forest products are projected to continue to deplete the world's forests. The Report estimates that these forests are now disappearing at rates as high as 18 to 20 million hectares—an area half the size of California—each year. As much as 40 percent of the remaining forests in poor countries may be gone by 2000. Most of the loss will occur in tropical and subtropical areas.

The loss of tropical forests, along with the impact of pollution and other pressures on habitats, could cause massive destruction of the planet's genetic resource base. Between 500,000 and two million plant and animal species—15 to 20 percent of all species on Earth—could become extinct by the year 2000. One-half to two-thirds of the extinctions will result from the clearing or deterioration of tropical forests. This would be a massive loss of potentially valuable sources of food, pharmaceutical chemicals, building materials, fuel sources, and other irreplaceable resources.

Deforestation and other factors will worsen severe regional water shortages and contribute to the deterioration of water quality. Population growth alone will cause demands for water to at least double from 1971 levels in nearly half of the world.

Industrial growth is likely to worsen air quality. Air pollution in some cities in less-developed countries is already far above levels considered safe by the World Health Organization. Increased burning of fossil fuels, especially coal, may contribute to acid rain damage to lakes, plantlife, and the exteriors of buildings. It also contributes to the increasing concentration of carbon dioxide in the Earth's atmosphere, which could possibly lead to climatic changes with highly disruptive effects on world agriculture. Depletion of the stratospheric ozone layer, attributed partly to chlorofluorocarbon emissions from aerosol cans and refrigeration equipment, could also have an adverse effect on food crops and human health.

Disturbing as these findings are, it is important to stress that the *Global 2000 Report's* conclusions represent not predictions of what will occur, but projections of what could occur if we do not respond. If there was any doubt before, there should be little doubt now—the nations of the world, industrialized and less developed alike, must act urgently and in concert to alter these dangerous trends before the projections of the *Global 2000 Report* become realities.

The warnings, then, are clear. Will we heed them, and will we heed them in time? For if our response is delayed, the costs could be great.

On these matters, I am cautiously optimistic. I like to think that the human race is *not* self-destructive—that it *is* paying, or can be made to pay, attention—that as people throughout the world come to realize the full dimensions of the challenge before us, we will take the actions needed to meet it.

Our efforts to secure the future must begin with a new appreciation for, and then an application of, three fundamental concepts. They are *conservation, sustainable development,* and *equity.* I am convinced that each of them is essential to the development of the kind of long-term global resource strategy we need to deal with the problems I have been discussing.

Conservation

The first thing we must do is to get serious about the conservation of resources—renewable and nonrenewable alike. We can no longer take for granted the renewability of renewable resources. The natural systems—the air and water, the forests, the land—that yield food, shelter, and the other necessities of life are susceptible to disruption, contamination, and destruction.

Indeed, one of the most troubling of the findings of the *Global 2000 Report* is the effect that rapid population growth and poverty are already having on the productivity of renewable natural resource systems. In some areas, particularly in the less-developed countries, the ability of biological systems to support human populations is already being seriously damaged by efforts of present populations to meet desperate immediate needs, such as the needs for grazing land, firewood, and building materials.

And these stresses, while most acute in the developing countries, are not confined to them. In recent years, the United States has been losing annually about 3 million acres of rural land—a third of it prime agricultural land—due to the spread of housing developments, highways, shopping malls, and the like. We are also losing annually the rough equivalent—in terms of production capability—of another 3 million acres due to soil degradation—erosion and salinization. Other serious resource threats in the United States include those posed by toxic chemicals and other pollutants to groundwater supplies, which provide drinking water for half of the American public, and directly affect both commercial and sport fishing.

Achieving the necessary restraint in the use of renewable resources will require new ways of thinking by the peoples and governments of the world. It will require the widespread adoption of a "Conserver Society" ethic—an approach to resources and environment that, while attuned to the needs of each society, recognizes not only the importance of resources and environment to our own sustenance, well-being, and security, but also our obligation to pass this vital legacy along to future generations. Perhaps the most arrogant attitude of which the human spirit is capable is the notion that the riches of the Earth are ours to plunder or carelessly destroy . . . that the needs and the lives of those who will follow us on this tiny and fragile planet are of no concern to us. "Future generations," someone once said "What have they done for us?"

Fortunately, we are beginning to see signs that people in the United States and in other nations *are* becoming aware of the limits to our resources and the importance of conserving them. Energy problems, for example, are pointing the way to a future in which conservation is the password. As energy supplies go down and prices go up, we are learning that conserving—getting more and more out of each barrel of oil or ton of coal—is the cheapest and safest approach. Learning to conserve nonrenewable resources like oil and coal is the first step toward building a Conserver Society that values, nurtures, and protects all of its resources. Such a society appreciates economy in design and avoidance of waste. It realizes the limits to low-cost resources and to the environment's carrying capacity. It insists that market prices reflect all costs, social as well as private, so that consumers are fully aware in the most direct way of the real costs of consumption.

The Conserver Society prizes recycling over pollution, durability over obsolescence, quality over quantity, diversity over uniformity. It knows that beauty—whether natural or man-made—is too precious to be destroyed and that the Earth's wild creatures demand our conserving restraint not simply for utilitarian reasons but because, as part of the community of life that has evolved here with us, they too call this place home.

In this, the United States must take the lead. We cannot expect the rest of the world to adopt a Conserver Society ethic if we ourselves do not set a strong, successful example.

Sustainable Development

But the Conserver Society ethic, by itself, is not enough. It is unrealistic to expect people living at the margin of existence—people fighting desperately for their own survival—to think about the long-term survival of the planet. When people need to burn wood to keep from freezing, they will cut down trees.

We must find a way to break the cycle of poverty, population growth, and environmental deterioration. We must find ways to improve the social and economic conditions of the poor nations and poor people of the world—their incomes, their access to productive land, their educational and employment opportunities. It is only through sustainable economic development that real progress can be made in alleviating hunger and poverty and in erasing the conditions that contribute so dangerously to the destruction of our planet's carrying capacity.

One of the most important lessons of the *Global 2000 Report* is that the conflict between development and environmental protection is, in significant part, a myth. Only a concerted attack on the roots of extreme poverty—one that provides people with the opportunity to earn a decent livelihood in a nondestructive manner—will enable us to protect the world's natural systems. It is also clear that development and economic reforms will have no lasting success unless they are suffused with concern for ecological stability and wise management of resources. The key concept here, of course, is *sustainable* development. Economic development, if it is to be successful over the long term, must proceed in a way that enhances the natural resource base of all the developing nations, instead of exploiting those resources for short-term economic or political gain.

Unfortunately, the realities of the current North-South dialogue between the developed and the developing nations suggest that achieving steady, sustainable development will be a difficult process—one that will require great patience and understanding on all sides. For our part here in the United States, we must resist the strong temptation to turn inward—to tune out the rest of the world's problems and to focus exclusively on our own economic difficulties. We must remember that, relatively speaking, we Americans luxuriate in the Earth's abundance, while other nations can barely feed and clothe their people. Unless we act, this disparity between rich and poor will tend to grow, increasing the possibilities for anger and resentment from those on the short end of the wealth equation—the great majority of mankind. One does not have to be particularly farsighted to see that the trends discussed in *Global 2000* heighten the chances for global instability—for exploitation of fears, resentments, and frustrations; for incitement to violence; for conflicts based on resources.

The *Global 2000 Report* itself discusses some of the destabilizing prospects that may be in store for us if we do not act decisively:

"The world will be more vulnerable both to natural disaster and to disruptions from human causes . . . Most nations are likely to be still more dependent on foreign sources of energy in 2000 than they are today. Food production will be more vulnerable to disruptions of fossil fuel energy supplies and to weather fluctuations as cultivation expands to more marginal areas. The loss of diverse germ plasm in local strains and wild progenitors of food crops, together with the increase of monoculture, could lead to greater risks of massive crop failures. Larger numbers of people will be vulnerable to higher food prices or even famine when adverse weather occurs. The world will be more vulnerable to the disruptive effects of war. The tensions that could lead to war will have multiplied. The potential for conflict over fresh water alone is underscored by the fact that out of 200 of the world's major river basins, 148 are shared by two countries and 52 are shared by three to ten countries."

The 1980 Report of the Brandt Commission on International Development Issues is eloquent in its plea for action: "War is often thought of in terms of military conflict, or even annihilation. But there is a growing awareness that an equal danger might be chaos—as a result of mass hunger, economic disaster, environmental catastrophes, and terrorism, so we should not think only of reducing the traditional threats to peace, but also of the need for change from chaos to order."

Equity

The late Barbara Ward, eminent British scholar, argued that the nations of the world can learn a valuable lesson from the experience of 19th-Century England, where the industrial revolution produced an appalling disparity in the distribution of wealth. It was a time when property owners and industrial managers reaped enormous profits while the laborers and mechanics—and their children—worked themselves into early graves.

Today, Ward observes: "The skew in world income is as great. The already developed peoples—North America, Europe, the Soviet Union, Japan—are the latter-day dukes, commanding over 70 percent of the planet's wealth for less than a quarter of the population. And in all too many developing countries the economic growth of the last two decades has been almost entirely appropriated by the wealthiest ten percent of the people. The comparisons in health, length of life, diet, literacy all work out on the old Victorian patterns of unbelievable injustice."

Ward recommends—and I heartily agree— that the developed nations of today follow the lead of men like Disraeli, who recognized the need to narrow the gap between rich and poor in 19th-Century England and to create a new social order which allowed every citizen a share of the nation's wealth. Without perceptive leaders like Disraeli and other men of conscience who saw the need for reform, Ward argues that the growing pressure for equality and social justice would have torn British society apart. The result would have been similar to that in other nations where far-thinking leadership and compassion were lacking: "social convulsion, violent revolution and an impetus to merciless worldwide war and conquest."

The situation we face in the world today is all too similar. While the humanitarian reasons for acting generously to alleviate global poverty and injustice are compelling enough in themselves, we must also recognize the extent to which global poverty and resource problems can contribute to regional and worldwide political instability—an instability that can

threaten the security of nations throughout the world.

Thus, along with conservation and sustainable development, the development of global resource strategy will require a much greater emphasis on *equity*—on a fair sharing of the means to development and the products of growth—not only among nations, but within nations as well.

Suggestions for Further Reading

Anthologies

Brown, Peter, and Shue, Henry. *Boundaries.* Totowa: Rowman and Littlefield, 1981.

Lucas, George R. Jr., and Ogletree, Thomas W. *Lifeboat Ethics.* New York: Harper & Row, 1976.

Luper-Foy, Steven. *Problems of International Justice.* Boulder: Westview, 1988.

Partridge, Ernest. *Responsibilities to Future Generations.* Buffalo: Prometheus, 1981.

Sikora, R. I., and Barry, Brian. *Obligation to Future Generations.* Philadelphia: Temple University Press, 1978.

Basic Concepts

Parfit, Derek. *Reasons and Persons.* Oxford: Oxford University Press, 1985.

Alternative Views

Amur, Samir. *Unequal Development.* New York: Monthly Review Press, 1976.

Bauer, P. T. *Equality, the Third World and Economic Delusion.* Cambridge: Harvard University Press, 1981.

Bayles, Michael D. *Morality and Population Policy.* Birmingham: University of Alabama Press, 1980.

Beitz, Charles R. *Political Theory and International Relations.* Princeton: Princeton University Press, 1979.

Elfstrom, Gerald. *Ethics for a Shrinking World.* New York: St. Martin's Press, 1990.

Hardin, Garrett. *Promethean Ethics.* Seattle: University of Washington Press, 1980.

Shue, Henry. *Basic Rights.* Princeton: Princeton University Press, 1980.

Practical Applications

Lappé, Frances Moore. *World Hunger: Twelve Myths.* New York: Grove Press, 1986.

Russett, Bruce, and Starr, Harvey. *World Politics: The Menu for Choice.* San Francisco: W. H. Freeman and Co., 1981.

Schumacher, E. F. *Small Is Beautiful.* New York: Harper & Row, 1973.

Abortion and Euthanasia

Basic Concepts

The problem of abortion and euthanasia has been as thoroughly discussed as any contemporary moral problem. As a result, the conceptual issues have been fairly well laid out, and there have been some interesting attempts to bridge the troublesome normative and practical disagreements that remain.

First of all, almost everyone agrees that the fundamental issue with respect to justifying abortion is the moral status of the fetus, although considerable disagreement exists as to what that status is.[1] Conservatives on the abortion question, like John Noonan (Selection 14), contend that from conception the fetus has full moral status and hence a serious right to life. Liberals on the abortion question, like Mary Anne Warren (Selection 15), hold that, at least until birth, the fetus has almost no moral status whatsoever and lacks a serious right to life.[2] Moderates on the abortion question adopt some position in between these two views. And still others, like Judith Jarvis Thomson (Selection 13) and Jane English (Selection 16), adopt for the sake of argument either the conservative or the liberal view on the moral status of the fetus and then try to show that such a view does not lead to the consequences its supporters assume.[3]

Second, almost everyone agrees that the position one takes on the moral status of the fetus has a bearing on whether one considers either the distinction between killing and letting die or the doctrine of double effect as relevant to the abortion question. For example, conservatives are quite interested in whether the killing and letting die distinction can be used to show that it is permissible to let the fetus die in certain contexts, even when it would be impermissible to kill it. However, liberals find the use of this distinction in such contexts to be completely unnecessary. Because liberals hold that the fetus has almost no moral status, they do not object to either killing it or letting it die. Similarly, although conservatives are quite interested in whether the doctrine of double effect can be used to permit the death of the fetus as a foreseen but unintended consequence of some legitimate course of action,

liberals find no use for the doctrine of double effect in such contexts.

Third, almost everyone agrees that either the killing and letting die distinction or the doctrine of double effect could prove useful in cases of euthanasia. Agreement is possible because most of the subjects of euthanasia are human beings who, in everyone's view, have full moral status and hence a serious right to life. Accordingly, despite the disagreement as to where it is useful to apply the killing and letting die distinction and the doctrine of double effect, everyone agrees that both of these conceptual tools deserve further examination.

The distinction between killing and letting die has its advocates and its critics. Advocates maintain that, other things being equal, killing is morally worse than letting die, with the consequence that letting die is justified in cases where killing is not. The critics of this distinction maintain that, other things being equal, killing is not morally worse than letting die, with the consequence that killing is morally justified whenever letting die is. Both advocates and critics agree that other things would not be equal if the killing were justified or deserved while the letting die unwanted and undeserved. They tend to disagree, however, over whether other things would be equal if the killing were in response to a patient's request to die while the letting die involved a prolonged and excruciatingly painful death, or if the killing resulted in the death of just a few individuals while the letting die resulted in the death of many people.

Yet whatever view one adopts as to when other things are equal, it is hard to defend the moral preferability of letting die over killing when both are taken to be intentional acts. As James Rachels so graphically illustrates (Selection 18), it seems impossible to judge the act of A, who intentionally lets Z die while standing ready to finish Z off if that proves necessary, as being morally preferable to the act of B, who with similar motive and intention kills Y. But it is far from clear whether advocates of the killing and letting die distinction are claiming that the distinction holds when the killing and the letting die are both intentional acts because it is unlikely in such cases that the letting die would be morally justified when the killing is not. Rather, as Bonnie Steinbock argues (Selection 19), advocates of the distinction seem to have in mind a contrast between *intentional* killing and *unintentional* letting die, or, more fully stated, a contrast between intentional killing and unintentional letting die when the latter is the foreseen consequence of an otherwise legitimate course of action.

Steinbock maintains that there are at least two types of cases in which letting die, distinguished in this way from killing, seems justified. In the first, a doctor ceases treatment at the patient's request, foreseeing that the patient will die or die sooner than otherwise, yet not intending that result. In the second, a doctor's intention is to avoid employing treatment that is extremely painful and has little hope of benefiting the patient, even though she foresees that this may hasten the patient's death. In addition, conservatives have argued that letting die, distinguished in this way from killing, can be justified in cases of ectopic pregnancy and cancer of the uterus because in such cases the fetus's death is the foreseen but unintended consequence of medical treatment that is necessary to preserve the basic well-being of the pregnant woman.

When the killing and letting die distinction is interpreted in this way, it has much in common with the doctrine of double effect. This doctrine places four restrictions on the permissibility of acting when some of the consequences of one's action are evil. These restrictions are as follows:

1. The act is good in itself or at least indifferent.
2. Only the good consequences of the act are intended.
3. The good consequences are not the effect of the evil.
4. The good consequences are commensurate with the evil consequences.

The basic idea of the killing and letting die distinction, as we have interpreted it, is expressed by restrictions 2 and 3.

When conservatives apply the doctrine of double effect to a case in which a pregnant woman has cancer of the uterus, the doctrine is said to justify an abortion because:

1. The act of removing the cancerous uterus is good in itself.
2. Only the removal of the cancerous uterus is intended.
3. The removal of the cancerous uterus is not a consequence of the abortion.
4. Preserving the life of the mother by removing the cancerous uterus is commensurate with the death of the fetus.

The doctrine is also said to justify unintentionally letting a person die, or "passive euthanasia," at least in the two types of cases described by Steinbock.

In recent moral philosophy, the main objection to the doctrine of double effect has been to question the necessity of its restrictions. Consider the following example. Imagine that a fat person who is leading a party of spelunkers gets herself stuck in the mouth of a cave in which flood waters are rising. The trapped party of spelunkers just happens to have a stick of dynamite with which they can blast the fat person out of the mouth of the cave; either they use the dynamite or they all drown, the fat person with them. It appears that the doctrine of double effect would *not* permit the use of the dynamite in this case because the evil consequences of the act are intended as a means to securing the good consequences in violation of restrictions 2 and 3. Yet it is plausible to argue in such a case that using the dynamite would be justified on the grounds that (a) the evil to be avoided (i.e., the evil of failing to save the party of spelunkers except for the fat person) is considerably greater than the evil resulting from the means employed (i.e., the evil of intentionally causing the death of the fat person) and/or that (b) the greater part of evil resulting from the means employed (i.e., the death of the fat person) would still occur regardless of whether those means were actually employed.

Some people might want to defend the doctrine of double effect against this line of criticism by maintaining that the spelunkers need not intend the death of the fat person, but only that "she be blown into little pieces" or that "the mouth of the cave be suitably enlarged." But how is the use of dynamite expected to produce these results except by way of killing the fat person? Thus, the death of the fat person is part of the means employed by the spelunkers to secure their release from the cave, and thus would be impermissible according to the doctrine of double effect. If, however, we think that bringing about the death of the fat person could be morally justified in this case, because, for example, (a) and/or (b) obtain, we are left with a serious objection to the necessity of the restrictions imposed by the doctrine of double effect for acting morally. And, as we shall see when considering the problem of national defense and military strategy, still other objections can be raised regarding the sufficiency of these restrictions.

Given these objections to the doctrine of double effect, Philippa Foot has suggested that we might more profitably deal with the moral questions at issue by distinguishing between negative and positive duties. *Negative duties* are said to be duties to refrain from doing certain sorts of actions. Typically, these are duties to avoid actions that inflict harm or injury on others. Thus, the duties not to kill or assault others are negative duties. By contrast, *positive duties* are duties to do certain actions, usually those that aid or benefit others. The duties to repay a debt and help others in need are positive duties. This distinction is used to resolve practical disputes by claiming that negative duties have priority over positive duties; accordingly, when negative and positive duties conflict, negative duties always take precedence over positive duties.

Applying this distinction, Foot claims that a doctor is justified in performing an abortion when nothing can be done to save the lives of both child and mother, but the life of the mother can be saved by killing the child. Obviously, this case is quite similar to the example of the fat person stuck in the mouth of the cave. But it is not clear how the distinction between positive and negative duties can help us in either situation. Since both the doctor and the group of spelunkers trapped by the fat person have a negative duty not to kill that takes precedence over any positive duty to help either themselves or others, it would seem that neither aborting the fetus nor blowing up the fat person could be justified on the basis of this distinction. Thus, the distinction

between negative and positive duties no more justifies evil consequences in such cases than does the doctrine of double effect. Accordingly, if we want to provide such a justification, we need to find some morally acceptable way of going beyond both of these requirements.

Alternative Views

As we mentioned earlier, conservatives hold that the fetus has full moral status and hence a serious right to life. As a consequence, conservatives oppose abortion in a wide range of cases. Hoping to undercut this antiabortion stance, Judith Jarvis Thomson adopts, for the sake of argument, the conservative position on the moral status of the fetus (Selection 13). She then tries to show that abortion is still justified in a wide range of cases. Thomson asks us to imagine that we are kidnapped and connected to an unconscious violinist who now shares the use of our kidneys. The situation is such that if we detach ourselves from the violinist before nine months transpire, the violinist will die. Thomson thinks it obvious that we have no obligation to share our kidneys with the violinist in such a case, and hence that, in analogous cases, abortion can be justified. Thomson's view has provoked so much discussion that the authors of each of the next four selections all feel compelled to consider her view in the course of developing their own positions.

In his selection, John Noonan objects to Thomson's use of fantasized examples (Selection 14). In place of Thomson's example of an unconscious violinist, Noonan offers a more realistic example found in the law. It is a case in which a family is found to be liable for the frostbite suffered by a dinner guest whom they refused to allow to stay overnight in their home, although it was very cold outside and the guest showed signs of being sick. But although Noonan is surely correct in pointing out the need for realistic examples, there still is an important difference between allowing a person to stay overnight in one's home and allowing a fetus to remain and develop in one's body for approximately nine months.

Mary Anne Warren also objects to Thomson's violinist example, but on grounds quite different from Noonan's (Selection 15). She claims that the example at most justifies abortion in cases of rape and hence will not provide the desired support for abortion on demand. Thomson, however, did provide additional examples and arguments in an attempt to show that abortion is justified in cases other than rape. Jane English has also argued that Thomson's case against abortion can be extended to a wider range of examples (Selection 16).

Convinced that Thomson's or anyone else's attempt to argue for abortion will prove unsuccessful if the fetus is assumed to have full moral status, Noonan wants to retain and support that assumption. His approach, however, is quite different from that usually adopted by conservatives.

Conservatives typically employ what are called "slippery slope arguments" to show that any attempt to draw a line—whether at implantation, or at quickening, or at viability, or at birth—for the purpose of separating those who do not have full moral status from those who do, fails to be nonarbitrary because of the continuity in the development of the fetus. Conservatives then contend that conception is the only point at which the line can be drawn nonarbitrarily.

By contrast, Noonan proposes to examine various models and methods employed in the debate on abortion, distinguishing those that do not work from those that do. We have already noted Noonan's objection to fantasized examples. In addition, he objects to any attempt to make exceptions for abortion when the fetus is known to be seriously defective or the result of a rape, arguing that exceptions in such cases would "eat up the rule." Surprisingly, Noonan also objects to the use of special metaphors such as direct and indirect, and in particular rejects the application of the doctrine of double effect to cases of ectopic pregnancy and the removal of a cancerous uterus containing a fetus. In such cases, Noonan claims, the doctor "necessarily intends to perform the abortion, he necessarily intends to kill." What legitimates abortion in such cases, claims Noonan, is not the doctrine of double effect, but rather the principle that whenever the fetus is a danger to the life of the mother, abortion is permissible on grounds of self-defense. But if the mother is justified on grounds of self-defense in aborting the fetus, surely some representative of the fetus would also be justified in defending the fetus against an abortion, given that in Noonan's view the fetus has a serious right to life. Consequently, Noonan has not provided us with a moral solution to such cases. At the same time, it is difficult to see how anyone could ignore the central plea of Noonan's article that we see what otherwise might be overlooked and respond to the full range of human experience.

Like Noonan, Warren wants to build a consensus on the abortion question. To achieve this, she proposes a set of criteria for being a person with full moral status that she thinks proabortionists and antiabortionists alike could accept. The criteria are (1) consciousness; (2) developed reasoning; (3) self-motivated activity; (4) a capacity to communicate; and (5) the presence of self-concepts and self-awareness. But although most people would certainly agree that these criteria are met in paradigm cases, conservatives would still reject them as necessary requirements for being a person. As Jane English (Selection 16) argues, the concept of a person is not sharp or decisive enough to bear the weight of a solution to the abortion controversy.

English, however, agrees with Thomson that even if we endorse the conservative view that the fetus is a full-fledged person, there are still cases where abortion would be justified to prevent serious harm or death to the pregnant woman. Similarly, she contends that even if we endorse the liberal view that the fetus is not a person, there are still cases, at least in the late months of pregnancy, where abortion would not be justified, because of the fetus's resemblance to a person.

Those who find both the conservative and liberal views on abortion unattractive might be inclined toward the moderate view. This view attempts to draw a line—typically at implantation, or at quickening, or at viability—for the purpose of separating those who do not have full moral status from those who do. The United States Supreme Court in *Wade* v. *Roe* (1973) has frequently been understood as supporting a moderate view on abortion. In this decision, the Court by a majority of 7 to 2 decided that the constitutional right to privacy, protected by the due process clause of the Fourteenth Amendment to the Constitution, entails that (1) no law may restrict the right of a woman to be aborted by a physician during the first three months (trimester) of her pregnancy; (2) during the second trimester abortion may be regulated by law only to the extent that the regulation is reasonably related to the preservation and protection of maternal health; and (3) when the fetus becomes viable (not before the beginning of the third trimester) a law may prohibit abortion, but only subject to an exception permitting abortion whenever necessary to protect the woman's life or health (including any aspects of her physical or mental health). But regardless of whether the Court's decision was intended to support the moderate view on abortion, some have argued that in the absence of reasonable constraints, the Court's decision has led to abortion on demand.

In her selection, Catharine MacKinnon situates the abortion debate within a feminist understanding of gender equality. She challenges the underlying assumption of the abortion debate that women significantly control sex. She argues that the limited right to abortion based on privacy recognized by the U.S. Supreme Court in *Roe* v. *Wade* not only accords with the restrictions on federal funding for abortion sanctioned by *Harris* v. *McRae,* but also fails to protect women from battery, marital rape, and exploited labor. What this shows is that a right to abortion based on a right to privacy may do little by itself to secure women's liberation. What it also suggests is that many aspects of women's liberation could be achieved without a right to abortion if men approached sex and the care and rearing of children more responsibly.

Although most of the contemporary discussion of abortion has focused on the moral status of the fetus, most of the discussion of euthanasia has focused on the killing and letting die distinction and the doctrine of double effect. As we noted before, advocates of the killing and letting die distinction and the doctrine of double effect tend to justify only passive euthanasia (i.e., letting a person die as a foreseen but unintended consequence of an

otherwise legitimate course of action). In contrast, critics of the killing and letting die distinction and the doctrine of double effect tend also to justify active euthanasia (i.e., intentional killing) on the basis of its consequences. Rachels (Selection 18) cites the case of a person suffering from cancer of the throat who has three options: (1) with continued treatment she will have a few more days of pain and then die; (2) if treatment is stopped but nothing else is done, it will be a few more hours; or (3) with a lethal injection she will die at once. In such a case, Rachels thinks, the third option—active euthanasia—is justified on the grounds that the person would be better off dying immediately.

But euthanasia is not only passive or active, it is also voluntary or involuntary. Voluntary euthanasia has the (informed) consent of the person involved. Involuntary euthanasia lacks such consent, usually but not always because the person involved is incapable of providing it. This means that at least four different types of euthanasia are possible: voluntary passive euthanasia, involuntary passive euthanasia, voluntary active euthanasia, and involuntary active euthanasia. Of the four types, voluntary passive euthanasia seems easiest to justify, involuntary active euthanasia the most difficult. But voluntary euthanasia, both passive and active, would seem more justifiable if it could be shown that there were a fundamental moral right to be assisted in bringing about one's own death if one so desired. Even if such a right could be supported, however, it would presumably only have force when one could reasonably be judged to be better off dead.

Practical Applications

It is not at all difficult to see how the various proposed solutions to the problem of abortion and euthanasia could be applied in contemporary societies. For example, in *Webster* v. *Reproductive Health Services* (Selection 20), a plurality of the U.S. Supreme Court in attempting to move closer to the conservative position on abortion threw out the trimester analysis of *Wade* v. *Roe* and ruled that the state's interest in protecting potential life justified requiring physicians to conduct viability tests prior to performing abortions. However, in dissent, Justice Blackmun, joined by Justices Brennan and Marshall, argued that there was no need to throw out the trimester analysis of *Wade* v. *Roe* because that analysis is consistent with requiring physicians to determine viability. Similarly, in *Cruzan* v. *Harmon* (Selection 21), the Missouri Supreme Court reviewed the legal history of a right to passive euthanasia and then decided to prohibit passive euthanasia when it involved withholding nutrition and hydration. Accordingly, if you think that different solutions to the problem of abortion and euthanasia are more morally defensible, you should favor other laws and judicial decisions.

But even as you begin to formulate the laws and social institutions, with their demands on social goods and resources, that are needed to enforce what you take to be the most morally defensible solution to the problem of abortion and euthanasia, you will still need to take into account the demands on social goods and resources that derive from solutions to other practical moral problems—such as the problem of sex equality, which is taken up in the next section.

Notes

1. The term "fetus" is understood to refer to any human organism from conception to birth.

2. Note that liberals on the abortion question need not be welfare liberals, although many of them are. Likewise, conservatives on the abortion question need not be libertarians or political conservatives.

3. Henceforth liberals, conservatives, and moderates on the abortion question are simply referred to as liberals, conservatives, and moderates.

13. A Defense of Abortion

Judith Jarvis Thomson

Judith Jarvis Thomson begins by assuming, for the sake of argument, that the fetus is a person. Using a series of examples, she then argues that even granting this assumption, a woman has a right to abortion in cases involving rape, in cases where the woman's life is endangered, and in cases in which the woman had taken reasonable precautions to avoid becoming pregnant. In these cases, Thomson claims, the fetus's assumed right not to be killed unjustly would not be violated by abortion. Thomson further distinguishes between cases in which it would be a good thing for a woman to forego an abortion and cases in which a woman has an obligation to do so.

Abridged from Judith Jarvis Thomson, "A Defense of Abortion," *Philosophy & Public Affairs* 1, no. 1 (Fall 1971). Copyright © 1971 by Princeton University Press. Excerpts, pp. 47–62, 65–66, reprinted by permission of Princeton University Press.

Most opposition to abortion relies on the premise that the fetus is a human being, a person, from the moment of conception. The premise is argued for, but, as I think, not well. Take, for example, the most common argument. We are asked to notice that the development of a human being from conception through birth into childhood is continuous; then it is said that to draw a line, to choose a point in this development and say "before this point the thing is not a person, after this point it is a person" is to make an arbitrary choice, a choice for which in the nature of things no good reason can be given. It is concluded that the fetus is, or anyway we had better say it is, a person from the moment of conception. But this conclusion does not follow. Similar things might be said about the development of an acorn into an oak tree, and it does not follow that acorns are oak trees or that we had better say they are. Arguments of this form are sometimes called "slippery slope arguments"—the phrase is perhaps self-explanatory—and it is dismaying that opponents of abortion rely on them so heavily and uncritically.

I am inclined to agree, however, that the prospects for "drawing a line" in the development of the fetus look dim. I am inclined to think also that we shall probably have to agree that the fetus has already become a human person well before birth. Indeed, it comes as a surprise when one first learns how early in its life it begins to acquire human characteristics. By the tenth week, for example, it already has a face, arms and legs, fingers and toes; it has internal organs, and brain activity is detectable.[1] On the other hand, I think that the premise is false, that the fetus is not a person from the moment of conception. A newly fertilized ovum, a newly implanted clump of cells, is no more a person than an acorn is an oak tree. But I shall not discuss any of this. For it seems to me to be of great interest to ask what happens if, for the sake of argument, we allow the premise. How, precisely, are we supposed to get from there to the conclusion that abortion is morally impermissible? Opponents of abortion commonly spend most of their time establishing that the fetus is a person, and hardly any time explaining the step from there to the impermissibility of abortion. Perhaps they think the step too simple and obvious to require much comment. Or perhaps instead they are simply being economical in argument. Many of those who defend abortion rely on the premise that the fetus is not a person, but only a bit of tissue that will become a person at birth; and why pay out more arguments than you have to? Whatever the explanation, I suggest that the step they take is neither easy nor obvious, that it calls for closer examination than it is commonly given, and that when we do give it this closer examination we shall feel inclined to reject it.

I propose, then, that we grant that the fetus is a person from the moment of conception. How does the argument go from here? Something like this, I take it. Every person has a right to life. So the fetus has a right to life. No doubt the mother has a right to decide what shall happen in and to her body; everyone would grant that. But surely a person's right to life is stronger and more stringent than the mother's right to decide what happens in and to her body, and so outweighs it. So the fetus may not be killed; an abortion may not be performed.

It sounds plausible. But now let me ask you to imagine this. You wake up in the morning and find yourself back to back in bed with an unconscious violinist. A famous unconscious violinist. He has been found to have a fatal kidney ailment, and the Society of Music Lovers has canvassed all the available medical records and found that you alone have the right blood type to help. They have therefore kidnapped you, and last night the violinist's circulatory system was plugged into yours, so that your kidneys can be used to extract poisons from his blood as well as your own. The director of the hospital now tells you, "Look, we're sorry the Society of Music Lovers did this to you—we would never have permitted it if we had known. But still, they did it, and the violinist now is plugged into you. To unplug you would be to kill him. But never mind, it's only for nine months. By then he will have recovered from his ailment, and can safely be unplugged from you." Is it morally incumbent on you to accede to this situation? No doubt it would be very nice of you if you did, a great kindness. But do you *have* to accede to it? What if it were not nine months, but nine years? Or longer still? What if the director of the hospital says, "Tough luck, I agree, but you've now got to stay in bed, with the violinist plugged into you, for the rest of your life. Because remember this. All persons have a right to life, and violinists are persons. Granted you have a right to decide what happens in and to your body, but a person's right to life outweighs your right to decide what happens in and to your body. So you cannot ever be unplugged from him." I imagine you would regard this as outrageous, which suggests that something really is wrong with that plausible-sounding argument I mentioned a moment ago.

In this case, of course, you were kidnapped; you didn't volunteer for the operation that plugged the violinist into your kidneys. Can those who oppose abortion on the ground I mentioned make an exception for a pregnancy due to rape? Certainly. They can say that persons have a right to life only if they didn't come into existence because of rape; or they can say that all persons have a right to life, but that some have less of a right to life than others, in particular, that those who came into existence because of rape have less. But these statements have a rather unpleasant sound. Surely the question of whether you have a right to life at all, or how much of it you have, shouldn't turn on the question of whether or not you are the product of a rape. And in fact the people who oppose abortion on the ground I mentioned do not make this distinction, and hence do not make an exception in case of rape.

Nor do they make an exception for a case in which the mother has to spend the nine months of her pregnancy in bed. They would agree that would be a great pity, and hard on the mother; but all the same, all persons have a right to life, the fetus is a person, and so on. I suspect, in fact, that they would not make an exception for a case in which, miraculously enough, the pregnancy went on for nine years, or even the rest of the mother's life.

Some won't even make an exception for a case in which continuation of the pregnancy is likely to shorten the mother's life; they regard abortion as impermissible even to save the mother's life. Such cases are nowadays very rare, and many opponents of abortion do not

accept this extreme view. All the same, it is a good place to begin: a number of points of interest come out in respect to it.

1. Let us call the view that abortion is impermissible even to save the mother's life "the extreme view." I want to suggest first that it does not issue from the argument I mentioned earlier without the addition of some fairly powerful premises. Suppose a woman has become pregnant, and now learns that she has a cardiac condition such that she will die if she carries the baby to term. What may be done for her? The fetus, being a person, has a right to life, but as the mother is a person too, so has she a right to life. Presumably they have an equal right to life. How is it supposed to come out that an abortion may not be performed? If mother and child have an equal right to life, shouldn't we perhaps flip a coin? Or should we add to the mother's right to life her right to decide what happens in and to her body, which everybody seems to be ready to grant—the sum of her rights now outweighing the fetus' right to life?

The most familiar argument here is the following. We are told that performing the abortion would be directly killing[2] the child, whereas doing nothing would not be killing the mother, but only letting her die. Moreover, in killing the child, one would be killing an innocent person, for the child has committed no crime, and is not aiming at his mother's death. And then there are a variety of ways in which this might be continued. (1) But as directly killing an innocent person is always and absolutely impermissible, an abortion may not be performed. Or, (2) as directly killing an innocent person is murder, and murder is always and absolutely impermissible, an abortion may not be performed.[3] Or, (3) as one's duty to refrain from directly killing an innocent person is more stringent than one's duty to keep a person from dying, an abortion may not be performed. Or, (4) if one's only options are directly killing an innocent person or letting a person die, one must prefer letting the person die, and thus an abortion may not be performed.[4]

Some people seem to have thought that these are not further premises which must be added if the conclusion is to be reached, but that they follow from the very fact that an innocent person has a right to life.[5] But this seems to me to be a mistake, and perhaps the simplest way to show this is to bring out that while we must certainly grant that innocent persons have a right to life, the theses in (1) through (4) are all false. Take (2), for example. If directly killing an innocent person is murder, and thus is impermissible, then the mother's directly killing the innocent person inside her is murder, and thus is impermissible. But it cannot seriously be thought to be murder if the mother performs an abortion on herself to save her life. It cannot seriously be said that she *must* refrain, that she *must* sit passively by and wait for her death. Let us look again at the case of you and the violinist. There you are, in bed with the violinist, and the director of the hospital says to you, "It's all most distressing, and I deeply sympathize, but you see this is putting an additional strain on your kidneys, and you'll be dead within the month. But you *have* to stay where you are all the same. Because unplugging you would be directly killing an innocent violinist, and that's murder, and that's impermissible." If anything in the world is true, it is that you do not commit murder, you do not do what is impermissible, if you reach around to your back and unplug yourself from that violinist to save your life.

The main focus of attention in writings on abortion has been on what a third party may or may not do in answer to a request from a woman for an abortion. This is in a way understandable. Things being as they are, there isn't much a woman can safely do to abort herself. So the question asked is what a third party may do, and what the mother may do, if it is mentioned at all, is deduced, almost as an afterthought, from what is concluded that the third parties may do. But it seems to me that to treat the matter in this way is to refuse to grant to the mother that very status of person which is so firmly insisted on for the fetus. For we cannot simply read off what a person may do from what a third party may do. Suppose you find yourself trapped in a tiny house with a growing child. I mean a very tiny house, and a rapidly growing child—you are already up against the wall of the house and in a few minutes you'll be crushed to death. The child

on the other hand won't be crushed to death; if nothing is done to stop him from growing he'll be hurt, but in the end he'll simply burst open the house and walk out a free man. Now I could well understand it if a bystander were to say, "There's nothing we can do for you. We cannot choose between your life and his, we cannot be the ones to decide who is to live, we cannot intervene." But it cannot be concluded that you too can do nothing, that you cannot attack it to save your life. However innocent the child may be, you do not have to wait passively while it crushes you to death. Perhaps a pregnant woman is vaguely felt to have the status of a house, to which we don't allow the right of self-defense. But if the woman houses the child, it should be remembered that she is a person who houses it.

I should perhaps stop to say explicitly that I am not claiming that people have a right to do anything whatever to save their lives. I think, rather, that there are drastic limits to the right of self-defense. If someone threatens you with death unless you torture someone else to death, I think you have not the right, even to save your life, to do so. But the case under consideration here is very different. In our case there are only two people involved, one whose life is threatened, and one who threatens it. Both are innocent: the one who is threatened is not threatened because of any fault, the one who threatens does not threaten because of any fault. For this reason we may feel that we bystanders cannot intervene. But the person threatened can.

In sum, a woman surely can defend her life against the threat to it posed by the unborn child, even if doing so involves its death. And this shows not merely that the theses in (1) through (4) are false; it shows also that the extreme view of abortion is false, and so we need not canvass any other possible ways of arriving at it from the argument I mentioned at the outset.

2. The extreme view could of course be weakened to say that while abortion is permissible to save the mother's life, it may not be performed by a third party, but only by the mother herself. But this cannot be right either. For what we have to keep in mind is that the mother and the unborn child are not like two

tenants in a small house which has, by an unfortunate mistake, been rented to both: the mother *owns* the house. The fact that she does adds to the offensiveness of deducing that the mother can do nothing from the supposition that third parties can do nothing. But it does more than this: it casts a bright light on the supposition that third parties can do nothing. Certainly it lets us see that a third party who says "I cannot choose between you" is fooling himself if he thinks this is impartiality. If Jones has found and fastened on a certain coat, which he needs to keep him from freezing, but which Smith also needs to keep him from freezing, then it is not impartiality that says "I cannot choose between you" when Smith owns the coat. Women have said again and again "This body is *my* body!" and they have reason to feel angry, reason to feel that it has been like shouting into the wind. Smith, after all, is hardly likely to bless us if we say to him, "Of course it's your coat, anybody would grant that it is. But no one may choose between you and Jones who is to have it. . . ."

3. Where the mother's life is not at stake, the argument I mentioned at the outset seems to have a much stronger pull. "Everyone has a right to life, so the unborn person has a right to life." And isn't the child's right to life weightier than anything other than the mother's own right to life, which she might put forward as ground for an abortion?

This argument treats the right to life as if it were unproblematic. It is not, and this seems to me to be precisely the source of the mistake.

For we should now, at long last, ask what it comes to, to have a right to life. In some views having a right to life includes having a right to be given at least the bare minimum one needs for continued life. But suppose that what in fact *is* the bare minimum a man needs for continued life is something he has no right at all to be given? If I am sick unto death, and the only thing that will save my life is the touch of Henry Fonda's cool hand on my fevered brow, then all the same, I have no right to be given the touch of Henry Fonda's cool hand on my fevered brow. It would be frightfully nice of him to fly in from the West Coast to provide it. It would be less nice, though no doubt well meant, if my friends flew out to the West Coast and carried Henry Fonda back with them. But I have no right at all against anybody that he should do this for me. Or again, to return to the story I told earlier, the fact that for continued life that violinist needs the continued use of your kidneys does not establish that he has a right to be given the continued use of your kidneys. He certainly has no right against you that *you* should give him continued use of your kidneys. For nobody has any right to use your kidneys unless you give him such a right; and nobody has the right against you that you shall give him this right—if you do allow him to go on using your kidneys, this is a kindness on your part, and not something he can claim from you as his due. Nor has he any right against anybody else that *they* should give him continued use of your kidneys. Certainly he had no right against the Society of Music Lovers that they should plug him into you in the first place. And if you now start to unplug yourself, having learned that you will otherwise have to spend nine years in bed with him, there is nobody in the world who must try to prevent you, in order to see to it that he is given something he has a right to be given.

Some people are rather stricter about the right to life. In their view, it does not include the right to be given anything, but amounts to, and only to, the right not to be killed by anybody. But here a related difficulty arises. If everybody is to refrain from killing that violinist, then everybody must refrain from doing a great many different sorts of things. Everybody must refrain from slitting his throat, everybody must refrain from shooting him—and everybody must refrain from unplugging you from him. But does he have a right against everybody that they shall refrain from unplugging you from him? To refrain from doing this is to allow him to continue to use your kidneys. It could be argued that he has a right against us that *we* should allow him to continue to use your kidneys. That is, while he had no right against us that we should give him the use of your kidneys, it might be argued that he anyway has a right against us that we shall not now intervene and deprive him of the use of your kidneys. I shall come back to third-party interventions later. But certainly the violinist has no right against you that *you* shall allow him to continue to use your kidneys. As I said, if you do allow him to use them, it is a kindness on your part, and not something you owe him.

The difficulty I point to here is not peculiar to the right to life. It reappears in connection with all the other natural rights; and it is something which an adequate account of rights must deal with. For present purposes it is enough just to draw attention to it. But I would stress that I am not arguing that people do not have a right to life—quite to the contrary, it seems to me that the primary control we must place on the acceptability of an account of rights is that it should turn out in that account to be a truth that all persons have a right to life. I am arguing only that having a right to life does not guarantee having either a right to be given the use of or a right to be allowed continued use of another person's body—even if one needs it for life itself. So the right to life will not serve the opponents of abortion in the very simple and clear way in which they seem to have thought it would.

4. There is another way to bring out the difficulty. In the most ordinary sort of case, to deprive someone of what he has a right to is to treat him unjustly. Suppose a boy and his small brother are jointly given a box of chocolates for Christmas. If the older boy takes the box and refuses to give his brother any of the chocolates, he is unjust to him, for the brother has been given a right to half of them. But suppose that, having learned that otherwise it means nine years in bed with that violinist, you unplug yourself from him. You surely are not being unjust to him, for you gave him no right to use your kidneys, and no one else can have given him any such right. But we have to notice that in unplugging yourself, you are killing him; and violinists, like everybody else, have a right to life, and thus in the view we were considering just now, the right not to be killed.

So here you do what he supposedly has a right you shall not do, but you do not act unjustly to him in doing it.

The emendation which may be made at this point is this: the right to life consists not in the right not to be killed, but rather in the right not to be killed unjustly. This runs a risk of circularity, but never mind: it would enable us to square the fact that the violinist has a right to life with the fact that you do not act unjustly toward him in unplugging yourself, thereby killing him. For if you do not kill him unjustly, you do not violate his right to life, and so it is no wonder you do him no injustice.

But if this emendation is accepted, the gap in the argument against abortion stares us plainly in the face: it is by no means enough to show that the fetus is a person, and to remind us that all persons have a right to life—we need to be shown also that killing the fetus violates its right to life, i.e., that abortion is unjust killing. And is it?

I suppose we may take it as a datum that in a case of pregnancy due to rape the mother has not given the unborn person a right to the use of her body for food and shelter. Indeed, in what pregnancy could it be supposed that the mother has given the unborn person such a right? It is not as if there were unborn persons drifting about the world, to whom a woman who wants a child says "I invite you in."

But it might be argued that there are other ways one can have acquired a right to the use of another person's body than by having been invited to use it by that person. Suppose a woman voluntarily indulges in intercourse, knowing of the chance it will issue in pregnancy, and then she does become pregnant; is she not in part responsible for the presence, in fact the very existence, of the unborn person inside her? No doubt she did not invite it in. But doesn't her partial responsibility for its being there itself give it a right to the use of her body? If so, then her aborting it would be more like the boy's taking away the chocolates, and less like your unplugging yourself from the violinist—doing so would be depriving it of what it does have a right to, and thus would be doing it an injustice.

And then, too, it might be asked whether or not she can kill it even to save her own life: If she voluntarily called it into existence, how can she now kill it, even in self-defense?

The first thing to be said about this is that it is something new. Opponents of abortion have been so concerned to make out the independence of the fetus, in order to establish that it has a right to life, just as its mother does, that they have tended to overlook the possible support they might gain from making out that the fetus is *dependent* on the mother, in order to establish that she has a special kind of responsibility for it, a responsibility that gives it rights against her which are not possessed by any independent person—such as an ailing violinist who is a stranger to her.

On the other hand, this argument would give the unborn person a right to its mother's body only if her pregnancy resulted from a voluntary act, undertaken in full knowledge of the chance a pregnancy might result from it. It would leave out entirely the unborn person whose existence is due to rape. Pending the availability of some further argument, then, we would be left with the conclusion that unborn persons whose existence is due to rape have no right to the use of their mothers' bodies, and thus that aborting them is not depriving them of anything they have a right to and hence is not unjust killing.

And we should also notice that it is not at all plain that this argument really does go even as far as it purports to. For there are cases and cases, and the details make a difference. If the room is stuffy, and I therefore open a window to air it, and a burglar climbs in, it would be absurd to say, "Ah, now he can stay, she's given him a right to the use of her house—for she is partially responsible for his presence there, having voluntarily done what enabled him to get in, in full knowledge that there are such things as burglars, and that burglars burgle." It would be still more absurd to say this if I had had bars installed outside my windows, precisely to prevent burglars from getting in, and a burglar got in only because of a defect in the bars. It remains equally absurd if we imagine it is not a burglar who climbs in, but an innocent person who blunders or falls in. Again, suppose it were like this: people-seeds drift about in the air like pollen, and if you open your windows, one may drift in and take root in your carpets or upholstery. You don't want children, so you fix up your windows with fine mesh screens, the very best you can buy. As can happen, however, and on very, very rare occasions does happen, one of

the screens is defective; and a seed drifts in and takes root. Does the person-plant who now develops have a right to the use of your house? Surely not—despite the fact that you voluntarily opened your windows, you knowingly kept carpets and upholstered furniture, and you knew that screens were sometimes defective. Someone may argue that you are responsible for its rooting, that it does have a right to your house, because after all you *could* have lived out your life with bare floors and furniture, or with sealed windows and doors. But this won't do—for by the same token anyone can avoid a pregnancy due to rape by having a hysterectomy, or anyway by never leaving home without a (reliable!) army.

It seems to me that the argument we are looking at can establish at most that there are *some* cases in which the unborn person has a right to the use of its mother's body, and therefore *some* cases in which abortion is unjust killing. There is room for much discussion and argument as to precisely which, if any. But I think we should sidestep this issue and leave it open, for at any rate the argument certainly does not establish that all abortion is unjust killing.

5. There is room for yet another argument here, however. We surely must all grant that there may be cases in which it would be morally indecent to detach a person from your body at the cost of his life. Suppose you learn that what the violinist needs is not nine years of your life, but only one hour: all you need do to save his life is to spend one hour in that bed with him. Suppose also that letting him use your kidneys for that one hour would not affect your health in the slightest. Admittedly you were kidnapped. Admittedly you did not give anyone permission to plug him into you. Nevertheless it seems to me plain you *ought* to allow him to use your kidneys for that hour—it would be indecent to refuse.

Again, suppose pregnancy lasted only an hour, and constituted no threat to life or health. And suppose that a woman becomes pregnant as a result of rape. Admittedly she did not voluntarily do anything to bring about the existence of a child. Admittedly she did nothing at all which would give the unborn person a right to the use of her body. All the same it might well be said, as in the newly emended violinist story, that she *ought* to allow it to remain for that hour—that it would be indecent in her to refuse.

Now some people are inclined to use the term "right" in such a way that it follows from the fact that you ought to allow a person to use your body for the hour he needs, that he has a right to use your body for the hour he needs, even though he has not been given that right by any person or act. They may say that it follows also that if you refuse, you act unjustly toward him. This use of the term is perhaps so common that it cannot be called wrong; nevertheless it seems to me to be an unfortunate loosening of what we would do better to keep a tight rein on. Suppose that box of chocolates I mentioned earlier had not been given to both boys jointly, but was given only to the older boy. There he sits, stolidly eating his way through the box, his small brother watching enviously. Here we are likely to say "You ought not to be so mean. You ought to give your brother some of those chocolates." My own view is that it just does not follow from the truth of this that the brother has any right to any of the chocolates. If the boy refuses to give his brother any, he is greedy, stingy, callous— but not unjust. I suppose that the people I have in mind will say it does follow that the brother has a right to some of the chocolates, and thus that the boy does act unjustly if he refuses to give his brother any. But the effect of saying this is to obscure what we should keep distinct, namely the difference between the boy's refusal in this case and the boy's refusal in the earlier case, in which the box was given to both boys jointly, and in which the small brother thus had what was from any point of view clear title to half.

A further objection to so using the term "right" that from the fact that A ought to do a thing for B, it follows that B has a right against A that A do it for him, is that it is going to make the question of whether or not a man has a right to a thing turn on how easy it is to provide him with it; and this seems not merely unfortunate, but morally unacceptable. Take the case of Henry Fonda again. I said earlier that I had no right to the touch of his cool hand on my fevered brow, even though I needed it to save my life. I said it would be

frightfully nice of him to fly in from the West Coast to provide me with it, but that I had no right against him that he should do so. But suppose he isn't on the West Coast. Suppose he has only to walk across the room, place a hand briefly on my brow—and lo, my life is saved. Then surely he ought to do it, it would be indecent to refuse. Is it to be said "Ah, well, it follows that in this case she has a right to the touch of his hand on her brow, and so it would be an injustice in him to refuse"? So that I have a right to it when it is easy for him to provide it, though no right when it's hard? It's rather a shocking idea that anyone's rights should fade away and disappear as it gets harder and harder to accord them to him.

So my own view is that even though you ought to let the violinist use your kidneys for the one hour he needs, we should not conclude that he has a right to do so—we should say that if you refuse, you are, like the boy who owns all the chocolates and will give none away, self-centered and callous, indecent in fact, but not unjust. And similarly, that even supposing a case in which a woman pregnant due to rape ought to allow the unborn person to use her body for the hour he needs, we should not conclude that he has a right to do so; we should conclude that she is self-centered, callous, indecent, but not unjust, if she refuses. The complaints are no less grave; they are just different. However, there is no need to insist on this point. If anyone does wish to deduce "he has a right" from "you ought," then all the same he must surely grant that there are cases in which it is not morally required of you that you allow that violinist to use your kidneys, and in which he does not have a right to use them, and in which you do not do him injustice if you refuse. And so also for mother and unborn child. Except in such cases as the unborn person has a right to demand it—and we were leaving open the possibility that there may be such cases— nobody is morally *required* to make large sacrifices, of health, of all other interests and concerns, of all other duties and commitments, for nine years, or even for nine months, in order to keep another person alive. . . .

8. My argument will be found unsatisfactory on two counts by many of those who want to regard abortion as morally permissible.

First, while I do argue that abortion is not impermissible, I do not argue that it is always permissible. I am inclined to think it a merit of my account precisely that it does *not* give a general yes or a general no. It allows for and supports our sense that, for example, a sick and desperately frightened fourteen-year-old schoolgirl, pregnant due to rape, may *of course* choose abortion, and that any law which rules this out is an insane law. And it also allows for and supports our sense that in other cases resort to abortion is even positively indecent. It would be indecent in the woman to request an abortion, and indecent in a doctor to perform it, if she is in her seventh month, and wants the abortion just to avoid the nuisance of postponing a trip abroad. The very fact that the arguments I have been drawing attention to treat all cases of abortion, or even all cases of abortion in which the mother's life is not at stake, as morally on a par ought to have made them suspect at the outset.

Secondly, while I am arguing for the permissibility of abortion in some cases, I am not arguing for the right to secure the death of the unborn child. It is easy to confuse these two things in that up to a certain point in the life of the fetus it is not able to survive outside the mother's body; hence removing it from her body guarantees its death. But they are importantly different. I have argued that you are not morally required to spend nine months in bed, sustaining the life of that violinist; but to say this is by no means to say that if, when you unplug yourself, there is a miracle and he survives, you then have a right to turn round and slit his throat. You may detach yourself even if this costs him his life; you have no right to be guaranteed his death, by some other means, if unplugging yourself does not kill him. There are some people who will feel dissatisfied by this feature of my argument. A woman may be utterly devastated by the thought of a child, a bit of herself, put out for adoption and never seen or heard of again. She may therefore want not merely that the child be detached from her, but more, that it die. Some opponents of abortion are inclined to regard this as beneath contempt—thereby showing insensitivity to what is surely a powerful source of despair. All the same, I agree that the desire for the child's death is not one which anybody

may gratify, should it turn out to be possible to detach the child alive.

At this place, however, it should be remembered that we have only been pretending throughout that the fetus is a human being from the moment of conception. A very early abortion is surely not the killing of a person, and so is not dealt with by anything I have said here.

Notes

---

1. Daniel Callahan, *Abortion: Law, Choice and Morality* (New York, 1970), p. 373. This book gives a fascinating survey of the available information on abortion. The Jewish tradition is surveyed in David M. Feldman, *Birth Control in Jewish Law* (New York, 1968), Part 5, the Catholic tradition in John T. Noonan, Jr., "An Almost Absolute Value in History," in *The Morality of Abortion*, ed. John T. Noonan, Jr. (Cambridge, Mass., 1970).

2. The term "direct" in the arguments I refer to is a technical one. Roughly, what is meant by "direct killing" is either killing as an end in itself, or killing as a means to some end, for example, the end of saving someone else's life. See note 5, below, for an example of its use.

3. Cf. *Encyclical Letter of Pope Pius XI on Christian Marriage,* St. Paul Editions (Boston, n.d.), p. 32: "however much we may pity the mother whose health and even life is gravely imperiled in the performance of the duty allotted to her by nature, nevertheless what could ever be a sufficient reason for excusing in any way the direct murder of the innocent? This is precisely what we are dealing with here." Noonan (*The Morality of Abortion,* p. 43) reads this as follows: "What cause can ever avail to excuse in any way the direct killing of the innocent? For it is a question of that."

4. The thesis in (4) is in an interesting way weaker than those in (1), (2), and (3): they rule out abortion even in cases in which both mother *and* child will die if the abortion is not performed. By contrast, one who held the view expressed in (4) could consistently say that one needn't prefer letting two persons die to killing one.

5. Cf. the following passage from Pius XII, *Address to the Italian Catholic Society of Midwives:* "The

baby in the maternal breast has the right to life immediately from God.—Hence there is no man, no human authority, no science, no medical, eugenic, social, economic or moral 'indication' which can establish or grant a valid juridical ground for a direct deliberate disposition of an innocent human life, that is a disposition which looks to its destruction either as an end or as a means to another end perhaps in itself not illicit.—The baby, still not born, is a man in the same degree and for the same reason as the mother" (quoted in Noonan, *The Morality of Abortion*, p. 45).

14. How to Argue About Abortion

John Noonan

John Noonan examines various models and methods used in the debate on abortion, distinguishing those that do not work from those that do. According to Noonan, those that do not work involve (1) fantasized examples, such as Thomson's unconscious violinist; (2) hard cases that are resolved in ways that ignore the child's interests; and (3) spatial metaphors, such as "direct" and "indirect," which obscure the moral distinctions involved. Those that do work are (1) balancing values in a nonquantitative manner; (2) seeing what might be otherwise overlooked; and (3) responding to the full range of human experience.

At the heart of the debate about abortion is the relation of person to person in social contexts. Analogies, metaphors, and methods of debate which do not focus on persons and which do not attend to the central contexts are mischievous. Their use arises from a failure to appreciate the distinctive character of moral argument—its requirement that values be organically related and balanced, its dependence on personal vision, and its rootedness in social experience. I propose here to examine various models and methods used in the debate on abortion distinguishing those such as fantasized situations, hard cases, and linear metaphors, all of which do not work, from the balancing, seeing, and appeal to human experience which I believe to be essential. I shall move from models and metaphors which take the rule against abortion as the expression of a single value to the consideration of ways of argument intended to suggest the variety of

From "Responding to Persons: Methods of Moral Argument in Debate over Abortion," *Theology Digest* (1973), pp. 291–307. Reprinted by permission of *Theology Digest*.

values which have converged in the formulation of the rule. The values embodied in the rule are various because abortion is an aspect of the relation of person to person, and persons are larger than single values; and abortion is an act in a social context which cannot be reduced to a single value. I write as a critic of abortion, with no doubt a sharper eye for the weaknesses of its friends than of its foes, but my chief aim is to suggest what arguments count.

Artificial Cases

One way of reaching the nub of a moral issue is to construct a hypothetical situation endowed with precisely the characteristics you believe are crucial in the real issue you are seeking to resolve. Isolated from the clutter of detail in the real situation, these characteristics point to the proper solution. The risk is that the features you believe crucial you will enlarge to the point of creating a caricature. The pedagogy of your illustration will be blunted by the uneasiness caused by the lack of correspondence between the fantasized situation and the real situation to be judged. Such is the case with recent efforts by philosopher Judith Jarvis Thomson to construct arguments justifying abortion.

Suppose, says Thomson, a violinist whose continued existence depends on acquiring new kidneys. Without the violinist's knowledge—he remains innocent—a healthy person is kidnapped and connected to him so that the violinist now shares the use of healthy kidneys. May the victim of the kidnapping break the connection and thereby kill the violinist? Thomson intuits that the normal judgment will be Yes. The healthy person should not be imposed upon by a lifelong physical connection with the violinist. This construct, Thomson contends, bears upon abortion by establishing that being human does not carry with it a right to life which must be respected by another at the cost of serious inconvenience.

This ingenious attempt to make up a parallel to pregnancy imagines a kidnapping; a serious operation performed on the victim of the kidnapping; and a continuing interference with many of the activities of the victim. It supposes that violinist and victim were unrelated. It supposed nothing by which the victim's initial aversion to his yoke-mate might be mitigated or compensated. It supposes no degree of voluntariness. The similitude to pregnancy is grotesque. It is difficult to think of another age or society in which a caricature of this sort could be seriously put forward as a paradigm illustrating the moral choice to be made by a mother.

While Thomson focuses on this fantasy, she ignores a real case from which American tort law has generalized. On a January night in Minnesota, a cattle buyer, Orlando Depue, asked a family of farmers, the Flateaus, with whom he had dined, if he could remain overnight at their house. The Flateaus refused and, although Depue was sick and had fainted, put him out of the house into the cold night. Imposing liability on the Flateaus for Depue's loss of his frostbitten fingers the court said, "In the case at bar defendants were under no contract obligation to minister to plaintiff in

his distress; but humanity demanded they do so, if they understood and appreciated his condition . . . The law as well as humanity required that he not be exposed in his helpless condition to the merciless elements." Depue was a guest for supper although not a guest after supper. The American Law Institute, generalizing, has said that it makes no difference whether the helpless person is a guest or a trespasser. He has the privilege of staying. His host has the duty not to injure him or put him into an environment where he becomes nonviable. The obligation arises when one person "understands and appreciates" the condition of the other. Although the analogy is not exact, the case seems closer to the mother's situation than the case imagined by Thomson; and the emotional response of the Minnesota judges seems to be a truer reflection of what humanity requires. . . .

Hard Cases and Exceptions

In the presentation of permissive abortion to the American public, major emphasis has been put on situations of great pathos—the child deformed by thalidomide, the child affected by rubella, the child known to suffer from Tay-Sachs disease or Downs syndrome, the raped adolescent, the exhausted mother of small children. These situations are not imagined, and the cases described are not analogies to those where abortion might be sought; they are themselves cases to which abortion is a solution. Who could deny the poignancy of their appeal?

Hard cases make bad law, runs the venerable legal adage, but it seems to be worse law if the distress experienced in situations such as these is not taken into account. If persons are to be given preeminence over abstract principle, should not exceptions for these cases be made in the most rigid rule against abortion? Does not the human experience of such exceptions point to a more sweeping conclusion—the necessity of abandoning any uniform prohibition of abortion, so that all the elements of a particular situation may be weighted by the woman in question and her doctor?

So far, fault can scarcely be found with this method of argumentation, this appeal to common experience. But the cases are oversimplified if focus is directed solely on the parents of a physically defective child or on the mother in the cases of rape or psychic exhaustion. The situations are very hard for the parents or the mother; they are still harder for the fetus who is threatened with death. If the fetus is a person as the opponents of abortion contend, its destruction is not the sparing of suffering by the sacrifice of a principle but by the sacrifice of a life. Emotion is a proper element in moral response, but to the extent that the emotion generated by these cases obscures the claims of the fetus, this kind of argumentation fosters erroneous judgment.

In three of the cases—the child deformed by drugs, disease, or genetic defect—the neglect of the child's point of view seems stained by hypocrisy. Abortion is here justified as putting the child out of the misery of living a less than normal life. The child is not consulted as to the choice. Experience, which teaches that even the most seriously incapacitated prefer living to dying, is ignored. The feelings of the parents are the actual consideration, and these feelings are treated with greater tenderness than the fetal desire to live. The common unwillingness to say frankly that the abortion is sought for the parents' benefit is testimony, unwillingly given, to the intuition that such self-preference by the parents is difficult for society or for the parents themselves to accept.

The other kind of hard case does not mask preference for the parent by a pretense of concern for the fetus. The simplest situation is that of a pregnancy due to rape—in presentations to some legislatures it was usual to add a racist fillip by supposing a white woman and a black rapist—but this gratuitous pandering to bias is not essential. The fetus, unwanted in the most unequivocal way, is analogized to an invader of the mother's body—is it even appropriate to call her a mother when she did nothing to assume the special fiduciary cares of motherhood? If she is prevented from having an abortion, she is being compelled for nine months to be reminded of a traumatic assault. Do not her feelings override the right to life of her unwanted tenant?

Rape arouses fear and a desire for revenge, and reference to rape evokes emotion. The emotion has been enough for the state to take the life of the rapist. Horror of the crime is easily extended to horror of the product, so that the fetal life becomes forfeit too. If horror is overcome, adoption appears to be a more humane solution than abortion. If the rape case is not being used as a stalking horse by proponents of abortion—if there is a desire to deal with it in itself—the solution is to assure the destruction of the sperm in the one to three days elapsing between insemination and impregnation.

Generally, however, the rape case is presented as a way of suggesting a general principle, a principle which could be formulated as follows: Every unintended pregnancy may be interrupted if its continuation will cause emotional distress to the mother. Pregnancies due to bad planning or bad luck are analogized to pregnancies due to rape; they are all involuntary. Indeed many pregnancies can without great difficulty be assimilated to the hard case, for how often do persons undertake an act of sexual intercourse consciously intending that a child be the fruit of that act? Many pregnancies are unspecified by a particular intent, are unplanned, are in this sense involuntary. Many pregnancies become open to termination if only the baby consciously sought has immunity.

This result is unacceptable to those who believe that the fetus is human. It is acceptable to those who do not believe the fetus is human, but to reach it they do not need the argument based on the hard case. The result would follow immediately from the mother's dominion over a portion of her body. Opponents of abortion who out of consideration for the emotional distress caused by rape will grant the rape exception must see that the exception can be generalized to destroy the rule. If, on other grounds they believe the rule good, they must deny the exception which eats it up.

Direct and Indirect

From the paradigmatic arguments, I turn to metaphors and especially those which, based on some spatial image, are misleading. I shall begin with "direct" and "indirect" and their cousins, "affirmative" and "negative." In the abortion argument "direct" and "indirect," "affirmative" and "negative" occur more frequently in these kinds of questions: If one denies that a fetus may be killed directly, but admits that indirect abortion is permissible, is he guilty of inconsistency? If one maintains that there is a negative duty not to kill fetuses, does he thereby commit himself to an affirmative obligation of assuring safe delivery of every fetus? If one agrees that there is no affirmative duty to actualize as many spermatic, ovoid, embryonic, or fetal potentialities as possible, does one thereby concede that it is generally permissible to take steps to destroy fertilized ova? The argumentative implications of these questions can be best unravelled by looking at the force of the metaphors invoked.

"Direct" and "indirect" appeal to our experience of linedrawing and of travel. You reach a place on a piece of paper by drawing a straight or crooked line—the line is direct or indirect. You go to a place without detours or you go in a roundabout fashion—your route is direct or indirect. In each instance, whether your path is direct or indirect your destination is the same. The root experience is that you can reach the same spot in ways distinguished by their immediacy and the amount of ground covered. "Indirectly" says you proceed more circuitously and cover more ground. It does not, however, say anything of the reason why you go circuitously. You may go indirectly because you want to cover more ground or because you want to disguise your destination.

The ambiguity in the reason for indirectness—an ambiguity present in the primary usage of the term—carries over when "indirect" is applied metaphorically to human intentions. There may be a reason for doing something indirectly—you want to achieve another objective besides the indirect action. You may also act indirectly to conceal from another or from yourself what is your true destination. Because of this ambiguity in the reason for indirection, "indirect" is apt to cause confusion when applied in moral analysis.

Defenders of an absolute prohibition of abortion have excepted the removal of a fertilized ovum in an ectopic pregnancy and the removal of a cancerous uterus containing an embryo. They have characterized the abortion involved as "indirect." They have meant that the surgeon's attention is focused on correcting a pathological condition dangerous to the mother and he only performs the operation because there is no alternative way of correcting it. But the physician has to intend to achieve not only the improvement of the mother but the performance of action by which the fertilized ovum becomes nonviable. He necessarily intends to perform an abortion, he necessarily intends to kill. To say that he acts indirectly is to conceal what is being done. It is a confusing and improper use of the metaphor.

A clearer presentation of the cases of the cancerous uterus and the ectopic pregnancy would acknowledge them to be true exceptions to the absolute inviolability of the fetus. Why are they not exceptions which would eat up the rule? It depends on what the rule is considered to be. The principle that can be discerned in them is, whenever the embryo is a danger to the life of the mother, an abortion is permissible. At the level of reason nothing more can be asked of the mother. The exceptions do eat up any rule of preferring the fetus to the mother—any rule of fetus first. They do not destroy the rule that the life of the fetus has precedence over other interests of the mother. The exceptions of the ectopic pregnancy and the cancerous uterus are special cases of the general exception to the rule against killing, which permits one to kill in self-defense. Characterization of this kind of killing as "indirect" does not aid analysis.

It is a basic intuition that one is not responsible for all the consequences of one's acts. By living at all one excludes others from the air one breathes, the food one eats. One cannot foresee all the results which will flow from any given action. It is imperative for moral discourse to be able to distinguish between injury foreseeably inflicted on another, and the harm which one may unknowingly bring about. "Direct" and "indirect" are sometimes used to distinguish the foreseen consequence from the unconsidered or unknown consequence. This usage does not justify terming abortion to save a mother's life "indirect." In the case of terminating the ectopic pregnancy, the cancerous uterus, the life-threatening fetus generally, one considers precisely the consequence, the taking of the fetal life.

Just as one intuits that one is not responsible for all the consequences, so one intuits that one is not called to right all wrongs. No one is bound to the impossible. There is, therefore, an intuitive difference between the duty to refrain from doing harm to anyone and the duty to help everyone in distress. The duty to refrain is possible of fulfillment if it refers only to conscious infliction of harm. The duty to help is impossible if one is going to develop as a human being, getting educated, earning a living, marrying, raising a family, and so forth. The needs of other human beings are subordinated or postponed by everyone to the fulfillment of many of one's own needs, and rightly so. The distinction between affirmative and negative duties, another linear metaphor, rests on this universal experience. The terms do have a basis in moral life. Their usefulness in moral analysis, however, is not great. The crucial distinction is not between negative and affirmative, but between limited and unlimited duty.

It is possible to state the duty not to kill the fetus as the duty to care for the fetus. Opponents of abortion, however, do not commit thereby themselves to the position that all fertilized ova must be born. A pregnant woman may, for example, take the chance of killing the baby by going for a walk or a drive instead of staying safely in bed. She is not responsible for all the consequences of her acts. She is not called to help the fetus in every possible way. The negative duty or the convertible affirmative duty excludes acts which have a high probability of death for the fetus, but not those with a low probability of death. Similarly, one has a duty not to kill one's older children, and a duty to care for them, but no duty to keep them free from all risk of harm. No inconsistency exists in not equating a limited negative duty with an unlimited affirmative duty; no inconsistency exists in rejecting high risk acts and approving low risk acts.

Linedrawing

The prime linear metaphor is, of course, linedrawing. It is late in the history of moral thought for anyone to suppose that an effec-

tive moral retort is, "Yes, but where do you draw the line?" or to make the inference that, because any drawing of a line requires a decision, all linedrawing is arbitrary. One variant or another of these old ploys is, however, frequently used in the present controversy. From living cell to dying corpse a continuum exists. Proponents of abortion are said to be committed to murder, to euthanasia, or, at a minimum, to infanticide. Opponents are alleged to be bound to condemn contraception—after all, spermatazoa are living human cells. Even if contraception is admitted and infanticide rejected, the range of choice is still large enough for the line drawn to be challenged—is it to be at nidation, at formation of the embryo, at quickening, at viability, at birth? Whoever adopts one point is asked why he does not move forward or backward by one stage of development. The difficulty of presenting apodictic reasons for preferring one position is made to serve as proof that the choice may be made as best suits the convenience of an individual or the state.

The metaphor of linedrawing distracts attention from the nature of the moral decision. The metaphor suggests an empty room composed of indistinguishable grey blocks. In whatever way the room is divided, there are grey blocks on either side of the line. Or if the metaphor is taken more mathematically, it suggests a series of points, which, wherever bisected, are fungible with each other. What is obscured in the spatial or mathematical model is the variety of values whose comparison enters into any moral decision. The model appeals chiefly to those novices in moral reasoning who believe that moral judgment is a matter of pursuing a principle to its logical limit. Single-mindedly looking at a single value, they ask, if this is good, why not more of it? In practice, however, no one can be so single-hearted. Insistence of this kind of logical consistency becomes the preserve of fanatics or of controversialists eager to convict their adversaries of inconsistency. If more than one good is sought by a human being, he must bring the goods he seeks into relationship with each other; he must limit one to maintain another; he must mix them.

The process of choosing multiple goods occurs in many particular contexts—in eating, in studying, in painting. No one supposes that those who take the first course must forego dessert, that the election of English means History shall not be studied, that the use of blue excludes red. Linear models for understanding choice in these matters are readily perceived as inappropriate. The commitment to values, the cutting off of values, and the mixing of values accompany each other.

Is, however, the choice of the stage of development which should not be destroyed by abortion a choice requiring the mixing of multiple goods? Is not the linear model appropriate when picking a point on the continuum of life? Are not the moral choices which require commitment and mixing made only after the selection of the stage at which a being becomes a person? To these related questions the answers must all be negative. To recognize a person is a moral decision; it depends on objective data but it also depends on the perceptions and inclinations and ends of the decision makers; it cannot be made without commitment and without consideration of alternative values. Who is a person? This is not a question asked abstractly, in the air, with no purpose in mind. To disguise the personal involvement in the response to personhood is to misconceive the issue of abortion from the start.

Those who identify the rational with the geometrical, the algebraic, the logical may insist that, if the fundamental recognition of personhood depends upon the person who asks, then the arbitrariness of any position on abortion is conceded. If values must be mixed even in identifying the human, who can object to another's mixture? The issue becomes like decisions in eating, studying, and painting, a matter of discretion. A narrow rationalism of this kind uses "taste" as the ultimate epithet for the non-rational. It does not acknowledge that each art has its own rules. It claims for itself alone the honorable term "reason."

As this sort of monopoly has become unacceptable in general philosophy, so it is unnecessary to accept it here. Taste, that is perceptiveness, is basic; and if it cannot be disputed, it can be improved by experience. Enology, painting, or moral reasoning all require basic aptitude, afford wide ranges of options, have limits beyond which a choice can

be counterproductive, and are better done by the experienced than by amateurs. Some persons may lack almost any capacity for undertaking one or another of them. Although all men are moral beings, not all are proficient at moral judgment, so that morality is not a democratic business. Selecting multiple goods, those who are capable of the art perceive, test, mix and judge. The process has little in common with linedrawing. In the case of abortion, it is the contention of its opponents that in such a process the right response to the data is that the fetus is a human being.

Balancing

The process of decisionmaking just described is better caught by the term "balancing." In contrast to linedrawing, balancing is a metaphor helpful in understanding moral judgment. Biologically understood, balancing is the fundamental metaphor for moral reasoning. A biological system is in balance when its parts are in the equilibrium necessary for it to live. To achieve such equilibrium, some parts—the heart, for example—must be preserved at all costs; others may be sacrificed to maintain the whole. Balance in the biological sense does not demand an egalitarian concern for every part, but an ordering and subordination which permit the whole to function. So in moral reasoning the reasoner balances values.

The mistaken common reading of this metaphor is to treat it as equivalent to weighing, so that balancing is understood as an act of quantitative comparison analogous to that performed by an assayer or a butcher. This view tacitly supposes that values are weights which are tangible and commensurate. One puts so many units on one pan of the scales and matches them with so many units on the other to reach a "balanced" judgment. To give a personal example, Daniel Callahan has questioned my position that the value of innocent life cannot be sacrificed to achieve the other values which abortion might secure. The "force of the rule," he writes, "is absolutist, displaying no 'balance' at all." He takes balancing in the sense of weighing and wonders how one value can be so heavy.

That justice often consists in the fair distribution or exchange of goods as in the familiar Aristotelian examples has no doubt worked to confirm a quantitative approach. Scales as the symbol of justice seem to suggest the antiquity of the quantitative meaning of balance. But the original sense of the scales was otherwise. In Egypt where the symbol was first used, a feather, the Egyptian hieroglyphic for truth, turned the balance. As put by David Daube in his illuminating analysis of the ancient symbolism, "The slightest turning of the scales—'but in the estimation of a hair'—will decide the issue, and the choice is between salvation and annihilation." Not a matching of weights, but a response to reality was what justice was seen to require, and what was at stake was not a slight overweighing in one direction or the other, but salvation. Moral choice, generally, has this character of a hair separating good from evil.

A fortiori then, in moral judgment, where more values are in play than in any system of strict law or commutative justice, balancing is a misleading metaphor if it suggests a matching of weights. It is an indispensable metaphor if it stands for the equilibrium of a living organism making the choices necessary for its preservation. A single value cannot be pursued to the point of excluding all other values. This is the caricature of moral argument I have already touched on in connection with the metaphor of linedrawing. But some values are more vital than others, as the heart is more vital to the body than the hand. A balanced moral judgment requires a sense of the limits, interrelations, and priority of values. It is the position of those generally opposed to abortion that a judgment preferring interests less than human life to human life is unbalanced, that a judgment denying a mother's fiduciary responsibility to her child is unbalanced, that a judgment making killing a principal part of the profession of a physician is unbalanced, that a judgment permitting agencies of the state to procure and pay for the destruction of the offspring of the poor or underprivileged is unbalanced. They contend that such judgments expand the right limits of a mother's responsibility for herself, destroy the fiduciary relation which is a central paradigm for the social bond, fail to relate to the physician's

service to life and the state's care for its citizens. At stake in the acceptance of abortion is not a single value, life, against which the suffering of the mother or parents may be balanced. The values to be considered are the child's life, the mother's faithfulness to her dependent, the physician's commitment to preserving life; and in the United States today abortion cannot be discussed without awareness that if law does not prohibit it, the state will fund it, so that the value of the state's abstention from the taking of life is also at issue. The judgment which accepts abortion, it is contended, is unbalanced in subordinating these values to the personal autonomy of the mother and the social interest in population control.

Seeing

The metaphor of balancing points to the process of combining values. But we do not combine values like watercolors. We respond to values situated in subjects. "Balancing" is an inadequate metaphor for moral thinking in leaving out of account the central moral transaction—the response of human beings to other human beings. In making moral judgments we respond to those human beings whom we see.

The metaphor of sight is a way of emphasizing the need for perception, whether by eyes or ears or touch, of those we take as subjects to whom we respond. Seeing in any case is more than the registration of a surface. It is a penetration yielding some sense of the other's structure, so that the experiencing of another is never merely visual or auditory or tactile. We see the features and comprehend the humanity at the same time. Look at the fetus, say the anti-abortionists, and you will see humanity. How long, they ask, can a man turn his head and pretend that he just doesn't see?

An accusation of blindness, however, does not seem to advance moral argument. A claim to see where others do not see is a usual claim of charlatans. "Illumination" or "enlightenment" appear to transcend experience and make moral disputation impossible. "Visionary" is often properly a term of disparagement. Is not an appeal to sight the end of rational debate?

In morals, as in epistemology, there is nonetheless no substitute for perception. Are animals within the range of beings with a right to life, and babies not, as Michael Tooley has recently suggested? Should trees be persons, as Christopher Stone has recently maintained? Questions of this kind are fundamentally frivolous for they point to the possibility of moral argument while attempting to deny the foundation of moral argument, our ability to recognize human persons. If a person could in no way perceive another person to be like himself, he would be incapable of moral response. If a person cannot perceive a cat or a tree as different from himself, he cuts off the possibility of argument. Debate should not end with pointing, but it must begin there.

Is there a contradiction in the opponents of abortion appealing to perception when fetuses are normally invisible? Should one not hold that until beings are seen they have not entered the ranks of society? Falling below the threshold of sight, do not fetuses fall below the threshold of humanity? If the central moral transaction is response to the other person, are not fetuses peculiarly weak subjects to elicit our response? These questions pinpoint the principal task of the defenders of the fetus—to make the fetus visible. The task is different only in degree from that assumed by defenders of other persons who have been or are "overlooked." For centuries, color acted as a psychological block to perception, and the blindness induced by color provided a sturdy basis for discrimination. Minorities of various kinds exist today who are "invisible" and therefore unlikely to be "heard" in the democratic process. Persons literally out of sight of society in prisons and mental institutions are often not "recognized" as fellow humans by the world with which they have "lost touch." In each of these instances those who seek to vindicate the rights of the unseen must begin by calling attention to their existence. "Look" is the exhortation they address to the callous and the negligent.

Perception of fetuses is possible with not substantially greater effort than that required to pierce the physical or psychological barriers to recognizing other human beings. The main difficulty is everyone's reluctance to accept the extra burdens of care imposed by an expansion of the numbers in whom humanity is recognized. It is generally more convenient to have to consider only one's kin, one's peers, one's country, one's race. Seeing requires personal attention and personal response. The emotion generated by identification with a human form is necessary to overcome the inertia which is protected by a vision restricted to a convenient group. If one is willing to undertake the risk that more will be required in one's action, fetuses may be seen in multiple ways—circumstantially, by the observation of a pregnant woman; photographically, by pictures of life in the womb; scientifically, in accounts written by investigators of prenatal life and child psychologists; visually, by observing a blood transfusion or an abortion while the fetus is alive or by examination of a fetal corpse after death. The proponent of abortion is invited to consider the organism kicking the mother, swimming peacefully in amniotic fluid, responding to the prick of an instrument, being extracted from the womb, sleeping in death. Is the kicker or swimmer similar to him or to her? Is the response to pain like his or hers? Will his or her own face look much different in death?

Response

Response to the fetus begins with grasp of the data which yield the fetus' structure. That structure is not merely anatomical form; it is dynamic—we apprehend the fetus' origin and end. It is this apprehension which makes response to the nameless fetus different from the conscious analogizing that goes on when we name a cat. Seeing, we are linked to the being in the womb by more than an inventory of shared physical characteristics and by more than a number of made-up psychological characteristics. The weakness of the being as potential recalls our own potential state, the helplessness of the being evokes the human condition of contingency. We meet another human subject.

Seeing is impossible apart from experience, but experience is the most imprecise of terms. What kind of experience counts, and whose? There are experiences which only women and usually only those within the ages of 14 to 46 who are fertile can have: conceiving a child, carrying a child, having an abortion, being denied an abortion, giving birth. There are experiences only a fetus can have: being carried, being aborted, being born. There is the experience of obstetricians who regularly deliver children and occasionally abort them; there is the differently-textured experience of the professional abortionist. There is the experience of nurses who prepare the mother for abortion, care for her after the abortion, and dispose of the aborted fetus. There is the experience of physicians, social workers, and ministers, who advise a woman to have an abortion or not to have one. There is the experience of those who enforce a law against abortion, and those who stealthily or openly, for profit or for conscience's sake, defy it. There is the experience of those who have sexual intercourse knowing that abortion is or is not a remedy if an accidental pregnancy should result. There is the experience of society at large of a pattern of uncontrolled abortion or of its regulation.

Some arguments are unduly exclusivist in the experience they will admit. Those who suggest that abortion is peculiarly a matter for women disqualify men because the unique experience of pregnancy is beyond their achievement. Yet such champions of abortion do not regularly disqualify sterile women whose experience of pregnancy must be as vicarious as a man's. Tertullian taught that only those who have known motherhood themselves have a right to speak from experience on the choices presented by abortion. Yet even Tertullian did not go so far as to say that only mothers who had both given birth and had had abortions were qualified to speak. Efforts of this sort to restrict those who are competent rest on a confusion between the relevant and the personal. You do not have to be a judge to know that bribery is evil or a slave to know that slavery is wrong. Vicarious experience, in this as in other moral matters, is a proper basis for judgment.

Vicarious experience appears strained to the outer limit when one is asked to consider the experience of the fetus. No one remembers being born, no one knows what it is like to die. Empathy may, however, supply for memory, as it does in other instances when we refer to the experience of infants who cannot speak or to the experience of death by those who cannot speak again. The experience of the fetus is no more beyond our knowledge than the experience of the baby and the experience of dying.

Participation in an abortion is another sort of experience relevant to moral judgment. Generals are not thought of as the best judges of the morality of war, nor is their experience thought to be unaffected by their profession, but they should be heard, when the permissibility of war is urged. Obstetricians are in an analogous position, their testimony subject to a discount. The testimony of professional abortionists is also relevant, although subject to an even greater discount. Nurses are normally more disinterested witnesses. They speak as ones who have empathized with the female patient, disposed of the fetal remains, and, like the Red Cross in wartime, have known what the action meant by seeing the immediate consequences.

The experience of individuals becomes a datum of argument through autobiography and testimony, inference and empathy. The experience of a society has to be captured by the effort of sociologists and novelists, historians and lawyers, psychologists and moralists; and it is strongly affected by the prism of the medium used. Typically the proponents of abortion have put emphasis on quantitative evidence—for example, on the number of abortions performed in the United States or in the world at large. The assumption underlying this appeal to experience is that what is done by a great many persons cannot be bad, is indeed normal. This assumption, often employed when sexual behavior is studied, is rarely favored when racial discrimination or war are considered. It is a species of natural law, identifying the usual with the natural. The experience appealed to counts as argument only for those who accept this identification and consider the usual the good.

Psychological evidence has been called upon by the opponents of abortion. Trauma and guilt have been found associated with the election of abortion. The inference is made that abortion is the cause of this unhappiness. As in many arguments based on social consequences, however, the difficulty is to isolate the cause. Do persons undergoing abortion have character predispositions which would in any event manifest themselves in psychic disturbance? Do they react as they do because of social conditioning which could be changed to encourage a positive attitude to abortion? Is the act of abortion at the root of their problems or the way in which the process is carried out? None of these questions is settled; the evidence is most likely to be convincing to those already inclined to believe that abortion is an evil.

Another kind of experience is that embedded in law. In Roman law where children generally had little status independent of their parents, the fetus was "a portion of the mother or her viscera." This view persisted in nineteenth century American tort law, Justice Holmes in a leading case describing the fetus as "a part of the body of the mother." In recent years, however, the tort cases have asked, in Justice Bok's phrase, if the fetus is a person; and many courts have replied affirmatively. The change, a striking revolution in torts law, came from the courts incorporating into their thought new biological data on the fetus as a living organism. Evidence on how the fetus is now perceived is also provided by another kind of case where abortion itself is not involved—the interpretation in wills and trusts of gifts to "children" or "issue." In these cases a basic question is, "What is the common understanding of people when they speak of children?" The answer, given repeatedly by American courts, is that "the average testator" speaking of children means to include a being who has been conceived but not born. Free from the distorting pressures of the conflict over abortion, this evidence of the common understanding suggests that social experience has found the fetus to be within the family of man.

The most powerful expression of common experience is that given by art and literature. Birth has almost everywhere been celebrated in painting. The Nativity has been a symbol of gladness not only because of its sacral signifi-

cance, but because of its human meaning—"joy that a man is born into the world." Abortion, in contrast, has rarely been the subject of art. Unlike other forms of death, abortion has not been seen by painters as a release, a sacrifice, or a victory. Characteristically it has stood for sterility, futility, and absurdity. Consider, for example, Orozco's mural, "Gods of the Modern World" in the Baker Library at Dartmouth College. Academia is savagely satirized by portraying professors as impotent attendants in an operating room in which truth is stillborn. Bottled fetuses in the foreground attest the professors' habitual failure. The entire force of the criticism of academic achievement comes from the painter's knowledge that everyone will recognize abortion as a grave defeat and the bottling of dead fetuses as a travesty of healthy birth. Whoever sees such a painting sees how mankind has commonly experienced abortion.

In contemporary American literature, John Updike's *Couples* comments directly upon abortion, using it at a crucial turn as both event and symbol. Piet Hanema, married to Angela, has promiscuously pursued other married women, among them Foxy Whitman, who is now pregnant by him. They have this exchange:

> All I know is what I honestly want. I want this damn thing to stop growing inside me.
>   Don't cry.
>   Nature is so stupid. It has all my maternal glands working, do you know what that means, Piet? You know what the great thing about being pregnant I found out was? It's something I just couldn't have imagined. You're never alone. When you have a baby inside you you are not alone. It's a person.

To procure the abortion it becomes necessary for Piet to surrender his own wife Angela to Freddy who has access to the abortionist. Embarked upon his course Piet does not stop at this act which destroys his own marriage irretrievably. Foxy's feelings at the time of the abortion are then described through Piet:

Not until days later, after Foxy had survived the forty-eight hours alone in the house with Toby and the test of Ken's return from Chicago, did Piet learn, not from Freddy but from her as told by Freddy, that at the moment of anesthesia she had panicked; she had tried to strike the Negress pressing the sweet, sweet mask to her face and through the first waves of ether had continued to cry that she should go home, that she was supposed to have this baby, that the child's father was coming to smash the door down with a hammer and would stop them.

Updike's only comment as an author is given as Piet then goes to Foxy's house: "Death, once invited in, leaves his muddy bootprints everywhere." The elements of the experience of abortion are here: the hatred of the depersonalized burden growing, willy-nilly, in the womb; the sense of a baby, a person, one's own child; the desperate desire to be rid of the burden extinguishing all other considerations; the ineffectual hope of delivery the moment before the child's death. A mask covers the human face of the mother. Symbolically the abortion seals a course of infidelity. Conclusively it becomes death personified. . . .

---

15. On the Moral and Legal Status of Abortion

Mary Anne Warren

Mary Anne Warren argues that if the fetus is assumed to be a person, there are a wide range of cases in which abortion cannot be defended. To provide such a defense, Warren sets out five criteria for being a person she feels should be acceptable to antiabortionists and proabortionists alike. Appealing to these criteria, she contends that fetuses, even when their potentiality is taken into account, do not sufficiently resemble persons to have a significant right to life.

In a "Postscript" to her article, she defends her view against the objection that it would justify infanticide. Although by her criteria newborn infants would not have a significant right to life, she claims that infanticide would still not be permissible, so long as there are people willing to care and provide for the well-being of such infants.

We will be concerned with both the moral status of abortion, which for our purposes we may define as the act which a woman performs in voluntarily terminating, or allowing another person to terminate, her pregnancy, and the legal status which is appropriate for this act. I will argue that, while it is not possible to produce a satisfactory defense of a woman's right to obtain an abortion without showing that a fetus is not a human being, in the morally

From "On the Moral and Legal Status of Abortion." Copyright 1973 The Monist, LaSalle, Illinois. Reprinted from vol. 57, no. 4, Oct. 1973 by permission; and "Postscript on Infanticide," in Today's Moral Problems, edited by Richard Wasserstrom (1979), pp. 135–136. Reprinted by permission of the author and the editor.

relevant sense of that term, we ought not to conclude that the difficulties involved in determining whether or not a fetus is human make it impossible to produce any satisfactory solution to the problem of the moral status of abortion. For it is possible to show that, on the basis of intuitions which we may expect even the opponents of abortion to share, a fetus is not a person, and hence not the sort of entity to which it is proper to ascribe full moral rights.

Of course, while some philosophers would deny the possibility of any such proof,[1] others will deny that there is any need for it, since the moral permissibility of abortion appears to them to be too obvious to require proof. But the inadequacy of this attitude should be evident from the fact that both the friends and the foes of abortion consider their position to be morally self-evident. Because proabortionists have never adequately come to grips with the conceptual issues surrounding abortion, most, if not all, of the arguments which they advance in opposition to laws restricting access to abortion fail to refute or even weaken the traditional antiabortion argument, i.e., that a fetus is a human being, and therefore abortion is murder.

These arguments are typically of one of two sorts. Either they point to the terrible side effects of the restrictive laws, e.g., the deaths due to illegal abortions, and the fact that it is poor women who suffer the most as a result of these laws, or else they state that to deny a woman access to abortion is to deprive her of her right to control her own body. Unfortunately, however, the fact that restricting access to abortion has tragic side effects does not, in itself, show that the restrictions are unjustified, since murder is wrong regardless of the consequences of prohibiting it; and the appeal to the right to control one's body, which is generally construed as a property right, is at best a rather feeble argument for the permissibility of abortion. Mere ownership does not give me the right to kill innocent people whom I find on my property, and indeed I am apt to be held responsible if such people injure themselves while on my property. It is equally unclear that I have any moral right to expel an innocent person from my property when I know that doing so will result in his death.

Furthermore, it is probably inappropriate to describe a woman's body as her property, since it seems natural to hold that a person is something distinct from her property, but not from her body. Even those who would object to the identification of a person with his body, or with the conjunction of his body and his mind, must admit that it would be very odd to describe, say, breaking a leg, as damaging one's property, and much more appropriate to describe it as injuring one*self*. Thus it is probably a mistake to argue that the right to obtain an abortion is in any way derived from the right to own and regulate property.

But however we wish to construe the right

to abortion, we cannot hope to convince those who consider abortion a form of murder of the existence of any such right unless we are able to produce a clear and convincing refutation of the traditional antiabortion argument, and this has not, to my knowledge, been done. With respect to the two most vital issues which that argument involves, i.e., the humanity of the fetus and its implication for the moral status of abortion, confusion has prevailed on both sides of the dispute.

Thus, both proabortionists and antiabortionists have tended to abstract the question of whether abortion is wrong to that of whether it is wrong to destroy a fetus, just as though the rights of another person were not necessarily involved. This mistaken abstraction has led to the almost universal assumption that if a fetus is a human being, with a right to life, then it follows immediately that abortion is wrong (except perhaps when necessary to save the woman's life), and that it ought to be prohibited. It has also been generally assumed that unless the question about the status of the fetus is answered, the moral status of abortion cannot possibly be determined. . . . John Noonan is correct in saying that "the fundamental question in the long history of abortion is, How do you determine the humanity of a being?"[2] He summarizes his own antiabortion argument, which is a version of the official position of the Catholic Church, as follows:

> . . . it is wrong to kill humans, however poor, weak, defenseless, and lacking in opportunity to develop their potential they may be. It is therefore morally wrong to kill Biafrans. Similarly, it is morally wrong to kill embryos.[3]

Noonan bases his claim that fetuses are human upon what he calls the theologians' criterion of humanity: that whoever is conceived of human beings is human. But although he argues at length for the appropriateness of this criterion, he never questions the assumption that if a fetus is human then abortion is wrong for exactly the same reason that murder is wrong.

Judith Thomson is, in fact, the only writer I am aware of who has seriously questioned this assumption; she has argued that, even if we grant the antiabortionist his claim that a fetus is a human being, with the same right to life as any other human being, we can still demonstrate that, in at least some and perhaps most cases, a woman is under no moral obligation to complete an unwanted pregnancy.[4] Her argument is worth examining, since if it holds up it may enable us to establish the moral permissibility of abortion without becoming involved in problems about what entitles an entity to be considered human, and accorded full moral rights. To be able to do this would be a great gain in the power and simplicity of the proabortion position, since, although I will argue that these problems can be solved at least as decisively as can any other moral problem, we should certainly be pleased to be able to avoid having to solve them as part of the justification of abortion.

On the other hand, even if Thomson's argument does not hold up, her insight, i.e., that it requires *argument* to show that if fetuses are human then abortion is properly classified as murder, is an extremely valuable one. The assumption she attacks is particularly invidious, for it amounts to the decision that it is appropriate, in deciding the moral status of abortion, to leave the rights of the pregnant woman out of consideration entirely, except possibly when her life is threatened. Obviously, this will not do; determining what moral rights, if any, a fetus possesses is only the first step in determining the moral status of abortion. Step two, which is at least equally essential, is finding a just solution to the conflict between whatever rights the fetus may have, and the rights of the woman who is unwillingly pregnant. While the historical error has been to pay far too little attention to the second step, Ms. Thomson's suggestion is that if we look at the second step first we may find that a woman has a right to obtain an abortion *regardless* of what rights the fetus has.

Our own inquiry will also have two stages. In Section I, we will consider whether or not it is possible to establish that abortion is morally permissible even on the assumption that a fetus is an entity with a full-fledged right to life. I will argue that in fact this cannot be established, at least not with the conclusiveness which is essential to our hopes of convincing those who are skeptical about the morality of

abortion, and that we therefore cannot avoid dealing with the question of whether or not a fetus really does have the same right to life as a (more fully developed) human being.

In Section II, I will propose an answer to this question, namely, that a fetus cannot be considered a member of the moral community, the set of beings with full and equal moral rights, for the simple reason that it is not a person, and that it is personhood, and not genetic humanity, i.e., humanity as defined by Noonan, which is the basis for membership in this community. I will argue that a fetus, whatever its stage of development, satisfies none of the basic criteria of personhood, and is not even enough *like* a person to be accorded even some of the same rights on the basis of this resemblance. Nor, as we will see, is a fetus's *potential* personhood a threat to the morality of abortion, since, whatever the rights of potential people may be, they are invariably overridden in any conflict with the moral rights of actual people.

I

We turn now to Professor Thomson's case for the claim that even if a fetus has full moral rights, abortion is still morally permissible, at least sometimes, and for some reasons other than to save the woman's life. Her argument is based upon a clever, but I think faulty, analogy. She asks us to picture ourselves waking up one day, in bed with a famous violinist. Imagine that you have been kidnapped, and your bloodstream hooked up to that of the violinist, who happens to have an ailment which will certainly kill him unless he is permitted to share your kidneys for a period of nine months. No one else can save him, since you alone have the right type of blood. He will be unconscious all that time, and you will have to stay in bed with him, but after the nine months are over he may be unplugged, completely cured, that is provided that you have cooperated.

Now then, she continues, what are your obligations in this situation? The antiabortionist, if he is consistent, will have to say that you are obligated to stay in bed with the violinist: for all people have a right to life, and violinists are people, and therefore it would be murder for you to disconnect yourself from him and let him die. But this is outrageous, and so there must be something wrong with the same argument when it is applied to abortion. It would certainly be commendable of you to agree to save the violinist, but it is absurd to suggest that your refusal to do so would be murder. His right to life does not obligate you to do whatever is required to keep him alive; nor does it justify anyone else in forcing you to do so. A law which required you to stay in bed with the violinist would clearly be an unjust law, since it is no proper function of the law to force unwilling people to make huge sacrifices for the sake of other people toward whom they have no such prior obligation.

Thomson concludes that, if this analogy is an apt one, then we can grant the anti-abortionist his claim that a fetus is a human being, and still hold that it is at least sometimes the case that a pregnant woman has the right to refuse to be a Good Samaritan towards the fetus, i.e., to obtain an abortion. For there is a great gap between the claim that x has a right to life, and the claim that y is obligated to do whatever is necessary to keep x alive, let alone that he ought to be forced to do so. It is y's duty to keep x alive only if he has somehow contracted a *special* obligation to do so; and a woman who is unwillingly pregnant, e.g., who was raped, has done nothing which obligates her to make the enormous sacrifice which is necessary to preserve the conceptus.

This argument is initially quite plausible, and in the extreme case of pregnancy due to rape is probably conclusive. Difficulties arise, however, when we try to specify more exactly the range of cases in which abortion is clearly justifiable even on the assumption that the fetus is human. Professor Thomson considers it a virtue of her argument that it does not enable us to conclude that abortion is *always* permissible. It would, she says, be "indecent" for a woman in her seventh month to obtain an abortion just to avoid having to postpone a trip to Europe. On the other hand, her argument enables us to see that "a sick and desperately frightened schoolgirl pregnant due to rape may *of course* choose abortion, and that

any law which rules this out is an insane law" (p. 65). So far, so good; but what are we to say about the woman who becomes pregnant not through rape but as a result of her own carelessness, or because of contraceptive failure, or who gets pregnant intentionally and then changes her mind about wanting a child? With respect to such cases, the violinist analogy is of much less use to the defender of the woman's right to obtain an abortion.

Indeed, the choice of a pregnancy due to rape, as an example of a case in which abortion is permissible even if a fetus is considered a human being, is extremely significant; for it is only in the case of pregnancy due to rape that the woman's situation is adequately analogous to the violinist case for our intuitions about the latter to transfer convincingly. The crucial difference between a pregnancy due to rape and the *normal* case of an unwanted pregnancy is that in the normal case we cannot claim that the woman is in no way responsible for her predicament; she could have remained chaste, or taken her pills more faithfully, or abstained on dangerous days, and so on. If, on the other hand, you are kidnapped by strangers, and hooked up to a strange violinist, then you are free of any shred of responsibility for the situation, on the basis of which it could be argued that you are obligated to keep the violinist alive. Only when her pregnancy is due to rape is a woman clearly just as nonresponsible.[5]

Consequently, there is room for the anti-abortionist to argue that in the normal case of unwanted pregnancy a woman has, by her own actions, assumed responsibility for the fetus. For if x behaves in a way which he could have avoided, and which he knows involves, let us say, a 1 percent chance of bringing into existence a human being, with a right to life, and does so knowing that if this should happen then that human being will perish unless x does certain things to keep him alive, then it is by no means clear that when it does happen x is free of any obligation to what he knew in advance would be required to keep that human being alive.

The plausibility of such an argument is enough to show that the Thomson analogy can provide a clear and persuasive defense of a woman's right to obtain an abortion only with respect to those cases in which the woman is in no way responsible for her pregnancy, e.g., where it is due to rape. In all other cases, we would almost certainly conclude that it was necessary to look carefully at the particular circumstances in order to determine the extent of the woman's responsibility, and hence the extent of her obligation. This is an extremely unsatisfactory outcome, from the viewpoint of the opponents of restrictive abortion laws, most of whom are convinced that a woman has a right to obtain an abortion regardless of how and why she got pregnant.

Of course a supporter of the violinist analogy might point out that it is absurd to suggest that forgetting her pill one day might be sufficient to obligate a woman to complete an unwanted pregnancy. And indeed it *is* absurd to suggest this. As we will see, the moral right to obtain an abortion is not in the least dependent upon the extent to which the woman is responsible for her pregnancy. But unfortunately, once we allow the assumption that a fetus has full moral rights, we cannot avoid taking this absurd suggestion seriously. Perhaps we can make this point more clear by altering the violinist story just enough to make it more analogous to a normal unwanted pregnancy and less to a pregnancy due to rape, and then seeing whether it is still obvious that you are not obligated to stay in bed with the fellow.

Suppose, then, that violinists are peculiarly prone to the sort of illness the only cure for which is the use of someone else's bloodstream for nine months, and that because of this there has been formed a society of music lovers who agree that whenever a violinist is stricken they will draw lots and the loser will, by some means, be made the one and only person capable of saving him. Now then, would you be obligated to cooperate in curing the violinist if you had voluntarily joined this society, knowing the possible consequences, and then your name had been drawn and you had been kidnapped? Admittedly, you did not promise ahead of time that you would, but you did deliberately place yourself in a position in which it might happen that a human life would be lost if you did not. Surely this is at least a prima facie reason for supposing that you have an obligation to stay in bed with the violinist. Suppose that you had gotten your name drawn deliberately; surely *that* would be quite a strong reason for thinking that you had such an obligation.

It might be suggested that there is one important disanalogy between the modified violinist case and the case of an unwanted pregnancy, which makes the woman's responsibility significantly less, namely, the fact that the fetus *comes into existence* as the result of the woman's actions. This fact might give her a right to refuse to keep it alive, whereas she would not have had this right had it existed previously, independently, and then as a result of her actions become dependent upon her for its survival.

My own intuition, however, is that x has no more right to bring into existence, either deliberately or as a foreseeable result of actions he could have avoided, a being with full moral rights (y), and then refuse to do what he knew beforehand would be required to keep that being alive, than he has to enter into an agreement with an existing person, whereby he may be called upon to save that person's life, and then refuse to do so when so called upon. Thus, x's responsibility for y's existence does not seem to lessen his obligation to keep y alive, if he is also responsible for y's being in a situation in which only he can save him.

Whether or not this intuition is entirely correct, it brings us back once again to the conclusion that once we allow the assumption that a fetus has full moral rights it becomes an extremely complex and difficult question whether and when abortion is justifiable. Thus the Thomson analogy cannot help us produce a clear and persuasive proof of the moral permissibility of abortion. Nor will the opponents of the restrictive laws thank us for anything less; for their conviction (for the most part) is that abortion is obviously *not* a morally serious and extremely unfortunate, even though sometimes justified act, comparable to killing in self-defense or to letting the violinist die, but rather is closer to being a morally neutral act, like cutting one's hair.

The basis of this conviction, I believe, is the realization that a fetus is not a person, and thus does not have a full-fledged right to life. Perhaps the reason why this claim has been so inadequately defended is that it seems self-evident to those who accept it. And so it is, insofar as it follows from what I take to be perfectly obvious claims about the nature of personhood, and about the proper grounds for ascribing moral rights, claims which ought, indeed, to be obvious to both the friends and foes of abortion. Nevertheless, it is worth examining these claims, and showing how they demonstrate the moral innocuousness of abortion, since this apparently has not been adequately done before.

II

The question which we must answer in order to produce a satisfactory solution to the problem of the moral status of abortion is this: How are we to define the moral community, the set of beings with full and equal moral rights, such that we can decide whether a human fetus is a member of this community or not? What sort of entity, exactly, has the inalienable rights to life, liberty, and the pursuit of happiness? Jefferson attributed these rights to all *men*, and it may or may not be fair to suggest that he intended to attribute them *only* to men. Perhaps he ought to have attributed them to all human beings. If so, then we arrive, first, at Noonan's problem of defining what makes a being human, and, second, at the equally vital question which Noonan does not consider, namely, What reason is there for identifying the moral community with the set of all human beings, in whatever way we have chosen to define that term?

1. On the Definition of 'Human'

One reason why this vital second question is so frequently overlooked in the debate over the moral status of abortion is that the term 'human' has two distinct, but not often distinguished, senses. This fact results in a slide of meaning, which serves to conceal the fallaciousness of the traditional argument that since (1) it is wrong to kill innocent human beings, and (2) fetuses are innocent human beings, then (3) it is wrong to kill fetuses. For if

'human' is used in the same sense in both (1) and (2) then, whichever of the two senses is meant, one of these premises is question-begging. And if it is used in two different senses then of course the conclusion doesn't follow.

Thus, (1) is a self-evident moral truth,[6] and avoids begging the question about abortion, only if 'human being' is used to mean something like "a full-fledged member of the moral community." (It may or may not also be meant to refer exclusively to members of the species *Homo sapiens*.) *We may call this the moral* sense of 'human'. It is not to be confused with what we will call the *genetic* sense, i.e., the sense in which *any* member of the species is a human being, and no member of any other species could be. If (1) is acceptable only if the moral sense is intended, (2) is non-question-begging only if what is intended is the genetic sense.

In "Deciding Who Is Human," Noonan argues for the classification of fetuses with human beings by pointing to the presence of the full genetic code, and the potential capacity for rational thought (p. 135). It is clear that what he needs to show, for his version of the traditional argument to be valid, is that fetuses are human in the moral sense, the sense in which it is analytically true that all human beings have full moral rights. But, in the absence of any argument showing that whatever is genetically human is also morally human, and he gives none, nothing more than genetic humanity can be demonstrated by the presence of the human genetic code. And, as we will see, the *potential* capacity for rational thought can at most show that an entity has the potential for *becoming* human in the moral sense.

2. Defining the Moral Community

Can it be established that genetic humanity is sufficient for moral humanity? I think that there are very good reasons for not defining the moral community in this way. I would like to suggest an alternative way of defining the moral community, which I will argue for only to the extent of explaining why it is, or should be, self-evident. The suggestion is simply that the moral community consists of all and only *people*, rather than all and only human beings;[7] and probably the best way of demonstrating its self-evidence is by considering the concept of personhood, to see what sorts of entity are and are not persons, and what the decision that a being is or is not a person implies about its moral rights.

What characteristics entitle an entity to be considered a person? This is obviously not the place to attempt a complete analysis of the concept of personhood, but we do not need such a fully adequate analysis just to determine whether and why a fetus is or isn't a person. All we need is a rough and approximate list of the most basic criteria of personhood, and some idea of which, or how many, of these an entity must satisfy in order to properly be considered a person.

In searching for such criteria, it is useful to look beyond the set of people with whom we are acquainted, and ask how we would decide whether a totally alien being was a person or not. (For we have no right to assume that genetic humanity is necessary for personhood.) Imagine a space traveler who lands on an unknown planet and encounters a race of beings utterly unlike any he has ever seen or heard of. If he wants to be sure of behaving morally toward these beings, he has to somehow decide whether they are people, and hence have full moral rights, or whether they are the sort of thing which he need not feel guilty about treating as, for example, a source of food.

How should he go about making this decision? If he has some anthropological background, he might look for such things as religion, art, and the manufacturing of tools, weapons, or shelters, since these factors have been used to distinguish our human from our prehuman ancestors, in what seems to be closer to the moral than the genetic sense of 'human'. And no doubt he would be right to consider the presence of such factors as good evidence that the alien beings were people, and morally human. It would, however, be overly anthropocentric of him to take the absence of these things as adequate evidence that they were not, since we can imagine people who have progressed beyond, or evolved without ever developing, these cultural characteristics.

I suggest that the traits which are most central to the concept of personhood, or humanity in the moral sense, are, very roughly, the following:

1. consciousness (of objects and events external and/or internal to the being), and in particular the capacity to feel pain;
2. reasoning (the *developed* capacity to solve new and relatively complex problems);
3. self-motivated activity (activity which is relatively independent of either genetic or direct external control);
4. the capacity to communicate, by whatever means, messages of an indefinite variety of types, that is, not just with an indefinite number of possible contents, but on indefinitely many possible topics;
5. the presence of self-concepts, and self-awareness, either individual or racial, or both.

Admittedly, there are apt to be a great many problems involved in formulating precise definitions of these criteria, let alone in developing universally valid behavioral criteria for deciding when they apply. But I will assume that both we and our explorer know approximately what (1)–(5) mean, and that he is also able to determine whether or not they apply. How, then, should he use his findings to decide whether or not the alien beings are people? We needn't suppose that an entity must have *all* of these attributes to be properly considered a person; (1) and (2) alone may well be sufficient for personhood, and quite probably (1)–(3) are sufficient. Neither do we need to insist that any one of these criteria is *necessary* for personhood, although once again (1) and (2) look like fairly good candidates for necessary conditions, as does (3), if 'activity' is construed so as to include the activity of reasoning.

All we need to claim, to demonstrate that a fetus is not a person, is that any being which satisfies *none* of (1)–(5) is certainly not a person. I consider this claim to be so obvious that I think anyone who denied it, and claimed that a being which satisfied none of (1)–(5) was a person all the same, would thereby demonstrate that he had no notion at all of what a person is—perhaps because he had confused the concept of a person with that of genetic humanity. If the opponents of abortion were to deny the appropriateness of these five criteria, I do not know what further arguments would convince them. We would probably have to admit that our conceptual schemes were indeed irreconcilably different, and that our dispute could not be settled objectively.

I do not expect this to happen, however, since I think that the concept of a person is one which is very nearly universal (to people), and that it is common to both proabortionists and antiabortionists, even though neither group has fully realized the relevance of this concept to the resolution of their dispute. Furthermore, I think that on reflection even the antiabortionists ought to agree not only that (1)–(5) are central to the concept of personhood, but also that it is a part of this concept that all and only people have full moral rights. The concept of a person is in part a moral concept; once we have admitted that x is a person we have recognized, even if we have not agreed to respect, x's right to be treated as a member of the moral community. It is true that the claim that x is a *human being* is more commonly voiced as part of an appeal to treat x decently than is the claim that x is a person, but this is either because 'human being' is here used in the sense which implies personhood, or because the genetic and moral senses of 'human' have been confused.

Now if (1)–(5) are indeed the primary criteria of personhood, then it is clear that genetic humanity is neither necessary nor sufficient for establishing that an entity is a person. Some human beings are not people, and there may well be people who are not human beings. A man or woman whose consciousness has been permanently obliterated but who remains alive is a human being which is no longer a person; defective human beings, with no appreciable mental capacity, are not and presumably never will be people; and a fetus is a human being which is not yet a person, and which therefore cannot coherently be said to have full moral rights. Citizens of the next century should be prepared to recognize highly advanced, self-aware robots or computers, should such be developed, and intelligent inhabitants of other worlds, should such be found, as people in the fullest sense, and to

respect their moral rights. But to ascribe full moral rights to an entity which is not a person is as absurd as to ascribe moral obligations and responsibilities to such an entity.

3. Fetal Development and the Right to Life

Two problems arise in the application of these suggestions for the definition of the moral community to the determination of the precise moral status of a human fetus. Given that the paradigm example of a person is a normal adult human being, then (1) How like this paradigm, in particular how far advanced since conception, does a human being need to be before it begins to have a right to life by virtue, not of being fully a person as of yet, but of being *like* a person? and (2) To what extent, if any, does the fact that a fetus has the *potential* for becoming a person endow it with some of the same rights? Each of these questions requires some comment.

In answering the first question, we need not attempt a detailed consideration of the moral rights of organisms which are not developed enough, aware enough, intelligent enough, etc., to be considered people, but which resemble people in some respects. It does seem reasonable to suggest that the more like a person, in the relevant respects, a being is, the stronger is the case for regarding it as having a right to life, and indeed the stronger its right to life is. Thus we ought to take seriously the suggestion that, insofar as "the human individual develops biologically in a continuous fashion . . . the rights of a human person might develop in the same way."[8] But we must keep in mind that the attributes which are relevant in determining whether or not an entity is enough like a person to be regarded as having some of the same moral rights are no different from those which are relevant to determining whether or not it is fully a person—i.e., are no different from (1)–(5)—and that being genetically human, or having recognizably human facial and other physical features, or detectable brain activity, or the capacity to survive outside the uterus, are simply not among these relevant attributes.

Thus it is clear that even though a seven- or eight-month fetus has features which make it apt to arouse in us almost the same powerful protective instinct as is commonly aroused by a small infant, nevertheless it is not significantly more personlike than is a very small embryo. It is *somewhat* more personlike; it can apparently feel and respond to pain, and it may even have a rudimentary form of consciousness, insofar as its brain is quite active. Nevertheless, it seems safe to say that it is not fully conscious, in the way that an infant of a few months is, and that it cannot reason, or communicate messages of indefinitely many sorts, does not engage in self-motivated activity, and has no self-awareness. Thus, in the *relevant* respects, a fetus, even a fully developed one, is considerably less personlike than is the average mature mammal, indeed the average fish. And I think that a rational person must conclude that if the right to life of a fetus is to be based upon its resemblance to a person, then it cannot be said to have any more right to life than, let us say, a newborn guppy (which also seems to be capable of feeling pain), and that a right of that magnitude could never override a woman's right to obtain an abortion, at any stage of her pregnancy.

There may, of course, be other arguments in favor of placing legal limits upon the stage of pregnancy in which an abortion may be performed. Given the relative safety of the new techniques of artificially inducing labor during the third trimester, the danger to the woman's life or health is no longer such an argument. Neither is the fact that people tend to respond to the thought of abortion in the later stages of pregnancy with emotional repulsion, since mere emotional responses cannot take the place of moral reasoning in determining what ought to be permitted. Nor, finally, is the frequently heard argument that legalizing abortion, especially late in the pregnancy, may erode the level of respect for human life, leading, perhaps, to an increase in unjustified euthanasia and other crimes. For this threat, if it is a threat, can be better met by educating people to the kinds of moral distinctions which we are making here than by limiting access to abortion (which limitation may, in its disregard for the rights of women, be just as damaging to the level of respect for human rights).

Thus, since the fact that even a fully developed fetus is not personlike enough to have

any significant right to life on the basis of its personlikeness shows that no legal restrictions upon the stage of pregnancy in which an abortion may be performed can be justified on the grounds that we should protect the rights of the older fetus; and since there is no other apparent justification for such restrictions, we may conclude that they are entirely unjustified. Whether or not it would be *indecent* (whatever that means) for a woman in her seventh month to obtain an abortion just to avoid having to postpone a trip to Europe, it would not, in itself, be *immoral,* and therefore it ought to be permitted.

4. Potential Personhood and the Right to Life

We have seen that a fetus does not resemble a person in any way which can support the claim that it has even some of the same rights. But what about its *potential*, the fact that if nurtured and allowed to develop naturally it will very probably become a person? Doesn't that alone give it at least some right to life? It is hard to deny that the fact that an entity is a potential person is a strong prima facie reason for not destroying it; but we need not conclude from this that a potential person has a right to life, by virtue of that potential. It may be that our feeling that it is better, other things being equal, not to destroy a potential person is better explained by the fact that potential people are still (felt to be) an invaluable resource, not to be lightly squandered. Surely, if every speck of dust were a potential person, we would be much less apt to conclude that every potential person has a right to become actual.

Still, we do not need to insist that a potential person has no right to life whatever. There may well be something immoral, and not just imprudent, about wantonly destroying potential people, when doing so isn't necessary to protect anyone's rights. But even if a potential person does have some prima facie right to life, such a right could not possibly outweigh the right of a woman to obtain an abortion, since the rights of any actual person invariably outweigh those of any potential person, whenever the two conflict. Since this may not be immediately obvious in the case of a human fetus, let us look at another case.

Suppose that our space explorer falls into the hands of an alien culture, whose scientists decide to create a few hundred thousand or more human beings, by breaking his body into its component cells, and using these to create fully developed human beings, with, of course, his genetic code. We may imagine that each of these newly created men will have all of the original man's abilities, skills, knowledge, and so on, and also have an individual self-concept, in short that each of them will be a bona fide (though hardly unique) person. Imagine that the whole project will take only seconds, and that its chances of success are extremely high, and that our explorer knows all of this, and also knows that these people will be treated fairly. I maintain that in such a situation he would have every right to escape if he could, and thus to deprive all of these potential people of their potential lives; for his right to life outweighs all of theirs together, in spite of the fact that they are all genetically human, all innocent, and all have a very high probability of becoming people very soon, if only he refrains from acting.

Indeed, I think he would have a right to escape even if it were not his life which the alien scientists planned to take, but only a year of his freedom, or, indeed, only a day. Nor would he be obligated to stay if he had gotten captured (thus bringing all these people-potentials into existence) because of his own carelessness, or even if he had done so deliberately, knowing the consequences. Regardless of how he got captured, he is not morally obligated to remain in captivity for *any* period of time for the sake of permitting any number of potential people to come into actuality, so great is the margin by which one actual person's right to liberty outweighs whatever right to life even a hundred thousand potential people have. And it seems reasonable to conclude that the rights of a woman will outweigh by a similar margin whatever right to life a fetus may have by virtue of its potential personhood.

Thus, neither a fetus's resemblance to a person, nor its potential for becoming a person provides any basis whatever for the claim that it has any significant right to life. Consequently, a woman's right to protect her health, happiness, freedom, and even her life,[9] by terminating an unwanted pregnancy, will always override whatever right to life it may be appropriate to ascribe to a fetus, even a fully developed one. And thus, in the absence of any overwhelming social need for every possible child, the laws which restrict the right to obtain an abortion, or limit the period of pregnancy during which an abortion may be performed, are a wholly unjustified violation of a woman's most basic moral and constitutional rights.[10] . . .

Postscript on Infanticide

Since the publication of this article, many people have written to point out that my argument appears to justify not only abortion, but infanticide as well. For a newborn infant is not significantly more personlike than an advanced fetus, and consequently it would seem that if the destruction of the latter is permissible so too must be that of the former. Inasmuch as most people, regardless of how they feel about the morality of abortion, consider infanticide a form of murder, this might appear to represent a serious flaw in my argument.

Now, if I am right in holding that it is only people who have a full-fledged right to life, and who can be murdered, and if the criteria of personhood are as I have described them, then it obviously follows that killing a newborn infant isn't murder. It does *not* follow, however, that infanticide is permissible, for two reasons. In the first place, it would be wrong, at least in this country and in this period of history, and other things being equal, to kill a newborn infant, because even if its parents do not want it and would not suffer from its destruction, there are other people who would like to have it, and would, in all probability, be deprived of a great deal of pleasure by its destruction. Thus, infanticide is wrong for reasons analogous to those which make it wrong to wantonly destroy natural resources, or great works of art.

Secondly, most people, at least in this country, value infants and would much prefer that they be preserved, even if foster parents are not immediately available. Most of us would rather be taxed to support orphanages than allow unwanted infants to be destroyed. So long as there are people who want an infant preserved, and who are willing and able to provide the means of caring for it, under reasonably humane conditions, it is, *ceteris parabis,* wrong to destroy it.

But, it might be replied, if this argument shows that infanticide is wrong, at least at this time and in this country, doesn't it also show that abortion is wrong? After all, many people value fetuses, are disturbed by their destruction, and would much prefer that they be preserved, even at some cost to themselves. Furthermore, as a potential source of pleasure to some foster family, a fetus is just as valuable as an infant. There is, however, a crucial difference between the two cases: so long as the fetus is unborn, its preservation, contrary to the wishes of the pregnant woman, violates her rights to freedom, happiness, and self-determination. Her rights override the rights of those who would like the fetus preserved, just as if someone's life or limb is threatened by a wild animal, his right to protect himself by destroying the animal overrides the rights of those who would prefer that the animal not be harmed.

The minute the infant is born, however, its preservation no longer violates any of its mother's rights, even if she wants it destroyed, because she is free to put it up for adoption. Consequently, while the moment of birth does not mark any sharp discontinuity in the degree to which an infant possesses the right to life, it does mark the end of its mother's right to determine its fate. Indeed, if abortion could be performed without killing the fetus, she would never possess the right to have the fetus destroyed, for the same reasons that she has no right to have an infant destroyed.

On the other hand, it follows from my argument that when an unwanted or defective infant is born into a society which cannot afford and/or is not willing to care for it, then its destruction is permissible. This conclusion will, no doubt, strike many people as heartless and immoral; but remember that the very existence of people who feel this way, and who are willing and able to provide care for unwanted infants, is reason enough to conclude that they should be preserved.

Notes

1. For example, Roger Wertheimer, who in "Understanding the Abortion Argument" (*Philosophy and Public Affairs,* 1, No. 1 [Fall, 1971], 67–95), argues that the problem of the moral status of abortion is insoluble, in that the dispute over the status of the fetus is not a question of fact at all, but only a question of how one responds to the facts.

2. John Noonan, "Abortion and the Catholic Church: A Summary History," *Natural Law Forum,* 12 (1967), 125.

3. John Noonan, "Deciding Who Is Human," *Natural Law Forum,* 13 (1968), 134.

4. "A Defense of Abortion."

5. We may safely ignore the fact that she might have avoided getting raped, e.g., by carrying a gun, since by similar means you might likewise have avoided getting kidnapped, and in neither case does the victim's failure to take all possible precautions against a highly unlikely event (as opposed to reasonable precautions against a rather likely event) mean that he is morally responsible for what happens.

6. Of course, the principle that it is (always) wrong to kill innocent human beings is in need of many other modifications, e.g., that it may be permissible to do so to save a greater number of other innocent human beings, but we may safely ignore these complications here.

7. From here on, we will use 'human' to mean genetically human, since the moral sense seems closely connected to, and perhaps derived from, the assumption that genetic humanity is sufficient for membership in the moral community.

8. Thomas L. Hayes, "A Biological View," *Commonweal,* 85 (March 17, 1967), 677–78; quoted by Daniel Callahan, in *Abortion, Law, Choice, and Morality* (London: Macmillan & Co., 1970).

9. That is, insofar as the death rate, for the woman, is higher for childbirth than for early abortion.

10. My thanks to the following people, who were kind enough to read and criticize an earlier version of this paper: Herbert Gold, Gene Glass, Anne Lauterbach, Judith Thomson, Mary Mothersill, and Timothy Binkley.

16. Abortion and the Concept of a Person

Jane English

According to Jane English, our concept of a person is not sharp or decisive enough to bear the weight of a solution to the abortion controversy. However, she argues that even if the fetus is a full-fledged person, there are still cases in which abortion would be justified to prevent harm or death to the pregnant woman. Similarly, English argues that even if the fetus is not a person, there are still cases, at least in the late months of pregnancy, in which abortion would not be justified because of the fetus's resemblance to a person.

The abortion debate rages on. Yet the two most popular positions seem to be clearly mistaken. Conservatives maintain that a human life begins at conception and that therefore abortion must be wrong because it is murder. But not all killings of humans are murders. Most notably, self defense may justify even the killing of an innocent person.

Liberals, on the other hand, are just as mistaken in their argument that since a fetus does not become a person until birth, a woman may do whatever she pleases in and to her own body. First, you cannot do as you please with your own body if it affects other people adversely.[1] Second, if a fetus is not a person, that does not imply that you can do to it anything you wish. Animals, for example, are not persons, yet to kill or torture them for no reason at all is wrong.

At the center of the storm has been the issue of just when it is between ovulation and adulthood that a person appears on the scene. Conservatives draw the line at conception, liberals at birth. In this paper I first examine our concept of a person and conclude that no single criterion can capture the concept of a person and no sharp line can be drawn. Next I argue that if a fetus is a person, abortion is still justifiable in many cases; and if a fetus is not a person, killing it is still wrong in many cases. To a large extent, these two solutions are in agreement. I conclude that our concept of a person cannot and need not bear the weight

From the *Canadian Journal of Philosophy* 5, no. 2 (October 1975), pp. 233–243. Reprinted with permission of the publisher.

that the abortion controversy has thrust upon it.

I

The several factions in the abortion argument have drawn battle lines around various proposed criteria for determining what is and what is not a person. For example, Mary Anne Warren[2] lists five features (capacities for reasoning, self-awareness, complex communication, etc.) as her criteria for personhood and argues for the permissibility of abortion because a fetus falls outside this concept. Baruch Brody[3] uses brain waves. Michael Tooley[4] picks having-a-concept-of-self as his criterion and concludes that infanticide and abortion are justifiable, while the killing of adult animals is not. On the other side, Paul Ramsey[5] claims a certain gene structure is the defining characteristic. John Noonan[6] prefers conceived-of-humans and presents counterexamples to various other candidate criteria. For instance, he argues against viability as the criterion because the newborn and infirm would then be non-persons, since they cannot live without the aid of others. He rejects any criterion that calls upon the sorts of sentiments a being can evoke in adults on the grounds that this would allow us to exclude other races as non-persons if we could just view them sufficiently unsentimentally.

These approaches are typical: foes of abortion propose sufficient conditions for personhood which fetuses satisfy, while friends of abortion counter with necessary conditions for personhood which fetuses lack. But these both presuppose that the concept of a person can be captured in a strait jacket of necessary and/or sufficient conditions.[7] Rather, "person" is a cluster of features, of which rationality, having a self concept and being conceived of humans are only part.

What is typical of persons? Within our concept of a person we include, first, certain biological factors: descended from humans, having a certain genetic makeup, having a head, hands, arms, eyes, capable of locomotion, breathing, eating, sleeping. There are psychological factors: sentience, perception, having a concept of self and of one's own interests and desires, the ability to use tools, the ability to use language or symbol systems, the ability to joke, to be angry, to doubt. There are rationality factors: the ability to reason and draw conclusions, the ability to generalize and to learn from past experience, the ability to sacrifice present interests for greater gains in the future. There are social factors: the ability to work in groups and respond to peer pressures, the ability to recognize and consider as valuable the interests of others, seeing oneself as one among "other minds," the ability to sympathize, encourage, love, the ability to evoke from others the responses of sympathy, encouragement, love, the ability to work with others for mutual advantage. Then there are legal factors: being subject to the law and protected by it, having the ability to sue and enter contracts, being counted in the census, having a name and citizenship, the ability to own property, inherit, and so forth.

Now the point is not that this list is incomplete, or that you can find counterinstances to each of its points. People typically exhibit rationality, for instance, but someone who was irrational would not thereby fail to qualify as a person. On the other hand, something could exhibit the majority of these features and still fail to be a person, as an advanced robot might. There is no single core of necessary and sufficient features which we can draw upon with the assurance that they constitute what really makes a person; there are only features that are more or less typical.

This is not to say that no necessary or sufficient conditions can be given. Being alive is a necessary condition for being a person, and being a U.S. Senator is sufficient. But rather than falling inside a sufficient condition or outside a necessary one, a fetus lies in the penumbra region where our concept of a person is not so simple. For this reason I think a conclusive answer to the question whether a fetus is a person is unattainable.

Here we might note a family of simple fallacies that proceed by stating a necessary condition for personhood and showing that a fetus has that characteristic. This is a form of the fallacy of affirming the consequent. For example, some have mistakenly reasoned from the premise that a fetus is human (after all, it is a human fetus rather than, say, a canine fetus), to the conclusion that it is *a* human. Adding an equivocation on "being," we get the fallacious argument that since a fetus is something both living and human, it is a human being.

Nonetheless, it does seem clear that a fetus has very few of the above family of characteristics, whereas a newborn baby exhibits a much larger proportion of them—and a two-year-old has even more. Note that one traditional anti-abortion argument has centered on pointing out the many ways in which a fetus resembles a baby. They emphasize its development ("It already has ten fingers. . . .") without mentioning its dissimilarities to adults (it still has gills and a tail). They also try to evoke the sort of sympathy on our part that we only feel toward other persons ("Never to laugh . . . or feel the sunshine?"). This all seems to be a relevant way to argue, since its purpose is to persuade us that a fetus satisfies so many of the important features on the list that it ought to be treated as a person. Also note that a fetus near the time of birth satisfies many more of these factors than a fetus in the early months of development. This could provide reason for making distinctions among the different stages of pregnancy, as the U.S. Supreme Court has done.[8]

Historically, the time at which a person has been said to come into existence has varied widely. Muslims date personhood from fourteen days after conception. Some medievals followed Aristotle in placing ensoulment at forty days after conception for a male fetus and eighty days for a female fetus.[9] In European common law since the Seventeenth Century, abortion was considered the killing of a person only after quickening, the time when a pregnant woman first feels the fetus move on its own. Nor is this variety of opinions surprising. Biologically, a human being develops gradually. We shouldn't expect there to be any specific time or sharp dividing point when a person appears on the scene.

For these reasons I believe our concept of a person is not sharp or decisive enough to bear the weight of a solution to the abortion controversy. To use it to solve that problem is to clarify *obscurum per obscurius*.

II

Next let us consider what follows if a fetus is a person after all. Judith Jarvis Thomson's landmark article, "A Defense of Abortion,"[10] correctly points out that some additional argumentation is needed at this point in the conservative argument to bridge the gap between the premise that a fetus is an innocent person and the conclusion that killing it is always wrong. To arrive at this conclusion, we would need the additional premise that killing an innocent person is always wrong. But killing an innocent person is sometimes permissible, most notably in self defense. Some examples may help draw out our intuitions or ordinary judgments about self defense.

Suppose a mad scientist, for instance, hypnotized innocent people to jump out of the bushes and attack innocent passers-by with knives. If you are so attacked, we agree you have a right to kill the attacker in self defense, if killing him is the only way to protect your life or to save yourself from serious injury. It does not seem to matter here that the attacker is not malicious but himself an innocent pawn, for your killing of him is not done in a spirit of retribution but only in self defense.

How severe an injury may you inflict in self defense? In part this depends upon the severity of the injury to be avoided: you may not shoot someone merely to avoid having your clothes torn. This might lead one to the mistaken conclusion that the defense may only equal the threatened injury in severity; that to avoid death you may kill, but to avoid a black eye you may only inflict a black eye or the equivalent. Rather, our laws and customs seem to say that you may create an injury somewhat, but not enormously, greater than the injury to be avoided. To fend off an attack whose outcome would be as serious as rape, a severe beating or the loss of a finger, you may shoot; to avoid having your clothes torn, you may blacken an eye.

Aside from this, the injury you may inflict should only be the minimum necessary to deter or incapacitate the attacker. Even if you know he intends to kill you, you are not justified in shooting him if you could equally well save yourself by the simple expedient of running away. Self defense is for the purpose of avoiding harms rather than equalizing harms.

Some cases of pregnancy present a parallel situation. Though the fetus is itself innocent, it may pose a threat to the pregnant woman's well-being, life prospects or health, mental or physical. If the pregnancy presents a slight threat to her interests, it seems self defense cannot justify abortion. But if the threat is on a par with a serious beating or the loss of a finger, she may kill the fetus that poses such a threat, even if it is an innocent person. If a lesser harm to the fetus could have the same defensive effect, killing it would not be justified. It is unfortunate that the only way to free the woman from the pregnancy entails the death of the fetus (except in very late stages of pregnancy). Thus a self defense model supports Thomson's point that the woman has a right only to be freed from the fetus, not a right to demand its death.[11]

The self defense model is most helpful when we take the pregnant woman's point of view. In the pre-Thomson literature, abortion is often framed as a question for a third party: do you, a doctor, have a right to choose between the life of the woman and that of the fetus? Some have claimed that if you were a passer-by who witnessed a struggle between the innocent hypnotized attacker and his equally innocent victim, you would have no reason to kill either in defense of the other. They have concluded that the self defense model implies that a woman may attempt to abort herself, but that a doctor should not assist her. I think the position of the third party is somewhat more complex. We do feel some inclination to intervene on behalf of the victim rather than the attacker, other things equal. But if both parties are innocent, other factors come into consideration. You would rush to the aid of your husband whether he was attacker or attackee. If a hypnotized famous violinist were attacking a skid row bum, we would try to save the individual who is of more value to society. These considerations would tend to support abortion in some cases.

But suppose you are a frail senior citizen who wishes to avoid being knifed by one of these innocent hypnotics, so you have hired a bodyguard to accompany you. If you are attacked, it is clear we believe that the bodyguard, acting as your agent, has a right to kill the attacker to save you from a serious beating. Your rights of self defense are transferred to your agent. I suggest that we should similarly view the doctor as the pregnant woman's agent in carrying out a defense she is physically incapable of accomplishing herself.

Thanks to modern technology, the cases are rare in which pregnancy poses as clear a threat to a woman's bodily health as an attacker brandishing a switchblade. How does self defense fare when more subtle, complex and long-range harms are involved?

To consider a somewhat fanciful example, suppose you are a highly trained surgeon when you are kidnapped by the hypnotic attacker. He says he does not intend to harm you but to take you back to the mad scientist who, it turns out, plans to hypnotize you to have a permanent mental block against all your knowledge of medicine. This would automatically destroy your career which would in turn have a serious adverse impact on your family, your personal relationships and your happiness. It seems to me that if the only way you can avoid this outcome is to shoot the innocent attacker, you are justified in so doing. You are defending yourself from a drastic injury to your life prospects. I think it is no exaggeration to claim that unwanted pregnancies (most obviously among teenagers) often have such adverse life-long consequences as the surgeon's loss of livelihood.

Several parallels arise between various views on abortion and the self defense model. Let's suppose further that these hypnotized attackers only operate at night, so that it is well known that they can be avoided completely by the considerable inconvenience of never leaving your house after dark. One view is that since you could stay home at night, therefore if you go out and are selected by one of these hypnotized people, you have no right to defend yourself. This parallels the view that abstinence is the only acceptable way to avoid pregnancy. Others might hold that you ought to take along some defense such as Mace which will deter the hypnotized person without killing him, but that if this defense fails, you are obliged to submit to the resulting injury, no matter how severe it is. This parallels the view that contraception is all right but abortion is always wrong, even in cases of contraceptive failure.

A third view is that you may kill the hypnotized person only if he will actually kill you, but not if he will only injure you. This is like the position that abortion is permissible only if it is required to save a woman's life. Finally we have the view that it is all right to kill the attacker, even if only to avoid a very slight inconvenience to yourself and even if you knowingly walked down the very street where all these incidents have been taking place without taking along any Mace or protective escort. If we assume that a fetus is a person, this is the analogue of the view that abortion is always justifiable, "on demand."

The self defense model allows us to see an important difference that exists between abortion and infanticide, even if a fetus is a person from conception. Many have argued that the only way to justify abortion without justifying infanticide would be to find some characteristic of personhood that is acquired at birth. Michael Tooley, for one, claims infanticide is justifiable because the really significant characterisics of person are acquired some time after birth. But all such approaches look to characteristics of the developing human and ignore the relation between the fetus and the woman. What if, after birth, the presence of an infant or the need to support it posed a grave threat to the woman's sanity or life prospects? She could escape this threat by the simple expedient of running away. So a solution that does not entail the death of the infant is available. Before birth, such solutions are not available because of the biological dependence of the fetus on the woman. Birth is the crucial point not because of any characteristics the fetus gains, but because after birth the woman can defend herself by a means less drastic than killing the infant. Hence self defense can be used to justify abortion without necessarily thereby justifying infanticide.

III

On the other hand, supposing a fetus is not after all a person, would abortion always be morally permissible? Some opponents of abortion seem worried that if a fetus is not a full-fledged person, then we are justified in treating it in any way at all. However, this does not follow. Non-persons do get some consideration in our moral code, though of course they do not have the same rights as persons have (and in general they do not have moral responsibilities), and though their interests may be overridden by the interests of persons. Still, we cannot just treat them in any way at all.

Treatment of animals is a case in point. It is wrong to torture dogs for fun or to kill wild birds for no reason at all. It is wrong Period, even though dogs and birds do not have the same rights persons do. However, few people think it is wrong to use dogs as experimental animals, causing them considerable suffering in some cases, provided that the resulting research will probably bring discoveries of great benefit to people. And most of us think it all right to kill birds for food or to protect our crops. People's rights are different from the consideration we give to animals, then, for it is wrong to experiment on people, even if others might later benefit a great deal as a result of their suffering. You might volunteer to be a subject, but this would be supererogatory; you certainly have a right to refuse to be a medical guinea pig.

But how do we decide what you may or may not do to non-persons? This is a difficult problem, one for which I believe no adequate

account exists. You do not want to say, for instance, that torturing dogs is all right whenever the sum of its effects on people is good—when it doesn't warp the sensibilities of the torturer so much that he mistreats people. If that were the case, it would be all right to torture dogs if you did it in private, or if the torturer lived on a desert island or died soon afterward, so that his actions had no effect on people. This is an inadequate account, because whatever moral consideration animals get, it has to be indefeasible, too. It will have to be a general proscription of certain actions, not merely a weighing of the impact on people on a case-by-case basis.

Rather, we need to distinguish two levels on which consequences of actions can be taken into account in moral reasoning. The traditional objections to Utilitarianism focus on the fact that it operates solely on the first level, taking all the consequences into account in particular cases only. Thus Utilitarianism is open to "desert island" and "lifeboat" counterexamples because these cases are rigged to make the consequences of actions severely limited.

Rawls' theory could be described as a teleological sort of theory, but with teleology operating on a higher level.[12] In choosing the principles to regulate society from the original position, his hypothetical choosers make their decision on the basis of the total consequences of various systems. Furthermore, they are constrained to choose a general set of rules which people can readily learn and apply. An ethical theory must operate by generating a set of sympathies and attitudes toward others which reinforces the functioning of that set of moral principles. Our prohibition against killing people operates by means of certain moral sentiments including sympathy, compassion and guilt. But if these attitudes are to form a coherent set, they carry us further: we tend to perform supererogatory actions, and we tend to feel similar compassion toward person-like non-persons.

It is crucial that psychological facts play a role here. Our psychological constitution makes it the case that for our ethical theory to work, it must prohibit certain treatment of non-persons which are significantly person-like. If our moral rules allowed people to treat some person-like non-persons in ways we do not want people to be treated, this would undermine the system of sympathies and attitudes that makes the ethical system work. For this reason, we would choose in the original position to make mistreatment of some sorts of animals wrong in general (not just wrong in the cases with public impact), even though animals are not themselves parties in the original position. Thus it makes sense that it is those animals whose appearance and behavior are most like those of people that get the most consideration in our moral scheme.

It is because of "coherence of attitudes," I think, that the similarity of a fetus to a baby is very significant. A fetus one week before birth is so much like a newborn baby in our psychological space that we cannot allow any cavalier treatment of the former while expecting full sympathy and nurturative support for the latter. Thus, I think that anti-abortion forces are indeed giving their strongest arguments when they point to the similarities between a fetus and a baby, and when they try to evoke our emotional attachment to and sympathy for the fetus. An early horror story from New York about nurses who were expected to alternate between caring for six-week premature infants and disposing of viable 24-week aborted fetuses is just that—a horror story. These beings are so much alike that no one can be asked to draw a distinction and treat them so very differently.

Remember, however, that in the early weeks after conception, a fetus is very much unlike a person. It is hard to develop these feelings for a set of genes which doesn't yet have a head, hands, beating heart, response to touch or the ability to move by itself. Thus it seems to me that the alleged "slippery slope" between conception and birth is not so very slippery. In the early stages of pregnancy, abortion can hardly be compared to murder for psychological reasons, but in the latest stages it is psychologically akin to murder.

Another source of similarity is the bodily continuity between fetus and adult. Bodies play a surprisingly central role in our attitudes toward persons. One has only to think of the philosophical literature on how far physical identity suffices for personal identity or Wittgenstein's remark that the best picture of the human soul is the human body. Even after death, when all agree the body is no longer a person, we still observe elaborate customs of respect for the human body; like people who torture dogs, necrophiliacs are not to be trusted with people.[13] So it is appropriate that we show respect to a fetus as the body continuous with the body of a person. This is a degree of resemblance to persons that animals cannot rival.

Michael Tooley also utilizes a parallel with animals. He claims that it is always permissible to drown newborn kittens and draws conclusions about infanticide.[14] But it is only permissible to drown kittens when their survival would cause some hardship. Perhaps it would be a burden to feed and house six more cats or to find other homes for them. The alternative of letting them starve produces even more suffering than the drowning. Since the kittens get their rights second-hand, so to speak, via the need for coherence in our attitudes, their interests are often overridden by the interests of fullfledged persons. But if their survival would be no inconvenience to people at all, then it is wrong to drown them, contra Tooley.

Tooley's conclusions about abortion are wrong for the same reason. Even if a fetus is not a person, abortion is not always permissible, because of the resemblance of a fetus to a person. I agree with Thomson that it would be wrong for a woman who is seven months pregnant to have an abortion just to avoid having to postpone a trip to Europe. In the early months of pregnancy when the fetus hardly resembles a baby at all, then, abortion is permissible whenever it is in the interests of the pregnant woman or her family. The reasons would only need to outweigh the pain and inconvenience of the abortion itself. In the middle months, when the fetus comes to resemble a person, abortion would be justifiable only when the continuation of the pregnancy or the birth of the child would cause harms—physical, psychological, economic or social—to the woman. In the late months of pregnancy, even on our current assumption that a fetus is not a person, abortion seems to be wrong except to save a woman from significant injury or death.

The Supreme Court has recognized similar gradations in the alleged slippery slope stretching between conception and birth. To this point, the present paper has been a discussion of the moral status of abortion only, not its legal status. In view of the great physical, financial and sometimes psychological costs of abortion, perhaps the legal arrangement most compatible with the proposed moral solution would be the absence of restrictions, that is, so-called abortion "on demand."

So I conclude, first, that application of our concept of a person will not suffice to settle the abortion issue. After all, the biological development of a human being is gradual. Second, whether a fetus is a person or not, abortion is justifiable early in pregnancy to avoid modest harms and seldom justifiable late in pregnancy except to avoid significant injury or death.[15]

Notes

1. We also have paternalistic laws which keep us from harming our own bodies even when no one else is affected. Ironically, antiabortion laws were originally designed to protect pregnant women from a dangerous but tempting procedure.

2. Mary Anne Warren, "On the Moral and Legal Status of Abortion," *Monist* 57 (1973), p. 55.

3. Baruch Brody, "Fetal Humanity and the Theory of Essentialism," in Robert Baker and Frederick Elliston, eds., *Philosophy and Sex* (Buffalo, N.Y., 1975).

4. Michael Tooley, "Abortion and Infanticide," *Philosophy and Public Affairs* 2 (1971).

5. Paul Ramsey, "The Morality of Abortion," in James Rachels, ed., *Moral Problems* (New York, 1971).

6. John Noonan, "Abortion and the Catholic Church: A Summary History," *Natural Law Forum* 12 (1967), pp. 125–131.

7. Wittgenstein has argued against the possibility of so capturing the concept of a game. *Philosophical Investigations* (New York, 1958), §66–71.

8. Not because the fetus is partly a person and so has some of the rights of persons, but rather because of the rights of person-like non-persons. This I discuss in part III below.

9. Aristotle himself was concerned, however, with the different question of when the soul takes form. For historical data, see Jimmye Kimmey, "How the Abortion Laws Happened," *Ms.* I (April, 1973), pp. 48ff, and John Noonan, *loc. cit.*

10. J. J. Thomson, "A Defense of Abortion," *Philosophy and Public Affairs* 1 (1971).

11. *Ibid.*, p. 52.

12. John Rawls, *A Theory of Justice* (Cambridge, Mass., 1971), §3–4.

13. On the other hand, if they can be trusted with people, then our moral customs are mistaken. It all depends on the facts of psychology.

14. *Op. cit.*, pp. 40, 60–61.

15. I am deeply indebted to Larry Crocker and Arthur Kuflik for their constructive comments.

17. A Feminist Perspective on the Right to Abortion

Catharine MacKinnon

Catharine MacKinnon situates the abortion debate within a feminist understanding of gender inequality. She argues that it is wrongly assumed in the abortion debate that women significantly control sex. She further contends that the liberal's proclaimed right to abortion is based on a concept of privacy that fails to protect women from battery, marital rape, and exploited labor.

Reprinted with permission from *Radical America* (Vol. 17, No. 4, August 1983).

In a society where women entered sexual intercourse willingly, where adequate contraception was a genuine social priority, there would be no "abortion issue." . . . Abortion is violence. . . . It is the offspring, and will continue to be the accuser of a more pervasive and prevalent violence, the violence of rapism.

Adrienne Rich
*Of Woman Born:
Motherhood as Experience
and Institution*

In 1973, Roe against Wade held that a statute that made criminal all abortions except to save the mother's life violated the constitutional right to privacy.[1] In 1980, Harris against McRae decided that this privacy right did not require public funding of medically necessary abortions for women who could not afford them.[2] Here I argue that the public/private line drawn in *McRae* sustains and reveals the meaning of privacy recognized in *Roe*.

First, the experience of abortion, and the terms of the struggle for the abortion right, is situated in a context of a feminist comprehension of gender inequality, to which a critique of sexuality is central.[3] Next, the legal concept of privacy is examined in the abortion context. I argue that privacy doctrine affirms what feminism rejects: the public/private split. Once the ideological meaning of the law of privacy is connected with a feminist critique of the public/private division, the *Roe* approach looks consistent with *McRae*'s confinement of its reach. To guarantee abortions as an aspect of the private, rather than of the public, sector is to guarantee women a right to abortion subject to women's ability to provide it for ourselves. This is to guarantee access to abortion only to some women on the basis of class, not to women *as women,* and therefore, under conditions of sex inequality, to guarantee it to *all* women only on male terms. The rest of this is an attempt to unpack what I mean by that.

I will neglect two important explorations, which I bracket now. The first is: what are babies to men? Sometimes men respond to women's right to abort as if confronting the possibility of their own potential nonexistence—at *women's* hands, no less. Men's issues of potency, of continuity as a compensation for mortality, of the thrust to embody themselves or the image of themselves in the world, seem to underlie their relation to babies, as well as to most everything else. The idea that women can undo what men have done to them on this level seems to provoke insecurity sometimes bordering on hysteria. To overlook these meanings of abortion to men as men is to overlook political and strategic as well as deep theoretical issues, is to misassess where much of the opposition to abortion is coming from, and to make a lot of mistakes. The second question I bracket is one that, unlike the first, has been discussed extensively in the abortion debate: the moral rightness of abortion itself. My view, which the rest of what I say on abortion reflects, is that the abortion choice should be available and must be *women's,* but not because the fetus is not a form of life. The more usual approach tends to make whether women should make the abortion decision somehow contingent on whether the fetus is a form of life. Why shouldn't women make life or death decisions? Which returns us to the first bracketed issue.

The issues I will discuss have largely not been discussed in the terms I will use. What has happened instead, I think, is that women's embattled need to survive in a system that is hostile to our survival, the desperation of our need to negotiate with whatever means that same system will respond to, has precluded our exploration of these issues in the way that I am about to explore them. That is, the terms on which we have addressed the issue of abortion have been shaped and constrained by the very situation that the abortion issue has put us in a position to need to address. We have not been able to risk thinking about these issues on our own terms because the terms have not been ours—either in sex, in social life in general, or in court. The attempt to grasp women's situation on our own terms, from our own point of view, defines the feminist impulse. If doing that is risky, our situation as women also makes it risky not to.

So, first feminism, then law.

Most women who seek abortions became pregnant while having sexual intercourse with men. Most did not mean or wish to conceive. In contrast to this fact of women's experience, the abortion debate has centered on the separation of control over sexuality from control over reproduction, and both from gender. Liberals have supported the availability of the abortion choice as if the woman just happened on the fetus.[4] The right recalls that intercourse precedes conception, only to urge abstinence, as if sex were up to women, while at the same time defending male authority, specifically including a wife's duty to submit to sex. Continuing this logic, many opponents of state funding of abortions, such as supporters of the Hyde Amendment, would permit funding of abortions when the pregnancy results from rape or incest.[5] These are exceptions for special occasions on which they presume women did not control sex. What I'm getting at is this convergence: many of abortion's proponents, who want to free women from reproduction in order to have sex, seem to share with abortion's opponents, who want to stick us with the consequences, the tacit assumption that women significantly *do* control sex.

Feminist investigations suggest otherwise. Sexual intercourse, the most common cause of pregnancy, cannot simply be presumed co-equally determined. Feminists have found that women feel compelled to preserve the appearance, which acted upon becomes the reality, of male direction of sexual expression, as if it is male initiative itself that we want, that turns us on. Men enforce this. It is much of what men want in a woman. It is what pornography eroticizes and prostitutes provide. Rape, by contrast, is intercourse with force that is recognized as force. The implicit standard against which rape is adjudicated, though, is not, I think, the power or even primarily the degree of force that the man wields or uses, but the degree of perceived intimacy between the parties. The more intimately acquainted you are with your accused rapist, the less likely a court is to find that what you think was rape is rape. Often indices of such intimacy include intercourse itself. If no can be taken as yes, depending on measures of familiarity rather than mutuality of desire, how free can yes be?

Under these conditions, women often do not use birth control because of its social meaning, a social meaning we did not make. Using contraception means acknowledging and planning and taking direction of intercourse, accepting one's sexual availability

and appearing nonspontaneous. It means appearing available to male incursions. A good user of contraception is a bad girl. She can be presumed sexually available, among other consequences; she can be raped with relative impunity. (If you think this isn't true, you should consider those rape cases in which the fact that a woman had a diaphragm in is taken as an indication that what happened to her was intercourse, not rape. Why did you have your diaphragm in?) Studies of abortion clinics have looked into circumstances surrounding abortions, including those of women who repeatedly seek abortions—the repeat offenders, high on the list of the right's villains, their best case for opposing abortion as female sexual irresponsibility. Ask such women why they are repeatedly pregnant, they say something like, the sex just happened. Like every night for over a year.[6] I wonder if a woman can be presumed to control access to her sexuality who feels unable to interrupt intercourse to insert a diaphragm; or worse, *cannot even want to,* aware that she risks a pregnancy she knows she doesn't want. Do you think she would stop the man for any other reason, such as, for instance—the real taboo—lack of desire? If not, how is sex, hence its consequences, meaningfully voluntary for women? Norms of sexual rhythm and romance that are felt interrupted by women's needs are constructed against women's interests. When it appears normatively less costly for women to risk an undesired, often painful, traumatic, dangerous, sometimes illegal, and potentially life-threatening procedure than it is to protect oneself in advance, sex doesn't look a whole lot like freedom. Yet the policy debate in the last twenty years has not explicitly approached abortion in the context of how women get pregnant, that is, as a consequence of sexual intercourse under conditions of gender inequality, that is, as an issue of forced sex.

Now, law. In 1973, Roe against Wade found the right to privacy "broad enough to encompass a woman's decision whether or not to terminate her pregnancy."[7] Privacy had previously been recognized as a constitutional principle in a case that decriminalized the prescription and use of contraceptives.[8] Note that courts implicitly connect contraception with abortion under the privacy rubric in a way that parallels the way I just did explicitly under the feminist rubric. In 1977, three justices observed, "In the abortion context, we have held that the right to privacy shields the woman from undue state intrusion in and external scrutiny of her very personal choice."[9] In 1980, the Supreme Court in Harris against McRae decided that this did not mean that federal Medicaid programs had to cover medically necessary abortions for poor women.[10] According to the Court, the privacy of the woman's choice was not unconstitutionally burdened by the government financing her decision to continue, but not her decision to end a conception. The Supreme Court reasoned that "although the government may not place obstacles in the path of a woman's exercise of her freedom of choice, it may not remove those not of its own creation."[11] Aside from holding the state exempt in any issue of the distribution of wealth, which is dubious, it was apparently a very short step from that which the government had a duty *not* to intervene in, as in *Roe*, and that which it has *no* duty to intervene in, as in *McRae*. That this distinction has consistent parallels in other areas of jurisprudence and social policy—such as in the distinction between negative and positive freedom[12] and in the state action requirement[13]—does not mean that the public/private line that forms their common dimension is not, there as well as here, the gender line. The result of government's stance is also the same throughout: an area of social life is cordoned off from the reach of explicitly recognized public authority. This does not mean, as they think, that government stays out really. Rather, this leaves the balance of forces where they are socially, so that government's patterns of intervention mirror and magnify, thus authorize, the existing social divisions of power.

The law of privacy, explicitly a public law *against* public intervention, is one such doctrine. Conceived as the outer edge of limited government, it embodies a tension between precluding public exposure or governmental intrusion on the one hand, and autonomy in the sense of protecting personal self-action on the other. This is a tension, not just two facets of one whole right. This tension is resolved from the liberal state's point of view—I am now moving into a critique of liberalism—by delineating the threshold of the state as its permissible extent of penetration (a term I use advisedly) into a domain that is considered free by definition: the private sphere. By this move the state secures what has been termed "an inviolable personality" by insuring what is called "autonomy or control over the intimacies of personal identity."[14] The state does this by centering its self-restraint on body and home, especially bedroom. By staying out of marriage and the family, prominently meaning sexuality, that is to say, heterosexuality, from contraception through pornography to the abortion decision, the law of privacy proposes to guarantee individual bodily integrity, personal exercise of moral intelligence, and freedom of intimacy.[15] What it actually does is translate traditional social values into the rhetoric of individual rights as a means of subordinating those rights to social imperatives.[16] In feminist terms, applied to abortion law, the logic of *Roe* consummated in *Harris* translates the ideology of the private sphere into individual women's collective needs to the imperatives of male supremacy.

This is my ten-year retrospective on Roe against Wade. Reproduction is sexual, men control sexuality, and the state supports the interest of men as a group. If *Roe* is part of this, why was abortion legalized? Why were women even imagined to have such a right as privacy? It is not an accusation of bad faith to answer that the interests of men as a social group converge here with the definition of justice embodied in law. The male point of view unites them. Taking this approach, one sees that the way the male point of view constructs a social event or legal notion is the way that event or notion is framed by state policy. For example, to the extent possession is the point of sex, illegal rape will be sex with a woman who is not yours unless the act makes her yours. If part of the kick of pornography involves eroticizing the putatively prohibited, illegal pornography—obscenity—will be prohibited enough to keep pornography desirable without ever making it truly illegitimate or unavailable. If, from the male standpoint, male is the implicit definition of human, maleness will be the implicit standard by which sex equality is measured in discrimination law. In parallel terms, the availability of abortion frames, and is framed by, the extent to which men, worked out among themselves, find it convenient to allow abortion—a reproductive consequence of intercourse—to occur. Abortion will then, to that extent, be available.

The abortion policy debate has construed the issues rather differently. The social problem posed by sexuality since Freud[17] has been seen as the problem of the repression of the innate desire for sexual pleasure by the constraints of civilization. Gender inequality arises as an issue in the Freudian context in women's repressive socialization to passivity and coolness (so-called frigidity), in women's so-called desexualization, and in the disparate consequences of biology, that is, pregnancy. Who defines what is seen as sexual, what sexuality therefore is, to whom what stimuli are erotic and why, and who defines the conditions under which sexuality is expressed—these issues are not available to be considered. "Civilization's" answer to these questions, in the Freudian context, instead fuses women's reproductivity with our attributed sexuality in its definition of what a woman is. We are, from a feminist standpoint, thus defined as women, as feminine, by the uses to which men want to put us. Seen this way, it becomes clear why the struggle for reproductive freedom, since Freud, has not included a woman's right to refuse sex. In the post-Freudian era, the notion of sexual liberation frames the sexual equality issue as a struggle for women to have sex with men on the same terms as men: "without consequences."

The abortion right, to the extent it has been admitted to have anything to do with sex, has been sought as freedom from the unequal reproductive consequences of sexual expression, with sexuality defined as centered on heterosexual genital intercourse. It has been as if it is biological organisms, rather than social relations, that have sex and reproduce the species, and sex itself is "really" a gender-neutral, hence sex-equal, activity. But if you see both sexuality and reproduction, hence gender, as socially situated, and your issue is less how more people can get more sex as it is than who, socially, defines what sexuality—hence pleasure and violation—is, the abortion right becomes situated within a very different

problematic: the social and political problematic of the inequality of the sexes. As Susan Sontag said, "Sex itself is not liberating for women. Neither is more sex. . . . The question is, what sexuality shall women be liberated to enjoy?"[18] To address this for purposes of abortion policy, from a feminist perspective, requires reconceiving the problem of sexuality from the repression of drives by civilization to the oppression of women by men.

Most arguments for abortion under the rubric of feminism have rested upon the right to control one's own body, gender-neutral. I think that argument has been appealing for the same reasons it is inadequate. Women's bodies have not socially been ours; we have not controlled their meanings and destinies. So feminists have needed to assert that control while feeling unable to risk pursuing the sense that something more than our bodies singular, something closer to a net of relations, relations in which we are (so far unescapedly) gendered, might be at stake.[19] Some feminists have noticed that our "right to decide" has become merged with an overwhelmingly male professional's right not to have his professional judgment second-guessed by the government.[20] But most abortion advocates have argued in rigidly and rigorously gender-neutral terms.

Consider, for instance, Judith Jarvis Thomson's celebrated hypothetical case justifying abortion, in which a gender-neutral abducted "you" has no obligation to be a life support system for the famous violinist ("he") one is forcibly connected to. On this basis, "one" is argued to have no obligation to support a fetus.[21] Never mind that no *woman* who needs an abortion, no woman period, is valued, no potential an actual woman's life might hold would be cherished, comparable to a male famous violinist's unencumbered possibilities. In the crunch, few women look like unborn Beethovens, even to sex-blind liberals. Not to mention that the underlying parallel to rape in the hypothetical—the origin in force, in abduction, that gives it weight while confining its application to instances in which force is recognized as force—is seldom interrogated in the abortion context for its applicability to the normal case. And abortion policy has to be made for the normal case. While the hypo-

thetical makes women's rights depend by analogy on what is not considered the normal case,
Thomson finds distinguishing rape from intercourse has "a rather unpleasant sound"
principally because *fetal* rights should not depend on the conditions of conception. My
point is that in order to apply even something
like Thomson's parallel to the usual case of
need for an abortion requires establishing
some relation between intercourse and rape—
sexuality—and conception. This issue has
been avoided in the abortion context by acting
as if *assuming* women are persons sexually will
make us persons reproductively, as if treating
women in gender-neutral terms analytically
will remove the social reality of gender from
the situation. By this sentimentality, liberal
feminism obscures the unequal gender basis
on which it attempts to construct women's
equal personhood.

Abortion without a sexual critique of gender inequality, I have said, promises women
sex with men on the same terms as men. Under conditions under which women do not
control access to our sexuality, this facilitates
women's heterosexual availability. It promises
men women on male terms. I mean, under
conditions of gender inequality, sexual liberation in this sense does not free women, it frees
male sexual aggression. Available abortion on
this basis removes one substantial legitimized
reason that women have had, since Freud, for
refusing sex besides the headache. Analyzing
the perceptions upon which initial male support for abortion was based, Andrea Dworkin
says: "Getting laid was at stake."[22] The Playboy
Foundation has supported abortion rights
from day one; it continues to, even with
shrinking disposable funds, on a level of priority comparable to its opposition to censorship.
There is also evidence that men eroticize abortion itself.[23]

Privacy doctrine is an ideal legal vehicle for
the process of sexual politics I have described.
The democratic liberal ideal of the private
holds that, so long as the public does not interfere, autonomous individuals interact freely and equally. Conceptually, this private is
hermetic. It means that which is inaccessible
to, unaccountable to, unconstructed by anything beyond itself. By definition, it is not part
of or conditioned by anything systematic or

outside itself. It is personal, intimate, autonomous, particular, individual, the original
source and final outpost of the self, gender-
neutral. Privacy is, in short, defined by everything that feminism reveals women have never
been allowed to be or to have, as well as by
everything that women have been equated
with and defined in terms of *men's* ability to
have. The liberal definition of the private does
not envisage public complaint of social inequality within it. In the liberal view, no act of
the state contributes to, hence properly should
participate in, shaping its internal alignments
or distributing its internal forces, including
inequalities among parties in private. Its inviolability by the state, framed as an individual
right, presupposes that it is not already an arm
of the state. It is not even a social sphere,
exactly. Intimacy is implicitly thought to
guarantee symmetry of power. Injuries arise
in violating the private sphere, not within and
by and because of it.

In private, consent tends to be presumed. It
is true that a showing of coercion voids this
presumption. But the problem is getting anything private perceived as coercive. Why one
would allow force in private—the "why doesn't
she leave" question raised to battered wom-
en—is a question given its urgency by the
social meaning of the private as a sphere of
equality and choice. But for women the measure of the intimacy has been the measure of
the oppression. This is why feminism has had
to explode the private. This is why feminism
has seen the personal as the political. In this
sense, for women as such there is no private,
either normatively or empirically. Feminism
confronts the reality that women have no
privacy to lose or to guarantee. We have no
inviolability. Our sexuality is not only violable,
it is, hence we are, seen in and as our violation.
To confront the fact that we have no privacy is
to confront the intimate degradation of
women *as* the public order.

In this light, recognizing abortion under
the legal right to privacy is a complicated
move. Freedom *from* public intervention coex-
ists uneasily with any right which requires
social preconditions to be meaningfully delivered. If inequality, for example, is socially pervasive and enforced, meaningful equality will
require intervention, not abdication. But the

right to privacy is not thought to require social change to be meaningful. It is not even thought to require any social preconditions, other than nonintervention by the public. The point for the abortion cases is not only that indigency, which was the specific barrier to effective choice in *McRae*, is well within public power to remedy, nor that the state, as I said, is hardly exempt in issues of the distribution of wealth. It is rather that Roe against Wade presumes that governmental nonintervention into the private sphere in itself amounts to, or at the least promotes, woman's freedom of choice. When the alternative is jail, there is much to be said for this argument. But the *McRae* result sustains the meaning of the privacy recognized in *Roe:* women are guaranteed by the public no more than what we can secure for ourselves in private. That is, what we can extract through our intimate associations with men. Women with privileges get rights.

Women got abortion as a private privilege, not as a public right. We got control over reproduction that is controlled by "a man or The Man,"[24] an individual man or (mostly male) doctors or the government. In this sense, abortion was not simply decriminalized, it was legalized; *Roe* set the stage for state regulation of the conditions under which women can have access to this right. Much of the control that women got out of legalization of abortion went directly into the hands of men socially—husbands, doctors, fathers. Much of the rest of it women have had to fight to keep from state attempts, both legislative and administrative, to regulate it out of existence.[25]

It is not inconsistent, in this light, that a woman's decision to abort, framed as a privacy right, would have no claim on public funding and might genuinely not be seen as burdened by that deprivation. Privacy conceived as a right from public intervention and disclosure is the conceptual *opposite* of the relief *McRae* sought for welfare women. State intervention would have provided a choice these women did *not* have in private. The women in *McRae*, poor women and women of color whose sexual refusal has counted for especially little,[26] needed something to make their privacy real. The logic of the court's response to them re-

sembles that by which women are supposed to consent to sex. Preclude the alternatives, then call the sole option remaining "her choice." The point is that the women's alternatives are precluded *prior* to the reach of the chosen remedy, the legal doctrine. They are precluded by conditions of sex, race, and class— the conditions the privacy frame not only assumes, but *works to guarantee*. These women were seen, essentially, as not having lost any privacy by having public funding for abortions withheld, as having no privacy to lose. In the bourgeois sense, in which you can have all the rights you can buy, converging with that dimension of male supremacy that makes the self-disposition money can buy a prerogative of masculinity, this was true. The *McRae* result certainly *made* it true.

The way the law of privacy restricts intrusions into intimacy also bars change in control over that intimacy. The existing distribution of power and resources within the private sphere will be precisely what the law of privacy exists to protect. Just as pornography is legally protected as individual freedom of expression without questioning whose freedom and whose expression and at whose expense, abstract privacy protects abstract autonomy without inquiring into whose freedom of action is being sanctioned, at whose expense. I think it is not coincidence that the very place (the body), the very relations (heterosexual), the very activities (intercourse and reproduction), and the very feelings (intimate) that feminism has found central to the subjection of women, form the core of privacy law's coverage. In this perspective, the legal concept of privacy can and has shielded the place of battery, marital rape, and women's exploited labor, preserved the central institutions whereby women are *deprived* of identity, autonomy, control, and self-definition, and protected the primary activities through which male supremacy is expressed and enforced.

To fail to recognize the meaning of the private in the ideology and reality of women's subordination by seeking protection behind a right *to* that privacy is to cut women off from collective verification and state support in the same act. When women are segregated in private, separated from each other, one at a time, a right *to* that privacy isolates us at once from each other and from public recourse, even as it provides the only form of that recourse made available to us. So defined, the right to privacy has included a right of men "to be let alone"[27] to oppress women one at a time. It embodies and reflects the private sphere's existing definition of womanhood. As an instance of liberalism—applied to women as if we *are* persons, gender-neutral—Roe against Wade reinforces the division between public and private, a division that is not gender-neutral. It is at once an ideological division that lies about women's shared experience and mystifies the unity among the spheres of women's violation, and a very material division that *keeps* the private beyond public redress and depoliticizes women's subjection within it. It keeps some men out of the bedrooms of other men.

There seems to be a social perception that the right has the high moral ground on abortion and the liberals have the high legal ground.[28] I have tried to sketch a feminist ground, a political ground critical of the common ground under the right's morals and liberals' laws.

References

1. *Roe* v. *Wade,* 410 U.S. 113 (1973).

2. *Harris* v. *McRae,* 448 U.S. 297 (1980).

3. I talk about this in "Feminism, Marxism, Method and the State: An Agenda for Theory," *Signs: Journal of Women in Culture and Society* 7, no. 3 (Spring 1982): 515–44.

4. See D. H. Reagan, "Rewriting *Roe* v. *Wade,*" *Michigan Law Review* 77 (August 1979): 1569–1646, in which the Good Samaritan, by analogy, happens upon the fetus.

5. As of 1973, ten states that made abortion a crime had exceptions for rape and incest; at least three had exceptions for rape only. Many of these exceptions were based on Model Penal Code Section 230.3 (Proposed Official Draft 1962), quoted in *Doe* v. *Bolton,* 410 U.S. 179, 205–7, app. B (1973), permitting abortion, *inter alia* in cases of "rape, incest, or other felonious intercourse." References to states with incest and rape exceptions can be found in *Roe* v. *Wade,* 410 U.S. 113, n. 37 (1973). Some versions of the Hyde Amendment, which prohibits use of public money to fund abortions, have contained exceptions for cases of rape or incest. Publ. L. No. 95-205, § 101, 91 stat. 1960 (1972); Pub. L. No. 95-480, § 210, 92 Stat. 1567, 1586 (1978); Pub. L. No. 96-123, 109, 93 Stat. 923, 926 (1979); Pub. L. No. 96-536, § 109, 94 Stat. 3166, 3170 (1980). All require immediate reporting of the incident.

6. Kristin Luker, *Taking Chances: Abortion and the Decision Not to Contracept* (Berkeley: University of California Press, 1975), p. 47.

7. *Roe,* 410 U.S. at 153.

8. *Griswold* v. *Connecticut,* 381 U.S. 479 (1965).

9. *H. L.* v. *Matheson,* 450 U.S. 398, 435 (dissent) (1981); see also *Whalen* v. *Roe,* 429 U.S. 589, 599–600 (1977).

10. *Harris* v. *McRae,* 448 U.S. 297 (1980).

11. *Harris,* 448 U.S. at 316.

12. Isiah Berlin, "Two Concepts of Liberty," in Berlin, *Four Essays on Liberty* (Oxford, 1969).

13. See Paul Brest, "State Action and Liberal Theory: A Casenote on *Flagg Brothers* v. *Brooks,*" 130 U. Pa L. Rev. 1296 (1982).

14. Tom Gerety, "Redefining Privacy," *Harvard Civil Rights—Civil Liberties Law Review* 12, no. 2 (Spring 1977): 236.

15. Thus the law of privacy wavers between protecting the institution of heterosexuality as such and protecting that which heterosexuality is at least theoretically only one instance of, that is, free choice in intimate behavior. For the first proposition, see, e.g., *Griswold* v. *Connecticut,* 381 U.S. 479 (1965) (distribution of contraceptives), *Loving* v. *Virginia,* 388 U.S. 1 (1967) (marriage partners), *Skinner* v. *Oklahoma,* 316 U.S. 535 (1942) (male fertility), as well as *Roe* v. *Wade, Doe* v. *Commonwealth's Attorney,* 403 F. Supp. 1199 (D. Va. 1975) (homosexual conduct not protected, since "no part of marriage, home or family life"). For the second, *New York* v. *Onofre,* 424 N.Y.S. 2d 566 (1980) (invalidating criminal sodomy statute). It is consistent with this analysis that homosexuality, when protected or found officially acceptable, would primarily be in private (i.e., in the closet) and primarily parodying rather than challenging the heterosexual model. Kenneth Karst attempts to include both approaches to privacy in his formation of "intimate association," yet implicitly retains the heterosexual model as central to his definition of the meaning of

intimacy. "By 'intimate association' I mean a close and familiar personal relationship with another that is in some significant way comparable to a marriage or family relationships . . . but in principle the idea of intimate association also includes close friendship, with or without any such links." K. L. Karst, "The Freedom of Intimate Association," *Yale Law Journal* 89, no. 4 (March 1980), p. 629. On pornography, see *Stanley* v. *Georgia*, 394 U.S. 557 (1969) and *Lovisi* v. *Slayton*, 539 F.2d 349 (5th Cir. 1976). Taken together, these cases suggest that Mr. Stanley's privacy rights encompass looking at pornography regardless of the intrusiveness of its production, while the women depicted in the pornography Mr. Stanley looks at have no privacy rights, if they could not have "reasonably expect[ed]" privacy to attach when they permitted "onlookers" to take sexual pictures. For a discussion of privacy law in the pornography context see Ruth Colker, "Pornography and Privacy: Towards the Development of a Group-Based Theory for Sex-Based Intrusions of Privacy," 1, 2 *Law and Equality: A Journal of Theory and Practice* (forthcoming, 1983).

16. This formulation learned a lot from Tom Grey, "Eros, Civilization and the Burger Court," *Law and Contemporary Problems* 43, no. 3 (Summer 1980): 83–99.

17. Nineteenth-century feminists connected the abortion right with control over access to their sexuality. See Linda Gordon, *Woman's Body, Woman's Right: A Social History of Birth Control in America* [New York: Grossman (Viking), 1976]: esp. 100–115.

18. S. Sontag, "The Third World of Women," *Partisan Review* 40, no. 2 (1973), p. 188.

19. Such a relation has at least two aspects: the women/men relation; and woman/fetus relation. To the latter, see Adrienne Rich on the fetus as "neither as me nor as not-me." *Of Woman Born: Motherhood as Experience Institution* (New York: W. W. Norton & Co., 1976), p. 64.

20. K. Glen, "Abortion in the Courts: A Lay Woman's Historical Guide to the New Disaster Area," *Feminist Studies* 4 (1978): 1.

21. Judith Jarvis Thomson, "A Defense of Abortion," *Philosophy and Public Affairs* 1, no. 1 (1971): 47–66.

22. A. Dworkin, *Right-Wing Women* (New York: Perigee, 1983). *You must read this book!* The support of men for abortion largely evaporated or became very equivocal when the women's movement produced, instead, women who refused sex with men and left men in droves. The fact that Jane Roe was pregnant from a gang rape, a fact which was not part of the litigation (" 'Jane Roe' Says She'd Fight Abortion Battle Again," *Minneapolis Star & Tribune*, Jan. 22, 1983), is emblematic of the sexual dimension of the issue. As further evidence, see Friedrich Engels arguing that removing private housekeeping into social industry would "remove all the anxiety about 'consequences,' which today is the most essential social—moral as well as economic—factor that prevents a girl from giving herself completely to the man she loves." *Origin of the Family, Private Property and the State* (New York: International Publishers, 1973, p. 139.

23. Andrea Dworkin's analysis of the Marquis de Sade's statements on abortion reveal that "Sade extolled the sexual value of murder and he saw abortion as a form of murder . . . abortion was a sexual act, an act of lust." *Pornography: Men Possessing Women* (New York: Perigee, 1981), p. 96. One woman complaining of sexual harassment said the codirector of the abortion clinic she worked at had asked to be present during her abortion: "He said he had a fantasy about having sexual intercourse with a woman on an examining table during an abortion," she reported. "Woman accuses clinic chief of sexual harassment," *Minneapolis Star & Tribune*, May 28, 1982. Ponder *Hustler*'s cartoon depicting a naked man masturbating enthusiastically reading a book labeled *Fetal Positions* in the corner of an operating room where a woman lies on the operating table, knees agape in stirrups. A male doctor is holding up what he has just delivered with tongs, saying "Want a piece of ass, Earl? This one's stillborn." WAVPM Slide Show. This slide show is described in Teresa Hommel, "Images of Women in Pornography and Medicine," VIII, 2 *NYU Review of Law and Social Change* (1978–79): 207–14.

24. Johnnie Tillmon, "Welfare is a Women's Issue," *Liberation News Service*, February 26, 1972, in *America's Working Women: A Documentary History, 1600 to the Present*, ed. Baxandall, Gordon, and Reverby (New York: Vintage Books, 1976), pp. 357–58.

25. *H. L.* v. *Matheson*, 450 U.S. 398 (1981) (up-

holding statute requiring physicians to notify parents of "dependent, unmarried minor girl" prior to performing an abortion), *Bellotti* v. *Baird,* 443 U.S. 672 (1977) (Bellotti II) (holding that parents may not have absolute veto power over their minor daughter's decision), *Doe* v. *Gerstein,* 517 F.2d 787 (5th Cir. 1975), *aff'd* 417 U.S. 281 (1974) (mandatory written consent requirements of husbands' parents unconstitutional). In *Planned Parenthood of Mo.* v. *Danforth,* 428 U.S. 52 (1976) the Supreme Court held that a state cannot by statute allow a man to veto a wife's abortion choice in part because the state cannot give a husband rights over the woman's reproductive choice that the state itself does not have. This leads one to wonder where the states got their power to regulate (under some circumstances preclude) abortions in the second and third trimesters, where apparently "public" considerations can weigh against the woman's "private" choice. Could states, by statutes, allow husbands to veto abortions then? Whether courts can do by injunction what states cannot do by statute is discussed if not resolved in *Hagerstown Reproductive Health Services and Bonny Ann Fritz* v. *Chris Allen Fritz,* 295 Md. 268, 454 A. 2d 846 (1983). See also, *City of Akron* v. *Akron Center for Reproductive Health,* 103 S. Ct. 2481 (1983) (invalidating five city ordinances regulating where abortions may be performed (hospitals), who needs written consent by a parent (girls younger

than 15), what doctors have to tell women prior to the procedure (e.g., tactile sensitivities of a fetus), when an abortion can be performed (24 hours after consent), and how the "fetal remains" must be disposed of).

26. The following statistics were reported in 1970: 79 percent of New York City's abortion deaths occurred among black and Puerto Rican women; the abortion death rate was 4.7 times as high for Puerto Rican women, and 8 times as high for black women as for white women. Lucinda Cisler, "Unfinished Business: Birth Control and Women's Liberation," in *Sisterhood Is Powerful: An Anthology of Writings from the Women's Liberation Movement,* ed. Robin Morgan (New York: Vintage, 1970), p. 291.

27. The classic article formulating privacy as "the right to be let alone" is S. D. Warren and L. D. Brandeis, "The Right to Privacy," *Harvard Law Review* 4 (1890), p. 205. But note that *state* constitutional privacy provisions are sometimes interpreted to require funding for abortions. *Committee to Defend Reproductive Rights* v. *Meyers,* 29 C. 3d 252, 172 Cal. Rptr. 866, 625 P. 2d 779 (1981), *Moe* v. *Society of Administration and Finance,* 417 N.E. 2d 387 (Mass. 1981).

28. I owe this conception of public debate to Jay Garfield, Hampshire College, Amherst, Massachusetts.

18. Euthanasia, Killing, and Letting Die

James Rachels

James Rachels criticizes a policy statement of the American Medical Association on the grounds that it endorses the doctrine that there is an important moral difference between active and passive euthanasia. Rachels denies that there is any moral difference between the two. He argues that once we judge a patient would be better off dead, it should not matter much whether that patient is killed or let die. He points out that both killing and letting die can be intentional and deliberate and can proceed from the same motives; further, that when killing and letting die are similar in these and other relevant respects, our moral assessment of these acts is also similar. Rachels concludes by considering a number of counterarguments to his view and finds them all wanting. In particu-

From *Ethical Issues Relating to Life and Death,* edited by John Ladd, pp. 146–161. Copyright © 1979 Oxford University Press, Inc. Reprinted by permission.

lar, Rachels rejects the idea that the killing and letting die distinction can be supported on the grounds that our duty to refrain from harming people is much stronger than our duty to help people in need. Rather, he contends that when conditions are similar our duty to refrain from harming people and our duty to help people in need have a similar moral force.

Dr. F. J. Ingelfinger, former editor of *The New England Journal of Medicine,* observes that

> This is the heyday of the ethicist in medicine. He delineates the rights of patients, of experimental subjects, of fetuses, of mothers, of animals, and even of doctors. (And what a far cry it is from the days when medical "ethics" consisted of condemning economic improprieties such as fee splitting and advertising!) With impeccable logic—once certain basic assumptions are granted—and with graceful prose, the ethicist develops his arguments. . . . Yet his precepts are essentially the products of armchair exercise and remain abstract and idealistic until they have been tested in the laboratory of experience.[1]

One problem with such armchair exercises, he complains, is that in spite of the impeccable logic and the graceful prose, the result is often an absolutist ethic which is unsatisfactory when applied to particular cases, and which is therefore of little use to the practicing physician. Unlike some absolutist philosophers, "the practitioner appears to prefer the principles of individualism. As there are few atheists in fox holes, there tend to be few absolutists at the bedside."[2]

I must concede at the outset that this chapter is another exercise in "armchair ethics" in the sense that I am not a physician but a philosopher. Yet I am no absolutist; and my purpose is to examine a doctrine that *is* held in an absolute form by many doctors. The doctrine is that there is an important moral difference between active and passive euthanasia, such that even though the latter is sometimes permissible, the former is always forbidden. This is an absolute which doctors hold "at the bedside" as well as in the seminar room, and the "principles of individualism" make little headway against it. But I will argue that this is an irrational dogma, and that there is no sound moral basis for it.

I will not argue, simply, that active euthanasia is all right. Rather, I will be concerned with the *relation* between active euthanasia and passive euthanasia: I will argue that there is no moral difference between them. By this I mean that there is no reason to prefer one over the other as a matter of principle—the fact that one case of euthanasia is active, while another is passive, is not *itself* a reason to think one morally better than the other. If you already think that passive euthanasia is all right, and you are convinced by my arguments, then you may conclude that active euthanasia must be all right, too. On the other hand, if you believe that active euthanasia is immoral, you may want to conclude that passive euthanasia must be immoral, too. Although I prefer the former alternative, I will not argue for it here. I will only argue that the two forms of euthanasia are morally equivalent—either both are acceptable or both are unacceptable.

I am aware that this will at first seem incredible to many readers, but I hope that this impression will be dispelled as the discussion proceeds. The discussion will be guided by two methodological considerations, both of which are touched on in the editorial quoted above. The first has to do with my "basic assumptions." My arguments are intended to appeal to all reasonable people, and not merely to those who already share my philosophical preconceptions. Therefore, I will try not to rely on any assumptions that cannot be accepted by any reasonable person. None of my arguments will depend on morally eccentric premises. Second, Dr. Ingelfinger is surely correct when he says that we must be as concerned with the realities of medical practice as with the more abstract issues of moral theory. As he notes, the philosopher's precepts "remain abstract and idealistic until they are tested in the laboratory of experience." Part of my argument will be precisely that, when "tested in the laboratory of experience," the doctrine in question has terrible results. I believe that if this doctrine were to be recognized as irrational, and rejected by the medical profession, the benefit to both doctors and patients would be enormous. In this sense, my paper is not intended as an "armchair exercise" at all.

The American Medical Association Policy Statement

"Active euthanasia," as the term is used, means taking some positive action designed to kill the patient; for example, giving him a lethal injection of potassium chloride. "Passive euthanasia," on the other hand, means simply refraining from doing anything to keep the patient alive. In passive euthanasia we withhold medication or other life-sustaining therapy, or we refuse to perform surgery, etc., and let the patient die "naturally" of whatever ills already afflict him.

Many doctors and theologians prefer to use the term "euthanasia" only in connection with active euthanasia, and they use other words to refer to what I am calling "passive euthanasia"—for example, instead of "passive euthanasia" they may speak of "the right to death with dignity." One reason for this choice of terms is the emotional impact of the words: it *sounds* so much better to defend "death with dignity" than to advocate "euthanasia" of any sort. And of course if one believes that there is a great moral difference between active and passive euthanasia—as most doctors and religious writers do—then one may prefer a terminology which puts as much psychological distance as possible between them. However, I do not want to become involved in a pointless dispute about terminology, because nothing of substance depends on which label is used. I will stay with the terms "active euthanasia" and "passive euthanasia" because they are the most convenient; but if the reader prefers a different terminology he may substitute his own throughout, and my arguments will be unaffected.

The belief that there is an important moral difference between active and passive euthanasia obviously has important consequences for medical practice. It makes a difference to what doctors are willing to do. Consider, for example, the following familiar situation. A patient who is dying from incurable cancer of the throat is in terrible pain that we can no longer satisfactorily alleviate. He is certain to die within a few days, but he decides that he does not want to go on living for those days since the pain is unbearable. So he asks the doctor to end his life now; and his family joins in the request. One way that the doctor might comply with this request is simply by killing the patient with a lethal injection. Most doctors would not do that, not only because of the possible legal consequences, but because they think such a course would be immoral. And this is understandable: the idea of killing someone goes against very deep moral feelings; and besides, as we are often reminded, it is the special business of doctors to save and protect life, not to destroy it. Yet, even so, the physician may sympathize with the dying patient's request and feel that it is entirely reasonable for him to prefer death now rather than after a few more days of agony. The doctrine that we are considering tells the doctor what to do: it says that although he may not administer the lethal injection—that would be "active euthanasia," which is forbidden—he *may* withhold treatment and let the patient die sooner than he otherwise would.

It is no wonder that this simple idea is so widely accepted, for it seems to give the doctor a way out of his dilemma without having to kill the patient, and without having to prolong the patient's agony. The idea is not a new one. What *is* new is that the idea is now being incorporated into official documents of medical ethics. What was once unofficially done is now becoming official policy. The idea is expressed, for example, in a 1973 policy statement of the American Medical Association, which says (in its entirety):

> The intentional termination of the life of one human being by another—mercy killing—is contrary to that for which the medical profession stands and is contrary to the policy of the American Medical Association.

The cessation of the employment of extraordinary means to prolong the life of the body when there is irrefutable evidence that biological death is imminent is the decision of the patient and/or his immediate family. The advice and judgment of the physician should be freely available to the patient and/or his immediate family.[3]

This is a cautiously worded statement, and it is not clear *exactly* what is being affirmed. I take it, however, that at least these three propositions are intended:

1. Killing patients is absolutely forbidden; however, it is sometimes permissible to allow patients to die.
2. It is permissible to allow a patient to die if
   a. there is irrefutable evidence that he will die soon anyway;
   b. "extraordinary" measures would be required to keep him alive; and
   c. the patient and/or his immediate family requests it.
3. Doctors should make their own advice and judgments available to the patient and/or his immediate family when the latter are deciding whether to request that the patient be allowed to die.

The first proposition expresses the doctrine which is the main subject of this paper. As for the third, it seems obvious enough, provided that 1 and 2 are accepted, so I shall say nothing further about it.

I do want to say a few things about 2. Physicians often allow patients to die; however, they do *not* always keep to the guidelines set out in 2. For example, a doctor may leave instructions that if a hopeless, comatose patient suffers cardiac arrest, nothing be done to start his heart beating again. "No-coding" is the name given to this practice, and the consent of the patient and/or his immediate family is not commonly sought. This is thought to be a medical decision (in reality, of course, it is a moral one) which is the doctor's affair. To take a different sort of example, when a Down's infant (a mongoloid) is born with an intestinal blockage, the doctor and parents may agree

that there will be no operation to remove the blockage, so that the baby will die.[4] (If the same infant were born without the obstruction, it certainly would not be killed. This is a clear application of the idea that "letting die" is all right even though killing is forbidden.) But in such cases it is clear that the baby is *not* going to die soon anyway. If the surgery were performed, the baby would proceed to a "normal" infancy—normal, that is, for a mongoloid. Moreover, the treatment required to save the baby—abdominal surgery—can hardly be called "extraordinary" by today's medical standards.

Therefore, all three conditions which the AMA statement places on the decision to let die are commonly violated. It is beyond the scope of this paper to determine whether doctors are right to violate those conditions. But I firmly believe that the second requirement—2b—is not acceptable. Only a little reflection is needed to show that the distinction between ordinary and extraordinary means is not important. Even a very conservative, religiously-oriented writer such as Paul Ramsey stresses this. Ramsey gives these examples:

> Suppose that a diabetic patient long accustomed to self-administration of insulin falls victim to terminal cancer, or suppose that a terminal cancer patient suddenly develops diabetes. Is he in the first case obliged to continue, and in the second case obliged to begin, insulin treatment and die painfully of cancer, or in either or both cases may the patient choose rather to pass into diabetic coma and an earlier death? . . . Or an old man slowly deteriorating who from simply being inactive and recumbent gets pneumonia: are we to use antibiotics in a likely successful attack upon this disease which from time immemorial has been called "the old man's friend"?[5]

I agree with Ramsey, and with many other writers, that in such cases treatment may be withheld even though it is not "extraordinary" by any reasonable standard. Contrary to what is implied by the AMA statement, the distinction between heroic and nonheroic means of treatment can *not* be used to determine when treatment is or is not mandatory.

Killing and Letting Die

I return now to the distinction between active and passive euthanasia. Of course, not every doctor believes that this distinction is morally important. Over twenty years ago Dr. D. C. S. Cameron of the American Cancer Society said that "Actually the difference between euthanasia [i.e., killing] and letting the patient die by omitting life-sustaining treatment is a moral quibble."[6] I argue that Cameron was right.

The initial thought can be expressed quite simply. In any case in which euthanasia seems desirable, it is because we think that the patient would literally be better off dead—or at least, no worse off dead—than continuing the kind of life available to him. (Without this assumption, even *passive* euthanasia would be unthinkable.) But, as far as the main question of ending the patient's life is concerned, it does not matter whether the euthanasia is active or passive: *in either case,* he ends up dead sooner than he otherwise would. And if the results are the same, why should it matter so much which method is used?

Moreover, we need to remember that, in cases such as that of the terminal cancer-patient, the justification for allowing him to die, rather than prolonging his life for a few more hopeless days, is that he is in horrible pain. But if we simply withhold treatment, it may take him *longer* to die, and so he will suffer *more* than he would if we were to administer the lethal injection. This fact provides strong reason for thinking that, once we have made the initial decision not to prolong his agony, active euthanasia is actually preferable to passive euthanasia rather than the reverse. It also shows a kind of incoherence in the conventional view: to say that passive euthanasia is preferable is to endorse the option which leads to more suffering rather than less, and is contrary to the humanitarian impulse which prompts the decision not to prolong his life in the first place.

But many people are convinced that there is an important moral difference between active and passive euthanasia because they think that, in passive euthanasia, the doctor does not really *do* anything. No action whatever is taken; the doctor simply does nothing, and the patient dies of whatever ills already afflict him. In active euthanasia, however, we *do something* to bring about the patient's death. We kill him. Thus, the difference between active and passive euthanasia is thought to be the difference between doing something to bring about someone's death, and not doing anything to bring about anyone's death. And of course if we conceive the matter in *this* way, passive euthanasia seems preferable. Ramsey, who denounces the view I am defending as "extremist" and who regards the active/passive distinction as one of the "flexibly wise categories of traditional medical ethics," takes just this view of the matter. He says that the choice between active and passive euthanasia "is not a choice between directly and indirectly willing and doing something. *It is rather the important choice between doing something and doing nothing,* or (better said) ceasing to do something that was begun in order to do something that is better because now more fitting."[7]

This is a very misleading way of thinking, for it ignores the fact that in passive euthanasia the doctor *does* do one thing which is very important: namely, he lets the patient die. We may overlook this obvious fact—or at least, we may put it out of our minds—if we concentrate only on a very restricted way of describing what happens: "The doctor does not administer medication or any other therapy; he does not instruct the nurses to administer any such medication; he does not perform any surgery"; and so on. And of course this description of what happens is correct, as far as it goes—these are all things that the doctor does not do. But the point is that the doctor *does* let the patient die when he could save him, and this must be included in the description, too.

There is another reason why we might fall into this error. We might confuse *not saving* someone with *letting him die.* Suppose a patient is dying, and Dr. X could prolong his life. But he decides not to do so and the patient dies. Now it is true of everyone on earth that he did not save the patient. Dr. X did not save him, and neither did you, and neither did I. So we might be tempted to think that all of us are in the same moral position, reasoning that since neither you nor I are responsible for the patient's death, neither is Dr. X. None of us did anything. This, however, is a mistake, for even though it is true that none of us saved the patient, it is *not* true that we all let him die. In order to let someone die, one must be *in a position* to save him. You and I were not in a position to save the patient, so we did not let him die. Dr. X, on the other hand, was in a position to save him, and did let him die. Thus the doctor is in a special moral position which not just everyone is in.

Here we must remember some elementary points, which are so obvious that they would not be worth mentioning except for the fact that overlooking them is a source of so much confusion in this area. The act of letting someone die may be intentional and deliberate, just as the act of killing someone may be intentional and deliberate. Moreover, the doctor is *responsible* for his decision to let the patient die, just as he would be responsible for giving the patient a lethal injection. The decision to let a patient die is subject to moral appraisal in the same way that a decision to kill is subject to moral appraisal: it may be assessed as wise or unwise, compassionate or sadistic, right or wrong. If a doctor deliberately let a patient die who was suffering from a routinely curable illness, then he would be to blame for what he did, just as he would be to blame if he had needlessly killed the patient. It would be no defense at all for him to insist that, *really,* he didn't "do anything" but just stand there. We would all know that he did do something very serious indeed, for he let the patient die.

These considerations show how misleading it is to characterize the difference between active and passive euthanasia as a difference between doing something (killing), for which the doctor may be morally culpable; and doing nothing (just standing there while the patient dies), for which the doctor is not culpable. The real difference between them is, rather, the difference between *killing* and letting die, both of which are actions for which a doctor, or anyone else, will be morally responsible.

Now we can formulate our problem more precisely. If there is an important moral difference between active and passive euthanasia,

it must be because *killing someone is morally worse than letting someone die.* But is it? Is killing, in itself, worse than letting die? In order to investigate this issue, we may consider two cases which are exactly alike except that one involves killing where the other involves letting someone die. Then we can ask whether this difference makes any difference to our moral assessments. It is important that the cases be *exactly* alike except for this one difference, since otherwise we cannot be confident that it is *this* difference which accounts for any variation in our assessments.

1. Smith stands to gain a large inheritance if anything should happen to his six-year-old cousin. One evening while the child is taking his bath, Smith sneaks into the bathroom and drowns the child, and then arranges things so that it will look like an accident.

2. Jones also stands to gain if anything should happen to his six-year-old cousin. Like Smith, Jones sneaks in planning to drown the child in his bath. However, just as he enters the bathroom Jones sees the child slip, hit his head, and fall face down in the water. Jones is delighted; he stands by, ready to push the child's head back under if it is necessary, but it is not necessary. With only a little thrashing about, the child drowns all by himself, "accidentally," as Jones watches and does nothing.

Now Smith killed the child, while Jones "merely" let the child die. That is the only difference between them. Did either man behave better, from a moral point of view? Is there a moral difference between them? *If the difference between killing and letting die were itself a morally important matter, then we should say that Jones's behavior was less reprehensible than Smith's.* But do we actually want to say that? I think not, for several reasons. In the first place, both men acted from the same motive, personal gain, and both had exactly the same end in view when they acted. We may infer from Smith's conduct that he is a bad man, although we may withdraw or modify that judgment if we learn certain further facts about him; for example, that he is mentally deranged. But would we not also infer the very same thing about Jones from his conduct? And would not the same further considerations also be relevant to any modification of that judgment? Moreover, suppose Jones pleaded in his defense, "After all, I didn't kill the child. I only stood there and let him die." Again, if letting die were in itself less bad than killing, this defense should have some weight. But—morally, at least—it does not. Such a "defense" can only be regarded as a grotesque perversion of moral reasoning.

Thus, it seems that when we are careful not to smuggle in any further differences which prejudice the issue, the mere difference between killing and letting die does not itself make any difference to the morality of actions concerning life and death.[8]

Now it may be pointed out, quite properly, that the cases of euthanasia with which doctors are concerned are not like this at all. They do not involve personal gain or the destruction of normal, healthy children. Doctors are concerned only with cases in which the patient's life is of no further use to him, or in which the patient's life has become or soon will become a positive burden. However, the point is the same in those cases: the difference between killing or letting die does not, *in itself*, make a difference, from the point of view of morality. If a doctor lets a patient die, for humane reasons, he is in the same moral position as if he had given the patient a lethal injection for humane reasons. If his decision was wrong—if, for example, the patient's illness was in fact curable—then the decision would be equally regrettable no matter which method was used to carry it out. And if the doctor's decision was the right one, then the method he used is not itself important.

The AMA statement isolates the crucial issue very well: "the intentional termination of the life of one human being by another." But then the statement goes on to deny that the cessation of treatment *is* the intentional termination of a life. This is where the mistake comes in, for what is the cessation of treatment, in those circumstances, if it is not "the intentional termination of the life of one human being by another"? Of course it is exactly that; if it were not, there would be no point to it.

Counter-Arguments

Our argument has now brought us to this point: we cannot draw any moral distinction between active and passive euthanasia on the grounds that one involves killing while the other only involves letting someone die, because that is a difference that does not make a difference, from a moral point of view. Some people will find this hard to accept. One reason, I think, is that they fail to distinguish the question of whether killing is, in itself, worse than letting die, from the very different question of whether most actual cases of killing are more reprehensible than most actual cases of letting die. Most actual cases of killing are clearly terrible—think of the murders reported in the newspapers—and we hear of such cases almost every day. On the other hand, we hardly ever hear of a case of letting die, except for the actions of doctors who are motivated by humanitarian reasons. So we learn to think of killing in a much worse light than letting die; and we conclude, invalidly, that there must be something about killing which makes it *in itself* worse than letting die. But this does not follow for it is not the bare difference between killing and letting die that makes the difference in these cases. Rather, it is the other factors—the murderer's motive of personal gain, for example, contrasted with the doctor's humanitarian motivation, or the fact that the murderer kills a healthy person while the doctor lets die a terminal patient racked with disease—that account for our different reactions to the different cases.

There are, however, some substantial arguments that may be advanced to oppose my conclusion. Here are two of them:

The first counter-argument focuses specifically on the concept of *being the cause of someone's death*. If we kill someone, then we are the cause of his death. But if we merely let someone die, we are not the cause; rather, he dies of whatever condition he already has. The doctor who gives the cancer patient a lethal injection will have caused his patient's death, and will have this on his conscience; whereas if he merely ceases treatment, the cancer and not the doctor is the cause of death. This is supposed to make a moral difference. This argument has been advanced many times. Ramsey, for example, urges us to remember that "In omission no human agent causes the patient's death, directly or indirectly."[9] And, writing in the *Villanova Law Review* for 1968, Dr. J. Russell Elkinton said that what makes the active/passive distinction important is that in passive euthanasia, "the patient does not die from the act [e.g. the act of turning off the respirator] but from the underlying disease or injury."[10]

This argument will not do, for two reasons. First, just as there is a distinction to be drawn between being and not being the cause of someone's death, there is also a distinction to be drawn between letting someone die and not letting anyone die. It is certainly desirable, in general, not to be the cause of anyone's death; but it is also desirable, in general, not to let anyone die when we can save them. (Doctors act on this precept every day.) Therefore, we cannot draw any special conclusion about the relative desirability of passive euthanasia just on these grounds. Second, the reason why we think it is bad to be the cause of someone's death is that we think that death is a great evil—and so it is. However, if we have decided that euthanasia, even passive euthanasia, is desirable in a given case, then we have decided that in *this* instance death is no greater an evil than the patient's continued existence. And if this is true, then the usual reason for not wanting to be the cause of someone's death simply does not apply. To put the point just a bit differently: There is nothing wrong with being the cause of someone's death if his death is, all things considered, a good thing. And if his death is *not* a good thing, then *no* form of euthanasia, active or passive, is justified. So once again we see that the two kinds of euthanasia stand or fall together.

The second counter-argument appeals to a favorite idea of philosophers, namely that our duty not to harm people is generally more stringent than our duty to help them. The law affirms this when it forbids us to kill people, or steal their goods, but does not require us in general to save people's lives or give them charity. And this is said to be not merely a point about the law, but about morality as well. We do not have a strict moral duty to help some poor man in Ethiopia—although it might be kind and generous of us if we did—but we *do* have a strict moral duty to refrain from doing anything to harm him. Killing someone is a violation of our duty not to harm, whereas letting someone die is merely a failure to give help. Therefore, the former is a more serious breach of morality than the latter; and so, contrary to what was said above, there is a morally significant difference between killing and letting die.

This argument has a certain superficial plausibility, but it cannot be used to show that there is a morally important difference between active and passive euthanasia. For one thing, it only seems that our duty to help people is less stringent than our duty not to harm them when we concentrate on certain sorts of cases: cases in which the people we could help are very far away, and are strangers to us; or cases in which it would be very difficult for us to help them, or in which helping would require a substantial sacrifice on our part. Many people feel that, in *these* types of cases, it may be kind and generous of us to give help, but we are not morally required to do so. Thus it is felt that when we give money for famine relief we are being especially big-hearted, and we deserve special praise—even if it would be immodest of us to seek such praise—because we are doing more than, strictly speaking, we are required to do.[11]

However, if we think of cases in which it would be very easy for us to help someone who is close at hand and in which no great personal sacrifice is required, things look very different. Think again of the child drowning in the bathtub: *of course* a man standing next to the tub would have a strict moral duty to help the child. Here the alleged asymmetry between the duty to help and the duty not to do harm vanishes. Since most of the cases of euthanasia with which we are concerned are of this latter type—the patient is close at hand, it is well within the professional skills of the physician to keep him alive—the alleged asymmetry has little relevance.

It should also be remembered, in considering this argument, that the duty of doctors toward their patients *is* precisely to help them; that is what doctors are supposed to do. Therefore, even if there were a general asymmetry between the duty to help and the duty not to harm—which I deny—it would not apply in the special case of the relation between doctors and their patients. Finally, it is not clear that killing such a patient *is* harming him, even though in other cases it certainly is a great harm to someone to kill him, for as I said before, we are going under the assumption that the patient would be no worse off dead than he is now; if this is so, then killing him is not harming him. For the same reason we should not classify letting such a patient die as failing to help him. Therefore, even if we grant that our duty to help people is less stringent than our duty not to harm them, nothing follows about our duties with respect to killing and letting die in the special case of euthanasia.

Practical Consequences

This is enough, I think, to show that the doctrine underlying the AMA statement is false. There is no general moral difference between active and passive euthanasia; if one is permissible, so is the other. Now if this were merely an intellectual mistake, having no significant consequences for medical practice, the whole matter would not be very important. But the opposite is true: the doctrine has terrible consequences for, as I have already mentioned—and as doctors know very well—the process of being "allowed to die" can be relatively slow and painful, while being given a lethal injection is relatively quick and painless. Dr. Anthony Shaw describes what happens when the decision has been made not to perform the surgery necessary to "save" a mongoloid infant:

> When surgery is denied [the doctor] must try to keep the infant from suffering while natural forces sap the baby's life away. As a surgeon whose natural inclination is to use the scalpel to fight off death, standing by and watching a salvageable baby die is the most emotionally exhausting experience I know. It is easy at a conference, in a theoretical discussion, to decide that such infants

should be allowed to die. It is altogether different to stand by in the nursery and watch as dehydration and infection wither a tiny being over hours and days. This is a terrible ordeal for me and the hospital staff—much more so than for the parents who never set foot in the nursery.[12]

Why must the hospital staff "stand by in the nursery and watch as dehydration and infection wither a tiny being over hours and days"? Why must they merely "try" to reduce the infant's suffering? The doctrine which says that the baby may be allowed to dehydrate and wither, but not be given an injection which would end its life without suffering, is not only irrational but cruel.

The same goes for the case of the man with cancer of the throat. Here there are three options: with continued treatment, he will have a few more days of pain, and then die; if treatment is stopped, but nothing else is done, it will be a few more hours; and with a lethal injection, he will die at once. Those who oppose euthanasia in all its forms say that we must take the first option, and keep the patient alive for as long as possible. This view is so patently inhumane that few defend it; nevertheless, it does have a certain kind of integrity. It is at least consistent. The third option is the one I think best. But the *middle* position—that, although the patient need not suffer for days before dying, he must nevertheless suffer for a few more hours—is a "moderate" view which incorporates the worst, and not the best, features of both extremes.

Let me mention one other practice that we would be well rid of if we stopped thinking that the distinction between active and passive euthanasia is important. About one in six hundred babies born in the United States is mongoloid. Most of these babies are otherwise healthy—that is, with only the usual pediatric care, they will proceed to a "normal" infancy. Some, however, are born with other congenital defects such as intestinal obstructions which require surgery if the baby is to live. As I have already mentioned, sometimes the surgery is withheld and the baby dies. But when there is no defect requiring surgery, the baby lives on.[13] Now surgery to remove an intestinal obstruction is not difficult; the reason why it is not performed in such cases is, clearly, that the child is mongoloid and the parents and doctor judge that because of *this* it is better for the child to die.

But notice that this situation is absurd, no matter what view one takes of the lives and potentials of such babies. If you think that the life of such an infant is worth preserving, then what does it matter if it needs a simple operation? Or, if you think it better that such a baby not live on, then what difference does it make if its intestinal tract is *not* blocked? In either case, the matter of life or death is being decided on irrelevant grounds. It is the mongolism, and not the intestine, that is the issue. The matter should be decided, if at all, on *that* basis, and not be allowed to depend on the essentially irrelevant question of whether the intestinal tract is blocked.

What makes this situation possible, of course, is the idea that when there is an intestinal obstruction we can "let the baby die," but when there is no such defect there is nothing we can do, for we must not "kill" it. The fact that this idea leads to such results as deciding life or death on irrelevant grounds is another good reason why it should be rejected.

Doctors may think that all of this is only of academic interest, the sort of thing which philosophers may worry about but which has no practical bearing on their own work. After all, doctors must be concerned about the legal consequences of what they do, and active euthanasia is clearly forbidden by the law. They are right to be concerned about this. There have not been many prosecutions of doctors in the United States for active euthanasia, but there have been some. Prosecutions for passive euthanasia, on the other hand, are virtually nonexistent, even though there are laws under which charges could be brought, and even though this practice is much more widespread. Passive euthanasia, unlike active euthanasia, is by and large tolerated by the law. The law may sometimes compel a doctor to take action which he might not otherwise take to keep a patient alive,[14] but of course this is very different from bringing criminal charges against him after the patient is dead.

Even so, doctors should be concerned with the fact that the law and public opinion are

forcing upon them an indefensible moral position, which has a considerable effect on their practices. Of course, most doctors are not now in the position of being coerced in this matter, for they do not regard themselves as merely going along with what the law requires. Rather, in statements such as the AMA statement that I quoted, they are endorsing the doctrine as a central point of medical ethics. In that statement, active euthanasia is condemned not merely as illegal but as "contrary to that for which the medical profession stands," while passive euthanasia is approved. However, if my arguments have been sound, there really is no intrinsic moral difference between them (although there may be morally important differences in their consequences, varying from case to case); so while doctors may have to discriminate between them to satisfy the law, they should not do any *more* than that. In particular, they should not give the distinction any added authority and weight by writing it into official statements of medical ethics.

Notes

1. F. J. Ingelfinger, "Bedside Ethics for the Hopeless Case," *The New England Journal of Medicine* 289 (25 October 1973), p. 914.

2. Ibid.

3. This statement was approved by the House of Delegates of the AMA on December 4, 1973. It is worth noting that some state medical societies have advised *patients* to take a similar attitude toward the termination of their lives. In 1973 the Connecticut State Medical Society approved a "background statement" to be signed by terminal patients which includes this sentence: "I value life and the dignity of life, so that I am not asking that my life be directly taken, but that my life not be unreasonably prolonged or the dignity of life be destroyed." Other state medical societies have followed suit.

4. A discussion of this type of case can be found in Anthony Shaw, " 'Doctor, Do We Have a Choice?' " *The New York Times Magazine*, 30 January 1972, pp. 44–54. Also see Shaw's "Dilemmas of 'Informed Consent' in Children," *The New*

England Journal of Medicine 289 (25 October 1973), pp. 885–90.

5. Paul Ramsey, *The Patient as Person* (New Haven, Conn.: Yale University Press, 1970), pp. 115–16.

6. D. C. S. Cameron, *The Truth About Cancer* (Englewood Cliffs, N.J.: Prentice-Hall, 1956), p. 116.

7. Ramsey, *The Patient as Person*, p. 151.

8. Judith Jarvis Thomson has argued that this line of reasoning is unsound. Consider, she says, this argument which is parallel to the one involving Smith and Jones:

Alfrieda knows that if she cuts off Alfred's head he will die, and wanting him to die, cuts it off; Bertha knows that if she punches Bert in the nose he will die—Bert is in peculiar physical condition—and, wanting him to die, punches him in the nose. But what Bertha does is surely every bit as bad as what Alfrieda does. So cutting off a man's head isn't worse than punching a man in the nose. ["Killing, Letting Die, and the Trolley Problem," *The Monist* 59 (1976), p. 204.]

She concludes that, since this absurd argument doesn't prove anything, the Smith/Jones argument doesn't prove anything either.

However, I think that the Alfrieda/Bertha argument is not absurd, as strange as it is. A little analysis shows that it is a sound argument and that its conclusion is true. We need to notice first that the reason why it is wrong to chop someone's head off is, obviously, that this causes death. The act is objectionable because of its consequences. Thus, a different act with the same consequences may be equally objectionable. In Thomson's example, punching Bert in the nose has the same consequences as chopping off Alfred's head; and, indeed, the two actions are equally bad.

Now the Alfrieda/Bertha argument presupposes a distinction between the act of chopping off someone's head, and the results of this act, the victim's death. (It is stipulated that, except for the fact that Alfrieda chops off someone's head, while Bertha punches someone in the nose, the two acts are "in all other respects alike." The "*other*" respects" include the act's consequence, the victim's death.) This is not a distinction we would normally think to make, since we cannot in fact cut off someone's head without killing him. Yet in thought the distinction can be drawn. The question raised in the argument, then, is whether, *considered apart from their consequences,*

head-chopping is worse than nose-punching. And the answer to *this* strange question is No, just as the argument says it should be.

The conclusion of the argument should be construed like this: The bare fact that one act is an act of head-chopping, while another act is an act of nose-punching, is not a reason for judging the former to be worse than the latter. At the same time—and this is perfectly compatible with the argument—the fact that one act causes death, while another does not, *is* a reason for judging the former to be worse. The parallel construal of my conclusion is: The bare fact that one act is an act of killing, while another act is an act of letting die, is not a reason for judging the former to be worse than the latter. At the same time—and this is perfectly compatible with my argument—the fact that an act (of killing, for example) prevents suffering, while another act (of letting die, for example) does not, *is* a reason for preferring one over the other. So once we see exactly how the Alfrieda/Bertha argument *is* parallel to the Smith/Jones argument, we find that Thomson's argument is, surprisingly, quite all right.

9. Ramsey, *The Patient as Person*, p. 151.

10. J. Russell Elkinton, "The Dying Patient, the Doctor, and the Law," *Villanova Law Review* 13 (Summer 1968), p. 743.

11. For the purposes of this essay we do not need to consider whether this way of thinking about "charity" is justified. There are, however, strong arguments that it is morally indefensible: see Peter Singer, "Famine, Affluence, and Morality," *Philosophy and Public Affairs* 1 (Spring 1972), pp. 229–43. Also see James Rachels, "Killing and Letting People Die of Starvation," forthcoming in *Philosophy,* for a discussion of the killing/letting die distinction in the context of world hunger, as well as further arguments that the distinction is morally unimportant.

12. Shaw, " 'Doctor, Do We Have a Choice?' " p. 54.

13. See the articles by Shaw cited in note 4.

14. For example, in February 1974 a Superior Court judge in Maine ordered a doctor to proceed with an operation to repair a hole in the esophagus of a baby with multiple deformities. Otherwise the operation would not have been performed. The baby died anyway a few days later. "Deformed Baby Dies Amid Controversy," *The Miami Herald,* 25 February 1974, p. 4-B.

19. The Intentional Termination of Life

Bonnie Steinbock

Bonnie Steinbock defends the policy statement of the American Medical Association on euthanasia against James Rachels's critique. She argues that the statement does not rest on the belief that there is a moral difference between active and passive euthanasia. Rather, she contends that the statement rejects both active and passive euthanasia but permits "the cessation of the employment of extraordinary means," which she claims is not the same as passive euthanasia. She points out that doctors can cease to employ extraordinary means to respect the wishes of the patient or because continued treatment is painful and has little chance of success, without intending to let the patient die. She allows, however, that in some cases, ceasing to employ extraordinary means does amount to intending to let the patient die and also that in other cases, killing may even be morally preferable to letting die.

According to James Rachels[1] a common mistake in medical ethics is the belief that there is a moral difference between active and passive euthanasia. This is a mistake, [he] argues, because the rationale underlying the distinction between active and passive euthanasia is the idea that there is a significant moral difference between intentionally killing and letting die. . . . Whether the belief that there is a significant moral difference (between intentionally killing and intentionally letting die) is mistaken is not my concern here. For it is far from clear that this distinction *is* the basis of the doctrine of the American Medical Association which Rachels attacks. And if the killing/letting die distinction is not the basis of the AMA doctrine, then arguments showing that the distinction has no moral force do not, in themselves, reveal in the doctrine's adherents either "confused thinking" or "a moral point of view unrelated to the interests of individuals". Indeed, as we examine the AMA doctrine, I think it will become clear that it appeals to and makes use of a number of overlapping distinctions, which may have moral significance in particular cases, such as the distinction between intending and foreseeing, or

Reprinted with permission from *Ethics in Science and Medicine*, pp. 59–64, Bonnie Steinbock, "The Intentional Termination of Life." Copyright 1979, Pergamon Press, Ltd.

between ordinary and extraordinary care. Let us then turn to the statement, from the House of Delegates of the American Medical Association, which Rachels cites:

> The intentional termination of the life of one human being by another—mercy-killing—is contrary to that for which the medical profession stands and is contrary to the policy of the American Medical Association.
>
> The cessation of the employment of extraordinary means to prolong the life of the body when there is irrefutable evidence that biological death is imminent is the decision of the patient and/or his immediate family. The advice and judgment of the physician should be freely available to the patient and/or his immediate family.[2]

Rachels attacks this statement because he believes that it contains a moral distinction between active and passive euthanasia. . . .

I intend to show that the AMA statement does not imply support of the active/passive euthanasia distinction. In forbidding the intentional termination of life, the statement rejects both active and passive euthanasia. It does allow for ". . . the cessation of the employment of extraordinary means . . ." to prolong life. The mistake Rachels makes is in identifying the cessation of life-prolonging treatment with passive euthanasia, or intentionally letting die. If it were right to equate the two, then the AMA statement would be self-contradictory, for it would begin by condemning, and end by allowing, the intentional termination of life. But if the cessation of life-prolonging treatment is not always or necessarily passive euthanasia, then there is no confusion and no contradiction.

Why does Rachels think that the cessation of life-prolonging treatment is the intentional termination of life? He says:

> The AMA policy statement isolates the crucial issue very well: the crucial issue is "the intentional termination of the life of one human being by another". But after identifying this issue, and forbidding "mercy-killing", the statement goes on to deny that the cessation of treatment is the intentional termination of a life. This is where the mistake comes in, for what is the cessation of treatment, in these circumstances, if it is not "the intentional termination of the life of one human being by another"? Of course it is exactly that, and if it were not, there would be no point to it.[3]

However, there *can* be a point (to the cessation of life-prolonging treatment) other than an endeavor to bring about the patient's death, and so the blanket identification of cessation of treatment with the intentional termination of a life is inaccurate. There are at least two situations in which the termination of life-prolonging treatment cannot be identified with the intentional termination of the life of one human being by another.

The first situation concerns the patient's right to refuse treatment. Rachels gives the example of a patient dying of an incurable disease, accompanied by unrelievable pain, who wants to end the treatment which cannot cure him but can only prolong his miserable existence. Why, they ask, may a doctor accede to the patient's request to stop treatment, but not provide a patient in a similar situation with a lethal dose? The answer lies in the patient's right to refuse treatment. In general, a competent adult has the right to refuse treatment, even where such treatment is necessary to prolong life. Indeed, the right to refuse treatment has been upheld even when the patient's reason for refusing treatment is generally agreed to be inadequate.[4] This right can be overridden (if, for example, the patient has dependent children) but, in general, no one may legally compel you to undergo treatment to which you have not consented. "Historically, surgical intrusion has always been considered a technical battery upon the person and one to be excused or justified by consent of the patient or justified by necessity created by the circumstances of the moment. . . ."[5]

At this point, it might be objected that if one has the right to refuse life-prolonging treatment, then consistency demands that one have the right to decide to end his life, and to obtain help in doing so. The idea is that the right to refuse treatment somehow implies a right to voluntary euthanasia, and we need to see why someone might think this. The right to refuse treatment has been considered by legal writers as an example of the right to privacy or, better, the right to bodily self-determination. You have the right to decide what happens to your own body, and the right to refuse treatment is an instance of that more general right. But if you have the right to determine what happens to your body, then should you not have the right to choose to end your life, and even a right to get help in doing so?

However, it is important to see that the right to refuse treatment is not the same as, nor does it entail, a right to voluntary euthanasia, even if both can be derived from the right to bodily self-determination. The right to refuse treatment is not itself a "right to die"; that one may choose to exercise this right even at the risk of death, or even *in order to die,* is irrelevant. The purpose of the right to refuse medical treatment is not to give persons a right to decide whether to live or die, but to protect them from the unwanted interferences of others. Perhaps we ought to interpret the right to bodily self-determination more broadly so as to include a right to die: but this would be a substantial extension of our present understanding of the right to bodily self-determination, and not a consequence of it. Should we recognize a right to voluntary euthanasia, we would have to agree that people have the right not merely to be left alone, but also the right to be killed. I leave to one side that substantive moral issue. My claim is simply that there can be a reason for terminating life-prolonging treatment other than "to bring about the patient's death".

The second case in which termination of treatment cannot be identified with intentional termination of life is where continued treatment has little chance of improving the patient's condition and brings greater discomfort than relief.

The question here is what treatment is appropriate to the particular case. A cancer specialist describes it in this way:

> My general rule is to administer therapy as long as a patient responds well and has the potential for a reasonably good quality of life. But when all feasible therapies have been administered and a patient shows signs of rapid deterioration, the continuation of therapy can cause more discomfort than the cancer. From that time I recommend surgery, radiotherapy, or chemotherapy only as a means of relieving pain. But if a patient's condition should once again stabilize after the withdrawal of active therapy and if it should appear that he could still gain some good time, I would immediately reinstitute active therapy. The decision to cease anticancer treatment is never irrevocable, and often the desire to live will push a patient to try for another remission, or even a few more days of life.[6]

The decision here to cease anticancer treatment cannot be construed as a decision that the patient die, or as the intentional termination of life. It is a decision to provide the most appropriate treatment for that patient at that time. Rachels suggests that the point of the cessation of treatment is the intentional termination of life. But here the point of discontinuing treatment is not to bring about the patient's death but to avoid treatment that will cause more discomfort than the cancer and has little hope of benefiting the patient. Treatment that meets this description is often called "extraordinary".[7] The concept is flexible, and

what might be considered "extraordinary" in one situation might be ordinary in another. The use of a respirator to sustain a patient through a severe bout with a respiratory disease would be considered ordinary; its use to sustain the life of a severely brain damaged person in an irreversible coma would be considered extraordinary.

Contrasted with extraordinary treatment is ordinary treatment, the care a doctor would normally be expected to provide. Failure to provide ordinary care constitutes neglect, and can even be construed as the intentional infliction of harm, where there is a legal obligation to provide care. The importance of the ordinary/extraordinary care distinction lies partly in its connection to the doctor's intention. The withholding of extraordinary care should be seen as a decision not to inflict painful treatment on a patient without reasonable hope of success. The withholding of ordinary care, by contrast, must be seen as neglect. Thus, one doctor says, "We have to draw a distinction between ordinary and extraordinary means. We never withdraw what's needed to make a baby comfortable, we would never withdraw the care a parent would provide. We never kill a baby. . . . But we may decide certain heroic intervention is not worthwhile."[8]

We should keep in mind the ordinary/extraordinary care distinction when considering an example given by Rachels to show the irrationality of the active/passive distinction with regard to infanticide. The example is this: a child is born with Down's syndrome and also has an intestinal obstruction which requires corrective surgery. If the surgery is not performed, the infant will starve to death, since it cannot take food orally. This may take days or even weeks, as dehydration and infection set in. Commenting on this situation, Rachels says:

> I can understand why some people are opposed to all euthanasia, and insist that such infants must be allowed to live. I think I can also understand why other people favor destroying these babies quickly and painlessly. But why should anyone favor letting "dehydration and infection wither a tiny being over hours and days"? The doctrine that says that a

baby may be allowed to dehydrate and wither, but may not be given an injection that would end its life without suffering, seems so patently cruel as to require no further refutation.[9]

Such a doctrine perhaps does not need further refutation; but this is not the AMA doctrine. For the AMA statement criticized by Rachels allows only for the cessation of extraordinary means to prolong life when death is imminent. Neither of these conditions is satisfied in this example. Death is not imminent in this situation, any more than it would be if a normal child had an attack of appendicitis. Neither the corrective surgery to remove the intestinal obstruction, nor the intravenous feeding required to keep the infant alive until such surgery is performed, can be regarded as extraordinary means, for neither is particularly expensive, nor does either place an overwhelming burden on the patient or others. (The continued existence of the child might be thought to place an overwhelming burden on its parents, but that has nothing to do with the characterization of the means to prolong its life as extraordinary. If it had, then *feeding* a severely defective child who required a great deal of care could be regarded as extraordinary.) The chances of success if the operation is undertaken are quite good, though there is always a risk in operating on infants. Though the Down's syndrome will not be alleviated, the child will proceed to an otherwise normal infancy.

It cannot be argued that the treatment is withheld for the infant's sake, unless one is prepared to argue that all mentally retarded babies are better off dead. This is particularly implausible in the case of Down's syndrome babies who generally do not suffer and are capable of giving and receiving love, of learning and playing, to varying degrees.

In a film on this subject entitled, "Who Should Survive?", a doctor defended a decision not to operate, saying that since the parents did not consent to the operation, the doctors' hands were tied. As we have seen, surgical intrusion requires consent, and in the case of infants, consent would normally come from the parents. But, as their legal guardians, parents are required to provide medical care

for their children, and failure to do so can constitute criminal neglect or even homicide. In general, courts have been understandably reluctant to recognize a parental right to terminate life-prolonging treatment.[10] Although prosecution is unlikely, physicians who comply with invalid instructions from the parents and permit the infant's death could be liable for aiding and abetting, failure to report child neglect, or even homicide. So it is not true that, in this situation, doctors are legally bound to do as the parents wish.

To sum up, I think that Rachels is right to regard the decision not to operate in the Down's syndrome example as the intentional termination of life. But there is no reason to believe that either the law or the AMA would regard it otherwise. Certainly the decision to withhold treatment is not justified by the AMA statement. That such infants have been allowed to die cannot be denied; but this, I think, is the result of doctors misunderstanding the law and the AMA position.

Withholding treatment in this case is the intentional termination of life because the infant is deliberately allowed to die; that is the point of not operating. But there are other cases in which that is not the point. If the point is to avoid inflicting painful treatment on a patient with little or no reasonable hope of success, this is not the intentional termination of life. The permissibility of such withholding of treatment, then, would have no implications for the permissibility of euthanasia, active or passive.

The decision whether or not to operate, or to institute vigorous treatment, is particularly agonizing in the case of children born with spina bifida, an opening in the base of the spine usually accompanied by hydrocephalus and mental retardation. If left unoperated, these children usually die of meningitis or kidney failure within the first few years of life. Even if they survive, all affected children face a lifetime of illness, operations and varying degrees of disability. The policy used to be to save as many as possible, but the trend now is toward selective treatment, based on the physician's estimate of the chances of success. If operating is not likely to improve significantly the child's condition, parents and doctors may agree not to operate. This is not the intentional termination of life, for again the purpose is not the termination of the child's life but the avoidance of painful and pointless treatment. Thus, the fact that withholding treatment is justified does not imply that killing the child would be equally justified.

Throughout the discussion, I have claimed that intentionally ceasing life-prolonging treatment is not the intentional termination of life unless the doctor has, as his or her purpose in stopping treatment, the patient's death.

It may be objected that I have incorrectly characterized the conditions for the intentional termination of life. Perhaps it is enough that the doctor intentionally ceases treatment, foreseeing that the patient will die; perhaps the reason for ceasing treatment is irrelevant to its characterization as the intentional termination of life. I find this suggestion implausible, but am willing to consider arguments for it. Rachels has provided no such arguments: indeed, he apparently shares my view about the intentional termination of life. For when he claims that the cessation of life-prolonging treatment *is* the intentional termination of life, his reason for making the claim is that "if it were not, there would be no point to it". Rachels believes that the point of ceasing treatment, "in these cases", is to bring about the patient's death. If that were not the point, he suggests, why would the doctor cease treatment? I have shown, however, that there can be a point to ceasing treatment which is not the death of the patient. In showing this, I have refuted Rachels' reason for identifying the cessation of life-prolonging treatment with the intentional termination of life, and thus his argument against the AMA doctrine.

Here someone might say: Even if the withholding of treatment is not the intentional termination of life, does that make a difference, morally speaking? If life-prolonging treatment may be withheld, for the sake of the child, may not an easy death be provided, for the sake of the child, as well? The unoperated child with spina bifida may take months or even years to die. Distressed by the spectacle of children "lying around waiting to die", one doctor has written, "It is time that society and medicine stopped perpetuating the fiction that withholding treatment is ethically different from terminating a life. It is time that society

began to discuss mechanisms by which we can alleviate the pain and suffering for those individuals whom we cannot help."[11]

I do not deny that there may be cases in which death is in the best interests of the patient. In such cases, a quick and painless death may be the best thing. However, I do not think that, once active or vigorous treatment is stopped, a quick death is always preferable to a lingering one. We must be cautious about attributing to defective children *our* distress at seeing them linger. Waiting for them to die may be tough on parents, doctors and nurses—it isn't necessarily tough on the child. The decision not to operate need not mean a decision to neglect, and it may be possible to make the remaining months of the child's life comfortable, pleasant and filled with love. If this alternative is possible, surely it is more decent and humane than killing the child. In such a situation, withholding treatment, foreseeing the child's death, is not ethically equivalent to killing the child, and we cannot move from the permissibility of the former to that of the latter. I am worried that there will be a tendency to do precisely that if active euthanasia is regarded as morally equivalent to the withholding of life-prolonging treatment.

Conclusion

The AMA statement does not make the distinction Rachels wishes to attack, i.e. that between active and passive euthanasia. Instead, the statement draws a distinction between the intentional termination of life, on the one hand, and the cessation of the employment of extraordinary means to prolong life, on the other. Nothing said by Rachels shows that this distinction is confused. It may be that doctors have misinterpreted the AMA statement, and that this had led, for example, to decisions to allow defective infants slowly to starve to death. I quite agree with Rachels that the decisions to which they allude were cruel and made on irrelevant grounds. Certainly it is worth pointing out that allowing someone to die can be the intentional termination of life, and that it can be just as bad as, or worse than, killing someone. However, the withholding of life-prolonging treatment is not necessarily the intentional termination of life, so that if it is permissible to withhold life-prolonging treatment, it does not follow that, other things being equal, it is permissible to kill. Furthermore, most of the time, other things are not equal. In many of the cases in which it would be right to cease treatment, I do not think that it would also be right to kill.

Notes

1. James Rachels, Active and passive euthanasia. *New Engl. J. Med.*, **292**, 78–80, 1975.

2. Rachels, p. 78.

3. Rachels, p. 79–80.

4. For example, *In re Yetter*, 62 Pa. D. & C. 2d 619, C.P., Northampton County Ct., 1974.

5. David W. Meyers, Legal aspects of voluntary euthanasia, *Dilemmas of Euthanasia* (Edited by John Behnke and Sissela Bok), p. 56. Anchor Books, New York, 1975.

6. Ernest H. Rosenbaum, MD., *Living with Cancer,* p. 27. Praeger, New York, 1975.

7. Cf. Tristam Engelhardt, Jr., Ethical issues in aiding the death of young children, *Beneficent Euthanasia* (Edited by Marvin Kohl), Prometheus Books, Buffalo, N.Y., 1975.

8. B. D. Colen, *Karen Ann Quinlan: Living and Dying in the Age of Eternal Life,* p. 115. Nash, 1976.

9. Rachels, p. 79.

10. Cf. Norman L. Cantor, Law and the termination of an incompetent patient's life-preserving care. *Dilemmas of Euthanasia, op. cit.,* pp. 69–105.

11. John Freeman, Is there a right to die—quickly?, *J. Pediat.* **80,** p. 905.

20. *Webster* v. *Reproductive Health Services*

Supreme Court of the United States

The issue before the Supreme Court of the United States was whether a Missouri law that prohibited the use of public facilities or employees to perform abortions and required physicians to conduct viability tests prior to performing abortions violated the First, Fourth, Ninth, and Fourteenth Amendments to the Constitution. Chief Justice Rehnquist, delivering the opinion of the Court, argued that the prohibition of the use of public facilities or employees did not violate the Constitution because the state is not required to provide abortions, but only to permit them. Rehnquist further argued that requiring physicians to conduct viability tests prior to performing abortions is justified because of the state's interest in protecting potential life. In dissent, Justice Blackmun, joined by Justices Brennan and Marshall, argued that the Missouri law is overrestrictive because it does not leave it up to the physician to determine whether or not to perform tests to determine viability. Blackmun further argued that the trimester analysis of *Wade* v. *Roe* is consistent with requiring physicians to determine viability and, hence, there was no need for the court to abandon that analysis.

Chief Justice *Rehnquist* announced the judgment of the Court.

I

In June 1986, the Governor of Missouri signed into law Missouri Senate Committee Substitute for House Bill No. 1596 (hereinafter Act or statute), which amended existing state law concerning unborn children and abortions. The Act consisted of 20 provisions, 5 of which are now before the Court. The first provision, or preamble, contains "findings" by the state legislature that "[t]he life of each human being begins at conception," and that "unborn children have protectable interests in life, health, and well-being." . . . The Act further requires that all Missouri laws be interpreted to provide unborn children with the same rights enjoyed by other persons, subject to the Federal Constitution and this Court's precedents. Among its other provisions, the Act requires that, prior to performing an abortion on any woman whom a physician has reason to believe is 20 or more weeks pregnant, the physician ascertain whether the fetus is viable by performing "such medical examinations and tests as are necessary to make a finding of the gestational age, weight, and lung maturity of the unborn child." The Act also prohibits the use of public employees and facilities to perform or assist abortions not necessary to save the mother's life, and it prohibits the use of public funds, employees, or facilities for the purpose of "encouraging or counseling" a woman to have an abortion not necessary to save her life. . . .

In July 1986, five health professionals employed by the State and two nonprofit corporations brought this class action in the United States District Court for the Western District of Missouri to challenge the constitutionality of the Missouri statute. Plaintiffs, appellees in this Court, sought declaratory and injunctive relief on the ground that certain statutory provisions violated the First, Fourth, Ninth, and Fourteenth Amendments to the Federal Constitution. . . . They asserted violations of various rights, including the "privacy rights of pregnant women seeking abortions"; the "woman's right to an abortion"; the "righ[t] to privacy in the physician-patient relationship"; the physician's "righ[t] to practice medicine"; the pregnant woman's "right to life due to inherent risks involved in childbirth"; and the woman's right to "receive . . . adequate medical advice and treatment" concerning abortions. . . .

Several weeks after the complaint was filed, the District Court temporarily restrained enforcement of several provisions of the Act. Following a 3-day trial in December 1986, the District Court declared seven provisions of the Act unconstitutional and enjoined their enforcement. . . . These provisions included the preamble, . . . the "informed consent" provision, which required physicians to inform the pregnant woman of certain facts before performing an abortion, . . . the requirement that post–16–week abortions be performed only in hospitals, . . . the mandated tests to determine viability, and the prohibition on the use of public funds, employees, and facilities to perform or assist nontherapeutic abortions, and the restrictions on the use of public funds, employees, and facilities to encourage or counsel women to have such abortions, . . .

. . . The Court of Appeals determined that Missouri's declaration that life begins at conception was "simply an impermissible state adoption of a theory of when life begins to justify its abortion regulations." . . . It further held that the requirement that physicians perform viability tests was an unconstitutional legislative intrusion on a matter of medical skill and judgment. . . . The Court of Appeals invalidated Missouri's prohibition on the use of public facilities and employees to perform or assist abortions not necessary to save the mother's life. . . . It distinguished our decisions in *Harris v. McRae*, . . . and *Maher v. Roe*, on the ground that " '[t]here is a fundamental difference between providing direct funding to effect the abortion decision and allowing staff physicians to perform abortions at an existing publicly owned hospital.' " . . . The Court of Appeals struck down the provision prohibiting the use of public funds for "encouraging or counseling" women to have nontherapeutic abortions, for the reason that this provision was both overly vague and inconsistent with the right to an abortion enunciated in *Roe v. Wade*. . . .

[The act] provides that "[i]t shall be unlawful for any public employee within the scope of his employment to perform or assist an abortion, not necessary to save the life of the mother," . . . [and] makes it "unlawful for any public facility to be used for the purpose of performing or assisting an abortion not necessary to save the life of the mother." The Court of Appeals held that these provisions contravened this Court's abortion decisions. . . . We take the contrary view.

As we said earlier this Term in *DeShaney v. Winnebago County Dept. of Social Services*, . . . "our cases have recognized that the Due Process Clauses generally confer no affirmative right to governmental aid, even where such aid may be necessary to secure life, liberty, or property interests of which the government itself may not deprive the individual." In *Maher v. Roe*, . . . the Court upheld a Connecticut welfare regulation under which Medicaid recipients received payments for medical services related to childbirth, but not for nontherapeutic abortions. The Court rejected the claim that this unequal subsidization of childbirth and abortion was impermissible under *Roe v. Wade*. As the Court put it:

> The Connecticut regulation before us is different in kind from the laws invalidated in our previous abortion decisions. The Connecticut regulation places no obstacles—absolute or otherwise—in the pregnant woman's path to an abortion. An indigent woman who desires an abortion suffers no disadvantage as a consequence of Connecticut's decision to fund childbirth; she continues as before to be dependent on private sources for the service she desires. The State may have made childbirth a more attractive alternative, thereby influencing the woman's decision, but it has imposed no restriction on access to abortions that was not already there. The indigency that may make it difficult—and in some cases,

perhaps, impossible—for some women to have abortions is neither created nor in any way affected by the Connecticut regulation. . . .

The Court of Appeals distinguished these cases on the ground that "[t]o prevent access to a public facility does more than demonstrate a political choice in favor of childbirth; it clearly narrows and in some cases forecloses the availability of abortion to women." . . . The court reasoned that the ban on the use of public facilities "could prevent a woman's chosen doctor from performing an abortion because of his unprivileged status at other hospitals or because a private hospital adopted a similar anti-abortion stance." *Ibid.* It also thought that "[s]uch a rule could increase the cost of obtaining an abortion and delay the timing of it as well." . . .

We think that this analysis is much like that which we rejected in *Maher, Poelker,* and *McRae*. As in those cases, the State's decision here to use public facilities and staff to encourage childbirth over abortion "places no governmental obstacle in the path of a woman who chooses to terminate her pregnancy." . . . Just as Congress' refusal to fund abortions in *McRae* left "an indigent woman with at least the same range of choice in deciding whether to obtain a medically necessary abortion as she would have had if Congress had chosen to subsidize no health care costs at all," . . . Missouri's refusal to allow public employees to perform abortions in public hospitals leaves a pregnant woman with the same choices as if the State had chosen not to operate any public hospitals at all. The challenged provisions only restrict a woman's ability to obtain an abortion to the extent that she chooses to use a physician affiliated with a public hospital. This circumstance is more easily remedied, and thus considerably less burdensome, than indigency, which "may make it difficult—and in some cases, perhaps, impossible—for some women to have abortions" without public funding. . . . Having held that the State's refusal to fund abortions does not violate *Roe v. Wade*, it strains logic to reach a contrary result for the use of public facilities and employees. If the State may "make a value judgment favoring childbirth over abortion and . . . implement that judgment by the allocation of public funds," . . . surely it may do so through the allocation of other public resources, such as hospitals and medical staff. . . .

The Missouri Act provides:

> Before a physician performs an abortion on a woman he has reason to believe is carrying an unborn child of twenty or more weeks gestational age, the physician shall first determine if the unborn child is viable by using and exercising that degree of care, skill, and proficiency commonly exercised by the ordinarily skillful, careful, and prudent physician engaged in similar practice under the same or similar conditions. In making this determination of viability, the physician shall perform or cause to be performed such medical examinations and tests as are necessary to make a finding of the gestational age, weight, and lung maturity of the unborn child and shall enter such findings and determination of viability in the medical record of the mother.

As with the preamble, the parties disagree over the meaning of this statutory provision. The State emphasizes the language of the first sentence, which speaks in terms of the physician's determination of viability being made by the standards of ordinary skill in the medical profession. . . . Appellees stress the language of the second sentence, which prescribes such "tests as are necessary" to make a finding of gestational age, fetal weight, and lung maturity. . . .

The Court of Appeals read [the Act] as requiring that after 20 weeks "doctors *must* perform tests to find gestational age, fetal weight and lung maturity." . . . The court indicated that the tests needed to determine fetal weight at 20 weeks are "unreliable and inaccurate" and would add $125 to $250 to the cost of an abortion. . . . It also stated that "amniocentesis, the only method available to determine lung maturity, is contrary to accepted medical practice until 28–30 weeks of gestation, expensive, and imposes significant health risks for both the pregnant woman and the fetus." . . .

We must first determine the meaning of [the Act] under Missouri law. Our usual practice is to defer to the lower court's construction of a state statute, but we believe the Court of Appeals has "fallen into plain error" in this case. . . .

We think the viability-testing provision makes sense only if the second sentence is read to require only those tests that are useful to making subsidiary findings as to viability. If we construe this provision to require a physician to perform those tests needed to make the three specified findings *in all circumstances*, including when the physician's reasonable professional judgment indicates that the tests would be irrelevant to determining viability or even dangerous to the mother and the fetus, the second sentence . . . would conflict with the first sentence's *requirement* that a physician apply his reasonable professional skill and judgment. It would also be incongruous to read this provision, especially the word "necessary," to require the performance of tests irrelevant to the expressed statutory purpose of determining viability. It thus seems clear to us that the Court of Appeals' construction of [the Act] violates well-accepted canons of statutory interpretation used in the Missouri courts. . . .

The viability-testing provision of the Missouri Act is concerned with promoting the State's interest in potential human life rather than in maternal health. [The Act] creates what is essentially a presumption of viability at 20 weeks, which the physician must rebut with tests indicating that the fetus is not viable prior to performing an abortion. It also directs the physician's determination as to viability by specifying consideration, if feasible, of gestational age, fetal weight, and lung capacity. The District Court found that "the medical evidence is uncontradicted that a 20-week fetus is *not* viable," and that "23½ to 24 weeks gestation is the earliest point in pregnancy where a reasonable possibility of viability exists." . . . But it also found that there may be a 4-week error in estimating gestational age, . . . which supports testing at 20 weeks.

In *Roe v. Wade,* the Court recognized that

the State has "important and legitimate" interests in protecting maternal health and in the potentiality of human life. . . . During the second trimester, the State "may, if it chooses, regulate the abortion procedure in ways that are reasonably related to maternal health." . . . After viability, when the State's interest in potential human life was held to become compelling, the State "may, if it chooses, regulate, and even proscribe, abortion except where it is necessary, in appropriate medical judgment, for the preservation of the life or health of the mother." . . .

In *Colautti v. Franklin*, . . . upon which appellees rely, the Court held that a Pennsylvania statute regulating the standard of care to be used by a physician performing an abortion of a possibly viable fetus was void for vagueness. . . . But in the course of reaching that conclusion, the Court reaffirmed its earlier statement in *Planned Parenthood of Central Missouri v. Danforth*, . . . that " 'the determination of whether a particular fetus is viable is, and must be, a matter for the judgment of the responsible attending physician.' " . . . The dissent, . . . 6, ignores the statement in *Colautti* that "neither the legislature nor the courts may proclaim one of the elements entering into the ascertainment of viability—be it weeks of gestation or fetal weight or any other single factor—as the determinant of when the State has a compelling interest in the life or health of the fetus." . . . To the extent that [the Act] regulates the method for determining viability, it undoubtedly does superimpose state regulation on the medical determination of whether a particular fetus is viable. The Court of Appeals and the District Court thought it unconstitutional for this reason. . . . To the extent that the viability tests increase the cost of what are in fact second-trimester abortions, their validity may also be questioned under *Akron*, . . . where the Court held that a requirement that second-trimester abortions must be performed in hospitals was invalid because it substantially increased the expense of those procedures.

We think that the doubt cast upon the Missouri statute by these cases is not so much a flaw in the statute as it is a reflection of the fact that the rigid trimester analysis of the course of a pregnancy enunciated in *Roe* has resulted in subsequent cases like *Colautti* and *Akron* making constitutional law in this area a virtual Procrustean bed. . . .

Stare decisis is a cornerstone of our legal system, but it has less power in constitutional cases, where, save for constitutional amendments, this Court is the only body able to make needed changes. . . . We have not refrained from reconsideration of a prior construction of the Constitution that has proved "unsound in principle and unworkable in practice." . . . We think the *Roe* trimester framework falls into that category.

In the first place, the rigid *Roe* framework is hardly consistent with the notion of a Constitution cast in general terms, as ours is, and usually speaking in general principles, as ours does. The key elements of the *Roe* framework—trimesters and viability—are not found in the text of the Constitution or in any place else one would expect to find a constitutional principle. Since the bounds of the inquiry are essentially indeterminate, the result has been a web of legal rules that have become increasingly intricate, resembling a code of regulations rather than a body of constitutional doctrine. As Justice *White* has put it, the trimester framework has left this Court to serve as the country's "*ex officio* medical board with powers to approve or disapprove medical and operative practices and standards throughout the United States." . . .

In the second place, we do not see why the State's interest in protecting potential human life should come into existence only at the point of viability, and that there should therefore be a rigid line allowing state regulation after viability but prohibiting it before viability. The dissenters in *Thornburgh*, writing in the context of the *Roe* trimester analysis, would have recognized this fact by positing against the "fundamental right" recognized in *Roe* the State's "compelling interest" in protecting potential human life throughout pregnancy. . . .

The tests that [the Act] requires the physician to perform are designed to determine viability. The State here has chosen viability as the point at which its interest in potential human life must be safeguarded. . . . It is true that the tests in question increase the expense of abortion, and regulate the discretion of the physician in determining the viability of the fetus. Since the tests will undoubtedly show in many cases that the fetus is not viable, the tests will have been performed for what were in fact second-trimester abortions. But we are satisfied that the requirement of these tests permissibly furthers the State's interest in protecting potential human life, and we therefore believe [the Act] to be constitutional.

The dissent takes us to task for our failure to join in a "great issues" debate as to whether the Constitution includes an "unenumerated" general right to privacy as recognized in cases such as *Griswold v. Connecticut,* . . . and *Roe*. But *Griswold v. Connecticut,* unlike *Roe*, did not purport to adopt a whole framework, complete with detailed rules and distinctions, to govern the cases in which the asserted liberty interest would apply. As such, it was far different from the opinion, if not the holding, of *Roe v. Wade*, which sought to establish a constitutional framework for judging state regulation of abortion during the entire term of pregnancy. That framework sought to deal with areas of medical practice traditionally subject to state regulation, and it sought to balance once and for all by reference only to the calendar the claims of the State to protect the fetus as a form of human life against the claims of a woman to decide for herself whether or not to abort a fetus she was carrying. The experience of the Court in applying *Roe v. Wade* in later cases, . . . suggests to us that there is wisdom in not unnecessarily attempting to elaborate the abstract differences between a "fundamental right" to abortion, as the Court described it in *Akron,* . . . a "limited fundamental constitutional right," which Justice Blackmun's dissent today treats *Roe* as having established, . . . or a liberty interest protected by the Due Process Clause, which we believe it to be. The Missouri testing requirement here is reasonably designed to ensure that abortions are not performed where the fetus is viable—an end which all concede is legitimate—and that is sufficient to sustain its constitutionality.

The dissent also accuses us, . . . of cowardice and illegitimacy in dealing with "the most po-litically divisive domestic legal issue of our time." . . . There is no doubt that our holding today will allow some governmental regulation of abortion that would have been prohibited under the language of cases such as *Colautti v. Franklin,* . . . and *Akron v. Akron Center for Reproductive Health.* . . . But the goal of constitutional adjudication is surely not to remove inexorably "politically divisive" issues from the ambit of the legislative process, whereby the people through their elected representatives deal with matters of concern to them. The goal of constitutional adjudication is to hold true the balance between that which the Constitution puts beyond the reach of the democratic process and that which it does not. We think we have done that today. The dissent's suggestion, . . . that legislative bodies, in a Nation where more than half of our population is women, will treat our decision today as an invitation to enact abortion regulation reminiscent of the dark ages not only misreads our views but does scant justice to those who serve in such bodies and the people who elect them. . . .

Justice *Blackmun,* with whom
Justice *Brennan* and Justice
Marshall join, concurring in part
and dissenting in part.

Today, *Roe v. Wade,* . . . and the fundamental constitutional right of women to decide whether to terminate a pregnancy, survive but are not secure. Although the Court extricates itself from this case without making a single, even incremental, change in the law of abortion, the plurality and Justice Scalia would overrule *Roe* (the first silently, the other explicitly) and would return to the States virtually unfettered authority to control the quintessentially intimate, personal, and life-directing decision whether to carry a fetus to term. Although today, no less than yesterday, the Constitution and the decisions of this Court prohibit a State from enacting laws that inhibit women from the meaningful exercise of that right, a plurality of this Court implicitly invites every state legislature to enact more and more restrictive abortion regulations in order to provoke more and more test cases, in the hope that sometime down the line the Court will return the law of procreative freedom to the severe limitations that generally prevailed in this country before January 22, 1973. Never in my memory has a plurality announced a judgment of this Court that so foments disregard for the law and for our standing decisions.

Nor in my memory has a plurality gone about its business in such a deceptive fashion. At every level of its review, from its effort to read the real meaning out of the Missouri statute, to its intended evisceration of precedents and its deafening silence about the constitutional protections that it would jettison, the plurality obscures the portent of its analysis. With feigned restraint, the plurality announces that its analysis leaves *Roe* "undisturbed," albeit "modif[ied] and narrow[ed]." . . . But this disclaimer is totally meaningless. The plurality opinion is filled with winks, and nods, and knowing glances to those who would do away with *Roe* explicitly, but turns a stone face to anyone in search of what the plurality conceives as the scope of a woman's right under the Due Process Clause to terminate a pregnancy free from the coercive and brooding influence of the State. The simple truth is that *Roe* would not survive the plurality's analysis, and that the plurality provides no substitute for *Roe's* protective umbrella.

I fear for the future. I fear for the liberty and equality of the millions of women who have lived and come of age in the 16 years since *Roe* was decided. I fear for the integrity of, and public esteem for, this Court. . . .

In the plurality's view, the viability-testing provision imposes a burden on second-trimester abortions as a way of furthering the State's interest in protecting the potential life of the fetus. Since under the *Roe* framework, the State may not fully regulate abortion in the interest of potential life (as opposed to maternal health) until the third trimester, the plurality finds it necessary, in order to save the Missouri testing provision, to throw out *Roe's* trimester framework. . . . In flat contradiction to *Roe*, . . . the plurality concludes that the State's interest in potential life is compelling before viability, and upholds the testing provision because it "permissibly furthers" that state interest. . . .

At the outset, I note that in its haste to limit abortion rights, the plurality compounds the errors of its analysis by needlessly reaching out to address constitutional questions that are not actually presented. The conflict between [the Act] and *Roe's* trimester framework, which purportedly drives the plurality to reconsider our past decisions, is a contrived conflict: the product of an aggressive misreading of the viability-testing requirement and a needlessly wooden application of the *Roe* framework. . . .

Abruptly setting aside the construction of [the Act] adopted by both the District Court and Court of Appeals as "plain error," the plurality reads the viability-testing provision as requiring only that before a physician may perform an abortion on a woman whom he believes to be carrying a fetus of 20 or more weeks gestational age, the doctor must determine whether the fetus is viable and, as part of that exercise, must, to the extent feasible and consistent with sound medical practice, conduct tests necessary to make findings of gestational age, weight, and lung maturity. . . . But the plurality's reading of the provision, according to which the statute requires the physician to perform tests only in order to determine *viability*, ignores the statutory language explicitly directing that "the physician *shall* perform or cause to be performed such medical examinations and tests as are *necessary to make a finding of the gestational age, weight, and lung maturity* of the unborn child and *shall* enter such findings" in the mother's medical record. . . . The statute's plain language requires the physician to undertake whatever tests are necessary to determine gestational age, weight, and lung maturity, regardless of whether these tests are necessary to a finding of viability, and regardless of whether the tests subject the pregnant woman or the fetus to additional health risks or add substantially to the cost of an abortion.

Had the plurality read the statute as written, it would have had no cause to reconsider the *Roe* framework. As properly construed, the viability-testing provision does not pass constitutional muster under even a rational-basis standard, the least restrictive level of review applied by this Court. . . . By mandating tests to determine fetal weight and lung maturity for every fetus thought to be more

than 20 weeks gestational age, the statute requires physicians to undertake procedures,
such as amniocentesis, that, in the situation
presented, have no medical justification, impose significant additional health risks on both
the pregnant woman and the fetus, and bear
no rational relation to the State's interest in
protecting fetal life. As written, [the Act] is an
arbitrary imposition of discomfort, risk, and
expense, furthering no discernible interest except to make the procurement of an abortion
as arduous and difficult as possible. Thus,
were it not for the plurality's tortured effort to
avoid the plain import of . . . [the Act], it could
have struck down the testing provision as
patently irrational irrespective of the *Roe*
framework.

The plurality eschews this straightforward
resolution, in the hope of precipitating a constitutional crisis. Far from avoiding constitutional difficulty, the plurality attempts to
engineer a dramatic retrenchment in our jurisprudence by exaggerating the conflict between its untenable construction of [the Act]
and the *Roe* trimester framework.

No one contests that under the *Roe*
framework the State, in order to promote its
interest in potential human life, may regulate
and even proscribe non-therapeutic abortions
once the fetus becomes viable. . . . If, as the
plurality appears to hold, the testing provision
simply requires a physician to use appropriate
and medically sound tests to determine
whether the fetus is actually viable when the
estimated gestational age is greater than 20
weeks . . . then I see little or no conflict with
Roe. Nothing in *Roe,* or any of its progeny,
holds that a State may not effectuate its compelling interest in the potential life of a viable
fetus by seeking to ensure that no viable fetus
is mistakenly aborted because of the inherent
lack of precision in estimates of gestational
age. A requirement that a physician make a
finding of viability, one way or the other, for
every fetus that falls within the range of possible viability does no more than preserve the
State's recognized authority. Although, as the
plurality correctly points out, such a testing
requirement would have the effect of imposing additional costs on second-trimester abortions where the tests indicated that the fetus
was not viable, these costs would be merely

incidental to, and a necessary accommodation
of, the State's unquestioned right to prohibit
nontherapeutic abortions after the point of
viability. In short, the testing provision, as construed by the plurality is consistent with the
Roe framework and could be upheld effort-
lessly under current doctrine.

How ironic it is, then, and disingenuous,
that the plurality scolds the Court of Appeals
for adopting a construction of the statute that
fails to avoid constitutional difficulties. . . . By
distorting the statute, the plurality manages to
avoid invalidating the testing provision on
what should have been noncontroversial constitutional grounds; having done so, however,
the plurality rushes headlong into a much
deeper constitutional thicket, brushing past an
obvious basis for upholding [the Act] in search
of a pretext for scuttling the trimester
framework. Evidently, from the plurality's
perspective, the real problem with the Court
of Appeals' construction of [the Act] is not that
it raised a constitutional difficulty, but that it
raised the wrong constitutional difficulty—one
not implicating *Roe.* The plurality has remedied that, traditional canons of construction and judicial forbearance notwithstanding.

Having set up the conflict between [the Act]
and the *Roe* trimester framework, the plurality
summarily discards *Roe's* analytic core as " 'unsound in principle and unworkable in practice.' " . . . This is so, the plurality claims,
because the key elements of the framework do
not appear in the text of the Constitution,
because the framework more closely resembles
a regulatory code than a body of constitutional
doctrine, and because under the framework
the State's interest in potential human life is
considered compelling only after viability,
when, in fact, that interest is equally compelling throughout pregnancy. . . . The plurality
does not bother to explain these alleged flaws
in *Roe.* Bald assertion masquerades as reasoning. The object, quite clearly, is not to persuade, but to prevail.

The plurality opinion is far more remarkable for the arguments that it does not advance than for those that it does. The plurality
does not even mention, much less join, the

true jurisprudential debate underlying this case: whether the Constitution includes an "unenumerated" general right to privacy as recognized in many of our decisions, most notably *Griswold v. Connecticut,* . . . and *Roe,* and, more specifically, whether and to what extent such a right to privacy extends to matters of childbearing and family life, including abortion. . . . These are questions of unsurpassed significance in this Court's interpretation of the Constitution, and mark the battleground upon which this case was fought, by the parties, by the Solicitor General as *amicus* on behalf of petitioners, and by an unprecedented number of *amici.* On these grounds, abandoned by the plurality, the Court should decide this case.

But rather than arguing that the text of the Constitution makes no mention of the right to privacy, the plurality complains that the critical elements of the *Roe* framework—trimesters and viability—do not appear in the Constitution and are, therefore, somehow inconsistent with a Constitution cast in general terms. . . . Were this a true concern, we would have to abandon most of our constitutional jurisprudence. As the plurality well knows, or should know, the "critical elements" of countless constitutional doctrines nowhere appear in the Constitution's text. The Constitution makes no mention, for example, of the First Amendment's "actual malice" standard for proving certain libels, . . . or of the standard for determining when speech is obscene. . . . Similarly, the Constitution makes no mention of the rational-basis test, or the specific verbal formulations of intermediate and strict scrutiny by which this Court evaluates claims under the Equal Protection Clause. The reason is simple. Like the *Roe* framework, these tests or standards are not, and do not purport to be, rights protected by the Constitution. Rather, they are judge-made methods for evaluating and measuring the strength and scope of constitutional rights or for balancing the constitutional rights of individuals against the competing interests of government.

With respect to the *Roe* framework, the general constitutional principle, indeed the fundamental constitutional right, for which it was developed is the right to privacy, . . . a species of "liberty" protected by the Due Process Clause, which under our past decisions safeguards the right of women to exercise some control over their own role in procreation. As we recently reaffirmed in *Thornburgh v. American College of Obstetricians and Gynecologists,* . . . few decisions are "more basic to individual dignity and autonomy" or more appropriate to that "certain private sphere of individual liberty" that the Constitution reserves from the intrusive reach of government than the right to make the uniquely personal, intimate, and self-defining decision whether to end a pregnancy. . . . It is this general principle, the " 'moral fact that a person belongs to himself and not others nor to society as a whole,' " . . . that is found in the Constitution. . . . The trimester framework simply defines and limits that right to privacy in the abortion context to accommodate, not destroy, a State's legitimate interest in protecting the health of pregnant women and in preserving potential human life. . . . Fashioning such accommodations between individual rights and the legitimate interests of government, establishing benchmarks and standards with which to evaluate the competing claims of individuals and government, lies at the very heart of constitutional adjudication. To the extent that the trimester framework is useful in this enterprise, it is not only consistent with constitutional interpretation, but necessary to the wise and just exercise of this Court's paramount authority to define the scope of constitutional rights.

The plurality next alleges that the result of the trimester framework has "been a web of legal rules that have become increasingly intricate, resembling a code of regulations rather than a body of constitutional doctrine." . . . Again, if this were a true and genuine concern, we would have to abandon vast areas of our constitutional jurisprudence. The plurality complains that under the trimester framework the Court has distinguished between a city ordinance requiring that second-trimester abortions be performed in clinics and a state law requiring that these abortions be performed in hospitals, or between laws requiring that certain information be furnished to a woman by a physician or his assistant and those requiring that such information be furnished by the physician exclusively. . . . Are these distinctions any finer, or more "regulatory," than the distinctions we have often drawn in our First Amendment jurisprudence, where, for example, we have held that a "release time" program permitting public-school students to leave school grounds during school hours to receive religious instruction does not violate the Establishment Clause, even though a release-time program permitting religious instruction on school grounds does violate the Clause? . . . Our Fourth Amendment jurisprudence recognizes factual distinctions no less intricate. Just this Term, for example, we held that while an aerial observation from a helicopter hovering at 400 feet does not violate any reasonable expectation of privacy, such an expectation of privacy would be violated by a helicopter observation from an unusually low altitude. . . . Similarly, in a Sixth Amendment case, the Court held that although an overnight ban on attorney-client communication violated the constitutionally guaranteed right to counsel, . . . that right was not violated when a trial judge separated a defendant from his lawyer during a 15-minute recess after the defendant's direct testimony. . . .

Finally, the plurality asserts that the trimester framework cannot stand because the State's interest in potential life is compelling throughout pregnancy, not merely after viability. The opinion contains not one word of rationale for its view of the State's interest. This "it-is-so-because-we-say-so" jurisprudence constitutes nothing other than an attempted exercise of brute force; reason, much less persuasion, has no place.

In answering the plurality's claim that the State's interest in the fetus is uniform and compelling throughout pregnancy, I cannot improve upon what Justice *Stevens* has written:

> I should think it obvious that the State's interest in the protection of an embryo— even if that interest is defined as 'protecting those who will be citizens' . . .— increases progressively and dramatically as the organism's capacity to feel pain, to experience pleasure, to survive, and to

react to its surroundings increases day by day. The development of a fetus—and pregnancy itself—are not static conditions, and the assertion that the government's interest is static simply ignores this reality. . . . [U]nless the religious view that a fetus is a 'person' is adopted . . . there is a fundamental and well-recognized difference between a fetus and a human being; indeed, if there is not such a difference, the permissibility of terminating the life of a fetus could scarcely be left to the will of the state legislatures. And if distinctions may be drawn between a fetus and a human being in terms of the state interest in their protection—even though the fetus represents one of 'those who will be citizens'—it seems to me quite odd to argue that distinctions may not also be drawn between the state interest in protecting the freshly fertilized egg and the state interest in protecting the 9–month–gestated, fully sentient fetus on the eve of birth. Recognition of this distinction is supported not only by logic, but also by history and by our shared experiences. . . .

For my own part, I remain convinced, as six other Members of this Court 16 years ago were convinced, that the *Roe* framework, and the viability standard in particular, fairly, sensibly, and effectively functions to safeguard the constitutional liberties of pregnant women while recognizing and accommodating the State's interest in potential human life. The viability line reflects the biological facts and truths of fetal development; it marks that threshold moment prior to which a fetus cannot survive separate from the woman and cannot reasonably and objectively be regarded as a subject of rights or interests distinct from, or paramount to, those of the pregnant woman. At the same time, the viability standard takes account of the undeniable fact that as the fetus evolves into its postnatal form, and as it loses its dependence on the uterine environment, the State's interest in the fetus' potential human life, and in fostering a regard for human life in general, becomes compelling. As a practical matter, because viability follows "quickening"—the point at which a woman feels movement in her womb—and because viability occurs no earlier than 23 weeks gestational age, it establishes an easily applicable standard for regulating abortion while providing a pregnant woman ample time to exercise her fundamental right with her responsible physician to terminate her pregnancy. Although I have stated previously for a majority of this Court that "[c]onstitutional rights do not always have easily ascertainable boundaries," to seek and establish those boundaries remains the special responsibility of this Court. . . . In *Roe,* we discharged that responsibility as logic and science compelled. The plurality today advances not one reasonable argument as to why our judgment in that case was wrong and should be abandoned.

Having contrived an opportunity to reconsider the *Roe* framework, and then having discarded that framework, the plurality finds the testing provision unobjectionable because it "permissibly furthers the State's interest in protecting potential human life." . . . This newly minted standard is circular and totally meaningless. Whether a challenged abortion regulation "permissibly furthers" a legitimate state interest is the *question* that courts must answer in abortion cases, not the standard for courts to apply. In keeping with the rest of its opinion, the plurality makes no attempt to explain or to justify its new standard, either in the abstract or as applied in this case. Nor could it. The "permissibly furthers" standard has no independent meaning, and consists of nothing other than what a majority of this Court may believe at any given moment in any given case. The plurality's novel test appears to be nothing more than a dressed-up version of rational-basis review, this Court's most lenient level of scrutiny. One thing is clear, however: were the plurality's "permissibly furthers" standard adopted by the Court, for all practical purposes, *Roe* would be overruled.

The "permissibly furthers" standard completely disregards the irreducible minimum of *Roe:* the Court's recognition that a woman has a limited fundamental constitutional right to decide whether to terminate a pregnancy. That right receives no meaningful recognition in the plurality's written opinion. Since, in the

plurality's view, the State's interest in potential life is compelling as of the moment of conception, and is therefore served only if abortion is abolished, every hindrance to a woman's ability to obtain an abortion must be "permissible." Indeed, the more severe the hindrance, the more effectively (and permissibly) the State's interest would be furthered. A tax on abortions or a criminal prohibition would both satisfy the plurality's standard. So, for that matter, would a requirement that a pregnant woman memorize and recite today's plurality opinion before seeking an abortion.

The plurality pretends that *Roe* survives, explaining that the facts of this case differ from those in *Roe:* here, Missouri has chosen to assert its interest in potential life only at the point of viability, whereas, in *Roe,* Texas had asserted that interest from the point of conception, criminalizing all abortions, except where the life of the mother was at stake. . . . This, of course, is a distinction without a difference. The plurality repudiates every principle for which *Roe* stands; in good conscience, it cannot possibly believe that *Roe* lies "undisturbed" merely because this case does not call upon the Court to reconsider the Texas statute, or one like it. If the Constitution permits a State to enact any statute that reasonably furthers its interest in potential life, and if that interest arises as of conception, why would the Texas statute fail to pass muster? One suspects that the plurality agrees. It is impossible to read the plurality opinion and especially its final paragraph, without recognizing its implicit invitation to every State to enact more and more restrictive abortion laws, and to assert their interest in potential life as of the moment of conception. All these laws will satisfy the plurality's non-scrutiny, until sometime, a new regime of old dissenters and new appointees will declare what the plurality intends: that *Roe* is no longer good law.

Thus, "not with a bang, but a whimper," the plurality discards a landmark case of the last generation, and casts into darkness the hopes and visions of every woman in this country who had come to believe that the Constitution guaranteed her the right to exercise some control over her unique ability to bear children. The plurality does so either oblivious or insensitive to the fact that millions of women, and their families, have ordered their lives around the right to reproductive choice, and that this right has become vital to the full participation of women in the economic and political walks of American life. The plurality would clear the way once again for government to force upon women the physical labor and specific and direct medical and psychological harms that may accompany carrying a fetus to term. The plurality would clear the way again for the State to conscript a woman's body and to force upon her a "distressful life and future." . . .

The result, as we know from experience, . . . would be that every year hundreds of thousands of women, in desperation, would defy the law, and place their health and safety in the unclean and unsympathetic hands of back-alley abortionists, or they would attempt to perform abortions upon themselves, with disastrous results. Every year, many women, especially poor and minority women, would die or suffer debilitating physical trauma, all in the name of enforced morality or religious dictates or lack of compassion, as it may be.

Of the aspirations and settled understandings of American women, of the inevitable and brutal consequences of what it is doing, the tough-approach plurality utters not a word. This silence is callous. It is also profoundly destructive of this Court as an institution. To overturn a constitutional decision is a rare and grave undertaking. To overturn a constitutional decision that secured a fundamental personal liberty to millions of persons would be unprecedented in our 200 years of constitutional history. Although the doctrine of *stare decisis* applies with somewhat diminished force in constitutional cases generally, . . . even in ordinary constitutional cases "any departure from *stare decisis* demands special justification." . . . This requirement of

justification applies with unique force where, as here, the Court's abrogation of precedent would destroy people's firm belief, based on past decisions of this Court, that they possess an unabridgeable right to undertake certain conduct.

As discussed at perhaps too great length above, the plurality makes no serious attempt to carry "the heavy burden of persuading . . . that changes in society or in the law dictate" the abandonment of *Roe* and its numerous progeny, . . . much less the greater burden of explaining the abrogation of a fundamental personal freedom. Instead, the plurality pretends that it leaves *Roe* standing, and refuses even to discuss the real issue underlying this case: whether the Constitution includes an unenumerated right to privacy that encompasses a woman's right to decide whether to terminate a pregnancy. . . .

This comes at a cost. The doctrine of *stare decisis* "permits society to presume that bedrock principles are founded in the law rather than in the proclivities of individuals, and thereby contributes to the integrity of our constitutional system of government, both in appearance and in fact." . . . Today's decision involves the most politically divisive domestic legal issue of our time. By refusing to explain or to justify its proposed revolutionary revision in the law of abortion, and by refusing to abide not only by our precedents, but also by our canons for reconsidering those precedents, the plurality invites charges of cowardice and illegitimacy to our door. I cannot say that these would be undeserved.

For today, at least, the law of abortion stands undisturbed. For today, the women of this Nation still retain the liberty to control their destinies. But the signs are evident and very ominous, and a chill wind blows.

I dissent.

21. *Cruzan v. Harmon*

Supreme Court of Missouri

The issue before the Supreme Court of Missouri was whether a guardian can order that all nutrition and hydration provided by a gastrostomy tube be withdrawn from an incompetent ward who is in a persistent vegetative state but not terminally ill. A majority of the Supreme Court held that the guardian did not have any independent authority to order a withdrawal of nutrition and hydration and that the evidence as to the patient's wishes was inherently unreliable and insufficient to support the guardian's claim to exercise substantial judgment on the patient's behalf. In dissent, Justice Higgens argues that the cases from other jurisdictions cited by the majority all supported a different judgment.

. . . At 12:54 A.M., January 11, 1983, the Missouri Highway Patrol dispatched Trooper Dale Penn to the scene of a single car accident in Jasper County, Missouri. Penn arrived six minutes later to find Nancy Beth Cruzan lying face down in a ditch, approximately thirty-five feet from her overturned vehicle. The trooper examined Nancy and found her without detectable respiratory or cardiac function.

At 1:09 A.M., Paramedics Robert Williams and Rick Maynard arrived at the accident scene; they immediately initiated efforts to revive Nancy. By 1:12 A.M., cardiac function and spontaneous respiration had recommenced. The ambulance crew transported Nancy to the Freeman Hospital where exploratory surgery revealed a laceration of the liver. A CAT scan showed no significant abnormalities of her brain. The attending physician diagnosed a probable cerebral contusion compounded by significant anoxia (deprivation of oxygen) of unknown duration. The trial judge found that a deprivation of oxygen to the brain approaching six minutes would result in permanent brain damage; the best estimate of the period of Nancy's anoxia was twelve to fourteen minutes.

Nancy remained in a coma for approximately three weeks following the accident. Thereafter, she seemed to improve somewhat and was able to take nutrition orally. Rehabilitative efforts began. In order to assist her recovery and to ease the feeding process, a gastrostomy feeding tube was surgically implanted on February 7, 1983, with the consent of her (then) husband.

Over a substantial period of time, valiant efforts to rehabilitate Nancy took place, without success. She now lies in the Mount Vernon State Hospital. She receives the totality of her nutrition and hydration through the gastrostomy tube.

The trial court found that (1) her respiration and circulation are not artificially maintained and are within the normal limits of a thirty-year-old female; (2) she is "oblivious to her environment except for reflexive responses to sound and perhaps painful stimuli"; (3) she suffered anoxia of the brain resulting in a "massive enlargement of the ventricles filling with cerebrospinal fluid in the area where the brain has degenerated" and that "cerebral cortical atrophy is irreversible, permanent, progressive and ongoing"; (4) "her highest cognitive brain function is exhibited by her grimacing perhaps in recognition of ordinarily painful stimuli, indicating the experience of pain and apparent response to sound"; (5) she is a spastic quadriplegic; (6) her four extremities are contracted with irreversible muscular and tendon damage to all extremities; (7) "she has no cognitive or reflexive ability to swallow food or water to maintain her daily essential needs" and that "she will never recover her ability to swallow sufficient [sic] to satisfy her needs." In sum, Nancy is diagnosed as in a persistent vegetative state. She is not dead.[1] She is not terminally ill. Medical experts testified that she could live another thirty years.

The trial court found that Nancy expressed, in "somewhat serious conversation" that if sick or injured she would not want to continue her life unless she could live "halfway normally." Based on this conversation, the trial court concluded that "she would not wish to continue with nutrition and hydration."

The court concluded that no state interest outweighed Nancy's "right to liberty" and that to deny Nancy's co-guardians authority to act under these circumstances would deprive Nancy of equal protection of the law. The court ordered state employees to "cause the request of the co-guardians to withdraw nutrition or hydration to be carried out."

As we said, this case presents a single issue for resolution: May a guardian order that food and water be withheld from an incompetent ward who is in a persistent vegetative state but who is otherwise alive . . . and not terminally ill? As the parties carefully pointed out in their thoughtful briefs, this issue is a broad one, invoking consideration of the authority of guardians of incompetent wards, the public policy of Missouri with regard to the termination of life-sustaining treatment and the amorphous mass of constitutional rights generally described as the "right to liberty", "the right to privacy", equal protection and due process.

This is also a case in which euphemisms readily find their way to the fore, perhaps to soften the reality of what is really at stake. But this is not a case in which we are asked to let someone die. Nancy is not dead. Nor is she terminally ill. This is a case in which we are asked to allow the medical profession to make Nancy die by starvation and dehydration. The debate here is thus not between life and death; it is between quality of life and death. We are asked to hold that the cost of maintaining Nancy's present life is too great when weighed against the benefit that life conveys both to Nancy and her loved ones and that she must die.

To be sure, no one carries a malevolent motive to this litigation. Only the coldest heart could fail to feel the anguish of these parents who have suffered terribly these many years.

They have exhausted any wellspring of hope which might have earlier accompanied their now interminable bedside vigil. And we understand, for these loving parents have seen only defeat through the memories they hold of a vibrant woman for whom the future held but promise.

Finally, we are asked to decide this case as a court of law. Neither this, nor any court lays proper claim to omniscience. We share the limits borne by all as human beings, only too aware of our earthbound perspective and frustrated by what we cannot now know. Our role is a limited one to which we remain true only if our decision is firmly founded on legal principles and reasoned analysis. And we must remember that we decide this case not only for Nancy, but for many, many others who may not be surrounded by the loving family with which she is blessed.

While this is a case of first impression in Missouri, the courts of some of our sister states have grappled with similar issues. Nearly unanimously, those courts have found a way to allow persons wishing to die, or those who seek the death of a ward, to meet the end sought.

The seminal case is . . . *Quinlan*. . . . Karen Quinlan suffered severe brain damage as a result of anoxia. Medical experts diagnosed her as terminally ill and in a persistent vegetative state. A respirator assisted her breathing; a feeding tube provided her nourishment. The experts believed that she could not survive without the respirator. The trial court found that there was no reasonable possibility that she would return to a cognitive or sapient life.

Karen's father sought judicial permission to disconnect the respirator, believing that death would follow quickly; the expert medical testimony so advised him. The New Jersey Supreme Court found a right of privacy in Karen to terminate her life under this "non-cognitive, vegetative existence". In striking a balance between Karen's right of privacy and the state's interest in life, the court said:

> We think that the State's interest *contra* weakens and the individual's right to privacy grows as the degree of bodily invasion increases and the prognosis dims. Ultimately there comes a point at which

the individual's rights overcome the State interest.

. . . In light of Karen's inability to exercise the right herself the court wrote:

> The only practical way to prevent destruction of the right is to permit the guardian and family of Karen to render their best judgment . . . as to whether she would exercise it in these circumstances. [W]e determine that Karen's right of privacy may be asserted in her behalf, in this respect, by her guardian and family under the particular circumstances presented by this record.

Superintendent of Belchertown State School v. Saikewicz . . . involved a mentally retarded resident of a state school suffering from acute myeloblastic monocytic leukemia, in need of chemotherapy, but incapable of giving informed consent for the treatment. The court recognized a general right to refuse medical treatment in appropriate circumstances and held that such a right extends to incompetents. Given Saikewicz' lifetime incompetency, the court adopted a substituted judgment standard for determining whether Saikewicz, if competent, would have elected to undergo chemotherapy. While recognizing that most persons in a similar situation would choose to lengthen their life through the treatments available, the court found that Saikewicz' inability to cooperate with the treatment and inability to understand the disruption in his routine, particularly the severe side effects produced by the drugs, rendered it likely that if Saikewicz could, he would decide against the treatment.

The court found a constitutional basis for the refusal-of-treatment decision, but eschewed the cognitive, sapient, quality of life considerations found in *Quinlan*. "To the extent that [quality of life even if treatment can bring about remission] equates the value of life with any measure of the quality of life, we firmly reject it." Instead, the Massachusetts court found the extraordinary nature of the treatment presented a sufficiently massive invasion of a person's privacy to warrant a decision against undergoing treatment.

In 1981, the New York Court of Appeals advanced a different theoretical approach to refusal-of-treatment decisions. . . .

In *Eichner*, Brother Joseph Fox, a member of the Society of Mary, suffered cardiac arrest during an operation. Oxygen depletion resulted in severe brain damage; Fox lost the ability to breathe without a respirator. In "formal" discussions consistent with his role as a teacher in a Catholic high school and a mission of promulgating Catholic moral principles, Fox discussed the Karen Quinlan case and stated that he wanted nothing extraordinary done to keep him alive. The court found his common law right to refuse treatment controlling under the circumstances, given the solemn and "formal" nature of Fox' expressed desire to forego extraordinary medical treatment.

[In *Storar*,] John Storar was a profoundly retarded 52-year-old suffering from metastatic cancer. His life expectancy was three to six months. He continually lost blood, requiring blood transfusions of two units every eight to fifteen days. Without the transfusions, medical experts believed Storar would bleed to death. His mother asked that the transfusions be stopped. Testimony at trial characterized the transfusions as "analogous to food—they would not cure the cancer, but would eliminate the risk of death from another treatable cause." . . .

The court recognized that Storar never possessed sufficient mental competency to render a decision as to extraordinary life sustaining procedures. Departing from the analysis in *Saikewicz*, the New York Court of Appeals found it "unrealistic to attempt to determine whether he would want to continue potentially life prolonging treatment if he were competent." . . . Instead, the court reasoned that Storar's condition was no different from that of any infant. A court would not allow a parent to deny a child all treatment for a condition which threatens his life; a parent's refusal to allow blood transfusions in the face of an infant bleeding to death presents a "classic" example of the court's power to order treatment in the face of parental refusal. Storar's blood transfusions could not be terminated.

Quinlan, *Saikewicz*, and *Eichner/Storar* provide the legal basis for all of the cases which followed. These three cases limit themselves to circumstances in which the patient is terminally ill. Cases which follow, however, recognize no such restraint, but extend the principles upon which the *Quinlan-Saikewicz-Eichner/Storar* trilogy rely, to persons who are not terminally ill.

In re Conroy, . . . (1985), attempted to determine the circumstances under which "life-sustaining treatment may be withheld or withdrawn from incompetent, institutionalized, elderly patients with severe and permanent mental and physical impairments and a limited life expectancy." . . . Specifically, 84-year-old Claire Conroy's guardian sought to remove a nasogastric feeding tube by which she received her nutrition.

The court formulated three tests to assist in making a determination as to the withdrawal of life-sustaining procedures. These tests are arguably the only ones adopted by a court which adequately consider the state's interest in life in the context of life-sustaining treatment. First, when clear and convincing evidence exists that an incompetent patient would refuse treatment under the circumstances were he able to do so, the guardian may exercise a substituted judgment to achieve that end. This is denominated the subjective test.

A second test, designated the limited objective test, is applied in the absence of clear and convincing evidence of the patient's wishes, but where there is a measure of trustworthy evidence that the patient would have refused the treatment. Noting that "it is naive to pretend that the right to self-determination serves as the basis for substituted decision making. . . ." . . . , the court went on to permit the termination of life support "if it is manifest that such action would further the patient's best interests. . . ."

Thus, where it is clear that the burden of the patient's unavoidable pain and suffering outweighs the benefits of continued life, termination could follow.

A third test, characterized as the pure objective test, is operable where there is no evidence of the patient's desires as to life-sustaining treatment. Where the "effect of

administering life-sustaining treatment would be inhumane" due to severe, recurring and unavoidable pain, treatment may be terminated. . . .

Ms. Conroy never expressed an opinion as to life-sustaining treatments, nor did the medical evidence show that feeding by the nasogastric tube was particularly painful. Since Ms. Conroy did not meet any of the three tests, the court would have refused to permit the withdrawal of the feeding tube.

Brophy v. New England Sinai Hospital, Inc., . . . (1986), went beyond *Conroy* on facts similar to Nancy's case. Paul Brophy suffered a ruptured aneurysm and due to oxygen deprivation to the brain, entered a persistent vegetative state. The trial court found that Brophy was neither dead, terminally ill, nor in danger of imminent death. His heart functioned without mechanical assistance as did his respiratory system. A gastrostomy tube provided food and water.

The court found that if Brophy were able to do so, he would decide to discontinue the feeding tube. While recognizing that the state's interest in life must be considered, the court reasoned that the state's interest could not overcome Brophy's right to discontinue treatment. The court allowed Brophy's guardian to exercise his substituted judgment to terminate feeding.

At about the time the Supreme Judicial Court of Massachusetts considered *Brophy,* the California Court of Appeals decided *Bouvia v. Superior Court,* . . . (1986). There a 28-year-old, quadriplegic woman afflicted with severe cerebral palsy sought removal of the nasogastric tube by which she was fed. The court characterized her as "intelligent, very mentally competent." . . . Finding it "immaterial that the removal of the nasogastric tube will hasten or cause Bouvia's eventual death," . . . , the court held that Bouvia's right to live her life in dignity and peace outweighed the state's interest in preserving life and preventing suicide.

In re Jobes, . . . (1987), presents facts similar to this case. Nancy Jobes was pregnant and in excellent health. Following an automobile accident and during surgery to remove the child killed in her womb in the accident, she lost oxygen flow to her brain. Irreversible brain damage followed; she needed assistance breathing and received nourishment through a tube inserted into the jejunum of her small intestine. Her husband sought permission to remove her feeding tube.

The tests established by this same court in *Conroy* were not applicable. The court found that Mrs. Jobes' previous statements about refusing life support under conditions like Karen Quinlan's were

> remote, general, spontaneous, and made in casual circumstances. Indeed, they closely track the examples of evidence that we have explicitly characterized as unreliable. . . .

Instead of relying on *Conroy,* the court determined that cases involving persistently vegetative patients required a return to *Quinlan.* Assuming again that a persistently vegetative patient would choose to have all life support terminated if able, the court determined that Ms. Jobes' family could make the determination to remove her life support. Given the court's reasoning, one must assume that the family's right to make that decision is unbridled given the patient's inability to voice objection. Again, the court was able to discount entirely the state's interest in the preservation of life, finding it "difficult to conceive of a case in which the State could have an interest strong enough to subordinate a *patient's right to choose* not to be sustained in a persistent vegetative state" . . . .

Against this background, we turn to consider the arguments of the parties in the case at hand.

On the dispositive point, the State argues that the trial court erred in "holding that a refusal to allow withdrawal of nutrition and hydration under the facts of this case would deny Nancy Cruzan's 'right to liberty' and that to deny the co-guardians the authority to act on her behalf would deprive her of equal protection of the laws." Respondents support the trial court's order by urging that Nancy has both a common law and constitutional right to be free from "invasive, unwanted and nonbeneficial" medical treatment, and that her

right to refuse such treatment survives incompetency and may be exercised by her guardians as substituted decisionmakers.

The Right to Refuse Treatment

The common law recognizes the right of individual autonomy over decisions relating to one's health and welfare. From this root of autonomy, the common law developed the principle that a battery occurs when a physician performs a medical procedure without valid consent. . . . The doctrine of informed consent arose in recognition of the value society places on a person's autonomy and as the primary vehicle by which a person can protect the integrity of his body. If one can consent to treatment, one can also refuse it. Thus, as a necessary corollary to informed consent, the right to refuse treatment arose. "The patient's ability to control his bodily integrity . . . is significant only when one recognizes that this right also encompasses a right to informed refusal." . . .

A decision as to medical treatment must be informed.

> There are three basic prerequisites for informed consent: the patient must have the capacity to reason and make judgments, the decision must be made voluntarily and without coercion, and the patient must have a clear understanding of the risks and benefits of the proposed treatment alternatives or nontreatment, along with a full understanding of the nature of the disease and the prognosis.

. . . In the absence of these three elements, neither consent nor refusal can be informed. Thus, it is definitionally impossible for a person to make an informed decision—either to consent or to refuse—under hypothetical circumstances; under such circumstances, neither the benefits nor the risks of treatment can be properly weighed or fully appreciated.

The Right to Privacy

Quinlan, and cases which follow it, announce that a patient's right to refuse medical treatment also arises from a constitutional right of privacy. Although some courts find that right embedded in their state constitutions, the privacy argument is most often founded on decisions of the United States Supreme Court, primarily *Roe v. Wade,* . . . (1973). Unfortunately, the bare statement that the right of privacy extends to treatment decisions is seldom accompanied by any reasoned analysis as to the scope of that right or its application to the refusal of life-sustaining treatment.

. . . We . . . find no unfettered right of privacy under our constitution that would support the right of a person to refuse medical treatment in every circumstance.

If Nancy possesses such a right, it must be found to derive from the federal constitutional right to privacy announced by the United States Supreme Court. That Court "has recognized that a right of personal privacy, or a guarantee of certain areas or zones of privacy, does exist under the [United States] Constitution." . . . . The Supreme Court has not, however, extended the right of privacy to permit a patient or her guardian to direct the withdrawal of food and water. We are left to determine for ourselves whether the penumbral right of privacy encompasses a right to refuse life-sustaining medical treatment.

Quinlan is the first case to apply a right of privacy to decisions regarding the termination of life-sustaining treatment. In deciding the applicability of the right to such determinations, *Quinlan* first cites *Griswold v. Connecticut,* . . . (1965), for the proposition that the right of privacy exists and, without further analysis states: "Presumably this right is broad enough to encompass a patient's decision to decline medical treatment under certain circumstances, in much the same way as it is broad enough to encompass a woman's decision to terminate a pregnancy under certain conditions." . . . The presumption invoked by the New Jersey Supreme Court provides the precedent for the extension of this right of privacy by other courts whose decisions permitting the termination of life-sustaining treatment is founded on privacy.

Yet *Roe* itself counsels against such a broad reading.

The privacy right involved, therefore, cannot be said to be absolute. In fact, it is not clear to us that the claim asserted by some amici that one has an unlimited right to do with one's body as one pleases bears a close relationship to the right of privacy previously articulated in the Court's decisions. The Court has refused to recognize an unlimited right of this kind in the past. . . .

The language in *Roe* is not an aberration. The Supreme Court's most recent privacy decision resisted expansion of the privacy right. In *Bowers v. Hardwick,* . . . (1986), the Supreme Court considered whether the right to privacy extended to the conduct of homosexuals. Noting that the prior right to privacy cases focused on a common theme of procreation and relationships within the bonds of marriage, the court refused to extend the right of privacy beyond those bounds, arguing that such an extension amounted to the discovery of a new right. . . .

Based on our analysis of the right to privacy decisions of the Supreme Court, we carry grave doubts as to the applicability of privacy rights to decisions to terminate the provision of food and water to an incompetent patient. As will be seen, however, even if we recognize such a broadly sweeping right of privacy, a decision by Nancy's co-guardians to withdraw food and water under these circumstances cannot be sustained. . . .

It is tempting to equate the state's interest in the preservation of life with some measure of quality of life. As the discussion which follows shows, some courts find quality of life a convenient focus when justifying the termination of treatment. But the state's interest is not in quality of life. The broad policy statements of the legislature make no such distinction; nor shall we. Were quality of life at issue, persons with all manner of handicaps might find the state seeking to terminate their lives. Instead, the state's interest is in life; that interest is unqualified.

Balancing the Patient's Rights and the State's Interest

1.

In casting the balance between the patient's common law right to refuse treatment/constitutional right to privacy and the state's interest in life, we acknowledge that the great majority of courts allow the termination of life-sustaining treatment. In doing so, these courts invariably find that the patient's right to refuse treatment outweighs the state's interest in preserving life. In some cases, that result is the product of a hopeless medical prognosis; in others, the court allows concerns with quality of life to discount the state's interest in life. *Quinlan*, of course, is the source in each instance. Although *Quinlan* dealt with a terminally-ill person, it did so in language sufficiently broad that courts cite it for much different purposes. . . .

Prior to *Quinlan*, the common law preferred to err on the side of life. Choices for incompetents were made to preserve life, not hasten death. *Quinlan* changed the calculus. Moving from the common law's prejudice in favor of life, *Quinlan* subtly recast the state's interest in life as an interest in the quality of life (cognitive and sapient), struck a balance between quality of life and Karen Quinlan's right to privacy and permitted the termination of a life-sustaining procedure. By the rhetorical device of replacing a concern for life with quality of life, the court managed "to avoid affronting previously accepted norms" in reaching its decision. . . .

As we previously stated, however, the state's interest is not in quality of life. The state's interest is an unqualified interest in life. . . .

. . . Nancy's counsel argues that her treatment is invasive. The invasion took place when the gastrostomy tube was inserted with con-

sent at a time when hope remained for recovery. Presently, the tube merely provides a conduit for the introduction of food and water. The *continuation* of feeding through the tube is not heroically invasive. . . .

. . . [T]he co-guardians argue that "Nancy's statements alone are enough to stop this artificial treatment." These statements are best summarized in the testimony of Nancy's roommate that she "would not want to continue her present existence without hope as it is." But "informally expressed reactions to other people's medical condition and treatment do not constitute clear proof of a patient's intent." . . .

Our earlier discussion about informed consent noted the requirements for consent or refusal to be truly informed. A decision to refuse treatment, when that decision will bring about death, should be as informed as a decision to accept treatment. If offered to show informed refusal, the evidence offered here "would be woefully inadequate. It is all the more inadequate to support a refusal that will result in certain death." . . . As the court said in *Jobes,* "All of the statements about life-support that were attributed to Mrs. Jobes were remote, general, spontaneous, and made in casual circumstances. Indeed they closely track the examples of evidence that we have explicitly characterized as unreliable." . . . Likewise, statements attributable to Nancy in this case are similarly unreliable for the purpose of determining her intent.

The state's relevant interest is in life, both its preservation and its sanctity. Nancy is not dead. Her life expectancy is thirty years.

Nancy's care requirements, while total, are not burdensome to Nancy. The evidence at trial showed that the care provided did not cause Nancy pain. Nor is that care particularly burdensome for her, given that she does not respond to it.

Finally, there is no evidence that Nancy is terminally ill. The quality of her life is severely diminished to be sure. Yet if food and water are supplied, she will not die.

Given the fact that Nancy is alive and that the burdens of her treatment are not excessive for her, we do not believe her right to refuse treatment, whether that right proceeds from a constitutional right of privacy or a common law right to refuse treatment, outweighs the immense, clear fact of life in which the state maintains a vital interest. . . .

Higgins, Judge, dissenting.

In my opinion, the decision in this important case of first impression in Missouri rests on an unsound opinion by a tenuous majority of judges sitting in the case. Accordingly, and with due respect, I dissent. . . .

. . . [T]he majority refinds facts to support its result, an inexcusable exercise for this Court. For example, the majority states, "the continuation of feeding through the tube is not heroically invasive." Yet the trial court found:

> a surgical procedure personally invasive to the body is required to implant the tube in the stomach and if repair or replacement of the tube should become necessary further surgical procedure would be required. Nutrition or hydration under these circumstances is medical treatment because it can only be and has for the past five years been maintained by the surgically implanted gastrostomy tube.

The majority's statement that subject medical treatment is not invasive is contrary to both the facts of this case and the cases that describe the use of a gastrostomy tube as "intrusive as a matter of law." . . .

For further example, the majority says, "the statements [in regard to whether Nancy would want to receive this medical treatment] attributable to Nancy in this case are similarly unreliable for the purpose of determining her intent." The trial court, however, found, by clear and convincing evidence, "given [Nancy's] present condition she would not want to continue on with her nutrition and hydration." The record is replete with evidence to

support this finding and the majority should not say otherwise. . . .

Finally, the majority says, "We further hold that the evidence offered at trial as to Nancy's wishes is inherently unreliable." This substitution of judgment for that of the trial court constitutes an incredible denial of the deference due the trial court's exclusive power to judge the credibility of witnesses. . . .

All parties agree this is a case of first impression. Accordingly, it is proper to look to the law of other jurisdictions that have ruled on the question in this case. Although the majority cites more than 50 cases from 16 states that support the judgment in this case, it rejects all and fails to point to a single case in support of its analysis and ultimate conclusion to reverse the judgment. Again, the irony in the majority view is its reversal on the ground of "erroneous declaration of law." Without exception, the cases cited in the majority's footnote 4 uphold a right to refuse life-sustaining medical treatment, either personally or through a guardian. . . .

Note

1. For all legal purposes, the occurrence of human death shall be determined in accordance with the usual and customary standards of medical practice, provided that death shall not be determined to have occurred unless the following minimal conditions have been met: (1) When respiration and circulation are not artificially maintained, there is an irreversible cessation of spontaneous respiration and circulation; or (2) When respiration and circulation are artificially maintained, and there is total and irreversible cessation of all brain function, including the brain stem and that such determination is made by a licensed physician.

Suggestions for Further Reading

Anthologies

Brody, Baruch, and Engelhardt, Tristan. *Bioethics.* Englewood Cliffs: Prentice-Hall, 1987.

Cohen, Marshall, and others. *The Rights and Wrongs of Abortion.* Princeton: Princeton University Press, 1974.

Feinberg, Joel. *The Problem of Abortion.* Belmont: Wadsworth Publishing Co., 1973.

Kohl, Marvin. *Beneficent Euthanasia.* Buffalo: Prometheus, 1975.

Ladd, John. *Ethical Issues Relating to Life and Death.* New York: Oxford University Press, 1979.

Munson, Ronald. *Interventions and Reflections.* Belmont: Wadsworth Publishing Co., 1979.

Basic Concepts

Devine, Philip. *The Ethics of Homicide.* Ithaca: Cornell University Press, 1978.

Glover, Jonathan. *Causing Death and Saving Lives.* New York: Penguin Books, 1977.

Steinbock, Bonnie, editor. *Killing and Letting Die.* Englewood Cliffs: Prentice-Hall, 1980.

Alternative Views

Callahan, Daniel. *Abortion: Law, Choice and Morality.* New York: Macmillan, 1970.

Grisez, Germain, and Boyle, Joseph. *Life and Death with Liberty and Justice.* Notre Dame: University of Notre Dame Press, 1979.

Kluge, Eike-Henner. *The Practice of Death.* New Haven: Yale University Press, 1975.

Luker, Kristin. *Abortion and the Politics of Motherhood.* Berkeley: University of California Press, 1984.

Nicholson, Susan. *Abortion and the Roman Catholic Church.* Knoxville: Religious Ethics, 1978.

Rachels, James. *The End of Life.* New York: Oxford University Press, 1986.

Ramsey, Paul. *The Patient as Person.* New Haven: Yale University Press, 1970.

Summer, L. W. *Abortion and Moral Theory.* Princeton: Princeton University Press, 1981.

Practical Applications

Denes, Magda. *In Necessity and Sorrow: Life and Death in an Abortion Hospital.* New York: Penguin Books, 1977.

Law Reform Commission of Canada. *Euthanasia, Aiding Suicide and Cessation of Treatment.* Working Paper 28, 1982.

Manier, Edward, and others, eds. *Abortion: New Directions for Policy Studies.* Notre Dame: University of Notre Dame Press, 1977.

Sex Equality

Basic Concepts

The problem of sex equality concerns the question of whether the sexes should be treated equally, and, if so, what constitutes equal treatment. This question was at the heart of the decade-long public debate on the Equal Rights Amendment to the Constitution (the ERA), which began in March 1972, when the Senate passed the amendment with a vote of 84 to 8, and ended in June 1982, when the extended deadline for the ERA expired—three states short of the 38 required for ratification.

The complete text of the ERA was as follows:

1. Equality of rights under the law shall not be denied or abridged by the United States or by any state on account of sex.
2. The Congress shall have the power to enforce by appropriate legislation the provisions of this article.
3. This amendment shall take effect two years after the date of ratification.

Public support for the ERA over this period, judging from opinion polls, hovered between 55 and 60 percent, but in key states anti-ERA forces were able to mount sufficient resistance to prevent its passage. In the end, Alabama, Arizona, Arkansas, Florida, Georgia, Illinois, Louisiana, Mississippi, Missouri, Nevada, North Carolina, Oklahoma, Utah, and Virginia failed to ratify the amendment.

Anti-ERA forces were able to block ratification because they successfully shifted the debate from equal rights to the substantive changes the ERA might bring about. This strategy was effective because support for the amendment generally came from individuals sympathetic to the notion of "equal rights" but not necessarily committed to substantive changes in women's roles.[1] For example, in one national survey, 67 percent of the people who claimed to have heard or read about the ERA favored it, 25 percent were opposed to it, and 8 percent had no opinion. Many people in the sample, however, had quite traditional views about women's roles. Two-thirds of the respondents thought that preschool children would suffer if their mothers worked, 62 percent thought married women should not hold jobs when jobs were scarce and their husbands could support them, and 55 percent thought it was more important for a woman to advance her husband's career than to have one of her own.

But what substantive changes would the ERA have brought about if it had been ratified in 1982? The surprising answer is not many, at least in the short run.[2] In 1970, when the ERA first reached the floor of Congress, a significant number of laws and official practices denied women "equality of rights under the law." For example, in 1970, eight states treated all property that a couple bought with their earnings during marriage as "community property," and these states normally gave the husband managerial control over such property. By 1976, most of these laws had been voluntarily changed or struck down by the Supreme Court's interpretation of the equal protection clause of the Fourteenth Amendment. Of course, supporters of the ERA did attempt to argue for the amendment on the grounds that it would bring about equal pay for equal work. Lobbyists for the ERA in state capitols wore buttons that said "59¢" to remind legislators that women who worked full time outside the home still typically earned only 59 cents for every dollar men earned—a ratio that has changed little since the federal government first began publishing such statistics in the 1950s. But the passage of the ERA would have had little immediate impact on that inequality. The ERA would have kept the federal or state governments from legally denying or abridging "equality of rights under the law." However, to help workers, the ERA would have had to do more than just make the law gender blind. It would have had to forbid wage discrimination by *private* organizations and individuals. And this it did not do.

Moreover, the ERA would have had few of the effects its opponents predicted. For example, Phyllis Schlafly frequently claimed that the ERA would require unisex public toilets and combat duty for women, but the Supreme Court would have found the first requirement an infringement of the right to privacy and the second would have run afoul of the war powers clause of the Constitution, which gives military commanders the freedom to decide how best to use their forces. Yet despite the fact that the immediate impact of the passage of the ERA would have been largely symbolic, neither proponents nor opponents sufficiently recognized this or, if they did, were not willing to surrender their exaggerated claims about the effects the amendment would have. Leaders on both sides of this debate may have feared the difficulty of motivating their followers if these exaggerated claims were abandoned.

Alternative Views

Yet regardless of what people believed the ERA would or would not have accomplished, is a commitment to equal rights justified? In the first selection (Selection 22), Elizabeth H. Wolgast argues that it is not. Wolgast claims that biological asymmetry with respect to fixing responsibility for parenthood undercuts the idea that men and women have equal basic rights. Wolgast shows that John Stuart Mill's defense of equal rights is compromised by his view that a woman who marries should make managing her household and raising her family her first duties and renounce all other occupations that are inconsistent with those duties. Wolgast also argues against Richard Wasserstrom's view that biological differences between men and women are not enough to nullify a claim to equal rights. Wolgast claims that in a good society, the biological asymmetry with respect to fixing responsibility for parenthood should be taken into account in determining the rights of men and women.

But why should this biological asymmetry with respect to fixing responsibility for parenthood (i.e., that we can more easily determine a child's mother than its father) be sufficient grounds for assigning unequal rights to men and women? When the child's father is known (the case in most instances), why shouldn't both parents share equal responsibility? And when the father isn't known, why shouldn't he still have the same rights and responsibilities as

the child's mother? The child's father may not be exercising those rights or assuming those responsibilities, but why should we claim he doesn't have them?

The next selection is by Gloria Steinem, the founder and editor of *Ms.* magazine. Steinem is usually taken to be a liberal feminist, that is, one who believes that equality between the sexes can be achieved by legal reform within a capitalist society. When Steinem wrote this piece for the *Time* essay of 1970, she was attempting to sketch the outlines of a liberal feminist utopia. Today, however, many of her goals seem as utopian as ever. Among those goals still to be reached are: (1) free access to the good jobs and decent pay for the bad ones, (2) equalization of parental responsibility, and (3) flexible work schedules. In the selections from her more recent work Steinem proposes a number of outrageous acts that would further the cause of women's liberation.

Although Steinem is careful not to remove the option of being a full-time housewife, one of the consequences of women increasingly joining the work force is their devaluation of the role of housewife.[3] This devaluation seems to be proportionate to education. Between 1957 and 1976, the percentage of college-educated women who said they enjoyed housework fell from 67 to 38 percent. The percentage fell from 66 to 54 percent among women with a high school education, but didn't change at all among women with only a grade school education (76 percent in both 1957 and 1976). The same pattern occurs vis-à-vis career aspirations. Among college-educated homemakers, 60 percent of the respondents in 1976 said they had at some point wanted a career, up from 48 percent in 1957. The percentage rose only slightly among homemakers with a high school education, from 37 to 40 percent. In homemakers with a grade school education, however, the percentage actually fell from 30 to 15 percent.

In the next selection (Selection 25), Evelyn Reed defends the Marxist feminist position that equality between the sexes can only be achieved by replacing capitalism with socialism. The inferior status of women, Reed claims, can be traced to the appearance of class-divided societies with their institutions of the patriarchal family, private property, and state power. On this account, Reed contends that the complete liberation of women can only come about as part of a social revolution that liberates the entire working class.

However, inequality between the sexes obviously predates capitalist and feudal societies, and although it may not predate the appearance of class-divided societies altogether (which takes us back to the beginnings of recorded history), it does seem to be a distinct problem from economic exploitation. After all, men from all economic classes have joined in the exploitation of women.

But given that the exploitation of women is a distinct problem from the exploitation of workers, aren't both problems equally fundamental? Not according to radical feminists such as Shulamith Firestone (Selection 26). Firestone argues that exploitation of women is the more fundamental problem because it is rooted in human biology and can only be changed by changing that biology. That change, she claims, would require us to introduce at least the option of artificial reproduction.

However, socialist feminists, such as Alison M. Jaggar (Selection 27), have criticized the radical feminist view for giving simply an ahistorical, biological explanation of the exploitation of women. Socialist feminists believe that the exploitation of women is rooted in both economic exploitation and human biology. Thus, according to socialist feminists, equality between the sexes can only be achieved by replacing capitalism with socialism *and* changing human biology. Radical feminists like Firestone also recognize the need to replace capitalism with socialism, but for them it is simply a means to the end of changing human biology. By contrast, socialist feminists regard replacing capitalism with socialism and changing human biology as equally important goals for achieving women's liberation. Socialist feminists also recognize an interaction between biology and economy not generally appreciated by radical feminists (i.e., that human biology is both the tool and the product of labor).

Jaggar also claims that the socialist feminist ideal can be described as an ideal of androgyny, but so understood, she hastens to add, it must involve a transformation of both physical and psychological capacities. Such a transformation might even include the capacities for insemination, lactation, and gestation so that, for instance, one woman could inseminate another, men and nonchild-bearing women could lactate, and fertilized ova could be transplanted into men's or women's bodies. Thus, given Jaggar's understanding of the view, socialist feminism would retain most of the commitments of radical feminism and simply integrate them with those of Marxist feminism.

Practical Applications

Turning to practical applications, we can see that, at least in the statement of the National Organization for Women (NOW) Bill of Rights (Selection 28), there was never any confusion that the ERA would achieve all the goals of the organization. In this Bill of Rights, the ERA is one of eight goals to be achieved.

Recently, maternity leave rights in employment, another of NOW's goals, was at stake in California Federal Savings and Loan vs. the Department of Fair Employment and Housing (Selection 29). Here the issue before the Supreme Court was whether Title VII of the Civil Rights Act of 1964 as amended by the Pregnancy Discrimination Act of 1978 (PDA) nullifies a California law that requires employers to provide leave and reinstatement to employees disabled by pregnancy. The majority of the court ruled that it did not nullify the law for two reasons. First, in passing PDA, Congress simply wanted to prohibit discrimination against pregnant women; there was no discussion of preferential treatment for pregnant women. In addition, by allowing both men and women to have families without losing their jobs, the California law did share with Title VII and PDA the goal of equal opportunity. Second, even if PDA did prohibit preferential treatment for pregnant women, an employer could avoid violating both PDA and the California statute by giving comparable benefits to all similarly disabled employees.

What is interesting is that NOW opposed the Court's decision in this case. Apparently, NOW's leaders were concerned that such preferential treatment might lead to a resurgence of nineteenth-century protective legislation that encouraged sexual stereotypes and restrained women from taking their rightful place in the workplace. Although this is a legitimate concern, it can be addressed by determining whether each particular piece of relevant legislation advances the goal of equal opportunity. If it does, as the California law seems to do, there shouldn't be any objection to it, at least from a welfare liberal, socialist, or communitarian point of view.

Notes

1. Jane J. Mansbridge, *Why We Lost the ERA* (Chicago: University of Chicago Press, 1986), Chapter 3.
2. *Ibid.*, Chapters 5–7.
3. *Ibid.*, pp. 106–107.

22. Women Are Different

Elizabeth H. Wolgast

In opposing a number of arguments for equal rights for men and women, Elizabeth Wolgast argues that a biological asymmetry with respect to fixing responsibility for parenthood undercuts the idea that men and women have exactly the same rights.

Equality is the key to arguments for many kinds of rights and against many kinds of injustices—against slavery, despotism, economic exploitation, the subjection of women, racial oppression. It is not surprising then that arguments for women's rights turn on the notion of equality. But it is wonderful that one idea can serve so many causes. Does it always work the same, for instance, in regard to race and sex? And particularly, what does equality mean when applied to men and women?

I

If people were all alike there would be no question about their equality. Thus the claim of human equality is often linked with the

assertion of human similarity. The philosopher John Locke, for instance, said that there is "nothing more evident than that creatures of the same species and rank, promiscuously born to all the same advantages of nature and the use of the same faculties, should also be equal one amongst another without subordination or subjection."[1] Insofar as they are similar in birth and faculties they should be equal in society.

From the equality of men it is natural to infer the equality of their principal rights. "Equals must be equal in rights," one scholar expressed it.[2] If men are equal, then none is privileged by nature, and their rights, like the men themselves, should be similar.

These ways of reasoning are very familiar in discussions of racial equality. Differences of race such as skin color and hair texture are superficial, it is argued; in the important respects the races are similar and therefore equal. To distinguish between the rights of one group and the rights of another when the only differences are these unimportant ones seems patently unjust. So an argument for racial equality based on similarity is tantamount to an argument for equal rights regardless of race.

Women's rights are commonly argued on the same lines. The first step is the assertion of their similarity with men, and the last step is the claim that they should have equal rights. The nineteenth-century philosopher John Stuart Mill argued in this way, long before most philosophers addressed the problem. "There is no natural inequality between the sexes," he claimed, "except perhaps in bodily strength." Women can be thought of as weak men. Now strength by itself is not a good ground for distinguishing among people's rights. Mill infers, "If nature has not made men and women unequal, still less ought the law to make them so." As in the case of race, similarity dictates similar treatment. "Men and women ought to be perfectly coequal," and "a woman ought not to be dependent on a man, more than a man on a woman, except so far as their affections make them so."[3]

If women are like men except perhaps for strength, the argument for sexual equality would be even more powerful than that for racial equality; for with race the differences are several and determined by heredity, while women and men may have the same genetic components and transmit the same ones. If strength alone differentiated women from men, sex equality would be perfectly apparent.

But of course women are not weak men, and Mill is not deceived. Women are talented like men and have imagination, determination, drive, and other capacities the same as men; but they are different in ways other than strength. Sometimes Mill acknowledges differences, even stresses their importance. He thinks that, while a woman should be able to support herself, "in the natural course of events she will *not*," but her husband will support them both. "It will be for the happiness of both that her occupation should rather be to adorn and beautify" their lives.[4] At the same time her commitment to the home is a large one.

> Like a man when he chooses a profession, so, when a woman marries, it may in general be understood that she makes choice of the management of a household and the bringing up of a family, as the first call upon her exertions, during as many years of her life as may be required for the purpose; and that she renounces . . . all [other occupations] which are not consistent with the requirements of this.[5]

Women should conform to an inflexible set of demands by household and family. Their role does not stem from their weakness—that wouldn't make sense. The real reason for women having this role is that they are the "opposite" sex and the ones to have children. That "coequality" Mill advocates turns out to be a "natural arrangement" with man and wife "each being absolute in the executive branch of their own department."[6] What happened to the equality nature provided? It was not so clear after all.

Mill is more convincing when he speaks of the particular virtues in which the sexes differ. Women have their distinctive contribution to make, he says: they bring depth to issues where men bring breadth; they are practical where men are theoretical; they introduce sentiment where it is needed and would otherwise be lacking; and of course women are especially apt in the care and training of children.[7] To extol these characteristics of women, Mill must put aside that similarity which first supported equality of rights; but here his respect for women is unequivocal and plain.

In sum, Mill is ambivalent about the similarity of the sexes. On the one hand he argues as if women were weak men, on the other, that they have their distinctive and important virtues. On the one hand he espouses legal equality; on the other he endorses a conventional dependent role for married women.

If Mill's claim for sexual equality rested entirely on similarity, it would seem that that equality is in jeopardy. But he has another defense ready. There is, he says, "an *a priori* assumption . . . in favour of freedom and impartiality . . . [and] the law should be no respecter of persons, but should treat all alike, save where dissimilarity of treatment is required by positive reasons."[8] Similar treatment is right by presumption, and dissimilar treatment will always need positive justification.

The argument from similarity was unnecessary then. But what kind of reason would justify differences of treatment? Mill doesn't say.

An argument for sex equality deriving from similarity is one that stresses the ways in which men and women are alike. But of course they are not exactly alike or there would not be a problem in the first place. It becomes necessary to make some such statement as: they are alike in all *important* respects, just as people of different races are importantly alike and only trivially different. But now it is necessary to consider whether differences of sex really are trivial.

In the case of race it seems clear that skin color and hair and features are unimportant, being superficial. They are mere physical marks. Can one say the same about the differences of sex? That is not so clear.

There is also a danger in using the argument from similarity, namely that, while it is meant to justify treating people alike, it implies that if people were importantly different they might need to be treated differently. So by implication it allows differences between individuals to justify *unequal* rights. This feature shows the importance for this kind of reasoning of maintaining that differences of sex are really trivial, for if they are not shown to be so, the argument can work against equality of rights. . . .

How can it be argued that sex is an unimportant difference? We can see the issue more clearly through a form of sex egalitarianism more sophisticated and modern than Mill's. Richard Wasserstrom, a philosopher and lawyer, argues that the good society would give no more recognition to sex or racial differences than we presently give to eye color. "Eye color is an irrelevant category" he argues, "nobody cares what color people's eyes are; it is not an important cultural fact; nothing turns on what eye color you have."[9] No laws or institutions distinguish between persons by eye color, nor do even personal decisions turn on it. The same would hold, in the good society, of racial and sexual differences. The good society would be "assimilationist" with respect to race and sex just as our society is with respect to eye color.

Race and sex and eye color would all be viewed in the same way if our society were just.

All three kinds of difference are biological, natural; but among them sex is "deeper," he concedes, and seems to have greater social implications:

> What opponents of assimilationism seize upon is that sexual difference appears to be a naturally occurring category of obvious and inevitable social relevance in a way, or to a degree, which race is not. . . . An analysis of the social realities reveals that it is the socially created sexual differences which tend in fact to matter the most. It is sex-role differentiation, not gender per se, that makes men and women as different as they are from each other.[10]

It is the way we recognize sex differences in socially created sex roles that gives them their great importance. If we stopped such artificial forms of recognition, we would see that the underlying difference of sex, like that of race, is trivial. Even though it is a naturally occurring difference, that in itself does not justify a social distinction, a distinction in roles. The principal difference of sex is social, not biological. And so sex is analogous to race: the difference allows for assimilation, given a change in laws, in institutions, and in social mores. Although there will still *be* a sexual difference, it will not make a difference.

To compare sex and race in this way implies that reproductive differences and reproduction itself should not much affect our social arrangements: "There appear to be very few, if any, respects in which the ineradicable, naturally occurring differences between males and females *must* be taken into account," Wasserstrom says.[11] The differences can just be ignored. But how do we ignore the reproductive differences? They are not many or very important, he argues, given the present state of medical knowledge:

> Sexual intercourse is not necessary, for artificial insemination is available. Neither marriage nor the family is required for conception or child rearing. Given the present state of medical knowledge and the natural realities of female pregnancy,

it is difficult to see why any important institutional or interpersonal arrangements must take the existing gender difference of *in utero* pregnancy into account.[12]

When you consider how many differences can be compensated for by medical innovations, there is only the nine months of *in utero* pregnancy left. And why should that make very much difference? Wasserstrom thinks it shouldn't. The sexes should be treated the same. . . .

In the good society there is sex equality: that is a primary consideration. For treating similar people the same would seem inherently just. If therefore it is within our means to make people more similar, through science and medicine, that course has much to recommend it; for with equality the goodness of society is assured. "Even though there are biological differences between men and women by nature, this fact does not determine the question of what the good society can and should make of these differences," Wasserstrom writes.[13] We don't need to be guided by nature; we can use our intelligence to control, adjust, and compensate for the differences nature produces.

Wasserstrom is not, like Mill, guided by existing similarities but is committed to create similarities wherever possible. Equality of the sexes is an ideal, an ideal of justice, and it requires similarities to exist. The good society, then, will create the similarities to go with its ideal, and that means it will create conditions under which its citizens will be, in all important ways, sexually similar.

I will not stop to consider whether this ideal is a pleasant or attractive one, for I want to ask the question: Is it true that merely biological differences of sex should not influence a good society?

II

Part of the egalitarian view expressed most commonly is the idea that biological differences of sex can be separated from social roles. Then the question is raised whether different

sex roles, which are social artifacts, are desirable. Put this way, it is difficult to see why the roles should be very different. But it is not clear that the biological differences and the social ones *are* so distinct and separate.

Take the one fact, mentioned by Wasserstrom as unalterable at present, that women bear children after a period of pregnancy. From this one fact of *in utero* pregnancy one consequence directly follows: a woman does not normally have occasion to wonder whether the baby she bears is hers. She does not wonder if she or someone else is the mother. The father stands in a different relation to his child at the outset; his position is logically more distant, depending on inferences a mother need not make. And it is possible that he may doubt and, doubting, even fail to acknowledge a child that is in fact his, while it is difficult to imagine a mother in just that position—to imagine her bearing a child and then wondering whose it can be.

It is easy to imagine confusion about babies in the context of a modern hospital nursery, of course, but what I call attention to is a deeper and inherent asymmetry in parenthood, one that does not stem from institutions but from reproduction itself. As parents mothers have a primary place, one that cannot be occupied by a father.

This fact in turn has consequences. From the fact that mothers are primary parents it is clear that in general a mother is the more easily identifiable of a child's parents. This is important because a child is a very dependent creature and dependent for a very long time. Someone must have responsibility for it, and most generally that responsibility is given to parents. So now, in assigning responsibility for a child, it is simpler and less equivocal to assign the responsibility to a mother than to a father. This is so because doubts can be raised about his parenthood that have no analogue for hers.

From the mere fact of the way children are born, then, there are consequences important to society. Society, in its need to recognize someone as responsible for a child, rightly makes use of this fact of reproduction, the *in utero* pregnancy, so it can identify one parent with reasonable certainty.

I am assuming that parents are responsible

for their children. However, this need not be part of the morality of a society, though it is part of the morality of most, and certainly part of ours. If this assumption is not made, the consequences would be different, depending on how society construes the relation of parent and child and places responsibility for the young. But it seems plausible that there will be some connection between parenthood and responsibility, and this connection will reflect the fact that mothers are primary parents.

That mothers are primary parents affects not only laws and institutions but also the way women look at their lives. The potential of pregnancy and motherhood are present from the time girls reach adolescence, and are part of a young female's life and thought in a way they cannot be for a male. She needs to consider parenthood's connection with her behavior, and this influences her options. It would be surprising if it did not also affect her relations with males, sharpening her sense of their polarity, arousing concern about the durability and stability of her relationships with them. In such ways the merely biological fact of *in utero* pregnancy comes to give different coloring to the sexual identity of males and females, laying the groundwork for some sex roles.

Nor is this all. In a society where paternal responsibility is recognized and valued, there is a need to identify males as fathers. Thus an institution that makes formal identification of fathers, such as marriage, becomes important. As a child has two biological parents, so it comes to have two parents in society, within a social structure. And it would be surprising if some mores involving chastity and fidelity did not arise as well. In this way the merely biological facts of reproduction will tend to influence both the form of society and its customs, even though the details of that influence will vary. Societies are not all formed alike; other influences are at work as well. My point is that the fact of *in utero* pregnancy will have some consequences connected with the asymmetry of parenthood. Wasserstrom complains that society "mistakenly leads many persons to the view that women are both naturally and necessarily better suited than men to be assigned the primary responsibilities of child rearing."[14] If he had said "better situated," the observation he attributes to society would be profoundly

right. The maternal role *is* more closely connected to parental responsibility than the paternal one, and neither talents nor conditioning nor tastes enter into it.

Suppose a society chooses not to acknowledge the asymmetry of parenthood. How would it do this? Would it assign equal responsibility to both parents? But what about the cases in which the father of an infant is unknown? It has a father, unless he is since deceased; but knowing this is no help. And what of the cases in which a mother refuses to acknowledge any father; is the child not then exclusively hers? In Hawthorne's *The Scarlet Letter,* Hester Prynne's Pearl is *hers,* although both she and the Reverend Dimmesdale know he is the father. How would the good society make that parenting equal?

I do not mean at all that fathers are less tender, less devoted, or less responsible than mothers, that parental solicitude and devotion are women's prerogatives. *That* kind of "sex role" is not implied by the primary parenthood of mothers. What is meant is that asymmetries of parenthood are neither small nor trivial. And because of this they will have asymmetrical effects on other aspects of a person's life, some only indirectly related to parenthood. In this sense of "sex role," it is difficult to understand how sex roles could be abolished or made alike. Would one have to ignore the asymmetries of reproduction? But that would be a pretense.

Since the parental roles are asymmetrical, a natural consequence is some asymmetry in the attitudes of young men and young women regarding both reproduction and sex. The same behavior, sexual intercourse for instance, will have different significance for each. A society that gives structure to these differences, that provides a context into which both genders are expected to fit, will thereby provide for differences in sex roles. A great deal may be embroidered here in the way of stereotypes, rituals, myths, and mores. But what I shall mean by sex roles is a minimal set of differences, differences in attitude and behavior and in life outlook, stemming from the asymmetries of reproduction and framed by a social context.

The answer to Wasserstrom then evolves: The biological differences of men and women do not determine what a good society should make of them, but a good society should take them into account, and probably must do so. In order to justify ignoring the asymmetries that characterize human reproduction, that form of reproduction would have to be drastically changed.

So long as babies develop *in utero* and not, for example, in bottles, parenthood will be an asymmetrical business. A good society will no more ignore it than it will ignore the fact that humans start out as babies and do not live forever.

Wasserstrom's next step may be the proposal that reproduction be changed so as to be more symmetrical, for example, by developing fetuses in the laboratory and delivering them at term to two symmetrically related parents. In this situation a child would have no primary parent; on both sides recognition of parenthood would depend on a similar inference. It is difficult to see that from either the child's point of view or society's this loss of a primary parent would be an improvement. . . .

In Wasserstrom's ideal, people will regard one another, even in personal matters, without distinguishing the sexes. We don't distinguish between people on the basis of eye color: "so the normal, typical adult in this kind of nonsexist society would be indifferent to the sexual, physiological differences of other persons for all interpersonal relationships. Bisexuality, not heterosexuality or homosexuality, would be the norm."[15] In order for the sexes to be really equal, he reasons, we need to treat them alike even in personal and private ways. For if there are sex distinctions regularly made in private, they will be echoed somehow in the public sphere, and this means there will be a sex-differentiated form of society. This cure for sexual injustice is extreme: what is required here is a society of individuals who behave and are treated as if they were sexually alike. It requires an androgynous society.

III

Sex equality based on the similarity of the sexes, as advocated by Wasserstrom, will lead to an assimilationist form of society, for insofar as people are similar, similar treatment of them will be justified, and the assimilationist society treats everyone alike. It ignores sex differences just as it ignores racial ones, and for the same reason—because they are unimportant. By this reasoning a nonassimilationist form of society will necessarily be unjust. Wasserstrom writes:

> Any . . . nonassimilationist society will make one's sexual identity an important characteristic, so that there are substantial psychological, role, and status differences between persons who are males and those who are females. . . . [But] sex roles, and all that accompany them, necessarily impose limits—restrictions on what one can do, be or become. As such, they are, I think, at least prima facie wrong.[16]

In restricting us sex roles are wrong. Through them "involuntarily assumed restraints have been imposed on the most central factors concerning the way one will shape and live one's life."[17] But sex roles in the narrow sense I mean them are reflections of restrictions; they do not create restrictions or impose them. Rather the restrictions come from the way human reproduction works and the kinds of responsibilities it entails in the framework of a real human society. It is hard to speak of the restrictions being imposed, just as it is hard to think of the character of human vision imposing restrictions on us. We cannot see what is behind our heads at any given moment; that is frustrating and certainly limits our freedom, restricting what we can do, be, or become. But one wouldn't for that reason call the visual system "wrong." Living in a society involves restrictions too, and so does being born to particular parents, in a particular place, in this century. These things too affect "the most central factors concerning the way one will shape and live one's life." But from what point of view can we term them "wrong"? We do not have an abstract viewpoint from which to measure the "wrongness" of such accidents.

Our difficulty with the assimilationist ideal has two sides: on the one, it seems to be based on human similarity, on the triviality of sex differences. But, as I argue, there is much reason to reject this and much justification for recognizing some form of sex roles. On the other hand, the assimilationist ideal seems to commit one to *creating* similarities, through medical and social measures, as if the ideal did not rest on anything, but were self-evident. If all sex roles are wrong, then only a unisex form of society will be just. But we are not unisex creatures; we are not androgynous or hermaphroditic. So assimilationism seems an inappropriate ideal, at least for human beings.

Having sex roles is natural to us and not the creation of society. As Midgley says, maternal instinct is not reducible to "cultural conditioning by the women's magazines."[18] If equality were adopted as an ideal, a massive effort at conditioning would be necessary to make us think like androgynous creatures with similar sex roles and sexual natures and so to fit that form of society. It is the androgynous role that is artificial, the product of a fictitious view of human nature. Instead of encouraging freedom and autonomy, the assimilationist society would thus restrict us to an androgynous form of life. It is a kind of Procrustean bed.

IV

Sex is a deeper phenomenon than race, Wasserstrom concedes. Its differences are more pervasive, more securely built into our institutions and practices. Nevertheless, he believes sex can be treated along the same lines as race, without qualitative adjustments. Lumping race and sex together is also common where there is talk of "group discrimination" and programs to combat it. But the cases are not alike.

One way to see the difference is to consider the way "assimilation" applies in the two cases. It is conceivable that, with less strictness in our mores, the races would come eventually to be assimilated to one. Differences in color and physiognomy would be so muted as to count only as individual ones, on a par with eye color. There is the possibility of real, genetic assimilation in the case of race. But with sex this is obviously not possible, and even if it were, we would have to think hard whether we

wanted it. To allow equality to determine the character of our species seems to show a wrong order of things.

Equality based on similarity is connected to the Aristotelian dictum that we should treat likes alike and unlikes differently. But which cases are alike and which different? The answer is not simple. In the matter of race we generally say the cases are alike; in the case of sex this is not at all obvious. The difference of sex is genetically nonassimilable and besides it is difficult to ignore. Perhaps Aristotle's rule should lead us to conclude that with sex the cases require different treatment.

Where similarity is a consideration, racial arguments and sexual ones need to be separated. A person's racial characteristics are not usually correlated with special concerns differentiating racial groups, while many of women's most important concerns, for instance those connected with pregnancy, are distinctive to women as a group. The fair treatment of the two sexes cannot be assumed to consist in the "assimilation" of their rights.

Less compelling is the fact that sex differences have a lot to do with our enjoyment of human relationships. *Could* we treat the sexes alike as Wasserstrom proposes? We normally respond differently to members of the opposite sex than to members of our own. Even putting sexual attraction aside, we still have different relations to members of different sexes. With members of our sex, we have and anticipate having, a good deal in common. To a child we say, "When I was a little girl . . ." (if we are women) with the implication that we lack the same identification with boys. While with members of the opposite sex we perceive contrasts and divergent points of view, for some areas of common experience are lacking. Understanding those other perspectives is often a tenuous matter, ignorance and mystery being the conditions it must work against; but it is also one that fascinates, challenges, delights, and amuses us.

Wasserstrom could respond that these differences are mostly the creation of society, and that the position I suggest amounts to an endorsement of present sex roles and stereotypes. This is not intended. What I propose is rather that biology differentiates us in ways that will have some implications for differentiated sex roles. It is not a "solution" to such differentiation to suggest that everyone have the same roles or pretend to have them. The feminist social critic Dorothy Dinnerstein argues in *The Mermaid and the Minotaur* that "gender symbiosis" is a neurotic condition that needs correcting.[19] Although I agree with many of her observations about sex roles in our society and the need for changes, I am arguing that asymmetry will persist in some form or other, that the implications of biology are pervasive. The idea that, under propitious conditions, sex differences can be flattened out or "nullified" does not seem either necessary or attractive.[20] Nor is it clearly possible. It may be no more possible for us to treat people of different sexes alike than it is for us to treat a baby as an adult, or an elderly man as a youth. Some differences cannot be discounted. . . .

Notes

1. John Locke, *Second Treatise on Civil Government*, Bk. I, ch. ii, para. 4. Locke added "unless the Lord and Master of them all should . . . set one above another, and confer on him . . . right to dominion and sovereignty." Americans in framing the Constitution used only the first part of Locke's principle.

2. Henry Alonzo Myers, *Are Men Equal?* (Ithaca: Cornell University Press, 1945), 136. The con-

nection between human equality and equality of rights in American political thought is carefully traced by J. R. Pole in *The Pursuit of Equality in American History* (Berkeley: University of California Press, 1978); see ch. 6 in particular.

3. J. S. Mill and Harriet Taylor Mill, *Essays on Sex Equality* (Chicago: University of Chicago Press, 1970), 73–74.

4. *Ibid.*, 74–75.

5. *The Subjection of Women* (Cambridge, Mass.: M.I.T. Press, 1970), 48.

6. *Ibid.*, 40.

7. *Ibid.*, 59–63.

8. *Ibid.*, 4.

9. Wasserstrom, "Racism, Sexism and Preferential Treatment: An Approach to the Topics," *U.C.L.A. Law Review*, 24 (July 1977), 586.

10. *Ibid.*, 609–610.

11. *Ibid.*, 611.

12. *Ibid.*, 611–612.

13. *Ibid.*, 610.

14. *Ibid.*, 611.

15. Wasserstrom, 606.

16. *Ibid.*, 615.

17. *Ibid.*, 615–616.

18. Midgley, 326.

19. New York: Harper, 1976.

20. "Nullifying sex differences" is used in Wasserstrom's book, *Philosophy and Social Issues: Five Studies* (Notre Dame: University of Notre Dame Press, 1980).

23. What It Would Be Like if Women Win

Gloria Steinem

When Gloria Steinem wrote this piece for the *Time* essay of 1970, she was sketching the outlines of a liberal feminist utopia. Among her utopian goals still to be reached are (1) free access to the good jobs and decent pay for the bad ones, (2) equalization of parental responsibility, and (3) flexible work schedules.

Abridged from *Time* (August 31, 1970), pp. 22–23. Reprinted by permission of Gloria Steinem.

Any change is fearful, especially one affecting both politics and sex roles, so let me begin these utopian speculations with a fact. To break the ice.

Women don't want to exchange places with men. Male chauvinists, science-fiction writers and comedians may favor that idea for its shock value, but psychologists say it is a fantasy based on ruling-class ego and guilt. Men assume that women want to imitate them, which is just what white people assumed about blacks. An assumption so strong that it may convince the second-class group of the need to imitate, but for both women and blacks that stage has passed. Guilt produces the question: What if they could treat us as we have treated them?

That is not our goal. But we do want to change the economic system to one more based on merit. In Women's Lib Utopia, there will be free access to good jobs—and decent pay for the bad ones women have been performing all along, including housework. Increased skilled labor might lead to a four-hour workday, and higher wages would encourage further mechanization of repetitive jobs now kept alive by cheap labor.

With women as half the country's elected representatives, and a woman President once in a while, the country's *machismo* problems would be greatly reduced. . . . I'm not saying that women leaders would eliminate violence. We are not more moral than men; we are only uncorrupted by power so far. When we do acquire power, we might turn out to have an equal impulse toward aggression. Even now, Margaret Mead believes that women fight less often but more fiercely than men, because women are not taught the rules of the war game and fight only when cornered. But for the next 50 years or so, women in politics will be very valuable by tempering the idea of manhood into something less aggressive and better suited to this crowded, post-atomic planet. Consumer protection and children's rights, for instance, might get more legislative attention.

Men will have to give up ruling-class privileges, but in return they will no longer be the only ones to support the family, get drafted, bear the strain of power and responsibility. Freud to the contrary, anatomy is not destiny,
at least not for more than nine months at a time. In Israel, women are drafted, and some have gone to war. In England, more men type and run switchboards. In India and Israel, a woman rules. In Sweden, both parents take care of the children. In this country, come Utopia, men and women won't reverse roles; they will be free to choose according to individual talents and preferences.

If role reform sounds sexually unsettling, think how it will change the sexual hypocrisy we have now. No more sex arranged on the barter system, with women pretending interest, and men never sure whether they are loved for themselves or for the security few women can get any other way. (Married or not, for sexual reasons or social ones, most women still find it second nature to [act servile].) No more men who are encouraged to spend a lifetime living with inferiors; with housekeepers, or dependent creatures who are still children. No more domineering wives, emasculating women, and "Jewish mothers," all of whom are simply human beings with all their normal ambition and drive confined to the home. No more unequal partnerships that eventually doom love and sex.

In order to produce that kind of confidence and individuality, child rearing will train according to talent. Little girls will no longer be surrounded by air-tight, self-fulfilling prophecies of natural passivity, lack of ambition and objectivity, inability to exercise power, and dexterity (so long as special aptitude for jobs requiring patience and dexterity is confined to poorly paid jobs; brain surgery is for males).

Schools and universities will help to break down traditional sex roles, even when parents will not. Half the teachers will be men, a rarity now at preschool and elementary levels; girls will not necessarily serve cookies or boys hoist up the flag. Athletic teams will be picked only by strength and skill. Sexually segregated courses like auto mechanics and home economics will be taken by boys and girls together. New courses in sexual politics will explore female subjugation as the model for political oppression, and women's history will be an academic staple, along with black history, at least until the white-male-oriented textbooks are integrated and rewritten.

As for the American child's classic problem—too much mother, too little father—that would be cured by an equalization of parental responsibility. Free nurseries, school lunches, family cafeterias built into every housing complex, service companies that will do household cleaning chores in a regular, businesslike way, and more responsibility by the entire community for the children: all these will make it possible for both mother and father to work, and to have equal leisure time with the children at home. For parents of very young children, however, a special job category, created by Government and unions, would allow such parents a shorter work day.

The revolution would not take away the option of being a housewife. A woman who prefers to be her husband's housekeeper and/or hostess would receive a percentage of his pay determined by the domestic relations courts. If divorced, she might be eligible for a pension fund, and for a job-training allowance. Or a divorce could be treated the same way that the dissolution of a business partnership is now.

If these proposals seem farfetched, consider Sweden, where most of them are already in effect. Sweden is not yet a working Women's Lib model; most of the role-reform programs began less than a decade ago, and are just beginning to take hold. But that country is so far ahead of us in recognizing the problem that Swedish statements on sex and equality sound like bulletins from the moon. . . .

What will exist is a variety of alternative life-styles. Since the population explosion dictates that childbearing be kept to a minimum, parents-and-children will be only one of many "families": couples, age groups, working groups, mixed communes, blood-related clans, class groups, creative groups. Single women will have the right to stay single without ridicule, without the attitudes now betrayed by "spinster" and "bachelor." Lesbians or homosexuals will no longer be denied legally binding marriages, complete with mutual-support agreements and inheritance rights. Paradoxically, the number of homosexuals may get smaller. With fewer overpossessive mothers and fewer fathers who hold up an impossibly cruel or perfectionist idea of manhood, boys will be less likely to be denied or reject their identity as males.

Changes that now seem small may get bigger:

Men's Lib

Men now suffer from more disease due to stress, heart attacks, ulcers, a higher suicide rate, greater difficulty living alone, less adaptability to change and, in general, a shorter life span than women. There is some scientific evidence that what produces physical problems is not work itself, but the inability to choose which work, and how much. With women bearing half the financial responsibility, and with the idea of "masculine" jobs gone, men might well feel freer and live longer.

Religion

Protestant women are already becoming ordained ministers; radical nuns are carrying out liturgical functions that were once the exclusive property of priests; Jewish women are rewriting prayers—particularly those that Orthodox Jews recite every morning thanking God they are not female. In the future, the church will become an area of equal participation by women. This means, of course, that organized religion will have to give up one of its great historical weapons: sexual repression. In most structured faiths, from Hinduism through Roman Catholicism, the status of women went down as the position of priests ascended. Male clergy implied, if they did not teach, that women were unclean, unworthy and sources of ungodly temptation, in order to remove them as rivals for the emotional forces of men. Full participation of women in ecclesiastical life might involve certain changes in theology, such as, for instance, a radical redefinition of sin.

Literary Problems

Revised sex roles will outdate more children's books than civil rights ever did. Only a few children had the problem of a *Little Black Sambo,* but most have the male-female stereotypes of "Dick and Jane." A boomlet of children's books about mothers who work has already begun, and liberated parents and editors are beginning to pressure for change in the textbook industry. Fiction writing will change more gradually, but romantic novels with wilting heroines and swashbuckling heroes will be reduced to historical value. Or perhaps to the sado-masochist trade. (*Marjorie Morningstar,* a romantic novel that took the '50s by storm, has already begun to seem as unreal as its '20s predecessor, *The Sheik.*) As for the literary plots that turn on forced marriages or horrific abortions, they will seem as dated as Prohibition stories. Free legal abortions and free birth control will force writers to give up pregnancy as the *deus ex machina.*

Manners and Fashion

Dress will be more androgynous, with class symbols becoming more important than sexual ones. Pro- or anti-Establishment styles may already be more vital than who is wearing them. Hardhats are just as likely to rough up antiwar girls as antiwar men in the street, and police understand that women are just as likely to be pushers or bombers. Dances haven't required that one partner lead the other for years, anyway. Chivalry will transfer itself to those who need it, or deserve respect: old people, admired people, anyone with an armload of packages. Women with normal work identities will be less likely to attach their whole sense of self to youth and appearance; thus there will be fewer nervous breakdowns when the first wrinkles appear. Lighting cigarettes and other treasured niceties will become gestures of mutual affection. "I like to be helped on with my coat," says one Women's Lib worker, "but not if it costs me $2,000 a year in salary."

For those with nostalgia for a simpler past, here is a word of comfort. Anthropologist Geoffrey Gorer studied the few peaceful human tribes and discovered one common characteristic: sex roles were not polarized. Differences of dress and occupation were at a minimum. Society, in other words, was not using sexual blackmail as a way of getting women to do cheap labor, or men to be aggressive.

Thus Women's Lib may achieve a more peaceful society on the way toward its other goals. That is why the Swedish government considers reform to bring about greater equality in the sex roles one of its most important concerns. As Prime Minister Olof Palme explained in a widely ignored speech delivered in Washington this spring: "It is *human beings* we shall emancipate. In Sweden today, if a politician should declare that the woman ought to have a different role from man's, he would be regarded as something from the Stone Age." In other words, the most radical goal of the movement is egalitarianism.

If Women's Lib wins, perhaps we all do.

24. Outrageous Acts and Everyday Rebellions

Gloria Steinem

In this selection Gloria Steinem proposes a number of outrageous acts that individuals and groups might undertake that serve the cause of feminist justice. They range from announcing a permanent refusal to contribute more money to a church or synagogue until women too can become priests, ministers, and rabbis to giving public awards and dinners to women (and men) who have helped advance the cause of women's liberation.

The great strength of feminism—like that of the black movement here, the Gandhian movement in India, and all the organic struggles for self-rule and simple justice—has always been encouragement for each of us to act, without waiting and theorizing about some future takeover at the top. It's no accident that, when some small group does accomplish a momentous top-down revolution, the change seems to benefit only those who made it. Even with the best intentions of giving "power to the people," the revolution is betrayed.

Power can be taken, but not given. The process of the taking is empowerment in itself.

So we ask ourselves: What might a spectrum of diverse, mutually supportive tactics really look like for us as individuals, for family and community groups, for men who care about equality, for children, and for political movements as a whole? Some actions will always be unique to particular situations and thus unforeseeable. Others will be suited to times of great energy in our lives, and still others will make sense for those who are burnt out and need to know that a time of contemplation and assessment is okay. But here are some that may inspire action, if only to say, "No, that's not right. But this is what I choose to do instead."

From *Outrageous Acts and Everyday Rebellions* (Holt, Rinehart, 1983). Reprinted by permission of the author.

As Individuals

In the early 1970s when I was traveling and lecturing with feminist lawyer and black activist Florynce Kennedy, one of her many epigrams went like this: "Unity in a movement situation is overrated. If you were the Establishment, which would you rather see coming in the door, five hundred mice or one lion?"

Mindful of her teaching, I now often end lectures with an organizer's deal. If each person in the room promises that in the twenty-four hours beginning the very next day she or he will do at least *one outrageous thing* in the cause of simple justice, then I promise I will, too. It doesn't matter whether the act is as small as saying, "Pick it up yourself" (a major step for those of us who have been our family's servants) or as large as calling a strike. The point is that, if each of us does as promised, we can be pretty sure of two results. First, the world one day later won't be quite the same. Second, we will have such a good time that we will never again get up in the morning saying, "*Will* I do anything outrageous?" but only "*What* outrageous act will I do today?"

Here are some samples I've recorded from the outrageous acts of real life.

- Announced a permanent refusal to contribute more money to a church or synagogue until women too can become priests, ministers, and rabbis.

• Asked for a long-deserved raise, or, in the case of men and/or white folks, refused an undeserved one that is being given over the heads of others because of their race or sex.

• Written a well-reasoned critique of a sexist or racist textbook and passed it out on campus.

• Challenged some bit of woman-hating humor or imagery with the seriousness more often reserved for slurs based on religion or race.

• Shared with colleagues the knowledge of each other's salaries so that unfairnesses can be calculated. (It's interesting that employers try to keep us from telling the one fact we know.)

• Cared for a child or children so that an overworked mother could have a day that is her own. (This is especially revolutionary when done by a man.)

• Returned to a birth name or, in the case of a man, gave his children both parents' names.

• Left home for a week so that the father of your young child could learn to be a parent. (As one woman later reported calmly, "When I came home, my husband and the baby had bonded, just the way women and babies do.")

• Petitioned for a Women's Studies section in a local library or bookstore.

• Checked a corporate employer's giving programs, see if they are really inclusive by benefiting women with at least half of their dollars, and made suggestions if not.

• Personally talked to a politician who needed persuasion to support, or reward for helping, issues of equality.

• Redivided a conventional house so that each person has a space for which he or she is solely responsible, with turns taken caring for kitchen, bathroom, and other shared rooms.

• Got married to an equal, or divorced from an unequal.

• Left a violent lover or husband.

• Led a walkout from a movie that presents rape scenes or other violence as titillating and just fine.

• Made a formal complaint about working (or living) in a white ghetto. White people are also being culturally deprived.

• Told the truth to a child, or a parent.

• Said proudly, "I am a feminist." (Because this word means a believer in equality, it's especially helpful when said by a man.)

• Organized a block, apartment house, or dormitory to register and vote.

• Personally picketed and/or sued a bigoted employer/teacher/athletic coach/foreman/union boss.

In addition to one-time outrageous acts, these are also the regular ones that should be the bottom line for each of us: writing five letters a week to lobby, criticize, or praise anything from TV shows to a senator; giving 10 percent of our incomes to social justice; going to one demonstration a month or one consciousness-raising group a week just to keep support and energy up; and figuring out how to lead our daily lives in a way that reflects what we believe. People who actually incorporate such day-by-day changes into their lives report that it isn't difficult: five lobbying letters can be written while watching "The Late Show"; giving 10 percent of their incomes often turns out to be the best investment they ever made; meetings create a free space, friends, and an antidote to isolation; and trying to transform a job or a family or a life-style in order to reflect beliefs, instead of the other way around, gives a satisfying sense of affecting the world.

If each of us only reached out and changed *five other people in our lifetimes*, the spiral of revolution would widen enormously—and we can do much more than that.

In Groups

Some of the most effective group actions are the simplest:

• Dividing membership lists according to political district, from precinct level up, so we can inform and get out the pro-equality vote.

• Asking each organization we belong to, whether community or professional, union or religious, to support issues of equality in their formal agendas.

- Making sure that the nonfeminist groups we're supporting don't have mostly women doing the work and mostly men on their boards.

- Making feminist groups *feminist;* that is, relevant to women of the widest diversity of age, race, economics, life-styles, and political labels practical for the work at hand. (An inclusiveness that's best begun among the founders. It's much tougher to start any group and only later reach out to "others.")

- Offering support where it's needed without being asked—for instance, to the school librarian who's fighting right-wing censorship of feminist and other books; or to the new family feeling racially isolated in the neighborhood. (Would you want to have to ask people to help you?)

- Identifying groups for coalitions and allies for issues.

- Streamlining communications. If there were an emergency next week—a victim of discrimination who needed defending, a piece of sinister legislation gliding through city council—could your membership be alerted?

- Putting the group's money where its heart is, and not where it isn't. That may mean contributing to the local battered women's shelter and protesting a community fund that gives far more to Boy Scouts than to Girl Scouts; or publishing a directory of women-owned businesses; or withholding student-activity fees from a campus program that invites mostly white male speakers. (Be sure and let the other side know how much money they're missing. To be more forceful, put your contributions in an escrow account, with payment contingent on a specific improvement.)

- Organizing speak-outs and press conferences. There's nothing like personal testimonies from the people who have experienced the problem firsthand.

- Giving public awards and dinners to women (and men) who've made a positive difference.

- Bringing in speakers or Women's Studies courses to inform your members; running speakers' bureaus so your group's message gets out to the community.

- Making sure new members feel invited and welcome once they arrive, with old members assigned to brief them and transfer group knowledge.

- Connecting with other groups like yours regionally or nationally for shared experience, actions, and some insurance against reinventing the wheel.

Obviously, we must be able to choose the appropriate action from a full vocabulary of tactics, from voting to civil disobedience, from supporting women in the trades to economic boycotts and tax revolts, from congressional hearings to zap actions with humor and an eye to the evening news.

Given the feminization of poverty, however, groups are also assuming another importance. Since women are an underdeveloped, undercapitalized labor force with an unequal knowledge of technology—in other words, a Third World country wherever we are—we're beginning to realize that the Horatio Alger model of individualistic economic progress doesn't work very well for us. Probably we have more to learn about economic development from our sisters in countries recognized as the Third World. Cooperative ownership forms and communal capital formation may be as important to our future as concepts of equal pay.

So far, these experiments have started small: three single mothers who combine children and resources to buy a house not one of them could afford alone; two women who buy a truck for long-distance hauling jobs; a dozen women who pool their savings to start a bakery or a housecleaning service, or single mothers and feminist architects who transform old buildings into new homes.

But we're beginning to look at Third World examples of bigger efforts. If the poorest women in rural Kenya can pool their savings for years, buy a bus, make money from passengers, and build a cooperative store, why can't we with our greater resources help each other to do the same? If illiterate women in India can found and run their own credit cooperative, thus giving them low-interest loans for the goods they sell in the streets, how dare American women be immobilized by a poor economy? It's also a healthy reversal of the usual flow of expertise from developed to underdeveloped country that may help feminists build bridges across national chasms of condescension and mistrust. Groups and organizations have been the base of our issue-oriented, electoral, consciousness-raising, and direct-action progress. In the future, they may be our economic base as well.

As Strategists

We've spent the first decade or so of the second wave of feminism on the riverbank, rescuing each other from drowning. In the survival areas of rape, battery, and other terrorist violence against women, for instance, we've begun to organize help through shelters, hot lines, pressure on police to provide protection, reforms in social services and legislation, and an insistence that society stop blaming the victim.

Now, some of us must go to the head of the river and keep the victims from falling in.

For instance, we can pursue new strategies that have proved effective in treating wife batterers and other violent men. Such strategies have been successful precisely because they came from experiences and feminist insight: violence is an addiction that a male-dominant society creates by teaching us that "real men" must dominate and control the world in general and women in particular. When some men inevitably become addicted to violence to prove their masculinity, conventional Freudian-style treatment has only said: "Yes, men are natural aggressors, but you must learn to control the degree." That's like telling a drug addict that he can have just a little heroin.

Treatment based on experience, on the other hand, says: "No, men are not natural aggressors; you must unhook your sense of identity and masculinity from violence, and kick the habit completely."

The few such programs that exist have been helpful to batterers, rapists and other violent men, criminals, and dangerous citizens who have been judged untreatable precisely because they saw themselves as normal men. This fundamental challenge to cultural ideas of masculinity might also hold hope for less violent ways of solving conflicts on this fragile Spaceship Earth.

That's one of hundreds of futurist examples. There are many other strategies centered around four great goals: *reproductive freedom; work redefined; democratic families; and depoliticized culture.*

Clearly, these goals can only be reached a long distance in the future. We are very far from the opposite shore.

But the image of crossing a river may be too linear to describe the reality we experience. In fact, we repeat similar struggles that seem cyclical and discouraging in the short run, yet each one is on slightly changed territory. One full revolution is not complete until it has passed through the superficiality of novelty and even law to become an accepted part of the culture. Only when we look back over a long passage of time do we see that each of these cycles has been moving in a direction. We see the spiral of history.

In my first days of activism, I thought I would do this ("this" being feminism) for a few years and then return to my real life (what my "real life" might be, I did not know). Partly, that was a naïve belief that injustice only had to be pointed out in order to be cured. Partly, it was a simple lack of courage.

But like so many others now and in movements past, I've learned that this is not just something we care about for a year or two or three. We are in it for life—and for our lives. Not even the spiral of history is needed to show the distance traveled. We have only to look back at the less complete people we ourselves used to be.

And that is the last Survival Lesson: *we look at how far we've come, and then we know—there can be no turning back.*

25. Women: Caste, Class or Oppressed Sex?

Evelyn Reed

Evelyn Reed argues that the inferior status of women did not result from any biological deficiency as a sex. Rather, its origins can be traced to the appearance of class-divided societies with their institutions of the patriarchal family, private property, and state power. Against those who claim that the oppression of women derives from their belonging to a separate caste or class, Reed points out that women have always belonged to both superior and inferior castes and classes. Reed concludes that the complete liberation of women can only come as part of a social revolution that liberates the entire working class.

The new stage in the struggle for women's liberation already stands on a higher ideological level than did the feminist movement of the last century. Many of the participants today respect the Marxist analysis of capitalism and subscribe to Engels's classic explanation of the origins of women's oppression. It came about through the development of class society, founded upon the family, private property and the state.

But there still remain considerable misunderstandings and misinterpretations of Marxist positions, which have led some women who consider themselves radicals or socialists to go off course and become theoretically disoriented. Influenced by the myth that women have always been handicapped by their childbearing functions, they tend to attribute the roots of women's oppression, at least in part, to biological sexual differences. In actuality its causes are exclusively historical and social in character.

Some of these theorists maintain that women constitute a special class or caste. Such definitions are not only alien to the views of Marxism but lead to the false conclusion that it is not the capitalist system but men who are the prime enemy of women. I propose to challenge this contention.

The findings of the Marxist method, which have laid the groundwork for explaining the

From "Women: Caste, Class or Oppressed Sex?" in *Problems of Women's Liberation* (1970), pp. 64–76. © 1970 by International Socialist Review. Reprinted by permission of Pathfinder Press, Inc.

genesis of woman's degradation, can be summed up in the following propositions:

First, women were not always the oppressed or "second" sex. Anthropology, or the study of prehistory, tells us the contrary. Throughout primitive society, which was the epoch of tribal collectivism, women were the equals of men and recognized by man as such.

Second, the downfall of women coincided with the breakup of the matriarchal clan commune and its replacement by class-divided society with its institutions of the patriarchal family, private property and state power.

The key factors which brought about this reversal in woman's social status came out of the transition from a hunting and food-gathering economy to a far higher mode of production based upon agriculture, stock raising and urban crafts. The primitive division of labor between the sexes was replaced by a more complex social division of labor. The greater efficiency of labor gave rise to a sizable surplus product, which led first to differentiations and then to deepgoing divisions among the various segments of society.

By virtue of the directing roles played by men in large-scale agriculture, irrigation and construction projects, as well as in stock raising, this surplus wealth was gradually appropriated by a hierarchy of men as their private property. This, in turn, required the institution of marriage and the family to fix the legal ownership and inheritance of a man's property. Through monogamous marriage the wife was brought under the complete control of her husband who was thereby assured of legitimate sons to inherit his wealth.

As men took over most of the activities of social production, and with the rise of the family institution, women became relegated to the home to serve their husbands and families. The state apparatus came into existence to fortify and legalize the institutions of private property, male dominion and the father-family, which later were sanctified by religion.

This, briefly, is the Marxist approach to the origins of woman's oppression. Her subordination did not come about through any biological deficiency as a sex. It was the result of the revolutionary social changes which destroyed the equalitarian society of the matriarchal gens or clan and replaced it with a patriarchal class society which, from its birth, was stamped with discriminations and inequalities of many kinds, including the inequality of the sexes. The growth of this inherently oppressive type of socioeconomic organization was responsible for the historic downfall of women.

But the downfall of women cannot be fully understood, nor can a correct social and political solution be worked out for their liberation, without seeing what happened at the same time to men. It is too often overlooked that the patriarchal class system which crushed the matriarchy and its communal social relations also shattered its male counterpart, the fratriarchy—or tribal brotherhood of men. Woman's overthrow went hand in hand with the subjugation of the mass of toiling men to the master class of men.

The import of these developments can be more clearly seen if we examine the basic character of the tribal structure which Morgan, Engels and others described as a system of "primitive communism." The clan commune was both a sisterhood of women and a brotherhood of men. The sisterhood of women, which was the essence of the matriarchy, denoted its collectivist character. The women worked together as a community of sisters: their social labors largely sustained the whole community. They also raised their children in common. An individual mother did not draw distinctions

between her own and her clan sisters' progeny, and the children in turn regarded all the older sisters as their mutual mothers. In other words, communal production and communal possessions were accompanied by communal child-raising.

The male counterpart of this sisterhood was the brotherhood, which was molded in the same communal pattern as the sisterhood. Each clan or phratry of clans comprising the tribe was regarded as a "brotherhood" from the male standpoint just as it was viewed as a "sisterhood" or "motherhood" from the female standpoint. In this matriarchal-brotherhood the adults of both sexes not only produced the necessities of life together but also provided for and protected the children of the community. These features made the sisterhood and brotherhood a system of "primitive communism."

Thus, before the family that had the individual father standing at its head came into existence, the functions of fatherhood were a *social*, not a *family* function of men. More than this, the earliest men who performed the services of fatherhood were not the mates or "husbands" of the clan sisters but rather their clan brothers. This was not simply because the processes of physiological paternity were unknown in ancient society. More decisively, this fact was irrelevant in a society founded upon collectivist relations of production and communal child-raising.

However odd it may seem to people today, who are so accustomed to the family form of child-raising, it was perfectly natural in the primitive commune for the clan brothers, or "mothers' brothers," to perform the paternal functions for their sisters' children that were later taken over by the individual father for his wife's children.

The first change in this sister-brother clan system came with the growing tendency for pairing couples, or "pairing families" as Morgan and Engels called them, to live together in the same community and household. However, this simple cohabitation did not substantially alter the former collectivist relations or the productive role of the women in the community. The sexual division of labor which had formerly been allotted between clan sisters and brothers became gradually transformed into a sexual division of labor between husbands and wives.

But so long as collectivist relations prevailed and women continued to participate in social production, the original equality between the sexes more or less persisted. The whole community continued to sustain the pairing units, just as each individual member of these units made his and her contribution to the labor activities.

Consequently, the pairing family, which appeared at the dawn of the family system, differed radically from the nuclear family of our times. In our ruthless competitive capitalist system every tiny family must sink or swim through its own efforts—it cannot count on assistance from outside sources. The wife is dependent upon the husband while the children must look to the parents for their subsistence, even if the wage earners who support them are stricken by unemployment, sickness or death. In the period of the pairing family, however, there was no such system of dependency upon "family economics," since the whole community took care of each individual's basic needs from the cradle to the grave.

This was the material basis for the absence, in the primitive commune, of those social oppressions and family antagonisms with which we are so familiar.

It is sometimes said or implied that male domination has always existed and that women have always been brutally treated by men. Contrariwise, it is also widely believed that the relations between the sexes in matriarchal society were merely the reverse of our own—with women dominating men. Neither of these propositions is borne out by the anthropological evidence.

It is not my intention to glorify the epoch of savagery nor advocate a romantic return to some past "golden age." An economy founded upon hunting and food-gathering is the lowliest stage in human development, and its living conditions were rude, crude and harsh. Nevertheless, we must recognize that male and female relations in that kind of society were fundamentally different from ours.

Under the clan system of the sisterhood of women and the brotherhood of men there was no more possibility for one sex to dominate the other than there was for one class to exploit another. Women occupied the most eminent position because they were the chief producers of the necessities of life as well as the procreators of new life. But this did not make them the oppressors of men. Their communal society excluded class, racial or sexual tyranny.

As Engels pointed out, with the rise of private property, monogamous marriage and the patriarchal family, new social forces came into play in both society at large and the family setup which destroyed the rights exercised by earliest womankind. From simple cohabitation of pairing couples there arose the rigidly fixed, legal system of monogamous marriage. This brought the wife and children under the complete control of the husband and father who gave the family his name and determined their conditions of life and destiny.

Women, who had once lived and worked together as a community of sisters and raised their children in common, now became dispersed as wives of individual men serving their lords and masters in individual households. The former equalitarian sexual division of labor between the men and women of the commune gave way to a family division of labor in which the woman was more and more removed from social production to serve as a household drudge for husband, home and family. Thus women, once "governesses" of society, were degraded under the class formations to become the governesses of a man's children and his chief housemaid.

This abasement of women has been a permanent feature of all three stages of class society, from slavery through feudalism to capitalism. So long as women led or participated in the productive work of the whole community, they commanded respect and esteem. But once they were dismembered into separate family units and occupied a servile position in home and family, they lost their prestige along with their influence and power.

Is it any wonder that such social changes should bring about intense and long-enduring antagonism between the sexes? As Engels says:

> Monogamy then does by no means enter history as a reconciliation of man and wife, and still less as the highest form of marriage. On the contrary, it enters as

the subjugation of one sex by the other, as the proclamation of an antagonism between the sexes unknown in all preceding history. . . . The first class antagonism appearing in history coincides with the development of the antagonism of man and wife in monogamy, and the first class oppression with that of the female by the male sex (Origin of the Family, Private Property, and the State).

Here it is necessary to note a distinction between two degrees of women's oppression in monogamous family life under the system of private property. In the productive farm family of the preindustrial age, women held a higher status and were accorded more respect than they receive in the consumer family of our own city life, the nuclear family.

So long as agriculture and craft industry remained dominant in the economy, the farm family, which was a large or "extended" family, remained a viable productive unit. All its members had vital functions to perform according to sex and age. The women in the family helped cultivate the ground and engaged in home industries as well as bearing children, while the children and older folks produced their share according to ability.

This changed with the rise of industrial and monopoly capitalism and the nuclear family. Once masses of men were dispossessed from the land and small businesses to become wage earners in factories, they had nothing but their labor power to sell to the capitalist bosses for their means of subsistence. The wives of these wage earners, ousted from their former productive farm and homecraft labors, became utterly dependent upon their husbands for the support of themselves and their children. As men became dependent upon their bosses, the wives became more dependent upon their husbands.

By degrees, therefore, as women were stripped of their economic self-dependence, they fell ever lower in social esteem. At the beginning of class society they had been removed from *social* production and social leadership to become farm-family producers, working through their husbands for home and family. But with the displacement of the productive farm family by the nuclear family

of industrial city life, they were driven from their last foothold on solid ground.

Women were then given two dismal alternatives. They could either seek a husband as provider and be penned up thereafter as housewives in city tenements or apartments to raise the next generation of wage slaves. Or the poorest and most unfortunate could go as marginal workers into the mills and factories (along with the children) and be sweated as the most downtrodden and underpaid section of the labor force.

Over the past generations women wage workers have conducted their own labor struggles or fought along with men for improvements in their wages and working conditions. But women as dependent housewives have had no such means of social struggle. They could only resort to complaints or wrangles with husband and children over the miseries of their lives. The friction between the sexes became deeper and sharper with the abject dependency of women and their subservience to men.

Despite the hypocritical homage paid to womankind as the "sacred mother" and devoted homemaker, the *worth* of women sank to its lowest point under capitalism. Since housewives do not produce commodities for the market nor create any surplus value for the profiteers, they are not central to the operations of capitalism. Only three justifications for their existence remain under this system: as breeders, as household janitors, and as buyers of consumer goods for the family.

While wealthy women can hire servants to do the dull chores for them, poor women are riveted to an endless grind for their whole lives. Their condition of servitude is compounded when they are obliged to take an outside job to help sustain the family. Shouldering two responsibilities instead of one, they are the "doubly oppressed."

Even middle-class housewives in the Western world, despite their economic advantages, are victimized by capitalism. The isolated, monotonous, trivial circumstances of their lives lead them to "living through" their children—a relationship which fosters many of the neuroses that afflict family life today. Seeking to allay their boredom, they can be played upon by the profiteers in the consumer goods fields. This exploitation of women as consumers is part and parcel of a system that grew up in the first place for the exploitation of men as producers.

The capitalists have ample reason for glorifying the nuclear family. Its petty household is a goldmine for all sorts of hucksters from real estate agents to the manufacturers of detergents and cosmetics. Just as automobiles are produced for individual use instead of developing adequate mass transportation, so the big corporations can make more money by selling small homes on private lots to be equipped with individual washing machines, refrigerators and other such items. They find this more profitable than building large-scale housing at low rentals or developing community services and child-care centers.

In the second place, the isolation of women, each enclosed in a private home and tied to the same kitchen and nursery chores, hinders them from banding together and becoming a strong social force or a serious political threat to the Establishment.

What is the most instructive lesson to be drawn from this highly condensed survey of the long imprisonment of womankind in the home and family of class society—which stands in such marked contrast to their stronger, more independent position in preclass society? It shows that the inferior status of the female sex is not the result of their biological makeup or the fact that they are the childbearers. Childbearing was no handicap in the primitive commune; it *became* a handicap, above all, in the nuclear family of our times. Poor women are torn apart by the conflicting obligations of taking care of their children at home while at the same time working outside to help sustain the family. Women, then, have been condemned to their oppressed status by the same social forces and relations which have brought about the oppression of one class by another, one race by another, and one nation by another. It is the capitalist system—the ultimate stage in the development of class society—which is the fundamental source of the degradation and oppression of women.

Some women in the liberation movement dispute these fundamental theses of Marxism. They say that the female sex represents a separate caste or class. Ti-Grace Atkinson, for example, takes the position that women are a separate *class:* Roxanne Dunbar says that they comprise a separate *caste.* Let us examine these two theoretical positions and the conclusions that flow from them.

First, are women a caste? The caste hierarchy came first in history and was the prototype and predecessor of the class system. It arose after the breakup of the tribal commune with the emergence of the first marked differentiations of segments of society according to the new divisions of labor and social functions. Membership in a superior or inferior station was established by being born into that caste.

It is important to note, however, that the caste system was also inherently and at birth a class system. Furthermore, while the caste system reached its fullest development only in certain regions of the world, such as India, the class system evolved far beyond it to become a world system, which engulfed the caste system.

This can be clearly seen in India itself, where each of the four chief castes—the Brahmans or priests, the soldiers, the farmers and merchants, and the laborers, along with the "out-castes" or pariahs—had their appropriate places in an exploitative society. In India today, where the ancient caste system survives in decadent forms, capitalist relations and power prevail over all the inherited precapitalist institutions, including the caste relics.

However, those regions of the world which advanced fastest and farthest on the road to civilization bypassed or overleaped the caste system altogether. Western civilization, which started with ancient Greece and Rome, developed from slavery through feudalism to the maturest stage of class society, capitalism.

Neither in the caste system nor the class system—nor in their combinations—have women comprised a separate caste or class. Women themselves have been separated into the various castes and classes which made up these social formations.

The fact that women occupy an inferior status as a sex does not *ipso facto* make women either an inferior caste or class. Even in ancient India women belonged to different castes, just as they belong to different classes in contemporary capitalist society. In the one case their social status was determined by birth into a caste; in the other it is determined by their own or their husband's wealth. But the two can be fused—for women as for men.

Both sexes can belong to a superior caste and possess superior wealth, power and status. . . .

Turning to the other position, it is even more incorrect to characterize women as a special "class." In Marxist sociology a class is defined in two interrelated ways: by the role it plays in the processes of production and by the stake it has in the ownership of property. Thus the capitalists are the major power in our society because they own the means of production and thereby control the state and direct the economy. The wage workers who create the wealth own nothing but their labor power, which they have to sell to the bosses to stay alive.

Where do women stand in relation to these polar class forces? They belong to all strata of the social pyramid. The few at the top are part of the plutocratic class: more among us belong to the middle class, most of us belong to the proletarian layers of the population. There is an enormous spread from the few wealthy women of the Rockefeller, Morgan and Ford families to the millions of poor women who subsist on welfare dole. *In short, women, like men, are a multiclass sex.*

This is not an attempt to divide women from one another but simply to recognize the actual divisions that exist. The notion that all women as a sex have more in common than do members of the same class with one another is false. Upper-class women are not simply bedmates of their wealthy husbands. As a rule they have more compelling ties which bind them together. They are economic, social and political bedmates, united in defense of private property, profiteering, militarism, racism—and the exploitation of other women.

To be sure, there can be individual exceptions to this rule, especially among young women today. We remember that Mrs. Frank Leslie, for example, left a $2 million bequest to further the cause of women's suffrage, and other upper-class women have devoted their means to secure civil rights for our sex. But it is quite another matter to expect any large number of wealthy women to endorse or support a revolutionary struggle which threatens their capitalist interests and privileges. Most of them scorn the liberation movement, saying openly or implicitly, "What do we need to be liberated from?". . .

It is true that all forms of class society have

been male-dominated and that men are trained from the cradle on to be chauvinistic. But it is not true that men as such represent the main enemy of women. This crosses out the multitudes of downtrodden, exploited men who are themselves oppressed by the main enemy of women, which is the capitalist system. These men likewise have a stake in the liberation struggle of the women: they can and will become our allies.

Although the struggle against male chauvinism is an essential part of the tasks that women must carry out through their liberation movement, it is incorrect to make that the central issue. This tends to conceal or overlook the role of the ruling powers who not only breed and benefit from all forms of discrimination and oppression but are also responsible for breeding and sustaining male chauvinism. Let us remember that male supremacy did not exist in the primitive commune, founded upon sisterhood and brotherhood. Sexism, like racism, has its roots in the private property system.

A false theoretical position easily leads to a false strategy in the struggle for women's liberation. Such is the case with a segment of the Redstockings who state in their *Manifesto* that "women are an oppressed *class*." If all women compose a class then all men must form a counterclass—the oppressor class. What conclusion flows from this premise? That there are no men in the oppressed class? Where does this leave the millions of oppressed white working men who, like the oppressed blacks, Chicanos and other minorities, are exploited by the monopolists? Don't they have a central place in the struggle for social revolution? At what point and under what banner do these oppressed peoples of all races and both sexes join together for common action against their common enemy? To oppose women as a class against men as a class can only result in a diversion of the real class struggle.

Isn't there a suggestion of this same line in Roxanne Dunbar's assertion that female liberation is the basis for social revolution? This is far from Marxist strategy since it turns the real situation on its head. Marxists say that social revolution is the basis for full female liberation—just as it is the basis for the liberation of the whole working class. In the last analysis the real allies of women's liberation are all those forces which are impelled for their own reasons to struggle against and throw off the shackles of the imperialist masters.

The underlying source of women's oppression, which is capitalism, cannot be abolished by women alone, nor by a coalition of women drawn from all classes. It will require a worldwide struggle for socialism by the working masses, female and male alike, together with every other section of the oppressed, to overthrow the power of capitalism, which is centered today in the United States.

In conclusion, we must ask, what are the connections between the struggle for women's liberation and the struggle for socialism?

First, even though the full goal of women's liberation cannot be achieved short of the socialist revolution, this does not mean that the struggle to secure reforms must be postponed until then. It is imperative for Marxist women to fight shoulder to shoulder with all our embattled sisters in organized actions for specific objectives from now on. This has been our policy ever since the new phase of the women's liberation movement surfaced a year or so ago, and even before.

The women's movement begins, like other movements for liberation, by putting forward elementary demands. These are: equal opportunities with men in education and jobs; equal pay for equal work; free abortions on demand; and child-care centers financed by the government but controlled by the community. Mobilizing women behind these issues not only gives us the possibility of securing some improvements but also exposes, curbs and modifies the worst aspects of our subordination in this society.

Second, why do women have to lead their own struggles for liberation, even though in the end the combined anticapitalist offensive of the whole working class will be required for the victory of the socialist revolution? The reason is that no segment of society which has been subjected to oppression, whether it consists of Third World people or of women, can delegate the leadership and promotion of their fight for freedom to other forces—even though other forces can act as their allies. We reject the attitude of some political tendencies that say they are Marxists but refuse to acknowledge that women have to lead and organize their own independent struggle for emancipation, just as they cannot understand why blacks must do the same.

The maxim of the Irish revolutionists—"who would be free themselves must strike the blow"—fully applies to the cause of women's liberation. Women must themselves strike the blows to gain their freedom. And this holds true after the anticapitalist revolution triumphs as well as before.

In the course of our struggle, and as part of it, we will reeducate men who have been brainwashed into believing that women are naturally the inferior sex due to some flaws in their biological makeup. Men will have to learn that, in the hierarchy of oppressions created by capitalism, their chauvinism and dominance is another weapon in the hands of the master class for maintaining its rule. The exploited worker, confronted by the even worse plight of his dependent housewife, cannot be complacent about it—he must be made to see the source of the oppressive power that has degraded them both.

Finally, to say that women form a separate caste or class must logically lead to extremely pessimistic conclusions with regard to the antagonism between the sexes in contrast with the revolutionary optimism of the Marxists. For unless the two sexes are to be totally separated, or the men liquidated, it would seem that they will have to remain forever at war with each other.

As Marxists we have a more realistic and hopeful message. We deny that women's inferiority was predestined by her biological makeup or has always existed. Far from being eternal, woman's subjugation and the bitter hostility between the sexes are no more than a few thousand years old. They were produced by the drastic social changes which brought the family, private property and the state into existence.

This view of history points up the necessity for a no less thoroughgoing revolution in socioeconomic relations to uproot the causes of inequality and achieve full emancipation for our sex. This is the purpose and promise of the socialist program, and this is what we are fighting for.

26. The Dialectic of Sex

Shulamith Firestone

According to Shulamith Firestone, the oppression of women is the most fundamental problem society faces. It is more fundamental than even economic oppression because human biology must be changed before it can be resolved. In particular, the biological family must be changed, and, Firestone claims, this change must include at least the option of artificial reproduction.

Sex class is so deep as to be invisible. Or it may appear as a superficial inequality, one that can be solved by merely a few reforms, or perhaps by the full integration of women into the labor force. But the reaction of the common man, woman, and child—"*That?* Why you can't change *that!* You must be out of your mind!"—is the closest to the truth. We are talking about something every bit as deep as that. This gut reaction—the assumption that, even when they don't know it, feminists are talking about changing a fundamental biological condition—is an honest one. That so profound a change cannot be easily fit into traditional categories of thought, e.g., "political," is not because these categories do not apply but because they are not big enough: radical feminism bursts through them. If there were another word more all-embracing than *revolution* we would use it.

Until a certain level of evolution had been reached and technology had achieved its present sophistication, to question fundamental biological conditions was insanity. Why should a woman give up her precious seat in the cattle car for a bloody struggle she could not hope to win? But, for the first time in some countries, the preconditions for feminist revolution exist—indeed, the situation is beginning to *demand* such a revolution.

The first women are fleeing the massacre, and, shaking and tottering, are beginning to find each other. Their first move is a careful joint observation, to resensitize a fractured consciousness. This is painful: No matter how many levels of consciousness one reaches, the problem always goes deeper. It is everywhere. The division yin and yang pervades all culture, history, economics, nature itself; modern Western versions of sex discrimination are only the most recent layer. To so heighten one's sensitivity to sexism presents problems far worse than the black militant's new awareness of racism: Feminists have to question, not just all of *Western* culture, but the organization of culture itself, and further, even the very organization of nature. Many women give up in despair: if *that's* how deep it goes they don't want to know. Others continue strengthening and enlarging the movement, their painful sensitivity to female oppression existing for a purpose: eventually to eliminate it.

Before we can act to change a situation, however, we must know how it has arisen and evolved, and through what institutions it now operates. Engels: "[We must] examine the historic succession of events from which the antagonism has sprung in order to discover in the conditions thus created the means of ending the conflict." For feminist revolution we shall need an analysis of the dynamics of sex war as comprehensive as the Marx-Engels analysis of class antagonism was for the economic revolution. More comprehensive. For we are dealing with a larger problem, with an oppression that goes back beyond recorded history to the animal kingdom itself.

In creating such an analysis we can learn a lot from Marx and Engels: Not their literal opinions about women—about the condition of women as an oppressed class they know next to nothing, recognizing it only where it overlaps with economics—but rather their analytic *method*.

Marx and Engels outdid their socialist forerunners in that they developed a method of analysis which was both *dialectical* and *materialist*. The first in centuries to view history dialectically, they saw the world as process, a natural flux of action and reaction, of opposites yet inseparable and interpenetrating. Because they were able to perceive history as movie rather than as snapshot, they attempted to avoid falling into the stagnant "metaphysical" view that had trapped so many other great minds. . . . They combined this view of the dynamic interplay of historical forces with a materialist one, that is, they attempted for the first time to put historical and cultural change on a real basis, to trace the development of economic classes to organic causes. By understanding thoroughly the mechanics of history, they hoped to show men how to master it.

Socialist thinkers prior to Marx and Engels, such as Fourier, Owen, and Bebel, had been able to do no more than moralize about existing social inequalities, positing an ideal world where class privilege and exploitation should not exist—in the same way that early feminist thinkers posited a world where male privilege and exploitation ought not exist—by mere virtue of good will. In both cases, because the early thinkers did not really understand how the social injustice had evolved, maintained itself, or could be eliminated, their ideas existed in a cultural vacuum, utopian. Marx and Engels, on the other hand, attempted a scientific approach to history. They traced the class conflict to its real economic origins, projecting an economic solution based on objective economic preconditions already present: the seizure by the proletariat of the means of production would lead to a communism in which government had withered away, no longer needed to repress the lower class for the sake of the higher. In the classless society the interests of every individual would be synonymous with those of the larger society.

But the doctrine of historical materialism, much as it was a brilliant advance over previous historical analysis, was not the complete answer, as later events bore out. For though Marx and Engels grounded their theory in reality, it was only a *partial* reality. Here is Engels' strictly economic definition of historical materialism from *Socialism: Utopian or Scientific:*

> Historical materialism is that view of the course of history which seeks the *ultimate* cause and the great moving power of all historical events in the economic development of society, in the changes of the modes of production and exchange, in the consequent division of society into distinct classes, and in the struggles of these classes against one another. (Italics mine)

Further, he claims:

> . . . that all past history with the exception of the primitive stages was the history of class struggles; that these warring classes of society are always the products of the modes of production and exchange—in a word, of the economic conditions of their time; that the *economic* structure of society always furnishes the real basis, starting from which we can alone work out the *ultimate* explanation of the whole superstructure of juridical and political institutions as well as of the religious, philosophical, and other ideas of a given historical period. (Italics mine)

It would be a mistake to attempt to explain the oppression of women according to this strictly economic interpretation. The class analysis is a beautiful piece of work, but limited: although correct in a linear sense, it does not go deep enough. There is a whole sexual substratum of the historical dialectic that Engels at times dimly perceives, but because he can see sexuality only through an economic filter, reducing everything to that, he is unable to evaluate in its own right.

Engels did observe that the original division of labor was between man and woman for the purposes of childbreeding; that within the family the husband was the owner, the wife the means of production, the children the labor; and that reproduction of the human species was an important economic system distinct from the means of production. . . .

But Engels has been given too much credit for these scattered recognitions of the oppression of women as a class. In fact he acknowledged the sexual class system only where it overlapped and illuminated his economic construct. Engels didn't do so well even in this respect. But Marx was worse: There is a growing recognition of Marx's bias against women (a cultural bias shared by Freud as well as all men of culture), dangerous if one attempts to squeeze feminism into an orthodox Marxist framework—freezing what were only incidental insights of Marx and Engels about sex class into dogma. Instead, we must enlarge historical materialism to *include* the strictly Marxian, in the same way that the physics of relativity did not invalidate Newtonian physics so much as it drew a circle around it, limiting its application—but only through comparison—to a smaller sphere. For an economic diagnosis traced to ownership of the means of production, even of the means of *re*production, does not explain everything. There is a level of reality that does not stem directly from economics.

The assumption that, beneath economics, reality is psychosexual is often rejected as ahistorical by those who accept a dialectical materialist view of history because it seems to land us back where Marx began: groping through a fog of utopian hypotheses, philosophical systems that might be right, that might be wrong (there is no way to tell), systems that explain concrete historical developments by *a priori* categories of thought; historical materialism, however, attempted to explain "knowing" by "being" and not vice versa.

But there is still an untried third alternative: We can attempt to develop a materialist view of history based on sex itself. . . .

Let us try to develop an analysis in which biology itself—procreation—is at the origin of the dualism. The immediate assumption of the layman that the unequal division of the sexes is "natural" may be well-founded. We need not immediately look beyond this. Unlike economic class, sex class sprang directly from a biological reality: men and women were created different, and not equally privileged. Although, as De Beauvoir points out, this

difference of itself did not necessitate the development of a class system—the domination of one group by another—the reproductive *functions* of these differences did. The biological family is an inherently unequal power distribution. The need for power leading to the development of classes arises from the psychosexual formation of each individual according to this basic imbalance, rather than, as Freud, Norman O. Brown, and others have, once again overshooting their mark, postulated, some irreducible conflict of Life against Death, Eros vs. Thanatos.

The *biological family*—the basic reproductive unit of male/female/infant, in whatever form of social organization—is characterized by these fundamental—if not immutable—facts:

1. That women throughout history before the advent of birth control were at the continual mercy of their biology—menstruation, menopause, and "female ills," constant painful childbirth, wetnursing and care of infants, all of which made them dependent on males (whether brother, father, husband, lover, or clan, government, community-at-large) for physical survival.

2. That human infants take an even longer time to grow up than animals, and thus are helpless and, for some short period at least, dependent on adults for physical survival.

3. That a basic mother/child interdependency has existed in some form in every society, past or present, and thus has shaped the psychology of every mature female and every infant.

4. That the natural reproductive difference between the sexes led directly to the first division of labor at the origins of class, as well as furnishing the paradigm of caste (discrimination based on biological characteristics).

These biological contingencies of the human family cannot be covered over with anthropological sophistries. Anyone observing animals mating, reproducing, and caring for their young will have a hard time accepting the "cultural relativity" line. For no matter how many tribes in Oceania you can find where the connection of the father to fertility is not known, no matter how many matrilineages, no matter how many cases of sex-role reversal, male housewifery, or even empathic labor pains, these facts prove only one thing: the amazing *flexibility* of human nature. But human nature is adaptable *to* something, it is, yes, determined by its environmental conditions. And the biological family that we have described has existed everywhere throughout time. Even in matriarchies where woman's fertility is worshipped, and the father's role is unknown or unimportant, if perhaps not on the genetic father, there is still some dependence of the female and the infant on the male. And though it is true that the nuclear family is only a recent development, one which, as I shall attempt to show, only intensifies the psychological penalties of the biological family, though it is true that throughout history there have been many variations on this biological family, the contingencies I have described existed in all of them, causing specific psychosexual distortions in the human personality.

But to grant that the sexual imbalance of power is biologically based is not to lose our case. We are no longer just animals. And the Kingdom of Nature does not reign absolute. . . .

The "natural" is not necessarily a "human" value. Humanity has begun to outgrow nature: we can no longer justify the maintenance of a discriminatory sex class system on grounds of its origins in Nature. Indeed, for pragmatic reasons alone it is beginning to look as if we *must* get rid of it.

The problem becomes political, demanding more than a comprehensive historical analysis, when one realizes that, though man is increasingly capable of freeing himself from the biological conditions that created his tyranny over women and children, he has little reason to want to give this tyranny up. As Engels said, in the context of economic revolution:

> It is the law of division of labor that lies at the basis of the division into classes [Note that this division itself grew out of a fundamental biological division]. But this does not prevent the ruling class, once having the upper hand, from consolidating its power at the expense of the

working class, from turning its social leadership into an intensified exploitation of the masses.

Though the sex class system may have originated in fundamental biological conditions, this does not guarantee once the biological basis of their oppression has been swept away that women and children will be freed. On the contrary, the new technology, especially fertility control, may be used against them to reinforce the entrenched system of exploitation.

So that just as to assure elimination of economic classes requires the revolt of the underclass (the proletariat) and, in a temporary dictatorship, their seizure of the means of *production*, so to assure the elimination of sexual classes requires the revolt of the underclass (women) and the seizure of control of *reproduction*: not only the full restoration to women of ownership of their own bodies, but also their (temporary) seizure of control of human fertility—the new population biology as well as all the social institutions of childbearing and childrearing. And just as the end goal of socialist revolution was not only the elimination of the economic class *privilege* but of the economic class *distinction* itself, so the end goal of feminist revolution must be, unlike that of the first feminist movement, not just the elimination of male *privilege* but of the sex *distinction* itself: genital differences between human beings would no longer matter culturally. (A reversion to an unobstructed *pansexuality*—Freud's "polymorphous perversity" —would probably supersede hetero/homo/bisexuality.) The reproduction of the species by one sex for the benefit of both would be replaced by (at least the option of) artificial reproduction: children would be born to both sexes equally, or independently of either, however one chooses to look at it; the dependence of the child on the mother (and vice versa) would give way to a greatly shortened dependence on a small group of others in general, and any remaining inferiority to adults in physical strength would be compensated for culturally. The division of labor would be ended by the elimination of labor altogether (cybernation). The tyranny of the biological family would be broken. . . .

Structural Imperatives

Before we talk about revolutionary alternatives, let's summarize—to determine the specifics that must be carefully excluded from any new structures. Then we can go on to "utopian speculation" directed by at least negative guidelines.

We have seen how women, biologically distinguished from men, are culturally distinguished from "human." Nature produced the fundamental inequality—half the human race must bear and rear the children of all of them—which was later consolidated, institutionalized, in the interests of men. Reproduction of the species cost women dearly, not only emotionally, psychologically, culturally but even in strictly material (physical) terms: before recent methods of contraception, continuous childbirth led to constant "female trouble," early aging, and death. Women were the slave class that maintained the species in order to free the other half for the business of the world—admittedly often its drudge aspects, but certainly all its creative aspects as well.

This natural division of labor was continued only at great cultural sacrifice: men and women developed only half of themselves, at the expense of the other half. The division of the psyche into male and female to better reinforce the reproductive division was tragic: the hypertrophy in men of rationalism, aggressive drive, the atrophy of their emotional sensitivity was a physical (war) as well as a cultural disaster. The emotionalism and passivity of women increased their suffering (we cannot speak of them in a symmetrical way, since they were victimized as a class by the division). Sexually men and women were channeled into a highly ordered—time, place, procedure, even dialogue—heterosexuality restricted to the genitals, rather than diffused over the entire physical being.

I submit, then, that the first demand for any alternative system must be:

1 *The freeing of women from the tyranny of their reproductive biology by every means available, and the diffusion of the childbearing and childrearing*

role to the society as a whole, men as well as women. There are many degrees of this. Already we have a (hard-won) acceptance of "family planning," if not contraception for its own sake. Proposals are imminent for day-care centers, perhaps even twenty-four-hour child-care centers staffed by men as well as women. But this, in my opinion, is timid if not entirely worthless as a transition. We're talking about *radical* change. And though indeed it cannot come all at once, radical goals must be kept in sight at all times. Day-care centers buy women off. They ease the immediate pressure without asking why that pressure is on *women.*

At the other extreme there are the more distant solutions based on the potentials of modern embryology, that is, artificial reproduction, possibilities still so frightening that they are seldom discussed seriously. We have seen that the fear is to some extent justified: in the hands of our current society and under the direction of current scientists (few of whom are female or even feminist), any attempted use of technology to "free" anybody is suspect. But we are speculating about post-revolutionary systems, and for the purposes of our discussion we shall assume flexibility and good intentions in those working out the change.

To thus free women from their biology would be to threaten the *social* unit that is organized around biological reproduction and the subjection of women to their biological destiny, the family. Our second demand will come also as a basic contradiction to the family, this time the family as an *economic* unit:

2 *The full self-determination, including economic independence, of both women and children.* To achieve this goal would require fundamental changes in our social and economic structure. This is why we must talk about a feminist socialism: in the immediate future, under capitalism, there could be at best a token integration of women into the labor force. For women have been found exceedingly useful and cheap as a transient, often highly skilled labor supply,[1] not to mention the economic value of their traditional function, the reproduction and rearing of the next generation of children, a job for which they are now patronized (literally and thus figuratively) rather than paid. But whether or not officially recognized, these are essential economic functions. Women, in this present capacity, are the very foundation of the economic superstructure, vital to its existence.[2] The paeans to self-sacrificing motherhood have a basis in reality: Mom *is* vital to the American way of life, considerably more than apple pie. She is an institution without which the system really *would* fall apart. In official capitalist terms, the bill for her economic services[3] might run as high as one-fifth of the gross national product. But payment is not the answer. To pay her, as is often discussed seriously in Sweden, is a reform that does not challenge the basic division of labor and thus could never eradicate the disastrous psychological and cultural consequences of that division of labor.

As for the economic independence of children, that is really a pipe dream, realized as yet nowhere in the world. And, in the case of children too, we are talking about more than a fair integration into the labor force; we are talking about the abolition of the labor force itself under a cybernetic socialism, the radical restructuring of the economy to make "work," i.e., wage labor, no longer necessary. In our post-revolutionary society adults as well as children would be provided for—irrespective of their social contributions—in the first equal distribution of wealth in history.

We have now attacked the family on a double front, challenging that around which it is organized: reproduction of the species by females and its outgrowth, the physical dependence of women and children. To eliminate these would be enough to destroy the family, which breeds the power psychology. However, we will break it down still further.

3 *The total integration of women and children into all aspects of the larger society.* All institutions that segregate the sexes, or bar children from adult society, e.g., the elementary school, must be destroyed. *Down with school!*

These three demands predicate a feminist revolution based on advanced technology. And if the male/female and the adult/child cultural distinctions are destroyed, we will no longer need the sexual repression that maintains these unequal classes, allowing for the first time a "natural" sexual freedom. Thus we arrive at:

4 *The freedom of all women and children to do whatever they wish to do sexually.* There will no longer be any reason *not* to. (Past reasons: Full sexuality threatened the continuous reproduction necessary for human survival, and thus, through religion and other cultural institutions, sexuality had to be restricted to reproductive purposes, all nonreproductive sex pleasure considered deviation or worse; The sexual freedom of women would call into question the fatherhood of the child, thus threatening patrimony; Child sexuality had to be repressed because it was a threat to the precarious internal balance of the family. These sexual repressions increased proportionately to the degree of cultural exaggeration of the biological family.) In our new society, humanity could finally revert to its natural polymorphous sexuality—all forms of sexuality would be allowed and indulged. The fully sexuate mind, realized in the past in only a few individuals (survivors), would become universal. Artificial cultural achievement would no longer be the only avenue to sexuate self-realization: one could now realize oneself fully, simply in the process of being and acting. . . .

Notes

---

1. Most bosses would fail badly had they to take over their secretaries' job, or do without them. I know several secretaries who sign without a thought their bosses' names to their own (often brilliant) solutions. The skills of college women especially would cost a fortune reckoned in material terms of male labor.

2. Margaret Benston ("The Political Economy of Women's Liberation," *Monthly Review,* September 1969), in attempting to show that women's oppression is indeed economic—though previous economic analysis has been incorrect—distinguishes between the male superstructure economy based on *commodity* production (capitalist ownership of the means of production, and wage labor), and the pre-industrial reduplicative economy of the family, production for immediate *use.* Because the latter is not part of the *official*

contemporary economy, its function at the basis of that economy is often overlooked. Talk of drafting women into the superstructure commodity economy fails to deal with the tremendous amount of necessary production of the traditional kind now performed by women without pay: Who will do it?

3. The Chase Manhattan Bank estimates a woman's over-all domestic work week at 99.6 hours. Margaret Benston gives her minimal estimate for a *childless* married woman at 16 hours, close to half of a regular work week; a *mother* must spend at least six or seven days a week working close to 12 hours.

27. Socialist Feminism and Human Nature

Alison M. Jaggar

According to Alison M. Jaggar, socialist feminism is best understood by distinguishing it from both Marxist feminism and radical feminism. On the one hand, socialist feminism shares with Marxist feminism a commitment to a historical materialist method but then denies that women's liberation can be achieved simply by replacing capitalism with socialism. On the other hand, socialist feminism shares with radical feminism a commitment to change human biology but then views such a change as only part of what is needed to bring about women's liberation.

. . . Like radical feminism, socialist feminism is a daughter of the contemporary women's liberation movement. It is a slightly younger daughter, born in the 1970s and, like most younger daughters, impressed by its elder sister, while wanting at the same time to avoid her mistakes. The central project of socialist feminism is the development of a political theory and practice that will synthesize the best insights of radical feminism and of the Marxist tradition and that simultaneously will escape the problems associated with each. So far, socialist feminism has made only limited progress toward this goal: "It is a commitment to the *development* of an analysis and political practice, rather than to one which already exists."[1] In spite of the programmatic nature of its achievement so far, I believe that socialist feminism constitutes a distinctive approach to political life, one that offers the most convincing promise of constructing an adequate theory and practice for women's liberation.

Any attempt to define socialist feminism faces the same problems as attempts to define liberal feminism, radical feminism or Marxism. Feminist theorists and activists do not al-

ways wear labels and, even if they do, they are not always agreed on who should wear which label. Moreover, there are differences even between those wearing the same label and, in addition, dialogue between feminists of different tendencies has led to modifications in all their views. Most Marxists, for instance, now take the oppression of women much more seriously than they did prior to the emergence of the women's liberation movement, while radical feminists are paying increasing attention to class, ethnic and national differences between women. As a result, the line between socialist feminism and other feminist theories is increasingly blurred, at least on the surface. For all these reasons, it is inevitable that my account of socialist feminism, like my account of the other feminist theories, will be stipulative as well as reportive. As in defining the other theories, I shall identify socialist feminism primarily by reference to its distinctive, underlying conception of human nature.

The easiest way to provide a preliminary outline of socialist feminism is in terms of its similarities and contrasts with the other feminist theories, especially with Marxism and radical feminism to which it is most closely linked. In a very general sense, all feminists address the same problem: what constitutes the op-

Abridged from *Feminist Politics and Human Nature* (1983), pp. 123–132. Reprinted by permission of Rowman and Allanheld. Notes renumbered.

pression of women and how can that oppression be ended? Both liberal feminists and traditional Marxists believe that this question can be answered in terms of the categories and principles that were formulated originally to deal with other problems. For them, the oppression of women is just one among a number of essentially similar types of problems. Socialist feminism shares with radical feminism the belief that older established political theories are incapable, in principle, of giving an adequate account of women's oppression and that, in order to do so, it is necessary to develop new political and economic categories.

Like radical feminists, socialist feminists believe that these new categories must reconceptualize not only the so-called public sphere, but also the hitherto private sphere of human life. They must give us a way of understanding sexuality, childbearing, childrearing and personal maintenance in political and economic terms. Unlike many American radical feminists, however, socialist feminists attempt to conceptualize these activities in a deliberately historical, rather than a universal and sometimes biologistic, way. A defining feature of socialist feminism is that it attempts to interpret the historical materialist method of traditional Marxism so that it applies to the issues made visible by radical feminists. To revise Juliet Mitchell's comment, it uses a feminist version of the Marxist method to provide feminist answers to feminist questions.[2]

Ever since its inception in the mid-1960s, the women's liberation movement has been split by a chronic dispute over the relation between feminism and Marxism. This dispute has taken a number of forms, but one of the most common ways of interpreting it has been in terms of political priorities. The political analysis of traditional Marxism has led to the position that the struggle for feminism should be subordinated to the class struggle, whereas a radical feminist analysis has implied that the struggle for women's liberation should take priority over the struggle for all other forms of liberation. Socialist feminism rejects this dilemma. Not only does it refuse to compromise socialism for the sake of feminism or feminism for the sake of socialism; it argues that either of these compromises ultimately would be self-defeating. On the socialist feminist analysis,

capitalism, male dominance, racism and imperialism are intertwined so inextricably that they are inseparable; consequently the abolition of any of these systems of domination requires the end of all of them. Socialist feminists claim that a full understanding of the capitalist system requires a recognition of the way in which it is structured by male dominance and, conversely, that a full understanding of contemporary male dominance requires a recognition of the way it is organized by the capitalist division of labor. Socialist feminists believe that an adequate account of "capitalist patriarchy" requires the use of the historical materialist method developed originally by Marx and Engels. They argue, however, that the conceptual tools of Marxism are blunt and biased until they are ground into precision on the sharp edge of feminist consciousness.

One question that arises from this preliminary characterization is whether socialist feminism is or is not a variety of Marxism. Obviously, the answer to this question depends both on one's understanding of socialist feminism and on one's interpretation of Marxism. Political motivations are also involved. Some Marxists do not want the honorific title of Marxism to be granted to what they see as heresy,[3] others want to appropriate for Marxism at least those aspects of socialist feminism that they perceive as correct. Similarly, some socialist feminists want to define themselves as Marxists in opposition to other types of socialists; others see no reason to give Marx credit for a theory and a practice that reveals a social reality ignored and obscured by traditional Marxism. My own view is that socialist feminism is unmistakably Marxist, at least insofar as it utilizes the method of historical materialism. I shall argue that socialist feminism is in fact the most consistent application of Marxist method and therefore the most "orthodox" form of Marxism. . . .

The Socialist Feminist Conception of Human Nature

Socialist feminism is commited to the basic Marxist conception of human nature as created historically through the dialectical interrelation between human biology, human society and the physical environment. This interrelation is mediated by human labor or praxis. The specific form of praxis dominant within a given society creates the distinctive physical and psychological human types characteristic of that society.

Traditional political theory has given theoretical recognition only to a very limited number of human types. It is true that liberals acknowledge individual human variation; indeed, this acknowledgment is a necessary part of their arguments for a firm limitation on the extent of state power. As we have seen, Locke and Mill explain the reasons for at least some of this variation in terms of the social opportunities available to different classes, and liberal feminists explain psychological differences between the sexes in terms of sex-role socialization. Ultimately, however, liberals view the differences between people as relatively superficial, and they assume that underlying these superficial differences is a certain fixed human nature which is modified but not fundamentally created by social circumstances. Marxists, by contrast, view human nature as necessarily constituted in society: they believe that specific historical conditions create distinctive human types. Within contemporary capitalism, they give theoretical recognition to two such types, the capitalist and the proletariat. However, the traditional Marxist conception of human nature is flawed by its failure to recognize explicitly that all human beings in contemporary society belong not only to a specific class; they also have a specific sex and they are at a specific stage in the life cycle from infancy to death. In addition, although this point was not emphasized earlier because it is not a specifically feminist point, all humans in modern industrial society have specific racial, ethnic and national backgrounds. Contemporary society thus consists of groups of individuals, defined simultaneously by age, sex, class, nationality and by racial and ethnic origin, and these groups differ markedly from each other, both physically and psychologically. Liberal political theory has tended to ignore or minimize all these differences. Marxist political theory has tended to recognize only differences of class.

The political theory of radical feminism has tended to recognize only differences of age and sex, to understand these in universal terms, and often to view them as determined biologically. By contrast, socialist feminism recognizes all these differences as constituent parts of contemporary human nature and seeks a way of understanding them that is not only materialist but also historical. In particular, it has insisted on the need for a more adequate theoretical understanding of the differences between women and men. Given that its methodological commitment is basically Marxist, it seeks this understanding through an examination of what it calls the sexual division of labor.[4] In other words, it focuses on the different types of praxis undertaken by women and men in order to develop a fully historical materialist account of the social construction of sex and gender.

The differences between women and men are both physical and psychological. Socialist feminists have begun to look at both these aspects of human nature. Some theorists, for instance, have studied variations in menstruation and menopause and have discovered that often these variations are socially determined.[5] Marian Lowe has begun to investigate the ways in which society influences women's sporting achievements, as well as their menstrual patterns.[6] Iris Young has explored some of the socially determined ways in which men and women move differently from each other and experience space, objects, and even their own bodies differently.[7] She has observed that women in sexist society are "physically handicapped." Interesting work has also been done on women's body language.[8] In undertaking these sorts of investigations, socialist feminists focus on the dialectical relationship between sex and society as it emerges through activity organized by gender norms. The methodological approach of socialist feminists makes it obvious that they have abandoned an ahistorical conception of human biology. Instead, they view human biology as being, in part, socially constructed. Biology is "gendered" as well as sexed.

In spite of their interest in the physical differences between women and men, contemporary feminists have been far more concerned with psychological differences, and socialist feminist theory has reflected that priority. Its main focus has been on the social construction not of masculine and feminine physical types, but rather of masculine and feminine character types. Among the many socialist feminist theorists who have worked on this project are Juliet Mitchell, Jane Flax, Gayle Rubin, Nancy Chodorow and, perhaps, Dorothy Dinnerstein.[9] All these theorists have been impressed by how early in life masculine and feminine character structures are established and by the relative rigidity of these structures, once established. To explain the mechanism by which psychological masculinity and femininity are imposed on infants and young children, all utilize some version of psychoanalysis. This is because they view psychoanalytic theory as providing the most plausible and systematic account of how the individual psyche is structured by gender. But unlike Freud, the father of psychoanalysis, socialist feminist theorists do not view psychological masculinity and femininity as the child's inevitable response to a fixed and universal biological endowment. Instead, they view the acquisition of gendered character types as the result of specific social practices, particularly procreative practices, that are not determined by biology and that in principle, therefore, are alterable. They want to de-biologize Freud and to reinterpret him in historical materialist terms. As Gayle Rubin puts it: "Psychoanalysis provides a description of the mechanisms by which the sexes are divided and deformed, of how bisexual, androgynous infants are transformed into boys and girls." . . .[10]

The distinctive aspect of the socialist feminist approach to human psychology is the way in which it synthesizes insights drawn from a variety of sources. Socialist feminism claims all of the following: that our "inner" lives, as well as our bodies and behavior, are structured by gender; that this gender-structuring is not innate but is socially imposed; that the specific characteristics that are imposed are related systematically to the historically prevailing system of organizing social production; that the gender-structuring of our "inner" lives occurs when we are very young and is reinforced throughout our lives in a variety of different spheres; and that these relatively rigid masculine and feminine character structures are a very important element in maintaining male dominance. Given this conception of human psychology, one of the major theoretical tasks that socialist feminism sets itself is to provide a historical materialist account of the relationship between our "inner" lives and our social praxis. It seeks to connect masculine and feminine psychology with the sexual division of labor. . . .

It is generally accepted, by non-feminists and feminists alike, that the most obvious manifestation of the sexual division of labor, in contemporary society if not in all societies, is marked by the division between the so-called public and private spheres of human life. The line between these two spheres has varied historically: in the political theory of ancient Greece, for instance, "the economy" fell within the private sphere, whereas in contemporary political theory, both liberal and Marxist, "the economy" is considered—in different ways—to be part of the public realm. Wherever the distinction has existed, the private realm has always included sexuality and procreation, has always been viewed as more "natural" and therefore less "human" than the public realm, and has always been viewed as the realm of women.[11] Although women have always done many kinds of work, they have been defined primarily by their sexual and procreative labor; throughout history, women have been defined as "sex objects" and as mothers.

Partly because of this definition of women's work and partly because of their conviction that an individual's gender identity is established very early in life, much socialist feminist theory has focused on the area of sexuality and procreation. Yet the theory has been committed to conceptualizing this area in terms that are historical, rather than biological, and specific, rather than universal. Socialist feminism has accepted the radical feminist insight that sexual activity, childbearing, and childrearing are social practices that embody power relations and are therefore appropriate subjects for political analysis. Because of its rejection of biological determinism, however, socialist feminism denies the radical feminist assumption that these practices are fundamentally invariant. On the contrary, socialist feminists have stressed historical variation both in the practices and in the categories by which they are understood. Zillah Eisenstein writes:

None of the processes in which a woman engages can be understood separate from the relations of the society which she embodies and which are reflected in the ideology of society. For instance, the act of giving birth to a child is only termed an act of motherhood if it reflects the relations of marriage and the family. Otherwise the very same act can be termed adultery and the child is "illegitimate" or a "bastard." The term "mother" may have a significantly different meaning when different relations are involved—as in "unwed mother." It depends on what relations are embodied in the act.[12]

In the same spirit, Ann Foreman writes that "fatherhood is a social invention . . . located in a series of functions rather than in biology."[13] Rayna Rapp writes that even "being a child is a highly variable social relation."[14] Using the same historical approach, Ann Ferguson has argued that the emergence of lesbianism, as a distinct sexual identity, is a recent rather than a universal phenomenon insofar as it presupposes an urban society with the possibility of economic independence for women.[15] More generally, "It was only with the development of capitalist societies that 'sexuality' and 'the economy' became separable from other spheres of society and could be counter-posed to one another as realities of different sorts."[16] Other authors have claimed that there is no transhistorical definition of marriage in terms of which the marital institutions of different cultures can be compared usefully.[17] Even within a single society, divisions of class mean that the working-class family unit is defined very differently from the upper-class family unit, and that it performs very different social functions.[18] One author denies that the family is a "bounded universe" and suggests that "we should extend to the study of 'family' [a] thoroughgoing agnosticism."[19] In general, socialist feminist theory has viewed human nature as constructed in part through the historically specific ways in which people have organized their sexual, childbearing and child-

rearing activities. The organization of these activities both affects and is affected by class and ethnic differences, but it is seen as particularly important in creating the masculine and feminine physiques and character structures that are considered appropriate in a given society.

The beginnings of this conception of human nature are already evident, to some extent, in the work of Marx and Engels. Engels' famous definition of the materialist conception of history in his introduction to *The Origin of the Family, Private Property and the State* states clearly:

The social organization under which the people of a particular historical epoch and a particular country live is determined by both kinds of production: by the state of development of labor on the one hand and of the family on the other.[20]

Moreover, Marx and Engels warn explicitly against conceptualizing procreation in an ahistorical way. In *The German Ideology,* they mock an ahistorical approach to "the concept of the family,"[21] and Engels' own work in *Origin* is designed precisely to demonstrate historical change in the social rules governing the eligibility of an individual's sexual partners. However, Marx and Engels view changes in the social organization of procreation as ultimately determined themselves by changes in the so-called mode of production, at least in postprimitive societies. Consequently, they see procreation as being now only of secondary importance in shaping human nature and society. One reason for this view may be that Marx and Engels still retain certain assumptions about the "natural," presumably biological, determination of much procreative activity. Thus, they do not give a symmetrical treatment to the human needs for food, shelter, and clothing, on the one hand, and to sexual, childbearing and childrearing needs, on the other. They view the former as changing historically, giving rise to new possibilities of social organization, but they regard human procreative needs as more "natural" and less open to historical transformation. Socialist feminists, by contrast, emphasize the social determination of sexual, childbearing and childrearing needs. They understand that these needs have developed historically in dialectical relation with changing procreative practices. Consequently, they are prepared to subject sexual and procreative practices to sustained political analysis and to reflect systematically on how changes in these practices could transform human nature.

Although socialist feminist theory stresses the importance of the so-called private sphere of procreation in constructing the historically appropriate types of masculinity and femininity, it does not ignore the so-called public sphere. It recognizes that women have always worked outside procreation, providing goods and services not only for their families but for the larger society as well. Socialist feminism claims that the conception of women as primarily sexual beings and/or as mothers is an ideological mystification that obscures the facts, for instance, that more than half the world's farmers are women,[22] and that, in the United States, women now make up almost half the paid labor force. Indeed, the Department of Labor projects that women will constitute 51.4 percent of the U.S. paid labor force by 1990.[23]

For socialist feminism, women, just as much as men, are beings whose labor transforms the non-human world. Socialist feminists view the slogan "A women's place is everywhere" as more than a call for change: for them, it is already a partial description of existing reality.

Only a partial description, however. Although socialist feminism recognizes the extent of women's productive work, it recognizes also that this work has rarely, if ever, been the same as men's. Even in contemporary market society, socialist feminism recognizes that the paid labor force is almost completely segregated by sex; at every level, there are "women's specialities." Within the contemporary labor force, moreover, women's work is invariably less prestigious, lower paid, and defined as being less skilled than men's, even when it involves such socially valuable and complex skills as dealing with children or sick people. Socialist feminism sees, therefore, that the sexual division of labor is not just a division *between* procreation and "production": it is also a division *within* procreation and *within* "production." Consequently, socialist feminism does

not view contemporary masculinity and femininity as constructed entirely through the social organization of procreation; these constructs are elaborated and reinforced in nonprocreative labor as well. . . .

We can now summarize the socialist feminist view of human nature in general and of women's nature in particular. Unlike liberalism and some aspects of traditional Marxism, socialist feminism does not view humans as "abstract, genderless" (and ageless and colorless) individuals,[24] with women essentially indistinguishable from men. Neither does it view women as irreducibly different from men, the same yesterday, today and forever. Instead, it views women as constituted essentially by the social relations they inhabit. "(T)he social relations of society define the particular activity a woman engages in at a given moment. Outside these relations, 'woman' becomes an abstraction."[25]

Gayle Rubin paraphrases Marx thus:

What is a domesticated woman? A female of the species. The one explanation is as good as the other. A woman is a woman. She only becomes a domestic, a wife, a chattel, a playboy bunny, a prostitute, or a human dictaphone in certain relations. Torn from these relationships, she is no more the helpmate of a man than gold in itself is money.[26]

To change these relationships is to change women's and so human nature.

Since history is never static, continuing changes in human nature are inevitable. As Marx himself remarked, "All history is nothing but a continuous transformation of human nature."[27] Socialist feminists want women to participate fully in taking conscious social control of these changes. They deny that there is anything especially natural about women's relationships with each other, with children or with men. Instead, they seek to reconstitute those relationships in such a way as to liberate the full power of women's (and human) creative potential.

No contemporary feminist would deny this goal, stated in the abstract. Just as at one time everyone was against sin, so now everyone is in favor of liberating human potential. Just as people used to disagree over how to identify sin, however, so now there is disagreement over what are human potentialities, which ones should be developed and how this development should be undertaken. Every conception of human nature implies an answer to these questions, and socialist feminism has its own distinctive answer. Unlike liberalism, the socialist feminist ideal of human fulfilment is not individual autonomy; for reasons that will be explained more fully later, socialist feminism views the ideal of autonomy as characteristically masculine as well as characteristically capitalist. The socialist feminist conception of human fulfilment is closer to the Marxist ideal of the full development of human potentialities through free productive labor, but socialist feminism construes productive labor more broadly than does traditional Marxism. Consequently, the socialist feminist ideal of human well-being and fulfilment includes the full development of human potentialities for free sexual expression, for freely bearing children and for freely rearing them.

To many Marxists, the theory of alienation expresses Marx's conception of human nature in capitalist society. As the theory is traditionally interpreted, alienation characterizes primarily workers' relation to wage labor; however, Marx saw that the way workers experience wage labor also affects the way they experience the rest of their lives. Because their wage labor is coerced, their activity outside wage labor seems free by contrast.

We arrive at the result that man (the worker) feels himself to be freely active only in his animal functions—eating, drinking and procreating, or at most also in his dwelling and in personal adornment—while in his human functions he is reduced to an animal. The animal becomes human and the human becomes animal.[28]

To socialist feminists, this conception of alienation is clearly male-biased. Men may feel free when eating, drinking, and procreating, but women do not. As the popular saying has it, "A woman's work is never done." An Englishman's home may be his castle, but it is his wife's prison. Women are compelled to do housework, to bear and raise children and to define themselves sexually in terms of men's wishes. The pressures on women to do this work are almost overwhelming:

When I say that women are subject to a form of compulsive labor, I mean that they may only resist with great difficulty, and that the majority succumb. The same may be said of non-owners when it comes to wage work. In both cases, it is not compulsive in the sense that one is driven to it with whips and chains (though that happens, too!), but in the sense that no real alternative is generally available to women, and that everything in society conspires to ensure that women do this work. While a nonowner may attempt small independent production, or simply refuse to work and live off begging or state welfare, that is not proof of his freedom. The same is true of women. While a woman may with great difficulty resist doing reproductive work, that is no proof that she is "free" not to do it.[29]

One way in which socialist feminists are attempting to conceptualize contemporary women's lack of freedom is by extending the traditional Marxist theory of alienation. . . . Iris Young's reflections on "the struggle for our bodies," cited earlier in this chapter, suggest that women suffer a special form of alienation from their bodies. Similarly, Sandra Bartky claims that women are alienated in cultural production, as mothers and sexual beings. She believes that feminine narcissism is the paradigm of a specifically feminine form of sexual alienation.[30] Ann Foreman argues that femininity as such is an alienated condition: "While alienation reduces the man to an instrument of labour within industry, it reduces the woman to an instrument for his sexual pleasure within the family."[31] One may define the goal of socialist feminism as being to overcome all forms of alienation but especially those that are specific to women.

If it is difficult to envision what nonalienated industry would be like, it seems almost impossible to foresee the form of nonalienated sexuality or parenthood. Because of the ideological dogma that these are determined biologically, it is even harder to envision alternatives to prevailing sexual and procreative practices than it is to the capitalist mode of production. Alternative ways of organizing procreation tend to be viewed as science fiction; indeed, they are considered more often in fiction than in political theory. A number of socialist feminists are experimenting with alternatives in procreation, but the extent and validity of those experiments is limited, of course, by their context in a society that is emphatically neither socialist nor feminist.

The one solid basis of agreement among socialist feminists is that to overcome women's alienation, the sexual division of labor must be eliminated in every area of life. Just as sexual segregation in nonprocreative work must be eliminated, so men must participate fully in childrearing and, so far as possible, in childbearing.[32] Normative heterosexuality must be replaced by a situation in which the sex of one's lovers is a matter of social indifference, so that the dualist categories of heterosexual, homosexual and bisexual may be abandoned. Some authors describe the ideal as androgyny,[33] but even this term is implicitly dualistic. If it is retained for the present, we must remember that the ultimate transformation of human nature at which socialist feminists aim goes beyond the liberal conception of psychological androgyny to a possible transformation of "physical" human capacities, some of which, until now, have been seen as biologically limited to one sex. This transformation might even include the capacities for insemination, for lactation and for gestation so that, for instance, one woman could inseminate another, so that men and nonparturitive women could lactate and so that fertilized ova could be transplanted into women's or even into men's bodies. These developments may seem farfetched, but in fact they are already on the technological horizon,[34] however, what is needed much more immediately than technological development is a substantial reduction in the social domination of women by men. Only such a reduction can ensure that these or alternative technological possibilities are used to increase women's control over their bodies and thus over their lives, rather than being used as an additional means for women's subjugation.

Gayle Rubin writes: "We are not only oppressed *as* women, we are oppressed by having to *be* women or men as the case may be."[35] The goal of socialist feminism is to abolish the social relations that constitute humans not only as workers and capitalists but also as women and men. Whereas one version of radical feminism takes the human ideal to be a woman, the ideal of socialist feminism is that women (and men) will disappear as socially constituted categories.

Notes

1. Margaret Page, "Socialist Feminism—a political alternative?", *m/f* 2 (1978):41.

2. Juliet Mitchell, a pioneering author whose work broke the ground for socialist feminism but whose basic orientation is ultimately Marxist, writes, "We should ask the feminist questions, but try to come up with Marxist answers." *Women's Estate* (New York: Pantheon Books, 1971), p. 99.

3. Pun intended. There is in fact an exciting journal named *Heresies: A Feminist Publication on Art & Politics.*

4. A clear statement of this methodological approach is given by Iris Young, "Socialist Feminism and the Limits of Dual Systems Theory," *Socialist Review* 50–51, pp. 169–88. Cf. also Iris Young "Beyond the Unhappy Marriage: A Critique of the Dual Systems Theory," in Lydia Sargent, ed., *Women and Revolution* (Boston: South End Press, 1981), pp. 43–69. Young in fact uses the term "gender division of labor", but I prefer to follow Nancy Hartsock in using the more familiar "sexual division of labor." Hartsock justifies her use of the latter term in part because of her belief that the division of labor between women and men is not yet entirely a social affair (women and not men still bear children), in part because she wishes to keep a firm hold of "the bodily aspect of existence." Nancy Hartsock, "The Feminist Standpoint: Developing the Ground for a Specifically Feminist Historical Materialism," in Sandra Harding and Merrill Hintikka, eds., *Discovering Reality: Feminist Perspectives on Epistemology, Metaphysics, Methodology*

and the Philosophy of Science (Dordrecht: Reidel Publishing Co.), 1983.

5. Janice Delaney, Mary Jane Lupton, and Emily Toth, *The Curse: A Cultural History of Menstruation* (New York: E. P. Dutton, 1976).

6. Marian Lowe, "The Biology of Exploitation and the Exploitation of Biology," paper read to the National Women's Studies Association Second National Conference, Indiana University, Bloomington, May 16–20, 1980.

7. Iris Marion Young, "Is There a Woman's World?—Some Reflections on the Struggle for Our Bodies," proceedings of *The Second Sex—Thirty Years Later: A Commemorative Conference on Feminist Theory* (New York: The New York Institute for the Humanities, 1979). See also Young's "Throwing Like a Girl: A Phenomenology of Feminine Body Comportment, Motility and Sexuality," *Human Studies* 3 (1980):137–56.

8. For example, see Nancy M. Henley, *Body Politics: Sex, Power and Non-Verbal Communication* (Englewood Cliffs, N.J.: Prentice-Hall, 1977).

9. Juliet Mitchell, *Psychoanalysis and Feminism* (New York: Vintage Books, 1975); Gayle Rubin, "The Traffic in Women: Notes on the 'Political Economy' of Sex," in Rayna R. Reiter, ed., *Toward an Anthropology of Women* (New York: Monthly Review Press, 1975), pp. 157–210; Nancy Chodorow, *Mothering: Psychoanalysis and the Sociology of Gender* (Berkeley and Los Angeles: University of California Press, 1978); Dorothy Dinnerstein, *The Mermaid and the Minotaur: Sexual Arrangements and Human Malaise* (New York: Harper & Row, 1977). Dinnerstein's work is idiosyncratic and consequently difficult to categorize. Many of her assumptions, however, are identical with the assumptions of the other theorists mentioned here.

10. Rubin, "Traffic," p. 185.

11. The significance of this distinction for feminist theory will be discussed later in this chapter and also elsewhere in the book. Other theorists who have examined the distinction include Jean Bethke Elshtain, "Moral Woman and Immoral Man: A Consideration of the Public-Private Split and its Political Ramifications," *Politics and Society,* 1974; Jean Bethke Elshtain, *Public Man, Private Woman: Women in Social and Political Thought* (Princeton: Princeton University Press, 1981); and Linda Nicholson, *Feminism as Political Philosophy* (in progress). Cf. also M. Z. Rosaldo, "The

Use and Abuse of Anthropology: Reflections on Feminism and Cross-Cultural Understanding," *Signs: Journal of Women in Culture & Society* 5, no. 3 (1980): esp. pp. 396–401.

12. Zillah Eisenstein, "Some Notes on the Relations of Capitalist Patriarchy," in Zillah Eisenstein, ed., *Capitalist Patriarchy and the Case for Socialist Feminism* (New York: Monthly Review Press, 1979), p. 47.

13. Ann Foreman, *Femininity as Alienation: Women and the Family in Marxism and Psychoanalysis* (London: Pluto Press, 1977), pp. 20 and 21.

14. Rayna Rapp, "Examining Family History," *Feminist Studies* 5, no 1 (Spring 1979):177.

15. Ann Ferguson, "Patriarchy, Sexual Identity and the Sexual Revolution," paper read at University of Cincinnati's Seventeenth Annual Philosophy Colloquium on "Philosophical Issues in Feminist Theory," November 13–16, 1980. This paper was later published in *Signs: Journal of Women in Culture and Society* 7, no. 1 (1981): 158–72.

16. Robert A. Padgug, "Sexual Matters: On Conceptualising Sexuality in History," *Radical History Review* 20 (Spring/Summer 1979):16.

17. Kathleen Gough, "The Nayars and the Definition of Marriage," in P. B. Hammond, ed., *Cultural and Social Anthropology* (London, New York: Collier-Macmillan, 1964).

18. Rayna Rapp, "Family & Class in Contemporary America: Notes Toward an Understanding of Ideology," *Science and Society* 52, no. 3 (Fall 1978).

19. Ellen Ross, "Rethinking 'the Family'," *Radical History Review* 20 (Spring/Summer 1979):83.

20. Frederick Engels, *The Origin of the Family, Private Property and the State* (New York: International Publishers, 1972), pp. 71–72.

21. Karl Marx and Frederick Engels, *The German Ideology* (New York: International Publishers, 1970), p. 49.

22. *Isis Bulletin* 11, Geneva, Switzerland.

23. U.S. Bureau of the Census, *A Statistical Portrait of Women in the U.S.* (Washington, D.C.: Department of Commerce, Bureau of the Census, 1977); Current Population Reports, Special Studies Series, P-23, no. 58, pp. 28, 30, 31.

24. Rubin, "Traffic," p. 171.

25. Eisenstein, "Capitalist Patriarchy," p. 47.

26. Rubin, "Traffic," p. 158.

27. Karl Marx, *The Poverty of Philosophy* (New York: International Publishers, 1963), p. 147.

28. Karl Marx, *Early Writings,* translated and edited by T. B. Bottomore (New York: McGraw-Hill, 1963), p. 125.

29. Lynda Lange, "Reproduction in Democratic Theory," in W. Shea and J. King-Farlow, eds., *Contemporary Issues in Political Philosophy,* vol. 2 (New York: Science History Publications, 1976), pp. 140–41.

30. Sandra L. Bartky, "Narcissism, Femininity and Alienation," *Social Theory and Practice* 8, no. 2 (Summer 1982):127–43.

31. Ann Foreman, *Femininity as Alienation,* p. 151.

32. Some feminists are beginning to speculate on whether advanced technology will ultimately make it possible for men to be equally involved with women in bearing children. Two authors who consider this question are Shulamith Firestone, *The Dialectic of Sex: The Case for Feminist Revolution* (New York: W. W. Morrow, 1970), and Marge Piercy, *Woman on the Edge of Time* (New York: Fawcett Books, 1977).

33. Ann Ferguson, "Androgyny as an Ideal for Human Development," in Mary Vetterling-Braggin, Frederick A. Elliston, and Jane English, eds., *Feminism and Philosophy* (Totowa, N.J.: Littlefield, Adams, 1977).

34. Barbara Katz Rothman, "How Science Is Redefining Parenthood," *Ms,* August 1982, pp. 154–58.

35. Rubin, "Traffic," p. 204.

28. National Organization for Women (NOW) Bill of Rights

  I **Equal Rights Constitutional Amendment**
 II **Enforce Law Banning Sex Discrimination in Employment**
III **Maternity Leave Rights in Employment and in Social Security Benefits**
 IV **Tax Deduction for Home and Child Care Expenses for Working Parents**
  V **Child Care Centers**
 VI **Equal and Unsegregated Education**
VII **Equal Job Training Opportunities and Allowances for Women in Poverty**
VIII **The Right of Women to Control Their Reproductive Lives**

We Demand:

I That the United States Congress immediately pass the Equal Rights Amendment to the Constitution to provide that "Equality of rights under the law shall not be denied or abridged by the United States or by any State on account of sex," and that such then be immediately ratified by the several States.

II That equal employment opportunity be guaranteed to all women, as well as men, by insisting that the Equal Employment Opportunity Commission enforces the prohibitions against sex discrimination in employment under Title VII of the Civil Rights Act of 1964 with the same vigor as it enforces the prohibitions against racial discrimination.

III That women be protected by law to ensure their rights to return to their jobs within a reasonable time after childbirth without loss of seniority or other accrued benefits, and be paid maternity leave as a form of social security and/or employee benefit.

IV Immediate revision of tax laws to permit the deduction of home and child care expenses for working parents.

V That child care facilities be established by law on the same basis as parks, libraries, and public schools, adequate to the needs of children from the pre-school years through adolescence, as a community resource to be used by all citizens from all income levels.

VI That the right of women to be educated to their full potential equally with men be secured by Federal and State Legislation, eliminating all discrimination and segregation by sex, written and unwritten, at all levels of education, including colleges, graduate and professional schools, loans and fellowships, and Federal and State training programs such as the Job Corps.

VII The right of women in poverty to secure job training, housing, and family allowances on equal terms with men, but without prejudice to a parent's right to remain at home to care for his or her children; revision of

welfare legislation and poverty programs which deny women dignity, privacy and self-respect.

VIII The right of women to control their own reproductive lives by removing from penal codes laws limiting access to contraceptive information and devices and laws governing abortion.

29. *California Federal Savings and Loan v. Department of Fair Employment and Housing*

Supreme Court of the United States

The issue before the Supreme Court was whether Title VII of the Civil Rights Act of 1964 as amended by the Pregnancy Discrimination Act of 1978 (PDA) nullified a California law requiring employers to provide leave and reinstatement to employees disabled by pregnancy. The majority of the Court ruled that it did not for two reasons. First, in passing PDA, Congress was concerned with prohibiting discrimination against pregnancy; preferential treatment, as found in the California law, was not discussed. Second, even if PDA did prohibit preferential treatment of pregnancy, an employer could avoid violating PDA and the California law by giving comparable benefits to all similarly disabled employees. In dissent, Justices White, Berger, and Powell argued that even though Congress did not explicitly consider the possibility of preferential treatment of pregnancy, the language of PDA ruled it out. In addition, they argued that if such preferential treatment were ruled out, those who wrote the California law could not have intended requiring comparable benefits for all similarly disabled employees.

Justice Marshall delivered the opinion of the Court.

The question presented is whether Title VII of the Civil Rights Act of 1964, as amended by the Pregnancy Discrimination Act of 1978, pre-empts a state statute that requires employers to provide leave and reinstatement to employees disabled by pregnancy.

California's Fair Employment and Housing Act (FEHA), Cal. Gov't Code Ann. § 12900 *et seq.* . . . is a comprehensive statute that prohibits discrimination in employment and housing. In September 1978, California amended the FEHA to proscribe certain forms of employment discrimination on the basis of pregnancy. . . . Subdivision (b)(2)—the provision at issue here—is the only portion of the statute that applies to employers subject to Title VII. . . . It requires these employers to provide female employees an unpaid pregnancy disability leave of up to four months. Respondent Fair Employment and Housing Commission, the state agency authorized to interpret the FEHA, has construed § 12945(b)(2) to require California employers to reinstate an employee returning from such pregnancy leave to the job she previously held, unless it is no longer available due to business necessity. In the latter case, the employer must make a reasonable, good faith effort to place the employee in a substantially similar job. The statute does not compel employers to provide *paid* leave to pregnant employees. Accordingly, the only benefit pregnant workers actually derive from § 12945(b)(2) is a qualified right to reinstatement.

Title VII of the Civil Rights Act of 1964 . . . also prohibits various forms of employment discrimination, including discrimination on the basis of sex. However, in *General Electric Co.* v. *Gilbert,* . . . this Court ruled that discrimination on the basis of pregnancy was not sex discrimination under Title VII. In response to the *Gilbert* decision, Congress passed the Pregnancy Discrimination Act of 1978 (PDA). . . . The PDA specifies that sex discrimination includes discrimination on the basis of pregnancy.

Petitioner California Federal Savings and Loan Association (Cal Fed) is a federally chartered savings and loan association based in Los Angeles; it is an employer covered by both Title VII and § 12945(b)(2). Cal Fed has a facially neutral leave policy that permits employees who have completed three months of service to take unpaid leaves of absence for a variety of reasons, including disability and pregnancy. Although it is Cal Fed's policy to try to provide an employee taking unpaid leave with a similar position upon returning, Cal Fed expressly reserves the right to terminate an employee who has taken a leave of absence if a similar position is not available.

Lillian Garland was employed by Cal Fed as a receptionist for several years. In January 1982, she took a pregnancy disability leave. When she was able to return to work in April of that year, Garland notified Cal Fed, but was informed that her job had been filled and that there were no receptionist or similar positions available. Garland filed a complaint with respondent Department of Fair Employment and Housing, which issued an administrative accusation against Cal Fed on her behalf. Respondent charged Cal Fed with violating § 12945(b)(2) of the FEHA. Prior to the scheduled hearing before respondent Fair Housing and Employment Commission, Cal Fed, joined by petitioners . . . , brought this action in the United States District Court for the Central District of California. They sought a declaration that § 12945(b)(2) is inconsistent with and

pre-empted by Title VII and an injunction against enforcement of the section. . . .

. . . In order to decide whether the California statute requires or permits employers to violate Title VII, as amended by the PDA, or is inconsistent with the purposes of the statute, we must determine whether the PDA prohibits the States from requiring employers to provide reinstatement to pregnant workers, regardless of their policy for disabled workers generally. . . .

Petitioners argue that the language of the federal statute itself unambiguously rejects California's "special treatment" approach to pregnancy discrimination, thus rendering any resort to the legislative history unnecessary. They contend that the second clause of the PDA forbids an employer to treat pregnant employees any differently than other disabled employees. . . .

The context in which Congress considered the issue of pregnancy discrimination supports this view of the PDA. Congress had before it extensive evidence of discrimination *against* pregnancy, particularly in disability and health insurance programs like those challenged in *Gilbert* and *Nashville Gas Co.* v. *Satty.* . . . The reports, debates, and hearings make abundantly clear that Congress intended the PDA to provide relief for working women and to end discrimination against pregnant workers. In contrast to the thorough account of discrimination against pregnant workers, the legislative history is devoid of any discussion of preferential treatment of pregnancy, beyond acknowledgments of the existence of state statutes providing for such preferential treatment. . . .

In support of their argument that the PDA prohibits employment practices that favor pregnant women, petitioners and several *amici* cite statements in the legislative history to the effect that the PDA does not *require* employers to extend any benefits to pregnant women that they do not already provide to other disabled employees. For example, the House Report explained that the proposed legislation "does not require employers to treat pregnant employees in any particular manner . . . ". We do not interpret these references to support petitioners' construction of the statute. On the contrary, if Congress had intended to *prohibit* preferential treatment, it would have been the height of understatement to say only that the legislation would not *require* such conduct. It is hardly conceivable that Congress would have extensively discussed only its intent not to require preferential treatment if in fact it had intended to prohibit such treatment.

We also find it significant that Congress was aware of state laws similar to California's but apparently did not consider them inconsistent with the PDA. In the debates and reports on the bill, Congress repeatedly acknowledged the existence of state antidiscrimination laws that prohibit sex discrimination on the basis of pregnancy. Two of the States mentioned then required employers to provide reasonable leave to pregnant workers. After citing these state laws, Congress failed to evince the requisite "clear and manifest purpose" to supersede them. . . . To the contrary, both the House and Senate Reports suggest that these laws would continue to have effect under the PDA.

Title VII, as amended by the PDA, and California's pregnancy disability leave statute share a common goal. The purpose of Title VII is "to achieve equality of employment opportunities and remove barriers that have operated in the past to favor an identifiable group of . . . employees over other employees." . . . Rather than limiting existing Title VII principles and objectives, the PDA extends them to cover pregnancy. As Senator Williams, a sponsor of the Act, stated: "The entire thrust . . . behind this legislation is to guarantee women the basic right to participate fully and equally in the workforce, without denying them the fundamental right to full participation in family life." . . .

Section 12945(b)(2) also promotes equal employment opportunity. By requiring employers to reinstate women after a reasonable pregnancy disability leave, § 12945(b)(2) ensures that they will not lose their jobs on account of pregnancy disability. . . . By "taking pregnancy into account," California's pregnancy disability leave statute allows women, as well as men, to have families without losing their jobs.

We emphasize the limited nature of the benefits § 12945(b)(2) provides. The statute is narrowly drawn to cover only the period of *actual physical disability* on account of pregnancy, childbirth, or related medical conditions. Accordingly, unlike the protective labor legislation prevalent earlier in this century, § 12945(b)(2) does not reflect archaic or stereotypical notions about pregnancy and the abilities of pregnant workers. A statute based on such stereotypical assumptions would, of course, be inconsistent with Title VII's goal of equal employment opportunity. . . .

Moreover, even if we agreed with petitioners' construction of the PDA, we would nonetheless reject their argument that the California statute requires employers to violate Title VII. . . . Section 12945(b)(2) does not compel California employers to treat pregnant workers *better* than other disabled employees; it merely establishes benefits that employers must, at a minimum, provide to pregnant workers. Employers are free to give comparable benefits to other disabled employees, thereby treating "women affected by pregnancy" no better than "other persons not so affected but similar in their ability or inability to work." Indeed, at oral argument, petitioners conceded that compliance with both statutes "is theoretically possible." . . .

Thus, petitioners' facial challenge to § 12945(b)(2) fails. The statute is not preempted by Title VII, as amended by the PDA, because it is not inconsistent with the purposes of the federal statute, nor does it require the doing of an act which is unlawful under Title VII.

The judgment of the Court of Appeals is

Affirmed

. . . Justice White, with whom The Chief Justice and Justice Powell join, dissenting.

I disagree with the Court that Cal. Gov't Code Ann. § 12945(b)(2) . . . is not pre-empted by the Pregnancy Discrimination Act of 1978 (PDA). . . . Section 703(a) of Title VII . . . forbids discrimination in the terms of employment on the basis of race, color, religion, sex, or national origin. The PDA gave added meaning to discrimination on the basis of sex:

The terms 'because of sex' or 'on the basis of sex' [in section 703(a) of this title] include, but are not limited to, because of or on the basis of pregnancy, childbirth or related medical conditions; and women affected by pregnancy, childbirth, or related medical conditions shall be treated the same for all employment-related purposes, including receipt of benefits under fringe benefit programs, as other persons not so affected but similar in their ability or inability to work. . . .

The second clause quoted above could not be clearer: it mandates that pregnant employees "shall be treated the same for all employment-related purposes" as nonpregnant employees similarly situated with respect to their ability or inability to work. . . .

Contrary to the mandate of the PDA, California law requires every employer to have a disability leave policy for pregnancy even if it has none for any other disability. An employer complies with California law if it has a leave policy for pregnancy but denies it for every other disability. On its face, § 12945(b)(2) is in square conflict with the PDA and is therefore pre-empted. . . .

The majority nevertheless would save the California law on two grounds. First, it holds that the PDA does not require disability from pregnancy to be treated the same as other disabilities; instead, it forbids less favorable, but permits more favorable, benefits for pregnancy disability. . . .

. . . Given the evidence before Congress of the wide-spread discrimination against pregnant workers, it is probable that most Congresspersons did not seriously consider the possibility that someone would want to afford preferential treatment to pregnant workers. The parties and their *amici* argued vigorously

to this Court the policy implications of preferential treatment of pregnant workers. In favor of preferential treatment it was urged with conviction that preferential treatment merely enables women, like men, to have children without losing their jobs. In opposition to preferential treatment it was urged with equal conviction that preferential treatment represents a resurgence of the 19th century protective legislation which perpetuated sex-role stereotypes and which impeded women in their efforts to take their rightful place in the workplace. . . . It is not the place of this Court, however, to resolve this policy dispute. . . .

Congress' acknowledgment of state antidiscrimination laws does not support a contrary inference. The most extensive discussion of state laws governing pregnancy discrimination is found in the House Report. . . . The Report did not in any way set apart the Connecticut and Montana statutes, on which the majority relies, from the other state statutes. The House Report gave no indication that these statutes required anything more than equal treatment. . . .

The Court's second, and equally strange, ground is that even if the PDA does prohibit special benefits for pregnant women, an employer may still comply with both the California law and the PDA: it can adopt the specified leave policies for pregnancy and at the same time afford similar benefits for all other disabilities. This is untenable. California surely had no intent to require employers to provide general disability leave benefits. It intended to prefer pregnancy and went no farther. . . .

In sum, preferential treatment of pregnant workers is prohibited by Title VII, as amended by the PDA. Section 12945(b)(2) of the California Gov't Code, which extends preferential benefits for pregnancy, is therefore pre-empted. . . .

Suggestions for Further Reading

Anthologies

Bishop, Sharon, and Weinzweig, Marjorie. *Philosophy and Women*. Belmont: Wadsworth Publishing Co., 1979.

Freeman, Jo. *Women: A Feminist Perspective*. 4th edition. Palo Alto: Mayfield Publishing Co., 1989.

Gould, Carol C., and Wartofsky, Marx W. *Women and Philosophy*. New York: G. P. Putnam & Sons, 1976.

Jaggar, Alison, and Struhl, Paula Rothenberg. *Feminist Frameworks*. New York: McGraw-Hill Co., 1981.

Vetterling-Braggin, Mary, Elliston, Frederick, and English, Jane. *Feminism and Philosophy*. Totowa: Littlefield, Adams, 1977.

Basic Concepts

Jaggar, Alison M. *Feminist Politics and Human Nature*. Totowa: Rowman & Allanheld, 1983.

Tong, Rosemarie. *Feminist Thought*. Boulder: Westview Press, 1989.

Alternative Views

DeCrow, Karen. *Sexist Justice*. New York: Vintage, 1975.

Eisenstein, Zellah. *Feminism and Sexual Equality*. New York: Monthly Review, 1984.

Friedan, Betty. *The Feminine Mystique*. New York: W. W. Norton & Co., 1963.

Frye, Marilyn. *The Politics of Reality*. New York: The Crossing Press, 1983.

Koedt, Anne, Levine, Ellen, and Rapone, Anita. *Radical Feminism*. New York: Quadrangle Press, 1973.

Okin, Susan. *Justice, Gender and the Family*. New York: Basic Books, 1989.

Pateman, Carole. *The Sexual Contract*. Stanford: Stanford University Press, 1988.

Practical Applications

Irving, John. *The World According to Garp*. New York: Dutton, 1978.

United States Commission on Civil Rights. *Statement on the Equal Rights Amendment*. Washington, D.C.: U.S. Government Printing Office, 1978.

Affirmative Action and Comparable Worth

Basic Concepts

Solutions to the problem of discrimination and prejudice tend to be either backward-looking or forward-looking. Backward-looking solutions seek to rectify and compensate for past injustices caused by discrimination or prejudice. Forward-looking solutions seek to realize an ideal of a society free from discrimination and prejudice. To justify a backward-looking solution to the problem of discrimination and prejudice, it is necessary to determine (1) who has committed or benefited from a wrongful act of discrimination or prejudice and (2) who deserves compensation for that act. To justify a forward-looking solution to the problem, it is necessary to determine (1) what a society free from discrimination and prejudice would be like and (2) how such a society might be realized. Solutions of both types have been proposed to deal with racism and sexism, the dominant forms of discrimination and prejudice in our times.

One useful way of approaching the topic of discrimination and prejudice is to note what particular solutions to the problem are favored by the political ideals of libertarianism, welfare liberalism, socialism, and communitarianism (see Section I).

Libertarians, for whom liberty is the ultimate political ideal, are not likely to recognize any need to rectify acts of discrimination and prejudice. Bad as these acts may be, they usually do not—according to libertarians—violate anyone's rights, and hence do not demand rectification. In particular, because no one can demand a right to equal basic educational opportunities (a person's educational opportunities being simply a function of the property he or she controls), no one can justify affirmative action or comparable worth on the basis that such a right was previously denied.

Socialists and communitarians, for whom equality and the common good, respectively, are the ultimate political ideals, recognize a need to correct for discrimination and prejudice. However, the corrective measures they favor are not limited to affirmative action or comparable worth; socialists ultimately want to socialize the means of production and do away

with private property, and communitarians ultimately want to establish and maintain the forms of community that are necessary for the common good.

Finally, affirmative action and comparable worth are central requirements of the political program of welfare liberals, whose ultimate political ideal is contractual fairness.

Proposed solutions to the problem of discrimination and prejudice usually involve favoring or compensating certain qualified individuals when there has been a wrongful denial of opportunities or benefits in the past. This practice is called affirmative action, preferential treatment, or reverse discrimination when what is provided are jobs or other desirable positions. It is called comparable worth when what is provided is equal pay for equal or comparable work. "Affirmative action" and "preferential treatment" are basically forward-looking designations employed by proponents of the practice. "Reverse discrimination" is basically a backward-looking designation employed by opponents of the practice. "Comparable worth" is a forward-looking designation employed by both proponents and opponents of the practice.

Alternative Views

In opposition to affirmative action programs, Charles Murray (Selection 30) argues that affirmative action for blacks has actually worked against their interests by encouraging a new form of racism. The old racism openly held that blacks are permanently less competent than whites. The new racism holds that blacks are temporarily less competent than whites. The main problem with the new racism, according to Murray, is that it tends to perpetuate the racial inequalities it purports to remedy. However, the examples of this new racism that Murray discusses are all composites drawn from personal observations and, hence, as even he seems to realize, do not by themselves support any generalizations. At the same time, Murray wants to conclude from his discussion that there is no such thing as good racial discrimination.

In Selection 31, Herman Schwartz begins by surveying the law on affirmative action from Bakke to Stotts, noting certain ambiguities in recent Supreme Court decisions and then analyzes the underlying moral issues involved in affirmative action. First, Schwartz charges that people who condemn affirmative action are hypocritical because they also use separate lists when making political appointments. Second, Schwartz argues that there is nothing inherently wrong with taking group identity into account as long as the people selected are qualified. In fact, in some cases, this might be necessary to achieve some legitimate goal, such as ethnic diversity for a university community or community cooperation with a police force. Third, Schwartz argues that it is an egregious mistake to equate affirmative action with the various forms of discrimination suffered by blacks. Fourth, to those who charge that affirmative action is unfair to white males, Schwartz stresses how few slots are actually allotted to affirmative action and how economically disadvantaged most blacks are in the United States today. What Schwartz seems to be saying is that although affirmative action is unfair to white males, it is nonetheless morally justified. In contrast, others have argued that white males have no right to the positions and opportunities allotted by affirmative action and, hence, are not treated unfairly when they are denied them for good reason.

While admitting that some of the pay disparity between women and men in the job market is unfair, Clifford Hackett in Selection 32 objects to using a program of comparable worth to correct for that disparity because he thinks that such a program would undermine a free market. Instead, he recommends that women either seek employment in the better-paying job categories where men now predominate or engage in various forms of job actions, like strikes, to gain higher pay. In contrast, Elaine Sorensen argues in Selection 33 that a program of comparable worth is needed because a free market does not eliminate discrimination. Historically, she points out, it took new laws and court rulings to eliminate some of the most blatant discriminatory practices that prevailed in the labor market.

But even if we were to agree with Sorensen that free markets don't always correct for discrimination, couldn't Hackett still be right that comparable worth would seriously undermine free markets? For example, suppose we raise the wages of secretaries, judging what they do is comparable to what truck drivers do. Won't that increase the supply of secretaries and decrease the supply of truck drivers, with the consequence that the wages of truck drivers will rise, leading to a new round of comparable worth wage adjustments? Not at all. Because even if more people would compete for secretarial positions if secretaries were paid more, it doesn't follow either that more secretaries would be hired or that the pool of would-be truck drivers would decrease as long as these jobs remained as sex segregated as they presently are. Of course, if the sex segregation were to end, there would no longer appear to be grounds for comparable worth.

Practical Applications

Assuming that we accept the need for affirmative action programs to compensate for past injustices, there remains the question of what form such programs should take. In a recent decision, *Sheet Metal Workers* v. *The Equal Opportunity Commission,* the majority of the U.S. Supreme Court ruled that in appropriate circumstances it was legitimate to order affirmative action that would benefit individuals who are not the actual victims of past discrimination. In this decision, the majority of the court attempted to eliminate the confusion and uncertainty caused by its ruling in *Firefighters* v. *Stotts,* where the court seemed to hold that remedies could be ordered only to people who had been the actual victims of illegal discrimination. In the Sheet Metal Workers case, the majority of the court ruled against this interpretation, claiming that when discrimination has been persistent and egregious, it is appropriate to employ remedies that benefit members of the relevant group even when they are not the identified victims of the past discrimination.

However, quite recently in *City of Richmond* v. *Croson,* the Supreme Court struck down an affirmative action plan of the city of Richmond that required that prime contractors awarded city construction contracts to subcontract at least 30 percent of the dollar amount of each contract to one or more "Minority Business Enterprises." Justice O'Connor in delivering the opinion of the Court argued that the City of Richmond's plan was not supported by the type of evidence of past discrimination in the city's construction industry that would authorize a race-based relief under the equal protection clause of the Fourteenth Amendment. Justice Marshall, with Justices Brennan and Blackmun concurring, argued that the national evidence of discrimination against minority contractors and the local evidence that only .67 percent of the dollar value of local construction contracts went to minority contractors, together with the Supreme Court's own *Fullilove* v. *Klutznick* decision, which allowed a 10 percent set-aside of federal contracts for minority contractors, justified the city's adoption of the plan.

Although the case for past discrimination presented by the dissenting justices does seem strong, the City of Richmond clearly erred in defining minority business members to include groups who most likely have not been discriminated against by the Richmond community. The city also erred in not determining the number of minority business enterprises in the Richmond area and whether they would be capable of handling the 30 percent set-aside.

But surely it is possible to fashion affirmative action programs that lack the negative features of the Richmond program but possess all its positive features. And surely welfare liberals along with socialists and communitarians would regard such programs as justified. Libertarians, of course, would strongly object to this application on the grounds that people lack a right to the relevant equal opportunity needed to justify any affirmative action program. Hence, our evaluation of the Supreme Court's decision depends on our evaluations of these alternative political ideals.

30. Affirmative Racism

Charles Murray

Charles Murray argues that preferential treatment for blacks has actually worked against their interest by encouraging a new form of racism that tacitly accepts the view that blacks are temporarily less competent than whites. The problem with this new form of racism, Murray claims, is that it perpetuates the race-based inequality it seeks to eliminate.

A few years ago, I got into an argument with a lawyer friend who is a partner in a New York firm. I was being the conservative, arguing that preferential treatment of blacks was immoral; he was being the liberal, urging that it was the only way to bring blacks to full equality. In the middle of all this he abruptly said, "But you know, let's face it. We must have

From *The New Republic* (December 31, 1984). Reprinted by permission of *The New Republic* © 1984, The New Republic, Inc.

hired at least ten blacks in the last few years, and none of them has really worked out." He then returned to his case for still stronger affirmative action, while I wondered what it had been like for those ten blacks. And if he could make a remark like that so casually, what remarks would he be able to make some years down the road, if by that time it had been fifty blacks who hadn't "really worked out"?

My friend's comment was an outcropping of a new racism that is emerging to take its place alongside the old. It grows out of preferential treatment for blacks, and it is not just the much-publicized reactions, for example, of the white policemen or firemen who are passed over for promotion because of an affirmative action court order. The new racism that is potentially most damaging is located among the white elites—educated, affluent, and occupying the positions in education, business, and government from which this country is run. It currently focuses on blacks; whether it will eventually extend to include Hispanics and other minorities remains to be seen.

The new racists do not think blacks are inferior. They are typically longtime supporters of civil rights. But they exhibit the classic behavioral symptom of racism: they treat blacks differently from whites, because of their race. The results can be as concretely bad and unjust as any that the old racism produces. Sometimes the effect is that blacks are refused an education they otherwise could have gotten. Sometimes blacks are shunted into dead-end jobs. Always, blacks are denied the right to compete as equals.

The new racists also exhibit another characteristic of racism: they *think* about blacks differently from the way they think about whites. Their global view of blacks and civil rights is impeccable. Blacks must be enabled to achieve full equality. They are still unequal, through no fault of their own (it is the fault of racism, it is the fault of inadequate opportunity, it is the legacy of history). But the new racists' local view is that the blacks they run across professionally are not, on the average, up to the white standard. Among the new racists, lawyers have gotten used to the idea that the brief a black colleague turns in will be a little less well-rehearsed and argued than the one they would have done. Businessmen expect that a black colleague will not read a balance sheet as subtly as they do. Teachers expect black students to wind up toward the bottom of the class.

The new racists also tend to think of blacks as a commodity. The office must have a sufficient supply of blacks, who must be treated with special delicacy. The personnel problems this creates are more difficult than most because whites barely admit to themselves what's going on.

What follows is a foray into very poorly mapped territory. I will present a few numbers that explain much about how the process gets started. But the ways that the numbers get translated into behavior are even more important. The cases I present are composites constructed from my own observations and taken from firsthand accounts. All are based on real events and real people, stripped of their particularities. But the individual cases are not intended as evidence, because I cannot tell you how often they happen. They have not been the kind of thing that social scientists or journalists have wanted to count. I am writing this because so many people, both white and black, to whom I tell such stories know immediately what I am talking about. It is apparent that a problem exists. How significant is it? What follows is as much an attempt to elicit evidence as to present it.

As in so many of the crusades of the 1960s, the nation began with a good idea. It was called "affirmative action," initiated by Lyndon Johnson through Executive Order 11246 in September 1965. It was an attractive label and a natural corrective to past racism: actively seek out black candidates for jobs, college, or promotions, without treating them differently in the actual decision to hire, admit, or promote. The term originally evoked both the letter and the spirit of the order.

Then, gradually, affirmative action came to mean something quite different. In 1970 a federal court established the legitimacy of quotas as a means of implementing Johnson's executive order. In 1971 the Supreme Court ruled that an employer could not use minimum credentials as a prerequisite for hiring if the credentials acted as a "built-in headwind" for minority groups—even when there was no discriminatory intent and even when the hiring procedures were "fair in form." In 1972 the Equal Employment Opportunity Commission acquired broad, independent enforcement powers.

Thus by the early 1970s it had become generally recognized that a good-faith effort to recruit qualified blacks was not enough—especially if one's school depended on federal grants or one's business depended on federal contracts. Even for businesses and schools not directly dependent on the government, the simplest way to withstand an accusation of violating Title VII of the Civil Rights Act of 1964 was to make sure not that they had not just interviewed enough minority candidates, but that they had actually hired or admitted enough of them. Employers and admissions committees arrived at a rule of thumb: if the blacks who are available happen to be the best candidates, fine; if not, the best available black candidates will be given some sort of edge in the selection process. Sometimes the edge will be small; sometimes it will be predetermined that a black candidate is essential, and the edge will be very large.

Perhaps the first crucial place where the edge applies is in admission to college. Consider the cases of the following three students: John, William, and Carol, 17 years old and applying to college, are all equal on paper. Each has a score of 520 in the mathematics section of the Scholastic Aptitude Test, which puts them in the top third—at the 67th percentile—of all students who took the test. (Figures are based on 1983 data.)

John is white. A score of 520 gets him into the state university. Against the advice of his high school counselor, he applies to a prestigious school, Ivy U., where his application is rejected in the first cut—its average white applicant has math scores in the high 600s.

William is black, from a middle-class family who sent him to good schools. His score of 520 puts him at the 95th percentile of all blacks who took the test. William's high school counselor points out that he could probably get into Ivy U. William applies and is admitted—Ivy U. uses separate standards for admission of whites and blacks, and William is among the top blacks who applied.

Carol is black, educated at an inner-city school, and her score of 520 represents an extraordinary achievement in the face of terrible schooling. An alumnus of Ivy U. who regularly looks for promising inner-city candidates finds her, recruits her, and sends her off with a full scholarship to Ivy U.

When American universities embarked on policies of preferential admissions by race, they had the Carols in mind. They had good reason to be optimistic that preferential treatment would work—for many years, the best universities had been weighting the test scores of applicants from small-town public schools

when they were compared against those of applicants from the top private schools, and had been giving special breaks to students from distant states to ensure geographic distribution. The differences in preparation tended to even out after the first year or so. Blacks were being brought into a long-standing and successful tradition of preferential treatment.

In the case of blacks, however, preferential treatment ran up against a large black-white gap in academic performance combined with ambitious goals for proportional representation. This gap has been the hardest for whites to confront. But though it is not necessary or even plausible to believe that such differences are innate, it is necessary to recognize openly that the differences exist. By pretending they don't, we begin the process whereby both the real differences and the racial factor are exaggerated.

The black-white gap that applies most directly to this discussion is the one that separates blacks and whites who go to college. In 1983, for example, the mean Scholastic Aptitude Test score for all blacks who took the examination was more than 100 points below the white score on both the verbal and the math sections. Statistically, it is an extremely wide gap. To convert the gap into more concrete terms, think of it this way: in 1983, the same Scholastic Aptitude Test math score that put a black at the 50th percentile of all blacks who took the test put him at the 16th percentile of all whites who took the test.

These results clearly mean we ought to be making an all-out effort to improve elementary and secondary education for blacks. But that doesn't help much now, when an academic discrepancy of this magnitude is fed into a preferential admissions process. As universities scramble to make sure they are admitting enough blacks, the results feed the new racism. Here's how it works:

In 1983, only 66 black students nationwide scored above 700 in the verbal section of the Scholastic Aptitude Test, and only 205 scored above 700 in the mathematics section. This handful of students cannot begin to meet the demand for blacks with such scores. For example, Harvard, Yale, and Princeton have in recent years been bringing an aggregate of about 270 blacks into each entering class. If the black students entering these schools had the same distribution of scores as that of the freshman class as a whole, then every black student in the nation with a verbal score in the 700s, and roughly 70 percent of the ones with a math score in the 700s, would be in their freshman classes.

The main problem is not that a few schools monopolize the very top black applicants, but that these same schools have much larger implicit quotas than they can fill with those applicants. They fill out the rest with the next students in line—students who would not have gotten into these schools if they were not black, who otherwise would have been showing up in the classrooms of the nation's less glamorous colleges and universities. But the size of the black pool does not expand appreciably at the next levels. The number of blacks scoring in the 600s on the math section in 1983, for example, was 1,531. Meanwhile, 31,704 nonblack students in 1983 scored in the 700s on the math section and 121,640 scored in the 600s. The prestige schools cannot begin to absorb these numbers of other highly qualified freshmen, and they are perforce spread widely throughout the system.

At schools that draw most broadly from the student population, such as the large state universities, the effects of this skimming produce a situation that confirms the old racists in everything they want most to believe. There are plenty of outstanding students in such student bodies (at the University of Colorado, for example, 6 percent of the freshmen in 1981 had math scores in the 700s and 28 percent had scores in the 600s), but the skimming process combined with the very small raw numbers means that almost none of them are black. What students and instructors see in their day-to-day experience in the classroom is a disproportionate number of blacks who are below the white average, relatively few blacks who are at the first rank. The image that the white student carries away is that blacks are less able than whites.

I am not exalting the SAT as an infallible measure of academic ability, or pointing to test scores to try to convince anyone that blacks are performing below the level of whites. I am simply using them to explain what instructors and students already notice, and talk about, among themselves.

They do not talk openly about such matters. One characteristic of the new racism is that whites deny in public but acknowledge in private that there are significant differences in black and white academic performance. Another is that they dismiss the importance of tests when black scores are at issue, blaming cultural bias and saying that test scores are not good predictors of college performance. At the same time, they watch anxiously over their own children's test scores.

The differences in academic performance do not disappear by the end of college. Far from narrowing, the gap separating black and white academic achievement appears to get larger. Various studies, most recently at Harvard, have found that during the 1970s blacks did worse in college (as measured by grade point average) than their test scores would have predicted. Moreover, the black-white gap in the Graduate Record Examination is larger than the gap in the Scholastic Aptitude Test. The gap between black and white freshmen is a bit less than one standard deviation (the technical measure for comparing scores). Black and white seniors who take the Graduate Record Examination reveal a gap of about one and a quarter standard deviations.

Why should the gap grow wider? Perhaps it is an illusion—for example, perhaps a disproportionate number of the best black students never take the examination. But there are also reasons for suspecting that in fact blacks get a worse education in college than whites do. Here are a few of the hypotheses that deserve full exploration.

Take the situation of William—a slightly above-average student who, because he is black, gets into a highly competitive school. William studies very hard during the first year. He nonetheless gets mediocre grades. He has a choice. He can continue to study hard and continue to get mediocre grades, and be seen by his classmates as a black who cannot do very well. Or he can explicitly refuse to engage in the academic game. He decides to opt out, and his performance gets worse as time goes on. He emerges from college with a poor education and is further behind the whites than he was as a freshman.

If large numbers of other black students at the institution are in the same situation as William, the result can be group pressure not to compete academically. (At Harvard, it is said, the current term among black students for a black who studies like a white is "incognegro.") The response is not hard to understand. If one subpopulation of students is conspicuously behind another population and is visibly identifiable, then the population that is behind must come up with a good excuse for doing poorly. "Not wanting to do better" is as good as any.

But there is another crucial reason why blacks might not close the gap with whites during college: thcy arc not taught as well as whites are. Racist teachers impeding the progress of students? Perhaps, but most college faculty members I know tend to bend over backward to be "fair" to black students—and that may be the problem. I suggest that inferior instruction is more likely to be a manifestation of the new racism than the old.

Consider the case of Carol, with outstanding abilities but deprived of decent prior schooling: she struggles the first year, but she gets by. Her academic skills still show the aftereffects of her inferior preparation. Her instructors diplomatically point out the more flagrant mistakes, but they ignore minor lapses, and never push her in the aggressive way they push white students who have her intellectual capacity. Some of them are being patronizing (she is doing quite well, considering). Others are being prudent: teachers who criticize black students can find themselves being called racists in the classroom, in the campus newspaper, or in complaints to the administration.

The same process continues in graduate school. Indeed, because there are even fewer blacks in graduate schools than in undergraduate schools, the pressure to get black students through to the degree, no matter what, can be still greater. But apart from differences in preparation and ability that have accumulated by the end of schooling, the process whereby we foster the appearance of black inferiority continues. Let's assume that William did not give up during college. He goes to business school, where he gets his Masters degree. He signs up for interviews with the corporate recruiters. There are 100 persons in his class, and William is ranked near the middle. But of the 5 blacks in his class, he ranks first (remember that he was at the 95th percentile of blacks taking the Scholastic Aptitude Test). He is hired on his first interview by his first-choice company, which also attracted the very best of the white students. He is hired alongside 5 of the top-ranking white members of the class.

William's situation as one of 5 blacks in a class of 100 illustrates the proportions that prevail in business schools, and business schools are by no means one of the more extreme examples. The pool of black candidates for any given profession is a small fraction of the white pool. This works out to a 20-to-1 edge in business; it is even greater in most of the other professions. The result, when many hiring institutions are competing, is that a major gap between the abilities of new black and white employees in any given workplace is highly likely. Everyone needs to hire a few blacks, and the edge that "being black" confers in the hiring decision warps the sequence of hiring in such a way that a scarce resource (the blacks with a given set of qualifications) is exhausted at an artificially high rate, producing a widening gap in comparison with the remaining whites from which an employer can choose.

The more aggressively affirmative action is enforced, the greater the imbalance. In general, the first companies to hire can pursue strategies that minimize or even eliminate the difference in ability between the new black and white employees. IBM and Park Avenue law firms can do very well, just as Harvard does quite well in attracting the top black students. But the more effectively they pursue these strategies, the more quickly they strip the population of the best black candidates.

To this point I have been discussing problems that are more or less driven by realities we have very little hope of manipulating in the short term except by discarding the laws regarding preferential treatment. People do differ in acquiring abilities. Currently, acquired abilities in the white and black populations are distributed differently. Schools and firms do form a rough hierarchy when they draw from these distributions. The results follow ineluctably. The dangers they represent are not a matter of statistical probabilities, but of day-to-day human reactions we see around us.

The damage caused by these mechanistic forces should be much less in the world of work than in the schools, however. Schools deal in a relatively narrow domain of skills, and "talent" tends to be assigned specific meanings and specific measures. Workplaces deal in highly complex sets of skills, and "talent" consists of all sorts of combinations of qualities. A successful career depends in large part upon finding jobs that elicit and develop one's strengths.

At this point the young black professional must sidestep a new series of traps laid by whites who need to be ostentatiously nonracist. Let's say that William goes to work for the XYZ Corporation, where he is assigned with another management trainee (white) to a department where much of the time is spent preparing proposals for government contracts. The white trainee is assigned a variety of scut work—proofreading drafts, calculating the costs of minor items in the bid, making photocopies, taking notes at conferences. William gets more dignified work. He is assigned portions of the draft to write (which are later rewritten by more experienced staff), sits in on planning sessions, and even goes to Washington as a highly visible part of the team to present the bid. As time goes on, the white trainee learns a great deal about how the company operates, and is seen as a go-getting young member of the team. William is perceived to be a bright enough fellow, but not much of a detail man and not really much of a self-starter.

Even if a black is hired under terms that put him on a par with his white peers, the subtler forms of differential treatment work against him. Particularly for any corporation that does business with the government, the new employee has a specific, immediate value purely because he is black. There are a variety of requirements to be met and rituals to be observed for which a black face is helpful. These have very little to do with the long-term career interests of the new employee; on the contrary, they often lead to a dead end as head of the minority-relations section of the personnel department.

Added to this is another problem that has nothing to do with the government. When the old racism was at fault (as it often still is), the newly hired black employee was excluded from the socialization process because the whites did not want him to become part of the group. When the new racism is at fault, it is because many whites are embarrassed to treat black employees as badly as they are willing to treat whites. Hence another reason that whites get on-the-job training that blacks do not: much of the early training of an employee is intertwined with menial assignments and mild hazing. Blacks who are put through these routines often see themselves as racially abused (and when a black is involved, old-racist responses may well have crept in). But even if the black is not unhappy about the process, the whites are afraid that he is, and so protect him from it. There are many variations, all having the same effect: the black is denied an apprenticeship that the white has no way of escaping. Without serving the apprenticeship, there is no way of becoming part of the team.

Carol suffers a slightly different fate. She and a white woman are hired as reporters by a major newspaper. They both work hard, but after a few months there is no denying it: neither one of them can write. The white woman is let go. Carol is kept on, because the paper cannot afford to have any fewer blacks than it already has. She is kept busy with reportorial work, even though they have to work around the writing problem. She is told not to worry—there's lots more to being a journalist than writing.

It is the mascot syndrome. A white performing at a comparable level would be fired. The black is kept on, perhaps to avoid complications with the Equal Employment Opportunity Commission (it can be very expensive to fire a black), perhaps out of a more diffuse wish not to appear discriminatory. Everybody pretends that nothing is wrong—but the black's career is at a dead end. The irony, of course, is that the white who gets fired and has to try something else has been forced into accepting a chance of making a success in some other line of work whereas the black is seduced into *not* taking the same chance.

Sometimes differential treatment takes an even more pernicious form: the conspiracy to promote a problem out of existence. As part of keeping Carol busy, the newspaper gives her some administrative responsibilities. They do not amount to much. But she has an impressive title on a prominent newspaper and she is black—a potent combination. She gets an offer from a lesser paper in another part of the country to take a senior editorial post. Her current employer is happy to be rid of an awkward situation and sends along glowing references. She gets a job that she is unequipped to handle—only this time, she is in a highly visible position, and within a few weeks the deficiencies that were covered up at the old job have become the subject of jokes all over the office. Most of the jokes are openly racist.

It is important to pause and remember who Carol is: an extremely bright young woman, not (in other circumstances) a likely object of condescension. But being bright is no protection. Whites can usually count on the market to help us recognize egregious career mistakes and to prevent us from being promoted too far from a career line that fits our strengths, and too far above our level of readiness. One of the most prevalent characteristics of white differential treatment of blacks has been to exempt blacks from these market considerations, substituting for them a market premium attached to race.

The most obvious consequence of preferential treatment is that every black professional, no matter how able, is tainted. Every black who is hired by a white-run organization that hires blacks preferentially has to put up with the knowledge that many of his coworkers believe he was hired because of his race; and he has to put up with the suspicion in his own mind that they might be right.

Whites are curiously reluctant to consider this a real problem—it is an abstraction, I am told, much less important than the problem that blacks face in getting a job in the first place. But black professionals talk about it, and they tell stories of mental breakdowns; of people who had to leave the job altogether; of long-term professional paralysis. What white would want to be put in such a situation? Of course it would be a constant humiliation to be resented by some of your coworkers and condescended to by others. Of course it would affect your perceptions of yourself and your self-confidence. No system that produces such side effects—as preferential treatment *must* do—can be defended unless it is producing some extremely important benefits.

And that brings us to the decisive question. If the alternative were no job at all, as it was for so many blacks for so long, the resentment and condescension are part of the price of getting blacks into the positions they deserve. But is that the alternative today? If the institutions of this country were left to their own devices now, to what extent would they refuse to admit, hire, and promote people because they were black? To what extent are American institutions kept from being racist by the government's intervention?

It is another one of those questions that are seldom investigated aggressively, and I have no evidence. Let me suggest a hypothesis that bears looking into: that the signal event in the struggle for black equality during the last thirty years, the one with real impact, was not the Civil Rights Act of 1964 or Executive Order 11246 or any other governmental act. It was the civil rights movement itself. It raised to a pitch of acute and lasting discomfort the racial consciousness of the generations of white Americans who are now running the country. I will not argue that the old racism is dead at any level of society. I will argue, however, that in the typical corporation or in the typical admissions office, there is an abiding desire to be not-racist. This need not be construed as brotherly love. Guilt will do as well. But the civil rights movement did its job. I suggest that the laws and the court decisions and the continuing intellectual respectability behind preferential treatment are not holding many doors open to qualified blacks that would otherwise be closed.

Suppose for a moment that I am right. Suppose that, for practical purposes, racism would not get in the way of blacks if preferential treatment were abandoned. How, in my most optimistic view, would the world look different?

There would be fewer blacks at Harvard and Yale; but they would all be fully competitive with the whites who were there. White students at the state university would encounter a cross-section of blacks who span the full range of ability, including the top levels, just as whites do. College remedial courses would no longer be disproportionately black. Whites rejected by the school they wanted would quit assuming they were kept out because a less-qualified black was admitted in their place. Blacks in big corporations would no longer be shunted off to personnel-relations positions, but would be left on the mainline tracks toward becoming comptrollers and sales managers and chief executive officers. Whites would quit assuming that black colleagues had been hired because they were black. Blacks would quit worrying that they had been hired because they were black.

Would blacks still lag behind? As a population, yes, for a time, and the nation should be mounting a far more effective program to improve elementary and secondary education for blacks than it has mounted in the last few decades. But in years past virtually every ethnic group in America has at one time or another lagged behind as a population, and has eventually caught up. In the process of catching up, the ones who breached the barriers were evidence of the success of that group. Now blacks who breach the barriers tend to be seen as evidence of the inferiority of that group.

And that is the evil of preferential treatment. It perpetuates an impression of inferiority. The system segments whites and blacks who come in contact with each other so as to maximize the likelihood that whites have the advantage in experience and ability. The system then encourages both whites and blacks to behave in ways that create self-fulfilling prophecies even when no real differences exist.

It is here that the new racism links up with the old. The old racism has always openly held that blacks are permanently less competent than whites. The new racism tacitly accepts that, in the course of overcoming the legacy of the old racism, blacks are temporarily less competent than whites. It is an extremely fine distinction. As time goes on, fine distinctions tend to be lost. Preferential treatment is providing persuasive evidence for the old racists, and we can already hear it *sotto voce:* "We gave you your chance, we let you educate them and push them into jobs they couldn't have gotten on their own and coddle them every way you could. And see: they still aren't as good as whites, and you are beginning to admit it yourselves." Sooner or later this message is going to be heard by a white elite that needs to excuse its failure to achieve black equality.

The only happy aspect of the new racism is that the corrective—to get rid of the policies encouraging preferential treatment—is so natural. Deliberate preferential treatment by race has sat as uneasily with America's equal-opportunity ideal during the post-1965 period as it did during the days of legalized segregation. We had to construct tortuous rationalizations when we permitted blacks to be kept on the back of the bus—and the rationalizations to justify sending blacks to the head of the line have been just as tortuous. Both kinds of rationalization say that sometimes it is all right to treat people of different races in different ways. For years, we have instinctively sensed this was wrong in principle but intellectualized our support for it as an expedient. I submit that our instincts were right. There is no such thing as good racial discrimination.

31. Affirmative Action

Herman Schwartz

Using a multifaceted argument for affirmative action, Herman Schwartz contends that there is nothing wrong with taking group identity into account so long as the persons selected are adequately qualified. While admitting that affirmative action may be unfair to white males, Schwartz argues that it is nonetheless morally justified.

The American civil rights struggle has moved beyond simply banning discrimination against blacks, women and others. It is now clear that centuries of discrimination cannot be undone by merely stopping bad practices. Some kind of affirmative action is necessary to provide members of the disadvantaged groups with equal opportunities to share in the good things society has to offer.

The question of what kind of affirmative action is appropriate has generated intense controversy in the United States. One view is that it is necessary to provide actual preferences to members of disadvantaged groups in hiring, educational opportunities, government benefits and programmes, and the like, often in arrangements calling for specific minimum goals and timetables or quotas to achieve certain proportions of jobs, or other benefits.

In the famous *Bakke* case, Justice Harry Blackmun wrote:

> I suspect that it would be impossible to arrange an affirmative action program in a racially neutral way and have it successful. To ask that this be so is to demand the impossible. In order to get beyond racism, we must first take account of race. There is no other way. And in order to treat some persons equally, we must treat them differently. We cannot—we dare not—let the Equal Protection Clause perpetuate racial supremacy.[1]

From *The Israeli Yearbook on Human Rights*, v. 14 (1984), pp. 120–133 by permission of the publisher. Copyright © 1984 Faculty of Law, Tel Aviv University, Israel. (Original title "Affirmative Action: The American Experience.")

And Justice Thurgood Marshall emphasized that "It is because of a legacy of unequal treatment that we now must permit the institutions of this society to give consideration to race in making decisions about who will hold the positions of influence, affluence and prestige in America."[2]

Others, including certain American Jewish organizations, find this kind of race or gender preference immoral and illegal, preferring instead to rely on finding and training disadvantaged group members for the desired opportunities. Thus, United States Civil Rights Commission Vice Chairman Morris Abram declared:

> I do not need any further study of a principle that comes from the basic bedrock of the Constitution, in which the words say that every person in the land shall be entitled to the equal protection of the law. Equal means equal. Equal does not mean you have separate lists of blacks and whites for promotion, any more than you have separate accommodations for blacks and whites for eating. Nothing will ultimately divide a society more than this kind of preference and this kind of reverse discrimination.[3]

Supreme Court Justice John Paul Stevens, who frequently votes with the liberal members of the Court, was so offended by a congressional enactment setting aside ten percent of public works contracts for minority contractors, that he compared it to the Nuremberg laws for its reliance on racial and ethnic identity.[4]

The Legal Issues

The constitutionality of governmental (constitutional limitations do not generally apply to private actions) affirmative action programmes involving race and gender-conscious goals and timetables or quotas seems quite firmly established. Voluntary private affirmative action plans also seem quite legal under the governing statutes. Language in the recent Memphis Fire Department case casts some doubt on whether federal statutory law permits a federal court to order such plans as a remedy for discrimination, but this latter situation seems to be the only situation in which such plans may be barred, and even that is uncertain for reasons to be discussed below.

There are four significant decisions.

1. The decision in *Regents of the University of California v. Bakke* represents a brilliant exercise in judicial statesmanship, engineered primarily by Justice Lewis F. Powell. In that case, the University of California Medical School at Davis had set aside sixteen places out of 100 for minority students. Allan Bakke, a white student, was denied admission because he did not qualify for one of the remaining 84 places; his grades and scores were higher than the average of the sixteen special admittees. He charged the University with racial discrimination against him.

Four Justices found the programme illegal under a federal statute and never reached the constitutional issue. Four other Justices—Brennan, Marshall, Blackmun and White—ruled that the normally strict scrutiny applicable to governmental classifications by race—characterized frequently in other contexts as " 'strict' in theory and fatal in fact"[5]—was inapplicable when the classification was designed to benefit groups suffering from societal discrimination. These four suggested that the "middle level" test—which requires only that the classification bear a substantial relation to an important governmental purpose[6]—was properly applicable, and for these Justices, the sixteen-seat set-aside met the standard.

Justice Powell walked a middle line. He first insisted that all racial classifications—even those favouring minorities—must meet the exacting strict scrutiny standard. He then declared that eradicating the general "societal" discrimination relied on by Justices Brennan *et al.* was an unacceptable goal and that fixed quotas were an unacceptable means. He found, however, that for a university, ethnic and racial diversity *was* an acceptable objective and that a flexible, individualized programme *taking race into account* was an acceptable means. Thus, Allan Bakke was admitted because the Davis plan was struck down, but race consciousness in university admission was also allowed.

While statesmanship in any setting can always be criticized for shortcomings in logic, accuracy, candor, and the like (and Justice Powell's opinion can be, and has been, on all of these grounds), the judgment was truly Solomonic: while criticizing "rigid quotas" and allowing Allan Bakke to enter, the decision also permitted state universities to continue affirmative action plans if they wanted to. A survey one year later found that the decision had not discouraged any affirmative action by schools and colleges. Moreover, in the course of his opinion, Justice Powell also approved various other preferential plans where prior discrimination had actually been found by an appropriate governmental body.

2. *Fullilove v. Klutznick* (1980). The significance of this latter point came out two years later in the minority set-aside case. During debate in 1977 on a public works bill, an amendment was attached requiring ten percent of the contracts to be given to minority business enterprises; such programmes have also become common on the state and local level. The minority set-aside was promptly challenged as discriminatory against white contractors, but six members of the Court, in opinions by Chief Justice Burger for three, and by Justices Powell and Marshall, had no difficulty upholding the programme as justified by the long history of discrimination in the construction industry. Justice Powell found that what might be called a "rigid" ten percent was still "reasonably necessary" enough to meet

even his conception of the strict scrutiny test.[7] The plan also survived criticisms from Justice Stevens in dissent that the beneficiaries were not themselves necessarily victims of the discrimination—this was a future-oriented plan where, as in most such programmes, the beneficiaries of the remedy may not be the same as the victims of the discrimination.

3. *United Steelworkers, Inc. v. Weber* (1979).[8] In the private sphere, a 5–2 majority of the Court has upheld a voluntarily adopted craft training programme which allocated half the trainee slots to blacks. No constitutional issue was at stake because all the parties were private entities, but the Court has subsequently declined opportunities to distinguish or overturn such voluntary employment plans when adopted by city agencies, which, like the University of California Regents in *Bakke,* are subject to constitutional restraints.

4. *Firefighters Local Union No. 1784 v. Stotts* (1984).[9] Finally, in the *Stotts* case in June 1984, the Court ruled that when it is necessary to lay off workers in a setting where a court had already ordered hiring goals and timetables, if there is an applicable seniority provision, seniority must be followed in the layoffs, even if that eliminates the gains for minorities achieved by the hiring plan.

This result, though deplored by many civil rights activists, was not unexpected. Although not always sacrosanct, seniority is nevertheless a hard-won goal for many workers, and is often indispensable to countering employer arbitrariness with respect to promotions, assignments and other employee benefits. For these reasons, the Supreme Court has frequently upheld seniority rights, particularly in the civil rights context.[10]

What shocked many, however, was a quite gratuitous two and a half page discussion of the general remedial powers of federal courts, which seems to announce that Title VII forbids federal courts from ordering goals and timetable hiring programmes even after a finding of discrimination: "[T]he policy behind § 706 (g) of Title VII, which affects the remedies available in Title VII litigation . . . is to provide make-whole relief only to those who have been actual victims of illegal discrimination",[11] is the way Justice White put it.

Until *Stotts,* the federal Courts of Appeal had unanimously ruled that in employment discrimination cases brought under Title VII of the Civil Rights Act of 1964, federal courts could order certain percentages of minority or female hiring or promotion.[12] Justice White's pronouncement, which was quite unnecessary to the result, as Justice Stevens emphasized, put a cloud on hundreds of orders going back to 1969, arguably affirmed by Congress in 1972 when it expanded Title VII, and never even questioned by the Supreme Court despite numerous opportunities over the last fifteen years to do so.

The Court's pronouncement on this issue is not a square holding, and it could be receded from in the next case without much difficulty. Even if that does happen, however, the opinion has created much confusion and uncertainty. It has removed pressure on employers and unions to hire and promote minorities and women, or to settle employment discrimination litigation. It has also encouraged the Justice Department to try to open up many of the scores of decrees entered during the last fifteen years ordering such relief.

Mr. Abram's constitutional opposition to such plans is thus in no way justified by the Supreme Court's view of "the basic bedrock of the Constitution." Nor is the history cited by Assistant Attorney General Reynolds any better. In January 1984, he told an audience of pre-law students that the Fourteenth Amendment was intended to bar taking race into account for any purpose at all—"we fought the Civil War" over that, he told *The New York Times.* If so, he knows something that the members of the 1865–66 Congress, who adopted that amendment and fought the war, did not: less than a month after Congress approved the Fourteenth Amendment in 1866, the very same Congress enacted eight laws exclusively for the freedmen, granting preferential benefits regarding land, education, banking facilities, hospitals, and more.[13] No comparable programmes existed or were established for whites. And that Congress did not act unthinkingly—the racial preferences involved in those programmes were vigorously debated with a vocal minority led by President Andrew Johnson, who argued that the preferences wrongly discriminated against whites.[14]

The Moral Issues

But law is not always the same as justice. If the case for affirmative action is morally flawed, then sooner or later, the law must change. What then is the moral case against preferences for disadvantaged groups in the allocation of opportunities and benefits?

The arguments are basically two-fold: (1) hiring and other distributional decisions should be made solely on the basis of "individual merit"; and (2) racial preferences are always evil and will take us back to *Plessy v. Ferguson*[15] and worse. Quoting Dr. Martin Luther King, Jr., Thurgood Marshall, and Roy Wilkins to support the claim that anything other than total race neutrality is "discriminatory", Assistant Attorney General Reynolds warns that race consciousness has "creat[ed] . . . a racial spoils system in America", "stifles the creative spirit", erects artificial barriers, and divides the society. It is, he says, unconstitutional, unlawful, and immoral. Ms. Midge Decter, writing in the *Wall Street Journal* a few years ago, sympathized with black and female beneficiaries of affirmative action programmes for the "self-doubts" and loss of "self-regard" that she is sure they suffer, "spiritually speaking", for their "unearned special privileges". Whenever we take race into account to hand out benefits, declares Linda Chavez, the Executive Director of the Reagan Civil Rights Commission, we "discriminate", "destroy[ing] the sense of self".

All of this represents the rankest form of hypocrisy. Despite Mr. Abram's condemnation of "separate lists", the Administration for which these people speak uses "separate lists" for blacks, Hispanics, women, Republicans, Democrats and any other group, whenever it finds that politically or otherwise useful. For example, does anyone believe that blacks like Civil Rights Commission Chairman Clarence Pendleton or Equal Employment Opportunities Commission Chairman Clarence Thomas were picked because of the color of their *eyes*? Or that Linda Chavez Gersten was made the new Executive Director of the Civil Rights Commission for reasons having nothing to do with the fact that her maiden and professional surname is Chavez?

Perhaps the most prominent recent example of affirmative action is President Reagan's selection of Sandra Day O'Connor for the Supreme Court. Obviously, she was on a "separate list", because on any unitary list this obscure lower-court state judge, with no federal experience and no national reputation, would never have come to mind as a plausible choice for the Nation's highest court. (Incidentally, despite Ms. Decter's, Mr. Reynolds', and Ms. Chavez's concern about the loss of "self-regard" suffered by beneficiaries of such preferences, "spiritually speaking" Justice O'Connor seems to be bearing her loss and "spiritual" pain quite easily.) And, like so many other beneficiaries of affirmative action given an opportunity that would otherwise be unavailable, she may indeed perform well. Mr. Reagan's fickleness on this issue has become so transparent that he was chastized for it by one of his own true believers, Civil Rights Commission Chairman Pendleton.

In fact, there is really nothing inherently wrong with taking group identity into account, so long as the person selected is qualified, a prerequisite that is an essential element of all affirmative action programmes. We do it all the time, with hardly a murmur of protest from anyone. We take group identity into account when we put together political slates, when a university gives preference to applicants from a certain part of the country or to the children of alumni, when Brandeis University restricts itself to Jews in choosing a president (as it did when it chose Morris Abram) or Notre Dame to Roman Catholics or Howard University to blacks, when this Administration finds jobs in government for children of cabinet members. Some of these examples are less laudable than others. But surely none of these seldom-criticized practices can be valued above the purpose of undoing the effects of past and present discrimination. In choosing a qualified applicant because of a race preference we merely acknowledge, as

Morton Horwitz has pointed out, "the burdens, stigmas, and scars produced by history . . . the injustices heaped on his ancestors and, through them, on him. The history and culture of oppression, transmitted through legally anonymous generations, is made antiseptic when each individual is treated as a separate being, disconnected from history."[16]

In some cases, moreover, group-oriented choices are necessary for effective performance of the job. Justice Powell in the *Bakke* case stressed the importance of ethnic and other diversity for a university, as a justification for taking race into account as one factor in university admissions. Such considerations are particularly important in police work, where police-community cooperation is indispensable, and the absence of a fair proportion of minority police in cities like Detroit and New York has not only hindered law enforcement, but has produced violent police-minority confrontations.

For these reasons, it is hard to take at face value this zeal for "individual merit", when it is group identity that determines so many choices on all our parts. As Justice Powell noted in *Bakke,* America is indeed "a Nation of minorities, . . . a 'majority' composed of various minority groups."[17] But as Burke Marshall has observed,

> The Constitution generally, and the Fourteenth Amendment specifically . . . do not mean that racial, cultural, ethnic, national, or even religious identification must be excluded from the considerations that lead to actions by government officials, or legislatures, reflecting the pluralism of American society. They cannot mean, for example, that decisions on judicial appointments, political candidates, cabinet officials at all levels, or even bureaucrats in the instrumentalities of the state can never reflect racial, ethnic, cultural, or religious constituencies. If these considerations are valid for the political apparatus of government, they must also be valid, so far as the constitutional command is concerned, for other state decisions with regard to who is, and who is not, included in the discretionary allocation of benefits and power.[18]

Is it not discriminatory against whites or males, however, to deny them something they might otherwise have gotten but for the color of their skin or their gender? Is it true, as Brian Weber's lawyer argued before the Supreme Court, that "you can't avoid discrimination by discriminating"? Will racially influenced hiring take us back to *Plessy v. Ferguson,* as Pendleton and Reynolds assert? Were Martin Luther King, Jr., Thurgood Marshall, Roy Wilkins, and other black leaders really against it?

Hardly. Indeed, it is hard to contain one's outrage at this perversion of what Dr. King, Justice Marshall, and others have said, at this manipulation of their often sorrow-laden eloquence, in order to deny a handful of jobs, school admissions, and other necessities for a decent life to a few disadvantaged blacks out of the many who still suffer from discrimination and would have few opportunities otherwise.

Can anyone honestly equate a remedial preference for a disadvantaged (and qualified) minority member with the brutality inflicted on blacks and other minorities by racist laws and practices? The preference may take away some benefits from some white men, but none of them is being beaten, lynched, denied the right to use a bathroom, a place to sleep or eat, being forced to take the dirtiest jobs or denied any work at all, forced to attend dilapidated and mind-killing schools, subjected to brutally unequal justice, or stigmatized as an inferior being. Setting aside, after proof of discrimination, a few places a year for qualified minorities out of hundreds and perhaps thousands of employees, as in the Kaiser plant in the *Weber* case, or sixteen medical school places out of 100 as in *Bakke,* or ten percent of all federal public work contracts as in *Fullilove,* or even 50 percent of new hires, cannot be mentioned in the same breath with the brutalities that racism and sexism inflicted on helpless minorities and women. It is nothing short of a shameful insult to the memory of the tragic victims of such oppression to equate the two.

Indeed, the real issue in all matters of equality and fairness is not reflected in the tautological "equal means equal" proclaimed by Mr. Abram. Rather, as H. L. A. Hart and so many others have pointed out, although the "leading precept" of justice "is often formulated as 'Treat like cases alike' . . . we need to add to the latter 'and treat different cases differently.' "[19] When some have been handicapped severely and unfairly by an accidental fact of birth, to treat such "different cases" no differently from others without that handicap is to treat them unjustly. It is not only on the golf course that it is necessary to consider handicaps.

But even if it is not discriminatory, is affirmative action unfair to innocent whites or males? Should a white policeman or fire fighter with ten years in the department be laid off when a black or a woman with less seniority is kept because an affirmative action decree is in force? Aren't those denied a job or opportunity because of an affirmative action programme often innocent of any wrong against the preferred group and just as much in need of the opportunities?

The last question is the most troubling. Brian Weber was not a rich man and he had to support a family on a modest salary, just like any black worker. A craft job would have been a significant step up in money, status, and working conditions. And *he* hadn't discriminated against anyone. Why should he pay for Kaiser's wrongs?

A closer look at the *Weber* case brings some other factors to light, however. Even if there had been no separate list for blacks, Weber would not have gotten the position, for there were too many other whites ahead of him anyway. Moreover, but for the affirmative action plan, there would not have been any craft training programme at the plant at all, for *any* whites. The white workers had been unsuccessfully demanding a craft-training programme for years, but they finally got it only when Kaiser felt it necessary to adopt the affirmative action plan.

Furthermore, even with the separate list, the number of whites adversely affected was really very small. The Kaiser plan contemplated hiring only three to four minority members a year, out of a craft work force of 275–300 and a total work force of thousands. In the first year of its operation, Kaiser still selected only a handful of blacks, because it also brought in 22 outside craftsmen, of whom only one was black. In the 1980 *Fullilove* case, upholding the ten percent set-aside of federal public works projects for minority contractors,

only 0.25 percent of the total annual expenditure for construction in the United States was involved. In *Bakke*, only sixteen places out of 100 at one medical school were set aside for minorities. A new Boston University special admissions programme for black medical students will start with three a year, with the hope of rising to ten, increasing the minority enrollment at the school by two percent.

The *Weber* case discloses another interesting aspect of affirmative action plans. Because such plans can adversely affect majority white males, creative ingenuity is often expended to prevent this from happening. In *Weber*, a new craft programme benefiting both whites and blacks was set up; in the lay-off cases, time sharing and other ways of avoiding the dismissals—including raising more money—can be devised. So much for Mr. Reynold's worries about "stifling" creativity.

Strains can and do result, especially if deliberately stirred up. But strain is not inevitable: broad-ranging goals and timetable programmes for women and blacks were instituted in the Bell Telephone Company with no such troubles. The same holds true elsewhere, especially when, as in *Weber*, the programme creates new, previously unavailable opportunities for whites. Conversely, even if, as the Reagan Administration urges, the remedies are limited to specific identifiable victims of discriminatory practices, some whites may be upset. If a black applicant can prove that an employer wrongly discriminated against him personally, he would be entitled to the seniority and other benefits that he would have had but for the discrimination—with the Administration's blessing—and this would give him competitive seniority over some white employees, regardless of those employees' innocence. The same thing happens constantly with veterans and other preferences, and few opponents of affirmative action seem to be upset by that.

Among some Jews, affirmative action brings up bitter memories of ceiling quotas, which kept them out of schools and jobs that could on merit have been theirs. This has produced a serious and nasty split within the American civil rights movement. But affirmative action goals and timetables are really quite different. Whereas quotas against Jews, Catholics, and others were ceilings to limit and keep these groups *out* of schools and jobs, today's "benign preferences" are designed to be floors that let minorities *into* a few places they would not ordinarily enter, and with relatively little impact on others. This distinction between inclusive and exclusionary practices is central.[20]

There is also a major confusion, exploited by opponents, resulting from the fact that we are almost all ethnic or religious minorities. Of course we are. And if it were shown that any minority is being victimized by intentional discrimination and that the only way to get more of that minority into a relatively representative portion of the work force or school is through an affirmative action plan, then these people would be entitled to such a remedy.

Group thinking is of course at odds with an individualistic strain that runs deep in American society. But individualism is only one strain among many. And what civil rights is all about, as many have emphasized, is an effort to undo a certain vicious strain of group thinking that established discriminatory *systems.* From *Brown v. Board of Education* on, civil rights decrees have been aimed at dismantling racist systems against groups. Obviously, these racist systems hurt individual group members, and individuals bring the law suits, but even in *Brown,* the "all deliberate speed" remedy gradually dismantling the segregated school systems was future-oriented, with the particular plaintiffs not necessarily the actual beneficiaries: in many cases, only future classes of black children would be allowed in a school to be gradually integrated, not the particular plaintiffs. The same logic applies to systems of allocating jobs and other benefits that systematically discriminated against and excluded people because they were members of minority groups.[21]

For the fact is that the centuries of injustice have created deeply imbedded abuses, and the plight of black Americans not only remains grave, but in many respects, it is getting worse. The black unemployment rate—21 percent in early 1983—is consistently double that for whites and the spread is not shrinking. For black males, the rate—an awful 30 percent—is almost triple that for whites; for black teenagers the rate approaches 50 percent. More than half of all black children under three years of

age live in homes below the poverty line. The gap between black and white family income, which prior to the '70s had narrowed a bit, has steadily edged wider, so that black family income is now only 55 percent that of whites. Only three percent of the nation's lawyers and doctors are black and only four percent of its managers, but over 50 percent of its maids and garbage collectors. Black life expectancy is about six years less than that of whites; the black infant mortality rate is nearly double.[22]

Although the situation for women, of all races, is not as bad, women generally still earned only 60–65 percent as much as their male counterparts, and in recent years black women have earned only 84 percent of the white females' incomes. The economic condition of black women, who now head 41 percent of the 6.4 million black families, is particularly bad. A recent Wellesley College study found that black women are not only suffering in the labour market, but they receive substantially less public assistance and child support than white women. The condition of female household heads of any race is troubling: 90 percent of the 8.4 million single parent homes are headed by women, and more than half are below the poverty line.

Affirmative action helps. For example, from 1974 to 1980 minority employment with employers subject to federal affirmative action requirements rose twenty percent, almost twice the increase elsewhere. The employment of women by covered contractors rose fifteen percent, but only two percent among others.[23] The number of black police officers nationwide rose from 24,000 in 1970 to 43,500 in 1980; that kind of increase in Detroit produced a sharp decline in citizen hostility toward the police and a concomitant increase in police efficiency. There were also large jumps in minority and female employment among fire fighters, and sheet metal and electrical workers.

Few other remedies work as well or as quickly. As the New York City Corporation Counsel told the Supreme Court about the construction industry in the *Fullilove* case, "less drastic means of attempting to eradicate and remedy discrimination have been repeatedly and continuously made over the past decade and a half. They have all failed." Where affirmative action is ended, progress often stops.[24]

An example from a state like Alabama illustrates the value of affirmative action quotas. Alabama, led by such arch-segregationists as George C. Wallace, had always excluded blacks from any but the most menial state jobs. In the late 1960s, a federal court found that only 27 of 3,000 clerical and managerial employees were black. Federal Judge Frank Johnson ordered extensive recruiting of blacks, as well as the hiring of the few specific identified individual blacks who could prove they were the victims of discrimination; these are, of course, the remedies currently urged by the Justice Department.

Nothing happened. Another suit was filed, this time just against the state police, and this time a 50 percent hiring quota was imposed, until blacks reached 25 percent of the force. Today, Alabama has the most thoroughly integrated state police force in the country, with 20–25 percent of the force black. A threat of such quotas in other agencies has also produced substantial improvements.[25]

Reasonable people will continue to differ about the appropriateness of affirmative action. Color blindness and neutrality are obviously the ultimate goal, and it was one of Martin Luther King, Jr.'s dreams. But it still remains only a dream, and until it comes closer to reality, affirmative action plans are necessary and appropriate. One cannot undo centuries of discrimination by simply saying "stop"—one has to take into account the harm that those centuries have brought, and try to make up for it. Otherwise, we in the United States will remain like Disraeli's "Two Nations".

Notes

1. University of California Regents v. Bakke, 438 U.S. 265, 407 (1978).

2. *Id.*, at 401 (Marshall, J., concurring).

3. *New York Times*, 18 January 1984, p. 1, col. 1.

4. Fullilove v. Klutznick, 448 *U.S.* 448, 534 n. 5 (Stevens, J., dissenting).

5. G. Gunther, "Foreword: In Search of Evolving Doctrine on a Changing Court: A Model for a Newer Equal Protection." 86 *Harv. L. Rev.* 1 (1972).

6. Craig v. Boren, 429 *U.S.* 190 (1976).

7. 448 *U.S.*, at 496–97 (Powell, J., concurring).

8. 443 *U.S.* 193 (1979).

9. 52 *U.S.L.W.* 4767 (12 June 1984).

10. International Brhd. of Teamsters v. U.S., 431 *U.S.* 324 (1977).

11. 52 *U.S.L.W.*, at 4772.

12. *See* cases cited by Justice Blackmun, *id.*, at 4781. n. 10.

13. *See, e.g.*, Act of 16 July 1866, 14 *Stat.* 173 (Freedmen's Bureau).

14. *See* the discussion in Justice Marshall's opinion in Bakke, 438 *U.S.*, at 396–98.

15. 163 *U.S.* 537 (1896).

16. M. J. Horwitz, "The Jurisprudence of *Brown* and the Dilemmas of Liberalism", 14 *Harv. Civ. Rts.-Civ. Libs. L. Rev.* 599, 610 (1979).

17. 438 *U.S.*, at 292.

18. B. Marshall, "A Comment on the Nondiscrimination Principle in a '*Nation of Minorities*',", 93 *Yale L.J.* 1006, 1011 (1984).

19. H. L. A. Hart, *The Concept of Law* 155 (1961).

20. Marshall, *supra* note 18, at 1011–1012.

21. *Id.*, at 1007–1008.

22. These statistics are drawn from various sources, but the primary source is the Urban League's annual, *The State of Black America*.

23. *Washington Post*, 20 June 1983, p. A3.

24. *Wall St. J.*, 10 August 1984. p. 31 (decline in minority government contracts upon termination of set-asides).

25. Huron, "But Government *Can* Help", *Washington Post*, 12 August 1984, p. B1.

32. Comparable Worth: Better From a Distance

Clifford Hackett

> While admitting that some of the pay disparity between women and men in the job market is unfair, Clifford Hackett objects to using a program of comparable worth to correct that disparity. Rather than seek some "objective criteria" for evaluating the jobs people have and then attempt to readjust their salaries according to these criteria, Hackett recommends either that women seek employment in the better-paying job categories where men now predominate or that women engage in various forms of job actions, like strikes, to gain higher pay. Hackett further argues that it is not possible, over the longer term, to have pockets of comparable worth in an otherwise competitive economy without creating serious problems.

Should women be paid for jobs on the basis of what men earn in entirely different jobs? The answer would seem to be yes following the federal equal-pay-for-equal-work law of 1963 which laid the ground for improved work opportunities for women. Yet the idea, called comparable worth, is finding it difficult to emerge, as some had predicted it would, as the "issue of the 80s" for women.

The appeal of comparable worth is considerable—especially from a distance. It seems to address a basic economic injustice: men earn more than women whether the measure is annual income, average hourly wages, starting salaries, or concentration in top-paying jobs. This differential also exists within jobs and professions, and persists even as women are moving into new job fields and upward in career tracks. Clearly, comparable worth defenders say, these discrepancies are unfair, perhaps illegal, and should be ended by law.

There is another broad appeal to justice related to the issue: the seeming inability of the free market economy to provide reasonable pay scales crossing vocational lines. Some of us are appalled by plumbers who get $40 for a house call; others are repelled by lawyers who earn $200 an hour. Johnny Carson and NFL football players prompt many to say, "No one can be worth that much!" An unstated comparison in our minds pits these "overpaid" exemplars against those of us who perform the hum-drum jobs which keep the economy going or who (and these are mostly women) undertake the most humane, compassionate, and bedeviling jobs in all societies: nursing, child care, and primary education—all low-paying labors. Is this pay disparity fair? Clearly not.

But the closer one looks at comparable worth, the more doubtful its real value appears. Instead of helping move women into new jobs as the equal-pay law did, comparable worth seems to give up that fight. It pleads for higher pay for women on two quite different, but equally dubious, bases: first, it argues that jobs women actually perform are undervalued and should be upgraded by law; second, it maintains that women's abilities, education, and experience are undervalued and they should get more money no matter *what* jobs they do.

Whatever happened to the premise of equal pay for women, that if women earned the same as men in a particular job category they would more surely compete for those jobs? For many reasons, women still do not always seek the same jobs men do. Comparable worth advocates conclude society must reevaluate the work women do choose. But this revaluing without regard to the job market is at the heart of the comparable worth dispute, the cause of dismay among almost everyone except those who think women would gain from a radical remaking of the economy.

Reprinted from *Commonweal* (May 31, 1985) with permission from the Commonweal Foundation.

Comparable worth entails assigning numbers to every important aspect of every paying job. Some incredible mechanism of government would then insure that everyone with the same numbers would get the same pay. Who assigns the numbers and weighs job skills against education, experience versus risks, and so on? A committee of personnel experts! But doesn't the open market already perform its own kind of valuation when people put their skills out for examination and competition? Yes, but unfairness results because women's work or women themselves are undervalued.

Let's be clear about what comparable worth is and isn't. It is not about the fact that football players and movie stars earn too much money, but that women make less money than men. Comparable worth is not concerned with the kinds of jobs women do, only how much they earn. Finally, comparable worth is not about job opportunity, job mobility, or job advancement, but about whether the open marketplace for jobs, with its flaws, should be abolished.

What is wrong with this new approach? First, it ignores the source of the problem: the labor pool has an oversupply of women who are available for too limited a number of entry-level jobs. Second, even admitting that economic life is not always fair, who is wise enough to evaluate continuously the varying worths which society applies to jobs? Who will decide, for instance, the worth of four years studying elementary education at a first-class university compared to four years studying engineering at a community college? Who will weigh the relative worth of a super-salesman who actually spends much of his time preparing for a few million-dollar sales a month and a senior secretary whose long hours and mental strain are usually endured under someone else's direct control?

The answer of comparable worth advocates is that these factors be judged by a committee of personnel experts who regularly analyze job content and make comparisons of skills and experience in large firms and within government. Yet such experts as Norman D. Willis, head of a personnel advisory firm which the state of Washington employed in one of the most famous comparable-worth cases, says he recoils at the possibility that his classifications, or anyone else's, should become law.

Even if large numbers of employers were persuaded to apply comparable worth, the concept could not be limited to women alone. It would have to apply to men's jobs as well. Would not church workers and writers, to take just two obvious examples of underpaid professions, have claims on higher pay based on the comparable worth of their education, skills, and contributions to society? It's not hard to see why private employers cannot take seriously the idea of actually setting pay by comparable worth rules.

Private employers pay the lowest possible wages needed to stay in competition. As long as the competition remains relatively open, workers benefit by maintaining the mobility and skills to move into better paying or more interesting jobs. The two are not always the same, but moving up usually means more demanding work. It may include not only greater skills but longer or irregular hours, and sometimes higher risks. Firefighters are paid for risking their lives in a pattern which alternates boredom with real danger. Most workers do not desire such a life, and those who do are thus able to demand higher wages and earlier retirements. Often the demands consist of entrance hurdles, like bar exams, advanced degrees and other qualifiers. Comparable worth proponents are sometimes accused of "credentialism" for seeking more pay for those women, like nurses and librarians, who also face educational hurdles for qualifications. But the pay which women, as well as men, receive is based not only on the credentials but also on market competition. If women want higher wages, they soon learn to avoid jobs with many qualified competitors, whether men or women. Why should employers pay librarians as much as electricians when the supply of the former will produce ample numbers at little more than the minimum white collar wage, while electricians are almost always scarce and, therefore, expensive?

Facing great hostility in the private sector, comparable worth has moved with some success into closed markets like state and local government where worker and union pressures combine with trendy political constituencies. Minnesota, a progressive state by most standards, recently passed laws requiring a study of job characteristics of all government jobs, state and local, and set aside money to start applying the program. In San Jose, California, a similar plan was initiated with $1.5 million for pay equity adjustments. What is wrong, then, with these plans, especially if they have public support?

The long-term problem is that comparable worth destroys the link between work and its marketplace evaluation. In the private sector, this linkage is vital to keep a company competitive. In government, paying secretaries without regard to their cost in the local job market destroys confidence in government's ability to match the efficiency of business. Eventually, elected officials will have to account for the pay of their secretaries and their plumbers. If the secretary earns premium pay in order to match the plumber's wage, private sector workers who pay the taxes will object. It is not possible, over the longer term, to have pockets of comparable worth in an otherwise competitive economy without problems.

Take the case of San Jose. It conducted a jobs study as the result of a strike over comparable worth. The study concluded that both librarians and electricians were worth $3,000 a month. In the local, competitive economy, however, librarians could be hired for much less while electricians in the area were paid more. The city must now pay electricians more than the study said they were "worth," while librarians are being paid above-market salaries. With victories like that, comparable worth will eventually fall of its own weight.

Behind all the arguments and the tactics of the comparable worth debate is the strong conviction that discrimination against women is a major factor in the labor market. But a careful look at female employment proves inconclusive on this point. Labor economists start by identifying known differentials on jobs and pay by sex, race, age, and occupational group. They weigh factors like intermittent and part-time work, interruptions for pregnancies, and other causes for lower pay for women. But because of the complexities in the job market there are always too many "other" or "unknown" factors of such analyses to explain the residual differential of lower pay for women. Yet, this inconclusive method of reductional analysis is at present the only "proof" of discrimination against women.

A recent article in a U.S. Labor Department journal by Janice Shack-Marquez, a federal economist, says, "Most of the studies of the pay disparity between men and women have been motivated by a desire to quantify the effects of discrimination in the labor market on women's earnings." Labor market discrimination, she notes, may be only one answer, of undetermined importance, in assessing women's lower pay. The pay difference, she says, is much smaller when narrowly-defined white collar jobs are compared for men and women than in broader studies. Ms. Shack-Marquez says "not enough is known" about individual earnings "to be confident that all the labor market variables in which men and women differ have been isolated."

No such caution animates the comparable worth advocates. Editors of a recent book *Comparable Worth and Wage Discrimination* . . . note that the authors, mostly women, represent a "broad spectrum" of views on the issue. Yet they agree that salary disparities between male- and female-dominated jobs "are based in large part on discrimination."

For the women's movement itself, comparable worth seems a very depressing course to take. To back the principle that women must be paid more because they are women implies a pessimism about the chances of full integration of women in the job market. If women can compete, this argument goes, they will; otherwise, they want to doctor the system so that the work they do gets more pay through government or judicial fiat.

Comparable worth advocates answer this argument in several ways, none fully cogent. First, they say, this competition of women in a men's job market will be enhanced if women in lower-paying jobs get the same pay as comparable men. Employers would then choose workers by merit, not gender. Second, the predominance of women in some low-paying jobs—retail clerking, secretarial and clerical work, child care and domestic work—has patterned so many women for so long that many are now too old to be retrained. Third, pay equity advocates say, these jobs are undervalued simply because women hold them. Why should women, who like to nurse or teach school, change jobs just to earn as much as men with comparable skills, education, and experience? Society is, in fact, subtly undervaluing jobs only because women perform them. And that, advocates say, is discrimination.

Correcting this discrimination will not bankrupt the country, proponents of comparable worth say, pointing to several cases where the system has been applied to government and private organizations. But these instances provide thin gruel to nourish the cause. While the only large-scale case, involving the state of Washington, is still in the courts, state taxpayers may have to pay over $1 billion if the suit prevails. The Washington state legislature's study of state jobs, which used the Willis scale, concluded that women's work was underpaid. Yet the governor's request for funds to implement the study was rejected in a budget crisis. The federal judge who heard the case decided that the state acted in bad faith by commissioning a study whose findings of pay discrimination were then not implemented. The state is certain to appeal the decision to the Supreme Court.

Even if the Washington state decision is sustained and the state government gets a huge bill for back wages, the case's impact on comparable worth remains unclear. Failure to pay, not the principles of comparable worth, are at issue here. Federal courts have, in several other cases, specifically excluded comparable worth from decisions about pay differences between men and women.

In a major decision in 1977 (*Christensen v. Iowa*), the Supreme Court cited the attempt to use the Civil Rights Act of 1964 as a basis for comparable worth. It rejected this approach saying: "We find nothing in the text and history of Title VII (of the Act) suggesting that Congress intended to abrogate the laws of supply and demand or other economic principles that determine wage rates for different kinds of work." Even in the 1981 *Gunther* case, cited most often by women as holding the door open for comparable worth actions, the Supreme Court said that the women prison guards' claim of lower pay because they were women "is not based on the controversial concept of 'comparable worth.' "

In order to make progress and to avoid another stalemate like the ERA, comparable worth advocates will have to either change the law or convince judges that existing laws require comparable worth interpretations. Neither the mood of the present Supreme Court, nor the explicit scorn of the Reagan administration is promising in this regard.

Over a dozen states have passed laws which refer to comparable worth, pay equity, or similar goals in their civil service systems, but most of these laws are too new or too vague to have established comparable worth up to now. Minnesota's 1982–83 laws on the subject were backed with an initial appropriation of $27 million to adjust state salaries. Until further studies are done, no one knows what the total cost to the state and its local governments, also covered, will be.

Comparable worth is like the parable of the golden egg. If its advocates insist on using political pressures to pay women in government more than wages in the private sector, cities and states will eventually react to increased costs by contracting much of "women's work" to the private sector.

In conclusion, if comparable worth seems such a mistaken solution for misconceived problems, here are several principles with which to insure that maximum benefits accrue to women in their search for true pay and job equity:

Not every difference between men and women in the job market comes from malevolent causes. Even if we reach the most perfect system of job access and pay for women, there may still be important differences in both the jobs they hold and what they earn. The values that women share may always be different from those of men. Anticipation of motherhood, its arrival, and its consequences will always affect women in the job market. Women's values, and the jobs they embody, are important for society and for the women who perform them, even when the pay is not high.

Economic rewards are not the only measure of job value for women or men. Many male-dominated jobs also pay less than others with lower investments of skills, education, and experience. The churches, the universities, art, and the government often pay less than business and industry. But pay, for these lesser-paid workers, is fortunately not the only consideration in their jobs.

Choosing motherhood may not be fully compatible with other career choices. This is such an old truth that it may *have* to be completely forgotten so we can learn it again. Yet many women know this before motherhood or shortly after. This fact of maternal life is not, in itself, unfair or a matter for the courts to handle. But motherhood should not bar the maximum participation a woman wants in the job marketplace. A genuine problem, worth some of the attention given to comparable worth, is how mothers of all ages can gain and hold such participation without sacrificing, jeopardizing, or postponing motherhood.

Comparable worth may have some benefits as an ideal if it leads toward better job integration. Even if most plumbers will always be men and most day-care workers women, society benefits when rigid job segregation by sex is softened. First, most women do not want to be shunted away, by gender, from certain jobs even if they choose other work. Second, men and women complement each other in social values, temperaments, and sensitivities. This relation may help and almost certainly does not hinder any workplace, even if not all jobs are interchangeable.

Women should consider more selective and specific approaches to better pay and job integration. In Colorado, nurses sought better wages through comparable worth action but lost in court. When they went on strike, however, they won. Job actions—whether in a single job, in one business or industry at a time, or nationwide—will probably command more attention and get more results in the long term than the murky concepts of comparable worth.

There will be no revolution in the workplace no matter what the strategy. There have been important changes this century in women's wages which have risen faster than men's since 1900, according to a recent Rand Corporation study. The sixty cents a woman earns today, on average, to a man's dollar, will rise to seventy-four cents by the end of the next decade. But the competing interests of blacks, Hispanics, and others who want to change the job market according to their legitimate grievances will prevent a clear field for women. Black women, for example, have now closed the wage gap with white women. Black men, however, hold many of the male-dominated blue collar jobs which comparable worth proponents cite as examples of unfairly high pay. Further, the private sector has so far largely ignored the comparable worth approach as a frothy concoction of no import. If state or court actions move toward serious implementation of the concept, a fierce reaction to the perceived threat against the free market will come. This assault against comparable worth could make the ERA debacle look mild by comparison. To avoid this course, more measured, more confident, and more reasonable goals are needed for women.

One unspoken premise of the comparable worth fight is resentment against the male domination of the political, social, and economic life of our society. However, the appropriate response to this male dominance is a realistic demand for fairness to women in the job market, not a casually conceived and marginally tenable idea like comparable worth.

33. The Comparable Worth Debate

Elaine Sorensen

In defense of comparable worth, Elaine Sorensen argues that the free market does not eliminate discrimination. Historically, it took new laws and court rulings to eliminate some of the most blatant discriminatory practices that prevailed in the labor market. She further argues that less than half of the sex- and race-based earning disparity between women and minorities and white men can be accounted for by differences in productivity-related characteristics such as the level of education or the willingness to choose a lower-paying job if it provides more flexible working hours. Responding to the objection that different jobs cannot be compared, Sorensen argues that all that comparable worth requires is the same job evaluation procedures currently used by management for different purposes.

Introduction

The U.S. Civil Rights Commission Chairman, Clarence Pendleton, denounced the concept as "the looniest idea since 'Looney Tunes.'" President Reagan called it "a cockamamie idea . . . [that] would destroy the basis of free enterprise." These men were referring to a strategy for rectifying economic inequities confronting women and minorities known as equal pay for comparable worth. Despite this opposition, comparable worth has gained considerable momentum during the past few years. Nearly every state government has taken initiative on this issue and at least fifteen have increased salaries for workers in occupations that have an over-representation of women or minorities. Numerous labor unions, feminist organizations, and the Democratic Party have also endorsed the idea.

As popular support for comparable worth policies has grown, so has its opposition. Conservative opponents of comparable worth argue that a comparable worth policy would undermine the "free market" system of wage

From *The Imperiled Economy Book II*, edited by Robert Cherry. Reprinted by permission.

determination, a system which they believe is above reproach both logically and legally. On the other hand, some progressive persons argue against a comparable worth strategy. They contend that it is divisive, pitting blue-collar and minority workers against their female co-workers. Furthermore, it is argued that comparable worth proposals do not reduce inequality and may even exacerbate it by increasing the salaries of skilled workers more than unskilled workers.

This essay will first introduce the concept of comparable worth. It will then survey the general objections to the concept and analyze their shortcomings.

Comparable Worth and Wage Discrimination

Comparable worth policies seek to counteract the persistent wage inequities that women and minorities experience in the labor market. White women's earnings relative to white men's earnings have remained disturbingly rigid during the past thirty years. In 1986, white women employed full-time still earned $.63 for every dollar that white men earned, the same ratio as in 1956 (U.S. Census 1987).

Although the earnings gap has improved slightly during this period for people of color, the earnings gap is greater for minority women than it is for white women (black women earn $.57 and Hispanic women earn $.53) and minority men still earn substantially less than white men (black men earn $.71 and Hispanic men earn $.65). Earnings increase with education for all workers, but women and minorities earn less than white men at every level of education. For example, women with four years of college education earn less on average than men who have not completed high school (black men with four years of college education earn about the same as white men who have completed high school).

Severe occupational segregation by sex and race also characterize the U.S. labor force. Nearly one out of three white women and one out of four women of color are employed as clerical workers. Another one-fourth of the white female work force is employed in service work and two professional classifications; teaching and nursing. Minority women are also heavily concentrated in service work (21 percent) and many work as machine operators (14 percent). Men of color are highly concentrated in different occupations than women and white men. For example, two out of three black men are employed in blue-collar and service work, and only one out of six are employed as managers or professionals. Within blue-collar work, 70 percent work as laborers and operators. One-fourth of white men, on the other hand, are employed as managers and professionals, and another one-fifth are employed as craft workers.

Proponents of comparable worth policies argue that extensive occupational segregation in the labor force contributes to the sex- and race-based earnings disparities that persist in the U.S. labor market. It allows firms to pay lower wages to workers in jobs with an over-representation of women and minorities. These jobs become identified as "women's work" or "minority men's work," and simply because of these labels firms pay workers less than they would if these jobs employed white men. For example, in the state of Washington a comparable worth study found that the job of licensed practical nurse was held primarily by women and that the job of correctional officer was dominated by men. It also found that these two jobs were equivalent with respect to the amount of knowledge, mental demands, accountability, and working conditions associated with the two jobs. However, in 1983, the state of Washington paid an entry level licensed practical nurse $985 per month while paying the correctional officer $1358 per month.

Proponents of comparable worth posit that if a single employer pays jobs with an over-representation of women or minorities less than jobs with an over-representation of white men, one that cannot be supported by corresponding differences in the requirements of the job, then the employer is guilty of sex- and race-based wage discrimination. The purpose of a comparable worth policy is to eliminate this type of discrimination. After it is implemented, wages for jobs with an over-representation of women or minorities will reflect job responsibilities, unencumbered by sexually or racially biased notions. Thus, in the state of Washington a comparable worth strategy would increase the salary of the licensed practical nurse to that received by comparable male dominated occupations such as that of correctional officer.

The Comparable Worth Debate

Conservative Arguments

Conservative opponents of comparable worth espouse three arguments against comparable worth policies all of which assume that the labor market is free and competitive: discrimination is not a major problem in today's labor market; the sex- and race-based earnings disparities are due to productivity differences between women (minorities) and men (whites); and jobs do not have intrinsic worth to a firm, their value is determined by supply and demand.

1. The Free Market Eliminates Discrimination

Conservative opponents of comparable worth argue that discrimination is not a principal factor contributing to the sex- and race-based earnings gaps. According to this view, a free market provides sufficient incentive to eliminate discrimination. In such a market, employers can not afford to discriminate against minority and female workers. If they did, an incentive would exist for some employer to hire them since discrimination would depress their market wage compared to that received by white men. With this cost advantage, the non-discriminating employer would outperform those who discriminate. Eventually, competitive forces would compel discriminating employers to discontinue such practices or lose their business, thus eliminating discrimination from the market.

Although in theory the free market ensures that employers do not discriminate, in fact, until the passage of the anti-discrimination laws of the early 1960s, the U.S. labor market was characterized by blatant discriminatory practices and institutions. Employers could pay women less than men for exactly the same work and they could refuse to hire blacks and other minorities, simply because of their race. These types of blatant discriminatory practices did not wither away under competitive pressures. Instead, legal prohibition was necessary to eliminate them. Thus, federal policies and court rulings have clearly reduced the discriminatory practices that are deeply imbedded in American labor markets. Unfortunately, however, these changes have not eliminated all types of discrimination. Proponents of comparable worth have identified yet another pervasive discriminatory pattern that causes workers in female or minority dominated jobs to receive less than they would if these jobs were dominated by white men. This form of discrimination deserves judicial and legislative attention, just as other forms have received.

2. Pay Gaps Are Caused by Productivity and Labor Supply Differences

Conservative opponents of comparable worth argue that women and minorities have different supply characteristics than white men and these differences explain their low relative earnings. They claim that women expect to drop-out of the labor force while raising their children, and thus choose low paying occupations that do not impose severe wage penalties for discontinuous labor market behavior. They also select occupations that are close to home, have convenient hours, and do not require overtime, to accommodate their family responsibilities. These choices limit women's labor supply and reduce their earnings potential. Conservative opponents of comparable worth also claim that minorities receive less education and poorer quality education, on average, than whites. This limits the types of occupations available to minorities and thus reduces their relative earnings.

Empirical research, however, has repeatedly shown that less than half of the sex- and race-based earnings disparities can be accounted for by differences in productivity-related characteristics between women and minorities and white men. In other words, differences in labor force attachment between women and men and differences in education between minorities and whites do not explain most of the earnings gaps. Consequently, existing research shows that even if women and minority men had identical labor market behavior as white men, they would still earn considerably less than white men. Comparable worth proposals attempt to eliminate that portion of the pay gaps which is unaccounted for by productivity-related differences, and which would remain even if women and minority men had identical labor force behavior to white men's.

In addition, an explanation of the earnings gap between women (minorities) and men (whites) that focuses upon productivity differences ignores the dramatic changes that have taken place in the productivity characteristics of women and minorities over the past thirty years. Between 1955 and 1977, the work life expectancy of a 20 year old woman increased from 14.5 to 26 years. In contrast, the work life expectancy of a 20 year old man drifted down from 41 to 37 years (Smith 1982). Thus, the number of years that women work in the labor force has clearly increased relative to men. Women are also marrying later, having fewer children and heading more of their own households than 30 years ago. All of these changes suggest an increased attachment to the labor force among women and yet their relative earnings have not improved.

The educational attainment of black men has also dramatically increased during the past 25 years. In 1962, white men in the civilian labor force had completed an average of 12.1 years of education; black men had completed an average of 9.0 years. By 1980, this education gap had almost disappeared: white men's average educational attainment increased to 12.7 years and black men's increased to 12.3 years (U.S. Department of Labor 1982). Yet, black men working full-time still earn 71 percent as much as white men. Thus, the productivity characteristics of women and minorities have changed, yet their pay persistently lags behind that of white men.

3. Different Jobs Can Not Be Compared

Opponents of comparable worth have expressed concern over the comparisons of dissimilar jobs that are made by comparable worth proposals. Can the job of nurse be compared to that of a tree trimmer to assess the relative worth of these jobs? They contend that job evaluations, the method used by comparable worth proposals to compare different jobs, are not an objective measure of a job's worth; the only objective measure is the salary that an employer must pay to attract workers to the job. Such a salary is determined by competitive market forces of supply and demand, forces external to an individual firm.

Advocates of comparable worth argue that wages are not exclusively determined by market forces; other factors, such as discrimination, also play a role. Furthermore, market forces themselves reflect and reproduce discrimination. This allows employers to pay workers in jobs with an over-representation of women and minorities less than if those jobs were held by white men. Advocates of comparable worth need a technique to measure the extent to which salaries are discriminatorily depressed in jobs with an over-representation of women and minorities.

Most comparable worth proposals have used an a priori factor-point job evaluation plan to assess jobs, the most commonly used plan in the United States. It consists of a set of factors and weights which are expected to re-

flect the requirements of a job. The factors generally fall into four broad categories: skill, effort, responsibility, and working conditions. Weights are applied to each factor and indicate their relative importance. Once the weights and factors are chosen, a basic set of procedures are followed to evaluate jobs. First, questionnaires specifically designed for the factor-point plan are completed. Based upon this information, jobs are evaluated on each factor. Jobs are assigned a level of points that is commensurate with the amount of each factor required to perform the job. These factor scores are summed for each job to produce a total score, which are used to establish an internal ranking of jobs according to their worth to the firm.

Comparable worth proposals do not alter the basic procedures of a job evaluation plan; they use the same techniques that management has traditionally used to evaluate jobs. The differences between comparable worth proposals and management's traditional practices do not take place during the evaluation of jobs, but during the determination of wages.

Management uses job evaluation plans as an instrument in wage determination, but they typically limit its use to comparisons within so-called job families. Job families consist of jobs that have similar skill requirements or are performed in the same division of the firm. Wages from the external labor market are pegged to a few occupations within each job family. Management determines the occupational salaries of other jobs within each job family by comparing job evaluation scores to those of the few occupations with external wages. For example, suppose the prevailing wage for a clerk/typist is $1000 per month, then all jobs within the clerk/typist job family would be adjusted around that salary according to their job evaluation score in comparison to that of the clerk/typist. Thus, the prevailing wages of other occupations outside of the clerk/typist job family, such as janitor or truck driver, would not enter into the determination of wages for this job family.

Comparable worth studies use the results of a job evaluation to examine a firm's existing salary practices for all jobs, regardless of their job family. Rather than using external wages for certain occupations, they use the salaries received by jobs dominated by white men as their set of comparison occupations. Salary comparisons are made between jobs with an over-representation of women or minorities and jobs that are dominated by white men. If the former salaries are less than the latter and the jobs are deemed comparable according to the criteria established by the job evaluation plan, then a comparable worth policy would increase the salaries of jobs with an over-representation of women or minorities.

Opponents of comparable worth argue that job evaluations can not be used in this way. Yet, numerous jurisdictions have already conducted such studies. Unfortunately, opponents of comparable worth tend to think that job evaluations are only capable of fulfilling their original purpose, which was to justify and perpetuate the existing wage structure. Clearly, comparable worth proposals alter the existing wage structure, by eliminating sex- and race-based wage discrimination. However, they do so by applying the basic procedures used by management to evaluate jobs.

Progressive Arguments

The progressive concerns regarding comparable worth legislation have focused upon its possible divisive nature and its reinforcement of existing salary practices.

Comparable Worth Would Lower Male Wages

Some have feared that comparable worth will benefit women at the expense of men, hindering attempts to unify male and female workers. Yet, in no instance has comparable worth been introduced in a form which has resulted in wage cuts for male workers. It is generally accepted by the courts and Congress that the elimination of wage discrimination is best accomplished by increasing the wages of those discriminated against, not by decreasing the wages of those unaffected by discrimination. Federal legislation mandating a comparable worth study of Federal pay practices (H.R. 5680-Oakar, 1984) specifically prohibited reducing anyone's pay because of this legislation. Similar prohibitions have been included in many state and local comparable worth proposals as well.

Employers may suggest lowering male salaries in particular jobs considered "overvalued" or they may suggest lower across-the-board increases for all workers in order to pay for higher wages in female dominated jobs. Advocates of comparable worth have consistently fought against these employer suggestions. For example, in May 1984, Donald Devine, then director of the federal Office of Personnel Management, held a private meeting of union officials representing federal employees and attempted to convince them that the wages of blue-collar workers would be lowered if a comparable worth bill before the House was enacted. The union officials were not convinced by Devine's arguments. They later testified before the Subcommittee on Compensation and Employee Benefits that unions were long familiar with employer "divide and conquer" tactics.

A policy of equal pay for comparable worth can be seen as a threat to those who are trying to maintain their *relative* wage or it can be seen as an egalitarian policy, one that can increase the likelihood that all workers receive a fair wage. As an egalitarian policy comparable worth can unite workers in their struggle with employers for decent wages for all workers. Advocates of comparable worth will most likely continue to fight against suggestions of lowering male wages to pay for comparable worth since this approach could undermine a general consensus for the policy.

Comparable Worth Will Decrease the Earnings of Minority Males

Some progressive and conservative opponents of comparable worth have argued that its implementation will decrease the earnings of men of color. This position was stated quite forcefully by Michael J. Horowitz, counsel to the director of the Office of Management and Budget, when he remarked that: "There is nothing that the Reagan Administration has done that holds as much long-term threat to the black community as comparable worth. The maintenance man will be paid less so the librarian can be paid more" (*New York Times*, 22 January, 1984).

This position ignores the wage discrimination that minority males experience due to race- and sex-based occupational segregation. Many public sector comparable worth studies have shown that a disproportionate number of minority males work in female or minority dominated jobs. Furthermore, they earn less than workers in comparable white male dominated jobs (NCPE 1987). A number of states, including New Jersey, New York, and Wisconsin, have already begun increasing the salaries of workers who are employed in minority or female dominated jobs. Clearly, additional research is needed in this area, but it would be rather surprising to find that occupational segregation by race does not contribute to the earnings disparities that minority workers face.

Comparable Worth Justifies Existing Wage Inequities

It is sometimes argued that comparable worth does not sufficiently challenge the present hierarchical wage structure. According to one opponent of comparable worth, "advocates of comparable worth don't want to achieve equality" (Cowley 1984:57). Instead, comparable worth will "enshrine" the existing earnings inequalities "by giving them the force of law" (Cowley 1984:57). Similar sentiments were echoed by a more sympathetic author when she stated that comparable worth "can have only a modest effect on the overall degree of inequality because it does not attack all forms of inequality" (Feldberg 1984:323). She later added that comparable worth "does not directly challenge the concept of a [wage] hierarchy; in fact, its insistence that jobs be evaluated implies a hierarchy" (Feldberg 1984:323).

Comparable worth proposals attack the existing hierarchical wage structure by arguing that it reflects wage discrimination against workers in female and minority dominated jobs and that this source of wage inequality should be eliminated. They do, however, accept a wage hierarchy as long as that hierarchy reflects job requirements and not the predominant sex or race of the worker in the occupation. In fact, job requirements are the criteria used to measure the extent to which female or minority dominated jobs are underpaid relative to comparable white male dominated jobs.

Some analysts argue that job requirements are the traditional criteria used by firms to justify wage inequity and thus its use by comparable worth proposals reinforces existing wage inequities. However, one of the most important findings of comparable worth studies is that employers have *not* applied this criteria uniformly to all occupations. Instead, they have applied a different set of standards for occupations with a disproportionate number of women or minorities than that used for occupations with a disproportionate number of white men.

Using job requirements to determine the extent of wage inequities does not imply that so-called unskilled female or minority dominated jobs will be unaffected by comparable worth proposals, in fact, quite the contrary. The largest disparities between current salaries and proposed comparable worth salaries typically occur among the lowest paid and supposedly unskilled female dominated occupations. For example, the occupational categories with the largest comparable worth pay disparities in the state of Washington were: telephone operator, laundry worker, nurse's assistant, general clerk, and secretary, three of which were the least skilled female dominated occupations examined.

It is true that comparable worth proposals would not cure all forms of inequality in U.S. society. However, they would reduce a serious source of earnings inequality in the United States, namely sex- and race-based wage discrimination against women and minorities. It would accomplish this by increasing the salaries of jobs with an over-representation of women or minorities, all of which tend to earn *less* than the average white male. For example, the highest paid female dominated job in the United States is the job of registered nurse and it pays less than the average salary received by white men. Thus, if the ideal is greater income equality, a comparable worth policy would certainly move the United States towards that goal.

Conclusion

The demand for comparable worth has emerged at an opportune moment. Many people have become increasingly aware of a disturbing trend towards greater inequality in the distribution of income in the United States. It is argued that the tax and budgets cuts under the Reagan Administration, as well as the relative decline of the smoke stack industries and the absolute rise in the service sector, have contributed to this trend. An increase in the poverty rate has also been noted. By 1986, 13.6 percent of the population lived in poverty, up from 11.4 percent in 1978. Women represent two-thirds of the poor adult population, while half of the families living in poverty are headed by women, the fastest growing type in the country. A comparable worth policy would increase the salaries of low paying traditionally female and minority dominated occupations within the service sector. Thus a comparable worth policy could alleviate the unfortunate trend toward greater income inequality.

References

Cowley, Geoffrey. 1984. Comparable Worth: Another Terrible Idea. *Washington Monthly* 15:52–57.

Feldberg, Roslyn L. 1984. Comparable Worth: Toward Theory and Practice in the United States. *Signs: Journal of Women in Culture and Society* 10(2):311–328.

Gregory, R. G. and R. C. Duncan. 1981. Segmented Labor Market Theories and the Australian Experience of Equal Pay for Women. *Journal of Post Keynesian Economics* III(3):403–428.

National Committee on Pay Equity (NCPE). 1987. *Pay Equity: An Issue of Race, Ethnicity, and Sex.* Washington, D.C.: NCPE.

Smith, Shirley J. 1982. New Worklife Estimates Reflect Changing Profile of Labor Force. *Monthly Labor Review* (March):15–20.

Sorensen, Elaine. 1986. Implementing Comparable Worth: A Survey of Recent Job Evaluation Studies. *American Economic Review* 76(2):364–368.

Treiman, Donald J. and Heidi I. Hartmann (ed.). 1981. *Women, Work, and Wages: Equal Pay for Jobs of Equal Value.* Washington, D.C.: National Academy Press.

U.S. Bureau of the Census. 1987. Money Income and Poverty Status of Families and Persons in the United States: 1986. *Current Population Reports.* P-60 Series, No. 157. Washington, D.C.: U.S. Government Printing Office.

U.S. Department of Labor. 1982. *Employment and Training Report of the President.* Washington, D.C.: U.S. Government Printing Office.

34. *City of Richmond v. Croson*

Supreme Court of the United States

The issue before the Supreme Court is whether the City of Richmond's plan requiring prime contractors awarded city construction contracts to subcontract at least 30 percent of the dollar amount of each contract to one or more "Minority Business Enterprises" was in violation of the equal protection clause of the Fourteenth Amendment. Justice O'Connor in delivering the opinion of the Court argued that the City of Richmond's plan was not supported by the type of evidence of past discrimination in the city's construction industry that would authorize a race-based relief under the equal protection clause of the Fourteenth Amendment. Justice Marshall, with Justices Brennan and Blackmun concurring, argued that the national evidence of discrimination against minority contractors and the local evidence that only .67 percent of the dollar value of local construction contracts went to minority contractors, together with the Supreme Court's own *Fullilove* v. *Klutznick* decision, which allowed a 10 percent set-aside of federal contracts for minority contractors, justified the city's adoption of the plan.

Justice O'Connor announced the judgment of the Court. . . .

On April 11, 1983, the Richmond City Council adopted the Minority Business Utilization Plan (the Plan). The Plan required prime contractors to whom the city awarded construction contracts to subcontract at least 30% of the dollar amount of the contract to one or more Minority Business Enterprises (MBEs). . . . The 30% set-aside did not apply to city contracts awarded to minority-owned prime contractors. . . .

The Plan defined an MBE as "[a] business at least fifty-one (51) percent of which is owned and controlled . . . by minority group members." . . . "Minority group members" were defined as "[c]itizens of the United States who are Blacks, Spanish-speaking, Orientals, Indians, Eskimos, or Aleuts." . . . There was no geographic limit to the Plan; an otherwise qualified MBE from anywhere in the United States could avail itself of the 30% set-aside. The Plan declared that it was "remedial" in nature, and enacted "for the purpose of promoting wider participation by minority business enterprises in the construction of public projects." . . . The Plan expired on June 30,

1988, and was in effect for approximately five years. . . .

The Plan authorized the Director of the Department of General Services to promulgate rules which "shall allow waivers in those individual situations where a contractor can prove to the satisfaction of the director that the requirements herein cannot be achieved." . . . To this end, the Director promulgated Contract Clauses, Minority Business Utilization Plan. . . . Section D of these rules provided:

> No partial or complete waiver of the foregoing [30% set-aside] requirement shall be granted by the city other than in exceptional circumstances. To justify a waiver, it must be shown that every feasible attempt has been made to comply, and it must be demonstrated that sufficient, relevant, qualified Minority Business Enterprises . . . are unavailable or unwilling to participate in the contract to enable meeting the 30% MBE goal. . . .

The Director also promulgated "purchasing procedures" to be followed in the letting of city contracts in accordance with the Plan. . . . Bidders on city construction contracts were provided with a "Minority Business Utilization Plan Commitment Form." . . . Within 10 days of the opening of the bids, the lowest otherwise responsive bidder was required to submit a commitment form naming the MBEs to be used on the contract and the percentage of the total contract price awarded to the minority firm or firms. The prime contractor's commitment form or request for a waiver of the 30% set-aside was then referred to the city Human Relations Commission (HRC). The HRC verified that the MBEs named in the commitment form were in fact minority owned, and then either approved the commitment form or made a recommendation regarding the prime contractor's request for a partial or complete waiver of the 30% set-aside. . . . The Director of General Services made the final determination on compliance with the set-aside provisions or the propriety of granting a waiver. . . . His discretion in this regard appears to have been plenary. There was no direct administrative appeal from the Director's denial of a waiver. Once a contract had been awarded to another firm a bidder denied an award for failure to comply with the MBE requirements had a general right of protest under Richmond procurement policies. . . .

The Plan was adopted by the Richmond City Council after a public hearing. . . . Seven members of the public spoke to the merits of the ordinance: five were in opposition, two in favor. Proponents of the set-aside provision relied on a study which indicated that, while the general population of Richmond was 50% black, only .67% of the city's prime construction contracts had been awarded to minority businesses in the 5-year period from 1978 to 1983. It was also established that a variety of contractors' associations, whose representatives appeared in opposition to the ordinance, had virtually no minority businesses within their membership. . . . The city's legal counsel indicated his view that the ordinance was constitutional under this Court's decision in *Fullilove v. Klutznick,* . . . Councilperson Marsh, a proponent of the ordinance, made the following statement:

There is some information, however, that I want to make sure that we put in the record. I have been practicing law in

this community since 1961, and I am familiar with the practices in the construction industry in this area, in the State, and around the nation. And I can say without equivocation, that the general conduct of the construction industry in this area, and the State, and around the nation, is one in which race discrimination and exclusion on the basis of race is widespread. . . .

There was no direct evidence of race discrimination on the part of the city in letting contracts or any evidence that the city's prime contractors had discriminated against minority-owned subcontractors. . . . ("[The public witnesses] indicated that the minority contractors were just not available. There wasn't a one that gave any indication that a minority contractor would not have an opportunity, if he were available").

Opponents of the ordinance questioned both its wisdom and its legality. They argued that a disparity between minorities in the population of Richmond and the number of prime contracts awarded to MBEs had little probative value in establishing discrimination in the construction industry. . . . Representatives of various contractors' associations questioned whether there were enough MBEs in the Richmond area to satisfy the 30% set-aside requirement. . . . Mr. Murphy noted that only 4.7% of all construction firms in the United States were minority owned and that 41% of these were located in California, New York, Illinois, Florida, and Hawaii. He predicted that the ordinance would thus lead to a windfall for the few minority firms in Richmond. . . . Councilperson Gillespie indicated his concern that many local labor jobs, held by both blacks and whites, would be lost because the ordinance put no geographic limit on the MBEs eligible for the 30% set-aside. . . . Some of the representatives of the local contractors' organizations indicated that they did not discriminate on the basis of race and were in fact actively seeking out minority members. . . . ("The company I work for belonged to all these [contractors'] organizations. Nobody that I know of, black, Puerto Rican or any minority, has ever been turned down. They're actually sought after to join, to become part of us"); see also *id.*, at 20 (statement of Mr. Watts). Councilperson Gillespie expressed his concern about the legality of the Plan, and asked that a vote be delayed pending consultation with outside counsel. His suggestion was rejected, and the ordinance was enacted by a vote of six to two, with councilmember Gillespie abstaining. . . .

We think it clear that the factual predicate offered in support of the Richmond Plan suffers from the same two defects identified as fatal in *Wygant.* The District Court found the city council's "findings sufficient to ensure that, in adopting the Plan, it was remedying the present effects of past discrimination in the *construction industry.*" . . . Like the "role model" theory employed in *Wygant,* a generalized assertion that there has been past discrimination in an entire industry provides no guidance for a legislative body to determine the precise scope of the injury it seeks to remedy. It "has no logical stopping point." . . . "Relief" for such an ill-defined wrong could extend until the percentage of public contracts awarded to MBEs in Richmond mirrored the percentage of minorities in the population as a whole.

Appellant argues that it is attempting to remedy various forms of past discrimination that are alleged to be responsible for the small number of minority businesses in the local contracting industry. Among these the city cites the exclusion of blacks from skilled construction trade unions and training programs. This past discrimination has prevented them "from following the traditional path from laborer to entrepreneur." . . . The city also lists a host of nonracial factors which would seem to face a member of any racial group attempting to establish a new business enterprise, such as deficiencies in working capital, inability to meet bonding requirements, unfamiliarity with bidding procedures, and disability caused by an inadequate track record. . . .

While there is no doubt that the sorry history of both private and public discrimination in this country has contributed to a lack of opportunities for black entrepreneurs, this observation, standing alone, cannot justify a rigid racial quota in the awarding of public contracts in Richmond, Virginia. Like the claim that discrimination in primary and secondary schooling justifies a rigid racial preference in medical school admissions, an amorphous claim that there has been past discrimination in a particular industry cannot justify the use of an unyielding racial quota.

It is sheer speculation how many minority firms there would be in Richmond absent past societal discrimination, just as it was sheer speculation how many minority medical students would have been admitted to the medical school at Davis absent past discrimination in educational opportunities. Defining these sorts of injuries as "identified discrimination" would give local governments license to create a patchwork of racial preferences based on statistical generalizations about any particular field of endeavor.

These defects are readily apparent in this case. The 30% quota cannot in any realistic sense be tied to any injury suffered by anyone. The District Court relied upon five predicate "facts" in reaching its conclusion that there was an adequate basis for the 30% quota: (1) the ordinance declares itself to be remedial; (2) several proponents of the measure stated their views that there had been past discrimination in the construction industry; (3) minority businesses received .67% of prime contracts from the city while minorities constituted 50% of the city's population; (4) there were very few minority contractors in local and state contractors' associations; and (5) in 1977, Congress made a determination that the effects of past discrimination had stifled minority participation in the construction industry. . . .

None of these "findings," singly or together, provide the city of Richmond with a "strong basis in evidence for its conclusion that remedial action was necessary." . . . There is nothing approaching a prima facie case of a constitutional or statutory violation by *anyone* in the Richmond construction industry. . . .

The District Court accorded great weight to the fact that the city council designated the Plan as "remedial." But the mere recitation of a "benign" or legitimate purpose for a racial classification, is entitled to little or no weight. . . . Racial classifications are suspect, and that means that simple legislative assurances of good intention cannot suffice.

The District Court also relied on the highly conclusionary statement of a proponent of the Plan that there was racial discrimination in the construction industry "in this area, and the State, and around the nation." . . . It also noted that the city manager had related his view that racial discrimination still plagued the construction industry in his home city of Pittsburg. . . . These statements are of little probative value in establishing identified discrimination in the Richmond construction industry. The fact-finding process of legislative bodies is generally entitled to a presumption of regularity and deferential review by the judiciary. . . . But when a legislative body chooses to employ a suspect classification, it cannot rest upon a generalized assertion as to the classification's relevance to its goals. . . . A governmental actor cannot render race a legitimate proxy for a particular condition merely by declaring that the condition exists. . . . The history of racial classifications in this country suggests that blind judicial deference to legislative or executive pronouncements of necessity has no place in equal protection analysis. . . .

Reliance on the disparity between the number of prime contracts awarded to minority firms and the minority population of the city of Richmond is similarly misplaced. There is no doubt that "[w]here gross statistical disparities can be shown, they alone in a proper case may constitute prima facie proof of a pattern or practice of discrimination" under Title VII. . . . But it is equally clear that "[w]hen special qualifications are required to fill particular jobs, comparisons to the general population (rather than to the smaller group of individuals who possess the necessary qualifications) may have little probative value." . . .

In the employment context, we have recognized that for certain entry level positions or positions requiring minimal training, statistical comparisons of the racial composition of an employer's workforce to the racial composition of the relevant population may be probative of a pattern of discrimination. . . . But where special qualifications are necessary, the relevant statistical pool for purposes of demonstrating discriminatory exclusion must

be the number of minorities qualified to undertake the particular task. . . .

In this case, the city does not even know how many MBEs in the relevant market are qualified to undertake prime or subcontracting work in public construction projects. . . . Nor does the city know what percentage of total city construction dollars minority firms now receive as subcontractors on prime contracts let by the city.

To a large extent, the set-aside of subcontracting dollars seems to rest on the unsupported assumption that white prime contractors simply will not hire minority firms. . . . Indeed, there is evidence in this record that overall minority participation in city contracts in Richmond is seven to eight percent, and that minority contractor participation in Community Block Development Grant *construction* projects is 17% to 22%. . . . Without any information on minority participation in subcontracting, it is quite simply impossible to evaluate overall minority representation in the city's construction expenditures.

The city and the District Court also relied on evidence that MBE membership in local contractors' associations was extremely low. Again, standing alone this evidence is not probative of any discrimination in the local construction industry. There are numerous explanations for this dearth of minority participation, including past societal discrimination in education and economic opportunities as well as both black and white career and entrepreneurial choices. Blacks may be disproportionately attracted to industries other than construction. See The State of Small Business: A Report of the President Transmitted to the Congress 201 (1986) ("Relative to the distribution of all businesses, black-owned businesses are more than proportionally represented in the transportation industry, but considerably less than proportionally represented in the wholesale trade, manufacturing, and finance industries"). The mere fact that black membership in these trade organizations is low, standing alone, cannot establish a prima facie case of discrimination. . . .

For low minority membership in these associations to be relevant, the city would have to link it to the number of local MBEs eligible for membership. If the statistical disparity between eligible MBEs and MBE membership were great enough, an inference of discriminatory exclusion could arise. In such a case, the city would have a compelling interest in preventing its tax dollars from assisting these organizations in maintaining a racially segregated construction market. . . .

Finally, the city and the District Court relied on Congress' finding in connection with the set-aside approved in *Fullilove* that there had been nationwide discrimination in the construction industry. The probative value of these findings for demonstrating the existence of discrimination in Richmond is extremely limited. By its inclusion of a waiver procedure in the national program addressed in *Fullilove*, Congress explicitly recognized that the scope of the problem would vary from market area to market area. . . .

Moreover, as noted above, Congress was exercising its powers under § 5 of the Fourteenth Amendment in making a finding that past discrimination would cause federal funds to be distributed in a manner which reinforced prior patterns of discrimination. While the States and their subdivisions may take remedial action when they possess evidence that their own spending practices are exacerbating a pattern of prior discrimination, they must identify that discrimination, public or private, with some specificity before they may use race-conscious relief. Congress has made national findings that there has been societal discrimination in a host of fields. If all a state or local government need do is find a congressional report on the subject to enact a set-aside program, the constraints of the Equal Protection Clause will, in effect, have been rendered a nullity. . . .

Justice Marshall apparently views the requirement that Richmond identify the discrimination it seeks to remedy in its own jurisdiction as a mere administrative headache, an "onerous documentary obligatio[n]." . . . We cannot agree. In this regard, we are in accord with Justice Stevens' observation in *Fullilove*, that "[b]ecause racial characteristics so seldom provide a relevant basis for disparate treatment, and because classifications based on race are potentially so harmful to the entire body politic, it is especially important that the reasons for any such classification be clearly

identified and unquestionably legitimate." . . . The "evidence" relied upon by the dissent, the history of school desegregation in Richmond and numerous congressional reports, does little to define the scope of any injury to minority contractors in Richmond or the necessary remedy. The factors relied upon by the dissent could justify a preference of any size or duration.

Moreover, Justice Marshall's suggestion that findings of discrimination may be "shared" from jurisdiction to jurisdiction in the same manner as information concerning zoning and property values is unprecedented. . . . We have never approved the extrapolation of discrimination in one jurisdiction from the experience of another. . . . ("Disparate treatment of white and Negro students occurred within the Detroit school system, and not elsewhere, and on this record the remedy must be limited to that system").

In sum, none of the evidence presented by the city points to any identified discrimination in the Richmond construction industry. We, therefore, hold that the city has failed to demonstrate a compelling interest in apportioning public contracting opportunities on the basis of race. To accept Richmond's claim that past societal discrimination alone can serve as the basis for rigid racial preferences would be to open the door to competing claims for "remedial relief" for every disadvantaged group. The dream of a Nation of equal citizens in a society where race is irrelevant to personal opportunity and achievement would be lost in a mosaic of shifting preferences based on inherently unmeasurable claims of past wrongs. "Courts would be asked to evaluate the extent of the prejudice and consequent harm suffered by various minority groups. Those whose societal injury is thought to exceed some arbitrary level of tolerability then would be entitled to preferential classifications. . . ." . . . We think such a result would be contrary to both the letter and spirit of a constitutional provision whose central command is equality. . . .

Justice Marshall, with whom Justice Brennan and Justice Blackmun join, dissenting.

It is a welcome symbol of racial progress

when the former capital of the Confederacy acts forthrightly to confront the effects of racial discrimination in its midst. In my view, nothing in the Constitution can be construed to prevent Richmond, Virginia, from allocating a portion of its contracting dollars for businesses owned or controlled by members of minority groups. Indeed, Richmond's set-aside program is indistinguishable in all meaningful respects from—and in fact was patterned upon—the federal set-aside plan which this Court upheld in *Fullilove v. Klutznick*, . . .

A majority of this Court holds today, however, that the Equal Protection Clause of the Fourteenth Amendment blocks Richmond's initiative. The essence of the majority's position is that Richmond has failed to catalogue adequate findings to prove that past discrimination has impeded minorities from joining or participating fully in Richmond's construction contracting industry. I find deep irony in second-guessing Richmond's judgment on this point. As much as any municipality in the United States, Richmond knows what racial discrimination is; a century of decisions by this and other federal courts has richly documented the city's disgraceful history of public and private racial discrimination. In any event, the Richmond City Council *has* supported its determination that minorities have been wrongly excluded from local construction contracting. Its proof includes statistics showing that minority-owned businesses have received virtually no city contracting dollars and rarely if ever belonged to area trade associations; testimony by municipal officials that discrimination has been widespread in the local construction industry; and the same exhaustive and widely publicized federal studies relied on in *Fullilove*, studies which showed that pervasive discrimination in the Nation's tight-knit construction industry had operated to exclude minorities from public contracting. These are precisely the types of statistical and testimonial evidence which, until today, this Court had credited in cases approving of race-conscious measures designed to remedy past discrimination.

More fundamentally, today's decision marks a deliberate and giant step backward in this Court's affirmative action jurisprudence.

Cynical of one municipality's attempt to redress the effects of past racial discrimination in a particular industry, the majority launches a grapeshot attack on race-conscious remedies in general. The majority's unnecessary pronouncements will inevitably discourage or prevent governmental entities, particularly States and localities, from acting to rectify the scourge of past discrimination. This is the harsh reality of the majority's decision, but it is not the Constitution's command.

As an initial matter, the majority takes an exceedingly myopic view of the factual predicate on which the Richmond City Council relied when it passed the Minority Business Utilization Plan. The majority analyzes Richmond's initiative as if it were based solely upon the facts about local construction and contracting practices adduced during the City Council session at which the measure was enacted. . . . In so doing, the majority downplays the fact that the City Council had before it a rich trove of evidence that discrimination in the Nation's construction industry had seriously impaired the competitive position of businesses owned or controlled by members of minority groups. It is only against this backdrop of documented national discrimination, however, that the local evidence adduced by Richmond can be properly understood. The majority's refusal to recognize that Richmond has proven itself no exception to the dismaying pattern of national exclusion which Congress so painstakingly identified infects its entire analysis of this case.

Six years before Richmond acted, Congress passed, and the President signed, the Public Works Employment Act of 1977, . . . a measure which appropriated $4 billion in federal grants to state and local governments for use in public works projects. Section 103(f)(2) of the Act was a minority business set-aside provision. It required state or local grantees to use 10% of their federal grants to procure services or supplies from businesses owned or controlled by members of statutorily identified minority groups, absent an administrative waiver. In 1980, in *Fullilove*, . . . this Court upheld the validity of this federal set-aside. Chief Justice Burger's opinion noted the importance of overcoming those "criteria, methods, or practices thought by Congress to have the effect of defeating, or substantially impairing, access by the minority business community to public funds made available by congressional appropriations." . . . Finding the set-aside provision properly tailored to this goal, the plurality concluded that the program was valid under either strict or intermediate scrutiny. . . .

The congressional program upheld in *Fullilove* was based upon an array of congressional and agency studies which documented the powerful influence of racially exclusionary practices in the business world. A 1975 report by the House Committee on Small Business concluded:

The effects of past inequities stemming from racial prejudice have not remained in the past. The Congress has recognized the reality that past discriminatory practices have, to some degree, adversely affected our present economic system.

'While minority persons comprise about 16 percent of the Nation's population, of the 13 million businesses in the United States, only 382,000, or approximately 3.0 percent, are owned by minority individuals. The most recent data from the Department of Commerce also indicates that the gross receipts of all businesses in this country totals about $2,540.8 billion, and of this amount only $16.6 billion, or about 0.65 percent was realized by minority business concerns.

These statistics are not the result of random chance. *The presumption must be made that past discriminatory systems have resulted in present economic inequities.*' . . .

A 1977 Report by the same Committee concluded:

'[O]ver the years, there has developed a business system which has traditionally excluded measurable minority participation. In the past more than the present, this system of conducting business transactions overtly precluded minority input. Currently, we more often encounter a

business system which is racially neutral on its face, but because of past overt social and economic discrimination is presently operating, in effect, to perpetuate these past inequities. Minorities, until recently, have not participated to any measurable extent, in our total business system generally, or in the construction industry in particular.' . . .

Congress further found that minorities seeking initial public contracting assignments often faced immense entry barriers which did not confront experienced nonminority contractors. A report submitted to Congress in 1975 by the United States Commission on Civil Rights, for example, described the way in which fledgling minority-owned businesses were hampered by "deficiencies in working capital, inability to meet bonding requirements, disabilities caused by an inadequate 'track record,' lack of awareness of bidding opportunities, unfamiliarity with bidding procedures, preselection before the formal advertising process, and the exercise of discretion by government procurement officers to disfavor minority businesses." . . .

Thus, as of 1977, there was "abundant evidence" in the public domain "that minority businesses ha[d] been denied effective participation in public contracting opportunities by procurement practices that perpetuated the effects of prior discrimination." . . . Significantly, this evidence demonstrated that discrimination had prevented existing or nascent minority-owned businesses from obtaining not only federal contracting assignments, but state and local ones as well. . . .

The members of the Richmond City Council were well aware of these exhaustive congressional findings, a point the majority, tellingly, elides. The transcript of the session at which the Council enacted the local set-aside initiative contains numerous references to the 6-year-old congressional set-aside program, to the evidence of nationwide discrimination barriers described above, and to the *Fullilove* decision itself. . . .

The City Council's members also heard testimony that, although minority groups made up half of the city's population, only

.67% of the $24.6 million which Richmond had dispensed in construction contracts during the five years ending in March 1983 had gone to minority-owned prime contractors. . . . They heard testimony that the major Richmond area construction trade associations had virtually no minorities among their hundreds of members. Finally, they heard testimony from city officials as to the exclusionary history of the local construction industry. As the District Court noted, not a single person who testified before the City Council denied that discrimination in Richmond's construction industry had been widespread. . . . So long as one views Richmond's local evidence of discrimination against the backdrop of systematic nationwide racial discrimination which Congress had so painstakingly identified in this very industry, this case is readily resolved.

The majority is wrong to trivialize the continuing impact of government acceptance or use of private institutions or structures once wrought by discrimination. When government channels all its contracting funds to a white-dominated community of established contractors whose racial homogeneity is the product of private discrimination, it does more than place its imprimatur on the practices which forged and which continue to define that community. It also provides a measurable boost to those economic entities that have thrived within it, while denying important economic benefits to those entities which, but for prior discrimination, might well be better qualified to receive valuable government contracts. In my view, the interest in ensuring that the government does not reflect and reinforce prior private discrimination in dispensing public contracts is every bit as strong as the interest in eliminating private discrimination—an interest which this Court has repeatedly deemed compelling. . . . The more government bestows its rewards on those persons or businesses that were positioned to thrive during a period of private racial discrimination, the tighter the dead-hand grip of prior discrimination becomes on the present and future. Cities like Richmond may not be constitutionally required to adopt set-aside plans. . . . But there can be no doubt that when Richmond acted affirmatively to stem the perpetuation of patterns of discrimination through its own decision-making, it served an interest of the highest order.

Had the majority paused for a moment on the facts of the Richmond experience, it would have discovered that the city's leadership is deeply familiar with what racial discrimination is. The members of the Richmond City Council have spent long years witnessing multifarious acts of discrimination, including, but not limited to, the deliberate diminution of black residents' voting rights, resistance to school desegregation, and publicly sanctioned housing discrimination. Numerous decisions of federal courts chronicle this disgraceful recent history. . . . [F]or example, this Court denounced Richmond's decision to annex part of an adjacent county at a time when the city's black population was nearing 50% because it was "infected by the impermissible purpose of denying the right to vote based on race through perpetuating white majority power to exclude Negroes from office." . . .

In *Bradley v. School Board of City of Richmond, Virginia*, . . . the Court of Appeals for the Fourth Circuit, sitting en banc, reviewed in the context of a school desegregation case Richmond's long history of inadequate compliance with *Brown v. Board of Education*, . . . and the cases implementing its holding. The dissenting judge elaborated:

The sordid history of Virginia's, and Richmond's attempts to circumvent, defeat, and nullify the holding of *Brown I* has been recorded in the opinions of this and other courts, and need not be repeated in detail here. It suffices to say that there was massive resistance and every state resource, including the services of the legal officers of the state, the services of private counsel (costing the State hundreds of thousands of dollars), the State police, and the power and prestige of the Governor, was employed to defeat *Brown I*. In Richmond, as has been mentioned, not even freedom of choice became actually effective until 1966, *twelve years after the decision of Brown I.* . . .

The Court of Appeals majority in *Bradley* used equally pungent words in describing public and private housing discrimination in Richmond. Though rejecting the black plaintiffs' request that it consolidate Richmond's school district with those of two neighboring counties, the majority nonetheless agreed with the plaintiffs' assertion that "within the City of Richmond there has been state (also federal) action tending to perpetuate apartheid of the races in ghetto patterns throughout the city." . . .

When the legislatures and leaders of cities with histories of pervasive discrimination testify that past discrimination has infected one of their industries, armchair cynicism like that exercised by the majority has no place. . . .

Finally, I vehemently disagree with the majority's dismissal of the congressional and Executive Branch findings noted in *Fullilove* as having "extremely limited" probative value in this case. . . . The majority concedes that Congress established nothing less than a "presumption" that minority contracting firms have been disadvantaged by prior discrimination. . . . The majority, inexplicably, would forbid Richmond to "share" in this information, and permit only Congress to take note of these ample findings. . . . In thus requiring that Richmond's local evidence be severed from the context in which it was prepared, the majority would require cities seeking to eradicate the effects of past discrimination within their borders to reinvent the evidentiary wheel and engage in unnecessarily duplicative, costly, and time-consuming factfinding. . . .

As for Richmond's 30% target, the majority states that this figure "cannot be said to be narrowly tailored to any goal, except perhaps outright racial balancing." . . . The majority ignores two important facts. First, the set-aside measure affects only 3% of overall city contracting; thus, any imprecision in tailoring has far less impact than the majority suggests. But more important, the majority ignores the fact that Richmond's 30% figure was patterned directly on the *Fullilove* precedent. Congress' 10% figure fell "roughly halfway between the present percentage of minority contractors and the percentage of minority group mem-

bers in the Nation." . . . The Richmond City Council's 30% figure similarly falls roughly halfway between the present percentage of Richmond-based minority contractors (almost zero) and the percentage of minorities in Richmond (50%). In faulting Richmond for not presenting a different explanation for its choice of a set-aside figure, the majority honors *Fullilove* only in the breach.

The majority today sounds a full-scale retreat from the Court's longstanding solicitude to race-conscious remedial efforts "directed toward deliverance of the century-old promise of equality of economic opportunity." . . . The new and restrictive tests it applies scuttle one city's effort to surmount its discriminatory past, and imperil those of dozens more localities. I, however, profoundly disagree with the cramped vision of the Equal Protection Clause which the majority offers today and with its application of that vision to Richmond, Virginia's, laudable set-aside plan. The battle against pernicious racial discrimination or its effects is nowhere near won. I must dissent.

Justice Blackmun, with whom
Justice Brennan joins, dissenting.

I join Justice Marshall's perceptive and incisive opinion revealing great sensitivity toward those who have suffered the pains of economic discrimination in the construction trades for so long.

I never thought that I would live to see the day when the city of Richmond, Virginia, the cradle of the Old Confederacy, sought on its own, within a narrow confine, to lessen the stark impact of persistent discrimination. But Richmond, to its great credit, acted. Yet this Court, the supposed bastion of equality, strikes down Richmond's efforts as though discrimination had never existed or was not demonstrated in this particular litigation. Justice Marshall convincingly discloses the fallacy and the shallowness of that approach. History is irrefutable, even though one might sympathize with those who—though possibly innocent in themselves—benefit from the wrongs of past decades.

So the Court today regresses. I am confident, however, that, given time, it one day again will do its best to fulfill the great promises of the Constitution's Preamble and of the guarantees embodied in the Bill of Rights—a fulfillment that would make this Nation very special.

Suggestions for Further Reading

Anthologies

Cohen, M., Nagel, T., and Scanlon, T. *Equality and Preferential Treatment.* Princeton, NJ: Princeton University Press, 1977.

Gould, C. C., and Wartofsky, M. W. *Women and Philosophy.* New York: G. P. Putnam & Sons, 1976.

Gross, B. *Reverse Discrimination.* Buffalo, NY: Prometheus, 1976.

Remick, H. *Comparable Worth and Wage Discrimination.* Philadelphia: Temple University Press, 1985.

Statham, Anne. *The Worth of Woman's Work.* Albany: State University of New York Press, 1988.

Alternative Views

Aaron, H. and Cameran, L. *The Comparable Worth Controversy.* Washington, D.C.: Brookings, 1986.

Bergman, Barbara. *The Economic Emergence of Women.* New York: Basic Books, 1986.

Fullinwider, R. *The Reverse Discrimination Controversy.* Totowa: Rowman and Littlefield, 1980.

Goldman, A. *Justice and Reverse Discrimination.* Princeton: Princeton University Press, 1979.

Paul, Ellen Frankel. *Equity and Gender: The Comparable Worth Debate.* New Brunswick: Transaction Publishers, 1989.

Sowell, T. *Markets and Minorities.* New York: Basic Books, 1981.

United States Comission on Civil Rights. *Comparable Worth: Issue for the 80's.* Washington, D.C.: U.S. Government Printing Office, 1984.

Practical Applications

United States Commission on Civil Rights. *Toward an Understanding of Bakke.* Washington, D.C.: U.S. Government Printing Office, 1979.

Pornography

Basic Concepts

The problem of pornography, as Catharine MacKinnon formulates it in Selection 35, is whether pornography should be prohibited for promoting discrimination and violence against women. But this has not been how the problem has been traditionally understood. In the Anglo-American legal tradition, pornography has always been identified with obscenity.[1] The test for obscenity set forth by the U.S. Supreme Court in *Roth* v. *United States* (1957) is "whether to the average person, applying contemporary community standards, the dominant theme of the material taken as a whole appeals to prurient interest." This test itself was an attempt to improve upon an 1868 test of obscenity that was taken over from English law. According to this earlier test, obscene materials are such that they have the tendency "to deprave and corrupt those whose minds are open to such immoral influences, and into whose hands a publication of this sort may fall." In *Roth* v. *United States,* the U.S. Supreme Court sought to remedy three defects in this 1868 test. First, the 1868 test permitted books to be judged obscene on the basis of isolated passages read out of context. In contrast, the Roth test requires that material be judged as obscene only if "the dominant theme of the material taken as a whole" is so judged. Second, the 1868 test allowed the obscenity of a work to be determined by its likely effects on unusually susceptible persons. By contrast, the Roth test judges material to be obscene on the basis of its likely effect on the "average person." Third, the 1868 test posited standards of obscenity fixed for all time. By contrast, the Roth test only appeals to "contemporary community standards."

Yet despite these advantages of the Roth test, problems remained. First, who was the average person to whose prurience the obscene materials has to appeal? In *Miskin* v. *New York* (1966), the Supreme Court needed to apply its Roth test to books that described sadomasochistic sexual acts, fetishism, lesbianism, and male homosexuality. Since these works did not appeal to the prurient interest of the average person in the population at large, the Supreme Court reformulated its Roth test so that when "material is designed for and primarily disseminated to a clearly defined deviant sexual group, . . . the prurient-appeal requirement of the Roth test is satisfied if the dominant theme of the material taken as a whole appeals to the prurient interest in sex of the members of that group." Second, how was the Supreme Court to avoid the task of having to determine what are community standards for an endless number of obscenity cases? In *Miller* v. *California* (1973), the Supreme Court dealt with the problem by delegating and relativizing the task of determining contemporary community standards to local communities. Henceforth, the application of local community standards determines whether material appeals to prurient interest. Obviously, this puts a severe burden on national publishers who now have to take into account local community standards for any work they distribute. For example, when Larry C. Flynt routinely mailed a copy of his publication *Hustler* to a person who had ordered it by mail from a town in Ohio, he was subsequently tried for a violation of the Ohio obscenity statutes and sentenced to 7 to 25 years in prison. So even with these improvements in the Supreme Court's test for obscenity, problems still remain.

Alternative Views

In Selection 35, Catharine MacKinnon takes an entirely new approach to pornography and obscenity. She sees pornography as a practice of sex discrimination, a violation of women's civil rights. She defines pornography "as the graphic sexually explicit subordination of women through pictures or words that also includes women dehumanized as sexual objects, things or commodities; enjoying pain or humiliation or rape; being tied up, cut up, mutilated, bruised, or physically hurt; in postures of sexual submission or servility or display; reduced to body parts, penetrated by objects or animals, or presented in scenarios of degradation, injury, torture; shown as filthy or inferior; bleeding, bruised or hurt in a context that makes these conditions sexual." By contrast, she defines erotica "as sexually explicit materials premised on equality." She argues that pornography is a harm of gender inequality that outweighs any social interest in its protection by recognized First Amendment standards. She points to recent experimental research that shows that pornography causes harm to women through increasing men's attitudes and behavior of discrimination in both violent and nonviolent forms.

In Selection 36, Lisa Duggan, Nan Hunter, and Carole Vance oppose MacKinnon's antipornography position. They argue that although the legislation she proposes claims to prohibit only material that is sexually explicit, violent, and sexist, it actually prohibits anything that is merely sexually explicit. They further argue that because of the diverse interests of those behind the antipornography movement, it is unlikely that these interests will unite behind a more limited notion of pornography. This latter objection, however, does not seem to touch the moral defensibility of a view modeled after MacKinnon's, which would aim at prohibiting only material that is sexually explicit, violent, and sexist, but would also employ better legal criteria for specifying material of this sort.

Duggan, Hunter, and Vance also question whether pornography harms women, but here they seem to have in mind a broader notion of pornography than the one we are considering. Yet even assuming that pornography more narrowly defined does harm women, Duggan, Hunter, and Vance further question whether it causes more harm than some other aspects of our sexist society that are not prohibited. But suppose that Duggan, Hunter, and Vance are right that pornography causes no more harm than some other aspects of our sexist society. What would that show? It may simply show that pornography as well as those other aspects of our sexist society should be prohibited.

Some opponents of any legal prohibition on pornography point to the Danish experience, where the legalization of pornography has not led to any increase in reported incidents of sexual assault against women. But even here the evidence is mixed because, for example, although the number of rapes reported to the authorities has decreased over the years, it is estimated that the number of actual rapes has increased.

Practical Application

In *American Booksellers* v. *Hudnutt* (Selection 37), the federal judiciary ruled against an Indianapolis ordinance that prohibited pornography. The judiciary denied that pornography causes sufficient harm to women to justify prohibition. But, of course, in MacKinnon's view, this is not surprising because much of the harm that pornography causes to women is not even seen in the sexist society in which we live. Yet if MacKinnon is right, treating women equally in this regard will require a radical transformation of our society that will also affect the solutions to the other moral problems discussed in this anthology. Moreover, this radical transformation would be the kind that libertarians would be expected to champion since they are so concerned with preventing harm to others.

Note

1. In ordinary usage, to call something obscene is to condemn that thing as blatantly disgusting, whereas to call something pornographic is simply to characterize it as sexually explicit. So in ordinary usage, unlike the law, it is an open question whether the pornographic is also obscene.

35. Pornography, Civil Rights and Speech

Catharine MacKinnon

Catharine MacKinnon argues that pornography is a practice of sex discrimination and, hence, a violation of women's civil rights. According to MacKinnon, pornography celebrates and legitimizes rape, battery, sexual harassment, and the sexual abuse of children. More generally, it eroticizes the dominance and submission that is the dynamic common to them all. She argues for the constitutionality of city ordinances, which she has helped design, that prohibit pornography.

. . . There is a belief that this is a society in which women and men are basically equals. Room for marginal corrections is conceded, flaws are known to exist, attempts are made to correct what are conceived as occasional lapses from the basic condition of sex equality. Sex discrimination law has concentrated most of its focus on these occasional lapses. It is difficult to overestimate the extent to which this belief in equality is an article of faith for most people, including most women, who wish to live in self-respect in an internal universe, even (perhaps especially) if not in the world. It is also partly an expression of natural law thinking: if we are inalienably equal, we can't "really" be degraded.

This is a world in which it is worth trying. In this world of presumptive equality, people make money based on their training or abilities or diligence or qualifications. They are employed and advanced on the basis of merit. In this world of just deserts, if someone is abused, it is thought to violate the basic rules of the community. If it doesn't, victims are seen to have done something they could have chosen to do differently, by exercise of will or better judgment. Maybe such people have placed themselves in a situation of vulnerability to physical abuse. Maybe they have done something provocative. Or maybe they were just unusually unlucky. In such a world, if such a person has an experience, there are words for it. When they speak and say it, they

Reprinted by permission of the publishers from *Feminism Unmodified* by Catharine MacKinnon, Cambridge, Mass.: Harvard University Press, copyright © 1987 by the President and Fellows of Harvard College.

are listened to. If they write about it, they will be published. If certain experiences are never spoken about, if certain people or issues are seldom heard from, it is supposed that silence has been chosen. The law, including much of the law of sex discrimination and the First Amendment, operates largely within the realm of these beliefs.

Feminism is the discovery that women do not live in this world, that the person occupying this realm is a man, so much more a man if he is white and wealthy. This world of potential credibility, authority, security, and just rewards, recognition of one's identity and capacity, is a world that some people do inhabit as a condition of birth, with variations among them. It is not a basic condition accorded humanity in this society, but a prerogative of status, a privilege, among other things, of gender.

I call this a discovery because it has not been an assumption. Feminism is the first theory, the first practice, the first movement, to take seriously the situation of all women from the point of view of all women, both on our situation and on social life as a whole. The discovery has therefore been made that the implicit social content of humanism, as well as the standpoint from which legal method has been designed and injuries have been defined, has not been women's standpoint. Defining feminism in a way that connects epistemology with power as the politics of women's point of view, this discovery can be summed up by saying that women live in another world: specifically, a world of *not* equality, a world of inequality.

Looking at the world from this point of view, a whole shadow world of previously invisible silent abuse has been discerned. Rape, battery, sexual harassment, forced prostitution, and the sexual abuse of children emerge as common and systematic. We find that rape happens to women in all contexts, from the family, including rape of girls and babies, to students and women in the workplace, on the streets, at home, in their own bedrooms by men they do not know and by men they do know, by men they are married to, men they have had a social conversation with, and, least often, men they have never seen before. Overwhelmingly, rape is something that men do or attempt to do to women (44 percent of American women according to a recent study) at some point in our lives. Sexual harassment of women by men is common in workplaces and educational institutions. Based on reports in one study of the federal workforce, up to 85 percent of women will experience it, many in physical forms. Between a quarter and a third of women are battered in their homes by men. Thirty-eight percent of little girls are sexually molested inside or outside the family. Until women listened to women, this world of sexual abuse was *not spoken* of. It was the unspeakable. What I am saying is, if you *are* the tree falling in the epistemological forest, your demise doesn't make a sound if no one is listening. Women did not "report" these events, and overwhelmingly do not today, because no one is listening, because no one believes us. This silence does not mean nothing happened, and it does not mean consent. It is the silence of women of which Adrienne Rich has written, "Do not confuse it with any kind of absence."

Believing women who say we are sexually violated has been a radical departure, both methodologically and legally. The extent and nature of rape, marital rape, and sexual harassment itself, were discovered in this way. Domestic battery as a syndrome, almost a habit, was discovered through refusing to believe that when a woman is assaulted by a man to whom she is connected, that it is not an assault. The sexual abuse of children was uncovered, Freud notwithstanding, by believing that children were not making up all this sexual abuse. Now what is striking is that when each discovery is made, and somehow made real in the world, the response has been: it happens to men too. If women are hurt, men are hurt. If women are raped, men are raped. If women are sexually harassed, men are sexually harassed. If women are battered, men are battered. Symmetry must be reasserted. Neutrality must be reclaimed. Equality must be reestablished.

The only areas where the available evidence supports this, where anything like what happens to women also happens to men, involve children—little boys are sexually abused—and prison. The liberty of prisoners is restricted, their freedom restrained, their humanity systematically diminished, their bodies and emotions confined, defined, and regulated. If paid at all, they are paid starvation wages. They can be tortured at will, and it is passed off as discipline or as means to a just end. They become compliant. They can be raped at will, at any moment, and nothing will be done about it. When they scream, nobody hears. To be a prisoner means to be defined as a member of a group for whom the rules of what can be done to you, of what is seen as abuse of you, are reduced as part of the definition of your status. To be a woman is that kind of definition and has that kind of meaning.

Men *are* damaged by sexism. (By men I mean the status of masculinity that is accorded to males on the basis of their biology but is not itself biological.) But whatever the damage of sexism to men, the condition of being a man is not defined as subordinate to women by force. Looking at the facts of the abuses of women all at once, you see that a woman is socially defined as a person who, whether or not she is or has been, can be treated in these ways by men at any time, and little, if anything, will be done about it. This is what it means when feminists say that maleness is a form of power and femaleness is a form of powerlessness.

In this context, all of this "men too" stuff means that people don't really believe that the things I have just said are true, though there really is little question about their empirical accuracy. The data are extremely simple, like women's pay figure of fifty-nine cents on the dollar. People don't really seem to believe that either. Yet there is no question of its empirical validity. This is the workplace story: what women do is seen as not worth much, or what is not worth much is seen as something for women to do. *Women* are seen as not worth much, is the thing. Now why are these basic realities of the subordination of women to men, for example, that only 7.8 percent of women have never been sexually assaulted, not effectively believed, not perceived as real in the face of all this evidence? Why don't *women* believe our own experiences? In the face of all this evidence, especially of systematic sexual abuse—subjection to violence with ·impunity is one extreme expression, although not the only expression, of a degraded status—the view that basically the sexes are equal in this society remains unchallenged and unchanged. The day I got this was the day I understood its real message, its real coherence: *This is equality for us.*

I could describe this, but I couldn't explain it until I started studying a lot of pornography. In pornography, there it is, in one place, all of the abuses that women had to struggle so long even to begin to articulate, all the *unspeakable* abuse: the rape, the battery, the sexual harassment, the prostitution, and the sexual abuse of children. Only in the pornography it is called something else: sex, sex, sex, sex, and sex, respectively. Pornography sexualizes rape, battery, sexual harassment, prostitution, and child sexual abuse; it thereby celebrates, promotes, authorizes, and legitimizes them. More generally, it eroticizes the dominance and submission that is the dynamic common to them all. It makes hierarchy sexy and calls that "the truth about sex" or just a mirror of reality. Through this process pornography constructs what a woman is as what men want from sex. This is what the pornography means.

Pornography constructs what a woman is in terms of its view of what men want sexually, such that acts of rape, battery, sexual harassment, prostitution, and sexual abuse of children become acts of sexual equality. Pornography's world of equality is a harmonious and balanced place. Men and women are perfectly complementary and perfectly bipolar. Women's desire to be fucked by men is equal to men's desire to fuck women. All the ways men love to take and violate women, women love to be taken and violated. The women who most love this are most men's equals, the most liberated; the most participatory child is the most grown-up, the most equal to an adult.

Their consent merely expresses or ratifies these preexisting facts.

The content of pornography is one thing. There, women substantively desire dispossession and cruelty. We desperately want to be bound, battered, tortured, humiliated, and killed. Or, to be fair to the soft core, merely taken and used. This is erotic to the male point of view. Subjection itself, with self-determination ecstatically relinquished, is the content of women's sexual desire and desirability. Women are there to be violated and possessed, men to violate and possess us, either on screen or by camera or pen on behalf of the consumer. On a simple descriptive level, the inequality of hierarchy, of which gender is the primary one, seems necessary for sexual arousal to work. Other added inequalities identify various pornographic genres or subthemes, although they are always added through gender: age, disability, homosexuality, animals, objects, race (including anti-Semitism), and so on. Gender is never irrelevant.

What pornography *does* goes beyond its content: it eroticizes hierarchy, it sexualizes inequality. It makes dominance and submission into sex. Inequality is its central dynamic; the illusion of freedom coming together with the reality of force is central to its working. Perhaps because this is a bourgeois culture, the victim must look free, appear to be freely acting. Choice is how she got there. Willing is what she is when she is being equal. It seems equally important that then and there she actually be forced and that forcing be communicated on some level, even if only through still photos of her in postures of receptivity and access, available for penetration. Pornography in this view is a form of forced sex, a practice of sexual politics, an institution of gender inequality.

From this perspective, pornography is neither harmless fantasy nor a corrupt and confused misrepresentation of an otherwise natural and healthy sexual situation. It institutionalizes the sexuality of male supremacy, fusing the erotization of dominance and submission with the social construction of male and female. To the extent that gender is sexual, pornography is part of constituting the meaning of that sexuality. Men treat women as who they see women as being. Pornography constructs who that is. Men's power over women means that the way men see women defines who women can be. Pornography is that way. Pornography is not imagery in some relation to a reality elsewhere constructed. It is not a distortion, reflection, projection, expression, fantasy, representation, or symbol either. It is a sexual reality.

In Andrea Dworkin's definitive work, *Pornography: Men Possessing Women,* sexuality itself is a social construct gendered to the ground. Male dominance here is not an artificial overlay upon an underlying inalterable substratum of uncorrupted essential sexual being. Dworkin presents a sexual theory of gender inequality of which pornography is a constitutive practice. The way pornography produces its meaning constructs and defines men and women as such. Gender has no basis in anything other than the social reality its hegemony constructs. Gender is what gender means. The process that gives sexuality its male supremacist meaning is the same process through which gender inequality becomes socially real.

In this approach, the experience of the (overwhelmingly) male audiences who consume pornography is therefore not fantasy or simulation or catharsis but sexual reality, the level of reality on which sex itself largely operates. Understanding this dimension of the problem does not require noticing that pornography models are real women to whom, in most cases, something real is being done; nor does it even require inquiring into the systematic infliction of pornography and its sexuality upon women, although it helps. What matters is the way in which the pornography itself provides what those who consume it want. Pornography *participates* in its audience's eroticism through creating an accessible sexual object, the possession and consumption of which *is* male sexuality, as socially constructed; to be consumed and possessed as which, *is* female sexuality, as socially constructed; pornography is a process that constructs it that way.

The object world is constructed according to how it looks with respect to its possible uses. Pornography defines women by how we look according to how we can be sexually used.

Pornography codes how to look at women, so you know what you can do with one when you see one. Gender is an assignment made visually, both originally and in everyday life. A sex object is defined on the basis of its looks, in terms of its usability for sexual pleasure, such that both the looking—the quality of the gaze, including its point of view—and the definition according to use become eroticized as part of the sex itself. This is what the feminist concept "sex object" means. In this sense, sex in life is no less mediated than it is in art. Men have sex with their image of a woman. It is not that life and art imitate each other; in this sexuality, they *are* each other.

To give a set of rough epistemological translations, to defend pornography as consistent with the equality of the sexes is to defend the subordination of women to men as sexual equality. What in the pornographic view is love and romance looks a great deal like hatred and torture to the feminist. Pleasure and eroticism become violation. Desire appears as lust for dominance and submission. The vulnerability of women's projected sexual availability, that acting we are allowed (that is, asking to be acted upon), is victimization. Play conforms to scripted roles. Fantasy expresses ideology, is not exempt from it. Admiration of natural physical beauty becomes objectification. Harmlessness becomes harm. Pornography is a harm of male supremacy made difficult to see because of its pervasiveness, potency, and, principally, because of its success in making the world a pornographic place. Specifically, its harm cannot be discerned, and will not be addressed, if viewed and approached neutrally, because it *is* so much of "what is." In other words, to the extent pornography succeeds in constructing social reality, it becomes invisible as harm. If we live in a world that pornography creates through the power of men in a male-dominated situation, the issue is not what the harm of pornography is, but how that harm is to become visible.

Obscenity law provides a very different analysis and conception of the problem of pornography. In 1973 the legal definition of obscenity became that which the average person, applying contemporary community standards, would find that, taken as a whole, appeals to the prurient interest; that which depicts or describes in a patently offensive way—you feel like you're a cop reading someone's *Miranda* rights—sexual conduct specifically defined by the applicable state law; and that which, taken as a whole, lacks serious literary, artistic, political or scientific value. Feminism doubts whether the average person gender-neutral exists; has more questions about the content and process of defining what community standards are than it does about deviations from them; wonders why prurience counts but powerlessness does not and why sensibilities are better protected from offense than women are from exploitation; defines sexuality, and thus its violation and expropriation, more broadly than does state law; and questions why a body of law that has not in practice been able to tell rape from intercourse should, without further guidance, be entrusted with telling pornography from anything less. Taking the work "as a whole" ignores that which the victims of pornography have long known: legitimate settings diminish the perception of injury done to those whose trivialization and objectification they contextualize. Besides, and this is a heavy one, if a woman is subjected, why should it matter that the work has other value? Maybe what redeems the work's value is what enhances its injury to women, not to mention that existing standards of literature, art, science, and politics, examined in a feminist light, are remarkably consonant with pornography's mode, meaning, and message. And finally—first and foremost, actually—although the subject of these materials is overwhelmingly women, their contents almost entirely made up of women's bodies, our invisibility has been such, our equation as a sex *with* sex has been such, that the law of obscenity has never even considered pornography a women's issue.

Obscenity, in this light, is a moral idea, an idea about judgments of good and bad. Pornography, by contrast, is a political practice, a practice of power and powerlessness. Obscenity is ideational and abstract; pornography is concrete and substantive. The two concepts represent two entirely different things. Nudity, excess of candor, arousal or excitement, prurient appeal, illegality of the acts depicted,

and unnaturalness or perversion are all qualities that bother obscenity law when sex is depicted or portrayed. Sex forced on real women so that it can be sold at a profit and forced on other real women; women's bodies trussed and maimed and raped and made into things to be hurt and obtained and accessed, and this presented as the nature of women in a way that is acted on and acted out, over and over; the coercion that is visible and the coercion that has become invisible—this and more bothers feminists about pornography. Obscenity as such probably does little harm. Pornography is integral to attitudes and behaviors of violence and discrimination that define the treatment and status of half the population.

At the request of the city of Minneapolis, Andrea Dworkin and I conceived and designed a local human rights ordinance in accordance with our approach to the pornography issue. We define pornography as a practice of sex discrimination, a violation of women's civil rights, the opposite of sexual equality. Its point is to hold those who profit from and benefit from that injury accountable to those who are injured. It means that women's injury—our damage, our pain, our enforced inferiority—should outweigh their pleasure and their profits, or sex equality is meaningless.

We define pornography as the graphic sexually explicit subordination of women through pictures or words that also includes women dehumanized as sexual objects, things, or commodities; enjoying pain or humiliation or rape; being tied up, cut up, mutilated, bruised, or physically hurt; in postures of sexual submission or servility or display; reduced to body parts, penetrated by objects or animals, or presented in scenarios of degradation, injury, torture; shown as filthy or inferior; bleeding, bruised, or hurt in a context that makes these conditions sexual. Erotica, defined by distinction as not this, might be sexually explicit materials premised on equality. We also provide that the use of men, children, or transsexuals in the place of women is pornography. The definition is substantive in that it is sex-specific, but it covers everyone in a sex-specific way, so is gender neutral in overall design. . . .

This law aspires to guarantee women's

rights consistent with the First Amendment by making visible a conflict of rights between the equality guaranteed to all women and what, in some legal sense, is now the freedom of the pornographers to make and sell, and their consumers to have access to, the materials this ordinance defines. Judicial resolution of this conflict, if the judges do for women what they have done for others, is likely to entail a balancing of the rights of women arguing that our lives and opportunities, including our freedom of speech and action, are constrained by—and in many cases flatly precluded by, in, and through—pornography, against those who argue that the pornography is harmless, or harmful only in part but not in the whole of the definition; or that it is more important to preserve the pornography than it is to prevent or remedy whatever harm it does.

In predicting how a court would balance these interests, it is important to understand that this ordinance cannot now be said to be either conclusively legal or illegal under existing law or precedent, although I think the weight of authority is on our side. This ordinance enunciates a new form of the previously recognized governmental interest in sex equality. Many laws make sex equality a governmental interest. Our law is designed to further the equality of the sexes, to help make sex equality real. Pornography is a practice of discrimination on the basis of sex, on one level because of its role in creating and maintaining sex as a basis for discrimination. It harms many women one at a time and helps keep all women in an inferior status by defining our subordination as our sexuality and equating that with our gender. It is also sex discrimination because its victims, including men, are selected for victimization on the basis of their gender. But for their sex, they would not be so treated.

The harm of pornography, broadly speaking, is the harm of the civil inequality of the sexes made invisible as harm because it has become accepted as the sex difference. Consider this analogy with race: if you see Black people as different, there is no harm to segregation; it is merely a recognition of that difference. To neutral principles, separate but equal was equal. The injury of racial separation to Blacks arises "solely because [they] choose to put that construction upon it." Epistemologically translated: how you see it is not the way it is. Similarly, if you see women as just different, even or especially if you don't know that you do, subordination will not look like subordination at all, much less like harm. It will merely look like an appropriate recognition of the sex difference.

Pornography does treat the sexes differently, so the case for sex differentiation can be made here. But men as a group do not tend to be (although some individuals may be) treated the way women are treated in pornography. As a social group, men are not hurt by pornography the way women as a social group are. Their social status is not defined as *less* by it. So the major argument does not turn on mistaken differentiation, particularly since the treatment of women according to pornography's dictates makes it all too often accurate. The salient quality of a distinction between the top and the bottom in a hierarchy is not difference, although top is certainly different from bottom; it is power. So the major argument is: subordinate but equal is not equal.

Particularly since this is a new legal theory, a new law, and "new" facts, perhaps the situation of women it newly exposes deserves to be considered on its own terms. Why do the problems of 53 percent of the population have to look like somebody else's problems before they can be recognized as existing? Then, too, they can't be addressed if they do look like other people's problems, about which something might have to be done if something is done about these. This construction of the situation truly deserves inquiry. Limiting the justification for this law to the situation of the sexes would serve to limit the precedential value of a favorable ruling.

Its particularity to one side, the *approach* to the injury is supported by a whole array of prior decisions that have justified exceptions to First Amendment guarantees when something that matters is seen to be directly at stake. What unites many cases in which speech interests are raised and implicated but not, on balance, protected, is harm, harm that counts. In some existing exceptions, the definitions are much more open-ended than ours. In some the sanctions are more severe, or potentially more so. For instance, ours is a civil law;

most others, although not all, are criminal. Almost no other exceptions show as many people directly affected. Evidence of harm in other cases tends to be vastly less concrete and more conjectural, which is not to say that there is necessarily less of it. None of the previous cases addresses a problem of this scope or magnitude—for instance, an eight-billion-dollar-a-year industry. Nor do other cases address an abuse that has such widespread legitimacy. Courts have seen harm in other cases. The question is, will they see it here, especially given that the pornographers got there first. I will confine myself here to arguing from cases on harm to people, on the supposition that, the pornographers notwithstanding, women are not flags. . . .

To reach the magnitude of this problem on the scale it exists, our law makes trafficking in pornography—production, sale, exhibition, or distribution—actionable. Under the obscenity rubric, much legal and psychological scholarship has centered on a search for the elusive link between harm and pornography defined as obscenity. Although they were not very clear on what obscenity was, it was its harm they truly could not find. They looked high and low—in the mind of the male consumer, in society or in its "moral fabric," in correlations between variations in levels of antisocial acts and liberalization of obscenity laws. The only harm they have found has been harm to "the social interest in order and morality." Until recently, no one looked very persistently for harm to women, particularly harm to women through men. The rather obvious fact that the sexes *relate* has been overlooked in the inquiry into the male consumer and his mind. The pornography doesn't just drop out of the sky, go into his head, and stop there. Specifically, men rape, batter, prostitute, molest, and sexually harass women. Under conditions of inequality, they also hire, fire, promote, and grade women, decide how much or whether we are worth paying and for what, define and approve and disapprove of women in ways that count, that determine our lives.

If women are not just born to be sexually used, the fact that we are seen and treated as though that is what we are born for becomes something in need of explanation. If we see

that men relate to women in a pattern of who they see women as being, and that forms a pattern of inequality, it becomes important to ask where that view came from or, minimally, how it is perpetuated or escalated. Asking this requires asking different questions about pornography than the ones obscenity law made salient.

Now I'm going to talk about causality in its narrowest sense. Recent experimental research on pornography shows that the materials covered by our definition cause measurable harm to women through increasing men's attitudes and behaviors of discrimination in both violent and nonviolent forms. Exposure to some of the pornography in our definition increases the immediately subsequent willingness of normal men to aggress against women under laboratory conditions. It makes normal men more closely resemble convicted rapists attitudinally, although as a group they don't look all that different from them to start with. Exposure to pornography also significantly increases attitudinal measures known to correlate with rape and self-reports of aggressive acts, measures such as hostility toward women, propensity to rape, condoning rape, and predicting that one would rape or force sex on a woman if one knew one would not get caught. On this latter measure, by the way, about a third of all men predict that they would rape, and half would force sex on a woman.

As to that pornography covered by our definition in which normal research subjects seldom perceive violence, long-term exposure still makes them see women as more worthless, trivial, nonhuman, and objectlike, that is, the way those who are discriminated against are seen by those who discriminate against them. Crucially, all pornography by our definition acts dynamically over time to diminish the consumer's ability to distinguish sex from violence. The materials work behaviorally to diminish the capacity of men (but not women) to perceive that an account of a rape is an account of a rape. The so-called sex-only materials, those in which subjects perceive no force, also increase perceptions that a rape victim is worthless and decrease the perception that she was harmed. The overall direction of current research suggests that the more expressly violent materials accomplish with less exposure what the less overtly violent—that is, the so-called sex-only materials—accomplish over the longer term. Women are rendered fit for use and targeted for abuse. The only thing that the research cannot document is which individual women will be next on the list. (This cannot be documented experimentally because of ethics constraints on the researchers—constraints that do not operate in life.) Although the targeting is systematic on the basis of sex, for individuals it is random. They are selected on a roulette basis. Pornography can no longer be said to be just a mirror. It does not just reflect the world or some people's perceptions. It *moves* them. It increases attitudes that are lived out, circumscribing the status of half the population.

What the experimental data predict will happen actually does happen in women's real lives. You know, it's fairly frustrating that women have known for some time that these things do happen. As Ed Donnerstein, an experimental researcher in this area, often puts it, "We just quantify the obvious." It is women, primarily, to whom the research results have been the obvious, because we live them. But not until a laboratory study predicts that these things *will* happen do people begin to believe you when you say they *did* happen to you. There is no—*not any*—inconsistency between the patterns the laboratory studies predict and the data on what actually happens to real women. Show me an abuse of women in society, I'll show it to you made sex in the pornography. If you want to know who is being hurt in this society, go see what is being done and to whom in pornography and then go look for them other places in the world. You will find them being hurt in just that way. We did in our hearings.

In our hearings women spoke, to my knowledge for the first time in history in public, about the damage pornography does to them. We learned that pornography is used to break women, to train women to sexual submission, to season women, to terrorize women, and to silence their dissent. It is this that has previously been termed "having no effect." The way men inflict on women the sex they experience through the pornography gives women no choice about seeing the pornography or doing the sex. Asked if anyone ever tried to

inflict unwanted sex acts on them that they knew came from pornography, 10 percent of women in a recent random study said yes. Among married women, 24 percent said yes. That is a lot of women. A lot more don't know. Some of those who do testified in Minneapolis. One wife said of her ex-husband, "He would read from the pornography like a textbook, like a journal. In fact when he asked me to be bound, when he finally convinced me to do it, he read in the magazine how to tie the knots." Another woman said of her boyfriend, "[H]e went to this party, saw pornography, got an erection, got me . . . to inflict his erection on . . . There is a direct causal relationship there." One woman, who said her husband had rape and bondage magazines all over the house, discovered two suitcases full of Barbie dolls with rope tied on their arms and legs and with tape across their mouths. Now think about the silence of women. She said, "He used to tie me up and he tried those things on me." A therapist in private practice reported:

> Presently or recently I have worked with clients who have been sodomized by broom handles, forced to have sex with over 20 dogs in the back seat of their car, tied up and then electrocuted on their genitals. These are children, [all] in the ages of 14 to 18, all of whom [have been directly affected by pornography,] [e]ither where the perpetrator has read the manuals and manuscripts at night and used these as recipe books by day or had the pornography present at the time of the sexual violence.

One woman, testifying that all the women in a group of ex-prostitutes were brought into prostitution as children through pornography, characterized their collective experience: "[I]n my experience there was not one situation where a client was not using pornography while he was using me or that he had not just watched pornography or that it was verbally referred to and directed me to pornography." "Men," she continued, "witness the abuse of women in pornography constantly and if they can't engage in that behavior with their wives, girl friends or children, they force a whore to do it."

Men also testified about how pornography hurts them. One young gay man who had seen *Playboy* and *Penthouse* as a child said of such heterosexual pornography: "It was one of the places I learned about sex and it showed me that sex was violence. What I saw there was a specific relationship between men and women. . . . [T]he woman was to be used, objectified, humiliated and hurt; the man was in a superior position, a position to be violent. In pornography I learned that what it meant to be sexual with a man or to be loved by a man was to accept his violence." For this reason, when he was battered by his first lover, which he described as "one of the most profoundly destructive experiences of my life," he accepted it.

Pornography also hurts men's capacity to relate to women. One young man spoke about this in a way that connects pornography—not the prohibition on pornography—with fascism. He spoke of his struggle to repudiate the thrill of dominance, of his difficulty finding connection with a woman to whom he is close. He said: "My point is that if women in a society filled by pornography must be wary for their physical selves, a man, even a man of good intentions, must be wary for his mind. . . . I do not want to be a mechanical, goose-stepping follower of the Playboy bunny, because that is what I think it is. . . . [T]hese are the experiments a master race perpetuates on those slated for extinction." The woman he lives with is Jewish. There was a very brutal rape near their house. She was afraid; she tried to joke. It didn't work. "She was still afraid. And just as a well-meaning German was afraid in 1933, I am also very much afraid."

Pornography stimulates and reinforces, it does not cathect or mirror, the connection between one-sided freely available sexual access to women and masculine sexual excitement and sexual satisfaction. The catharsis hypothesis is fantasy. The fantasy theory is fantasy. Reality is: pornography conditions male orgasm to female subordination. It tells men what sex means, what a real woman is, and codes them together in a way that is behaviorally reinforcing. This is a real five-dollar sentence, but I'm going to say it anyway: pornography is a set of hermeneutical equivalences that work on the epistemological level.

Substantively, pornography defines the meaning of what a woman is seen to be by connecting access to her sexuality with masculinity through orgasm. What pornography means *is* what it does.

So far, opposition to our ordinance centers on the trafficking provision. This means not only that it is difficult to comprehend a group injury in a liberal culture—that what it *means* to be a woman is defined by this and that it is an injury for all women, even if not for all women equally. It is not only that the pornography has got to be accessible, which is the bottom line of virtually every objection to this law. It is also that power, as I said, is when you say something, it is taken for reality. If you talk about rape, it will be agreed that rape is awful. But rape is a conclusion. If a victim describes the facts of a rape, maybe she was asking for it or enjoyed it or at least consented to it, or the man might have thought she did, or maybe she had had sex before. It is now agreed that there is something wrong with sexual harassment. But describe what happened to you, and it may be trivial or personal or paranoid, or maybe you should have worn a bra that day. People are against discrimination. But describe the situation of a real woman, and they are not so sure she wasn't just unqualified. In law, all these disjunctions between women's perspective on our injuries and the standards we have to meet go under dignified legal rubrics like burden of proof, credibility, defenses, elements of the crime, and so on. These standards all contain a definition of what a woman is in terms of what sex is and the low value placed on us through it. They reduce injuries done to us to authentic expressions of who we are. Our silence is written all over them. So is the pornography.

We have as yet encountered comparatively little objection to the coercion, force, or assault provisions of our ordinance. I think that's partly because the people who make and approve laws may not yet see what they do as that. They *know* they use the pornography as we have described it in this law, and our law defines that, the reality of pornography, as a harm to women. If they suspect that they might on occasion engage in or benefit from coercion or force or assault, they may think that the victims won't be able to prove it—and they're right. Women who charge men with sexual abuse are not believed. The pornographic view of them is: they want it; they all want it. When women bring charges of sexual assault, motives such as veniality or sexual repression must be invented, because we cannot really have been hurt. Under the trafficking provision, women's lack of credibility cannot be relied upon to negate the harm. There's no woman's story to destroy, no credibility-based decision on what happened. The hearings establish the harm. The definition sets the standard. The grounds of reality definition are authoritatively shifted. Pornography is bigotry, *period*. We are now—*in* the world pornography has decisively defined—having to meet the burden of proving, once and for all, for all of the rape and torture and battery, all of the sexual harassment, all of the child sexual abuse, all of the forced prostitution, *all* of it that the pornography is part of and that is part of the pornography, that the harm *does happen* and that when it happens it looks like this. Which may be why all this evidence never seems to be enough.

It is worth considering what evidence has been enough when other harms involving other purported speech interests have been allowed to be legislated against. By comparison to our trafficking provision, analytically similar restrictions have been allowed under the First Amendment, with a legislative basis far less massive, detailed, concrete, and conclusive. Our statutory language is more ordinary, objective, and precise and covers a harm far narrower than the legislative record substantiates. Under *Miller*, obscenity was allowed to be made criminal in the name of the "danger of offending the sensibilities of unwilling recipients, or exposure to juveniles." Under our law, we have direct evidence of harm, not just a conjectural danger, that unwilling women in considerable numbers are not simply offended in their sensibilities, but are violated in their persons and restricted in their options. Obscenity law also suggests that the applicable standard for legal adequacy in measuring such connections may not be statistical certainty. The Supreme Court has said that it is not their job to resolve empirical uncertainties that underlie state obscenity legis-

lation. Rather, it is for them to determine whether a legislature could reasonably have determined that a connection might exist between the prohibited material and harm of a kind in which the state has legitimate interest. Equality should be such an area. The Supreme Court recently recognized that prevention of sexual exploitation and abuse of children is, in their words, "a governmental objective of surpassing importance." This might also be the case for sexual exploitation and abuse of women, although I think a civil remedy is initially more appropriate to the goal of empowering adult women than a criminal prohibition would be.

Other rubrics provide further support for the argument that this law is narrowly tailored to further a legitimate governmental interest consistent with the goals underlying the First Amendment. Exceptions to the First Amendment—you may have gathered from this—exist. The reason they exist is that the harm done by some speech outweighs its expressive value, if any. In our law a legislature recognizes that pornography, as defined and made actionable, undermines sex equality. One can say—and I have—that pornography is a causal factor in violations of women; one can also say that women will be violated so long as pornography exists; but one can also say simply that pornography violates women. Perhaps this is what the woman had in mind who testified at our hearings that for her the question is not just whether pornography causes violent acts to be perpetrated against some women. "Porn is already a violent act against women. It is our mothers, our daughters, our sisters, and our wives that are for sale for pocket change at the newsstands in this country." *Chaplinsky v. New Hampshire* recognized the ability to restrict as "fighting words" speech which, "by [its] very utterance inflicts injury." Perhaps the only reason that pornography has not been "fighting words"—in the sense of words that by their utterance tend to incite immediate breach of the peace—is that women have seldom fought back, yet.

Some concerns that are close to those of this ordinance underlie group libel laws, although the differences are equally important. In group libel law, as Justice Frankfurter's opinion in *Beauharnais* illustrates, it has been understood that an individual's treatment and alternatives in life may depend as much on the reputation of the group to which that person belongs as on their own merit. Not even a partial analogy can be made to group libel doctrine without examining the point made by Justice Brandeis and recently underlined by Larry Tribe: would more speech, rather than less, remedy the harm? In the end, the answer may be yes, but not under the abstract system of free speech, which only enhances the power of the pornographers while doing nothing substantively to guarantee the free speech of women, for which we need civil equality. The situation in which women presently find ourselves with respect to the pornography is one in which more *pornography* is inconsistent with rectifying or even counterbalancing its damage through speech, because so long as the pornography exists in the way it does there *will not be more speech by women*. Pornography strips and devastates women of credibility, from our accounts of sexual assault to our everyday reality of sexual subordination. We are stripped of authority and reduced and devalidated and silenced. Silenced here means that the purposes of the First Amendment, premised upon conditions presumed and promoted by protecting free speech, do not pertain to women because they are not our conditions. Consider them: individual self-fulfillment—how does pornography promote our individual self-fulfillment? How does sexual inequality even permit it? Even if she can form words, who listens to a woman with a penis in her mouth? Facilitating consensus—to the extent pornography does so, it does so one-sidedly by silencing protest over the injustice of sexual subordination. Participation in civic life—central to Professor Meiklejohn's theory—how does pornography enhance women's participation in civic life? Anyone who cannot walk down the street or even lie down in her own bed without keeping her eyes cast down and her body clenched against assault is unlikely to have much to say about the issues of the day, still less will she become Tolstoy. Facilitating change—*this law* facilitates the change that existing First Amendment theory had been used to throttle. Any system of freedom of expression that does not address a problem where the free speech of men silences the free speech

of women, a real conflict between speech interests as well as between people, is not serious about securing freedom of expression in this country.

For those of you who still think pornography is only an idea, consider the possibility that obscenity law got one thing right. Pornography is more actlike than thoughtlike. The fact that pornography, in a feminist view, furthers the idea of the sexual inferiority of women, which is a political idea, doesn't make the pornography itself into a political idea. One can express the idea a practice embodies. That does not make that practice into an idea. Segregation expresses the idea of the inferiority of one group to another on the basis of race. That does not make segregation an idea. A sign that says "Whites Only" is only words. Is it therefore protected by the First Amendment? Is it not an act, a practice, of segregation because what it means is inseparable from what it does? *Law* is only words.

The issue here is whether the fact that words and pictures are the central link in the cycle of abuse will immunize that entire cycle, about which we cannot do anything without doing something about the pornography. As Justice Stewart said in *Ginsburg*, "When expression occurs in a setting where the capacity to make a choice is absent, government regulation of that expression may coexist with and *even implement* First Amendment guarantees." I would even go so far as to say that the pattern of evidence we have closely approaches Justice Douglas' requirement that "freedom of expression can be suppressed if, and to the extent that, it is so closely brigaded with illegal action as to be an inseparable part of it." Those of you who have been trying to separate the acts from the speech—that's an act, that's an act, there's a law against that act, regulate that act, don't touch the speech—notice here that the illegality of the acts involved doesn't mean that the speech that is "brigaded with" it *cannot* be regulated. This is when it *can* be.

I take one of two penultimate points from Andrea Dworkin, who has often said that pornography is not speech for women, it is the silence of women. Remember the mouth taped, the woman gagged, "Smile, I can get a lot of money for that." The smile is not her expression, it is her silence. It is not her expression not because it didn't happen, but because it *did* happen. The screams of the women in pornography are silence, like the screams of Kitty Genovese, whose plight was misinterpreted by some onlookers as a lovers' quarrel. The flat expressionless voice of the woman in the New Bedford gang rape, testifying, is silence. She was raped as men cheered and watched, as they do in and with the pornography. When women resist and men say, "Like this, you stupid bitch, here is how to do it" and shove their faces into the pornography, this "truth of sex" is the silence of women. When they say, "If you love me, you'll try," the enjoyment we fake, the enjoyment we learn is silence. Women who submit because there is more dignity in it than in losing the fight over and over live in silence. Having to sleep with your publisher or director to get access to what men call speech is silence. Being humiliated on the basis of your appearance, whether by approval or disapproval, because you have to look a certain way for a certain job, whether you get the job or not, is silence. The absence of a woman's voice, everywhere that it cannot be heard, is silence. And anyone who thinks that what women say in pornography is women's speech—the "Fuck me, do it to me, harder," all of that—has never heard the sound of a woman's voice.

The most basic assumption underlying First Amendment adjudication is that, socially, speech is free. The First Amendment says Congress shall not abridge the freedom of speech. Free speech, get it, *exists*. Those who wrote the First Amendment *had* speech—they wrote the Constitution. *Their* problem was to keep it free from the only power that realistically threatened it: the federal government. They designed the First Amendment to prevent government from constraining that which, if unconstrained by government, was free, meaning *accessible to them*. At the same time, we can't tell much about the intent of the framers with regard to the question of women's speech, because I don't think we crossed their minds. It is consistent with this analysis that their posture toward freedom of speech tends to presuppose that whole segments of the population are not systematically silenced socially, prior to government action. If everyone's power were equal to theirs, if this were a nonhierarchical society, that might make sense. But the place of pornography in the inequality of the sexes makes the assumption of equal power untrue.

This is a hard question. It involves risks. Classically, opposition to censorship has involved keeping government off the backs of people. Our law is about getting some people off the backs of other people. The risks that it will be misused have to be measured against the risks of the status quo. Women will never have that dignity, security, compensation that is the promise of equality so long as the pornography exists as it does now. The situation of women suggests that the urgent issue of our freedom of speech is not primarily the avoidance of state intervention as such, but getting affirmative access to speech for those to whom it has been denied.

36. Feminist Antipornography Legislation

Lisa Duggan, Nan Hunter, and Carole Vance

Lisa Duggan, Nan Hunter, and Carole Vance challenge the recent legal attempt to prohibit pornography as a form of sex discrimination. They claim that although such legislation aims at prohibiting only material that is sexually explicit, violent, and sexist, in fact, it prohibits anything that is merely sexually explicit and, hence, it could contribute to an antifeminist crusade. Duggan, Hunter, and Vance also question whether pornography causes any more harm to women than other aspects of our sexist society that are not prohibited.

In the United States, after two decades of increasing community tolerance for dissenting or disturbing sexual or political materials, there is now growing momentum for retrenchment. In an atmosphere of increased conservatism, evidenced by a wave of book banning and anti-gay harassment, support for new repressive legislation of various kinds—from an Oklahoma law forbidding schoolteachers from advocating homosexuality to new antipornography laws passed in Minneapolis and Indianapolis—is growing.

The antipornography laws have mixed roots of support, however. Though they are popular with the conservative constituencies that traditionally favor legal restrictions on sexual expression of all kinds, they were drafted and are endorsed by antipornography feminists who oppose traditional obscenity and censorship laws. The model law of this type, which is now being widely copied, was drawn up in the politically progressive city of Minneapolis by two radical feminists, author Andrea Dworkin and attorney Catharine MacKinnon. It was passed by the city council there, but vetoed by the mayor. A similar law was also passed in Indianapolis, but later declared unconstitutional in federal court, a ruling that the city will appeal. Other versions of the legislation are being considered in numerous cities, and Pennsylvania senator Arlen Specter has introduced legislation modeled on

From *Women Against Censorship*, edited by Varda Burstyn (Vancouver: Groundwood Books/Douglas & McIntyre, 1985). Reprinted by permission of the publisher.

parts of the Dworkin-MacKinnon bill in the U.S. Congress.

Dworkin, MacKinnon and their feminist supporters believe that the new antipornography laws are not censorship laws. They also claim that the legislative effort behind them is based on feminist support. Both of these claims are dubious at best. Though the new laws are civil laws that allow individuals to sue the makers, sellers, distributors or exhibitors of pornography, and not criminal laws leading to arrest and imprisonment, their censoring impact would be substantially as severe as criminal obscenity laws. Materials could be removed from public availability by court injunction, and publishers and booksellers could be subject to potentially endless legal harassment. Passage of the laws was therefore achieved with the support of right-wing elements who expect the new laws to accomplish what censorship efforts are meant to accomplish. Ironically, many antifeminist conservatives backed these laws, while many feminists opposed them. In Indianapolis, the law was supported by extreme right-wing religious fundamentalists, including members of the Moral Majority, while there was *no* local feminist support. In other cities, traditional procensorship forces have expressed interest in the new approach to banning sexually explicit materials. Meanwhile, anticensorship feminists have become alarmed at these new developments and are seeking to galvanize feminist opposition to the new antipornography legislative strategy pioneered in Minneapolis.

One is tempted to ask in astonishment, how

can this be happening? How can feminists be entrusting the patriarchal state with the task of legally distinguishing between permissible and impermissible sexual images? But in fact this new development is not as surprising as it at first seems. . . . [P]ornography has come to be seen as a central cause of women's oppression by a significant number of feminists. Some even argue that pornography is the root of virtually all forms of exploitation and discrimination against women. It is a short step from such a belief to the conviction that laws against pornography can end the inequality of the sexes. But this analysis takes feminists very close—indeed far too close—to measures that will ultimately support conservative, anti-sex, procensorship forces in American society, for it is with these forces that women have forged alliances in passing such legislation.

The first feminist-inspired antipornography law was passed in Minneapolis in 1983. Local legislators had been frustrated when their zoning restrictions on porn shops were struck down in the courts. Public hearings were held to discuss a new zoning ordinance. The Neighborhood Pornography Task Force of South and South Central Minneapolis invited Andrea Dworkin and Catharine MacKinnon, who were teaching a course on pornography at the University of Minnesota, to testify. They proposed an alternative that, they claimed, would completely eliminate, rather than merely regulate, pornography. They suggested that pornography be defined as a form of sex discrimination, and that an amendment to the city's civil rights law be passed to proscribe it. City officials hired Dworkin and MacKinnon to develop their new approach and to organize another series of public hearings.

The initial debate over the legislation in Minneapolis was intense, and opinion was divided within nearly every political grouping. In contrast, the public hearings held before the city council were tightly controlled and carefully orchestrated; speakers invited by Dworkin and MacKinnon—sexual abuse victims, counselors, educators and social scientists—testified about the harm pornography does women. (Dworkin and MacKinnon's agenda was the compilation of a legislative record that would help the law stand up to its inevitable court challenges.) The legislation passed, supported by antipornography feminists, neighborhood groups concerned about the effects of porn shops on residential areas, and conservatives opposed to the availability of sexually explicit materials for "moral" reasons.

In Indianapolis, the alignment of forces was different. For the previous two years, conservative antipornography groups had grown in strength and public visibility, but they had been frustrated in their efforts. The police department could not convert its obscenity arrests into convictions; the city's zoning law was also tied up in court challenges. Then Mayor William Hudnutt III, a Republican and a Presbyterian minister, learned of the Minneapolis law. Mayor Hudnutt thought Minneapolis's approach to restricting pornography might be the solution to the Indianapolis problems. Beulah Coughenour, a conservative Republican stop-ERA activist, was recruited to sponsor the legislation in the city-county council.

Coughenour engaged MacKinnon as consultant to the city—Dworkin was not hired, but then, Dworkin's passionate radical feminist rhetoric would not have gone over well in Indianapolis. MacKinnon worked with the Indianapolis city prosecutor (a well-known anti-vice zealot), the city's legal department and Coughenour on the legislation. The law received the support of neighborhood groups, the Citizens for Decency and the Coalition for a Clean Community. There were no crowds of feminist supporters—in fact, there were no feminist supporters at all. The only feminists to make public statements opposed the legislation, which was nevertheless passed in a council meeting packed with 300 religious fundamentalists. All 24 Republicans voted for its passage; all five Democrats opposed it to no avail.

A group of publishers and booksellers challenged the law in Federal District Court, where they won the first round. This legal setback for the ordinance may cause some other cities considering similar legislation to hold off until the final resolution of the appeal of the Indianapolis decision; meanwhile, however, mutated versions of the Dworkin-MacKinnon bill have begun to appear. A version of the law introduced in Suffolk County on Long Island in New York emphasized its conservative potential—pornography was said to cause "sodomy" and "disruption" of the family unit, in addition to rape, incest, exploitation and other acts "inimical to the public good." In Suffolk, the law was put forward by a conservative, anti-ERA male legislator who wishes to "restore ladies to what they used to be." The Suffolk County bill clearly illustrates the repressive, antifeminist potential of the new antipornography legislation. The appearance of a federal bill, together with the possibility of a new, Reagan-appointed commission to study new antipornography legislation, indicates how widespread the repressive effects of the ordinances may become.

Yet it is true that some of the U.S. laws have been proposed and supported by antipornography feminists. This is therefore a critical moment in the feminist debate over sexual politics. As anticensorship feminists work to develop alternatives to antipornography campaigns, we also need to examine carefully the new laws and expose their underlying assumptions. We need to know why these laws, for all their apparent feminist rhetoric, actually appeal to conservative antifeminist forces, and why feminists should be preparing to move in a different direction.

Definitions: The Central Flaw

The antipornography ordinances passed in Minneapolis and Indianapolis were framed as amendments to municipal civil rights laws. They provide for complaints to be filed against pornography in the same manner that complaints are filed against employment discrimination. If enforced, the laws would make illegal public or private availability (except in libraries) of any materials deemed pornographic.

Such material could be the object of a lawsuit on several grounds. The ordinance would penalize four kinds of behavior associated with pornography: its production, sale, exhibition or distribution ("trafficking"); coercion into

pornographic performance; forcing pornography on a person; and assault or physical attack due to pornography. . . .

Although proponents claim that the Minneapolis and Indianapolis ordinances represent a new way to regulate pornography, the strategy is still laden with our culture's old, repressive approach to sexuality. The implementation of such laws hinges on the definition of pornography as interpreted by the court. The definition provided in the Minneapolis legislation is vague, leaving critical phrases such as "the sexually explicit subordination of women," "postures of sexual submission" and "whores by nature" to the interpretation of the citizen who files a complaint and to the civil court judge who hears the case. The legislation does not prohibit just the images of gross sexual violence that most supporters claim to be its target, but instead drifts toward covering an increasingly wide range of sexually explicit material.

The most problematic feature of this approach, then, is a conceptual flaw embedded in the law itself. Supporters of this type of legislation say that the target of their efforts is misogynist, sexually explicit and violent representation, whether in pictures or words. Indeed, the feminist antipornography movement is fueled by women's anger at the most repugnant examples of pornography. But a close examination of the wording of the model legislative text, and examples of purportedly actionable material offered by proponents of the legislation in court briefs suggest that the law is actually aimed at a range of material considerably broader than what proponents claim is their target. The discrepancies between the law's explicit and implicit aims have been almost invisible to us, because these distortions are very similar to distortions about sexuality in the culture as a whole. The legislation and supporting texts deserve close reading. Hidden beneath illogical transformations, nonsequiturs, and highly permeable definitions are familiar sexual scripts drawn from mainstream, sexist culture that potentially could have very negative consequences for women.

The Venn diagram [on the next page] illustrates the three areas targeted by the law, and represents a scheme that classifies words or images that have any of three characteristics: violence, sexual explicitness or sexism.

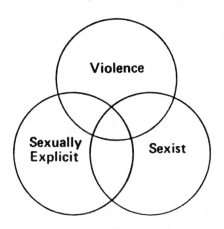

Clearly, a text or an image might have only one characteristic. Material can be violent but not sexually explicit or sexist: for example, a war movie in which both men and women suffer injury or death without regard to or because of their gender. Material can be sexist but not sexually explicit and violent. A vast number of materials from mainstream media—television, popular novels, magazines, newspapers—come to mind, all of which depict either distraught housewives or the "happy sexism" of the idealized family, with mom self-sacrificing, other-directed and content. Finally, material can be sexually explicit but not violent or sexist: for example, the freely chosen sexual behavior depicted in sex education films or women's own explicit writing about sexuality.

As the diagram illustrates, areas can also intersect, reflecting a range of combinations of the three characteristics. Images can be violent and sexually explicit without being sexist—for example, a narrative about a rape in a men's prison, or a documentary about the effect of a rape on a woman. The latter example illustrates the importance of context in evaluating whether material that is sexually explicit and violent is also sexist. The intent of the maker, the context of the film and the perception of the viewer together render a depiction of a rape sympathetic, harrowing, even educational, rather than sensational, victim-blaming and laudatory.

Another possible overlap is between material that is violent and sexist but not sexually explicit. Films or books that describe violence directed against women by men in a way that clearly shows gender antagonism and inequality, and sometimes strong sexual tension, but no sexual explicitness fall into this category—for example, the popular genre of slasher films in which women are stalked, terrified and killed by men, or accounts of mass murder of women, fueled by male rage. Finally, a third point of overlap arises when material is sexually explicit and sexist without being violent—that is, when sex is consensual but still reflects themes of male superiority and female abjectness. Some sex education materials could be included in this category, as well as a great deal of regular pornography.

The remaining domain, the inner core, is one in which the material is simultaneously violent, sexually explicit and sexist—for example, an image of a naked woman being slashed by a knife-wielding rapist. The Minneapolis law, however, does not by any means confine itself to this material.

To be actionable under the law as pornography, material must be judged by the courts to be "the sexually explicit subordination of women, graphically depicted whether in pictures or in words that also includes at least one or more" of nine criteria. Of these, only four involve the intersection of violence, sexual explicitness and sexism, and then only arguably. ... Even in these cases, many questions remain about whether images with all three characteristics do in fact cause violence against women. ... And the task of evaluating material that is ostensibly the target of these criteria becomes complicated—indeed, hopeless—because most of the clauses that contain these criteria mix actions or qualities of violence with those that are not particularly associated with violence.

The section that comes closest to the stated purpose of the legislation is clause (iii): "women are presented as sexual objects who experience sexual pleasure in being raped." This clause is intended to cover depictions of rape that are sexually explicit and sexist; the act of rape itself signifies the violence. But other clauses are not so clearcut, because the list of characteristics often mixes signs or byproducts of violence with phenomena that are unrelated or irrelevant to judging violence. We might be willing to agree that clause (ii)—"women are presented as sexual objects who enjoy pain"—signifies the conjunction of all three characteristics, with violence the presumed cause of pain, but the presence of the words "and humiliation" at the end of the clause is problematic. Humiliation may be offensive or disagreeable, but it does not necessarily imply violence.

A similar problem occurs with clause (iv): "women are presented as sexual objects tied up or cut up or mutilated or bruised or physically hurt." All these except the first, "tied up," generally occur as a result of violence. "Tied up," if part of consensual sex, is not violent and, for some practitioners, not particularly sexist. Women who are tied up may be participants in nonviolent sex play involving bondage, a theme in both heterosexual and lesbian pornography. (See, for example, *The Joy of Sex* and *Coming to Power*.) Clause (ix) contains another mixed list, in which "injury," "torture," "bleeding," "bruised" and "hurt" are combined with words such as "degradation" and "shown as filthy and inferior," neither of which is violent. Depending on the presentation, "filthy" and "inferior" may constitute sexually explicit sexism, although not violence. "Degradation" is a sufficiently inclusive term to cover most acts of which a viewer disapproves.

Several other clauses have little to do with violence at all; they refer to material that is sexually explicit and sexist, thus falling outside the triad of characteristics at which the legislation is supposedly aimed. For example, movies in which "women are presented as dehumanized sexual objects, things, or commodities" may be infuriating and offensive to feminists, but they are not violent.

Finally, some clauses describe material that is neither violent nor necessarily sexist. Clause (v), "women . . . in postures of sexual submission or sexual servility, including by inviting penetration," and clause (viii), "women . . . being penetrated by objects or animals," are sexually explicit, but not violent and not obviously sexist unless one believes that penetration—whether heterosexual, lesbian, or autoerotic masturbation—is indicative of gender inequality and female oppression. Sim-

ilarly problematic are clauses that invoke representations of "women . . . as whores by nature" and "women's body parts . . . such that women are reduced to those parts."

Texts filed in support of the Indianapolis law show how broadly it could be applied. In the amicus brief filed on behalf of Linda Marchiano ("Linda Lovelace," the female lead in *Deep Throat*) in Indianapolis, Catharine MacKinnon offered *Deep Throat* as an example of the kind of pornography covered by the law. *Deep Throat* served a complicated function in this brief, because the movie, supporters of the ordinance argue, would be actionable on two counts: coercion into pornographic performance, because Marchiano alleges that she was coerced into making the movie; and trafficking in pornography, because the content of the film falls within one of the categories in the Indianapolis ordinance's definition—that which prohibits presenting women as sexual objects "through postures or positions of servility or submission or display." Proponents of the law have counted on women's repugnance at allegations of coerced sexual acts to spill over and discredit the sexual acts themselves in this movie.

The aspects of *Deep Throat* that MacKinnon considered to be indicative of "sexual subordination" are of particular interest, since any movie that depicted similar acts could be banned under the law. MacKinnon explained in her brief that the film "subordinates women by using women . . . sexually, specifically as eager servicing receptacles for male genitalia and ejaculate. The majority of the film represents 'Linda Lovelace' in, minimally, postures of sexual submission and/or servility." In its brief, the City of Indianapolis concurred: "In the film *Deep Throat* a woman is being shown as being ever eager for oral penetration by a series of men's penises, often on her hands and knees. There are repeated scenes in which her genitalia are graphically displayed and she is shown as enjoying men ejaculating on her face."

These descriptions are very revealing, since they suggest that multiple partners, group sex and oral sex subordinate women and hence are sexist. The notion that the female character is "used" by men suggests that it is improbable that a woman would engage in fellatio of her own accord. *Deep Throat* does draw on several sexist conventions common in advertising and the entire visual culture—the woman as object of the male gaze, and the assumption of heterosexuality, for example. But it is hardly an unending paean to male dominance, since the movie contains many contrary themes. In it, the main female character is shown as both actively seeking her own pleasure and as trying to please men; a secondary female character is shown as actually directing encounters with multiple male partners. Both briefs described a movie quite different from the one viewers see.

At its heart, this analysis implies that heterosexual sex itself is sexist; that women do not engage in it of their own volition; and that behavior pleasurable to men is repugnant to women. In some contexts, for example, the representation of fellatio and multiple partners can be sexist, but are we willing to concede that they always are? If not, then what is proposed as actionable under the Indianapolis law includes merely sexually explicit representation (the traditional target of obscenity laws), which proponents of the legislation vociferously insist they are not interested in attacking.

Some other examples offered through exhibits submitted with the City of Indianapolis brief and also introduced in the public hearing further illustrate this point. Many of the exhibits are depictions of sadomasochism. The court briefs treat SM material as depicting violence and aggression, not consensual sex, in spite of avowals to the contrary by many SM practitioners. With this legislation, then, a major question for feminists that has only begun to develop would be closed for discussion. Instead, a simplistic reduction has been advanced as the definitive feminist position. The description of the material in the briefs focused on submissive women and implied male domination, highlighting the similarity proponents would like to find between all SM narratives and male/female inequality. The actual exhibits, however, illustrated plots and power relations far more diverse than the descriptions provided by MacKinnon and the City of Indianapolis would suggest, including SM between women and female dominant/male submissive SM. For example, the In-

dianapolis brief stated that in the magazine *The Bitch Goddesses*, "women are shown in torture chambers with their nude body parts being tortured by their 'master' for 'even the slightest offense'. . . . The magazine shows a woman in a scenario of torture." But the brief failed to mention that the dominants in this magazine are all female, with one exception. This kind of discrepancy characterized many examples offered in the briefs.

This is not to say that such representations do not raise questions for feminists. The current lively discussion about lesbian SM clearly demonstrates that this issue is still unresolved. But in the Indianapolis briefs all SM material was assumed to be male dominant/female submissive, thereby squeezing a nonconforming reality into prepackaged, inadequate—and therefore dangerous—categories. This legislation would virtually eliminate all SM pornography by recasting it as violent, thereby attacking a sexual minority while masquerading as an attempt to end violence against women.

Analysis of clauses in the Minneapolis ordinance and several examples offered in court briefs filed in connection with the Indianapolis ordinance show that the law targets material that is sexually explicit and sexist, but ignores material that is violent and sexist, violent and sexually explicit, only violent or only sexist.

Certain troubling questions arise here, for if one claims, as some antipornography activists do, that there is a direct relationship between images and behavior, why should images of violence against women or scenarios of sexism in general not be similarly proscribed? Why is sexual explicitness singled out as the cause of women's oppression? For proponents to exempt violent and sexist images, or even sexist images, from regulation is inconsistent, especially since they are so pervasive.

Even more difficulties arise from the vagueness of certain terms crucial in interpreting the ordinances. The term "subordination" is especially important, since pornography is defined as the "sexually explicit subordination of women." The authors of this legislation intend it to modify each of the clauses, and they appear to believe that it provides a definition of sexism that each example must meet. The term is never defined in the legislation, yet the Indianapolis brief, for example, suggests that the average viewer, on the basis of "his or her common understanding of what it means for one person to subordinate another" should be able to decide what is pornographic. But what kind of sexually explicit acts place a woman in an inferior status? To some, *any* graphic sexual act violates women's dignity and therefore subordinates them. To others, consensual heterosexual lovemaking within the boundaries of procreation and marriage is acceptable, but heterosexual acts that do not have reproduction as their aim lower women's status and hence subordinate them. Still others accept a wide range of nonprocreative, perhaps even nonmarital, heterosexuality but draw the line at lesbian sex, which they view as degrading.

The term "sex object" is also problematic. The City of Indianapolis's brief maintains that "the term sexual object, often shortened to sex object, has enjoyed a wide popularity in mainstream American culture in the past fifteen years, and is used to denote the objectification of a person on the basis of their sex or sex appeal. . . . People know what it means to disregard all aspects of personhood but sex, to reduce a person to a thing used for sex." But, indeed, people do not agree on this point. The definition of "sex object" is far from clear or uniform. For example, some feminist and liberal cultural critics have used the term to mean sex that occurs without strong emotional ties and experience. More conservative critics maintain that any detachment of women's sexuality from procreation, marriage and family objectifies it, removing it from its "natural" web of associations and context. Unredeemed and unprotected by domesticity and family, women—and their sexuality—become things used by men. In both these views, women are never sexually autonomous agents who direct and enjoy their sexuality for their own purposes, but rather are victims. In the same vein, other problematic terms include "inviting penetration," "whores by nature" and "positions of display."

Through close analysis of the proposed legislation one sees how vague the boundaries of the definitions that contain the inner core of the Venn diagram really are. Their dissolution does not happen equally at all points, but only at some: the inner core begins to include sexually explicit and sexist material, and finally expands to include purely sexually explicit material. Thus "sexually explicit" becomes identified and equated with "violent" with no further definition or explanation.

It is also striking that so many feminists have failed to notice that the laws (as well as examples of actionable material) cover so much diverse work, not just that small and symbolic epicentre where many forms of opposition to women converge. It suggests that for us, as well as for others, sexuality remains a difficult area. We have no clearly developed framework in which to think about sex equivalent to the frameworks that are available for thinking about race, gender and class issues. Consequently, in sex, as in few other areas of human behavior, unexamined and unjustifiable prejudice passes itself off as considered opinion about what is desirable and normal. And finally, sex arouses considerable anxiety, stemming from both the meeting with individual difference and from the prospect—suggested by feminists themselves—that sexual behavior is constructed socially and is not simply natural.

The law takes advantage of everyone's relative ignorance and anxious ambivalence about sex, distorting and oversimplifying what confronts us in building a sexual politic. For example, antipornography feminists draw on several feminist theories about the role of violent, aggressive or sexist representations. The first is relatively straightforward: that these images trigger men into action. The second suggests that violent images act more subtly, to socialize men to act in sexist or violent ways by making this behavior seem commonplace and more acceptable, if not expected. The third assumption is that violent, sexually explicit or even sexist images are offensive to women, assaulting their sensibilities and sense of self. Although we have all used metaphor to exhort women to action or illustrate a point, antipornography proponents have frequently used these conventions of speech as if they were literal statements of fact. But these metaphors have gotten out of hand, as Julie Abraham has noted, for they fail to recognize that the assault committed by a wife beater is quite different from the visual "assault" of a sexist ad on TV. The nature of that difference is still being clarified in a complex debate within feminism that must continue; this law cuts off speculation, settling on a causal relationship between image and action that is starkly simple, if unpersuasive.

This metaphor also paves the way for reclassifying images that are merely sexist as also violent and aggressive. Thus, it is no accident that the briefs supporting the legislation first invoke violent images and rapidly move to include sexist and sexually explicit images without noting that they are different. The equation is made more easy by the constant shifts back to examples of depictions of real violence, almost to draw attention away from the sexually explicit or sexist material that in fact would be affected by the laws.

Most important, what underlies this legislation and the success of its analysis in blurring and exceeding boundaries is an appeal to a very traditional view of sex: sex is degrading to women. By this logic, any illustrations or descriptions of explicit sexual acts that involve women are in themselves affronts to women's dignity. In its brief, the City of Indianapolis was quite specific about this point: "The harms caused by pornography are by no means limited to acts of physical aggression. The mere existence of pornography in society degrades and demeans all women." Embedded in this view are several other familiar themes: that sex is degrading to women, but not to men; that men are raving beasts; that sex is dangerous for women; that sexuality is male, not female; that women are victims, not sexual actors; that men inflict "it" on women; that penetration is submission; that heterosexual sexuality, rather than the institution of heterosexuality, is sexist.

These assumptions, in part intended, in part unintended, lead us back to the traditional target of obscenity law: sexually explicit material. What initially appeared novel, then, is really the reappearance of a traditional theme. It's ironic that a feminist position on pornography incorporates most of the myths about sexuality that feminism has struggled to displace.

The Dangers of Application

The Minneapolis and Indianapolis ordinances embody a political view that holds pornography to be a central force in "creating and maintaining" the oppression of women. This view appears in summary form in the legislative findings section at the beginning of the Minneapolis bill, which describes a chain reaction of misogynistic acts generated by pornography. The legislation is based on the interweaving of several themes: that pornography constructs the meaning of sexuality for women and, as well, leads to discrete acts of violence against women; that sexuality is the primary cause of women's oppression; that explicitly sexual images, even if not violent or coerced, have the power to subordinate women; and that women's own accounts of force have been silenced because, as a universal and timeless rule, society credits pornographic constructions rather than women's experiences. Taking the silencing contention a step further, advocates of the ordinance effectively assume that women have been so conditioned by the pornographic world view that if their own experiences of the sexual acts identified in the definition are not subordinating, then they must simply be victims of false consciousness.

The heart of the ordinance is the "trafficking" section, which would allow almost anyone to seek the removal of any materials falling within the law's definition of pornography. Ordinance defenders strenuously protest that the issue is not censorship because the state, as such, is not authorized to initiate criminal prosecutions. But the prospect of having to defend a potentially infinite number of privately filed complaints creates at least as much of a chilling effect against pornographic or sexual speech as does a criminal law. And as long as representatives of the state—in this case, judges—have ultimate say over the interpretation, the distinction between this ordinance and "real" censorship will not hold.

In addition, three major problems should dissuade feminists from supporting this kind of law: first, the sexual images in question do not cause more harm than other aspects of misogynist culture; second, sexually explicit speech, even in male-dominated society, serves positive social functions for women; and third, the passage and enforcement of antipornography laws such as those supported in Minneapolis and Indianapolis are more likely to impede, rather than advance, feminist goals.

Ordinance proponents contend that pornography does cause violence because it conditions male sexual response to images of violence and thus provokes violence against women. The strongest research they offer is based on psychology experiments that employ films depicting a rape scene, toward the end of which the woman is shown to be enjoying the attack. The ordinances, by contrast, cover a much broader range of materials than this one specific heterosexual rape scenario. Further, the studies ordinance supporters cite do not support the theory that pornography causes violence against women. . . .

In addition, the argument that pornography itself plays a major role in the general oppression of women contradicts the evidence of history. It need hardly be said that pornography did not lead to the burning of witches or the English common law treatment of women as chattel property. If anything functioned then as the prime communication medium for woman-hating, it was probably religion. Nor can pornography be blamed for the enactment of laws from at least the eighteenth century that allowed a husband to rape or beat his wife with impunity. In any period, the causes of women's oppression have been many and complex, drawing on the fundamental social and economic structures of society. Ordinance proponents offer little evidence to explain how the mass production of pornography—a relatively recent phenomenon—could have become so potent a causative agent so quickly.

The silencing of women is another example of the harm attributed to pornography. Yet if this argument were correct, one would expect that as the social visibility of pornography has increased, the tendency to credit women's accounts of rape would have decreased. In fact, although the treatment of women complainants in rape cases is far from perfect, the last 15 years of work by the women's movement has resulted in marked improvements. In many places, the corroboration requirement has now been abolished; cross-examination of victims as to past sexual experiences has been prohibited; and a number of police forces have developed specially trained units and procedures to improve the handling of sexual assault cases. The presence of rape fantasies in pornography may in part reflect a backlash against these women's movement advances, but to argue that most people routinely disbelieve women who file charges of rape belittles the real improvements made in social consciousness and law.

The third type of harm suggested by the ordinance backers is a kind of libel: the maliciously false characterization of women as a group of sexual masochists. Like libel, the City of Indianapolis brief argues pornography is "a lie [which] once loosed" cannot be effectively rebutted by debate and further speech.

To claim that all pornography as defined by the ordinance is a lie is a false analogy. If truth is a defence to charges of libel, then surely depictions of consensual sex cannot be thought of as equivalent to a falsehood. For example, some women (and men) do enjoy being tied up or displaying themselves. The declaration by fiat that even sadomasochism is a "lie" about sexuality reflects an arrogance and moralism that feminists should combat, not engage in. When mutually desired sexual experiences are depicted, pornography is not "libelous." . . .

These laws, which would increase the state's regulation of sexual images, present many dangers for women. Although the ordinances draw much of their feminist support from women's anger at the market for images of sexual violence, they are aimed not at violence, but at sexual explicitness. Far-right elements recognize the possibility of using the full potential of the ordinances to enforce their sexually conservative world view, and have supported them for that reason. Feminists should therefore look carefully at the text of these "model" laws in order to understand why many believe them to be a useful tool in *anti*feminist moral crusades.

The proposed ordinances are also dangerous because they seek to embody in law an analysis of the role of sexuality and sexual images in the oppression of women with which even all feminists do not agree. Underlying virtually every section of the proposed laws there is an assumption that sexuality is a realm of unremitting, unequaled victimization for women. Pornography appears as the monster that made this so. The ordinances' authors seek to impose their analysis by putting state power behind it. But this analysis is not the only feminist perspective on sexuality. Feminist theorists have also argued that the sexual terrain, however power-laden, is actively contested. Women are agents, and not merely victims, who make decisions and act on them, and who desire, seek out and enjoy sexuality.

Acknowledgments

For stimulating discussion and political comradeship, thanks to FACT (Feminist Anti-Censorship Task Force), New York, and to members of the Scholar and the Feminist IX study group (Julie Abraham, Hannah Alderfer, Meryl Altman, Jan Boney, Frances Doughty, Kate Ellis, Faye Ginsburg, Diane Harriford, Beth Jaker, Barbara Kerr, Mary Clare Lennon, Marybeth Nelson, Ann Snitow, Paula Webster and Ellen Willis). Special thanks to Rayna Rapp and Janice Irvine for comments and criticisms, to Lawrence Krasnoff for graphics and to Ann Snitow for aid above and beyond the call of duty. We are grateful to Varda Burstyn for her helpful suggestions and patience. We remain responsible for the opinions expressed here.

37. *American Booksellers v. Hudnutt*

United States District Court and Court of Appeals

The issue before the federal judiciary was whether the Indianapolis ordinance that sought to prohibit pornography as a practice that discriminated against women was restricting speech rather than conduct, and if it was restricting speech whether it was restricting speech that was protected by the First Amendment to the United States Constitution. The federal judiciary ruled that the ordinance was restricting speech rather than conduct and that the speech it was restricting was in fact protected by the First Amendment.

Indianapolis enacted an ordinance defining "pornography" as a practice that discriminates against women. "Pornography" is to be redressed through the administrative and judicial methods used for other discrimination. . . .

"Pornography" under the ordinance is "the graphic sexually explicit subordination of women, whether in pictures or in words, that also includes one or more of the following:

(1) Women are presented as sexual objects who enjoy pain or humiliation; or

(2) Women are presented as sexual objects who experience sexual pleasure in being raped; or

(3) Women are presented as sexual objects tied up or cut up or mutilated or bruised or physically hurt, or as dismembered or truncated or fragmented or severed into body parts; or

(4) Women are presented as being penetrated by objects or animals; or

(5) Women are presented in scenarios of degradation, injury, abasement, torture, shown as filthy or inferior, bleeding, bruised, or hurt in a context that makes these conditions sexual; or

(6) Women are presented as sexual objects for domination, conquest, violation, exploitation, possession, or use, or through postures or positions of servility or submission or display." . . .

First Amendment Requirements

This Ordinance cannot be analyzed adequately without first recognizing this: the drafters of the Ordinance have used what appears to be a legal term of art, "pornography," but have in fact given the term a specialized meaning which differs from the meanings ordinarily assigned to that word in both legal and common parlance. In Section 16-3(v) (page 6), the Ordinance states:

> Pornography shall mean the sexually explicit subordination of women, graphically depicted, whether in pictures or in words, that includes one or more of the following: . . .

There follows at that point a listing of five specific presentations of women in various settings which serve as examples of "pornography" and as such further define and describe that term under the Ordinance.

As is generally recognized, the word "pornography" is usually associated, and sometimes synonymous, with the word, "obscenity." "Obscenity" not only has its own separate and specialized meaning in the law, but in laymen's use also, and it is a much broader meaning than the definition given the word "pornography" in the Ordinance which is at issue in this action. There is thus a considerable risk of confusion in analyzing this ordinance unless care and precision are used in that process.

The Constitutional analysis of this Ordinance requires a determination of several underlying issues: first, the Court must determine whether the Ordinance imposes restraints on speech or behavior (content versus conduct); if the Ordinance is found to regulate speech, the Court must next determine whether the subject speech is protected or not protected under the First Amendment; if the speech which is regulated by this Ordinance is protected speech under the Constitution, the Court must then decide whether the regulation is constitutionally permissible as being based on a compelling state interest justifying the removal of such speech from First Amendment protections.

Do the Ordinances Regulate Speech or Behavior (Content or Conduct)?

It appears to be central to the defense of the Ordinance by defendants that the Court accept their premise that the City-County Council has not attempted to regulate speech, let alone protected speech. Defendants repeat throughout their briefs the incantation that their Ordinance regulates conduct, not speech. They contend (one senses with a certain sleight of hand) that the production, dissemination, and use of sexually explicit words and pictures is the actual subordination of women and not an expression of ideas deserving of First Amendment protection. . . .

Defendants claim support for their theory by analogy, arguing that it is an accepted and established legal distinction that has allowed other courts to find that advocacy of a racially "separate but equal" doctrine in a civil rights context is protected speech under the First Amendment though "segregation" is not constitutionally protected behavior. Accordingly, defendants characterize their Ordinance here as a civil rights measure, through which they seek to prevent the distribution, sale, and exhibition of "pornography," as defined in the Ordinance, in order to regulate and control the underlying unacceptable conduct.

The content-versus-conduct approach espoused by defendants is not persuasive, however, and is contrary to accepted First Amendment principles. Accepting as true the City-County Council's finding that pornography conditions society to subordinate women, the means by which the Ordinance attempts to combat this sex discrimination is nonetheless through the regulation of speech.

For instance, the definition of pornography, the control of which is the whole thrust of the Ordinance, states that it is "the sexually explicit subordination of women, graphically *depicted,* whether in *pictures* or in *words,* that includes one or more of the following:" (emphasis supplied) and the following five descriptive subparagraphs begin with the words, "Women are *presented* . . . ." . . .

The unlawful acts and discriminatory practices under the Ordinance are set out in Section 16-3(g):

(4) Trafficking in pornography: the production, sale, exhibition, or distribution of pornography. . . .
(5) Coercion into pornographic performance: coercing, intimidating or fraudulently inducing any person . . . into performing for pornography. . . .
(6) Forcing pornography on a person:
    . . . .
(7) Assault or physical attack due to pornography: the assault, physical attack, or injury of any woman, man, child or transsexual in a way that is directly caused by specific pornography. . . .

Section (7), *supra,* goes on to provide a cause of action in damages against the perpetrators, makers, distributors, sellers and exhibitors of pornography and injunctive relief against the further exhibition, distribution or sale of pornography.

In summary, therefore, the Ordinance establishes through the legislative findings that pornography causes a tendency to commit these various harmful acts, and outlaws the pornography (that is, the "depictions"), the activities involved in the production of pornography, and the behavior caused by or resulting from pornography.

Thus, though the purpose of the Ordinance is cast in civil rights terminology—"to prevent and prohibit all discriminatory practices of sexual subordination or inequality through pornography" . . .—it is clearly aimed at controlling the content of the speech and ideas which the City-County Council has found harmful and offensive. Those words and pictures which depict women in sexually subordinate roles are banned by the Ordinance. Despite defendants' attempt to redefine offensive speech as harmful action, the clear wording of the Ordinance discloses that they seek to control speech, and those restrictions must be analyzed in light of applicable constitutional requirements and standards.

Is the Speech Regulated by the Ordinance Protected or Unprotected Speech Under the First Amendment?

The First Amendment provides that government shall make no law abridging the freedom of speech. However, "the First and Fourteenth Amendments have never been thought to give absolute protection to every individual to speak whenever or wherever he pleases or to use any form of address in any circumstances that he chooses." *Cohen v. California,* . . . (1971). Courts have recognized only a "relatively few categories of instances," . . . where the government may regulate certain forms of individual expression. The traditional categories of speech subject to permissible government regulation include "the lewd and obscene, the profane, the libelous, and the insulting or 'fighting' words—those which by their very utterance inflict injury or tend to incite an immediate breach of the peace." *Chaplinsky v. State of New Hampshire,* . . . (1942). In addition, the Supreme Court has recently upheld legislation prohibiting the dissemination of material depicting children engaged in sexual conduct. *New York v. Ferber,* . . . (1982).

Having found that the Ordinance at issue here seeks to regulate speech (and not conduct), the next question before the Court is whether the Ordinance, which seeks to restrict the distribution, sale, and exhibition of "pornography" as a form of sex discrimination against women, falls within one of the established categories of speech subject to permissible government regulation, that is, speech deemed to be unprotected by the First Amendment.

It is clear that this case does not present issues relating to profanity, libel, or "fighting words." In searching for an analytical "peg," the plaintiffs argue that the Ordinance most closely resembles obscenity, and is, therefore, subject to the requirements set forth in *Miller v. California,* . . . (1973). . . . But the defendants admit that the scope of the Ordinance is not limited to the regulation of legally obscene material as defined in *Miller.* . . . In fact, defendants concede that the "pornography" they seek to control goes beyond obscenity, as defined by the Supreme Court and excepted from First Amendment protections. Accordingly, the parties agree that the materials encompassed in the restrictions set out in the Ordinance include to some extent what have traditionally been protected materials.

The test under *Miller* for determining whether material is legal obscenity is:

> (a) whether 'the average person, applying contemporary community standards' would find that the work, taken as a whole, appeals to the prurient interest, . . . ; (b) whether the work depicts or describes, in a patently offensive way, sexual conduct specifically defined by the applicable state law; and (c) whether the work, taken as a whole, lacks serious literary, artistic, political, or scientific value. . . .

It is obvious that this three-step test is not directly applicable to the present case, because, as has been noted, the Ordinance goes beyond legally obscene material in imposing its controls. The restrictions in the Indianapolis ordinance reach what has otherwise traditionally been regarded as protected speech under the *Miller* test. Beyond that, the Ordinance does not speak in terms of a "community standard" or attempt to restrict the dissemination of material that appeals to the "prurient interest." Nor has the Ordinance been drafted in a way to limit only distributions of "patently offensive" materials. Neither does it provide for the dissemination of works which, though "pornographic," may have "serious literary, artistic, political or scientific value." Finally, the Ordinance does not limit its reach to "hard core sexual conduct," though conceivably "hard core" materials may be included in its proscriptions.

Because the Ordinance spans so much more broadly in its regulatory scope than merely "hard core" obscenity by limiting the distribution of "pornography," the proscriptions in the Ordinance intrude with defendants' explicit approval into areas of otherwise protected speech. Under ordinary constitutional analysis, that would be sufficient grounds to overturn the Ordinance, but defendants argue that this case is not governed by any direct precedent, that it raises a new issue for the Court and even though the Ordinance regulates protected speech, it does so in a constitutionally permissible fashion.

Does Established First Amendment Law Permit the Regulation Provided for in the Ordinance of Otherwise Protected Speech?

In conceding that the scope of this Ordinance extends beyond constitutional limits, it becomes clear that what defendants actually seek by enacting this legislation is a newly-defined class of constitutionally unprotected speech, labeled "pornography" and characterized as sexually discriminatory.

Defendants vigorously argue that *Miller* is not the " 'constitutional divide' separating protected from unprotected expression in this area." . . . Defendants point to three cases which allegedly support their proposition that *Miller* is not the exclusive guideline for disposing of pornography/obscenity cases, and that the traditional obscenity test should not be applied in the present case. . . .

Defendants first argue that the Court must use the same reasoning applied by the Supreme Court in *New York v. Ferber*, . . . which upheld a New York statute prohibiting persons from promoting child pornography by distributing material which depicted such activity, and carve out another similar exception to protected speech under the First Amendment.

Defendants can properly claim some support for their position in *Ferber*. There the Supreme Court allowed the states "greater leeway" in their regulation of pornographic depictions of children in light of the State's compelling interest in protecting children who, without such protections, are extraordinarily vulnerable to exploitation and harm. The Court stated in upholding the New York statute:

> "The prevention of sexual exploitation and abuse of children constitutes a government objective of surpassing importance. The legislative findings

accompanying passage of the New York laws reflect this concern: . . . ."

. . . The Supreme Court continued in *Ferber* by noting that the *Miller* standard for legal obscenity does not satisfy the unique concerns and issues posed by child pornography where children are involved; it is irrelevant, for instance, that the materials sought to be regulated contain serious literary, artistic, political or scientific value. In finding that some speech, such as that represented in depictions of child pornography, is outside First Amendment protections, the *Ferber* court stated:

> When a definable class of material, . . . , bears so heavily and pervasively on the welfare of children engaged in its production, we think the balance of competing interests is clearly struck and that it is permissible to consider these materials as without the protection of the First Amendment.

Defendants, in the case at bar, argue that the interests of protecting women from sex-based discrimination are analogous to and every bit as compelling and fundamental as those which the Supreme Court upheld in *Ferber* for the benefit of children. But *Ferber* appears clearly distinguishable from the instant case on both the facts and law.

As has already been shown, the rationale applied by the Supreme Court in *Ferber* appears intended to apply solely to child pornography cases. In *Ferber,* the court recognized "that a state's interest in 'safeguarding the physical and psychological well-being of a minor' is 'compelling.' " . . . Also, the obscenity standard in *Miller* is appropriately abandoned in child pornography cases because it "[does] not reflect the State's particular and more compelling interest in prosecuting those who promote the sexual exploitations of children." . . . Since a state's compelling interest in preventing child pornography outweighs an individual's First Amendment rights, the Supreme Court held that "the states are entitled to greater leeway in the regulation of pornographic depictions of children." . . .

In contrast, the case at bar presents issues more far reaching than those in *Ferber*. Here, the City-County Council found that the distribution, sale, and exhibition of words and pictures depicting the subordination of women is a form of sex discrimination and as such is appropriate for governmental regulation. The state has a well-recognized interest in preventing sex discrimination, and, defendants argue, it can regulate speech to accomplish that end.

But the First Amendment gives primacy to free speech and any other state interest (such as the interest of sex based equality under law) must be so compelling as to be fundamental; only then can it be deemed to outweigh the interest of free speech. This Court finds no legal authority or public policy argument which justifies so broad an incursion into First Amendment freedoms as to allow that which defendants attempt to advance here. *Ferber* does not open the door to allow the regulation contained in the Ordinance for the reason that adult women as a group do not, as a matter of public policy or applicable law, stand in need of the same type of protection which has long been afforded children. This is true even of women who are subject to the sort of inhuman treatment defendants have described and documented to the Court in support of this Ordinance. The Supreme Court's finding in *Ferber* of the uncontroverted state interest in "safeguarding the physical and psychological well being of a minor" and its resultant characterization of that interest as "compelling," . . . is an interest which inheres to children and is not an interest which is readily transferrable to adult women as a class. Adult women generally have the capacity to protect themselves from participating in and being personally victimized by pornography, which makes the State's interest in safeguarding the physical and psychological well-being of women by prohibiting "the sexually explicit subordination of women, graphically depicted, whether in pictures or in words" not so compelling as to sacrifice the guarantees of the First Amendment. In any case, whether a state interest is so compelling as to be a fundamental interest sufficient to warrant an exception from constitutional protections, therefore, surely must turn on something other than mere legislative dictate, which issue is discussed more fully further on in this Opinion. . . .

The second case relied upon by defendants to support their contention that *Miller* is not controlling in the present case is *FCC v. Pacifica Foundation*, . . . (1978). According to defendants, *Pacifica* exemplifies the Supreme Court's refusal to make obscenity the sole legal basis for regulating sexually explicit conduct.

In *Pacifica*, the Supreme Court was faced with the question of whether a broadcast of patently offensive words dealing with sex and excretion may be regulated on the basis of their content. . . . The Court held that this type of speech was not entitled to absolute constitutional protection in every context. . . . Since the context of the speech in *Pacifica* was broadcasting, it was determined only to be due "the most limited First Amendment protection." . . . The reason for such treatment was two-fold:

> First, the broadcast media have established a uniquely pervasive presence in all the lives of all Americans. Patently offensive, indecent material presented over the airwaves confronts the citizen, not only in public, but also in the privacy of the home, where the individual's right to be left alone plainly outweighs the First Amendment rights of an intruder.
>
> Second, broadcasting is uniquely accessible to children, even those too young to read. . . .

Although the defendants correctly point out that the Supreme Court did not use the traditional obscenity test in *Pacifica,* this Court is not persuaded that the rule enunciated there is applicable to the facts of the present case. The Ordinance does not attempt to regulate the airwaves; in terms of its restrictions, it is not even remotely concerned with the broadcast media. The reasons for the rule in *Pacifica,* that speech in certain contexts should be afforded minimal First Amendment protection, are not present here, since we are not dealing with a medium that "invades" the privacy of the home. In contrast, if an individual is offended by "pornography," as defined in the Ordinance, the logical thing to do

is avoid it, an option frequently not available to the public with material disseminated through broadcasting.

In addition, the Ordinance is not written to protect children from the distribution of pornography, in contrast to the challenged FCC regulation in *Pacifica*. Therefore, the peculiar state interest in protecting the "well being of its youth," . . . does not underlie this Ordinance and cannot be called upon to justify a decision by this Court to uphold the Ordinance.

The third case cited by defendants in support of their proposition that the traditional obscenity standard in *Miller* should not be used to overrule the Ordinance is *Young v. American Mini Theatres, Inc.,* . . . (1976). In *Young* the Supreme Court upheld a city ordinance that restricted the location of movie theatres featuring erotic films. The Court, in a plurality opinion, stated that "[e]ven though the First Amendment protects communication in this area from total suppression, we hold that the State may legitimately use the content of these materials as the basis for placing them in a different classification from other motion pictures." . . . The Court concluded that the city's interest in preserving the character of its neighborhoods justified the ordinance which required that adult theatres be separated, rather than concentrated, in the same areas as it is permissible for other theaters to do without limitation. . . .

Young is distinguishable from the present case because we are not here dealing with an attempt by the City-County Council to restrict the time, place, and manner in which "pornography" may be distributed. Instead, the Ordinance prohibits completely the sale, distribution, or exhibition of material depicting women in a sexually subordinate role, at all times, in all places and in every manner.

The Ordinance's attempt to regulate speech beyond one of the well-defined exceptions to protected speech under the First Amendment is not supported by other Supreme Court precedents. The Court must, therefore, examine the underlying premise of the Ordinance: that the State has so compelling an interest in regulating the sort of sex discrimination imposed and perpetuated through "pornography" that it warrants an exception to free speech.

Is Sex Discrimination a Compelling State Interest Justifying an Exception to First Amendment Protections?

It is significant to note that the premise of the Ordinance is the sociological harm, *i.e.,* the discrimination, which results from "pornography" to degrade women as a class. The Ordinance does not presume or require specifically defined, identifiable victims for most of its proscriptions. The Ordinance seeks to protect adult women, as a group, from the diminution of their legal and sociological status as women, that is, from the discriminatory stigma which befalls women *as women* as a result of "pornography." On page one of the introduction to defendants' *Amicus Brief,* counsel explicitly argues that the harm which underlies this legislation is the "harm to the treatment and *status* of women . . . on the basis of sex." . . .

This is a novel theory advanced by the defendants, an issue of first impression in the courts. If this Court were to accept defendants' argument—that the State's interest in protecting women from the humiliation and degradation which comes from being depicted in a sexually subordinate context is so compelling as to warrant the regulation of otherwise free speech to accomplish that end—one wonders what would prevent the City-County Council (or any other legislative body) from enacting protections for other equally compelling claims against exploitation and discrimination as are presented here. Legislative bodies, finding support here, could also enact legislation prohibiting other unfair expression—the publication and distribution of racist material, for instance, on the grounds that it causes racial discrimination,* or legislation prohibiting ethnic or religious slurs on the grounds that they cause discrimination against particular ethnic or religious groups, or legislation barring literary depictions which are uncomplimentary or oppressive to handicapped persons on the grounds that they cause discrimination against that group of people, and so on. If this Court were to extend to this case the rationale in *Ferber* to uphold the Amendment, it would signal so great a potential encroachment upon First Amendment freedoms that the precious liberties reposed within those guarantees would not survive. The compelling state interest, which defendants claim gives constitutional life to their Ordinance, though important and valid as that interest may be in other contexts, is not so fundamental an interest as to warrant a broad intrusion into otherwise free expression.

Defendants contend that pornography is not deserving of constitutional protection because its harms victimize all women. It is argued that "pornography" not only negatively affects women who risk and suffer the direct abuse of its production, but also, those on whom violent pornography is forced through such acts as compelled performances of "dangerous acts such as being hoisted upside down by ropes, bound by ropes and chains, hung from trees and scaffolds or having sex with animals. . . ." It is also alleged that exposure to pornography produces a negative impact on its viewers, causing in them an increased willingness to aggress toward women, *ibid.* . . . , and experience self-generated rape fantasies, increases in sexual arousal and a rise in the self-reported possibility of raping. . . . In addition, it causes discriminatory attitudes and behavior toward all women. . . . The City-County Council, after considering testimony and social research studies, enacted the Ordinance in order to "combat" pornography's "concrete and tangible harms to women." . . .

Defendants rely on *Paris Adult Theatre I v. Slaton,* . . . (1973), to justify their regulation of "pornography." In that case the Supreme Court held "that there are legitimate state interests at stake in stemming the tide of commercialized obscenity . . . [which] include the

---

*In *Beauharnais v. Illinois,* . . . (1952), the Supreme Court upheld an Illinois libel statute prohibiting the dissemination of materials promoting racial or religious hatred and which tended to produce a breach of the peace and riots. It has been recognized that "the rationale of that decision turns quite plainly on the strong tendency of the prohibited utterances to cause violence and disorder." *Collin v. Smith,* . . . (7th Cir. 1978). The Supreme Court has recognized breach of the peace as the traditional justification for upholding a criminal libel statute. *Beauharnais,* . . . Therefore, a law preventing the distribution of material that causes racial discrimination, an attitude, would be upheld under this analysis. Further, the underlying reasoning of the *Beauharnais* opinion, that the punishment of libel raises no constitutional problems, has been questioned in many recent cases. . . .

interest of the public in the quality of life and the total community environment, the tone of commerce in the great city centers, and, possibly, the public safety itself." . . .

The Georgia Legislature had determined that in that case exposure to obscene material adversely affected men and women, that is to say, society as a whole. Although the petitioners argued in that case that there was no scientific data to conclusively prove that proposition, the Court said, "[i]t is not for us to resolve empirical uncertainties underlying state legislation, save in the exceptional case where that legislation plainly impinges upon rights protected by the constitution itself." . . .

Based on this reasoning, defendants argue that there is more than enough "empirical" evidence in the case at bar to support the City-County Council's conclusion that "pornography" harms women in the same way obscenity harms people, and, therefore, this Court should not question the legislative finding. As has already been acknowledged, it is not the Court's function to question the City-County Council's legislative finding. The Court's solitary duty is to ensure that the Ordinance accomplishes its purpose without violating constitutional standards or impinging upon constitutionally protected rights. In applying those tests, the Court finds that the Ordinance cannot withstand constitutional scrutiny.

It has already been noted that the Ordinance does not purport to regulate legal obscenity, as defined in *Miller*. Thus, although the City-County Council determined that "pornography" harms women, this Court must and does declare the Ordinance invalid without being bound by the legislative findings because "pornography," as defined and regulated in the Ordinance, is constitutionally protected speech under the First Amendment and such an exception to the First Amendment protections is constitutionally unwarranted. This Court cannot legitimately embark on judicial policy-making, carving out a new exception to the First Amendment simply to uphold the Ordinance, even when there may be many good reasons to support legislative action. To permit every interest group, especially those who claim to be victimized by unfair expression, their own legislative exceptions to the First Amendment so long as they succeed in obtaining a majority of legislative votes in their favor demonstrates the potentially predatory nature of what defendants seek through this Ordinance and defend in this lawsuit.

It ought to be remembered by defendants and all others who would support such a legislative initiative that, in terms of altering sociological patterns, much as alteration may be necessary and desirable, free speech, rather than being the enemy, is a long-tested and worthy ally. To deny free speech in order to engineer social change in the name of accomplishing a greater good for one sector of our society erodes the freedoms of all and, as such, threatens tyranny and injustice for those subjected to the rule of such laws. The First Amendment protections presuppose the evil of such tyranny and prevent a finding by this Court upholding the Ordinance. . . .

Suggestions for Further Reading

Anthologies

Copp, D. and Wendell, S. *Pornography and Censorship.* Buffalo: Prometheus Press, 1983.

Donnerstein, E., Linz, D., and Pernod S. *The Question of Pornography.* New York: Free Press, 1987.

Alternative Views

Dworkin, A. *Pornography: Men Possessing Women.* New York: Perigee, 1981.

Griffin, S. *Pornography and Silence.* New York: Harper & Row, 1981.

Lovelace, L. and McGrady, M. *Ordeal.* New York: Berkeley Books, 1980.

Soble, A. *Pornography.* New Haven: Yale University Press, 1986.

Practical Applications

Report of the Attorney General's Commission on Pornography. Washington, D.C.: Government Printing Office, 1986.

Privacy, Drug Testing, and AIDS

Basic Concepts

Do programs for drug testing and testing for AIDS violate people's right to privacy? In order to answer this question, we need first to get clear about what sort of privacy it is to which we can claim a right. Privacy, as defined by W. A. Parent (Selection 38), is the condition of not having undocumented personal knowledge about one possessed by others. Parent criticizes a number of other definitions. First, he contends that privacy does not consist of simply being let alone because we can fail to let people alone by forcefully interfering with them or insulting them without invading their privacy. Second, he argues that privacy is not a form of autonomy or control over significant personal matters because we can have this form of autonomy even when we choose to give up our privacy by revealing all sorts of undocumented personal information about ourselves. Third, Parent argues that privacy is not a limitation on access to oneself. Rather, he contends that such a limitation would protect privacy while not itself being privacy.

Yet notice that it is not the disclosure of just any undocumented information about oneself, such as one's hat size, that interferes with privacy. Rather, privacy is at issue when the information that is disclosed is important to one's personal life. So, for example, if someone were to reveal accounts of friends and associates found in your diary, that would clearly infringe upon your privacy. Nor is privacy interfered with only when undocumented information that is important to one's personal life is made public. Some documented information may only be known to a small number of people, so that bringing that information to a larger audience may also infringe upon privacy.

But obviously other things can have an important impact upon one's personal life than other people's knowledge of it, and some of these other ways of affecting one's personal life have been thought to infringe upon privacy as well. For example, the Supreme Court considered prohibiting the use of contraceptives an unjustified infringement on people's privacy in *Griswold* v. *Connecticut,* and the Court also considered anti-abortion laws an unjustified infringement on the privacy of women in *Roe* v. *Wade*. So it would seem that the question of whether one's privacy has been infringed upon turns upon whether there has been a significant negative impact on one's personal life either by the disclosure of personal information or by direct interference with one's life.

Alternative Views

Once we know what constitutes an infringement of privacy, the next question is when such infringements are unjustified because they violate a person's right to privacy. Currently, this question is being debated in the area of drug testing and testing for AIDS. In Selection 39, Susan Dentzer and coauthors survey various examples of job testing that are presently in use, such as honesty tests, drug tests, personality tests, and tests for AIDS, bringing out the conflicting interests of employees and employers in each case. The authors claim that society has much to gain from careful and sophisticated testing, but the challenge, as they see it, is whether this gain can be attained without unwarranted encroachment on the rights and freedoms that Americans hold dear.

In Selection 40, James Felman and Christopher Petrini argue that drug testing as it is practiced in public employment violates the Fourth Amendment's prohibition on unreasonable searches and seizures. They present a statistical overview of the nature and scope of illegal drug use in the United States. While drug use has been declining since 1979, it was estimated in 1982 that 3 to 5 percent of the U.S. work force used drugs regularly. It has also been determined that poverty and affluence correlate with drug use, but not race and ethnicity.

Felman and Petrini discuss two types of drug tests: the EMIT and the GC/MS. The EMIT is inexpensive and easy to administer on the job, but is inherently inaccurate. The GC/MS is more expensive and requires laboratory conditions to evaluate, but is highly accurate. Yet even when EMIT positive results are confirmed by GC/MS testing, the likelihood that a given positive result is correct depends entirely upon the extent to which the testing group actually uses drugs. If one assumes that 5 percent of a group of employees uses illegal drugs and an employer uses a drug testing program with 95 percent accuracy to screen the group, the program will yield one false positive for every true positive. If only 2 percent of the group uses illegal drugs, three out of every four positives will be false.

Felman and Petrini point out that the main governmental interests in drug testing are to maintain (1) the safety and efficiency in the workplace and (2) the integrity of the employment institution as perceived by the public. Yet they argue that a general drug testing program is both an overinclusive and underinclusive means of reaching these goals. They argue that, in general, a better and less intrusive means of reaching these goals is a supervision program that focuses on employees who make more mistakes, are frequently absent, and suffer from drug-related health problems.

Yet the courts seem less concerned with whether drug testing programs are a good means of reaching these goals as they are with whether the programs violate anyone's rights. Since the courts do not consider a job something to which people have a right, imposing drug testing as a condition for initial or continued employment does not seem objectionable to them.* By contrast in criminal cases where people's rights to life and liberty are clearly at issue, "probable cause" is generally required to justify search and seizure. Of course, it could be argued that what the courts are failing to appreciate in these cases is the extent to which a person's right to privacy is at issue.

Obviously, testing for AIDS raises somewhat different questions than testing for illegal drugs. A major controversy over testing for AIDS concerns whether insurance companies should be allowed to test for AIDS. In Selection 41, Karen Clifford and Russel Iuculano argue that insurance is founded on the princi-

ple that policyholders with the same expected risk of loss should be treated equally. They further argue that AIDS antibody tests are sufficiently reliable to be valid underwriting tools for the insurance industry. What they would hope to do is separate out those applicants for insurance who have the HTLV-III virus and have their insurance needs met by state and federal governments.

In Selection 42, Benjamin Schatz argues that because AIDS has been popularly associated with gay men, some insurers have responded to AIDS by discriminating against gays in insuring policies. Despite its medical reliability, Schatz argues against the use of HIV testing. The issue, as he sees it, is who should bear the costs: the industry or the government. Since in arguing against proposals for national health insurance the industry has long insisted that it is in a better position to manage the health care costs, Schatz contends that it should not be now allowed to shift a burden that it deems unprofitable to the government. Nevertheless, Schatz agrees with Clifford and Iuculano that some state and federal help is still required to deal with the insurance needs of those with AIDS.

Practical Application

In *Schaill* v. *Tippecanoe School Corporation* (Selection 43), the issue before the United States Court of Appeals was whether a random urinalysis program at a school operated by the Tippecanoe County School Corporation violated the right of student athletes not to be subjected to reasonable searches and seizures under the Fourth Amendment. The court argues that the urinalysis program was a search and seizure under the Fourth Amendment, but that it was justified because a standard of reasonableness rather than "probable cause" is all that has to be met by such a program. Here the court is arguing in much the same way that other courts have argued with respect to drug testing for employment and insurance. The court contends that because participation in interscholastic athletics is a

*Notice that this is the same type of reasoning that was employed by the Supreme Court in *Wyman* v. *James*, an earlier Fourth Amendment case concerning welfare.

good to which student athletes do not have a right, "reasonable" restrictions on access to that good do not violate a right to privacy. So it would seem that as the court interprets a right to privacy, it rides "piggy-back," so to speak, on other rights. If then, as libertarians claim, people do not have a right to employment, insurance, or participation in interscholastic athletics, restricting access to these goods does not violate their right to privacy. But if welfare liberals or socialists are correct that people do have a right to employment and insurance and maybe even to participate in interscholastic athletics, then it would seem that what the courts have permitted in these cases does violate a right to privacy.

38. Privacy, Morality, and the Law

W. A. Parent

According to W. A. Parent, privacy is the condition of not having undocumented personal knowledge about one possessed by others. Parent criticizes a number of other definitions of privacy and then argues that privacy, as he defines it, is a fundamental moral value that people have a right to have protected. Finally, he develops a set of questions for determining when a right to privacy has been wrongfully invaded.

The Definition of Privacy

Defining privacy requires a familiarity with its ordinary usage, of course, but this is not enough since our common ways of talking and using language are riddled with inconsistencies, ambiguities, and paradoxes. What we need is a definition which is by and large consistent with ordinary language, so that capable speakers of English will not be genuinely surprised that the term "privacy" should be defined in this way, but which also enables us to talk consistently, clearly, and precisely about the family of concepts to which privacy belongs. Moreover the definition must not usurp or encroach upon the basic meanings and functions of the other concepts within this family. Drawing useful and legitimate distinctions between different values is the best

W. A. Parent, "Privacy, Morality, and the Law," *Philosophy and Public Affairs* 12, No. 4 (Fall 1983). Copyright © 1983 by Princeton University Press. Excerpts reprinted with permission of Princeton University Press.

antidote to exploitation and evisceration of the concept of privacy.

Let me first state and then elaborate on my definition. Privacy is the condition of not having undocumented personal knowledge about one possessed by others. A person's privacy is diminished exactly to the degree that others possess this kind of knowledge about him. I want to stress that what I am defining is the condition of privacy, not the right to privacy. I will talk about the latter shortly. My definition is new, and I believe it to be superior to all of the other conceptions that have been proffered when measured against the desiderata of conceptual analysis above.

A full explication of the personal knowledge definition requires that we clarify the concept of personal information. My suggestion is that it be understood to consist of *facts* about a person which most individuals in a given society at a given time do not want widely known about themselves. They may not be concerned that a few close friends, relatives, or professional associates know these facts, but they would be very much concerned if the information passed beyond this limited circle.

In contemporary America facts about a person's sexual preferences, drinking or drug habits, income, the state of his or her marriage and health belong to the class of personal information. Ten years from now some of these facts may be a part of everyday conversation; if so their disclosure would not diminish individual privacy.

This account of personal information, which makes it a function of existing cultural norms and social practices, needs to be broadened a bit to accommodate a particular and unusual class of cases of the following sort. Most of us don't care if our height, say, is widely known. But there are a few persons who are extremely sensitive about their height (or weight or voice pitch). They might take extreme measures to ensure that other people not find it out. For such individuals height is a very personal matter. Were someone to find it out by ingenious snooping we should not hesitate to talk about an invasion of privacy.

Let us, then, say that personal information consists of facts which most persons in a given society choose not to reveal about themselves (except to close friends, family, . . .) or of facts about which a particular individual is acutely sensitive and which he therefore does not choose to reveal about himself, even though most people don't care if these same facts are widely known about themselves.

Here we can question the status of information belonging to the public record, that is, information to be found in newspapers, court proceedings, and other official documents open to public inspection. (We might discover, for example, that Jones and Smith were arrested many years ago for engaging in homosexual activities.) Should such information be excluded from the category of personal information? The answer is that it should not. There is, after all, nothing extraordinary about public documents containing some very personal information. I will hereafter refer to personal facts belonging to the public record as documented.

My definition of privacy excludes knowledge of documented personal information. I do this for a simple reason. Suppose that A is browsing through some old newspapers and happens to see B's name in a story about child prodigies who unaccountably failed to succeed as adults. B had become an obsessive gambler

and an alcoholic. Should we accuse A of invading B's privacy? No. An affirmative answer blurs the distinction between the public and the private. What belongs to the public domain cannot without glaring paradox be called private; consequently it should not be incorporated within our concept of privacy.

But, someone might object, A might decide to turn the information about B's gambling and drinking problems over to a reporter who then publishes it in a popular news magazine. Isn't B's privacy diminished by this occurrence? No. I would certainly say that his reputation might well suffer from it. And I would also say that the publication is a form of gratuitous exploitation. But to challenge it as an invasion of privacy is not at all reasonable since the information revealed was publicly available and could have been found out by anyone, without resort to snooping or prying. In this crucial respect, the story about B no more diminished his privacy than would have disclosures about his property interests, say, or about any other facts concerning him that belonged to the public domain.

I hasten to add that a person does lose a measure of privacy at the time when personal information about him first becomes a part of the public record, since the information was until that time undocumented. It is also important not to confuse documented facts as I define them here with facts about individuals which are kept on file for special purposes but which are not available for public consumption, for example, health records. Publication of the latter does imperil privacy; for this reason special precautions are usually taken to ensure that the information does not become public property.

I believe the personal knowledge definition isolates the conceptual one of privacy, its distinctive and unique meaning. It does not appropriate ideas which properly belong to other concepts. Unfortunately the three most popular definitions do just this, confusing privacy with quite different values.

Privacy Consists of Being Let Alone

Warren and Brandeis were the first to advocate this broad definition. Brandeis movingly appealed to it again in his celebrated dissent to the U.S. Supreme Court's majority ruling in *Olmstead v. U.S.* Objecting to the Court's view that telephone wiretapping does not constitute a search and seizure, Brandeis delivered an impassioned defense of every citizen's right to be let alone, which he called our most cherished entitlement. Several other former U.S. Supreme Court Justices have endorsed this conception of privacy, among them Douglas, Fortas, and Steward. And a number of distinguished law professors have done likewise.

What proponents of the Brandeis definition fail to see is that there are innumerable ways of failing to let a person alone which have nothing to do with his privacy. Suppose, for instance, that A clubs B on the head or repeatedly insults him. We should describe and evaluate such actions by appeal to concepts like force, violence, and harassment. Nothing in the way of analytical clarity and justificatory power is lost if the concept of privacy is limited, as I have suggested that it be, to cases involving the acquisition of undocumented personal knowledge. Inflationary conceptions of privacy invite muddled reasoning.

Privacy Consists of a Form of Autonomy or Control over Significant Personal Matters

"If the right to privacy means anything, it is the right of the individual, married or single, to be free from unwarranted government invasion into matters so fundamentally affecting a person as the decision whether to bear or beget a child." With these words, from the Supreme Court case of *Eisenstadt v. Baird,* Mr. Justice Brennan expresses a second influential theory of privacy.

Indeed, definitions of privacy in terms of control dominate the literature. Perhaps the most favored among them equates privacy with the control over personal information about oneself. Fried, Wasserstrom, Gross, and Beardsley all adopt it or a close variation of it. Other lawyers and philosophers, including Van Den Haag, Altman, and Parker, identify privacy with control over access to oneself, or in Parker's words, "control over when and by whom the various parts of us can be sensed by others."

All of these definitions should be jettisoned.

To see why, consider the example of a person who voluntarily divulges all sorts of intimate, personal, and undocumented information about himself to a friend. She is doubtless exercising control, in a paradigm sense of the term, over personal information about herself as well as over (cognitive) access to herself. But we would not and should not say that in doing so she is preserving or protecting her privacy. On the contrary, she is voluntarily relinquishing much of her privacy. People can and do choose to give up privacy for many reasons. An adequate conception of privacy must allow for this fact. Control definitions do not.

I believe the voluntary disclosure counterexample is symptomatic of a deep confusion underlying the thesis that privacy is a form of control. It is a conceptual confusion, the mistaking of privacy for a part of liberty. The defining idea of liberty is the absence of external restraints or coercion. A person who is behind bars or locked in a room or physically pinned to the ground is unfree to do many things. Similarly a person who is prohibited by law from making certain choices should be described as having been denied the liberty or freedom to make them. The loss of liberty in these cases takes the form of a deprivation of autonomy. Hence we can meaningfully say that the right to liberty embraces in part the right of persons to make fundamentally important choices about their lives and therewith to exercise significant control over different aspects of their behavior. It is clearly distinguishable from the right to privacy, which condemns the unwarranted acquisition of undocumented personal knowledge.

Privacy Is the Limitation on Access to the Self

This definition, defended by Garrett and Gavison among others, has the virtue of separating privacy from liberty. But it still is unsatisfactory. If we understand "access" to mean something like "physical proximity," then the difficulty becomes that there are other viable concepts which much more precisely describe what is at stake by limiting such access. Among these concepts I would include personal property, solitude, and peace. If, on the other hand, "access" is interpreted as referring to the acquisition of personal knowledge, we're still faced with a seemingly intractable counterexample. A taps B's phone and overhears many of her conversations, including some of a very intimate nature. Official restraints have been imposed on A's snooping, though. He must obtain permission from a judge before listening in on B. This case shows that limitation of cognitive access does not imply privacy.

A response sympathetic with the Garrett-Gavison conception to the above criticism might suggest that they really meant to identify privacy with certain kinds of limitations on access to the self. But why then didn't they say this, and why didn't they tell us what relevant limitations they had in mind?

Let us suppose that privacy is thought to consist of certain normal limitations on cognitive access to the self. Should we accept this conception? I think not, since it confuses privacy with the existential conditions that are necessary for its realization. To achieve happiness I must have some good luck, but this doesn't mean that happiness is good luck. Similarly, if I am to enjoy privacy there have to be limitations on cognitive access to me, but these limitations are not themselves privacy. Rather privacy is what they safeguard.

The Value of Privacy

Is privacy a basic human value? There are many unpersuasive arguments that it is. Consider one of the most well-known, that given by Fried: "to respect, love, trust, feel affection for others, and to regard ourselves as the objects of love, trust, and affection is at the heart of our notion of ourselves as persons among persons, and privacy is the necessary atmosphere for these attitudes and actions, as oxygen is for combustion." Privacy is essential for intimate relationships because, in Fried's view, their defining mark is the sharing of information about oneself that is not shared with others, and without privacy this would be impossible.

The difficulty with Fried's argument is that it relies on a skewed conception of intimacy.

Intimacy involves much more than the exclusive sharing of information. It also involves the sharing of one's total self—one's experiences, aspirations, weaknesses, and values. This kind of emotional commitment, and concomitant giving, is entirely overlooked by Fried. He furnishes no argument for the claim that it cannot survive the loss of privacy.

Several so-called functional arguments on behalf of privacy also fail. Thus it is sometimes said that privacy is needed for relaxation, emotional release, self-reflection, and self-analysis, but this account confuses privacy with solitude, that is, the condition of being physically alone. Granted A might not be able to relax or think about her life unless she is left by herself, we are still not being told why *privacy* is important. Of course A might have to believe that her privacy is being respected if she is to relax and reflect successfully, but this still doesn't show that privacy itself (as opposed to the belief that we have it) is necessary to do these things.

Nor should we buy the thesis that privacy is necessary for individuality and freedom. It is easy to imagine a person who has little or no privacy but who nonetheless possesses the determination and strength of will to think and act individually. Even those lacking in such determination might still be able to think and act for themselves so long as they believe (rightly or wrongly) that their privacy is intact. Similarly, persons without privacy might still enjoy considerable freedom. This will be true in cases where A is not aware of and has no reason for thinking that someone else is watching her every move and so is not deterred from pursuing various activities. It will also be true in cases where A simply doesn't care whether anyone else is watching her.

Lest you now begin to wonder whether privacy has any value at all, let me quickly point to several very good reasons why people in societies like ours desire privacy as I have defined it. First of all, if others manage to obtain sensitive personal knowledge about us they will by that very fact acquire power over us. Their power could then be used to our disadvantage. The possibilities for exploitation become very real. The definite connection between harm and the invasion of privacy explains why we place a value on not having undocumented personal information about ourselves widely known.

Second, as long as we live in a society where individuals are generally intolerant of life styles, habits, and ways of thinking that differ significantly from their own, and where human foibles tend to become the object of scorn and ridicule, our desire for privacy will continue unabated. No one wants to be laughed at and made to feel ashamed of himself. And we all have things about us which, if known, might very well trigger these kinds of unfeeling and wholly unwarranted responses.

Third, we desire privacy out of a sincere conviction that there are certain facts about us which other people, particularly strangers and casual acquaintances, are not entitled to know. This conviction is constitutive of "the liberal ethic," a conviction centering on the basic thesis that individuals are not to be treated as mere property of the state but instead are to be respected as autonomous, independent beings with unique aims to fulfill. These aims, in turn, will perforce lead people down life's separate paths. Those of us educated under this liberal ideology feel that our lives are our own business (hence the importance of personal liberty) and that personal facts about our lives are for the most part ours alone to know. The suggestion that all personal facts should be made available for public inspection is contrary to this view. Thus, our desire for privacy is to a large extent a matter of principle.

For most people, this desire is perfectly innocent. We are not seeking to hurt or disadvantage anyone by exercising it. Unquestionably some people at times demand privacy for fraudulent purposes, for example, to hide discreditable facts about themselves from future employers who are entitled to this information. Posner emphasizes this motive for privacy. But not everyone values privacy for this reason, and, even for those who do, misrepresentation is most often not the only or the overriding motive.

So there are several good reasons why we hold privacy to be an important value, one worth arguing for, and defending from unwarranted invasion. Now I want to suggest that anyone who deliberately and without justification frustrates or contravenes our desire for privacy violates the distinctively liberal, moral principle of respect for persons. Let us say that A frustrates B's desire for privacy if he invades B's privacy and B knows it. A acts in contravention of B's desire for privacy if he invades B's privacy without B's knowing it. Assuming that A has no justification for doing either, we can and should accuse him of acting in disregard of B's own desires and interests. A's action displays contempt for B in the sense that it is undertaken with no effort to identify with her life purposes or to appreciate what the fulfillment of these purposes might mean to her. Specifically by gratuitously or indiscriminately invading B's privacy (I will explain these terms shortly) A manifests disrespect for B in the sense that he ignores or counts as having no significance B's desire, spawned and nurtured by the liberal values of her society, not to have personal facts about herself known by ingenious or persistent snooping.

The Moral Right to Privacy

The above argument establishes that privacy is indeed a moral value for persons who also prize freedom and individuality. That we should seek to protect it against unwarranted invasion should come, then, as no surprise. Advocating a moral right to privacy comprises an integral part of this effort. It expresses our conviction that privacy should only be infringed under exigent circumstances and for the most compelling reasons, for example, law enforcement and health care provision.

The moral right to privacy does not embody the rule "privacy may never be invaded." It is important to emphasize that there are such things as justifiable invasions of privacy. Our concern is not to condemn invasions but to declare our right not to become the victims of wrongful invasions. Discussion of a right to privacy presupposes that privacy is a good, vulnerable to loss by human contrivance. It does not presuppose that such loss is always bad.

Davis and Thomson have recently tried to deflate the right to privacy. The latter's essay is the better known so I will now discuss it.

Thomson wants us to believe that there is no one independently identifiable right to privacy. Instead there are a number of diverse rights under "privacy" each of which is a right of some other kind. Moreover, the right to privacy is derivative in the sense that we can explain why we possess each of the rights subsumable under privacy without ever mentioning the right of privacy itself. And we can also explain the wrongness of every violation of the right to privacy without once mentioning it. So according to Thomson we really don't need to talk about a distinct right to privacy at all. She supports her argument with the following analyses.

(1) A owns a pornographic picture which he keeps locked up in a safe. B trains his special X-ray device on the safe and sees the picture. Thomson concedes that B has violated A's right to privacy, but she thinks a more fundamental explanation of why B acted wrongly is in terms of A's right that others not do certain things with what he owns. These include looking at them and selling them. These are property rights and it is by infringing one of them that B wrongs A.

(2) B finds out by entirely legitimate means that A owns the pornographic picture. He proceeds to publish this fact in a newspaper. If anyone thinks that B has invaded A's right to privacy, a very simple explanation is available: A has the right not to be caused mental distress, and it is this right that B's action violates.

(3) A doesn't want her face looked at and so keeps it covered. B uses his X-ray device to look at A's face through the covering. In doing so B violates A's right that her face not be looked at (how simple!). This is one of the rights over our person that we possess.

(4) A is a great opera singer who no longer wants to be listened to. She only sings quietly behind closed doors and soundproof walls. B trains an amplifier on A's home and listens to her sing. In so doing B transgresses A's right not to be listened to, which according to Thomson is another one of those basic rights over the person we possess. Here, as in each of the preceding cases, we have no need to invoke the right to privacy.

Thomson's attempt to diminish the status of the right to privacy fails to persuade. It requires that we recognize a plethora of rights whose status is certainly more problematic than that of the right whose significance she wants to impugn. Do we really think of ourselves as possessing the rights not to be looked at and listened to? Must we talk about a right not to have our property looked at? Thomson's claim that we waive these rights all the time—a claim she has to make to avoid the absurd implication that our rights are violated thousands of times every day—flies in the face of common sense and common experience. Just ask whether you thought of yourself as having waived the right not to be listened to before speaking with people today. The idea seems preposterous. I certainly didn't conceive of myself as waiving a right not to be looked at before entering the classroom this morning. And I venture to add that it would bemuse my students to hear me speak of my right not to be looked at.

Thomson's simplifying strategy is unmistakably convoluted. It is possible to deal in a much less ad hoc and tortuous manner with her examples once we have settled on an adequate definition of privacy.

(1) If B's looking at A's picture is unjustified, and if A is entitled to possess the pornographic picture, then by my account of the moral right to privacy B does violate this right in A. We could also say that A has a concrete moral right that her picture not be looked at which can be deduced from the more fundamental right of privacy when applied to the particular circumstances of this case.

(2) If B has no justification for publishing the fact that A possesses a pornographic picture, then he has violated A's right to privacy. And it is by virtue of violating this right that B causes A mental distress.

(3) If A has no evil intention in covering her face and if B has no substantial reason for peeking at it, then B's intrusion violates A's right to privacy. We could express this point by saying that A's right to privacy when applied to the particular circumstances of this case yields her concrete right not to be looked at. (Remember that a person's physical appearance can constitute personal information.)

(4) If B's snooping is without justification it should be condemned as a violation of A's right to privacy.

The basic failing of Thomson's essay is that she makes no attempt to define privacy. We have good reason to ask how she hopes to convince anyone that the right to privacy is derivative and quite dispensable without first telling us what the right means. My position is that once the meaning of privacy is clarified and its value articulated no one will have cause to question the legitimacy of our talk about a fundamental right of privacy.

Criteria of Wrongful Invasion

Which invasions of privacy are justifiable and which are not? A complete conception of the right to privacy must address this question, providing general criteria of wrongful invasion, which will then have to be applied to specific cases. Whether the right to privacy has been violated in a specific case can often only be answered through a process of making difficult and controversial value judgments. No conception of the right to privacy, no matter how detailed and sophisticated will allow us to eliminate or bypass this process.

The following questions are central to assessing alleged violations of the right to privacy:

(1) For what purpose(s) is the undocumented personal knowledge sought?
(2) Is this purpose a legitimate and important one?
(3) Is the knowledge sought through invasion of privacy relevant to its justifying purpose?
(4) Is invasion of privacy the only or the least offensive means of obtaining the knowledge?
(5) What restrictions or procedural restraints have been placed on the privacy-invading techniques?
(6) What protection is to be afforded the personal knowledge once it has been acquired?

The first four questions all have to do with the rationale for invading privacy. We can say that the right to privacy is violated by *gratuitous* invasions and that these occur when: there is no purpose at all to them; when the purpose is less than compelling; when the personal facts sought have nothing to do with the justifying purposes; when the personal information could have been obtained by less intrusive measures. Among the legitimate purposes for acquiring undocumented personal information are efficient law enforcement, confirmation of eligibility criteria set forth in various government welfare programs, and the compilation of statistical data concerning important behavioral trends.

Question (5) pertains to the actual invasion of privacy itself. We can say that the right to privacy is violated by *indiscriminate* invasions and that these occur when insufficient procedural safeguards have been imposed on the techniques employed so that either: all sorts of personal information, some germane to the investigation but some totally irrelevant thereto, is obtained; or persons with no business knowing the personal facts acquired are allowed to gain cognitive access to them. One can argue against a proposed invasion of privacy on the grounds that it is too likely to be indiscriminate in either of these two senses.

Question (6) pertains to postinvasion safeguards. We can say that the right to privacy is violated when the undocumented personal information acquired is not adequately protected against unwarranted cognitive intrusion or unauthorized uses. It is also violated, of course, by actual instances of such intrusions and uses.

Let us look at a concrete example. Suppose a large city is faced with the growing problem of welfare fraud. It decides that to combat this problem an elaborate system of surveillance must be initiated. Personal information regarding welfare recipients' income, family status, sexual habits, and spending habits is to be obtained. Search warrants are obtained permitting unlimited surveillance and specifying the kind of information being sought. Once obtained the information is to be stored on magnetic tapes and kept in the welfare department.

Any person who takes the right to privacy

seriously will raise the following questions and make the following observations about this city's (C's) action:

(i) C presents no arguments or evidence in support of its belief that the problem of welfare fraud can be solved by resorting to large-scale surveillance. We should demand that C do so.

(ii) C presents no arguments or evidence showing that surveillance is the only way to acquire the relevant personal information. Did it first try to obtain knowledge of welfare recipients' life styles by asking them about it or sending them questionnaires? Were there other, less intensive measures available for acquiring this knowledge?

(iii) Search warrants permitting unlimited surveillance are insufficiently discriminating. So are warrants which do not particularly describe the places to be observed and the facts to be gathered. C should have insisted that the warrants place restrictions on the time periods of surveillance as well as on its scope.

(iv) Why is it necessary to acquire information about welfare recipients' sexual habits? How is this knowledge relevant to the objective of eradicating fraud?

(v) What kind of security does C intend to provide for the magnetic tapes containing the acquired information? Who will enjoy access to these tapes? Will they eventually be erased or destroyed? C has the duty to guard against the potential abuse of the stored facts.

I hope this brief analysis is helpful in isolating some of the crucial issues and difficult questions that must be confronted when applying the right of privacy to particular cases. Often there will be strong disagreement over whether proposed programs of physical, psychological, and data surveillance are gratuitous or indiscriminate. This is to be expected. The results of these disputes will determine the contours of the privacy right.

39. Can You Pass the Job Test?

Susan Dentzer, Bob Cohn, George Raine, Ginny Carroll, and Vicki Quade

> In this selection the authors survey various examples of job testing that are currently in use, such as honesty tests, drug tests, personality tests, and tests for AIDS, and bring out the conflicting interests of employees and employers with respect to each case.

When Arlo Guthrie sang his Vietnam-era ballad "Alice's Restaurant," his tormentor was that era's answer to Big Brother—the military draft board. Today John Sexton might cast someone else in the role of snooping archvillain: his former employer. Last year [1985] Sexton, then a $30,000-a-year dispatcher at Federal Express Corp. in Atlanta, was one of a

From *Newsweek* (5 May 1986): 46–53; story prepared by Susan Dentzer, Bob Cohn, George Raine, Ginny Carroll, and Vicki Quade.

group of employees ordered to submit urine samples for a drug test. Sexton tested positive; he says he had smoked marijuana at a party two weeks earlier, but he didn't appear impaired at the time of the test. Next he was ordered to take a lie-detector test or face suspension—but when he denied using drugs on the job or knowing anyone who did, the polygrapher running the test concluded he was holding something back. Fired last May, the 29-year-old college graduate hasn't been able to land another job since. Federal Express declines to comment on the episode but suggests that Sexton's firing was appropriate. Sexton, meanwhile, is preparing to sue Federal for wrongful discharge—and the American Civil Liberties Union (ACLU) of Georgia says he has a strong case.

Sexton's situation isn't unusual: in corporations across the United States, a frenzy of inspecting, detecting, selecting and rejecting is under way. Plans to test baseball players for illegal drug use have created a stir, but nearly a third of the corporations in the Fortune 500 also screen employees for abuse of even casual intake of such substances as marijuana and cocaine. Countless other firms monitor workers' honesty with lie detectors or written exams or probe their psyches with an array of personality tests. Some corporations have begun monitoring employees for diseases such as AIDS. And in quest of the perfect employee, many firms may one day be able to screen out workers with hundreds of genetic traits that could predispose them to serious and costly illnesses.

The boom in testing is fueling the growth of what was once a cottage industry: an array of labs, consulting firms, security specialists and other testing companies that together take in hundreds of millions of dollars in revenue each year. At the same time, it pits employees against management in a debate over whose interests tip the scales of justice. Which set of rights is paramount: those of companies seeking a productive and safe work force—or those of employees trying to protect their privacy? Does testing really identify drug abusers, in-house thieves and other undesirables, or are the innocent and employable also caught in the net? Is testing of employees the key to U.S. industrial competitiveness, or is it worsening labor-management relations at a time when more cooperation is needed? Does testing protect the commonweal, or does it run against the grain of American society—smacking of the oppressive utopias of Aldous Huxley's *Brave New World* or George Orwell's *1984*?

. . . Lawsuits and union grievances challenging the use of drug testing are on the rise; California has barred testing for the AIDS virus or antibody as a condition of employment, and Congress may soon approve legisla-tion to outlaw the use of lie detectors by most private employers. But whether these developments will dampen the current enthusiasm for testing is unclear. Many companies, alarmed by growing drug use and fearful of everything from wrongful-discharge suits to liability for faulty products, are embracing the use of testing as a vital defense. And advances in technology have made testing almost irresistible, yielding procedures that are "good enough and cheap enough that they are now an [inexpensive] management tool," says Bill Maher, a San Francisco supervisor who helped draft a city ordinance that bars most blanket drug testing.

Testing employees and job applicants is hardly new; in fact, the 1950s may have marked an earlier zenith of testing, as companies gathered reams of information on their prospective workers through psychological profiles, employment histories, criminal records and personal data. The shifting values and mores of the 1960s and 1970s changed all that, says Columbia University professor of public law Alan Westin. Federal equal-employment-opportunity guidelines put the onus on employers to ensure that testing was a scientifically valid selection tool and that it didn't discriminate against specific racial or social groups. As privacy laws were passed to protect the public from intrusive or discriminatory data collection by government and institutions such as credit agencies, private employers also began weeding out their personnel files and testing less.

Now that companies are turning to testing again, the privacy issue is back with a vengeance. Through the Fourth Amendment, only government workers have constitutional protection against unreasonable searches and seizures by their employer—a by-product of the Founding Fathers' fear that unchecked government posed the greatest threat to citizens' rights. Nonetheless, many legal scholars believe that there also exists in society "a certain essential right of individuals to be left alone, and not to be subjected to . . . invasive activities without justification," as Geoffrey Stone, a professor of constitutional law at the University of Chicago, puts it. "Can you imagine the Founding Fathers saying that the major source of authority in [your] life"—your employer—"can make you drop your pants and urinate as a condition of getting or keeping a job?" asks Gene Guerrero, director of the Georgia ACLU. "It's ludicrous." But while employers argue that it's necessary, that's in a sense what many are compelling employees to do.

Honesty Tests: Are They Valid?

The late Sen. Sam Ervin called them "20th-century witchcraft," but that hasn't stopped many employers from administering lie detectors, or polygraph tests. Almost 2 million are given to employees and job applicants each year—and they can be "a very effective tool in stopping employee crime," says Mark A. de Bernardo, a labor lawyer at the U.S. Chamber of Commerce. Brokerage firms such as E. F. Hutton and banks like Citicorp routinely give polygraphs—Hutton to all employees and Citicorp to most workers who physically handle money. Days Inns of America, a national motel chain based in Atlanta, testified in Congress last year that use of lie detectors helped cut its losses from employee crime to $115,000 in 1984, down from $1 million in 1975.

But polygraphs are undoubtedly more of a deterrent to crime than an effective means of determining an employee's guilt or innocence. The federal Office of Technology Assessment determined in 1983 that the scientific validity of lie-detector results couldn't be established. The American Psychological Association charges that polygraphs turn up "an unacceptable number of false positives"—that is, the subjects had not been lying. Because of these and other factors, few American courts will admit polygraph data as evidence.

Following the pattern of similar legislation in about 20 states, the House of Representatives last March passed the Polygraph Protection Act, which would prohibit private employers from giving lie-detector tests to most current or prospective employees. (Many utility workers, pharmaceutical workers handling controlled substances, day-care workers and employees of private security companies could

still be polygraphed). Last week hearings were held on a similar measure introduced in the Senate by Republican Orrin Hatch of Utah, a conservative, and liberal Democrat Ted Kennedy. Opposed by the likes of attorney F. Lee Bailey—as well as polygraphers and many employers, who would prefer tighter regulation of the polygraph industry—the measure seems likely to pass.

To avoid the cost (about $40 to $50 per test) and ambiguity of polygraph tests, many companies have turned instead to written honesty tests. John E. Reid & Associates of Chicago, a pioneer in the field, markets its $9 tests to about 2,000 clients nationwide: Stanton Corp., based in Charlotte, N.C., sells about a million tests each year to hotel chains, clothing retailers, convenience stores and other companies whose workers regularly handle money or merchandise for sale. Jim Walls, vice president of Stanton, contends that such screening is a necessity in an age when people move or change jobs frequently. "There's no way that [companies] can ever get to know the people they're hiring before they're hired," he says.

Many honesty-test questions are almost disarmingly ingenuous. Dr. Homer B. C. Reed, a neuropsychologist at Tufts University's New England Medical Center and a consultant to Stanton, singles out one sample question: "The amount I stole from my employer was (a) 0 (b) $5 (c) $25 (d) $100 (e) $500," accompanied by a space for an explanation. Reed says many job applicants actually circle one of the last four answers. "You would think you can't identify scoundrels by asking them if they're scoundrels, but you can," he says.

Prompted by concerns that employers would use written tests to pry too much into employees' backgrounds, as some lie-detector tests have done, a new Massachusetts state law prohibits employers from giving honesty tests that amount to "paper and pencil" polygraphs. Many experts are troubled for different reasons, calling some tests a useless tool that could actually screen out capable, honest employees. Columbia Professor Westin derides the absolutism of some tests in requiring "a Fearless Fosdick, Dick Tracy response to every situation"; he thinks they may be used to screen out "people more likely to join a union or challenge something on a job as being morally or ethically improper." Michael Merbaum, a psychologist with St. Louis-based Psychological Associates Inc., a management-consulting and training firm, concurs. He believes that the "correct" answers to many tests are too often based on strict definitions of honesty that may not be shared by test takers: for example, an employee who admits he once took office supplies may not believe he did anything wrong. A far better approach, says Merbaum, is interviewing prospective employees carefully to determine their level of emotional maturity—and to discover whether they have "the capability to appraise situations . . . judiciously so they will make the proper decisions."

Drug Tests: Legal Challenges

When guards conducted an early-morning drug sweep of the Albuquerque Publishing Co. last January, company officials said it was for good reason: an estimated 20 percent of the firm's employees have "an abuse problem," says company president Thompson Lang—and of all the job applicants who've taken drug tests in recent months, "no one has passed." Few companies face problems quite so dramatic, but drug use does take a serious toll: the U.S. Chamber of Commerce estimates that drug and alcohol abuse among workers costs employers $60 billion a year—the total tab for lost productivity, accidents, higher medical claims, increased absenteeism and theft of company property (the means by which many workers finance their drug habits). Relatively few companies seem to be tackling alcohol abuse with as much conviction, but concern about drugs is plainly growing, and it has spread well beyond the private workplace. Last week Boston's police commissioner called for mandatory drug testing of all officers, and in a recommendation hotly disputed by some panel members, President Reagan's Commission on Organized Crime recently called for testing of all federal workers in an attempt to control the spread of drugs.

To root out drug abusers among applicants or employees, meanwhile, companies such as Michigan-based Consumers Power Co., Westinghouse Electric Corp., the Du Pont Co. and Albuquerque Publishing have turned to relatively inexpensive urine tests, such as the EMIT (Enzyme Multiplied Immunoassay Test) manufactured by Syva Co., a subsidiary of Syntex Corp. of Palo Alto, Calif. But whether use of these tests does much to control drug abuse is a matter of fierce debate. A major flaw of the most widely used tests is that they don't measure an employee's degree of impairment or level of job performance at the time of the test but show only traces of drugs in the urine. Cocaine may show up as much as three days after consumption; marijuana may be present from five days to three weeks afterward. A drug test, then, may nab even drug users who don't use them at the workplace. "What someone does outside the job isn't a concern for the employer unless it affects what they do on the job," argues Erwin Chemerensky, professor of constitutional law at the University of Southern California (USC).

An even bigger problem is that the tests aren't always accurate. Results can vary widely with the skills of the individuals carrying out the tests or the laboratories analyzing the results. Over-the-counter drugs such as Advil and Nuprin have shown up as illegal drugs on some tests, notes Kerry Shannon, marketing director of Bio-Analytical Technologies, a Chicago lab that conducts urinalysis tests. The most widely used tests claim a 95 to 99 percent accuracy rate; in companies where blanket testing is carried out, this means that, on average, 1 to 5 out of every 100 tests will produce inaccurate results. A recent Northwestern University study suggests an even worse record: it found that 25 percent of all EMIT tests that came up positive were really "false positives." And James Woodford, a forensic chemist in Atlanta and a consultant to the U.S. Public Health Service, contends that urinalysis tests may be racially biased. The reason: test results may be skewed by blacks' higher concentrations of the pigment melanin, which has an ion identical to THC, the active ingredient in marijuana—and which may also soak up body substances similar to THC.

Manufacturers of urine tests acknowledge some of their deficiencies. Michelle Klaich, a spokeswoman for Syntex, stresses that a positive reading on one test shouldn't by itself be a ground for firing: she says Syntex recommends follow-up tests and other measures to verify the results. To improve accuracy, meanwhile, some companies are at work on the next generation of testing devices. National Patent Analytical Systems, Inc., of Roslyn Heights, N.Y., is awaiting results of clinical tests of its Veritas 100 Analyzer, which uses computer hardware and software to analyze the electrical stimuli given off by the brain in the presence of certain drugs. Company president Joseph Boccuzi says the device measures only the presence of drugs at the time of the test and cuts the false-positive rate to less than 5 percent.

But Ira Glasser, executive director of the ACLU, worries that the growing testing industry will become its own reason for being, propounding the use of testing to justify its existence. He recommends "an unused method for detecting [drug abuse]—it's called 'two eyes'." Most employees who are drug abusers reveal telltale signs of their problem, such as erratic behavior or inability to concentrate. A watchful supervisor, says Glasser, should be able to spot drug use and help an employee into a drug-rehabilitation program—an approach that ultimately may be most helpful in eliminating drug abuse.

Despite a growing number of lawsuits, courts so far have generally upheld the legality of drug testing. But some state and local legislatures are moving to restrict and regulate it. California Assemblyman Johan Klehs has proposed a bill that would require a company's testing policy to be in writing; test results would be kept confidential, and all labs that analyze tests of employees and job applicants would be licensed. The Civil Liberties Union of Massachusetts is drafting a bill that would allow testing of only those employees whose performance had a bearing on public safety—nuclear-plant operators, school-bus drivers and the like—and who show some signs of impairment. Similarly, in San Francisco, a new ordinance prohibits drug testing by private employers unless there is a high degree of what's known as individualized suspicion—that the employees to be tested are not only impaired but also pose a "clear and present danger" to themselves or others. Only through such measures will companies be barred from "rummaging through another person's biology," says San Francisco supervisor Maher, unless testing is absolutely necessary.

Personality Tests: Probing the Psyche

Wanted: people with "kinetic energy," "emotional maturity" and the ability to "deal with large numbers of people in a fairly chaotic situation." No, not to be cohost of "Wheel of Fortune"; American Multi Cinema, the third largest theater chain in America, wants to hire candidates with these qualities to manage its movie houses. To identify the right employees, AMC is one of an increasing number of companies that administer personality or psychological tests to job applicants. Meanwhile, dozens of others such as General Motors, American Cyanamid, J. C. Penney and Westinghouse now rely on personality-assessment programs to evaluate and promote many current employees.

The tests that companies administer run the gamut. Some are standard psychological tests such as the 46-year-old MMPI (Minnesota Multiphasic Personality Inventory). Long used by psychiatrists and psychologists to test individuals for an array of personality traits, the MMPI consists of up to 566 statements and requires the answers "true," "false" or "cannot say" to questions such as "I avoid getting together with people" or "I have a great deal of self-confidence." Simpler tests include AMC's timed personality-profile exam, known as the PEP test, which among other things examines an applicant's level of mechanical interest and aptitude; people who score well "will be more likely to cope if the butter machine or the projection equipment develops problems," says an AMC district manager, Mario Marques.

Praendix Inc. of Wellesley Hills, Mass., produces a personality-assessment test that consists of a list of phrases and adjectives—including "life of the party," "sympathetic" and "aggressive"—and two questions: "Which of these adjectives describes how you think you are expected to act by others?" and "Which of these adjectives describes who you really are?" Arnold Daniels, founder of Praendix, explains that people who select "patient" as an apt description of themselves might be good "detail" workers, such as researchers, and comfortable reporting to a higher authority. But those who select "impatient"—and think others expect them to be less so—might be good managers, focused on the big picture and eager to see tasks completed.

Many companies swear by the tests. Bobbi Ciarfella, an administrator of Yankee Cos., Inc., an oil-and-gas firm based in Massachusetts, says the Praendix test has helped the firm cut its high turnover rate and hire employees who thrive in a fast-paced environment. "You can't afford to make a mistake when you're hiring somebody in the $45,000 range," she says. Others insist the objectivity of many tests benefits applicants by being even fairer than the typically subjective job interview.

Yet some employees may not fare so well. "For a large number of people, [tests] can predict" roughly who will perform a given job well, says Alexandra Wigdor of the National Research Council, which is currently conducting a study to devise an advanced testing system for the U.S. military. But for any one person, especially one who doesn't test well, "they can be hopeless," she concedes. Moreover, the human personality is so complex that not even the MMPI—considered by many psychiatrists to be the most objective of psychological tests—can give anything like a full and accurate reflection of the individual, says New York psychologist Juliet Lesser. Finally, there's the danger that employers will substitute test results for background checks or even old-fashioned intuition. "Anyone relying too much on tests is abdicating his responsibility as a manager," says New York industrial psychologist Brian Schwartz.

Genetic Tests: Screening for Diseases

At Enserch Corp., a diversified energy company based in Dallas, officials were horrified:

last summer the *maître d' hôtel* of the executive dining room was discovered to have AIDS. When the company summarily ordered mandatory AIDS tests for its other food-service workers, another was discovered to have the AIDS antibody. Both employees were suspended with full pay and medical benefits and escorted from the premises.

The consternation that followed among gay-rights groups and civil libertarians pointed up the controversy around a growing area of testing: monitoring employees' health. Examining blood or tissue samples for signs of disease or certain genetic traits could protect employees and the public from health risks—while sparing employers higher medical-insurance costs and reduced productivity. But as tests get increasingly sophisticated, they could also provide a powerful tool for discrimination against homosexuals, women, those predisposed to diseases or other groups of employees.

Testing for AIDS is especially problematic. Most of the tests offered have high rates of both false positives and "false negatives" (incorrect negative results)—traumatic with AIDS. Nor is it clear just what AIDS testing accomplishes, given most experts' belief that the disease isn't spread through the casual contact typical of the workplace but through sexual relations or contact with AIDS-contaminated blood. Yet so far, only California has acted to prohibit AIDS testing as a condition of employment.

Looming on the horizon is genetic testing. Each year 390,000 workers contract occupational illnesses including lung, bladder and other cancers; about 100,000 die. The belief that some workers possessed genetic "hyper-susceptibility" to some of these conditions that could be triggered by exposure to toxins in the workplace led companies like Du Pont and Dow Chemical to conduct tests on workers beginning in the 1970s. But "after a number of years we were not seeing what we thought we might find," says Dr. John Venable, medical director of Dow. Negative publicity about tests—particularly Du Pont's testing of workers for sickle-cell trait, which leads to a condition that affects many blacks—further dampened corporate enthusiasm for testing. By the time a 1983 report by the Office of Technology Assessment determined that existing genetic tests couldn't predict what might happen on the job, most companies had quit the field.

Recently, however, biologists have discovered genetic "markers" for a number of genetic diseases such as cystic fibrosis and are now searching for others for more commonplace conditions such as Alzheimer's disease and breast cancer. "We're still many years away" from the time when genetic tests for such conditions could come into widespread use, asserts Alexander Morgan Capron, professor of law and medicine at USC. But since so many people may be prone to these diseases, there is the distant prospect that companies could one day undertake genetic screening—declining to hire employees who seem likely to become sick on the job, use up expensive medical benefits or die young.

As the technology of testing advances, say the experts, so must the public's attention to the range of economic, ethical and legal issues it raises. Columbia's Westin is confident that such awareness will increase; as a consequence, he predicts, within 10 years a "latticework of legislation" will be in place to balance employers' aims with employees' rights. Society has much to gain from careful and sophisticated testing—a potentially more productive corps of workers whose skills more closely match the requirements of their jobs. But the preeminent challenge for on-the-job testing will be whether it can avoid unwarranted encroachment on the rights and freedoms Americans hold dear.

40. Drug Testing and Public Employment

James Felman and Christopher Petrini

James Felman and Christopher Petrini present a statistical overview of the nature and scope of illegal drug use in America. They also examine the prevalence of drug testing in the workplace and describe the forms and accuracy of drug testing. They then consider the major constitutional issue: whether drug testing of a public employee without any individualized suspicion of drug use is an unreasonable search and seizure in violation of the Fourth Amendment. They argue that it is.

I. Introduction

In the absence of legislative action, the fourth amendment to the Constitution provides the most important barrier to "the progress of science." Fourth amendment analysis inevitably involves a balancing of competing interests— the collective needs of the society must be tempered by the interests of individual human

dignity and privacy. As these interests change and science progresses, new balances must be struck. The issue of drug testing in public employment presents a controversial example of such a new balance to be struck.

Significant societal interests are advanced in support of drug testing of public employees. Drug testing may increase employee safety and efficiency, enhance the perceived integrity of the particular public entity, as well as help reduce society's overall demand for illegal drugs. The individual interests implicated by drug testing are also formidable. Being told by the government to urinate into a jar brushes up against normal expectations of individual privacy. Moreover, the tests are sometimes inaccurate, falsely implicating innocent employees, and they reveal a broad array of private facts, such as pregnancy, medication for a psychological condition, and other similar information that is not of legitimate concern to employers.

This article focuses on the fourth amendment issues presented by the drug testing of public employees. This issue, in a nutshell, is whether an individual may be subjected to a highly intrusive bodily search in the absence of any individualized suspicion to ensure that she does not use drugs, whether at home or on the job. If upheld, drug testing will represent the first instance in the history of the fourth amendment in which a highly intrusive bodily search has been permitted without any measure of individualized suspicion. Such an erosion of the fourth amendment should not be allowed without a critical inquiry into the interests at stake, and the extent to which they are served by drug testing. The authors believe that this inquiry leads to the conclusion that testing public employees should be impermissible in the absence of individualized suspicion.

Even if the reader disagrees with the authors' conclusion, however, perhaps the more important point is that a critical examination of the competing interests involved should be used to draw the fourth amendment line between permissible and impermissible bodily searches in the absence of individualized suspicion. If this critical analysis is not adhered to, there may be no further fourth amendment lines left to draw, and the "progress of science" is surely not complete.

Part II of the article presents a brief statistical overview of the nature and scope of illegal drug use in America. It discusses how many illegal drug users there are, who they are, and what costs they are estimated to impose upon American society. Part II also examines the prevalence of drug testing in the workplace, describes the forms of drug testing, and details the accuracy of drug testing. Part III of the article presents the major constitutional issue: whether drug testing of a public employee without any individualized suspicion of drug use is an unreasonable search and seizure in violation of the fourth amendment. . . .

II. The Lines of Battle: Drug Use and Drug Testing in the Public Workplace

A. The Nature and Scope of the American Drug Problem

1. *How Many Drug Users Are There?* Unfortunately, there is a dearth of reliable scientific evidence detailing the extent of illegal drug use in America, although it is undoubtedly a serious problem. Illicit drug use per capita in this country is estimated to exceed that of any other industrialized nation. The permissiveness and experimentation of the 1960's included the use and acceptance of numerous illegal drugs. American illicit drug use increased throughout the 1960's and the 1970's, peaking by some estimates in 1979. Between 1979 and 1986 there was a statistically significant decline in illegal drug use. Accurate measurement of illicit drug use is difficult, however, because the relative popularity of illegal drugs fluctuates when inexpensive substitutes or new, more potent varieties of existing drugs reach the market. In 1982, narcotics officials estimated that 3 to 5 percent of the American work force used drugs regularly.

To some extent, persons of all races, ethnicities, and socioeconomic backgrounds use illegal drugs. Ironically, however, studies identify the two extremes of poverty and affluence as characteristics often correlating with drug abuse. In a study examining whether particular ethnic and racial groups are more prone to alcohol or drug abuse, it was found that the percentage breakdown of ethnic and racial groups in drug or alcohol treatment programs merely reflected their percentage in the general population. In fact, prior use of alcohol or drugs was found to be a stronger predictor of abuse than race or ethnicity.

2. *At What Cost?* Employees who use illegal drugs regularly may use drugs on the job or report to work under the influence of drugs. There is little evidence regarding the number of employees who may be impaired on the job, but those who use drugs on the job un-

doubtedly inflict upon employers increased costs from inefficiency, greater absenteeism, accidents, and insurance claims. The workplace costs of employee drug use are, however, difficult to estimate, in part because it is not always clear whether drug use by employees is a cause of inefficiency or merely a symptom of an already inefficient employee. The only study of the issue seems to have overlooked this difficulty, assuming all costs imposed by drug-using employees to have been caused by the drugs, not the employee. This study, by the Research Triangle Institute, estimated that employee drug use cost American industry $25.7 billion in 1980, and that alcohol and drug use together cost American society as a whole an estimated $136.4 billion. One drug consulting firm has reported that the average drug user is likely to be tardy three times as often as nonusers, request time off during work 2.2 times more often, and have 2.5 times as many absences of eight days or more. Other experts, however, dispute these statistics.

Drug use on the job is also believed to increase workplace accidents. One writer suggests that drug users are three times as likely as nonusers to injure themselves or someone else on the job. Since 1975, investigators have attributed about fifty train accidents to workers impaired by drugs or alcohol. Medical and property insurance claims are estimated to be somewhat higher because of employee drug use. There may also be a connection between employee drug use and increased workplace theft and embezzlement. Authorities have uncovered several large-scale drug selling operations in employment settings.

Although illegal drug use is a serious problem, its significance must be kept in proper perspective. By any standard of measurement, the more pervasive national drug problem is the abuse of alcohol, tobacco, and legal prescription and over-the-counter drugs. Each year 15,000 Americans die from misuse of legal prescription drugs. The National Institute on Drug Abuse (NIDA) estimates that legal prescription drugs cause sixty percent of emergency room admissions for drug overdoses and seventy percent of all drug-related deaths. Compared to the staggering number of deaths caused each year by alcohol and tobacco abuse, the yearly number of deaths

attributable to illegal drug use appears small indeed. The Research Triangle Institute estimates that the costs imposed upon American industry by employee alcohol use are nearly two times that caused by illegal drug use. Employees with an alcohol problem are an estimated 21 percent less productive than other employees. Yet despite the tremendous costs of alcohol use to American industry, very few drug testing programs currently screen employees for alcohol abuse.

B. The Employers' Response: The Use and Variety of Drug Testing

1. *The Increased Implementation of Drug Testing Programs.* Many employers have responded to workplace costs of employee drug use by implementing drug testing programs. Currently, about 40 percent of the Fortune 500 companies have instituted such programs or plan to do so, and some professional sports leagues have proposed player drug testing programs.

Federal, state, and local public employers have increasingly developed employee drug testing programs. Such programs for all federal agencies are currently being developed in response to an Executive Order issued by President Reagan. This order seeks to make the federal workforce a model for eliminating drug use in the national workplace by requiring implementation of such programs. In addition, drug testing programs are already in place in all four branches of the military, the Coast Guard, and several administrative agencies.

In addition to requiring testing of certain public employees, government regulations require some private companies in highly regulated industries to test their employees for illegal drug use. For example, most railroads now test employees under regulations issued by the Federal Railroad Administration, and 90 percent of all nuclear power plants have instituted testing programs on a voluntary basis under guidelines issued by the Nuclear Regulatory Commission. In addition, many public utilities such as electric power companies and gas companies have voluntarily established drug testing programs, and a 1986 study revealed that nearly three-fourths of major police departments surveyed require urine testing for all job applicants.

2. *The Variety of Drug Testing Programs.* When employers test and what they do with the results varies significantly among employers. Testing may be conducted randomly or upon a possible drug-related incident, such as an accident. Testing may be required for all job applicants, for all promotions, or as part of periodically required physicals. Some programs focus upon only specific types of employees. Of the Fortune 500 companies with testing programs, 80 percent test job applicants, 47 percent test employees after accidents, and 13 percent test employees at random.

Drug testing programs also vary in terms of the actions taken toward employees testing positive for illegal drug use. Many simply dismiss all employees who test positive. A few testing programs, however, require employees who test positive to enter drug treatment or counseling programs paid for by the company or employee health insurance. About 30 percent of Fortune 500 companies with testing programs have established in-house employee assistance programs which refer drug abusing employees to hospitals or clinics for treatment.

3. *The Variety of Urine Tests.* Drug testing programs may employ a variety of different types of tests to evaluate the physiological components of urine. Two of the most commonly used tests are the enzyme multiplied immunoassay test (EMIT), and the gas chromatography-mass spectrometer test (GC/MS). The tests differ significantly in chemical evaluation process, accuracy, and cost.

The EMIT is highly popular because it is inexpensive and because it is portable, easy to administer on the job location. The EMIT relies upon a process known as competitive displacement and bonding, in which metabolites of illegal drugs present in the subject's urine displace preexisting bonds in the testing reagent and create new molecular configurations which indicate prior illegal drug use. For reasons discussed below, the EMIT suffers from inherent inaccuracy problems that make reliance on its results ill-advised without confirmation by GC/MS testing.

The much more expensive GC/MS test requires laboratory conditions to evaluate, but is highly accurate. In the GC/MS test, compounds present in urine are classified in a gas chromatographer and fragmented by bombarding them with high energy particles in a mass spectrometer. Different compounds split apart at different times, and the fragments' ionic weights vary. The time of fragmentation and the fragments' ionic weights are then compared to data stored in a computer library of compounds. If the fragmentation time and ionic weights match the computer data for a particular compound, a molecular "fingerprint" exists which is regarded as a highly accurate confirmation of that compound's presence. For optimum efficiency and accuracy, the EMIT should be used for initial screening. Positive EMIT results should then be subjected to GC/MS testing for more reliable confirmation.

C. A Critical Review of the Employers' Response: The Scientific Limitations of Drug Testing Programs

Is drug testing a reasonable response by employers to the problem of employee drug use? To answer this question, one must examine the scientific limitations of drug testing programs.

1. *The Inherent Inaccuracy of EMIT Testing.* While the GC/MS test is quite accurate, the EMIT is to some degree inherently inaccurate, even when properly administered. The EMIT may yield a "false positive" by mistaking legal substances for illegal drugs due to "cross-reactivity," which occurs when compounds present in urine react with the testing solution and displace its preexisting chemical bonds in the same manner as by-products of the targeted drug. Courts examining testing programs have recognized the serious accuracy problems of the EMIT, and many have suggested the need for confirmation by a more accurate test.

The substances that the EMIT may mistake for various illegal drugs are numerous. Legal prescription and over-the-counter drugs such as aspirin, Contac, and Nyquil may cause a false positive result. Also, certain foods may trigger a false positive EMIT finding. For example, poppy seeds may be mistaken for opiates such as heroin and morphine, and herbal teas may be confused with cocaine. Bodily enzymes with which the EMIT testing reagent may react are excreted through the urine. If an individual happens to discharge above-average amounts of those enzymes, the EMIT may register a false positive. The same problem may occur with the polar acids present in urine. The concentration and bonding properties of these acids vary with the body chemistry of the subject, and they may cross-react with the EMIT testing reagent. Some scientific evidence also suggests that higher concentrations of the pigment melanin present in the bodies of blacks and Hispanics may cause false positives. Because of cross-reactivity, it is estimated that 5 percent to 25 percent of the positive results indicated by EMIT testing are incorrect, even if the EMIT is properly administered and evaluated. The EMIT may also register false *negative* readings, thus failing to identify those subjects who have used illegal drugs.

2. *The Administrative Inaccuracy of Drug Testing.* While the EMIT is inaccurate even when properly administered, an EMIT positive result confirmed by GC/MS testing is quite reliable. This level of scientific accuracy, however, may be obtained only if testing administrators carefully observe strict processing procedures. Administrative errors may result from incorrect collection processes, sample mislabeling, improper training of administrators and lab technicians, dirty or uncalibrated laboratory equipment, or failure to keep urine specimens at the proper temperature. Since even the most accurate test is administered by fallible humans, errors are bound to occur in any large-scale testing program.

The Centers for Disease Control (CDC) in Atlanta conducted a nine year study of thirteen independent laboratories which revealed that some field testing programs had a false-positive rate ranging from 6 to 60 percent depending upon the drug being tested for. The error rate for false negatives was even

higher. The factors of operator error, inadequate testing protocol, and poor laboratory quality control are, of course, to some extent correctable. Nevertheless, the CDC study indicates that even established companies with professional technicians and comprehensive testing controls remain subject to remarkably high rates of error. The study concluded that these randomly selected laboratories displayed "serious shortcomings" in quality control even though they knew they were being monitored.

3. *Limitations on the Probative Value of Drug Testing.* Having discussed the extent to which drug tests are able to detect illicit substances, it is useful, in order to assess the probative value of urinalysis, to examine what the tests do *not* show. First, even a correct positive test result for marijuana use does not prove that the test subject ever used marijuana himself. Depending upon what concentration of an illicit substance metabolite constitutes a positive test result, a positive result could be caused by the subject's passive inhalation of smoke from marijuana used by someone else.

Second, urine testing shows neither intoxication nor actual job impairment. Rather, it indicates only that the subject ingested the detected drug within the preceding days or weeks. The tests cannot identify the presence of an illicit drug directly; instead, they determine prior use of an illicit drug inferentially by screening for the presence of its by-products in the urine.

For instance, prior use of marijuana is determined by screening not for the intoxicating chemical itself, tetrahydrocannabinol (THC), but for its by-product metabolite, which appears only after THC breaks down and its intoxicating effects disappear. Because the target metabolite does not appear until intoxication passes, testing "can establish only marijuana *use*, not *intoxication*." The metabolite is detectable in the body of a casual user for several days and even longer in the chronic user. The use of other drugs can have a similar effect, permitting detection of by-products long after intoxication has passed.

Because urine testing cannot detect present intoxication or the time that the illegal drugs were taken, it cannot measure job impairment accurately. These serious shortcomings necessarily permit an employer's drug testing to scrutinize an employee's off-duty drug use, whether or not that use impairs her job performance.

In addition, testing may fail to identify those drug-using employees who avoid or manipulate tests. If employees learn of the testing date, drug users may merely abstain from drug use in order to test negative. Drug users may also neutralize evidence of drug use by adulterating their samples with substances as common as table salt. A drug-using employee may even substitute a drug-free urine sample for her own.

The most telling limitation on the probative value of drug testing is its statistical unreliability. The likelihood that a given positive result is correct depends entirely upon the extent to which the tested group actually uses drugs. If one assumes that 5 percent of a group of employees uses illegal drugs and that an employer uses a drug testing program with 95 percent accuracy to screen the group, the employer's "accurate" program will yield one false positive result for every correct positive result. If only 2 percent of the group uses illegal drugs, three out of every four positive results will be incorrect.* If all 2.8 million federal workers are tested as suggested by the President's Commission on Organized Crime, an estimated 140,000 workers will be accused and disciplined unjustly.

III. Drug Testing and the Fourth Amendment

But even if the front door of the house is no longer protected by the Constitution, surely it had been thought until now that the bathroom door is.

*This analysis is illustrated by the following table:

Prevalence, %	Predictive Value of a Positive Result, %
0.1	2
1.0	16
2.0	28
5.0	50
10.0	68
50.0	95

A. The Purpose and Scope of the Fourth Amendment

Against this factual background, careful application of fourth amendment doctrine to random drug testing programs in the public sector reveals that such programs are unconstitutional searches and seizures under most circumstances. The fourth amendment to the United States Constitution provides:

> The right of the people to be secure in their persons, houses, papers, and effects, against unreasonable searches and seizures, shall not be violated, and no Warrants shall issue, but upon probable cause, supported by Oath or affirmation, and particularly describing the place to be searched and the persons or things to be seized.

"The fundamental command of the Fourth Amendment is that searches and seizures be reasonable. . . ." The amendment prohibits only *unreasonable* searches and seizures. What is reasonable, however, depends on the context of the search. The prevailing test for "reasonableness" was set forth by the Supreme Court in *Bell v. Wolfish:* "The test of reasonableness under the Fourth Amendment is not capable of precise definition or mechanical application. In each case it requires a balancing of the need for the particular search against the invasion of personal rights that the search entails."

It is difficult to predict with certainty, however, the exact test the Supreme Court will use when confronted with the testing of public employees. Most recently, in *O'Connor v. Ortega,* the Court indicated that searches of

> government employees for noninvestigatory, work-related purposes, as well as for investigations of work-related misconduct, should be judged by the standard of reasonableness under all the circumstances. Under this reasonableness standard, both the inception and the scope of the intrusion must be reasonable.

The Court explicitly did not, however, "address the proper Fourth Amendment analysis for drug and alcohol testing of employees." It is difficult to discern what independent meaning is communicated by this most recent formulation of the test. Depending upon the context, it may be impossible to determine whether a search is justified at its inception without first considering the scope of the search. For example, the "scope" of a drug test is the compelled tender of a urine specimen. It may be compelled under direct or indirect observation. All of these considerations seem appropriate to take into account when determining whether the drug test was justified at its inception.

Whether the inception and scope of a search are reasonable would seem in the final analysis to depend upon a balancing of the interests outlined in *Bell*. Even if the Court utilizes the recent *O'Connor* formulation, it appears inevitable that the same balancing of governmental interests against individual privacy rights articulated in *Bell* will in the end determine the constitutionality of public employee drug testing programs. Thus, to determine the constitutionality of such drug testing, the state interests advanced by testing must be balanced against its intrusiveness upon employees' privacy interests; the greater the intrusion occasioned by the search, the greater must be the governmental interest in conducting the search.

B. The Threshold Issue: A Drug Test Is a Search

The threshold issue in fourth amendment analysis is whether a drug test is a search. If the test is not a search, then no fourth amendment objection arises, which obviates the need to balance state and individual privacy interests. Whether a drug test is a search generally depends upon whether there exists a "reasonable expectation of privacy" in the act of urination.

Evaluating reasonable expectations of privacy for purposes of determining whether an intrusion constitutes a fourth amendment search is an abstract, non-case-specific inquiry which focuses upon whether society is prepared to recognize that the employee has a legitimate expectation of privacy from drug tests. In response to this question, the courts have uniformly found that a drug test is a search within the meaning of the fourth amendment. Despite the novelty of the tech-

nology, the courts have recognized that drug testing implicates central fourth amendment values, and that individuals have legitimate expectations of privacy in the act of urination.

C. The Individual Interests: The Intrusiveness of Drug Testing

Once courts determine that a drug test is a search, they must balance the intrusiveness of the search against the government's need for the information that the search will reveal. In focusing on the intrusiveness of a search, courts first examine the context of an individual's expectation of privacy. What is reasonable in one context may not be reasonable in another. Although most public employees legitimately have very strong expectations of privacy both in the act of urination and in its contents, an employee's expectations of privacy may be diminished if she enters an occupation which requires significant preparedness and discipline, such as the military, intensely regulated industries, nuclear power plants, prisons, public transportation, or law enforcement. On the other hand, public employees whose occupations do not directly implicate public safety or other similar governmental interests retain the same level of privacy enjoyed by the ordinary citizen.

After courts assess the context of the employee's expectations of privacy, they examine the intrusiveness of the search. Because an individual generally has the highest expectations of privacy in her body, searches violating the integrity of the body are greater invasions of privacy than inspections of personal effects. The Supreme Court has observed that "even a limited search of the person is a substantial invasion of privacy."

There are three compelling reasons why drug tests are very intrusive, even when compared with other bodily searches. First, the tests reveal not only past drug use, but also numerous other physiological facts that are of no legitimate interest to the employer. While exposing past illegal drug use, drug tests also expose the use of legally prescribed medications, including oral contraceptives and medication to treat physical and psychiatric conditions previously recognized as within the traditional confidentiality of medical records.

Drug testing also exposes otherwise private medical conditions, including diabetes, epilepsy, urinary tract infections, venereal disease, and pregnancy.

Second, drug tests necessarily scrutinize a broad array of off-duty activities. As observed in *American Federation of Government Employees v. Weinberger*, "[t]hese tests enable the individual or organization administering them to monitor the off-duty conduct of employees, and represent a technological advance that . . . could threaten much of the privacy most citizens now take for granted."

Third, the manner in which urine specimens are obtained is quite intrusive. Urination is a personal bodily function usually performed in solitude. In fact, many municipal ordinances prohibit the act in public. Some testing programs require a government official's direct observation of the act of urination to assure the accuracy of the test and to prevent adulteration of the samples. Urination under the direct observation of another "necessarily includes exposing one's private parts, an experience which even if courteously supervised can be humiliating and degrading."

Even if urine samples are not collected under direct observation, many testing programs require at least indirect observation, which may be equally embarrassing and insulting. Regardless of whether testing requires any observation, the experience of being forced to produce a urine sample at the behest of an employer offends normal expectations of dignity. As one court noted, "the very taking of the sample makes for a quite substantial intrusion that could not be negated even if an employee were allowed to produce his urine sample in the privacy of an executive washroom, with no observation whatsoever." Drug tests have been described as more intrusive than a search of the home; equal to or more intrusive than a blood test; and equal to the intrusiveness of a strip search or even a body cavity search. In light of the private bodily information that drug testing can reveal, the potential days of off-duty activity it can scrutinize, and the highly offensive and degrading process of collecting the specimen itself, it is fair to conclude that drug testing is a highly invasive search that requires a proportionally weighty state interest to justify it.

D. The Governmental Interests

The magnitude of the invasion upon individual liberties caused by drug testing must be balanced against the governmental interests furthered by the tests. Three distinct governmental interests have been advanced in support of drug testing: (1) the identification of drug-using employees to further efficiency and safety in the workplace; (2) the integrity of the particular employment institution as perceived by the public; and (3) the enforcement of the criminal laws against drug trade and use by reducing the demand for illegal drugs. While these are certainly legitimate objectives of governmental action, the fourth amendment question is not the legitimacy of the goals themselves, but whether the goals properly may be achieved by means of drug testing. Each of the asserted governmental interests must be examined critically with this question in mind.

1. *The Safety/Efficiency Interest.* The governmental interest most commonly advanced in support of drug testing is to increase efficiency and safety in the workplace through detection of employees who use drugs on the job. Mistakes made by drug-using employees may endanger themselves or others, and under some circumstances, may result in the employer's liability. But while the governmental interest in efficiency and safety is an important one, the extent to which drug testing promotes this interest is limited for three reasons.

First, it is worthwhile to note that the safety/efficiency interest suggests a great deal more than testing for illegal drugs. If the efficiency of the workforce is the issue, employers should logically test for other influences that affect efficiency. Recently, Representative Patricia Schroeder argued:

> [I]f [efficiency and on-the-job performance] is the reason for the [proposed urine testing], why did the Commission [on organized crime] not recommend testing for off-duty use of the two most addictive and destructive drugs known to society—alcohol and tobacco? Alcoholism has ruined the careers and families of hundreds of thousands of Americans. As

for smoking, the Surgeon General has documented that cigarette smoking results in greater illness and use of sick leave. If our goal is to regulate off-duty conduct which could hurt performance, alcohol and tobacco would be prime candidates. I, however, along with most Americans, would find such restrictions abhorrent.

Second, the governmental interest in safety varies greatly with the context. The government has a significant safety interest in preventing the use of drugs by employees whose drug use would ordinarily pose situations of grave public danger, such as air traffic controllers and police officers. But this safety interest is not significant in other contexts, where danger to life does not result, as a matter of course, from the conduct of drug-using employees.

Third, the strength of the government's safety/efficiency interest depends upon the extent to which employees now engage in drug use. If drug use is widespread, then some additional efficiency and safety might be achieved by drug testing. On the other hand, if no employees use drugs, then drug testing will not enhance efficiency or safety *at all*. The courts should not rest content with the mere assertion that a drug problem exists; given the intrusiveness of drug testing, the employer should be required to produce evidence on the extent of employee drug use to justify drug testing. Without such evidence, ordering drug testing is "an act of pure bureaucratic caprice."

Even in those circumstances in which the employer has a strong safety and efficiency interest in identifying drug users, the question remains whether drug testing is a reasonable means of furthering that interest. As Judge Vietor explained:

There is no doubt about it—searches and seizures can yield a wealth of information useful to the searcher. (That is why King George III's men so frequently searched the colonists.) That potential, however, does not make a governmental employer's search of an employee a constitutionally reasonable one.

Even where an employer is able to assert a strong safety/efficiency interest, drug testing is both an over- and underinclusive means of advancing that interest. Drug testing is overinclusive because the tests do not reveal whether or when the illicit substance was ingested. Drug testing does not indicate whether an individual was intoxicated or impaired on the job or at the time the test was given. It does not indicate whether an individual is drug-dependent, a regular user, or likely to ingest the drug during working hours. If employers discipline an employee based upon a positive urine test, the employer in effect regulates the employee's off-duty behavior. In these respects, drug testing is no less overinclusive than random searches of employees' homes or wire-taps placed on employees' phones.

Drug testing to detect on-the-job drug use by employees is also an underinclusive means of advancing safety and efficiency, due to its inaccuracy. Tests may be manipulated, and studies show that properly administered urine tests have very high rates of false negatives. Even those employees who have used drugs immediately prior to a test may not be detected.

Finally, drug testing is not only extremely overinclusive and somewhat underinclusive, but also is not the least intrusive means of furthering the governmental interest. A properly designed and implemented program of employee supervision will in many contexts lead to the detection of virtually all drug-using employees. Given that scientific studies are able to generate statistical and scientific evidence of the absenteeism, mistakes, and health problems caused by drug use, one wonders why employers do not simply take disciplinary action against those employees who make more mistakes, are frequently absent, or suffer from drug-related health problems? "Certainly one so under the influence of drugs as to impair the performance of his or her duties must manifest some outward symptoms. . . ." While it is possible that an employee on drugs may escape detection for a while, risking injury to himself or another, there is certainly no guarantee that drug testing would prevent such an accident.

Drug testing is a much more intrusive action than is necessary to serve the governmental safety/efficiency interest. To the extent that it does so, it is both over- and underinclusive. Accordingly, the governmental interest in safety and efficiency in the workplace has only a marginal nexus with drug testing.

2. *The Integrity Interest.* Wholly apart from the actual effects of drug use, the government's ability to do its job may be impaired if the public perceives governmental workers as drug users. Under this line of reasoning, the imposition of drug testing will comfort the public and contribute to the perception that public employees are drug-free. Because of this perception the government arguably will be able to carry out its duties more effectively.

The strength of the integrity interest, like the safety/efficiency interest discussed above, depends entirely upon context. Only in some employment situations is the public's perception critical to the ability of an employee to do his job effectively. The integrity interest is most commonly advanced as a justification for testing law enforcement officers.

The argument that the perceived use of drugs by law enforcement officers will affect their ability to carry out their duties is attenuated at best. In the absence of any empirical evidence to the contrary, it is equally plausible to infer that most citizens obey law enforcement officers even if they have some vague suspicion that some officers, although not necessarily the officers they are dealing with, use illegal drugs. Furthermore, the establishment by way of testing that law enforcement officers do not use drugs can only serve to heighten respect for the officers to the extent that it is already perceived that the officers use drugs. That is, if no one thinks law enforcement officers use drugs, then confirming that they do not serves little purpose. Accordingly, the mere assertion of an unfavorable public perception must not suffice to trigger the government's integrity interest. To prove that drug testing is needed to preserve the integrity of law enforcement officers, the government must be required to make at least some evidentiary showing that perceived drug use actually has compromised law enforcement integrity.

Even if the public actually perceives that its law enforcement officers use illegal drugs, it is doubtful that drug testing will eliminate that perception. Although it is true that drug testing may serve to comfort the public, this comforting effect inevitably will be to some extent undermined by the report of positive test results, which will likely receive a lot of attention and strengthen the public's impression that the public employees are drug users.

The governmental interest in employee integrity does not exist in other contexts where the performance of its employees is not affected by public perception. In those areas of employment, the integrity interest should never be allowed as a justification for drug testing.

3. *Policing Drug Use.* The government occasionally asserts that it should be permitted to conduct employee drug testing programs to advance its interest in eliminating the use and trade of illegal drugs. While it may be true, at the margin, that drug use and trade may be attacked by reducing demand for drugs through employee drug testing, the extent to which demand and trade may be reduced by drug testing is certainly speculative. The difficulty with this justification for drug testing is that it presents no reason to stop with public employees. If the elimination of drug demand is the goal, then there is no rational basis for testing only employees, let alone public employees. An equal state interest would support random drug testing at roadway blockades, election booths, street corners, and so on. Because there is no reason to believe that public employees are more likely to support the drug trade than any other citizen, random drug testing for this purpose limited to public employees as a class raises profound equal protection problems. Government cannot legitimately promote its interest in eliminating drug use and trade by testing public employees only.

E. Balancing the Competing Interests

After examining the intrusiveness of drug testing and the countervailing state interests, courts must balance these competing values to arrive at the appropriate level of suspicion or cause required to make the testing of an individual employee reasonable under the fourth amendment. Unfortunately, courts have given rather hasty treatment to this portion of the analysis, arriving at results in a rather conclusory fashion. While only a few courts have allowed drug testing without any individualized suspicion, none have gone so far as to require probable cause. Most of the courts have instead held that "reasonable suspicion" is the constitutionally required standard. "Reasonable suspicion" is often defined as suspicion that is based on specific objective facts and reasonable inferences that a particular employee has used drugs on the job. That so many courts have adopted the reasonable suspicion standard without any detailed analysis when confronted with many different factual scenarios suggests that a spirit of compromise is in the air. Though many courts oppose random testing plans, they do not want to appear to promote employee drug use by requiring probable cause. The lesser "reasonable suspicion" standard allows courts to stop random testing programs while politically saving face. Because the governmental interests in testing necessarily vary with the context, constitutional standards which reflect these factual distinctions would be more analytically satisfying. The authors offer the following framework as a rough guide to achieve a more thoughtful balancing of interests.

When the governmental interest in integrity is irrelevant because the public's perception of the institution does not affect its ability to function, and when the governmental interest in safety is less important, as in situations where drug use would not inevitably present public danger, the government should not be allowed to test an employee for illegal drug use without *probable cause* to believe that she uses illegal drugs on the job. In such a situation, absent evidence of widespread drug use among employees, there is simply no compelling reason to alter the probable cause standard.

When the government demonstrates a strong integrity interest, by proving that (1) public perception is critical to the ability of the employees to perform their functions, and (2) there is an accurate general public perception of drug use among those employees, then the government should be allowed to test an employee based on *reasonable suspicion* of drug use on the job. However, courts must not accept mere assertions of unfavorable public perception. Without proof that such a perception impairs the employee's performance, drug testing is a remedy without a wrong.

Alternatively, when the government shows a strong safety interest by demonstrating that employee drug use would as a matter of course present situations of grave public danger, then the government should be permitted to test an employee based upon *reasonable suspicion*. As with the integrity interest, however, courts must require evidence of extensive employee drug use on the job and accurate confirmatory test procedures. Without such evidence, the government may advance its safety interest adequately by implementing a well-designed program of supervision.

Drug testing is so intrusive, over- and underinclusive, and of such limited utility in detecting drug use on the job that testing without reasonable suspicion must not be allowed under any circumstances.

F. Consent?

Even if a testing program violates the fourth amendment, an employer could attempt to obtain employee consent to the search. In several drug testing programs challenged in the courts, employees were required to sign consent forms before testing.

There are two reasons why these consent forms may not validate an otherwise unreasonable search. First, consent is not voluntary where each employee knows that her refusal to consent will result in disciplinary action. Second, even if employees signed the forms voluntarily, the government should never be allowed to condition public employment upon the waiver of constitutional rights.

Whether the consent of an employee is voluntary, and not the result of duress or coercion, express or implied, is a question of fact to be determined from all the circumstances. The critical consideration in consent form situations is what the employee reasonably believes will happen if she does not sign the form. If it is obvious under the circumstances that disciplinary action will result from a failure to sign the form, then clearly any decision to sign results from coercion.

Regardless of the voluntariness with which consent is given, the government should not be permitted to require a waiver of fourth amendment rights as a condition of public employment. If government could do this, it could by the same reasoning require the relinquishment of other fundamental rights. In *Frost & Frost Trucking Company v. Railroad Commission,* the Supreme Court observed:

> If the state may compel the surrender of one constitutional right as a condition of its favor, it may, in like manner, compel a surrender of all. It is inconceivable that guarantees embedded in the Constitution of the United States may thus be manipulated out of existence.

The point is perhaps best captured by Judge Vietor in *McDonell v. Hunter:* "Advance consent to future *unreasonable* searches is not a reasonable condition of employment."

G. The Government As Employer

A separate but related argument that has been advanced in support of drug testing is that the government in its role as employer, as contrasted with its role as law enforcer, should be given the same latitude in dealing with its employees as any other employer in the private sector. Upon first examination this argument appears seductively simple and sound: Because private employers generally may institute employee drug testing programs, the government as employer arguably should be permitted to do the same. Upon closer analysis, however, the argument is compelling only from the government's perspective; from the employee's perspective, his fourth amendment rights may depend upon whether his employer suspects him of criminal activity. Nevertheless, several courts have adopted some form of the "government-as-employer" rationale in upholding drug testing programs.

The courts' utilization of the rationale, however, has been analytically confusing; some courts view the doctrine as rendering the fourth amendment totally inapplicable to governmental searches for work-related misconduct while others view the fourth amendment as applicable to such searches, but to a lesser extent.

In *Allen v. City of Marietta,* for example, the court considered a fourth amendment challenge by a public employee to a drug test imposed on reasonable suspicion of drug use. The *Allen* court determined at the outset that the drug test was a "search" within the meaning of the fourth amendment. Further, the court recognized that "[g]overnment employees do not surrender their fourth amendment rights merely because they go to work for the government. They have as much of a right to be free from warrantless government searches as any other citizens." Nevertheless, the court drew a distinction between governmental searches for evidence of crime and searches for noncriminal work-related misconduct. As to the latter type of search, the court stated: "Because the government as employer has the same rights to discover and prevent employee misconduct relevant to the employee's performance of her duties [as a private employer], the employee cannot really claim a legitimate expectation of privacy from searches of that nature." Although the *Allen* court stated that fourth amendment protection extends to government employees, the logical result of its holding that government employees have no reasonable expectation of privacy from searches for work-related misconduct is that the fourth amendment does *not* protect government employees from work-related searches. This is because where there is no legitimate expectation of privacy to be free from a search, there is no fourth amendment protection. Accordingly, the *Allen* court's analysis, focusing on the government as employer's need to search, leads to the conclusion that the fourth amendment has no application *at all* to searches for employment-related misconduct. This holding would appear to be squarely at odds with Supreme Court precedent, particularly the Court's latest pronouncement in *O'Connor v. Ortega* that "[s]earches and seizures by government employers or supervisors of the private property of their employees . . . are subject to the restraints of the Fourth Amendment."

The government-as-employer argument was stated somewhat differently in *National Treasury Employees Union v. Von Raab*. In that case, the court seemed to focus on the employee's need to be free from governmental searches: "While the fourth amendment protects against invasions for civil as well as criminal investigatory purposes, *the need for protection against governmental intrusion diminishes if the investigation is neither designed to enforce criminal laws nor likely to be used to bring criminal charges against the person investigated.*" Under the Fifth Circuit's view, the fourth amendment continues to apply to governmental searches for work-related misconduct, but in a somewhat less robust form.

At least two criticisms of this position may be made. First, it is entirely unclear *why* the need to be free from searches "diminishes" where the search is not intended to enforce criminal laws. It is equally plausible that a citizen's "need" to be free from a search depends upon the intrusiveness of the search itself, rather than upon whether the evidence sought is proscribed by a statute instead of an employment regulation.

Second, it is unclear why the focus of inquiry should be on the employee's "need for protection *against* governmental intrusion" rather than on the government's need *for* the intrusion. That is, the *Von Raab* court's proposition seems no more inherently appealing than the proposition that "the need for [the governmental intrusion itself] diminishes if the investigation is neither designed to enforce criminal laws nor likely to be used to bring criminal charges. . . ." This is because it is difficult to classify the "need" for a search (or to be free from one) by whether the object of the search is to be used in civil or criminal proceedings. On the civil side, the government-as-employer may have a great need to discover whether an air traffic controller is impaired by alcohol, whereas it may have little need to discover that he is double parked. On the other hand, searching an employee's car for a murder weapon will be of greater neces-

sity than a search of the car for a box of pencils taken from the office.

The civil/criminal distinction is equally unavailing when viewed from an employee's perspective. Many employees would prefer to have a search yield evidence of a minor criminal infraction than evidence causing their employment to be terminated. As this brief discussion indicates, it is of little help in determining the reasonableness of a search to focus on whether the evidence sought to be obtained relates to criminal or civil matters.

Regardless of the manner in which the government-as-employer theory is applied, however, it rests upon an extremely problematic interpretation of the fourth amendment. The doctrine makes sense, if at all, only from the perspective of the government. From an employee's perspective, the theory allows fourth amendment protections "to fluctuate with the 'intent' of the invading officers." If an employee is subjected to a drug test because he is suspected of criminal activity, the test is illegal. But if a test is administered merely to evaluate his fitness for a job, the same urine test is legal. Clearly, this turns the fourth amendment on its head. As the Supreme Court commented in *Camara v. Municipal Court*, "It is surely anomalous to say that the individual and his private property are fully protected by the Fourth Amendment only when the individual is suspected of criminal behavior."

This anomaly should be foreclosed by the language of the amendment itself. As Justice Brennan noted:

The Amendment states its own purpose, the protection of the privacy of the individual and of his property against the incursions of officials: the "right of the people to be secure in their persons, houses, papers, and effects." Like most of the Bill of Rights it was not designed to be a shelter for criminals, but a basic protection for everyone; to be sure, it must be upheld when asserted by criminals, in order that it may be at all effective, but it "reaches all alike, whether accused of crime or not."

H. Administrative Searches

Several courts have upheld the drug testing of public employees under the administrative search exception to the warrant requirement. This exception is based upon a line of Supreme Court decisions allowing warrantless searches of commercial premises in closely regulated industries. In these decisions the Court has recognized significant state interests in regulating industries such as coal mining, firearms sales, junkyards, and the sale of alcoholic beverages. Because such regulation tends to reduce expectations of privacy, the Court has allowed warrantless searches of commercial property where authorized by specific statutory authority. The Court has made it clear, however, that the exception does not excuse warrantless searches of personal property outside of the commercial context, especially warrantless searches of private homes. In *Donovan v. Dewey,* the Court explicitly distinguished searches of private residences from searches of commercial premises for purposes of the administrative search exception.

The Court's most recent case on administrative searches, *New York v. Burger,* set forth three criteria which must be met in order for a warrantless search of commercial premises to be permissible. There must be a "substantial" government interest supported by the regulatory scheme permitting the search; "warrantless inspections must be 'necessary to further [the] regulatory scheme';" and "the statute's inspection program, in terms of the certainty and regularity of its application, [must] provid[e] a constitutionally adequate substitute for a warrant." The Court has also required a nexus between the purposes for the regulation and the interests involved in the search, although it did not articulate it as a formal criterion.

On its face, the administrative search exception to the warrant requirement does not apply to bodily searches of public employees. The Court has taken great pains to explicitly limit the doctrine to searches of commercial *property*. Nevertheless, several courts have extended the doctrine to apply to drug testing employees in regulated industries. In effect, these courts have taken a relatively narrow

doctrine permitting warrantless searches of commercial property in a few historically and pervasively regulated industries and applied it to highly intrusive bodily fluid searches of individual employees who work in regulated industries. There is little that can be said about this development except that it represents a radical departure from precedent. The Sixth Circuit has noted this point quite forcefully:

> To allow widespread mandatory drug testing of individuals by analogizing it to the relaxed standards governing the less intrusive searches of places allowed under the administrative search warrant exception fundamentally misapprehends that doctrine.
>
> Given the origins of the administrative search warrant exception, it seems incredible that the argument in favor of mandatory drug testing should be based on this doctrine.

The application of the administrative search doctrine to bodily searches is particularly unfortunate in view of the relaxation of the doctrine itself in *Burger.* There, the Court found a "substantial" state interest in the regulation of junkyards. Warrantless searches were considered necessary to further the regulatory scheme because a warrant requirement might impair the "surprise" found crucial to the Court in order to enforce the regulatory scheme. Finally, the Court found that the regulatory scheme provided a "constitutionally adequate substitute for a warrant." As Justice Brennan noted in his dissent, however, the only real restriction on the searches was that they must occur during the business hours of junkyards. That the search actually conducted was unrelated to the administrative regulations that initially justified the search, but rather was aimed at criminal law enforcement, was not viewed as a sufficient difficulty to remove the search from the administrative search exception.

In the wake of *Burger,* it becomes clear that almost any regulatory scheme may validly authorize a warrantless search as long as the legislature is able to articulate some plausible significant interest and at least one restriction on the time, place, and scope of the authorized searches. Moreover, the search will not be objectionable merely because its sole purpose is criminal law enforcement. As Justice Brennan observed, "[t]he implications of the Court's opinion, if realized, will virtually eliminate Fourth Amendment protection of commercial entities in the context of administrative searches." Applying the administrative search doctrine to bodily searches of individual employees will have the further effect of virtually eliminating fourth amendment protection of individuals employed in commercial entities. The implications of this result may be to allow a legislature to effectively abrogate much of traditional fourth amendment protection by regulatory fiat.

41. The Rationale for AIDS-Related Testing

Karen Clifford and Russel Iuculano

Karen Clifford and Russel Iuculano argue that insurance is founded on the principle that policyholders with the same expected risk of loss should be treated equally. They further argue that AIDS antibody tests are sufficiently reliable to be valid underwriting tools for the insurance industry. To deal with the problem of uninsurables, they support state and federal government initiatives.

Acquired Immune Deficiency Syndrome (AIDS) is potentially the most serious health threat the United States has ever faced. The disease, although unknown in this nation until 1981, may afflict as many as 270,000 Americans by 1991, causing an estimated 179,000 deaths. Most of these deaths will occur among the 1 to 1.5 million Americans already infected with the virus, many of whom do not yet show signs of illness.

Although the immediate danger posed by AIDS to Americans has understandably attracted a great deal of attention, the epidemic also threatens the country's economic well-being and the solvency of its health care system. In the rush to ensure that persons with AIDS are treated fairly, some legislatures have enacted and others are considering laws which, by mandating the abandonment of time-honored and sensible underwriting principles, endanger the financial stability of many insurers.

From the *Harvard Law Review* Vol. 100 (1987). Reprinted by permission.

The United States Public Health Service estimates that the annual direct cost of health care for the estimated 171,000 AIDS patients expected to be alive in 1991 will be between eight billion and sixteen billion dollars. This figure assumes a per case cost of $46,000 to $92,000. Some studies predict considerably higher costs. A large portion of these health care costs will be borne by insurance companies. Yet, high as they are, these figures underestimate the total impact of AIDS on the insurance industry because they do not include the cost of outpatient health care, including counseling and home health care costs. Moreover, these studies do not reflect claims incurred for loss of income due to disability, and they do not in any way measure the impact on the life insurance business. Insurers expect to pay billions of dollars for AIDS-related claims over the next several years as they fulfill contractual responsibilities to policyholders who are or become AIDS patients. Estimates indicate that the insurance community has already paid a significant portion of the health care costs associated with

AIDS, from thirteen to sixty-five percent in some hospitals.

Insurance is founded on the principle that policyholders with the same expected risk of loss should be treated equally. Infection with the AIDS virus is now known to be a highly significant risk factor, one that cannot be ignored by any actuarially sound insurance system. Yet some lawmakers, understandably motivated by sympathy for persons with AIDS, are giving serious consideration to a prohibition on any use of AIDS-related testing for insurance purposes, a ban that would seriously distort the fair and equitable functioning of the insurance pricing system.

This Commentary argues that insurers must be allowed to continue using AIDS-related testing to determine insurability. Part I begins with an explanation of some fundamental principles of insurance and examines how these principles might apply to individuals at risk for developing AIDS. Parts II through IV then review both the legal and medical rationales behind testing by insurers and set forth recent actions by several jurisdictions that have prohibited AIDS-related testing for insurance purposes. Part V concludes that such actions present potential dangers to both insurers and the insurance-buying public. Finally, Part VI suggests an alternative means of financing the AIDS-related costs of individuals who are denied insurance.

I. Basics of Insurance Underwriting

Even a cursory review of the fundamentals of insurance underwriting underscores the unprecedented challenges and implications the AIDS crisis holds for the life and health insurance industry. Underwriting is generally defined as the "process by which an insurer determines whether or not and on what basis it will accept an application for insurance." The primary goal of underwriting is the accurate prediction of future mortality and morbidity costs. An insurance company has the re-

sponsibility to treat all its policyholders fairly by establishing premiums at a level consistent with the risk represented by each individual policyholder. As one observer has noted, "[b]asic to the concept of providing insurance to persons of different ages, sexes, . . . occupations and health histories . . . [is] the right of the insurer to create classifications to recognize the many differences which exist among individuals." Individual characteristics that have an impact on risk assessment, such as age, health history and general physical condition, gender, occupation, and use of alcohol and tobacco, are analyzed separately and in combination to determine their effects on mortality. "It is the understanding of the way these various [characteristics] influence mortality that enables companies to classify applicants into groups or classes with comparable mortality risks to be charged appropriate premium rates."

At last count, some 158 million Americans under the age of sixty-five were covered by some form of group health insurance, and nine million more were covered solely by individual health insurance. About ninety percent of the insured population is covered by group health insurance, and forty-seven percent is covered by group life insurance. Group insurance underwriting involves an evaluation of the risk of a *group*—for example, employees, members of a labor union, or members of an association—to determine the terms on which the insurance contract will be acceptable to the insurer.

In contrast to underwriting for individual insurance, insurers underwriting group life and health insurance consider only the relevant characteristics of the *group*, not of the individuals who comprise the group. Such an approach operates "on the premise that in any large group of individuals there will only be a few individuals who have medical conditions of [significant] severity and frequency which would, using individual underwriting standards, make them either a substandard or noninsurable risk." Thus, the issue of testing for the presence of the AIDS virus, its antibodies, AIDS-related complex (ARC), or the active presence of AIDS relates only to new coverage for which evidence of insurability is required.

II. Fairness and Equity Required by Insurance Law

The insurance industry has long been subject to statutory rules requiring the fair and equitable treatment of insured parties in the underwriting process. The Unfair Trade Practices Act (UTPA), developed by the National Association of Insurance Commissioners (NAIC), was, by 1960, enacted in some form in all states and the District of Columbia. The central tenet of the UTPA is its distinction between fair and unfair discrimination. State insurance laws modeled on the NAIC Act both compel discrimination in certain situations and prohibit unfair discrimination in others. For example, the Act deems it inequitable to charge identical premiums for life insurance to a sixty-year-old man in poor health and a twenty-year-old woman in good health. In such a case, an insurer must differentiate between the two to determine an equitable premium: "[r]ates should be adequate but not excessive and should discriminate fairly between insureds . . . so that each insured will pay in accordance with the quality of his risk."

Likewise, section 4(7)(a) of the UTPA prohibits any insurer from "making or permitting any *unfair* discrimination between individuals of the same class and equal expectation of life in the rates charged for any contract of life insurance." Section 4(7)(b) contains a similar provision for health insurance that proscribes "unfair discrimination between individuals of the same class and having essentially the same hazard." We contend that persons who have been infected by the AIDS virus are not of the same class and risk as those who have not been infected.

The proper definition of "fairness" in the underwriting context has been the subject of litigation. In *Physicians Mutual Insurance Co. v. Denenberg,* for example, the Pennsylvania Insurance Commissioner had revoked his approval of several of Physicians Mutual's health insurance policy forms. Each of the policy forms in question provided for an initial premium of one dollar, regardless of the type of risk insured. The Commissioner's action was based on his determination that the policy forms "effected unfair discrimination and . . . were not in accord with sound actuarial principles." Agreeing with the Commissioner's ruling, a Pennsylvania state court found that "[t]he $1.00 premium in the first month in no way relate[d] actuarially to the risk involved and [was] discriminatory." To underwrite within the spirit of state antidiscrimination laws, an insurer is bound to accord similar treatment in the underwriting process to those representing similar health risks.

Last year, Washington became the first state to address the practical application of its Unfair Trade Practices Act to the underwriting of AIDS. The state's insurance department had promulgated a rule establishing minimum standards to be met by insurers in underwriting the AIDS risk. The regulation construed the state's UTPA "to *require* grouping of insureds into classes of like risk and exposure" and the "charg[ing of] a premium commensurate with the risk and exposure." The department's rule stresses the Act's mandate that underwriting considerations for AIDS be consistent with underwriting considerations for other diseases. It notes, by way of example, that "policies issued on a standard basis should not be surcharged to support those issued to insureds suffering from an ailment."

The Washington regulation illustrates that although, on its face, the UTPA seems to impose only a negative duty on insurers, closer examination reveals that under the Act insurers have a positive duty to separate insureds with identifiable, serious health risks from the pool of insureds without those risks. Failure to do so represents a forced subsidy from the healthy to the less healthy. To meet the fundamental fairness requirements of the UTPA and to address the concern for unfair discrimination, insurers must continue to use objective, accurate, and fair standards for appraising the risk of AIDS. As will be shown below, the tests for infection by the AIDS virus indisputably identify an actuarially significant risk of developing AIDS. If the insuring process is to remain fair to other applicants and policyholders, insurers must be permitted to treat tests for infection by the AIDS virus in the same manner as they treat medical tests for other diseases. To ignore the risk levels associated with infection and treat a seropositive individual on the same terms as one not similarly infected would constitute unfair discrimination against noninfected insureds and, therefore, violate the states' Unfair Trade Practices Acts.

III. AIDS Antibody Tests Are Valid Underwriting Tools

AIDS is caused by a virus that has been given various scientific designations but is chiefly known as HTLV-III. When the HTLV-III virus enters the bloodstream, it begins to attack certain white blood cells (T-lymphocytes) which are vital to the body's immune defenses. In response to infection with the virus, the white blood cells produce antibodies. A person generally develops antibodies two weeks to three months after infection.

A protocol of tests, known as the ELISA-ELISA-Western blot (WB) series, is considered highly accurate for determining the presence of infection with the HTLV-III virus. A person with two positive ELISA tests and a positive WB is a true confirmed positive with 99.9% reliability. The insurance industry and the medical profession commonly administer the ELISA-ELISA-WB series of tests. . . .

Nonetheless, when analyzing a test's validity for underwriting purposes, reliability, in and of itself, is not sufficient. A test must also be established as an effective and accurate predictor of future mortality and morbidity costs. In June 1986, the CDC estimated that 20% to 30% of those infected will develop the invariably fatal disease over the next five years. In July of the same year, the National Institutes of Health predicted that, over the next six to eight years, as many as 35% of HTLV-III antibody positive persons may develop AIDS. On October 29, 1986, the Institute of Medicine of the National Academy of Sciences issued a

374-page report, *Confronting AIDS*, which estimated that up to 50% of all those infected with the virus might develop full-scale AIDS within ten years.

Quite apart from signaling the risk of developing AIDS itself, HTLV-III infection may herald the onset of other illnesses such as ARC or neurological disease. Studies cited by the CDC found that 25% of those who were confirmed positive with the HTLV-III antibody developed ARC within two to five years. An individual suffering from ARC may have a weakened immune system and manifest such symptoms as night sweats, weight loss, fatigue, fever, gastrointestinal symptoms, and enlargement of the lymph nodes, and may become disabled as a result. Due to the chronic nature of these ailments, ARC may, in and of itself, give rise to substantial medical expenses.

Despite the wealth of medical data that lends support to AIDS-related testing for insurance purposes, utilization of such tests is sometimes questioned because there are a significant number of individuals who have tested positive but have not yet developed AIDS. This viewpoint, however, demonstrates a fundamental lack of familiarity with basic insurance principles. Underwriting is, by its very nature, concerned with probabilities, not certainties; no one knows how many infected people will eventually develop AIDS. Even assuming that "only" twenty percent will contract AIDS during the first five years, there is a demonstrable risk that a large percentage of infected individuals will develop AIDS in year six and beyond.

A twenty percent assumption implies that 200 of each 1000 applicants testing positive on the ELISA-ELISA-WB series will develop AIDS within five years and, therefore, die within approximately seven years. In comparison, life insurance mortality tables estimate that, of a standard group of 1000 persons aged thirty-four, only about seven and one-half (as opposed to 200 in 1000) will die within the first seven years from any cause.

The substantially greater risk represented by persons who test positive for HTLV-III infection is obvious. The comparison of 200 deaths to seven and one-half deaths indicates that a person infected with the AIDS virus is, over a seven-year period, twenty-six times more likely to die than is someone in "standard" health. The actuarial significance of these percentages is overwhelming and cannot be ignored. Because such tests are reliable, accurate, and effective predictors of risk, they must be considered appropriate as underwriting tools.

IV. Legislative Restrictions on AIDS-Related Testing

Until recently, the right of insurance companies to inquire into and test for health conditions affecting mortality and morbidity was generally accepted within the industry and rarely questioned outside of it. However, a fundamental misunderstanding of insurance principles, coupled with the desire to prevent discrimination against homosexuals, has led to the passage of laws in several jurisdictions granting individuals infected with AIDS a favored status in the underwriting process. These laws substantially impede the insurance industry's ability to assess risk, thereby undercutting the industry's financial stability and compromising its ability to pay future claims.

In April 1985, for example, the California legislature enacted a law that provided that "the results of a blood test to detect antibodies to the probable causative agent of acquired immune deficiency syndrome . . . shall not be used in any instance for the determination of insurability or suitability for employment." In July 1985, the Wisconsin legislature enacted a similar but more restrictive measure. Most recently, in 1986, the District of Columbia enacted D.C. Act 6-170, the most restrictive legislation of its kind in the country. It prohibits the use of *all* AIDS-related tests for a five-year period, including tests for the AIDS antibody, tests to appraise the condition of the immune system, and tests to identify the existence of the AIDS virus itself. The Act further forbids the use of personal characteristics such as age, marital status, geographic area of residence, occupation, sex, or sexual orientation for the purpose of predicting whether an individual will develop AIDS or ARC.

On August 5, 1986, the American Council of Life Insurance (ACLI) and the Health Insurance Association of America (HIAA) brought suit against the District of Columbia in the United States District Court for the District of Columbia, arguing that the Act violated both the fifth amendment and the District of Columbia's Home Rule Act. On September 19, 1986, in *American Council of Life Insurance v. District of Columbia,* a district court upheld the Act, though it did not do so on the basis of the city council's allegations regarding the reliability, accuracy, or predictive value of the AIDS tests. In fact, the court appeared to agree with the plaintiffs that presently available evidence refuted those premises upon which the city council based the Act. For example, the court stated that the plaintiffs had offered "persuasive evidence that the tests accurately target a group of individuals with significantly higher risks." The court upheld the constitutionality of the law, however, because the evidence presented by the plaintiffs, ACLI and HIAA, had not been available to the city council at the time the bill was under consideration. The court further observed: "[a]lthough [we] agree[] that in light of this evidence the D.C. Council should be encouraged to reconsider its decision, this report was not before the Council last spring and therefore cannot prove the irrationality of the law."

The court seriously questioned the wisdom of the Act's five-year moratorium on all AIDS-related testing:

The nature of the rapidly changing landscape of AIDS research suggests that the D.C. Council may have acted too hastily in imposing the five-year moratorium on rate increases. . . . [T]he court agrees with the plaintiffs that *new evidence on the accuracy of AIDS tests for insurance purposes and the everchanging breakthroughs in AIDS research raise serious questions about imposing a five-year ban on screening applicants for AIDS. . . .*

This decision thus calls into question whether similar legislation recently introduced in other jurisdictions will pass constitutional muster in light of the medical and scientific data that now supports the credibility of the ELISA-ELISA-WB series.

A major impetus behind these restrictive laws has been the concern that insurance companies be prevented from discriminating against homosexuals. The life and health insurance industry share that concern. In fact, the ACLI and HIAA have endorsed guidelines, adopted by the NAIC in December 1986, that set forth two general propositions:

> No inquiry in an application for health or life insurance coverage, or in an investigation conducted by an insurer or insurance support organization on its behalf in connection with an application for such coverage, shall be directed toward determining the applicant's sexual orientation. . . . Sexual orientation may not be used in the underwriting process or in the determination of insurability.

The insurance industry, by supporting these guidelines, refutes the contentions of certain groups that sexual orientation has a place in the underwriting process. Rather, the industry seeks only to use the best medical knowledge available to assess accurately the level of risk an applicant represents. Although members of the industry are in substantial agreement that an applicant's sexual orientation is not an appropriate underwriting tool, they are in equally strong agreement that current state-of-the-art tools for predicting the AIDS risk, as exemplified by the ELISA-ELISA-WB sequence, are valid for that purpose and should be used accordingly in a responsible fashion. . . .

VI. Availability of Health Insurance

As representatives of an industry that endorses AIDS-related blood testing to ensure the equitable treatment of all insurance applicants in the underwriting process, we must address an inevitable consequence of effective underwriting—the denial of health insurance to some high-risk applicants, particularly those

with HTLV-III infection. For those covered by group health insurance, various laws operate to prevent an interruption in coverage when an individual is no longer eligible for group coverage, such as upon termination of employment. The availability of continued insurance protection was significantly bolstered by the ninety-ninth Congress. Federal law now requires, with some minor exceptions, that all employers with twenty or more employees provide continuation of health coverage for up to eighteen months to employees after termination of their employment (for reasons other than gross misconduct) or a reduction in hours. Several states also require continuation of group coverage, at the group rate, for varying periods of time. Given that most AIDS patients die within two years of the manifestation of AIDS-related symptomatology, federal and state continuation laws effectively assure that a significant portion of AIDS-related health care costs will be borne by the health insurance industry. In the face of current projections on the spread of AIDS, these laws will, in all probability, take on added significance by ensuring the continued availability of health insurance coverage for many Americans.

A. Pools for Uninsurables

Despite the fact that a majority of Americans have private health coverage, some individuals do not have access to group coverage and are medically uninsurable for individual health insurance. Medical uninsurability is not, however, a phenomenon suffered exclusively by those at risk for developing AIDS. Individuals suffering from developmental disabilities, physical or mental impairments, or chronic health conditions account for a large number of those who are unable to obtain individually purchased health insurance. Estimates place the number of uninsurables in the country today at one million.

Some argue that a quick and easy solution to this problem would be to force insurers to discard the underwriting process and to assume all future health care costs of AIDS patients, thereby ignoring the risk these individuals represent. Although the goal of ensuring accessibility to quality health care is certainly a laudable one, this simplistic and ill-founded approach demonstrates a basic misunderstanding of the insurance mechanism. Further, it fails to provide for the intake of premiums sufficient to cover the expected claims. If the insurance industry cannot collect premiums commensurate with the underlying risk, it will simply not have the money to satisfy the inevitable claims that are submitted. If such a policy were implemented, some companies would surely face major solvency problems. Indeed, if risk assessment were abandoned and if it were generally understood by all that insurance could be purchased after the development of an illness, the public would have no incentive whatsoever to purchase health insurance. Such a policy could have grave and serious consequences for this country's health care system.

State pools for uninsurables have been suggested as one solution to the problem. Common sense indicates—and indeed experience has shown—that such pools can reasonably be expected to sustain substantial losses. Once such losses are determined, insurance companies contribute assessments based on their pro rata share of premium volume in that state. Eleven states have enacted into law such pools.

A recognized difficulty in financing these pools, however, is that the losses from each pool cannot be shared equally by all health insurance providers—the commercial insurers, Blue Cross and Blue Shield, health maintenance organizations, and self-insured employers—because of the Employee Retirement Income Security Act (ERISA) of 1974. In short, plans that are self-funded—those that finance benefits by paying claims directly out of the assets of the employer or union trust fund rather than through the purchase of group insurance coverage—may not be treated as insurers. Under state law, employers who choose to insure employee benefits must comply with the multitude of legislative and regulatory requirements, such as state risk pools. However, section 514 of ERISA preempts state law as it relates to employee benefit plans. A state law requiring a self-funded employer to participate in a pool would be a law that "relates to" employee benefit plans and would, therefore, be subject to federal preemption. Thus, the self-insurance community is shielded by federal law from participation in the state pools.

The establishment of state pools could, therefore, serve as a strong incentive for employers to self-insure to avoid assessments by the pool, premium taxes by the state, and the need to comply with other state laws and regulations. As more insured plans switch to the self-insurance mechanism, a shrinking of the available insurance base upon which to impose assessments to pay for AIDS claims and other claims handled by that state's pool would occur. Consequently, the assessments per policy or group would steadily rise, thereby encouraging even more plans to switch to the self-insured market.

An intelligent approach to the national problem of uninsurability does not necessitate, nor is it well-served by, threatening the underpinnings of the private health insurance industry, an industry currently responsible for the payment of $113.6 billion of this nation's health care bill. To prevent the inevitable loss of state revenue and regulatory control, a solution could appropriately be sought at the federal level. Indeed, the ninety-ninth Congress was witness to the introduction of just such legislation. Had it been enacted, this legislation would have imposed a tax on most employers who did not voluntarily participate in state pools that meet certain minimum standards. Thus, the bill would have established tax incentives for the states to establish pools that offer comprehensive health insurance to all citizens regardless of their health status, thereby assuring that the social responsibility of providing coverage to the uninsurable population would be fairly apportioned.

Unless and until appropriate state and/or federal laws are passed, legislation that requires only the insurance industry to engage in health care pooling for those medically uninsurable will represent a financial burden on the health insurance industry that is unshared by self-insurers, resulting in a dislocation of the forces of marketplace competition. Absent such initiatives, state pools for uninsurables fail to address effectively the problem of insuring potential AIDS patients and could, in fact, create other significant problems in the process.

VII. Conclusion

To operate in a voluntary market, insurance underwriting must appraise the risk of an unknown and unanticipated occurrence and spread that risk over a large number of individuals. The risk must be assessed as accurately as possible because the whole price structure of insurance depends on the principle that individuals who present the same expected risk of loss pay the same premium. When an insurer is able to estimate accurately the risk to which it is exposed, it can, in turn, be more precise in pricing the cost of the insurance.

Contrary to this principle, several jurisdictions have imposed legal constraints which place AIDS outside the normal medical and regulatory rules pertaining to underwriting for other diseases. Although it is legally permissible for an insurer to obtain medical information about an applicant who may contract any other disease, such as heart disease or cancer, some states grant AIDS carriers special treatment by completely exempting them from relevant tests.

The tests for infection by the AIDS virus are extremely accurate in the same sense that any tests used in the insurance business can be accurate: they provide a basis for an objective determination of significantly higher risks and, hence, risk-based pricing. Legislation intended to force life and health insurers to ignore reliable, scientific evidence of a person's increased risk of contracting a fatal disease will result in significant inequities to policyholders. Given the potential magnitude of the AIDS epidemic and the substantial likelihood that gay rights advocates will seek additional legal constraints on AIDS-related testing by insurers, the financial consequences of AIDS to all involved—insurers, policyholders, and the public—will become even more severe.

Because the life and health insurance industry's livelihood is dependent on insuring persons against premature death and the costs of disability, it is as concerned as the public health community with curbing this tragic disease. Although the industry is fully cognizant of the concerns of those who have been infected with the AIDS virus, it must also consider its responsibility to those who have not been infected. If projections of AIDS cases materialize, public policy makers will be faced with an increasingly pressing need to achieve a balance between competing concerns. This balance need not, and indeed should not, be achieved at the expense of an industry that will inevitably bear a substantial amount of the costs associated with the AIDS crisis.

42. The AIDS Insurance Crisis

Benjamin Schatz

Benjamin Schatz argues that because AIDS has been associated with gay men, some insurers have responded to AIDS by discriminating against gays in insuring policies. He further contends that the use of HIV testing by insurance companies is likely to increase this discrimination against gays. Moreover, he argues that it will also shift AIDS-related costs from the highly profitable insurance industry to the government. Schatz points out that the insurance industry has long resisted legislative proposals for national health insurance, insisting that it is in a better position than the government to manage health care costs. Accordingly,

From the *Harvard Law Review* Vol. 100 (1987). Reprinted by permission.

he argues that the insurance industry should not now be allowed to use underwriting policies that shift onto the government a burden that it deems unprofitable.

As of February 1987, over 30,000 Americans have been diagnosed with Acquired Immune Deficiency Syndrome (AIDS). An even larger number of people—perhaps five to ten times the number with AIDS—suffer from a related illness called AIDS-related complex (ARC). Like people with AIDS—but unlike the majority of people only *exposed* to HIV, the virus believed to cause AIDS—people with ARC also experience medical problems. Although these symptoms are often virtually unnoticeable, ARC can sometimes lead to severe disability and even death.

Frighteningly, these numbers pale in comparison to future projections. The United States Public Health Service (PHS) estimates that 270,000 Americans will develop AIDS by 1991. Yet the actual numbers will likely be far higher: the PHS projections are based solely upon the number of people already infected with HIV and do not take into account the millions likely to be infected in the future.

Seventy-three percent of all Americans diagnosed with AIDS have been men who have had same-gender sexual experience. Unfortunately, this statistical association has reinforced societal animosity toward an already unpopular group—an animosity intensified by a fear that the usually fatal illness can be spread through casual contact. The result has been a steady increase in discrimination and violence directed at gay men and even lesbians.

Yet medical evidence overwhelmingly demonstrates that AIDS is spread only in utero or through sexual intercourse or shared blood products. Furthermore, AIDS is not a "gay disease." According to current projections, the vast majority of gay and bisexual men will not develop AIDS. Moreover, in many countries, AIDS is largely a heterosexual phenomenon. Here in the United States, the percentage of cases resulting from heterosexual transmission is rising significantly.

The fact is that gay and bisexual men represent only one of several AIDS "high risk groups" identified by the United States Centers for Disease Control (CDC): other groups include past recipients of blood transfusions, intravenous drug users, prostitutes and their clients, and hemophiliacs. When we add one last group—persons who have had "unsafe" sexual contact with anyone in the categories named above—we see that many if not most Americans are considered to be at risk.

Ironically, the increasing public perception that AIDS threatens all Americans has only heightened the panic and prejudice accompanying the disease. People who have or are perceived to be at risk for AIDS have been fired from their jobs, evicted from their homes, refused services by businesses and government agencies, and denied visitation privileges with their children. Doctors have been evicted from their offices for treating people with AIDS, while other medical personnel have refused to offer treatment. Discrimination may persist even after death; some funeral homes have refused to accommodate the bodies of people who have died from the disease.

Much of the discrimination associated with AIDS involves the use—or, more appropriately, the misuse—of the HIV antibody test. As its name implies, the test is not a test for AIDS, nor even the AIDS virus; instead, it detects antibodies to the virus and thus indicates previous viral exposure and an *increased risk* of developing AIDS. As of this writing, only one antibody test, known as "ELISA," has been licensed by the United States Food and Drug Administration (FDA). Because this test was designed to eliminate potentially infected blood used by blood banks, it is oversensitive, and false positive results often occur. Thus, the FDA cautions that "[i]t is inappropriate to use this test as a screen for AIDS or as a screen for members of groups at increased risk for AIDS in the general population."

Despite this warning, the test has been widely abused. People with positive test results have been denied employment, child visitation privileges, and even bail. In addition, the military and the United States Foreign Service have established a policy of rejecting all job applicants who test positive for HIV antibodies. Such discrimination has been legitimized by the United States Department of Justice, which declared in a recent memorandum that the federal law prohibiting discrimination on the basis of physical handicap does not forbid discrimination based on HIV antibody test results.

It is within this context that we must analyze current insurance industry reactions to the AIDS epidemic. Is the industry behaving fairly, or is it, as some charge, overreacting?

One fact cannot be disputed: the sudden arrival of AIDS has forced health and life insurers to assume large, unanticipated costs. Unfortunately, many insurers have attempted to limit these costs through unscrupulous "post-claim underwriting," that is, by denying financial responsibility after a person already insured is diagnosed with AIDS. Thus, some insurers have relied upon contractual language precluding payments for "experimental treatments" to avoid paying for promising AIDS therapies. Others have expanded the definition of clauses that exclude payment for "pre-existing conditions" to justify withholding life or health benefits to policyholders who exhibited any medical ailments prior to being diagnosed. Finally, some insurers have made it difficult for people with AIDS who have employer-provided group life or health insurance to convert to an individual plan upon leaving their jobs. People with AIDS who lose insurance in this manner will be unable to purchase new insurance because of their poor health.

An even greater problem is the use of questionable underwriting practices prior to the issuance of a policy. A growing number of insurers have sought to limit future liability for AIDS by rejecting all applicants thought to be gay or bisexual, or by declining to issue group insurance plans to employers believed to have a large gay workforce. In addition, many insurers are attempting to learn the HIV antibody status of their applicants so that they can reject those who test positive.

It is the issue of AIDS-related underwriting that is the focus of this Commentary. Part I analyzes the legal and public policy implications of underwriting on the basis of sexual orientation. Part II explores the current

debate over insurer use of the HIV antibody test. The Commentary concludes by arguing that the financial concerns of the insurance industry are not sufficient to outweigh the social, medical, and moral costs of sexual orientation discrimination or HIV antibody testing.

I. Sexual Orientation Discrimination

Because AIDS has been popularly associated with gay men, some members of the insurance industry have responded to AIDS with calls for anti-gay discrimination in issuing policies. One industry spokesman, for example, was quoted as saying that "[i]f an applicant is a potential homosexual, the underwriters have ways to find out. We can deny coverage. We wouldn't tell them why."

Insurance industry attempts to refuse coverage to gay and bisexual men have not been limited to declarations of intent. One health insurance company, for example, distributed an "AIDS Profile," which required its agents to segregate applications from "single males without dependents that are engaged in occupations that do not require physical exertion." The occupations named—"restaurant employees, antique dealers, interior decorators, consultants, florists, and people in the jewelry or fashion business"—were evidently those stereotyped as the professional interests of gay men. Another company issued "underwriting guidelines for AIDS" urging agents to scrutinize applicants who are unmarried, who name as a life insurance beneficiary someone other than a spouse or child, or who show evidence of a "sexually promiscuous or illicit lifestyle." Insurance companies have also used information about living arrangements, residence or zip codes, medical history, and even "morals," in an attempt to identify and then reject those applicants thought to be gay or bisexual.

Discrimination of this nature is dangerous in several ways. The exclusion of gay and bisexual men from the insurance pool can lead to employment discrimination, denial of credit or home mortgages, and an increased financial burden on government medical assistance programs. Discrimination also threatens to drive gay and bisexual men back into the closet. Although such a result may be ideologically pleasing to some, its implications are medically disastrous. A climate of homophobia deters frank discussion with physicians and discourages people from seeking out AIDS prevention information that may "implicate" them as gay or bisexual. Moreover, gay and bisexual men who fear discrimination may become unwilling to risk honesty with sexual partners, and may instead feel compelled to seek the protection of sham marriages—a possibility that could increase the spread of AIDS among heterosexuals.

Yet the most powerful argument against the denial of insurance to gay and bisexual men is a moral one. To decline coverage to an entire social class because a small percentage of its members are expected to develop a disease represents stereotyping at its worst. Unfortunately, the current phenomenon of anti-gay discrimination by insurers is part of a long history of religious, racial, and gender discrimination by the insurance industry. In the 1860s, for example, insurance companies often refused to sell fire insurance to Jews. Ninety years later, insurers used race-based mortality and medical tables to charge blacks more than whites for health and life insurance. Although problems persist, many states have now passed laws prohibiting insurers from using race in rating or underwriting. Regrettably, however, most insurers continue to charge men and women differing amounts for identical coverage.

Surprisingly, the two leading insurance trade organizations, the Health Insurance Association of America (HIAA) and the American Council of Life Insurance (ACLI), have agreed to oppose the use of sexual orientation in underwriting. As recently as December 1986, both groups endorsed a "model bulletin" forbidding life and health insurers to inquire into an applicant's sexual orientation or to use such information in the underwriting process. Drafted by the National Association of Insurance Commissioners (NAIC), the nation's organization of insurance regulators, the bulletin also prohibits the use of information about gender, marital status, living arrangements, occupation, medical history, beneficiaries, and zip codes or other territorial classifications to determine an applicant's sexual orientation.

The impact of this model bulletin is uncertain. In the first place, bulletins are not a formal regulatory device, but are only an informal means by which regulators inform insurers of the interpretations of existing law that they intend to adopt. Moreover, approval of a bulletin by the NAIC does not compel insurance regulators to implement it in their own states. Yet even where insurance commissioners have not adopted the bulletin, insurers are likely to consider themselves bound by it; once a fairly small number of states endorse a model law or bulletin of the NAIC, most insurers comply. This does not mean, of course, that all insurers will abandon anti-gay discrimination, but rather that the bulletin and relevant nondiscrimination laws will encourage compliance once discrimination is detected.

The readiness of the HIAA and ACLI to oppose discrimination on the basis of sexual orientation and race, but not gender, seems puzzling. The likely explanation for the industry's inconsistent approaches to race and gender may simply be that the black civil rights movement has been more successful than the women's movement in making such discrimination socially unacceptable. Yet in the case of sexual orientation discrimination, it is simple logistics, and not politics, that appear to have motivated the industry's stand. Insurers generally prefer underwriting criteria that are easy to identify, inexpensive to administer, and clearly predictive. Thus, they have refused to abandon gender-based rating because other variables that might indicate risk, such as eating patterns and exercise habits, are less "administratively convenient" to use.

By contrast, sexual orientation is usually difficult if not impossible to identify. Most gay and bisexual men have developed the ability to conceal their sexual orientation in order to protect themselves from discrimination and ostracism. They work in all professions, belong to all races and religions, and live in every region of every state. Many are married. Because gay and bisexual men, as a class, cannot be identified, it is impossible to demonstrate that they live either longer or shorter than others.

Ironically, it is the very pervasiveness of discrimination that has caused many gay and bisexual men to remain invisible, and thereby has made it difficult for insurers to discriminate against them effectively. A culture that has historically divided its members into racial and gender categories has facilitated the creation of race- and gender-based mortality tables, which make it easy and "logical" for insurers to evaluate applicants on these bases. Because this same culture has suppressed discussion of homosexuality, insurers lack similar tools for evaluating applicants who are gay or bisexual—or lesbian.

Yet even if insurers could identify gay and bisexual men, to deny all of them insurance because a small percentage is likely to develop a disease would still be problematic. The essential question remains whether insurers should be allowed to use the claim of "economic necessity" to exempt themselves from the prohibitions against discrimination that are imposed upon the rest of society. The primary argument that insurers use to justify such an exemption—that discrimination is needed in order to make actuarially valid determinations—has been firmly rejected in the context of race. And generally, the courts have rejected the argument that financial concerns alone justify discriminatory behavior: courts have refused to allow landlords and employers to discriminate against blacks, Jews, women, and others, even though the prejudice of neighbors, customers or coworkers makes a policy of nondiscrimination more costly.

Socially-charged insurance classifications do not become morally neutral simply because they are—or are thought to be—statistically based. Indeed, by treating blacks, women, or gay and bisexual men unfavorably, the insurance industry both reflects and reinforces social inequality. The fundamental issue in employment, housing, *and* insurance is one of access. Our society has determined that the stereotypes that have polarized us should not be used to deny basic needs and opportunities, even when it is more costly to the private sector to provide these necessities on a nondiscriminatory basis. Insurance is just such a ne-

cessity, and should be treated accordingly in the context of AIDS.

II. HIV Testing

A. Framing the Debate

The rejection of sexual orientation discrimination as a basis for underwriting necessarily raises another question: what forms of underwriting are appropriate? Gay and lesbian civil rights organizations, by endorsing the NAIC model bulletin on AIDS, have recognized that insurers have a legal right to decline applicants with AIDS, just as they may decline applicants with cancer, tuberculosis, or other serious illnesses. The model bulletin also permits underwriting on the basis of symptoms associated with ARC or prior history of sexually transmitted disease.

Enormous disagreement, however, has erupted over the appropriateness of use of the HIV antibody test by insurers. The NAIC, for example, was unable to reach a consensus on the subject in fashioning its model bulletin. Nevertheless, insurers point to a recent policy shift in Wisconsin to justify their use of the test. Although a law passed in 1985 originally barred insurers from using the test, the act was amended to allow testing if the state epidemiologist found the test "medically significant and . . . reliable." The state epidemiologist has made such a finding, and testing by insurers is likely to resume.

Although some opponents of HIV antibody testing by insurers question the test's accuracy, the primary argument against such testing is one of social policy, not medical reliability. Thus, industry opponents have increasingly focused on the perceived *social* costs of allowing insurers to use the test. For this reason, the argument against HIV antibody testing also applies to tests that may soon be developed for the virus itself.

Several insurance departments have responded favorably to these arguments and have taken action to limit insurer use of the antibody test. Yet with the amendment of Wisconsin's law, only California and the District of Columbia have statutes that forbid insurers to test applicants or ask them for the results of prior tests. A third state, Maine, allows insurer testing but outlaws questioning about prior tests.

The power of states to enact such legislation was recently affirmed in an important federal court ruling. In *American Council of Life Insurance v. District of Columbia,* the U.S. District Court for the District of Columbia rejected the argument of the ACLI that the District's ban on HIV-related testing constitutes an arbitrary and irrational denial of due process under the fifth amendment. Although questioning the wisdom of the Act, the court found the statute constitutional.

The decision in *American Council of Life Insurance* implicitly endorses the view that insurers do not have an absolute right to use information simply because it is actuarially valid. Similarly, another court has recognized that "actuarial justification does not operate without limit." Indeed, even the American Academy of Actuaries (AAA) acknowledges this fact. In a 1986 report entitled "Risk Classification and AIDS," the AAA declared that "laws, regulations, and public opinion all constrain risk classification systems within the broad guidelines of social acceptability." Legislatures and insurance regulators, they declared, "must balance . . . public acceptability against the potential economic side effects" on the insurance industry.

It is just such a balancing that this Commentary undertakes. Any public policy analysis of the issue of HIV antibody (or viral) testing must weigh the cost to insurers of forbidding the test against the cost to society of allowing it. An approach that fails to consider societal concerns in addition to insurance industry interests is hopelessly one-sided: it is the equivalent of analyzing the problem of air pollution by asking only how much it would cost manufacturers to install emission control devices, while ignoring the costs society pays by not having them installed.

B. Ban on Testing— The Cost to Insurers

The motivation of insurers to test for HIV is largely economic. A joint report by the ACLI and the HIAA states that "if people who have

tested positive for antibodies to the AIDS virus apply for large amounts of life and health insurance and companies are not allowed to identify them as high risks, there will be a potential for large uncontrollable financial liabilities [that could] . . . undermine insurers' ability to remain financially stable."

The economic concerns of the insurance industry should not be casually dismissed. Nonetheless, industry claims that HIV antibody testing is compelled by economic necessity do not withstand scrutiny. In the first place, insurers have greatly exaggerated the cost of AIDS. A study commissioned by the CDC estimates the cost of treating people with AIDS to be only 0.2% of the nation's total personal health care expenditures in 1985, with a projected rise to 1.4% by 1991. The same authors estimate the average cost of treating people with AIDS in 1986 to be $60,000 to 75,000 per person, far less than many other illnesses. The ACLI and HIAA continue, however, to cite an outdated CDC cost estimate of $147,000, even suggesting that it may be "conservative." This assertion is particularly outrageous when compared with the industry's own research: a 1986 ACLI/HIAA survey of 372 companies reveals an average health insurance claim paid for people with AIDS of $36,159 and an average life insurance claim of $33,471.

Second, it is not at all clear that HIV testing will significantly reduce the AIDS-related expenses of insurers. As the ACLI and the HIAA have admitted, "AIDS-testing by insurers has largely been confined to individual policies of insurance." Because eighty-five percent of all medical insurance is purchased on a *group* basis, however, it is clear that health insurers can eliminate only a small percentage of potential AIDS-related expenses by testing individual applicants. Thus, if AIDS threatens the solvency of the insurance industry, the elimination of such a small fraction of the cost is unlikely to prevent insolvency. The fact that the HIV antibody test is not crucial to insurance company survival has been borne out by industry spokespersons, who have conceded that insurers have been able to operate without disruption in states that ban use of the test.

Third, insurers may use other underwriting techniques besides HIV antibody testing to reduce their AIDS-related costs. Many insurers, for example, now include questions on their applications about swollen glands, weight loss, and night sweats—symptoms that often precede diagnosis with AIDS or ARC, but are less stigmatizing than a positive test result. Insurers may also make use of general blood tests that are not designed specifically to detect HIV and are therefore less likely to discourage voluntary HIV testing or to result in employment discrimination. Thus, routine blood panels may indicate abnormal white blood cell counts and other factors often associated with HIV-related immunodeficiency, without actually branding the individual as an HIV antibody carrier. Similarly, the "T-Cell" test, although less precise than an HIV antibody test, can measure actual damage to the immune system, especially when testing is repeated over time.

Fourth, underwriting is by no means the only way for insurers to decrease their AIDS-related expenses. For example, AIDS-related medical costs can be significantly reduced when alternatives to hospital care are explored. Yet the ACLI/HIAA survey reveals that barely half of the nation's insurers allow individual (nongroup) claimants to be reimbursed for home health care and that fewer than 30% pay for hospice care. By expanding coverage of these less expensive forms of treatment, insurance companies could cut costs considerably while continuing to cover people with AIDS.

Similarly, health insurers can limit their AIDS-related losses the way they limit losses due to other major expenses—by spreading their costs. One easy way of doing this is to increase premiums (or to reduce dividends). A more sophisticated concept, known as risk pooling, would accomplish the same goal. Under a mandatory pooling system, each health insurer in a given state is required to accept a share of previously rejected applicants proportionate to its share of the state's insurance market. Premiums for risk pool participants are usually statutorily limited to 150% to 200% of the average premium in a given state for healthy insureds. The medical costs of risk pool participants often exceed this cap, and these excess costs are passed on to other policyholders.

By 1986, at least thirteen states had passed risk pool legislation; two bills recently introduced in Congress would provide other states with financial incentives to adopt similar legislation. If adopted, this vitally important legislation would make health insurance available to the millions of Americans now considered uninsurable because of risk for AIDS or other illnesses. Such legislation would also help the industry by spreading the financial burden of poor health risks equitably among insurers, while diffusing criticism that our system of insurance is unable or unwilling to respond adequately to the nation's health care needs.

The most effective way for insurers to reduce the cost of AIDS, however, is to help prevent the spread of the disease. To that end, AIDS service organizations and gay community groups have struggled on meager budgets to educate people about the risks of contracting the disease by sharing hypodermic needles or engaging in unprotected sex. Yet it was not until 1986, long after the HIAA and ACLI began lobbying to use the HIV antibody test, that these insurance industry groups made their first AIDS-related charitable contribution. Because of the financial threat posed by the disease, it is in the economic self-interest of the insurance industry to increase dramatically its contributions to such efforts and to pressure elected officials to do the same.

In addition to expressing concern about the financial implications of a prohibition on testing, insurers have argued that such a ban "would create an entirely new, special set of rules for one class of applicants." Insurer investigations to discover applicants with HIV antibodies, they claim, are analogous to permitted assessments of factors such as smoking, obesity, or hypertension—all of which indicate increased risk, although not necessarily bad health. Thus, insurers assert, any prohibition on industry use of the HIV antibody test "discriminates . . . against persons with other diseases."

The industry's argument is flawed in two respects. In the first place, it is factually incorrect. Several states have banned the use of other tests by insurers in deference to public policy considerations, even though the tests involved have clear predictive value. A number of states have constrained insurers from denying coverage on the basis of exposure to DES or the presence of sickle cell, Tay-Sachs, and hemoglobin C traits.

Second, the analogy simply does not hold. Obesity, smoking, and hypertension are all risks that an individual may be able to eliminate. Insurance industry rating of these factors may be positively motivating and, therefore, medically constructive. It is impossible, however, to reverse one's antibody status, just as it is impossible to "undo" a mother's use of DES or change one's genetic traits. Furthermore, genetic traits for sickle cell anemia and Tay-Sachs, like AIDS, are popularly associated with social groups that have long been the targets of discrimination. The ban on the use of predictive tests for these diseases thus reflects a laudable belief that medical tests must not be used to discriminate against unpopular groups.

The true motivation for the industry's "no special treatment" argument appears not to be a desire to avoid "unfair" discrimination against smokers or people with high blood pressure, but rather a desire to test without regard to social cost. The rejection of persons testing HIV antibody positive is, after all, likely to bring little comfort to those declined because of coronary risk. The real fear of insurers is not that those at coronary risk will want others to be rejected but rather that they will lobby to be insured as well.

In short, insurers are fearful that the AIDS crisis will highlight the increasing problem of uninsurability in America. Ironically, medical advances threaten to make this situation worse. With the expected development of tests to detect genetic predispositions toward cancer, alcoholism, and hundreds of other illnesses, more individuals will fall into high risk categories every year. Thus, the Congressional Office of Technology Assessment (OTA), spurred in part by concerns over HIV testing by insurers, has launched an investigation into the "implications of greatly expanded use" of diagnostic and predictive tests by the insurance industry. According to the OTA, Congress is concerned about both "the possibility of increased Federal health care costs if insurers use these tests to substantially decrease their financial risks," and "the social con-

sequences of identifying persons at risk for untreatable diseases."

C. Use of the Test by Insurers—The Cost to Society

Testing by insurers is socially harmful in at least four ways. First, insurer testing is almost certain to be applied in a manner that discriminates against gay and bisexual men. An August 1985 report of the chair of an ACLI/HIAA committee on AIDS declares:

The major threat to insurance companies at present is largely confined to the homosexual population. . . . If we could somehow use [antibody] testing on this population, results could be expected to be VERY reliable. . . . On the other hand to use [antibody testing] in a nonselective, random screening, manner seems to be very much a mistake at this time. We would not want to lobby for this privelege [sic]. Our efforts should be to push for the right to use [antibody testing] in "high prevelence [sic] settings."

The NAIC model bulletin forbidding sexual orientation discrimination is an important step in combatting discriminatory testing, but it is naive to believe that this effort will eliminate the problem. Because testing can be costly, insurers are likely to want to test only those applicants whom they believe to be "high risk." Thus, they may be tempted to scrutinize the medical records of applicants believed to be gay or bisexual in order to find a pretext that justifies testing. Unfortunately, it would be difficult for an applicant in this position to prove that other applicants with similar medical histories are not being tested or to show that any difference in treatment is based on sexual orientation.

Second, insurers have ignored their obligation to include counseling as part of the testing process, thereby shifting to underfunded AIDS service organizations the responsibility for helping people to live with the results of these tests. Public officials have repeatedly warned that "[c]ounseling and education programming *must* be in place before any testing is contemplated. . . . Once the test results are known, the *person requesting the test* should be prepared to counsel the patient and to help him/her interpret the results." Similarly, an unpublished FDA memorandum declares that "[t]he determination that a person's serum contains antibodies to HTLV-III has such extensive medical, social, psychological, and economic implications for the person concerned that appropriate counseling and medical evaluation . . . must be considered an *essential aspect* of the testing sequence."

Counseling of applicants who submit to the test is essential for two reasons. First, it is valuable in educating people about what test results mean, what AIDS is, and how to avoid it. Indeed, fifty-seven percent of the subjects surveyed anonymously through San Francisco's "alternative test sites" stated that the counseling that they received was important in clarifying the meaning of their test results; the same percentage stated that it was helpful in encouraging conformance with risk reduction guidelines.

Second, counseling often helps to alleviate the emotional difficulties that accompany taking the test. Individuals who submit to the test have been found to exhibit "disruptions in personal relationships, depression and anxiety, impotence, alienation, sleeping disorders, and other troubling feelings." These difficulties can be particularly acute for people who test positive, because they cannot be offered medical intervention—only general advice about risk reduction that ought to be followed irrespective of test outcome. Counseling may help such individuals by providing them with accurate information, reassurance, and referrals to therapists and community organizations with appropriate expertise. People who are tested involuntarily and without counseling may be especially vulnerable to severe emotional strain; in the military, at least one recruit committed suicide after learning that he had tested positive in a mass screening.

A third problem with testing by insurers is that it will inevitably lead to discrimination. Although insurers argue that they have "a long history of effectively dealing with highly sensitive medical information," the confidentiality of AIDS-related records simply cannot be guaranteed. For example, employees who are rejected for individually

screened small group coverage because they have tested positive risk having this information made known to employers. The small-group applicant is therefore vulnerable not only to AIDS-based employment discrimination, but, given prevailing assumptions, to sexual orientation discrimination as well.

There are additional confidentiality problems. The NAIC's model privacy act, for example, permits insurers to exchange information in some circumstances without the knowledge of their insureds. In addition, the medical records of both insurance companies and the Medical Information Bureau (MIB), an industry-funded organization that shares computerized information about applicants, are subject to subpoena. Moreover, as of December 1986, six states required the names of people testing HIV antibody positive to be reported to state officials. Some of these states have also considered legislation that would deny employment to teachers, restaurant workers, medical personnel, and others with positive test results. Thus, it is easy to envision a scenario in which an unsuspecting insurance applicant tests positive, has his or her test results reported to the state, and, as a consequence, loses his or her job. Even somebody whose test results are not involuntarily reported may unwittingly expose himself or herself to discrimination. Because insurance applicants generally take the test unwillingly and without expecting a positive result, they are especially likely to react by confiding in people who may later violate their trust. But for testing by insurers, these breaches would not occur.

Fourth, and finally, testing by insurers will endanger the public health. There is an inherent conflict between the threatening character of insurer testing and the efforts of public health officials to convince people that testing can be personally beneficial. Testing by insurers, which is "voluntary" only in the most strained sense of the word, increases the atmosphere of fear and mistrust that already surrounds AIDS-related testing. In part for this reason, leading AIDS researchers and public health experts have concluded that testing should be performed only on a voluntary or clinical basis.

Perhaps more medically dangerous than direct testing by insurers is the more common industry practice of questioning applicants about the results of tests that the applicant has already taken. Although questioning about prior tests involves many of the same risks associated with insurer testing, it is even more problematic because it directly discourages people from taking the test voluntarily as part of an AIDS prevention program. One study of gay and bisexual men in San Francisco, for example, showed that fear of discrimination by employers, insurers, and the government was the most commonly cited reason for not taking the test. The possibility of becoming uninsurable may also deter high risk women considering pregnancy from abiding by the PHS recommendation to take the test. Blood donations may also decline if potential donors decide that they do not want to risk becoming uninsurable upon being notified by a blood bank that they tested positive. In addition, high risk individuals may be unwilling to participate in the numerous epidemiological and medical studies that require volunteers to be tested for HIV antibodies.

The danger of questioning by insurers about prior tests was highlighted in a landmark study on AIDS by the National Academy of Sciences (NAS). In its report, the NAS warned that "[t]he general threat of *discrimination in employment or insurance . . . may deter individuals in high-risk groups from being tested* to ascertain their antibody status. Since knowledge of antibody status may prompt some individuals to adopt healthier behavior, *social disincentives to testing should be minimized.*"

The insurance industry itself has admitted the danger of investigating the prior test results of applicants. In 1985, the ACLI declared that "our position is to not try to obtain from blood banks, plasma centers, or alternative testing sites the results of blood tests given by them, since to do so might discourage people from donating blood." It is hypocritical, however, for the ACLI at the same time to demand this information from applicants themselves. The disincentive, after all, is identical in both cases: a penalty for being tested. The industry's continued insistence that it has a right to ask applicants about prior test results, even though it has recognized the dangers involved in such inquiries, calls into ques-

tion its professed concern for the public health when profits are at stake.

III. Conclusion

In a private system of insurance, insurance companies need to be able to develop underwriting schemes that assess the risk of their applicants. In addition to helping insurers, however, these underwriting practices have a broad social impact: they substantially determine who can receive quality health care and may affect access to credit and employment as well. Thus, it is not sufficient merely to ask whether insurance classification schemes are statistically accurate or generally helpful to insurers. The fundamental question is whether they are, on balance, socially beneficial or harmful.

Clearly, the two industry practices analyzed—discrimination on the basis of sexual orientation and HIV testing—are socially destructive. Each is likely to increase both the extent and perceived legitimacy of discrimination against an already ostracized group. Even more alarming, insurer use of the HIV antibody test penalizes participation in critical research studies while discouraging voluntary testing among people who might wish to use the results to prompt themselves to adopt safer behavior. In addition, sexual orientation discrimination by insurers and others inevitably forces gay and bisexual men to return to the paralyzing dishonesty of the closet, where a climate of fear, denial, and self-hatred makes open discussion with physicians and between sexual partners increasingly unlikely.

The insistence of the insurance industry that it has a "right" to take actions that will ultimately endanger the public health calls into question the industry's very purpose. This demand might be more understandable if industry survival hinged on its ability to test for HIV or to screen on the basis of social stereotypes. But, to paraphrase Mark Twain, rumors of the industry's death have been greatly exaggerated.

Indeed, the more the insurance industry successfully evades responsibility for AIDS-related expenses, the more this financial burden will be shifted onto the government. Although the HIAA claims that "other policyholders will bear the brunt of paying" for AIDS if insurers cannot exclude high risk applicants, this argument ignores the fact that most people with AIDS are forced to rely upon government-funded programs such as Medicare, Medicaid, and public hospitals if they are uninsured. Thus, if health insurance premiums are not increased to cover the costs of AIDS, taxes may have to be raised instead. The federal government, although saddled with budget deficits, has already spent hundreds of millions of dollars on AIDS research and education—whereas the highly profitable insurance industry has contributed little to such efforts.

The real question, then, is who should pay for AIDS-related medical expenses. For two important reasons, it is clearly preferable to place primary responsibility on the insurance industry and not on the government. First, insurers have the ability to spread more evenly the costs of AIDS, costs that thus far have been borne disproportionately by a few cities and states. Second, the very function of health insurance is to pay for medical care. Ironically, the insurance industry has long resisted legislative proposals for national health in-

surance, insisting that it is in a better position than the government to manage health care costs. It should not be allowed now to use socially harmful underwriting methods to shift onto the government a burden that it deems unprofitable.

Even if insurers cease their efforts to avoid the costs of AIDS through testing for HIV and discriminating against gay and bisexual men, they are almost certain to use other criteria to identify and reject "high risk" applicants. This possibility highlights the fundamental irony of an insurance system run exclusively for profit: those who most need insurance to pay for medical care or to protect their dependants are the least able to obtain it. Thus, the problems of sexual orientation discrimination and HIV testing suggest broader problems inherent in a privately underwritten insurance system and point to the need for some form of guaranteed health insurance for all Americans.

Until such a scheme is available, however, we must work with the system we have. Within this system, the desire of the insurance industry to guarantee its fiscal solvency must be balanced against society's need to maintain its moral solvency. Insurance companies' unjustified fears about the former should not lead us to sacrifice the latter.

43. *Schaill* v. *Tippecanoe School Corporation*

Court of Appeals of the United States

The issue before the United States Court of Appeals was whether a random urinalysis program at a school operated by the Tippecanoe County School Corporation violated the right of student athletes not to be subject to reasonable searches and seizures under the Fourth Amendment. The court argued that the urinalysis program was a search and seizure under the Fourth Amendment, but that it was justified because a standard of reasonableness rather than "probable cause" is all that has to be met by such a program. In this case, the court claimed that this standard was met because, among other things, there is a much diminished expectation of privacy in interscholastic athletics.

The essential facts of this case are undisputed, and can be stated quite briefly. TSC operates Harrison and McCutcheon High Schools in Indiana. In the spring of 1986, based on information concerning possible drug use by

athletes on the McCutcheon High School baseball team, the team's coach ordered sixteen team members to provide urine samples. Of the sixteen students tested, five students' tests produced positive results for the presence of marijuana. Based on these results, other reports of drug use among participants in the TSC athletic program, and their concern over the high incidence of drug abuse among high school students nationwide, the board of trustees of TSC decided to institute a random urine testing program for interscholastic athletes and cheerleaders in the TSC school system.

Under the program, all students desiring to participate in interscholastic athletics and their parent or guardian are required to sign a consent form agreeing to submit to urinalysis if chosen on a random basis. Each student selected for an athletic team is assigned a number. The athletic director and head coach of each athletic team are authorized to institute random urine tests during the athletic season. In order to select individuals to be tested, the number assigned to each athlete is placed in a box, and a single number is drawn.

The student selected for testing is accompanied by a school official of the same sex to a bathroom, where the student is provided with an empty specimen bottle. The student is then allowed to enter a lavatory stall and close the door in order to produce a sample. The student is not under direct visual observation while producing the sample; however, the water in the toilet is tinted to prevent the student from substituting water for the sample, the monitor stands outside the stall to listen for normal sounds of urination and the monitor checks the temperature of the sample by hand in order to assure its genuineness.

The chain of custody of the sample is designed to insure the accuracy and anonymity of the testing procedure. The sample is sent to a private testing laboratory, where it is initially tested for the presence of controlled substances or performance-enhancing drugs using the enzyme multiplied immunoassay technique ("EMIT"). Any sample which tests positive is then retested using the more accurate, and more expensive, gas chromatography/mass spectrometry ("GC/MS") method.

If a sample tests positive under both the EMIT and GC/MS analyses, the student and his or her parent or guardian are informed of the results. They then have the opportunity to have the remaining portion of the sample tested at a laboratory of their choice. The stu-

dent and his or her parent or guardian may also present the athletic director with any evidence which suggests an innocent explanation for the positive result, such as the fact that the athlete legally takes prescription or over-the-counter medication.

Barring a satisfactory explanation, the student is then suspended from participation in a portion of the varsity competitions held during the athletic season. A first positive urinalysis test results in a suspension from 30% of the athletic contests, a second positive results in a 50% suspension, a third positive causes a suspension for a full calendar year and a fourth positive results in the student's being barred from all interscholastic athletic competitions during the remainder of the student's high school career. No other penalties are imposed, and a student may decrease the specified punishment by participating in an approved drug counselling program.

In the spring of 1987, appellants Darcy Schaill and Shelley Johnson were 15-year-old sophomores at Harrison High School. Shelley had been a member of the varsity swim team as a freshman. Both appellants attended an organizational meeting for students desiring to participate in interscholastic athletics in the fall of 1987, at which time they were first informed of the proposed implementation of the TSC urinalysis program. Both appellants were offended by the thought of having to undergo urinalysis as a condition of participation in interscholastic athletics, and both decided that they would forego the opportunity to compete in interscholastic athletics if required to sign a form consenting to random urine testing. . . .

As a threshold matter, we must consider whether TSC's random urine testing program involves a "search" as that term is employed in the fourth amendment. The Supreme Court has held that "[a] 'search' occurs when an expectation of privacy that society is prepared to consider reasonable is infringed." . . .

There can be little doubt that a person engaging in the act of urination possesses a reasonable expectation of privacy as to that act, and as to the urine which is excreted. In our society, it is expected that urination be performed in private, that urine be disposed of in private and that the act, if mentioned at all, be described in euphemistic terms. . . .

The fact that urine is voluntarily discharged from the body and treated as a waste product does not eliminate the expectation of privacy which an individual possesses in his or her urine. While urine is excreted from the body, it is not "knowingly expose[d] to the public," . . . ; instead, the highly private manner by which an individual disposes of his or her urine demonstrates that it is not intended to be inspected or examined by anyone. . . .

Having determined that urine testing constitutes a "search" in the constitutional sense, we must consider what level of suspicion is required to authorize urinalysis of any particular student. Appellants first argue that individual student's urine may not be tested unless TSC officials have probable cause to believe that the particular student has consumed the drugs which the test is designed to detect, and have obtained a warrant authorizing the test from a neutral and detached judicial officer. Determining the level of suspicion required before the government may conduct a search requires "balanc[ing] the nature and quality of the intrusion on the individual's Fourth Amendment interests against the importance of the governmental interests alleged to justify the intrusion." . . . Unfortunately for appellants, we believe that the Supreme Court has already struck the appropriate balance in the context of school searches, and has determined that the probable cause and warrant requirements do not apply. . . .

In the present case, TSC plans to conduct a search not only without probable cause or a warrant, but in the absence of any individualized suspicion of drug use by the students to be tested. In these circumstances, TSC bears a heavier burden to justify its contemplated actions. In a criminal law enforcement context, the Supreme Court has been extremely hesitant to condone searches performed without any articulable basis for suspecting the particular individual of unlawful conduct. However, in several carefully defined situations, the Court has recognized that searches may be conducted in the absence of any grounds to believe that the individual searched has violated the law. The Court has stressed that "[i]n those situations in which the balance of interests precludes insistence upon 'some quantum of individualized suspicion,' other safeguards are generally relied upon to assure that the individual's reasonable expectation of privacy is not 'subject to the discretion of the officer in the field.' " . . .

In general, there is a substantial expectation of privacy in connection with the act of urination. However, the privacy considerations are somewhat mitigated on the facts before us because the provider of the urine sample enters a closed lavatory stall and the person monitoring the urination stands outside listening for the sounds appropriate to what is taking place. The invasion of privacy is therefore not nearly as severe as would be the case if the monitor were required to observe the subject in the act of urination.

We also find great significance in the fact that the drug testing program in this case is being implemented solely with regard to participants in an interscholastic athletic program. In the first place, in athletic programs in general there is a much diminished expectation of privacy and, in particular, privacy with respect to urinalysis. There is an element of "communal undress" inherent in athletic participation, which suggests reduced expectations of privacy. In addition, physical examinations are integral to almost all athletic programs. In fact, athletes and cheerleaders desiring to participate in the TSC athletic program have long been required to produce a urine sample as part of a mandatory medical examination. This sample is not produced under monitored conditions, is only tested for the presence of sugar in the urine and is given to the athlete's physician of choice rather than a school official; however, the fact that such samples are required suggests that legitimate expectations of privacy in this context are diminished.

Further, in the case before us, we are dealing with *interscholastic* athletics. In these programs the Indiana High School Athletic Association has extensive requirements which it imposes upon schools and individuals participating in interscholastic athletics. These include minimum grade, residency and eligibility requirements. In addition to IHSAA regulations, participants in interscholastic athletics are also subject to training rules, including prohibitions on smoking, drinking and drug use both on and off school premises.

Perhaps even more demonstrative of the special characteristics of athletics is the high visibility and pervasiveness of drug testing in professional and collegiate athletics in this country and in the Olympic Games. The suspension and disqualification of prominent athletes on the basis of positive urinalysis results has been the subject of intense publicity all over the world. . . .

The combination of these factors makes it quite implausible that students competing for positions on an interscholastic athletic team would have strong expectations of privacy with respect to urine tests. We can, of course, appreciate that monitored collection and subsequent testing of urine samples may be distasteful (although plaintiffs' subjective evidence on this point was not powerful), but such procedures can hardly come as a great shock or surprise under present-day circumstances. For this reason, we believe that sports are quite distinguishable from almost any other activity. Random testing of athletes does not necessarily imply random testing of band members or the chess team. . . .

The convergence of several important factors convinces us that the searches involved here take place in one of the relatively unusual environments in which suspicionless searches are permissible: interscholastic athletes have diminished expectations of privacy, and have voluntarily chosen to participate in an activity which subjects them to pervasive regulation of off-campus behavior; the school's interest in preserving a drug-free athletic program is substantial, and cannot adequately be furthered by less intrusive measures; the TSC program adequately limits the discretion of the officials performing the search; and the information sought is intended to be used solely for noncriminal educational and rehabilitative purposes. Based on a careful and considered weighing of these factors, we conclude that the TSC urinalysis program does not violate the fourth amendment. . . .

Appellants' final contention is that the procedures provided in the TSC program for a student to challenge a positive urinalysis test are insufficient under the due process clause of the fourteenth amendment. . . .

Appellants fault the TSC program for placing on the student the burden of proving that the twice-confirmed test result is erroneous, for requiring the student to hire his own toxicologist or testing laboratory to conduct a further evaluation of the TSC urine test and for allowing the athletic director, who was personally involved in the collection, labeling and storage of the initial sample, to serve as the adjudicator of the student's claim that the initial result was erroneous.

There was evidence before the district court indicating that TSC's urine testing program, which requires confirmation of any positive result using the gas chromatography/mass spectrometry method, would produce results with a 95% confidence level. Based on this evidence, the district court concluded that the "possible pitfalls involved in EMIT screening have been avoided, as much as possible, by [GC/MS] followup." . . . Given the high degree of accuracy inhering in TSC's testing procedures, we cannot conclude that the school system has violated the due process clause by placing the burden to disprove a confirmed positive result on the student. Further, after providing a confirmatory test using the most accurate technology available at no cost to the student, TSC cannot be faulted for requiring a student to bear the cost of any further testing which the student may desire to perform. . . .

In our consideration and decision of this case, we have been mindful of the Supreme Court's admonition that public school students "do not shed their constitutional rights . . . at the schoolhouse gate." . . . We are also cognizant of the trenchant observation of Justice Jackson: "That [schools] are educating the young for citizenship is reason for scrupulous protection of Constitutional freedoms of the individual, if we are not to strangle the free mind at its source and teach youth to discount important principles of our government as mere platitudes." . . .

However, we recognize that, if students are to be educated at all, an environment conducive to learning must be maintained. The plague of illicit drug use which currently threatens our nation's schools adds a major dimension to the difficulties the schools face in fulfilling their purpose—the education of our children. If the schools are to survive and prosper, school administrators must have reasonable means at their disposal to deter conduct which substantially disrupts the school environment. In this case, we believe that the Tippecanoe County School Corporation has chosen a reasonable and limited response to a serious evil. In formulating its urinalysis program, the school district has been sensitive to the privacy rights of its students, and has sought to emphasize rehabilitation over punishment. We cannot conclude that this approach is inconsistent with the mandates of the Constitution. The judgment of the district court is therefore

Affirmed.

Suggestions for Further Reading

Anthologies

Pennock, J. R. and Chapman, J. *Privacy.* New York: Atherton Press. 1971.

Pierce, C. and Van DeVeer, D. *AIDS: Ethics and Public Policy.* Belmont: Wadsworth Publishing Co., 1988.

"What Science Knows About AIDS." *Scientific American,* October, 1988.

Alternative Views

Arthur, J. *The Unfinished Constitution.* Belmont: Wadsworth Publishing Co., 1989.

Hollowell, E. and Eldridge, J. "AIDS and the Insurance Industry." *The Journal of Legal Medicine* (1989), pp. 77–87.

Oppenheimer, G. and Padgug, R. "AIDS: The Risks to Insurers, the Threat to Equity." *Hastings Center Report* (1986), pp. 18–22.

Research Triangle Institute. *Economic Costs to Society of Alcohol and Drug Abuse.* Research Triangle Park, N.C., 1984.

Rubenfeld, J. "The Right to Privacy." *Harvard Law Review* (1989), pp. 737–807.

Winston, M. "AIDS, Confidentiality and the Right to Know." *Public Affairs Quarterly* (1988), pp. 91–104.

Practical Applications

Boggan, C. *The Rights of Gay People: The Basic ACLU Guide to a Gay Person's Rights.* New York: Avon, 1975.

Gay and Lesbian Rights

Basic Concepts

Prohibitions against homosexuality have ancient roots, but the enforcement of such prohibitions has most always been haphazard at best. This is because when one is dealing with acts between consenting adults, it can be difficult to find a complainant. Even so, twenty-four states and the District of Columbia still have statutes on the books prohibiting homosexual acts. Penalties range from three months in prison or one year's probation to life imprisonment.

Moreover, what these statutes prohibit is sodomy, which involves more than just homosexual acts. For example, the Georgia statute whose constitutionality was upheld by the Supreme Court in *Bowers* v. *Hardwick* (see Selection 46) holds that "a person commits the offense of sodomy when he performs or submits to any sexual act involving the sex organs of one person and the mouth or anus of another." The reason why sodomy is defined so broadly here is that the main complaint against homosexual acts—that they are unnatural—also applies to a range of other acts. More specifically, the complaint applies to oral and anal intercourse between heterosexuals, masturbation, and bestiality, as well as homosexual acts.

Now it is important to understand what is considered unnatural about these acts. One sense of *natural* refers to what is found in nature as contrasted with what is artificial or the product of human artifice. In this sense, homosexuality would seem to be natural because it is found in virtually every human society. But even if homosexuality is understood to be a product of a certain type of upbringing or socialization and hence artificial, that would hardly seem to be grounds for condemning it, because a great deal of human behavior has a similar origin.

Another sense of natural refers to what is common or statistically normal as contrasted with what is uncommon or statistically abnormal. In this sense, homosexuality would not be natural because most people are not homosexuals, despite the fact that according to one study about half of all American males have

engaged in homosexual acts at some time of their lives. But being unnatural in this sense could not be grounds for condemning homosexuality because many traits we most value in people are also statistically abnormal and, hence, unnatural in this sense.

Still another sense of natural refers to a thing's proper function, and it is this sense of natural that is frequently used to condemn homosexuality. Because if we maintain that the proper function of human sexual organs is simply procreation, then any use of those organs for a purpose other than procreation would be unnatural. Hence, homosexuality, contraception, masturbation, and bestiality would all be unnatural. But clearly the proper function of human sexual organs is not limited to procreation. These organs are also used to express love and to provide pleasure for oneself and others. Given that our sexual organs can be properly used for these other purposes, we would need to argue that every use of these organs must serve their procreative function in order to be able to condemn homosexuality. But no nontheologically based argument has succeeded in establishing this conclusion.[1] Moreover, once we grant that, for example, contraception and masturbation can be morally permissible, there seems to be no ground left, based on the proper functioning of our sexual organs, for denying that homosexuality can be morally permissible as well.

Alternative Views

Other arguments against homosexuality do not depend on characterizing it as unnatural in the sense just defined. One such argument is developed by Paul Cameron in Selection 44. Cameron begins with the assumption that human sexuality is totally learned. According to Cameron, homosexuality and heterosexuality are equally the products of socialization. Cameron further argues that there are a number of factors favoring the adoption of homosexuality: (1) the extreme homosociality of children starting around age

[1]Clearly if there is to be freedom of religion, a nontheologically based argument is needed here.

five, (2) the greater attraction males have for sex than females, (3) the superiority of homosexual sex as sex, and (4) the self-servingness/egocentricity of the young. Cameron argues that we need to overcome these factors because heterosexuality leads to more permanent social relationships, greater altruism, and more social cohesion than homosexuality.

Yet although the social problems that Cameron focuses on are real enough, these problems can be combated without criminalizing homosexuality. First, homosexuals would probably form more permanent social relationships among themselves if they were not denied the social and legal means for maintaining such relationships. Second, the extreme homosociality of children can be effectively combated by providing the same socialization for girls and boys. Third, the egocentricity of the young, which manifests itself not in harming but simply in failing to benefit others, is probably best combated with positive altruistic ideals rather than threatened criminalization, except where the basic needs of others are at stake.

In Selection 45, Richard D. Mohr surveys various ways in which homosexuals are discriminated against in our society. He cites one study in which 90 percent of gays and lesbians report that they have been victimized because of their sexual orientation and another study according to which there are 307 occupations that are prohibited to them. In opposition to Cameron, Mohr argues that being gay or lesbian is not a matter of choice, making it difficult, if not impossible to change one's sexual orientation. Obviously then, what sodomy statutes demand of homosexuals is that they not act as they are. A difficult charge indeed! Moreover, it is a charge that does not appear to be supported by a defensible account of what is wrong with homosexual behavior.

Practical Application

The most recent Supreme Court case dealing with homosexuality is *Bowers* v. *Hardwick* (1986). In this case, the issue before the Supreme Court was whether the Georgia sodomy statute violates the federal Constitution. In delivering the opinion of the court, Justice White argues that the statute does not violate the Constitution because the Constitution does not confer a fundamental right on homosexuals to engage in sodomy. While in previous cases, the Constitution was interpreted to confer a right to decide whether or not to beget or bear a child and a right not to be convicted for possessing and reading obscene material in the privacy of one's home, White argues that the Constitution cannot analogously be interpreted to confer a fundamental right on homosexuals to engage in sodomy. Justice Burger concurs, stressing the ancient roots of sodomy statutes. Justice Blackmun joined by Justices Brennan and Marshall argues that notwithstanding the ancient roots of prohibitions against homosexuality, a right to be let alone that is the underpinning of previous court decisions justifies in this case a right to engage in sodomy at least in the privacy of one's home.

In this case, the majority of the Supreme Court seem to reach their conclusion by interpreting previous decisions in an excessively literal manner in much the same way that the majority of the court ruled in *Olmstead* v. *United States* (1928) that warrantless wiretapping did not violate the Fourth Amendment prohibitions against search and seizure because the framers of the amendment were not explicitly prohibiting this method of obtaining incriminating evidence. One can only hope that just as the Supreme Court later repudiated its decision in *Olmstead* v. *United States,* the Supreme Court will someday return to the issue of the criminalization of homosexuality and address the relevant privacy concern it raises.

It is also important to note that adherents of four of our political ideals generally tend to favor granting homosexuals the same rights as heterosexuals. Libertarians favor this view because to do otherwise would deny homosexuals important basic liberties. Welfare liberals favor this view because to do otherwise would deny homosexuals fundamental fairness. Socialists favor this view because to do otherwise would deny homosexuals basic equality, and communitarians favor this view because to do otherwise would deny homosexuals an appropriate share of the common good.

44. A Case Against Homosexuality

Paul Cameron

Beginning with the assumption that human sexuality is totally learned, Paul Cameron argues that there are a number of factors favoring the adoption of homosexuality: (1) the extreme homosociality of children starting around age five, (2) the greater attraction males have for sex than females, (3) the superiority of homosexual sex as sex, and (4) the self-servingness/egocentricity of the young. To overcome these factors, Cameron argues that discrimination against homosexuals is justified, especially in view of the fact that heterosexuality leads to more permanent social relationships, greater altruism, and more social cohesion.

In some segments of the mass media, the homosexuality issue takes on the appearance of a struggle between orange juice peddlers and bathhouse owners. At a different level individual rights vs. the interests of society provide the conflict. Some argue that adult homosexuals ought to be allowed to do what they want behind closed doors. Others, often seeing the issue in terms of rights, honesty, and overpopulation, seek to grant homosexuality equal status with heterosexuality. The school system of San Francisco, apparently resonating with the latter tack, is offering a course including "homosexual life-styles." Liberals attempt to shame as unenlightened all who oppose complete equality as vigorously as conservative Bible-thumpers threaten wrath from above.

No known human society has ever granted equal status to homo and heterosexuality. What information do those who desire social equivalence for these two sexual orientations possess that assures them that this new venture in human social organization is called for at this time? Have the cultures of the past practiced discrimination against homosexuality out of a mere prejudice, or was there substance to their bias? At the risk of seeming rather out of step with the academic community, no new information has surfaced that would lead me

From the *Human Life Review* (1978), pp. 17–49. Reprinted by permission of the Human Life Foundation and the author.

to discount the social policies of the past. On the contrary, the policies of the past in regard to homosexuality appear generally wise, and considerable discrimination against homosexuality and for heterosexuality, marriage and parenthood appears needful for the social good.

Discrimination

Discrimination is something all humans and all human communities do. Individually we discriminate for certain things and against others, e.g., movies over T.V. Collectively we discriminate for and against selected: 1) acts (pleasantries, sharing vs. murder, robbery), 2) traits (generous, kind vs. whiny, hostile) and 3) life-styles (independent, productive vs. gambling, indolent). Prejudice is unwarranted discrimination. The issue is not whether discrimination should exist—for human society to exist, it must. The issues are always: 1) is discrimination called for? and 2) how much is necessary? Reasonable people can and do disagree on what ought to be discriminated for and against, to what degree, and even if discrimination is prejudicial rather than called for. But reasoned opinion *can* hold that homosexuality and homosexuals ought to be discriminated against. . . .

The Case Against Homosexuality/Wisdom of the Ages

No contemporary society accords homosexuality equivalent status with heterosexuality. No known society has accorded equivalent status in the past (Karlen, 1971). No current or ancient religion of any consequence has failed to teach discrimination against homosexuality. The Judeo-Christian tradition is no exception to this rule. The Old Testament made homosexuality a capital offense, and while the New Testament writers failed to invoke capital punishment for any offense, they did manage to consign homosexuals to eternal hell for the practice. Church fathers and traditions have stayed in line with this position until recently. To the degree that tradition and agreed-upon social policy ought to carry weight in our thinking about issues, the weight of tradition is preponderately on the side of discrimination. The same is true if we "poll" famous thinkers of the past: Plato, for instance, who at one time of his life provided some endorsement of homosexuality, but switched to a strongly negative vote by the end of his career. Aristotle simply considered homosexuality a depravity and Plutarch noted that "no wise father would permit a notable Greek philosopher near his sons." St. Augustine condemned homosexuality and St. Thomas Aquinas ranked homosexuality just a rung above bestiality.

While it is somewhat fashionable to claim that the ancient Greeks legalized and practiced homosexuality, it rather appears that this was, at most, true for only a short time, and only for the leisure class (Karlen, 1971). Similarly, while a number of American Indian societies had a place for the homosexual, it was, all in all, a rather unpleasant one (the Mohave interchanged the word for "coward" and "queer"). Most of the anthropological information that alludes to common practicing of homosexuality among males of various tribes neglects to note that the members of the tribe didn't consider what they were doing sexual, much less homosexual (various touching customs among males featured no erections,

etc). Further, the common anti-female bias of the Greeks and other philosophic systems is not fairly construed as homosexuality. Aristotle claimed that the best forms of friendship and love were found "between men," but condemned homosexuality. One can be pro-male without necessitating elimination of copulation between the sexes. It is quite possible to keep love and sex, or friendship and sex, almost completely separate.

While one cannot carry the "wisdom of the ages" argument too far—just because all peoples up to a certain point in time believed something does not necessarily mean that it was so—yet it appears more than a little injudicious to cast it aside as merely "quaint." Probably no issue has occupied man's collective attentions more than successful living together. That such unanimity of opinion and practice should exist must give one pause. Certainly such congruence "puts the ball in the changer's court." As in so many spheres of human endeavor, when we know that we can get on in a particular way, the burden of proof that we can get on as well or better by following a different custom falls upon those seeking the change. The "fallacy of the ages" is that we "got here because we did X" (we might have gotten here just as well, thank you, by doing K) but that we are regarding fallacy rather than wisdom must still be *proven* by those seeking change.

To date, those seeking change have not been flush with scientific evidence that homosexuality is not socially disruptive. On the contrary, the arguments that have been advanced have been little more than "people ought not to be discriminated against; homosexuals are people; ergo homosexuals ought not to be discriminated against" shouted larger and louder. No one to my knowledge has ever claimed that homosexuals were not people, and one would have to be a dunce to believe that being a person qualifies one, *ipso facto*, for nondiscrimination. Aside from this argument repeated in endless variations and *ad nauseam*, the evidence is simply not there. I'll admit to a charm in residing in a society undergoing dramatic change. You get to stand at the end of the tunnel of history and help dig a new hole (something that particularly excites the modern scholar and local news team). But let us be sure we are not digging new holes just for our amusement. Meddling with procreation and heterosexuality is considerably more than a parlor game in which the stakes are but a trifle. Because what we are about is so very serious, if anything, an even better set of evidence needs to be produced by those seeking change, not, as is the case today, mere syllogistic flatus.

Homosociality Coupled with Increasing Self-Centeredness Could Lead to Widespread Homosexuality

. . . Jimmy Carter said: "I don't see homosexuality as a threat to the family." . . . His sentiments probably echo those of the educated class of our society. They trust that "only deviants" are really into homosexuality anyway, and, more importantly, that "mother nature" will come through in the last analysis. Biology, they assume, has a great deal to do with sexuality and sexual attraction, and millions of years of heterosexuality has firmly engraved itself on the genetic code.

Such thinking betrays a lack of appreciation of the enormous component of learning that goes into human sexuality. The point that anthropology has made over the past hundred years is the *tremendous diversity of human social organization.* Marvelously varied are the ways man rears his young, honors his dead, plays the game of procreation, or practices dental hygiene. While the onset of the events of puberty vary relatively little from one society to another, the onset of copulation varies over a full quarter of the life-span—from 5 or 6 years of age to mid-20s. While three-spine sticklebacks predictably go into paroxysms of delight over a given colored shape, the object of man's sexual desires varies from car mufflers, to animals, to various ages, and sexes of his own kind. Many mammals practice sex for only a few days or weeks in the year, but man varies from untrammeled lust to studied virginity. While I have enumerated my reasons more fully elsewhere (Cameron, 1977), I believe that

the most reasonable construal of the evidence to date suggests that *human sexuality is totally learned.*

There are really only three ways for human sexuality to develop. Humans are among, if not *the,* most gregarious creatures. We are reared by our kind, schooled with and by our kind, and just generally like to be around other humans (my research into the contents of consciousness suggests that, world-wide, *the* most frequent topic of thought is other humans). We prefer to do just about anything with one or more other humans. We prefer to eat with another human, we would rather go to the movies, picnic, take walks with another, etc. We are firmly gregarious. The same is true for sexuality. For all but the kinkiest of us, we would rather "do it" with another human. Bestiality, necrophilia, vacuum cleaners, dolls, you name it, none of these sexual aberrations will ever become modal sex—they will always appeal to only a few. Since modal human sexuality must needs be confined to other humans, the three ways to "fly" are obvious modes: heterosexuality, homosexuality, or bisexuality. Because human sexuality is totally learned, humans must be pointed in the "right" direction, and taught how and with whom to perform. And there's the rub. Homosexuality and heterosexuality do not start off on the same footing. *Au contraire,* one gets a number of important boosts in the scheme of things. In our society the developmental process is decidedly *tilted toward the adoption of homosexuality!*

Part of the homosexual tilt is the extreme homosociality of children starting around the age of 5. As everyone is aware, boys want to play with boys and girls with girls, and they do so with a vengeance. It's quite reasonable, on their part. First, boys' and girls' bodies are different and they are aware that their bodies-to-be will differ still more. In part because of this the games, sports and skills they practice differ. As if in anticipation of the differing roles they will have, their interests and proclivities differ. Even if they try, few girls can do as well as most boys at "boy things" and few boys can do as well as girls at "girl things." They almost inhabit different worlds. Not surprisingly for members of two different

"races," poles apart psychologically, socially, and physically, they "stick to their own kind."
. . .

There are three other components that contribute to the homosexual tilt. First, on the average in our society, males are considerably more taken with sex than females are. In my 1975 survey of 818 persons on the east coast of the U.S., respondents were asked to rate the degree of pleasure they obtained from 22 activities including "being with one's family," "listening to music," "being out in nature," "housework," and "sexual activity." Between the late teens through middle age, sexual activity topped the male list as the "most pleasurable activity." It did manage to rank as high as fifth place for young adult women (aged 18 to 25), but, overall for the female life span, was outscored by almost everything including "housework" (which, incidentally ranked dead last among males). . . .

How well suited are "hot" males to "cool" females? Not very. One of (if not *the*) most common problems in marital counseling is sexual incompatibility. *Females pay sex as the price of love/companionship and males pay love for sex.* While this is rather too aphoristic to capture all that goes on in the male-female struggle, there is a great deal of truth to it. Even among homosexuals, the males probably out sex lesbians by a factor of 5 to 1 (see Tripp's sympathetic treatment for elaboration on this theme). Where is a male most apt to find his counterpart, among maledom or femaledom? If he wants hot, dripping sex, what better place to find it than with another of similar bent? If she wants tender companionship, which sex is most apt to provide the partner? The answers are obvious.

The second part of the homosexual tilt derives from the fact that *homosexual encounter offers better sex,* on the average, *than heterosexual sex.* If pleasure is what you are after, who better to fulfill you than a partner who has a body and predilections like yours? One of the things that both the male homosexual and lesbian societies advertise is that "they satisfy." The Greek literature of yore also contains the "better sex" claim of homosexuals. And why not? A male, who has the same basic equipment and rhythms is most able to satisfy—par-

ticularly initially (heterosexual "one nite stands" are frequently exciting, but just as frequently lacking in sexual satisfaction for both participants—not so homosexual "one niters"). Who better to understand "what you need" than someone whose needs are as your own? From a sexual standpoint, a female can offer little extra orifice as compensation for her: ignorance, timidity, desire for companionship first, etc. Further, sex between members of a sex assures that there will be no pregnancy problems further on down the line.

Another developmental boost for homosexuality comes from the self-servingness/egocentricity of the young. Humans are born with, at best, rudimentary consciousness. Then, over time and experience, they learn to differentiate themselves from the environment. From about the age of 5 or 6 onward for the next decade or so of life, they are engrossed in themselves, in the service of themselves, their pleasures, their interests, their ways. Reciprocity of interaction is rendered begrudgingly, certainly far from spontaneously. My research, involving the interviewing of over 8,000 respondents from the U.S. and five other nations, in which we asked persons to tell us: 1) whose interests they had just been thinking about serving—their own or another's or others' and 2) whether they had just been thinking about themselves, things, or other people, indicated that younger persons more frequently reported themselves in a self-serving attitude and thinking about themselves than adults did. In the U.S., adults of both sexes typically reported themselves in an other-serving attitude. But U.S. males "switched" from self-servingness to other-servingness around age 26 while for females the switch occurred in the middle teens. If one is after self-fulfillment, pleasure for self, which sexual orientation "fits" better? Homosexuality, obviously. One can have his homosociality and sex too. One can comfortably neglect the painful transformation from self-interest to other-interest. Me and mine to the fore.

Which kind of sexuality is the more compelling? The one that can say "come, sex my way and I will show you a life of complexity. Of children and responsibility. Of getting on with 'that other kind.' I will offer you poorer sex initially, and, who knows, perhaps you will just have to satisfy yourself with poorer sex permanently. But you will be able to 'glimpse immortality in your children' (Plato)." Or "come, sex my way and I will give it to you straight and hot. Pleasures of the best quality, almost on demand, with persons with whom you already share a great deal, and I will enable you to share more. It will not be difficult, in fact, it will be fun. You will not have to change or adapt your personality style or your egocentric orientation. You'll fit right in immediately. None of this hemming and hawing—you'll get what you want when you want it. Motto? Pleasure—now. The future? Who knows, but the present is going to be a dilly." Which kind of sexuality is the more compelling? Does anyone doubt which way most youth would turn if equivalent social status attended homosexuality and heterosexuality? . . .

The myths about love and romance that grace our society have been almost 100% heterosexual. From children's readers to tube fare, heterosexuality has been the "only game in town." Tom and Jane live with their parents Dick and Sue, *not* Tim and Jim. Dagwood has Blondie, and the odd couple is squarely heterosexual. Yet even in the glare of the massive efforts of religions, customs, laws, and example, about 2% of the citizenry fail to accomplish the mental gymnastic of separating sexual object from social object. They go the developmentally "easy way," and add sexuality to homosociality. What if society offered an honest to goodness *choice* between the two sexual orientations? The current lock on the myth-making, image-providing process by heterosexuality may be an instance of overkill. Perhaps an 80/20 hetero-homosexuality split would still result in 96% heterosexuality. Maybe even a 60/40 split would. But we've got 2% now with something like a 99/1 split, and somewhere up the line, growth in homosexual mythology and literature *has* to have an effect (unless one can seriously believe that that to which people are exposed does not influence them).

It appears that once a solid choice for either homo or heterosexuality is made, the "other way" becomes unlikely, and, in fact, disgust-

ing. True, with the current pro-heterosexual bias in the psychiatric community, about a third of homosexuals in treatment can, with considerable effort, be "switched." But as "even-steven" literature grows and becomes incorporated into the psychiatric community's consciousness, the attempt to convert will be made less frequently. Tripp's *The Homosexual Matrix* is a well-received work that melds the myths of love, sex, homo and heterosexuality. It certainly constitutes a solid start toward "even-steven" in myth-making. The resolutions of the American Psychiatric and American Psychological Associations calling for equality or near equality of treatment of professionals and clients with either homo or hetero orientations, further movement toward equality of the sexual orientations. Pre-teens and teens are the battle ground. With the exception of the San Francisco school system, students' official fare is still 100% heterosexual. In my opinion, heterosexuality "needs all the help it can get," and these current developments portend a much more homosexual future. . . .

A Cluster of Undesirable Traits Is Disproportionately Associated with Homosexuality

Though some may shriek that "my personality traits are my business," let us acknowledge that some traits are society's business. A person's traits can lead to actions which affect the collectivity. Megalomania often proves socially disruptive, and sometimes, as in the case of Hitler, leads to incredible human destruction. It is obviously in society's interest to encourage those social roles and traits that tend to social cohesion and betterment. Similarly, it is in the social interest to discourage those that tend to produce disruption and harm. Any life-style that leads to, or is more frequently associated with, undesirable personality traits suitably receives discouragement. Most traits, e.g. intelligence, appear unsystematically related to either homo or heterosexuality, but those that are systematically related are socially important.

It would be as silly to contend that each of the following traits is associated with each homosexual as to argue that none of these appear in heterosexuals (or even worse, that the obverse of these traits always accompanies heterosexuality). However, for social policy formulation, it is enough to demonstrate disproportionate "loading" of undesirable traits within a given subgroup or subculture to justify social discrimination.

The Egocentric/ Supercilious/Narcissistic/ Self-Oriented/Hostile Complex

This cluster of traits appears to "go together" with homosexuality. . . . A person who, in part, seeks more of himself in his lover, is more apt to remain in the egocentric/self-centered orientation of youth. Such a person is more apt to gravitate toward those kinds of professions in which he can be a "star" and be noticed. . . .

The "star" lives for gratification of self. *My* way is his motto. . . . The star need not accommodate himself to the needs of others to the same degree as most folk. If a current love is "not working out" he can be discarded and a more suitable one found. . . .

Superciliousness—an attitude of aloof, hostile disdain—is also consonant with the egocentric person. If you will not realize his marvelous qualities and pay homage, he still has you one down. After all he treated you with contempt *first*. Even if you become hostile, his preceded yours. I am well aware that much of what I have written frequently applies to notable Hollywood and Broadway actors. Adoration-seekers disproportionately frequently make poor models for marriages. As the columnists often put it, "there was too much ego to go around." . . .

The greater component of the childish "I want it my way" associated with homosexuality

stems, in part, from the greater ease connected with homosexual attachments. Developmentally, both hetero and homosexuals want things "their way." But the kinds of accommodations and adjustment necessary for successful heterosexuality assure participants that it won't be all their way. Just because so much of the time things don't work out perfectly in the face of such effort helps wean one from the coddled security of childhood. Parents and the rest of society work to "make the world nice" for children. Every childhood painting is worthy of note, as is every musical note. But adulthood is strewn with disappointments. Heterosexuality is a "maturing" sexual orientation. . . .

. . . It appears to me that homosexuality leads to a shallower commitment to society and its betterment. Such shallowness comes about both because of a lack of children and the ease of sexual gratification. The *effort* involved in being heterosexual, the *effort* expended in being a parent—these are denied the homosexual. As he *has* less responsibility and commitment, so he *is* or becomes less responsible and committed. It is difficult to develop personality characteristics that fail to resonate with one's environment. While we are not totally creatures of our environment, it is far easier to "swim with the tide."

It is difficult to find anything like "hard" scientific evidence to substantiate the notion that homosexuals are on the average, less responsible/trustworthy than heterosexuals. The Weinberg and Williams sample of homosexuals was asked a question that bears upon the issue. Do you agree or disagree with the statement "most people can be trusted?" To a degree, since a person cannot know "most people" it appears reasonable to assume that he might project his own personality onto "most people" and/or assume that those people with whom he comes in contact are like "most people." While 77% of a reasonably representative sample of the U.S. population chose "agree," only 47% of the homosexuals ticked the same response. Because of the ambiguity of such items, I would not make too much of the difference. But it could suggest that homosexuals are less trustworthy.

Homosexuality Is Associated with Personal Lethality

One of the more troubling traits associated with homosexuality is personal lethality. Extending back in time to classical Greece, a lethal theme shines through. In Greece, if historical sources are to be believed, companies of homosexual warriors were assembled because it was believed that they made better killers.

. . . In our society the childless are more apt to suicide and childless couples are more apt to be involved in homicide.

Heterosexuality Provides the Most Desirable Model of Love

Myths are created not only by storytellers but by people living within the myth. Almost all (95% or so) heterosexuals get married, and 75%–80% stay married to their original partner till death. To be sure, there are marriage "hogs" within the heterosexual camp who play serial monogamy and assure that a third of all marriages end in divorce. Further, about half of all married men and about a third of all married women admit to one or more infidelities over the duration of their marriage (probably the greater bulk of the "cheaters" come from the serial monogamy camp). While heterosexuality's colors are far from simon pure, the relationship heterosexuality spawns is among, if not *the,* most enduring of human bonds. . . .

Homosexuality offers no comparison in durability. While "slam, bam, thank you ma'am" occurs in heterosexuality, few heterosexuals could more than fantasize about what occurs in homosexual bathhouses or tearooms. As Weinberg and Williams note, the homosexual community typically features "sex for sex's sake." Their survey in which two thirds of their respondents chose to respond "no" to whether they had limited their ". . . sexual relationships primarily to (another)" is telling. Names and banter are typically neglected in bathhouses. . . .

When people are merely "getting their jollies," and fantasizing perfection while doing so, reduced communication is an asset. If you discover that your beautiful lover holds political views antithetical to your own, how can you really enjoy him/her? The "less known the better" is fantasy sex. Communicating, mutually knowledgeable people often have to "work it out" before attempts at sex can even occur. But while typically short on durability, some homosexual relationships are more lasting. The quality of even these is often questionably desirable. Part of the problem lies in the lack of commitment that follows lower effort in the homosexual pairing. Tripp, for instance, opines that part ". . . of the reason many homosexual relationships do not survive the first serious quarrel is that one or both partners simply find it much easier to remarket themselves than work out conflicts (p. 155)." In heterosexuality, no matter how similar the participants, there is always a considerable gap between them. To stay together takes great effort, and the expenditure of this effort prompts both personal and social commitment to the partner.

. . . Because the heterosexual partners are so dissimilar, accommodation and adjustment are their key strategies. Because mutually satisfying heterosexual sexing takes so long and so much effort, both participants have to "hang in there" long after "sane people" would have toddled off in frustration. *We become the way we act. The heterosexual relationship places a premium on "getting on" and thus provides a model to smooth countless other human interactions.* The homosexual model is a considerably less satisfactory one upon which to build a civilization. Note Tripp again (p. 167): ". . . the problems encountered in balancing heterosexual and homosexual relationships are strikingly different. The *heterosexual blend tends to be rich in stimulating contrasts and short on rapport*—so much so that popular marriage counseling literature incessantly hammers home the advice that couples should develop common interests and dissolve their conflicts by increasing their 'communication.' By comparison, homosexual relationships are over-close, fatigue-prone, and are often adjusted to such narrow, trigger-sensitive tolerances that a mere whisper of disrapport can jolt the partners into making repairs, or into conflict." . . .

Our social system also features large components of delay of gratification. The heterosexual "carrot" is hard to get and requires a lot of input before successful outcome is achieved. The homosexual model is too immediate and influences people to expect instant results. . . .

In short, heterosexuality is effortful, durable, and demands delay of gratification. While any human relationship takes effort, homosexuality pales in comparison to heterosexuality on each count. . . .

No one is rich enough, powerful enough, or attractive enough to guarantee himself personal happiness. Incredibly wealthy, fabulously beautiful people have taken their lives in despair. *Nothing* guarantees happiness. On the other hand, extremely poor, grotesquely ugly people have achieved personal life-satisfaction. So it can likewise be said that nothing guarantees misery. More than any other single factor, happiness or life-satisfaction is an *achievement*. (The greatest "secret" to happiness is a dogged determination to wrest happiness from the cards life deals.)

Both degree of determination to be happy and the stage upon which happiness is pursued are influential in life-satisfaction. Since the stage is important, the prudent person attempts to include "props" that aid rather than hinder his pursuit of happiness. From the prudent perspective, it is foolish to neglect one's body or engage in needlessly hazardous pursuits. Similarly, it is wise to seek sufficient wherewithal to be free of nagging financial concern. From the prudent standpoint, homosexuality is an obstacle in the pursuit of happiness.

The best evidence on the question of homosexuals' happiness is, like most of what is known about homosexuality, not the best. But it is "fair" evidence from a social science standpoint. In their survey of 1,117 homosexuals, Weinberg & Williams asked respondents to answer "yes" or "no" to "I am a happy person." In an earlier poll of over 3,000 citizens, 92.8% had chosen "yes" to this question, but only 68.8% of the homosexuals did the same. Now I would not argue that 92.8% of Americans

are "happy persons" because they chose "yes" rather than "no" to this kind of item—such questions probably can be used to suggest differences between groups of persons, but hardly deserve to be considered precise. Answering such questions is rather like being asked "do you like ice cream, yes or no?" Both the person who LOVES ice cream and those who merely think its "OK" probably check "yes" rather than "no." And those who HATE ice cream check "no" along with those who just feel indifferent to it. But even with this caveat, and it's an important one, the way the responses fell suggests that homosexuals *are* less happy, on-the-average, than heterosexuals are. My educated guess is that most homosexuals are "happy" with life, just as most heterosexuals are. It probably works both ways—that is, unhappy people may be attracted to homosexuality and/or homosexuality may be a "negative prop" on the "life-satisfaction stage." But, either way, evidence such as Weinberg and Williams report cannot just be tossed aside. Even if their findings only mean that homosexuality attracts unhappy, less cheery sorts of people, a person "buying into" homosexuality is going to have to run his "happiness play" on a stage disproportionately filled with "unhappy props."

Does homosexuality make being happy more difficult? In the Weinberg and Williams study, homosexuals were asked to respond "yes" or "no" to the statement "no one cares what happens to you." While a general population sample had chosen "yes" 23% of the time, 34% of homosexuals chose "yes." . . . Heterosexuality helps generate the very kinds of props and reasons that contribute toward making life-satisfaction more possible. *In the long run,* heterosexuality has a lot more to offer as a life-style than homosexuality. . . .

Summary

In sum, there are a number of reasons why homosexuality is best treated as a deviant sexual mode. I do not believe that homosexuality ought to be placed on an even-keel with heterosexuality. Further, homosexuals ought not, in my opinion, to be permitted to openly ply their sexual orientation and retain influential positions in the social system. Thus teachers, or pastors who "come out," ought, in my opinion, to lose their claim to the roles they occupy.

Reasonable people can and do differ on the degree and kind of discrimination that is to be laid against undesirable life-styles. There are a number of issues that appear substantive and weigh against the liberalization of social policy toward homosexuality. The burden of proof always justly falls upon those who would change the social system. If the homosexual community and/or those who endorse the liberalization of social policy toward homosexuality have evidence that bears upon these points, by all means bring it forward and let us reason together. But mere cries of "we are being discriminated against" are not evidence. The collection of decent evidence takes organized time and effort. I am weary of those who feel that a case has been made just because they have gotten blisters on the streets or their voices are louder.

References

Allport, G. W. *The Person in Psychology*. NY: Beacon, 1961.

Atkins, J. *Sex in Literature*. NY: Grove Press, 1970.

Bergler, E. *Homosexuality: Disease or Way of Life?* NY: Macmillan, 1956.

Bieber, I. *Homosexuality: A Psychoanalytic Study*. NY: Basic Books, 1962.

Cameron, P. "Immolations to the Juggernaut," *Linacre Quarterly*, 1977, *44*, 64–74.

Cameron, P. *The Life-Cycle: Perspectives and Commentary*. NY: General Health, 1977.

Cameron, P. & Oeschger, D. "Homosexuality in the Mass Media as Indexed by Magazine Literature over the Past Half Century in the U.S." Paper presented at Eastern Psychological Association Convention, New York, April 4, 1975.

Davis, N. & Graubert, J. *Heterosexual*. NY: Vantage Press, 1975.

Freud, S. "Three Contributions to Sexual Theory," *Nervous and Mental Disease Monograph Series*, 1925, 7.

Gubrium, J. F. "Being Single in Old Age," *International Journal of Aging and Human Development*, 1975, *6*, 29–41.

Hunt, M. *Sexual Behavior in the 1970s*. Chicago: Playboy Press, 1974.

Karlen, A. *Sexuality and Homosexuality*. NY: Norton, 1971.

Kastenbaum, R. J. & Costa, P. T. "Psychological Perspectives on Death," *Annual Review of Psychology*, 1977, *28*, 225–49.

Maugham, S. *El Greco*. NY: Doubleday, 1950.

Sears, R. R. "Sources of Life Satisfactions of the Terman Gifted Man," *American Psychologist*, 1977, *32*, 119–128.

Tripp, C. A. *The Homosexual Matrix*. NY: McGraw-Hill, 1975.

Weinberg, M. S. & Williams, C. J. *Male Homosexuals: Their Problems and Adaptations*. NY: Oxford University Press, 1974.

45. Gay Basics: Some Questions, Facts, and Values

Richard D. Mohr

Richard D. Mohr begins by noting that although gays are a significant percentage of the American population, they are characterized by stereotypes based on false generalizations. He cites one study in which 90 percent of gays and lesbians report that they have been victimized because of their sexual orientation and another study according to which there are 307 occupations that are prohibited to them. Mohr also questions whether a correct understanding of Christianity would condemn homosexuality, and he denies that any argument from nature supports such a condemnation. He further argues that if gays were socially accepted, society would be enriched and a step closer to its goal of "liberty and justice for all."

Who Are Gays Anyway?

A recent Gallup poll found that only one in five Americans reports having a gay or lesbian acquaintance.[1] This finding is extraordinary given the number of practicing homosexuals in America. Alfred Kinsey's 1948 study of the sex lives of 5,000 white males shocked the nation: 37 percent had at least one homosexual experience to orgasm in their adult lives; an additional 13 percent had homosexual fantasies to orgasm; 4 percent were exclusively homosexual in their practices; another 5 percent had virtually no heterosexual experience; and nearly one-fifth had at least as many homosexual as heterosexual experiences.[2]

Two out of five men one passes on the street have had orgasmic sex with men. Every second family in the country has a member who is essentially homosexual, and many more people regularly have homosexual experiences. Who are homosexuals? They are your friends, your minister, your teacher, your bank teller, your doctor, your mail carrier, your secretary, your congressional representative, your sibling, parent, and spouse. They are everywhere, virtually all ordinary, virtually all unknown.

Several important consequences follow. First, the country is profoundly ignorant of the actual experience of gay people. Second, social attitudes and practices that are harmful to gays have a much greater overall harmful impact on society than is usually realized. Third, most gay people live in hiding—in the closet—making the "coming out" experience the central fixture of gay consciousness and invisibility the chief characteristic of the gay community.

Ignorance, Stereotype, and Morality

Ignorance about gays, however, has not stopped people from having strong opinions about them. The void which ignorance leaves has been filled with stereotypes. Society holds chiefly two groups of antigay stereotypes; the two are an oddly contradictory lot. One set of stereotypes revolves around alleged mistakes in an individual's gender identity: Lesbians are women who want to be, or at least look and act like, men—bulldykes, diesel dykes; while gay men are those who want to be, or at least look and act like, women—queens, fairies, limp-wrists, nellies. These stereotypes of mismatched genders provide the materials through which gays and lesbians become the butts of ethnic-like jokes. These stereotypes and jokes, though derisive, basically view gays and lesbians as ridiculous.

Another set of stereotypes revolves around gays as a pervasive sinister conspiratorial threat. The core stereotype here is the gay

Reprinted with the permission of Richard D. Mohr.

person as child molester and, more generally, as sex-crazed maniac. These stereotypes carry with them fears of the very destruction of family and civilization itself. Now, that which is essentially ridiculous can hardly have such a staggering effect. Something must be afoot in this incoherent amalgam.

Sense can be made of this incoherence if the nature of stereotypes is clarified. Stereotypes are not *simply* false generalizations from a skewed sample of cases examined. Admittedly, false generalizing plays some part in the stereotypes a society holds. If, for instance, one takes as one's sample homosexuals who are in psychiatric hospitals or prisons, as was done in nearly all early investigations, not surprisingly one will probably find homosexuals to be of a crazed and criminal cast. Such false generalizations, though, simply confirm beliefs already held on independent grounds, ones that likely led the investigator to the prison and psychiatric ward to begin with. Evelyn Hooker, who in the late '50s carried out the first rigorous studies to use nonclinical gays, found that psychiatrists, when presented with case files including all the standard diagnostic psychological profiles—but omitting indications of sexual orientation—were unable to distinguish gay files from straight ones, even though they believed gays to be crazy and supposed themselves to be experts in detecting craziness.[3] These studies proved a profound embarrassment to the psychiatric establishment, the financial well-being of which has been substantially enhanced by "curing" allegedly insane gays. The studies led the way to the American Psychiatric Association finally dropping homosexuality from its registry of mental illnesses in 1973.[4] Nevertheless, the stereotype of gays as sick continues apace in the mind of America.

False generalizations *help maintain* stereotypes, they do not *form* them. As the history of Hooker's discoveries shows, stereotypes have a life beyond facts; their origin lies in a culture's ideology—the general system of beliefs by which it lives—and they are sustained across generations by diverse cultural transmissions, hardly any of which, including slang and jokes, even purport to have a scientific basis. Stereotypes, then, are not the products of bad science but are social constructions that perform central functions in maintaining society's conception of itself.

On this understanding, it is easy to see that the antigay stereotypes surrounding gender identification are chiefly means of reinforcing still powerful gender roles in society. If, as this stereotype presumes and condemns, one is free to choose one's social roles independently of gender, many guiding social divisions, both domestic and commercial, might be threatened. The socially gender-linked distinctions between breadwinner and homemaker, boss and secretary, doctor and nurse, protector and protected would blur. The accusations "fag" and "dyke" exist in significant part to keep women in their place and to prevent men from breaking ranks and ceding away theirs.

The stereotypes of gays as child molesters, sex-crazed maniacs, and civilization destroyers function to displace (socially irresolvable) problems from their actual source to a foreign (and so, it is thought, manageable) one. Thus, the stereotype of child molester functions to give the family unit a false sheen of absolute innocence. It keeps the unit from being examined too closely for incest, child abuse, wife battering, and the terrorism of constant threats. The stereotype teaches that the problems of the family are not internal to it, but external.[5]

One can see these cultural forces at work in society's and the media's treatment of current reports of violence, especially domestic violence. When a mother kills her child or a father rapes his daughter—regular Section B fare even in major urbane papers—this is never taken by reporters, columnists, or pundits as evidence that there is something wrong with heterosexuality or with traditional families. These issues are not even raised. But when a homosexual child molestation is reported, it is taken as confirming evidence of the way homosexuals are. One never hears of heterosexual murders, but one regularly hears of "homosexual" ones. Compare the social treatment of Richard Speck's sexually motivated mass murder of Chicago nurses with that of John Wayne Gacy's murders of Chicago youths. Gacy was in the culture's mind taken as symbolic of gay men in general. To prevent the possibility that "The Family" was viewed as anything but an innocent victim in this affair, the mainstream press knowingly failed to mention that most of Gacy's adolescent victims were homeless hustlers. That knowledge would be too much for the six o'clock news and for cherished beliefs.

Because "the facts" largely don't matter when it comes to the generation and maintenance of stereotypes, the effects of scientific and academic research and of enlightenment generally will be, at best, slight and gradual in the changing fortunes of lesbians and gay men. If this account of stereotypes holds, society has been profoundly immoral. For its treatment of gays is a grand scale rationalization, a moral sleight-of-hand. The problem is not that society's usual standards of evidence and procedure in coming to judgments of social policy have been misapplied to gays; rather, when it comes to gays, the standards themselves have simply been ruled out of court and disregarded in favor of mechanisms that encourage unexamined fear and hatred.

Are Gays Discriminated Against? Does It Matter?

Partly because lots of people suppose they don't know any gay people and partly through willful ignorance of its own workings, society at large is unaware of the many ways in which gays are subject to discrimination in consequence of widespread fear and hatred. Contributing to this social ignorance of discrimination is the difficulty for gay people, as an invisible minority, even to complain of discrimination. For if one is gay, to register a complaint would suddenly target one as a stigmatized person, and so in the absence of any protections against discrimination, would simply invite additional discrimination. Further, many people, especially those who are persistently downtrodden and so lack a firm sense of self to begin with, tend either to blame themselves for their troubles or to view injustice as a matter of bad luck rather than as indicating something wrong with society. The latter recognition would require doing something to rectify wrong, and most people, es-

pecially the already beleaguered, simply aren't up to that. So for a number of reasons discrimination against gays, like rape, goes seriously underreported.

First, gays are subject to violence and harassment based simply on their perceived status rather than because of any actions they have performed. A recent extensive study by the National Gay Task Force found that over 90 percent of gays and lesbians had been victimized in some form on the basis of their sexual orientation.[6] Greater than one in five gay men and nearly one in ten lesbians had been punched, hit, or kicked, a quarter of all gays had had objects thrown at them, a third had been chased, a third had been sexually harassed, and 14 percent had been spit on—all just for being perceived as gay.

The most extreme form of antigay violence is queerbashing—where groups of young men target a person who they suppose is a gay man and beat and kick him unconscious and sometimes to death amid a torrent of taunts and slurs. Such seemingly random but in reality socially encouraged violence has the same social origin and function as lynchings of blacks—to keep a whole stigmatized group in line. As with lynchings of the recent past, the police and courts have routinely averted their eyes, giving their implicit approval to the practice.

Few such cases with gay victims reach the courts. Those that do are marked by inequitable procedures and results. Frequently judges will describe queerbashers as "just all-American boys." Recently a District of Columbia judge handed suspended sentences to queerbashers whose victim had been stalked, beaten, stripped at knife point, slashed, kicked, threatened with castration, and pissed on, because the judge thought the bashers were good boys at heart—after all, they went to a religious prep school.[7]

Police and juries will simply discount testimony from gays; they typically construe assaults on and murders of gays as "justified" self-defense—the killer need only claim his act was a panicked response to a sexual overture. Alternatively, when guilt seems patent, juries will accept highly implausible "diminished capacity" defenses, as in the case of Dan White's 1978 assassination of openly gay San

Francisco city [supervisor] Harvey Milk—Hostess Twinkies made him do it.[8]

These inequitable procedures and results collectively show that the life and liberty of gays, like those of blacks, simply count for less than the life and liberty of members of the dominant culture.

The equitable rule of law is the heart of an orderly society. The collapse of the rule of law for gays shows that society is willing to perpetrate the worst possible injustices against them. Conceptually there is only a difference in degree between the collapse of the rule of law and systematic extermination of members of a population simply for having some group status independently of any act an individual has performed. In the Nazi concentration camps, gays were forced to wear pink triangles as identifying badges, just as Jews were forced to wear yellow stars. In remembrance of that collapse of the rule of law, the pink triangle has become the chief symbol of the gay rights movement.[9]

Gays are subject to widespread discrimination in employment—the very means by which one puts bread on one's table and one of the chief means by which individuals identify themselves to themselves and achieve personal dignity. Governments are leading offenders here. They do a lot of discriminating themselves, require that others do it ([such as] government contractors), and set precedents favoring discrimination in the private sector. The federal government explicitly discriminates against gays in the armed forces, the CIA, FBI, National Security Agency, and the State Department. The federal government refuses to give security clearances to gays and so forces the country's considerable private-sector military and aerospace contractors to fire known gay employees. State and local governments regularly fire gay teachers, policemen, firemen, social workers, and anyone who has contact with the public. Further, states through licensing laws officially bar gays from a vast array of occupations and professions—everything from doctors, lawyers, accountants, and nurses to hairdressers, morticians, and used car dealers. The American Civil Liberties Union's handbook *The Rights of Gay People* lists 307 such prohibited occupations.[10]

Gays are subject to discrimination in a wide variety of other ways, including private-sector employment, public accommodations, housing, immigration and naturalization, insurance of all types, custody and adoption, and zoning regulations that bar "singles" or "nonrelated" couples. All of these discriminations affect central components of a meaningful life; some even reach to the means by which life itself is sustained. In half the states, where gay sex is illegal, the central role of sex to meaningful life is officially denied to gays.

All these sorts of discriminations also affect the ability of people to have significant intimate relations. It is difficult for people to live together as couples without having their sexual orientation perceived in the public realm and so becoming targets for discrimination. Illegality, discrimination, and the absorption by gays of society's hatred of them all interact to impede or block altogether the ability of gays and lesbians to create and maintain significant personal relations with loved ones. So every facet of life is affected by discrimination. Only the most compelling reasons could justify it.

But Aren't They Immoral?

Many people think society's treatment of gays is justified because they think gays are extremely immoral. To evaluate this claim, different senses of *moral* must be distinguished. Sometimes by *morality* is meant the overall beliefs affecting behavior in a society—its mores, norms, and customs. On this understanding, gays certainly are not moral: Lots of people hate them and social customs are designed to register widespread disapproval of gays. The problem here is that this sense of morality is merely a *descriptive* one. On this understanding *every* society has a morality—even Nazi society, which had racism and mob rule as central features of its "morality" understood in this sense. What is needed in order to use the notion of morality to praise or condemn behavior is a sense of morality that is *prescriptive* or *normative*—a sense of morality whereby, for instance, the descriptive morality of the Nazis is found wanting.

As the Nazi example makes clear, that something is descriptively moral is nowhere near enough to make it normatively moral. [The fact that] a lot of people in a society say something is good, even over eons, does not make it so. Our rejection of the long history of socially approved and state-enforced slavery is another good example of this principle at work. Slavery would be wrong even if nearly everyone liked it. So consistency and fairness require that we abandon the belief that gays are immoral simply because most people dislike or disapprove of gays or gay acts, or even because gay sex acts are illegal.

Furthermore, recent historical and anthropological research has shown that opinion about gays has been by no means universally negative. Historically, it has varied widely even within the larger part of the Christian era and even within the church itself.[11] There are even societies—current ones—where homosexuality is not only tolerated but a universal compulsory part of social maturation.[12] Within the last thirty years, American society has undergone a grand turnabout from deeply ingrained, near total condemnation to near total acceptance on two emotionally charged "moral" or "family" issues: contraception and divorce. Society holds its current descriptive morality of gays not because it has to, but because it chooses to.

If popular opinion and custom are not enough to ground moral condemnation of homosexuality, perhaps religion can. Such argument[s] proceed along two lines. One claims that the condemnation is a direct revelation of God, usually through the Bible; the other claims to be able to detect condemnation in God's plan as manifested in nature.

One of the more remarkable discoveries of recent gay research is that the Bible may not be as univocal in its condemnation of homosexuality as has been usually believed.[13] Christ never mention[ed] homosexuality. Recent interpreters of the Old Testament have pointed out that the story of Lot at Sodom is probably intended to condemn inhospitality rather than homosexuality. Further, some of the Old Testament condemnations of homosexuality seem simply to be ways of tarring those of the Israelites' opponents who happen to accept homosexual practices when the Israelites themselves did not. If so, the condemnation is merely a quirk of history and rhetoric rather than a moral precept.

What does seem clear is that those who regularly cite the Bible to condemn an activity like homosexuality do so by reading it selectively. Do ministers who cite what they take to be condemnations of homosexuality in Leviticus maintain in their lives all the hygienic and dietary laws of Leviticus? If they cite the story of Lot at Sodom to condemn homosexuality, do they also cite the story of Lot in the cave to praise incestuous rape? It seems then not that the Bible is being used to ground condemnations of homosexuality as much as society's dislike of homosexuality is being used to interpret the Bible.[14]

Even if a consistent portrait of condemnation could be gleaned from the Bible, what social significance should it be given? One of the guiding principles of society, enshrined in the [U.S.] Constitution as a check against the government, is that decisions affecting social policy are not made on religious grounds. If the real ground of the alleged immorality invoked by governments to discriminate against gays is religious (as it has explicitly been even in some recent court cases involving teachers and guardians), then one of the major commitments of our nation is violated.

But Aren't They Unnatural?

The most noteworthy feature of the accusation of something being unnatural (where a moral rather than an advertising point is being made) is that the plaint is so infrequently made. One used to hear the charge leveled against abortion, but that has pretty much faded as antiabortionists have come to lay all their chips on the hope that people will come to view abortion as murder. Incest used to be considered unnatural but discourse now usually assimilates it to the moral machinery of rape and violated trust. The charge comes up now in ordinary discourse only against homosexuality. This suggests that the charge is highly idiosyncratic and has little, if any, explanatory force. It fails to put homosexuality in a class with anything else so that one can learn by comparison with clear cases of the class just exactly what it is that is allegedly wrong with it.

Though the accusation of unnaturalness looks whimsical, in actual ordinary discourse when applied to homosexuality, it is usually delivered with venom of forethought. It carries a high emotional charge, usually expressing disgust and evincing queasiness. Probably it is nothing but an emotional charge. For people get equally disgusted and queasy at all sorts of things that are perfectly natural—to be expected in nature apart from artifice—and that could hardly be fit subjects for moral condemnation. Two typical examples in current American culture are some people's responses to mothers' suckling in public and to women who do not shave body hair. When people have strong emotional reactions, as they do in these cases, without being able to give good reasons for them, we think of them not as operating morally, but rather as being obsessed and manic. So the feelings of disgust that some people have to gays will hardly ground a charge of immorality. People fling the term *unnatural* against gays in the same breath and with the same force as when they call gays "sick" and "gross." When they do this, they give every appearance of being neurotically fearful and incapable of reasoned discourse.

When *nature* is taken in *technical* rather than ordinary usage, it looks like the notion also will not ground a charge of homosexual immorality. When *unnatural* means "by artifice" or "made by humans," it need only be pointed out that virtually everything that is good about life is unnatural in this sense, that the chief feature that distinguishes people from other animals is their very ability to make over the world to meet their needs and desires, and that their well-being depends upon these departures from nature. On this understanding of human nature and the natural, homosexuality is perfectly unobjectionable.

Another technical sense of *natural* is that something is natural, and so, good, if it fulfills some function in nature. Homosexuality on this view is unnatural because it allegedly violates the function of genitals, which is to produce babies. One problem with this view is that lots of bodily parts have lots of functions and just because some one activity can be fulfilled by only one organ (say, the mouth for eating) this activity does not condemn other functions of the organ to immorality (say, the mouth for talking, licking stamps, blowing bubbles, or having sex). So the possible use of the genitals to produce children does not, without more, condemn the use of the genitals for other purposes, say, achieving ecstasy and intimacy.

The functional view of nature will only provide a morally condemnatory sense to the unnatural if a thing which might have many uses has but one proper function to the exclusion of other possible functions. But whether this is so cannot be established simply by looking at the thing. For what is seen is all its possible functions. The notion of function seemed like it might ground moral authority, but instead it turns out that moral authority is needed to define proper function. Some people try to fill in this moral authority by appeal to the "design" or "order" of an organ, saying, for instance, that the genitals are designed for the purpose of procreation. But these people cheat intellectually if they do not make explicit *who* the designer and orderer is. If it is God, we are back to square one—holding others accountable for religious beliefs.

Further, ordinary moral attitudes about childrearing will not provide the needed supplement, which, in conjunction with the natural function view of bodily parts, would produce a positive obligation to use the genitals for procreation. Society's attitude toward a childless couple is that of pity not censure—even if the couple could have children. The pity may be an unsympathetic one, that is, not registering a course one would choose *for oneself,* but this does not make it a course one would *require* of others. The couple who discovers it cannot have children is viewed not as having thereby had a debt canceled, but rather as having to forgo some of the richness of life, just as a quadriplegic is not viewed as absolved from some moral obligation to hop, skip, and jump, but is viewed as missing some of the richness of life. Consistency requires then that, at most, gays who do not or cannot have children are to be pitied rather than condemned. What *is* immoral is the willful preventing of people from achieving the richness of life. Immorality in this regard lies with those social customs, regulations, and statutes that prevent lesbians and gay men from establishing blood or adoptive families, not with gays themselves.

Sometimes people attempt to establish authority for a moral obligation to use bodily parts in a certain fashion simply by claiming that moral laws are natural laws and vice versa. On this account, inanimate objects and plants are good in that they follow natural laws by necessity, animals by instinct, and persons by a rational will. People are special in that they must first discover the laws that govern them. Now, even if one believes the view—dubious in the post-Newtonian, post-Darwinian world—that natural laws in the usual sense ($e = mc^2$, for instance) have some moral content, it is not at all clear how one is to discover the laws in nature that apply to people.

If, on the one hand, one looks to people themselves for a model—and looks hard enough—one finds amazing variety, including homosexuality as a social ideal (upper-class 5th-century Athenians) and even as socially mandatory (Melanesia today). When one looks to people, one is simply unable to strip away the layers of social custom, history, and taboo in order to see what's really there to any degree more specific than that people are the creatures that make over their world and are capable of abstract thought. That this is so should raise doubts that neutral principles are to be found in human nature that will condemn homosexuality.

On the other hand, if one looks to nature apart from people for models, the possibilities are staggering. There are fish that change gender over their lifetimes: Should we "follow nature" and be operative transsexuals? Orangutans, genetically our next of kin, live completely solitary lives without social organization of any kind: Ought we to "follow nature" and be hermits? There are many species where only two members per generation reproduce: Shall we be bees? The search in nature for people's purpose—far from finding sure models for action—is likely to leave one morally rudderless.

But Aren't Gays Willfully the Way They Are?

It is generally conceded that if sexual orientation is something over which an individual—for whatever reason—has virtually no control, then discrimination against gays is especially deplorable, as it is against racial and ethnic classes, because it holds people accountable without regard for anything they themselves have done. And to hold a person accountable for that over which the person has no control is a central form of prejudice.

Attempts to answer the question whether or not sexual orientation is something that is reasonably thought to be within one's own control usually appeal simply to various claims of the biological or "mental" sciences. But the ensuing debate over genes, hormones, twins, early childhood development, and the like is as unnecessary as it is currently inconclusive.[15] All that is needed to answer the question is to look at the actual experience of gays in current society, and it becomes fairly clear that sexual orientation is not likely a matter of choice. For coming to have a homosexual identity simply does not have the same sort of structure that decision-making has.

On the one hand, the "choice" of the gender of a sexual partner does not seem to express a trivial desire which might be as easily well fulfilled by a simple substitution of the desired object. Picking the gender of a sex partner is decidedly dissimilar, that is, to such activities as picking a flavor of ice cream. If an ice-cream parlor is out of one's flavor, one simply picks another. And if people were persecuted, threatened with jail terms, shattered careers, loss of family and housing and the like for eating, say, rocky road ice cream, no one would ever eat it; everyone would pick another easily available flavor. That gay people abide in being gay even in the face of persecution shows that being gay is not a matter of easy choice.

On the other hand, even if establishing a sexual orientation is not like making a relatively trivial choice, perhaps it is nevertheless relevantly like making the central and serious life choices by which individuals try to establish themselves as being of some type. Again, if one examines gay experience, this seems not to be the case. For one never sees anyone setting out to become a homosexual, in the way one does see people setting out to become doctors, lawyers, and bricklayers. One does not find gays-to-be picking some end—"At some point in the future, I want to become a homosexual"—and then set[ting] about planning and acquiring the ways and means to that end, in the way one does see people deciding that they want to become lawyers, and then sees them plan[ning] what courses to take and what sort of temperaments, habits, and skills to develop in order to become lawyers. Typically gays-to-be simply find themselves having homosexual encounters and yet at least initially resisting quite strongly the identification of being homosexual. Such a person even very likely resists having such encounters but ends up having them anyway. Only with time, luck, and great personal effort, but sometimes never, does the person gradually come to accept her or his orientation, to view it as a given material condition of life, coming as materials do with certain capacities and limitations. The person begins to act in accordance with his or her orientation and its capacities, seeing its actualization as a requisite for an integrated personality and as a central component of personal well-being. As a result, the experience of coming out to oneself has for gays the basic structure of a discovery, not the structure of a choice. And far from signaling immorality, coming out to others affords one of the few remaining opportunities in ever more bureaucratic, mechanistic, and socialistic societies to manifest courage.

How Would Society at Large Be Changed If Gays Were Socially Accepted?

Suggestions to change social policy with regard to gays are invariably met with claims that to do so would invite the destruction of civilization itself: After all, isn't that what did Rome in? Actually Rome's decay paralleled not the flourishing of homosexuality, but its repression under the later Christianized emperors.[16] Predictions of American civilization's imminent demise have been as premature as they have been frequent. Civilization has shown itself rather resilient here, in large part because of the country's traditional commitments to a respect for privacy, to individual liberties, and especially to people minding their own business. These all give society an open texture and the flexibility to try out things to see what works. And because of this one now need not speculate about what changes reforms in gay social policy might bring to society at large. For many reforms have already been tried.

Half the states have decriminalized homosexual acts. Can you guess which of the following states still have sodomy laws? Wisconsin, Minnesota; New Mexico, Arizona; Vermont, New Hampshire; Nebraska, Kansas. One from each pair does and one does not have sodomy laws. And yet one would be hard pressed to point out any substantial difference between the members of each pair. (If you're interested: It is the second of each pair with them.) Empirical studies have shown that there is no increase in other crimes in states that have decriminalized [homosexual acts].[17] Further, sodomy laws are virtually never enforced. They remain on the books not to "protect society" but to insult gays and, for that reason, need to be removed.

Neither has the passage of legislation barring discrimination against gays ushered in the end of civilization. Some 50 counties and municipalities, including some of the country's largest cities (like Los Angeles and Boston) have passed such statutes and among the states and [counties] Wisconsin and the District of Columbia have model protective codes. Again, no more brimstone has fallen in these places than elsewhere. Staunchly antigay cities, like Miami and Houston, have not been spared the AIDS crisis.

Berkeley, California, has even passed domestic partner legislation giving gay couples the same rights to city benefits as married couples, and yet Berkeley has not become more weird than it already was.

Seemingly hysterical predictions that the American family would collapse if such reforms would pass proved false, just as the same dire predictions that the availability of divorce would lessen the ideal and desirability of marriage proved completely unfounded. Indeed, if current discriminations, which drive gays into hiding and into anonymous relations, were lifted, far from seeing gays raze American families, one would see gays forming them.

Virtually all gays express a desire to have a permanent lover. Many would like to raise or foster children—perhaps [from among the] alarming number of gay kids who have been beaten up and thrown out of their "families" for being gay. But currently society makes gay coupling very difficult. A life of hiding is a pressure-cooker existence not easily shared with another. Members of nongay couples are here asked to imagine what it would take to erase every trace of their own sexual orientation for even just a week.

Even against oppressive odds, gays have shown an amazing tendency to nest. And those gay couples who have survived the odds show that the structure of more usual couplings is not a matter of destiny but of personal responsibility. The so-called basic unit of society turns out not to be a unique immutable atom but can adopt different parts, be adapted to different needs, and even be improved. Gays might even have a thing or two to teach others about divisions of labor, the relation of sensuality and intimacy, and stages of development in such relations.

If discrimination ceased, gay men and lesbians would enter the mainstream of the human community openly and with self-respect. The energies that the typical gay person wastes in the anxiety of leading a day-to-day existence of systematic disguise would be released for use in personal flourishing. From this release would be generated the many spin-off benefits that accrue to a society when its individual members thrive.

Society would be richer for acknowledging another aspect of human richness and diversity. Families with gay members would develop relations based on truth and trust rather than lies and fear. And the heterosexual majority would be better off for knowing that they are no longer trampling their gay friends and neighbors.

Finally and perhaps paradoxically, in extending to gays the rights and benefits it has reserved for its dominant culture, America would confirm its deeply held vision of itself as a morally progressing nation, a nation itself advancing and serving as a beacon for others—especially with regard to human rights. The words with which our national pledge ends—"with liberty and justice for all"—are not a description of the present but a call for the future. Ours is a nation given to a prophetic political rhetoric which acknowledges that morality is not arbitrary and that justice is not merely the expression of the current collective will. It is this vision that led the black civil rights movement to its successes. Those congressmen who opposed that movement and its centerpiece, the 1964 Civil Rights Act, on obscurantist grounds, but who lived long enough and were noble enough came in time to express their heartfelt regret and shame at what they had done. It is to be hoped and someday to be expected that those who now grasp at anything to oppose the extension of that which is best about America to gays will one day feel the same.

Notes

1. "Public Fears—and Sympathies," *Newsweek* (August 12, 1985), p. 23.

2. Alfred C. Kinsey, *Sexual Behavior in the Human Male* (Philadelphia: Saunders, 1948), pp. 650–51. On the somewhat lower incidences of lesbianism, see Alfred C. Kinsey, *Sexual Behavior in the Human Female* (Philadelphia: Saunders, 1953), pp. 472–75.

3. Evelyn Hooker, "The Adjustment of the Male Overt Homosexual," *Journal of Projective Techniques* 21 (1957), pp. 18–31, reprinted in Hendrik M. Ruitenbeek, ed., *The Problem of Homosexuality* (New York: Dutton, 1963), pp. 141–61.

4. See Ronald Bayer, *Homosexuality and American Psychiatry* (New York: Basic Books, 1981).

5. For studies showing that gay men are no more likely—indeed, are less likely—than heterosex-

uals to be child molesters and that the largest classes and most persistent sexual abusers of children are the children's fathers, stepfathers, or mother's boyfriends, see Vincent De Francis, *Protecting the Child Victim of Sex Crimes Committed by Adults* (Denver: The American Humane Association, 1969), pp. *vii*, 38, 69–70; A. Nicholas Groth, "Adult Sexual Orientation and Attraction to Underage Persons," *Archives of Sexual Behavior* 7 (1978), pp. 175–81; Mary J. Spencer, "Sexual Abuse of Boys," *Pediatrics* 78:1 (July 1986), pp. 133–38.

6. See National Gay Task Force, *Antigay/Lesbian Victimization* (New York: NGTF, 1984).

7. "2 St. John's Students Given Probation in Assault on Gay," *The Washington Post* (May 15, 1984), p. 1.

8. See Randy Shilts, *The Mayor of Castro Street: The Life and Times of Harvey Milk* (New York: St. Martin's, 1982), pp. 308–25.

9. See Richard Plant, *The Pink Triangle: The Nazi War Against Homosexuals* (New York: Holt, 1986).

10. E. Carrington Boggan, *The Rights of Gay People: The Basic ACLU Guide to a Gay Person's Rights*, 1st ed. (New York: Avon, 1975), pp. 211–35.

11. John Boswell, *Christianity, Social Tolerance, and Homosexuality: Gay People in Western Europe from the Beginning of the Christian Era to the Fourteenth Century* (Chicago: The University of Chicago Press, 1980).

12. See Gilbert Herdt, *Guardians of the Flute: Idioms of Masculinity* (New York: McGraw-Hill, 1981), pp. 232–39, 284–88, and see generally Gilbert Herdt, ed., *Ritualized Homosexuality in Melanesia* (Berkeley: University of California Press, 1984). For another eye-opener, see Walter J. Williams, *The Spirit and the Flesh: Sexual Diversity in American Indian Culture* (Boston: Beacon, 1986).

13. See especially Boswell, *op. cit.*, Chapter 4.

14. For Old Testament condemnations of homosexual acts, see Leviticus 18:22, 21:3. For hygienic and dietary codes, see, for example, Leviticus 15:19–27 (on the uncleanliness of women) and Leviticus 11:1–47 (on not eating rabbits, pigs, bats, finless water creatures, legless creeping creatures, and so on). For Lot at Sodom, see Genesis 19:1–25. For Lot in the cave, see Genesis 19:30–38.

15. The preponderance of the scientific evidence supports the view that homosexuality is either genetically determined or a permanent result of early childhood development. See the Kinsey Institute's study by Alan Bell, Martin Weinberg, and Sue Hammersmith, *Sexual Preference: Its Development in Men and Women* (Bloomington: Indiana University Press, 1981); Frederick Whitam and Robin Mathy, *Male Homosexuality in Four Societies* (New York: Praeger, 1986), Chapter 7.

16. See Boswell, *op. cit.*, Chapter 3.

17. See Gilbert Geis, "Reported Consequences of Decriminalization of Consensual Adult Homosexuality in Seven American States," *Journal of Homosexuality* 1:4 (1976), pp. 419–26; Ken Sinclair and Michael Ross, "Consequences of Decriminalization of Homosexuality: A Study of Two Australian States," *Journal of Homosexuality* 12:1 (1985), pp. 119–27.

46. *Bowers v. Hardwick*

The Supreme Court of the United States

The issue before the Supreme Court was whether the Georgia sodomy statute violates the Federal Constitution. In delivering the opinion of the Court, Justice White argues that the statute does not violate the Constitution because the Constitution does not confer a fundamental right on homosexuals to engage in sodomy. While in previous cases, the Constitution was interpreted to confer a right to decide whether or not to beget or bear a child and a right not to be convicted for possessing and reading obscene material in the privacy of one's home, White argues that the Constitution cannot be analogously interpreted to confer a fundamental right on homosexuals to engage in sodomy. Justice Burger concurs, stressing the ancient roots of sodomy statutes. Justice Blackmun joined by Justices Brennan and Marshall argues that notwithstanding the ancient roots of prohibitions against homosexuality, a right to be let alone that is the underpinning of previous court decision justifies in this case a right to engage in sodomy at least in the privacy of one's home.

Justice White delivered the opinion of the Court.

In August 1982, respondent Hardwick . . . was charged with violating the Georgia statute criminalizing sodomy by committing that act with another adult male in the bedroom of respondent's home. After a preliminary hearing, the District Attorney decided not to present the matter to the grand jury unless further evidence developed.

Respondent then brought suit in the Federal District Court, challenging the constitutionality of the statute insofar as it criminalized consensual sodomy. He asserted that he was a practicing homosexual, that the Georgia sodomy statute, as administered by the defendants, placed him in imminent danger of arrest, and that the statute for several reasons violates the Federal Constitution. . . .

This case does not require a judgment on whether laws against sodomy between consenting adults in general, or between homosexuals in particular, are wise or desirable. It raises no question about the right or propriety of state legislative decisions to repeal their laws that criminalize homosexual sodomy, or of state-court decisions invalidating those laws on state constitutional grounds. The issue presented is whether the Federal Constitution confers a fundamental right upon homosexuals to engage in sodomy and hence invalidates the laws of the many States that still

make such conduct illegal and have done so for a very long time. The case also calls for some judgment about the limits of the Court's role in carrying out its constitutional mandate.

We first register our disagreement with the Court of Appeals and with respondent that the Court's prior cases have construed the Constitution to confer a right of privacy that extends to homosexual sodomy and for all intents and purposes have decided this case. . . . [Three] cases were interpreted as construing the Due Process Clause of the Fourteenth Amendment to confer a fundamental individual right to decide whether or not to beget or bear a child. . . .

Accepting the decisions in these cases . . . we think it evident that none of the rights announced in those cases bears any resemblance to the claimed constitutional right of homosexuals to engage in acts of sodomy that is asserted in this case. No connection between family, marriage, or procreation on the one hand and homosexual activity on the other has been demonstrated, either by the Court of Appeals or by respondent. Moreover, any claim that these cases nevertheless stand for the proposition that any kind of private sexual conduct between consenting adults is constitutionally insulated from state proscription is unsupportable. . . .

Precedent aside, however, respondent

would have us announce, as the Court of Appeals did, a fundamental right to engage in homosexual sodomy. This we are quite unwilling to do. It is true that despite the language of the Due Process Clauses of the Fifth and Fourteenth Amendments, which appears to focus only on the processes by which life, liberty, or property is taken, the cases are legion in which those Clauses have been interpreted to have substantive content, subsuming rights that to a great extent are immune from federal or state regulation or proscription. Among such cases are those recognizing rights that have little or no textual support in the constitutional language. . . .

Striving to assure itself and the public that announcing rights not readily identifiable in the Constitution's text involves much more than the imposition of the Justices' own choice of values on the States and the Federal Government, the Court has sought to identify the nature of the rights qualifying for heightened judicial protection. In *Palko v. Connecticut,* . . . it was said that this category includes those fundamental liberties that are "implicit in the concept of ordered liberty," such that "neither liberty nor justice would exist if [they] were sacrificed." A different description of fundamental liberties appeared in *Moore v. East Cleveland,* . . . where they are characterized as those liberties that are "deeply rooted in this Nation's history and tradition." . . .

It is obvious to us that neither of these formulations would extend a fundamental right to homosexuals to engage in acts of consensual sodomy. Proscriptions against that conduct have ancient roots. . . . Sodomy was a criminal offense at common law and was forbidden by the laws of the original thirteen States when they ratified the Bill of Rights. In 1868, when the Fourteenth Amendment was ratified, all but 5 of the 37 States in the Union had criminal sodomy laws. In fact, until 1961, all 50 States outlawed sodomy, and today, 24 States and the District of Columbia continue to provide criminal penalties for sodomy performed in private and between consenting adults. . . . Against this background, to claim that a right to engage in such conduct is "deeply rooted in this Nation's history and tradition" or "implicit in the concept of ordered liberty" is, at best, facetious.

Nor are we inclined to take a more expansive view of our authority to discover new fundamental rights imbedded in the Due Process Clause. The Court is most vulnerable and comes nearest to illegitimacy when it deals with judge-made constitutional law having little or no cognizable roots in the language or design of the Constitution. That this is so was painfully demonstrated by the face-off between the Executive and the Court in the 1930's, which resulted in the repudiation of much of the substantive gloss that the Court had placed on the Due Process Clauses of the Fifth and Fourteenth Amendments. There should be, therefore, great resistance to expand the substantive reach of those Clauses, particularly if it requires redefining the category of rights deemed to be fundamental. Otherwise, the Judiciary necessarily takes to itself further authority to govern the country without express constitutional authority. The claimed right pressed on us today falls far short of overcoming this resistance.

Respondent, however, asserts that the result should be different where the homosexual conduct occurs in the privacy of the home. He relies on *Stanley v. Georgia,* . . . where the Court held that the First Amendment prevents conviction for possessing and reading obscene material in the privacy of one's home: "If the First Amendment means anything, it means that a State has no business telling a man, sitting alone in his house, what books he may read or what films he may watch." . . .

Stanley did protect conduct that would not have been protected outside the home, and it partially prevented the enforcement of state obscenity laws; but the decision was firmly grounded in the First Amendment. The right pressed upon us here has no similar support in the text of the Constitution, and it does not qualify for recognition under the prevailing principles for construing the Fourteenth Amendment. Its limits are also difficult to discern. Plainly enough, otherwise illegal conduct is not always immunized whenever it occurs in the home. Victimless crimes, such as the possession and use of illegal drugs, do not escape the law where they are committed at home. *Stanley* itself recognized that its holding offered no protection for the possession in the home of drugs, firearms, or stolen goods. . . . And if respondent's submission is limited to the voluntary sexual conduct between consenting adults, it would be difficult, except by fiat, to limit the claimed right to homosexual conduct while leaving exposed to prosecution adultery, incest, and other sexual crimes even though they are committed in the home. We are unwilling to start down that road.

Even if the conduct at issue here is not a fundamental right, respondent asserts that there must be a rational basis for the law and that there is none in this case other than the presumed belief of a majority of the electorate in Georgia that homosexual sodomy is immoral and unacceptable. This is said to be an inadequate rationale to support the law. The law, however, is constantly based on notions of morality, and if all laws representing essentially moral choices are to be invalidated under the Due Process Clause, the courts will be very busy indeed. Even respondent makes no such claim, but insists that majority sentiments about the morality of homosexuality should be declared inadequate. We do not agree, and are unpersuaded that the sodomy laws of some 25 States should be invalidated on this basis.

Accordingly, the judgment of the Court of Appeals is
Reversed.

Chief Justice Burger, concurring.

I join the Court's opinion, but I write separately to underscore my view that in constitutional terms there is no such thing as a fundamental right to commit homosexual sodomy.

As the Court notes, . . . the proscriptions against sodomy have very "ancient roots." Decisions of individuals relating to homosexual conduct have been subject to state intervention throughout the history of Western civilization. Condemnation of those practices is firmly rooted in Judaeo-Christian moral and ethical standards. Homosexual sodomy was a capital crime under Roman law. . . . During the English Reformation when powers of the ecclesiastical courts were transferred to the King's Courts, the first English statute criminalizing sodomy was passed. . . . Blackstone described "the infamous *crime against nature*" as an offense of "deeper malignity" than rape, a heinous act "the very mention of which is a disgrace to human nature," and "a crime not

fit to be named." . . . The common law of England, including its prohibition of sodomy, became the received law of Georgia and the other Colonies. In 1816 the Georgia Legislature passed the statute at issue here, and that statute has been continuously in force in one form or another since that time. To hold that the act of homosexual sodomy is somehow protected as a fundamental right would be to cast aside millennia of moral teaching.

This is essentially not a question of personal "preferences" but rather of the legislative authority of the State. I find nothing in the Constitution depriving a State of the power to enact the statute challenged here. . . .

Justice Blackmun, with whom Justice Brennan, Justice Marshall, and Justice Stevens join, dissenting.

This case is no more about "a fundamental right to engage in homosexual sodomy," as the Court purports to declare, . . . than *Stanley v. Georgia* . . . was about a fundamental right to watch obscene movies, or *Katz v. United States,* . . . was about a fundamental right to place interstate bets from a telephone booth. Rather, this case is about "the most comprehensive of rights and the right most valued by civilized men," namely, "the right to be let alone." . . .

The statute at issue, . . . denies individuals the right to decide for themselves whether to engage in particular forms of private, consensual sexual activity. The Court concludes that [the statute] is valid essentially because "the laws of . . . many States . . . still make such conduct illegal and have done so for a very long time." . . . But the fact that the moral judgments expressed by statutes like . . . [the Georgia statute] may be " 'natural and familiar . . . ought not to conclude our judgment upon the question whether statutes embodying them conflict with the Constitution of the United States.' " . . . Like Justice Holmes, I believe that "[i]t is revolting to have no better reason for a rule of law than that so it was laid down in the time of Henry IV. It is still more revolting if the grounds upon which it was laid down have vanished long since, and the rule simply persists from blind imitation of the past." . . . I believe we must analyze Hardwick's claim in the light of the values that underlie the constitutional right to privacy. If that right means anything, it means that, before Georgia can prosecute its citizens for making choices about the most intimate aspects of their lives, it must do more than assert that the choice they have made is an " 'abominable crime not fit to be named among Christians.' " . . .

In its haste to reverse the Court of Appeals and hold that the Constitution does not "confe[r] a fundamental right upon homosexuals to engage in sodomy," . . . the Court relegates the actual statute being challenged to a footnote and ignores the procedural posture of the case before it. A fair reading of the statute and of the complaint clearly reveals that the majority has distorted the question this case presents.

. . . [T]he Court's almost obsessive focus on homosexual activity is particularly hard to justify in light of the broad language Georgia has used. Unlike the Court, the Georgia Legislature has not proceeded on the assumption that homosexuals are so different from other citizens that their lives may be controlled in a way that would not be tolerated if it limited the choices of those other citizens. . . . Rather, Georgia has provided that "[a] person commits the offense of sodomy when he performs or submits to any sexual act involving the sex organs of one person and the mouth or anus of another." . . . The sex or status of the persons who engage in the act is irrelevant as a matter of state law. In fact, to the extent I can discern a legislative purpose for Georgia's 1968 enactment . . . that purpose seems to have been to broaden the coverage of the law to reach heterosexual as well as homosexual activity. I therefore see no basis for the Court's decision to treat this case . . . solely on the grounds that it prohibits homosexual activity. Michael Hardwick's standing may rest in significant part on Georgia's apparent willingness to enforce against homosexuals a law it seems not to have any desire to enforce against heterosexuals. . . . But his claim that . . . [the Georgia statute] involves an unconstitutional intrusion into his privacy and his right of intimate association does not depend in any way on his sexual orientation. . . .

"Our cases long have recognized that the Constitution embodies a promise that a certain private sphere of individual liberty will be kept largely beyond the reach of government." . . . In construing the right to privacy, the Court has proceeded along two somewhat distinct, albeit complementary, lines. First, it has recognized a privacy interest with reference to certain *decisions* that are properly for the individual to make. . . . Second, it has recognized a privacy interest with reference to certain *places* without regard for the particular activities in which the individuals who occupy them are engaged. . . . The case before us implicates both the decisional and the spatial aspects of the right to privacy.

The Court concludes today that none of our prior cases dealing with various decisions that individuals are entitled to make free of governmental interference "bears any resemblance to the claimed constitutional right of homosexuals to engage in acts of sodomy that is asserted in this case." . . . While it is true that these cases may be characterized by their connection to protection of the family, . . . the Court's conclusion that they extend no further than this boundary ignores the warning in *Moore v. East Cleveland,* . . . against "clos[ing] our eyes to the basic reasons why certain rights associated with the family have been accorded shelter under the Fourteenth Amendment's Due Process Clause." We protect those rights not because they contribute, in some direct and material way, to the general public welfare, but because they form so central a part of an individual's life. "[T]he concept of privacy embodies the 'moral fact that a person belongs to himself and not others nor to society as a whole.' " . . . And so we protect the decision whether to marry precisely because marriage "is an association that promotes a way of life, not causes; a harmony in living, not political faiths; a bilateral loyalty, not commercial or social projects." . . . We protect the decision whether to have a child because parenthood alters so dramatically an individual's self-definition, not because of demographic considerations or the Bible's command to be fruitful and multiply. . . . And we protect the family because it contributes so powerfully to the happiness of individuals, not because of a preference for stereotypical households. . . . The Court recognized in *Roberts* . . . that the "ability independently to define one's identity that is central to any concept of liberty" cannot truly be exercised in a vacuum; we all depend on the "emotional enrichment from close ties with others."

Only the most willful blindness could obscure the fact that sexual intimacy is "a sensitive, key relationship of human existence, central to family life, community welfare, and the development of human personality," . . . The fact that individuals define themselves in a significant way through their intimate sexual relationships with others suggests, in a Nation as diverse as ours, that there may be many "right" ways of conducting those relationships, and that much of the richness of a relationship will come from the freedom an individual has to *choose* the form and nature of these intensely personal bonds. . . .

In a variety of circumstances we have recognized that a necessary corollary of giving individuals freedom to choose how to conduct their lives is acceptance of the fact that different individuals will make different choices. For example, in holding that the clearly important state interest in public education should give way to a competing claim by the Amish to the effect that extended formal schooling threatened their way of life, the Court declared: "There can be no assumption that today's majority is 'right' and the Amish and others like them are 'wrong.' A way of life that is odd or even erratic but interferes with no rights or interests of others is not to be condemned because it is different." . . . The Court claims that its decision today merely refuses to recognize a fundamental right to engage in homosexual sodomy; what the Court really has refused to recognize is the fundamental interest all individuals have in controlling the nature of their intimate associations with others.

The behavior for which Hardwick faces prosecution occurred in his own home, a place to which the Fourth Amendment attaches special significance. The Court's treatment of this aspect of the case is symptomatic of its overall refusal to consider the broad principles that have informed our treatment of privacy in specific cases. Just as the right to privacy is more than the mere aggregation of a number

of entitlements to engage in specific behavior, so too, protecting the physical integrity of the home is more than merely a means of protecting specific activities that often take place there. Even when our understanding of the contours of the right to privacy depends on "reference to a 'place,' " . . . "the essence of a Fourth Amendment violation is 'not the breaking of [a person's] doors, and the rummaging of his drawers,' but rather is 'the invasion of his indefeasible right of personal security, personal liberty and private property.' " . . .

The Court's interpretation of the pivotal case of *Stanley v. Georgia,* . . . is entirely unconvincing. *Stanley* held that Georgia's undoubted power to punish the public distribution of constitutionally unprotected, obscene material did not permit the State to punish the private possession of such material. According to the majority here, *Stanley* relied entirely on the First Amendment, and thus, it is claimed, sheds no light on cases not involving printed materials. . . . But that is not what *Stanley* said. Rather, the *Stanley* Court anchored its holding in the Fourth Amendment's special protection for the individual in his home:

> " 'The makers of our Constitution undertook to secure conditions favorable to the pursuit of happiness. They recognized the significance of man's spiritual nature, of his feelings and of his intellect. They knew that only a part of the pain, pleasure and satisfactions of life are to be found in material things. They sought to protect Americans in their beliefs, their thoughts, their emotions and their sensations.'
>
> "These are the rights that appellant is asserting in the case before us. He is asserting the right to read or observe what he pleases—the right to satisfy his intellectual and emotional needs in the privacy of his own home." . . . quoting *Olmstead v. United States* . . .

The central place that *Stanley* gives Justice Brandeis' dissent in *Olmstead,* a case raising *no* First Amendment claim, shows that *Stanley* rested as much on the Court's understanding of the Fourth Amendment as it did on the

First. Indeed, in *Paris Adult Theatre I v. Slaton,* . . . the Court suggested that reliance on the Fourth Amendment not only supported the Court's outcome in *Stanley* but actually was *necessary* to it: "If obscene material unprotected by the First Amendment in itself carried with it a 'penumbra' of constitutionally protected privacy, this Court would not have found it necessary to decide *Stanley* on the narrow basis of the 'privacy of the home,' which was hardly more than a reaffirmation that 'a man's home is his castle.' " . . . "The right of the people to be secure in their . . . houses," expressly guaranteed by the Fourth Amendment, is perhaps the most "textual" of the various constitutional provisions that inform our understanding of the right to privacy, and thus I cannot agree with the Court's statement that "[t]he right pressed upon us here has no . . . support in the text of the Constitution," . . . Indeed, the right of an individual to conduct intimate relationships in the intimacy of his or her own home seems to me to be the heart of the Constitution's protection of privacy. . . .

. . . Petitioner asserts that the acts made criminal by the statute may have serious adverse consequences for "the general public health and welfare," such as spreading communicable diseases or fostering other criminal activity. . . . Inasmuch as this case was dismissed by the District Court on the pleadings, it is not surprising that the record before us is barren of any evidence to support petitioner's claim. In light of the state of the record, I see no justification for the Court's attempt to equate the private, consensual sexual activity at issue here with the "possession in the home of drugs, firearms, or stolen goods," . . . to which *Stanley* refused to extend its protection. . . . None of the behavior so mentioned in *Stanley* can properly be viewed as "[v]ictimless," . . . : drugs and weapons are inherently dangerous, . . . and for property to be "stolen," someone must have been wrongfully deprived of it. Nothing in the record before the Court provides any justification for finding the activity forbidden [by the Georgia statute] to be physically dangerous, either to the persons engaged in it or to others.

The core of petitioner's defense . . . however, is that respondent and others who engage in the conduct prohibited . . . interfere with Georgia's exercise of the " 'right of the Nation and of the States to maintain a decent society,' " . . . Essentially, petitioner argues, and the Court agrees, that the fact that the acts described . . . "for hundreds of years, if not thousands, have been uniformly condemned as immoral" is a sufficient reason to permit a State to ban them today. . . .

I cannot agree that either the length of time a majority has held its convictions or the passions with which it defends them can withdraw legislation from this Court's scrutiny. . . . As Justice Jackson wrote so eloquently . . . "we apply the limitations of the Constitution with no fear that freedom to be intellectually and spiritually diverse or even contrary will disintegrate the social organization. . . . [F]reedom to differ is not limited to things that do not matter much. That would be a mere shadow of freedom. The test of its substance is the right to differ as to things that touch the heart of the existing order." . . . It is precisely because the issue raised by this case touches the heart of what makes individuals what they are that we should be especially sensitive to the rights of those whose choices upset the majority.

The assertion that "traditional Judeo-Christian values proscribe" the conduct involved, . . . cannot provide an adequate justification. . . . That certain, but by no means all, religious groups condemn the behavior at issue gives the State no license to impose their judgments on the entire citizenry. The legitimacy of secular legislation depends instead on whether the State can advance some justification for its law beyond its conformity to religious doctrine. . . . Thus, far from buttressing his case, petitioner's invocation of Leviticus, Romans, St. Thomas Aquinas, and sodomy's heretical status during the Middle Ages undermines his suggestion that [the Georgia statute] represents a legitimate use of secular coercive power. A State can no more punish private behavior because of religious intolerance than it can punish such behavior because of racial animus. "The Constitution cannot control such prejudices, but neither can it tolerate them. Private biases may be outside the reach of the law, but the law cannot, directly or indirectly, give them effect." . . . No matter how uncomfortable a certain group may make the majority of this Court, we have held that "[m]ere public intolerance or animosity cannot constitutionally justify the deprivation of a person's physical liberty." . . .

. . . Reasonable people may differ about whether particular sexual acts are moral or immoral, but "we have ample evidence for believing that people will not abandon morality, will not think any better of murder, cruelty and dishonesty, merely because some private sexual practice which they abominate is not punished by the law." . . . Petitioner and the Court fail to see the difference between laws that protect public sensibilities and those that enforce private morality. Statutes banning public sexual activity are entirely consistent with protecting the individual's liberty interest in decisions concerning sexual relations: the same recognition that those decisions are intensely private which justifies protecting them from governmental interference can justify protecting individuals from unwilling expo-

sure to the sexual activities of others. But the mere fact that intimate behavior may be punished when it takes place in public cannot dictate how States can regulate intimate behavior that occurs in intimate places. . . .

This case involves no real interference with the rights of others, for the mere knowledge that other individuals do not adhere to one's value system cannot be a legally cognizable interest, . . . let alone an interest that can justify invading the houses, hearts, and minds of citizens who choose to live their lives differently.

. . . I can only hope that . . . the Court soon will reconsider its analysis and conclude that depriving individuals of the right to choose for themselves how to conduct their intimate relationships poses a far greater threat to the values most deeply rooted in our Nation's history than tolerance of nonconformity could ever do. Because I think the Court today betrays those values, I dissent.

Suggestions for Further Reading

Anthologies

Batchelor, E. *Homosexuality and Ethics*. New York: Pilgrims Press, 1980.

Marmor, J. *Homosexual Behavior*. New York: Basic Books, 1980.

Basic Concepts

"Survey on the Constitutional Right to Privacy in the Context of Homosexual Activity." *Miami Law Review* (1986), pp. 521–657.

Alternative Views

du Mas, F. *Gay Is Not Good*. Nashville: Thomas Nelson Publishers, 1979.

Friedman, R. *Male Homosexuality*. New Haven: Yale University Press, 1988.

Harrigan, J. *Homosexuality: The Test Case for Christian Ethics*. New Jersey: Paulist Press, 1988.

Malloy, E. *Homosexuality and the Christian Way of Life*. Lanham: University Press of America, 1981.

Mohr, R. *Gays/Justice*. New York: Columbia University Press, 1988.

Animal Liberation and Environmental Concern

Basic Concepts

The problem of animal liberation and environmental concern has begun to attract widespread public attention. Beginning with the 1973 publication of Peter Singer's article, "Animal Liberation," in the *New York Review of Books,* followed by the publication two years later of his book of the same title, people have become increasingly concerned with two of the most serious forms of animal exploitation: animal experimentation and factory farming.

Animal experimentation is a big business, involving 60 to 100 million animals a year. Two experiments alone—the rabbit-blinding Draize eye test and the LD50 toxicity test designed to find the lethal dose for 50 percent of a sample of animals—cause the deaths of more than 5 million animals per year in the United States alone. In factory farming, millions of animals are raised in such a way that their short lives are dominated by pain and suffering. Veal calves are put in narrow stalls and tethered with a chain so that they cannot turn around, lie down comfortably, or groom themselves. They are fed a totally liquid diet to promote rapid weight gain, and they are given no water because thirsty animals eat more than those who drink water.

In recent years, environmental concern has focused on a myriad of problems from acid rain to the destruction of the rain forests and the ozone layer. For example, the acidity of rainfall over the northeastern United States has quadrupled since 1900. Moreover, just last year, an estimated 12,350 square miles of Brazilian rain forest—an area larger than Belgium—was reduced to ashes, and over the past decade, ozone levels over Antarctica have diminished by 50 percent. In many cases, resolving these problems will require extensive programs and international cooperation. For example, in the Montreal protocol of 1987, dozens of nations agreed to cut their chlorofluorocarbon emissions (which are thought to be the major cause of ozone depletion) in half by the end of the century, and several countries and the major chlorofluorocarbon manufacturers have more recently announced their intentions to eliminate the chemicals by that deadline.

At the most general level, the problem of animal liberation and environmental concern raises the question of what should be our policies for treating animals and preserving the environment, or alternatively, what is the moral status of nonhuman living things. One possible answer is that nonhuman living things have no independent moral status at all, but that their moral status depends completely on the impact they have on human welfare. Another possible answer is that nonhuman living things have an independent moral status such that their welfare has to be weighed against, and at least sometimes outweigh, considerations of human welfare.

Obviously, supporters of animal liberation favor the view that animals have independent moral status, but they disagree as to the grounds for this independent moral status. Some claim that animals have independent moral status because taking their welfare into account would maximize overall utility. Others claim that the independent moral status of animals rests on a nonutilitarian foundation.

This conflict among supporters of animal liberation reflects a general conflict among utilitarians and nonutilitarians with respect to a wide range of practical problems (see the General Introduction to this anthology). However, with respect to this particular problem, supporters of animal liberation cannot rely on some form of social contract theory to reach an acceptable resolution because most animals are incapable of forming either an actual or hypothetical contract with human beings for the purpose of securing their common welfare. Social contract theory, however, is only a means to a goal, which is to achieve a fair resolution of morally relevant interests. Consequently, if nonhuman living things do have morally relevant interests, then to achieve that goal some means other than social contract theory will have to be employed.

This is not to say that social contract theory is not useful for achieving a fair resolution of conflicts when only human interests pertain. In fact, it would seem that a fair resolution of conflicts among human and nonhuman interests would mirror a fair resolution of conflicts among purely human interests. For example, if a utilitarian (or a nonutilitarian) resolution were fair when only human interests are taken into account, a utilitarian (or a nonutilitarian) resolution would seem to be fair when both human and nonhuman interests are considered.

With respect to environmental concern, supporters do not agree that all nonhuman living things have independent moral status. Those who maintain that only sentient beings have independent moral status attempt to ground human concern for other living things on the impact they have on the welfare of sentient beings. Accordingly, to resolve the problem of animal liberation and environmental concern, we must determine which living beings have independent moral status and what sort of justification best accounts for that status.

Alternative Views

In Selection 47, Peter Singer argues for the independent moral status of animals by comparing the bias against animals, which he calls "speciesism," with biases against blacks and women. According to Singer, the grounds we have for opposing racism and sexism are also grounds for opposing speciesism because all forms of discrimination run counter to the principle of equal consideration. Racists violate this principle by giving greater weight to the interests of members of their own race in cases of conflict; sexists violate this principle by favoring the interests of their own specific sex; and speciesists violate this principle by allowing the interests of their own species to override the greater interests of other species.

Animals have interests, Singer maintains, because they have a capacity for suffering and enjoyment. According to the principle of equal consideration, there is no justification for regarding the pain animals feel as less important than the same amount of pain (or pleasure) humans feel. As for the practical requirements of this view, Singer contends that we cannot go astray if we give the same respect to the lives of animals that we give to the lives of humans at a similar mental level. In

the end, Singer thinks, this requires a utilitarian weighing of both human and animal interests.

In the next selection, R. G. Frey argues that utilitarianism does not ultimately support a strong case for animal rights for several reasons. First of all, by Singer's own omission, it is permissible to eat farm animals, typically cattle and sheep, that are reared and killed without suffering. Second, Singer's objection to the suffering inflicted on animals in factory farms can be overcome by reforming the practices used on such farms rather than by requiring that we become vegetarians. Third, a radical turn to vegetarianism would probably result in the elimination of most farm animals as we know them because they certainly cannot survive in the wild. This would seriously disrupt and/or eliminate many industries and social practices, resulting in significant disutility.

Responding to these criticisms in an article in the *New York Review of Books*, Singer makes two points. He first claims that adopting vegetarianism would improve people's general health, eliminate Third World poverty, and create new and beneficial industries and social practices. Second, Singer claims that in political campaigning, opposition to the current techniques of factory farming is not taken seriously unless one is also a committed vegetarian. According to Singer, only vegetarians can silence that invariable objection to reforming our treatment of animals: But don't you eat them?

Nevertheless, Singer's response turns on the political effectiveness of being a vegetarian and the effects vegetarianism would have on human welfare rather than its effects on animal welfare. However, it is in terms of animal welfare that the case for animal rights must ultimately be made.

In Selection 49, Paul W. Taylor argues that all living beings have independent moral status. He grounds his view on two central claims: (1) that each individual organism is a teleological center of life, pursuing its own good in its own way, and (2) that whether we are concerned with standards of merit or with the concept of inherent worth, there is no grounds for believing that humans by their very nature are superior to other species. Taylor's argument for his second claim is similar to the argument used in the General Introduction to support morality against rational egoism. Both claim that their view represents a non-question-begging solution.

The main difficulty with Taylor's view concerns how we are to weigh human welfare against the good of other living beings if we were to grant that human beings are not superior to other species. In a later book that develops the argument of this essay, Taylor distinguishes between basic and nonbasic interest of living beings, but because he doesn't hold that the basic interests always have priority over nonbasic interests, it is difficult to know how decisions should be made when there is conflict between human and nonhuman interests.

In opposition to Taylor, Bernard E. Rollin (Selection 50) argues that only sentient beings have independent moral status. According to Rollin, the ground for that status is that what we do to such beings matters to them. But while denying that other living things have any independent moral status, Rollin contends that they still have instrumental value that in some cases is enormous. For that reason, he thinks that the argument against their destruction can be extremely strong.

But why should we agree with Rollin that the fact that what we do to sentient beings matters to them supports the view that sentient beings have independent moral status, and not agree with Taylor that the fact that each individual organism is a teleological center of life pursuing its own good in its own way supports the view that all living things have independent moral status? Obviously, we wouldn't need to answer this question if the instrumental value of nonsentient living beings is so great that in valuing them instrumentally we would be required to treat them in just the same way we would if we thought they had independent moral status. Unfortunately, we can hardly expect this coincidence of interest to obtain.

Practical Applications

The next two selections come from the only federal law in the United States pertaining to the treatment of animals. The provisions of the Animal Welfare Act pertain only to the transportation of animals and the treatment of animals for research and experimentation. The act does not mention the treatment of animals in factory farms. The amendments to the Animal Welfare Act passed in 1985 represent a considerable strengthening of the original act. Specifically, the amendments call for a national data bank that will list the results of all animal experiments and thus prevent needless repetition. All laboratories using live animals are also required, under the amendments, to set up animal-care committees and submit to annual inspections. Facilities housing dogs must let them exercise, and those housing primates must provide for their "psychological well-being." Unfortunately, the implementation of these amendments is currently held up by the federal budget office.

In *Tennessee Valley Authority* v. *Hill* (Selection 53), the issue before the Supreme Court is whether the Endangered Species Act of 1973 prohibited the completion of a dam whose operation would destroy the habitat of the snail darter, an endangered species, despite the fact that the dam was virtually completed and that Congress continued to appropriate large sums of money to the project even after the congressional appropriations committees were appraised of the project's apparent impact upon the survival of the snail darter. The Court held that the Endangered Species Act did prohibit the completion of the dam because the language of the act and the history that led to its passage required that its provisions be applied without exceptions. Immediately after this Supreme Court decision, however, Congress amended the Endangered Species Act to provide a "review" process designed to relax the protection accorded endangered species in some circumstances. In the case of the snail darter, protection was relaxed because it was possible to transport snail darters to another river. It was also discovered that additional populations of snail darters existed in other rivers. An interesting sidelight to this case, however, was that an economic study conducted in the interim revealed that the construction of the dam was a pork barrel project. Its benefits to the Tennessee economy could have been achieved in much less costly ways while at the same time preserving the natural state of the river.

Although there is no denying that existing federal laws protecting animals and the environment are quite limited in scope, it seems clear that any solution to the problem of an-imal liberation and environmental concern that gives independent moral status to all living beings, or even just to all sentient beings will, if implemented, have a significant impact on the way we live and work and, accordingly, on how we will be able to solve the other practical problems discussed in this anthology.

47. All Animals Are Equal

Peter Singer

Peter Singer begins his defense of animal liberation by comparing the bias against animals with biases against blacks and women. According to Singer, all of these forms of discrimination violate the principle of equal consideration. According to this principle, there is no justification for regarding the pain or pleasure that animals feel as less important than the same amount of pain or pleasure felt by humans.

"Animal Liberation" may sound more like a parody of other liberation movements than a serious objective. The idea of "The Rights of Animals" actually was once used to parody the case for women's rights. When Mary Wollstonecraft, a forerunner of today's feminists, published her *Vindication of the Rights of Women* in 1792, her views were widely regarded as absurd, and before long an anonymous publication appeared entitled *A Vindication of the Rights of Brutes*. The author of this satirical work (now known to have been Thomas Taylor, a distinguished Cambridge philosopher) tried to refute Mary Wollstonecraft's arguments by showing that they could be carried one stage further. If the argument for equality was sound when applied to women, why should it not be applied to dogs, cats, and horses? The reasoning seemed to hold for these "brutes" too; yet to hold that brutes had rights was manifestly absurd; therefore the reasoning by which this conclusion had been reached must be unsound, and if unsound when applied to brutes, it must also be un-

From *Animal Liberation* (New York: New York Review, 1975), pp. 1–22. Reprinted by permission of Peter Singer.

sound when applied to women, since the very same arguments had been used in each case.

In order to explain the basis of the case for the equality of animals, it will be helpful to start with an examination of the case for the equality of women. Let us assume that we wish to defend the case for women's rights against the attack by Thomas Taylor. How should we reply?

One way in which we might reply is by saying that the case for equality between men and women cannot validly be extended to nonhuman animals. Women have a right to vote, for instance, because they are just as capable of making rational decisions about the future as men are; dogs, on the other hand, are incapable of understanding the significance of voting, so they cannot have the right to vote. There are many other obvious ways in which men and women resemble each other closely, while humans and animals differ greatly. So, it might be said, men and women are similar beings and should have similar rights, while humans and nonhumans are different and should not have equal rights.

The reasoning behind this reply to Taylor's analogy is correct up to a point, but it does not go far enough. There *are* important differences between humans and other animals, and these differences must give rise to *some* differences in the rights that each have. Recognizing this obvious fact, however, is no barrier to the case for extending the basic principle of equality to nonhuman animals. The differences that exist between men and women are equally undeniable, and the supporters of Women's Liberation are aware that these differences may give rise to different rights. Many feminists hold that women have the right to an abortion on request. It does not follow that since these same feminists are campaigning for equality between men and women they must support the right of men to have abortions too. Since a man cannot have an abortion, it is meaningless to talk of his right to have one. Since a dog can't vote, it is meaningless to talk of its right to vote. There is no reason why either Women's Liberation or Animal Liberation should get involved in such nonsense. The extension of the basic principle of equality from one group to another does not imply that we must treat both groups in exactly the same way, or grant exactly the same rights to both groups. Whether we should do so will depend on the nature of the members of the two groups. The basic principle of equality does not require equal or identical *treatment;* it requires equal *consideration.* Equal consideration for different beings may lead to different treatment and different rights.

So there is a different way of replying to Taylor's attempt to parody the case for women's rights, a way that does not deny the obvious differences between humans and nonhumans but goes more deeply into the question of equality and concludes by finding nothing absurd in the idea that the basic principle of equality applies to so-called "brutes." At this point such a conclusion may appear odd; but if we examine more deeply the basis on which our opposition to discrimination on grounds of race or sex ultimately rests, we will see that we would be on shaky ground if we were to demand equality for blacks, women, and other groups of oppressed humans while denying equal consideration to nonhumans. To make this clear we need to see, first, exactly why racism and sexism are wrong.

When we say that all human beings, whatever their race, creed, or sex, are equal, what is it that we are asserting? Those who wish to defend hierarchical, inegalitarian societies have often pointed out that by whatever test we choose it simply is not true that all humans are equal. Like it or not we must face the fact that humans come in different shapes and sizes; they come with different moral capacities, different intellectual abilities, different amounts of benevolent feeling and sensitivity to the needs of others, different abilities to communicate effectively, and different capacities to experience pleasure and pain. In short, if the demand for equality were based on the actual equality of all human beings, we would have to stop demanding equality.

Still, one might cling to the view that the demand for equality among human beings is based on the actual equality of the different races and sexes. Although, it may be said, humans differ as individuals there are no differences between the races and sexes *as such.* From the mere fact that a person is black or a woman we cannot infer anything about that person's intellectual or moral capacities. This, it may be said, is why racism and sexism are wrong. The white racist claims that whites are superior to blacks, but this is false—although there are differences among individuals, some blacks are superior to some whites in all of the capacities and abilities that could conceivably be relevant. The opponent of sexism would say the same: a person's sex is no guide to his or her abilities, and this is why it is unjustifiable to discriminate on the basis of sex.

The existence of individual variations that cut across the lines of race or sex, however, provides us with no defense at all against a more sophisticated opponent of equality, one who proposes that, say, the interests of all those with IQ scores below 100 be given less consideration than the interests of those with ratings over 100. Perhaps those scoring below the mark would, in this society, be made the slaves of those scoring higher. Would a hierarchical society of this sort really be so much better than one based on race or sex? I think not. But if we tie the moral principle of equality to the factual equality of the different races or sexes, taken as a whole, our opposition to racism and sexism does not provide us with any basis for objecting to this kind of in-egalitarianism.

There is a second important reason why we ought not to base our opposition to racism and sexism on any kind of actual equality, even the limited kind that asserts that variations in capacities and abilities are spread evenly between the different races and sexes: we can have no absolute guarantee that these capacities and abilities really are distributed evenly, without regard to race or sex, among human beings. So far as actual abilities are concerned there do seem to be certain measurable differences between both races and sexes. These differences do not, of course, appear in each case, but only when averages are taken. More important still, we do not yet know how much of these differences is really due to the different genetic endowments of the different races and sexes, and how much is due to poor schools, poor housing, and other factors that are the result of past and continuing discrimination. Perhaps all of the important differences will eventually prove to be environmental rather than genetic. Anyone opposed to racism and sexism will certainly hope that this will be so, for it will make the task of ending discrimination a lot easier; nevertheless it would be dangerous to rest the case against racism and sexism on the belief that all significant differences are environmental in origin. The opponent of, say, racism who takes this line will be unable to avoid conceding that *if* differences in ability do after all prove to have some genetic connection with race, racism would in some way be defensible.

Fortunately there is no need to pin the case for equality to one particular outcome of a scientific investigation. The appropriate response to those who claim to have found evidence of genetically based differences in ability between the races or sexes is not to stick to the belief that the genetic explanation must be wrong, whatever evidence to the contrary may turn up: instead we should make it quite clear that the claim to equality does not depend on intelligence, moral capacity, physical strength, or similar matters of fact. Equality is a moral idea, not an assertion of fact. There is no logically compelling reason for assuming that a factual difference in ability between two people justifies any difference in the amount of consideration we give to their needs and interests. *The principle of the equality of human beings is not a description of an alleged actual equality among humans: it is a prescription of how we should treat humans.*

Jeremy Bentham, the founder of the reforming utilitarian school of moral philosophy, incorporated the essential basis of moral equality into his system of ethics by means of the formula: "Each to count for one and none for more than one." In other words, the interests of every being affected by an action are to be taken into account and given the same weight as the like interests of any other being. A later utilitarian, Henry Sidgwick, put the point in this way: "The good of any one individual is of no more importance, from the point of view (if I may say so) of the Universe, than the good of any other." More recently the leading figures in contemporary moral philosophy have shown a great deal of agreement in specifying as a fundamental presupposition of their moral theories some similar requirement which operates so as to give everyone's interests equal consideration—although these writers generally cannot agree on how this requirement is best formulated.[1]

It is an implication of this principle of equality that our concern for others and our readiness to consider their interests ought not to depend on what they are like or on what abilities they may possess. Precisely what this concern or consideration requires us to do may vary according to the characteristics of those affected by what we do: concern for the well-being of a child growing up in America would require that we teach him to read; concern for the well-being of a pig may require no more than that we leave him alone with other pigs in a place where there is adequate food and room to run freely. But the basic element—the taking into account of the interests of the being, whatever those interests may be —must, according to the principle of equality, be extended to all beings, black or white, masculine or feminine, human or nonhuman.

Thomas Jefferson, who was responsible for writing the principle of the equality of men into the American Declaration of Independence, saw this point. It led him to oppose slavery even though he was unable to free himself fully from his slaveholding background. He wrote in a letter to the author of a book that emphasized the notable intellectual achievements of Negroes in order to refute the then common view that they had limited intellectual capacities:

> Be assured that no person living wishes more sincerely than I do, to see a complete refutation of the doubts I have myself entertained and expressed on the grade of understanding allotted to them by nature, and to find that they are on a par with ourselves . . . but whatever be their degree of talent it is no measure of their rights. Because Sir Isaac Newton was superior to others in understanding, he was not therefore lord of the property or person of others.[2]

Similarly when in the 1850s the call for women's rights was raised in the United States a remarkable black feminist named Sojourner Truth made the same point in more robust terms at a feminist convention:

> . . . they talk about this thing in the head; what do they call it? ["Intellect," whispered someone near by.] That's it. What's that got to do with women's rights or Negroes' rights? If my cup won't hold but a pint and yours holds a quart, wouldn't you be mean not to let me have my little half-measure full?[3]

It is on this basis that the case against racism and the case against sexism must both ultimately rest; and it is in accordance with this principle that the attitude that we may call "speciesism," by analogy with racism, must also be condemned. Speciesism—the word is not an attractive one, but I can think of no better term—is a prejudice or attitude of bias toward the interests of members of one's own species and against those of members of other species. It should be obvious that the fundamental objections to racism and sexism made by Thomas Jefferson and Sojourner Truth apply equally to speciesism. If possessing a higher

degree of intelligence does not entitle one human to use another for his own ends, how can it entitle humans to exploit nonhumans for the same purpose?[4]

Many philosophers and other writers have proposed the principle of equal consideration of interests, in some form or other, as a basic moral principle; but not many of them have recognized that this principle applies to members of other species as well as to our own. Jeremy Bentham was one of the few who did realize this. In a forward-looking passage written at a time when black slaves had been freed by the French but in the British dominions were still being treated in the way we now treat animals, Bentham wrote:

> The day *may* come when the rest of the animal creation may acquire those rights which never could have been withholden from them but by the hand of tyranny. The French have already discovered that the blackness of the skin is no reason why a human being should be abandoned without redress to the caprice of a tormentor. It may one day come to be recognized that the number of the legs, the villosity of the skin, or the termination of the *os sacrum* are reasons equally insufficient for abandoning a sensitive being to the same fate. What else is it that should trace the insuperable line? Is it the faculty of reason, or perhaps the faculty of discourse? But a full-grown horse or dog is beyond comparison a more rational, as well as a more conversable animal, than an infant of a day or a week or even a month, old. But suppose they were otherwise, what would it avail? The question is not, Can they *reason?* nor Can they *talk?* but, *Can they suffer?*[5]

In this passage Bentham points to the capacity for suffering as the vital characteristic that gives a being the right to equal consideration. The capacity for suffering—or more strictly, for suffering and/or enjoyment or happiness—is not just another characteristic like the capacity for language or higher mathematics. Bentham is not saying that those who try to mark "the insuperable line" that determines whether the interests of a being should be considered happen to have chosen the wrong characteristic. By saying that we must consider the interests of all beings with the capacity for suffering or enjoyment Bentham does not arbitrarily exclude from consideration any interests at all—as those who draw the line with reference to the possession of reason or language do. The capacity for suffering and enjoyment is *a prerequisite for having interests at all,* a condition that must be satisfied before we can speak of interests in a meaningful way. It would be nonsense to say that it was not in the interests of a stone to be kicked along the road by a schoolboy. A stone does not have interests because it cannot suffer. Nothing that we can do to it could possibly make any difference to its welfare. A mouse, on the other hand, does have an interest in not being kicked along the road, because it will suffer if it is.

If a being suffers there can be no moral justification for refusing to take that suffering into consideration. No matter what the nature of the being, the principle of equality requires that its suffering be counted equally with the like suffering—in so far as rough comparisons can be made—of any other being. If a being is not capable of suffering, or of experiencing enjoyment or happiness, there is nothing to be taken into account. So the limit of sentience (using the term as a convenient if not strictly accurate shorthand for the capacity to suffer and/or experience enjoyment) is the only defensible boundary of concern for the interests of others. To mark this boundary by some other characteristic like intelligence or rationality would be to mark it in an arbitrary manner. Why not choose some other characteristic, like skin color?

The racist violates the principle of equality by giving greater weight to the interests of members of his own race when there is a clash between their interests and the interests of those of another race. The sexist violates the principle of equality by favoring the interests of his own sex. Similarly the speciesist allows the interests of his own species to override the greater interests of members of other species. The pattern is identical in each case.

Most human beings are speciesists. The following chapters show that ordinary human be-

ings—not a few exceptionally cruel or heartless humans, but the overwhelming majority of humans—take an active part in, acquiesce in, and allow their taxes to pay for practices that require the sacrifice of the most important interests of members of other species in order to promote the most trivial interests of our own species.

There is, however, one general defense of the practices to be described in the next two chapters that needs to be disposed of before we discuss the practices themselves. It is a defense which, if true, would allow us to do anything at all to nonhumans for the slightest reason, or for no reason at all, without incurring any justifiable reproach. This defense claims that we are never guilty of neglecting the interests of other animals for one breathtakingly simple reason: they have no interests. Nonhuman animals have no interests, according to this view, because they are not capable of suffering. By this is not meant merely that they are not capable of suffering in all the ways that humans are—for instance, that a calf is not capable of suffering from the knowledge that it will be killed in six months time. That modest claim is, no doubt, true; but it does not clear humans of the charge of speciesism, since it allows that animals may suffer in other ways—for instance, by being given electric shocks, or being kept in small, cramped cages. The defense I am about to discuss is the much more sweeping, although correspondingly less plausible, claim that animals are incapable of suffering in any way at all; that they are, in fact, unconscious automata, possessing neither thoughts nor feelings nor a mental life of any kind.

Although, as we shall see in a later chapter, the view that animals are automata was proposed by the seventeenth-century French philosopher René Descartes, to most people, then and now, it is obvious that if, for example, we stick a sharp knife into the stomach of an unanesthetized dog, the dog will feel pain. That this is so is assumed by the laws in most civilized countries which prohibit wanton cruelty to animals. . . . Implausible as it is, though, for the sake of completeness this skeptical position must be discussed.

Do animals other than humans feel pain? How do we know? Well, how do we know if anyone, human or nonhuman, feels pain? We know that we ourselves can feel pain. We know this from the direct experiences of pain that we have when, for instance, somebody presses a lighted cigarette against the back of our hand. But how do we know that anyone else feels pain? We cannot directly experience anyone else's pain, whether that "anyone" is our best friend or a stray dog. Pain is a state of consciousness, a "mental event," and as such it can never be observed. Behavior like writhing, screaming, or drawing one's hand away from the lighted cigarette is not pain itself; nor are the recordings a neurologist might make of activity within the brain observations of pain itself. Pain is something that we feel, and we can only infer that others are feeling it from various external indications.

In theory, we *could* always be mistaken when we assume that other human beings feel pain. It is conceivable that our best friend is really a very cleverly constructed robot, controlled by a brilliant scientist so as to give all the signs of feeling pain, but really no more sensitive than any other machine. We can never know, with absolute certainty, that this is not the case. But while this might present a puzzle for philosophers, none of us has the slightest real doubt that our best friends feel pain just as we do. This is an inference, but a perfectly reasonable one, based on observations of their behavior in situations in which we would feel pain, and on the fact that we have every reason to assume that our friends are beings like us, with nervous systems like ours that can be assumed to function as ours do, and to produce similar feelings in similar circumstances.

If it is justifiable to assume that other humans feel pain as we do, is there any reason why a similar inference should be unjustifiable in the case of other animals?

Nearly all the external signs which lead us to infer pain in other humans can be seen in other species, especially the species most closely related to us—other species of mammals, and birds. Behavioral signs—writhing, facial contortions, moaning, yelping or other forms of calling, attempts to avoid the source of pain, appearance of fear at the prospect of its repetition, and so on—are present. In addition, we know that these animals have nervous systems very like ours, which respond physiologically as ours do when the animal is in circumstances in which we would feel pain: an initial rise of blood pressure, dilated pupils, perspiration, an increased pulse rate, and, if the stimulus continues, a fall in blood pressure. Although humans have a more developed cerebral cortex than other animals, this part of the brain is concerned with thinking functions rather than with basic impulses, emotions, and feelings. These impulses, emotions, and feelings are located in the diencephalon, which is well developed in many other species of animals, especially mammals and birds.[6]

We also know that the nervous systems of other animals were not artificially constructed to mimic the pain behavior of humans, as a robot might be artificially constructed. The nervous systems of animals evolved as our own did, and in fact the evolutionary history of humans and other animals, especially mammals, did not diverge until the central features of our nervous systems were already in existence. A capacity to feel pain obviously enhances a species' prospects of survival, since it causes members of the species to avoid sources of injury. It is surely unreasonable to suppose that nervous systems which are virtually identical physiologically, have a common origin and a common evolutionary function, and result in similar forms of behavior in similar circumstances should actually operate in an entirely different manner on the level of subjective feelings.

It has long been accepted as sound policy in science to search for the simplest possible explanation of whatever it is we are trying to explain. Occasionally it has been claimed that it is for this reason "unscientific" to explain the behavior of animals by theories that refer to the animal's conscious feelings, desires, and so on—the idea being that if the behavior in question can be explained without invoking consciousness or feelings, that will be the simpler theory. Yet we can now see that such explanations, when placed in the over-all context of the behavior of both human and nonhuman animals, are actually far more complex than their rivals. For we know from our own experience that explanations of our own behavior that did not refer to consciousness and the feeling of pain would be incomplete; and it is simpler to assume that the similar behavior of animals with similar nervous systems is to be explained in the same way than to try to invent some other explanation for the behavior of nonhuman animals as well as an explanation for the divergence between humans and nonhumans in this respect.

The overwhelming majority of scientists who have addressed themselves to this question agree. Lord Brain, one of the most eminent neurologists of our time, has said:

> I personally can see no reason for conceding mind to my fellow men and denying it to animals. . . . I at least cannot doubt that the interests and activities of animals are correlated with awareness and feeling in the same way as my own, and which may be, for aught I know, just as vivid.[7]

While the author of a recent book on pain writes:

> Every particle of factual evidence supports the contention that the higher mammalian vertebrates experience pain sensations at least as acute as our own. To say that they feel less because they are lower animals is an absurdity; it can easily be shown that many of their senses are far more acute than ours—visual acuity in certain birds, hearing in most wild animals, and touch in others; these animals depend more than we do today on the sharpest possible awareness of a hostile environment. Apart from the complexity of the cerebral cortex (which does not directly perceive pain) their nervous systems are almost identical to ours and their reactions to pain remarkably similar, though lacking (so far as we know) the philosophical and moral overtones. The emotional element is all too evident, mainly in the form of fear and anger.[8]

In Britain, three separate expert government committees on matters relating to animals have accepted the conclusion that animals feel pain. After noting the obvious behavioral evidence for this view, the Committee on Cruelty to Wild Animals said:

> . . . we believe that the physiological, and more particularly the anatomical, evidence fully justifies and reinforces the commonsense belief that animals feel pain.

And after discussing the evolutionary value of pain they concluded that pain is "of clear-cut biological usefulness" and this is "a third type of evidence that animals feel pain." They then went on to consider forms of suffering other than mere physical pain, and added that they were "satisfied that animals do suffer from acute fear and terror." In 1965, reports by British government committees on experiments on animals, and on the welfare of animals under intensive farming methods, agreed with this view, concluding that animals are capable of suffering both from straightforward physical injuries and from fear, anxiety, stress, and so on.[9]

That might well be thought enough to settle the matter; but there is one more objection that needs to be considered. There is, after all, one behavioral sign that humans have when in pain which nonhumans do not have. This is a developed language. Other animals may communicate with each other, but not, it seems, in the complicated way we do. Some philosophers, including Descartes, have thought it important that while humans can tell each other about their experience of pain in great detail, other animals cannot. (Interestingly, this once neat dividing line between humans and other species has now been threatened by the discovery that chimpanzees can be taught a language.)[10] But as Bentham pointed out long ago, the ability to use language is not relevant to the question of how a being ought to be treated—unless that ability can be linked to the capacity to suffer, so that the absence of a language casts doubt on the existence of this capacity.

This link may be attempted in two ways. First, there is a hazy line of philosophical thought, stemming perhaps from some doctrines associated with the influential philosopher Ludwig Wittgenstein, which maintains that we cannot meaningfully attribute states of consciousness to beings without language. This position seems to me very implausible. Language may be necessary for abstract thought, at some level anyway; but states like pain are more primitive, and have nothing to do with language.

The second and more easily understood way of linking language and the existence of pain is to say that the best evidence that we can have that another creature is in pain is when he tells us that he is. This is a distinct line of argument, for it is not being denied that a non-language-user conceivably *could* suffer, but only that we could ever have sufficient reason to *believe* that he is suffering. Still, this line of argument fails too. As Jane Goodall has pointed out in her study of chimpanzees, *In the Shadow of Man*, when it comes to the expressions of feelings and emotions language is less important than in other areas. We tend to fall back on nonlinguistic modes of communication such as a cheering pat on the back, an exuberant embrace, a clasp of the hands, and so on. The basic signals we use to convey pain, fear, anger, love, joy, surprise, sexual arousal, and many other emotional states are not specific to our own species.[11]

Charles Darwin made an extensive study of this subject, and the book he wrote about it, *The Expression of the Emotions in Man and Animals*, notes countless nonlinguistic modes of expression. The statement "I am in pain" may be one piece of evidence for the conclusion that the speaker is in pain, but it is not the only possible evidence, and since people sometimes tell lies, not even the best possible evidence.

Even if there were stronger grounds for refusing to attribute pain to those who do not have a language, the consequences of this refusal might lead us to reject the conclusion. Human infants and young children are unable to use language. Are we to deny that a year-old child can suffer? If not, language cannot be crucial. Of course, most parents understand the responses of their children better than they understand the responses of other animals; but this is just a fact about the relatively greater knowledge that we have of our own species, and the greater contact we have with infants, as compared to animals. Those who have studied the behavior of other animals, and those who have pet animals, soon learn to understand their responses as well as we understand those of an infant, and sometimes better. Jane Goodall's account of the chimpan-

zees she watched is one instance of this, but the same can be said of those who have observed species less closely related to our own. Two among many possible examples are Konrad Lorenz's observations of geese and jackdaws, and N. Tinbergen's extensive studies of herring gulls.[12] Just as we can understand infant human behavior in the light of adult human behavior, so we can understand the behavior of other species in the light of our own behavior—and sometimes we can understand our own behavior better in the light of the behavior of other species.

So to conclude: there are no good reasons, scientific or philosophical, for denying that animals feel pain. If we do not doubt that other humans feel pain we should not doubt that other animals do so too.

Animals can feel pain. As we saw earlier, there can be no moral justification for regarding the pain (or pleasure) that animals feel as less important than the same amount of pain (or pleasure) felt by humans. But what exactly does this mean, in practical terms? To prevent misunderstanding I shall spell out what I mean a little more fully.

If I give a horse a hard slap across its rump with my open hand, the horse may start, but it presumably feels little pain. Its skin is thick enough to protect it against a mere slap. If I slap a baby in the same way, however, the baby will cry and presumably does feel pain, for its skin is more sensitive. So it is worse to slap a baby than a horse, if both slaps are administered with equal force. But there must be some kind of blow—I don't know exactly what it would be, but perhaps a blow with a heavy stick—that would cause the horse as much pain as we cause a baby by slapping it with our hand. That is what I mean by "the same amount of pain" and if we consider it wrong to inflict that much pain on a baby for no good reason then we must, unless we are speciesists, consider it equally wrong to inflict the same amount of pain on a horse for no good reason.

There are other differences between humans and animals that cause other complications. Normal adult human beings have mental capacities which will, in certain circumstances, lead them to suffer more than animals would in the same circumstances. If, for instance, we decided to perform extremely painful or lethal scientific experiments on normal adult humans, kidnaped at random from public parks for this purpose, every adult who entered a park would become fearful that he would be kidnaped. The resultant terror would be a form of suffering additional to the pain of the experiment. The same experiments performed on nonhuman animals would cause less suffering since the animals would not have the anticipatory dread of being kidnaped and experimented upon. This does not mean, of course, that it would be right to perform the experiment on animals, but only that there is a reason, which is *not* speciesist, for preferring to use animals rather than normal adult humans, if the experiment is to be done at all. It should be noted, however, that this same argument gives us a reason for preferring to use human infants—orphans perhaps—or retarded humans for experiments, rather than adults, since infants and retarded humans would also have no idea of what was going to happen to them. So far as this argument is concerned nonhuman animals and infants and retarded humans are in the same category; and if we use this argument to justify experiments on nonhuman animals we have to ask ourselves whether we are also prepared to allow experiments on human infants and retarded adults; and if we make a distinction between animals and these humans, on what basis can we do it, other than a barefaced—and morally indefensible—preference for members of our own species?

There are many areas in which the superior mental powers of normal adult humans make a difference: anticipation, more detailed memory, greater knowledge of what is happening, and so on. Yet these differences do not all point to greater suffering on the part of the normal human being. Sometimes an animal may suffer more because of his more limited understanding. If, for instance, we are taking prisoners in wartime we can explain to them that while they must submit to capture, search, and confinement they will not otherwise be harmed and will be set free at the conclusion of hostilities. If we capture a wild animal, however, we cannot explain that we are not threatening its life. A wild animal cannot distinguish an attempt to overpower and confine from an attempt to kill; the one causes as much terror as the other.

It may be objected that comparisons of the sufferings of different species are impossible to make, and that for this reason when the interests of animals and humans clash the principle of equality gives no guidance. It is probably true that comparisons of suffering between members of different species cannot be made precisely, but precision is not essential. Even if we were to prevent the infliction of suffering on animals only when it is quite certain that the interests of humans will not be affected to anything like the extent that animals are affected, we would be forced to make radical changes in our treatment of animals that would involve our diet, the farming methods we use, experimental procedures in many fields of science, our approach to wildlife and to hunting, trapping and the wearing of furs, and areas of entertainment like circuses, rodeos, and zoos. As a result, a vast amount of suffering would be avoided.

So far I have said a lot about the infliction of suffering on animals, but nothing about killing them. This omission has been deliberate. The application of the principle of equality to the infliction of suffering is, in theory at least, fairly straightforward. Pain and suffering are bad and should be prevented or minimized, irrespective of the race, sex, or species of the being that suffers. How bad a pain is depends on how intense it is and how long it lasts, but pains of the same intensity and duration are equally bad, whether felt by humans or animals.

The wrongness of killing a being is more complicated. I have kept, and shall continue to keep, the question of killing in the background because in the present state of human tyranny over other species the more simple, straightforward principle of equal consideration of pain or pleasure is a sufficient basis for identifying and protesting against all the major abuses of animals that humans practice. Nevertheless, it is necessary to say something about killing.

Just as most humans are speciesists in their readiness to cause pain to animals when they would not cause a similar pain to humans for the same reason, so most humans are speciesists in their readiness to kill other animals when they would not kill humans. We need to proceed more cautiously here, however, because people hold widely differing views about when it is legitimate to kill humans, as the continuing debates over abortion and euthanasia attest. Nor have moral philosophers been able to agree on exactly what it is that makes it wrong to kill humans, and under what circumstances killing a human being may be justifiable.

Let us consider first the view that it is always wrong to take an innocent human life. We may call this the "sanctity of life" view. People who take this view oppose abortion and euthanasia. They do not usually, however, oppose the killing of nonhumans—so perhaps it would be more accurate to describe this view as the "sanctity of *human* life" view.

The belief that human life, and only human life, is sacrosanct is a form of speciesism. To see this, consider the following example.

Assume that, as sometimes happens, an infant has been born with massive and irreparable brain damage. The damage is so severe that the infant can never be any more than a "human vegetable," unable to talk, recognize other people, act independently of others, or develop a sense of self-awareness. The parents of the infant, realizing that they cannot hope for any improvement in their child's condition and being in any case unwilling to spend, or ask the state to spend, the thousands of dollars that would be needed annually for proper care of the infant, ask the doctor to kill the infant painlessly.

Should the doctor do what the parents ask? Legally, he should not, and in this respect the law reflects the sanctity of life view. The life of every human being is sacred. Yet people who would say this about the infant do not object to the killing of nonhuman animals. How can they justify their different judgments? Adult chimpanzees, dogs, pigs, and many other species far surpass the brain-damaged infant in their ability to relate to others, act independently, be self-aware, and any other capacity that could reasonably be said to give value to life. With the most intensive care possible, there are retarded infants who can never achieve the intelligence level of a dog. Nor can we appeal to the concern of the infant's parents, since they themselves, in this imaginary

example (and in some actual cases), do not want the infant kept alive.

The only thing that distinguishes the infant from the animal, in the eyes of those who claim it has a "right to life," is that it is, biologically, a member of the species Homo sapiens, whereas chimpanzees, dogs, and pigs are not. But to use *this* difference as the basis for granting a right to life to the infant and not to the other animals is, of course, pure speciesism.* It is exactly the kind of arbitrary difference that the most crude and overt kind of racist uses in attempting to justify racial discrimination.

This does not mean that to avoid speciesism we must hold that it is as wrong to kill a dog as it is to kill a normal human being. The only position that is irredeemably speciesist is the one that tries to make the boundary of the right to life run exactly parallel to the boundary of our own species. Those who hold the sanctity of life view do this because while distinguishing sharply between humans and other animals they allow no distinctions to be made within our own species, objecting to the killing of the severely retarded and the hopelessly senile as strongly as they object to the killing of normal adults.

To avoid speciesism we must allow that beings which are similar in all relevant respects have a similar right to life—and mere membership in our own biological species cannot be a morally relevant criterion for this right. Within these limits we could still hold that, for instance, it is worse to kill a normal adult human, with a capacity for self-awareness, and the ability to plan for the future and have meaningful relations with others, than it is to kill a mouse, which presumably does not share

*I am here putting aside religious views, for example the doctrine that all and only humans have immortal souls, or are made in the image of God. Historically these views have been very important, and no doubt are partly responsible for the idea that human life has a special sanctity. Logically, however, these religious views are unsatisfactory, since a reasoned explanation of why it should be that all humans and no nonhumans have immortal souls is not offered. This belief too, therefore, comes under suspicion as a form of speciesism. In any case, defenders of the "sanctity of life" view are generally reluctant to base their position on purely religious doctrines, since these doctrines are no longer as widely accepted as they once were.

all of these characteristics; or we might appeal to the close family and other personal ties which humans have but mice do not have to the same degree; or we might think that it is the consequences for other humans, who will be put in fear of their own lives, that makes the crucial difference; or we might think it is some combination of these factors, or other factors altogether.

Whatever criteria we choose, however, we will have to admit that they do not follow precisely the boundary of our own species. We may legitimately hold that there are some features of certain beings which make their lives more valuable than those of other beings; but there will surely be some nonhuman animals whose lives, by any standards, are more valuable than the lives of some humans. A chimpanzee, dog, or pig, for instance, will have a higher degree of self-awareness and a greater capacity for meaningful relations with others than a severely retarded infant or someone in a state of advanced senility. So if we base the right to life on these characteristics we must grant these animals a right to life as good as, or better than, such retarded or senile humans.

Now this argument cuts both ways. It could be taken as showing that chimpanzees, dogs, and pigs, along with some other species, have a right to life and we commit a grave moral offense whenever we kill them, even when they are old and suffering and our intention is to put them out of their misery. Alternatively one could take the argument as showing that the severely retarded and hopelessly senile have no right to life and may be killed for quite trivial reasons, as we now kill animals.

Since the focus of this book is on ethical questions concerning animals and not on the morality of euthanasia I shall not attempt to settle this issue finally. I think it is reasonably clear, though, that while both of the positions just described avoid speciesism, neither is entirely satisfactory. What we need is some middle position which would avoid speciesism but would not make the lives of the retarded and senile as cheap as the lives of pigs and dogs now are, nor make the lives of pigs and dogs so sacrosanct that we think it wrong to put them out of hopeless misery. What we must do is bring nonhuman animals within our sphere of moral concern and cease to treat their lives as expendable for whatever trivial purposes we may have. At the same time, once we realize that the fact that a being is a member of our own species is not in itself enough to make it always wrong to kill that being, we may come to reconsider our policy of preserving human lives at all costs, even when there is no prospect of a meaningful life or of existence without terrible pain.

I conclude, then, that a rejection of speciesism does not imply that all lives are of equal worth. While self-awareness, intelligence, the capacity for meaningful relations with others, and so on are not relevant to the question of inflicting pain—since pain is pain, whatever other capacities, beyond the capacity to feel pain, the being may have—these capacities may be relevant to the question of taking life. It is not arbitrary to hold that the life of a self-aware being, capable of abstract thought, of planning for the future, of complex acts of communication, and so on, is more valuable than the life of a being without these capacities. To see the difference between the issues of inflicting pain and taking life, consider how we would choose within our own species. If we had to choose to save the life of a normal human or a mentally defective human, we would probably choose to save the life of the normal human; but if we had to choose between preventing pain in the normal human or the mental defective—imagine that both have received painful but superficial injuries, and we only have enough painkiller for one of them—it is not nearly so clear how we ought to choose. The same is true when we consider other species. The evil of pain is, in itself, unaffected by the other characteristics of the being that feels the pain; the value of life is affected by these other characteristics.

Normally this will mean that if we have to choose between the life of a human being and the life of another animal we should choose to save the life of the human; but there may be special cases in which the reverse holds true, because the human being in question does not have the capacities of a normal human being. So this view is not speciesist, although it may appear to be at first glance. The preference, in normal cases, for saving a human life over the life of an animal when a choice *has* to be made is a preference based on the characteristics that normal humans have, and not on the mere fact that they are members of our own species. This is why when we consider members of our own species who lack the characteristics of normal humans we can no longer say that their lives are always to be preferred to those of other animals. This issue comes up in a practical way in the following chapter. In general, though, the question of when it is wrong to kill (painlessly) an animal is one to which we need give no precise answer. As long as we remember that we should give the same respect to the lives of animals as we give to the lives of those humans at a similar mental level, we shall not go far wrong.

Notes

1. For Bentham's moral philosophy, see his *Introduction to the Principles of Morals and Legislation,* and for Sidgwick's see *The Methods of Ethics* (the passage quoted is from the seventh edition, p. 382). As examples of leading contemporary moral philosophers who incorporate a requirement of equal consideration of interests, see R. M. Hare, *Freedom and Reason* (New York: Oxford University Press, 1963) and John Rawls, *A Theory of Justice* (Cambridge: Harvard University Press, Belknap Press, 1972). For a brief account of the essential agreement on this issue between these and other positions, see R. M. Hare, "Rules of War and Moral Reasoning," *Philosophy and Public Affairs,* vol. 1, no. 2 (1972).

2. Letter to Henri Gregoire, February 25, 1809.

3. Reminiscences by Francis D. Gage, from Susan B. Anthony, *The History of Woman Suffrage,* vol. 1; the passage is to be found in the extract in Leslie Tanner, ed., *Voices from Women's Liberation* (New York: Signet, 1970).

4. I owe the term "speciesism" to Richard Ryder.

5. *Introduction to the Principles of Morals and Legislation,* chapter 17.

6. Lord Brain, "Presidential Address" in C. A. Keele and R. Smith, eds., *The Assessment of Pain in Men and Animals* (London: Universities Federation for Animal Welfare, 1962).

7. Ibid., p. 11.

8. Richard Serjeant, *The Spectrum of Pain* (London: Hart-Davis, 1969), p. 72.

9. See the reports of the Committee on Cruelty to Wild Animals (Command Paper 8268, 1951), paragraphs 36–42; the Departmental Committee on Experiments on Animals (Command Paper 2641, 1965), paragraphs 179–182; and the Technical Committee to Enquire into the Welfare of Animals Kept under Intensive Livestock Husbandry Systems (Command Paper 2836, 1965), paragraphs 26–28 (London: Her Majesty's Stationery Office).

10. One chimpanzee, Washoe, has been taught the sign language used by deaf people, and acquired a vocabulary of 350 signs. Another, Lana, communicates in structured sentences by pushing buttons on a special machine. For a brief account of Washoe's abilities, see Jane van Lawick-Goodall, *In the Shadow of Man* (Boston: Houghton Mifflin, 1971), pp. 252–254; and for Lana, see *Newsweek,* 7 January 1974, and *New York Times,* 4 December 1974.

11. *In the Shadow of Man,* p. 225; Michael Peters makes a similar point in "Nature and Culture," in Stanley and Roslind Godlovitch and John Harris, eds., *Animals, Men and Morals* (New York: Taplinger Publishing Co., 1972).

12. Konrad Lorenz, *King Solomon's Ring* (New York: T. Y. Crowell, 1952); N. Tinbergen, *The Herring Gull's World,* rev. ed. (New York: Basic Books, 1974).

48. Pain, Amelioration, and the Choice of Tactics

R. G. Frey

R. G. Frey argues that utilitarianism does not provide a strong case for animal rights because (1) some animals are already reared and killed without suffering, (2) factory farming could be reformed, and (3) the widespread practice of vegetarianism would cause great disutility.

The Argument and the Concerned Individual

If the pain food animals undergo and the period over which they undergo it were insignificant, then I suspect many people would not be unduly worried by factory farming, with the result that they might well either see no need for the argument from pain and suffering, or see it as a manifestation of an undue sensitivity. Either way, the chances of the argument serving as the vehicle of widespread dietary change would recede.

The above, however, is certainly not the picture of factory farming which Singer paints, which, whether one considers *Animal Liberation, Practical Ethics,* or (with James Mason) *Animal Factories,*[1] is in the blackest terms. As we saw in the last chapter, he thinks, and would have us think, of factory farming in terms of animals who 'are so crowded together and restricted in their movements that their lives seem to be more of a burden than a benefit to them'[2] and who 'do not have pleasant lives'.[3] His view is that these animals lead miserable lives, that, in short, the pain inflicted upon them is substantial and its duration prolonged.

The argument itself points the direction in which the meat-eater will try to move: since what is held to be wrong with the particular farming practices objected to is that they are

Abridged from *Rights, Killing and Suffering* (Oxford: Basil Blackwell, 1983), pp. 175–189. Reprinted by permission of R. G. Frey. Notes renumbered.

productive of pain, the meat-eater will, among other things, try to make improvements in and to find alternatives to these practices. It is by no means obvious that such improvements and alternatives are not to be had, so that the only remaining course is to abolish intensive farming. Nothing whatever in, say, *Animal Liberation* rules out such improvements and alternatives; thus, any conclusion to the effect that the only way to mitigate, reduce, or eliminate the pains of food animals is to abolish factory farming is simply not licensed by that book.

If we do think of factory farming as Singer would have us, then . . . vast numbers of intensively farmed food animals, such as cattle, cows, sheep, a great many hogs, some pigs, elude the argument from pain and suffering. For vast numbers of commercially-farmed animals lead lives which are not, on balance, miserable, nor are those methods of rearing which are held to produce misery in the cases of laying hens and veal calves used on all food animals. Singer concedes the point: he remarks that, for example, 'as long as sheep and cattle graze outdoors . . . arguments directed against factory farming do not imply that we should cease eating meat altogether'.[4]

Two things follow. First, even if the argument from pain and suffering were successful, it would demand only that we abstain from the flesh of those creatures leading miserable lives; and even if we did so, large-scale, technology-intensive, commercial farming would by no means disappear, since there are numerous food animals so farmed who do not lead miserable lives.

Second, the amelioration argument becomes applicable. The more animals that can be brought to lead pleasant lives, the more animals that escape the argument from pain and suffering and so may be eaten. A concerned individual, therefore, can perfectly consistently strive, not for the abolition of factory farming, but for improvements and alternative methods on factory farms, in order that the animals no longer lead, on balance, miserable lives. With this the case, factory farming could continue, consistently with the application of the argument to it.

In short, if the argument demands that we abstain from the flesh of creatures whose lives are a burden to them, then a perfectly consistent response from the concerned individual, besides pointing to the huge numbers of commercially-farmed as well as traditionally-farmed animals which escape the argument, is to do his best to reduce the misery incurred on factory farms. Thus, when Singer has us think of factory farms in terms of the quality of life being lived upon them (and remarks such as 'our society tolerates methods of meat production that confine sentient animals in cramped, unsuitable conditions for the entire duration of their lives'[5] leave little doubt that, at least for those animals covered by his argument, he regards the quality of their lives as very low), the task of the concerned individual is to improve the quality of the lives being lived on those farms. It is just not true, however, that the only way to do this, the only tactic available, is to abolish large-scale, commercial farming.

One can always insist, of course, that the quality of life of the commercially farmed animals in question (remember, vast numbers of such animals are not in question) will never rise high enough; but this sort of issue cannot be decided *a priori*. Precisely how high a quality of life must be reached before animals may be said to be leading pleasant lives is, as we have seen, a contentious and complex issue; but we may at least use as a benchmark the situation at present. As improvements in and alternatives to the particular farming practices objected to arise, we can reasonably regard the pain associated with these practices as diminishing, if the improvements and alternatives are of the sort our concerned individual is seeking.

We have here, then, two parties, the Singer vegetarian and the concerned individual, both of whom are concerned to reduce the pain and suffering involved in factory farming. The Singer vegetarian's way is to adopt vegetarianism; the concerned individual's way is, among other things, to seek improvements in and alternatives to those practices held to be the source of the pain and suffering in question.

Suffering: Miserable Life and Single Experience Views

Singer's remarks on suffering in farming are not always of the sort depicted in the previous section. In both *Animal Liberation* and *Practical Ethics*, he occasionally writes as if any amount of suffering whatever sufficed, in terms of his argument, to condemn some method of rearing animals for food. For instance, he remarks that his 'case against using animals for food is at its strongest when animals are made to lead miserable lives . . .',[6] with the implication that his argument applies even when food animals suffer on a few or even a single occasion. Again, of traditional livestock farming, he maintains that it involves suffering, even if one has on occasion to go to such things as the breaking up of herds in order to find it, and he remarks in *Animal Liberation,* of these and other aspects of traditional farming, that 'it is difficult to imagine how animals could be raised for food without suffering in any of these ways'.[7]

Passages such as these suggest that Singer believes his argument condemns any method of rearing animals for food which causes them any suffering, however transient, however low-level, indeed, which causes them even a single, isolated painful experience. When he speaks of the permissibility of eating only 'the flesh of animals reared and killed without suffering',[8] therefore, he might be taken to mean by 'without suffering', not suffering of an amount and duration short of that required to make a life miserable, but any suffering whatever, so that the permissibility claim extends only to animals who have not had a single painful experience, a single trace of suffering in being bred and killed for food. But if this is what he means, how can he allow, as we have seen that he does, that sheep and cattle (these he cites as examples only,[9] so there may well, even in his eyes, be others) escape his argument? For it seems extremely unlikely that sheep and cattle are reared for food without a single painful experience. So either he is inconsistent to allow these exceptions, because he is operating with something like the single experience view of suffering, or he consistently allows them, but only because he is operating with something like the miserable life view of suffering.

These two views of suffering plainly do not come to the same thing. In order to lead, on balance, a pleasant life, pain, even significant pain, need not be absent from that life; indeed, it can recur on a daily basis, provided it falls short of that quantity over that duration required to tip the balance in the direction of a miserable life. Certainly, isolated, painful experiences or, for that matter, painful interludes, cannot, without further argument, be said to produce a miserable life.

Singer's whole position is affected by this ambiguity, if not inconsistency, over suffering. For instance, one of the most important points he wants to make concerns the possibility of rearing animals painlessly:

> Whatever the theoretical possibilities of rearing animals without suffering may be, the fact is that the meat available from butchers and supermarkets comes from animals who did suffer while being reared. So we must ask ourselves, not: is it *ever* right to eat meat? but: is it right to eat *this* meat?[10]

In *Practical Ethics,* he says that the question is not 'whether animal flesh *could* be produced without suffering, but whether the flesh we are considering buying *was* produced without suffering'.[11] But he has already allowed that vegetarianism is not demanded of us with respect to sheep and beef cattle, precisely because they do not lead miserable lives; so how can he say of all meats that it is a fact 'that the meat available from butchers and supermarkets comes from animals who did suffer while being reared'? Again, there is a question of

consistency. The problem can be favourably resolved, of course, if Singer shifts from the miserable life view of suffering to something like the single experience view; for he can be reasonably certain that the meat on display in supermarkets, including that from sheep and beef cattle, has come from animals who have had at least one painful experience, in being reared for food.

Without this shift, Singer has difficulty in discouraging you from buying the meat in question. If you are standing before the meats from sheep and beef cattle in your supermarket, if you have read Singer's book, and if you put to yourself the question of whether the meats before you have come from animals who have suffered in the course of being reared for food, then, on the miserable life view of suffering, you may cite Singer's own works to justify your purchase of the meats. You have every reason to believe that sheep and beef cattle do not lead miserable lives and so escape his argument; you have no reason whatever to believe, of course, that commercially- and traditionally-farmed food animals of any sort have not suffered at least once at human hands.

We have here, then, two views of suffering and, accordingly, two views on the argument from pain and suffering of what counts as a morally unacceptable method of rearing animals for food. On one, a method is unacceptable if it so affects an animal's quality of life as to make it miserable. This is why Singer so often stresses confinement in cramped conditions: this has the effect, which isolated painful experiences or interludes do not, of converting a life from a benefit to a burden. This view of suffering is compatible, however, with farm animals experiencing pain. On the second view, a method of rearing is unacceptable if it produces any pain or suffering whatever, whether or not the animal's general quality of life is affected thereby.

This division over unacceptable methods has several obvious implications here. First, to see one's task as reducing suffering in commercial farming is on one view of suffering, at least in many cases, not really to the point. Since the reduction of suffering is nevertheless compatible with the presence of suffering, only if the method of reduction eliminates all suffering in rearing may reduction, on something like the single experience view, really be to the point. On the miserable life view, however, any reduction in suffering is *prima facie* to the point, since that view is concerned with the quality of life of animals. That is, though it is tempting to think one method of rearing more acceptable than another if it involves considerably less suffering, this is only true on the miserable life view, at least if the method which causes less suffering causes any suffering; for reduction in suffering is very likely to affect animals' quality of life. This is true of any attempt to reduce suffering in farming, whether it succeeds partially or wholly, since, extraordinary circumstances aside, any decrease in suffering represents an increase or a contributory factor to an increase in quality of life.

Second, a meat-eater will not respond to both views of suffering in the same way; in the case of the miserable life view, his response will be much more varied. Broadly speaking, there are the methods of rearing themselves and the animals, and the meat-eater will, for example, seek ever gradual reduction in suffering through, for example, ever better improvements in and alternatives to (very) painful methods and the development of new pain-preventing and pain-killing drugs. He will seek development on these fronts simultaneously. In the case of something like the single experience view, however, since it is unlikely that any improvements in or alternatives to present methods would not involve even a single painful experience, a single trace of suffering, there may seem little point in seeking continuous evolution in rearing methods, beyond, say, those initial measures which substantially improve on the methods under attack. Accordingly, the meat-eater will be forced to rely primarily on pain-preventing and pain-killing drugs, an area in which he will seek continuous technological advances.

There is also the further possibility of genetic engineering to consider, to which both John Rodman[12] and Michael Martin[13] have drawn attention. So far as something like the single experience view is concerned, genetic engineering would have to take the form of the development of food animals which lacked the ability to feel pain. Precisely how feasible

that is, I do not know; but given the incredible advances in genetic engineering during the past 30 years, it would be rash to dismiss the idea out of hand. On the miserable life view, however, nothing so dramatic is required; here, the development of animals who felt pain less intensively or who felt it only in some minimal sense or who felt it only above a certain threshold would, especially given evolution in rearing methods and pain-preventing and pain-killing drugs, suffice to ensure the animals did not have miserable lives.

Finally, though the single experience view may strike some readers as reflecting an undue sensitivity, I shall not pursue this claim; rather, I want to draw attention to a rather curious upshot of the view. If the only acceptable method of rearing animals for food is one free of even a single painful experience or trace of suffering, then it is hard to see why the same should not be said of pets. It is extremely unlikely, however, that any method of rearing and keeping pets could be entirely without pain and suffering; so if we must give up farming animals because there are no morally acceptable ways of doing so, then it would appear that we must give up rearing and keeping pets on the same ground. But if the only acceptable method of rearing animals, whether for food or companionship, is one free of all pain and suffering, then it is hard to see why the same should not be said of our own children. It is extremely unlikely, however, that any method of rearing children could be entirely without pain or suffering; so if we must give up farming animals because there are no morally acceptable methods of doing so, then it would appear that we must give up having children on the same ground.

On the other hand, if it is acceptable to rear children by painful methods, why is it unacceptable to rear food animals by painful methods? Nothing is gained by saying that the pain we inflict upon children is in order to benefit them (this, I think, is questionable anyway, a good portion of the time), whereas the pain we inflict upon food animals is in order to benefit ourselves, i.e., in order to eat them; for, so far, it has not been shown that it is wrong to benefit ourselves in this way, that the end of eating meat is immoral. Indeed, it was the infliction of pain that was to have shown this. Nor is anything gained by saying that, in the case of children, we at least seek, or, probably more accurately, ought to seek to rear them by methods as painless as we can devise, since the concerned individual I have been describing is quite prepared to consent to this in the case of animals. Nor will it do to say that the level of pain and suffering in food animals cannot be brought to a level commensurate with their leading pleasant lives; not only is one not entitled to legislate in this way on what is not a conceptual matter but it is also not at all obvious, if the concerned individual pursues evolution in rearing methods, drugs, and genetic engineering, that this claim is true.

It is tempting to say that the suffering of children is necessary whereas that of food animals is unnecessary, but it is not at all clear that this is the case. If there is no method of rearing children which is free of all suffering, and if there is no method of rearing animals for food or as pets which is free of all suffering, then the suffering in each case is necessary. If there were a way to rear children or to turn them into responsible, upright citizens without suffering, then it would be incumbent upon us to adopt it; and if there were a way of turning animals into food without suffering, it would be equally incumbent upon us to take it. Certainly, my concerned individual concurs in this; so, on this score, if the suffering in the one case is necessary, then so is it in the other. If we shift the terms of the argument to a different level, so that suffering is necessary *only if* it is inflicted in order for us to live, then the suffering in both cases is unnecessary. Just as I can live without meat, so I can live without children; they are as superfluous to my existence, to my carrying on living, as cars, houses, rose bushes, and pets. In this sense, then, if the only way to avoid unnecessary suffering in pets and food animals is to give them up entirely and cease breeding them, then it seems that we should give up having children for the same reason.

Now I am not suggesting that one cannot draw any differences among these cases; that would be silly. On something like the single experience view of suffering, however, the criterion of acceptability in rearing methods is pitched so high that we appear barred from rearing any feeling creature, including our own children. Readers may well believe, therefore, that we must cast our sights lower. To do so, however, is to settle for a criterion of acceptability which permits some suffering. Precisely how much will be a matter of dispute; but a strong contender for the criterion, in both man and beast, will be the miserable life view. This in turn makes the varied course advocated by the concerned individual into an option on all fours with Singer's option of vegetarianism.

The Concerned Individual's Tactic as a Response to the Argument

The concerned individual's tactic is a direct response to Singer's argument: it addresses itself precisely to what the argument from pain and suffering objects to in factory farming. Indeed, it arises directly out of the terms of that argument. This fact enables us to appreciate several further points about the two tactics before us.

First, someone who took *Animal Liberation* and Singer's argument seriously might maintain that what Singer has shown is not that it is wrong to eat meat but that it is wrong to rear and kill animals by (very) painful methods; and this same reader might very well go on to conclude, not that we must all become vegetarians, but rather that we must (a) strive to improve conditions on factory farms, to eradicate some of the devices and practices upon them, and to replace these devices and practices with more humane ones, (b) divert resources into the development of new and relatively painless methods of breeding, feeding, and killing animals, of new pain-preventing and pain-killing drugs, of new types of tranquillizers and sedatives, etc., and (c) seek further appropriate breakthroughs in genetic engineering. After all, as we have seen, if we could be practically certain that the meat before us did not come from an animal bred and/or killed by (very) painful methods, and if we ate the meat, then Singer's argument would provide no ground for complaint against us. Accordingly, why not seek to obtain that practical certainty? The problem would then be how to go about this, and the concerned individual's tactic arises as an option.

Once we see that the concerned individual's tactic arises out of the terms of Singer's argument, we are in a position to appreciate that, even if we take that argument in its own terms and take it seriously, vegetarianism is not the obvious conclusion to draw from it. The course advocated by the concerned individual could equally well be the conclusion drawn. One needs some further reason for picking the one tactic as opposed to the other.

Second, as the meat-eater's option flourishes, Singer's case for vegetarianism is progressively undercut. That case loses its applicability, as the amount and intensity of pain produced on factory farms diminish. In other words, his case for vegetarianism hinges upon the actual state of evolution in rearing methods, drugs, and genetic engineering: each development in these areas which reduces pain in farming undercuts Singer's position still further.

If it is true that pain in farming has been drastically reduced or eliminated, however, why should the erosion of his position bother Singer? Whether or not it bothers Singer, it certainly is going to bother countless other vegetarians. For the concerned individual's tactic envisages the continuation of meat-eating and, with (some) changed methods, intensive farming; and the whole point is that, under the conditions set out, the argument from pain and suffering is compatible with, and places no further barrier in the way of, these things.

Third, the meat-eater's option must be faced by all readers of *Animal Liberation* who feel the force of the argument from pain and suffering; *per se*, there is nothing about Singer's position which enables them to avoid a choice between the two tactics I have described. A concerned reader of *Animal Liberation* may well feel impelled by what he reads there about factory farming to take up the cudgels and seek among people at large for a commitment to evolution in rearing methods, drugs, and genetic engineering. Could he not thereby be said to be following the book's lesson, that what is seriously wrong is not eating meat but raising and killing animals by painful

methods? Certainly, this individual, who seeks the elimination of (very) painful devices and practices on factory farms and their replacement with more humane ones, who seeks technological advances on all fronts likely to be relevant to the diminution of pain in farming, and who actively tries to stir people up to commit themselves to these ends, is responding directly to Singer's message.

Accordingly, anyone convinced by Singer's argument, anyone convinced that we must reduce, if not eliminate, pain in farming faces a choice between the concerned individual's tactic and vegetarianism as the way to go about this. Neither tactic is *per se* more favoured than the other.

Attempts to Prejudice the Choice between Tactics

Finally, before turning to Singer's reasons for choosing vegetarianism as one's tactic for combating the pains of food animals, I want to consider two ways in which one might try at the outset to prejudice this choice in tactics between Singer and the concerned individual.

A Life Proper to Their Species

One way of trying to compromise the concerned individual's tactic involves a quite specific use of a very broad sense of pain or suffering.[14] It might be suggested, that is, that to deprive animals of the sort of life proper to their species is a form of pain or suffering in some broad sense, even if the means involved in carrying out this deprivation are, as the result of the concerned individual's option flourishing, so far as new rearing methods and new advances in technology are concerned, free of all pain or suffering in the narrow sense. Thus, even if the concerned individual's tactic was entirely successful in its aims, so long as some intensive methods of rearing were held to deprive some food animals of the sort of life proper to their species, it might be suggested that these animals would continue to have pain or suffering inflicted upon them.

Singer's argument from pain and suffering

takes these terms, in the light of the above distinction, in the narrow sense; and I myself do not find much value in inflating their extension, in the way the broad sense envisages.

So far as the concerned individual's tactic is concerned, one must not focus upon his concern with technology to the exclusion of his concern with improvements in and alternatives to some present rearing methods. Take confinement in cruelly narrow spaces, which is by far the most commonly cited reason not only for food animals' miserable lives but also, so it is claimed, for their not leading lives proper to their species: this is a cardinal instance where the concerned individual will seek improvements and alternatives. Already there is some movement in the right direction. For example, in perhaps the most widely cited case of abuse, veal calves, Quantock Veal, which dominates the British veal market, has introduced a new method of rearing these calves.[15] They are not kept alone but in groups of 30; they are not kept in narrow stalls with slatted bottoms but in straw-filled pens in which they can move around freely; they are not kept in darkness but in light; they are not fed an iron-deficient diet but can obtain iron-laced milk from automatic feeders at any time. In this particular case, too, Quantock Veal maintains that this method of rearing veal calves, particularly given the availability of the European Community's dairy surplus, is cheaper than the objectionable method. Plainly, a development of this sort is likely to have a profound, positive effect on the quality of veal calves' lives; as well, it moves to meet the claim that, under present conditions, veal calves are not allowed to lead lives proper to their species.

Or consider the other, major case of abuse commonly cited, laying hens: one development in this area has been the Aviary method. It does not confine hens in cages but allows them to roam freely in poultry sheds, as a result of which they can scratch, flap about, and exercise; they lay in nest boxes or shelves above the ground. So far as I know, debeaking forms no part of the method. This development is not the end of evolution in rearing laying hens, but it seems a beginning.

I give these two examples as instances of the sorts of developments the concerned in-

dividual will favour, but I do not pretend either that they are the end of the process of evolution or that they are representative of recent developments as a whole in intensive farming. Rather, they are but two sorts of developments for which the concerned individual must lobby and work, examples of the kinds of evolution in rearing methods for which he must press.

It may be objected, however, that while the concerned individual is pressing for such developments and for advances in technology, food animals are still suffering. But so they are on the other tactic, vegetarianism.

If you face up to the choice of tactics I have been delineating, and you opt for vegetarianism, you would be wrong to think the suffering of food animals is going to come to a halt. In fact, of course, you are going to be left waiting for a sufficient number of others to make a similar choice, in order to give your act any efficacy whatever on the rearing of food animals. And, clearly, you are in for a long wait: even as the number of vegetarians in the United States has grown, the amount of meat consumed there has reached even more colossal heights. It was estimated in December, 1979, that meat consumption in the United States would amount to 214.4 pounds per person during 1980.[16] For a more homely example, a single hamburger establishment in Oxford reported in mid-1981 that it had, since it had opened only six or seven years previously, sold more than 5½ million hamburgers. That is a single establishment, in a single, relatively small city, with a host of fast-food and other restaurants. In facing up to the decision before you, you know beyond doubt that, if you decide in favour of vegetarianism, food animals are going to continue to suffer.[17] On this score, you have no real basis for choosing one tactic over the other.

In sum, evolution in rearing methods seems likely to meet the objection that some methods do not permit some food animals to lead lives proper to their species, if only because improvements in and alternatives to these methods can be sought specifically on this basis. And this moves to meet another objection: it might be charged that the concerned individual's tactic is uncharitable to food animals because it only tries to relieve and not abolish their pains; but this is not true. While the concerned individual does want to relieve animal pain, his response to that pain is varied and includes, through his stress on evolution in rearing methods, the search for improvements in and alternatives to precisely those rearing methods held to be the primary source of the pain in question.

I am also unhappy with this first attempt to prejudice the choice between tactics on another count as well. This has to do with the expression 'the sort of life proper to their species'.

The contemporary *penchant* for studying animals in the wild, in order to find out what they are really like, and, therefore, what sort of life is proper to their respective species, cannot be indulged here, since virtually none of our food animals are found in the wild. Beef, ham, pork, chicken, lamb, mutton, and veal all come from animals who are completely our own productions, bred by us in ways we select to ends we desire. Indeed, the gene pools of these creatures of ours have been manipulated by us to a point today where we can in a great many respects produce the type and strain of creature we want,[18] and the amount of research presently going on in this area is enormous. My point is this: it is a mistake to use expressions like 'the sort of life proper to their species' as if this sort of life were itself immune to technological advance; for by manipulating the gene pools of food animals, by varying our drugs and breeding practices, and by having funded research for progressive advances in all these areas, we already breed these animals to a sort of life which to their bred species—there is no other—is proper.

For example, chickens have been bred with weak leg and wing muscles and with shorter necks, both to reduce their mobility and so to help fatten them and to reduce the sheer amount of each chicken which cannot be turned into food. Even a variation in the size of their bones can now be bred into them. In a word, the descendants of these bred chickens have had bred out of them many of the traits which food producers have wanted eliminated, and they are characterized by reduced mobility, a larger appetite, increased lethargy,

significantly increased (or decreased) size, etc. We have manipulated them to this end, and we are carrying on research in this area, funded by major food interests, government organizations, international bodies, and universities, at an accelerated pace. Thus, one very recent development has been a featherless chicken, for use in warm climates. In the southern United States, for example, plumed birds succumb to the heat at a sufficient rate to be a significant cost to farmers, and the featherless bird has in part been developed to meet this problem.[19] (Developments to meet specific problems are increasingly commonplace. For example, cows have a slightly longer gestation period than women, which has meant that they can have only one calf a year; farmers have long wanted more. A procedure has now been developed, which involves the use of multiple ovulation hormones, artificial insemination, and the non-surgical implantation of fertilized eggs in other cows, to solve this problem.)

What sort of life is proper to these chickens? One cannot appeal to chickens in the wild or 'non-developed' chickens for an answer, since there are none; chickens are, to repeat, developments or productions of our own, produced in order to satisfy the fast-food chains and the demands of our Sunday lunches and school picnics. But if one asks what sort of life is proper to 'developed' chickens, we get the above answer. Or are we to turn back the clock and say that the sort of life proper to chickens is the sort they enjoyed when, say, they were first introduced into the United States, long before the first of the developmental farms and any thought of mass-producing them arose? Unless we artificially select some time as that time which reveals to us what chickens are really like, to ask 'What is it in the nature of chickens to be like?' is to ask a question the answer to which must be framed in the light of 'developed' chickens and of technological change.

Now the manipulation of animal gene pools to the extent that we have long since affected the very species of animal in question may well be repugnant to many, and I can easily imagine it being condemned as tampering with nature (and, through nature, with our kith and kin) or with God's handiwork. But I do not really see how it can be condemned on the grounds of inflicting pain and suffering, unless the extension of these terms is simply bloated, not merely beyond anything Singer envisages, but beyond any reasonable degree. There does not seem to be much difference, in fact, between the animal and human cases in this regard: much of the genetic research being conducted with respect to human beings, including experiments involving determination of sex and number of children, test-tube breeding, cloning, and eliminating an extra Y chromosome in males, is widely condemned; but no one condemns it on the ground of inflicting pain and suffering. . . .

Valuing Suffering but Not Life

A second way of trying to compromise the concerned individual's tactic is, in a quite specific way, to try to reduce it to absurdity. The concerned individual seeks to relieve, minimize, and eliminate the pains of food animals but continues to eat meat; it is tempting to portray him, therefore, as valuing animal suffering but not valuing animal life, and then, on the basis of this portrayal, to force him to draw the unpalatable conclusion that, since every animal is going to suffer at some time in its life, he ought now to exterminate all animals painlessly.[20]

I do not myself think well of this argument, which I believe Michael Martin has shown how to answer;[21] but, I contend, if it works against anyone, it works against Singer.

The difficulty with the argument, apart from the very obvious fact that the concerned individual is in no way whatever committed to giving animal life a value of zero, is that, in typically simplistic fashion, it makes it appear that minimizing animal suffering is the only factor applicable to the situation. This is obviously false. For example, to destroy all animals now would result in financial collapse of the meat markets, in financial ruin for food producers and those in related and support industries, in massive unemployment in these industries as well as among farmers, in financial loss to rail and road haulage firms, in a substantial loss in television, newspaper, and

magazine advertising revenues, with consequent effect upon the media's viability and profitability, and so on. Here, in quite mercenary terms, is one good reason why the concerned individual will not exterminate all animals. It is the effects upon human beings and their interests, financial and otherwise, which are here held to outweigh minimizing animal suffering through total extermination or are held at least to be applicable to the situation. Other factors come to mind with equal facility. To kill all animals now would mean the collapse of all experimentation upon animals for human benefit, would depopulate our zoos, which so many children and adults enjoy visiting, and would deprive countless lonely people of their companions. Here, it is human well-being and enjoyment which are held to outweigh minimizing animal suffering through total extermination, or are held at least to be applicable to the situation.

I must stress again, however, that the concerned individual is not compelled to give animal life *no value whatever;* all he has to do is to give human interests, human well-being, and human enjoyment the same or a higher value than minimizing animal suffering through complete extermination.

I do not, then, think much of this argument. But what is little recognized, is that, if the argument applies to anyone, it applies to Singer. His case for vegetarianism, as we have seen, turns exclusively upon minimizing animal pain and suffering, and not in the least upon the value of animal life, which, for the purposes of his case, he is prepared to allow to be anything you like, including zero. Again, he openly endorses the view that a genuine concern for the pains of animals demands that we become vegetarians, without in the least endorsing a view about the value of animal life demanding that we become vegetarians. Pain alone is the basis of his case, and its diminution, minimization, and elimination is his goal. Surely, if anyone must now envisage the complete extermination of animals, because of a concern with the minimization of their suffering, if anyone is forced to conclude that all animals should now be painlessly eliminated, it is Singer?

I am not concerned here to go into possible

ways in which Singer might resist this conclusion, except to emphasize that, if they begin even partially to include or make reference to those already sketched, he will be using human interests, well-being, and enjoyment to justify restraint in slaughtering animals, a surprising result in his case.

Notes

1. Peter Singer and James Mason, *Animal Factories*, New York, Crown Publishers Inc., 1980.

2. Peter Singer, 'Killing humans and killing animals', p. 149.

3. Peter Singer, *Practical Ethics*, p. 105.

4. Ibid., p. 56.

5. Ibid., p. 55.

6. Ibid.

7. Peter Singer, *Animal Liberation*, p. 165.

8. Ibid.

9. 'These arguments do not take us all the way to a vegetarian diet, since some animals, for instance sheep and beef cattle, still graze freely outdoors' (Peter Singer, *Practical Ethics*, p. 56).

10. Peter Singer, *Animal Liberation*, p. 165 (italics in original).

11. Peter Singer, *Practical Ethics*, pp. 56–7 (italics in original).

12. John Rodman, 'The liberation of nature?', *Inquiry*, vol. 20, 1977, pp. 90 ff, 103 ff, 112ff.

13. Michael Martin, 'A critique of moral vegetarianism', *Reason Papers No. 3*, Fall 1976, pp. 16, 18, 20.

14. See, e.g., John Benson, 'Duty and the beast', *Philosophy*, vol. 53, 1978, p. 532.

15. See Hugh Clayton, 'Veal farmers aim to erase the stigma of cruelty', *The Times*, 8 May 1980; Ena Kendall, ' "Welfare" for veal calves', *Observer*, 4 May 1980.

16. See Sue Shellenbarger, 'Pork Gains on Beef as Meat Choice in U.S.', *International Herald Tribune*, December 23, 1979.

17. In the next chapter, I take up Singer's recent statement that he envisages (his argument working over) a considerable period of time in bringing a halt to the meat industry. Had this statement appeared in *Animal Liberation* alongside the picture of the effects of becoming vegetarians sketched there, I think readers might have found it at odds with that picture.

18. See Rodman, 'The liberation of nature', pp. 90–1; Martin, 'A critique of moral vegetarianism', pp. 18, 20; Benson, 'Duty and the beast', p. 531.

19. See, for example, 'Plucky US poultry experts breed featherless fowl for better eating', *International Herald Tribune*, 28 December 1979.

20. See A. Linzey, *Animal Rights* (London, SCM Press, 1976), pp. 29 ff; and R. Godlovitch, 'Animals and morals', in S. and R. Godlovitch, J. Harris, (eds), *Animals, Men and Morals* (London, Gollancz, 1971), pp. 167 ff.

21. Michael Martin, 'A critique of moral vegetarianism', pp. 31–2.

49. The Ethics of Respect for Nature

Paul W. Taylor

According to Paul W. Taylor, the ethics of respect for nature is made up of three elements: a belief system, an ultimate moral attitude, and a set of rules of duty and standards of character. The belief system is said to justify the adoption of the attitude of respect for nature, which in turn requires a set of rules and standards of character. Two central elements of the belief system are (1) that each individual organism is a teleological center of life, pursuing its own good in its own way, and (2) that whether we are concerned with standards of merit or with the concept of inherent worth, the claim that humans by their very nature are superior to other species is groundless.

Human-Centered and Life-Centered Systems of Environmental Ethics

In this paper I show how the taking of a certain ultimate moral attitude toward nature, which I call "respect for nature," has a central place in the foundations of a life-centered system of environmental ethics. I hold that a set of moral norms (both standards of character and rules of conduct) governing human treatment of the natural world is a rationally grounded set if and only if, first, commitment to those norms is a practical entailment of adopting the attitude of respect for nature as an ultimate moral attitude, and second, the adopting of that attitude on the part of all rational agents can itself be justified. When the basic characteristics of the attitude of respect for nature are made clear, it will be seen that a life-centered system of environmental ethics need not be holistic or organicist in its conception of the kinds of entities that are deemed the appropriate objects of moral concern and consideration. Nor does such a system require that the concepts of ecological homeostasis, equilibrium, and integrity provide us with

From "The Ethics of Respect for Nature," *Environmental Ethics* (1986), pp. 197–218. Reprinted by permission of the publisher. Notes renumbered.

normative principles from which could be derived (with the addition of factual knowledge) our obligations with regard to natural ecosystems. The "balance of nature" is not itself a moral norm, however important may be the role it plays in our general outlook on the natural world that underlies the attitude of respect for nature. I argue that finally it is the good (well-being, welfare) of individual organisms, considered as entities having inherent worth, that determines our moral relations with the Earth's wild communities of life.

In designating the theory to be set forth as life-centered, I intend to contrast it with all anthropocentric views. According to the latter, human actions affecting the natural environment and its nonhuman inhabitants are right (or wrong) by either of two criteria: they have consequences which are favorable (or unfavorable) to human well-being, or they are consistent (or inconsistent) with the system of norms that protect and implement human rights. From this human-centered standpoint it is to humans and only to humans that all duties are ultimately owed. We may have responsibilities *with regard to* the natural ecosystems and biotic communities of our planet, but these responsibilities are in every case based on the contingent fact that our treatment of those ecosystems and communities of life can further the realization of human values and/or human rights. We have no obligation to promote or protect the good of nonhuman living things, independently of this contingent fact.

A life-centered system of environmental ethics is opposed to human-centered ones precisely on this point. From the perspective of a life-centered theory, we have prima facie moral obligations that are owed to wild plants and animals themselves as members of the Earth's biotic community. We are morally bound (other things being equal) to protect or promote their good for *their* sake. Our duties to respect the integrity of natural ecosystems, to preserve endangered species, and to avoid environmental pollution stem from the fact that these are ways in which we can help make it possible for wild species populations to achieve and maintain a healthy existence in a natural state. Such obligations are due those living things out of recognition of their inherent worth. They are entirely additional to and independent of the obligations we owe to our fellow humans. Although many of the actions that fulfill one set of obligations will also fulfill the other, two different grounds of obligation are involved. Their well-being, as well as human well-being, is something to be realized *as an end in itself*.

If we were to accept a life-centered theory of environmental ethics, a profound reordering of our moral universe would take place. We would begin to look at the whole of the Earth's biosphere in a new light. Our duties with respect to the "world" of nature would be seen as making prima facie claims upon us to be balanced against our duties with respect to the "world" of human civilization. We could no longer simply take the human point of view and consider the effects of our actions exclusively from the perspective of our own good.

The Good of a Being and the Concept of Inherent Worth

What would justify acceptance of a life-centered system of ethical principles? In order to answer this it is first necessary to make clear the fundamental moral attitude that underlies and makes intelligible the commitment to live by such a system. It is then necessary to examine the considerations that would justify any

rational agent's adopting that moral attitude.

Two concepts are essential to the taking of a moral attitude of the sort in question. A being which does not "have" these concepts, that is, which is unable to grasp their meaning and conditions of applicability, cannot be said to have the attitude as part of its moral outlook. These concepts are, first, that of the good (well-being, welfare) of a living thing, and second, the idea of an entity possessing inherent worth. I examine each concept in turn.

(1) Every organism, species population, and community of life has a good of its own which moral agents can intentionally further or damage by their actions. To say that an entity has a good of its own is simply to say that, without reference to any *other* entity, it can be benefited or harmed. One can act in its overall interest or contrary to its overall interest, and environmental conditions can be good for it (advantageous to it) or bad for it (disadvantageous to it). What is good for an entity is what "does it good" in the sense of enhancing or preserving its life and well-being. What is bad for an entity is something that is detrimental to its life and well-being.[1]

We can think of the good of an individual nonhuman organism as consisting in the full development of its biological powers. Its good is realized to the extent that it is strong and healthy. It possesses whatever capacities it needs for successfully coping with its environment and so preserving its existence throughout the various stages of the normal life cycle of its species. The good of a population or community of such individuals consists in the population or community maintaining itself from generation to generation as a coherent system of genetically and ecologically related organisms whose average good is at an optimum level for the given environment. (Here *average good* means that the degree of realization of the good of *individual organisms* in the population or community is, on average, greater than would be the case under any other ecologically functioning order of interrelations among those species populations in the given ecosystem.)

The idea of a being having a good of its own, as I understand it, does not entail that the being must have interests or take an interest in what affects its life for better or for worse. We can act in a being's interest or contrary to its interest without its being interested in what we are doing to it in the sense of wanting or not wanting us to do it. It may, indeed, be wholly unaware that favorable and unfavorable events are taking place in its life. I take it that trees, for example, have no knowledge or desires or feelings. Yet is is undoubtedly the case that trees can be harmed or benefited by our actions. We can crush their roots by running a bulldozer too close to them. We can see to it that they get adequate nourishment and moisture by fertilizing and watering the soil around them. Thus we can help or hinder them in the realization of their good. It is the good of trees themselves that is thereby affected. We can similarly act so as to further the good of an entire tree population of a certain species (say, all the redwood trees in a California valley) or the good of a whole community of plant life in a given wilderness area, just as we can do harm to such a population or community.

When construed in this way, the concept of a being's good is not coextensive with sentience or the capacity for feeling pain. William Frankena has argued for a general theory of environmental ethics in which the ground of a creature's being worthy of moral consideration is its sentience. I have offered some criticisms of this view elsewhere, but the full refutation of such a position, it seems to me, finally depends on the positive reasons for accepting a life-centered theory of the kind I am defending in this essay.[2]

It should be noted further that I am leaving open the question of whether machines—in particular, those which are not only goal-directed, but also self-regulating—can properly be said to have a good of their own.[3] Since I am concerned only with human treatment of wild organisms, species populations, and communities of life as they occur in our planet's natural ecosystems, it is to those entities alone that the concept "having a good of its own" will here be applied. I am not denying that other living things, whose genetic origin and environmental conditions have been produced, controlled, and manipulated by humans for human ends, do have a good of their own in the same sense as do wild plants and animals. It is not my purpose in this essay, however,

to set out or defend the principles that should guide our conduct with regard to their good. It is only insofar as their production and use by humans have good or ill effects upon natural ecosystems and their wild inhabitants that the ethics of respect for nature comes into play.

(2) The second concept essential to the moral attitude of respect for nature is the idea of inherent worth. We take that attitude toward wild living things (individuals, species populations, or whole biotic communities) when and only when we regard them as entities possessing inherent worth. Indeed, it is only because they are conceived in this way that moral agents can think of themselves as having validly binding duties, obligations, and responsibilities that are *owed* to them as their *due*. I am not at this juncture arguing why they *should* be so regarded; I consider it at length below. But so regarding them is a presupposition of our taking the attitude of respect toward them and accordingly understanding ourselves as bearing certain moral relations to them. This can be shown as follows:

What does it mean to regard an entity that has a good of its own as possessing inherent worth? Two general principles are involved: the principle of moral consideration and the principle of intrinsic value.

According to the principle of moral consideration, wild living things are deserving of the concern and consideration of all moral agents simply in virtue of their being members of the Earth's community of life. From the moral point of view their good must be taken into account whenever it is affected for better or worse by the conduct of rational agents. This holds no matter what species the creature belongs to. The good of each is to be accorded some value and so acknowledged as having some weight in the deliberations of all rational agents. Of course, it may be necessary for such agents to act in ways contrary to the good of this or that particular organism or group of organisms in order to further the good of others, including the good of humans. But the principle of moral consideration prescribes that, with respect to each being an entity having its own good, every individual is deserving of consideration.

The principle of intrinsic value states that,

regardless of what kind of entity it is in other respects, if it is a member of the Earth's community of life, the realization of its good is something *intrinsically* valuable. This means that its good is prima facie worthy of being preserved or promoted as an end in itself and for the sake of the entity whose good it is. Insofar as we regard any organism, species population, or life community as an entity having inherent worth, we believe that it must never be treated as if it were a mere object or thing whose entire value lies in being instrumental to the good of some other entity. The well-being of each is judged to have value in and of itself.

Combining these two principles, we can now define what it means for a living thing or group of living things to possess inherent worth. To say that it possesses inherent worth is to say that its good is deserving of the concern and consideration of all moral agents, and that the realization of its good has intrinsic value, to be pursued as an end in itself and for the sake of the entity whose good it is.

The duties owed to wild organisms, species populations, and communities of life in the Earth's natural ecosystems are grounded on their inherent worth. When rational, autonomous agents regard such entities as possessing inherent worth, they place intrinsic value on the realization of their good and so hold themselves responsible for performing actions that will have this effect and for refraining from actions having the contrary effect.

The Attitude of Respect for Nature

Why should moral agents regard wild living things in the natural world as possessing inherent worth? To answer this question we must first take into account the fact that, when rational, autonomous agents subscribe to the principles of moral consideration and intrinsic value and so conceive of wild living things as having that kind of worth, such agents are *adopting a certain ultimate moral attitude toward the natural world*. This is the attitude I call "respect for nature." It parallels the attitude of

respect for persons in human ethics. When we adopt the attitude of respect for persons as the proper (fitting, appropriate) attitude to take toward all persons as persons, we consider the fulfillment of the basic interests of each individual to have intrinsic value. We thereby make a moral commitment to live a certain kind of life in relation to other persons. We place ourselves under the direction of a system of standards and rules that we consider validly binding on all moral agents as such.[4]

Similarly, when we adopt the attitude of respect for nature as an ultimate moral attitude we make a commitment to live by certain normative principles. These principles constitute the rules of conduct and standards of character that are to govern our treatment of the natural world. This is, first, an *ultimate* commitment because it is not derived from any higher norm. The attitude of respect for nature is not grounded on some other, more general, or more fundamental attitude. It sets the total framework for our responsibilities toward the natural world. It can be justified, as I show below, but its justification cannot consist in referring to a more general attitude or a more basic normative principle.

Second, the commitment is a *moral* one because it is understood to be a disinterested matter of principle. It is this feature that distinguishes the attitude of respect for nature from the set of feelings and dispositions that comprise the love of nature. The latter stems from one's personal interest in and response to the natural world. Like the affectionate feelings we have toward certain individual human beings, one's love of nature is nothing more than the particular way one feels about the natural environment and its wild inhabitants. And just as our love for an individual person differs from our respect for all persons as such (whether we happen to love them or not), so love of nature differs from respect for nature. Respect for nature is an attitude we believe all moral agents ought to have simply as moral agents, regardless of whether or not they also love nature. Indeed, we have not truly taken the attitude of respect for nature ourselves unless we believe this. To put it in a Kantian way, to adopt the attitude of respect for nature is to take a stance that one wills it to be a universal law for all rational beings. It is to hold that stance categorically, as being validly applicable to every moral agent without exception, irrespective of whatever personal feelings toward nature such an agent might have or might lack.

Although the attitude of respect for nature is in this sense a disinterested and universalizable attitude, anyone who does adopt it has certain steady, more or less permanent dispositions. These dispositions, which are themselves to be considered disinterested and universalizable, comprise three interlocking sets: dispositions to seek certain ends, dispositions to carry on one's practical reasoning and deliberation in a certain way, and dispositions to have certain feelings. We may accordingly analyze the attitude of respect for nature into the following components. (a) The disposition to aim at, and to take steps to bring about, as final and disinterested ends, the promoting and protecting of the good of organisms, species populations, and life communities in natural ecosystems. (These ends are "final" in not being pursued as means to further ends. They are "disinterested" in being independent of the self-interest of the agent.) (b) The disposition to consider actions that tend to realize those ends to be prima facie obligatory *because* they have that tendency. (c) The disposition to experience positive and negative feelings toward states of affairs in the world *because* they are favorable or unfavorable to the good of organisms, species populations, and life communities in natural ecosystems.

The logical connection between the attitude of respect for nature and the duties of a life-centered system of environmental ethics can now be made clear. Insofar as one sincerely takes that attitude and so has the three sets of dispositions, one will at the same time be disposed to comply with certain rules of duty (such as nonmaleficence and noninterference) and with standards of character (such as fairness and benevolence) that determine the obligations and virtues of moral agents with regard to the Earth's wild living things. We can say that the actions one performs and the character traits one develops in fulfilling these moral requirements are the way one *expresses* or *embodies* the attitude in one's conduct and character. In his famous essay, "Justice as Fairness," John Rawls describes the rules of the duties of human morality (such as fidelity, gratitude, honesty, and justice) as "forms of conduct in which recognition of others as persons is manifested."[5] I hold that the rules of duty governing our treatment of the natural world and its inhabitants are forms of conduct in which the attitude of respect for nature is manifested.

The Justifiability of the Attitude of Respect for Nature

I return to the question posed earlier, which has not yet been answered: why *should* moral agents regard wild living things as possessing inherent worth? I now argue that the only way we can answer this question is by showing how adopting the attitude of respect for nature is justified for all moral agents. Let us suppose that we were able to establish that there are good reasons for adopting the attitude, reasons which are intersubjectively valid for every rational agent. If there are such reasons, they would justify anyone's having the three sets of dispositions mentioned above as constituting what it means to have the attitude. Since these include the disposition to promote or protect the good of wild living things as a disinterested and ultimate end, as well as the disposition to perform actions for the reason that they tend to realize that end, we see that such dispositions commit a person to the principles of moral consideration and intrinsic value. To be disposed to further, as an end in itself, the good of any entity in nature just because it is that kind of entity, is to be disposed to give consideration to *every* such entity and to place intrinsic value on the realization of its good. Insofar as we subscribe to these two principles we regard living things as possessing inherent worth. Subscribing to the principles is what it *means* to so regard them. To justify the attitude of respect for nature, then, is to justify commitment to these principles and thereby to justify regarding wild creatures as possessing inherent worth.

We must keep in mind that inherent worth is not some mysterious sort of objective property belonging to living things that can be discovered by empirical observation or scientific investigation. To ascribe inherent worth to an entity is not to describe it by citing some feature discernible by sense perception or inferable by inductive reasoning. Nor is there a logically necessary connection between the concept of a being having a good of its own and the concept of inherent worth. We do not contradict ourselves by asserting that an entity that has a good of its own lacks inherent worth. In order to show that such an entity "has" inherent worth we must give good reasons for ascribing that kind of value to it (placing that kind of value upon it, conceiving of it to be valuable in that way). Although it is humans (persons, valuers) who must do the valuing, for the ethics of respect for nature, the value so ascribed is not a human value. That is to say, it is not a value derived from considerations regarding human well-being or human rights. It is a value that is ascribed to nonhuman animals and plants themselves, independently of their relationship to what humans judge to be conducive to their own good.

Whatever reasons, then, justify our taking the attitude of respect for nature as defined above are also reasons that show why we *should* regard the living things of the natural world as possessing inherent worth. We saw earlier that, since the attitude is an ultimate one, it cannot be derived from a more fundamental attitude nor shown to be a special case of a more general one. On what sort of grounds, then, can it be established?

The attitude we take toward living things in the natural world depends on the way we look at them, on what kind of beings we conceive them to be, and on how we understand the relations we bear to them. Underlying and supporting our attitude is a certain *belief system* that constitutes a particular world view or outlook on nature and the place of human life in it. To give good reasons for adopting the attitude of respect for nature, then, we must first articulate the belief system which underlies and supports that attitude. If it appears that the belief system is internally coherent and well-ordered, and if, as far as we can now tell, it is consistent with all known scientific truths relevant to our knowledge of the object of the attitude (which in this case includes the whole

set of the Earth's natural ecosystems and their communities of life), then there remains the task of indicating why scientifically informed and rational thinkers with a developed capacity of reality awareness can find it acceptable as a way of conceiving of the natural world and our place in it. To the extent we can do this we provide at least a reasonable argument for accepting the belief system and the ultimate moral attitude it supports.

I do not hold that such a belief system can be *proven* to be true, either inductively or deductively. As we shall see, not all of its components can be stated in the form of empirically verifiable propositions. Nor is its internal order governed by purely logical relationships. But the system as a whole, I contend, constitutes a coherent, unified, and rationally acceptable "picture" or "map" of a total world. By examining each of its main components and seeing how they fit together, we obtain a scientifically informed and well-ordered conception of nature and the place of humans in it.

This belief system underlying the attitude of respect for nature I call (for want of a better name) "the biocentric outlook on nature." Since it is not wholly analyzable into empirically confirmable assertions, it should not be thought of as simply a compendium of the biological sciences concerning our planet's ecosystems. It might best be described as a philosophical world view, to distinguish it from a scientific theory or explanatory system. However, one of its major tenets is the great lesson we have learned from the science of ecology: the interdependence of all living things in an organically unified order whose balance and stability are necessary conditions for the realization of the good of its constituent biotic communities.

Before turning to an account of the main components of the biocentric outlook, it is convenient here to set forth the overall structure of my theory of environmental ethics as it has now emerged. The ethics of respect for nature is made up of three basic elements: a belief system, an ultimate moral attitude, and a set of rules of duty and standards of character. These elements are connected with each other in the following manner. The belief system provides a certain outlook on nature which supports and makes intelligible an autonomous agent's adopting, as an ultimate moral attitude, the attitude of respect for nature. It supports and makes intelligible the attitude in the sense that, when an autonomous agent understands its moral relations to the natural world in terms of this outlook, it recognizes the attitude of respect to be the only *suitable* or *fitting* attitude to take toward all wild forms of life in the Earth's biosphere. Living things are now viewed as *the appropriate objects of the attitude of respect* and are accordingly regarded as entities possessing inherent worth. One then places intrinsic value on the promotion and protection of their good. As a consequence of this, one makes a moral commitment to abide by a set of rules of duty and to fulfill (as far as one can by one's own efforts) certain standards of good character. Given one's adoption of the attitude of respect, one makes that moral commitment because one considers those rules and standards to be validly binding on all moral agents. They are seen as embodying forms of conduct and character structures in which the attitude of respect for nature is manifested.

This three-part complex which internally orders the ethics of respect for nature is symmetrical with a theory of human ethics grounded on respect for persons. Such a theory includes, first, a conception of oneself and others as persons, that is, as centers of autonomous choice. Second, there is the attitude of respect for persons as persons. When this is adopted as an ultimate moral attitude it involves the disposition to treat every person as having inherent worth or "human dignity." Every human being, just in virtue of her or his humanity, is understood to be worthy of moral consideration, and intrinsic value is placed on the autonomy and well-being of each. This is what Kant meant by conceiving of persons as ends in themselves. Third, there is an ethical system of duties which are acknowledged to be owed by everyone to everyone. These duties are forms of conduct in which public recognition is given to each individual's inherent worth as a person.

This structural framework for a theory of human ethics is meant to leave open the issue of consequentialism (utilitarianism) versus nonconsequentialism (deontology). That issue concerns the particular kind of system of rules defining the duties of moral agents toward persons. Similarly, I am leaving open in this paper the question of what particular kind of system of rules defines our duties with respect to the natural world.

The Biocentric Outlook on Nature

The biocentric outlook on nature has four main components. (1) Humans are thought of as members of the Earth's community of life, holding that membership on the same terms as apply to all the nonhuman members. (2) The Earth's natural ecosystems as a totality are seen as a complex web of interconnected elements, with the sound biological functioning of each being dependent on the sound biological functioning of the others. (This is the component referred to above as the great lesson that the science of ecology has taught us.) (3) Each individual organism is conceived of as a teleological center of life, pursuing its own good in its own way. (4) Whether we are concerned with standards of merit or with the concept of inherent worth, the claim that humans by their very nature are superior to other species is a groundless claim and, in the light of elements (1), (2), and (3) above, must be rejected as nothing more than an irrational bias in our own favor. . . .

The Denial of Human Superiority

This fourth component of the biocentric outlook on nature is the single most important idea in establishing the justifiability of the attitude of respect for nature. Its central role is due to the special relationship it bears to the first three components of the outlook. This relationship will be brought out after the concept of human superiority is examined and analyzed.[6]

In what sense are humans alleged to be superior to other animals? We are different from them in having certain capacities that they lack. But why should these capacities be a mark of superiority? From what point of view are they judged to be signs of superiority and what sense of superiority is meant? After all, various nonhuman species have capacities that humans lack. There is the speed of a cheetah, the vision of an eagle, the agility of a monkey. Why should not these be taken as signs of *their* superiority over humans?

One answer that comes immediately to mind is that these capacities are not as *valuable* as the human capacities that are claimed to make us superior. Such uniquely human characteristics as rational thought, aesthetic creativity, autonomy and self-determination, and moral freedom, it might be held, have a higher value than the capacities found in other species. Yet we must ask: valuable to whom, and on what grounds?

The human characteristics mentioned are all valuable to humans. They are essential to the preservation and enrichment of our civilization and culture. Clearly it is from the human standpoint that they are being judged to be desirable and good. It is not difficult here to recognize a begging of the question. Humans are claiming human superiority from a strictly human point of view, that is, from a point of view in which the good of humans is taken as the standard of judgment. All we need to do is to look at the capacities of nonhuman animals (or plants, for that matter) from the standpoint of *their* good to find a contrary judgment of superiority. The speed of the cheetah, for example, is a sign of its superiority to humans when considered from the standpoint of the good of its species. If it were as slow a runner as a human, it would not be able to survive. And so for all the other abilities of nonhumans which further their good but which are lacking in humans. In each case the claim to human superiority would be rejected from a nonhuman standpoint.

When superiority assertions are interpreted in this way, they are based on judgments of *merit*. To judge the merits of a person or an organism one must apply grading or ranking standards to it. (As I show below, this distinguishes judgments of merit from judgments of inherent worth.) Empirical investigation then determines whether it has the "good-making

properties" (merits) in virtue of which it fulfills the standards being applied. In the case of humans, merits may be either moral or nonmoral. We can judge one person to be better than (superior to) another from the moral point of view by applying certain standards to their character and conduct. Similarly, we can appeal to nonmoral criteria in judging someone to be an excellent piano player, a fair cook, a poor tennis player, and so on. Different social purposes and roles are implicit in the making of such judgments, providing the frame of reference for the choice of standards by which the nonmoral merits of people are determined. Ultimately such purposes and roles stem from a society's way of life as a whole. Now a society's way of life may be thought of as the cultural form given to the realization of human values. Whether moral or nonmoral standards are being applied, then, all judgments of people's merits finally depend on human values. All are made from an exclusively human standpoint.

The question that naturally arises at this juncture is: why should standards that are based on human values be assumed to be the only valid criteria of merit and hence the only true signs of superiority? This question is especially pressing when humans are being judged superior in merit to nonhumans. It is true that a human being may be a better mathematician than a monkey, but the monkey may be a better tree climber than a human being. If we humans value mathematics more than tree climbing, that is because our conception of civilized life makes the development of mathematical ability more desirable than the ability to climb trees. But is it not unreasonable to judge nonhumans by the values of human civilization, rather than by values connected with what it is for a member of *that* species to live a good life? If all living things have a good of their own, it at least makes sense to judge the merits of nonhumans by standards derived from *their* good. To use only standards based on human values is already to commit oneself to holding that humans are superior to nonhumans, which is the point in question.

A further logical flaw arises in connection with the widely held conviction that humans are *morally* superior beings because they possess, while others lack, the capacities of a moral agent (free will, accountability, deliberation, judgment, practical reason). This view rests on a conceptual confusion. As far as moral standards are concerned, only beings that have the capacities of a moral agent can properly be judged to be *either* moral (morally good) *or* immoral (morally deficient). Moral standards are simply not applicable to beings that lack such capacities. Animals and plants cannot therefore be said to be morally inferior in merit to humans. Since the only beings that can have moral merits *or be deficient in such merits* are moral agents, it is conceptually incoherent to judge humans as superior to nonhumans on the ground that humans have moral capacities while nonhumans don't.

Up to this point I have been interpreting the claim that humans are superior to other living things as a grading or ranking judgment regarding their comparative merits. There is, however, another way of understanding the idea of human superiority. According to this interpretation, humans are superior to nonhumans not as regards their merits but as regards their inherent worth. Thus the claim of human superiority is to be understood as asserting that all humans, simply in virtue of their humanity, have *a greater inherent worth* than other living things.

The inherent worth of an entity does not depend on its merits.[7] To consider something as possessing inherent worth, we have seen, is to place intrinsic value on the realization of its good. This is done regardless of whatever particular merits it might have or might lack, as judged by a set of grading or ranking standards. In human affairs, we are all familiar with the principle that one's worth as a person does not vary with one's merits or lack of merits. The same can hold true of animals and plants. To regard such entities as possessing inherent worth entails disregarding their merits and deficiencies, whether they are being judged from a human standpoint or from the standpoint of their own species.

The idea of one entity having more merit than another, and so being superior to it in merit, makes perfectly good sense. Merit is a grading or ranking concept, and judgments of comparative merit are based on the different degrees to which things satisfy a given standard. But what can it mean to talk about one

thing being superior to another in inherent worth? In order to get at what is being asserted in such a claim it is helpful first to look at the social origin of the concept of degrees of inherent worth.

The idea that humans can possess different degrees of inherent worth originated in societies having rigid class structures. Before the rise of modern democracies with their egalitarian outlook, one's membership in a hereditary class determined one's social status. People in the upper classes were looked up to, while those in the lower classes were looked down upon. In such a society one's social superiors and social inferiors were clearly defined and easily recognized.

Two aspects of these class-structured societies are especially relevant to the idea of degrees of inherent worth. First, those born into the upper classes were deemed more worthy of respect than those born into the lower orders. Second, the superior worth of upper class people had nothing to do with their merits nor did the inferior worth of those in the lower classes rest on their lack of merits. One's superiority or inferiority entirely derived from a social position one was born into. The modern concept of a meritocracy simply did not apply. One could not advance into a higher class by any sort of moral or nonmoral achievement. Similarly, an aristocrat held his title and all the privileges that went with it just because he was the eldest son of a titled nobleman. Unlike the bestowing of knighthood in contemporary Great Britain, one did not earn membership in the nobility by meritorious conduct.

We who live in modern democracies no longer believe in such hereditary social distinctions. Indeed, we would wholeheartedly condemn them on moral grounds as being fundamentally unjust. We have come to think of class systems as a paradigm of social injustice, it being a central principle of the democratic way of life that among humans there are no superiors and no inferiors. Thus we have rejected the whole conceptual framework in which people are judged to have different degrees of inherent worth. That idea is incompatible with our notion of human equality based on the doctrine that all humans, simply in virtue of their humanity, have the same inherent worth. (The belief in universal human rights is one form that this egalitarianism takes.)

The vast majority of people in modern democracies, however, do not maintain an egalitarian outlook when it comes to comparing human beings with other living things. Most people consider our own species to be superior to all other species and this superiority is understood to be a matter of inherent worth, not merit. There may exist thoroughly vicious and depraved humans who lack all merit. Yet because they are human they are thought to belong to a higher class of entities than any plant or animal. That one is born into the species *Homo sapiens* entitles one to have lordship over those who are one's inferiors, namely, those born into other species. The parallel with hereditary social classes is very close. Implicit in this view is a hierarchical conception of nature according to which an organism has a position of superiority or inferiority in the Earth's community of life simply on the basis of its genetic background. The "lower" orders of life are looked down upon and it is considered perfectly proper that they serve the interests of those belonging to the highest order, namely humans. The intrinsic value we place on the well-being of our fellow humans reflects our recognition of their rightful position as our equals. No such intrinsic value is to be placed on the good of other animals, unless we choose to do so out of fondness or affection for them. But their well-being imposes no moral requirement on us. In this respect there is an absolute difference in moral status between ourselves and them.

This is the structure of concepts and beliefs that people are committed to insofar as they regard humans to be superior in inherent worth to all other species. I now wish to argue that this structure of concepts and beliefs is completely groundless. If we accept the first three components of the biocentric outlook and from that perspective look at the major philosophical traditions which have supported that structure, we find it to be at bottom nothing more than the expression of an irrational bias in our own favor. The philosophical traditions themselves rest on very questionable assumptions or else simply beg the question. I briefly consider three of the main traditions to

substantiate the point. These are classical Greek humanism, Cartesian dualism, and the Judeo-Christian concept of the Great Chain of Being.

The inherent superiority of humans over other species was implicit in the Greek definition of man as a rational animal. Our animal nature was identified with "brute" desires that need the order and restraint of reason to rule them (just as reason is the special virtue of those who rule in the ideal state). Rationality was then seen to be the key to our superiority over animals. It enables us to live on a higher plane and endows us with a nobility and worth that other creatures lack. This familiar way of comparing humans with other species is deeply ingrained in our Western philosophical outlook. The point to consider here is that this view does not actually provide an argument *for* human superiority but rather makes explicit the framework of thought that is implicitly used by those who think of humans as inherently superior to nonhumans. The Greeks who held that humans, in virtue of their rational capacities, have a kind of worth greater than that of any nonrational being, never looked at rationality as but one capacity of living things among many others. But when we consider rationality from the standpoint of the first three elements of the ecological outlook, we see that its value lies in its importance for *human* life. Other creatures achieve their species-specific good without the need of rationality, although they often make use of capacities that humans lack. So the humanistic outlook of classical Greek thought does not give us a neutral (nonquestion-begging) ground on which to construct a scale of degrees of inherent worth possessed by different species of living things.

The second tradition, centering on the Cartesian dualism of soul and body, also fails to justify the claim to human superiority. That superiority is supposed to derive from the fact that we have souls while animals do not. Animals are mere automata and lack the divine element that makes us spiritual beings. I won't go into the now familiar criticisms of this two-substance view. I only add the point that, even if humans are composed of an immaterial, unextended soul and a material, extended body, this in itself is not a reason to deem them of greater worth than entities that are only bodies. Why is a soul substance a thing that adds value to its possessor? Unless some theological reasoning is offered here (which many, including myself, would find unacceptable on epistemological grounds), no logical connection is evident. An immaterial something which thinks is better than a material something which does not think only if thinking itself has value, either intrinsically or instrumentally. Now it is intrinsically valuable to humans alone, who value it as an end in itself, and it is instrumentally valuable to those who benefit from it, namely humans.

For animals that neither enjoy thinking for its own sake nor need it for living the kind of life for which they are best adapted, it has no value. Even if "thinking" is broadened to include all forms of consciousness, there are still many living things that can do without it and yet live what is for their species a good life. The anthropocentricity underlying the claim to human superiority runs throughout Cartesian dualism.

A third major source of the idea of human superiority is the Judeo-Christian concept of the Great Chain of Being. Humans are superior to animals and plants because their Creator has given them a higher place on the chain. It begins with God at the top, and then moves to the angels, who are lower than God but higher than humans, then to humans, positioned between the angels and the beasts (partaking of the nature of both), and then on down to the lower levels occupied by nonhuman animals, plants, and finally inanimate objects. Humans, being "made in God's image," are inherently superior to animals and plants by virtue of their being closer (in their essential nature) to God.

The metaphysical and epistemological difficulties with this conception of a hierarchy of entities are, in my mind, insuperable. Without entering into this matter here, I only point out that if we are unwilling to accept the metaphysics of traditional Judaism and Christianity, we are again left without good reasons for holding to the claim of inherent human superiority.

The foregoing considerations (and others like them) leave us with but one ground for the assertion that a human being, regardless of

merit, is a higher kind of entity than any other living thing. This is the mere fact of the genetic makeup of the species *Homo sapiens*. But this is surely irrational and arbitrary. Why should the arrangement of genes of a certain type be a mark of superior value, especially when this fact about an organism is taken by itself, unrelated to any other aspect of its life? We might just as well refer to any other genetic makeup as a ground of superior value. Clearly we are confronted here with a wholly arbitrary claim that can only be explained as an irrational bias in our own favor.

That the claim is nothing more than a deep-seated prejudice is brought home to us when we look at our relation to other species in the light of the first three elements of the biocentric outlook. Those elements taken conjointly give us a certain overall view of the natural world and of the place of humans in it. When we take this view we come to understand other living things, their environmental conditions, and their ecological relationships in such a way as to awake in us a deep sense of our kinship with them as fellow members of the Earth's community of life. Humans and nonhumans alike are viewed together as integral parts of one unified whole in which all living things are functionally interrelated. Finally, when our awareness focuses on the individual lives of plants and animals, each is seen to share with us the characteristic of being a teleological center of life striving to realize its own good in its own unique way.

As this entire belief system becomes part of the conceptual framework through which we understand and perceive the world, we come to see ourselves as bearing a certain moral relation to nonhuman forms of life. Our ethical role in nature takes on a new significance. We begin to look at other species as we look at ourselves, seeing them as beings which have a good they are striving to realize just as we have a good we are striving to realize. We accordingly develop the disposition to view the world from the standpoint of their good as well as from the standpoint of our own good. Now if the groundlessness of the claim that humans are inherently superior to other species were brought clearly before our minds, we would not remain intellectually neutral toward that claim but would reject it as being fundamentally at variance with our total world outlook. In the absence of any good reasons for holding it, the assertion of human superiority would then appear simply as the expression of an irrational and self-serving prejudice that favors one particular species over several million others.

Rejecting the notion of human superiority entails its positive counterpart: the doctrine of species impartiality. One who accepts that doctrine regards all living things as possessing inherent worth—the *same* inherent worth, since no one species has been shown to be either "higher" or "lower" than any other. Now we saw earlier that, insofar as one thinks of a living thing as possessing inherent worth, one considers it to be the appropriate object of the attitude of respect and believes that attitude to be the only fitting or suitable one for all moral agents to take toward it.

Here, then, is the key to understanding how the attitude of respect is rooted in the biocentric outlook on nature. The basic connection is made through the denial of human superiority. Once we reject the claim that humans are superior either in merit or in worth to other living things, we are ready to adopt the attitude of respect. The denial of human superiority is itself the result of taking the perspective on nature built into the first three elements of the biocentric outlook.

Now the first three elements of the biocentric outlook, it seems clear, would be found acceptable to any rational and scientifically informed thinker who is fully "open" to the reality of the lives of nonhuman organisms. Without denying our distinctively human characteristics, such a thinker can acknowledge the fundamental respects in which we are members of the Earth's community of life and in which the biological conditions necessary for the realization of our human values are inextricably linked with the whole system of nature. In addition, the conception of individual living things as teleological centers of life simply articulates how a scientifically informed thinker comes to understand them as the result of increasingly careful and detailed observations. Thus, the biocentric outlook recommends itself as an acceptable system of concepts and beliefs to anyone who

is clear-minded, unbiased, and factually enlightened, and who has a developed capacity of reality awareness with regard to the lives of individual organisms. This, I submit, is as good a reason for making the moral commitment involved in adopting the attitude of respect for nature as any theory of environmental ethics could possibly have.

Moral Rights and the Matter of Competing Claims

I have not asserted anywhere in the foregoing account that animals or plants have moral rights. This omission was deliberate. I do not think that the reference class of the concept, bearer of moral rights, should be extended to include nonhuman living things. My reasons for taking this position, however, go beyond the scope of this paper. I believe I have been able to accomplish many of the same ends which those who ascribe rights to animals or plants wish to accomplish. There is no reason, moreover, why plants and animals, including whole species populations and life communities, cannot be accorded *legal* rights under my theory. To grant them legal protection could be interpreted as giving them legal entitlement to be protected, and this, in fact, would be a means by which a society that subscribed to the ethics of respect for nature could give public recognition to their inherent worth.

There remains the problem of competing claims, even when wild plants and animals are not thought of as bearers of moral rights. If we accept the biocentric outlook and accordingly adopt the attitude of respect for nature as our ultimate moral attitude, how do we resolve conflicts that arise from our respect for persons in the domain of human ethics and our respect for nature in the domain of environmental ethics? This is a question that cannot adequately be dealt with here. My main purpose in this paper has been to try to establish a base point from which we can start working toward a solution to the problem. I have shown why we cannot just begin with an initial presumption in favor of the interests of our own species. It is after all within our power as moral beings to place limits on human population and technology with the deliberate intention of sharing the Earth's bounty with other species. That such sharing is an ideal difficult to realize even in an approximate way does not take away its claim to our deepest moral commitment.

Notes

1. The conceptual links between an entity *having* a good, something being good *for* it, and events doing good *to* it are examined by G. H. Von Wright in *The Varieties of Goodness* (New York: Humanities Press, 1963), chaps. 3 and 5.

2. See W. K. Frankena, "Ethics and the Environment," in K. E. Goodpaster and K. M. Sayre, eds., *Ethics and Problems of the 21st Century* (Notre Dame, University of Notre Dame Press, 1979), pp. 3–20. I critically examine Frankena's views in "Frankena on Environmental Ethics," *Monist*, forthcoming.

3. In the light of considerations set forth in Daniel Dennett's *Brainstorms: Philosophical Essays on Mind and Psychology* (Montgomery, Vermont:

Bradford Books, 1978), it is advisable to leave this question unsettled at this time. When machines are developed that function in the way our brains do, we may well come to deem them proper subjects of moral consideration.

4. I have analyzed the nature of this commitment of human ethics in "On Taking the Moral Point of View," *Midwest Studies in Philosophy,* vol. 3, *Studies in Ethical Theory* (1978), pp. 35–61.

5. John Rawls, "Justice As Fairness," *Philosophical Review* 67 (1958): 183.

6. My criticisms of the dogma of human superiority gain independent support from a carefully reasoned essay by R. and V. Routley showing the many logical weaknesses in arguments for human-centered theories of environmental ethics. R. and V. Routley, "Against the Inevitability of Human Chauvinism," in K. E. Goodpaster and K. M. Sayre, eds., *Ethics and Problems of the 21st Century* (Notre Dame: University of Notre Dame Press, 1979), pp. 36–59.

7. For this way of distinguishing between merit and inherent worth, I am indebted to Gregory Vlastos, "Justice and Equality," in R. Brandt, ed., *Social Justice* (Englewood Cliffs, N. J.: Prentice-Hall, 1962), pp. 31–72.

50. Environmental Ethics and International Justice

Bernard E. Rollin

According to Bernard E. Rollin, sentient beings have intrinsic value and moral rights because what we do to such beings matters to them. By contrast, Rollin argues that rivers, mountains, forests, plants, and ecosystems do not have intrinsic value or moral rights. Even so, Rollin contends that they do have instrumental value that in some cases is enormous. For that reason, he thinks that the argument against their destruction can be extremely strong.

The past two decades have witnessed a major revolutionary thrust in social moral awareness, one virtually unknown in mainstream Western ethical thinking, although not unrecognized in other cultural traditions; for example, the Navajo, whose descriptive language for nature

From *Problems of International Justice,* edited by Steven Luper-Foy (Boulder: Westview Press, 1988), pp. 124–153. Reprinted by permission of the publisher. Notes renumbered.

and animals is suffused with ethical nuances; the Australian Aboriginal people; and the ancient Persians. This thrust is the recognition that nonhuman entities enjoy some moral status as objects of moral concern and deliberation. Although the investigation of the moral status of nonhuman entities has sometimes been subsumed under the global rubric of environmental ethics, such a blanket term does not do adequate justice to the substantial conceptual differences of its components.

The Moral Status of Nonhuman Things

As a bare minimum, environmental ethics comprises two fundamentally divergent concerns—namely, concern with individual nonhuman animals as direct objects of moral concern and concern with species, ecosystems, environments, wilderness areas, forests, the biosphere, and other nonsentient natural or even abstract objects as direct objects of moral concern. Usually, although with a number of major exceptions,[1] those who give primacy to animals have tended to deny the moral significance of environments and species as direct objects of moral concern, whereas those who give moral primacy to enviro-ecological concerns tend to deny or at least downplay the moral significance of individual animals.[2] Significant though these differences are, they should not cloud the dramatic nature of this common attempt to break out of a moral tradition that finds loci of value only in human beings and, derivatively, in human institutions.

Because of the revolutionary nature of these attempts, they also remain somewhat undeveloped and embryonic. Writings in this area by and large have tended to focus more on making the case for the attribution of moral status to these entities than in working out detailed answers to particular issues.[3] Thus, in order to assess these thrusts in relation to international justice, one must first attempt to articulate a consensus concerning the basic issue of attributing moral status to nonhumans, an attribution that, prima facie, flies in the face of previous moral tradition. In attempting such an articulation, one cannot hope to capture all approaches to these issues, but rather to glean what appears most defensible when assessed against the tribunal of common moral practice, moral theory attempting to explain that practice, and common moral discourse.

The most plausible strategy in attempting to revise traditional moral theory and practice is to show that the seeds of the new moral notions or extensions of old moral notions are, in fact, already implicit in the old moral machinery developed to deal with other issues. Only when such avenues are exhausted will it make sense to recommend major rebuilding of the machinery, rather than putting it to new uses. The classic examples of such extensions are obviously found in the extension of the moral/legal machinery of Western democracies to cover traditionally disenfranchised groups such as women and minorities. The relatively smooth flow of such applications owes much of its smoothness to the plausibility of a simple argument of the form:

Our extant moral principles ought to cover all humans.
Women are humans.
_____

∴ Our extant moral principles ought to cover women.

On the other hand, conceptually radical departures from tradition do not lend themselves to such simple rational reconstruction. Thus, for example, the principles of *favoring* members of traditionally disenfranchised groups at the expense of innocent members of nondisenfranchised groups for the sake of rectifying historically based injustice is viewed as much more morally problematic and ambivalent than simply according rights to these groups. Thus, it would be difficult to construct a simple syllogism in defense of this practice that would garner universal acquiescence with the ease of the one indicated previously.

Thus, one needs to distinguish between moral revolutionary thrusts that are ostensibly paradoxical to common sense and practice because they have been ignored in a wholesale fashion, yet are in fact logical extensions of common morality, and those revolutionary thrusts that are genuinely paradoxical to previous moral thinking and practice because they are not implicit therein. Being genuinely paradoxical does not invalidate a new moral thrust—it does, however, place upon its proponents a substantially greater burden of proof. Those philosophers, like myself, who have argued for a recognition of the moral status of individual animals and the rights and legal status that derive therefrom, have attempted to place ourselves in the first category. We recognize that a society that kills and eats billions of animals, kills millions more in research, and disposes of millions more for relatively frivolous reasons and that relies economically on animal exploitation as a mainstay of social wealth, considers talk of elevating the moral status of animals as impossible and paradoxical. But this does not mean that such an elevation does not follow unrecognized from moral principles we all hold. Indeed, the abolition of slavery or the liberation of women appeared similarly paradoxical and economically impossible, yet gradually both were perceived as morally necessary, in part because both were implicit, albeit unrecognized, in previously acknowledged assumptions.[4]

My own argument for elevating the status of animals has been a relatively straightforward deduction of unnoticed implications of traditional morality. I have tried to show that no morally relevant grounds for excluding animals from the full application of our moral machinery will stand up to rational scrutiny. Traditional claims that rely on notions such as animals have no souls, are inferior to humans in power or intelligence or evolutionary status, are not moral agents, are not rational, are not possessed of free will, are not capable of language, are not bound by social contract to humans, and so forth, do not serve as justifiable reasons for excluding animals and their interests from the moral arena.

By the same token, morally relevant similarities exist between us and them in the case of the "higher" animals. Animals can suffer, as Jeremy Bentham said; they have interests; what we do to them matters to them; they can feel pain, fear, anxiety, loneliness, pleasure, boredom, and so on. Indeed, the simplicity and power of the argument calling attention to such morally relevant similarities has led Cartesians from Descartes to modern physiologists with a vested interest against attributing moral status to animals to declare that animals are machines with no morally relevant modes of awareness, a point often addressed today against moral claims such as mine. In fact, such claims have become a mainstay of what I have elsewhere called the "common sense of science." Thus, one who argues for an augmented moral status for animals finds it necessary to establish philosophically and scientifically what common sense takes for granted—namely, that animals *are* conscious.[5] Most people whose common sense is intact are not Cartesians and can see that moral talk cannot be withheld from animals and our treatment of them.

In my own work, appealing again to common moral practice, I have stressed our society's quasi-moral, quasi-legal notion of rights as a reflection of our commitment to the moral primacy of the individual, rather than the state. Rights protect what are hypothesized as the fundamental interests of human beings from cavalier encroachment by the common good—such interests as speech, assembly, belief, property, privacy, freedom from torture, and so forth. But those animals who are conscious also have fundamental interests arising out of *their* biologically given natures (or *teloi*), the infringement upon which matters greatly to them, and the fulfillment of which is central to their lives. Hence, I deduce the notion of animal rights from our common moral theory and practice and attempt to show that conceptually, at least, it is a deduction from the moral framework of the status quo rather than a major revision therein. Moral concern for individual animals follows from the hitherto ignored presence of morally relevant characteristics, primarily sentience, in animals. As a result, I am comfortable in attributing what Immanuel Kant called "intrinsic value," not merely use value, to animals if we attribute it to people.[6]

The task is far more formidable for those who attempt to make nonsentient natural objects, such as rivers and mountains, or, worse, quasi-abstract entities, such as species and ecosystems, into direct objects of moral concern. Interestingly enough, in direct opposition to the case of animals, such moves appear prima facie plausible to common morality, which has long expressed concern for the value and preservation of some natural objects, while condoning wholesale exploitation of others. In the same way, common practice often showed extreme concern for certain favored kinds of animals, while systematically exploiting others. Thus, many people in the

United States strongly oppose scientific research on dogs and cats, but are totally unconcerned about such use of rodents or swine. What is superficially plausible, however, quite unlike the case of animals, turns out to be deeply paradoxical given the machinery of traditional morality.

Many leading environmental ethicists have attempted to do for nonsentient natural objects and abstract objects the same sort of thing I have tried to do for animals—namely, attempted to elevate their status to direct objects of intrinsic value, ends in themselves, which are morally valuable not only because of their relations and utility to sentient beings, but in and of themselves.[7] To my knowledge, none of these theorists has attempted to claim, as I do for animals, that the locus of such value lies in the fact that what we do to these entities matters to them. No one has argued that we can harm rivers, species, or ecosystems in ways that matter to them.

Wherein, then, do these theorists locate the intrinsic value of these entities? This is not at all clear in the writings, but seems to come down to one of the following doubtful moves:

1. Going from the fact that environmental factors are absolutely essential to the well-being or survival of beings that are loci of intrinsic value to the conclusion that environmental factors therefore enjoy a similar or even higher moral status. Such a move is clearly fallacious. Just because I cannot survive without insulin, and I am an object of intrinsic value, it does not follow that insulin is, too. In fact, the insulin is a paradigmatic example of instrumental value.

2. Going from the fact that the environment "creates" all sentient creatures to the fact that its welfare is more important than theirs. This is really a variation on (1) and succumbs to the same sort of criticism, namely, that this reasoning represents a genetic fallacy. The cause of something valuable need not itself be valuable and certainly not necessarily more valuable than its effect—its value must be established independently of its result. The Holocaust may have caused the state of Israel; that does not make the Holocaust more valuable than the state of Israel.

3. Confusing aesthetic or instrumental value for sentient creatures, notably humans, with intrinsic value and underestimating aesthetic value as a category. We shall return to this shortly, for I suspect it is the root confusion in those attempting to give nonsentient nature intrinsic value.

4. Substituting rhetoric for logic at crucial points in the discussions and using a poetic rhetoric (descriptions of natural objects in terms such as "grandeur," "majesty," "novelty," "variety") as an unexplained basis for according them "intrinsic value."

5. Going from the metaphor that infringement on natural objects "matters" to them in the sense that disturbance evokes an adjustment by their self-regulating properties, to the erroneous conclusion that such self-regulation, being analogous to conscious coping in animals, entitles them to direct moral status.

In short, traditional morality and its theory do not offer a viable way to raise the moral status of nonsentient natural objects and abstract objects so that they are direct objects of moral concern on a par with or even higher than sentient creatures. Ordinary morality and moral concern take as their focus the effects of actions on beings who can be helped and harmed, in ways that matter to them, either directly or by implication. If it is immoral to wreck someone's property, it is because it is someone's; if it is immoral to promote the extinction of species, it is because such extinction causes aesthetic or practical harm to humans or to animals or because a species is, in the final analysis, a group of harmable individuals.

There is nothing, of course, to stop environmental ethicists from making a recommendation for a substantial revision of common and traditional morality. But such recommendations are likely to be dismissed or whittled away by a moral version of Occam's razor: Why grant animals rights and acknowledge in animals intrinsic value? Because they are conscious and what we do to them matters to them? Why grant rocks, or trees, or species, or ecosystems rights? Because these objects have great aesthetic value, or are essential to us, or are basic for survival? But these are paradigmatic examples of *instrumental* value. A conceptual confusion for a noble purpose is still a conceptual confusion.

There is nothing to be gained by attempting to elevate the moral status of nonsentient natural objects to that of sentient ones. One can develop a rich environmental ethic by locating the value of nonsentient natural objects in their relation to sentient ones. One can argue for the preservation of habitats because their destruction harms animals; one can argue for preserving ecosystems on the grounds of unforeseen pernicious consequences resulting from their destruction, a claim for which much empirical evidence exists. One can argue for the preservation of animal species as the sum of a group of individuals who would be harmed by its extinction. One can argue for preserving mountains, snail darters, streams, and cockroaches on aesthetic grounds. Too many philosophers forget the moral power of aesthetic claims and tend to see aesthetic reasons as a weak basis for preserving natural objects. Yet the moral imperative not to destroy unique aesthetic objects and even nonunique ones is an onerous one that is well ingrained into common practice—witness the worldwide establishment of national parks, preserves, forests, and wildlife areas.

Rather than attempting to transcend all views of natural objects as instrumental by grafting onto nature a mystical intrinsic value that can be buttressed only by poetic rhetoric, it would be far better to nurture public appreciation of subtle instrumental value, especially aesthetic value. People can learn to appreciate the unique beauty of a desert, or of a fragile ecosystem, or even of a noxious creature like a tick, when they understand the complexity and history therein and can read the story each life form contains. I am reminded of a colleague in parasitology who is loath to destroy worms he has studied upon completing his research because he has aesthetically learned to value their complexity of structure, function, and evolutionary history and role.

It is important to note that the attribution of value to nonsentient natural objects as a relational property arising out of their significance (recognized or not) for sentient beings does not denigrate the value of natural objects. Indeed, this attribution does not even imply that the interests or desires of individual sentient beings always trump concern for nonsentient ones. Our legal system has, for example,

valuable and irreplaceable property laws that forbid owners of aesthetic objects, say a collection of Vincent Van Gogh paintings, to destroy them at will, say by adding them to one's funeral pyre. To be sure, this restriction on people's right to dispose of their own property arises out of a recognition of the value of these objects to other humans, but this is surely quite sensible. How else would one justify such a restriction? Nor, as we said earlier, need one limit the value of natural objects to their relationship to humans. Philosophically, one could, for example, sensibly (and commonsensically) argue for preservation of acreage from the golf-course developer because failure to do so would mean the destruction of thousands of sentient creatures' habitats—a major infringement of their interests—while building the golf course would fulfill the rarefied and inessential interests of a few.

Thus, in my view, one would accord moral concern to natural objects in a variety of ways, depending on the sort of object being considered. Moral status for individual animals would arise from their sentience. Moral status of species and their protection from humans would arise from the fact that a species is a collection of morally relevant individuals; moral status also would arise from the fact that humans have an aesthetic concern in not letting a unique and irreplaceable aesthetic object (or group of objects) disappear forever from our *Umwelt* (environment). Concern for wilderness areas, mountains, deserts, and so on would arise from their survival value for sentient animals as well as from their aesthetic value for humans. (Some writers have suggested that this aesthetic value is so great as to be essential to human mental/physical health, a point perfectly compatible with my position.[8])

Nothing in what I have said as yet tells us how to weigh conflicting interests, whether between humans and other sentient creatures or between human desires and environmental protection. How does one weigh the aesthetic concern of those who oppose blasting away part of a cliff against the pragmatic concern of those who wish to build on a cliffside? But the problem of weighing is equally thorny in traditional ethics—witness lifeboat questions or questions concerning the allocation of scarce medical resources. Nor does the intrinsic value approach help in adjudicating such issues. How does one weigh the alleged intrinsic value of a cliffside against the interests of the (intrinsic-value-bearing) homebuilders?

Furthermore, the intrinsic value view can lead to results that are repugnant to common sense and ordinary moral consciousness. Thus, for example, it follows from what has been suggested by one intrinsic value theorist that if a migratory herd of plentiful elk were passing through an area containing an endangered species of moss, it would be not only permissible but obligatory to kill the elk in order to protect the moss because in one case we would lose a species, in another "merely" individuals.[9] In my view, such a case has a less paradoxical resolution. Destruction of the moss does not matter to the moss, whereas elk presumably care about living or being injured. Therefore, one would give prima facie priority to the elk. This might presumably be trumped if, for example, the moss were a substratum from which was extracted an ingredient necessary to stop a raging, lethal epidemic in humans or animals. But such cases—and indeed most cases of conflicting interests—must be decided on the actual occasion. These cases are decided by a careful examination of the facts of the situation. Thus, our suggestion of a basis for environmental ethics does not qualitatively change the situation from that of current ethical deliberation, whereas granting intrinsic value to natural objects would leave us with a "whole new ball game"—and one where we do not know the rules.

In sum, then, the question of environmental ethics in relation to international justice must be analyzed into two discrete components. First are those questions that pertain to direct objects of moral concern—nonhuman animals whose sentience we have good reason to suspect—and that require the application of traditional moral notions to a hitherto ignored domain of moral objects. Second are those questions pertaining to natural objects or abstract natural objects. Although it is nonsensical to attribute intrinsic or direct moral value to these objects, they nonetheless must become (and are indeed becoming) central to our social moral deliberations. This centrality derives from our increasing recognition of the far-reaching and sometimes subtle instrumental value these objects have for humans and animals. Knowing that contamination of remote desert areas by pollutants can destroy unique panoplies of fragile beauty, or that dumping wastes into the ocean can destroy a potential source of antibiotics, or that building a pipeline can have undreamed-of harmful effects goes a long way toward making us think twice about these activities—a far longer way than endowing them with quasi-mystical rhetorical status subject to (and begging for) positivistic torpedoing.

The Environment and International Justice

How do both of these newly born areas of moral concern relate to issues of international justice? In the case of issues pertaining to moral awareness of the questions involved in the preservation and despoliation of nonsentient natural objects, processes, and abstract objects, the connection becomes increasingly clear as our knowledge increases. The interconnectedness of all things occupying the biosphere, the tenuousness and violability of certain natural objects and events whose permanence and invulnerability were long taken for granted have become dramatically clearer as environmental science has developed and the results of cavalier treatment of nature have become known.

Even those lacking any moral perspective on the instrumental values in nature now ought to have some prudential ones. Thus, even if one does not care about poisoning the air that other people and animals breathe, prudential reason would dictate that one realize that one is also poisoning oneself. Thus, the question of control of the actions of those who would or could harm another or everyone for the sake of selfish interests begins to loom large as our knowledge of environmental impact of individual actions begins to grow. These effects therefore enter into the dialectic of social justice. What constraints can legitimately be placed upon my freedoms in order to protect the environment? What social or individual benefits balance what costs to the environment or to natural objects? How much ought aesthetic values weigh against economic ones? Whole bureaucracies like the Environmental Protection Agency in the United States exist to ponder and regulate such questions in almost all civilized countries, and recent legal thinking has sought ways to codify the importance of natural objects in the law—for example, by granting them legal standing.[10] (Such a granting can and should be based on a realization of their instrumental value, not on intrinsic value; we already have such a precedent in legal standing for ships, cities, and corporations.)

Nevertheless, increased environmental knowledge has driven home a major but often ignored point: Environmental effects do not respect national boundaries. I recall traveling more than twenty years ago to the northernmost regions of eastern Canada that can be reached by road—areas inhabited almost exclusively by Native Americans to whom the benefits accruing from technological progress were manifestly limited. I was appalled to discover that in this land of few roads and fewer amenities, atmospheric pollutants such as sulfur dioxide and hydrogen sulfide reigned supreme—an unwelcome gift from factories hundreds of miles away across the U.S. border. I had no doubt that the respiratory systems of those native people were paying a heavy, and totally unjustified, price for another country's prosperity in which they did not share.

Similar examples abound. When propellant gases released by people in affluent societies (possibly) succeed in tearing a hole in the ozone layer, which hole then has cataclysmic effects on global weather, penetration of noxious rays, and so on, we again see that environmental damage does not respect national boundaries.

In a slightly different vein, one can consider underdeveloped countries struggling to raise the living standards of their populace. To do so, they must exploit and perhaps despoil resources and environments that, from the point of view of a detached observer, ought to be left alone or whose exploitation will or may in some measure ultimately threaten the whole biosphere. The detached observer may well be (and probably is) where he is in virtue of similar despoliation routinely engaged in by his country generations before environmental consciousness had dawned. Is the underdeveloped country to bear a burden of poverty just because its awakening is happening a hundred years late? Or is the new environmental knowledge to count for naught in the face of the need for development?

An excellent example of this point was recently given by an environmental scientist, Michael Mares, in an article in *Science*. Echoing the point we just made, Mares asserts that "broad-scale ecological problems have little to do with national boundaries. In our complex world, where multiple links of commerce, communications, and politics join all countries to a remarkable degree, the suggestion that ecological problems of large magnitude can or should be solved only at a local level is unrealistic. We are all involved in biospheric problems."[11]

Using the case of South America, for which massive extinction of species has been predicted and where wholesale destruction of rain forests has occurred, Mares points out that one cannot look at this situation strictly as South America's problem, but as one caused by global as well as local pressures with global and local consequences. With South American countries in economic difficulties, can one really expect governments there to take a long-run ecological perspective rather than acceding to short-term gain? If other countries in an immediate position to adopt a long-run perspective wish to do so, they must help South America with the requisite expertise as well as with significant financial assistance. . . .

The ultimate example is, of course, the ecological catastrophe of the nuclear winter that is projected to follow nuclear war. Those who would suffer from the effects of such a winter far outnumber the belligerents. Thus, nuclear war becomes a pressing matter not only to those nations with a penchant for annihilating one another, but even to those simple innocents thousands of miles and cultural light years away from the principals who have no notion of the ideological and economic disputes leading to the conflagration and no allegiance to either side.

Yet another striking example of the need for international cooperation and justice in environmental matters comes from the burgeoning area of biotechnology and genetic engineering. For some time, the United States has led in genetic engineering and also in attempts to create rules and guidelines for its regulation. Interest groups have brought suit against projects that might have untoward and unpredictable environmental consequences—for example, the ice nucleation experiments in California that use genetically engineered bacteria to protect crops from frost.[12] Demands for stringent federal regulation of such work have persisted, primarily on the grounds that such activities could wreak havoc with the environment in undreamed-of ways. What is all too often forgotten is that genetic engineering is a problem for international regulation, not merely for national rules. By and large, the technology for doing pioneering work in genetic engineering is relatively inexpensive, compared, for example, to the need for enormous amounts of capital to build particle accelerators. Thus, stringent regulation or even abolition of genetic engineering in a country such as the United States would not alone solve the problem; regulation would merely move genetic engineering into countries less concerned with potential national and global catastrophe. The net effect is that probably riskier, less supervised work would be done under less stringent conditions. Thus, by its very nature, genetic engineering must be controlled internationally if national control is to be effective.

The point about genetic engineering can be made even more strongly when one contemplates its use for military purposes. If there is a real possibility of environmental disaster arising adventitiously out of benign applications of biotechnology, this is a fortiori the case regarding those uses whose avowed purpose is destructive and whose sphere of effect is unpredictable. So much is manifest in the ratification of the Biological Weapons Convention of 1975, widely cited as the world's first disarmament treaty, "since it is the only one that outlaws the production and use of an entire class of weapons of mass destruction."[13] In October 1986, steps were taken to strengthen the verificational procedures of the treaty, but these essentially boil down to merely voluntary compliance, with no system of sanctions or enforcement.

The final example of environmental problems depending for their solution on some system of international justice concerns the extinction of species. Such problems fall into two distinct categories given the argument we have developed, although this distinction has traditionally been ignored. In my view, we must distinguish between threats of extinction involving sentient and nonsentient species. In the case of sentient species, the fact that a species is threatened is trumped by the fact that its members are sentient. First and foremost, the issue involves harming individual, direct objects of moral concern, just as genocide amounts to mass murder, not the elimination of an abstract entity.

Thus, from the point of view of primary loci of moral concern, killing *any* ten Siberian tigers is no different than killing the *last* ten. Our greater horror at the latter stems from invoking the relational value dimension to humans—no human will ever again be able to witness the beauty of these creatures; our world is poorer in the same way that it would be if one destroyed the last ten Van Goghs, not just any ten; the loss of the last ten tigers may lead to other losses of which we are not aware. But we should not lose sight of the fact that the greater harm is to the animals, not to us. For this reason, I will discuss the destruction of sentient species separately, along with cases where individual animals are destroyed and hurt without endangering the species.

This still leaves us with the case of species extinction involving nonsentient species—plants or animals in whom we have no reason to suspect the presence of consciousness. Such extinction is not necessarily an evil. Few (albeit some) bemoaned the eradication of the smallpox virus, and David Baltimore recently remarked that, in his view, all viruses could be eradicated with no loss (save perhaps to intrinsic value theorists).[14] On the other hand, most cases of extinction presumably would be cases of (relational) evil because nonsentient species that do not harm us or other sentient creatures directly or indirectly are at worst neutral, and their loss is both an aesthetic loss for their uniqueness and beauty (the humblest organisms often contain great beauty—in symmetry, adaptation, complexity, or whatever, as my friend the parasitologist discovered), or a loss of a potential tool whose value is not yet detected (as a source of medicine, dye, and so on), or as crucial to the ecosystem in some unrecognized way.

The destruction of myriad species is a major problem. The greatest threat lies in the tropics, where species diversity is both the richest and under the greatest threat. It has been estimated that only one in ten to one in twenty species in the tropics are known to science.[15] A hectare of land in the Peruvian Amazon rain forest contains 41,000 species of insect alone, according to a recent count.[16] A *single tree* contained 43 species of ant. In ten separate hectare plots in Borneo, 700 species of tree were identified, matching the count for all of North America![17] According to a report in *Science,* "The continued erosion of tropical rain forests—through small-scale slash and burn agriculture at one extreme to massive timber operations at the other—is . . . closing in on perhaps half the world's natural inventory of species. Most biologists agree that the world's rain forests will be all but obliterated at some point in the next century."[18] Furthermore, small parks and preserves could not harbor numbers and varieties of species proportional to their size. Thus, standard conservation compromises do not represent a viable solution to the problem.

Other habitats holding a large diversity of species also are threatened. These include coral reefs, coastal wetlands, such as those in California, and large African lakes. The last have been especially threatened by the attempt to cultivate within them varieties of fish not indigenous to the area. A mere documentation of species unknown to science and possibly threatened would require the life work of twenty-five thousand taxonomists; currently there are a mere fifteen hundred such individuals at work.[19] Standard techniques of conserving representative members of such species in zoos and herbaria or preserving germ plasm in essence represent the proverbial drop in the bucket, although they are of course better than nothing.

Scientists who have devoted a great deal of study to these issues again echo the point cited earlier from Mares: These concerns are not local, but international. Michael Robinson puts the point dramatically: "We are facing 'the enlightenment fallacy.' The fallacy is that if you educate the people of the Third World, the problem will disappear. It won't. The problems are not due to ignorance and stupidity. The problems . . . derive from the poverty of the poor and the greed of the rich."[20] *Science,* in concluding its analysis, asserted that "the problems are those of economics and politics. Inescapably, therefore, the solutions are to be found in those same areas."[21]

Some recognition of this politico-economic dimension of environmental problems has been slowly forthcoming politically. There are, for example, indications that policies of the World Bank, which lends development money to countries, are being restructured to take more cognizance of environmental concerns. The bank has been criticized for funding the Polonoroeste project in Brazil, which would have destroyed large forest areas in Brazil in order to allow mass migration of farmers from impoverished areas, and for funding cattle ranching projects in Africa that promote desertification.[22]

Thus, even a cursory examination of some major environmental issues affecting the nonsentient environment indicates that those problems are insoluble outside of the context of international justice. The question then becomes: What, if any, philosophical basis exists for a system of international justice in this area? History has shown, after all, that attempts to create viable machinery of international justice in any area, ranging from an end to genocide to the prevention of war, have run the gamut from laughable to ineffectual. Self-interest has always trumped justice; the situation among nations, it is often remarked, is essentially the Hobbesian "war of each against all." This historical point again blunts even the pragmatic justification for attributing intrinsic value to the nonsentient environment. After all, widespread recognition in the Western tradition of the intrinsic value of humans has not at all assisted in the development of effective mechanisms to ensure that such value is respected.

Ironically, if we begin with the Hobbesian insight, it actually may be easier to provide a rational (and pragmatically effective) basis for a system of international justice regarding environmental concerns rather than human rights. After all, there is no pragmatic reason for a nation to sacrifice its sovereignty in the international arena regarding matters of human rights. If a given country benefits significantly from oppressing all or some of its citizenry, what positive incentive is there for that nation to respond to other nations' protests, and what incentive is there for other nations to protest? In the latter case, of course, there may be moral or ideological reasons for a nation to protest another's human rights policies, but such concerns usually give way to more pragmatic pressures—for example, if the oppressive country stands in a mutually beneficial trade or defensive relationship with the concerned nation.

In the case of global environmental concerns—destruction of the ozone, pollution of air and water, nuclear winter, dangers arising out of genetic engineering, loss of species—*everyone* loses (or might lose) if these concerns are not addressed. A leitmotif of our discussion has been precisely the global nature of such concerns. We have, in the case of all of the examples cited previously, something closer to what game theorists call a game of cooperation rather than a game of competition. That is, if one nation loses its fight with an environmental problem, or simply does not address it, any other nation could, and in many cases would, be likely to suffer as well. Thus, if the United States, through excessive use of fluorocarbons, weakens the ozone barrier, the results will not be restricted to the United States, but will have global impact.

By the same token, even if a given nation X stands to gain by ignoring environmental despoliation, others may lose and, without a system of regulation, may in turn bear the brunt of Y's or Z's cavalier disregard of other aspects of the environment. Furthermore, there is good reason to believe that the short-run gains accruing to a nation by a disregard of environmental concerns may well be significantly outweighed in the long run by unforeseen or ignored consequences. Thus, the wholesale conversion of African grasslands into grazing lands for domestic animals not ecologically adapted to such an environment may yield short-term profits, but in the long run lead to desertification, which leaves the land of no use at all. By the same token, cavalier disregard of species loss in the deforestation of the tropics may certainly provide short-term windfall profits, but at the expense of far richer resources. *Time* magazine recounted a number of examples of these riches.

These threatened ecosystems have already proved a valuable source of medicines, foods and new seed stock for crops. Nine years ago, for example, a strain of perennial, disease-resistant wild maize named *Zea diploperennis* was found in a Mexican mountain forest, growing in three small plots. Crossing domestic corn varieties with this maize produces hardy hybrids that should ultimately be worth billions of dollars to farmers. A great many of the prescription drugs sold in the U.S. are based on unique chemical compounds found in tropical plants. For example, vincristine, originally isolated from the Madagascan periwinkle, is used to treat some human cancers. Scientists are convinced that still undiscovered forest plants could be the source of countless new natural drugs.[23]

The fundamental argument, however, is still the Hobbesian one of rational self-interest. Any country, if utterly unbridled in its pursuit of short-term economic gains, or in its cavalier disregard for the impact of its activities on other nations, can permanently harm the interests of other nations. An irresponsibly genetically engineered microorganism does not respect national boundaries or military power, nor does oceanic or atmospheric pollution. The consequences of lack of control of environmental damage can range from loss of potential benefits—such as loss of new medication derived from plants, or loss of the delight and wonder in seeing a fragile tundra aglow in wildflowers—to positive and serious harm—the dramatic rise in cancers or other diseases produced by environmental despoliation of air, water, or the food chain, or even to a new ice age or tidal waves resulting from destruction of the ozone. Given modern technology, virtually any nation can damage any or all nations in any number of these ways; hence, a situation ripe for Hobbesian contractualism is reached.

In Hobbesian terms, of course, individuals engaged in a war of each against all are rendered equal by their ultimate vulnerability to harm and death by action on the part of others or combinations of others. Thus, we rationally relinquish our natural tendency toward rapaciousness in recognition of others' similar tendency, and our vulnerability thereto. Unrestricted greed is sacrificed for security and protection from the unrestricted greed of others, and a sovereign who, as it were, builds fences protecting each from all is constituted by each individual surrendering a portion of his or her unbridled autonomy. As we have seen, a precisely analogous situation exists regarding environmental vulnerability, and thus rationality would dictate that each nation surrender some of its autonomy to an international authority in order to protect itself, or the whole world including itself, from major disaster. This is of course especially clear, as we have seen earlier, in matters pertaining to biological warfare, where any nation can effectively annihilate any or all others.

In summary, then, the relevance of a viable mechanism of international justice to environmental ethical concerns is manifest. Indeed, many if not most environmental issues, and certainly the most vexing and important ones, entail major global consequences and thus cannot be restricted to local issues of sovereignty. An environmental ethics is inseparable from a system of international justice, not only in terms of policing global dangers and verifying and monitoring compliance with international agreements, but also in terms of implementing the distributive justice necessary to prevent poor countries from looking only at short-term gains. The rain forests are not only a problem for the countries in which they are found; if other developed nations are to benefit from the continued existence of the rain forests, we must be prepared to pay for that benefit. No country should be expected to bear the full brunt of environmental concerns. Classical economics does not work for ecological and environmental concerns; each unit pursuing its own interest will not enrich the biosphere, but deplete and devastate it. As E. O. Wilson put it in a recent conference on biodiversity, "The time has come to link ecology to economic and human development. . . . What is happening to the rain forests of Madagascar and Brazil will affect us all."[24] In other words, if a tree is felled in a primeval forest and there is no one else around, one should care about it anyway. . . .

Nonetheless, the situation is not hopeless. The case of the Canadian harp seal hunt dramatically illustrates that nations can be motivated by a moral concern that is actually inimical to self-interest. The European Economic Community recently banned the importation of seal products derived from the barbaric Newfoundland hunt. This was done despite the fact that at least some European nations derived economic benefit from the seal hunt and despite the fact that the European public was a major traditional consumer of seal products. This case dramatically illustrates that human consciousness is being increasingly sensitized to the suffering and interests of animals.

Cynics might argue that the seal case derives from the sentiment attached to the furry cuteness of baby seals and the jarring image of their slaughter by clubbing—big eyes and blood on the white snow. Although there is some truth in this claim, it is by no means all. Until recently, moral concern as embodied in the "humane ethic" was highly selective and favored the cute, cuddly, and familiar. Thus, for example, the Animal Welfare Act of 1966 and 1970, the only legal constraint on animal research in the United States, exempted from its very limited purview (it concerned itself only with food, caging, transport, and so on and disavowed concern with the actual content and conduct of research) rats, mice, and farm animals, in fact, 90 percent of the animals used in research. For purposes of the act, a dead dog was defined as an animal, a live mouse was not. Recently, however, things have changed. With the rise of an articulated moral concern for sentient beings by philosophers such as Peter Singer, Tom Regan, Steven Sapontzis,[25] and myself, that concern has captured the social imagination nationally and internationally.

New guidelines and laws extend concern even to the more prosaic and unlovely animals, and a new amendment to the Animal Welfare Act in the United States, which I helped to draft, now mandates control of pain, suffering, and distress, which is a direct insult to the ideology of science that treated these as unknowable. Similar thrusts have occurred in other countries; in Germany, a new law bans animal research for military and cosmetic purposes, as does a new Dutch law. By the same token, many countries, such as Britain, Switzerland, and Denmark, have put constraints on confinement agriculture—"factory farming"—even though a price is paid in "efficiency" and cost to the consumer.

We sometimes forget that there is an international dimension even to animal research and factory farming. Unilateral and major constraints on such practices by one country for the sake of moral concern for animals, with other countries not making similar moves, can lead, for example, to an erosion of the legislating country's agricultural economy if the constraints make its products prohibitively more expensive and drastically reduce a market for them. But a universal constraint applicable to all countries would merely put all competitors back at the same starting gate. Public education also can convince consumers to "put their money where their morality is."

In the case of animals in science, a parallel problem arises. Multinational corporations, and even individual researchers, when unable to do a particular kind of experiment in one country will simply go to another. Given that experimenters then are shifting the suffering from one animal to another who is not different morally, this is not a just solution. Here we cannot even use the rationalization we do with humans—"Their culture makes things tolerable to them that are not tolerable to us"—because, as a Dutch colleague of mine said, "All dogs bark in the same language." Thus, scientific research must also be regulated by internationally accepted rules, else the burden of injustice is merely shifted from one innocent animal to another who happens to be living in a different place. For this reason, the European Economic Community member nations are drafting rules designed to govern all member nations, which is a step in the right direction because it would probably be impractical for companies smarting under such rules to move out of Europe altogether to less enlightened countries.

There are many areas of animal abuse where the network of interests and thus the need for rules are obviously international. There are other cases—for example, a horrendous blood sport practiced in a small country—where there are fewer international connections and implications. Nonetheless, the key to stopping all such evils is, in the final analysis, the same. It lies in a widespread philosophical extension of widespread moral notions. Thus, the philosophical basis for a system of international justice that can stop, for example, the slaughter of rhinoceroses for frivolous consumer goods such as ornamental knives and aphrodisiacs (which reduced the black rhino population from 65,000 in 1970 to 4,500 today),[26] or the killing of the snow leopard for fur, lies in the expanded moral vision of many people in diverse nations. Such expanded awareness is contagious and creates a new gestalt on animals that finds expression in legislation, boycotts, embargos, and the like. Such concern is likely to manifest first on a national level, with demands for regulation of research and mandated protection of research animals (including recent demands for housing that respects their telos); legal constraints on agricultural practices that yield efficiency at the expense of animals' suffering; restriction of frivolous and painful testing on animals, such as the LD 50 and Draize tests used in developing cosmetics and the like; tighter controls imposed over zoos, circuses, and rodeos; and so on.

But as I said, animal exploitation does not stop at national boundaries, nor does moral concern for animals. Thus, such abuses as traffic in rare birds where vast shipments of them arrive dead and dying; unregulated transport of all varieties of animals; the murder of porpoises in pursuit of tuna; the slaughter of migrating whales in the Faroe Islands as a sport and "cultural tradition," will—whether happening in any or all countries—be subjected to international pressures for regulation. These inevitably will result in tighter monitoring and restriction of such activities, which in turn will require international cooperation of the sort that is starting to develop in order to control the drug traffic.

It is perhaps not totally utopian to suggest that expanded concern for animals, a concern crossing geopolitical barriers, may lead to expanded concern for other human beings in countries not one's own, in a lovely dialectical reversal of the traditional wisdom preached by St. Thomas Aquinas and Immanuel Kant, suggesting that concern for animals is merely disguised concern for human beings.

Notes

1. See the chapters in Tom Regan, *All That Dwell Therein* (Berkeley: University of California Press, 1982).

2. See Aldo Leopold, *A Sand County Almanac* (Oxford: Oxford University Press, 1949); J. Baird Callicott, "Animal Liberation: A Triangular Affair," *Environmental Ethics* 2 (1980):311–338; Holmes Rolston III, *Philosophy Gone Wild* (Buffalo, N.Y.: Prometheus Books, 1986).

3. There are exceptions to this generalization—for example, my own work in abolishing multiple use of animals as a standard teaching practice in medical and veterinary schools and my efforts in writing and promoting new legislation on proper care of laboratory animals.

4. See the discussions of this point in Peter Singer, *Animal Liberation* (New York: New York Review of Books, 1975); and B. Rollin, *Animal Rights and Human Morality* (Buffalo, N.Y.: Prometheus Books, 1981).

5. See my "Animal Pain," in M. Fox and L. Mickley (eds.), *Advances in Animal Welfare Science 1985* (The Hague: Martinus Nijhoff, 1985); and my "Animal Consciousness and Scientific Change," *New Ideas in Psychology* 4, no. 2 (1986):141–152, as well as the replies to the latter by P. K. Feyerabend, H. Rachlin, and T. Leahey in the same issue, p. 153. See also my *Animal Consciousness, Animal Pain, and Scientific Change* (tentative title) (Oxford: Oxford University Press, forthcoming).

6. See my *Animal Rights,* Part I.

7. See the works mentioned in footnotes 1 and 2.

8. This point is made with great rhetorical force in Edward Abbey, *Desert Solitaire* (New York: Ballantine Books, 1971).

9. See Holmes Rolston, "Duties to Endangered Species," *Philosophy Gone Wild.*

10. See the seminal discussion in Christopher Stone, *Should Trees Have Standing? Toward Legal Rights for Natural Objects* (Los Altos, Calif.: William Kaufmann, 1974).

11. Michael Mares, "Conservation in South America: Problems, Consequences, and Solutions." *Science* 233 (1986):734.

12. For a discussion of various ethical issues surrounding genetic engineering, see my "The Frankenstein Thing," in J. W. Evans and A. Hollaender (eds.), *Genetic Engineering of Agricultural Animals* (New York: Plenum, 1986).

13. *Science* 234 (1986):143.

14. *Time,* November 3, 1986, p. 74.

15. *Science* 234 (1986):149.

16. Ibid.

17. Ibid.

18. Ibid.

19. Ibid., p. 150.

20. Ibid.

21. Ibid.

22. *Science* 234 (1986):813.

23. *Time,* October 13, 1986, p. 80.

24. Ibid.

25. Steven Sapontzis, *Morals, Reason, and Animals* (Philadelphia: Temple University Press, 1987).

26. *Science* 234 (1986):147.

51. From the Animal Welfare Act

Congress of the United States

"Sec. 13. The Secretary shall promulgate standards to govern the humane handling, care, treatment, and transportation of animals by dealers, research facilities, and exhibitors. Such standards shall include minimum requirements with respect to handling, housing, feeding, watering, sanitation, ventilation, shelter from extremes of weather and temperatures, adequate veterinary care, including the appropriate use of anesthetic, analgesic or tranquilizing drugs, when such use would be proper in the opinion of the attending veterinarian of such research facilities, and separation by species when the Secretary finds such separation necessary for the humane handling, care, or treatment of animals. In promulgating and enforcing standards established pursuant to this section, the Secretary is authorized and directed to consult experts, including outside consultants where indicated. Nothing in this Act shall be construed as authorizing the Secretary to promulgate rules, regulations, or orders with regard to design, outlines, guidelines, or performance of actual research or experimentation by a research facility as determined by such research facility: *Provided* That the Secretary shall require, at least annually, every research facility to show that professionally acceptable standards governing the care, treatment, and use of animals, including appropriate use of anesthetic, analgesic, and tranquilizing drugs, during experimentation are being followed by the research facility during actual research or experimentation."

52. Amendments to the Animal Welfare Act

Congress of the United States

The bill amends the Animal Welfare Act as follows:

1. Expands the definition of the term "research facility" to include each department, agency or instrumentality of the United States which uses animals for research or experimentation; defines the term "Federal agency" to mean any Executive agency from which a research facility has received or may receive Federal funds to support the conduct of research, experimentation, or testing involving the use of animals; and, makes it clear that the definition of "animal" is the same as that provided under the current Act.

2. Deletes the language stating that minimum requirements be applied to the standards promulgated by the Secretary of Agriculture to govern the humane handling, care, treatment, and transportation of animals by dealers, research facilities and exhibitors; adds exercise for dogs as a standard; and, allows the Secretary to make exceptions to the standards, but only when such exceptions are specified by the research protocol.

3. Requires the Secretary to promulgate standards for research facilities, including requirements for animal care, treatment, and practices in experimental procedures, to ensure that animal pain and distress are minimized. Requires each research facility, in its annual statement of compliance, to provide the Secretary of Agriculture with assurances that such standards are being followed. Also requires the research facility to provide annual training sessions for personnel involved with animal care and treatment.

4. Provides that any State (or political subdivision of that State) may promulgate standards in addition to those promulgated by the Secretary.

5. Mandates the establishment and make-up of an animal research committee of three or more members within each research facility. Makes it unlawful for any member of the committee to release trade secrets or confidential information. The committee must make inspections at least semiannually of all animal study areas of the research facility and file an inspection report which must remain on file at the research facility for three years. The committee must notify, in writing, the Animal and Plant Health Inspection Service (APHIS) of the Department of Agriculture and the funding Federal agency of any unacceptable conditions that are not corrected despite notification. Federal support for a particular project can be suspended or revoked for continued failure by a research facility to comply with the standards of animal care,

treatment or practices; such suspension or revocation may be appealed.

6. The inspection results of the animal research committee must be available to the Department of Agriculture's inspectors for review during inspection. These inspectors must forward to APHIS and the funding Federal agency any inspection records of the committee which include reports of any deficient conditions of animal care or treatment and any deviations of research practices from the originally approved proposal that adversely affect animal welfare.

7. Prohibits the Secretary from promulgating rules, regulations, or orders that may require a research facility to disclose trade secrets or commercial or financial information which is privileged or confidential.

8. Mandates the establishment of an information service on improved methods of animal experimentation at the National Agricultural Library. . . .

---

53. *Tennessee Valley Authority* v. *Hill*

Supreme Court of the United States

The issue before the Supreme Court was whether the Endangered Species Act of 1973 prohibited the completion of a dam whose operation would destroy the habitat of the snail darter, an endangered species, despite the fact that the dam was virtually completed and that Congress continued to appropriate large sums of money to the project even after the congressional appropriations committees were appraised of the project's apparent impact upon the survival of the snail darter. Chief Justice Burger, delivering the opinion of the Court, held that the Endangered Species Act did prohibit the completion of the dam because the language of the act and the history that led to its passage required that its provisions be applied without exceptions.

We begin with the premise that operation of the Tellico Dam will either eradicate the known population of snail darters or destroy their critical habitat. Petitioner does not now seriously dispute this fact. In any event, . . . the Secretary of the Interior is vested with exclusive authority to determine whether a species such as the snail darter is "endangered" or

"threatened" and to ascertain the factors which have led to such a precarious existence. . . . Congress has authorized—indeed commanded—the Secretary to "issue such regulations as he deems necessary and advisable to provide for the conservation of such species." . . . As we have seen, the Secretary promulgated regulations which declared the snail darter an endangered species whose critical habitat would be destroyed by creation of the Tellico Dam. Doubtless petitioner would prefer not to have these regulations on the books, but there is no suggestion that the Secretary exceeded his authority or abused his discretion in issuing the regulations. Indeed, no judicial review of the Secretary's determinations has ever been sought and hence the validity of his actions are not open to review in this Court. . . .

It may seem curious to some that the survival of a relatively small number of three-inch fish among all the countless millions of species extant would require the permanent halting of a virtually completed dam for which Congress has expended more than $100 million. The paradox is not minimized by the fact that Congress continued to appropriate large sums of public money for the project, even after congressional Appropriations Committees were apprised of its apparent impact upon the survival of the snail darter. We conclude, however, that the explicit provisions of the Endangered Species Act require precisely that result. . . .
. . . By 1973, when Congress held hearings on what would later become the Endangered Species Act of 1973, it was informed that species were still being lost at the rate of about one per year, . . . and "the pace of disappearance of species" appeared to be "accelerating." Moreover, Congress was also told that the primary cause of this trend was something other than the normal process of natural selection:

"[M]an and his technology has [sic] continued at any ever-increasing rate to disrupt the natural ecosystem. This has resulted in a dramatic rise in the number and severity of the threats faced by the world's wildlife. The truth in this is apparent when one realizes that half of the recorded extinctions of mammals over the past 2,000 years have occurred in the most recent 50-year period." . . .

That Congress did not view these developments lightly was stressed by one commentator:

"The dominant theme pervading all Congressional discussion of the proposed [Endangered Species Act of 1973] was the overriding need *to devote whatever effort and resources were necessary* to avoid further diminution of national and worldwide wildlife resources. Much of the testimony at the hearings and much debate was devoted to the biological problem of extinction. Senators and Congressmen uniformly deplored the irreplaceable loss to aesthetics, science, ecology, and the national heritage should more species disappear." . . .

The legislative proceedings in 1973 are, in fact, replete with expressions of concern over the risk that might lie in the loss of *any* endangered species. Typifying these sentiments is the Report of the House Committee on Merchant Marine and Fisheries on . . . a bill which contained the essential features of the subsequently enacted Act of 1973; in explaining the need for the legislation, the Report stated:

"As we homogenize the habitats in which these plants and animals evolved, and as we increase the pressure for products that they are in a position to supply (usually unwillingly) we threaten their— and our own—genetic heritage.
"*The value of this genetic heritage is, quite literally, incalculable.*
"From the most narrow possible point of view, *it is in the best interests of mankind to minimize the losses of genetic variations.* The reason is simple: they are potential resources. They are keys to puzzles which we cannot solve, and may provide answers to questions which we have not yet learned to ask.
"To take a homely, but apt, example: one of the critical chemicals in the regulation of ovulations in humans was found in a common plant. Once discovered, and analyzed, humans could duplicate it synthetically, but had it never existed—or had it been driven out of existence before we knew its potentialities—we would never have tried to synthesize it in the first place.

"Who knows, or can say, what potential cures for cancer or other scourges, present or future, may lie locked up in the structures of plants which may yet be undiscovered, much less analyzed? . . . Sheer self-interest impels us to be cautious." . . .

As the examples cited here demonstrate, Congress was concerned about the *unknown* uses that endangered species might have and about the *unforeseeable* place such creatures may have in the chain of life on this planet. . . .

. . . Representative Dingell, provided an interpretation of what the Conference bill would require, making it clear that the mandatory provisions . . . were not casually or inadvertently included:

. . . "A recent article . . . illustrates the problem which might occur absent this new language in the bill. It appears that the whooping cranes of this country, perhaps the best known of our endangered species, are being threatened by Air Force bombing activities along the gulf coast of Texas. Under existing law, the Secretary of Defense has some discretion as to whether or not he will take the necessary action to see that this threat disappears . . . . [O]nce the bill is enacted, [the Secretary of Defense] *would be required to take the proper steps.* . . .

"Another example . . . [has] to do with the continental population of grizzly bears which may or may not be endangered, but which is surely threatened. . . . Once this bill is enacted, the appropriate Secretary, whether of Interior, Agriculture or whatever, *will have to take action* to see that this situation is not permitted to worsen, and that these bears are not driven to extinction. The purposes of the bill included the conservation of the species and of the ecosystems upon which they depend, and *every agency of government is committed* to see that those purposes are carried out. . . . [T]he agencies of Government can no longer plead that they can do nothing about it. *They can, and they must. The law is clear.*"

. . .

Notwithstanding Congress' expression of intent in 1973, we are urged to find that the continuing appropriations for Tellico Dam constitute an implied repeal of the 1973 Act, at least insofar as it applies to the Tellico Project. In support of this view, TVA points to the statements found in various House and Senate Appropriations Committees' Reports. . . . Since we are unwilling to assume that these latter Committee statements constituted advice to ignore the provisions of a duly enacted law, we assume that these Committees believed that the Act simply was not applicable in this situation. But even under this interpretation of the Committees' actions, we are unable to conclude that the Act has been in any respect amended or repealed. . . .

. . . The starting point in this analysis must be the legislative proceedings leading to the 1977 appropriations since the earlier funding of the dam occurred prior to the listing of the snail darter as an endangered species. In all successive years, TVA confidently reported to the Appropriations Committees that efforts to transplant the snail darter appeared to be successful; this surely gave those Committees some basis for the impression that there was no direct conflict between the Tellico Project and the Endangered Species Act. Indeed, the special appropriation for 1978 of $2 million for transplantation of endangered species supports the view that the Committees saw such relocation as the means whereby collision between Tellico and the Endangered Species Act could be avoided. . . .

. . . Here we are urged to view the Endangered Species Act "reasonably," and hence shape a remedy "that accords with some modicum of common sense and the public weal." . . . But is that our function? We have no expert knowledge on the subject of endangered species, much less do we have a mandate from the people to strike a balance of equities on the side of the Tellico Dam. Congress has spoken in the plainest of words, making it abundantly clear that the balance has been struck in favor of affording endangered species the highest of priorities, thereby adopting a policy which it described as "institutionalized caution."

Our individual appraisal of the wisdom or unwisdom of a particular course consciously selected by the Congress is to be put aside in the process of interpreting a statute. Once the meaning of an enactment is discerned and its constitutionality determined, the judicial process comes to an end. We do not sit as a committee of review, nor are we vested with the power of veto. The lines ascribed to Sir Thomas More by Robert Bolt are not without relevance here:

"The law, Roper, the law. I know what's legal, not what's right. And I'll stick to what's legal. . . . I'm *not* God. The currents and eddies of right and wrong, which you find such plain-sailing, I can't navigate, I'm no voyager. But in the thickets of the law, oh there I'm a forester. . . . What would you do? Cut a great road through the law to get after the De-

vil? . . . And when the last law was down, and the Devil turned round on you— where would you hide, Roper, the laws all being flat? . . . This country's planted thick with laws from coast to coast— Man's laws, not God's—and if you cut them down . . . d'you really think you could stand upright in the winds that would blow then? . . . Yes, I'd give the Devil benefit of law, for my own safety's sake." R. Bolt, A Man for All Seasons, . . .

We agree with the Court of Appeals that in our constitutional system the commitment to the separation of powers is too fundamental for us to pre-empt congressional action by judicially decreeing what accords with "common sense and the public weal." Our Constitution vests such responsibilities in the political branches.

Suggestions for Further Reading

Anthologies

Managing the Planet Earth. Special Issue, *Scientific American* (1989).

Miller, H., and Williams, W. (eds.). *Ethics and Animals.* Clifton, NJ: Humana Press, 1983.

Regan, T., and Singer, P. (eds.). *Animal Rights and Human Obligation.* Englewood Cliffs, NJ: Prentice-Hall, 1976.

Alternative Views

Atfield, R. *The Ethics of Environmental Concern.* New York: Columbia University Press, 1983.

Clark, S. *The Moral Status of Animals.* Oxford, England: Clarendon Press, 1977.

Dombrowski, D. *The Philosophy of Vegetarianism.* Amherst, MA: The University of Massachusetts Press, 1984.

Francis, L., and Norman, R. "Some Animals Are More Equal than Others." *Philosophy* (1978) pp. 507–527.

Frey, R. G. *Rights, Killing and Suffering.* Oxford, England: Basil Blackwell, 1983.

Regan, T. *The Case for Animal Rights.* Berkeley: University of California Press, 1984.

Singer, P. *Animal Liberation.* New York: New York Review, 1975.

Stone, C. *Earth and Other Ethics.* New York: Harper & Row 1987.

Taylor, P. *Respect for Nature.* Princeton: Princeton University Press, 1988.

Practical Applications

Akers, K. *A Vegetarian Sourcebook.* New York: G. P. Putnam and Sons, 1983.

Boas, M., and Chain, S. *Big Mac: The Unauthorized Story of McDonald's.* New York: New American Library, 1976.

Swanson, W., and Schultz, G. *Prime Rip.* Englewood Cliffs, NJ: Prentice-Hall, 1982.

Punishment and Responsibility

Basic Concepts

The problem of punishment and responsibility is the problem of who should be punished and in what their punishment should consist. It is a problem of punishment *and* responsibility because determining who should be punished and in what their punishment should consist involves an assessment of responsibility. However, before discussing alternative justifications for assigning punishment, it is important to first clarify the concepts of punishment and responsibility.

Let us begin with the concept of punishment. Consider the following definition:

(*a*) Punishment is hardship inflicted on an offender by someone entitled to do so.

This definition certainly seems adequate to many standard cases of punishment. For example, suppose you pursue and capture a young man who has just robbed a drug store. The police then arrive and arrest the fellow. He is tried, convicted, and sentenced to two years in prison. Surely it would seem that a sentence of two years in prison in this case would constitute punishment, and obviously the sentence meets the conditions of (*a*).

But suppose we vary the example a bit. Suppose that, as before, you pursue the robber, but this time he gets away and in the process drops the money he took from the drug store, which you then retrieve. Suppose further that two eyewitnesses identify you as the robber, and you are arrested by the police, tried, and sentenced to two years in prison. Surely we would like to say that in this example it is you who are being punished, albeit unjustly; however, according to (*a*), this is not the case. For according to this definition, punishment can only be inflicted on offenders, and you are not an offender. But this simply shows that (*a*) is too narrow a definition of punishment. There clearly are cases, like our modified example, in which we can truly say that nonoffenders, that is, innocent people, are being punished. Accordingly, an accept-

able definition of punishment should allow for such cases.

Let us consider, then, the following definition of punishment, which does allow for the possibility that nonoffenders can be punished:

(*b*) Punishment is hardship inflicted on a person by someone entitled to do so.

Although (*b*) clearly represents an advance over (*a*) in that it allows for the possibility that innocent people can be punished, serious difficulties remain. For according to (*b*), paying taxes is punishment, as is civil commitment of mentally ill persons who have not committed any offense. And even though we may have good reasons for opposing taxation and even good reasons for opposing civil commitment it is usually not because we regard such impositions as punishments. Clearly, then, a definition of punishment that includes paying taxes and civil commitment as punishments is simply too broad; what is needed is a definition that is narrower than (*b*) but broader than (*a*).

Consider the following possibility:

(*c*) Punishment is hardship inflicted on a person who is found guilty of an offense by someone entitled to do so.

This definition, like (*b*), allows that innocent people can be punished, because it is possible that a person can be found guilty by some procedure or other without really being guilty. Yet (*c*), unlike (*b*), does not allow that just any hardship imposed by someone entitled to do so is punishment. Rather, only a hardship imposed *for an offense* can be a punishment.

But is this definition adequate? It would seem it is not. For, according to (*c*), paying a $5 parking ticket or suffering a 15-yard penalty in a football game are both punishments. Yet in both cases, the hardship imposed lacks the moral condemnation and denunciation that is characteristic of punishment. This suggests the following definition:

(*d*) Punishment is hardship involving moral condemnation and denunciation inflicted on a person who is found guilty of an offense by someone entitled to do so.

Examples like the $5 parking ticket and the 15-yard penalty indicate that we need to distinguish between punishments proper, which satisfy the conditions of (d), and mere penalties, which only satisfy the conditions of (c). When we impose mere penalties, we are claiming that a person has done something wrong, perhaps even something morally wrong, but, because of the insignificant nature of the offense, we don't attempt to determine whether the person is morally blameworthy for so acting. Because we don't make this determination, we don't go on to morally condemn and denounce those we penalize. By contrast, when we impose punishments proper, we do make such a determination and, as a consequence, we do condemn and denounce those we penalize.

Turning to the concept of responsibility, we find that this concept is employed in a variety of different but related ways. For example, in everyday usage, we say that people are responsible for their actions if they could have acted otherwise than they did. In making this claim, we usually assume that people could have acted otherwise than they did in two respects. First, we assume that they could have acted otherwise if they had the ability to do so; for example, as presumably most varsity athletes have even when they play badly. Second, we assume that people could have acted otherwise if they had the opportunity to do so; for example, as you or I might have, even if we lacked the relevant ability, when, by chance, we were substituted in some varsity game and performed miserably. Thus, we can say that people are responsible for their actions if they had the ability and opportunity to act otherwise than they did.

Lawyers, however, usually approach the concept of responsibility differently. They are typically concerned with determining whether people have "mens rea," which translated means "a guilty mind." When people are said to have mens rea, they are held responsible for their actions.

Mens rea is said to involve three conditions:

1. Knowledge of circumstances
2. Foresight of consequences
3. Voluntariness

The first condition of mens rea is said to be absent when, for example, you didn't know the gun was loaded, or you didn't know the person you shot breaking into your home was a plainclothes police officer operating on a false lead. In such a case, lawyers would say you lacked mens rea because you lacked the knowledge of the relevant circumstances. The second condition of mens rea is said to be absent when, for example, you had no reason to suspect the person you shot would be wandering behind your target in a fenced-off range. In such a case, lawyers would say you lacked mens rea because you lacked foresight of the relevant consequences. The third condition of mens rea is said to be absent when, for example, you are having an epileptic fit or being attacked by a swarm of bees. This third condition is the least understood of the three conditions of mens rea.

But actually this weakness of the lawyer's mens rea notion of responsibility with respect to its third condition seems to be the strength of the everyday notion. This is because the everyday notion of responsibility is an unpacking of what it is for an action to be voluntary. Consequently, if we put the two notions together, we arrive at the following more adequate analysis:

People are responsible for their action if they have:

1. Knowledge of circumstances
2. Foresight of consequences
3. The ability and opportunity to act otherwise than they did.

Armed with a clearer understanding of the notions of punishment and responsibility, we should be in a better position to examine alternative justifications for assigning punishment in society.

Forward-Looking and Backward-Looking Views

There are basically two kinds of justifications for punishment: forward-looking and backward-looking. Forward-looking justifications maintain that punishment is justified because of its relationship to what *will occur*. Backward-looking justifications maintain that punishment is justified because of its relationship to what *has occurred*. An example of a forward-looking justification would be the claim that punishment is justified because it deters or reforms persons from crime. An example of a backward-looking justification would be the claim that punishment is justified because it fits or is proportionate to a crime or because it is applied to a person who is responsible for a crime. Those who adopt forward-looking justifications for punishment view punishment from the point of view of a social engineer seeking to produce certain good consequences in society. By contrast, those who adopt backward-looking justifications view punishment from the point of view of a stern balancer seeking to achieve a moral balance between punishment and the crime.

Karl Menninger provides us with a forceful example of a forward-looking justification for punishment—one that is directed at the reform of the offender (Selection 54). Menninger criticizes the existing criminal justice system as ineffective at preventing crime, grounded as it is on a theory of human motivation that fails to recognize the similarities between the motives of offenders and nonoffenders. In its place, Menninger advocates a therapeutic treatment program that would detain offenders, and possibly potential offenders, until they are reformed. Thus, Menninger would replace vengeful punishment—which he regards as itself a crime—with humanitarian reform.

One prerequisite for the justification of Menninger's system of humanitarian reform that is not generally recognized is that the opportunities open to offenders for leading a good life must be reasonably adequate, or at least arguably just and fair. If this is not the case, there would be little justification for asking criminal offenders to live their lives within the bounds of the legal system. Nor for that matter could we expect any attempt at implementing a system of reform like Menninger's to be generally effective in a society characterized by basic social and economic injustices. In such a society, criminal offenders who perceive these injustices will have a strong moral reason to resist any attempt to turn them into law-abiding citizens.

Richard B. Brandt (Selection 55), however, argues that a system of punishment similar to the actual systems found in the United States and Great Britain can be justified on utilitarian or forward-looking grounds. Such a system would be justified, Brandt claims, because it would secure the good consequences of both reform and deterrence. Yet, C. S. Lewis (Selection 56) claims that the goals of both reform and deterrence are opposed to a fundamental requirement of justice—giving people what they deserve. Obviously, if Lewis's critique is sound, it presents a serious difficulty for both Menninger's and Brandt's views, as well as for any other forward-looking view.

Needless to say, raising difficulties for forward-looking justifications for punishment is not the same as directly defending backward-looking justifications. Hence the importance of the attempt by Edmund L. Pincoffs (Selection 57) to provide us with such a defense. Pincoffs begins by setting out the following three principles, which, he claims, are characteristic of a traditional backward-looking justification for punishment:

1. The only acceptable reason for punishing a person is that he or she has committed a crime.
2. The only acceptable reason for punishing a person in a given manner and degree is that the punishment is equal to the crime.
3. Whoever commits a crime must be punished in accordance with his or her desert.

Pincoffs claims that the underlying rationale for these principles can be expressed as follows:

(*a*) A proper justification for punishment is one that justifies it to the criminal.
(*b*) Punishment is justified because the criminal has willed the punishment he or she now suffers.

But how can criminals be said to will their own punishment if they do not like or want to be punished? One possible answer, which seems consistent with Pincoffs's analysis, is that criminals, by deliberately violating the rights of others (e.g., by harming others in some way), imply that they think it is reasonable for them to do so. But if this were the case, it would be reasonable for anyone else in similar circumstances to do the same. As a result, criminals would be implicitly conceding that it is all right for others to violate their rights by punishing them, and in this sense they could be said to will their own punishment.

In response to such a defense of a backward-looking justification for punishment, supporters of the forward-looking view might claim that the above principles and their underlying rationale are only proximate answers to the question of why punishment is justified, the ultimate answer to which is still given by the forward-looking view. Since Pincoffs's principles and their underlying rationale do not seem to be compatible with Menninger's system of humanitarian reform, such a response does imply that the ultimate forward-looking justification for punishment is to be found more in general deterrence, as in Brandt's system, than in humanitarian reform. But even if this were the case, the ultimate justification for punishment would still be forward-looking.

To meet this response, supporters of a backward-looking view need to show why Pincoffs's principles and their underlying rationale cannot be subsumed under a forward-looking justification. This might be done by showing that Pincoffs's principles and their underlying rationale can be grounded in a social contract theory of corrective justice analogous to the social contract theory of distributive justice discussed in Section I. Because many philosophers believe that a social contract theory of distributive justice conflicts with forward-looking goals, it should be possible to argue that a social contract theory of corrective justice does the same.[1]

Practical Applications

Obviously, a crucial area for the application of forward-looking and backward-looking views is that of capital punishment. Ernest van den Haag and Louis Schwartz state briefly some of the main arguments for and against capital punishment (Selection 58). Sometimes van den Haag and Schwartz present their arguments simply by way of example, in which case

we must ask ourselves about the generality of the examples they give.

In 1976 the Supreme Court of the United States (Selection 59) examined the question of whether capital punishment violates the Eighth Amendment prohibition of cruel and unusual punishment. The majority of the Court held that it does not violate that prohibition. In support of its ruling, the majority maintained that capital punishment does not offend against contemporary standards of decency as shown by recent legislation in this area. But with regard to the harder question of whether capital punishment is contrary to human dignity and so lacks either a forward-looking or a backward-looking justification, the Court simply deferred to state legislatures. That left the Court with the easier task of deciding whether the procedures for imposing capital punishment, as provided by the Georgia statute that was under review, were capricious and arbitrary. On this score the Court found no reason to fault the Georgia statute.

In more recent cases, however, the Court has gone beyond this purely procedural issue and ruled that the imposition of capital punishment for rape (*Coker* v. *Georgia*) and the imposition of capital punishment on anyone who did not fire the fatal shot or intend the death of the victim (*Locket* v. *Ohio*) would be unconstitutional. Given that the Court has not seen fit to defer to the judgment of state legislatures in these matters, it is not clear why the Court should continue to defer to their judgment with regard to the question of whether capital punishment can be supported by an adequate forward-looking or backward-looking justification.

In any case, once you have faced that question yourself and worked out a theory of corrective justice, you will still not know exactly how to apply that theory unless you also know how just the distribution of goods and resources is in your society. This is because regardless of whether you adopt an essentially forward-looking or backward-looking theory of corrective justice, you will need to know what economic crimes—that is, crimes against property—should be punished according to your theory; and in order to know that, you will need to know what demands are placed on the available goods and resources by solutions to the other moral problems discussed in this anthology. Of course, some crimes (e.g., many cases of murder and rape) are crimes against people rather than property. And presumably these crimes would be proscribed by your theory of corrective justice independent of the solutions to other contemporary moral problems. Nevertheless, because most crimes are crimes against property, the primary application of your theory will still depend on solutions to the other moral problems discussed in this anthology. In particular, you will need to know to what extent goods and resources can legitimately be expended for military de-fense—which just happens to be the moral problem taken up in the next section of this anthology.

Note

1. James P. Sterba, "Retributive Justice," *Political Theory* (1977); "Social Contract Theory and Ordinary Justice," *Political Theory* (1981); "Is There a Rationale for Punishment?" *American Journal of Jurisprudence* (1984); "A Rational Choice Justification for Punishment," *Philosophical Topics* (1990).

---

54. The Crime of Punishment

Karl Menninger

Karl Menninger argues that the reason crime is so difficult to eradicate is that it serves the needs of offenders and nonoffenders alike. In fact, according to Menninger, the motives of offenders and nonoffenders are quite similar; what distinguishes serious offenders is simply a greater sense of helplessness and hopelessness in the pursuit of their goals. Menninger concludes that we must find better ways to enable people to realize their goals. Menninger also argues that punishment as a vengeful response to crime does not work because crime is an illness requiring treatment by psychiatrists and psychologists. Thus, Menninger finds vengeful punishment itself to be a crime.

Few words in our language arrest our attention as do "crime," "violence," "revenge," and "injustice." We abhor crime; we adore justice; we boast that we live by the rule of law. Violence and vengefulness we repudiate as unworthy of our civilization, and we assume this sentiment to be unanimous among all human beings.

Yet crime continues to be a national disgrace and a world-wide problem. It is threatening, alarming, wasteful, expensive, abundant, and apparently increasing! In actuality it is decreasing in frequency of occurrence, but it is certainly increasing in visibility and the reactions of the public to it.

Our system for controlling crime is ineffective, unjust, expensive. Prisons seem to oper-

From "The Crime of Punishment," *Saturday Review* (September 7, 1968). Copyright © 1968 by *Saturday Review*. All rights reserved. Reprinted by permission.

ate with revolving doors—the same people going in and out and in and out. *Who cares?*

Our city jails and inhuman reformatories and wretched prisons are jammed. They are known to be unhealthy, dangerous, immoral, indecent, crime-breeding dens of iniquity. Not everyone has smelled them, as some of us have. Not many have heard the groans and the curses. Not everyone has seen the hate and despair in a thousand blank, hollow faces. But, in a way, we all know how miserable prisons are. *We want them to be that way.* And they are. *Who cares?*

Professional and big-time criminals prosper as never before. Gambling syndicates flourish. White-collar crime may even exceed all others, but goes undetected in the majority of cases. We are all being robbed and we know who the robbers are. They live nearby. *Who cares?*

The public filches millions of dollars worth

of food and clothing from stores, towels and sheets from hotels, jewelry and knick-knacks from shops. The public steals, and the same public pays it back in higher prices. *Who cares?*

Time and time again somebody shouts about this state of affairs, just as I am shouting now. The magazines shout. The newspapers shout. The television and radio commentators shout (or at least they "deplore"). Psychologists, sociologists, leading jurists, wardens, and intelligent police chiefs join the chorus. Governors and mayors and Congressmen are sometimes heard. They shout that the situation is bad, bad, bad, and getting worse. Some suggest that we immediately replace obsolete procedures with scientific methods. A few shout contrary sentiments. Do the clear indications derived from scientific discovery for appropriate changes continue to fall on deaf ears? Why is the public so long-suffering, so apathetic and thereby so continuingly self-destructive? How many Presidents (and other citizens) do we have to lose before we do something?

The public behaves as a sick patient does when a dreaded treatment is proposed for his ailment. We all know how the aching tooth may suddenly quiet down in the dentist's office, or the abdominal pain disappear in the surgeon's examining room. Why should a sufferer seek relief and shun it? Is it merely the fear of pain of the treatment? Is it the fear of unknown complications? Is it distrust of the doctor's ability? All of these, no doubt.

But, as Freud made so incontestably clear, the sufferer is always somewhat deterred by a kind of subversive, internal opposition to the work of cure. He suffers on the one hand from the pains of his affliction and yearns to get well. But he suffers at the same time from traitorous impulses that fight against the accomplishment of any change in himself, even recovery! Like Hamlet, he wonders whether it may be better after all to suffer the familiar pains and aches associated with the old method than to face the complications of a new and strange, even though possibly better way of handling things.

The inescapable conclusion is that society secretly *wants* crime, *needs* crime, and gains definite satisfactions from the present mishandling of it! We condemn crime; we punish offenders for it; but we need it. The crime and punishment ritual is a part of our lives. We need crimes to wonder at, to enjoy vicariously, to discuss and speculate about, and to publicly deplore. We need criminals to identify ourselves with, to envy secretly, and to punish stoutly. They do for us the forbidden, illegal things we *wish* to do and, like scapegoats of old, they bear the burdens of our displaced guilt and punishment—"the iniquities of us all."

We have to confess that there is something fascinating for us all about violence. That most crime is not violent we know but we forget, because crime is a breaking, a rupturing, a tearing—even when it is quietly done. To all of us crime seems like violence.

The very word "violence" has a disturbing, menacing quality. . . . In meaning it implies something dreaded, powerful, destructive, or eruptive. It is something we abhor—or do we? Its first effect is to startle, frighten—even to horrify us. But we do not always run away from it. For violence also intrigues us. It is exciting. It is dramatic. Observing it and sometimes even participating in it gives us acute pleasure.

The newspapers constantly supply us with tidbits of violence going on in the world. They exploit its dramatic essence often to the neglect of conservative reporting of more extensive but less violent damage—the flood disaster in Florence, Italy, for example. Such words as crash, explosion, wreck, assault, raid, murder, avalanche, rape, and seizure evoke pictures of eruptive devastation from which we cannot turn away. The headlines often impute violence metaphorically even to peaceful activities. Relations are "ruptured," a tie is "broken," arbitration "collapses," a proposal is "killed."

Meanwhile on the television and movie screens there constantly appear for our amusement scenes of fighting, slugging, beating, torturing, clubbing, shooting, and the like which surpass in effect anything that the newspapers can describe. Much of this violence is portrayed dishonestly; the scenes are only semirealistic; they are "faked" and romanticized.

Pain cannot be photographed; grimaces indicate but do not convey its intensity. And wounds—unlike violence—are rarely shown. This phony quality of television violence in its mentally unhealthy aspect encourages irrationality by giving the impression to the observer that being beaten, kicked, cut, and stomped, while very unpleasant, are not very painful or serious. For after being slugged and beaten the hero rolls over, opens his eyes, hops up, rubs his cheek, grins, and staggers on. The *suffering* of violence is a part both the TV and movie producers *and* their audience tend to repress.

Although most of us *say* we deplore cruelty and destructiveness, we are partially deceiving ourselves. We disown violence, ascribing the love of it to other people. But the facts speak for themselves. We do love violence, all of us, and we all feel secretly guilty for it, which is another clue to public resistance to crime-control reform.

The great sin by which we all are tempted is the wish to hurt others, and this sin must be avoided if we are to live and let live. If our destructive energies can be mastered, directed, and sublimated, we can survive. If we can love, we can live. Our destructive energies, if they cannot be controlled, may destroy our best friends, as in the case of Alexander the Great, or they may destroy supposed "enemies" or innocent strangers. Worst of all—from the standpoint of the individual—they may destroy us.

Over the centuries of man's existence, many devices have been employed in the effort to control these innate suicidal and criminal propensities. The earliest of these undoubtedly depended upon fear—fear of the unknown, fear of magical retribution, fear of social retaliation. These external devices were replaced gradually with the law and all its machinery, religion and its rituals, and the conventions of the social order.

The routine of life formerly required every individual to direct much of his aggressive energy against the environment. There were trees to cut down, wild animals to fend off, heavy obstacles to remove, great burdens to lift. But the machine has gradually changed all of this. Today, the routine of life, for most people, requires no violence, no fighting, no killing, no life-risking, no sudden supreme exertion: occasionally, perhaps, a hard pull or a strong push, but no tearing, crushing, breaking, forcing.

And because violence no longer has legiti-mate and useful vents or purposes, it must *all* be controlled today. In earlier times its expression was often a virtue, today its control is the virtue. The control involves symbolic, vicarious expressions of our violence—violence modified; "sublimated," as Freud called it; "neutralized," as Hartmann described it. Civilized substitutes for direct violence are the objects of daily search by all of us. The common law and the Ten Commandments, traffic signals and property deeds, fences and front doors, sermons and concerts, Christmas trees and jazz bands—these and a thousand other things exist today to help in the control of violence.

My colleague, Bruno Bettelheim, thinks we do not properly educate our youth to deal with their violent urges. He reminds us that nothing fascinated our forefathers more. The *Iliad* is a poem of violence. Much of the Bible is a record of violence. One penal system and many methods of child-rearing express violence—"violence to suppress violence." And, he concludes [in the article "Violence: A Neglected Mode of Behavior"]: "We shall not be able to deal intelligently with violence unless we are first ready to see it as a part of human nature, and then we shall come to realize the chances of discharging violent tendencies are now so severely curtailed that their regular and safe draining-off is not possible anymore."

Why aren't we all criminals? We all have the impulses; we all have the provocations. But becoming civilized, which is repeated ontologically in the process of social education, teaches us what we may do with impunity. What then evokes or permits the breakthrough? Why is it necessary for some to bribe their consciences and do what they do not approve of doing? Why does all sublimation sometimes fail and overt breakdown occur in the controlling and managing machinery of the personality? Why do we sometimes lose self-control? Why do we "go to pieces"? Why do we explode?

These questions point up a central problem in psychiatry. Why do some people do things they do not want to do? Or things we do not want them to do? Sometimes crimes are motivated by a desperate need to act, to do *something* to break out of a state of passivity, frustration, and helplessness too long endured, like a child who shoots a parent or a teacher after some apparently reasonable act. Granting the universal presence of violence within us all, controlled by will power, conscience, fear of punishment, and other devices, granting the tensions and the temptations that are also common to us all, why do the mechanisms of self-control fail so completely in some individuals? Is there not some pre-existing defect, some moral or cerebral weakness, some gross deficiency of common sense that lets some people tumble or kick or strike or explode, while the rest of us just stagger or sway?

When a psychiatrist examines many prisoners, writes [Seymour] Halleck [in *Psychiatry and the Dilemmas of Crime*], he soon discovers how important in the genesis of the criminal outbreak is the offender's previous *sense of helplessness or hopelessness*. All of us suffer more or less from infringement of our personal freedom. We fuss about it all the time; we strive to correct it, extend it, and free ourselves from various oppressive or retentive forces. We do not want others to push us around, to control us, to dominate us. We realize this is bound to happen to some extent in an interlocking, interrelated society such as ours. No one truly has complete freedom. But restriction irks us.

The offender feels this way, too. He does not want to be pushed around, controlled, or dominated. And because he often feels that he is thus oppressed (and actually is) and because he does lack facility in improving his situation without violence, he suffers more intensely from feelings of helplessness.

Violence and crime are often attempts to escape from madness; and there can be no doubt that some mental illness is a flight from the wish to do the violence or commit the act. Is it hard for the reader to believe that suicides are sometimes committed to forestall the commiting of murder? There is no doubt of it. Nor is there any doubt that murder is sometimes committed to avert suicide.

Strange as it may sound, many murderers do not realize whom they are killing, or, to put it another way, that they are killing the wrong people. To be sure, killing anybody is reprehensible enough, but the worst of it is that the person who the killer thinks should die (and he has reasons) is not the person he attacks. Sometimes the victim himself is partly responsible for the crime that is committed against him. It is this unconscious (perhaps sometimes conscious) participation in the crime by the victim that has long held up the very humanitarian and progressive-sounding program of giving compensation to victims. The public often judges the victim as well as the attacker.

Rape and other sexual offenses are acts of violence so repulsive to our sense of decency and order that it is easy to think of rapists in general as raging, oversexed, ruthless brutes (unless they are conquering heroes). Some rapists are. But most sex crimes are committed by undersexed rather than oversexed individuals, often undersized rather than oversized, and impelled less by lust than by a need for reassurance regarding an impaired masculinity. The unconscious fear of women goads some men with a compulsive urge to conquer, humiliate, hurt, or render powerless some available sample of womanhood. Men who are violently afraid of their repressed but nearly emergent homosexual desires, and men who are afraid of the humiliation of impotence, often try to overcome these fears by violent demonstrations.

The need to deny something in oneself is frequently an underlying motive for certain odd behavior—even up to and including crime. Bravado crimes, often done with particular brutality and ruthlessness, seem to prove *to the doer* that "I am no weakling! I am no sissy! I am no coward. I am no homosexual! I am a tough man who fears nothing." The Nazi storm troopers, many of them mere boys, were systematically trained to stifle all tender emotions and force themselves to be heartlessly brutal.

Man perennially seeks to recover the magic of his childhood days—the control of the mighty by the meek. The flick of an electric light switch, the response of an automobile throttle, the click of a camera, the touch of a match to a skyrocket—these are keys to a sudden and magical display of great power induced by the merest gesture. Is anyone already so blasé that he is no longer thrilled at the opening of a door specially for him by a magic-eye signal? Yet for a few pennies one can purchase a far more deadly piece of magic—a stored explosive and missile encased within a shell which can be ejected from a machine at the touch of a finger so swiftly that no eye can follow. A thousand yards away something falls dead—a rabbit, a deer, a beautiful mountain sheep, a sleeping child, or the President of the United States. Magic! Magnified, projected power. "Look what I can do. I am the greatest!"

It must have come to every thoughtful person, at one time or another, in looking at the revolvers on the policemen's hips, or the guns soldiers and hunters carry so proudly, that these are instruments made for the express purpose of delivering death to someone. The easy availability of these engines of destruction, even to children, mentally disturbed people, professional criminals, gangsters, and even high school girls is something to give one pause. The National Rifle Association and its allies have been able to kill scores of bills that have been introduced into Congress and state legislatures for corrective gun control since the death of President Kennedy. Americans still spend about $2 billion on guns each year.

Fifty years ago, Winston Churchill declared that the mood and temper of the public in regard to crime and criminals is one of the unfailing tests of the civilization of any country. Judged by this standard, how civilized are we?

The chairman of the President's National Crime Commission, Nicholas de B. Katzenbach, declared . . . that organized crime flourishes in America because enough of the public wants its services, and most citizens are apathetic about its impact. It will continue uncurbed as long as Americans accept it as inevitable and, in some instances, desirable.

Are there steps that we can take which will reduce the aggressive stabs and self-destructive lurches of our less well-managing fellow men? Are there ways to prevent and control the grosser violations, other than the clumsy traditional maneuvers which we have inherited? These depend basically upon intimidation and slow-motion torture. We call it punishment, and justify it with our "feeling." We know it doesn't work.

Yes, there *are* better ways. There are steps that could be taken; some *are* taken. But we move too slowly. Much better use, it seems to me, could be made of the members of my profession and other behavioral scientists than having them deliver courtroom pronunciamentos. The consistent use of a diagnostic clinic would enable trained workers to lay what they can learn about an offender before the judge who would know best how to implement the recommendation.

This would no doubt lead to a transformation of prisons, if not to their total disappearance in their present form and function. Temporary and permanent detention will perhaps always be necessary for a few, especially the professionals, but this could be more effectively and economically performed with new types of "facility" (that strange, awkward word for institution).

I assume it to be a matter of common and general agreement that our object in all this is to protect the community from a repetition of the offense by the most economical method consonant with our other purposes. Our "other purposes" include the desire to prevent these offenses from occurring, to reclaim offenders for social usefulness, if possible, and to detain them in protective custody, if reclamation is *not* possible. But how?

The treatment of human failure or dereliction by the infliction of pain is still used and believed in by many nonmedical people. "Spare the rod and spoil the child" is still considered wise counsel by many.

Whipping is still used by many secondary schoolmasters in England, I am informed, to stimulate study, attention, and the love of learning. Whipping was long a traditional treatment for the "crime" of disobedience on the part of children, pupils, servants, apprentices, employees. And slaves were treated for centuries by flogging for such offenses as weariness, confusion, stupidity, exhaustion, fear, grief, and even overcheerfulness. It was assumed and stoutly defended that these "treatments" cured conditions for which they were administered.

Meanwhile, scientific medicine was acquiring many new healing methods and devices. Doctors can now transplant organs and limbs; they can remove brain tumors and cure incipient cancers; they can halt pneumonia, meningitis, and other infections; they can correct deformities and repair breaks and tears and scars. But these wonderful achievements are accomplished on *willing* subjects, people who voluntarily ask for help by even heroic measures. And the reader will be wondering, no doubt, whether doctors can do anything with or for people who *do not want* to be treated at all, in any way! Can doctors cure willful aberrant behavior? Are we to believe that crime is a *disease* that can be reached by scientific measures? Isn't it merely "natural meanness" that makes all of us do wrong things at times even when we "know better"? And are not self-control, moral stamina, and will power the things needed? Surely there is no medical treatment for the lack of those!

Let me answer this carefully, for much misunderstanding accumulates here. I would say that according to the prevalent understanding of the words, crime is *not* a disease. Neither is it an illness, although I think it *should* be! It *should* be treated, and it could be; but it mostly isn't.

These enigmatic statements are simply explained. Diseases are undesired states of being which have been described and defined by doctors, usually given Greek or Latin appellations, and treated by long-established physical and pharmacological formulae. Illness, on the other hand, is best defined as a state of impaired functioning of such a nature that the public expects the sufferer to repair to the physician for help. The illness may prove to be a disease; more often it is only vague and nameless misery; but something which doctors, not lawyers, teachers, or preachers, are supposed to be able and willing to help.

When the community begins to look upon the expression of aggressive violence as the symptom of an illness or as indicative of illness, it will be because it believes doctors can do something to correct such a condition. At present, some better-informed individuals do believe and expect this. However angry at or sorry for the offender, they want him "treated" in an effective way so that he will cease to be a danger to them. And they know that the traditional punishment, "treatment-punishment," will not effect this.

What *will*? What effective treatment is there for such violence? It will surely have to begin with motivating or stimulating or arousing in a cornered individual the wish and hope and intention to change his methods of dealing with the realities of life. Can this be done by education, medication, counseling, training? I would answer *yes*. It can be done successfully in a majority of cases, if undertaken in time.

The present penal system and the existing legal philosophy do not stimulate or even expect such a change to take place in the criminal. Yet change is what medical science always aims for. The prisoner, like the doctor's other patients, should emerge from his treatment experience a different person, differently equipped, differently functioning, and headed in a different direction than when he began the treatment.

It is natural for the public to doubt that this can be accomplished with criminals. But remember that the public *used* to doubt that change could be effected in the mentally ill. No one a hundred years ago believed mental illness to be curable. Today *all* people know (or should know) that *mental illness is curable* in the great majority of instances and that the prospects and rapidity of cure are directly related to the availability and intensity of proper treatment.

The forms and techniques of psychiatric treatment used today number in the hundreds. No one patient requires or receives all forms, but each patient is studied with respect to his particular needs, his basic assets, his interests, and his special difficulties. A therapeutic team may embrace a dozen workers—as in a hospital setting—or it may narrow down to the doctor and the spouse. Clergymen, teachers, relatives, friends, and even fellow patients often participate informally but helpfully in the process of readaptation.

All of the participants in this effort to bring about a favorable change in the patient—i.e., in his vital balance and life program—are imbued with what we may call a *therapeutic attitude*. This is one in direct antithesis to attitudes of avoidance, ridicule, scorn, or punitiveness. Hostile feelings toward the subject, however justified by his unpleasant and even destructive behavior, are not in the curriculum of therapy or in the therapist. This does not mean that therapists approve of the offensive and obnoxious behavior of the patient; they distinctly disapprove of it. But they recognize it as symptomatic of continued imbalance and disorganization, which is what they are seeking to change. They distinguish between disapproval, penalty, price, and punishment.

Doctors charge fees; they impose certain "penalties" or prices, but they have long since put aside primitive attitudes of retaliation toward offensive patients. A patient may cough in the doctor's face or may vomit on the office rug; a patient may curse or scream or even struggle in the extremity of his pain. But these acts are not "punished." Doctors and nurses have no time or thought for inflicting unnecessary pain even upon patients who may be difficult, disagreeable, provocative, and even dangerous. It is their duty to care for them, to try to make them well, and to prevent them from doing themselves or others harm. This requires love, not hate. This is the deepest meaning of the therapeutic attitude. Every doctor knows this; every worker in a hospital or clinic knows it (or should).

There is another element in the therapeutic attitude. It is the quality of hopefulness. If no one believes that the patient can get well, if no one—not even the doctor—has any hope, there probably won't be any recovery. Hope is just as important as love in the therapeutic attitude.

"But you were talking about the mentally ill," readers may interject, "those poor, confused, bereft, frightened individuals who yearn for help from you doctors and nurses. Do you mean to imply that willfully perverse individuals, our criminals, can be similarly reached and rehabilitated? Do you really believe that effective treatment of the sort you visualize can be applied to people *who do not want any help,* who are so willfully vicious, so well aware of the wrongs they are doing, so lacking in penitence or even common decency that punishment seems to be the only thing left?"

Do I believe there is effective treatment for offenders, and that they *can* be changed? *Most certainly and definitely I do.* Not all cases, to be sure; there are also some physical afflictions which we cannot cure at the moment. Some provision has to be made for incurables— pending new knowledge—and these will include some offenders. But I believe the majority of them would prove to be curable. The willfulness and the viciousness of offenders are part of the thing for which they have to be treated. These must not thwart the therapeutic attitude.

It is simply not true that most of them are "fully aware" of what they are doing, nor is it true that they want no help from anyone, although some of them say so. Prisoners are individuals: some want treatment, some do not. Some don't know what treatment is. Many are utterly despairing and hopeless. Where treatment is made available in institutions, many prisoners seek it even with the full knowledge that doing so will not lessen their sentences. In some prisons, seeking treatment by prisoners is frowned upon by the officials.

Various forms of treatment are even now being tried in some progressive courts and prisons over the country—educational, social, industrial, religious, recreational, and psychological treatments. Socially acceptable behavior, new work-play opportunities, new identity and companion patterns all help toward community reacceptance. Some parole officers and some wardens have been extremely ingenious in developing these modalities of rehabilitation and reconstruction— more than I could list here even if I knew them all. But some are trying. The secret of success in all programs, however, is the replacement of the punitive attitude with a therapeutic attitude.

Offenders with propensities for impulsive and predatory aggression should not be permitted to live among us unrestrained by some kind of social control. *But the great majority of offenders, even "criminals," should never become prisoners if we want to "cure" them.*

There are now throughout the country many citizens' action groups and programs for the prevention and control of crime and delinquency. With such attitudes of inquiry and concern, the public could acquire information (and incentive) leading to a change of feeling about crime and criminals. It will discover how unjust is much so-called "justice," how baffled and frustrated many judges are by the ossified rigidity of old-fashioned, obsolete laws and state constitutions which effectively prevent the introduction of sensible procedures to replace useless, harmful ones.

I want to proclaim to the public that things are not what it wishes them to be, and will only become so if it will take an interest in the matter and assume some responsibility for its own self-protection.

Will the public listen?

If the public does become interested, it will realize that we must have more facts, more trial projects, more checked results. It will share the dismay of the President's Commission in finding that no one knows much about even the incidence of crime with any definiteness or statistical accuracy.

The average citizen finds it difficult to see how any research would in any way change his mind about a man who brutally murders his children. But just such inconceivably awful acts most dramatically point up the need for research. Why should—how can—a man become so dreadful as that in our culture? How is such a man made? Is it comprehensible that he can be born to become so depraved?

There are thousands of questions regarding crime and public protection which deserve scientific study. What makes some individuals maintain their interior equilibrium by one kind of disturbance of the social structure rather than by another kind, one that would have landed him in a hospital? Why do some individuals specialize in certain types of crime? Why do so many young people reared in areas of delinquency and poverty and bad example never become habitual delinquents? (Perhaps this is a more important question than why some of them do.)

The public has a fascination for violence, and clings tenaciously to its yen for vengeance, blind and deaf to the expense, futility, and dangerousness of the resulting penal system. But we are bound to hope that this will yield in time to the persistent, penetrating light of intelligence and accumulating scientific knowledge. The public will grow increasingly ashamed of its cry for retaliation, its persistent demand to punish. This is its crime, *our* crime against criminals—and, incidentally, our crime against ourselves. For before we can diminish our sufferings from the ill-controlled aggressive assaults of fellow citizens, we must renounce the philosophy of punishment, the obsolete, vengeful penal attitude. In its place we would seek a comprehensive constructive social attitude—therapeutic in some instances, restraining in some instances, but preventive in its total social impact.

In the last analysis this becomes a question of personal morals and values. No matter how glorified or how piously disguised, vengeance as a human motive must be personally repudiated by each and every one of us. This is the message of old religions and new psychiatries. Unless this message is heard, unless we, the people—the man on the street, the housewife in the home—can give up our delicious satisfactions in opportunities for vengeful retaliation on scapegoats, we cannot expect to preserve our peace, our public safety, or our mental health.

---

55. A Utilitarian Theory of Punishment

Richard B. Brandt

Richard B. Brandt argues that a system of punishment similar to that found in the United States and Great Britain can be justified on utilitarian or forward-looking grounds. He rejects the view that a utilitarian theory cannot approve of any excuses for criminal liability. He also denies that a utilitarian theory must approve of occasionally punishing the innocent provided the theory is understood in an extended sense to require a principle of equal distribution.

The ethical foundations of the institution and principles of criminal justice require examination just as do the ethical foundations of systems of economic distribution. In fact, the two

Abridged from *Ethical Theory* (1959), pp. 480, 489–495, 503–505. Reprinted by permission of Richard B. Brandt. Notes renumbered.

problems are so similar that it is helpful to view either one in the light of conclusions reached about the other. It is no accident that the two are spoken of as problems of "justice," for the institution of criminal justice is essentially a mode of allocating welfare (or "illfare," if we prefer). Also, just as an economic return can be regarded as a reward for past services, the punishment of criminals can be regarded as punishment for past disservices. Moreover, just as a major reason for differences in economic reward is to provide motivation for promoting the public welfare by industrious effort, so a major reason for a system of punishment for criminals is to give motivation for not harming the public by crime. The two topics, then, are very similar; but they are also sufficiently different to require separate discussion. . . .

The broad questions to be kept in the forefront of discussion are the following: (1) What justifies anyone in inflicting pain or loss on an individual on account of his past acts? (2) Is there a valid general principle about the punishments proper for various acts? (Possibly there should be no close connection between offense and penalty; perhaps punishment should be suited to the individual needs of the criminal, and not to his crime.) (3) What kinds of defense should excuse from punishment? An answer to these questions would comprise prescriptions for the broad outlines of an ideal system of criminal justice. . . .

The Utilitarian Theory of Criminal Justice

. . . It is convenient to begin with the utilitarian theory. Since we have tentatively concluded that an "extended" rule-utilitarianism is the most tenable form of theory, we shall have this particular type of theory in mind. For present purposes, however, it would make no difference, except at two or three points where we shall make note of the fact, if we confined our attention to a straight rule-utilitarian principle. There is no harm in thinking of the matter in this way. . . .

The essence of the rule-utilitarian theory, we recall, is that our actions, whether legislative or otherwise, should be guided by a set of prescriptions, the conscientious following of which by all would have maximum net expectable utility. As a result, the utilitarian is not, just as such, committed to any particular view about how anti-social behavior should be treated by society—or even to the view that society should do anything at all about im-

moral conduct. It is only the utilitarian principle *combined* with statements about the kind of laws and practices which will maximize expectable utility that has such consequences. Therefore, utilitarians are free to differ from one another about the character of an ideal system of criminal justice; some utilitarians think that the system prevalent in Great Britain and the United States essentially corresponds to the ideal, but others think that the only system that can be justified is markedly different from the actual systems in these Western countries. We shall concentrate our discussion, however, on the more traditional line of utilitarian thought which holds that roughly the actual system of criminal law, say in the United States, is morally justifiable, and we shall follow roughly the classic exposition of the reasoning given by Jeremy Bentham[1]—but modifying this freely when we feel amendment is called for. At the end of the chapter we shall look briefly at a different view.

Traditional utilitarian thinking about criminal justice has found the rationale of the practice, in the United States, for example, in three main facts. (Those who disagree think the first two of these "facts" happen not to be the case.) (1) People who are tempted to misbehave, to trample on the rights of others, to sacrifice public welfare for personal gain, can usually be deterred from misconduct by fear of punishment, such as death, imprisonment, or fine. (2) Imprisonment or fine will teach malefactors a lesson; their characters may be improved, and at any rate a personal experience of punishment will make them less likely to misbehave again. (3) Imprisonment will certainly have the result of physically preventing past malefactors from misbehaving, during the period of their incarceration.

In view of these suppositions, traditional utilitarian thinking has concluded that having laws forbidding certain kinds of behavior on pain of punishment, and having machinery for the fair enforcement of these laws, is justified by the fact that it maximizes expectable utility. Misconduct is not to be punished just for its own sake; malefactors must be punished for their past acts, according to law, as a way of maximizing expectable utility.

The utilitarian principle, of course, has implications for decisions about the severity of punishment to be administered. Punishment is itself an evil, and hence should be avoided where this is consistent with the public good. Punishment should have precisely such a degree of severity (not more or less) that the probable disutility of greater severity just balances the probable gain in utility (less crime because of the more serious threat). The cost, in other words, should be counted along with the value of what is bought; and we should buy protection up to the point where the cost is greater than the protection is worth. How severe will such punishment be? Jeremy Bentham had many sensible things to say about this. Punishment, he said, must be severe enough so that it is to no one's advantage to commit an offense even if he receives the punishment; a fine of $10 for bank robbery would give no security at all. Further, since many criminals will be undetected, we must make the penalty heavy enough in comparison with the prospective gain from crime, that a prospective criminal will consider the risk hardly worth it, even considering that it is not certain he will be punished at all. Again, the more serious offenses should carry the heavier penalties, not only because the greater disutility justifies the use of heavier penalties in order to prevent them, but also because criminals should be motivated to commit a less serious rather than a more serious offense. Bentham thought the prescribed penalties should allow for some variation at the discretion of the judge, so that the actual suffering caused should roughly be the same in all cases; thus, a heavier fine will be imposed on a rich man than on a poor man.

Bentham also argued that the goal of maximum utility requires that certain facts should *excuse* from culpability, for the reason that punishment in such cases "must be inefficacious." He listed as such (1) the fact that the relevant law was passed only after the act of the accused, (2) that the law had not been made public, (3) that the criminal was an infant, insane, or was intoxicated, (4) that the crime was done under physical compulsion, (5) that the agent was ignorant of the probable consequences of his act or was acting on the basis of an innocent misapprehension of the facts, such that the act the agent thought he was performing was a lawful one, and (6) that the motivation to commit the offense was so strong that no threat of law could prevent the crime. Bentham also thought that punishment should be remitted if the crime was a collective one and the number of the guilty so large that great suffering would be caused by its imposition, or if the offender held an important post and his services were important for the public, or if the public or foreign powers would be offended by the punishment; but we shall ignore this part of his view.

Bentham's account of the logic of legal "defenses" needs amendment. What he should have argued is that *not* punishing in certain types of cases (cases where such defenses as those just indicated can be offered) reduces the amount of suffering imposed by law and the insecurity of everybody, and that failure to impose punishment in these types of case will cause only a negligible increase in the incidence of crime.

How satisfactory is this theory of criminal justice? Does it have any implications that are far from being acceptable when compared with concrete justified convictions about what practices are morally right?[2]

Many criminologists, as we shall see at the end of this chapter, would argue that Bentham was mistaken in his facts: The deterrence value of [the] threat of punishment, they say, is much less than he imagined, and criminals are seldom reformed by spending time in prison. If these contentions are correct, then the ideal rules for society's treatment of malefactors are very different from what Bentham thought, and from what actual practice is today in the United States. To say all this, however, is not to show that the utilitarian *principle* is incorrect, for in view of these facts presumably the attitudes of a "qualified" person would not be favorable to criminal justice as practiced today. Utilitarian theory might still be correct, but its implications would be different from what Bentham thought—and they might coincide with justified ethical judgments. We shall return to this.

The whole utilitarian approach, however, has been criticized on the ground that it ought not in consistency to approve of *any* excuses from criminal liability.[3] Or at least, it should do so only after careful empirical inquiries. It is not obvious, it is argued, that we increase net expectable utility by permitting such defenses. At the least, the utilitarian is committed to defend the concept of "strict liability." Why?

Because we could get a more strongly deterrent effect if everyone knew that *all behavior* of a certain sort would be punished, irrespective of mistaken supposals of fact, compulsion, and so on. The critics admit that knowledge that all behavior of a certain sort will be punished will hardly deter from crime the insane, persons acting under compulsion, persons acting under erroneous beliefs about facts, and others, but, as Professor Hart points out, it does not follow from this that general knowledge that certain acts will always be punished will not be salutary.

The utilitarian, however, has a solid defense against charges of this sort. We must bear in mind (as the critics do not) that the utilitarian principle, *taken by itself, implies nothing whatever* about whether a system of law should excuse persons on the basis of certain defenses. What the utilitarian does say is that, when we *combine* the principle of utilitarianism with *true* propositions about a certain thing or situation, then we shall come out with true statements about obligations. The utilitarian is certainly not committed to saying that one will derive true propositions about obligations if one starts with *false* propositions about fact or about what will maximize welfare, or with *no* such propositions at all. Therefore the criticism sometimes made (for example, by Hart), that utilitarian theory does not render it "obviously" or "necessarily" the case that the recognized excuses from criminal liability should be accepted as excusing from punishment, is beside the point. Moreover, in fact the utilitarian can properly claim that we do have excellent reason for believing that the general public would be no better motivated to avoid criminal offenses than it now is, if the insane and others were also punished along with intentional wrong-doers. Indeed, he may reasonably claim that the example of punishment of these individuals could only have a hardening effect—like public executions. Furthermore, the utilitarian can point out that abolition of the standard exculpating excuses would lead to serious insecurity. Imagine the pleasure of driving an automobile if one knew one could be executed for running down a child whom it was absolutely impossible to avoid striking! One certainly does not maximize expectable utility by eliminating the traditional excuses. In general, then, the utilitarian theory is not threatened by its implications about exculpating excuses.

It might also be objected against utilitarianism that it cannot recognize the validity of *mitigating* excuses (which presumably have the support of "qualified" attitudes). Would not consequences be better if the distinction between premeditated and impulsive acts were abolished? The utilitarian can reply that people who commit impulsive crimes, in the heat of anger, do not give thought to legal penalties; they would not be deterred by a stricter law. Moreover, such a person is unlikely to repeat his crime, so that a mild sentence saves an essentially good man for society.[4] Something can also be said in support of the practice of judges in giving a milder sentence when a person's temptation is severe: at least the *extended* rule-utilitarian can say, in defense of the practice of punishing less severely the crime of a man who has had few opportunities in life, that a judge ought to do what he can to repair inequalities in life, and that a mild sentence to a man who has had few opportunities is one way of doing this. There are, then, utilitarian supports for recognizing the mitigating excuses. . . .

Another popular objection to the utilitarian theory is that the utilitarian must approve of prosecutors or judges occasionally withholding evidence known to them, for the sake of convicting an innocent man, if the public welfare really is served by so doing. Critics of the theory would not deny that there *can* be circumstances where the dangers are so severe that such action is called for; they only say that utilitarianism calls for it all too frequently. Is this criticism justified? Clearly, the utilitarian is not committed to advocating that a provision should be written into the *law* so as to permit punishment of persons for crimes they did not commit if to do so would serve the public good. Any such provision would be a shattering blow to public confidence and security. The question is only whether there should be an informal moral rule to the same effect, for the guidance of judges and prosecutors. Will the rule-utilitarian necessarily be committed to far too sweeping a moral rule on this point? We must recall that he is not in the position of the act-utilitarian, who must say that an innocent man must be punished if in *his particular case* the public welfare would be served by his punishment. The rule-utilitarian rather asserts only that an innocent man should be punished if he falls within a class of cases such that net expectable utility is maximized if *all* members of the class are punished, taking into account the possible disastrous effects on public confidence if it is generally known that judges and prosecutors are guided by such a rule. Moreover, the "extended" rule-utilitarian has a further reason for not punishing an innocent man unless he has had more than his equal share of the good things of life already; namely, that there is an obligation to promote equality of welfare, whereas severe punishment is heaping "illfare" on one individual person. When we take these considerations into account, it is *not* obvious that the rule-utilitarian (or the "extended" rule-utilitarian) is committed to action that we are justifiably convinced is immoral.[5] . . .

Utilitarianism and Reform

Some thinkers today believe that criminal justice in Great Britain and the United States is in need of substantial revision. If we agree with their proposals, we have even less reason for favoring the retributive principle; but we must also question the traditional utilitarian emphasis on deterrence as the primary function of the institution of criminal justice.

Their proposal, roughly, is that we should extend, to all criminal justice, the practices of juvenile courts and institutions for the reform of juvenile offenders. Here, retributive concepts have been largely discarded at least in theory, and psychiatric treatment and programs for the prevention of crime by means of slum clearance, the organization of boys' clubs, and so forth, have replaced even deterrence as guiding ideas for social action.

The extension of these practices to criminal justice as a whole would work somewhat as follows: First, the present court procedure would be used to determine whether an offense has actually been committed. Such procedure would necessarily include ordinary rules about the admission of evidence, trial by jury, and the exculpating justifications and excuses for offenses (such as wrong suppositions about the facts). Second, if an accused were adjudged guilty, decisions about his treatment would then be in the hands of the experts, who would determine what treatment was called for and when the individual was ready for return to normal social living. The trial court might, of course, set some maximum period during which such experts would have a right to control the treatment of the criminal. What the experts would do would be decided by the criminal's condition; it would be criminal-centered treatment, not crime-centered treatment.

One might object to this proposal that it overlooks the necessity of disagreeable penalties for crime, in order to deter prospective criminals effectively. But it is doubtful whether threats of punishment have as much deterrent value as is often supposed. Threats of punishment will have little effect on morons, or on persons to whom normal living offers few prospects of an interesting existence.[6] Moreover, persons from better economic or social circumstances will be deterred sufficiently by the prospect of conviction in a public trial and being at the disposal of a board for a period of years.

Such proposals have their difficulties. For instance, would the police be as safe as they are, if criminals knew that killing a policeman would be no more serious in its consequences than the crime for which the policeman was trying to arrest them? However, there is much factual evidence for answering such questions, since systems of criminal justice along such lines are already in operation in some parts of the world, in particular among the Scandinavian countries. In fact, in some states the actual practice is closer to the projected system than one might expect from books on legal theory.

Another objection that many would raise is that psychiatry and criminology have not yet advanced far enough for such weighty decisions about the treatment of criminals to be placed in their hands. The treatment of criminals might vary drastically depending on the particular theoretical predilections of a given theorist, or on his personal likes and dislikes. One can probably say as much, or more, however, about the differences between judges, in their policies for picking a particular sentence within the range permitted by law.

An institution of criminal justice operating on such basic principles would come closer to our views about how parents should treat their children, or teachers their students, than the more traditional practices of criminal justice today.

We should repeat that this view about the ideal form for an institution of criminal justice is not in conflict with utilitarianism; in fact it is utilitarian in outlook. The motivation behind advocating it is the thought that such a system would do more good. It differs from the kind of institution traditionally advocated by utilitarians like Bentham only in making different factual assumptions, primarily about the deterrence value of threat of imprisonment, and the actual effect of imprisonment on the attitudes of the criminal.

Notes

1. In *Principles of Morals and Legislation.*

2. Act-utilitarians face some special problems. For instance, if I am an act-utilitarian and serve on a jury, I shall work to get a verdict that will do the most good, irrespective of the charges of the judge, and of any oath I may have taken to give a reasonable answer to certain questions on the basis of the evidence presented—unless I think my doing so will have indirect effects on the institution of the jury, public confidence in it, and so on. This is certainly not what we think a juror should do. Of course, neither a juror nor a judge can escape his prima facie obligation to do what good he can; this obligation is present in some form in every theory. The act-utilitarian, however, makes this the whole of one's responsibility.

3. See H. L. A. Hart, "Legal Responsibility and Excuses," in Sidney Hook (ed.), *Determinism and Freedom* (New York: New York University Press, 1958), pp. 81–104; and David Braybrooke, "Professor Stevenson, Voltaire, and the Case of Admiral Byng," *Journal of Philosophy,* LIII (1956), 787–96.

4. The utilitarian must admit that the same thing is true for many deliberate murders; and probably he should also admit that some people who commit a crime in the heat of anger would have found time to think had they known that a grave penalty awaited them.

5. In any case, a tenable theory of punishment must approve of punishing persons who are *morally* blameless. Suppose someone commits treason for moral reasons. We may have to say that his deed is not reprehensible at all, and might even (considering the risk he took for his principles) be morally admirable. Yet we think such persons must be punished no matter what their motives; people cannot be permitted to take the law into their own hands.

6. It is said that picking pockets was once a capital offense in England, and hangings were public, in order to get the maximum deterrent effect. But hangings in public had to be abolished, because such crimes as picking pockets were so frequent during the spectacle! See N. F. Cantor, *Crime, Criminals, and Criminal Justice* (New York: Henry Holt & Company, Inc., 1932).

56. A Critique of the Humanitarian Theory of Punishment

C. S. Lewis

C. S. Lewis argues that the humanitarian theory of punishment is not in the interests of the criminal. According to Lewis, this is because the humanitarian theory is concerned with the goals of reform and deterrence and not the requirements of justice. Hence, the theory permits the violation of the criminal's rights as a way of promoting these goals. Moreover, Lewis claims, deciding what promotes reform and deterrence, unlike deciding what is required by justice, seems best left to experts. Yet these experts, Lewis argues, even with the best of intentions, may act "as cruelly and unjustly as the greatest tyrants."

In England we have lately had a controversy about Capital Punishment. I do not know whether a murderer is more likely to repent and make a good end on the gallows a few weeks after his trial or in the prison infirmary thirty years later. I do not know whether the fear of death is an indispensable deterrent. I need not, for the purpose of this article, decide whether it is a morally permissible deterrent. Those are questions which I propose to leave untouched. My subject is not Capital Punishment in particular, but that theory of punishment in general which the controversy showed to be almost universal among my fellow-countrymen. It may be called the Humanitarian theory. Those who hold it think that it is mild and merciful. In this I believe that they are seriously mistaken. I believe that the "Humanity" which it claims is a dangerous illusion and disguises the possibility of cruelty and injustice without end. I urge a return to the traditional or Retributive theory not solely, not even primarily, in the interests of society, but in the interests of the criminal.

According to the Humanitarian theory, to punish a man because he deserves it, and as much as he deserves, is mere revenge, and, therefore, barbarous and immoral. It is maintained that the only legitimate motives for punishing are the desire to deter others by

From "The Humanitarian Theory of Punishment," *Res Judicatae* (1953), pp. 224–230. Reprinted by permission of the *Melbourne University Law Review* and the Trustee for the C. S. Lewis Estate.

example or to mend the criminal. When this theory is combined, as frequently happens, with the belief that all crime is more or less pathological, the idea of mending tails off into that of healing or curing and punishment becomes therapeutic. Thus it appears at first sight that we have passed from the harsh and self-righteous notion of giving the wicked their deserts to the charitable and enlightened one of tending the psychologically sick. What could be more amiable? One little point which is taken for granted in this theory needs, however, to be made explicit. The things done to the criminal, even if they are called cures, will be just as compulsory as they were in the old days when we called them punishments. If a tendency to steal can be cured by psychotherapy, the thief will no doubt be forced to undergo the treatment. Otherwise, society cannot continue.

My contention is that this doctrine, merciful though it appears, really means that each one of us, from the moment he breaks the law, is deprived of the rights of a human being.

The reason is this. The Humanitarian theory removes from Punishment the concept of Desert. But the concept of Desert is the only connecting link between punishment and justice. It is only as deserved or undeserved that a sentence can be just or unjust. I do not here contend that the question "Is it deserved?" is the only one we can reasonably ask about a punishment. We may very properly ask whether it is likely to deter others and to reform the criminal. But neither of these two last questions is a question about justice. There is no sense in talking about a "just deterrent" or a "just cure". We demand of a deterrent not whether it is just but whether it will deter. We demand of a cure not whether it is just but whether it succeeds. Thus when we cease to consider what the criminal deserves and consider only what will cure him or deter others, we have tacitly removed him from the sphere of justice altogether; instead of a person, a subject of rights, we now have a mere object, a patient, a "case".

The distinction will become clearer if we ask who will be qualified to determine sentences when sentences are no longer held to derive their propriety from the criminal's deservings. On the old view the problem of fixing the right sentence was a moral problem. Accordingly, the judge who did it was a person trained in jurisprudence: trained, that is, in a science which deals with rights and duties, and which, in origin at least, was consciously accepting guidance from the Law of Nature, and from Scripture. We must admit that in the actual penal code of most countries at most times these high originals were so much modified by local custom, class interests, and utilitarian concessions, as to be very imperfectly recognizable. But the code was never in principle, and not always in fact, beyond the control of the conscience of the society. And when (say, in eighteenth-century England) actual punishments conflicted too violently with the moral sense of the community, juries refused to convict and reform was finally brought about. This was possible because, so long as we are thinking in terms of Desert, the propriety of the penal code, being a moral question, is a question on which every man has the right to an opinion, not because he follows this or that profession, but because he is simply a man, a rational animal enjoying the Natural Light. But all this is changed when we drop the concept of Desert. The only two questions we may now ask about a punishment are whether it deters and whether it cures. But these are not questions on which anyone is entitled to have an opinion simply because he is a man. He is not entitled to an opinion even if, in addition to being a man, he should happen also to be a jurist, a Christian, and a moral theologian. For

they are not questions about principle but about matter of fact; and for such *cuiquam in sua arte credendum*. Only the expert "penologist" (let barbarous things have barbarous names), in the light of previous experiment, can tell us what is likely to deter: only the psychotherapist can tell us what is likely to cure. It will be in vain for the rest of us, speaking simply as men, to say, "but this punishment is hideously unjust, hideously disproportionate to the criminal's deserts". The experts with perfect logic will reply, "but nobody was talking about deserts. No one was talking about *punishment* in your archaic vindictive sense of the word. Here are the statistics proving that this treatment deters. Here are the statistics proving that this other treatment cures. What is your trouble?"

The Humanitarian theory, then, removes sentences from the hands of jurists whom the public conscience is entitled to criticize and places them in the hands of technical experts whose special sciences do not even employ such categories as rights or justice. It might be argued that since this transference results from an abandonment of the old idea of punishment, and, therefore, of all vindictive motives, it will be safe to leave our criminals in such hands. I will not pause to comment on the simple-minded view of fallen human nature which such a belief implies. Let us rather remember that the "cure" of criminals is to be compulsory; and let us then watch how the theory actually works in the mind of the Humanitarian. The immediate starting point of this article was a letter I read in one of our Leftist weeklies. The author was pleading that a certain sin, now treated by our laws as a crime, should henceforward be treated as a disease. And he complained that under the present system the offender, after a term in gaol, was simply let out to return to his original environment where he would probably relapse. What he complained of was not the shutting up but the letting out. On his remedial view of punishment the offender should, of course, be detained until he was cured. And of course the official straighteners are the only people who can say when that is. The first result of the Humanitarian theory is, therefore, to substitute for a definite sentence (reflecting to some extent the community's moral judgment on the degree of ill-desert involved) an indefinite sentence terminable only by the word of those experts—and they are not experts in moral theology nor even in the Law of Nature—who inflict it. Which of us, if he stood in the dock, would not prefer to be tried by the old system?

It may be said that by the continued use of the word punishment and the use of the verb "inflict" I am misrepresenting Humanitarians. They are not punishing, not inflicting, only healing. But do not let us be deceived by a name. To be taken without consent from my home and friends; to lose my liberty; to undergo all those assaults on my personality which modern psychotherapy knows how to deliver; to be re-made after some pattern of "normality" hatched in a Viennese laboratory to which I never professed allegiance; to know that this process will never end until either my captors have succeeded or I grown wise enough to cheat them with apparent success— who cares whether this is called Punishment or not? That it includes most of the elements for which any punishment is feared—shame, exile, bondage, and years eaten by the locust—is obvious. Only enormous ill-desert could justify it; but ill-desert is the very conception which the Humanitarian theory has thrown overboard.

If we turn from the curative to the deterrent justification of punishment we shall find the new theory even more alarming. When you punish a man *in terrorem*, make of him an "example" to others, you are admittedly using him as a means to an end; someone else's end. This, in itself, would be a very wicked thing to do. On the classical theory of Punishment it was of course justified on the ground that the man deserved it. That was assumed to be established before any question of "making him an example" arose. You then, as the saying is, killed two birds with one stone; in the process of giving him what he deserved you set an example to others. But take away desert and the whole morality of the punishment disappears. Why, in Heaven's name, am I to be sacrificed to the good of society in this way?—unless, of course, I deserve it.

But that is not the worst. If the justification of exemplary punishment is not to be based on desert but solely on its efficacy as a deterrent,

it is not absolutely necessary that the man we punish should even have committed the crime. The deterrent effect demands that the public should draw the moral, "If we do such an act we shall suffer like that man." The punishment of a man actually guilty whom the public think innocent will not have the desired effect; the punishment of a man actually innocent will, provided the public think him guilty. But every modern State has powers which make it easy to fake a trial. When a victim is urgently needed for exemplary purposes and a guilty victim cannot be found, all the purposes of deterrence will be equally served by the punishment (call it "cure" if you prefer) of an innocent victim, provided that the public can be cheated into thinking him guilty. It is no use to ask me why I assume that our rulers will be so wicked. The punishment of an innocent, that is, an undeserving, man is wicked only if we grant the traditional view that righteous punishment means deserved punishment. Once we have abandoned that criterion, all punishments have to be justified, if at all, on other grounds that have nothing to do with desert. Where the punishment of the innocent can be justified on those grounds (and it could in some cases be justified as a deterrent) it will be no less moral than any other punishment. Any distaste for it on the part of a Humanitarian will be merely a hang-over from the Retributive theory.

It is, indeed, important to notice that my argument so far supposes no evil intentions on the part of the Humanitarian and considers only what is involved in the logic of his position. My contention is that good men (not bad men) consistently acting upon that position would act as cruelly and unjustly as the greatest tyrants. They might in some respects act even worse. Of all tyrannies a tyranny sincerely exercised for the good of its victims may be the most oppressive. It may be better to live under robber barons than under omnipotent moral busybodies. The robber baron's cruelty may sometimes sleep, his cupidity may at some point be satiated; but those who torment us for our own good will torment us without end for they do so with the approval of their own conscience. They may be more likely to go to Heaven yet at the same time likelier to make a Hell of earth. Their very kindness stings with intolerable insult. To be "cured" against one's will and cured of states which we may not regard as disease is to be put on a level with those who have not yet reached the age of reason or those who never will; to be classed with infants, imbeciles, and domestic animals. But to be punished, however severely; because we have deserved it, because we "ought to have known better", is to be treated as a human person made in God's image.

In reality, however, we must face the possibility of bad rulers armed with a Humanitarian theory of punishment. A great many popular blue prints for a Christian society are merely what the Elizabethans called "eggs in moonshine" because they assume that the whole society is Christian or that the Christians are in control. This is not so in most contemporary States. Even if it were, our rulers would still be fallen men, and, therefore, neither very wise nor very good. As it is, they will usually be unbelievers. And since wisdom and virtue are not the only or the commonest qualifications for a place in the government, they will not often be even the best unbelievers. The practical problem of Christian politics is not that of drawing up schemes for a Christian society, but that of living as innocently as we can with unbelieving fellow-subjects under unbelieving rulers who will never be perfectly wise and good and who will sometimes be very wicked and very foolish. And when they are wicked the Humanitarian theory of punishment will put in their hands a finer instrument of tyranny than wickedness ever had before. For if crime and disease are to be regarded as the same thing, it follows that any state of mind which our masters choose to call "disease" can be treated as crime; and compulsorily cured. It will be vain to plead that states of mind which displease government need not always involve moral turpitude and do not therefore always deserve forfeiture of liberty. For our masters will not be using the concepts of Desert and Punishment but those of disease and cure. We know that one school of psychology already regards religion as a neurosis. When this particular neurosis becomes inconvenient to government, what is to hinder government from proceeding to "cure" it? Such "cure" will, of course, be compulsory; but under the Humanitarian theory it will not be called by the shock-

ing name of Persecution. No one will blame us for being Christian, no one will hate us, no one will revile us. The new Nero will approach us with the silky manners of a doctor, and though all will be in fact as compulsory as the *tunica molesta* or Smithfield or Tyburn, all will go on within the unemotional therapeutic sphere where words like "right" and "wrong" or "freedom" and "slavery" are never heard. And thus when the command is given, every prominent Christian in the land may vanish overnight into Institutions for the Treatment of the Ideologically Unsound, and it will rest with the expert gaolers to say when (if ever) they are to reemerge. But it will not be persecution. Even if the treatment is painful, even if it is life-long, even if it is fatal, that will be only a regrettable accident; the intention was purely therapeutic. Even in ordinary medicine there were painful operations and fatal operations; so in this. But because they are "treatment", not punishment, they can be criticized only by fellow-experts and on technical grounds, never by men as men and on grounds of justice.

This is why I think it essential to oppose the Humanitarian theory of punishment, root and branch, wherever we encounter it. It carries on its front a semblance of mercy which is wholly false. That is how it can deceive men of good will. The error began, perhaps, with Shelley's statement that the distinction between mercy and justice was invented in the courts of tyrants. It sounds noble, and was indeed the error of a noble mind. But the distinction is essential. The older view was that mercy "tempered" justice, or (on the highest level of all) that mercy and justice had met and kissed. The essential act of mercy was to pardon; and pardon in its very essence involves the recognition of guilt, and ill-desert in the recipient. If crime is only a disease which needs cure, not sin which deserves punishment, it cannot be pardoned. How can you pardon a man for having a gumboil or a club foot? But the Humanitarian theory wants simply to abolish Justice and substitute Mercy for it. This means that you start being "kind" to people before you have considered their rights, and then force upon them supposed kindnesses which they in fact had a right to refuse, and finally kindnesses which no one but you will recognize as kindnesses and which the recipient will feel as abominable cruelties. You have overshot the mark. Mercy, detached from Justice, grows unmerciful. That is the important paradox. As there are plants which will flourish only in mountain soil, so it appears that Mercy will flower only when it grows in the crannies of the rock of Justice: transplanted to the marshlands of mere Humanitarianism, it becomes a man-eating weed, all the more dangerous because it is still called by the same name as the mountain variety. But we ought long ago to have learned our lesson. We should be too old now to be deceived by those humane pretensions which have served to usher in every cruelty of the revolutionary period in which we live. These are the "precious balms" which will "break our heads."

There is a fine sentence in Bunyan: "It came burning hot into my mind, whatever he said, and however he flattered, when he got me home to his house, he would sell me for a slave." There is a fine couplet, too, in John Ball:

Be ware ere ye be woe
Know your friend from your foe.

One last word. You may ask why I sent this to an Australian periodical. The reason is simple and perhaps worth recording: I can get no hearing for it in England.

57. Classical Retributivism

Edmund L. Pincoffs

Edmund L. Pincoffs begins by setting out three principles that, he holds, express the essence of a Kantian retributive theory of punishment. He then claims that the underlying rationale for these principles is to provide a justification of the punishment to the criminal on the grounds that she has willed the punishment she now suffers. Pincoffs concludes by noting two difficulties for the retributive theory of punishment that he has not addressed: how to make punishment equal to the crime and how to distinguish punishment from revenge.

I

The classification of Kant as a retributivist[1] is usually accompanied by a reference to some part of the following passage from the *Rechtslehre*, which is worth quoting at length.

> Juridical punishment can never be administered merely as a means for promoting another good either with regard to the criminal himself or to civil society, but must in all cases be imposed only because the individual on whom it is in-

From *The Rationale of Legal Punishment* (1966), pp. 2–16. Reprinted by permission of Humanities Press, Inc., Atlantic Highlands, N.J., 07716.

flicted *has committed a crime*. For one man ought never to be dealt with merely as a means subservient to the purpose of another, nor be mixed up with the subjects of real right. Against such treatment his inborn personality has a right to protect him, even though he may be condemned to lose his civil personality. He must first be found guilty and *punishable* before there can be any thought of drawing from his punishment any benefit for himself or his fellow-citizens. The penal law is a categorical imperative; and woe to him who creeps through the serpent-windings of utilitarianism to discover some advantage that may discharge him from the justice of punishment, or even from the due measure of it, according to the Pharisaic maxim: "It is better that *one* man should die than the whole people should perish." For if justice and righteousness perish, human life would no longer have any value in the world.

. . .

But what is the mode and measure of punishment which public justice takes as its principle and standard? It is just the principle of equality, by which the pointer of the scale of justice is made to incline no more to the one side than the other. It may be rendered by saying that the undeserved evil which any one commits on another, is to be regarded as perpetrated on himself. Hence it may be said: "If you slander another, you slander yourself; if you steal from another, you steal from yourself; if you strike another, you strike yourself; if you kill another, you kill yourself." This is the Right of RETALIATION (*jus talionis*); and properly understood, it is the only principle which in regulating a public court, as distinguished from mere private judgment, can definitely assign both the quality and the quantity of a just penalty. All other standards are wavering and uncertain; and on account of other considerations involved in them, they contain no principle conformable to the sentence of pure and strict justice.[2]

Obviously we could mull over this passage for a long time. What, exactly, is the distinction between the Inborn and the Civil Personality? How is the Penal Law a Categorical Imperative: by derivation from one of the five formulations in the *Grundlegung*, or as a separate formulation? But we are on the trail of the traditional retributive theory of punishment and do not want to lose ourselves in niceties. There are two main points in this passage to which we should give particular attention:

i. The only acceptable reason for punishing a man is that he has committed a crime.

ii. The only acceptable reason for punishing a man in a given manner and degree is that the punishment is "equal" to the crime for which he is punished.

These propositions, I think it will be agreed, express the main points of the first and second paragraphs respectively. Before stopping over these points, let us go on to a third. It is brought out in the following passage from the *Rechtslehre*, which is also often referred to by writers on retributivism.

Even if a civil society resolved to dissolve itself with the consent of all its members—as might be supposed in the case of a people inhabiting an island resolving to separate and scatter themselves throughout the whole world—the last murderer lying in prison ought to be executed before the resolution was carried out. This ought to be done in order that every one may realize the desert of his deeds, and that bloodguiltiness may not remain upon the people; for otherwise they will all be regarded as participators in the murder as a public violation of justice.[3]

It is apparent from this passage that, so far anyway as the punishment of death for murder is concerned, the punishment awarded not only may but must be carried out. If it must be carried out "so that everyone may realize the desert of his deeds," then punishment for deeds other than murder must be carried out too. We will take it, then, that Kant holds that:

iii. Whoever commits a crime must be punished in accordance with his desert.

Whereas (i) tells us what kind of reason we must have *if* we punish, (iii) now tells us that we must punish *whenever* there is desert of punishment. Punishment, Kant tells us elsewhere, is "The *juridical* effect or consequence of a culpable act of Demerit."[4] Any crime is a culpable act of demerit, in that it is an "*intentional* transgression—that is, an act accompanied with the consciousness that it is a transgression."[5] This is an unusually narrow definition of crime, since crime is not ordinarily limited to intentional acts of transgression but may also include unintentional ones, such as acts done in ignorance of the law, and criminally negligent acts. However, Kant apparently leaves room for "culpable acts of demerit" outside of the category of crime. These he calls "faults," which are unintentional transgressions of duty, but "are nevertheless imputable to a person."[6] I can only suppose, though it is a difficulty in the interpretation of the *Rechtslehre*, that when Kant says that punishment must be inflicted "only because he has committed a crime," he is not including in "crime" what he would call a fault. Crime would, then, refer to any *intentional* imputable transgressions of duty; and these are what must be punished as involving ill desert. The difficulties involved in the definition of crime as the transgression of duty, as opposed to the mere violation of a legal prohibition, will be taken up later.

Taking the three propositions we have isolated as expressing the essence of the Kantian retributivistic position, we must now ask a direct and obvious question. What makes Kant hold this position? Why does he think it apparent that consequences should have *nothing to do* with the decision whether, and how, and how much to punish? There are two directions an answer to this question might follow. One would lead us into an extensive excursus on the philosophical position of Kant, the relation of this to his ethical theory, and the relation of his general theory of ethics to his philosophy of law. It would, in short, take our question as one about the consistency of Kant's position concerning the justification of punishment with the whole of Kantian philosophy. This would involve discussion of Kant's reasons for believing that moral laws must be universal and categorical in virtue of their form alone, and divorced from any empirical content; of his attempt to make out a moral decision-procedure based upon an "empty" categorical imperative; and, above all, of the concept of freedom as a postulate of practical reason, and as the central concept of the philosophy of law. This kind of answer, however, we must forego here; for while it would have considerable interest in its own right, it would lead us astray from our purpose, which is to understand as well as we can the retributivist position, not as a part of this or that philosophical system but for its own sake. It is a position taken by

philosophers with diverse philosophical systems; we want to take another direction, then, in our answer. Is there any *general* (nonspecial, nonsystematic) reason why Kant rejects consequences in the justification of punishment?

Kant believes that consequences have nothing to do with the justification of punishment partly because of his assumptions about the *direction* of justification; and these assumptions are, I believe, also to be found underlying the thought of Hegel and Bradley. Justification is not only *of* something, it is also *to* someone: it has an addressee. Now there are important confusions in Kant's and other traditional justifications of punishment turning on the question what the "punishment" *is* which is being justified. . . . But if we are to feel the force of the retributivist position, we can no longer put off the question of the addressee of justification.

To whom is the Kantian justification of punishment directed? The question may seem a difficult one to answer, since Kant does not consider it himself as a separate issue. Indeed, it is not the kind of question likely to occur to a philosopher of Kant's formalistic leanings. A Kantian justification or rationale stands, so to speak, on its own. It is a structure which can be examined, tested, probed by any rational being. Even to speak of the addressee of justification has an uncomfortably relativistic sound, as if only persuasion of A or B or C is possible, and proof impossible. Yet, in practice, Kant does not address his proffered justification of punishment so much to any rational being (which, to put it otherwise, is to address it not at all), as to the being most affected: the criminal himself.

It is the criminal who is cautioned not to creep through the serpent-windings of utilitarianism. It is the criminal's rights which are in question in the debate with Beccaria over capital punishment. It is the criminal we are warned not to mix up with property or things: the "subjects of Real Right." In the *Kritik der Praktischen Vernunst*, the intended direction of justification becomes especially clear.

> Now the notion of punishment, as such, cannot be united with that of becoming a partaker of happiness; for

although he who inflicts the punishment may at the same time have the benevolent purpose of directing this punishment to this end, yet it must be justified in itself as punishment, that is, as mere harm, so that if it stopped there, and the person punished could get no glimpse of kindness hidden behind this harshness, he must yet admit that justice was done him, and that his reward was perfectly suitable to his conduct. In every punishment, as such, there must first be justice, and this constitutes the essence of the notion. Benevolence may, indeed, be united with it, but the man who has deserved punishment has not the least reason to reckon upon this.[7]

Since this matter of the direction of justification is central in our understanding of traditional retributivism, and not generally appreciated, it will be worth our while to pause over this paragraph. Kant holds here, as he later holds in the *Rechtslehre*, that once it has been decided that a given "mode and measure" of punishment is justified, then "he who inflicts punishment" may do so in such a way as to increase the long-term happiness of the criminal. This could be accomplished, for example, by using a prison term as an opportunity for reforming the criminal. But Kant's point is that reforming the criminal has nothing to do with justifying the infliction of punishment. It is not inflicted because it will give an opportunity for reform, but because it is merited. The passage does not need my gloss; it is transparently clear. Kant wants the justification of punishment to be such that the criminal "who could get no glimpse of kindness behind this harshness" would have to admit that punishment is warranted.

Suppose we tell the criminal, "We are punishing you for your own good." This is wrong, because it is then open to him to raise the question whether he deserves punishment, and what you consider good to be. If he does not deserve punishment, we have no right to inflict it, especially in the name of some good of which the criminal may not approve. So long as we are to treat him as rational—a being with dignity—we cannot force our judgments of good upon him. This is what makes the appeal to supposedly good consequences "wavering and uncertain." They waver because the criminal has as much right as anyone to question them. They concern ends which he may reject, and means which he might rightly regard as unsuited to the ends.

In the "Supplementary Explanations of the Principles of Right" of the *Rechtslehre*, Kant distinguishes between "punitive justice *(justitia punitiva)*, in which the ground of the penalty is moral *(quia peccatum est),*" and "punitive expediency, the foundation of which is merely pragmatic *(ne peccetur)* as being grounded upon the experience of what operates most effectively to prevent crime." Punitive justice, says Kant, has an "entirely distinct place *(locus justi)* in the topical arrangement of the juridical conceptions." It does not seem reasonable to suppose that Kant makes this distinction merely to discard punitive expediency entirely, that he has no concern at all for the *ne peccetur*. But he does hold that there is no place for it in the justification of punishment proper: for this can only be to show the criminal that the punishment is just.

How is this to be done? The difficulty is that on the one hand the criminal must be treated as a rational being, an end in himself; but on the other hand the justification we offer him cannot be allowed to appear as the opening move in a rational discussion. It cannot turn on the criminal's acceptance of some premise which, as rational being, he has a perfect right to question. If the end in question is the well-being of society, we are assuming that the criminal will not have a different view of what that well-being consists in, and we are telling him that he should sacrifice himself *to* that end. As a rational being, he can question whether any end we propose is a good end. And we have no right to demand that he sacrifice himself to the public well-being, even supposing he agrees with us on what that consists in. No man has a duty, on Kant's view, to be benevolent.[8]

The way out of the quandary is to show the criminal that we are not inflicting the punishment on him for some questionable purpose of our own choice, but that he, as a free agent, has exercised *his* choice in such a way as to make the punishment a necessary consequence. "His own evil deed draws the punishment upon himself."[9] "The undeserved evil which anyone commits on another, is to be regarded as perpetuated on himself."[10] But may not the criminal rationally question this asserted connection between crime and punishment? Suppose he wishes to regard the punishment *not* as "drawn upon himself" by his own "evil deed?" Suppose he argues that no good purpose will be served by punishing him? But this line of thought leads into the "serpent-windings of utilitarianism," for if it is good consequences that govern, then justice goes by the board. What may not be done to him in the name of good consequences? What proportion would remain between what he has done and what he suffers?[11]

But punishment is *inflicted*. To tell the criminal that he "draws it upon himself" is all very well, only how do we justify *to ourselves* the infliction of it? Kant's answer is found early in the *Rechtslehre*.[12] There he relates punishment to crime *via* freedom. Crime consists in compulsion or constraint of some kind: a hindrance of freedom.[13] If it is wrong that freedom should be hindered, it is right to block this hindrance. But to block the constraint of freedom it is necessary to apply constraint. Punishment is a "hindering of a hindrance of freedom." Compulsion of the criminal is, then, justified only to the extent that it hinders his compulsion of another.

But how are we to understand Kant here? Punishment comes after the crime. How can it hinder the crime? The reference cannot be to the hindrance of future crime, or Kant's doctrine reduces to a variety of utilitarianism. The picture of compulsion *vs.* compulsion is clear enough, but how are we to apply it? Our answer must be somewhat speculative, since there is no direct answer to be found in the *Rechtslehre*. The answer must begin from yet another extension of the concept of a crime. For the crime cannot consist merely in an act. What is criminal is acting in accordance with a wrong maxim: a maxim which would, if made universal, destroy freedom. The adoption of the maxim is criminal. Should we regard punishment, then, as the hindrance of a wrong maxim? But how do we hinder a maxim? We show, exhibit, its wrongness by taking it at face value. If the criminal has adopted it, he is claiming that it can be universalized. But if it is

universalized it warrants the same treatment of the criminal as he has accorded to his victim. So if he murders he must be executed; if he steals we must "steal from" him.[14] What we do to him he willed, in willing to adopt his maxim as universalizable. To justify the punishment to the criminal is to show him that the compulsion we use on him proceeds according to the same rule by which he acts. This is how he "draws the punishment upon himself." In punishing, we are not adopting his maxim but demonstrating its logical consequences if universalized: We show the criminal *what* he has willed. This is the positive side of the Kantian rationale of punishment.

II

Hegel's version of this rationale has attracted more attention, and disagreement, in recent literature. It is the Hegelian metaphysical terminology which is in part responsible for the disagreement, and which has stood in the way of an understanding of the retributivist position. The difficulty turns around the notions of "annulment of crime," and of punishment as the "right" of the criminal. Let us consider "annulment" first.

In the *Philosophie des Rechts*[15] Hegel tells us that

Abstract right is a right to coerce, because the wrong which transgresses it is an exercise of force against the existence of my freedom in an external thing. The maintenance of this existent against the exercise of force therefore itself takes the form of an external act and an exercise of force annulling the force originally brought against it.[16]

Holmes complains that by the use of his logical apparatus, involving the negation of negations (or annulment), Hegel professes to establish what is only a mystic (though generally felt) bond between wrong and punishment.[17] Hastings Rashdall asks how any rational connection can be shown between the evil of the pain of punishment, and the twin evils of the suffering of the victim and the moral evil which "pollutes the offender's soul," unless appeal is made to the probable good consequences of punishment. The notion that the "guilt" of the offense must be, in some mysterious way, wiped out by the suffering of the offender does not seem to provide it.[18] Crime, which is an evil, is apparently to be "annulled" by the addition to it of punishment, which is another evil. How can two evils yield a good?[19]

But in fact Hegel is following the *Rechtslehre* quite closely here, and his doctrine is very near to Kant's. In the notes taken at Hegel's lectures,[20] we find Hegel quoted as follows:

> If crime and its annulment . . . are treated as if they were unqualified evils, it must, of course, seem quite unreasonable to will an evil merely because "another evil is there already." . . . But it is not merely a question of an evil or of this, that, or the other good; the precise point at issue is wrong, and the righting of it. . . . The various considerations which are relevant to punishment as a phenomenon and to the bearing it has on the particular consciousness, and which concern its effects (deterrent, reformative, etcetera) on the imagination, are an essential topic for examination in their place, especially in connection with modes of punishment, but all these considerations presuppose as their foundation the fact that punishment is inherently and actually just. In discussing this matter the only important things are, first, that crime is to be annulled, not because it is the producing of an evil, but because it is the infringing of the right as right, and secondly, the question of what that positive existence is which crime possesses and which must be annulled; it is this existence which is the real evil to be removed, and the essential point is the question of where it lies. So long as the concepts here at issue are not clearly apprehended, confusion must continue to reign in the theory of punishment.[21]

While this passage is not likely to dethrone confusion, it does bring us closer to the basically Kantian heart of Hegel's theory. To "annul

crime" should be read "right wrong." Crime is a wrong which consists in an "infringement of the right as right."[22] It would be unjust, says Hegel, to allow crime, which is the invasion of a right, to go unrequited. For to allow this is to admit that the crime is "valid": that is, that it is not in conflict with justice. But this is what we do want to admit, and the only way of showing this is to pay back the deed to the agent: coerce the coercer. For by intentionally violating his victim's rights, the criminal in effect claims that the rights of others are not binding on him; and this is to attack *das Recht* itself: the system of justice in which there are rights which must be respected. Punishment not only keeps the system in balance, it vindicates the system itself.

Besides talking about punishment's "annulment" of crime, Hegel has argued that it is the "right of the criminal." The obvious reaction to this is that it is a strange justification of punishment which makes it someone's right, for it is at best a strange kind of right which no one would ever want to claim! McTaggart's explanation of this facet of Hegel's theory is epitomized in the following quotation:

> What, then, is Hegel's theory? It is, I think, briefly this: In sin, man rejects and defies the moral law. Punishment is pain inflicted on him because he has done this, and in order that he may, by the fact of his punishment, be forced into recognizing as valid the law which he rejected in sinning, and so repent of his sin—really repent, and not merely be frightened out of doing it again.[23]

If McTaggart is right, then we are obviously not going to find in Hegel anything relevant to the justification of legal punishment, where the notions of sin and repentance are out of place. And this is the conclusion McTaggart of course reaches. "Hegel's view of punishment," he insists, "cannot properly be applied in jurisprudence, and . . . his chief mistake regarding it lay in supposing that it could."[24]

But though McTaggart may be right in emphasizing the theological aspect of Hegel's doctrine of punishment, he is wrong in denying it a jurisprudential aspect. In fact, Hegel is only saying what Kant emphasized: that to justify punishment to the criminal is to show him that *he* has chosen to be treated as he is being treated.

> The injury (the penalty) which falls on the criminal is not merely *implicitly* just— as just, it is *eo ipso* his implicit will, an embodiment of his freedom, his right; on the contrary, it is also a right *established* within the criminal himself, that is, in his objectively embodied will, in his action. The reason for this is that his action is the action of a rational being and this implies that it is something universal and that by doing it the criminal has laid down a law which he has explicitly recognized in his action and under which in consequence he should be brought as under his right.[25]

To accept the retributivist position, then, is to accept a thesis about the burden of proof in the justification of punishment. Provided we make the punishment "equal" to the crime it is not up to us to justify it to the criminal, beyond pointing out to him that it is what he willed. It is not that he initiated a chain of events likely to result in his punishment, but that in willing the crime he willed that he himself should suffer in the same degree as his victim. But what if the criminal simply wanted to commit his crime and get away with it (break the window and run, take the funds and retire to Brazil, kill but live?) Suppose we explain to the criminal that *really* in willing to kill he willed to lose his life; and, unimpressed, he replies that *really* he wished to kill and save his skin. The retributivist answer is that to the extent that the criminal understands freedom and justice he will understand that his punishment was made inevitable by his own choice. No moral theory can hope to provide a justification of punishment which will seem such to the criminal merely as a nexus of passions and desires. The retributivist addresses him as a rational being, aware of the significance of his action. The burden of proof, the retributivist would argue, is on the theorist who would not start from this assumption. For to assume from the beginning that the criminal is not rational is to treat him, from the beginning, as merely a "harmful animal."

What is involved in the action of the criminal is not only the concept of crime, the rational aspect present in crime as such whether the individual wills it or not, the aspect which the state has to vindicate, but also the abstract rationality of the individual's *volition*. Since that is so, punishment is regarded as containing the criminal's right and hence by being punished he is honored as a rational being. He does not receive this due of honor unless the concept and measure of his punishment are derived from his own act. Still less does he receive it if he is treated as a harmful animal who has to be made harmless, or with a view to deterring and reforming him.[26]

To address the criminal as a rational being aware of the significance of his action is to address him as a person who knows that he has not committed a "bare" act; to commit an act is to commit oneself to the universalization of the rule by which one acted. For a man to complain about the death sentence for murder is as absurd as for a man to complain that when he pushed down one tray of the scales, the other tray goes up; whereas the action, rightly considered, is of pushing down *and* up. "The criminal gives his consent already by his very act."[27] "The Eumenides sleep, but crime awakens them, and hence it is the very act of crime which vindicates itself."[28]

F. H. Bradley's contribution to the retributive theory of punishment adds heat but not much light. The central, and best-known, passage is the following:

> If there is any opinion to which the man of uncultivated morals is attached, it is the belief in the necessary connection of Punishment and guilt. Punishment is punishment, only where it is deserved. We pay the penalty because we owe it, and for no other reason; and if punishment is inflicted for any other reason whatever than because it is merited by wrong, it is a gross immorality, a crying injustice, an abominable crime, and not what it pretends to be. We may have regard for whatever considerations we please—our own convenience, the good

of society, the benefit of the offender; we are fools, and worse, if we fail to do so. Having once the right to punish, we may modify the punishment according to the useful and the pleasant; but these are external to the matter, they cannot give us a right to punish, and nothing can do that but criminal desert. This is not a subject to waste words over; if the fact of the vulgar view is not palpable to the reader, we have no hope, and no wish, to make it so.[29]

Bradley's sympathy with the "vulgar view" should be apparent. And there is at least a seeming variation between the position he expresses here and that we have attributed to Kant and Hegel. For Bradley can be read here as leaving an open field for utilitarian reasoning, when the question is how and how much to punish. Ewing interprets Bradley this way, and argues at some length that Bradley is involved in an inconsistency.[30] However, it is quite possible that Bradley did not mean to allow kind and quantity of punishment to be determined by utilitarian considerations. He could mean, as Kant meant, that once punishment is awarded, then "it" (what the criminal must suffer: time in jail, for example) may be made use of for utilitarian purposes. But, it should by this time go without saying, the retributivist would then wish to insist that we not argue backward from the likelihood of attaining these good purposes to the rightness of inflicting the punishment.

Bradley's language is beyond question loose when he speaks, in the passage quoted, of our "modifying" the punishment, "having once the right to punish." But when he says that "we pay the penalty because we owe it, and for no other reason," Bradley must surely be credited with the insight that we may owe more or less according to the gravity of the crime. The popular view, he says, is "that punishment is justice; that justice implies the giving what is due."[31] And, "punishment is the complement of criminal desert; is justifiable only so far as deserved."[32] If Bradley accepts this popular view, then Ewing must be wrong in attributing to him the position that kind and degree of punishment may be determined by utilitarian considerations.[33]

III

Let us sum up traditional retributivism, as we have found it expressed in the paradigmatic passage we have examined. We have found no reason in Hegel or Bradley to take back or qualify importantly the *three propositions* we found central in Kant's retributivism:

i. The only acceptable reason for punishing a man is that he has committed a crime.
ii. The only acceptable reason for punishing a man in a given manner and degree is that the punishment is "equal" to the crime.
iii. Whoever commits a crime must be punished in accordance with his desert.

To these propositions should be added *two underlying assumptions:*

i. An assumption about the direction of justification: to the criminal.
ii. An assumption about the nature of justification: to show the criminal that it is he who has willed what he now suffers.

Though it may have been stated in forbidding metaphysical terms, traditional retributivism cannot be dismissed as unintelligible, or absurd, or implausible.[34] There is no obvious contradiction in it; and there are no important disagreements among the philosophers we have studied over what it contends. Yet in spite of the importance of the theory, no one has yet done much more than sketch it in broad strokes. If, as I have surmised, it turns mainly on an assumption concerning the direction of justification, then this assumption should be explained and defended.

And the key concept of "desert" is intolerably vague. What does it mean to say that punishment must be proportionate to what a man *deserves*? This seems to imply, in the theory of the traditional retributivists, that there is some way of measuring desert, or at least of balancing punishment against it. How this measuring or balancing is supposed to be done, we will discuss later. What we must recognize here is that there are alternative criteria of "desert," and that it is not always clear which of these the traditional retributivist means to imply.

When we say of a man that he "deserves severe punishment" how, if at all, may we support our position by arguments? What kind of considerations tend to show what a man does or does not deserve? There are at least two general sorts: those which tend to show that what he has done is a member of a class of action which is especially heinous; and those which tend to show that his doing of this action was, in (or because of) the circumstances, particularly wicked. The argument that a man deserves punishment may rest on the first kind of appeal alone, or on both kinds. Retributivists who rely on the first sort of consideration alone would say that anyone who would do a certain sort of thing, no matter what the circumstances may have been, deserves punishment. Whether there are such retributivists I do not know. Kant, because of his insistence on *intention* as a necessary condition of committing a crime, clearly wishes to bring in considerations of the second sort as well. It is not, on his view, merely *what* was done, but the intention of the agent which must be taken into account. No matter what the intention, a man cannot commit a crime deserving punishment if his deed is not a transgression. But if he does commit a transgression, he must do so intentionally to commit a crime; and all crime is deserving of punishment. The desert of the crime is a factor both of the seriousness of the transgression, considered by itself, and the degree to which the intention to transgress was present. If, for Kant, the essence of morality consists in knowingly acting from duty, the essence of immorality consists in knowingly acting against duty.

The retributivist can perhaps avoid the question of how we decide that one crime is morally more heinous than another by hewing to his position that no such decision is necessary so long as we make the punishment "equal" to the crime. To accomplish this, he might argue, it is not necessary to argue to the *relative* wickedness of crimes. But at best this leaves us with the problem how we *do* make punishments equal to crimes, a problem which

will not stop plaguing retributivists. And there is the problem *which* transgressions, intentionally committed, the retributivist is to regard as crimes. Surely not every morally wrong action!

And how is the retributivist to fit in appeals to punitive expediency? None of our authors denies that such appeals may be made, but where and how do they tie into punitive justice? It will not do simply to say that justifying punishment to the criminal is one thing, and justifying it to society is another. Suppose we must justify in both directions at once? And who are "we" anyway—the players of which roles, at what stage of the game? And has the retributivist cleared himself of the charge, sure to arise, that the theory is but a cover for a much less commendable motive than respect for justice: elegant draping for naked revenge?

Notes

1. . . . [S]ince in our own time there are few defenders of retributivism, the position is most often referred to by writers who are opposed to it. This does not make for clarity. In the past few years, however, there has been an upsurge of interest, and some good articles have been written. Cf. esp. J. D. Mabbott, "Punishment," *Mind*, XLVIII (1939), pp. 152–67; C. S. Lewis, "The Humanitarian Theory of Punishment," *20th Century* (Australian), March, 1949; C. W. K. Mundle, "Punishment and Desert," *The Philosophical Quarterly*, IV (1954), pp. 216–28; A. S. Kaufman, "Anthony Quinton on Punishment," *Analysis*, October, 1959; and K. G. Armstrong, "The Retributivist Hits Back," *Mind*, LXX (1961), pp. 471–90.

2. *Rechtslehre*. Part Second, 49, E. Hastie translation, Edinburgh, 1887, pp. 195–7.

3. *Ibid.*, p. 198. Cf. also the passage on p. 196 beginning "What, then, is to be said of such a proposal as to keep a Criminal alive who has been condemned to death . . ."

4. *Ibid.*, Prolegomena, General Divisions of the Metaphysic of Morals, IV. (Hastie, p. 38).

5. *Ibid.*, p. 32.

6. *Ibid.*, p. 32.

7. Book I, Ch. I, Sect. VIII, Theorem IV, Remark II (T. K. Abbott translation, 5th ed., revised, London, 1898, p. 127).

8. *Rechtslehre.*

9. "Supplementary Explanation of The Principles of Right," V.

10. Cf. long quote from the *Rechtslehre*, above.

11. How can the retributivist allow utilitarian considerations even in the administration of the sentence? Are we not then opportunistically imposing our conception of good on the convicted man? How did we come by this right, which we did not have when he stood before the bar awaiting sentence? Kant would refer to the loss of his "Civil Personality;" but what rights remain with the "Inborn Personality," which is not lost? How is human dignity modified by conviction of crime?

12. Introduction to The Science of Right, General Definitions and Divisions, D. Right is Joined with the Title to Compel. (Hastie, p. 47).

13. This extends the definition of crime Kant has given earlier by specifying the nature of an imputable transgression of duty.

14. There are serious difficulties in the application of the "Principle of Equality" to the "mode and measure" of punishment. This will be considered. . . .

15. I shall use this short title for the work with the formidable double title of *Naturrecht und Stattswissenschaft in Grundrisse; Grundlinien der Philosophie des Rechts (Natural Law and Political Science in Outline: Elements of The Philosophy of Right.)* References will be to the T. M. Knox translation (*Hegel's Philosophy of Right,* Oxford, 1942).

16. *Philosophie des Rechts,* Sect. 93 (Knox, p. 67).

17. O. W. Holmes, Jr., *The Common Law,* Boston, 1881, p. 42.

18. Hastings Rashdall, *The Theory of Good and Evil,* 2nd. Edn., Oxford, 1924, vol. 1, pp. 285–6.

19. G. E. Moore holds that, consistently with his doctrine of organic wholes, they might; or at least they might yield that which is less evil than the sum of the constituent evils. This indicates for him a possible vindication of the Retributive theory of punishment. (*Principia Ethica,* Cambridge, 1903, pp. 213–4).

20. Included in the Knox translation.

21. Knox translation, pp. 69–70.

22. There is an unfortunate ambiguity in the German word *Recht,* here translated as "right." The word can mean either that which is a right or that which is in accordance with the law. So when Hegel speaks of "infringing the right as right" it is not certain whether he means a right as such or the law as such, or whether, in fact, he is aware of the ambiguity. But to say that the crime infringes the law is analytic, so we will take it that Hegel uses *Recht* here to refer to that which is right. But what the criminal does is not merely to infringe a right, but "the right *(das recht)* as right," that is, to challenge by his action the whole system of rights. (On *"Recht,"* Cf. J. Austin, *The Province of Jurisprudence Determined,* (London, Library of Ideas Edition, 1954), Note 26, pp. 285–8 esp. pp. 287–8).

23. J. M. E. McTaggart, *Studies in The Hegelian Cosmology,* Cambridge, 1901, Ch. V, p. 133.

24. *Ibid.,* p. 145.

25. *Op Cit.,* Sect. 100 (Hastie, p. 70.)

26. *Ibid.,* Lecture-notes on Sect. 100, Hastie, p. 71.

27. *Ibid.,* Addition to Sect. 100, Hastie, p. 246.

28. *Ibid.,* Addition to Sect. 101, Hastie, p. 247. There is something ineradicably *curious* about retributivism. We keep coming back to the metaphor of the balance scale. Why is the metaphor powerful and the same time strange? Why do we agree so readily that "the assassination" cannot "trammel up the consequence," that "evenhanded justice commends the ingredients of our poisoned chalice to our own lips?"

29. F. H. Bradley, *Ethical Studies,* Oxford, 1952, pp. 26–7.

30. A. C. Ewing, *The Morality of Punishment,* London, 1929, pp. 41–42.

31. *Op. Cit.,* p. 29.

32. *Ibid.,* p. 30.

33. *Op. Cit.,* p. 41.

34. Or, more ingeniously, "merely logical," the "elucidation of the use of a word;" answering the question, "When (logically) *can* we punish?" as opposed to the question answered by the utilitarians, "When (morally) *may* or *ought* we to punish?" (Cf. A. M. Quinton, "On Punishment," *Analysis,* June, 1954, pp. 133–42).

58. The Death Penalty: For and Against

Ernest van den Haag and Louis Schwartz

Ernest van den Haag favors the death penalty because (1) it is the indispensable deterrent for certain crimes, (2) some evidence seems to support its deterrent value, (3) imposing the death penalty is the least risky alternative, and (4) it is a requirement of justice.

Louis B. Schwartz opposes the death penalty because (1) mistakes occur in our trial system, (2) having the death penalty makes it difficult to get convictions, (3) some evidence seems to indicate that the death penalty does not deter, (4) having the death penalty can in certain cases stimulate a criminal to kill, and (5) the process of choosing those to be executed is inevitably arbitrary.

Q Professor van den Haag, why do you favor the use of the death penalty?

A For certain kinds of crimes it is indispensable.

Thus: The federal prisons now have custody of a man sentenced to life imprisonment who, since he has been in prison, has committed three more murders on three separate occasions—both of prison guards and inmates. There is no further punishment that he can receive. In effect, he has a license to murder.

Take another case: When a man is threatened with life imprisonment for a crime he has already committed, what reason has he not to kill the arresting officer in an attempt to escape? His punishment would be the same.

In short, there are many cases where the death penalty is the only penalty available that could possibly deter.

I'll go a step further. I hold life sacred. Because I hold it sacred, I feel that anyone who takes someone else's life should know that thereby he forsakes his own and does not just suffer an inconvenience about being put into prison for some time.

Q Could the same effect be achieved by putting the criminal in prison for life?

A At present, "life imprisonment" means anything from six months—after which the parole board in Florida can release the man—to 12 years in some States. But even if it were real life imprisonment, its deterrent effect will never be as great as that of the death penalty. The death penalty is the only actually irrevocable penalty. Because of that, it is the one that people fear most. And because it is feared, it is the one that is most likely to deter.

Q Authorities seem to differ as to whether the death sentence really does deter crime—

A Usually the statistics quoted were compiled more than 10 years ago and seem to indicate that the absence or presence of the death penalty made no difference in murder rates.

However, in the last 10 years there have been additional investigations. The results indicate, according to Isaac Ehrlich's recent article in the *American Economic Review:* Over the period 1933 to 1969, "an additional execution per year . . . may have resulted on the average in seven or eight fewer murders."

In New York in the last six years, the murder rate went up by 60 percent. Previous to the abolition of the death penalty, about 80 per cent of all murders committed in New York were so-called crimes of passion, defined as crimes in which the victim and the murderer were in some way involved with each other. Right now, only 50 per cent of all murders in New York are crimes of passion.

Q How do you interpret those figures?

A As long as the death penalty existed, largely only people in the grip of passion could not be deterred by the threat of the death penalty. Now that there's no death penalty, people who previously were deterred—who are not in the grip of passion—are no longer deterred from committing murder for the sake of gain. Murder is no longer an irrational act, least of all for juveniles for whom it means at most a few months of inconvenience.

Even if you assume the evidence for the deterrent effect of the death penalty is not clear—I make this point in my book "Punishing Criminals"—you have two risks. Risk 1: If you impose the death penalty and it doesn't have an additional deterrent effect, you have possibly lost the life of a convicted murderer without adding to deterrence and thereby sparing future victims. Risk 2: If you fail to execute the convicted murderer and execution would have had an additional deterrent effect, you have failed to spare the lives of a number of future victims.

Between the two risks, I'd much rather execute the convicted murderer than risk the lives of innocent people who could have been saved.

Q You noted that the death penalty is irrevocable once it is imposed. Does this make death such a different penalty that it should not be used?

A It makes it a different penalty. This is why it should be used when the crime is different—so heinous and socially dangerous to call for this extreme measure. When you kill a man with premeditation, you do something very different from stealing from him. I think the punishment should be appropriate. I favor the death penalty as a matter of justice and human dignity even apart from deterrence. The penalty must be appropriate to the seriousness of the crime.

Q Can you elaborate on your statement that the penalty should match the seriousness of the crime?

A Our system of punishment is based not just on deterrence but also on what is called "justice"—namely, that we feel a man who has committed a crime must be punished in proportion to the seriousness of the crime. Since the crime that takes a life is irrevocable, so must be the punishment.

All religions that I'm aware of feel that human life is sacred and that its sacredness must be enforced by depriving of life anyone who deprives another person of life. Once we make it clear to a person that if he deprives someone else of life he will suffer only minor in-

convenience, we have cheapened human life. We are at that point today.

Q Some argue that capital punishment tends to brutalize and degrade society. Do you agree?

A Many of the same people also argue that the death penalty is legalized murder because it inflicts on the criminal the same situation that he inflicted on his victim. Yet most punishments inflict on the criminal what he inflicted on the victim. The difference between the punishment and the crime is that one is a legal measure and the other is not.

As for brutalizing, I think that people are more brutalized by their daily TV fare. At any rate, people are not so much brutalized by punishment as they are brutalized by our failure to seriously punish brutal acts.

Q Professor Schwartz, why do you oppose the death penalty?

A For a number of reasons. In the first place, mistakes do occur in our trial system. And, if the victim of a mistake has been executed, that mistake is irremediable.

For example: I myself once represented a man who had been frightened into confessing a murder. He was afraid he'd get the electric chair if he stood trial. So he pleaded guilty and got life imprisonment. Twelve years later I was able to prove he was innocent. That would have been too late if he had been executed.

In the second place—and, for me, very important—the death penalty, rarely administered as it is, distorts the whole penal system. It makes the criminal procedure so complex that it turns the public off.

Q How does it do that?

A People are so reluctant to administer the death penalty until every last doubt is eliminated that the procedural law gets encumbered with a lot of technical rules of evidence. You not only get this in the trial, but you get habeas corpus proceedings after the trial.

This highly technical procedure is applied not only to capital cases but to other criminal cases as well. So it makes it hard to convict anybody.

I believe the death penalty actually does more harm to security in this country than it does good. Without it, we would be safer from criminals than with it.

Q Do you think the death penalty is a deterrent to crime?

A The evidence is inconclusive about that.

The best studies I know, done by Thorsten Sellin, Marvin Wolfgang and their students at the University of Pennsylvania, would indicate that there is no deterrent effect. This study compared States using the death penalty with next-door States that did not use it. They also compared the homicide rates in the same State during periods when it used the death penalty and when it did not. And they found no statistical differences in homicide rates—with or without the death penalty.

I agree that there may be cases where a robber will not shoot because he doesn't want to risk "the hot seat." But, in my opinion, there are also situations where the death penalty stimulates a criminal to kill. I'm talking about cases, for instance, where a kidnaper decides to kill the only witness who could identify him, or where witnesses or informers get wiped out because the criminal says: "If I'm convicted, I'm going to get the chair anyway, and I'm safer if I kill him."

So if the death penalty is not demonstrably helpful in saving innocent lives, I don't think we ought to use it—especially considering the risk of mistakes.

Q Are there no criminals who commit crimes so heinous that they ought to be executed for society's safety?

A My view is that society is not well enough organized to make a list of those people who ought to be executed. Sometimes I think if I were permitted to make up the list of those to be executed I wouldn't mind eliminating some people. But the list that society or the Government might make would probably not be the same as my list. Who is to decide who should live and who should die?

Now we're getting to the essential basis of what the Supreme Court must decide. This is whether the processes for choosing the ones to be killed are inevitably irrational, arbitrary and capricious.

Q Do you think this element of arbitrariness or capriciousness can ever be eliminated—even by making the death penalty mandatory for certain crimes, as many States have?

A No, I don't. No society has ever been able to make the death-penalty system operate fairly, even by making it mandatory. Look at the British system, which operated for a century with mandatory death penalties. They found juries just wouldn't convict in many cases where the conviction meant execution. And even if the death penalty was imposed, the Home Office eventually decided who would actually be killed by granting or withholding clemency.

Taking human nature as it is, I know of no way of administering a death penalty which would be fair. Not every problem has a solution, you know—and I think this is one of those insoluble problems.

Q Have we given the death penalty a chance to prove its deterrent effect? It hasn't been applied in this country in recent years—

A Not just in recent years. Use of the death penalty has been declining for decades. In 1933, there were something like 233 people executed in the United States. Since then, the figures have been going down steadily. And, of course, there haven't been any executions since 1967 because of the litigation over the death penalty's legality. But even before that, the American public was turning against the death penalty.

If you take a poll, you find people overwhelmingly in favor of the death penalty. But when you ask a person to sit on a jury and vote to execute a defendant, you find a great reluctance—increasingly so in the modern era.

Q It has been suggested that jurors and judges who impose a death penalty be required to push the buttons that would carry out the execution—

A Of course, society would reject that at once. You couldn't get 12 or 13 people who would do it. They may be willing to vote for it to be done, but they don't want to be a part of it. If you really want to make execution a deterrent, make it public—put it on TV—so people can see what it can be like if they kill someone. But, of course, we won't do that. We keep it hidden away from ourselves.

Q Do you regard it as immoral to execute a criminal?

A I steer away from that question because I know people's views on the morality of it are varied—and almost unchangeable. I'm a pragmatist. I just don't think it can be made fair or workable.

59. *Gregg* v. *Georgia*

Supreme Court of the United States

The issue before the Supreme Court of the United States was whether capital punishment violates the Eighth Amendment prohibition of cruel and unusual punishment. The majority of the Court held that it does not violate this prohibition because (1) capital punishment accords with contemporary standards of decency, (2) capital punishment may serve some deterrent or retributive purpose that is not degrading to human dignity, and (3) in the case of the Georgia law under review, capital punishment is no longer arbitrarily applied. Dissenting Justice Brennan argued that (1) through (3) do not suffice to show that capital punishment is constitutional; it would further have to be shown that capital punishment is not degrading to human dignity. Dissenting Justice Marshall objected to the majority's decision on the grounds that capital punishment is not necessary for deterrence and that a retributive purpose for capital punishment is not consistent with human dignity. He also contended that contemporary standards of decency with respect to capital punishment are not based on informed opinion.

We address initially the basic contention that the punishment of death for the crime of murder is, under all circumstances, "cruel and unusual" in violation of the Eighth and Fourteenth Amendments of the Constitution. . . .

The Court on a number of occasions has both assumed and asserted the constitutionality of capital punishment. In several cases that assumption provided a necessary foundation for the decision, as the Court was asked to decide whether a particular method of carrying out a capital sentence would be allowed to stand under the Eighth Amendment. But until *Furman* v. *Georgia*, (1972), the Court never confronted squarely the fundamental claim that the punishment of death always, regardless of the enormity of the offense or the procedure followed in imposing the sentence, is cruel and unusual punishment in violation of the Constitution. Although this issue was presented and addressed in *Furman*, it was not resolved by the Court. Four Justices would have held that capital punishment is not unconstitutional *per se;* two Justices would have reached the opposite conclusion; and three Justices, while agreeing that the statutes then before the Court were invalid as applied, left open the question whether such punishment may ever be imposed. We now hold that the punishment of death does not invariably violate the Constitution. . . .

It is clear from the foregoing precedents that the Eighth Amendment has not been regarded as a static concept. As Mr. Chief Justice Warren said, in an oft-quoted phrase, "[t]he Amendment must draw its meaning from the evolving standards of decency that mark the progress of a maturing society." . . . Thus, an assessment of contemporary values concerning the infliction of a challenged sanction is relevant to the application of the Eighth Amendment. As we develop below more fully, this assessment does not call for a subjective judgment. It requires, rather, that we look to objective indicia that reflect the public attitude toward a given sanction.

But our cases also make clear that public perceptions of standards of decency with respect to criminal sanctions are not conclusive. A penalty also must accord with "the dignity of man," which is the "basic concept underlying the Eighth Amendment." This means, at least, that the punishment not be "excessive." When a form of punishment in the abstract (in this case, whether capital punishment may ever be imposed as a sanction for murder) rather than in the particular (the propriety of death as a penalty to be applied to a specific defendant for a specific crime) is under consideration, the inquiry into "excessiveness" has two aspects. First, the punishment must not involve the unnecessary and wanton infliction of pain. Second, the punishment must not be grossly out of proportion to the severity of the crime.

Of course, the requirements of the Eighth Amendment must be applied with an awareness of the limited role to be played by the courts. This does not mean that judges have no role to play, for the Eighth Amendment is a restraint upon the exercise of legislative power. . . .

But, while we have an obligation to insure that constitutional bounds are not overreached, we may not act as judges as we might as legislators.

> "Courts are not representative bodies. They are not designed to be a good reflex of a democratic society. Their judgment is best informed, and therefore most dependable, within narrow limits. Their essential quality is detachment, founded on independence. History teaches that the independence of the judiciary is jeopardized when courts become embroiled in the passions of the day and assume primary responsibility in choosing between competing political, economic and social pressures." *Dennis* v. *United States* (1951)

Therefore, in assessing a punishment selected by a democratically elected legislature against the constitutional measure, we presume its validity. We may not require the legislature to select the least severe penalty possible so long as the penalty selected is not cruelly inhumane or disproportionate to the crime involved. And a heavy burden rests on those who would attack the judgment of the representatives of the people.

This is true in part because the constitutional test is intertwined with an assessment of contemporary standards and the legislative judgment weighs heavily in ascertaining such standards. "[I]n a democratic society legislatures, not courts, are constituted to respond to the will and consequently the moral values of the people." *Furman* v. *Georgia*. The deference we owe to the decisions of the state legislatures

under our federal system, is enhanced where the specification of punishments is concerned, for "these are peculiarly questions of legislative policy." *Gore* v. *United States*. . . . A decision that a given punishment is impermissible under the Eighth Amendment cannot be reversed short of a constitutional amendment. The ability of the people to express their preference through the normal democratic processes, as well as through ballot referenda, is shut off. Revisions cannot be made in the light of further experience.

. . . We now consider specifically whether the sentence of death for the crime of murder is a *per se* violation of the Eighth and Fourteenth Amendments to the Constitution. We note first that history and precedent strongly support a negative answer to this question.

The imposition of the death penalty for the crime of murder has a long history of acceptance both in the United States and in England. The common-law rule imposed a mandatory death sentence on all convicted murderers. And the penalty continued to be used into the 20th century by most American States, although the breadth of the common-law rule was diminished, initially by narrowing the class of murders to be punished by death and subsequently by widespread adoption of laws expressly granting juries the discretion to recommend mercy.

It is apparent from the text of the Constitution itself that the existence of capital punishment was accepted by the Framers. At the time the Eighth Amendment was ratified, capital punishment was a common sanction in every State. Indeed, the First Congress of the United States enacted legislation providing death as the penalty for specified crimes. . . .

For nearly two centuries, this Court, repeatedly and often expressly, has recognized that capital punishment is not invalid *per se*. . . .

Four years ago, the petitioners in *Furman* and its companion cases predicated their argument primarily upon the asserted proposition that standards of decency had evolved to the point where capital punishment no longer could be tolerated. The petitioners in those cases said, in effect, that the evolutionary process had come to an end, and that standards of decency required that the Eighth Amendment be construed finally as prohibiting capital punishment for any crime regardless of its depravity and impact on society. This view was accepted by two Justices. Three other Justices were unwilling to go so far; focusing on the procedures by which convicted defendants were selected for the death penalty rather than on the actual punishment inflicted, they joined in the conclusion that the statutes before the Court were constitutionally invalid.

The petitioners in the capital cases before the Court today renew the "standards of decency" argument, but developments during the four years since *Furman* have undercut substantially the assumptions upon which their argument rested. Despite the continuing debate, dating back to the 19th century, over the morality and utility of capital punishment, it is now evident that a large proportion of American society continues to regard it as an appropriate and necessary criminal sanction.

The most marked indication of society's endorsement of the death penalty for murder is the legislative response to *Furman*. The legislatures of at least 35 States have enacted new statutes that provide for the death penalty for at least some crimes that result in the death of another person. And the Congress of the United States, in 1974, enacted a statute providing the death penalty for aircraft piracy that results in death. These recently adopted statutes have attempted to address the concerns expressed by the Court in *Furman* primarily (i) by specifying the factors to be weighed and the procedures to be followed in deciding when to impose a capital sentence, or (ii) by making the death penalty mandatory for specified crimes. But all of the post-*Furman* statutes make clear that capital punishment itself has not been rejected by the elected representatives of the people. . . .

As we have seen, however, the Eighth Amendment demands more than that a challenged punishment be acceptable to contemporary society. The Court also must ask whether it comports with the basic concept of human dignity at the core of the Amendment. Although we cannot "invalidate a category of penalties because we deem less severe penalties adequate to serve the ends of penology," the sanction imposed cannot be so totally without penological justification that it results in the gratuitous infliction of suffering.

The death penalty is said to serve two principal social purposes: retribution and deterrence of capital crimes by prospective offenders.

In part, capital punishment is an expression of society's moral outrage at particularly offensive conduct. This function may be unappealing to many, but it is essential in an ordered society that asks its citizens to rely on legal processes rather than self-help to vindicate their wrongs.

> "The instinct for retribution is part of the nature of man, and channeling that instinct in the administration of criminal justice serves an important purpose in promoting the stability of a society governed by law. When people begin to believe that organized society is unwilling or unable to impose upon criminal offenders the punishment they 'deserve,'" then there are sown the seeds of anarchy—of self-help, vigilante justice, and lynch law."
> *Furman* v. *Georgia*.

"Retribution is no longer the dominant objective of the criminal law," but neither is it a forbidden objective nor one inconsistent with our respect for the dignity of men. Indeed, the decision that capital punishment may be the appropriate sanction in extreme cases is an expression of the community's belief that certain crimes are themselves so grievous an affront to humanity that the only adequate response may be the penalty of death.

Statistical attempts to evaluate the worth of the death penalty as a deterrent to crimes by potential offenders have occasioned a great deal of debate. The results simply have been inconclusive. As one opponent of capital punishment has said:

> "[A]fter all possible inquiry, including the probing of all possible methods of inquiry, we do not know; and for systematic and easily visible reasons cannot know; what the truth about this 'deterrent' effect may be. . . .
>
> "The inescapable flaw is . . . that social conditions in any state are not constant through time, and that social conditions are not the same in any two states. If an

effect were observed (and the observed effects, one way or another, are not large) then one could not at all tell whether any of this effect is attributable to the presence or absence of capital punishment. A 'scientific'—that is to say, a soundly based—conclusion is simply impossible, and no methodological path out of this tangle suggests itself." C. Black, Capital Punishment: The Inevitability of Caprice and Mistake 25–26 (1974).

Although some of the studies suggest that the death penalty may not function as a significantly greater deterrent than lesser penalties, there is no convincing empirical evidence either supporting or refuting this view. We may nevertheless assume safely that there are murderers, such as those who act in passion, for whom the threat of death has little or no deterrent effect. But for many others, the death penalty undoubtedly is a significant deterrent. There are carefully contemplated murders, such as murder for hire, where the possible penalty of death may well enter into the cold calculus that precedes the decision to act. And there are some categories of murder, such as murder by a life prisoner, where other sanctions may not be adequate.

The value of capital punishment as a deterrent of crime is a complex factual issue the resolution of which properly rests with the legislatures, which can evaluate the results of statistical studies in terms of their own local conditions and with a flexibility of approach that is not available to the courts. . . .

In sum, we cannot say that the judgment of the Georgia Legislature that capital punishment may be necessary in some cases is clearly wrong. Considerations of federalism, as well as respect for the ability of a legislature to evaluate, in terms of its particular State, the moral consensus concerning the death penalty and its social utility as a sanction, require us to conclude, in the absence of more convincing evidence, that the infliction of death as a punishment for murder is not without justification and thus is not unconstitutionally severe.

Finally, we must consider whether the punishment of death is disproportionate in relation to the crime for which it is imposed. There is no question that death as a punishment is unique in its severity and irrevocability. When a defendant's life is at stake, the Court has been particularly sensitive to insure that every safeguard is observed. But we are concerned here only with the imposition of capital punishment for the crime of murder, and when a life has been taken deliberately by the offender, we cannot say that the punishment is invariably disproportionate to the crime. It is an extreme sanction, suitable to the most extreme of crimes.

We hold that the death penalty is not a form of punishment that may never be imposed, regardless of the circumstances of the offense, regardless of the character of the offender, and regardless of the procedure followed in reaching the decision to impose it.

We now consider whether Georgia may impose the death penalty on the petitioner in this case. . . .

The basic concern of *Furman* centered on those defendants who were being condemned to death capriciously and arbitrarily. Under the procedures before the Court in that case, sentencing authorities were not directed to give attention to the nature or circumstances of the crime committed or to the character or record of the defendant. Left unguided, juries imposed the death sentence in a way that could only be called freakish. The new Georgia sentencing procedures, by contrast, focus the jury's attention on the particularized nature of the crime and the particularized characteristics of the individual defendant. While the jury is permitted to consider any aggravating or mitigating circumstances, it must find and identify at least one statutory aggravating factor before it may impose a penalty of death. In this way the jury's discretion is channeled. No longer can a jury wantonly and freakishly impose the death sentence; it is always circumscribed by the legislative guidelines. In addition, the review function of the Supreme Court of Georgia affords additional assurance that the concerns that prompted our decision in *Furman* are not present to any significant degree in the Georgia procedure applied here.

For the reasons expressed in this opinion, we hold that the statutory system under which Gregg was sentenced to death does not violate the Constitution. Accordingly, the judgment of the Georgia Supreme Court is affirmed. . . .

Mr. Justice Brennan, dissenting.*

The Cruel and Unusual Punishments Clause "must draw its meaning from the evolving standards of decency that mark the progress of a maturing society." The opinions of Mr. Justice Stewart, Mr. Justice Powell, and Mr. Justice Stevens today hold that "evolving standards of decency" require focus not on the essence of the death penalty itself but primarily upon the procedures employed by the State to single out persons to suffer the penalty of death. Those opinions hold further that, so viewed, the Clause invalidates the mandatory infliction of the death penalty but not its infliction under sentencing procedures that Mr. Justice Stewart, Mr. Justice Powell, and Mr. Justice Stevens conclude adequately safeguard against the risk that the death penalty was imposed in an arbitrary and capricious manner.

In *Furman* v. *Georgia,* I read "evolving standards of decency" as requiring focus upon the essence of the death penalty itself and not primarily or solely upon the procedures under which the determination to inflict the penalty upon a particular person was made. . . .

This Court inescapably has the duty, as the ultimate arbiter of the meaning of our Constitution, to say whether, when individuals condemned to death stand before our Bar, "moral concepts" require us to hold that the law has progressed to the point where we should declare that the punishment of death, like punishments on the rack, the screw, and the wheel, is no longer morally tolerable in our civilized society. My opinion in *Furman* v. *Georgia* concluded that our civilization and the law had progressed to this point and that therefore the punishment of death, for whatever crime and under all circumstances, is "cruel and unusual" in violation of the Eighth and Fourteenth Amendments of the Constitution. I shall not again canvass the reasons that led to that conclusion. I emphasize only that foremost among the "moral concepts" recognized in our cases and inherent in the Clause is the primary moral principle that the State, even as it punishes, must treat its citizens in a manner consistent with their intrinsic worth as human beings—a punishment must not be so severe as to be degrading to human dignity. A judicial determination whether the punishment of death comports with human dignity is therefore not only permitted but compelled by the Clause.

. . . Death for whatever crime and under all circumstances "is truly an awesome punishment. The calculated killing of a human being by the State involves, by its very nature, a denial of the executed person's humanity. . . . An executed person has indeed 'lost the right to have rights.' " Death is not only an unusually severe punishment, unusual in its pain, in its finality, and in its enormity, but it serves no penal purpose more effectively than a less severe punishment; therefore the principle inherent in the Clause that prohibits pointless infliction of excessive punishment when less severe punishment can adequately achieve the same purposes invalidates the punishment. . . .

Mr. Justice Marshall, dissenting.

. . . My sole purposes here are to consider the suggestion that my conclusion in *Furman* has been undercut by developments since then, and briefly to evaluate the basis for my Brethren's holding that the extinction of life is a permissible form of punishment under the Cruel and Unusual Punishments Clause.

In *Furman* I concluded that the death penalty is constitutionally invalid for two reasons. First, the death penalty is excessive. And second, the American people, fully informed as to the purposes of the death penalty and its liabilities, would in my view reject it as morally unacceptable.

Since the decision in *Furman,* the legislatures of 35 States have enacted new statutes authorizing the imposition of the death sentence for certain crimes, and Congress has enacted a law providing the death penalty for air piracy resulting in death. I would be less than candid if I did not acknowledge that these developments have a significant bearing on a realistic assessment of the moral acceptability of the death penalty to the American people. But if the constitutionality of the death penalty turns, as I have urged, on the opinion of an *informed* citizenry, then even the enactment of new death statutes cannot be viewed as conclusive. In *Furman,* I observed that the American people are largely unaware of the information critical to a judgment on the

*[This opinion applies also to No. 75-5706, *Proffitt* v. *Florida, post,* p. 242, and No. 75-5394, *Jurek* v. *Texas, post,* p. 262.]

morality of the death penalty, and concluded that if they were better informed they would consider it shocking, unjust, and unacceptable. A recent study, conducted after the enactment of the post-*Furman* statutes, has confirmed that the American people know little about the death penalty, and that the opinions of an informed public would differ significantly from those of a public unaware of the consequences and effects of the death penalty.

Even assuming, however, that the post-*Furman* enactment of statutes authorizing the death penalty renders the prediction of the views of an informed citizenry an uncertain basis for a constitutional decision, the enactment of those statutes has no bearing whatsoever on the conclusion that the death penalty is unconstitutional because it is excessive. An excessive penalty is invalid under the Cruel and Unusual Punishments Clause "even though popular sentiment may favor" it. The inquiry here, then, is simply whether the death penalty is necessary to accomplish the legitimate legislative purposes in punishment, or whether a less severe penalty—life imprisonment—would do as well.

The two purposes that sustain the death penalty as nonexcessive in the Court's view are general deterrence and retribution. In *Furman*, I canvassed the relevant data on the deterrent effect of capital punishment. The state of knowledge at that point, after literally centuries of debate, was summarized as follows by a United Nations Committee:

> "It is generally agreed between the retentionists and abolitionists, whatever their opinions about the validity of comparative studies of deterrence, that the data which now exist show no correlation between the existence of capital punishment and lower rates of capital crime."

The available evidence, I concluded in *Furman*, was convincing that "capital punishment is not necessary as a deterrent to crime in our society."

The Solicitor General in his *amicus* brief in these cases relies heavily on a study by Isaac Ehrlich, reported a year after *Furman*, to support the contention that the death penalty does not deter murder. . . .

. . . Ehrlich found a negative correlation between changes in the homicide rate and changes in execution risk. His tentative conclusion was that for the period from 1933 to 1967 each additional execution in the United States might have saved eight lives.

The methods and conclusions of the Ehrlich study have been severely criticized on a number of grounds. . . .

. . . Analysis of Ehrlich's data reveals that all empirical support for the deterrent effect of capital punishment disappears when the five most recent years are removed from his time series—that is to say, whether a decrease in the execution risk corresponds to an increase or a decrease in the murder rate depends on the ending point of the sample period. This finding has cast severe doubts on the reliability of Ehrlich's tentative conclusions. . . .

The Ehrlich study, in short, is of little, if any, assistance in assessing the deterrent impact of the death penalty. The evidence I reviewed in *Furman* remains convincing, in my view, that "capital punishment is not necessary as a deterrent to crime in our society." The justification for the death penalty must be found elsewhere.

The other principal purpose said to be served by the death penalty is retribution. The notion that retribution can serve as a moral justification for the sanction of death finds credence in the opinion of my Brothers Stewart, Powell, and Stevens, and that of my Brother White in *Roberts* v. *Louisiana*. It is this notion that I find to be the most disturbing aspect of today's unfortunate decisions.

The concept of retribution is a multifaceted one, and any discussion of its role in the criminal law must be undertaken with caution. On one level, it can be said that the notion of retribution or reprobation is the basis of our insistence that only those who have broken the law be punished, and in this sense the notion is quite obviously central to a just system of criminal sanctions. But our recognition that retribution plays a crucial role in determining who may be punished by no means requires approval of retribution as a general justification for punishment. It is the question whether retribution can provide a moral justification for punishment—in particular, capital punishment—that we must consider. . . .

The . . . contentions—that society's expression of moral outrage through the imposition of the death penalty pre-empts the citizenry from taking the law into its own hands and reinforces moral values—are not retributive in the purest sense. They are essentially utilitarian in that they portray the death penalty as valuable because of its beneficial results. These justifications for the death penalty are inadequate because the penalty is, quite clearly I think, not necessary to the accomplishment of those results.

There remains for consideration, however, what might be termed the purely retributive justification for the death penalty—that the death penalty is appropriate, not because of its beneficial effect on society, but because the taking of the murderer's life is itself morally good. . . .

The mere fact that the community demands the murderer's life in return for the evil he has done cannot sustain the death penalty, for . . . "The Eighth Amendment demands more than that a challenged punishment be acceptable to contemporary society." To be sustained under the Eighth Amendment, the death penalty must "compor[t] with the basic concept of human dignity at the core of the Amendment"; the objective in imposing it must be "[consistent] with our respect for the dignity of [other] men." Under these standards, the taking of life "because the wrongdoer deserves it" surely must fall, for such a punishment has as its very basis the total denial of the wrongdoer's dignity and worth.

The death penalty, unnecessary to promote the goal of deterrence or to further any legitimate notion of retribution, is an excessive penalty forbidden by the Eighth and Fourteenth Amendments. I respectfully dissent from the Court's judgment upholding the sentences of death imposed upon the petitioners in these cases.

Suggestions for Further Reading

Anthologies

Acton, H. B. *The Philosophy of Punishment.* London: Macmillan & Co., 1969.

Cains, Huntington. *Legal Philosophy from Plato to Hegel.* Baltimore: Johns Hopkins Press, 1967.

Ezorsky, Gertrude. *Philosophical Perspectives on Punishment.* Albany: State University of New York Press, 1972.

Feinberg, Joel, and Gross, Hyman. *Philosophy of Law.* Belmont: Wadsworth Publishing Co., 1980.

Gerber, Rudolph J., and McAnany, Patrick D. *Contemporary Punishment.* Notre Dame: University of Notre Dame Press, 1972.

Murphy, Jeffrie G. *Punishment and Rehabilitation.* Belmont: Wadsworth Publishing Co., 1984.

Basic Concepts

Golding, Martin P. *Philosophy of Law.* Englewood Cliffs: Prentice-Hall, 1975.

Richards, David A. J. *The Moral Criticism of Law.* Belmont: Dickenson Publishing Co., 1977.

The Forward-Looking and Backward-Looking Views

Andenaes, Johannes. *Punishment and Deterrence.* Ann Arbor: The University of Michigan Press, 1974.

Gross, Hyman. *A Theory of Criminal Justice.* New York: Oxford University Press, 1979.

Menninger, Karl. *The Crime of Punishment.* New York: The Viking Press, 1968.

Murphy, Jeffrie G. *Retribution, Justice and Therapy.* Boston: D. Reidel Publishing Co., 1979.

Packer, Herbert. *The Limits of the Criminal Sanction.* Stanford: Stanford University Press, 1968.

Von Hirsh, Andrew. *Doing Justice.* New York: Hill and Wang, 1976.

Practical Application

Bedau, Hugo. *The Death Penalty in America.* New York: Oxford University Press, 1982.

Black, Charles L., Jr. *Capital Punishment.* New York: W.W. Norton & Co., 1974.

———. "Reflections on Opposing the Penalty of Death." *St. Mary's Law Journal* (1978), pp. 1–12.

Van den Haag, Ernest. *Punishing Criminals.* New York: Basic Books, 1975.

National Defense and Military Strategy

Basic Concepts

The problem of national defense and military strategy is simply the problem of determining the moral limits of military defense. *Just war theories* attempt to specify what these moral limits are. Such theories have two components: a set of criteria that establish a right to go to war *(jus ad bellum)*, and a set of criteria that determine legitimate conduct in war *(jus in bello)*. The first set of criteria can be grouped under the label "just cause," the second under "just means."

Consider the following specification of just cause:

> There must be substantial aggression, and nonbelligerent correctives must be hopeless or too costly.

This specification of just cause implicitly contains a number of criteria, for example, last resort, formal declaration, and reasonable hope of success. It does, however, exclude the criterion of legitimate authority, which has had a prominent place in just war theories. That criterion is excluded because it has the character of a second-order requirement; it is a requirement that must be satisfied whenever there is a question of group action with respect to any moral problem whatsoever. For example, with respect to the problem of the distribution of goods and resources in a society, we can certainly ask who has the (morally legitimate) authority to distribute or redistribute goods and resources in a society; with respect to the problem of punishment and responsibility, we can ask who has the (morally legitimate) authority to punish offenders in a society. But before we ask such questions with respect to particular moral problems, it is important to understand first what are the morally defensible solutions to these problems because a standard way of identifying morally legitimate authorities is by their endorsement of such solutions. With respect to the problem of nuclear deterrence and strategic defense, we first need to determine the nature and existence of just causes before we try to iden-

tify morally legitimate authorities by their endorsement of such causes.

Regardless of whether we define just cause independently of legitimate authority, pacifists will simply deny that there are any just causes that ought to be recognized. Pacifists hold that it is never morally too costly to use nonbelligerent correctives against aggression. According to pacifists, people should never defend themselves against aggression by intentionally killing other human beings.

But military actions can be condemned for failing to satisfy the criteria of just means as well as the criteria of just cause. Consider the following specification of just means:

1. The harm inflicted on the aggressor must not be disproportionate to the aggression.
2. Harm to innocents should not be directly intended as an end or a means.
3. Harm to innocents must be minimized by accepting risks (costs) to oneself that would not doom the military venture.

The first criterion is a widely accepted requirement of just means. The second criterion is also widely accepted and contains the main requirement of the doctrine of double effect (see the introduction to Section III). Many philosophers seem willing to endorse the application of the doctrine in this context given that those to whom the doctrine applies are generally recognized to be persons with full moral status.

The doctrine of double effect, however, does not require (3), which incorporates an even stronger safeguard against harming innocents in warfare than (2).

To evaluate these requirements of just war theory, we need to determine to what degree they can be supported by the moral approaches to practical problems presented in the General Introduction. Of course, one or more of these approaches may ultimately favor the pacifist position, but assuming that these approaches favored some version of a just war theory, which version would that be?

Obviously, the utilitarian approach would have little difficulty accepting the requirement of just cause and requirement (1) on just means because these requirements can be interpreted as having a utilitarian backing. However, this approach would only accept requirements (2) and (3) on just means conditionally, because occasions would surely arise when violations of these requirements would maximize net utility.

Unlike the Utilitarian Approach, the Human Nature Approach is relatively indeterminate in its requirements. All that is certain, as I have interpreted the approach, is that it would be absolutely committed to requirement (2) on just means.[1] Of course, the other requirements on just cause and just means would be required by particular versions of this approach.

The Social Contract Approach is distinctive in that it seeks to combine and compromise both the concern of the Utilitarian Approach for maximal net utility and the concern of the Human Nature Approach for the proper development of each individual.[2] In its hypothetical choice situation, persons would clearly favor the requirement of just cause and requirement (1) on just means, although they would not interpret them in a strictly utilitarian fashion.

Yet what about the requirements (2) and (3) on just means? Because persons behind a veil of ignorance would not be committed simply to whatever maximizes net utility, they would want to put a stricter limit on the harm that could be inflicted on innocents in defense of a just cause than could be justified on utilitarian grounds alone. This is because persons behind a veil of ignorance would be concerned not only with what maximizes net utility, but also with the distribution of utility to particular individuals. Persons imagining themselves to be ignorant of what position they are in would be particularly concerned that they might turn out to be in the position of those who are innocent, and, consequently, they would want strong safeguards against harming those who are innocent, such as requirements (2) and (3) on just means.

Yet even though persons behind a veil of ignorance would favor a differential restriction on harm to innocents, they would not favor an absolute restriction on intentional harm to innocents. They would recognize as exceptions to such a restriction cases where intentional harm to innocents is either:

1. Trivial (e.g., stepping on someone's foot to get out of a crowded subway).
2. Easily reparable (e.g., lying to a temporarily depressed friend to keep her from committing suicide).
3. Sufficiently outweighed by the consequences of the action (e.g., shooting one of two hundred civilian hostages to prevent in the only way possible the execution of all two hundred).

Accordingly, while persons behind a veil of ignorance would favor requirement (2) on just means, their commitment to this requirement would also have to incorporate the above exceptions. Even so, these exceptions are far more limited than those that would be tolerated by the Utilitarian Approach.

In sum, the Social Contract Approach would strongly endorse the requirement of just cause and requirements (1), (2), and (3) on just means. Yet its commitment to requirement (2) on just means would fall short of the absolute commitment that is characteristic of the Human Nature Approach to practical problems.

It is clear, therefore, that our three moral approaches to practical problems differ significantly with respect to their requirements for a just war theory. The Utilitarian Approach strongly endorses the requirement of just cause and requirement (1) on just means, but only conditionally endorses requirements (2) and (3) on just means. The Human Nature Approach endorses requirement (2) on just means as an absolute requirement, but is indeterminate with respect to the other requirements of just war theory. Only the Social Contract Approach strongly endorses all of the basic requirements of a traditional just war theory, although it does not regard requirement (2) on just means as an absolute requirement. Fortunately for traditional just war theory, there are good reasons for favoring the Social Contract Approach over each of the other two moral approaches to practical problems.

One reason for favoring the Social Contract Approach over the Utilitarian Approach is that its requirements are derived from a veil of ignorance decision-procedure that utilitarians and contractarians alike recognize to be fair. It is not surprising, therefore, to find such utilitarians as John Harsanyi and R. M. Hare simply endorsing this decision-procedure and then trying to show that the resulting requirements would maximize utility.[3] Yet we have just seen how the concern of persons behind a veil of ignorance with the distribution of utility would lead them to impose a stricter limit on the harm that could be inflicted on innocents in defense of a just cause than could be justified on grounds of maximizing utility alone. At least with respect to just war theory, therefore, the Utilitarian Approach and the Social Contract Approach differ significantly in their practical requirements.

Utilitarians who endorse this decision-procedure are faced with a difficult choice; give up their commitment to this decision-procedure or modify their commitment to utilitarian goals. Utilitarians cannot easily choose to give up their commitment to this decision-procedure because the acceptability of utilitarianism as traditionally conceived has always depended on showing that fairness and utility rarely conflict, and that when they do, it is always plausible to think that the requirements of utility are morally overriding. Consequently, when a fair decision-procedure significantly conflicts with utility, which it is not plausible to think can always be morally overridden by the requirements of utility, that procedure exposes the inadequacy of the Utilitarian Approach to practical problems.

These reasons for favoring the Social Contract Approach over the Utilitarian Approach to practical problems are also reasons for favoring the human nature approach, because the Human Nature Approach is also concerned with fairness and the distribution of utility to particular individuals. Nevertheless, there are other reasons for favoring the Social Contract Approach over the Human Nature Approach.

One reason is that the Social Contract Approach does not endorse any absolute requirements. In particular, the Social Contract Approach does not endorse an absolute requirement not to intentionally harm innocents. The Social Contract Approach recognizes that if the harm is trivial, easily repara-

ble, or sufficiently outweighed by the consequences, such harm can be morally justified.

Another reason for favoring the Social Contract Approach over the Human Nature Approach is that the Social Contract Approach is determinate in its requirements; it actually leads to a wide range of practical recommendations. By contrast, the Human Nature Approach lacks a deliberative procedure that can produce agreement with respect to practical requirements. This is evident because supporters of this approach tend to endorse radically different practical requirements. In this regard, the veil of ignorance decision-procedure employed by the Social Contract Approach appears to be just the sort of morally defensible device needed to achieve determinate requirements.

Finally, the particular requirements of just war theory endorsed by the Social Contract Approach are further supported by the presence of analogous requirements for related areas of conduct. Thus, the strong legal prohibitions that exist against punishing the innocent provide support for the strong prohibition against harming innocents expressed by requirements (2) and (3) on just means. This is the type of correspondence we would expect from an adequate moral theory; requirements in one area of conduct would be analogous to those in related areas of conduct.

Alternative Views

In the first selection (Selection 60), James P. Sterba attempts to answer a number of challenges that have been directed at just war theory. Against the pacifist challenge to just cause, Sterba argues that killing in self-defense can be morally justified provided either that the killing is the foreseen consequence of an action whose intended consequence is stopping an attempt on one's life or that the killing is not morally evil because those engaging in the attempt on one's life have already forfeited their right to life. Against the conventionalist challenge to just means, Sterba argues that there is a perfectly acceptable convention-independent way of supporting condition (2) of just means. Sterba also argues against the collectivist challenge that not just any contribution to the unjust actions of one's leaders opens one to attack or the threat of attack. Rather, one's contribution must be significant enough to justify such a response. Finally, against the feminist challenge to both components of just war theory, Sterba concedes that the only way of meeting the challenge is to rid society of its sexist and militarist attitudes and practices so as to increase the chances that just war theory will be applied correctly in the future.

In this selection, Sterba then applies the requirements of just war theory to the use and threat to use nuclear weapons and concludes that, under present conditions, the United States and the Soviet Union are only morally justified in simply possessing a survivable nuclear force to be able to threaten quickly or bluff nuclear retaliation should conditions change for the worse. If conditions do worsen, however, Sterba claims that it would be morally justified at some point for the United States or the Soviet Union to threaten a form of limited nuclear retaliation or bluff a form of massive nuclear retaliation.

Sterba even allows that under certain conceivable but very unlikely conditions, a limited retaliatory use of nuclear weapons against tactical and strategic targets would be morally justified to restore deterrence.

In Selection 61, McGeorge Bundy argues that given the recent events in Eastern Europe and the Soviet Union, it is now possible to end the cold war and move toward a trusting peace. He contends that the hardest problem of all will be how to implement German unification in a way that respects the legitimate interests of everyone involved. He then discusses the superpower relationship and argues for a substantial reduction of conventional and nuclear forces.

Bundy does not specify exactly what reductions in conventional and nuclear forces he would want to see made, although he does single out the Stealth bomber for unfavorable mention. Yet clearly he would be unhappy with the limited cuts in the United States defense budget proposed by Dick Cheney in

Selection 62. Cheney defends these limited cuts on the grounds that it is possible that the policies of Mikhail Gorbachev could be reversed by his successor. However, Cheney's view has recently been criticized from within the Bush administration by William Webster, Director of the CIA.[4] Even a top expert within Cheney's own Department of Defense has agreed with Webster that there is little chance of renewed Soviet domination over Eastern Europe even if Gorbachev is ousted by hardliners.[5] The expert, Philip A. Peterson, also said that the Warsaw Pact has already ceased to exist as an effective military organization, and will be maintained as a political "fiction" in the future.

In Selection 63, the Center for Defense Information gives some additional reasons for cutting the U.S. defense budget. The center argues that (1) deep-rooted flaws in the procedures for developing and buying new weapons waste billions of dollars every year, (2) the Pentagon has provided no military rationale for many new weapons such as nuclear-war fighting missiles and Stealth bombers, (3) jobs and profits have increasingly become the reason for the development and production of weapons, and (4) the desire to acquire the most advanced weapons systems has resulted in the acquisition of complex weapons that are costly, unreliable, and difficult for crews to maintain and operate. The only response that administration officials seem to offer to critiques of this sort is that they are trying to do better. For example, without admitting any previous mistakes, Cheney has just recently announced a new plan to improve the defense acquisition and the management of the Pentagon.[6]

Practical Applications

The readings in this section have already suggested a number of practical solutions to the problem of national defense and military strategy. However, two of the more sweeping solutions are included in the final two selections. The solution offered by Rear Admiral Gene R. La Rocque would provide an enormous "peace dividend" by reducing the U.S. military budget from $300 to $200 billion almost overnight. Gorbachev's solution of Nuclear Disarmament by the year 2000 was the basis for the Soviet negotiating stance at the Reykjavik Summit. By drawing on the previous readings in this section, you should be in a better position to assess the moral defensibility of these practical proposals.

Nevertheless, it is important to recognize that a solution to this practical problem cannot stand alone; it requires solutions to the other practical problems discussed in this anthology as well. For example, a solution to the problem of the distribution of income and wealth may show that it is morally illegitimate to increase military security by sacrificing the basic needs of the less advantaged members of a society rather than by sacrificing the nonbasic needs of the more advantaged members of the society. Accordingly, it is impossible to reach a fully adequate solution to this or any other practical problem discussed in this anthology without solving the other practical problems as well.

Notes

1. See General Introduction.

2. See General Introduction.

3. See John Harsanyi, *Rational Behavior and Bargaining Equilibrium in Games and Social Situations* (Cambridge: Cambridge University Press, 1977), and R. M. Hare, "Justice and Equality," in *Justice: Alternative Political Perspectives,* edited by James P. Sterba (Belmont, CA: Wadsworth Publishing Co., 1980).

4. *The New York Times,* March 7, 1990.

5. *The New York Times,* March 8, 1990.

6. *Defense,* Special Issue (1989).

60. Just War Theory and Nuclear Strategy

James P. Sterba

This article defends just war theory against pacifist, conventionalist, collectivist, and feminist challenges that have recently been directed against it. Just war theory is then applied to the use of and threat to use nuclear weapons, and the article concludes that under present conditions the possession of, but not the threat to use, nuclear weapons is morally justified.

In traditional just war theory, there are two basic components: a set of criteria which establish a right to go to war (*jus ad bellum*) and a set of criteria which determine legitimate conduct in war (*jus in bello*). The first set of criteria can be grouped under the label "just cause," the second under the label "just means." In recent years, the just cause component of just war theory has been subjected to a pacifist challenge, the just means component has been subjected to conventionalist and collectivist challenges and both components have been subject to a feminist challenge. In this paper,

From "Just War Theory and Nuclear Strategy," *Analyse & Kritik* (Special Issue), 1987. Reprinted by permission.

I will attempt to respond to each of these challenges in turn and then go on to determine the practical implications of just war theory for nuclear strategy.

The Pacifist Challenge to Just Cause

In traditional just war theory, just cause is usually specified as follows:

Just Cause   There must be substantial aggression and nonbelligerent correctives must be hopeless or too costly.

Needless to say, the notion of substantial aggression is a bit fuzzy, but it is generally understood to be the type of aggression that violates people's most fundamental rights. To suggest some specific examples of what is and what is not substantial aggression, usually nationalization of particular firms owned by foreigners is not regarded as substantial aggression while the taking of hostages is so regarded. But even when substantial aggression occurs, frequently nonbelligerent correctives are neither hopeless nor too costly.

However, according to the pacifist challenge to just war theory nonbelligerent correctives, or at least nonlethal correctives, are never hopeless or too costly. Thus, for pacifists there aren't any just causes.

But this pacifist challenge to just war theory is sometimes claimed to be incoherent. In a well-known article, Jan Narveson rejects pacifism as incoherent because it recognizes a right to life yet rules out any use of force in defense of that right.[1] The view is incoherent, Narveson claims, because having a right entails the legitimacy of using force in defense of that right at least on some occasions. But as Cheyney Ryan has pointed out Narveson's argument only works against the following extreme form of pacifism:

Pacifism I Any use of force is morally prohibited.

It doesn't touch the form of pacifism that Ryan thinks is most defensible, which is the following:

Pacifism II Any lethal use of force is morally prohibited.[2]

This form of pacifism only prohibits the use of lethal force in defense of people's rights.

Ryan goes on to argue that there is a substantial issue between the pacifist and the nonpacifist concerning whether we can or should create the necessary distance between ourselves and other human beings in order to make the act of killing possible. To illustrate, Ryan cites George Orwell's reluctance to shoot at an enemy soldier who jumped out of a trench and ran along the top of a parapet half-dressed and holding up his trousers with both hands. Ryan contends that what kept Orwell from shooting was that he couldn't think of the soldier as a thing rather than a fellow human being.

But do we have to objectify other human beings in order to kill them? If we do, this would seem to tell in favor of the form of pacifism Ryan defends. However, it is not clear that Orwell's encounter supports such a view. For it may be that what kept Orwell from shooting the enemy soldier was not his inability to think of the soldier as a thing rather than a fellow human being but rather his inability to think of the soldier who was holding up his trousers with both hands as a threat or a combatant. Under this interpretation, Orwell's decision not to shoot would accord well with the requirements of just war theory.

Let us suppose, however, that someone is attempting to take your life. Why does that permit you, the pacifist might ask, to kill the person making the attempt? Isn't such killing prohibited by the principle that one should never intentionally do evil that good may come of it? Of course, someone might not want to endorse this principle as an absolute requirement, but surely it cannot be reasonable to regard all cases of justified killing in self-defense as exceptions to this principle.

One response to this pacifist objection is to allow that killing in self-defense can be morally justified provided that the killing is the foreseen consequence of an action whose intended consequence is the stopping of the attempt upon one's life. Another response is to allow that intentional killing in self-defense can be morally justified provided that you are reasonably certain that your attacker is wrongfully engaged in an attempt upon your life. It is claimed that in such a case the intentional killing is not evil, or at least not morally evil, because anyone who is wrongfully engaged in an attempt upon your life has already forfeited her or his right to life by engaging in such aggression.

Taken together, these two responses seem to constitute an adequate reply to the pacifist challenge. The first response is theoretically closer to the pacifist's own position since it rules out all intentional killing, but the second response is also needed when it does not seem possible to stop a threat to one's life without intentionally killing one's attacker.

The Conventionalist Challenge to Just Means

Now the just means component of just war theory can be specified as follows:

Just Means

1) The harm resulting from the belligerent means employed should not be disproportionate to the military objective to be attained.
2) Harm to innocents should not be directly intended as an end or a means.
3) Harm to innocents should be minimized by accepting risks (costs) to oneself that would not render it impossible to attain the military objective.

Obviously, the notion of what is disproportionate is a bit fuzzy in (1), but the underlying idea is that the harm resulting from the belligerent corrective should not outweigh the benefit to be achieved from attaining the military objective. By contrast, (2) is a relatively precise requirement. Where it was obviously violated was in the antimorale terror bombing of Dresden and Hamburg and in the use of atomic bombs against Hiroshima and Nagasaki in World War II.[3]

Some people think that (1) and (2) capture the essential requirements of just means. Others maintain that something like (3) is also required. Michael Walzer provides an example from Frank Richard's memoir of World War I which shows the attractiveness of (3).

When bombing dug-outs or cellars, it was always wise to throw the bombs into them first and have a look around after. But we had to be very careful in this village as there were civilians in some of the cellars. We shouted down to them to make sure. Another man and I shouted down one cellar twice and receiving no reply were just about to pull the pins out of our bomb when we heard a woman's voice and a young lady came up the cellar steps. . . . She and the members of her family . . . had not left (the cellar) for some days. They guessed an attack was being made and when we first shouted down had been too frightened to answer. If the young lady had not cried out when she did we would have innocently murdered them all.[4]

Many restrictions on the operation of police forces also seem to derive from a requirement like (3).

As one would expect, these criteria of just means have been incorporated to some degree in the military codes of different nations and adopted as international law. Yet rarely has anyone contended that the criteria ought to be met simply because they have been incorporated into military codes or adopted as international law. Recently, however, George Mavrodes has defended just such a conventionalist view.[5] Mavrodes arrives at this conclusion largely because he finds the standard attempts to specify the convention-independent basis for (2) and (3) to be so totally unsuccessful. All such attempts, Mavrodes claims, are based on an identification of innocents with noncombatants. But by any plausible standard of guilt and innocence that has moral content, Mavrodes contends, noncombatants can be guilty and combatants innocent. For example, noncombatants who are doing everything in their power to financially support an unjust war would be morally guilty, and combatants who were forced into military service and intended never to fire their weapons at anyone would be morally innocent. Consequently, the guilt/innocence distinction will not support the combatant/noncombatant distinction.

Hoping to still support the combatant/noncombatant distinction, Mavrodes suggests that the distinction might be grounded on a convention to observe it. This would mean that our obligation to morally abide by (2) and (3) would be a convention-dependent obligation. Nevertheless, Mavrodes does not deny that we have some convention-independent obligations. Our obligation to refrain from wantonly murdering our neighbors is given as an example of a convention-independent obligation, as is our obligation to reduce the pain and death involved in combat. But to refrain from harming noncombatants when harming them would be the most effective way of pursuing a just cause is not included among our convention-independent obligations.

Yet Mavrodes does not claim that our obligation to refrain from harming noncombatants is *purely* convention-dependent. He allows that in circumstances in which the convention of refraining from harming noncombatants does not exist, we might still have an obligation to unilaterally refrain from harming noncombatants provided that our action will help give rise to a convention prohibiting such harm with its associated good consequences. According to Mavrodes, our primary obligation is to maximize good consequences, and this obligation requires that we refrain from harming noncombatants when that will help bring about a convention prohibiting such harm. By contrast, someone who held that our obligation to refrain from harming noncombatants was purely convention-dependent would never recognize an obligation to unilaterally refrain from harming noncombatants. On a purely convention-dependent account, obligations can only be derived from existing conventions; the expected consequences from establishing a particular convention could never ground a purely convention-dependent obligation. But while Mavrodes does not claim that our obligation to refrain from harming noncombatants is purely convention-dependent, he does claim that this obligation generally arises only when there exists a convention prohibiting such harm. According to Mavrodes, the reason for this is that generally only when there exists a convention prohibiting harm to noncombatants will our refraining from harming them, while pursuing a just cause, actually maximize good consequences.

But is there no other way to support our obligation to refrain from harming noncombatants? Mavrodes would deny that there is. Consider, however, Mavrodes's own example of the convention-independent obligation not to wantonly kill our neighbors. There are at least two ways to understand how this obligation is supported. Some would claim that we ought not to wantonly kill our neighbors because this would not maximize good consequences. This appears to be Mavrodes's view. Others would claim that we ought not to wantonly kill our neighbors, even if doing so would maximize good consequences, simply because it is not reasonable to believe that our neighbors are engaged in an attempt upon our lives. Both these ways of understanding how the obligation is supported account for the convention-independent character of the obligation, but the second approach can also be used to show how our obligation to refrain from harming noncombatants is convention-independent. According to this approach since it is not reasonable to believe that noncombatants are engaged in an attempt upon our lives, we have an obligation to refrain from harming them. So interpreted, our obligation to refrain from harming noncombatants is itself convention-independent, although it will certainly give rise to conventions.

Of course, some may argue that whenever it is not reasonable to believe that persons are engaged in an attempt upon our lives, an obligation to refrain from harming such persons will also be supported by the maximization of good consequences. Yet even if this were true, which seems doubtful, all it would show is that there exists a utilitarian or forward-looking justification for a convention-independent obligation to refrain from harming noncombatants; it would not show that such an obligation is a convention-dependent obligation, as Mavrodes claims.

The Collectivist Challenge to Just Means

Now according to the collectivist challenge to just means, more people should be included under the category of combatants than the standard interpretation of (2) allows. The reason for this is that the standard interpretation of (2) does not assume, as the advocates of the collectivist challenge do, that the members of a society are collectively responsible for the actions of their leaders unless they have taken radical steps to oppose or disassociate themselves from those actions, e.g., by engaging in civil disobedience or emigration. Of course, those who are unable to take such steps, particularly children, would not be responsible in any case, but, for the rest, advocates of the collectivist challenge contend that failure to take the necessary radical steps, when one's leaders are acting aggressively, has the consequence that one is no longer entitled to full protection as a noncombatant. Some of those who press this objection against the just means component of just war theory, like Gregory Kavka, contend that the members of a society can be directly threatened with nuclear attack to secure deterrence but then deny that carrying out such an attack could ever be morally justified.[6] Others, like James Child, contend that the members of a society who fail to take the necessary radical steps can be both indirectly threatened and indirectly attacked with what would otherwise be a disproportionate attack.[7]

In response to this collectivist challenge, the first thing to note is that people are more responsible for disassociating themselves from the unjust acts of their leaders than they are for opposing those same acts. For there is no general obligation to oppose all unjust acts, even all unjust acts of one's leaders. Nevertheless, there is a general obligation to disassociate oneself from unjust acts and to minimize one's contribution to them. Of course, how much one is required to disassociate oneself from the unjust acts of one's leaders depends upon how much one is contributing to those actions. If one's contribution is insignificant, as presumably a farmer's or a teacher's would be, only a minimal effort to disassociate oneself would be required, unless one's action could somehow be reasonably expected, in cooperation with the actions of others, to put a stop to the unjust actions of one's leaders. However, if one's contribution is significant, as presumably a soldier's or a munitions worker's would be, a maximal effort at disassociating oneself would

be immediately required, unless by delaying, one could reasonably expect to put a stop to the unjust actions of one's leaders.

In support of the collectivist challenge, James Child offers the following example:

> A company is considering engaging in some massively immoral and illegal activity—pouring large quantities of arsenic into the public water supply as a matter of ongoing operations, let us say. A member of the board of directors of the company, when the policy is before the board, votes no but does nothing else. Later, when sued in tort (or charged in crime) with these transgressions of duty, she pleads that she voted no. What would our reaction be? The answer is obvious! We would say, you are responsible as much, or nearly as much, as your fellow board members who voted yes. You should have blown the whistle, gone public or to regulatory authorities, or at the very least, resigned from the board of so despicable a company. Mere formal dissent in this case does almost nothing to relieve her liability, legal or moral.[8]

But while one might agree with Child that in this case the member of the board of directors has at least the responsibility to disassociate herself from the actions of the board by resigning, this does not show that farmers and teachers are similarly responsible for disassociating themselves from the unjust actions of their leaders either by engaging in civil disobedience or by emigration. This is because neither their contributions to the unjust actions of their leaders nor the effect of their disassociation on those unjust actions would typically be significant enough to require such a response.

This is not to deny that some other response (e.g., political protest or remunerations at the end of the war) would not be morally required. However, to meet the collectivist challenge, it suffices to show that not just any contribution to the unjust actions of one's leaders renders the contributor subject to attack or threat of attack; one's contribution must be significant enough to morally justify such a response.

The Feminist Challenge to Just Cause and Just Means

According to the feminist challenge to both components of just war theory, sexism and militarism are inextricably linked in society. They are linked, according to Betty Reardon, because sexism is essentially a prejudice against all manifestations of the feminine, and militarism is a policy of excessive military preparedness and eagerness to go to war that is rooted in a view of human nature as limited to masculine characteristics.[9] Seen from a militarist perspective, other nations are competitive, aggressive and adverse to cooperation, the same traits that tend to be fostered exclusively in men in a sexist society. By contrast, the traits of openness, cooperativeness and nurturance which promote peaceful solutions to conflicts tend to be fostered exclusively in women who are then effectively excluded from positions of power and decision-making in a sexist society. Consequently, if we are to rid society of militarism, Reardon argues, we need to rid society of sexism as well.

But even granting that sexism and militarism are inextricably linked in society in just the way Reardon maintans, how does this affect the validity of just war theory? Since just war theory expresses the values of proportionality and respect for the rights of innocents, how could it be linked to militarism and sexism? The answer is that the linkage is practical rather than theoretical. It is because the leaders in a militarist/sexist society have been socialized to be competitive, aggressive and adverse to cooperation that they will tend to misapply just war theory when making military decisions. This represents an important practical challenge to just war theory. And, the only way of meeting this challenge, as far as I can tell, is to rid society of its sexist and militarist attitudes and practices so as to increase the chances that just war theory will be correctly applied in the future.

Practical Implications for the Use of Nuclear Weapons

The requirements for just war theory that have been defended so far are directly applicable to the question of the morality of nuclear war. In particular, requirements (2) and (3) on just means would prohibit any counter-city or counter-population use of nuclear weapons. While this prohibition need not be interpreted as absolute, it is simply not foreseeable that any use of nuclear weapons could ever be a morally justified exception to this prohibition.

But what about a counter-force use of nuclear weapons? Consider the massive use of nuclear weapons by the United States or the Soviet Union against industrial and economic centers. Such a strike, involving three to five thousand warheads, could destroy between 70–80% of each nation's industry and result in the immediate death of as many as 165 million Americans and 100 million Russians respectively, in addition to running a considerable risk of a retaliatory nuclear strike by the opposing superpower.[10] It has also been estimated by Carl Sagan and others that such a strike is very likely to generate firestorms which would cover much of the earth with sooty smoke for months, creating a "nuclear winter" that would threaten the very survival of the human species.[11] Applying requirement (1) on just means, there simply is no foreseeable military objective which could justify such morally horrendous consequences.

The same holds true for a massive use of nuclear weapons against tactical and strategic targets. Such a strike, involving two to three thousand warheads, directed against only ICBMs and submarine and bomber bases could wipe out as many as 20 million Americans and 28 million Russians respectively, in addition to running a considerable risk of a retaliatory nuclear strike by the opposing superpower.[12] Here too there is a considerable risk of a "nuclear winter" occurring. This being the case what military objective might foreseeably justify such a use of nuclear weapons?

Of course, it should be pointed out that the above argument does not rule out a limited use of nuclear weapons at least against tactical and strategic targets. Such a use is still possible. Yet practically it would be quite difficult for either superpower to distinguish between a limited and a massive use of nuclear weapons, especially if a full-scale conventional war is raging. In such circumstances, any use of nuclear weapons is likely to be viewed as part of a massive use of such weapons, thus increasing the risk of a massive nuclear retaliatory strike.[13] In addition, war games have shown that if enough tactical nuclear weapons are employed over time in a limited area, such as Germany, the effect on noncombatants in that area would be much the same as in a massive nuclear attack.[14] As Bundy, Kennan, McNamara and Smith put the point in their recent endorsement of a doctrine of no first use of nuclear weapons:

> Every serious analysis and every military exercise, for over 25 years, has demonstrated that even the most restrained battlefield use would be enormously destructive to civilian life and property. There is no way for anyone to have any confidence that such a nuclear action will not lead to further and more devastating exchanges. Any use of nuclear weapons in Europe, by the Alliance or against it, carries with it a high and inescapable risk of escalation into the general nuclear war which would bring ruin to all and victory to none.[15]

For these reasons, even a limited use of nuclear weapons generally would not meet requirement (1) on just means.

Nevertheless, there are some circumstances in which a limited use of nuclear weapons would meet all the requirements on just means. For example, suppose that a nation was attacked with a massive nuclear counterforce strike and it was likely that, if the nation did not retaliate with a limited nuclear strike on tactical and strategic targets, a massive attack on its industrial and population centers would follow. Under such circumstances, it can be argued, a limited nuclear retaliatory

strike would satisfy all the requirements on just means. Of course, the justification for such a strike would depend on what foreseen effect the strike would have on innocent lives and how likely it was that the strike would succeed in deterring a massive attack on the nation's industrial and population centers. But assuming a limited nuclear retaliatory strike on tactical and strategic targets was the best way of avoiding a significantly greater evil, it would be morally justified according to the requirements on just means.

Practical Implications for the Threat to Use Nuclear Weapons

Yet what about the morality of threatening to use nuclear weapons to achieve nuclear deterrence? Obviously, the basic requirements of just war theory are not directly applicable to threats to use nuclear weapons. Nevertheless, it seems clear that the just war theory would support the following analogous requirements of what we could call "just threat theory."

Just Cause   There must be a substantial threat or the likelihood of such a threat and nonthreatening correctives must be hopeless or too costly.

Just Means

1) The risk of harm resulting from the use of threats (or bluffs) should not be disproportionate to the military objective to be attained.

2) Actions that are prohibited by just war theory cannot be threatened as a end or a means.

3) The risk of harm to innocents from the use of threats (bluffs) should be minimized by accepting risks (costs) to oneself that would not render it impossible to attain the military objective.

Now if we assume that the requirement of just cause is met, the crucial restriction of just threat theory is requirement (2) on just means.

This requirement puts a severe restriction on what we can legitimately threaten to do, assuming, that is, that threatening implies an intention to carry out under appropriate conditions what one has threatened to do. In fact, since, as we have seen, only a limited use of nuclear weapons could ever foreseeably be morally justified, it follows from requirement (2) that only such a use can be legitimately threatened. Obviously, this constitutes a severe limit on the use of threats to achieve nuclear deterrence.

Nevertheless, it may be possible to achieve nuclear deterrence by other means, for example, by bluffing. Now there are two ways that one can be bluffing while proclaiming that one will do actions that are prohibited by just war theory. One way is *by not being committed to doing* what one proclaims one will do should deterrence fail. The other is *by being committed not to do* what one proclaims one would do should deterrence fail. Of course, the first form of bluffing is more morally problematic than the second since it is less of a barrier to the subsequent formation of a commitment to do what would be prohibited by just war theory, but since it lacks a present commitment to carry out actions prohibited by just war theory should deterrence fail, it still has the form of a bluff rather than a threat.[16]

The possibility of achieving nuclear deterrence by bluffing, however, has not been sufficiently explored because it is generally not thought to be possible to institutionalize bluffing. But suppose we imagine bluffing to include deploying a survivable nuclear force and preparing that force for possible use in such a way that leaders who are bluffing a morally prohibited form of nuclear retaliation need outwardly distinguish themselves from those who are threatening such retaliation only in their strong moral condemnation of this use of nuclear weapons. Surely this form of bluffing is capable of being institutionalized.

This form of bluffing can also be effective in achieving deterrence because it is subject to at least two interpretations. One interpretation is that the leaders of a nation are actually bluffing because while the leaders do deploy nuclear weapons and do appear to threaten to use them in certain ways, they also morally condemn those uses of nuclear weapons, so

they can't really be intending to so use them. The other interpretation is that the leaders are not bluffing but are in fact immoral agents intentionally committed to doing what they regard as a grossly immoral course of action. But since the leaders of other nations can never be reasonably sure which interpretation is correct, a nation's leaders can effectively bluff under these conditions.

Moreover, citizens who think that only a bluffing strategy with respect to certain forms of nuclear retaliation can ever be morally justified would look for leaders who express their own views on this issue in just this ambiguous manner. It is also appropriate for those who are in places of high command within a nation's nuclear forces to express the same ambiguous views; only those low in the command structure of a nation's nuclear forces need not express the same ambiguous views about the course of action they would be carrying out, assuming they can see themselves as carrying out only (part of) a limited nuclear retaliatory strike. This is because, as we noted earlier, such a strike would be morally justified under certain conceivable but unlikely conditions.

Yet even granting that a threat of limited nuclear retaliation and a bluff of massive nuclear retaliation can be justified by the requirements of just means, it would not follow that we are presently justified in so threatening or bluffing unless there presently exists a just cause for threatening or bluffing. Of course, it is generally assumed that such a cause does presently exist. That is, it is generally assumed that both superpowers have a just cause to maintain a state of nuclear deterrence vis-à-vis each other by means of threats and bluffs of nuclear retaliation.

But to determine whether this assumption is correct, let us consider two possible stances a nation's leaders might take with respect to nuclear weapons:

1) A nation's leaders might be willing to carry out a nuclear strike *only* in response to either a nuclear first strike or a massive conventional first strike on itself or its principal allies.

2) A nation's leaders might be willing to carry out a massive conventional strike *only* in response to either a nuclear first strike or a

massive conventional first strike on itself or its principal allies.

Now assuming that a nation's leaders were to adopt (1) and (2) then threats or bluffs of nuclear retaliation could not in fact be made against them! For a threat or bluff must render less eligible something an agent might otherwise want to do, and leaders of nations who adopt (1) and (2) have a preference structure that would not be affected by any attempt to threaten or bluff nuclear retaliation. Hence, such threats or bluffs could not be made against them either explicitly or implicitly.

Of course, a nation's leaders could try to threaten or bluff nuclear retaliation against another nation but if the intentions of the leaders of that other nation are purely defensive then although they may succeed in restricting the liberty of the leaders of that other nation by denying them a possible option, they would not have succeeded in threatening them for that would require that they render less eligible something those leaders might otherwise want to do.[17]

Now if we take them at their word, the leaders of both superpowers seem to have adopted (1) and (2). As Caspar Weinberger recently characterized U.S. policy:

> Our strategy is a defensive one, designed to prevent attack, particularly nuclear attack, against us or our allies.[18]

And a similar statement of Soviet policy can be found in Mikhail Gorbachev's recent appeal for a return to a new era of detente.[19] Moreover, since 1982 Soviet leaders appear to have gone beyond simply endorsing (1) and (2) and have ruled out the use of a nuclear first strike under any circumstances.[20]

Assuming the truth of these statements, it follows that the present leaders of the U.S. and the Soviet Union could not be threatening or bluffing each other with nuclear retaliation despite their apparent attempts to do so. This is because a commitment to (1) and (2) rules out the necessary aggressive intentions that it is the purpose of such threats or bluffs to deter. Leaders of nations whose strategy is a

purely defensive one would be immune from threats or bluffs of nuclear retaliation. In fact, leaders of nations who claim their strategy is purely defensive yet persist in attempting to threaten or bluff nuclear retaliation against nations whose proclaimed strategy is also purely defensive eventually throw into doubt their own commitment to a purely defensive strategy. It is for these reasons that a just cause for threatening or bluffing nuclear retaliation does not exist under present conditions.

Of course, the leaders of a superpower might claim that threatening or bluffing nuclear retaliation would be morally justified under present conditions on the grounds that the proclaimed defensive strategy of the other superpower is not believable. Surely this stance would be reasonable if the other superpower had launched an aggressive attack against the superpower or its principal allies. But neither U.S. intervention in Nicaragua nor Soviet intervention in Afghanistan nor other military actions taken by either superpower are directed against even a principal ally of the other superpower. Consequently, in the absence of an aggressive attack of the appropriate sort and in the absence of an opposing military force that could be used without risking unacceptable losses from retaliatory strikes, each superpower is morally required to provisionally place some trust in the proclaimed defensive strategy of the other superpower.

Nevertheless, it would still be morally legitimate for both superpowers to retain a retaliatory nuclear force so as to be able to threaten or bluff nuclear retaliation in the future should conditions change for the worse. For as long as nations possess nuclear weapons, such a change could occur simply with a change of leadership bringing to power leaders who can only be deterred by a threat or bluff of nuclear retaliation.

For example, suppose a nation possesses a survivable nuclear force capable of inflicting unacceptable damage upon its adversary, yet possession of such a force alone would not suffice to deter an adversary from carrying out a nuclear first strike unless that possession were combined with a threat of limited nuclear retaliation or a bluff of massive nuclear retaliation. (With respect to massive nuclear retaliation, bluffing would be required here since leaders who recognize and respect the above just war constraints on the use of nuclear weapons could not in fact threaten such retaliation.) Under these circumstances, I think the required threat or bluff would be morally justified. But I also think that there is ample evidence today to indicate that neither the leadership of the United States nor that of the Soviet Union requires such a threat or bluff to deter them from carrying out a nuclear first strike.[21] Consequently, under present conditions, such a threat or bluff would not be morally justified.

Nevertheless, under present conditions it would be legitimate for a nation to maintain a survivable nuclear force in order to be able to deal effectively with a change of policy in the future. Moreover, if either superpower does in fact harbor any undetected aggressive intentions against the other, the possession of a survivable nuclear force by the other superpower should suffice to deter a first strike since neither superpower could be sure whether in response to such strike the other superpower would follow its moral principles or its national interest.[22]

Of course, if nuclear forces were only used to retain the capacity for threatening or bluffing in the future should conditions change for the worse then surely at some point this use of nuclear weapons could also be eliminated. But its elimination would require the establishment of extensive political, economic and cultural ties between the superpowers so as to reduce the present uncertainty about the future direction of policy, and obviously the establishment of such ties, even when it is given the highest priority, which it frequently is not, requires time to develop.

In the meantime a nuclear force deployed for the purpose of being capable of threatening or bluffing in the future should conditions change for the worse, should be capable of surviving a first strike and then inflicting either limited or massive nuclear retaliation on an aggressor. During the Kennedy-Johnson years, Robert McNamara estimated that massive nuclear retaliation required a nuclear force capable of destroying one-half of a nation's industrial capacity along with one-quarter of its population, and comparable figures have been suggested by others. Clearly,

ensuring a loss in this neighborhood should constitute unacceptable damage from the perspective of any would-be aggressor.

Notice, however, that in order for a nation to maintain a nuclear force capable of inflicting such damage, it is not necessary that components of its land-, its air- and its sea-based strategic forces all be survivable. Accordingly, even if all of the land-based ICBMs in the United States were totally destroyed in a first strike, surviving elements of the U.S. air and submarine forces could easily inflict the required degree of damage and more. In fact, any one of the 37 nuclear submarines maintained by the United States, each with up to 192 warheads, could almost single-handedly inflict the required degree of damage. Consequently, the U.S. submarine force alone should suffice as a force capable of massive nuclear retaliation.

But what about a nuclear force capable of limited nuclear retaliation? At least with respect to U.S. nuclear forces, it would seem that as Trident I missiles replace less accurate Poseidon missiles, and especially when Trident II missiles come on line in the next few years, the U.S. submarine force will have the capacity for both limited and massive nuclear retaliation. However, until this modernization is complete, the U.S. will still have to rely, in part, on survivable elements of its air- and land-based strategic forces for its capacity to inflict limited nuclear retaliation. And it would seem that the Soviet Union is also in a comparable situation.[23]

A nuclear force retained for this purpose, however, would not be as large as the forces currently maintained by both superpowers. Consequently, sizable reductions in the size of the nuclear arsenals of both superpowers are clearly required in a world where the only need for nuclear weapons is to secure nuclear deterrence in the future in case it was ever required.

But obviously these reductions are not being made. Why is this the case? I think the answer to this question does not lie in any weakness in the foregoing moral argument that I have just presented against the existing nuclear strategies of both superpowers that mindlessly pursue a presently unattainable nuclear deterrence, but rather the answer is to be found in the size and political strength of the military-industrial complexes of both superpowers. So many careers and jobs in both nations are tied to a continuation and expansion of military production that it is very difficult to gain sufficient support for cutbacks and reductions in nuclear weapons, even when such cutbacks and reductions are supported by the best moral arguments. In the end, therefore, the main obstacle to establishing a morally acceptable nuclear strategy is the narrow self-interest of certain groups of citizens within each superpower.

But where moral argument has failed to motivate, nonmoral arguments might yet succeed to do so. Recently, there has been much work done on the economic costs of military expenditures. The idea is that after a certain point, military expenditures weaken rather than strengthen a nation. Put another way, after a certain point, what is good for the military-industrial complex is not good for the nation. One noted historian even claims to have discovered a trend in history to the effect that major powers have caused or contributed to their decline by overspending on their military forces.[24] Currently, economic indicators in both the United States and the Soviet Union may be signally just this sort of decline. In the Soviet Union, people have been experiencing a decline in living standard over the last few years (e.g., longer lines at shops and more shortages of this or that item). In the United States, the national debt has doubled because of military expenditures, the number of commercial inventions is down, and the living standard has experienced little gain since the 1970s. Maybe national leaders who have so far failed to heed the moral argument against current nuclear strategy will be willing to take a more courageous stance now that both moral and economic arguments support changes in that strategy.

Notes

1. Jan Narveson, "Pacifism: A Philosophical Analysis," *Ethics* Vol. 75 (1965).

2. Cheyney Ryan, "Self-Defense and Pacifism," in *The Ethics of War and Nuclear Deterrence*, edited by James P. Sterba (Belmont, Wadsworth Publishing Co., 1985).

3. Even if these bombings did help shorten World War II, and there is considerable evidence that they did not, they would have still been in violation of requirement (2) on just means.

4. See Michael Walzer, *Just and Unjust Wars* (New York, 1977), p. 152.

5. George Mavrodes, "Conventions and the Morality of War," in *Morality in Practice*, 1st ed., edited by James P. Sterba (Belmont, 1983), pp. 302–310.

6. Gregory Kavka, "Nuclear Deterrence: Some Moral Perplexities," in *The Ethics of War and Nuclear Deterrence*, edited by James P. Sterba (Belmont, 1985), pp. 127–138.

7. James Child, *Nuclear War: The Moral Dimension* (Bowling Green, 1986), especially pp. 140–149.

8. Child, p. 142.

9. Betty Reardon, *Sexism and the War System* (New York, 1985), especially Chapter 3.

10. *The Effects of Nuclear War*, Office of Technology Assessment (Washington, D.C., U.S. Government Printing Office, 1979), pp. 94, 100; Nigel Calder, *Nuclear Nightmare* (New York, Viking, 1979), p. 150; Sidney Lens, *The Day Before Doomsday* (Boston, Beacon Press, 1977), p. 102.

11. Carl Sagan, "Nuclear War and Climate Catastrophe: Some Policy Implications," *Foreign Affairs* Vol. 62 (1983), pp. 257–292.

12. *The Effects of Nuclear War*, pp. 83, 91; Jerome Kahan, *Security in the Nuclear Age* (Washington, D.C., The Brookings Institution, p. 202; Lens, pp. 98, 99, 102.

13. Lens, pp. 78–79; Spurgeon Keeny and Wolfgang Panofsky, "MAD verse NUTS," *Foreign Affairs* Vol. 60 (1981–2), pp. 297–298; Ian Clark, *Limited Nuclear War* (Princeton, Princeton University Press, 1982), p. 242.

14. Lens, p. 73.

15. McGeorge Bundy, George F. Kennan, Robert S. McNamara and Gerald Smith, "Nuclear Weapons and the Atlantic Alliance," *Foreign Affairs* Vol. 61 (1982), p. 757. It should be noted that Bundy, Kennan, McNamara and Smith believed that their endorsement of a doctrine of no first use of nuclear weapons *may* involve increased spending for conventional forces in Europe. Others, however, have found NATO's ex-

isting conventional strength to be adequate to meet a Soviet attack. See David Barash and Judith Lipton, *Stop Nuclear War* (New York, Gwne Press, 1982), pp. 138–140; Harold Brown, *Department of Defense, Annual Report* (1981).

16. For a defense of this second form of bluffing although mistakenly classified as a form of threatening, see Kenneth Kemp, "Nuclear Deterrence and the Morality of Intentions," *The Monist* (1987).

17. On my view to succeed in threatening two conditions must be met:

1) One must have the intention to carry out the action one is purporting to threaten under the stated conditions, that is, one must expect that if the stated conditions do obtain then one will carry out that action.

2) The preference structure of the party that one is trying to threaten must be so affected that something the party might otherwise have wanted to do is rendered less eligible.

18. Caspar Weinberger, "Why We Must Have Nuclear Deterrence," *Defense* (March 1983), p. 3.

19. *The New York Times*, May 9, 1985.

20. See Leonid Brezhnev's message to the U.N. General Assembly on June 2, 1982.

21. See Kahan, *Security in the Nuclear Age*; Lens, *The Day Before Doomsday*; Henry Kendall and others, *Beyond the Freeze* (Boston, Beacon Press, 1982); George Kistiakowsky, "False Alarm: The Story Behind Salt II," *The New York Review of Books* (April 1, 1979); Les Aspin, "How to Look at the Soviet-American Balance," *Foreign Policy* Vol. 22 (1976); Gordon Adams, "The Iron Triangle,"

The Nation (October, 1981), pp. 425, 441–444. Much of this evidence is reviewed in my paper "How to Achieve Nuclear Deterrence Without Threatening Nuclear Destruction," included in *The Ethics* of *War and Nuclear Deterrence*.

22. It might be objected that this proposed policy is hypocritical because it allows a nation following it to benefit from an adversary's uncertainty as to whether that nation would follow its moral principles or its national interest. But it seems odd to deny a nation such a benefit. For we all know that moral people can lose out in so many ways to those who are immoral. Occasionally, however, being immoral does have its liabilities and one such liability is that it is hard for immoral people to believe that others will not act in just the way they themselves do, especially when the benefits from doing so are quite substantial. Why then should not moral people be allowed to extract some benefit from the inability of immoral people to believe that moral people are as good as they say they are. After all, it is not the fault of moral people that immoral people are blinded in their judgment in this regard. Consequently, I see no reason to allow a nation to benefit from its adversary's uncertainty as to whether it will follow the requirements of morality or those of national interest.

23. *Soviet Military Power*, U.S. Department of Defense (Washington, D.C., U.S. Government Printing Office, 1983); David Holloway, *The Soviet Union and the Arms Race* (New Haven, Yale University Press, 1983); Andrew Cockburn, *The Threat* (New York, Random House, 1983) Chapter 12.

24. Paul Kennedy, *The Decline of Nations* (New York, 1988).

61. From Cold War Toward Trusting Peace

McGeorge Bundy

In this selection, McGeorge Bundy argues that given the recent events in Eastern Europe and the Soviet Union, it is now possible to end the cold war and move toward a trusting peace. He contends that the hardest problem of all will be how to implement German unification in a way that respects the legitimate interests of everyone involved. He then discusses the superpower relationship and argues for a substantial reduction of conventional and nuclear forces.

The *annus mirabilis* 1989 has made it clear that the Soviet Union and the United States now have it in their power to put an end to the cold war—the most important, expensive and dangerous phenomenon of the second half of our tumultuous century. It is too soon for historians to say that the cold war is over. There are still many unresolved tensions where mistakes on one side or the other could revive it. Moreover, excessive optimism could again be a cause of failure as it has been in the past.

Disappointed hopes about Joseph Stalin were one reason for the intensity of American responses in 1946 and 1947, and disappointed hopes for détente more than 25 years later led to the renewal of the cold war in the decade of 1975–85. If these two great nations are to make durably strong the stable peace between them that is so clearly in prospect as we enter the 1990s, the first point for both to keep in mind is that this task will take continued effort by both parties. The December meeting in Malta between Mikhail Gorbachev and George Bush seems to have been a hopeful step toward such a joint effort.

Nonetheless it is right to celebrate the great events that made 1989 the best year for East-West relations since World War II. At the end of the year in Eastern Europe there was one splendid surprise after another. The Poles had a government led by the men and women of Solidarity; the Hungarians were preparing for free elections after their Communist Party

Reprinted by permission of *Foreign Affairs* (Fall 1989). Copyright 1989 by the Council on Foreign Relations, Inc.

changed its name and lost most of its members; the old man who had ruled Bulgaria for 35 years was forced to quit; the massive demonstrations of those who would be free ended neo-Stalinism in Czechoslovakia and overthrew Nicolae Ceauşescu in Romania. In the largest surprise of all, the East Germans decisively rejected their own hard-line leaders and an interim regime responded to millions of peaceful demonstrators by opening the Berlin Wall.

Every one of those great events has been accepted, and most have been explicitly encouraged, by the government of the Soviet Union. More astonishing still, those massive changes—except in Romania—have taken place with less violence than we have come to fear from a single soccer game.

I

If the cold war could be ended as easily as it began, we could readily argue that the changes in Eastern Europe are in themselves enough to finish it off: It started there, and it is ending there.

The single set of events that was decisive in ending wartime hopes for lasting Soviet-American friendship was the Stalinization of Eastern Europe between the arrival of the Red Army in 1945 and the death of Jan Masaryk in 1948. Franklin Roosevelt had tried to prevent what happened, but the words of the Yalta declaration—clear in their pledge of free elections in all the countries set free from Hitler, and hailed by Americans left, right and center—were overridden by Stalin's army and his local henchmen. The Yalta conference is misunderstood when it is remembered as a meeting in which Roosevelt and Winston Churchill gave away the freedom of East Europeans. That freedom was never theirs to give. Both leaders may have put more trust in words than they should have, but were they wrong to try? At the very least, as I argued 40 years ago in this journal, the words of that declaration set a standard by which Stalin's actions could be judged.* The great events of 1989 have precisely this meaning: If the rush to freedom is carried through, "the test of Yalta" will finally be passed, and the principles of the Yalta declaration will be realized.

The revolutions of 1989 have undermined the cold war in another way. They have given a massive and final blow to the appeal of international communism as the political wave of the future. Those of us who are old enough remember how much the cold war owed, in its beginnings, to fear of communists everywhere. Some of that fear was wildly exaggerated, though not all of it, but we need not here review that balance. What matters for the 1990s is that international communism has now plainly lost its missionary appeal. The communists who have been thrown out in Eastern Europe stand exposed as corrupt, tyrannical and incompetent, and their repudiation is plainly the work of the masses for whom they claimed to speak. The unfinished contest for China's future leaves that country without political appeal beyond its borders. Even Gorbachev, attractive as he is as a politician, has no exportable ideology. Individual communist tyrants can still oppress their own people and trouble those nearby, as in North Korea, Vietnam and Cuba. But communism as a worldwide political movement died in 1989. There will be a parallel decline in the political appeal of anticommunism; not many will persist in endless war against the dead.

The peoples of Eastern Europe are themselves the primary authors of the great events of 1989. Without the clear consent and the general approval of Gorbachev those changes

*McGeorge Bundy, "The Test of Yalta," *Foreign Affairs*, July 1949.

could not have come as they have. It is right that his name should have been cheered in East Berlin, but what is forcing change, amazingly, is the will of the peoples. I know of no one, expert or not, who foresaw these events, but their unexpectedness can only increase our admiration for the people who brought them to pass. In that number we must include those in government who have been willing to bend. If in 1776 there had been such men in power in London, our own revolution might have been fast and peaceful.

Still we must not suppose that the overthrow of tyranny is the same thing as the establishment of stable and peaceful democracies. Within each East European country there are deeply rooted antagonisms, and there is almost none without its memories of land and people now beyond its boundaries. Almost everywhere there is economic distress, and the task of economic turnaround will be harder than it was 45 years ago in Western Europe. External assistance is already in prospect, most generously from Western Europe, and it is probable that local wars can be prevented by the weight of Soviet power on the side of the territorial status quo. Nonetheless there will be a time of testing for all of the self-liberated countries.

II

The hardest problems of all—and the most important in terms of European peace—are those that lie ahead for East Germany. The apparently durable regime of Walter Ulbricht and Erich Honecker did seem to stand in the way of major change. In its way it was thus a guarantor of a strangely stable central Europe, where two world wars had been let loose in 25 years.

It is distressing, but not really surprising, that some of those who are habituated to the predictabilities of the cold war have displayed withdrawal pangs over the fall of the Iron Curtain. And it is entirely natural, indeed politically essential, that the future choices of both West and East Germans should take account of the interests of all their neighbors and of both superpowers. In terms of international law those interests are justified by the absence, still, of a German peace treaty. In terms of international politics they are more decisively justified by the reality that all the concerned parties must be reliably assured that there will never be a third world war caused by Germany.

My own conviction is that there is no such danger. I believe that the people of West and East Germany, perhaps more than any others, are now immunized from war-making. I also believe that one citizenry has learned from success, and the other from failure, that the real rewards of today and of the future are to be found in the arts of peaceful and productive work. I also believe, on a question that would be decisive by itself, that no German government, West or East or united, will ever develop its own nuclear weapons. I believe that such propositions would be widely accepted both by Germans and by those who know them best.

We cannot limit our interest in that enormous question, however, only to what will in fact happen. We must be concerned also with possibilities that will be feared. And what Germans might do in those matters will indeed be feared, even after forty years of West German statesmanship and East German obedience. That is the inheritance, unwanted but unavoidable, that we all have from Adolf Hitler.

It follows that the arrangements of the Germans must include safeguards that will adequately take the place of the vanished Iron Curtain as a guarantor of the German commitment to peace. I do not here venture to suggest what those arrangements should be. The variables are many, and since the central concern must be with what does and does not prevent fear, we must allow for the likelihood that what is needed will change over time.

What deserves emphasis right at the start, however, is that the requirement of reassurance against what Germany might do is not a judgment against the Germans. It is not even a requirement placed on Germany only in the interest of others. The Germans, as much as any other people, need the same reassurance; except for the Jews, the people who in the end suffered most from Hitler were the Germans themselves.

One great guarantee of peace remains in place for the present—the armies of NATO and the Warsaw Pact. It is more than likely that there will be some early cutbacks in the forces deployed on both sides; there has already been progress in 1989 toward agreement on large-scale reductions in military forces, and there should be more in 1990. There is good reason, however, for both armies to maintain for some time the military presence that has been customary for so long. It will be appropriate for the two superpowers to reduce to a minimum the inconvenience that their presence imposes on those who live in the two Germanys. Training exercises in particular can be cut back. The professional readiness of those forces simply does not have the urgency now that it was thought to have in earlier years.

The political rearrangement of Germany will take time, and it would be a mistake for any government to pretend to certainty about what that eventual rearrangement should be. In the first weeks after the Berlin Wall was opened, it was easy and natural for individual commentators to express themselves in sweeping terms—that German reunification was inevitable, or impossible. In truth, no one yet knows the answer. . . . What we all need to remember here is what both German governments know very well. They have been actively negotiating the German future with each other for two decades now, and while there will be much more to discuss in the future than in the past, there is a great deal to be learned from their experiences.

The great innovator here was the former West German Chancellor Willy Brandt, who led the way to the set of agreements that opened the way to serious relations between the two Germanys in 1972. Brandt had the courage to reverse the priorities of West Germany—from an insistence on unconditional and therefore unobtainable reunification to an acceptance of the boundaries of the two Germanys as they were, along with a new Soviet guarantee for the security of West Berlin and a new acceptance by each German government of the other's existence. He then set out, and his successors have followed him, along a course using modest economic concessions—relatively easy for the rich West Germans—to increase the human and economic connections across the Iron Curtain. By 1989 those small steps had covered a lot of ground; the annual contribution of the rich West to the straitened East was running about six-to-seven billion deutsche marks, and the overall advantage to East Germany of its preferred trading relation with its larger and richer brother-state was even greater.

In the autumn of 1989, with change the order of the day in the East, the government of Helmut Kohl made it clear that further steps, and larger ones, could and would be taken in response to the East German abandonment of one-party dictatorship. In effect the West Germans are offering massive reinforcement to their fellow Germans insofar as they commit themselves to free and democratic elections by May 1990. No one can predict with precision the kind of relations that a freely elected government will and will not want with its neighbors. It is a safe assumption that East Germany will want and get large-scale economic help from Bonn, and that there will be large-scale movements of Germans back and forth in both directions, for work and for play.

Over time the free movement of Germans, the free elections of a new East German government, and the offer and acceptance of a new economic partnership are likely to lead on to political relations that will go beyond those that are usual in separate states. If the winners of the East German elections should come in with a mandate for reunification, both the speed and the magnitude of such political change would almost surely increase. Obviously it will remain possible for the Soviet Union to prevent such change, but only at very high cost to its own objectives of lower tension, lower defense bills and greater economic connection. Moreover, there is much that German leaders can do to reduce the likelihood of a Soviet veto. First they can make it wholly clear that their new political arrangements reflect the commitment to democracy and human rights that have so strongly marked both the forty-year tradition of Bonn and the people's revolution of 1989 in the East. The Gorbachev government is not likely to believe that a Germany with that kind of political base is eager for conflict.

The Germans can also draw on the examples of Konrad Adenauer and Brandt to reaffirm and deepen two great commitments already part of their own history: the rejection of German nuclear weapons and the acceptance of the Oder-Neisse line between East Germany and Poland. Both decisions were not so much a matter of right and wrong as a matter of good sense. The underlying reality is that neither boundary changes nor nuclear weapons would ever be as valuable to Germany as the international reassurance that has come from the decisions by both Adenauer and Brandt to keep those issues off the German agenda. The wisdom of their actions is amply demonstrated by the evident reality of political, economic and societal success in the Federal Republic. The newly connected Germany now on the horizon, whether or not in the end it becomes a single unified or federated state, will greatly reinforce its own peaceful future by unilateral and unconditional reaffirmation of those decisions.

As they address the future of the two Germanys, the leaders of West Germany will be concerned not only with what will give reassurance to all their neighbors, but also with the maintenance of their notable and constructive role in Western Europe. The West Germans will have the enormous asset of their solid record as good citizens of Western Europe, an honored and well-tended inheritance from Adenauer. The ways and means of community in Western Europe have a complexity that defies summary, but it is notable that there is not a single working organization in the region in which the West Germans are not active, effective and trusted. Every postwar German chancellor has been a good European; what Adenauer understood first is now understood almost across the board in Bonn, and it is backed by a profoundly *European* electorate.

For that reason it is natural, in West Germany, to think about "the German question" as part of "the European question." Even in its first passionate response to the opening of the Berlin Wall the government in Bonn did not lose sight of its interest in Poland's future; it has been responsive also to the reality that Hungary, by a timely opening of borders, played a most important role in the retirement of Honecker. Other European leaders, like French President François Mitterrand, have been quick to recognize that the right response to new freedoms in the East is self-confident generosity from the emerging Europe of the West. The West Germans, by wealth and location and self-interest, will have a great role in all this—all the more so because their credentials as loyal Europeans have been validated by more than forty years of commitment and performance.

Finally, there is the relation between the Federal Republic and the United States. At the end of the year in which John McCloy died it is natural to remember that in the forty years since he went to Germany as U.S. high commissioner, each country has been the other's most important friend. For us the Japanese are now even more important economically and the British are even closer, but the Germans have been the most important to us and we to them. A breakdown of German-American trust at any time in all those years could have meant the end of freedom in the center of Europe.

Are we to suppose that this great connection no longer matters? The question answers itself. The relationship will evolve—fewer American soldiers on the scene, not so many angels (or devils) dancing on the head of the pin of nuclear policy, a need for cooperation in durable détente with Moscow, as against solidarity in standing up to threats. But there is no substitute available to either government for its partnership with the other. There may come a day when the peace of Europe does not need the Americans, or even a day when the peace between the superpowers is so strong that Europe can relax in its shade, but along the way to such distant goals the Americans and the Germans will still need each other.

III

Let us return to the two superpowers and remind ourselves that just as the Americans will still have a guarantor's role in the West, so the Soviet Union will insist on remaining a guarantor of its own security in the East. We can go clear back to the Yalta conference and remind ourselves that one large element in what Roosevelt and Churchill were attempting

there rested on their own awareness and acceptance of the Soviet need for unthreatening neighbors. We can also remember that not every ardent Polish nationalist of that generation would have seemed a good neighbor even to a less black-and-white Soviet judge than Stalin. There will always be watchful Soviet eyes on the new leaders of Eastern Europe, but there are also great differences between 1945 and 1990. So far those new leaders have shown sensitivity to the requirement to avoid threatening the Soviets' power. Moreover, the Soviets appear to have reached a clear decision that they need neighboring governments that make them feel secure, but not governments that hold their own peoples in a neo-Stalinist grip.

We do not know—and quite probably Gorbachev himself does not know—just what is meant by his requirement that those newly awakened societies remain both socialist and loyal to the Warsaw Pact. If, as I think, it is right to expect that both Gorbachev and the new leaders of Eastern Europe will strongly prefer genuinely peaceful coexistence to any renewal of ancient quarrels, then it is also reasonable to expect that Gorbachev will succeed in finding enough socialism and reliability among his neighbors to satisfy his announced standards. There is no more elastic word than socialism, unless it is the word market, and it may well be that in the long run the new socialism of Eastern Europe, and the perestroika of the Soviet Union, will all be definable as cases of market socialism.

As for reliability, if it be defined as a relationship that ensures peace both within the group and with others in Europe, then it can be found in many arrangements less expensive than that of allied armies fully deployed. Obviously the rearrangement here must be careful and it must take place in both alliances, but there is nothing in the declared purposes of either side that requires the two sets of deployments to remain as they are. No leader understands that reality more plainly than Gorbachev; none has less need for the postural rigidities that hardened in both alliances during the cold war years.

It is not yet clear that there is a parallel subtlety of understanding on the Western side. In December, as he visited NATO after

Malta, President Bush appeared to share the general view of NATO leaders that if Germany is to be reunited, it should be reunited inside NATO. It is unlikely that such a formula would be acceptable to Moscow and it does not really make sense for Washington either. Does anyone really suppose that the détente so skillfully nourished at Malta would survive the incorporation of all of Germany in NATO and the arrival of American forces at the Polish border? Even supposing that the Russians would in fact withdraw in our favor from an occupation we have accepted for 45 years, do we really want to generate the fear and mistrust that would result if we took their place?

Those who talk of a united Germany as a member of NATO have not really decided what that would mean or how it could be acceptable to the Soviet Union. It is a shorthand way of asserting that a Germany rooted in Western Europe and linked to the United States is better for all than a Germany not so rooted and linked. That more general assertion is correct, but it is also incomplete if it does not respect the equally correct assertion that the Soviet Union, with its own intense memories of the war against Germany, will insist on safeguards more direct than those offered by the self-restraint of a self-consciously righteous NATO embracing all of Germany.

Fortunately the problem presented here is more apparent than real. Sooner or later it will be clear to all that the liberation of the six former satellite countries totally changes the calculus of danger in Europe. Those countries, in their new freedom, constitute a wide and strong buffer zone protecting both the Soviets and the West Europeans from their historical fears of one another.

In that situation the roles of both American and Soviet forces must change over time because the level of fear is so greatly reduced. It then becomes entirely reasonable to expect that there need be no more Americans in West Germany than the Germans truly want, and no more Soviet forces in liberated Europe than the liberated Europeans are willing to accept. It becomes quite likely that there should be no foreign troops at all in what is now East Germany. Sobered by all that was unexpected in 1989, I do not venture to foretell the eventual result. What does seem pre-dictable, however, is that any result that is satisfactory to the free people on the spot will also be a stable reassurance to all concerned. Already in 1989 we have seen that interconnection, as the lowering of tension in the East decisively reduced the West German interest in modernizing short-range nuclear weapons. Each such demonstration of Western moderation is likely in its turn to help the men and women in Moscow feel at ease with change in Eastern Europe.

The reduction of American and Soviet forces in Europe will also help to increase the confidence of each superpower in the peaceful intentions of the other. In 1989 there was a gradual but significant shift in Washington from wariness to confidence about the reality of Moscow's commitment to major reductions in conventional forces. By the end of the year Secretary of Defense Dick Cheney was planning American reductions on a scale that he would have denounced as dangerous folly when he took office. The Malta meeting reaffirmed the commitment of both governments to the early conclusion of a broad agreement on conventional arms reductions. Both the negotiations and the design of reduced military budgets will be demanding on the defense leaders of both countries, and it may well turn out that the rate of change is less rapid than optimists hope. But here as elsewhere in the new world of the 1990s it is the general direction of change, and not its magnitude in any one season, that matters most.

There is a busy season ahead, then, as each of the two superpowers rearranges its relations with the part of Germany and Europe to which it has been connected. What is striking about that prospect is if the two countries continue as they have begun, the changes required in the interest of good relations with allies will also be changes that improve the direct relations between the United States and the Soviet Union. We have here the exact converse of what happened in the first years after World War II, when the abrasive impact of oppressive Soviet expansion in Eastern Europe was rapidly countered by the integration of Adenauer's Germany into a recovering West.

Yet it is also right to emphasize the magnitude of the changes of 1989. It is hard to overestimate the value, both to the self-confidence of Europe and to the direct relations between Moscow and Washington, of the reduction in the Soviet threat in Europe that has resulted from the combination of multiple national revolutions and Soviet conventional restraint. By the end of the year there was official acceptance of what was already obvious to public opinion throughout the Atlantic alliance: Warsaw Pact countries, large and small, had neither the intent nor the capability for rapid assault on the West, and there would be ample advance warning of any large-scale move to change that reality.

IV

In strictly bilateral terms there is a special importance to the strategic nuclear arms race. In Soviet memory it is almost surely the American atomic bomb, not the Iron Curtain, that marked the beginning of the cold war, and the first Soviet nuclear test in 1949 sharply increased cold war tension in Washington. It remains true today, as it has been since the 1950s, that each of the two nations lives in constant awareness that its whole society could be smashed in a day by the missiles of the other.

Strategic arms control had a thin decade in the 1980s. The second Strategic Arms Limitation Talks (SALT II) Treaty was signed in 1979 by Jimmy Carter but never ratified by Congress. Ronald Reagan never understood what was and was not possible in the nuclear competition, so he committed himself recklessly to the unattainable goal of a leakproof space shield and then in his summit meeting with Gorbachev flirted briefly with a misconceived "abolition" of strategic missiles, thus making Reykjavik a permanent word of warning to his successor. In the end, when Gorbachev's good sense and the responsive diplomacy of George Shultz and Paul Nitze brought an excellent strategic agreement within plain reach, Reagan stubbornly preferred his dream of effective defense. That decision made a messy legacy for President Bush, and it is not all bad that 1989 has been a year of deliberation.

Yet much more is now possible and there are new forces on the side of large-scale strategic reductions. The most powerful, for both governments, may be the pressure on military budgets. New systems, pressing as they do against the limits of what is technologically feasible, come in at prices hard to defend at a time when the strategic stalemate is sturdy and the charge of dangerous imbalance long since dismissed by Reagan himself. What exactly is it that makes a single Stealth Bomber worth half-a-billion dollars? As the year ended, the Stealth program was being stretched out. Still more significantly, the appropriation for strategic defense was repeatedly cut from Reagan's last proposals—by President Bush, the Senate and the House. No one now claims that there can be a leakproof shield, and those who proclaim the value of enormously expensive partial protection are each year less persuasive in Washington.

There is some tension between the downward pressure on military budgets and the complex process of agreed reduction by arms control agreements. It is often supposed that the only way to get agreements is to have good systems you can trade away—the most notable examples may be the primitive antiballistic missile deployments that were limited in the SALT I treaty and the Pershing missiles that were traded for Soviet SS-20s in 1987. Such build-and-bargain tactics, however, are not the only way of getting balanced and mutually reassuring reductions. In the new political environment that we all owe primarily to Gorbachev, it becomes entirely possible to make a virtue of moderation and to count it as a part of the process of constructive bilateral reductions.

It is also reasonable to hope that both great governments are beginning to escape from the pressure of the war-fighting doctrines embraced by military leaders on both sides in earlier years. The low point in the U.S. discussion on that issue came in the late 1970s when conservative civilians, with some help from retired military men, argued that Soviet leaders committed to victory in nuclear warfare were in fact acquiring a strategic superiority, which they would be able to use as nuclear blackmail to obtain a decisive cold war advantage.

It was one of Reagan's most valuable contributions as president that he made mincemeat of those false fears with a single sentence, first uttered in 1982 and then repeated regularly and in his last years jointly with Gorbachev: A nuclear war cannot be won and must never be fought. The proposition is both deeply correct and highly constructive. Its practical meaning is that most of the new weapons systems developed by both sides in the last twenty years have been unnecessary or even destabilizing. Because nuclear war is unwinnable, only weapons (such as better submarines and single-warhead mobile missiles) that add significantly to overall survivability are worth buying, and even then not too many of them.

Yet not even a president with a gift for phrase-making and an earned immunity to criticism from conservatives can undo a whole strategic mindset by a single sentence. There is much serious work to be done in thinking through what it means, in terms of strategic doctrine, planning and procurement, to start from the proposition that a nuclear war cannot be won. The central tradition of military thought in both countries is that what you must do in war is win. In the particular version adopted as a formal service credo by the U.S. Air Force, you must win by the resolute and decisive application of strategic air power—nuclear since 1945 and including submarine-launched missiles since 1960. Unless Reagan and Gorbachev are all wrong about nuclear war, such pursuit of victory is quite literally nonsensical. You cannot win, and if you try to, you will only commit national suicide.

Senior military men are obviously not blind to that reality. In practical terms what they expect from strategic strength is deterrence, not victory. Nonetheless they have been slow to address the habits of mind that lead planners and service leaders to seek ways and means of attack that might in some numerical sense "win"; this creates, for example, a demand for ever more numerous "prompt hard-target killers." There will never be enough to win—that is the meaning of Reagan's statement—and building more and more only stimulates the new deployments of the opponent. What you need is enough to deter, as Dwight Eisenhower was the first president to say, and both sides have vastly more than enough as the 1990s begin. I believe that the president who tells his senior commanders to apply common sense to strategic doctrine will find a ready response; many military men understand that there is an unbridgeable gap between inherited doctrine and the reality of strategic stalemate.

The stalemate of today would be a stalemate even if one side were to go on building while the other cut back by half its many survivable warheads. The band of parity, in Robert McNamara's phrase, is very wide. In such a situation there is no need for either government to be greatly troubled by the exact numbers of vehicles and warheads agreed in the Strategic Arms Reduction Talks treaty now so near to completion. What is needed on both sides is political determination, and here the words from Malta are encouraging.

There is also room on both sides for acts of unilateral moderation. Over time of course, such acts must be roughly matched if there is to be a sustained process of two-sided restraint, but it helps a lot not to have to worry about precise balances at every step. Indeed in that situation, once it is clearly understood, the side that takes the lead in moderation is doing itself a favor. It is saving money without risk. Bilateral moderation, with or without formal agreements, will be reinforcing to mutual trust. The two superpowers cannot abolish nuclear danger, but they can greatly strengthen their confidence in each other's rejection of nuclear war and by doing so reinforce each other's acceptance of stable peace.

Each side has much to learn about those realities. Budget pressures, improved doctrines, sensible restraint in procurement and new formal agreements will take time to have their effect on each other and on the overall attitudes of both governments. There will always be voices for caution in both capitals. On the American side there is a particular hazard of rigidity among those who really believe in the nuclear orthodoxies of NATO planners. Fortunately there is also a much more impressive tradition in NATO, the one represented among American leaders by General Eisenhower and his best student, Andrew Goodpaster. In that tradition the underlying purpose is always the political reassurance of allies, not the deployment of this or that specific weapons system. Precisely because political reassurance will be much easier in the emerging post-Stalinist Europe, it will also be easier to avoid renewed entrapment in "requirements" that have their basis in dated doctrine, not in nuclear or political reality. American nuclear moderation, across the board from battlefield weapons to intercontinental missiles, will be reinforcing to Western self-confidence in the coming decade.

The most uncertain of all the relationships between the two superpowers are those that occur not in their direct encounters over strategic weaponry or over Europe, but in their relations to other countries, most of them in the Third World. Except for the important and welcome Soviet withdrawal from Afghanistan, we cannot call 1989 a year of great improvement in those relations. It is not surprising that the Malta summit produced no visible progress on the question of large-scale Soviet support for the unrepentantly old-fashioned dictator Fidel Castro and, through him, for communists in Central America. American policy in that region remains narrow, and much of the U.S. concern about turmoil in those small countries is absurdly exaggerated. Central America is not the soft underbelly of American security—Panama is an exception because of U.S. interests in the canal (and because of the viciousness of the fallen Panamanian leader, General Manuel Antonio Noriega).

As the year ends, the large Soviet role that is played in and through Cuba remains a source of mistrust and a serious constraint on other improvements in bilateral relations. Nothing would do more to ease the way for such improvement than a visible and sustained reduction in the Soviet subsidy to Castro, and it will be entirely understandable if that happens only by independent Soviet choice, not by superpower negotiation.

V

Underlying the Soviet-American relationship—whether in Europe, in strategic weaponry, in Third World countries or indeed in matters of economics and human rights—is the question of communication and understanding between the two governments and their societies. In that broad field 1989 was a good year and, as in the case of freedom in Eastern Europe, we must give decisive importance to the role of President Gorbachev. Glasnost is not the same as free speech, because it goes only as far as authority permits, and there are still limits that are not unimportant merely because they are unspecified. Nonetheless the change since 1985 has been large and good, perhaps as great in those four years as in all the decades between the death of Stalin and Gorbachev's succession.

The new openness both in Soviet diplomacy and in political discourse is both a major element in the easing of the cold war and a major reinforcement of the prospect for stable and confidently peaceful relations between the two superpowers. In 1989 we had a striking demonstration of the constructive power of glasnost when Foreign Minister Eduard Shevardnadze made a formal public acknowledgment that the radar at Krasnoyarsk violated the 1972 Antiballistic Missile Treaty, thus ending years in which implausible Soviet denials had interacted destructively with wildly overstated American claims that this one misplaced radar was of decisive strategic importance. Shevardnadze's courageous statement reflected a new level of Soviet understanding that systematic deception is the enemy of trust between nations. Conversely, when great governments deal openly with one another, and when they do what they say they will do, the reinforcement of their mutual trust can be both quick and strong.

Before the cold war began, the great nuclear physicist Niels Bohr tried to persuade Roosevelt and Churchill that the first requirement of the nuclear age had to be openness—above all between the great powers, and most of all between the United States and the Soviet Union. He was not heeded at the time, and it is far from clear that what he wanted could have happened while Stalin lived. Nonetheless, Bohr was right. As the 1990s begin, the most important single source of new hope is that both governments do now seem to have leaders who expect to be open with each other and with their friends, to the common advantage of all. As a matter of history we cannot yet say that the cold war is over. But looking ahead from where we are now it is not wrong to say that the last decade of the century bids fair to be a time of steadily stronger peace, both in Europe and in the overall relations between the two great protagonists of the years since 1945.

62. Where We Must Cut the Defense Budget and Why

Dick Cheney

In this selection, Secretary of Defense Dick Cheney argues that the United States should make only limited cuts in its defense budget because it is possible that the policies of Mikhail Gorbachev could be reversed by his successor. Cheney then goes on to indicate precisely where these limited cuts should be made.

This is a very challenging time from the standpoint of the United States if we look at our foreign and defense policies—a period of great ferment in the Soviet Union and Eastern Europe. Clearly, there is fundamental change under way. Look at what's transpiring not only in the Soviet Union, but in Eastern Europe with the Polish government's recognition of Solidarity and its commitment to hold free elections.

I have moved from a posture of skepticism about Mikhail Gorbachev to one of believing that he does, in fact, seek fundamental change in the Soviet system, that his effort to reform the Soviet economy and Soviet society may, in fact, have positive effects in terms of U.S. relations, that we'll end up possibly with a less hostile, less threatening Soviet Union than we've been faced with before. I think his intentions seem clear, but it's not at all clear to me that he'll be able to pull it off.

What does all of this mean for U.S. national security policy? While we certainly can point to benign intentions on the part of the stated posture of Gorbachev, my problem is that I have to deal with the capabilities that the Soviet Union still possesses. From a military standpoint, it is still the most formidable power in the world, relative to the United States, with enormous nuclear and conventional military capability. The perception of a reduced threat to NATO creates special problems for us, because this perception makes it more difficult for us to maintain the kind of cohesion and unity within the alliance that's been the cornerstone of the success of our strategy for 40 years.

There's a great debate under way with respect to whether or not the changes that we see in the Soviet Union are historically inevitable or are simply the result of the policies of one man. Can his policies be easily reversed by his successor, whenever that individual takes office?

Based on those general views, I am of the opinion that U.S. policy at this time has to be firmly consistent, not only because of the uncertainties about the future direction of Soviet policy, but also because within the alliance it's absolutely essential the United States provide the stability around which the rest of the alliance can rally, while we maintain a forthright posture with respect to the potential problems that could occur if the Soviets should reverse course.

It's not the time for us unilaterally to reduce our commitments or our capabilities. Such reductions should only be taken on a careful step-by-step basis in conjunction with our allies and as a result of reduced Soviet capabilities. Gorbachev has announced a 14.2 percent reduction in the Soviet defense budget. It's difficult to know exactly what that means, because we don't know precisely how much they're spending on defense.

But with our budget, we will have implemented a 12 percent reduction in U.S. defense spending over the last four years. He's proposed a reduction of 10,000 tanks in Eastern Europe, but they're still producing 3,400 new tanks every new year. We've gone from a level of 1,200 tanks per year down to a level of fewer than 700 tanks per year, already accomplished.

So the notion that somehow Gorbachev is moving in the direction of adopting a less hostile and a less threatening posture—reducing the defense budget, reducing commitments—the fact is that we already, in many cases, have matched him, if not exceeded him, in terms of decisions that the Congress has had to make in recent years.

Budget Cuts

The task at hand is budget cuts. In January, the proposed Reagan budget called for 2 percent real growth. President George Bush recommended 0 percent real growth to keep pace with inflation. Many in Congress preferred a reduction of 2 percent in real terms. Ultimately, a compromise was reached of approximately 1 percent real decline in defense spending in fiscal 1990 over fiscal 1989. What that means in terms of budget authority for fiscal 1990 is a reduction of $10 billion. If you look at it over the course of the five-year defense program, it is in excess of $64 billion.

Since January 1987, just a little over two years ago, reductions in defense spending for fiscal 1988 through fiscal 1994 totaled $373 billion. Stated another way, if the original five-year defense program approved in 1986 had been implemented, we'd be here today talking about a defense budget of approximately $479 billion for next year. Instead, we're talking about a defense budget of $305 billion for next year.

That's an enormous change. It constitutes a fundamental shift in direction. And I think everybody can understand why, with cuts of that magnitude, the decisions to be made are not easy ones.

It is very hard, in spite of what everybody may think, to come up with $65 billion out of a five-year defense program or $10 billion in the next year. It's very, very painful. Everybody needs to understand that. The Congress needs to understand that; the press needs to understand that; and the public needs to understand that. You do not buy more defense capability with less money. There may be ways down the road that we can save money and do our job as efficiently or more efficiently than we have in the past. I think there is. But the bottom line is when you have reductions of the magnitude that we've seen over the last few years, the result is significantly less military capability than had originally been anticipated.

My former colleagues have been great. I've heard from a lot of them in the last couple of weeks, all of them interested in making certain that I don't close their base or cut their weapon system or cancel a program that they believe is absolutely essential to national defense. There isn't any way for me to do what I'm expected to do without offending somebody, without breaking some china, without stepping on some toes.

They are tough decisions. We've done the best we could, I think, on relatively short notice to put together a responsible budget under the guidance that we've been given.

I'd like to talk about the philosophy I tried to pursue as we undertook this review of programs and decided which areas we wanted to cut. From a philosophical standpoint, I approached the problem of coming up with $10 billion for next year with the basic, fundamental belief that it's better to cancel lower-priority systems outright and to reduce force structure than it is to keep up the fiction that somehow we can have just as effective forces with less money—or to move back, if you will, to the notion of the hollow forces of the late 1970s.

From a priority standpoint, my first was people. I thought personnel questions were foremost, and I'll come back to that in a minute. Secondly, I felt it was important that we maintain our forward strategy, our forward-deployed strategy. It is not an appropriate time for us to make unilateral reductions in Europe. My third priority was maintaining the readiness of those forward-deployed forces. My fourth was the question of strategic modernization, which you've all heard so much about. My fifth was the notion that we ought to procure what we do procure at efficient rates.

Personnel

From a personnel standpoint, I steered clear of all proposals that would have had a negative impact on our ability to recruit and retain topflight people. I am tremendously impressed—based on prior exposure to the military before I took the job, as well as conversations with career civilian and military personnel since—at the quality of today's armed forces. It might, in fact, be a cliche to say it, but it's absolutely true, that we've never had people of as high a caliber, capability, as we do consistently across all the forces today.

I think it's essential when we talk about our military posture in the years ahead that we do nothing to make it more difficult to recruit those kinds of people or to retain them in the force. So pay raises are in the budget, they're absolutely essential, they shouldn't be trimmed. If I could, I'd raise them. . . .

Forward Strategy

In terms of forward strategy, I really think it's essential—with respect to Europe especially, but also to our other forward-deployed forces—that we not make unilateral cuts in that posture under the guise of budget reductions. And there's one exception to that that I'll talk about in a minute when I get into the force structure changes. But the fact of the matter is, we should not be bringing home forces in significant numbers until we've arrived at some kind of an accord with the Soviets in terms of conventional forces in Europe.

I also think that it's extremely important, from the standpoint of the alliance, that now, more than ever, strong leadership is required on our part. The United States cannot exert that strong leadership or provide that kind of guidance if the first act of its administration, under budget pressure from the Congress, is to significantly reduce our presence in Europe. . . .

Strategic Modernization

In terms of strategic modernization, let me explain what we propose with respect to our overall strategic posture. The Trident program will continue unchanged. The Navy proposed that we reject—that we take down—two Tridents from the planned construction program. I rejected that proposition. No change in the Trident program.

With respect to the B-2 bomber, I have slipped it by a year. That's a reflection of reality in part; it's an enormously complex new technology; it's an enormously expensive technology. I find, as I looked at the program, that there are a lot of unresolved questions there about how ultimately we are going to finance it and what it ultimately will cost. So, I have asked for a review by the Defense Acquisition Board of the entire B-2 program. But I would be less than forthright if I didn't acknowledge that we've got problems with the B-2, and a lot of work is required before we're going to be in a position to be able to say how much it's going to cost or when it will be available.

With respect to land-based ICBM forces, I recommended to the president that the proper course of action would be to take the 50 Peacekeeper missiles currently deployed in silos and go to the rail-garrison scheme. I made that recommendation because it was the low-cost option. It was the cheapest way to get mobility built into our land-based ICBM force. And I also made the point that it's the way to achieve the earliest initial operational capability for a mobile missile. We can have that system on the rail, some of those missiles actually deployed, ready to go, by 1992.

The president decided that he also wanted the Small ICBM. Now, in effect, that's what we're going to do. That's the decision. The basic problem we have is one of budget and fitting both programs in a tight fiscal situation.

The amount of money available for the Small ICBM in fiscal 1990 is only approximately $100 million. We do have some money, another $100 million roughly, that we can reprogram in 1989 into the Small ICBM account, part of the funds left over after the ICBM compromise of last year.

The numbers, then, would wrap up on the Small ICBM from $100 million spent in 1990, $200 million in 1992, $250 million, $300 million, $350 million over the five-year defense budget. We may want to change that. One of the problems with that particular set of numbers is that it's not the most efficient spending profile on the program. It is budget-driven, especially in the early years. We may want to make some changes in that profile to get greater economy and more efficiency, but the basic theory and concept is that we'll first build and deploy rail-garrison. We'll keep the Small ICBM alive, but it will come in behind the rail-garrison procurement, with the Small ICBM and we will end up, in fact, ultimately deploying both systems.

I think the arguments for that approach are as follows: Obviously, more than anything else, we acquire a significant element of mobility in our land-based ICBM forces. This will end, if it's agreed to by the Congress, a 10-year impasse over how to deal with the so-called "window of vulnerability." We've spent 10 years in that debate since I came to Congress, trying to figure out how we were going to deal with the vulnerability of those land-based systems; this proposal would do it.

If we deploy both systems in that mode, with strategic warning we'd have 1,000 survivable warheads; with tactical warning, we'd have at least 500 survivable warheads. And I think there's a strong argument to be made for that posture, based on the notion that this is the best way to proceed from the standpoint of the Strategic Arms Reduction Talks. It does, in fact, parallel what the Soviets are deploying with the SS-25 and the SS-24 and the strongest posture we could be in in Geneva would be to have similar systems of our own.

With respect to the Strategic Defense Initiative, we've made some changes there as well. In part, this is a reflection of the reality of the technical complexity of the programs we're trying to deal with. President Ronald Reagan had proposed a level of funding for fiscal 1990 at $5.6 billion; our proposal is to fund SDI in fiscal 1990 at $4.6 billion.

The package over the five-year program moves from $40 billion under the Reagan proposal to $33 billion under the Bush proposal. This will give us a robust program to continue to pursue both ground-based and space-based interceptors. It will buy us the capability to look aggressively at the Brilliant Pebbles concept; if we can make Brilliant Pebbles work, that would add significantly to our capacity to reduce the cost of the total space-based part of the program.

If, after aggressive testing and development of the concept over the next year or two, Brilliant Pebbles doesn't work out, one of the byproducts of the recommended funding levels is that the ultimate deployment date on the current space-based interceptor concept would be slipped by about two years. So there is a cost to be paid for that reduction in overall spending on SDI.

I have been a strong advocate of SDI. I would also argue that SDI is very important because of the extent to which we've got resources dedicated to some fundamental research and development questions. Some of the technology that is coming out of that with other applications besides SDI itself is, I think, fascinating, and I think it would be a grave mistake for us to shortchange SDI.

Efficient Procurement

As a general proposition, I rejected proposals to stretch out procurement if it significantly increased cost. For example, the AH-64 Apache helicopter—the Army came in with a proposal to slip the procurement on it, to reduce the buy, that would have had the effect in that one instance of raising the cost of each helicopter from $12 million to $19 million.

I tried to avoid those kinds of stretchouts. Now this is not a hard-and-fast rule. Obviously, old rules are meant to have exceptions. But in terms again of guidance as we put the budget together, I tried to avoid interfering with, or interrupting, on-going production lines of the existing systems.

So where, in effect, did we cut? Primarily what got hit was procurement—$5.4 billion out of the $10 billion—and also, force structure, which doesn't show up in exactly those terms. Most of the personnel changes relate to force structure.

I did not take the approach in cutting the budget of making certain that every service ponied up exactly the same percentage, since I didn't think that made a lot of sense. And while the marks originally went back down to the services before I arrived on the scene for *pro rata* reductions, I took the approach that I wasn't going to worry about how those numbers came out until I had looked at each program that was offered for revision.

When you look at top line under the Army, basically what I've directed that the service do is to save the approximately 8,000 slots that had been committed to the intermediate-range nuclear forces in Europe. We've eliminated the Pershing IIs as a result of the INF accord. That frees up approximately 8,000 slots—some 7,900, to be exact. The original plan was to have all of those personnel assigned new missions in Europe.

In effect, I told the Army that it had to take down its end strength by 4,000 slots. I did not want it all to come out of Europe or any other single spot. I wanted part of it to come out of the continental United States. The result was a recommendation from the Army, which I have approved, that we take about half of it out of personnel who would have otherwise been reassigned from the Pershing II mission in Europe to other assignments—that's a total of about 4,000—and that simultaneously we deactivate one mechanized brigade, 4th Infantry Division, here in the continental United States.

With respect to the Navy, one of the toughest decisions I had to make had to do with the size of our carrier fleet. We're currently at 14 aircraft carriers. We're scheduled to go to 15. Fifteen is a goal that many of us liked and supported in the past. I voted for all of those increments when I served as a member of Congress. But in my judgment, we can do the job we have to do with those 14 carriers that we currently have. So, in effect, what I have instructed is that we will not have the already planned increase from 14 to 15 carrier groups.

We'll do that by taking the USS *Coral Sea* out early, and eventually the USS *Midway* will be retired early as well.

We are accelerating the retirement of DDG-2s and 37-class destroyers, some of our least capable vessels. They were scheduled to come out of the force anyway; we're going to accelerate that retirement. We're going to deactivate 73 of the P-3A and P-3B anti-submarine warfare aircraft and make some other changes in the program there. Specifically, with respect to the P-3s, we'll end up with 24 active and nine Reserve P-3C squadrons, and the Reserves will also operate 10 squadrons of the P-3B aircraft.

We're also going to move 10 frigates the first year, a total of 24 frigates ultimately, to the Reserves from the active force. These are the 1052s.

With respect to the Air Force, a relatively minor change. We still have a WC-130 hurricane unit. That's nice to have, but the fact is that with satellites and the National Oceanic and Atmospheric Administration, we cover hurricanes perfectly adequately; and that struck me as a unit that could, in fact, be deactivated and saved. And we also restructured the TR-1 program, details of which are classified.

Program Cuts

I made decisions to terminate programs. My decisions in these cases were not necessarily based on the proposition that these are bad programs, that there's anything fundamentally wrong with the contractor or that there wasn't wisdom in buying these originally. Some of them are already established programs. We've already acquired a number of items. Others are new and not yet on the books. But I came back to the proposition that I had to cut somewhere, and rather than stretch out all the programs and run everything at an inefficient rate, I opted for knocking specific programs out of the budget.

On the AH-64 helicopter, we will end up with a total of 807 aircraft, which we think is sufficient to equip 40 battalions of 15 helicopters each. The program would be terminated after the fiscal 1991 deliveries.

The Army Helicopter Improvement Program helicopter is also a nice piece of equipment—we'll have about 207 of them in the inventory once all the deliveries currently in the works are completed. The problem is that we're producing the AH-64 helicopter for the Army and the Army Helicopter Improvement Program helicopter for the Army, and we're trying to get started on the LHX new light attack helicopter for the Army.

And it didn't all fit into the pot, so the result is, we terminate the AH-64 program after two more years, cancel the Army Helicopter Improvement Program in 1990 and put a major effort into bringing the LHX on line as soon as possible.

In addition to that, I canceled the M-88 recovery vehicle. Frankly, it had never served its purpose in terms of being able to perform the mission assigned to it, and I couldn't find very many advocates of the M-88 recovery vehicle for tanks.

The V-22 Osprey aircraft for the Marine Corps is an important program, and I think the V-22 is an interesting concept. I think it's probably a good aircraft, but I could not justify spending the amount of money that was proposed to be spent when we were just getting ready to move into procurement on the V-22 to perform a very narrow mission that I think can be performed in another fashion, specifically by using helicopters instead of the V-22.

I know the V-22 has a lot of commercial appeal. Maybe it's possible to find some way to keep that effort on line and going. But the fact is, it costs a couple of billion dollars a year in terms of procurement, and to perform that specific, fairly narrow mission in moving Marines from ship to shore, it seemed to me that this was a capability that, if we had to give someplace, this was one we could do without.

With respect to the F-14D, again, a first-class aircraft, I have no problems at all with the capability that it has provided for us over the years. In effect, what we're proposing is that we terminate new production on the F-14D. That's scheduled in 1990, but we would retain the remanufacture program. Now we've got two production lines there: one to build new

F-14Ds, the other to remanufacture F-14As and the older aircraft into F-14Ds, with new engines and so forth. We'll keep the remanufacturing process going. We're operating the new line at the rate of 12 per year; one a month. Each one of those aircraft is costing well over $50 million. By keeping the remanufacturing operation going, we'll ramp up over the course of the five-year defense budget to the point where we will be remanufacturing 60 aircraft a year. That costs about half of what a new one does. I think it's a way to maintain the force structure and, at the same time, save some bucks. The Phoenix missile, of course, is associated with the F-14D.

On the SSN-688 (Los Angeles-class) submarine, the Navy, when it came in with its response to the need to cut, recommended that we take out one of the SSN-21s, one of the new attack submarines scheduled for procurement in the early 1990s. I rejected that offer on the grounds that that was supposed to be an extremely capable submarine, far more capable than the SSN-688. And instead of taking out one of the SSN-21s, put that back in the budget, and we will simply stop our buy of SSN-688s. We only had two more to go anyway, now we're going to buy only one additional SSN-688.

With respect to the Air Force, the F-15E is obviously a great aircraft, one much in demand by the commanders in chief. In effect, what this proposal does is to terminate the program after the procurement of 200 F-15E aircraft. This will leave us, obviously, with the emphasis on developing the A-12 aircraft later on, and the advanced tactical fighter coming down the road. But while the F-15E is extremely capable, 200 of them seem sufficient from my standpoint. It will give us two full active wings plus some spares. Again, that was a place where we could stop a current existing production line and save some money.

Now we did, in fact, reschedule some programs, as I mentioned earlier. I tried to do it in a way that would not harm efficient production rates or interfere with multiyear programs. But, again, as a general proposition, we tried to maintain existing efficient rates of production, except in cases where technology problems and problems of developing complex new systems made it necessary for us to defer procurement.

In some areas, I generally felt it was important for us not to accept the recommendations that were made. Again, it's relatively self-explanatory. On the C-17 aircraft, if you think in terms of the long-term strategic developments that may occur in the next decade, with a significantly reduced presence in Europe, the C-17 becomes even more important in terms of our capacity to reinforce and keep our commitments there. If you look at our capacity to operate elsewhere in the world, on that basis, I rejected proposals to stretch out the C-17 as well.

There were proposals to stretch out the buy on the M-1 tank. Well, we're already down, getting ready to operate with only one factory, and to run that one at an efficient rate; proposed cuts in the Abrams buy didn't strike me as making any sense at all from an economic standpoint. The same held true with respect to the Bradley fighting vehicle.

Conclusion

These were not easy decisions. If anyone thinks it's pleasant, with my record of unqualified support for the Defense Department and the services and the various systems that we've voted for over the years, it's not. But we do have to make some of these calls, and I look forward to having the opportunity to structure the wisest and best possible budget we can for our military services, in light of the very important challenges that we face as a nation and in light of the fact of life of a constrained budget.

63. Wasteful Weapons

Center for Defense Information

In this selection, the Center for Defense Information argues that (1) deep-rooted flaws in the procedures for developing and buying new weapons waste billions of dollars every year, (2) the Pentagon has provided no military rationale for many new weapons such as nuclear war-fighting missiles and Stealth bombers, (3) jobs and profits have increasingly become the reason for the development and production of weapons, and (4) the desire to acquire the most advanced weapons systems has resulted in the acquisition of complex weapons that are costly, unreliable, and difficult for crews to maintain and operate.

The United States weapons industry is the biggest in the world. The Pentagon spends about $6 Billion per week and executes about 56,000 contracts per working day. But over the past several decades the weapons bought by the Pentagon have become increasingly unrelated to the nation's military needs.

More and more, *the U.S. is buying weapons it does not need and is spending too much for the weapons it does buy.*

From the *Defense Monitor* (Vol. XVIII, No. 7). Reprinted with the permission of the Center for Defense Information.

For example, the Pentagon buys costly and deadly weapons such as super-accurate nuclear missiles, binary chemical artillery shells, and $600 million Stealth bombers for use in a war nobody could win.

Since World War II six major governmental commissions have examined how the Pentagon buys weapons. All have found serious flaws resulting in enormous waste. Their criticisms included issues such as a lack of professionalism in the management of weapons contracts and conflicts of interest involving those who leave government jobs to work for the same companies they previously supervised. But these commissions failed to take into account basic policies which have perpetuated many of the problems we now face. Consequently, past reform efforts proved unsuccessful because they only tinkered at the margins of the problem and ignored the root causes prompting the Pentagon to buy unneeded weapons in the first place.

Obsolete Goals

Weapons should be bought to meet clear and important military goals. If the goals change, the old weapons often become obsolete. The fundamental fault with our current weapons-buying decisions is the Pentagon's reluctance to recognize that our military needs have changed. The goals dictating which weapons we buy today were developed in the Cold War era after World War II.

Since the 1950s weapons have been produced by private companies on a scale previously unimaginable. The idea took hold that in order to intimidate and contain the Soviet Union the U.S. needed to keep its armed forces at something close to a wartime level indefinitely. Today, the prospect of going to war against the Soviet Union around the world appears to be receding.

The Pentagon has very ambitious and expensive military goals. Because of this, there is an inevitable gap between what the military wants to do (or thinks it is required to do) and the resources which are available.

Currently the U.S. builds nuclear weapons to fight and prevail in a nuclear war. The military trains to fight in every corner of the world, from the arctic to the tropics. The Navy seeks to control all the world's oceans. The U.S. plans to provide military aid to 114 countries. The U.S. promises to preserve the world military "balance," a term that has never been defined with any precision.

The U.S. has military agreements with some 60 foreign governments and has long supported anticommunist insurgencies around the world. Thus, we find ourselves in a situation similar to that which Frederick the Great, the eighteenth-century Prussian monarch, warned against when he said, "He who attempts to defend too much defends nothing."

The U.S. seeks to buy complex weapons that allegedly allow it to accomplish these goals. Yet buying increasingly complex weapons at ever higher costs cannot achieve the goal of being able to fight and win at any time and place. This pursuit means the U.S. gets weapons that often do not work and are inappropriate for real world needs.

Trying to Do Everything

Since the end of World War II the U.S. has prepared to fight under all sorts of circumstances, ranging from prolonged nuclear war to conventional war in Europe to intervention in developing nations. The current call for U.S. military forces to interdict drugs is just the latest example of "we can do everything" thinking. Planning to fight everywhere, the Pentagon's solution has been to ask for money to buy complex and costly weapons of all kinds. Since it is unable to devise clearly defined military goals, *the U.S. has opted for an approach in which national security is measured in terms of how much money the military spends.* But this ignores more crucial questions such as: Is there a valid military need for the weapons, or, if there is, can they be produced at acceptable costs?

Currently, the U.S. and the Soviet Union are conducting negotiations to reduce their nuclear weapons on long-range missiles and bombers. The Soviet Union is beginning to restructure its conventional military forces to reduce their size and offensive capabilities and to make them less well-suited for a surprise attack. In December 1988 Soviet President Mikhail Gorbachev announced the decision to unilaterally reduce Soviet troop strength by 500,000. Some of the world's regional conflicts are being resolved. Soviet troops have withdrawn from Afghanistan, Vietnamese troops have withdrawn from Cambodia, and Cuban troops have been leaving Angola. Furthermore, our allies are no longer the weak, poor countries they were at the end of World War II.

Thus, it is no longer sensible for the "business-as-usual" Cold War assumptions which governed the weapons buying decisions for the past 40 years to drive today's weapons procurement. These assumptions were based on the premise that the Soviet Union was an expansionist state bent on world domination and that the U.S. had to be the world's policeman. At a time when Soviet forces have left Afghanistan, when a Soviet bloc nation such as Poland votes its Communist government out of office, and when the Berlin Wall has been opened, such a proposition cannot be accepted.

Money, Money, Money

There has been an overemphasis on money as a way to increase military strength. *To an alarming degree during the 1980s the U.S. has focused on how much money could be spent, not how well it is spent.* Attention has been paid to what portion of the Gross National Product (GNP) should be devoted to the military or what the annual percentage increases should be, not whether more money is necessary or would significantly contribute to the nation's security.

The Reagan Administration spent a total of $2.2 Trillion dollars on the military. Even taking inflation into account, the 1984 military budget was greater than the 1969 military budget, the peak spending year of the Vietnam War. Never before had the U.S. military budget experienced a 50 percent increase during peacetime. By fanning fears of American military weakness, the Reagan Administration was able to persuade Congress to provide these huge sums of money to the military.

In the 1980s money was spent in haste and without a coherent plan, resulting in inevitable and predictable waste. John Tower, the chairman of the Senate Armed Services Committee in the early 1980s, now states "I regret my part in front-loading the budget."

"In Every Corner"

The Pentagon still wants to do too much. As recently as 1987 Defense Secretary Caspar Weinberger said, "In every corner of the globe, America's vital interests are threatened by an evergrowing Soviet military threat." He gave first priority to increasing the Pentagon's budget, largely leaving decisions over what to buy and how much to pay to the services. Even those increases, however, proved insufficient to pay for the ambitious military goals of the Reagan Administration. The Joint Chiefs of Staff argued they would need an additional $750 Billion to carry out the missions specified by the Administration, over and above the $1.6 Trillion requested by the Secretary of Defense for the military in the 1984–1988 5-year defense plan. The results are that *Americans pay far too much to the military and receive too little security in return.*

Clearly, the Pentagon cannot expect the sort of money it received during the Reagan Administration. Nor should it, since spending is still at a peacetime high. *According to the Pentagon's latest calculations, the total program cost of 98 major weapons programs currently in production is approximately $819 Billion,* a sum that is higher than the GNP of almost every country in the world. Military officials have yet to appreciate that the unrestricted military spending of the Reagan years is over. In 1989 the General Accounting Office (GAO) found that President Bush's 5-year defense plan is at least $100 Billion short of the money needed to buy weapons already started. In large part this is due to the desire of the services to buy more weapons than the military budget provides. Chronic gaps between plans and reality are a built-in source of inefficiency and waste.

Burdensome Weapons

During the past 20 years a disturbing situation has developed. The U.S. military shows reduced interest in already-proven conventional weapons. In many respects an already-proven weapon is preferable to a new technologically complex one due to the inherent reliability and lower cost of maintenance and support. Such weapons also make rapid production by a contractor easier if more weapons are needed.

Today's weapons, such as aircraft carriers, take so long to produce and have become so expensive that their protection becomes the foremost priority.

A little-recognized consequence of over-reliance on technology is the effect on military troops. Even if complex weapons work as promised, their potential will not be realized unless military personnel are up to the task of operating and maintaining them. Currently we buy weapons developed by Ph.D.s and expect them to be operated by high school graduates. A 1985 study by the Army Research Institute concluded, *"the Army is not developing weapons systems that work well when they get into the field. These problems are going to worsen because weapons are becoming more complex while the supply of capable soldiers is decreasing."*

Wrong Choices

Service traditions cause the development of new and unnecessary weapons. The Navy's tradition of carrying the fight to the enemy has caused the Pentagon to produce bigger and extremely expensive aircraft carriers. They are used frequently for intervening overseas. Yet, in the nuclear missile age, carriers represent extremely vulnerable targets.

In addition, according to current Navy strategy, carrier aircraft would be used to attack targets in the Soviet Union. The high vulnerability of our carriers resulting from such a plan is pointed out by many senior naval officers who question whether any rational military commander would ever risk their loss in such attacks. Such vulnerability makes it questionable whether we need more carriers, let alone the 15 the Navy has currently. The cost of buying just one carrier and the additional warships and aircraft to protect it is about $18 Billion.

The Air Force plans to buy 132 Stealth bombers to add to the B-1B and B-52 bombers during the 1990s and eventually replace them. In the age of nuclear-armed missiles which can destroy the Soviet Union in 30 minutes, the role of the manned bomber is obsolete if not dead. The desire to have more bombers really reflects the traditional importance the Air Force gives to manned strategic bombing. But $72 Billion for Stealth bombers is a high price to pay for an outmoded tradition.

Service Competition

Competition between different military services is yet another reason why we buy unnecessary weapons. The U.S. does not have one air force, it has four: one each for the Air Force, Army, Navy, and Marine Corps. The U.S. has at least half a dozen different ways to attack the Soviet Union with nuclear weapons. Since the end of World War II there have been continuous struggles between the different branches of the military over which services would control which tasks. This has led to duplication and waste in weapons development as the services fight for control of a specific job by seeking to outdo rival services in developing weapons for that task.

Political Spending

Of course, responsibility for decisions to procure unnecessary weapons does not lie only with the military. Another factor is the pressure by contractors who manufacture them and from members of Congress who promote systems built in their districts and states. The motivation of the contractors is easily understood. In many cases the ability of a military contractor to make big profits depends on receiving a contract from the Pentagon. Without one, it may lose money and face financial difficulties.

The Pentagon wants to preserve the vast

array of contractors and subcontractors who collectively produce the huge quantities of equipment needed to fight around the world. A contract is often awarded to a particular company to ensure that it stays in business. The awarding of the M-1 tank production contract to the Chrysler Corporation in November 1976 was such a case. This can be expected in *a system where the major motivation for building weapons is profit.*

Military-Industrial Complex

The top 20 contractors have annual sales to the Pentagon exceeding a Billion dollars each and cumulatively capture about 50 percent of the total Pentagon spending on weapons each year. In turn, some of these firms monopolize the production of a specific type of weapon. The percentages of business done by the top four firms are: nuclear submarines (99%), fighter aircraft (97%), attack aircraft (97%), helicopters (93%).

Since the Pentagon generally finds the loss of any major contractor unacceptable, due to concern over maintaining an industrial production base for wartime production, contracts are parceled out selectively to firms. Buying weapons primarily to preserve a bloated "defense industrial base" for war with the Soviet Union seems outmoded, particularly as any U.S.-Soviet war would be a short nuclear war.

General Dynamics was awarded the F-111 aircraft contract in 1962 immediately following cancellation of production of its B-58 bomber and was awarded the F-16 in 1974 when F-111 production was ending. McDonnell Douglas was awarded the F-15 fighter aircraft contract in 1970 as the F-4 program was being phased down. Production of the C-5A transport aircraft began at Lockheed as C-141 production ended. For 30 years, Lockheed has provided all of the Navy's submarine ballistic missiles—moving from the Polaris to the Poseidon to the Trident I and now to the Trident II—all on an essentially noncompetitive basis.

Pork Barrel Weapons

Members of Congress often press for new weapons or continuing production of old weapons out of concern for jobs in their districts. Fearing their constituents will be angry if a contractor in their district starts laying off workers, many congressmen go to great lengths to ensure that local companies obtain contracts. Rockwell had 5,200 subcontracts in 48 states, a fact it used to great effect to gain support for the B-1B bomber in Congress.

More recently, legislators from Long Island have lobbied to continue production of the F-14D fighter made by Grumman, while legislators from Pennsylvania and Texas have fought to save the V-22 tilt-rotor aircraft made by Bell Helicopter/Textron, aircraft the Secretary of Defense recommended canceling.

Congressmen frequently accept political action committee (PAC) contributions and other favors from defense contractors. They are also extensively lobbied by contractors' representatives. *These three—the congressman, the contractor, and the military service—form a powerful trinity that brings tremendous pressure to bear to ensure that money for building new weapons keeps flowing.*

Also, the Pentagon promises to deploy new weapons to military bases in the states of its supporters. The B-1B was deployed to Dyess Air Force Base in Texas in part to reward former Senate Armed Services chairman John Tower for his past support. The B-1B was also stationed at McConnell Air Force Base in Kansas to ensure the support of Sen. Robert Dole, who was Senate majority leader. In purely military terms, other sites were more suitable.

Although contractor selection is supposed to be insulated from outside pressures, the pattern of awards has shown a definite tendency to favor firms with political clout. Besides making PAC contributions, firms gain influence by paying honoraria to members of Congress for speeches and by arranging to farm out work to as many subcontractors as possible in key districts and states.

Restoring money for weapons that even the Pentagon does not want is a traditional practice. In 1981 the Defense Department requested no funds for the Cobra/TOW helicopter, but the delegation from Texas where the helicopters were made restored 17 of them to the budget at a cost of $44.5 million. That same year the Administration requested no money for the A-6E attack plane, made by Grumman on Long Island, but the New York delegation saw to it that 12 planes were included in the budget at a cost of $186.7 million. These aircraft were then produced with astonishing inefficiency, the A-6E at the rate of one per month and the Cobra at the rate of 1.5 per month, which pushed costs per weapon to new highs.

In 1989 the Northrop Corporation, with the cooperation of the Pentagon, issued a news release defending the B-2 bomber as a jobs program, stating, "The U.S. Air Force's B-2 program is supported nationwide by tens of thousands of men and women at prime contractor Northrop Corporation, key subcontractors Boeing, LTV, General Electric and Hughes, and other suppliers and subcontractors in 46 states." Buying $600 million aircraft to create jobs is a gross waste of tax dollars.

Weapons Testing

Even if the government buys an unnecessary weapon, one would expect it to test weapons rigorously to ensure that they perform properly in combat. Unfortunately, this has not been the case. Far too frequently the Pentagon relies heavily on laboratory testing. This sort of testing is done to determine how well various systems and parts meet theoretical requirements, but such testing does not address the critical question of how well it will perform in combat. Speaking about tests designed to show the "lethality" of Star Wars weapons, Dr. Roger Hagengruber of Sandia National Laboratory, said, "These demonstrations have the potential to be what we call strap-down chicken tests, where you strap the chicken down, blow it apart with a shotgun, and say shotguns kill chickens. But that's quite different from trying to kill a chicken in a dense forest while it's running away."

To determine combat capabilities, one must conduct operational testing. Such testing is done in the field under conditions which realistically reflect the harsh demands of the battlefield.

Frequently, weapons testing is flawed in two ways: it is not realistic, and it is not finished before production decisions are made. Because the Pentagon is obsessed with gaining congressional funding for new weapons it often objects to subjecting its weapons to operational tests for fear of being embarrassed by the results. The embarrassments are avoided by rigging the tests or manipulating the test results.

As a result, the Pentagon often starts producing weapons before it has finished developing and testing them. This results in long-term problems that cost big bucks to fix. The B-1B bomber was produced in that fashion and as a result the U.S. has a bomber plagued by numerous performance problems. The Congressional Budget Office (CBO) and the GAO estimate that it might cost up to another $7 or $8 Billion to fix existing problems. The B-2 Stealth bomber program is also being produced in this fashion.

In addition, if the final design is not determined before a weapon is put into production, one cannot predict how much the final product will cost. By putting such weapons into production, huge cost increases become almost inevitable.

When operational testing is done the results are of great importance. A recent GAO report found that tests showed the combat effectiveness of the Advanced Medium Range Air-to-Air Missile (AMRAAM) had not been demonstrated and recommended the Pentagon not proceed with production until serious problems were fixed. Another GAO report found that the military is not realistically testing its aircraft against bird collisions.

When operational testing is not done properly, the result can be disastrous. The Sergeant York Division Air Defense (DIVAD) gun, which was supposed to protect ground forces against aerial attack, was never operationally tested, which helps explain why it was ultimately canceled in 1985. The tests that were performed were highly unrealistic and unfavorable results of those tests were hidden from superior officers who continued to promote DIVAD.

Recently, Senator David Pryor (D-Arkansas) charged the Pentagon with a cover-up with regard to the Airborne Self-Protection Jammer (ASPJ). This is a new joint Navy-Air Force system for jet fighters intended to deceive and jam enemy radar. Sen. Pryor noted that production approval was given for the $4.8 Billion program despite the fact that ASPJ failed many of its operational tests.

Many managers are reluctant to test new weapons realistically. If the results show a weapon is unreliable, the manager is likely to risk having money for the weapon cut off and find his chances for career advancement ended.

Weapons Limitations

The high cost of weapons often means not enough are available for training. This unavailability is compounded by the complexity of many weapons which often generate high training costs and require a longer training time to allow operators to learn to maintain and employ them properly. One example is the B-1B bomber, which costs $21,000 per flying hour to operate. Also, such weapons often need additional support, requiring more money to be spent for operating and maintenance purposes, and may be out of service for repair more often.

The turbine engine of the M-1 tank has limited the tank's mobility by frequently breaking down. In 1986 operational testing of the M-1E1 tank revealed it malfunctioned once every 58 miles. The Army considers one combat day to be 120 miles. That means the tank broke down twice a day. It also costs three and a half times as much per mile to maintain than its predecessor, the M-60.

Because it takes longer to develop and produce complex weapons, there is a greater risk of leaving troops short of the equipment they need. In turn, because of the delay in replacing equipment lost due to normal wear and tear of the inventory, the average age of the force increases.

Illegal Means

Getting a major weapons contract is very profitable and the competition for many contracts is extremely fierce. Thus, at times contractors will resort to illegal means to try to gain an edge in bidding for a contract. This too often results in an unqualified company winning a contract. Consequent delays and attempts to fix problems caused by their own inadequacies increase the price. The trafficking in inside information by defense consultants revealed in the Ill Wind investigation made public in 1988 is a recent example. So far, there have been 2 indictments and 24 guilty pleas from this one investigation.

Unrealistic Planning

The Pentagon frequently puts forward a low estimate of the price of a weapon in order to win congressional approval and arranges contracts in order to build support for the weapon. If people knew how much weapons were really going to cost they might not buy them. The current debate over the B-2 Stealth bomber is a case in point. A GAO report found that underestimating weapons costs is a major factor in the creation of greatly unrealistic cost projections for military programs.

For controversial weapons, the Pentagon sometimes inflates its own requests as a form of insurance to allow for inevitable congressional cuts. The Strategic Defense Initiative (SDI) is typical of this practice. Each year, Administration officials complain Congress is cutting the SDI budget, but up until FY 1990 money for SDI had gone up every year since its inception.

Goldplating

One of the most serious problems facing the U.S. in attempting to produce useful weapons at reasonable prices is that achievable goals are not set. The problem starts at the very outset of the process, when the military seeks new weapons capable of fighting many kinds of wars all around the world. Congress is not provided the information it needs to judge the need for such weapons. Military contractors make big money by pushing the most expensive, high-tech weapons and aid the military in lobbying Congress to buy new weapons.

This often leads to a process known as "goldplating," *the incorporation into a weapon of the newest and most expensive technologies regardless of their battlefield effectiveness or cost.* It was this inclination which led to the fiasco of the DIVAD, a system that was so flawed that former Defense Secretary Weinberger was forced to cancel its production after an expenditure of $1.8 Billion. Norman Augustine, a defense industry official and former Assistant Secretary of the Army, has said, "The last ten percent of performance sought generates one-third of the cost and two-thirds of the problems."

Another weapon which has been afflicted by the "goldplating" syndrome is the Bradley infantry fighting vehicle. The Bradley was to replace the Army's M-113 personnel carrier and was conceived as a motorized infantry combat vehicle which would allow troops to fight while inside. The design kept changing after development began. The TOW antitank missile was attached and a complex turret was added. As a result, the weight rose, causing problems with the vehicle's power train and reducing its ability to ford streams. The TOW turret leaves less room for infantrymen, forcing a reduction in squad size to 7 rather than the 9 soldiers judged necessary. The armor is made of aluminum, which is a reactive metal. When it is hit by an antitank round the aluminum vaporizes, becoming chemical fuel for the explosion and intensifying the deadly blast effects.

Understated Costs

When a new weapon finally receives approval from Congress, the promised capabilities for the program are often highly overstated and the costs are greatly

understated. This is due in large part to powerful political pressures. Understating costs enables a contractor to submit an artificially low bid in the hope of winning a contract, subsequently making his profits through price increases, spare parts, training programs, and repair programs. The 1986 Reagan-appointed Packard Commission reported that military planners pursue unneeded weapons capabilities. The Commission noted that this tendency "has led to overstated specifications, which have led to higher equipment costs. Such so-called 'goldplating' has become deeply embedded in our system today."

After a design is approved, the next step is allowing firms to compete for contracts for the weapon. Contractors are discouraged from requesting modifications of or pointing out problems with the design. Since a contractor must promise that it will fully satisfy the blueprint, the competition is based mainly on the contractor's optimism. To make a profit, the contractor always remains optimistic. In order to sell their products they often resort to standard marketing techniques: they advertise, they exaggerate, and they criticize their competitors. Yet a low bid is required to win the contract. The usual result is that the company bids low to win the contract and comes back later asking for more.

United Technologies promised to deliver Black Hawk helicopters to the Army for only $2.6 million apiece in the late 1970s, but jacked up the price to $4.7 million each when the deliveries started. Predictably, a major weapon takes too long to produce (10–15 years) and has many cost overruns.

Congress can also drive up costs by calling for cuts in the overall quantity of a particular weapon as a way of dealing with budget limitations. A CBO report noted that stretching out production of weapons over a longer period of time adds to the total cost by preventing manufacturers from producing efficiently and introducing cost-saving manufacturing innovations. The report also noted that stretch-outs often occur because the military services seek to develop and acquire too many different weapons simultaneously.

The Pentagon understands that *Congress will rarely stop a major weapon program once a large amount of money has already been spent* on research and development. For example, since approximately $23 Billion has already been spent on the B-2 bomber, it is probable the program will continue despite current congressional criticism. Senator Dan Quayle, later to become Vice-President, said in 1985, "From a political point of view, Congress cannot and does not cut procurement programs; it is what is known as the camel's-nose-under-the-tent syndrome, and it is adroitly practiced by military planners."

Faulty Management

Yet another problem with the way we buy our weapons is that *the people charged with buying weapons are often unqualified*. Despite the fact that procurement involves extraordinarily complex technologies and Billions of dollars, the personnel are not considered "professionals" by the Office of Personnel Management. Thus, they are not required to have the same degree of administrative skills found in their counterparts in the private sector. As a result there are far too many people involved in buying weapons who do not have the necessary technical or management skills. Only half of the contract specialists have business-related college degrees.

The Packard Commission found that "lasting progress in the performance of the acquisition system demands dramatic improvements in our management of acquisition personnel at all levels within the Department of Defense."

Too many people in the military involved in this area see it as a dead-end job. The GAO found in a 1986 survey that the average tenure of a program manager, including his time as a deputy program manager, was just over 2 years. Thus, during the 8–12 years of its development, a weapon system is likely to have 4 or 5 different military officers as program managers, an extremely inefficient way to run a business.

The lack of incentives for those military and civilian personnel involved in buying weapons to pay the lowest prices and obtain the most reliable product is one reason why there has

been such a serious conflict of interest, also known as the "revolving door," in the military-industrial sector. Many military officers in charge of buying weapons face retirement by the time they reach their early forties. At this time they have children going to college and mortgages to pay and cannot afford a big cut in income. It is usually at this time that a representative of a military contractor pays a visit and says that a job will be available after retirement. If an officer stands up and makes a fuss about the overruns and lack of quality of a weapon being produced there will be no job offer.

The GAO reported that more than 30,000 senior military and civilian employees left the DoD in 1983 and 1984. More than 6,000 of these later held industrial security clearances and approximately 5,700 were thought to be working for companies contracting with the Pentagon.

What to Do

The U.S. cannot tolerate a "business-as-usual" approach toward military spending any longer. Changing international conditions, constraints on money, growing technological complexity, and the drive for profits have all combined to produce weapons that are becoming irrelevant to our military needs.

Without appropriate military goals, it is unlikely the Pentagon will buy the weapons truly needed for defending the country. Buying weapons to fight nuclear wars or to defend countries capable of defending themselves does not contribute to the defense of the U.S.

To help ensure that the U.S. buys the weapons it needs and does not pay too much for them we should *eliminate the present piecemeal oversight of military affairs by Congress.* The military sections of different congressional support agencies—such as the General Accounting Office, Congressional Budget Office, Office of Technology Assessment, and the Congressional Research Service—could be pulled together into a Congressional Office of Defense Appraisal (CODA) with a clear mandate to help Congress assess defense needs and monitor the military. An immediate task for CODA would be to reassess American military strategy and the force levels needed to carry it out in a world of rapidly changing conditions.

The U.S. would be more likely to buy truly necessary weapons if decisions were not distorted by the desire of contractors to make huge profits from government contracts. To help achieve that, consideration should be given to *making it illegal for contractors to contribute money to members of Congress.*

Effective Weapons

No matter how technologically complex a weapon is, its effectiveness is only as good as its ability to operate under actual battlefield conditions. U.S. soldiers and sailors should not have to risk their lives operating a weapon whose reliability is based on a contractor's advertising. To ensure combat effectiveness, the military should not produce any weapons until they have been fully tested. This means testing out in the field by the same troops who would actually operate them, not computer tests done in some antiseptic laboratory.

In the past decade the Pentagon bought weapons that were not needed because the military and defense contractors had more money than they could spend effectively. In the future it is likely the U.S. will be reducing both its military spending and the size of its armed forces. This will have at least two very positive effects. *Smaller military budgets will hopefully restore a sense of discipline in spending taxpayers' dollars.* As the U.S. moves to a leaner military force the Pentagon should be able to pay service members more and train them better to operate today's and tomorrow's weapons.

64. National Security in the 1990s

Rear Admiral Gene R. La Rocque, U.S. Navy (Ret.)

Soviet Military Changes

The sweep of announced and actual change in the Soviet military is impressive. The military role in Soviet foreign policy is being de-emphasized. Military strategy and forces are being shifted from offensive to defensive. Big unilateral cuts are being made in Soviet conventional forces. Extraordinary concessions have been extended to the United States in arms control negotiations to reduce nuclear, chemical, and conventional arms. *Cuts have been undertaken in military spending and produc-*

From the *Defense Monitor* (Vol. XVIII, No. 7). Reprinted with the permission of the Center for Defense Information.

tion of some weapons, such as tanks. There is far less secrecy about military matters in the Soviet Union. Civilian control of the military has been strengthened and there is now growing public criticism of the military.

Where once we spoke of "the Russians are coming," we can now speak of *"the Russians are going."* Soviet troops have left Afghanistan. Hundreds of thousands of Soviet troops are leaving Eastern Europe. The Brezhnev Doctrine is replaced by the Sinatra Doctrine. The slogan of "wars of national liberation" has disappeared from Soviet rhetoric.

The Soviets have been driven to these big changes by a number of factors. The most important one is that the enormous burden of the Cold War military competition was destroying the Soviet economy and undermining the quality of life for all Soviet citizens. The

United States is much richer than the Soviet Union but *we also have paid a very heavy price for the Cold War.* Our own economic situation is precarious in part because of excessive military spending.

Clinging to the Past

Why is it so hard for us to surrender unnecessary, wasteful, and damaging military burdens? *Emotionally we refuse to give up the Cold War.* We refuse to see that the need for new weapons has decreased. We refuse to see that Japan and Germany no longer need us. We refuse to stop squandering our money on useless, egregiously expensive weapons like the B-2 Stealth bomber and the SDI enterprise.

Large numbers of Americans benefit from the continuation of the Cold War. These include the arms manufacturers, uniformed and civilian Defense officials, and members of Congress. Many Americans are economically dependent on military bases, military industry jobs, and the profits of military corporations. *The Cold War has been good for an influential segment of our society.*

Cold War mobilization and distraction has diverted our attention from other important aspects of our lives. Housing, health, education, transportation, the environment, care of the young, all have suffered and continue to suffer because of lack of money. We fail to take seriously the truth that our nation's security rests not alone on the force of arms, but on a strong economy and a healthy, educated, well-housed people.

Drifting

Washington is drifting along because the inhabitants are doing quite well and *the old Cold Warriors are still in charge.* Military spending is staying at extraordinarily inflated peacetime levels. Just about every new weapon the Pentagon wants gets funded by the Congress. Nuclear weapons for war-fighting such as the MX and Trident II missiles continue to have a high priority. Congress and the Bush Administra-

tion show little interest in really reducing military spending.

Why should they? Defense contractors keep them in office with honoraria, campaign funds, and gifts. The military establishment in Washington and its military industry allies have become a bloated bureaucracy stealing the wealth of the nation.

My respect for the Congress has diminished in recent years but we cannot give up on our representatives. Our system of government and our economic system are the best in the world but we need a vision of the future that demonstrates that we know where we are going and the kind of world we want. If we are to retain our influence in the world we must demonstrate our ability to control our own internal affairs. In particular, *we must restrain the power of the military industrial complex over our elected representatives.* It should be illegal for military contractors to give money or services to any member of Congress or candidate for political office.

CDI Proposals

The time has come to conform our military posture with the realities of the present era. We at the Center for Defense Information have carefully analyzed the nuclear and conventional forces the United States will need in the future.

With regard to the nuclear forces, these are our specific recommendations for the United States:

1. Today the Pentagon has 12,000 strategic nuclear warheads. The total number of U.S. nuclear weapons required to completely destroy the Soviet Union as a functioning society is 1000, all of which can be carried on at-sea invulnerable missile submarines. With 20 strategic submarines carrying about *3000 nuclear warheads* the U.S. would have a strong retaliatory nuclear force.
2. Stop building new nuclear weapons.
3. Stop construction of new bomb factories.
4. Stop all nuclear weapons test explosions.
5. Phase out the SDI program.
6. Cancel the B-2 Stealth bomber program.

Our proposals for U.S. conventional forces are:

1. Maintain sufficient forces to defend the United States and its territories.
2. Shut down chemical weapons production.
3. Return all U.S. troops based in foreign countries to the U.S. by the year 2000.
4. *Reduce U.S. troop strength to 1.2 million* (a cut of about 1 million from today's force).

$200 Billion for Defense

The cost of our proposed U.S. military force would be about $200 Billion a year, $100 Billion less than the $300 Billion spent on the military today. *For $200 Billion the country would have a powerful, versatile military force* that would be both adequate and reasonably priced.

Such a force means neither a return to isolation nor disarmament. The U.S. would still have the most powerful military in the world. But it does mean that we will have the money in a strengthened economy to provide for the components of our society which make us more secure. It also enhances our ability, if we so chose, to help those less fortunate in the third world. Our capacity to exercise constructive influence around the world would be enhanced.

Our country could take a quantum leap forward. But it will require action to reduce and ultimately remove the powerful, corrosive influence of the military establishment.

65. Nuclear Disarmament by the Year 2000

Mikhail S. Gorbachev

. . . The Soviet Union proposes that a step-by-step, consistent process of ridding the earth of nuclear weapons be implemented and completed within the next 15 years, before the end of this century.

. . . How does the Soviet Union envisage today in practical terms the process of reducing nuclear weapons, both delivery vehicles and warheads, up to their complete elimination? Our proposals on this subject can be summarized as follows.

Stage One. Within the next 5 to 8 years the USSR and the USA will reduce by one half the nuclear weapons that can reach each other's territory. As for the remaining delivery vehicles of this kind, each side will retain no more than 6,000 warheads.

It stands to reason that such a reduction is possible only if both the USSR and the USA renounce the development, testing and deployment of space strike weapons. As the Soviet Union has repeatedly warned, the de-

Reprinted by permission of the Information Department of the USSR Embassy in Washington, D.C.

velopment of space strike weapons will dash the hopes for a reduction of nuclear armaments on earth.

The first stage will include the adoption and implementation of a decision on the complete elimination of medium-range missiles of the USSR and the USA in the European zone—both ballistic and cruise missiles—as a first step towards ridding the European conflict of nuclear weapons.

At the same time the United States should undertake not to transfer its strategic and medium-range missiles to other countries, while Great Britain and France should pledge not to build up their respective nuclear arsenals.

The USSR and the USA should from the very beginning agree to stop all nuclear explosions and call upon other states to join in such a moratorium as soon as possible.

The reason why the first stage of nuclear disarmament should concern the Soviet Union and the United States is that it is they who should set an example for the other nuclear powers. We said that very frankly to President

Reagan of the United States during our meeting in Geneva.

Stage Two. At this stage, which should start no later than 1990 and last for 5 to 7 years, the other nuclear powers will begin to join the process of nuclear disarmament. To start with, they would pledge to freeze all their nuclear arms and not to have them on the territories of other countries.

In this period the USSR and the USA will continue to carry out the reductions agreed upon during the first stage and also implement further measures aimed at eliminating their medium-range nuclear weapons and freezing their tactical nuclear systems.

Following the completion by the USSR and the USA of a 50 percent reduction of their respective armaments at the second stage, another radical step will be taken: All nuclear powers will eliminate their tactical nuclear weapons, i.e., weapons having a range (or radius of action) of up to 1,000 kilometres.

At this stage the Soviet-U.S. accord on the prohibition of space strike weapons would become multilateral, with the mandatory participation in it of major industrial powers.

All nuclear powers would stop nuclear tests.

There would be a ban on the development of nonnuclear weapons based on new physical principles, whose destructive power is close to that of nuclear arms or other weapons of mass destruction.

Stage Three will begin no later than 1995. At this stage the elimination of all remaining nuclear weapons will be completed. By the end of 1999 there will be no nuclear weapons on earth. A universal accord will be drawn up that such weapons should never again come into being.

We envisage that special procedures will be worked out for the destruction of nuclear weapons as well as for the dismantling, re-equipment or scrapping of delivery vehicles. In the process, agreement will be reached on the number of weapons to be scrapped at each stage, the sites of their destruction, and so on.

Verification of the destruction or limitation of arms should be carried out both by national technical means and through on-site inspections. The USSR is ready to reach agreement on any other additional verification measures. . . .

Suggestions for Further Reading

Anthologies

Marrin, Albert. *War and the Christian Conscience.* Chicago: Henry Regnery Co., 1971.

Sterba, James, P. *The Ethics of War and Nuclear Deterrence.* Belmont: Wadsworth, 1985.

Thompson, W. Scott. *From Weakness to Strength.* San Francisco: Institute for Contemporary Studies, 1980.

Wakin, Malham. *War, Morality and the Military Profession.* Boulder: Westview Press, 1979.

Wasserstrom, Richard A. *War and Morality.* Belmont: Wadsworth Publishing Co., 1970.

Basic Concepts

Walters, LeRoy. *Five Classic Just-War Theories.* Ann Arbor: University Microfilms, 1971.

Walzer, Michael. *Just and Unjust Wars.* New York: Basic Books, 1977.

Alternative Views

Allison, Graham T. *Essence of Decision.* Boston: Little, Brown & Co., 1971.

Boston Study Group. *Winding Down.* San Francisco: W. H. Freeman, 1982.

Catudal, H. *Soviet Nuclear Strategy from Stalin to Gorbachev.* Atlantic Highlands: Humanities Press, 1989.

Clayton, J. L. *On the Brink: Defense Deficits and Welfare Spending.* New York: Ramapo Press, 1984.

Cohen, S. *Arms and Judgment.* Denver: Westview Press, 1989.

Fallow, James. *National Defense.* New York: Vintage Books, 1981.

Kahan, Jerome H. *Security in the Nuclear Age.* Washington, D.C.: The Brookings Institution, 1975.

Lens, Sidney. *The Day Before Doomsday.* Boston: Beacon Press, 1977.

McNaugher, T. *New Weapons, Old Politics: American Military Procurement Muddle.* Washington, D.C.: The Brookings Institution, 1989.

Union of Concerned Scientists. *Empty Promise.* Boston: Beacon, 1986.

Practical Application

Brembeck, H. *The Civilized Defense Plan.* Goshen: Fourth Freedom Foundation, 1989.

Ground Zero. *Nuclear War.* New York: Pocket Books, 1982.

Kennedy, Edward M., and Hatfield, Mark O. *Freeze.* New York: Bantam Books, 1982.